Poetry Criticism

Guide to Gale Literary Criticism Series

For criticism on	Consult these Gale series
Authors now living or who died after December 31, 1999	*CONTEMPORARY LITERARY CRITICISM (CLC)*
Authors who died between 1900 and 1999	*TWENTIETH-CENTURY LITERARY CRITICISM (TCLC)*
Authors who died between 1800 and 1899	*NINETEENTH-CENTURY LITERATURE CRITICISM (NCLC)*
Authors who died between 1400 and 1799	*LITERATURE CRITICISM FROM 1400 TO 1800 (LC)* *SHAKESPEAREAN CRITICISM (SC)*
Authors who died before 1400	*CLASSICAL AND MEDIEVAL LITERATURE CRITICISM (CMLC)*
Authors of books for children and young adults	*CHILDREN'S LITERATURE REVIEW (CLR)*
Dramatists	*DRAMA CRITICISM (DC)*
Poets	*POETRY CRITICISM (PC)*
Short story writers	*SHORT STORY CRITICISM (SSC)*
Literary topics and movements	*HARLEM RENAISSANCE: A GALE CRITICAL COMPANION (HR)* *THE BEAT GENERATION: A GALE CRITICAL COMPANION (BG)* *FEMINISM IN LITERATURE: A GALE CRITICAL COMPANION (FL)* *GOTHIC LITERATURE: A GALE CRITICAL COMPANION (GL)*
Asian American writers of the last two hundred years	*ASIAN AMERICAN LITERATURE (AAL)*
Black writers of the past two hundred years	*BLACK LITERATURE CRITICISM (BLC)* *BLACK LITERATURE CRITICISM SUPPLEMENT (BLCS)*
Hispanic writers of the late nineteenth and twentieth centuries	*HISPANIC LITERATURE CRITICISM (HLC)* *HISPANIC LITERATURE CRITICISM SUPPLEMENT (HLCS)*
Native North American writers and orators of the eighteenth, nineteenth, and twentieth centuries	*NATIVE NORTH AMERICAN LITERATURE (NNAL)*
Major authors from the Renaissance to the present	*WORLD LITERATURE CRITICISM, 1500 TO THE PRESENT (WLC)* *WORLD LITERATURE CRITICISM SUPPLEMENT (WLCS)*

ISSN 1052-4851

Poetry Criticism

Excerpts from Criticism of the Works of the Most Significant and Widely Studied Poets of World Literature

Volume 100

Michelle Lee
Project Editor

GALE
CENGAGE Learning™

Detroit • New York • San Francisco • New Haven, Conn • Waterville, Maine • London

Poetry Criticism, Vol. 100

Project Editor: Michelle Lee

Editorial: Dana Barnes, Kathy D. Darrow, Kristen Dorsch, Jeffrey W. Hunter, Jelena O. Krstović, Thomas J. Schoenberg, Lawrence J. Trudeau

Content Conversion: Katrina D. Coach, Gwen Tucker

Indexing Services: Factiva, Inc.

Rights and Acquisitions: Margaret Chamberlain-Gaston, Kelly Quin, and Aja Perales

Composition and Electronic Capture: Gary Leach

Manufacturing: Rhonda Dover

Product Manager: Janet Witalec

For product information and technology assistance, contact us at
Gale Customer Support, 1-800-877-4253.
For permission to use material from this text or product,
submit all requests online at **www.cengage.com/permissions.**
Further permissions questions can be emailed to
permissionrequest@cengage.com

Gale
27500 Drake Rd.
Farmington Hills, MI, 48331-3535

LIBRARY OF CONGRESS CATALOG CARD NUMBER 81-640179

ISBN-13: 978-1-4144-4177-1
ISBN-10: 1-4144-4177-0

ISSN 1052-4851

Printed in the United States of America
1 2 3 4 5 6 7 13 12 11 10 09

Contents

Preface vii

Acknowledgments ix

Literary Criticism Series Advisory Board xi

Preface

*P*oetry Criticism (*PC*) presents significant criticism of the world's greatest poets and provides supplementary biographical and bibliographical material to guide the interested reader to a greater understanding of the genre and its creators. Although major poets and literary movements are covered in such Gale Literary Criticism series as *Contemporary Literary Criticism* (*CLC*), *Twentieth-Century Literary Criticism* (*TCLC*), *Nineteenth-Century Literature Criticism* (*NCLC*), *Literature Criticism from 1400 to 1800* (*LC*), and *Classical and Medieval Literature Criticism* (*CMLC*), *PC* offers more focused attention on poetry than is possible in the broader, survey-oriented entries on writers in these Gale series. Students, teachers, librarians, and researchers will find that the generous excerpts and supplementary material provided by *PC* supply them with the vital information needed to write a term paper on poetic technique, to examine a poet's most prominent themes, or to lead a poetry discussion group.

Scope of the Series

PC is designed to serve as an introduction to major poets of all eras and nationalities. Since these authors have inspired a great deal of relevant critical material, *PC* is necessarily selective, and the editors have chosen the most important published criticism to aid readers and students in their research. Each author entry presents a historical survey of the critical response to that author's work. The length of an entry is intended to reflect the amount of critical attention the author has received from critics writing in English and from foreign critics in translation. Every attempt has been made to identify and include the most significant essays on each author's work. In order to provide these important critical pieces, the editors sometimes reprint essays that have appeared elsewhere in Gale's Literary Criticism Series. Such duplication, however, never exceeds twenty percent of a *PC* volume.

Organization of the Book

Each *PC* entry consists of the following elements:

- The **Author Heading** cites the name under which the author most commonly wrote, followed by birth and death dates. Also located here are any name variations under which an author wrote, including transliterated forms for authors whose native languages use nonroman alphabets. If the author wrote consistently under a pseudonym, the pseudonym will be listed in the author heading and the author's actual name given in parenthesis on the first line of the biographical and critical introduction. Uncertain birth or death dates are indicated by question marks. Single-work entries are preceded by the title of the work and its date of publication.

- The **Introduction** contains background information that introduces the reader to the author and the critical debates surrounding his or her work.

- The list of **Principal Works** is ordered chronologically by date of first publication and lists the most important works by the author. The first section comprises poetry collections and book-length poems. The second section gives information on other major works by the author. For foreign authors, the editors have provided original foreign-language publication information and have selected what are considered the best and most complete English-language editions of their works.

- Reprinted **Criticism** is arranged chronologically in each entry to provide a useful perspective on changes in critical evaluation over time. All individual titles of poems and poetry collections by the author featured in the entry are printed in boldface type. The critic's name and the date of composition or publication of the critical work are given at the beginning of each piece of criticism. Unsigned criticism is preceded by the title of the source in which it appeared. Footnotes are reprinted at the end of each essay or excerpt. In the case of excerpted criticism, only those footnotes that pertain to the excerpted texts are included.

- Critical essays are prefaced by brief **Annotations** explicating each piece.

- A complete **Bibliographical Citation** of the original essay or book precedes each piece of criticism.

- An annotated bibliography of **Further Reading** appears at the end of each entry and suggests resources for additional study. In some cases, significant essays for which the editors could not obtain reprint rights are included here. Boxed material following the further reading list provides references to other biographical and critical sources on the author in series published by Gale.

Cumulative Indexes

A **Cumulative Author Index** lists all of the authors that appear in a wide variety of reference sources published by Gale, including *PC*. A complete list of these sources is found facing the first page of the Author Index. The index also includes birth and death dates and cross references between pseudonyms and actual names.

A **Cumulative Nationality Index** lists all authors featured in *PC* by nationality, followed by the number of the *PC* volume in which their entry appears.

A **Cumulative Title Index** lists in alphabetical order all individual poems, book-length poems, and collection titles contained in the *PC* series. Titles of poetry collections and separately published poems are printed in italics, while titles of individual poems are printed in roman type with quotation marks. Each title is followed by the author's last name and corresponding volume and page numbers where commentary on the work is located. English-language translations of original foreign-language titles are cross-referenced to the foreign titles so that all references to discussion of a work are combined in one listing.

Citing *Poetry Criticism*

When citing criticism reprinted in the Literary Criticism Series, students should provide complete bibliographic information so that the cited essay can be located in the original print or electronic source. Students who quote directly from reprinted criticism may use any accepted bibliographic format, such as University of Chicago Press style or Modern Language Association (MLA) style. Both the MLA and the University of Chicago formats are acceptable and recognized as being the current standards for citations. It is important, however, to choose one format for all citations; do not mix the two formats within a list of citations.

The examples below follow recommendations for preparing a bibliography set forth in *The Chicago Manual of Style,* 14th ed. (Chicago: The University of Chicago Press, 1993); the first example pertains to material drawn from periodicals, the second to material reprinted from books:

Linkin, Harriet Kramer. "The Language of Speakers in *Songs of Innocence and of Experience.*" *Romanticism Past and Present* 10, no. 2 (summer 1986): 5-24. Reprinted in *Poetry Criticism.* Vol. 63, edited by Michelle Lee, 79-88. Detroit: Thomson Gale, 2005.

Glen, Heather. "Blake's Criticism of Moral Thinking in *Songs of Innocence and of Experience.*" In *Interpreting Blake,* edited by Michael Phillips, 32-69. Cambridge: Cambridge University Press, 1978. Reprinted in *Poetry Criticism.* Vol. 63, edited by Michelle Lee, 34-51. Detroit: Thomson Gale, 2005.

Suggestions are Welcome

Readers who wish to suggest new features, topics, or authors to appear in future volumes, or who have other suggestions or comments are cordially invited to call, write, or fax the Associate Product Manager:

Product Manager, Literary Criticism Series
Gale
27500 Drake Road
Farmington Hills, MI 48331-3535
1-800-347-4253 (GALE)
Fax: 248-699-8054

Acknowledgments

The editors wish to thank the copyright holders of the criticism included in this volume and the permissions managers of many book and magazine publishing companies for assisting us in securing reproduction rights. Following is a list of the copyright holders who have granted us permission to reproduce material in this volume of *PC*. Every effort has been made to trace copyright, but if omissions have been made, please let us know.

COPYRIGHTED MATERIAL IN *PC*, VOLUME 100, WAS REPRODUCED FROM THE FOLLOWING PERIODICALS:

ANQ, v. 17, summer, 2004. Copyright © 2004 by the Helen Dwight Reid Educational Foundation. Reproduced with permission of the Helen Dwight Reid Educational Foundation, published by Heldref Publications, 1319 18th Street, NW, Washington, DC 20036-1802.—*Charles Lamb Bulletin,* October, 1995 for "The Ancient Mariner Controversy" by Seamus Perry. Copyright © 1995 by the Charles Lamb Society and the contributors. All rights reserved. Reproduced by permission of the author.—*Chicago Review,* v. 53, spring, 2007. Copyright © 2007 by the *Chicago Review*. Reproduced by permission.—*Dalhousie Review,* v. 69, fall, 1989 for "Sydney Dobell: Sunk without Trace" by Martha Westwater. Reproduced by permission of the publisher and the author.—*ELH,* v. 65, 1998. Copyright © 1998 by the Johns Hopkins University Press. Reproduced by permission.—*Explicator,* v. 63, fall, 2004; v. 65, fall, 2006; v. 65, summer, 2007. Copyright © 2004, 2006, 2007 by the Helen Dwight Reid Educational Foundation. All reproduced with permission of the Helen Dwight Reid Educational Foundation, published by Heldref Publications, 1319 18th Street, NW, Washington, DC 20036-1802.—*Kenyon Review,* v. 24, winter, 2002 for "Beowulf and 'Heaneywulf'" by Howell Chickering. Reproduced by permission of the author.—*New Hibernia Review,* v. 9, summer, 2005 for "Making a Dantean Poetic: Seamus Heaney's 'Ugolino'" by Joseph Heininger; v. 11, summer, 2007 for "From Winter Seeds to Wintering Out: The Evolution of Heaney's Third Collection" by Michael Parker; v. 12, spring, 2008 for "Violence and Silence in Seamus Heaney's 'Mycenae Lookout'" by Elizabeth Lunday. Copyright © 2005, 2007, 2008 by the University of St. Thomas. All rights reserved. All reproduced by permission of the publisher and the respective authors.—*Papers on Language and Literature,* v. 37, spring, 2001. Copyright © 2001 by the Board of Trustees, Southern Illinois University at Edwardsville. Reproduced by permission.—*Parnassus: Poetry in Review,* v. 26, 2002 for "Steady under Strain and Strong through Tension" by Dennis O'Driscoll. Copyright © 2002 by the Poetry in Review Foundation, NY. Reproduced by permission of the publisher and the author.—*Philological Quarterly,* v. 70, spring, 1991. Copyright © 1991 by the University of Iowa. Reproduced by permission.—*Philosophy and Literature,* v. 26, 2002. Copyright © 2002 by the Johns Hopkins University Press. Reproduced by permission.—*Southern Review,* v. 38, spring, 2002 for "Heaney at Play" by Don Johnson. Reproduced by permission of the author.—*Southwest Review,* v. 92, 2007. Copyright © 2007 by Southern Methodist University. All rights reserved. Reproduced by permission.—*Studies in English Literature, 1500-1900,* v. 38, autumn, 1998. Copyright © 1998 by William Marsh Rice University. Reproduced by permission.—*Studies in Philology,* v. 86, winter, 1989. Copyright © 1989 by the University of North Carolina Press. Used by permission.—*Studies in Romanticism,* v. 43, fall, 2004. Copyright © 2004 by the Trustees of Boston University. Reproduced by permission.—*Twentieth-Century Literature,* v. 51, fall, 2005; v. 54, spring, 2008. Copyright © 2005, 2008 by Hofstra University Press. Both reproduced by permission.—*Victorian Poetry,* v. 42, winter, 2004 for "Rhythmic Numinousness: Sydney Dobell and 'The Church,'" by Emma Mason; v. 42, winter, 2004 for "Rhythmic Intimacy, Spasmodic Epistemology" by Jason R. Rudy. Copyright © 2004 by West Virginia University. Reproduced by permission of the authors.—*Wordsworth Circle,* v. 30, spring, 1999. Copyright © 1999 by Marilyn Gaull. Reproduced by permission of the editor.—*Yearbook of English Studies,* v. 35, 2005. Copyright © 2005 by Modern Humanities Research Association. Reproduced by permission of the publisher.

COPYRIGHTED MATERIAL IN *PC*, VOLUME 100, WAS REPRODUCED FROM THE FOLLOWING BOOKS:

Armstrong, Charles I. From "Touch and Go: Seamus Heaney and the Transcendence of the Aesthetic," in *The Body and Desire in Contemporary Irish Poetry.* Edited by Irene Gilsenan Nordin. Irish Academic Press, 2006. Copyright © by this edition Irish Academic Press, for chapter, individual contributor, 2006. Reproduced by permission.—Engell, James. From "Coleridge (and His Mariner) on the Soul: 'As an exile in a Far Distant Land,'" in *The Fountain Light: Studies in Romanticism and Religion.* Edited by J. Robert Barth, S. J. Fordham University Press, 2002. Copyright © 2002 by

Gale Literature Product Advisory Board

The Rime of the Ancient Mariner

Samuel Taylor Coleridge

Poem, first published in *Lyrical Ballads* in 1798.

INTRODUCTION

Considered one of Coleridge's three major works of imaginative poetry—along with *Kubla Khan* and *Christabel*—*The Rime of the Ancient Mariner* tells of the fantastic and hellish torments experienced by a seaman after he shoots an albatross. Written in ballad form, the poem is comprised of seven parts and takes the form of a dramatic monologue, as the elderly Mariner relates his haunting tale to a spellbound Wedding Guest. Many scholars believe that the poem reveals the poet's fascination with the imaginative capabilities of the mind, pointing to the preponderance of supernatural elements in the poem, including the presence of cherubic and saintly spirits along with demonic beings and extraordinary occurrences. Christian overtones pervade the poem as well, as the Mariner's experiences are typically viewed as a journey of the soul as he undergoes a form of penance in reparation for his sin.

BIOGRAPHICAL INFORMATION

Born in October of 1772 in Ottery St. Mary, Devonshire, Coleridge was the youngest of ten children born to Ann Bowdon and the Reverend John Coleridge, a minister of the Church of England and head master of the local school. When his father died in 1781, Coleridge was sent to Christ's Hospital, a London boarding school. There he distinguished himself academically, earning a scholarship in 1791 to Jesus College, Cambridge; however, he attended the university for a very short time and left without earning a degree. Deeply in debt, he joined the Light Dragoons under an assumed name; when his identity was discovered, his friends and family secured his discharge. He returned to Cambridge but left again in 1795. That same year, Coleridge married Sara Fricker, and a year later the couple moved to the Lake District. His close friends included Charles Lamb, Robert Southey, and William Wordsworth, with whom he collaborated on the 1798 collection *Lyrical Ballads*, containing Coleridge's *The Rime of the Ancient Mariner*. The poet's success was marred by his unhappy marriage and increasing dependence on opium, which he had been taking for years to treat a variety of ailments. By 1806 he had developed a full-blown addiction to opium and alcohol and had virtually abandoned poetry, although he wrote an occasional short lyric. A few years later, in 1810, he suffered a devastating and acrimonious break with Wordsworth, due in part to Coleridge's erratic behavior caused by his drug and alcohol use. Isolated and suffering financially, he relied on his skill as a powerful and gifted speaker, giving lectures throughout London on matters involving philosophy, literature, and textual analysis. By 1828, he had reconciled with both his wife and Wordsworth and was again writing. Coleridge died on July 25, 1834, due to complications from his opium dependency.

PLOT AND MAJOR CHARACTERS

In *The Rime of the Ancient Mariner*, Coleridge employed the first-person voice of the elderly Mariner to recount the supernatural experiences he had endured at sea many years earlier. Part 1 opens as the Mariner detains a Wedding Guest on his way to the ceremony and compels him to listen to his "ghastly tale." According to the Mariner, his ship and its crew of two hundred men were sailing south from England toward the Equator when violent storms forced the ship farther south into the Antarctic. The ship becomes stuck in the ice and the sailors, having seen no signs of life, welcome the appearance of an Albatross. Since its arrival brings the breakup of the ice and a return of the breeze, the sailors believe the bird has brought them luck and feed it as it trails the ship. However, the Mariner, suddenly and without explanation, kills the Albatross with his crossbow. Part 2 opens as the ship is traveling north, toward the equator. Though the men initially condemn the Mariner's act, when the fog is erased by the sun, they decide his actions were just after all. Abruptly, however, the wind dies and the ship becomes motionless. Suffering from dehydration, some sailors suspect that the ship has been followed by the Polar Spirit, seeking to avenge the senseless death of the Albatross. The seamen curse the Mariner and replace the cross around his neck with the dead Albatross. By Part 3, all the seamen are in agony and tormented with thirst when the Mariner spies an approaching ship, one that moves despite the lack of wind. Their initial joy turns to horror when they realize it appears to be the skeleton of a ship, with only two figures on board: Life-in-Death and her partner, Death, playing a dice game, which Life-in-Death wins. Death subsequently takes the lives of all two hundred sailors, leaving the Mariner to Life-in-Death.

In Part 4, the Mariner laments being alone at sea with two hundred dead bodies heaped around, all seeming to stare at the Mariner. After seven days of this torment, the Mariner expresses joy at the beauty of the water-snakes—which he had previously despised as "slimy things"—surrounding the motionless ship. He is immediately set free by the love that permeates his soul, and the dead bird drops from his neck into the water. In Part 5, the Mariner believes he is under the shelter of a saintly presence granting him rest and refreshing rain. Soon thereafter, the winds begin to roar, lightning and black storm clouds appear, and the dead men's bodies rise up, and begin to man the ship which is propelled from beneath the sea by the Polar Spirit. In Part 6 the Mariner enters a trance as the ship crosses the ocean at high speeds. When he awakens, he sees his home harbor in the distance. The dead bodies now lay strewn on the deck of the ship, each with an angelic being standing over him. The Mariner sees an approaching boat containing three occupants, one of them a Hermit whom the Mariner hopes will hear his confession and absolve him from his sin. In Part 7 the approaching boat nears as a mighty sound emanates from the sea, sinking the ship. The Mariner is saved by the passengers of the boat and when they reach land, the Mariner begs the Hermit to hear his confession. The Mariner tells his story and is free, but from then on is compelled to wander, telling and retelling his saga of despair and loneliness, recounting a time when he could hardly believe there was a God and averring that "He prayeth well, who loveth well / Both man and bird and beast."

MAJOR THEMES

Many scholars see in *The Rime of the Ancient Mariner* an emphasis on the Christian doctrines of penance and suffering, relating both to the sin of the individual and to the communal sin of mankind, in particular as this collective sin relates to the notions of Original Sin and the Fall of Man. In fact, the voyage of the Mariner is often viewed as the shared journey of Man, with the poem dramatizing mankind's fall into sin, the judgment and purgation of the soul, and the mercy of God's plan of salvation. Another theme is the notion of the wanderer; according to some scholars, Coleridge modeled the Mariner on the idea of the fugitive or outcast, one who exists outside the community of the living. They point to possible sources, including the medieval legend of the Wandering Jew, who, for doubting Jesus' divinity and mocking him on his way to his crucifixion,

is cursed by having to traverse the earth in perpetuity until the Second Coming. The idea that the recognition of beauty and love leads to the ability to pray is seen as a motif as well, with some critics maintaining that the capacity to pray, and the subsequent power of that prayer, is elevated in the poem above reason. Looking at issues contemporary to Coleridge's time, some historians believe that the poem centers on colonialism and slavery, representing the poet's commentary on the horrors and atrocities linked with these activities. Among the numerous other themes identified by scholars are an admonition against relying on superstition, a reliance bordering on idolatry and resulting in horror and death; obsessive guilt; despair; eternal hope versus rejection and abandonment by God; the power and beauty of nature; remorse and responsibility; and the intrusion and intervention of supernatural beings and forces, both good and evil.

CRITICAL RECEPTION

A central discussion in scholarship on *The Rime of the Ancient Mariner* revolves around its theology, sometimes viewed as a conflict between Unitarianism and Trinitarian Christianity. Coleridge's biographers note that the poet firmly embraced Unitarianism during the time he was writing the poem, and some critics find this religious allegiance reflected in the work's emphasis on the love and appreciation of the natural world, in keeping with the Unitarian belief in the idea of God-in-nature. Reflected in the poem as well is Coleridge's adherence to the theory of Necessity, in which divine providence is coupled with a belief in the natural order of the universe and the freedom of the human will. This freedom of will is represented, critics claim, by the Mariner's vicious act, which is seen as an aberration in a pure, good soul but an act that nevertheless divides the Mariner from God. Conversely, many others see the poem as Christian in its understanding of the idea of redemptive suffering and the saving grace of God, enacted through the crucifixion. In addition, some scholars speculate that the poem is modeled after Dante Alighieri's *Inferno*, drawing parallels between the two works, both of which emphasize a spiritual pilgrimage, the incorporation of a spiritual guide, judgment, the intercession of saints or supernatural beings, and rebirth.

Opposed to this line of critical analysis is the notion that the work contains no moral foundation and is purely a work of the poet's imagination. Critics espousing this view see in the irrational and miraculous events no defense of any moral law and, in fact, perceive in the arbitrary slaying of the Albatross solid evidence that moral laws are nonexistent. An additional area of study is the instability of the text, a consequence of the countless revisions Coleridge made—around one hundred versions according to many critics. Versions published during Coleridge's lifetime appeared in 1798, 1800, and 1817, with the 1817 version—the most widely cited in scholarly studies—containing the most significant revisions, including an increased emphasis on Coleridge's religious concerns. In other examinations of the poem scholars speak of the work as an incomplete epic and maintain that its lofty, grandiose poetry about the journey of a hero fails as an epic because the voice of the sailor cannot fully comprehend the magnitude of events. Critics find its conclusion unsatisfactory, claiming that the Mariner is left in pain and forced to continually retell his story. Moreover, several commentators argue that there is no sense that the Mariner reaches a spiritual understanding or achieves redemption.

While some scholars continue to debate whether or not the poem's ending is ambiguous, others focus on the political and historical backdrop to the poem, particularly in light of Coleridge's social activism. Interested in political, public, and religious affairs throughout his professional life, Coleridge was fervently opposed to slavery and other human subjugation, including that brought about by colonial domination. Many see the Mariner as emblematic of Europe's participation in the slave trade and view the slaying of the Albatross as the enslavement of the indigenous Caribbean people. Believing that in the poem Coleridge equated human subjugation with disease, they also maintain that the torment of the sailors mark them as being afflicted with yellow fever, a devastating and horrific disease common to white slave traders, seamen, soldiers, and visitors who traveled to the Caribbean during the late 1700s and into the early 1800s.

PRINCIPAL WORKS

Poetry

Poems on Various Subjects [with Charles Lamb and Robert Southey] 1796; revised and enlarged as *Poems* [with Lamb and Charles Lloyd] 1797; revised 1803

Ode on the Departing Year 1797

Fears in Solitude, Written in 1798 during the alarm of an invasion. To Which Are Added, France, an Ode; and Frost at Midnight 1798

*Lyrical Ballads, with a Few Other Poems [anonymous; with William Wordsworth] 1798; revised and enlarged edition, 2 vols. 1800; second revised edition, 1802

Dejection: An Ode 1802

Christabel; Kubla Khan, a Vision; The Pains of Sleep 1816

Sibylline Leaves: A Collection of Poems 1817; republished in part as *Selections from the Sibylline Leaves of S. T. Coleridge* 1827

The Poetical Works of Samuel Taylor Coleridge Including the Dramas of Wallenstein, Remorse, and Zapolya. 3 vols. (poetry and plays) 1828; revised edition, 1829

The Poetical Works of S. T. Coleridge 1835

The Literary Remains in Prose and Verse of Samuel Taylor Coleridge. 4 vols. (poetry, plays, and essays) 1836-39

The Complete Works of Samuel Taylor Coleridge. 7 vols. (poetry, plays, essays, and translations) 1853

The Complete Poetical Works of Samuel Taylor Coleridge. 2 vols. 1912

The Poems of Samuel Taylor Coleridge: Including Poems and Versions of Poems Herein Published for the First Time, Edited with Textual and Bibliographical Notes by Ernest Hartley Coleridge 1961

Poems 1963

The Collected Works of Samuel Taylor Coleridge. 16 vols. (poetry, plays, lectures, translations, essays, sermons, criticism, and other prose) 1969-2002

Coleridge's Verse: A Selection 1972

Poetical Works. 3 vols. 2001

Other Major Works

The Fall of Robespierre. An Historic Drama [with Robert Southey] (play) 1794

Osorio (play) 1797; revised as *Remorse, A Tragedy, in Five Acts* 1813

Wallenstein (translation; from the plays *Die piccolomini* and *Wallensteins Tod* by Johann Christoph Friedrich von Schiller) 1800

The Friend: A Literary, Moral, and Political Weekly Paper, Excluding Personal and Party Politics, and the Events of the Day 27 parts, plus one supernumerary (newspaper) 1809-10; republished as *The Friend: A Series of Essays* 1812; revised and enlarged as *The Friend: A Series of Essays, In Three Volumes, To Aid in the Formation of Fixed Principles in Politics, Morals, and Religion, with Literary Amusements Interspersed* 1818

The Statesman's Manual; or, The Bible the Best Guide to Political Skill and Foresight: A Lay Sermon, Addressed to the Higher Classes of Society, With an Appendix, Containing Comments and Essays Connected with the Study of the Inspired Writings (essay) 1816

Biographia Literaria; or, Biographical Sketches of My Literary Life and Opinions. 2 vols. (essays) 1817

Zapolya: A Christmas Tale, in Two Parts (play) 1817

Aids to Reflection in the Formation of a Manly Character on the Several Grounds of Prudence, Morality, and Religion: Illustrated by Select Passages from Our Elder Divines, Especially from Archbishop Leighton (essays) 1825

On the Constitution of Church and State, according to the Idea of Each: with Aids toward a Right Judgment on the Late Catholic Bill (essay) 1830; revised edition, 1830

Specimens of the Table Talk of the Late Samuel Taylor Coleridge. 2 vols. (conversations) 1835

Confessions of an Inquiring Spirit (essays and other prose) 1840

Hints towards the Formation of a more Comprehensive Theory of Life (essay) 1848

Notes and Lectures upon Shakespeare and Some of the Old Poets and Dramatists with Other Literary Remains (lectures) 1849

Essays on His Own Times; forming a second series of "The Friend." 3 vols. 1850

Seven Lectures upon Shakespeare and Milton (lectures) 1856

The Letters of Samuel Taylor Coleridge. 2 vols. (letters) 1895

Unpublished Letters of Samuel Taylor Coleridge. 2 vols. (letters) 1932

The Philosophical Lectures of Samuel Taylor Coleridge (lectures) 1949

Collected Letters of Samuel Taylor Coleridge. 6 vols. (letters) 1956-71

The Notebooks of Samuel Taylor Coleridge. 6 vols. to date (notebooks) 1957-

Coleridge on Shakespeare: The Text of the Lectures of 1811-12 (lectures) 1971

Samuel Taylor Coleridge: Selected Letters (letters) 1987

*Lyrical Ballads, a collaboration between Coleridge and Wordsworth, was published anonymously in 1798; the identities of the authors were not revealed until the 1800 edition. The collection was revised and enlarged in both 1800 and 1802. The Rime of the Ancient Mariner is the first poem in the 1798 edition.

CRITICISM

Dorothy Bilik (essay date winter 1989)

SOURCE: Bilik, Dorothy. "Josephus, Mosollamus, and the Ancient Mariner." *Studies in Philology* 86, no. 1 (winter 1989): 87-95.

[*In the following essay, Bilik locates a possible source for the figure of the Mariner in the ancient cavalryman and marksman Mosollamus whose bold act of killing a bird believed to possess divine powers was recorded by first-century Jewish historian Josephus.*]

John Livingston Lowes unearthed the sources that fed Coleridge's imagination and thus illuminated Coleridge's poetry. Lowes' method, in part, is to raise rhetorical questions concerning the cruces in the poem and to answer the questions qualifiedly in a fluid, wide-ranging, associative style like Coleridge's own. In discussing the gloss to **The Rime of the Ancient Mariner,** Lowes asks, "But what is the learned Jew, Josephus, doing in that galley?" Josephus (c. C.E. 37-100), unlike the Neoplatonist Michael Psellus with whom he is coupled, is not an authority on demonology.[1] However, Lowes points out that Josephus and others wrote about Cain; and Cain, together with the Wandering Jew, combined with Wordsworth's suggestions and other influences, culminated, because of Coleridgean magic, in the haunting figure of the ancient Mariner.[2] Coleridge's notebook entries for 1796 include excerpts, in Greek, from Josephus' *Antiquities*; in an 1802 entry Coleridge refers to Josephus' *The Jewish Wars*.[3]

It would be reasonable to assume that Coleridge was reading *Against Apion* along with Josephus' other works. There is a direct mention of *Against Apion* in an 1815 letter to William Lisle Bowles which suggests Coleridge's familiarity with the work:

> Besides it is supposed that before his controversy with Apion Josephus had forsaken the Pharisaic, and passed over to the Patrician, Party. Yet in this work are the strongest evidences to be found of the whole Canon of the O.T. as we now have it: as all alike inspired by God himself.[4]

Whether Coleridge read all Josephus' works in Greek or used William Whiston's English translation which first appeared in 1737, he appears to have regarded Josephus with respect. But respect for Josephus as historian or even as occasional demonologist does not fully account for the presence of "the learned Jew" in **The Rime of the Ancient Mariner.** Indeed, Josephus' importance to the **Rime** may be in his relation to a question raised by the poem itself and asked by many of its critics: Why did the Mariner shoot the Albatross?[5]

Given Coleridge's poetic world, perhaps the question should remain unanswerable, at least in terms of ascribing a motive to the Mariner. Nevertheless, a clear analogue for the slaying of the Albatross is found in *Against Apion*. Josephus cites a Greek historian, Hecataeus of Abdera (4th century B.C.E.), who allegedly witnessed the following incident while on the march with Alexander the Great. During a march to the Red Sea there was, among an escort of Jewish cavalry, a robust, intelligent man, one Mosollamus, who was considered by all the best bowman. Mosollamus noted that the force was halted and discovered that a seer was watching a bird in order to determine what the army should do next. The seer told Mosollamus that if the bird stood still, they ought all to stand still; that if the bird flew onward, they ought all to move forward; that if the bird flew backward, they ought all to retreat.

> The Jew, without saying a word, drew this bow, shot and struck the bird and killed it. The seer and some others were indignant, and heaped curses upon him.

'Why so mad, you poor wretches' he retorted; and then, taking the bird in his hands, continued, 'Pray, how could any sound information about our march be given by this creature, which could not provide for its own safety? Had it been gifted with divination, it would not have come to this spot, for fear of being killed by an arrow of Mosollamus the Jew.'[6]

Despite obvious differences in tone and form, there are striking parallels between Hecataeus' anecdote and the rime. For, while the Greek tale may be characterized as a comic and didactic analogue of the Mariner's rime, the issues confronting both protagonists are strangely similar.

What primarily differentiates Mosollamus from Coleridge's Mariner is the former's complete control of events and awareness of his actions. What overwhelmingly characterizes the Mariner is his unawareness. He appears to be unaware when he shoots the Albatross. He is unaware (as he says twice) when he performs the blessing that is to free him (IV. 285-7).[7] Mosollamus is ever aware and alert and secure in his faith. His tale is no paradigm for original sin as Robert Penn Warren sees Coleridge's poem;[8] nor does it contain the neurotic guilt which William Empson posits as part of the Mariner's burden.[9] Mosollamus is quite proud of his action. He has a motive and message. His jealous God has commanded him: Thou shalt have no other Gods before me. (Ex:20:3) This is the first commandment and all the evidence in Leviticus and Deuteronomy points to its overwhelming importance. Admonitions against signs, portents, oracles, auguries, wizards, necromancers and such abound in the Pentateuch. Such heathen practices lead to the greatest danger—idolatry—the worship of gods other than Jehovah. Mosollamus has practical reasons for his deed; the seer and the auguries are holding up the war. So Mosollamus kills two birds with one arrow, thereby ridding the army of a roadblock and teaching the pagans a Jewish lesson.[10]

As an ex-cavalryman himself, albeit one who could not stay on a horse, Coleridge would have found the stalwart Jew appealing. Mosollamus was sure of himself, sure of his ability as a marksman and sure of his God. The army undoubtedly soon marched again and most likely was victorious. In such a context the killing of the bird is hardly a moral question.

Yet no matter how much the poem and the tale differ in tone and characterization, there are telling similarities in action and theme. Most striking is the attitude of the "others" toward the bird. The seer and his fellow Greeks believe the bird's actions are portentous, and that by following the bird a correct decision can be made in relation to the forthcoming battle. In the eyes of the Mariner's companions the arrival of the Albatross is related to the breaking up of the ice. As the glosser tells us, "the Albatross proveth a bird of good omen" (I. 70-

5). As the rest of the poem graphically demonstrates, the bird "proveth" nothing of the kind. In the dream/nightmare world of the rime, chance operates with customary neutrality. Two hundred men are killed seemingly to avenge the death of the Albatross while the bird-killer is "saved" from death to serve a "death-in-life" sentence because of a roll of the dice. The Mariner dreams that the reason for vengeance is that the particular bird happens to be the favorite of a peculiar Polar Spirit. It cannot be assumed that the bird, though friendly, was a good omen. In Coleridge's poetic world the laws of cause and effect are frequently suspended in order to allow for poetic impact. Like the soldiers in Hecataeus' tale, the mariners and the glosser appear to be incorrect about bird prophecy. In poetic fact, the mariners are punished just because they are superstitious about the bird.

The poem records no immediate reaction to the slaying of the Albatross. Coleridge gives the impression of time passing (II. 82-90). The mariners, literal fair weather friends, change their minds about the bird and the deed when the wind blows or the fog appears. They leap to simplistic cause-effect conclusions.

> For all averred, I had killed the bird
> That made the breeze to blow.
> Ah wretch! said they, the bird to slay,
> That made the breeze to blow!

> (II. 93-6)

After the wind shifts,

> Then all averred, I had killed the bird
> That brought the fog and mist
> 'Twas right, said they, such birds to slay
> That bring the fog and mist.

> (II. 99-102)

The almost sing-song repetition, the twinned diction, the internal rhyme and the heavy use of monosyllables contribute to an effect of nursery rhyme simplicity and superficiality. The childish solipsism of the mariners' response is made manifest in their callous opportunism which has no concern for the bird except as it might affect them.

The mariners are described by the glosser as "accomplices in the crime" because of their perfidy. But the crime involved is more serious than opportunism, at least according to the Pentateuch. Like the soldiers in the earlier tale, the mariners stand accused of anthropomorphism and idolatry. The Albatross was hailed "as if it had been a Christian soul" (I. 65), and it is fed human food. What the mariners admire about the Albatross are what they consider to be its human qualities, with all the condescension involved in the relationship of an owner to a pet. They domesticate the wild, innocent creature. Then they anthropomorphically ascribe religious motives to the presence of the bird. Even for the pious glosser the Albatross becomes "the pious bird of good omen" which, in traditional religious terms, is idolatrous.

Paradoxically, the "fair breeze" which the mariners now childishly attribute to the *death* of the Albatross (II. 103) enables the company to perform the Promethean action of being "the first that ever burst / Into that silent sea" (II. 105-6). Even here the internal rhyme combines solipsism with the pride of discovery. The hubris of being "first," usually a mixed curse, is related to the egocentricity of the attitude toward the Albatross.

The mariners do not punish the Ancient Mariner for his action until well after the killing of the bird and the entry into the silent sea. Only after natural calamities dog their ship do they elect the Mariner scapegoat. In their primitive, simplistic and superstitious action they are attempting to absolve themselves and thereby pacify the various deities they feel they have offended. Ironically, instead of sacrificing the Mariner to appease a group of angry deities, they are themselves sacrificed.

"Even the worship of one God becomes idolatry in my convictions," says Coleridge, "when instead of the Eternal & Omnipresent, in whom we live and move, and *have* our Being, we set up a distinct Jehovah tricked out in the *anthropomorphic* Attributes of Time & *Successive* Thoughts—& think of him, as a PERSON *from* whom we *had* our Being. The tendency to *Idolatry* seems to me to lie at the root of all our human Vices—it is our Original Sin."[11]

William Marshall looks at ***The Rime of the Ancient Mariner*** in relation to these comments.

> For a few years following the composition of the poem Coleridge still regarded anthropomorphism or any notion of a personal deity as a form of idolatry. . . . By *anthropomorphism* Coleridge appears to have meant *animism* as well. Actually they are similar in that each confuses levels of being: in anthropomorphism one moves downward from the idea of God to the image of man, and in animism one moves upward from the sensation of object to the image of animal or (in personification) of man.[12]

Marshall also cites a frequently omitted section of Coleridge's famous comments to Mrs. Barbauld. Coleridge demurs when Mrs. Barbauld finds no moral in the ***Rime,*** "the only fault in the poem is that there is *too much*. In a work of such pure imagination I ought not to have stopped to give reasons for things, or inculcate [sic] humanity to beasts."[13]

The need "to give reasons for things" is the Mariner's rather than Coleridge's. Marshall stresses the irony of the simple, primitive Mariner's understanding of his

experience and its distinct difference from Coleridge's. Robert Penn Warren's important essay does not concern itself with irony but it does point out the relation between Coleridge's thoughts on idolatry and the action of the poem. Warren describes the Mariner's deed as a crime against Nature and hence against God. Warren cites Coleridge's observations on Man's "Satanic pride and rebellious self-idolatry [which] . . . by the fearful resolve to find in itself alone the one absolute motive of action" characterizes those whom Coleridge cites as "the mighty hunters of mankind, from Nimrod to Bonaparte."[14]

Coleridge's mention of Nimrod in this context brings Josephus, idolatry and the ***Rime*** together once more. For the 1796 notebook entries from Josephus indicate that Coleridge was reading about Nimrod who was perhaps the first Biblical embodiment of the secularization of power. The sons of Noah, according to Josephus, were incited by Nimrod to believe that they alone were responsible for their happiness and plenty. Nimrod wanted to turn men away from the fear of God and to bring them into his power.[15]

Not unlike Warren, M. H. Abrams associates the slaying of the Albatross with "the Mariner's prideful self-sufficiency, his readiness to cut himself off from the universal community of life and love."[16] In a sense the Mariner's "god-like" act enables the ship and its crew to perform the Promethean action of discovering the Pacific. The Mariner says proudly "we were the first." Coleridge's characterization of idolatry as "Original Sin" and "Satanic" may influence him toward a negative view of the discovery. That characteristically Coleridgean fear and ambivalence toward creativity that is manifested in ***Kubla Khan*** may also be manifested here. In contrast to Mosollamus' iconoclasm, neither "god-like" action (neither slaying nor discovery) is done in God's name. Jehovah is the jealous God when man dares to usurp God-like functions, and the Hebraic context of the poem has been noted by many.

Frederick Pottle notes that the rime "is not unlike a story from the Old Testament recording the exceeding fierce wrath of the Lord; for example, how He smote the men of Bethshemesh because, through no malice at all, they had looked into the ark."[17] And Edward Botstetter says in reference to the throw of the dice determining life and death: "The Moral conception here is primitive and savage—utterly arbitrary in its ruthlessness . . . it is the Old Testament morality of the avenging Jehovah."[18] But what is being avenged? In the dream, the typically Coleridgean evasion, the Mariner "learns" that the death of the Albatross is being avenged by the Polar Spirit—hardly a surrogate for Jehovah. The Mariner needs reasons; for Coleridge to ascribe such "reasons" to God would be idolatrous. And it is idolatry, in its animistic and anthropomorphic forms and in its manifestation as human hubris, that is being avenged in the poem. Arbitrary boundaries have been transgressed but they have not been recognized as boundaries until after they have been violated.

Paradoxically, despite the "evil" of the Mariner's deed there is something in it of *felix culpa,* a fortunate fall which gives him more wisdom than his companions who die unshrieved and in ignorance. The Mariner does not attribute magic powers of weather control to the Albatross. Although he does say "As if it had been a Christian soul, / We hailed it in God's name" he does not appear to participate in the domesticating of the bird. "It ate the food it ne'er had eat" (II. 67) replaced the earlier version "The Mariners gave it biscuit worms." The Mariner seems isolated from his companions even before the action. Perversely, although he kills the Albatross, he does not attempt to exploit the bird for human purposes. The mariner may not necessarily be an unwitting instrument of Jehovah's wrath but he is moving, albeit with some loss, from paganism to piety.

Within the Hebraic tradition, man and nature are differentiated. Nature within the poem, with its ice storms, deadly calms, and treacherous winds, is neither benign nor subservient to man. These natural phenomena take place in the transgression areas where man does not usually venture. The "Hermit good" who represents a kind of norm in the poem, is specifically depicted as living in harmony with nature, in the wood with moss as his cushion. When the ear-splitting sounds "split the bay," when the terrifying figure of the Mariner emerges from the strangely sinking ship, the Pilot falls into a fit, the Pilot's boy "doth crazy go"—but the Hermit prays. The Hermit has already described the natural universe where he is at home where "the owlet whoops to the wolf below / That eats the she-wolf's young" (VII.536-7). The Hermit neither condemns nor approves. All of nature is accepted for what it is.

> He prayeth well who loveth well
> Both man and bird and beast.
> He prayeth best, who loveth best
> All things both great and small
> For the dear God who loveth us,
> He made and loveth all.

The Mariner's "moral" presents a God who does not appear in the Mariner's universe as experienced within the poem. He persists in creating God in his own image and may thus still be idolatrous. However, he is now passive rather than active, humble rather than proud, accepting rather than questioning. Within the world of the poem, the love that he expresses at its end is arbitrary like his "crime." After the violence and the terror, the Mariner's sense of his experience is inadequate and anticlimactic. Such is the perception of a simple, primitive and frightened man in need of explanation.

The Mariner's simplicity and need for a moral contribute to the wedding guest's wisdom and sorrow. The Mariner, no wise man, taught better than he knew. The more fortunate reader experiences the extraordinary power of the poem that transcends its sources, analyses and even its deconstruction.

To the distinguished company which includes Cain and other diverse wanderers, the Old Navigator and other sailors, Nimrod and other hunters may be added the cavalryman-archer Mosollamus who, transformed by Coleridge's shaping powers of imagination, adds a paradoxically orthodox yet outrageous quality that represents a similar paradox in Josephus, the Ancient Mariner, and, most important, in his creator.[19]

Notes

1. *The Road to Xanadu: A Study in the Ways of the Imagination* (1927; rpt. Boston: Houghton Mifflin, 1955), 216-17. However, a few scholars interpret some comments made by Josephus in *Antiquities* 18:1, 3 and *Jewish Wars* 2:8 as referring to *gilgul*—transmigration of souls and not resurrection. Given Coleridge's "cormorant's reading and tenacious and systematizing memory" (Lowes, 39) the possibility exists that Coleridge may have known of this. The phrase "tenacious and systematizing memory" is Coleridge's own and Lowes quotes it often.

2. Lowes, Ch. xiv, "How an Old Navigator Met Strange Company in Limbo," 220-338. According to his note on "We Are Seven," Wordsworth made a number of suggestions about *The Ancient Mariner,* among them that the mariner kill the bird.

3. *The Notebooks of Samuel Taylor Coleridge,* ed., Kathleen Coburn, Bollingen Series L., Vol. 1, 1794-1804 (New York: Pantheon Books, 1957), entries 277; 279; 280; 851.

4. *Collected Letters of Samuel Taylor Coleridge,* ed. Earl Leslie Griggs (Oxford: Clarendon Press, 1959), Vol. 4, 166.

5. Lowes, 277, discusses the importance of "the very triviality of the act." A. M. Buchan calls the act "a miracle of evil. If such an act can occur, sanity is threatened and the moral law disappears." "The Sad Wisdom of the Mariner," *SP* [*Studies in Philology*], 61 (1964): 673. Robert Penn Warren finds the question itself too literal, "A Poem of Pure Imagination: An Experiment in Reading," in *The Rime of the Ancient Mariner* by Samuel Taylor Coleridge, illus. Alexander Calder (New York: Reynal and Hitchcock, 1946), 78.

6. Josephus, *Against Apion,* trans. H. St. John Thackerary; Loeb Classical Library (Cambridge: Harvard University Press, 1961), 244-7.

7. All citations from *The Rime of the Ancient Mariner* are from *The Poems of Samuel Taylor Coleridge,* ed. Ernest Hartley Coleridge (Oxford: Clarendon Press, 1912), Vol. I, 187-209; Vol. II, 1030-40.

8. Warren, 80-5.

9. *Coleridge's Verse: A Selection,* eds. William Empson and David Pirie (New York: Schocken Books, 1972). Mr. Empson's Introduction and Appendix (27-100) are largely concerned with his basic view that "the poem is therefore about Neurotic Guilt; it is the first major study of that condition, recognized as such" (39).

10. The Mosollamus story is a typical example of what probably was the only early "Jewish joke." Rabbi Nachman warns that "all scoffing is forbidden except scoffing at idols which is permitted." *The Babylonian Talmud,* Sanhedrin, ed. Isador Epstein, trans. H. Freedman (London: Soncino 1935), I, 63. A well-known Talmudic tale is equally iconoclastic. Abraham as a young boy smashes every one of his father's idols except one, in whose hands he places a stick. When the father asks who did the idol smashing Abraham says it was the idol with the stick in his hands. The father says "But these gods can't do anything!" And Abraham says "Let your ears hear what your mouth is saying."

11. Letter to John Prior Estlin, 7 December 1802, Griggs, Vol. 2, 893. Italics are Coleridge's.

12. "Coleridge, The Mariner, and Dramatic Irony." *Personalist,* 42 (1961): 526.

13. Marshall, 527-8. Marshall is citing *The Quarterly Review,* 52 (1834): 28.

14. *The Statesman's Manual* in *The Complete Works of Samuel Taylor Coleridge,* ed. W. G. T. Shedd (New York: Harper and Brothers, 1853), Vol. 1, 458-9.

15. *The Works of Flavius Josephus, Antiquities of the Jews,* trans. William Whiston, (Philadelphia: J. Gregg, 1829) Vol. I. IV: 19-20.

16. *Natural Supernaturalism: Tradition and Revolution in Romantic Literature* (New York: W. W. Norton & Co., 1971), 273.

17. From "Modern Criticism of *The Ancient Mariner,*" reprinted in *Twentieth Century Interpretations of the Rime of the Ancient Mariner,* ed. James D. Boulger (Englewood Cliffs, New Jersey: Prentice Hall, 1969), 113.

18. "The Nightmare World of the Ancient Mariner," *Twentieth Century Views: Coleridge, A Collection of Critical Essays,* ed. Kathleen Coburn (Englewood Cliffs, New Jersey: Prentice Hall, 1967), 69.

19. A Coleridgean controversy surrounds the authenticity of Josephus' source for the story of Mosollamus. Ben Zion Wacholder, writing in the *Encyclopedia Judaica* (Jerusalem, 1971), ascribes the Mosollamus story to Pseudo-Hecataeus I, an ardent Jew who took on the identity of the Greek historian in order to counteract the anti-Semitism of the time. Menaham Stern in a more recent study (*Greek and Latin Authors on Jews and Judaism,* Jerusalem, 1974, 21-5), offers extensive evidence for Josephus' use of a slightly revised version of the authentic book of Hecataeus.

The creator of Satyrane's letters and the "person from Porlock" who himself used the pseudonym Silas Tomkyn Comberbacke, would have appreciated the controversy surrounding the authenticity of Mosollamus.

John Ower (essay date spring 1991)

SOURCE: Ower, John. "The 'Death-Fires,' the 'Fire-Flags' and the Corposant in *The Rime of the Ancient Mariner.*" *Philological Quarterly* 70, no. 2 (spring 1991): 199-218.

[*In the following essay, Ower argues that the "death-fires" and the "fire-flags" in* Mariner *serve as ambivalent signs of God's wrath as well as his divine protection.*]

Neither entirely correct nor complete exegeses seem yet to have been given of two complex and richly significant images in **The Rime of the Ancient Mariner**. These are the "death-fires" of line 128, and the "fire-flags" of line 314.[1] The former is according to John Livingston Lowes a conflation of the "corpo santo, or St. Elmo's fire;"[2] the *ignis fatuus,* or Will o' the Wisp; and the lights produced in graveyards by decaying cadavers (*Road* [*The Road to Xanadu*], pp. 85-86). Lowes further suggests that the "fire-flags" are literally the frequent and intense flashes of lightning from a tropical thunderstorm (*Road,* pp. 186-89). That phenomenon is in turn for Lowes imaginatively "telescoped" in the flags with an auroral display (*Road,* pp. 187-190). Lowes's explanations of the "death-fires" and the flags are presumably the sources for M. H. Abrams's footnotes to lines 128 and 314 of the **Ancient Mariner** in *The Norton Anthology. . . .*[3] Here, Abrams identifies the "death-fires" as the "corposant, or St. Elmo's fire" (*Norton,* 2:339 n.), and the "fire-flags" as the "Aurora Australis, or Southern Lights" (*Norton,* 2:344 n.).

Lowes and Abrams would both seem partly wrong about the "death-fires" and the flags in ways which involve the corposant.[4] Thus, the accounts of St. Elmo's fire in Coleridge's possible authorities for the phenomenon are variously incongruous with both the physical setting and the spiritual context of line 128.[5] Such multiple inconsistencies make it unlikely that the "death-fires" have on the material plane as significant a relation with the corposant as either Lowes or Abrams believed. Instead, the flames of line 128 would seem to be literally the *ignis fatuus,* to which the corposant and graveyard lights could stand as "vehicles" in two implicit (or, one could say, "submerged") similes or metaphors.[6] Turning now to the "fire-flags," these do not appear to be literally either lightning or the aurora. Those phenomena would instead seem to function in the "flags" as "vehicles" in two other "submerged" figures of comparison, of which the literal "tenor" is St. Elmo's fire. This last conclusion is suggested by the physical particulars of the "fire-flags" and their setting, all of which jibe with Coleridge's sources for the corposant. Again, the spiritual circumstances in which the flags appear are consistent with several beliefs about St. Elmo's fire in Coleridge's authorities. In this regard, the "fire-flags" as corposant could render as possibly do also the flames of line 128 certain dualities in the Mariner's spiritual situation.

As I have indicated, Coleridge's authorities for St. Elmo's fire are variously inconsistent with both the physical setting and the spiritual circumstances in which the "death-fires" appear. To begin with, most of Coleridge's sources link the corposant at sea with stormy conditions.[7] Such foul weather is described by some of Coleridge's authorities with a forcefulness that would for the poet have strongly associated St. Elmo's fire with high winds, rain and storm clouds:

> a sudden storm bursting upon us one night, with a terrible east wind, drove us with such violence, that . . . without any sail at all, we made more way than we had done for seven days before. During this tempest we saw a light, which the mariners call the fire of St. Elme. . . .
>
> (Adanson, p. 102)

> In this sort wee lay driving for the space of two dayes and two nights together, with a continuall storme and fowle weather with rayne. The same night we saw uppon the maine yarde . . . a certaine signe, which the Portingalles call *Corpo Santo.* . . .
>
> (Linschoten, p. 167)

> This storme continued for the space of two dayes, and two nights most fearfull and dangerous, with raine, lightning, and thunder. . . . In the extremitie of our storme appeared to us in the night, upon our maine Top-mast head, a flame . . . which the Portugals call Corpo Sancto. . . .
>
> (Purchas, 2:351)

The weather conditions in these and similar accounts of the corposant are in sharp contrast with the dead calm, "utter drought" (135) and sunny days during the period in which the "death-fires" occur:[8]

All in a hot and copper sky,
The bloody Sun, at noon,
Right up above the mast did stand,
No bigger than the Moon.

Day after day, day after day,
We stuck, nor breath nor motion;
As idle as a painted ship
Upon a painted ocean.

Water, water, every where,
And all the boards did shrink;
Water, water, every where,
Nor any drop to drink.

(111-22)

There are not in lines 107-262 even the thunderstorms that sometimes occur in tropical sea-calms (*Road,* p. 186).[9] The weather in line 128 is thus completely wrong for St. Elmo's fire according to the collective testimony of most of Coleridge's authorities. Furthermore, the "death-fires" dance "About, about" (127), which presumably means that the flames are on or above the waters *around* the Mariner's vessel. However, the corposant is specifically located upon the ship itself in most of Coleridge's sources.

If the physical circumstances under which the "death-fires" occur seem to be wrong for the corposant, so likewise do the most evident aspects of the spiritual situation in line 128. Here, the Mariner has recently killed in the albatross a minister of divine mercy that is associated with both Christ and the Holy Spirit.[10] Such a heinous transgression (which perhaps verges upon the unforgivable "blasphemy" against the Holy Ghost, Matt. 12:31-32)[11] has to all appearances deeply alienated God and His saints (234-35 and 599-600). Thus, the Deity in lines 107-262 has seemingly withdrawn from the Mariner except to manifest His anger at the sinner.[12] This doubly negative relationship of God with the Mariner is expressed in an apparent hell,[13] where the offender is tormented as if he were damned.

The seemingly negative spiritual context in which the "death-fires" appear is indeed consistent with the tradition that St. Elmo's fire is a bad omen.[14] However, this significance is generally attributed by Coleridge's authorities to the corposant when it occurs either singly or on a ship's deck.[15] Seemingly neither circumstance applies to the "death-fires," which are multiple and apparently not on the Mariner's vessel. Moreover, the spiritual situation in line 128 is incongruous with the positive beliefs about the corposant which predominate over the negative in Coleridge's sources. Thus, the majority of those writers state that St. Elmo's fire was regarded as propitious.[16] Such a favorable sign is further taken in many of Coleridge's authorities to manifest a special heavenly care.[17] In this connection, the corposant is associated with a number of saints.[18] These include the Virgin Mary, whose protection was thought by Portuguese sailors to be indicated by five corposants appearing together:

> Those five lights the Portingals cal *Coroa de nossa Senhora*, that is, deere Ladies Crowne, and have great hope therein when they see it.
>
> (Linschoten, p. 167)[19]

The positive beliefs about the corposant are incongruous with some particulars of the spiritual situation in line 128. Here, the Mariner has recently rejected in the "pious bird of good omen" (gloss on lines 81-82) a precise equivalent to St. Elmo's fire as an auspicious token of heaven's regard. Moreover, the slaying of the "pious bird" seemingly alienates from the Mariner the company of saints with which the corposant is connected. In this regard, Mary's estrangement from the Mariner is hinted in a way that opposes the "death-fires" to the corposant as a sign of Our Lady's care. Thus, the flames of line 128 are intimately associated with Mary's evil antithesis in the **Ancient Mariner**: the "Night-mare LIFE-IN-DEATH" (193).[20] That malignant figure is connected with the "death-fires" (1) by the occurrence of the first and last words of her name in line 128, and (2) by the "witch's oils" of line 129. This linking of the "death-fires" to Mary's demonic opposite renders them contrary to the corposant as indicating Our Lady's protection.

The flames of line 128 are also opposed to the corposant as a sign of heaven's care by being linked with (1) the fierce tropical sun which seems to express God's wrath towards the Mariner,[21] and (2) with the absence of wind and rain as vehicles of the divine life and love.[22] All of these aspects of the Mariner's inferno are given a powerful poetic emphasis just before the "death-fires" appear. Thus, the blazing equatorial sun is vividly evoked in lines 111-14, while the utter calm and drought are strikingly rendered in lines 115-22. In this way, God's apparent angry estrangement from the Mariner is closely associated with the flames of line 128. Such a connection would presumably render the "death-fires" antithetical to the corposant as a sign of heaven's regard.[23]

In sum, it appears that the "death-fires" are not literally the corposant, nor yet on the material level as significantly related to St. Elmo's fire as Lowes believed. If such be the case, what physically speaking are the flames of line 128? The answer would seem to be that the "death-fires" are literally the *ignis fatuus*. This conclusion is suggested by Joseph Priestley's "Of Light Proceeding from Putrescent Substances . . . ,"[24] which as Lowes has demonstrated (*Road*, pp. 80-86) was a seminal influence upon lines 123-30 of the **Ancient Mariner**:

> The very deep did rot: O Christ!
> That ever this should be!

> Yea, slimy things did crawl with legs
> Upon the slimy sea.

> About, about, in reel and rout
> The death-fires danced at night;
> The water, like a witch's oils,
> Burnt green, and blue and white.

The chief source for these lines seems to have been Priestley's explanations of marine phosphorescence and the *ignis fatuus*. These, when viewed in relation to one another and to lines 123-30, suggest that the "death-fires" are most probably an oceanic Will o' the Wisp:

> The observations of Father Bourzes . . . make it extremely probable that the luminousness of the sea arises from slimy and other putrescent matter with which it abounds. . . .
>
> ("Light" [*Vision, Light, and Colours*], p. 576)

> It seems probable that some kinds of putrescent matter, capable of giving a considerable degree of light, are *volatile*, and that this is the cause of that luminous appearance which goes by the name of *ignis fatuus*, or in common English *Will with a wisp*, to which the credulous vulgar ascribe . . . mischievous powers. This phenomenon is chiefly visible in damp places, and is also said to be very often seen in burying grounds, and near dunghills.
>
> ("Light," pp. 579-80)

These passages are in fairly close textual proximity, and both centrally involve light and "putrescent matter." Those linkages between Priestley's two explanations apparently resulted in their becoming interconnected for Coleridge in such a way as to leave in the poet's memory a nexus involving three associations. The first two (the parallel causal relations of "putrescent matter" to marine luminescence[25] and the *ignis fatuus*) together generate the third (the analogy between oceanic phosphorescence and the "Will with a wisp" as lucent phenomena with similar origins). This network of connections would seem to constitute the basis of lines 123-30 of the **Ancient Mariner.** Here, Priestley's "slimy and other putrescent matter" becomes the "rot" in Coleridge's "slimy sea." That such decomposition produces the luminescence of lines 129-30 is hinted by the two phenomena being respectively mentioned in successive stanzas. In this way, Coleridge implies the first of the three linkings suggested to him by Priestley. The other two are both intimated in lines 123-30 by the "death-fires." Their generation from the "rot" in the "deep" is hinted by their appearing immediately after the Mariner mentions the "slimy sea." The flames of line 128 are furthermore an obvious analog to the burning phosphorescence of lines 129-30. The "death-fires" accordingly complete in lines 123-30 the pattern suggested to Coleridge by Priestley. Since the "death-fires" do so as a counterpart of the *ignis fatuus*, they are most probably that phenomenon. More specifically, the flames of line 128 would presumably be the "Will with a wisp" as explained by Priestley: "*volatile . . . luminous*" substances which are emitted by the "putrescent matter" in the "rotting sea" (240).

That Coleridge indeed derived his "death-fires" from Priestley's consideration of the *ignis fatuus* is suggested by the multiple parallels between the scientist's discussion and the flames of line 128. Just as Priestley notes that the "Will with a wisp" is "chiefly visible in damp places," and often occurs "near dunghills," so the fires of line 128 apparently play over water which "rots." Again, Priestley's observation that the *ignis fatuus* frequently appears in "burying grounds" has a counterpart in Coleridge's notion of "death-fires" (*Road*, p. 86). Furthermore, those flames with their lively dancing recall Priestley's description of an *ignis fatuus* which "kept skipping about a dead thistle" ("Light," p. 580; *Road*, p. 86). Finally, Priestley's statement that the "vulgar ascribe . . . mischievous powers" to the "Will with a wisp" corresponds to the sinister associations of the "death-fires."

It would thus appear in the light of evidence from Priestley that the flames of line 128 are literally an oceanic *ignis fatuus*. In that case, the "death-fires" are not physically speaking as Lowes has suggested a figmental fusion of the Will o' the Wisp, the graveyard lights and the corposant. However, the last two phenomena could still be connected to the *ignis fatuus* of line 128 as its "vehicles" in a pair of "submerged" similes or metaphors. In this regard, the corposant might well have been suggested to Coleridge as a term of comparison for the Will o' the Wisp by Priestley (*Road*, p. 86). Thus, the scientist immediately after discussing the *ignis fatuus* describes St. Elmo's fire as "luminous appearances, which, at sea, skip about the masts and yards of ships" ("Light," p. 584). Priestley's corposant as "luminous," "skip[ping]" and "at sea" may have struck Coleridge as an appropriate "vehicle" for his "*volatile . . . luminous*" substances that dance over the ocean.[26] Again, the graveyard lights could have seemed to Coleridge an apposite term of comparison for the Will o' the Wisp. Thus, both are "luminous appearances," and both Priestley suggests ("Light," pp. 576 and 579-580) originate in "putrescent matter."

The "death-fires" as combining the *ignis fatuus*, the graveyard lights and the corposant could intimate the Mariner's spiritual situation in line 128. This is, as I have previously suggested, to all appearances negative. The Mariner has been condemned to a seeming inferno, where he experiences the agonies of the damned. In this regard, the flames of line 128 would appear to be a kind of hellfire that expresses God's anger with the Mariner by tormenting his sensibilities.[27] Such affliction seemingly combines[28] (1) the overpowering sense of in-

ner decay and death which is rendered by much of the external setting of lines 107-262, and (2) the perception of being subjected to a malicious mockery that is variously suggested by the Mariner's inferno.[29] The first of these tortures is intimated by the "death-fires" as including two phenomena (viz., the *ignis fatuus* and the graveyard lights) which originate in "putrescent matter." The second torment is hinted in the flames of line 128 by the *ignis fatuus* as in folklore a mischievous spirit who leads the foolish astray.[30]

The "death-fires" could thus doubly afflict the Mariner's spirit in visiting upon him the divine wrath. However, the flames of line 128 might also have a redemptive function which is intimated by St. Elmo's fire with its connotations of heavenly care. In this regard, the "death-fires" could minister to the Mariner God's saving grace[31] by mortifying his soul in preparation for the spiritual rebirth of lines 263-308.[32] If the flames of line 128 indeed have such a redemptive role, then the apparent inferno of lines 107-262 would be at least partly a purgatory in disguise.[33] The Mariner himself would be both (1) a reprobate who is punished for his crime by God's righteous anger, and (2) a penitent being regenerated through his very infernal sufferings by grace.[34]

Let us now turn from the "death-fires" to the flames of line 314. If the former are not on the material plane as significantly related to St. Elmo's fire as Lowes or Abrams believed, the corposant does appear central to the "fire-flags." These would seem to be literally St. Elmo's fire rather than lightning as Lowes has argued, or the aurora as Abrams maintains. The two last explanations of the flags might indeed appear to be supported by evidence marshalled by Lowes. He has most convincingly demonstrated from Coleridge's sources (*Road*, pp. 186-90) that the "fire-flags" are in some manner connected with both the aurora and lightning. However, each of these phenomena would if it were literally the flags entail some bothersome inconsistencies on the physical plane.[35] To begin with, auroral displays occur not at the equator where the "fire-flags" seemingly appear, but instead in the upper latitudes.[36] This latter fact is variously conveyed by Coleridge's most likely sources for the northern and southern lights.[37] Moreover, the poet himself specifically locates an aurora in Finland (3) in **"To William Godwin"** (1795), and in Lapland (64-80) in **"The Destiny of Nations"** (1796).

The "fire-flags" as literally an aurora would be inconsistent not just with their equatorial setting, but seemingly also with line 317 of the **Ancient Mariner**. Here, the "wan stars" are described as dancing "between" the "fire-flags." That preposition would be inappropriate were the flags an auroral display, which typically consists of diffuse "arcs" and "draperies" filling much of the sky.[38] The stars of line 317 should accordingly shine not "between" but rather *through* the "fire-flags" were these an aurora. In this regard, the correct description is significantly given by two of Coleridge's likely sources. Thus, Erasmus Darwin notes in *The Botanic Garden* that "the light of small stars . . . [is] seen undiminished through . . . the aurora borealis."[39] Again, George Forster observes in his account of Captain Cook's second voyage that "The stars were . . . sometimes faintly to be seen through . . . these southern lights" (G. Forster, 1:116).

If the "fire-flags" as literally an aurora would involve some apparent inconsistencies on the physical plane, so too would the flags as literally flashes of lightning. The latter identification presupposes that lines 313-15 refer to an intense tropical thunderstorm in the "upper air" above the Mariner's ship (*Road*, pp. 188-89).[40] The presence of such a storm in lines 313-15 is, however, seemingly incompatible with the Mariner's observation in line 320 that there is "*one* black cloud" [italics mine] in the sky. This thunderhead as the only cloud present just after the "fire-flags" occur should presumably also be the storm postulated for lines 313-15. If that is so, then the "one black cloud" should be above the Mariner's vessel when he first sees the flags. This unfortunately does not appear to be the case in view of line 318. Here, what is seemingly the squall from the "black cloud" is (1) described as a "coming wind," and (2) is roaring "more loud[ly]" than in lines 309-12. Those two details placed where they are both imply that the storm of line 320 is still only approaching the Mariner's ship *after* the "fire-flags" occur.[41] Thus, if there be just a single cloud in lines 313-20, it is not in lines 313-15 where it should be to create the "fire-flags" as lightning. However, a separate thunderstorm to produce the flags would it appears be inconsistent with the Mariner's reference to "one . . . cloud" in line 320.

There are still further problems with assuming a tropical lightning storm is above the Mariner's ship in lines 313-15. That disturbance should involve torrential rain and loud thunder, since both are emphasized by Coleridge's sources for lower-latitude electrical storms.[42] However, neither a downpour nor thunder-claps are noted specifically by the Mariner in immediate connection with the "fire-flags." These omissions would be rather unlikely were there really a thunderstorm in lines 313-15. Thus, the Mariner after enduring a long period of "utter drought" and "silence" (110) is in lines 297-326 unusually aware of both precipitation and sound. In this connection, the Mariner mentions twice showers of rain, and twice also the roaring of the wind (300, 309-12 and 318-20). Given these references, the Mariner would surely also note both the cloudburst and the stentorian thunder from a tropical lightning storm above his ship.[43] Such a tempest would furthermore, if of sufficient magnitude to produce a "hundred" lightning flashes, involve a heavy cloud cover throughout the "upper air." In that case, the "wan stars" would presumably not be

visible to dance "between" the flags as in fact happens in lines 316-17.[44]

In sum, the existence of a thunderstorm in lines 313-15 of the *Ancient Mariner* to produce "fire-flags" of lightning would seem variously inconsistent with lines 316-20. The flags are therefore no more liable to be literally flashes of lightning that literally an aurora. These two phenomena would nonetheless appear to be somehow connected with the "fire-flags" given the evidence presented by Lowes. Both of the just-noted considerations regarding the aurora and lightning must apparently be taken into account if the "fire-flags" are to be satisfactorily explained. This can be done by assuming that the flags involve two other "submerged" similes or metaphors, in which the aurora and lightning are "vehicles" for St. Elmo's fire.[45] In that case, the flags would be literally a multiple appearance of corposants on the Mariner's vessel.

Such an explanation of the "fire-flags" is consonant with the various physical details of lines 309-17. To start with, the weather in line 314 is tempestuous as in most of Coleridge's sources when the corposant appears. Thus, a "roaring" wind has arisen in line 309, and this heralds besides the approach of an intense electrical storm. Furthermore, the Mariner in line 314 is quite likely to be looking just where the flags would be situated were they indeed St. Elmo's fire. In this regard, the attention of Coleridge's protagonist has in lines 311-13 been drawn first to his ship's sails and then to the "upper air." The Mariner is accordingly when the flags occur quite probably looking aloft upon his vessel. That is where the corposant appears in the great majority of Coleridge's sources, who locate St. Elmo's fire upon a ship's masts, spars, sails and rigging.[46] The corposant as so situated is implied by the image of "fire-flags." This is suggestive of St. Elmo's fire as spatially close and hence metaphorically connected to a ship's pennants.[47]

Again, the physical particulars of lines 315-17 seem in accord with the "fire-flags" being the corposant. Thus, the flags as "hurried" "To and fro" (315) recall the lively movements of St. Elmo's fire in several of Coleridge's sources. For instance, Priestley ("Light," p. 584) describes the corposant as "skip[ping] about the masts and yards of ships." Similarly, Sir Thomas Gates speaks of "a little round light, like a faint Starre . . . streaming along with a sparkling blaze . . . and shooting sometimes from Shroud to Shroud" (Purchas, 19:11). Such accounts of St. Elmo's fire are consonant with the "hurried" motions of Coleridge's flags.[48] Moreover, the likening by Gates and others of the corposant to a star fits with the implicit visual parallel in lines 315-17:[49]

. . . a hundred fire-flags sheen,
To and fro they were hurried about!

And to and fro, and in and out,
The wan stars danced between.

In creating this scene, Coleridge might well have been
inspired by Gates and others among his sources to
imagine a "dance" upon the Mariner's ship of star-like
corposants. Such discharges could have been envisioned
by Coleridge as either (1) intermediate in their shape
and size between a flag and a star, or (2) changing from
one of those forms to the other. In either case, the corposants in motion upon the Mariner's vessel would
parallel visually the "dance" of the "wan stars" in the
sky surrounding the ship. This latter movement is
presumably that of the stars relative to the Mariner's
vessel as she pitches and rolls in the waves from the
coming storm.

In sum, the physical details of lines 309-17 would seem
consistent with the "fire-flags" being the corposant. The
spiritual circumstances in which the flags occur are
likewise right for St. Elmo's fire. Thus, the "fire-flags"
appear shortly after the Mariner has begun to be
reconciled with heaven. A "kind saint" (286) has moved
Coleridge's protagonist to bless the water-snakes,
thereby enabling him to pray (288). His petition is
answered by Mary's gifts of sleep and rain (292-300).
The latter with the "roaring wind" of line 309 returns
both manifestations of God that were absent in lines
107-299.[50] Therefore, the spiritual context of line 314 is
eminently suitable for St. Elmo's fire as a token of
heaven's care. More specifically, the "fire-flags" as the
corposant associated by tradition with the "kind" saints
would reaffirm their mercy and favor toward the
Mariner. In particular, the "hundred" (314) flags might
show Mary's special regard for the Mariner by multiply-
ing twentyfold the corposants of "deere Ladies
Crowne."[51] The flags as St. Elmo's fire could likewise
signify the return of the Holy Spirit to Coleridge's
protagonist. This would be implied by the corposants of
line 314 and the "roaring wind" as recalling the
"tongues . . . of fire" and "rushing mighty wind" at
Pentecost (Acts 2:2-3).[52]

The "fire-flags" as corposant would thus fit with the
indications in lines 263-312 of the Mariner's atonement
with heaven. However, the flags could also jibe as partly
the corposant of ill-omen with the suggestions in lines
309-409 that God is not entirely reconciled with the
Mariner.[53] In this regard, the killing of the albatross is
an offense so heinous that it has not (as we learn in
lines 408-09) been completely expiated by the torments
of lines 107-262. God accordingly still seems incensed
with the Mariner when the "fire-flags" occur. This divine
wrath is suggested just before the flags appear by the
roaring of the wind, and just after by the fierce tropical
thunderstorm.[54] In thus "framing" the flags, Coleridge
intimates that they too in part express God's burning
ire. This negative significance for the "fire-flags" might

be hinted through their being in part the corposant as
boding ill. Such an inauspicious sign in the flags as
connected with God's anger may portend additional
sufferings to be visited upon the Mariner by the divine
wrath. That affliction could well be an element in the
further "penance" for the Mariner which is mentioned
in lines 408-09.

The "fire-flags" as corposant could thus like the "death-
fires" render the contraries of divine love and divine
anger, of retribution and redemption. These same
antitheses may likewise be intimated by the flags
through their secondary elements of lightning and the
aurora. The former could tie in with the violent
thunderstorm of lines 320-26 to suggest God's continuing anger with the Mariner. The aurora in the "fire-
flags" may for its part hint that ultimately the Mariner
will be brought to heaven by divine grace. In this connection, the northern lights were associated for Coleridge with a celestial beatitude for the human soul
after death. Such a connection was established in the
poet's mind by primitive beliefs which were recorded
by David Crantz, Hans Egede, and Samuel Hearne
(*Road*, pp. 97-98 and 487):[55]

> Others [among the Greenland Eskimos], that are more
> charmed with the beauty of the celestial bodies, soar
> . . . to the loftiest sky to seek their paradise there; and
> they imagine the flight thither is so easy and rapid, that
> the soul rests the very same evening in the mansion of
> the Moon, . . . and there it can dance and play at ball
> with the rest of the souls; for they interpret the Northern
> Lights to be the dance of sportive souls.
>
> . . . the Southern Indians . . . believe . . . [the aurora]
> to be the spirits of their departed friends dancing in the
> clouds; and when the *Aurora Borealis* is remarkably
> bright, . . . they say, their deceased friends are very
> merry.

Since these passages inspired lines 75-80 of **"The
Destiny of Nations"** (*Road*, pp. 96-98 and 487), they
are presumably also part of the complex intertextual
background of the "fire-flags." Therefore, the flags as
involving an aurora could be a sign that the Mariner's
redemption will ultimately be fulfilled in celestial bliss.
Such a happy portent would tie in with other nearby
intimations of the Mariner's heavenly destiny. Thus, he
feels in lines 306-08 "almost" as if he had died and
become a "blessèd ghost." Again, lines 329-66 obliquely
hint that the Mariner will finally join the heavenly
company by associating Coleridge's protagonist with a
"troop of spirits blest" (349).

To conclude, the "death-fires" and the "fire-flags" would
both seem worthy in various ways of their great creator.
In this regard, our two images apparently reflect Coleridge's wide-ranging studies, and his remarkably reten-
tive memory for the details of his reading. Concerning

the latter, the "death-fires" and the flags both seem scrupulously faithful to the facts of natural history as these are presented by Coleridge's sources.[56] Such a "scientific" accuracy could in the "death-fires" and the flags be accompanied by some richness of spiritual implication. Thus, the flames of lines 128 and 314 may both suggest the antitheses of divine love and divine anger, of retribution and redemption.[57] In the case, still further complexity would be generated by the "death-fires" and the flags when they are taken together. The latter image would present its theological opposites with a reversal of their negative relative emphases in the "death-fires," thereby hinting the Mariner's spiritual progress between line 128 and line 314. This possibility well illustrates how the "death-fires" and the flags could both contribute to the intricate and subtle nexus of ideas and images by which Coleridge develops the religious themes of the **Ancient Mariner.**

Notes

1. All quotations from and line references to the *Ancient Mariner* and others of Coleridge's poems conform to the texts in *The Complete Poetical Works of Samuel Taylor Coleridge,* ed. Ernest Hartley Coleridge, 2 vols. (Oxford U. Press, 1912). This will be referred to subsequently as *Works.* There are no significant textual variations in the different versions of the *Ancient Mariner* with regard to the "death-fires" or to their immediate poetic context. There is, however, one textual variant in lines 309-30 of the *Ancient Mariner* that is germane to my discussion of the "fire-flags." This variant is mentioned in endnote 43 below.

2. John Livingston Lowes, *The Road to Xanadu* (Boston: Houghton, 1927). This work will be referred to subsequently as *Road.*

3. M. H. Abrams, et al., eds., *The Norton Anthology of English Literature,* 5th ed., 2 vols. (New York: Norton, 1986). This will subsequently be referred to as *Norton.* Martin Gardner in the *Annotated Ancient Mariner* (New York: Potter, 1965) likewise follows *Road* in his explanations of the "death-fires" and "fire-flags." See Martin Gardner, pp. 56 and 76-77.

4. St. Elmo's fire as described by Coleridge's authorities (See note 5) is an electrical point discharge induced by the negative charge on storm clouds. It typically appears at elevated locations. See *Encyclopedia Americana,* 1989, s.v. "Saint Elmo's Fire."

5. For some accounts of St. Elmo's fire which Coleridge may have read, see Michel Adanson, *A Voyage to Senegal. . . .* (London, 1759), pp. 102-03; Fletcher S. Bassett, *Sea Phantoms . . . ,* rev. ed. (Chicago, 1892), pp. 302-12; Stephen Batman,

The Golden Booke of the Leaden Gods (London, 1577; reprint, New York: Garland, 1976), p. 22; Robert Burton, *The Anatomy of Melancholy,* ed. Floyd Dell and Paul Jordan-Smith (New York: Tudor, 1927), p. 166; George C. Carey, "The Tradition of the St. Elmo's Fire," *The American Neptune* 23 (1963): 29-38; Awnsham Churchill, *A Collection of Voyages and Travels . . . ,* 3d ed., 6 vols. (London, 1744-46), 1:293; and 2:526; William Dampier, *A New Voyage Round the World . . . ,* 2d ed. (London, 1697), pp. 414-15; Richard Eden, *The First Three English Books on America . . . ,* ed. Edward Arber (Birmingham, Eng., 1885), p. 250; Amédée François Frézier, *A Voyage to the South-Sea . . .* (London, 1717), p. 37; Richard Hakluyt, *The Principal Navigations, Voyages, Traffiques & Discoveries of the English Nation . . . ,* 12 vols. (Glasgow: MacLehose; New York: Macmillan, 1903-05; reprint, New York: Kelley, 1969), 9:345-46; Sir Thomas Herbert, *Some Yeares Travels into . . . Africa, and Asia the Great . . .* (London, 1677), p. 11; John Josselyn, *An Account of Two Voyages to New-England . . .* (Boston, 1865), p. 8; Jan Huygen van Linschoten, *John Huighen van Linschoten. His Discours of Voyages into the Easte & West Indies* (London, 1598; reprint, Norwood, N. J.: Walter J. Johnson and Amsterdam: Theatrum Orbis, 1974), p. 167; Joseph Priestley, *The History and Present State of Discoveries Relating to Vision, Light, and Colours* (London, 1772), p. 584; Samuel Purchas, *Hakluytus Posthumus, or Purchas His Pilgrimes . . . ,* 20 vols. (Glasgow: MacLehose; New York: Macmillan, 1905-07), 2:86, 2:351, 14:81, and 19:11-12; Seneca, *Naturales Quaestiones,* 2 vols. (Loeb Classical Library, 1971), 1:21; William Shakespeare, *The Tempest,* ed. Stephen Orgel, *The Oxford Shakespeare* (Oxford U. Press, 1987), pp. 112-13; and Antonio de Ulloa, *A Voyage to South America . . . ,* 2d ed. (London, 1760), pp. 350-51. Subsequent references to these works will be by their authors' names.

6. By these terms, I mean figurative connections (whether of similitude or identity) that could have been suggested to Coleridge's highly associative mind by his sources for the "death-fires." Such figures (1) would have been at least in the back of Coleridge's mind when creating l. 128 of the *Ancient Mariner,* and (2) suggest themselves to the student of Coleridge's sources (as does, for example, the symbolic significance of an image like the albatross to the more sophisticated reader). Implicit similes and metaphors seem as likely in the "death-fires" as the conflation posited by Lowes. This is so especially in view of the many explicit similes or metaphors in the *Ancient Mariner.*

7. See, for example, Adanson, pp. 102-03; Bassett, pp. 303 and 305; Burton, p. 166; Carey, p. 37; Churchill, 1:293 and 2:526; Dampier, pp. 413-15; Eden, p. 250; Frézier, p. 37; Hakluyt, 9:345-46; Herbert, p. 11; Josselyn, p. 8; Linschoten, p. 167; Purchas, 2:86, 2:351, 14:81, and 19:6-12; Seneca 1:21; and Shakespeare, p. 112.

8. For some other particularly forceful descriptions of stormy weather with which the corposant is connected, see Churchill 1:293, and 2:526; Dampier pp. 413-14; and Purchas, 19:6-12. These descriptions, like those just quoted in the text, would doubtless have especially impressed Coleridge as the first-hand accounts of actual seafarers.

9. Such conditions seem to have prevailed during two appearances of the corposant described by Ulloa (pp. 350-51).

10. For these associations of the albatross, see W. H. Auden, *The Enchafèd Flood* (New York: Random, 1950), p. 75; L. D. Berkoben, *Coleridge's Decline as a Poet* (The Hague: Mouton, 1975), pp. 86-87; Alice Chandler, "Structure and Symbol in 'The Rime of the Ancient Mariner,'" *MLQ* [*Modern Language Quarterly*] 26 (1965): 409; W. H. Gardner, "The Poet and the Albatross," *English Studies in Africa* 1 (1958): 111-13; Bernard Martin, *The Ancient Mariner and the Authentic Narrative* (London: Heinemann, 1949), p. 19; Charles H. Rowell, "Coleridge's Symbolic Albatross," *CLA Journal* 6 (1962): 133-35; Robert Penn Warren, "A Poem of Pure Imagination . . . ," in *Selected Essays* (New York: Random, 1958), p. 230; and Geoffrey Yarlott, *Coleridge and the Abyssinian Maid* (London: Methuen, 1967), pp. 156 and 161. All critical commentaries on the *Ancient Mariner* other than *Road* will be referred to after their first citation by their authors' names.

11. Bernard Martin, p. 19, notes "how very real was the crime of blasphemy in the eighteenth century."

12. J. B. Beer (*Coleridge the Visionary,* London: Chatto, 1959) apparently does not believe that God responds to the Mariner's sin in part with anger. The critic suggests (p. 155) that what seems the divine wrath in ll. 107-262 of the *Ancient Mariner* is really God's love misperceived by the "diseased imagination" of Coleridge's protagonist. However, the torments inflicted upon the Mariner by the tropical sun are not merely a product of his own subjective spiritual state. Therefore, if the sun does represent the divine ire, this anger possesses an objective existence apart from the Mariner's spiritual condition.

13. See J. Robert Barth, S.J., *Coleridge and the Power of Love* (U. of Missouri Press, 1988), p. 68; Walter Jackson Bate, *Coleridge* (New York: Macmillan, 1968), p. 61; Chandler, p. 404; and W. H. Gardner, p. 115.

14. Abrams refers to this tradition (*Norton,* 2:339 n.) in connection with the "death-fires."

15. See, for example, Bassett, pp. 302, 305 and 312; Churchill, 1:293; Dampier, p. 414; Purchas, 19:11; and *Road,* pp. 484-85.

16. See, for example, Adanson, pp. 102-03; Bassett, pp. 302, 305, 306, and 312; Batman, p. 22; Churchill 1:293 and 2:526; Dampier, pp. 414-15; Eden, p. 250; Hakluyt, 9:345; Herbert, p. 11; Josselyn, p. 8; Linschoten, p. 167; Purchas, 2:351; Seneca, 1:21; and Ulloa, p. 350. Some of these same writers also mention negative beliefs about the corposant.

17. See, for example, Bassett, pp. 302-03; Carey, p. 30; Churchill, 2:526; Dampier, p. 415; Hakluyt, 9:345; Linschoten, p. 167; Purchas, 2:351; and Seneca, 1:21.

18. These include Saints Clare, Elmo, Nicholas of Myra, Peter Gonzales, and Ursula. St. Elmo, or Erasmus, is "the patron saint of Mediterranean sailors" (*Encyclopaedia Britannica,* 1972, s.v. "Saint Elmo's Fire"). The word corposant comes from "cuerpo santo" (Spanish, Portuguese) or "corpo santo" (Italian) = holy, blessed or sacred body.

19. For another account of this belief which may have been familiar to Coleridge, see Bassett, p. 312.

20. Coleridge implicitly establishes this antithesis in l. 178 of the *Ancient Mariner.* Here, the Mariner reacts to his memory of the sinister approach of the "Night-mare's" ship by exclaiming "Heaven's Mother send us grace!"

21. See Beer, pp. 154-55; W. H. Gardner, p. 115; and Elliott B. Gose, Jr., "Coleridge and the Luminous Gloom: An Analysis of the 'Symbolical Language' in *The Rime of the Ancient Mariner,*" *PMLA* 75 (1960): 241.

22. See W. H. Gardner, pp. 113 and 115; Florence Marsh, "The Ocean-Desert: *The Ancient Mariner* and *The Waste Land,*" *Essays in Criticism* 9 (1959): 127-28; H. W. Piper, *Nature and the Supernatural in "The Ancient Mariner"* (Sydney: Halstead, 1955), p. 13; and Maren-Sofie Røstvig, "*The Rime of the Ancient Mariner* and the Cosmic System of Robert Fludd," *Tennessee Studies in Literature* 12, (1967): 75-76. The wind and rain are both ambivalent symbols in the *Ancient Mariner.* Thus, the "Storm-Blast" of ll. 41-50 suggests a wrathful or otherwise terrible God. The same negative meaning is implied by the downpour of l. 320, which recalls the biblical Flood.

23. In this connection, the flames of l. 128 might be a cognate of the burning solar rays as manifesting God's wrath. Thus, the "death-fires" seem to torment the Mariner's sensibilities by night as the sun's burning, parching heat tortures his body by day.

24. This essay appears as a chapter in Priestley, *Vision, Light, and Colours.* Priestley's essay will be subsequently referred to as "Light."

25. For the idea that marine phosphorescence is produced by organic decay, Coleridge could well have had two sources in addition to "Light." These are Erasmus Darwin, *The Botanic Garden* (London, 1791; reprint, Menston, Yorkshire: Scholar Press, 1973), Part 1, "Additional Notes," p. 18; and Johann Reinhold Forster, *Observations Made during a Voyage Round the World.* . . . (London, 1778), pp. 66-67. These possible sources are noted respectively in Piper, *Nature,* pp. 16-17; and Bernard Smith, "Coleridge's *Ancient Mariner* and Cook's Second Voyage," *Journal of the Warburg and Courtauld Institutes* 19 (1956): 144.

26. There are two further links between Priestley's corposant and the "death-fires." First, the scientist in his account of St. Elmo's fire uses the word "Corpusanse" ("Light," p. 584). This in phonetically suggesting a combination of "corpse" and "putrescence" ties in with the notion of "death-fires." Also, just as the flames of l. 128 dance "About, about," so Priestley's corposant skips "about."

27. This interpretation may be supported by the occurrence of the "death-fires" at night. That detail could relate the flames of l. 128 to the motif in Coleridge's poetry of a nocturnal hell for the human spirit. See "Dejection: An Ode," ll. 94-116, and "The Pains of Sleep."

28. Besides the two torments to be mentioned, there might also be a third inflicted upon the Mariner by the "death-fires." This is a sense of overwhelming defeat suggested punningly by the "reel and rout" (127) of the "death-fires." Such an anguish might be obliquely hinted in the flames of l. 128 by the corposant as sometimes portending "disaster" (*Norton,* 2:339n.).

29. A malicious mockery of Coleridge's protagonist seems implicit in ll. 121-22 ("Water, water, every where, / Nor any drop to drink."), in the quashing of the Mariner's hope of rescue by the "Nightmare's" ship (167-94), and in her curse of "life-in-death." The motif of mockery is also suggested by ll. 267-68 ("Her beams bemocked the sultry main, / Like April hoar-frost spread;").

30. See *Folklore, Myths and Legends of Britain* (London: Reader's Digest Association, 1973), p.

118; and Gertrude Jobes, *Dictionary of Mythology Folklore and Symbols,* 3 vols. (New York: Scarecrow, 1962), 1:821.

31. In this connection, Coleridge in creating the "death-fires" may have been influenced by a passage from Bishop Berkeley's *Siris* . . . (Beer, p. 144; subsequent page references to *Siris* . . . are to *The Works of George Berkeley,* ed., Alexander Fraser, 4 vols., Oxford U. Press, 1901, vol. 3). Berkeley in discussing the "vital flame" (p. 220) in the human body states that such fire "being extremely subtle, might not be seen any more than . . . *ignes fatui* by daylight" (p. 221). If this passage be a source for the "death-fires" as *ignis fatuus,* then they may be in part Berkeley's "vital flame." This is for the philosopher one manifestation of the "pure fire" (p. 205) which is the primary and universal instrument of the divine Mind when acting upon and within creation (pp. 199-200). As such, "pure fire" is creative and life-giving as well as destructive: "And it is very remarkable that this same element, so fierce and destructive, should yet be so . . . tempered . . . as to be withal the salutary warmth, the genial, cherishing, and vital flame of all living creatures" (p. 206). Such a "genial, cherishing . . . flame" could in the "death-fires" be the instrument of God's grace in redeeming the Mariner.

32. By thus preparing the Mariner, the flames of l. 128 might anticipate the manifestation of God's regenerative love in the fires of ll. 270-71 and 280-81 of the *Ancient Mariner.* See Gose, pp. 240-41.

33. For the influence of Dante's *Divine Comedy* upon the *Ancient Mariner,* see A. A. Mendilow, "Symbolism in Coleridge and the Dantesque Element in *The Ancient Mariner,*" *Scripta Hierosolymitana* 2 (1955): 25-81.

34. Any such regenerative process is quite unapparent to the tormented and spiritually alienated (244-47) Mariner during his agony. That concealment might reflect an ironic divine mockery towards Coleridge's protagonist, or perhaps the sinner's own spiritual blindness (Beer, p. 149).

35. That Coleridge in general took care that the *Ancient Mariner* should be faithful in detail to the physical/phenomenal realm is suggested by his 1817 emendation of l. 104 (*Works,* 1:190 n.): "In the former editions the line was, The furrow follow'd free: But I had not been long on board a ship, before I perceived that this was the image as seen by a spectator from the shore, or from another vessel. From the ship itself, the *Wake* appears like a brook flowing off from the stern."

36. This problem is noted by Martin Gardner, p. 76. As a solution, Gardner suggests (p. 76) that

"While the Mariner slept, his ship may have been driven north far enough to see the *aurora borealis,* or south far enough to see the *aurora australis.*" However, there is nothing to support such a conjecture in either the relevant lines of the *Ancient Mariner* (292-312) or in their marginal glosses. Rather, Gardner's hypothesis would seem to be countered by the Mariner's statement in l. 328: "Yet *now* the ship moved on" (italics mine). Here, the Mariner implies that his vessel has remained stationary until after the "strange sights and commotions" (gloss to ll. 309-26) which include the "fire-flags." Moreover, a relocation of the Mariner's ship in ll. 292-310 to the upper latitudes would seem to be inconsistent with ll. 320-26. That passage apparently describes (as Lowes cogently argues in *Road,* pp. 186-88) an intense tropical thunderstorm.

For an explanation of why Coleridge might locate an aurora at the equator despite the facts of nature, see Arden Reed, *Romantic Weather: The Climates of Coleridge and Baudelaire* (U. Press of New England, 1983), pp. 161-62. Reed notes (p. 161) that in Parts 2-4 of the *Ancient Mariner,* "Coleridge collapses the distance between the pole and the Line, turning their antipodal climates into another set of doubles."

37. For some of these, see *Road,* pp. 97-100, 187-90 and 517; and Smith, pp. 148-50. With one exception, all of Coleridge's sources for the *aurora borealis* that are mentioned in *Road* are works that deal with far northern regions such as Lapland, Greenland, Finland, and arctic Canada. Coleridge would accordingly have strongly associated the *aurora borealis* with high northern latitudes. The *aurora australis* was apparently first observed during Captain Cook's second voyage. Several of the published accounts of that voyage which Coleridge probably read (Smith, pp. 123-24) locate the sightings of the *aurora australis* in far southern latitudes. See, for example, James Cook, *A Voyage Towards the South Pole . . . ,* 2 vols. (London, 1777), 1:53-55, 1:64-65, and 2:166; George Forster, *A Voyage Round the World . . . ,* 2 vols. (London, 1777), 1:115-16 and 118; and J. R. Forster, pp. 120-21.

38. *Encyclopaedia Britannica,* 1972, s.v. "Aurora Polaris."

39. Part 1, "Additional Notes," p. 9.

40. The evidence for this hypothesis is not especially convincing. Thus, l. 313 of the *Ancient Mariner* ("The upper air burst into life!") is not very specific. The Mariner could in l. 313 be referring not to a thunderstorm, but rather back to the "roaring wind" of ll. 309-12. In this regard, Coleridge might in l. 313 be attempting to clear up for the reader an apparent inconsistency in the preceding stanza. Thus, while the "loud wind" (327) does not "come anear" (310) the Mariner's vessel, the blast still shakes the sails with its "sound" (311). How could such an effect be produced by even a loudly "roaring" wind if it remains at some distance from the Mariner's ship? This apparent difficulty would be resolved should the squall be blowing in the "upper air" right above the vessel. It would then be close enough to the sails to shake them with its "roaring," but still "not . . . anear" to the Mariner himself upon the ship's deck.

The only other suggestion that the "fire-flags" may be flashes of lightning is provided by the gloss to ll. 309-26: "He [i.e. the Mariner] heareth sounds and seeth strange sights and commotions in the sky and the element." If Coleridge be here describing the "fire-flags" as a "commotion" in the "sky," then they are very probably lightning flashes. However, such a reading of the gloss is by no means certain due to its vagueness and ambiguity. Thus, the referents of "sights" and "commotions" cannot be unequivocally determined. Are the two words intended to be synonyms in apposition which denote the same phenomena? If so, do "sights" and "commotions" each comprehend all of the various apparitions in ll. 309-26, or just some of these? Alternatively, could not "sights" and "commotions" each denote different things? In that case, it would seem most logical to assume that Coleridge in his gloss is speaking of the phenomena of ll. 309-26 in the order of their appearance. Combining this supposition with the most plausible guesses about the referents of Coleridge's words, we could identify (1) the "sounds" with the "roaring wind" of ll. 309-12; (2) the "sights" with the "fire-flags" and dancing stars of ll. 314-17, and (3) the "commotions" with the thunderstorm of ll. 320-26. If this reading be correct, then Coleridge is describing the flags simply as a "sight" in the "sky" or "element." This is not sufficiently specific to provide any real clue as to the nature of the "fire-flags."

41. The Mariner's ship is not specifically described as being under the "one black cloud" until ll. 329-30. By that time, not only has the "one black cloud" presumably moved from its position in ll. 313-15, but the Mariner's vessel itself has changed location (328). Since both motions were apparently necessary to place the ship beneath the "one black cloud," that storm was seemingly at some distance from the vessel in ll. 313-15.

42. For these sources, see *Road,* pp. 186-87. For the emphasis of these authorities upon the torrential rain and/or loud thunder in lower latitude lightning

storms, see William Bartram, *The Travels of William Bartram,* ed. Mark van Doren (New York: Macy, 1928), pp. 39, 132-33, 279, and 311; and Purchas 2:124 and 2:352.

43. It might be argued against this supposition that the Mariner does not mention thunder in connection with the storm of ll. 320-26. However, the 1798 version of what was finally l. 322 of the *Ancient Mariner* ("Hark! hark! the thick black cloud is cleft," *Works,* p. 199 n.) suggests that the Mariner does in fact hear thunder.

44. It could of course be assumed that the "fire-flags" are discharges of lightning from separate thunder-heads. However, this is in no way suggested by Coleridge, and may in any case be precluded by the Mariner's reference to "one black cloud" in l. 320.

45. In this regard, Coleridge as we shall see appears to have imagined the corposants of l. 314 as being in motion aloft upon the Mariner's ship (i.e., in or against the sky from the viewpoint of the Mariner upon the vessel's deck). Such illuminations would resemble both the aurora and multiple flashes of lightning in being lights in the sky which display considerable activity.

46. See, for example, Adanson, p. 102; Bassett, pp. 302 and 312; Burton, p. 166; Churchill, 1:293 and 2:526; Dampier, p. 414; Eden, p. 250; Frézier, p. 37; Hakluyt, 9:345-46; Herbert, p. 11; Josselyn, p. 8; Linschoten, p. 167; Purchas, 2:351 and 19:11; Seneca, 1:21; and Ulloa, p. 350.

47. In this connection, Coleridge could possibly have been influenced in creating the image of "fire-flags" by the plate from Erasmus Francisci's *Der Wunder-reiche . . .* (Nürnberg, 1680) that is the frontispiece of *Road.* In this illustration, a multiple display of corposants in a ship's rigging are visually paralleled by highlights upon pennants flying from the mast-tops. The two parallel images could have been merged by Coleridge's imagination to produce the metaphor of "fire-flags."

48. For some other accounts of the "antics" (*Road,* p. 85) of St. Elmo's fire, see Bassett, pp. 305 and 312; Batman, p. 22; Eden, p. 250; Hakluyt, 9:345; Herbert, p. 11; Linschoten, p. 167; and Shakespeare, p. 112.

49. For some other comparisons of the corposant to a star, see Bassett, pp. 302 and 303; Burton, p. 166; Carey, p. 30; Dampier, p. 414; and Seneca, 1:21.

50. See H. W. Piper, *The Singing of Mount Abora* (Fairleigh Dickinson U. Press and Associated U. Presses, 1987), pp. 53-54.

51. The star-like corposants as "deere Ladies Crowne" could have been associated in Coleridge's mind with Mary's crown of stars in Rev. 12:1.

52. In this regard, ll. 311 and 313 together recall Acts 2:2. In the former, the Mariner hears the "sound" of the wind in the "upper air." In the latter, the "sound" of the wind comes "from heaven."

53. See Chandler, p. 408. She notes that the "incompleteness of the Mariner's redemption is reinforced by the ambivalent imagery" of ll. 309-20 of the *Ancient Mariner.* However, Chandler does not in this connection mention the "fire-flags."

54. The storm suggests the divine wrath through its blackness, its intense lightning, and its downpour of rain (320) which recalls the biblical Flood.

55. The two following quotes are from David Crantz, *The History of Greenland . . . ,* 2 vols. (London, 1767), 1:202; and Samuel Hearne, *A Journey from Prince of Wales's Fort . . . ,* ed., Richard Glover (Toronto: Macmillan, 1958), p. 222 n . . . .

56. This would reflect both Coleridge's romantic interest in the details of nature, and also the poet's respect for empirical reality that arose from his grounding in 18th Century philosophy and science.

57. Coleridge's use of the corposant in the "fire-flags" as an ambivalent spiritual symbol is paralleled by Melville's later employment of St. Elmo's fire in the famous Chapter 118 ("The Candles") of *Moby-Dick.* Melville (besides having seen the corposant himself at sea during a voyage in 1849) was apparently familiar with St. Elmo's fire from some of the same literary sources known to Coleridge. These include Burton, Hakluyt, Pliny, Purchas, and Seneca. See Kenneth Walter Cameron, "A Note on the Corpusants in *Moby-Dick,*" *The Emerson Society Quarterly,* no. 19 (1960): 22-23; and Howard P. Vincent, *The Trying-Out of Moby-Dick* (Boston: Houghton, 1949), pp. 376-79. From his literary sources, Melville apparently knew like Coleridge that the corposant was traditionally regarded as both an ill-omen and a favorable sign of heaven's care (Cameron, p. 23; and Vincent, pp. 377-79). Thus, in "The Candles," Stubb sees St. Elmo's fire as a favorable portent, while Starbuck takes it as a negative omen. There opposing beliefs about the corposant may have suggested to Melville as they did to Coleridge that St. Elmo's fire could be used as an *"ambiguous* symbol" (Vincent, p. 379). In this regard, just as Coleridge's "fire-flags" imply both God's love and God's anger, so Melville uses the corposant to suggest the contrarities of good and evil in the divine nature. See Mukhtar Ali Isani, "Zoroastrianism and the Fire Symbolism in *Moby-Dick,*" *American Literature* 44 (1972): 395-96; and Charles Child Walcutt, "The Fire Symbol in *Moby Dick,*" *MLN* [*Modern Language Notes*] 49 (1944): 305-09.

An earlier version of this paper was read at the February 1990 meeting of the South Central Conference on Christianity and Literature. I would like to dedicate my paper to the memory of my late colleague Professor Malcolm Ware (1927-81).

Jack Stillinger (essay date 1992)

SOURCE: Stillinger, Jack. "The Multiple Versions of Coleridge's Poems: How Many *Mariner*s Did Coleridge Write?" In *Romantic Complexity: Keats, Coleridge, and Wordsworth,* pp. 166-82. Urbana, Ill.: University of Illinois Press, 2006.

[*In the following excerpt, originally published in 1992, Stillinger argues against the critical notion that regards an author's latest version of a text as his most authoritative, emphasizing the significance of each of the numerous drafts of Coleridge's best-known poems and speculating as to the poet's motives for these multiple revisions.*]

Each of Coleridge's best-known poems exists not just in a single text but in several separate versions, some of which differ drastically from others, and every one of which is independently authoritative in the sense that it was authored by Coleridge himself.[1] Thus we have sixteen or more manuscript and printed texts of *The Eolian Harp,* twelve distinct texts of *This Lime-Tree Bower My Prison,* eighteen or more texts of *The Rime of the Ancient Mariner,* and similar numbers for *Frost at Midnight, Kubla Khan, Christabel,* and the *Dejection* ode. The multiplicity of versions considerably complicates any attempt to read and interpret the poems. In this chapter I shall describe some of the versions of Coleridge's most frequently anthologized poems and discuss some of the complications that these versions introduce into Coleridge criticism.

One of our most deeply ingrained notions about Coleridge's poetic texts is that there should be—somewhere, whether already existing or yet to be constructed by scholars—a single "best" or "most authoritative" text for each of Coleridge's poems and that it is the job of the modern textual scholar to determine what that single best or most authoritative text is (and, if the scholar is doing an edition of the poems, to construct and print that text as the standard to which all earlier variant texts lead up and from which all later variant texts descend).

Traditionally, the best or most authoritative text of an author's work has been thought to be some form of "final" version, most often the latest text written or printed during the author's lifetime—the last that the author *could* or *might* have had a hand in. All earlier versions of the work, whether in manuscript or printed form, were routinely assigned inferior status, as so many temporary stages on the way to the final version. When they were given any recognition at all, these earlier versions were usually reported fragmentarily, in textual apparatuses at the foot of the page or in the back of an edition. In the rare instances where an edition presented early and late versions on facing pages, it was usually understood that the version on the left-hand side was some kind of incomplete preliminary text that stood as a milepost on the way toward the perfection of the text on the right-hand side.[2] Thus in the case of *The Rime of the Ancient Mariner,* the text in one or another of Coleridge's late *Poetical Works*—1828, 1829, or 1834 (this last in the year in which the poet died)—was *the* best, *the* most authoritative, version. All earlier versions were viewed as texts preliminary to the one Coleridge most wanted us to read ever after, the version of the late *Poetical Works.*

Another, more recent view of textual authority—a view associated in Romantic studies with Jonathan Wordsworth, Stephen Parrish, and the Cornell edition of Wordsworth's poems, and in the field of American literature vigorously argued by Hershel Parker—is the idea that the most authoritative version of a work is the *earliest* rather than the latest and is usually (where manuscripts are available) a manuscript form of the work rather than an early printed text. Thus Wordsworth's tale of poor Margaret is seen as "best" in the early text called *The Ruined Cottage,* and this form of the story is (aesthetically as well as theoretically) preferred over the more complicated versions in *The Pedlar* and book 1 of *The Excursion.* In the much-discussed instance of *The Prelude,* a number of influential critics are on record as preferring one or another earlier version rather than the latest recoverable text in which Wordsworth himself had a hand—that is, the thirteen-book text of 1805 over the fourteen-book text of 1850, and then a hypothetical five-book version of 1804 over the thirteen books of 1805, and, to move even further backward, a two-part version of 1798-99 over the hypothetical five books of 1804.[3] (Jeffrey Baker [1982, 79] commented some years ago that the best text of all, earlier than any known manuscript, would be the version heard by Wordsworth's dog as the poet composed orally during his walks.) In the example of *The Rime of the Ancient Mariner,* for which we have no extant manuscript, the best—because earliest—version would be that of the first edition of *Lyrical Ballads,* and this is the basis of the text that William Empson and David Pirie concocted, without marginal glosses but with modernized spelling and passages taken over from later versions, in their selected edition, *Coleridge's Verse,* published by Faber in 1972.

Both of these views—the preference for the author's final text and the countering preference for a first or early text—alike depend on the belief that there is, whether late or early, some single version that is best or most authoritative. This is a belief that is being challenged, and gradually replaced, by an idea first proposed by James Thorpe in the 1960s and then developed and championed in Germany by Hans Zeller; in the United States by Jerome McGann, Donald Reiman, Peter Shillingsburg, and myself (among others); and in Britain by James McLaverty and the most recent serious editor of Coleridge's poems, J. C. C. Mays.[4] This newest idea is that every individual version of a work is a distinct text in its own right, with unique aesthetic character and unique authorial intention.

The concept of multiple versions has more practical relevance to some writers than to others. Keats, who died young and had no time to revise over a long lifetime the way Wordsworth and Coleridge did, is generally a single-version author. He does not seem to have been interested in revising even where he had plenty of time to make changes, and frequently when one is looking around for the best, most authoritative version of a Keats poem (say, of *Ode on a Grecian Urn*) there is really only a single substantive text to choose.[5] But with Wordsworth and Coleridge, compulsive revisers who lived three or four decades after first drafting their most admired poems, there are plenty of versions competing for attention. The theory of versions—the idea that every separate version is a work in its own right and that all authoritative versions are equally authoritative—allows for some interesting new ways of looking at their works.

Thus, where before we might have thought we had only one or two *Rimes of the Ancient Mariner*—for example, the well-glossed, well-epigraphed text of one of the late *Poetical Works* (or of J. D. Campbell's and E. H. Coleridge's editions based on one or another of those late texts) and the sparer, more archaic version of the first printed text in the *Lyrical Ballads* of 1798—it is now possible to say that Coleridge authored (and, in authoring, *authorized*) a great many separate versions of *The Ancient Mariner*. I count at least eighteen but feel certain that there are others still to be discovered.

Let me go into a little detail concerning the multiple versions of Coleridge's major poems. Every student of Romanticism knows that Coleridge modernized the spelling and some of the language of *The Ancient Mariner* for the second publication of the poem, in the next edition of *Lyrical Ballads* in 1800, and that he added the Latin epigraph and the prose marginal glosses fifteen or more years after that. It is similarly well known that he added the lines celebrating "the one Life within us and abroad" to *The Eolian Harp* twenty-two years after he completed the first version of that poem and that there are striking differences between the original and revised texts of the Dejection ode, which at

one time or another was addressed to Sara Hutchinson, Wordsworth, a fictional character called "Edmund," and an unnamed "Lady." And the best critics working on individual poems—say, *Frost at Midnight* or *Kubla Khan*—regularly make use of the manuscripts, successive printings, and annotated copies to support their interpretations. Even so, I think that students of Coleridge in general have very little idea of the frequency of variation among the texts or of the multiplicity of versions of the works they are studying and the complexity of relationships among the versions. And I also think that these same students continue, in large numbers, to regard the so-called final texts as the principal versions, slighting or entirely ignoring the earlier authoritative versions.

Here are some textual facts concerning the seven best-known works in the canon.[6] For *The Eolian Harp* we have sixteen or more separate manuscripts and printed versions dating from 1796 through 1828. Coleridge drafted at least part of the poem in August 1795, a few weeks before his marriage to Sara Fricker, and had a complete first version in hand sometime before the end of the year. The earliest surviving forms of the poem are the first printed text, in Coleridge's *Poems on Various Subjects,* published in April 1796, and the holograph manuscripts associated with that text at the University of Texas and Haverford College (*CoS* [Manuscripts in the Coleridge Section of Rosenbaum and White (1982)] 119, 120, 124). Subsequently there are attempts at revision by Coleridge in other holographs at Texas and Cornell (*CoS* 121-23); then a second printed text, in the next edition of Coleridge's *Poems,* published in October 1797; a version constituted by Coleridge's request to his publisher to cancel three lines comparing melodies to footless birds of Paradise (*CL* [*Collected Letters of Samuel Taylor Coleridge*] (Coleridge 1956b)], 1:331); and another printed text, in the third edition of Coleridge's *Poems,* published in 1803. After the *Poems* of 1803, there are Coleridge's manuscript alterations of the text in a copy of the 1797 *Poems* now at Yale (*CoS* 515), then two distinct versions in the volume published in 1817 titled *Sibylline Leaves*—the first version consisting of the original printed text in the body of the book, the second consisting of this text as corrected and expanded in the errata items listed at the front of the book (errata items that included, among other things, the insertion of the lines about "the one Life within us and abroad"). The latest authoritative version is that in Coleridge's *Poetical Works* of 1828 (though there are additional changes in minor details in the final lifetime edition, the *Poetical Works* of 1834).

These amount, as I said, to sixteen different versions of the poem, ranging from fifty-one to sixty-four lines in length—sometimes written or printed as a single paragraph, sometimes divided into three, four, or five paragraphs—and variously titled **"Effusion XXXV"** or

"Composed at Clevedon, Somersetshire" or *The Eolian Harp.* There are too many differences to enumerate in this essay. In general terms, they change the tone, the philosophical and religious ideas, and the basic structure rather drastically. The first recoverable version, **"Effusion XXXV,"** recounts an amusing incident of early married life, while the latest version is a much more serious affair—and one of the most frequently discussed poems of the Coleridge canon.

For *This Lime-Tree Bower My Prison,* which Coleridge first drafted in the summer of 1797 and then revised and expanded over the next year or so, there is a much simpler array—only twelve separate versions. The first of these is in a letter to Robert Southey of July 1797, the same month in which Sara Coleridge spilled the boiling milk on Samuel's foot (*CL,* 1:334-36). The second is in a letter to Charles Lloyd now in the Berg Collection of the New York Public Library (*CoS* 680). The third version is represented by an extract of lines 38-43 quoted in a letter to John Thelwall, October 1797 (*CL,* 1:349-50). The fourth is the earliest printed text, in Southey's *Annual Anthology* in 1800, and the fifth is constituted by manuscript alterations that Coleridge made sometime between 1800 and 1810 in a copy of the *Annual Anthology* now at Yale (*CoS* 682).[7] The sixth version is a text reprinted with only very minor changes from the *Annual Anthology* in William Frederick Mylius's *The Poetical Class-Book* (1810). The seventh and eighth versions are the uncorrected and corrected texts in *Sibylline Leaves* of 1817, and the ninth is constituted by Coleridge's further alterations of the poem in a copy of *Sibylline Leaves* now at Harvard (*CoS* 606). There are still more minor substantive changes in the *Poetical Works* of 1828, 1829, and 1834.

These versions vary from fifty-five to seventy-seven lines in length. The most interesting differences among the versions appear in the manuscript texts, in two of which (the letters to Southey and Lloyd) the exquisitely detailed description of the roaring dell that we admire so much in the printed texts is mostly left out and the wide prospect—the second of the three landscapes described in the standard text—is missing entirely. But manuscript and printed versions alike show important differences concerning the spiritual significance of nature: in several earlier texts, all nature is "a living thing / Which acts upon the mind"; a middle version replaces this idea with a description of the "soul / Kindling unutterable Thanksgivings / And Adorations" (*CoS* 682); and in subsequent texts Coleridge dropped both the idea of nature as a "living thing" (*Sibylline Leaves* errata) and the lines about "the Almighty Spirit . . . [making] Spirits perceive his presence" (*CoS* 606).

For *Frost at Midnight,* written in 1798, I know of ten distinct versions beginning with the first printed text, in the quarto volume containing *Fears in Solitude,*

France: An Ode, and *Frost at Midnight* published in the fall of 1798. After this comes a version constituted by manuscript changes that Coleridge made probably about a decade later in an annotated copy of the 1798 quarto.[8] Subsequently, we have two different printed versions in 1812 (in the *Poetical Register,* vol. 7, and the pamphlet *Poems, by S. T. Coleridge, Esq.* issued by Law and Gilbert), three others in the proofs and the uncorrected and corrected published texts of *Sibylline Leaves* in 1817, a substantial set of variants in a letter that Coleridge wrote in 1820 (*CL,* 5:111-12), and the texts of the *Poetical Works* of 1828, 1829, and 1834 (1828 agrees substantively with the corrected *Sibylline Leaves;* 1829 and 1834 together constitute the final lifetime version).

These versions range from eighty-five to seventy-three lines in length, and in this case Coleridge shortened the poem, cutting out half a dozen lines from the end so as to conclude with the "silent icicles, / Quietly shining to the quiet Moon." He continually worked at revising the description and evaluation of the speaker's mental activity in the first paragraph of the poem. One text mentions the speaker's "delights . . . volition . . . deep faith" and emphasizes the playfulness of the interaction of the speaker's mind with the objective world (1798 quarto). Another text describes this playfulness as "wild reliques of our childish Thought" and associates it with the speaker's life in the past rather than his situation in the present (*Poetical Register*). A still later text removes all the self-belittling phrases of the description (*Sibylline Leaves*). And the latest text substitutes an almost negative description for the positive, with emphasis on the triviality of the experience and the bizarre, solipsistic character of the "puny flaps and freaks" of the idling spirit, everywhere seeking of itself, making a toy of thought.

The eighteen versions that I mentioned of *The Rime of the Ancient Mariner* consist of the first printed text, in the original *Lyrical Ballads* of 1798; then a version constituted by revisions that Coleridge requested in a letter to the publisher of mid-July 1800 (*CL,* 1:598-602), and another version, earlier or later than this, represented by Coleridge's annotations in a copy of *Lyrical Ballads* now at Trinity College, Cambridge (*CoS* 577). Subsequently there are three more printed texts, each different from the others, in the *Lyrical Ballads* of 1800, 1802, and 1805; two more versions in the uncorrected and corrected texts of *Sibylline Leaves;* at least six further versions represented by Coleridge's handwritten changes in copies of *Sibylline Leaves* at Columbia, Harvard, Yale, Duke, Stanford, and in a private collection (*CoS* 598-603, 605);[9] and finally the versions of Coleridge's late *Poetical Works* in 1828, 1829, and 1834.

The poem loses some thirty-nine lines in the course of revision, most of its archaic spellings, and the prose

"Argument" that was printed on a separate page before the beginning of the poem in the first two editions of *Lyrical Ballads*; undergoes changes of title; gains a Latin epigraph from Thomas Burnet; and gains fifty-eight prose glosses printed in the margins beside and beneath the verses. (All commentators, regardless of whether or not they approve of Coleridge's addition of the glosses, agree that the glosses produced major changes in our reading of the poem.)[10]

Kubla Khan has the smallest number of versions among the major poems. It is not difficult to imagine an initial stage of the work consisting of the first thirty-six lines—the description of Kubla Khan the triumphant creator, or arrogant tyrant, decreeing his stately pleasure dome in a place sacred to the river Alph, producing a miracle of rare device—and then a later stage of composition in which Coleridge added the remaining eighteen lines expressing a fervent desire to re-create "that dome in air." Among extant versions, however, as opposed to imagined ones, there are only five: the holograph fair copy in the British Library (*CoS* 288); the first printing of the poem, in the *Christabel* volume of 1816; a slightly altered version in the form of a marked copy of this printed text at Harvard (*CoS* 62); and the texts in Coleridge's *Poetical Works* of 1828 and 1834.

The manuscript differs in wording from the first printed text in about one-fifth of the lines, but the manuscript variants, like those that occur in later printings, are of relatively minor importance. The more interesting differences among the versions have to do with the organization (rather than the wording) of the lines—in particular, the successive changes in the structure of the poem that are created by the changing positions of the paragraph divisions—and with Coleridge's prose accompanying the verse. Concerning this first matter, the manuscript text consists of two paragraphs of verse, the 1816 text is in four paragraphs, the final versions are printed as three or four paragraphs (there is an ambiguous page-break in 1834)—and each scheme of divisions produces a different way of reading the poem.[11] Concerning the other matter, Coleridge's first (extant) explanation of the circumstances, in a short note at the end of the manuscript, gives the place and date and mentions the influence of opium but says nothing about Purchas's *Pilgrimage,* or the composition of "two to three hundred lines," or the interruption by a person on business from Porlock. This is then expanded into the much longer version, containing all those now-famous details, that formed the preface to the poem in the first printing of 1816. It has been sensibly remarked that were it not for the preface we would never know that the poem was a fragment. The preface controls our reading from beginning to end: when it is removed, the poetic lines clearly emphasize creativity and inspiration, but coming after the preface, the lines emphasize the poet's *failure* at creativity.[12]

For *Christabel,* which Coleridge began in 1798, expanded in 1800, further enlarged in 1801, and then tinkered with, but never completed, all the rest of his life, I have identified eighteen versions, but probably there are several more than that number. To begin with, we know of nine manuscript versions (or partial versions) earlier than the first printed text, which was in the *Christabel* volume of 1816.[13] That first printed text can count as the tenth version. Then there are at least five subsequent versions in the form of manuscript changes that Coleridge made in copies of the edition of 1816.[14] Three more versions are constituted by the texts in the *Poetical Works* of 1828, 1829, and 1834.

Christabel is the longest of Coleridge's best-known works, and it is not possible here to go into the numerous details of substantive difference among the manuscripts and printed texts. I shall just mention a couple of interesting revisions in two annotated copies of the 1816 text that survive at Harvard and Princeton. In the first (*CoS* 62), at the point at which the witch Geraldine removes her robe and vest and the narrator exclaims, "Behold! her bosom and half her side," Coleridge inserted a rhyming line to describe what Christabel saw: "It was dark and rough as the Sea Wolf's hide." In the annotated copy at Princeton (*CoS* 63), Coleridge added a series of prose glosses in the margin, written in the same style as those in *The Ancient Mariner,* to explain what was happening in the lines of verse beside them. For lines 204-9, for example, Coleridge writes, "The Mother of Christabel, who is now her Guardian Spirit, appears to Geraldine, as in answer to her wish. Geraldine fears the Spirit, but yet has power over it for a time." And for lines 262-70: "As soon as the wicked Bosom, with the mysterious sign of Evil stamped thereby, touches Christabel, she is deprived of the power of disclosing what had occurred." There are five such glosses for the text of part 1, and four for the text of part 2, and in them Coleridge assumes the role and the voice of one of the earliest interpreters of the action taking place in the verse.

Finally (in this skimming survey) we come to the *Dejection* ode, which Coleridge wrote and rewrote several times in 1802 and then, just as with his other poems, continued to revise over the next three decades. For this work we have at least fifteen distinct versions—the first four in manuscripts and a transcript written before the initial publication of the poem, in the *Morning Post* of 4 October 1802; then several more versions in manuscripts and transcripts of late 1802, 1803, and 1804-5;[15] a partial version constituted by two long quotations in an essay by Coleridge in *Felix Farley's Bristol Journal* in 1814; then three more versions in the proof sheets and the uncorrected and corrected published texts of *Sibylline Leaves*; further revisions in some annotated copies of *Sibylline Leaves*; and finally, as usual, the texts included in the late *Poetical Works.*

The earliest version of **Dejection** is 339 or 340 lines long—two and a half times the length of the latest version—and it is so different in theme and tone from the latest that some scholars consider it a separate work in the Coleridge canon. John Beer, for example, in his Everyman edition of Coleridge's poems, prints both an early and a late text, with separate titles (Coleridge 1974), and Stephen Parrish, in the preface to his study of the manuscripts, insists that the earliest version is "an altogether different poem" (1988a). These scholars are quite right. One of the points of the present [essay] is simply that all the other versions of **Dejection** are separate works as well. Not least among the interesting revisions is the changing identity of the person addressed in the poem: the famous lines at the beginning of what we usually think of as the fourth stanza—"O Lady! we receive but what we give, / And in our life alone does Nature live"—are successively uttered to Sara, to Wordsworth, to Edmund, to William, to Edmund again, and finally to the unnamed "Lady." The revisions change the poem from a passionate love lament to an almost academic dissertation on the shaping spirit of imagination. The beloved Sara of the letter becomes something like a Spenserian or Miltonic muse in the shorter, more dignified text of the late **Poetical Works.**

My enumeration of the multiple versions of Coleridge's seven best-known poems adds up to ninety-four separate texts. But even this expanded canon of versions does not take into account the thousands of differences in the lesser details of punctuation, capitalization, spelling, and paragraphing among the texts. Such lesser differences can have considerable effects. The first printing of **The Eolian Harp,** for example, made frequent use of the old long *s,* while the second printing, just a year later, uses only the modern *s*—with the result that the first text looks much more like an eighteenth-century poem and the second looks much more like a work of the nineteenth century. The paragraph divisions in **Christabel** continually change from version to version, and so, as a result, does the reader's idea of how Coleridge structured this narrative fragment.[16]

This multiplicity of versions constitutes a type of textual *instability* that makes interpretation of Coleridge far more difficult than it would be if we had only one version per work. Practical criticism—the day-to-day business of reading and interpretation—has always needed two things: first, a single author of the work that is being read and interpreted, and, second, a single text. Notwithstanding its far greater literary sophistication, critical theory also depends on single authors and fixed texts. With Coleridge there is no problem about the single author. But with so many versions of his poems, there does seem to be a problem in identifying the work that the critic is to read and interpret. Coleridge is usually the sole author of the poems we are concerned

with, but he himself undermines the concept of a stable text by his continuous revising.

Coleridge made no secret of his idea that revision is an essential part of the creation of poetry. In his twenty-year plan for an epic poem, as he outlines it in a letter of early April 1797, the final five years were to be devoted to revision—an amount of time equal to the five years that he says he would give to the original drafting of the work (*CL,* 1:320-21, 6:1009). In another letter, this time in early October 1800, he says that his "taste in judging" is "far more perfect than [his] power to execute": "I do nothing, but almost instantly it's defects & sillinesses come upon my mind, and haunt me, till I am completely disgusted with my performance" (*CL,* 1:629). The implication is that he immediately sets about to remedy, by revising, what he perceives as "defects & sillinesses."

But while these remarks in Coleridge's letters would cover the ordinary practices that we see in many poets who want to alter and improve their works, there is something extraordinary about the frequency with which Coleridge revised his texts. I suggest that Coleridge changed his texts at least partly in order to create the very instability that would make his poems and their meanings elusive. Certainly his public practice called attention to textual fluctuations in his poetry.

He was, for example (as I pointed out at the beginning of chapter 9 [of *Romantic Complexity: Keats, Coleridge, and Wordsworth*]), conspicuously casual about his poetic accomplishments. He classed the first version of **The Eolian Harp** among his "Effusions" when he published it in his volume of 1796; he gave **Reflections on Having Left a Place of Retirement** the subtitle "A Poem Which Affects Not to Be Poetry"; he characterized **Fears in Solitude** as "a sort of middle thing between Poetry and Oratory"; he offered **Kubla Khan** to the public, as he says in the preface, "rather as a psychological curiosity, than on the ground of any supposed *poetic* merits" (Coleridge 1912, 1:100 n., 106 n., 257 n., 295). **Sibylline Leaves** begins with a preface mentioning "the fragmentary and widely scattered state" of the poems herein collected, and the final piece in the volume, **The Destiny of Nations,** is pointedly fragmentary, breaking off almost in midsentence with the beginning of a wild and desolate landscape that is never further described.[17] In such practices Coleridge intentionally presents himself to the public as a writer who is not wholly serious in his endeavors and perhaps not even competent. The emphasis is on the amateur qualities of the performance, its rough and unfinished character—the transitory, provisional nature of the work that the reader is holding in hand.

This public casualness seems to go together with Coleridge's almost flaunting display of the instability of his texts. As he kept revising his works, he also called attention to his revising in notes and prefaces to the poems. And he frequently changed his texts right before the reader's eyes (as it were) by means of printed errata lists, which both emphasize the fact that the revisions were made since the poems were set in type for the book and also provide a second version of the printed poem to accompany the first. In *Sibylline Leaves,* where the errata revisions are the most extensive of all, the errata pages are prominently placed at the beginning rather than the end of the volume. Then there are the handwritten changes and revisions that Coleridge wrote in the margins and above and beneath the lines in copies of his works that he gave to friends and acquaintances. The abundance of such annotated copies—J. C. C. Mays has located two dozen annotated copies just of *Sibylline Leaves*—suggests that Coleridge was typically unwilling to give away his works without making changes by hand to show that the printed text alone would not do.

For the critic who inherits this entire poetic ensemble, the existence of these many versions creates a number of important theoretical and practical problems. In the first place, it certainly has the potential of expanding the Coleridge canon dramatically (this is the issue implied in the subtitle of this chapter, "How Many *Mariners* Did Coleridge Write?"). If every separate version is a work in its own right and all authoritative versions of a work are equally authoritative, then the Coleridge canon contains not just a single *Eolian Harp* but sixteen or more works variously entitled **"Effusion XXXV"** or **"Composed at Clevedon, Somersetshire"** or *The Eolian Harp*; contains twelve separate works titled *This Lime-Tree Bower My Prison*; contains at least eighteen works titled *The Rime of the Ancient Mariner*; and so on through the list.

Another way of thinking about the Coleridge canon is to question the *identity* of any specific work in it. When we speak of *The Eolian Harp* or *The Ancient Mariner,* are we speaking of a single version of a work or of all the versions taken together? And if we are speaking of all the versions taken together, are we thinking of a series of stages in which the work is defined by the *process* of its successive revisions, or are we thinking of all the versions as existing simultaneously, as they might in a variorum edition giving a complete account of successive readings? Theorists who worry about the identity of a literary work are primarily concerned with the elements of the work that make the same impression on all readers alike (as opposed to elements that impress each reader differently according to the individual reader's interpretation).[18] But these theorists always start with some specific text at hand. The more basic question raised by a theory of versions is how to identify a work in the first place so as to have a specific text to theorize about.

There are of course practical questions about editorial procedure—most obviously the question of which version we shall choose for reprinting (for example, in a standard edition or in an anthology) when we are allowed only one version per title. The old concept of choosing or constructing a text according to the author's final intentions was a handy solution to the problem. But as James Thorpe remarked more than three decades ago, saying that the author's final text is the most authoritative "is much like saying that an author's last poem (or novel, or play) is . . . [the author's] best one; it may be, and it may not be" (1972, 47). The newer idea of taking the earliest text as most authoritative is similarly handy but also similarly suspect when several versions exist.

The newest idea that all authoritative versions are equally authoritative makes editing considerably more difficult, because scholars now have to make choices not necessarily indicated by the authors—involving themselves in what Thorpe called "the aesthetics of textual criticism" (1965, 1972) or choosing versions on such grounds as historical importance or "representativeness." John Beer defied convention by printing the earliest (rather than the latest) text of *The Eolian Harp* in his Everyman edition of Coleridge's poems, and, as I have already mentioned, he included there both early and late versions of *Dejection.* Many more such departures from the old standard may be predicted, and future editors will have some tough choices to make in presenting a single reading text for each of the several hundred titles in the Coleridge canon.

Most important, there are a number of ways in which these multiple versions complicate the problems of interpreting the poems, whether individually or all the poems taken together as a unified (or, as the case may be, *dis*unified) body of work constituting the poet "Coleridge." The editorial choice of the latest texts may well be artistically justifiable. Coleridge, just like Wordsworth, seems to have been an amazingly shrewd reviser, and I think most critics would agree, even if they couldn't logically defend their preferences, that his later versions are almost always richer, more complex, better structured, more pleasing aesthetically. But when we come to interpretation (as opposed to reading and admiring), there are serious liabilities in working—as we usually do—solely or even primarily with those latest texts.

For one thing, any view of Coleridge's poetry based only on the latest texts—a view that one might get, for example, from reading selections in an anthology that arranges them in chronological order—certainly results in a distorted idea of Coleridge's development as a poet. We conventionally read *The Eolian Harp* in its chronological position for the summer or autumn of 1795, *This Lime-Tree Bower My Prison* in its chronological position for July 1797, *Frost at Midnight* and *The Ancient Mariner* in their positions for the spring of 1798, and so on, all the while imagining that Coleridge wrote what we are reading in just this order and at just the times represented by the dates of original composition. In fact, in such a situation, we are reading a text of *The Eolian Harp* that dates either from 1817 or from 1828 (depending on when the 1817 errata revisions are considered to have become a part of the complete poem), but in any case a text that Coleridge first arrived at some twenty or more years after the first-draft date of August 1795. Similarly we are reading a *Lime-Tree Bower* and an *Ancient Mariner* that date not from 1797 and 1798 but again from 1817 or later—that is, from a time when Coleridge was in his forties rather than in his twenties—and a *Frost at Midnight* that dates not from 1798 but from 1829, when Coleridge was in his later fifties. (And since I am supposing that many of us are still reading texts based on E. H. Coleridge's Oxford edition, in matters of punctuation and other accidentals we are reading versions that date from the very end of Coleridge's life—and even beyond, since there were numerous further small changes introduced into Coleridge's poems by the twentieth-century editor and the Oxford printers.)

In a like manner, by working with the latest texts we run the risk of misunderstanding or even being entirely ignorant of Coleridge's changes of interest and emphasis in subject matter, idea, and theme. We customarily read *The Eolian Harp* as a serious meditation on "the one Life within us and abroad," while the poem in fact began as a relatively frivolous "effusion" and only gradually developed into the philosophical poem that we have today. *Lime-Tree Bower* undergoes significant changes in religious sentiment in the course of revision. The structural and thematic opposition that makes *Frost at Midnight* so successful a poem was arrived at only toward the end of Coleridge's life. *The Ancient Mariner* seems to become a much more theologically minded work in its later versions. And so on through the list.

It is clearly a mistake to think that all these latest texts existed together before the end of Coleridge's career, and any idea of unity in Coleridge's work that is based on these latest texts can apply only to the late period in which they were perfected. With an understanding of multiple versions, the critic can begin to grasp the biographical and historical reality of Coleridge's work—can do a kind of archaeological excavation, as it were, in which versions actually existing at the same time can be connected to form layers of Coleridgean textual history.[19]

For an example of such a Coleridgean archaeological layer, consider the following. In the early summer of 1798, just before Wordsworth wrote *Tintern Abbey,* the canon of major poems that I am surveying stood as fol-

lows: *The Eolian Harp* was in the state represented by the text in Coleridge's *Poems* of 1797—no longer an effusion but still a long way from the more serious philosophical meditation that we read in the standard text. The state of *Lime-Tree Bower* is somewhat in question. Coleridge may have arrived at the text with the three successive landscapes that he published in 1800, but it is possible that the work was still in the more rudimentary form represented by the letters of the summer and autumn of 1797. *Frost at Midnight* at this time was presumably in the state represented by the quarto text of 1798—more ambiguous in its attitude toward the speaker's mental activity in the opening lines and concluding not with the "silent icicles, / Quietly shining to the quiet Moon" but with the infant Hartley's shouts of eagerness as he tries to escape his mother's arms (a rather discordant note in relation to the tone of the rest of the midnight meditation). The just-completed *Ancient Mariner* was probably in its earliest known form—sans epigraph, sans gloss, sans everything except the plot itself (which Wordsworth criticized as "having no necessary connection") and the imagery (which Wordsworth thought "somewhat too laboriously accumulated").[20] Presumably at least some of the lines of *Kubla Khan* had been drafted by this time, perhaps the first thirty-six, as I surmised earlier in this [essay]. Some of all of part 1 of *Christabel* had been drafted. The *Dejection* ode would not begin to take shape for another three years.

Such an array as I have described is a far more accurate representation of the state of Coleridge's poetry just before Wordsworth wrote *Tintern Abbey* in the summer of 1798 and presumably is more useful as a background for discussion of such topics as Coleridge's influence on Wordsworth and Coleridge's development of the blank-verse meditation that marks the beginning of what we now admire as the so-called greater Romantic lyric. Coleridge, as he himself was well aware,[21] did invent the greater Romantic lyric, because *The Eolian Harp, This Lime-Tree Bower,* and *Frost at Midnight* are all earlier than *Tintern Abbey* and other works in this mode by Wordsworth, and also earlier than any that we single out by other writers, such as the odes of Keats. But *The Eolian Harp, Lime-Tree Bower,* and *Frost at Midnight* as they existed in the early summer of 1798 were quite different poems from the ones we know today.

It is of course the late texts that we read, interpret, and find unity in (and among). There remains, however, for author-centered critics, a nagging question concerning the poet's intentions in his continuous remaking of the poems. A favorable view of Coleridge as artist and thinker might wish to take the line that he had a deliberate plan in his revisions: to create, in his poems taken all together, the kind of unity in multeity—the harmonious whole made out of the separate parts—that he described in *Biographia Literaria* and elsewhere as the ideal of poetic art and that has become, not coincidentally, the kind of unity that critics have generally placed a high premium on ever since (Deconstruction notwithstanding).

Coleridge changed his poems at every period of his life, but he did some especially significant revising in 1815, when he was preparing his works for publication in *Sibylline Leaves.* The date coincides neatly with two important publications by Wordsworth around the same time: first, *The Excursion,* perhaps just a few months earlier (August 1814), with the highly publicized preface in which Wordsworth explains the unity and interrelatedness of all his works together, and second, Wordsworth's first collected *Poems* (April 1815) with another preface explaining the principles by which the poems were classified and arranged into categories. It would be a nice piece of biographical and textual criticism to explain Coleridge's most significant revisions as a reaction to these publications by Wordsworth. Such an explanation would inevitably involve seeing Coleridge the critical theorist turning theory into practical self-criticism as he revises to achieve in his own work the same kind of unity of effect that Wordsworth was in the process of accomplishing in his.

It requires only a medium amount of ingenuity to see Coleridge's alterations as tending toward this unity of effect. In *The Eolian Harp* Coleridge adds the lines celebrating "the one Life within us and abroad," thus giving us ever afterward a memorable passage to help explain the action and theme of *The Ancient Mariner*: the Mariner's abrupt and seemingly motiveless shooting of the albatross now becomes a violation of the "one Life" principle. Similarly, this same passage added to *The Eolian Harp* helps explain why it is that the poet's lime-tree bower, in the next Conversation poem, can be correctly seen as no prison at all but instead as a part of the "one Life" available wherever one looks. *This Lime-Tree Bower My Prison* is revised to make the religious significance of nature more compatible with that conveyed in *The Eolian Harp* and *Frost at Midnight. Frost at Midnight* is revised so as to place more emphasis on the interactions between the human mind and nature and to strengthen the contrast between what is in effect a failure of imagination in the opening paragraph and the successful working of the same faculty later on in the poem, a contrast that parallels the nonfunctioning and subsequent functioning of imagination in *The Ancient Mariner* and relates to similar concerns with the imagination in other works.

The Ancient Mariner itself is made much more complex by the addition of voices, most notably the voice of the theologically minded, scholarly annotater who supplies commentary in the margins and thereby sharpens the logic of the story, expands the religious and moral significances, and adds to the unity of the work. *Kubla Khan* becomes, with the addition of Coleridge's preface, a poem not so much about Kubla's glorious (perhaps we should say arrogant) decree of the stately pleasure dome as it is a poem about creating, or failing to create, unity. Kubla Khan did create a unity, as we can tell from all the images of mingling and merging in the first part of the poem, culminating in the shadow of the dome floating midway on the waves of the sacred river and the "mingled measure" heard from fountain and caves: "It was a miracle of rare device, / A sunny pleasure-dome with caves of ice" (31-36). The question suggested by Coleridge's preface is whether the speaker, desperately wanting to "build that dome in air," can accomplish a similar act of unification. The most important revisions of the *Dejection* ode heighten the emphasis on Coleridge's concerns with perception of nature, with imagination, and with creativity and thus make that poem more obviously relatable to principal concerns of the others.

Only *Christabel,* at this level of medium ingenuity, does not conveniently connect with the others I have discussed, though I feel sure that a slightly greater-than-medium degree of ingenuity could make suitable connections there as well. Perhaps one could solve the problem for the time being simply by exempting all fragments of any sort in this scheme. *Christabel* is the only real, as opposed to purported, fragment among the works I have mentioned so far. One could give it a place similar to that occupied by *Hyperion* among Keats's otherwise well-integrated poetical works: *Hyperion* fails to fit any scheme for the unity of Keats's poems taken all together, and so, we might say, *Christabel* doesn't have to fit either.

In this favorable view that I have sketched out, Coleridge appears to have been a genius at revising his poems. The main tendency of his changes, with or without the model of Wordsworth before him, was to create unity out of the diversity of his compositions in their numerous earlier forms, and the unity that he created provides license and authority for modern critics to explain—however diversely—the unity they discover as a quality that genuinely exists in the poetry.

A less favorable view of the poetry as a unified body is also possible. In this view, the revisions do not really support the progress of unity out of diversity after all. The alterations were made randomly, some much earlier than others, and some in an opposite or contrary direction (for example, the religious sentiments of one of the later versions of *Lime-Tree Bower* actually conflict, rather than harmonize, with the tendency of changes made in other Conversation poems, and the insertion of the lines about "the one Life within us and abroad" seriously damaged the structure and therefore the meaning of *The Eolian Harp*). Coleridge as reviser seems compulsive, willful, out of control, and the bulk of the revisions have to be judged as arbitrary tinkering, minor adjusting, alteration for the mere sake of alteration, rather than the results of any sober attempt to integrate the poems in the way I described just above. The bottom line of this kind of thinking is that Coleridge the famous advocate of unity may in fact have been one of the most scattered and *dis*unified poets in all of English literature.

Yet a third, and again favorable, view of the alterations may be constructed on the basis of my earlier observations about Coleridge's conspicuous featuring of his poetry's instability. Coleridge may have wished to imply that his poems were always in progress toward a never-to-be-attained but increasingly approached perfection. Or, equally, he may have wished to suggest that the perfect poem was a chimera and that authority itself was therefore a fiction. That is to say, he may have been either a Whig or a Deconstructionist, for both of these positions could require a demonstration of textual instability.

There is evidence to support all three of these different views of Coleridge as reviser. But judgments of this kind are ultimately critical constructs—at best, informed opinions—while the multiplicity of versions, being a matter of textual fact, is in a different category of information. It is a matter of fact with which Coleridgeans should become better acquainted.

Notes

Originally published in *Studies in Romanticism* 31 (1992): 127-46. The essay is a preliminary statement of details and theory later incorporated into my *Coleridge and Textual Instability: The Multiple Versions of the Major Poems* (1994).

1. In theoretical writings on the subject (see note 4 below), there is no agreed-on definition of the degree of difference necessary to distinguish one version of a work from another. On the present occasion, I have used Shillingsburg's definition in *Scholarly Editing*: "A version has no substantial existence, but it is represented more or less well or completely by a single text as found in a manuscript, proof, book, or some other written or printed form" (1986, 47). In my subsequent study, *Coleridge and Textual Instability* (1994, 130), I incorporated Hans Zeller's more specific idea ("A New Approach to the Critical Constitution of Literary Texts," 1975) that a single substantive variant is sufficient to separate one version from another.

2. Parrish (1988b, 344), making an analogy with "the Whig interpretation of history," has described this traditional thinking as "textual Whiggery." As, in Whig history, events progress to ever better states of existence, so textual Whiggery has a retrospective view of a succession of texts "moving in an ordered, coherent way by a process of 'unfolding logic' toward completion of a great design."

3. See my "Textual Primitivism and the Editing of Wordsworth," chapter 8 in the present collection [*Romantic Complexity: Keats, Coleridge, and Wordsworth*].

4. See Thorpe (1965), esp. pp. 32-47; Zeller (1975); McGann (1983); Reiman (1987), chap. 10, "'Versioning': The Presentation of Multiple Texts"; Shillingsburg (1986), esp. pp. 44-55, 99-106; Stillinger (1991a), chap. 9, "Implications for Theory"; Stillinger (1991b); McLaverty (1984); and Mays (1992).

5. While this is true generally, there are still many situations of multiple versions with relatively minor differences among them. I discuss Keats's methods of composing (and not revising very much) in chapter 5 in the present collection [*Romantic Complexity*] and give details concerning his multiple texts in the second section of chapter 6 [of *Romantic Complexity*].

6. In parenthetical documentation, *CoS* refers to items in the Coleridge section of Rosenbaum and White (1982). Mays (1992, 138) calculates that he has "uncovered some twenty to thirty per cent more material" than is listed in *Index of English Literary Manuscripts*.

7. The alterations are given in Coleridge's *Marginalia* (1980, 1:94-95).

8. See Evans (1935).

9. These annotated copies are described by Johnson (1975).

10. For example (among critics of the last three decades), Dyck (1973); Lipking (1977); Simpson (1979), esp. pp. 98-101; Mellor (1980), esp. pp. 143-48; McGann (1981); Wheeler (1981, 42-64); Wallen (1986); and Wall (1987).

11. None of these schemes agrees exactly with the three-paragraph arrangement in E. H. Coleridge's Oxford edition (Coleridge 1912).

12. See Perkins (1990).

13. The nine manuscripts are the lost holograph lent to J. P. Collier (see Coleridge 1856, xxxix-xliii) plus *CoS* 51-53, 55, 57-59 and Coleridge's quotation of lines 656-77 in a letter to Southey of May 1801 (*CL* [*Collected Letters of Samuel Taylor Coleridge* (Coleridge 1956b)], 2:728).

14. These are listed in Rosenbaum and White (1982) as *CoS* 60-64. The annotations in *CoS* 63, now in

the Robert H. Taylor Collection at Princeton, and *CoS* 64, owned by John Murray, are given by Rooke (1974).

15. The manuscripts are *CoS* 82-85, prior to first publication, and *CoS* 86-88, afterward. Stephen Parrish (1988a) provides facsimiles and annotated reading texts of the most important versions.

16. As Paul Magnuson pointed out when I delivered an early version of this [essay] at the 1990 Coleridge Summer Conference in Cannington, Somerset, versions can also differ significantly from one another—quite independently of verbal and accidental variants—according to differences in the *contexts* in which the versions appear: for example, newspaper versus collected works, rare book versus modern anthology, and a change in position (relative to the rest of the contents) within a volume or set of volumes. Magnuson's own paper at the same Coleridge Conference, on the political context of the 1798 version of *Frost at Midnight* (in a volume issued by the radical publisher Joseph Johnson and containing, for the rest of the contents, two political pieces on the French Revolution, *Fears in Solitude* and *France: An Ode*) provided a telling illustration. For the paper, see Magnuson (1991), and for the larger study on the same idea, see Magnuson (1998).

17. See Dyer (1989).

18. See Jonathan Culler's introduction to Valdés and Miller's *Identity of the Literary Text* (1985, 3-15).

19. In the process of organizing my information, I constructed a large grid consisting of seven vertical columns (one for each of the seven works whose versions I was tracing) and a series of forty vertical lines across the columns (one for each year of Coleridge's life from 1795 to 1834) and entered notes detailing the successive revisions of the poems in the seven vertical columns. I could then, for any year of Coleridge's poetic career, by reading horizontally across the grid, see at a glance which version of a poem existed at the same time as which versions of the others. This simple device—which one might think would be used routinely by anyone engaged in critical work grounded in biography and history—seemed to arouse considerable interest when I explained it in a related lecture on Coleridge's texts ("The Unity of Coleridge's Poetry and the Instability of the Texts") at the 1990 Wordsworth Summer Conference in Grasmere.

20. Wordsworth's comments occur in a note at the end of vol. 1 of *Lyrical Ballads* in the edition of 1800 (only).

21. In a manuscript note written above the beginning of *The Eolian Harp* in the copy of *Sibylline Leaves*

formerly owned by Arthur A. Houghton, Coleridge speaks of "having first introduced this species of short blank verse poems—of which Southey, Lamb, Wordsworth, and others have since produced so many exquisite specimens" (Johnson 1975, 472).

References

Baker, Jeffrey. 1982. "Prelude and Prejudice." *The Wordsworth Circle* 13: 79-86.

Beer, John. 1959. *Coleridge the Visionary.* London: Chatto and Windus.

————. 1974. "A Stream by Glimpses: Coleridge's Later Imagination." In *Coleridge's Variety: Bicentenary Studies,* ed. Beer, 219-42. London: Macmillan, 1974.

————. 1977. *Coleridge's Poetic Intelligence.* London: Macmillan.

Coleridge, Samuel Taylor. 1856. *Seven Lectures on Shakespeare and Milton.* Transcribed and introduced by J. P. Collier. London: Chapman and Hall.

————. 1893. *The Poetical Works of Samuel Taylor Coleridge.* Ed. James Dykes Campbell. London: Macmillan.

————. 1912. *The Complete Poetical Works of Samuel Taylor Coleridge.* Ed. Ernest Hartley Coleridge. 2 vols. Oxford, UK: Clarendon.

————. 1956b. *Collected Letters of Samuel Taylor Coleridge.* Ed. Earl Leslie Griggs. 6 vols. Oxford, UK: Clarendon, 1956-71.

————. 1972. *Coleridge's Verse: A Selection.* Ed. William Empson and David Pirie. London: Faber.

————. 1974. *Poems.* Ed. John Beer. Everyman Library. London: Dent.

————. 1980. *Marginalia,* Vol. 1, ed. George Whalley. Princeton, N.J.: Princeton University Press.

————. 2001. *Poetical Works.* Ed. J. C. C. Mays. No. 16 of *The Collected Works of Samuel Taylor Coleridge.* 3 vols. (in 6). Princeton, N.J.: Princeton University Press.

Dyck, Sarah. 1973. "Perspective in *The Rime of the Ancient Mariner.*" *Studies in English Literature* 13: 591-604.

Dyer, Gary. 1989. "Unwitnessed by Answering Deeds: 'The Destiny of Nations' and Coleridge's *Sibylline Leaves.*" *The Wordsworth Circle* 20: 148-55.

Evans, B. Ifor. 1935. "Coleridge's Copy of 'Fears in Solitude.'" *Times Literary Supplement,* 18 April, p. 255.

Johnson, Mary Lynn. 1975. "How Rare Is a 'Unique Annotated Copy' of Coleridge's *Sibylline Leaves?*" *Bulletin of the New York Public Library* 78: 451-81.

Lipking, Lawrence. 1977. "The Marginal Gloss." *Critical Inquiry* 3: 609-55.

Magnuson, Paul. 1991. "The Politics of 'Frost at Midnight.'" *The Wordsworth Circle* 22: 3-11.

———. 1998. *Reading Public Romanticism.* Princeton, N.J.: Princeton University Press.

Mays, J. C. C. 1992. "Reflections on Having Edited Coleridge's Poems." In *Romantic Revisions,* ed. Robert Brinkley and Keith Hanley, 136-53. Cambridge: Cambridge University Press.

McGann, Jerome J. 1981. "The Meaning of *The Ancient Mariner.*" *Critical Inquiry* 8: 35-67. (Reprinted in McGann's *The Beauty of Inflections: Literary Investigations in Historical Method and Theory.* Oxford, UK: Clarendon, 1985, 135-72.)

———. 1983. *A Critique of Modern Textual Criticism.* Chicago: University of Chicago Press.

McLaverty, James. 1984. "The Concept of Authorial Intention in Textual Criticism." *Library,* 6th ser., 6: 121-38.

Mellor, Anne K. 1980. *English Romantic Irony.* Cambridge: Harvard University Press.

Parrish, Stephen Maxfield. 1988a. *Coleridge's "Dejection": The Earliest Manuscripts and the Earliest Printings.* Ithaca, N.Y.: Cornell University Press.

———. 1988b. "The Whig Interpretation of Literature." *TEXT* 4: 343-50.

Perkins, David. 1990. "The Imaginative Vision of *Kubla Khan*: On Coleridge's Introductory Note." In *Coleridge, Keats, and the Imagination: Romanticism and Adam's Dream,* ed. J. Robert Barth and John L. Mahoney, 97-108. Columbia: University of Missouri Press.

Reiman, Donald H., ed. 1972. *The Romantics Reviewed, Part C, Shelley, Keats, and London Radical Writers.* New York: Garland.

———. 1987. *Romantic Texts and Contexts.* Columbia: University of Missouri Press.

Rooke, Barbara E. 1974. "An Annotated Copy of Coleridge's 'Christabel.'" *Studia Germanica Gandensia* 15: 179-92.

Rosenbaum, Barbara, and Pamela White, compilers. 1982. *Index of English Literary Manuscripts,* Vol. 4, 1800-1900, Part 1. London: Mansell.

Shillingsburg, Peter L. 1986. *Scholarly Editing in the Computer Age: Theory and Practice.* Athens: University of Georgia Press.

Simpson, David, 1979. *Irony and Authority in Romantic Poetry.* London: Macmillan.

Stillinger, Jack. 1991a. *Multiple Authorship and the Myth of Solitary Genius.* New York: Oxford University Press.

———. 1991b. "Multiple Authorship and the Question of Authority." *TEXT* 5: 283-93.

———. 1994. *Coleridge and Textual Instability: The Multiple Versions of the Major Poems.* New York: Oxford University Press.

Thorpe, James. 1965. "The Aesthetics of Textual Criticism." *PMLA* 80: 465-82.

———. 1972. *Principles of Textual Criticism.* San Marino, Calif.: Huntington Library.

Valdés, Mario J., and Owen Miller, eds. 1985. *Identity of the Literary Text.* Toronto: University of Toronto Press.

Wall, Wendy. 1987. "Interpreting Poetic Shadows: The Gloss of *The Rime of the Ancient Mariner.*" *Criticism* 29: 179-95.

Wallen, Martin. 1986. "Return and Representation: The Revisions of *The Ancient Mariner.*" *The Wordsworth Circle* 17: 148-56.

Wheeler, K. M. 1981. *The Creative Mind in Coleridge's Poetry.* London: Heinemann.

Wordsworth, William. 1940. *The Poetical Works of William Wordsworth.* Ed. Ernest de Selincourt and Helen Darbishire. 5 vols. Oxford, UK: Clarendon, 1940-49.

———. 1970. *The Prelude or Growth of a Poet's Mind (Text of 1805).* Ed. Ernest de Selincourt. New ed., corr. by Stephen Gill. London: Oxford University Press.

———. 1971. *The Prelude: A Parallel Text.* Ed. J. C. Maxwell. Harmondsworth, UK: Penguin.

———. 1977. *"The Prelude," 1798-1799.* Ed. Stephen Parrish. Ithaca, N.Y.: Cornell University Press.

———. 1985a. *The Fourteen-Book "Prelude."* Ed. W. J. B. Owen. Ithaca, N.Y.: Cornell University Press.

———. 1991. *The Thirteen-Book "Prelude."* Ed. Mark L. Reed. 2 vols. Ithaca, N.Y.: Cornell University Press.

———. 1992. *"Lyrical Ballads," and Other Poems, 1797-1800.* Ed. James Butler and Karen Green. Ithaca, N.Y.: Cornell University Press.

Zeller, Hans. 1975. "A New Approach to the Critical Constitution of Literary Texts." *Studies in Bibliography* 28: 231-64.

Seamus Perry (essay date October 1995)

SOURCE: Perry, Seamus. "The Ancient Mariner Controversy." *Charles Lamb Bulletin,* no. 92 (October 1995): 208-23.

[*In the following essay, Perry discusses Coleridge's many revisions of the poem in light of Wordsworth's and Coleridge's conflicting poetic theories and Coleridge's belief in the religious doctrine of the "One Life."*]

(I)

Throughout his life, Coleridge returns to the poem, more so than to any other, continually making textual changes, often very substantial ones, as if unable to leave the thing alone. This returning and retouching, which goes on for over 30 years, happily creates the kind of controversy textual scholars dream about: Jack Stillinger, for example, has recently calculated that at least 18 different texts of the poem exist, each of which naturally has its proper claim on the Coleridgean student, and the exhibition of all of which naturally requires the protracted labour of textual scholars.[1] But the editorial controversy is not my concern here: that whole issue is a tortuous question of pragmatics, including the pragmatics of recognizing the reader's mortality; and I am almost tempted to say that it would be wrong for a Coleridgean to dwell too much on anything pragmatic, since Coleridge's own life was so shining an example of what you can still get done while making almost no allowances whatsoever to pragmatism of any kind.

Yet for all that, the kind of behaviour on Coleridge's part that gives rise to the editorial controversy is not unconnected with my subject. Such compulsive returning to the poem might suggest that the idea of controversy has a different kind of relevance: a private one, as if the poem embodied a controversy or division within Coleridge himself, one which successive revisions to the text might promise to work out or to clarify. The sporadic compulsiveness of Coleridge's returns to this disastrous story oddly mirror the Mariner's own compulsive need to tell and re-tell his tale: 'at an uncertain hour, / The agony returns: / And till my ghastly tale is told, / This heart within me burns' (ll. 582-5).[2] Coleridge is frequently identified with the Mariner in the memoirs of his circle, and quite quickly came himself to think of the figure he chose to re-christen with affectionate familiarity 'the Old Navigator' as a kind of *alter ego*. So, in a characteristically oblique way, the protracted history of Coleridge's revisions may be rather like the serial, retrospective redefinitions of belief and identity which one can read in the successive stages of Wordsworth's confessional epic, *The Prelude*.

The obliquity, though, is what matters. One can deplore, or enjoy, the Anglican accretions in *The Prelude,* but, even if the resulting work is a confusing collage of old and new, one can have little doubt about the broad direction of the movement in Wordsworth's beliefs. With the changing *Ancient Mariner* on the other hand, as so often with Coleridge, nothing is so sure. Admittedly, the great Empson read the major changes of 1817 as

evidence of a massive Trinitarian reaction, Coleridge hastily seeking to cover the tracks of an earlier, heretical self;[3] but one wonders whether Empson's own disgust at the Trinitarian God led him to find out too readily an exemplary tale of young genius corrupted by awful orthodoxy. For in truth no-one has more honest scruples about the implications of the traditional Christian beliefs than Coleridge, or more openly entertains heterodoxies; and this includes the later Coleridge, much later even than the 1817 additions to *The Ancient Mariner*: for example, in *Aids to Reflection,* as John Beer has argued, it is the *continuity* of so many of the terms and patterns of thinking which is more striking and stirring than any stark, revolutionary rupture.[4] This makes a certain intuitive sense: how permanently interesting a mind would Coleridge have if his career were quite so broken-backed an affair as all that? To be sure, Coleridge may, like (to choose some very different poets) John Donne or Wystan Auden, portray his own intellectual lifestory as a sort of Pauline 'conversion', away from a shabby, sophistic empiricist Unitarianism and towards the enlightened Tory spirituality of an Anglican 'Plato-Plotino-Proclian Idealism'.[5] But the very extremity of such a self-representation may suggest a degree of wishfulness, a wishfulness expressing itself, perhaps, in kinds of self-dramatizating invention.

The Ancient Mariner is one of the places where this kind of driven self-dramatization can be seen at work. I think Coleridge returns to the poem so often because it contains, by a sort of accident, some of the central intellectual divisions of his life, divisions which he is forever attempting, and failing, to resolve into orderliness and reconciliation. What these are, and why they should still be interesting to us, I hope at least to suggest; and one approach to the task is to describe the odd occasion of the poem's genesis, part of Coleridge's brief, doomed, perfectly happy collaboration with Wordsworth in Somerset in the last half of 1797 and the first half of 1798. Like many elements of Coleridge's thinking, the relationship with Wordsworth seems crucial in working out the full implications (rather more crucial, I would argue, than modern accounts of Coleridge usually allow for; but that is an argument for another place).

The poem first came into being, as did almost all Coleridge's important works, by a kind of fruitful accident. The first version of the poem was written between November 1797 and May 1798, and was originally intended as a magazine poem, the fee for which would subsidize an excursion Coleridge was to take with the Wordsworths. The impulse for the project was, it seems, an enthusiasm on Coleridge's part for collaboration with his newly established friend. An earlier attempt at such partnership, to write a poem in three cantos on the death of Abel, had foundered when Wordsworth found himself quite unable to produce anything toward the line tally; the garrulous Coleridge, meanwhile, had scribbled off a complete canto. The scheme was abandoned. A few days later, during an eight-mile walk to Watchet, 'William and Coleridge employ[ed] themselves in laying the plan of a ballad, to be published with some pieces of William's', as Dorothy wrote, the ballad in question being *The Ancient Mariner*.[6] But this attempt at collaboration was no more successful: later in life, Wordsworth remembered contributing 'certain parts' of the plot, and some isolated lines, but recalled that '[a]s we endeavoured to proceed conjointly our respective manners proved so widely different that it would have been quite presumptuous in me to do anything but separate from an undertaking upon which I could only have been a clog'.[7] *The Ancient Mariner* 'grew and grew till it became too important for our object, which was limited to our expectation of five pounds, and we began to talk of a Volume'.[8] So, it appears, from the attempt at collaboration on this poem two quite distinct kinds of 'manner' separated out, to be retrospectively rationalized in Coleridge's *Biographia Literaria* as the two voices of *Lyrical Ballads*: one focussing on 'common subjects' and the other on 'supernatural subjects', the first Wordsworth's, the second Coleridge's. Distinction, to reverse a favourite Coleridgean maxim, was here proving itself to be division, even if it was a fruitful sort of division.

This failure of the poets successfully to collaborate on the poem can be seen not only as the contingent origin of the *Lyrical Ballads* volume, but also as sign of the first stirrings of a deep controversy about poetic theory between the two men. It seems important that it is *Coleridge* who proposes collaboration, as if seeking to enact literally a partnership of powers: for it is exactly the way in which the poem embodies the controversial forces within Coleridge's own thinking which made it so provocative a poem for him. To see what elements are opposed in this internal controversy, spilling out into more public controversy with Wordsworth, we should turn to Coleridge before the Mariner. Both formally and thematically we will be able to see already there the competing elements of his thinking which fall, as it were accidentally, into the open, given narrative occasion of *The Ancient Mariner* and there assume their intrinsic, oppositional, Coleridgean pattern.

(II)

Even a keen watcher of modern poetry in the 1790s would not have guessed that Coleridge was set to write anything like *The Ancient Mariner*: the last thing one would have expected was a ballad, and least of all one in medieval fancy dress. Insofar as one would have associated him with any particular verse form, it would probably have been the thumping Miltonics of his biggest and most ambitious work, *Religious Musings*; one might have him marked down as a charming, if not terribly substantial, follower of William Lisle Bowles, the

writer of some charming 'effusions'; or, if one had a sharp eye, as the poet of an interesting new kind of blank verse meditation which sought to bring together the description of landscape and natural beauty with abstract theological speculation. (Alternatively, of course, if one were a more political animal, one might dismiss him as a provocative left-winger who had stirred up a good deal of trouble and whose name stank.)[9]

From his own point of view, Coleridge's literary ambitions in 1797 had been most immediately directed toward theatrical tragedy. He had been writing a play, *Osorio*, since receiving what seemed like a commission from Sheridan at Drury Lane in February, and read the two-and-a-half acts he had finished to the Wordsworths when he visited Racedown in June; Wordsworth made positive noises and read Coleridge his own tragedy, *The Borderers*, the following morning. He also read Coleridge an early version of *The Ruined Cottage*, but this, interestingly, seems to have made less impact at the time: their minds, clearly, were on other kinds of poetry. Coleridge clearly made a deep impression: 'You had a great loss in not seeing Coleridge', wrote Dorothy to Mary Hutchinson, 'He is a wonderful man';[10] and Coleridge was no less amazed, particularly at the qualities of Wordsworth's play—'absolutely wonderful' he thought it, and later pulled strings for it to be considered for performance by Covent Garden.[11]

Neither play prospered: when *Osorio* had at last been ground out of an increasingly unenthused Coleridge, it was only to receive a rejection from Drury Lane: Sheridan's apparent commission proved nothing like so firm a commitment as Coleridge had thought. At about the same time *The Borderers* met a similar fate at Covent Garden: the contemporary stage was evidently not a likely forum for the kinds of poetry either man wanted or seemed best able to write. Rejection of the plays also implied, rather more vulgarly but importantly, that the stage was not going to be a source of income: Wordsworth's financial worries feature largely in his letters of the period, and, despite Dorothy's unconvincing protest before *The Borderers* was submitted that '[w]e have not the faintest expectation that it will be accepted', its rejection proved rather a great set-back.[12]

In fact, the shortage of cash exerts a perhaps unexpectedly important influence on the kind of poem *The Ancient Mariner* turned out to be. For it is, generically, however subtle and individual Coleridge's variations on the generic norm are, a supernatural romantic ballad, and in that deliberately set to chime in with an enthusiasm for the gothic and weird: this taste was all the rage in the theatre too, 'Monk' Lewis's play *The Castle Spectre* being a particular current hit. A letter Coleridge writes to Wordsworth from Shrewsbury in late January 1798 suggests that the superb and galling success of *The Castle Spectre* particularly exercised

Wordsworth after his own play's failure; Coleridge adopts a more judiciously even-handed tone, even singling out Lewis's 'great & peculiar excellence' at writing ballad songs, though he agrees that Lewis's stock gothic sensationalism is pretty deplorable.[13] But by this time, money was not anything like so pressing for Coleridge, and so Lewis's success would not have been so irritating a contrast with the fortunes of *Osorio* as it evidently was with *The Borderers* for Wordsworth: for by then Coleridge had successfully won the heart of Tom Wedgwood, erratic, drug-taking, manic-depressive and rich, and had accepted a lifetime annuity of £150 from him and his brother.[14] How calculating Coleridge's cultivation of his philanthropist had been is not clear; Wordsworth, who it seems was never much liked by Wedgwood, appears to have felt some irritation about his friend's spectacular good fortune: the disgruntlement, perhaps, of one too stubborn to be much good at that kind of charm offensive.

However that may be, the painful contrast Wordsworth draws between his own bad luck and the popularity of Lewis's meretricious gothicism is interesting. In March, several months after *The Borderers* had been turned down, Wordsworth is still grumbling on to Tobin, about the now heavily symbolic success of *The Castle Spectre,* moodily telling his correspondent 'if I had no other method of employing myself Mr Lewis's success would have thrown me into despair' (the brave tone of rather self-admiring stoicism seems so exclusively Wordsworth's). 'No doubt you have heard of the munificence of the Wedgwoods towards Coleridge', he writes a few lines later, almost as if listing another example of aesthetic dismerit rewarded, adding grimly: 'I hope the fruit will be good as the seed is noble'.[15] With £150 a year for life, he may well have thought, Coleridge could afford to be disinterestedly even-handed about Monk Lewis. For Gothic was coming to represent all the Wordsworth's new poetic set itself against: sensational, not meditative; an affair of extraordinary narrative, not internal, probing self-exploration. More generally, as Stephen Gill remarks, from this time on he is predisposed to think of popular success as intrinsically artistically compromised.[16]

Wordsworth's distrust of Gothic effect plays its part in the mixed feelings he comes to bear toward **The Ancient Mariner.** It was, after all, like Wordsworth's ballads (or at least so Wordsworth protested when Southey published his mean-spirited review) written specifically to make money: the serious creative energies were being put elsewhere, into the newly-conceived philosophical epic, *The Recluse.* Although he became more protective towards them in later life—and even came to hold up approval of *The Idiot Boy* as a sign of true literary judgment—at the time the ballads were poems (and **The Ancient Mariner,** particularly, a poem) purposely designed to play off the vulgarities of public taste and

get published for money: in a sense, they were imaginatively compromised from the start. Conversely, Coleridge's qualified indulgence towards Lewis's spooky play comes when he is midway through his own exercise in preternatural literature; so there may be reasons other than the diffuse good feeling brought by unexpected wealth to account for his generosity towards Lewis's tenuous merits.

What is emerging in the spring of 1798 is the first sign of what Coleridge will call 'a radical Difference' between the two men as to the nature of poetry, a sense of difference which Coleridge internalizes and makes the subject of his criticism:[17] their different attitudes towards the kind of vulgar gothicism represented by Lewis are symptomatic, but do not really exhaust the matter. Yet, only months before, during that excited encounter at Racedown in June, it must have seemed that their creative ambitions were extraordinarily in step, and that they were made for collaboration. This was not only indicated by their recent attempts to write drama modelled on Shakespeare: Wordsworth was apparently interested in the possibilities of the epic too, a kind of poetry drawing its model from Milton; and the writing of an epic had frequently featured in the lists of prospective masterpieces that the young Coleridge set out for himself in his notebooks.

Coleridge's epic has inevitably taken up its place in the mythology alongside all his other planned—and even publicized—but unexecuted works; but it seems to have appeared a perfectly viable possibility at the time: Lamb, for example, had no illusions about Coleridge's habit of 'taking up splendid schemes . . . only to lay them down again', yet could still seriously counsel his friend 'to write an Epic poem. . . . Nothing but it can satisfy the vast capacity of your true poetic genius'.[18] Moreover, while Wordsworth's epic aspirations do not seem to have been focussed about a particular work until Coleridge presented him with one in the spring of 1798,[19] Coleridge's own epic hopes, on the other hand, appear to have been centred more specifically on a long poem called *The Brook.*[20] This poem was, apparently, to integrate philosophical reflections and the scenery of the Quantocks in a fusion or juxtaposition of landscape and internal consciousness anticipating that part of Wordsworth's aborted epic which his executors chose to call *The Prelude*: hidden connections like this make you recall Garrod's *bon mot,* that in a sense Coleridge's greatest single work was Wordsworth.[21]

Coleridge's appearance at Racedown in June 1797 was a return visit: Wordsworth had visited Stowey in April, cheering Coleridge out of a gloom about (again) money; and soon after Wordsworth had left to rejoin Dorothy, Coleridge was writing to Cottle about the true nature of epic, in what sounds very like the summary of his recent conversations with Wordsworth. Their discussion seems to have started with the subject of Southey, an attractive target, no doubt, for he was rapidly becoming successful, while Coleridge worried about bread and cheese and Wordsworth lived on a diet which he heroically described as 'the essence of carrots, cabbages, turnips and other esculent vegetables'.[22] Still, there was comfort to be had from the manifest inadequacy of Southey's poetry; and this inadequacy stemmed from 'rely[ing] too much on *story* and *event* in his poems, to the neglect of those *lofty imaginings,* that are peculiar to, and definitive of, the poet. The *story* of Milton might be told in two pages—it is this which distinguishes an *Epic Poem* from a *Romance in metre*.'[23] In contrast to Southey's uninformed stumblings, Coleridge stipulated enormous, indeed self-disablingly large, criteria for the writer of epic to fulfil, telling Cottle that a proper epic would take at least 20 years to research, write and correct—perhaps *not* the most tactful thing to tell one's publisher, waiting for copy. Unsurprisingly, given the extent of the necessary groundwork, *The Brook* remained almost completely unwritten.

No such programmatic preparation marked **The Ancient Mariner,** of course; but the duration of Coleridge's imaginative engagement with the poem otherwise easily attained his stipulated epic dimensions. In other ways, too, it gestures towards the condition of epic: like the *Odyssey,* it is a poem about proving adventures at sea and an eventual return home; like *Paradise Lost,* it is about, or seems to be about, a fall from grace; and like *The Prelude,* it is an epic of consciousness, in which the important events of the poem are not military adventures, nor taken from scripture, but occurrences within an individual mind or heart. There is a kind of aspirant epic stature or grandiloquence to many of the descriptions: 'All in a hot and copper sky, / The bloody Sun, at noon . . .' (ll. 111-12); or 'And ice, mast-high, came floating by, / As green as emerald' (ll. 53-4).

But it is an epic *manqué* in Coleridge's own terms, for its form is manifestly indebted to the kind of (small 'r') romantic narrative ballads to be found in Bishop Percy's *Reliques of English Poetry,* a work which lies behind the idiom of **Christabel** too (a *'Romance in metre'*). **The Ancient Mariner** is also an epic *manqué* in that the poet maintains not the impersonal authority of one inspired by a muse or the Holy Ghost, nor the sovereign confidence of one exploring the private territories of his own growth, nor even of one bearing the fruit of ten years' solid research in all human knowledge; but rather the untrustworthy voice of an old man who quite probably does not really understand the significance of what it is that he went through those many years before.

For the poem, while obviously not a piece of drama either, is in an important way strongly dramatized in its structure; and in this way, we can see it inheriting

aspects of Coleridge's current desires to write the drama as well. For it is not, as we perhaps tend to think of it, a poem about a man who goes on a disastrous sea voyage, but a poem about a man hearing about another man's disastrous sea voyage, just as *Heart of Darkness* is not about travelling up the Congo but about sitting on a barge on the Thames hearing a man talk about making a trip up the Congo. (A similar shift of emphasis away from a description of a series of events and towards the reception of those events in the mind of a dramatically 'placed' character can be seen in Wordsworth's reworking of *The Ruined Cottage* during the spring of 1798.) And so, although Coleridge's hopes for the drama were frustrated and he grew quickly bored of writing *Osorio* anyway, his mighty epic never left the ground and he signed it over to Wordsworth in the Spring, one might see elements of both surviving in the formal conception of the poem financial need encouraged him to write.

(III)

Those are issues of poetic form or *genre*. But what matter was it that found its best expression in this oddly hybrid poetic idiom, in which Coleridge played off the authoritative voice and ambition of symbolic, narrative epic against the 'placed' speech of a dramatized monologue?

Here, too, we must return to the hopes and achievements of the earlier Coleridge. In the letter to Cottle outlining his notion of the ideal epic, Coleridge speaks of another project he has going besides 'my Tragedy': this is 'a book of Morals in answer to Godwin'. This is another example of an unwritten Coleridgean masterpiece: the ambition to scotch Godwin's materialist, atheistical rationalism with an alternative, drawn from Coleridge's religious convictions, which would yet align itself with the forces of liberty, is a recurring project in the early notebooks and letters; and the connection between his own Christian position and the progressive amelioration of suffering naturally puts the theological problem of worldly evil high in his thoughts. Godwin has a sound theory about the existence of evil: it is caused by political injustice; but while accepting the point, Coleridge could not agree that it exhausted the matter, and set out to find a more specifically Christian way of discussing the presence of suffering.

It is, of course, a difficult point for anyone who believes at once in an omnipotent, benevolent deity and in the evidence of their eyes, one of the most famous cruces in Christian theology; but it is especially testing for the young Coleridge, for whom God had an almost material ubiquity throughout the world: the 'One Life'. The upside of this belief was that it provided a good reason for thinking the universe one, answering the deep need for unity which is so familiar a feature of Coleridge's fraught emotional and religious life: ''Tis God / Diffused through all, that doth make all one whole', as he put it in *Religious Musings,* where God is 'Nature's Essence, Mind, and Energy' (ll. 139-40). A further consequence of such an immanent and quasi-physical belief in the vibrating presence of God was a radical re-conceptualisation of human consciousness: as Coleridge puts it, with appropriate hesitancy, in *The Destiny of Nations*:

> Others boldlier think
> That as one body seems the aggregate
> Of atoms numberless, each organized;
> So by a strange and dim similitude
> Infinite myriads of self-conscious minds
> Are one all-conscious Spirit, which informs
> With absolute ubiquity of thought . . .
> All his involvéd Monads, that yet seem
> With various province and apt agency
> Each to pursue its own self-centering end.
>
> (ll. 39-49)

It is difficult, and not remarkably elegant, but seems to say: self-conscious minds (that is, you and me) are *in fact* mere fragments of a bigger, 'all-conscious Spirit', God of course, Who composes the tiny component consciousnesses of His Monads (Monads being a rather less aggrandizing title for you and me). We persist in our lives, apparently acting of our free volition, but that's only what 'seem[s]'; the reality is that our will as much as our mental autonomy are subsumed as parts of the divine One Life.

This doctrine has its clear attractions: one's sense of proximity with God is complete, for one is part of God; religious illumination consists then of knowing oneself 'Part and proportion of one wond'rous whole' (*Religious Musings* 137). Moreover, you are no longer ultimately responsible for what you do, for those actions are simply part of the ongoing multiform existence of God, Who is, we trust, well-intentioned and infinitely wise: Coleridge was a weak rather than a bad man, a sinner (as Humphry House remarks)[24] of the unsensationally familiar variety—certainly no Byron—and this doctrine of divine necessity was no doubt temperamentally a vast relief, or, perhaps, temptation.[25]

But surprising kinds of ethical strength break through in Coleridge all the time, like rock breaking through hillside turf, and the downside of these necessitarian beliefs was not lost to him either. The most obvious drawback to such theistic inevitablism is the dark interpretation of one of its appeals: the denial of free will. Coleridge, who, unlike most theorists, actually tried to live out the theories he entertained, found this drawback out in practice. When Southey sprung the news that he was thinking of becoming a Church of England vicar, Coleridge was understandably shocked, but consoled himself with the thought that if that was

what the Infinite Spirit had decided to do with the finite Monad known as Robert Southey, it would by definition work out for the best. Southey (deftly or obtusely is hard to say, as often the case with Southey) replied that he was grateful for Coleridge's good wishes; at which Coleridge exasperatedly responded that he hadn't meant to express anything like good wishes, but was obliged to believe, against all logic, that God knew what he was up to.[26] Necessitarianism is, clearly, an unreliable tool of persuasion. Moreover, if you are politically active, as Coleridge had been, righteously, properly enraged by social injustice and anxious for change and reform, to attribute the state of things so unreservedly to the enacted wisdom of God is, logically, quite incongruous.[27] An awful notion: Pitt was a Monad of the Infinite Spirit like Coleridge.

Another drawback, and a more interesting one perhaps, is that the manifest variety and difference of which the world is, to our eyes, composed does not readily tally with a conviction of Unity behind or within it. The position would seem to drift in one of two directions: either the unity is a kind of truth which rises in moments of illumination through the befuddling chaos of ordinary experience; or the divine unity is itself to be thought of as somehow fragmented amongst its monadic representatives. The first of these alternatives presents the variety of the world as a kind of illusion or bad faith, a position unlikely to appeal spontaneously to the young Coleridge, whose early notebooks are at times an implicit running eulogy to the world's rich, particulate variety, from leaf-shapes to the appearance of urine in a chamber-pot.[28] Placing the emphasis on diversity, on the other hand, obviously undermines the supreme unity of God: as Coleridge asked a Christian friend, if God is and does everything, then where is the unity of His personality?[29] More to the point, if God is composed, in part, of the events of the world, doesn't that imply that He is, in odd minutiae of His composition, wicked? Not only does this theology risk giving Pitt *carte blanche* to carry on with divine approval, but also seems to blacken God's name by making Him, in tiny part, Pitt—which is, I suppose, the same horror seen from God's point of view.

But the appeals of the doctrine are too strong for it to be wholly renounced for some years, and so, unsurprisingly, the subject Coleridge singles out for his epic several times in the early notebooks is the nature or origin of evil: the topic would presumably, therefore, have featured in *The Brook*; the religious counselling offered to true imagination by the divine presence in nature would no doubt have played a prominent part in the structure of the poem, as it does, on a smaller scale, in *This Lime Tree Bower My Prison* or *Frost at Midnight.* Coleridge's mighty precursor in vernacular epic, Milton, had similarly undertaken the massive task of justifying God's apparently erratic behaviour to an humanity puzzled at His decision to let them suffer; so the theme would have seemed especially appropriate for an epic. As several critics have pointed out, this interest also links **The Ancient Mariner** with the projected poem on the murder of Abel and also with the related, contemporary prose fragment, *The Wanderings of Cain.* So, **The Ancient Mariner** absorbs Coleridge's epic interest in evil and associates it with the evocation of utter isolation which forms one of the better bits of *Osorio*:

> And is it then
> An enviable lot to waste away
> With inward wounds, and like the spirit of chaos
> To wander on disquietly thro' the earth,
> Cursing all lovely things?

> (V ii 295-9)[30]

Isolation could be interpreted as exclusion from the inclusive, divine society of the One Life: so might come together the epic theme of evil and Coleridge's recent practice dramatising burdensome solitariness.

One does not need to probe so deeply to grasp that a conviction and fear of isolation was a prominent part of Coleridge's psychology:[31] the desire to be consumed in the vast, Monad-absorbing unity of God would itself be one response to such a conviction; the desire to write in partnership with 'the Giant Wordsworth' another.[32] Immersed in this rich and testing mixture of abstract speculation and personal compulsion, Coleridge stumbled on the Mariner, taking up the happy contingency of plot suggested by Wordsworth, and freed from the burdens of his epic aspirations by the deliberate assumption of that least weighty genre, the magazine romantic ballad, one written, moreover, as a kind of medieval pastiche; and into this sudden, unmediated space, initially created by his requiring some cash, the young Coleridge poured himself: the poem, as Wordsworth says, 'grew and grew', like a fairy-tale beanstalk.

(IV)

One question critics ask (and, subsequently, divide over) is, as one might ask of *The Turn of the Screw*: does it really happen? We only have one person's account of what goes on during that terrible journey, and that is the Mariner's, who was hardly in his right state of mind for much of it; and, until 1817 at any rate, we only have one moralising interpretation offered us, and that is also the Mariner's:

> Farewell, farewell! but this I tell
> To thee, thou Wedding-guest!
> He prayeth well, who loveth well
> Both man and bird and beast.

> He prayeth best, who loveth best
> All things both great and small;

> For the dear God who loveth us,
> He made and loveth all.

> (ll. 610-17)

Many readers have found these lines to be an inadequate summary of the kinds of moral lesson we have been learning in the poem; but, like the final chorus in *Don Giovanni*, in which the survivors sing of the recently hell-sent Don, 'This is the end of all those who do evil', the inadequacy of the *moralitas* seems too emphatic to be anything other than dramatically deliberate. The point of such poised insufficiency would be the *impossibility* of reducing certain kinds of experience to the univocal summary and lesson-to-be-drawn which a fable or allegory normally demands.

The structure of the poem takes up what seems very like a crime-penance-redemption shape: the Mariner kills the albatross, suffers terribly, but, upon unconsciously blessing the water snakes begins a process by which, culminating in his confession and shrieving by the hermit, he acquires the spiritual wisdom and authority with which he ends his story. Certainly, when, presumably in or soon before 1817, Coleridge adds the marginal comments, this shape is apparently emphasized and the 'parable' nature of the work stressed. 'The ancient Mariner inhospitably killeth the pious bird of good omen'; 'By the light of the Moon he beholdeth God's creatures of the great calm. . . . Their beauty and happiness. . . . He blesseth them in his heart. . . . The spell begins to break'; 'The curse is finally expiated'; 'to teach by his own example, love and reverence to all things that God made and loveth', writes the man in the margin, who seems an editorial commentator of positively Jamesian unreliability.

However, critics, knowing that in the 1790s Coleridge expresses belief in the unifying presence of God throughout the universe (the 'One Life'), are drawn to transplant those terms into the manifest structure of the poem and find it a fable of transgression against, and ultimate reconciliation with, that One Life. The most influential reading of this kind would be, I suppose, Robert Penn Warren's;[33] something like it is also proposed in M. H. Abrams's *Natural Supernaturalism.*[34] There is, however, something unfitting about the reading. First, the allegory is not neat at the moments when it should be: the killing of the albatross is followed, after a little time, by a fair breeze, and the Mariner is thanked by the crew for ridding the ship of the ill-omened bird's fog; then, when the rot does set in it is rather noticeably the Mariner's shipmates, whose only sin was momentarily to misinterpret the kind of omen attached to the albatross, who die *en masse.* As Leslie Stephen remarked, the main moral would then seem to be: don't be on board with a man who inhospitably shoots albatrosses.[35] Then again, the fitness of the allegorical shape is manifestly undercut by the dice-throwing arbitrariness deciding the Mariner's own fate: as Einstein said, in rather different circumstances, God doesn't play dice. Arguably, the kind of redemptive moment the Mariner experiences is curiously unmomentous: pugnacious Irving Babbitt for one thought a spiritual restitution that could be effected by noticing how well sea creatures caught the light was a fairly trivial affair;[36] and, anyway, things only get worse still for a time after the moment of the snakes, unless one considers the springing-up of the crew's animated corpses a welcome respite from horror. Finally, the Mariner's return home is, to put it mildly, not the happily reintegrative event he must have been hoping for: the pilot's boy promptly loses his sanity upon seeing him, thinking he's the devil, hardly a hopeful sign; there is at least some doubt that the Mariner ever receives the 'shrieving' for which he petitions so earnestly (we never actually see it); his supposedly benevolent message of nature's sanctity is not passed on as a piece of evangelism, nor yet a piece of avuncular advice, but periodically wrenched out in a state of agony (an odd kind of state to still be in after the 'expiation' of a curse);[37] and the Wedding Guest is left, quite unlike the enlightened Wordsworth-figure of *The Ruined Cottage,* stunned and forlorn and gets up the next morning wiser, though about what exactly is hard to say, and sadder, about more, presumably, than missing the wedding feast.

But more even than all this, the testing point, especially for one so interested in the origin of evil, is how on earth, within the 'One Life', an evil act *could ever have been committed in the first place.* The One Life is not something one can opt out of, like national insurance; it is the very ground of being, of the universe itself. The Mariner's shooting of the albatross is as unpremeditated and spontaneous as is his blessing of the water snakes: one could not even claim the sin to be the—inexplicable—Luciferan self-assertion of the Monad against the Unifying Spirit. Coleridge's ideas about God clearly must play a part in the poem: there is enough sense of spiritual order vestigially present to make us doubt accounts of the poem as simply a nightmarishly parodic inversion of an otherwise well-held faith in a divinely ordered universe;[38] but it is clear that that God's part is not anything doctrinally straightforward.

That critics are so drawn to make of the poem a kind of parable is itself, perhaps, a clue. A parable is a way of reading as much as a style of writing: *The Song of Songs* can gain a place in the Bible if a parabolist or allegorist reads it with sufficient interpretative ingenuity and propagates his interpretation with sufficient persuasiveness; and what the 1817 marginal comments pick up and amplify is the Mariner's own tendency to think of his experience in symbolic terms. Why should he do this?

An important observation is that whatever Coleridge believes, the Mariner himself does not believe in the One Life: he is not a late eighteenth-century nonconformist Protestant who knows about Dr Priestley; he is, presumably, within the dramatic structure of the piece, a fifteenth-century Catholic. This is more puzzling even than it might seem. For, through all his theological changes and shifts of heart, one thing can be firmly asserted about Coleridge's religious thought and this is that it was never much attracted by Catholicism. For an example: on Malta in 1804, Lady Ball, his chief's wife, seems to have made the kind of casual, inane comment which dinners require, causing (one imagines) Coleridge to bite his lip before pouring his withering anger out to his notebook in the privacy of his rooms:

> Well! (says [Lady Ball]) the Catholic Religion is better than none / Why, to be sure, it is called a Religion: but the [question] is, is it, a Religion? Sugar of Lead / Well! better that than no sugar. Put Oil of Vitriol into my Sallad—well, better that than no oil at all—or a fellow vends a poison under the name of James's powders—well! we must get the best we can—better that than none! So did not our noblest ancestors reason, or feel—or we should now be Slaves, and even as the Sicilians are at this day—or worse: for even they have been made less foolish in spite of themselves by others' wisdom.[39]

Yet the references in the poem to Maria, and the Catholic pattern of sin, penance and confession, so alien to Coleridge's Unitarianism, leave us in no doubt as to the kind of theological universe the Mariner himself inhabits. The poem is open in this way to all the imaginative possibilities of wrongness, like the narrator of *Christabel* asking 'For what can ail the mastiff bitch?' or 'Can she the bodiless dead espy?': a man clearly in the dark. Perhaps one way of reading both poems, then, is as finely dramatic studies in superstition and its misinterpretations. Coming to terms with his own bewildering, inexplicable, hallucinatory experience, the Mariner reaches naturally for the ways of explaining spiritual experience with which he is most familiar and tries to apply them to his own case: of course, they do not fit, penance is never effected and redemption never arises.

Yet, still, the needy ghost of redemption and confession flits about the poem like the bat in Maud's garden, half-answering not to Coleridgean theory, but to Coleridgean need. It is as if Coleridge adopts a Catholic framework in *The Ancient Mariner* (and *Christabel*) to exercise—and, perhaps, ideally, to exorcise—the deep anxieties lurking incongruously in his optimistic Christian determinism. Thus, he seeks to dramatize what are his properly illegitimate feelings of isolation and remorse and his longings for homecomings and atonement as the superstitious responses of his unenlightened spokesman. It is perfectly fitting that Lamb should have been one of the poem's earliest champions, for Lamb is of all the romantics most aware of the freeing imaginative possibilities created when the writer at once shields and exposes himself in the equivocal, dramatized half-light of 'middle emotions' and 'half-reality'.[40]

Now, this was not at all the scheme Wordsworth proposed as a good story for a spooky magazine poem on that walk to Watchet in the Autumn of 1797: that, in striking bad faith, was going to be real Monk Lewis stuff with genuine, thrilling gothic circumstances and, presumably, the uninspired ethical scheme, derived from *Faustus,* that most Gothic relies upon. 'Certain parts I myself suggested', he modestly told Miss Fenwick in later life; but it is startling to realize that almost all the ostensibly objective events of the poem which seem to take up an allegorical shape are Wordsworth's contribution: the crime, the punishment of the crime by supernatural agencies, his wanderings about the sea; the specific detail of an albatross being the victim and of the ship being sailed by the dead men. When Wordsworth adds 'but [I] do not recollect I had anything more to do with the scheme of the poem,' one wonders what more to do with the 'scheme' there might be.[41] Significantly, the main Coleridgean contributions to the scheme seem to have been the allegory-complicating dice-game between Death and Life-in-Death and the brilliantly irresolved homecoming.

For Coleridge's alterations to Wordsworth's more normally gothic scheme of accepted spookiness make the poem, like *The Turn of the Screw* or, more so, Hogg's *Memoirs and Confessions of a Justified Sinner,* deliberately ambiguous. *The Ancient Mariner* exploits the fallibility of a first-person narrative of extreme events to play off the illusory inventions of the fevered brain against the objective supernaturalism of magical forces, leaving the reader, along with the Wedding Guest, caught between those rival interpretations and finding himself wrong-footed. '"Nay, if thou'st got a laughsome tale, / "Marinere, come with me",' (ll. 11-12) says the misinterpreting Wedding Guest in 1798 and 1800 texts, after the bearded figure has button-holed him: he thinks the Mariner is going to tell him a funny story. '"I fear thee, ancient Mariner! I fear thy skinny hand"' (ll. 224-5), he cries at the beginning of Part IV, not unreasonably getting the wrong end of the stick again and thinking the Mariner dropped down with the rest of the crew and is walking dead. It is interesting to see that, in March 1798, as Coleridge's poem was coming to completion, Wordsworth began to write his own ballads illustrating the power of the mind to create its own, properly illusory, kinds of reality, like *The Thorn,* itself a psychological reworking of a true gothic chiller ballad by Bürger, or that portrait of psychosomatic disease, *Goody Blake and Harry Gill*: he has been learning from Coleridge again.

One cannot say with certainty, as one probably can of *The Turn of the Screw,* that **The Ancient Mariner** is a study in what Empson called 'neurotic guilt':[42] for the quality of religious feeling in the poem seems to militate against so simple and secular a reading: 'O Wedding-Guest! this soul hath been / Alone on a wide wide sea: / So lonely 'twas, that God himself / Scarce seeméd there to be' (ll. 597-600)—a powerfully ambiguous stanza, adroitly manoeuvering itself between the neurotic subjectivity of the isolated Mariner ('It was so lonely in that place that I felt, absurdly, that God was not there, whereas I know that He is everywhere') and a more universal claim of powerful metaphysical assertiveness ('So lonely that even the existence of God suddenly revealed itself to be utterly implausible'). For it is the equivocation, at once fraught and effortless, between the two kinds of reading which Coleridge exploits so brilliantly; by contrast, *The Thorn* is an ingenious, almost Browningesque, dramatic monologue exemplifying the distorting lens of neurosis, but ultimately a simple enough affair, and winning its success by that simplicity.

When published in the 1800 edition, **The Ancient Mariner** is shifted out of its pride of place at the front of the book, and placed number 23 in what was now the first of two volumes, between *The Mad Mother* and the great conclusive Wordsworthian *vox humana* swell of *Tintern Abbey* at the close of the volume one. One can sense Wordsworth taking over completely in the 1800 edition: only his name appears on the title-page, despite the fact that several of Coleridge's poems appeared (**The Ancient Mariner** did not appear under Coleridge's own name until 1817); and Coleridge himself wrote in a letter of 1800 that Wordsworth had sent off to the printers '*his* Lyrical Ballads'.[43] Wordsworth's increasing power manifests itself most startlingly in his successful petitions to Coleridge to move north, to nothing, and leave London, where he was set on a well-paid, highly prestigious career in journalism; Coleridge's adoration of his mighty friend—and neglect of his wife—is evident enough in his going. Once there, naturally, Wordsworth rather abandoned him in Keswick, suitably distant, where Coleridge grew ill and depressed: thus proving that authorship, as the excellent Lamb wrote, is a kind of warfare.

As if this were not sign enough of Coleridge's now secondary place in the once collaboratory partnership, the 1800 text of **The Ancient Mariner** was accompanied by a note by Wordsworth obligingly explaining to the reader all the poem's many faults, as well as its few admitted merits. There is no record of what Coleridge thought of this; other things may have preoccupied him, if we consider that his inability to finish **Christabel** had inspired Wordsworth to drop the poem altogether, thus effecting, as Stephen Parrish amongst others has argued, a disastrous blow to Coleridge's self-confidence as a poet.[44] The note by Wordsworth, which I am gratified to see its most recent editor calls 'controversial',[45] says, amongst other things:

> The Poem of my Friend has indeed great defects; first, that the principal person has no distinct character, either in his profession of Mariner, or as a human being who having been long under the control of supernatural impressions might be supposed himself to partake of something supernatural; secondly, that he does not act, but is continually acted upon; thirdly, that the events having no necessary connection do not produce each other; and lastly, that the imagery is somewhat too laboriously accumulated.

Can any poem of comparable stature have received so bad a press from a fellow labourer? It is like Pound publishing a bad review of *The Waste Land* or Isherwood putting in an appendix pointing out the defects of Auden's *Look Stranger!*. Wordsworth makes several points here. The lack of volition is, as we have seen, exactly the theological doctrine which Coleridge is examining, at least in part because of a terribly self-aware understanding of his own 'Strength without Power', a subject he is very likely to have discussed with his friend: we may be seeing in Wordsworth's note an uncharitable reproduction of Coleridge's own self-destructive insight.[46] The Wordsworth note's major complaint seems to be that Coleridge's poem is neither one thing nor the other. It was not clearly a tale of objective hauntings, as Wordsworth had probably proposed; nor did the Mariner seem to have learnt from the experience, as one might expect of a story with allegorical significance, for he was still stumbling round in the dark, vainly seeking to interpret his story, years later. Yet nor was it a piece of complete dramatization, as his own ballads had been, in which we would have seen the way the Mariner's nature as a seaman created his way of superstitiously misinterpreting things (a bizarre notion, surely, of what would have made a better poem). This latter course, it might be mentioned, would have made the poem much more like Wordsworth's *The Thorn*, for which Wordsworth helpfully provided another new note in the 1800 edition, later much ridiculed, not unreasonably, by Byron. The suspicion that Wordsworth was impatient with the equivocal nature of the work seems to be confirmed by the subtitle the poem acquired in the 1800 edition: 'A Poet's Reverie'. It pushes the work more emphatically towards the status of dramatic monologue and implies its theme to be the inventiveness of subjectivity and was almost certainly Wordsworth's idea—at any rate Lamb thought so and wrote him a furious letter on the subject. Lamb's sense that Wordsworth disapproved of the poem was characteristically shrewd: to have a 'reverie', presumably a lowgrade sort of dream, sums up just about everything Wordsworth opposed in his 1800 Preface, which championed the real language of men and the passions of humans, not angels.

Wordsworth is not just being obtuse about Coleridge's poem, nor simply rivalrous, nor obliquely acknowledging the inadequate dramatization of his own *The Thorn*, though he is certainly doing these things as well; there is a radical difference in their world-views which is expressing itself in a disagreement about poetry. Coleridge's poem is haunted by an illicit sense of the denied possibility of atonement, a word which Coleridge himself was later to gloss, fancifully, as 'at-one-ment', the being-made-at-one with things: 'at-one', as Coleridge speculates, as flowers are selflessly at one with the global energies of God's nature, and, I suppose, water-snakes equally.[47] It is something like this that the marginal commentator in the 1817 text seems wishfully to claim for the Mariner, though the poet knows better. What is the use of responding to the variety of the world's enormous provision if one's soul is homeless and aimless? What if the brilliant apprehension of the world's diverse particularity—the sheer vibrant quiddity of the water-snakes—keeps feeling like the experience of a sheer, disunified, manifold chaos? What if one's conviction of the sublime, vital unity of all only serves to confirm one's own feeling of individual exclusion from that otherwise all-inclusive life? That quintessentially Coleridgean construction, 'And what if . . . ?', by which religious hope and personal dejection come into unstable union, seems to find its perfect narrative form in the competing epic and dramatic perspectives of *The Ancient Mariner*.

Such deeply, tragically religious aspirations had no acknowledged home in Wordsworth's poetry: his flirtation around the turn of the century with the One Life, picked up from Coleridge, is brief and curiously non-committal in one sense, while being complete in another; and talking to Henry Crabb Robinson in 1812 Wordsworth famously announced himself in no need of a redeemer.[48] No comment could be more properly an optimist determinist's, yet no comment could seem less Coleridgean. The way the 1805 *Prelude* muscles in on Miltonic territory and seizes its Christian structures of thought for the Wordsworthian imagination is amply suggestive of Wordsworth's appropriative attitude towards the patterns of the spiritual life which Coleridge introduced with such poised dramatic equivocation in *The Ancient Mariner*, as if aware of their proper incongruity for a good Unitarian. The mere play of human perspectives, Wordsworth's foremost amongst them, is enough for the deeply, stoically humanistic vision which is Wordsworth's; the stubborn objectivity against which the individualizing subjectivities of the men and women of his *Lyrical Ballads* are measured is not the whole scheme of redemption and sacrifice, but the empiricist objectivity of the material world. One thinks of the young Wordsworth clinging onto the stone wall to convince himself of its external existence; or of the obsessional lines from *The Thorn*: 'I've measured it from side to side: / 'Tis three feet long, and two feet wide' (ll. 32-3). This Wordsworth, at his most moving, speaks of 'the very world which is the world / Of all of us, the place in which, in the end, / We find our happiness, or not at all', in a uniquely Wordsworthian voice, in which the message of secularism acquires a practically Miltonic authority and forebearance.[49]

And there is a side of the young Coleridge which might assert itself for this world and commit himself to the obvious moral of his poem. This side would set itself against Babbitt, say that one *might* seek salvation in the sheer concreteness of its variety and the particularity of its diverse fecundity—that the water-snakes *are* enough—and agree with Louis MacNeice that the world is benevolently crazier and more of it than we think, incorrigibly plural.[50] (As he excitedly urges himself in an early notebook entry, 'But go & look & look!'.)[51] This side of Coleridge finds in the effortless, atoning innocence of the objective world, 'something out of me', what John Beer calls so well 'a whole world of relief':[52] 'The silly buckets on the deck, / That had so long remained, / I dreamt that they were filled with dew' (ll. 297-9). The One Life holds out for the young Coleridge all this world and blesses it with the organising inspiration of the deity.

But there is another side to Coleridge, one which says with Wallace Stevens, 'that we live in a place / That is not our own and, much more, not ourselves / And hard it is in spite of blazoned days', and finds that MacNeice's generously pluralistic craziness is but a kind of chaotic lunacy.[53] One loses a sense of that deep unity which should make sense of the diversity of experience and restore it all, oneself included, to the benevolence of order. This homeless, suffering Coleridge will come to search for routes to atonement altogether elsewhere, out of nature, coming eventually to see the natural world as nothing less than a wily witch set to confuse and obfuscate the spiritual life, and the redemption apparently brought by water-snakes to be simply an illusory fantasy. The full development of this position is a later phenomenon, but its seeds are already there in the equivocations of the early poem. *The Ancient Mariner* is poised unrepeatably between a conviction of hope and an awareness of hopelessness, between the conviction of an allegorical structure and the implication that that structure is quite subjectively perceived and actually misrepresents a quite arbitrary, meaningless series of events. Coleridge is uniquely enabled by the simultaneous authority and non-committedness of dramatized epic at once to preach a natural atonement and secretly to confess an implicit sense of isolated neediness. His compulsive returning to it is a compulsive returning to the difficult, anxious uncertainties which the later, more corpulent Highgate Sage garrulously strove to talk himself through, but of which the perpetually present evidence of his young poem must have stood as permanent reminder.

Notes

1. Jack Stillinger, 'The Multiple Versions of Coleridge's Poems: How Many *Mariners* Did Coleridge Write?', *Studies in Romanticism* 31 (1992) 127-146, p. 127. Martin Wallen's elaborate and useful *Coleridge's Ancient Mariner: An Experimental Edition of Texts and Revision 1798-1828* (New York, 1993) presents 1798, 1800 and 1817 texts with other variants noted. (Since this paper was read at Grasmere, Professor J. C. C. Mays, editor of the poems for the Bollingen *Coleridge* has told us there are over 100 versions of the poem: the difficulties multiply.)

2. All quotations from the poem are taken from Samuel Taylor Coleridge, *Poems* ed. John Beer (1963; repr., London, 1991).

3. William Empson, Introduction to Samuel Taylor Coleridge, *Selected Poems* ed. William Empson and David Pirie (1972; repr., Manchester, 1989) (hereafter Empson).

4. See the editor's introduction to Samuel Taylor Coleridge, *Aids to Reflection* ed. John Beer (Princeton, NJ, 1993) (hereafter *Aids to Reflection*), p. xcv ff.

5. *The Notebooks of Samuel Taylor Coleridge* ed. Kathleen Coburn et al. (4 vols. to date; London and New York, 1957-) (hereafter *Notebooks*), ii. 2784.

6. *The Letters of William and Dorothy Wordsworth: The Early Years 1787-1805* ed. E. de Selincourt, rev. Chester L. Shaver (Oxford, 1967) (hereafter *EY*), p. 194.

7. The Fenwick note to *We are Seven*; reproduced in *Lyrical Ballads* ed. Michael Mason (London, 1992) (hereafter Mason), pp. 368-9.

8. Mason 368.

9. Coleridge himself appreciated the stink his name might bring with it and warned his publisher not to use it on the title page: *The Collected Letters of Samuel Taylor Coleridge* ed. E. L. Griggs (6 vols., Oxford, 1956-71) (hereafter Griggs), i. 412.

10. *EY* 188.

11. Griggs i. 324, 358.

12. *EY* 194.

13. Griggs i. 379.

14. Griggs i. 371.

15. *EY* 210-11.

16. Stephen Gill, *William Wordsworth: A Life* (Oxford, 1989), p. 133.

17. Griggs ii. 830.

18. *The Letters of Charles and Mary Anne Lamb* ed. Edwin W. Marrs Jr. (3 vols., Ithaca, NY, 1975-8), i. 51.

19. See Jonathan Wordsworth, *William Wordsworth: The Borders of Vision* (Oxford, 1982), pp. 352-6.

20. Samuel Taylor Coleridge, *Biographia Literaria* ed. Walter Jackson Bate and James Engell (2 vols., Princeton, NJ, 1983), i. 197-8.

21. H. W. Garrod, *Wordsworth: Lectures and Essays* (Oxford, 1927), p. 30.

22. *EY* 178.

23. Griggs i. 320.

24. *Coleridge: The Clark Lectures, 1951-52* (London, 1962), pp. 18-19.

25. See Basil Willey, *Samuel Taylor Coleridge* (London, 1972), p. 39.

26. Griggs i. 159, 168.

27. See the editors' introduction to Samuel Taylor Coleridge, *Lectures 1795 On Politics and Religion* ed. Lewis Patton and Peter Mann (Princeton, NJ, 1971) (hereafter *Lectures 1795*), p. lxiii.

28. For a fine account of this too-often neglected aspect of Coleridge's intelligence see House, *Coleridge,* 47-50.

29. '. . . if God *be* every Thing, every Thing is God—' (Griggs i. 192).

30. *Osorio* is naturally not included in Beer's edition of the *Poems*; I quote here from *The Poetical Works of Samuel Taylor Coleridge* ed. E. H. Coleridge (2 vols., Oxford, 1912), ii. 596.

31. For a good, wide-ranging account of Coleridge's neuroses, see 'Coleridge's Anxiety' in Thomas McFarland, *Romanticism and the Forms of Ruin: Wordsworth, Coleridge, and the Modalities of Fragmentation* (Princeton, 1980), pp. 104-36.

32. Griggs i. 391.

33. 'A Poem of Pure Imagination: An Experiment in Reading' in Robert Penn Warren, *Selected Essays* (New York, 1958).

34. *Natural Supernaturalism: Tradition and Revolution in Romantic Literature* (London, 1971), pp. 272-5.

35. 'Indeed, the moral, which would apparently be that people who sympathise with a man who shoots an albatross will die in prolonged torture of thirst, is open to obvious objections' ('Coleridge' in Leslie Stephen, *Hours in a Library* [3 vols., London, 1909], iii. 316-43, 335).

36. '. . . the Ancient Mariner . . . it will be remembered, is relieved of the burden of his transgression by admiring the color of water-snakes!' (Babbitt, *Rousseau and Romanticism* [Boston, 1919], p. 287).

37. 'The curse is finally expiated', the marginal commentator announces beside line 442.

38. As argued by E. Bostetter, 'The Nightmare World of *The Ancient Mariner*' in *Coleridge: A Collection of Critical Essays* ed. Kathleen Coburn (Englewood Cliffs, 1967), pp. 65-77.

39. *Notebooks* ii. 2324. (I have clarified some of Coleridge's informal shorthand.) And see, e.g., *Lectures 1795* 209-11, and *Aids to Reflection* 212-13, for other expressions of this anti-Papism.

40. 'On the Artificial Comedy of the Last Century', in Charles Lamb, *Elia and The Last Essays of Elia* ed. Jonathan Bate (Oxford, 1987), pp. 161, 164.

41. Mason 368.

42. Empson 39ff.

43. Griggs i. 658.

44. Coleridge's pain at his treatment by Wordsworth is described in Stephen M. Parrish, *The Art of the Lyrical Ballads* (Cambridge, Mass., 1973), p. 52.

45. Mason 39.

46. A suggestion made in conversation by Dr Jonathan Wordsworth.

47. *The Statesman's Manual* in Samuel Taylor Coleridge, *Lay Sermons* ed. R. J. White (Princeton, NJ, 1972), pp. 55, 71.

48. *Henry Crabb Robinson on Books and their Writers* ed. Edith J. Morley (3 vols., London, 1938), i. 87, 158.

49. *The Thirteen-Book Prelude* x 725-7, in *The Prelude: 1799, 1805, 1850* ed. Jonathan Wordsworth, Stephen Gill and M. H. Abrams (New York, 1979).

50. *Snow* in Louis MacNeice, *Selected Poems* ed. Michael Longley (London, 1988), p. 23.

51. *Notebooks* ii. 2102.

52. Coleridge, *Poems* 172.

53. *Notes Toward a Supreme Fiction*, in Wallace Stevens, *Collected Poems* (London, 1955), p. 383.

Debbie Lee (essay date fall 1998)

SOURCE: Lee, Debbie. "Yellow Fever and the Slave Trade: Coleridge's *The Rime of the Ancient Mariner*." *ELH* 65, no. 3 (fall 1998): 675-700.

[*In the following essay, Lee demonstrates how in* The Ancient Mariner *Coleridge metaphorically linked England's involvement in the slave trade with disease—*

specifically yellow fever—focusing on the poet's treat-ment of such pressing, contemporary issues as "foreign-ers," colonialism, miscegenation, commerce, social hierarchies, and guilt.]

Yellow fever of the West Indies, a plague that attacked like an army during the height of British colonial slavery, swept through the body with shocking symp-toms. The fever attacked suddenly, with fits of hot and cold, and violent pain in the head, neck, and back. Not only would the patient's eyes turn watery and yellow, but the whole face would change, appearing "un-natural," denoting "anxiety" and "dejection of mind."[1] Finally, it produced delirium and sometimes madness. During its progress, doctors noted changes "in the great mass of blood itself," which became putrefied and then oozed from the gums, nose, ears, and anus.[2] The skin turned from flush to yellow or light brown. But it was in the final stages that patients underwent the worst of all symptoms: the black vomit, described variously by medical experts as resembling coffee grounds, black sand, kennel water, soot, or the meconium of newborn children.

Throughout the late eighteenth and early nineteenth centuries, medical workers and lay people alike considered yellow fever a disease to which Africans were miraculously immune. Dr. Thomas Trotter, a naval doctor famous for implementing mandatory smallpox vaccination in the British armed forces, claimed that "African negroes" appeared immune to "contagious fever[s]," while the poet Robert Southey explicitly stated that "yellow fever will not take root in a negro."[3] If yellow fever graciously spared Africans and slaves, it just as ferociously attacked white Europeans who visited Africa and the Caribbean. Yet it was not merely the "newcomers from Europe, in high health" that were "singularly affected with the yellow fever."[4] Many medi-cal experts emphasized British susceptibility. "Britons," noted Dr. Hillary, were "by the great increased Heat of the Climate, usually not long after their Arrival" in the Caribbean "seized with a Fever."[5] The great Dr. Hume, expert on tropical medicine, even went so far as to cre-ate a catalog of likely British yellow fever candidates: "Strong muscular men are most liable to it, and suffer most."[6]

Yellow fever's insistence on attacking the British body wreaked havoc with the nation's military plans. Since the fever was considered one of Britain's biggest obstacles to successful commerce with Africa and the Caribbean, it was often discussed using terms from military rhetoric. In 1797, for example, Dr. Trotter is-sued a pamphlet called *Medicina Nautica: An Essay on the Diseases of Seamen*, where he wrote concerning the yellow fever:

> The ravages which this fatal Disease have made . . . in our fleets and armies, are beyond all precedent: the insidious mode of attack, the rapid strides by which it

advances to an incurable stage, point it out as one of the most formidable opponents of medical skill. It has offered the severest obstacle to military operations, which the history of modern warfare can produce.[7]

This fever turned the British body against itself by turn-ing it into its own foreign enemy. And it did so on an epic scale. Throughout the late eighteenth and early nineteenth centuries, aggressive fever pathogens ac-counted for seventy-one percent of all European deaths in the Caribbean, and most of these were from yellow fever.[8]

More than yellow fever's military power, it was the geographical movement of this disease that determined its interpretive implications. Because these early medi-cal studies nearly always referred to yellow fever as a Caribbean disease, and since the Caribbean was synonymous with the slave trade and colonial slavery, yellow fever itself became intimately tied to the physi-cal and philosophical effects of slavery. Together, the medical study of yellow fever and the debate on the abolition of the slave trade and of slavery kindled a series of specific concerns—especially among British writers—about what happened when "foreign" matter, or "foreigners," became part of the physical or political body.

No one work is more important for defining the poetic as well as the political concerns for British writers dur-ing this period than Samuel Taylor Coleridge's *The Rime of the Ancient Mariner. The Ancient Mariner* opened the 1798 *Lyrical Ballads* and so established itself as a first among a new poetics. But when he composed the poem, Coleridge himself was thoroughly engaged in the social and political issues of the day, from the latest theories of epidemic disease to the debates on abolition and slavery. Coleridge, along with Robert Southey, was an active abolitionist in Bristol from 1795 until at least the year he wrote *The Ancient Mariner.* The poem, in fact, has frequently and convinc-ingly been interpreted as a poem about the slave trade by writers who, in the tradition of John Livingston Lowes, contextualize the poem's major tropes using Coleridge's material concerns with travel literature, colonialism, and the slave trade. J. R. Ebbotson is just one of a number of readers to view the poem as an indictment of British maritime expansion, where "the central act of *The Ancient Mariner,* the shooting of the albatross, may be a symbolic rehearsal of the crux of colonial expansion, the enslavement of native peoples."[9] Patrick Keane, in a recent book on Coleridge, has traced most of *The Ancient Mariner*'s images to their sources in debates on abolition and emancipation.[10]

What has not been exposed in these studies is the extent to which *The Ancient Mariner* takes up issues of slavery and race along with the material conditions of fever, particularly the yellow fever.[11] For example, in the initial stages of the ballad—after the mariner's albatross murder dislodges the ship from the icy fields of the South Pole—fever sets the poem afire.[12] Coleridge takes the reader from climatic realities (the "broad bright sun," the standing water, and the Western wave "all aflame") to bodily symptoms ("parched throats and "cold sweat[s]") to symbolic fever: the "charmed water" that "burnt always / A still and awful red" (3.174, 3.171, 3.144). But even more dramatic than this is the fever of the British imagination, the "uncertain hour" when "agony returns: / And till my ghastly tale is told, / This heart within me burns" (7.582-85).

Coleridge was certainly not alone in setting fever to poetry. William Roscoe's "The Wrongs of Africa" (1797) described the effects of contagion during the slave voyage and in the "polluted islands" of the voyage's destination. But this is nothing compared to Roscoe's final warning. He insists that British consumption will result in both national stagnation and universal pain. Though the "copious stream / Of universal bliss" might seem to flow to every nation, it will "stagnate in its course" and spread "foul and putrid . . . corruption round."[13] British avarice—witnessed so clearly in the case of slavery—was, according to Roscoe, "in nature's breast a dagger" that debilitated all of nature. Hannah More's "Slavery" (1788) portrayed the voice of British liberty in a similar way: "convulsed . . . and pestilent her breath, / She raves for mercy, while she deals out death."[14] Such writing emphasized how the consciousness of slavery as pestilence partly defined British identity during this time.

But how was it that disease, slavery, and the consciousness of slavery as disease operated in early nineteenth-century British culture, only to be taken up by Coleridge in an extraordinary tale of guilt and redemption? *The Ancient Mariner,* like abolitionist and emancipation literature of the period, draws on early nineteenth-century medical and ecological models used to analyze yellow fever—the most deadly and widespread disease for British seamen on slave voyages. But discussion of fever within the discourse of slavery, and discussion of slavery within the discourse of yellow fever, really addresses a wider question: could Britain establish a social system free from the diseases of tyranny and subjection?

I. FEVER AND THE PROXIMITY OF CULTURES

When reading Coleridge's various writings, one has the sense that he could actually imagine a process where British "self" and foreign "other" could unite in harmony. He certainly contemplated the philosophic working out of such a process. In his *Marginalia,* for instance, he wrote that "the copula" of "identity" and "alterity" meant "losing self in another form by loving the self of another as another."[15] It was in the context of British masters and African slaves, however, where the concepts of "identity" and "alterity" took on a blatant, material reality, and where "losing self in another" by taking on the alterity of that other had complex consequences for both British and African subjectivity. If *The Ancient Mariner* is read through the lens of this potent topic, it must be read as a process where the mariner tries to reconcile identity and alterity in a political, as well as a philosophical, way.[16]

In both medical literature and abolitionist poetry, the intersection of slavery and disease nearly always ended in a rethinking of philosophical definitions of identity and alterity. The work of Julia Kristeva provides some help in understanding this rather complex phenomenon.[17] Taken together, Kristeva's work on the abject in *Powers of Horror* and on foreigners in *Strangers to Ourselves* and *Nations Without Nationalism* offer a compelling theory linking bodily disease and foreign travel through the category of alterity.

Kristeva's writings revolve around a fundamental distinction between "self" and "not-self." Everything that is horrifying, everything that signals our possible inhumanity, everything that reminds us of our mortality, is not-self. As Kristeva has it, the diseased, decaying body (the yellow fever victim's black vomit and bleeding orifices, for example) is the most potent form of the not-self, or what she calls "the abject." And the abject itself, because it is the ultimate expression of the flesh, is an explicit manifestation of sin (at least from the perspective of dominant culture). Blood, urine, excrement, and the human corpse, these are the raw materials of the abject:

> corpses *show me* what I permanently thrust aside in order to live. These body fluids, this defilement, this shit are what life withstands, hardly and with difficulty on the part of death. There, I am at the border of my condition as a living being. My body extricates itself, as being alive, from that border . . . If dung signifies the other side of the border, the place where I am not and which permits me to be, the corpse, the most sickening of wastes, is a border that has encroached upon everything.[18]

We constitute ourselves, according to Kristeva, through abjection by excluding what is not-self. Yet the abject is always part of us, even though it must constantly be ignored, buried, or thrown over the edge of consciousness. The abject is, in this way, the cornerstone of personal subjectivity.

The process by which an individual constitutes personal subjectivity is, for Kristeva, also worked out on a national level. Just as the individual tries to evade death as symbolized in the corpse, so national character shies away from that which is foreign to it:

Hatred of others who do not share my origins and who affront me personally, economically, and culturally: I then move back among "my own," I stick to an archaic, primitive "common denominator," the one of my frailest childhood, my closest relatives, hoping they will be more trustworthy than foreigners.[19]

Foreigners, like Coleridge's mariner, who transgress borders and break taboos, who identify with and touch otherness, are culturally abject. Kristeva maintains a distinctly Coleridgean position by arguing that the unity of the self, though impossible, may be glimpsed by realizing we are all, in some sense, "strangers to ourselves." She sees the encounter with foreigners very like Coleridge's notion of "losing self in another," a process that involves self-alteration and loss of direction:

Confronting the foreigner whom I reject and with whom at the same time I identify, I lose my boundaries, I no longer have a container, the memory of experiences which I had abandoned overwhelm me, I lose my composure. I feel "lost," "indistinct," "hazy."[20]

Throughout her writings, Kristeva describes the marriage of identity and alterity as a boundary-dissolving process, whether those boundaries are individual or national, material or metaphysical.

If nineteenth-century systems of medicine and slavery were about anything, they were about boundaries, or boundary-dissolving processes. In fact, it might be said that these systems of medicine and slavery were designed to reestablish borders that were in the process of dissolving with the increased foreign travel that the slave trade instigated. Dissolving both personal and national borders, after all, is how yellow fever first gained attention. Medical writers warned that epidemics in the Caribbean could spread throughout Europe, conjuring up images of the Black Plague of the fourteenth century, which wiped out one third of the European population.[21] In the meantime, European heads of state put doctors in the service of deflecting national panic. Dr. Blane reported that Britain, Russia and Prussia, had held conferences to dispel the public and medical fear of "importation of this pestilential epidemic [yellow fever], which in the end of last century, and beginning of this, had so afflicted the West Indies, North America, and Spain."[22] In 1797, Dr. Trotter likewise assured a potentially panicky British audience that there was no danger whatsoever of yellow fever "becoming active on this side of the Atlantic."[23]

The presence of yellow fever could not only disintegrate national borders, it could also redefine political alliances. Dr. Blane recounted an example of French war ships that had captured British frigates carrying crews seized with yellow fever. The epidemic spread quickly among the French crews who were then quarantined with British prisoners, despite their status as French enemies.[24] In times of epidemic, it seemed, national identity was as unreliable as the body itself. Unlucky victims were the embodiment of alterity, no matter what their skin color or national status. Not surprisingly, slaves in the Caribbean were even more aware of fever's ability to cross boundaries and render Europeans powerless. In 1799, Robert Renny recalled being greeted on the shore of Jamaica by a canoe full of slave women sarcastically chanting:

New come buckra,
He get sick,
He tak fever,
He be die,
He be die, & etc.[25]

Yellow fever often killed European individuals who were involved in the slave trade, but what seemed worse to legislators and plantation owners was the imminent death of the slave system itself. With increased pressure from abolitionists like Southey and Coleridge, British culture faced the possibility of a social system that no longer divided itself neatly into masters and slaves. This heightened national anxiety about economic consequences existed most vocally among Caribbean proprietors, many of whom owned failing plantations as it was. But underneath this fiscal fear lay a deeper worry over how the change in the status of African slaves—from foreigners to citizens—would not only infect Europeans, but deplete any differences between the races. Coleridge would later confront this fear in his planned lecture on the "Origins of the Human Race." In this lecture, he opposed Blumenbach's implication that Africans resembled orangutans.[26] But this changing view of the slave from inferior to moral equal threatened to dissolve the fragile border of the British self. For there was nothing quite like the abjection of the African slave against which British national character defined itself in the early part of the nineteenth century.

In *The Rime of the Ancient Mariner* Coleridge merges this fear of miscegenation with the fear of fever. The poem, which would have been more widely read than either the discourse of medicine or the debate on slavery, expresses anxieties about dissolving borders. For example, at the very beginning of the poem, the mariner relates in his story to the unhappy wedding guest how the ship set sail from a British port. But as soon as it moved "below the kirk, below the hill, / Below the lighthouse top" (1.23-24) and thus beyond Britain's geographical borders, other borders turned suddenly fragile. The result of this movement into the waters of foreignness and abjection is a narrative standstill when mariner and crew encounter "Nightmare Life-in-Death" upon her "spectre bark" (3.193, 202), a vessel William Empson (among others) calls "the premonition of a slaver."[27] This encounter turns the crew into a feverish image of the living dead, "for a charnel dungeon fitter" (6.435), and so has them dancing on the most unbreakable and abject boundary in human experience, that between life and death.

By marrying the tropes of fever and slavery, *The Ancient Mariner* also explores slippages between the walled-off categories of self and otherness. In the heat of the poem's fever, the mariner is identified with Englishmen *and* slaves, even though yellow fever underscored what were perceived as natural differences between Britons and Africans in how their bodies weathered forces of nature.[28] The mariner's implied nationality and the wedding guest's response to his "long, and lank, and brown" body (4.226) links him to British sailors who had been yellow fever victims. Because these victims were (according to the Caribbean traveler Robert Renny) "exposed to the burning sun, and a sultry atmosphere by day; chilling dews, and unhealthful employments, new food, and new clothing," their bodies took on a ghostly, unnatural appearance. They became "irritable and weak" and were thus "readily affected" with the fever.[29] During this time, there was also an acute awareness that yellow fever (or "imported contagion") traveled by way of sun-scorched mariners and soldiers from one tropical shore to another.[30] When mariners arrived home, people seemed naturally afraid of touching these potentially unclean victims of seafaring diseases. It is thus not surprising to find this fear openly erupting in the beginning lines of *The Ancient Mariner.* Who can blame the wedding-guest for voicing an immediate prohibition against bodily contact, ordering the mariner to "Hold off! Unhand me, grey-beard loon!" (1.11) Like the British seaman whose body changed color in the heat of a yellow fever outbreak, the ancient mariner's shadowy weakness and brown "skinny hand" emerge repeatedly throughout the poem, as if to remind readers that yellow fever took its name from its ability to change the skin color of European victims.

But in the poem's infected environment, the very markers that identify the mariner as a British sailor (the "brown hand"), also designate him a slave. He is linked to the bodies of Africans not only through his color, but also through his health. When the mariner assures his listener, "Fear not, fear not, thou Wedding Guest! / This body dropt not down" (3.230-31), he acknowledges his own immunity to the fever that struck down all two hundred shipmates, an immunity that implicitly aligns him with the alterity of the slave. For when medical writers, such as Henry Clutterbuck M.D., observed that infectious fevers were "communicable from one individual to another, either by actual contact, or by the effluvia escaping from the bodies of the sick," they were referring to communication between European and European, not European and African.[31] The wedding guest's fear of touching the Mariner's "skinny hand, so brown" (3.229), then, also demonstrates a fear of "los-ing self in another," of being infected and thus profoundly changed by the alterity carried in the blood under dark skin.

This boundary-dissolving process that *The Ancient Mariner* articulates so powerfully was also a central issue in the early nineteenth-century medical search for the origin of yellow fever. Medical experts agreed that every disease had its own geographical habitat. For example, Dr. Thomas Beddoes—Coleridge's friend and correspondent—represented a common opinion when he said "small-pox, yellow fever, and the plague" came from a certain "effluvia" produced in the air of hot regions.[32] Tropical climates—Africa and the Caribbean particularly—were thus carriers of disease, and natives of Britain and America who came in contact with these climates could carry the disease back with them and so become foreigners in their homeland. The search for yellow fever's origin could help reestablish borders between "self" and "other," between "us" and "them," between British and African, which yellow fever itself obliterated.[33]

The search for origins, it seems, was everybody's business. In 1802, a writer named William Deverell published a book proposing to locate yellow fever's origin through a study of Milton, Virgil, and "thence to [the poetry] of Homer, and to the times when the temples of Egypt were founded; and I think it will be seen that the same or a similar disease, arising from the same causes and in the same places, prevailed in each of those ages."[34] Using the *Aenied,* Deverell established a one-to-one correspondence between Ortygia and Britain, Cycladas and the Caribbean, and "the tabida lues, affecting both animate and inanimate nature" was "most clearly a West Indian or American fever."[35] Coleridge also had an interest in the origin of epidemic disease. He located the origin of smallpox—the seafaring disease most closely associated with yellow fever—and demonstrated its coincidence with commerce, war, and the movement of Africans:

> Small pox . . . was first introduced by the Abyssinians into Arabia when they conquered the Province of Hemyen [Yemen]; & they called it the Locust-plague, believing it to have originated in the huge heaps of putrefying Locusts in the Desart.—From Arabia it was carried by Greek merchants to Constantinople—& from thence by the armies of Justinian in his Goth War to Italy, Switzerland, & France.[36]

Coleridge's theory supports the period's belief that, though the instigators of most diseases came from nature, from heaps of putrefying Locusts, from "effluvia" of hot climates, or from "decomposing vegetable matter," the growth of disease turned truly epidemic only through cross-cultural interaction.[37]

II. The Contagion of Consumption and Guilt

During the early part of the century, a radical change took place in the interaction between Britons and Africans. Up until the late eighteenth century, most segments of society accepted, without too many questions, racial hierarchies that placed white Europeans in a superior position to people of color. These hierarchies naturalized the slave system. Africans were considered inferior, and so slavery was justified. But things changed in the 1780s and 90s. Largely because of the abolitionist movement, but also because of increased slave uprisings, the majority of British people, for the first time in centuries, began to consider Africans as moral others instead of "things." Coleridge articulated a fairly common opinion in an article intended for the *Courier* where he wrote, "A slave is a Person perverted into a Thing; Slavery therefore is not so properly a deviation from Justice as an absolute subversion of all morality."[38] As one can imagine, this "subversion of all morality" by the British brought with it an overwhelming sense of guilt. Coleridge and other writers began to see European guilt in the same way doctors saw yellow fever's black vomit: as a primary symptom.

Guilt defined Britain as a sick society. And nowhere is the guilt of slavery and the punishment of disease more apparent than in abolitionist literature. Helen Maria Williams's 1788 "Poem on the bill lately passed" presents a vision of slavery where the "beams direct, that on each head / The fury of contagion shed."[39] The "beams" in this case radiate from the "guilty man" in charge of a slave vessel. While Williams located the origin of contagion in the guilt of British slave traders, Coleridge located the origin of slavery in the guilt of the British consumer. Slavery, he contended, was "evil in the form of guilt."[40] Those who consumed the products of the trade were just as guilty as slave traders and plantation owners themselves. After all, Coleridge argued, the trade's "final effect" and "first Cause" was "self-evidently the consumption of its Products! and does not the Guilt rest on the Consumers? and is it not an allowed axiom in Morality that Wickedness may be multiplied but cannot be divided and that the Guilt of all attaches to each one who is knowingly an accomplice?"[41] Wickedness multiplied and spread through the social body, like so many germs, leaving the collective British consumer with an all-consuming guilt.

The Rime of the Ancient Mariner struggles with guilt through disease, too. The poem suggests that it is possible to atone for the commerce of slavery, wipe out European guilt, and therefore stop disease from wiping out Europeans. *The Ancient Mariner,* according to James McKusick, sails in the shadow of guilt associated with the Western "civilizing" mission. McKusick suggests that the albatross is "an emblematic representation of all the innocent lives destroyed by European conquest," including the guilt associated with the slave trade.[42] But the albatross is just one emblem of guilt. Although the poem does not pinpoint any one source for the mariner's guilt, it seems related more to the deathly-ill state of the crew than it does to the killing of the bird. Similarly, what arrests the ship "day after day, day after day" (2.115) is not so much the storm-blast or the navigational disaster at the South Pole as it is the outbreak of disease and death. If the ship is on a commercial mission, especially one dealing in slaves, Coleridge implies a moral cause for the epidemic.

Coleridge was well aware of the natural causes of epidemics. But he, like many other writers, turned these natural causes into moral ones. For example, according to many medical experts of the day, stagnant waters combined with the torrid climate of the tropics to produce the yellow fever infection so common to slave vessels. The physician-poet Erasmus Darwin imported this well-known medical tidbit into his exotically charged diatribe *The Botanic Garden*. The poem rails against "Britannia's sons" who invaded the coasts of Africa "with murder, rapine, theft,—and call it Trade!"[43] The poem builds towards a genuine Old Testament plague, put into the modern context of contagion emanating from stagnant waters:

> Sylphs! with light shafts you pierce the drowsy FOG,
> That lingering slumbers on the sedge-wove bog,
> With webbed feet o'er midnight meadows creeps,
> Or flings his hairy limbs on stagnant deeps,
> You meet CONTAGION issuing from afar,
> And dash the baleful conqueror from his car[44]

Not just contagion, it was believed, but yellow fever in particular, targeted those like the mariner and his crew, floating on an ocean where "the very deep did rot . . . Yea, slimy things did crawl with legs / Upon the slimy sea" (2.123-26). A slave vessel stuck without "breath" or "motion" beneath a "hot and copper sky" (2.116; 2.111) was especially vulnerable from a medical as well as a moral point of view. Yellow fever was God's just punishment for the atrocities of the slave trade in James Montgomery's 1807 poem *The West Indies*:

> The Eternal makes his dread displeasure known,
> At his command the pestilence abhorr'd
> Spared poor slaves, and smites the haughty lord[45]

Similarly, one British traveler to the Caribbean said that "the new world, indeed, appears to be surrounded with the flaming sword of the angel, threatening destruction to all those, who venture within its reach."[46]

In *The Ancient Mariner*'s diseased climate, then, it is not just the albatross murder that prompts the crew to hang the bird around the mariner's neck as a symbol of guilt and death. It is the outbreak itself, the "spirit that plagued" them with suffocating symptoms: tongues "withered at the root" and "choked with soot," "throats unslaked, with black lips baked," "glazed" eyes reflecting the "bloody sun" and "death-fires" of the stagnant waters (2.132; 2.136; 3.157; 3:146; 2.112; 2.128). In fact before he wrote the poem Coleridge explained how by way of disease the slave trade destroyed the British national body by destroying individual bodies. Following Thomas Clarkson, who argued that the slave trade was infeasible because of the diseases to which crews were exposed, Coleridge said that "from the unwholesomeness of the Climate through which [crews] pass, it has been calculated that every slave vessel from the Port of Bristol loses on average almost a fourth of the whole crew" (W [The Watchman], 238). The slave trade, he said, turned British mariners into "rather shadows in their appearance than men" (W, 238), just as in The Ancient Mariner disease changes the mariners into a shadowy, "ghastly crew."

But Coleridge emphasizes this point when he locates the source of the disease in the skin of a ghostly, white woman. As soon as the crew hangs the dead white bird around the mariner's neck, the woman-specter, who is "white as leprosy" emerges on a "western wave" (3.192; 3.171), and the sailors drop dead:

> One after one, by the star-dogged Moon,
> Too quick for groan or sigh,
> Each turned his face with a ghastly pang,
> And cursed me with his eye.
> Four times fifty living men,
> (And I heard nor sigh nor groan)
> With a heavy thump, a lifeless lump,
> They dropped down one by one.
>
> (2.212-19)

Coleridge thus deviates from the medical community's indictment of the African and Caribbean atmosphere as a carrier of disease for Westerners. In a dramatic reversal, he places foreignness in a white, western woman, who becomes the expression of alterity through disease.

In his notebooks, Coleridge also pictured a white woman as a carrier of disease and moral depravity. In what is now a well-known account of one of his dreams, he told of being "followed up and down by a frightful pale woman who, I thought, wanted to kiss me, and had the property of giving a shameful Disease by breathing on the face" (CNB [The Notebooks of Samuel Taylor Coleridge], 1:1250).[47] In this case, the diseased white woman is quite clearly the cargo of his fevered mind. But the link between this diseased woman and the pale woman of The Ancient Mariner is the link between Western seafaring diseases and sexually transmitted, morally reprehensible diseases such as syphilis.

For Coleridge, at least, there was more to whiteness than met the eye. In The Ancient Mariner, he folds disease in the envelope of whiteness and thus highlights the extent to which he was conversant with the operations of disease and guilt within anti-slavery literature. When Coleridge called the slave trade "a commerce which is blotched all over with one leprosy of evil" (W, 236), he drew on the same theme as Thomas Pringle did in an anti-slavery sonnet, which suggested that sugar "taints with leprosy the white man's soul."[48] Sugar sifted down English channels and dissolved in their tea-cups, but it remained symbolically as a disease of white culture. Its cultural twin, leprosy, poisoned instead of sweetened, rotted away white flesh instead of increasing it. Thus abolitionist writers began to see sugar's deceptive sweetness, like the illusive whiteness of European skin, as something that tainted rather than purified. No wonder that in The Ancient Mariner the two apparent hosts of contagion—the leprous white woman and the decaying white bird—destroy the myth of white purity that the British bride symbolizes. The poem, after all, opens in the epithalamic tradition, with the promise of a wedding-image of purity, but the mariner's tale nervously disrupts the wedding story. He replaces it with the Life-in-Deathness of white disease. The wedding, in fact, is not just contaminated, but completely obliterated from view by the mariner's tale of rot, slime, sickness, and death.

It is not at all surprising that writers like Coleridge and Pringle brought sugar and disease together in literature, given sugar's whiteness and its economic position as the country's foremost slave-produced import. In its refined whiteness, sugar was synonymous with the addiction of the British consumer. And according to Coleridge, guilt sprang not just from consumption of slave products, but from addiction to them. By funneling a variety of such substances into Britain, international trade fed what Coleridge saw as the addictive British personality. "Perhaps from the beginning of the world," he wrote, "the evils arising from the formation of imaginary wants have been in no instance so dreadfully exemplified as in the Slave Trade and West India Commerce! We receive from the West Indias Sugars, Rum, Cotton, log-wood, cocoa, coffee, pimento, ginger, mahogany, and conserves—not one of these are necessary—" (W, 236).[49]

Coleridge was just one of many writers to move the medical to the political level by designating slavery a European disease. Robert Southey's vaccination poem A Tale of Paraguay imagined smallpox as an act of African reprisal. According to the poem's opening lines, Edward Jenner—who had pioneered work on cowpox inoculation to combat smallpox the same year that Coleridge wrote The Ancient Mariner—defeated epidemic disease and thus the vengeance of slavery:

> Jenner! for ever shall thy honored name
> Among the children of mankind be blest,
> Who by thy skill hast taught us how to tame

One dire disease,—the lamentable pest
Which Africa sent forth to scourge the West,
As if in vengeance for her sable brood
So many an age remorselessly oppressed.[50]

But if smallpox was a scourge from Africa that could be conquered through British medical technology, yellow fever could not. And so it was most often that abolitionists used the symptoms of yellow fever, as opposed to those of smallpox or other contagious diseases, to demonstrate the interminable vengeance Africa would have on European bodies. In James Stanfield's *The Guinea Voyage* (1789), for instance, yellow fever eats the crew alive. It leaves behind putrid bodies as spoils of war, as condemnation for the "remorseless oppression" of slavery. In militaristic fashion, the "troops of wan disease begin their march":

Now droops the head in faint dejection hung,
Now raging thirst enflames the dry parch'd tongue;
In yellow films the rayless eye is set,
With chilling dews the loaded brow is wet[51]

The guilt that bleeds through the lines of poems like Stanfield's, Southey's, and Coleridge's is in some sense a logical response to the horrors of slavery. Guilt signaled the beginnings of a dismantling of the slave system that had been in place for so many hundreds of years. Guilt was nothing less than the initial pangs of remorse felt upon recognizing the inhumanity of the British self against the humanity of the African other. Though it would still be hundreds of years until the British and Americans truly changed their behavior towards others, guilt reflected a new social ethos that eventually altered Britain's relations with peoples from other parts of the world.

III. DISEASE AND THE ECOLOGY OF SLAVERY

Interestingly enough, recognition of slaves as more than "things" coincided with recognition that slavery created a biological and psychological rift in the natural environment. From its beginnings in the fifteenth century to its peak in the early nineteenth century, the slave trade represented the largest migration of people in human history. It was clear to medical writers of the period that the movement of millions of people from native to foreign shores disturbed the atmosphere. When Dr. Clark noted that the activity of the slave trade caused "a deranged state of the atmosphere" and thus "excited this mortal disease in our island," he was saying that the slave trade disturbed environmental balances, which in turn produced yellow fever.[52]

Moving bodies turned the earth in a dangerous and often fatal direction. Since Africans and slaves appeared to be immune to yellow fever, the only way epidemics spread was among gatherings of freshly arrived Europeans in a tropical locale. As Philip Curtin explains in his book *Death by Migration* the yellow fever pathogen *A. aegypti* needed groups of non-immune subjects "concentrated within the flight range" of the virus in order to survive. If not, the disease would creep back into the recesses of the tropical jungle, where animals kept it active until a new crop of Europeans arrived.[53] Of course, early nineteenth-century medical workers did not have germ theories, and they did not even consider the mosquito as a carrier of the virus. But they did understand at some level yellow fever's mode of existence. They knew that the disease stemmed from the European encounter with the tropics. Dr. Thomas Dancer, for one, observed how yellow fever "first visits the abodes of wretchedness and squalor, and disappears for a season, or diminishes in virulence to return again and expend its fury over the community at large."[54] American doctors, reporting on the yellow fever epidemic of Philadelphia, recognized that the fever "exists in the West Indies particularly in times of war, when great numbers of strangers are to be found there."[55] The "great number of strangers" referred to the interaction of different nationalities—French, Spanish, British, African, and every miscegenized variation in between.

These early medical men clearly believed that the breakdown of the Caribbean ecosystem caused yellow fever to break out. When Dr. Clark insisted in 1799 that yellow fever ran rampant in the Caribbean the more it was "crowded with strangers," he gestured towards the cultural suspicion that yellow fever was the result of environmental trauma.[56] Although Britain had its own socio-environmental problems (the poverty of the city, the fear of French invasion), nothing of the sort was happening at home. In contrast to the environment of the Quantock Mountains, where Coleridge and Wordsworth first conceived of *The Ancient Mariner,* the abolitionist poet William Hutchenson wrote of the Caribbean in 1792:

New cargoes crowd our shores, and on the beach
The squalid multitudes are pouring forth,
From over-loaded ships, which, like the curse
Of vile Pandora's box, bring forth disease,
With misery, and pallid want,
Crippled and maimed, whose ulcerating sores
Cling to the canker'd chains, that rankle deep.[57]

If the yellow fever outbreaks of the Caribbean frightened Europeans, outbreaks in America created real alarm. The 1793 outbreak in Philadelphia was by far the most widely discussed and terrifying nineteenth-century yellow fever epidemic precisely because it proved that the disease could be imported like so many slaves and goods. Dr. Trotter blamed the fever on "damaged coffee, that was left to rot on the wharfs, and from which noxious exhalations were spread that first affected the neighbourhood, and afterwards more distant parts of the city."[58] The Americans insisted that this "imported" fever had transgressed the national boundary and thus altered the American environment. Jackson and Redman, two prominent American doctors, led public opinion in the matter. Yellow fever, said Jackson, had been "imported into Philadelphia from some foreign country" and was "propagated afterwards solely by contagion."[59] Redman traced the infection to "imported clothing of persons who died in the West Indies"; at the very least, the disease stemmed directly from "the neighbourhood of shipping or among persons connected with vessels."[60] So it was that doctors blamed commerce for destroying environmental balances that otherwise kept epidemics at bay. People who carried on the national dirty work of commerce brought fever home. Those, like the mariner, "connected with vessels" were literally on the national border and were somehow held responsible for importing the wrong thing. On the one hand, countries like England and America relied heavily on people associated with the seafaring industry, yet on the other, these individuals were seen as diseased, disturbing and abject, because of their inevitable contact with foreign cultures.

Many bystanders, however, could not help but use the outbreak of European-contracted disease in tropical climates to condemn the slave trade for deforming the environment. The unnatural system of slavery, according to Helen Maria Williams:

> Deforms Creation with the gloom
> Of crimes, that blot its cheerful bloom;
> Darkens a work so perfect made,
> And casts the Universe in shade!—[61]

Though the moral universe condemned the British slavery system with plagues of yellow fever, the natural universe ultimately paid the price. In James Montgomery's abolitionist poem, yellow fever destroys the British body and thus the entire cosmos:

> Foreboding melancholy sinks his min,
> Soon at his heart he feels the monster's fangs,
> They tear his vitals with convulsive pangs . . .
> Now frenzy-horrors rack his whirling brain,
> Tremendous pulses throb through every vein;
> The firm earth shrinks beneath his torture-bed,
> The sky in ruins ruses o'er his head;
> He rolls, he rages in consuming fires,
> Till nature, spent with agony, expires.[62]

Wordsworth also spoke of slavery in ecological terms. It was, he said, the "most rotten branch of human shame" that ought to "fall together with its parent tree."[63] From what came to be seen as the center of the Romantic poetic tradition, Wordsworth called the structures of slavery a disease that could out-rot the worst atrocities of the French Revolution. Medical experts reinforced this view. "Since the abolition of the slave-trade," wrote Dr. Henderson, "some disorders of African origin, and highly contagious, have almost disappeared."[64]

In *The Ancient Mariner,* Coleridge captures sharply the ruination of the universe that the slave trade instigated. His mariner finds disease and thus nightmarish deformation everywhere: it appears not just in the rotting bodies of birds, men, and a white woman, but in heavenly bodies as well, such as the "bloody Sun . . . with broad and burning face (2.111). Even the body of the ship is diseased: "The planks look warped and see those sails, / How thin they are and sere!" (7.529-30). The Hermit—who is also a figure for decay as he prays at a "rotted old oak stump" (7.522)—likens the ship to the rotting skeletal leaves of the forest, decaying like the planks of the vessel, which Coleridge had already designated as a feature of a slave ship. In his "[Lecture] on the Slave Trade," he noted that slaves were "crammed into the hold of a ship with so many fellow-victims, that the heat and stench arising from [their] diseased bodies [would] rot the very planks" (*W,* 248-49).

Surrounded as he is by disease and deformation, it is no wonder that when the mariner and his ship pull up to the British bay, only the mariner is alive. By this time, the bay does not seem as pure as it did at the voyage's beginning. Described as "white with silent light," the bay swallows up the mass of contagion that is now practically synonymous with the doubly-identified mariner. Yet the ship settles in an ambiguous space, neither this side or nor that side of Britain's national boundary. It sinks just below the surface of the water. But, like the mariner's tale of guilt, or like the slave population itself, it could emerge at anytime.

Just as the outbreak on the ship coincides with a catastrophic deformation of nature, the rift between the mariner and his environment increases during the journey itself. Coleridge's gloss to the poem indicates how "horror follows" the mariner's meeting of the spectre-bark. And indeed, the mariner is horrified most of all by the living-death of the crew and the quarantined solitude the mariner himself experiences after the crew dies. His hollow repetition, "Alone, alone, all, all alone, / Alone on a wide wide sea!" (4.232-33) echoes back through the poem as through a chasm. He is both nowhere and nothing—neither self nor other. He is disconnected from his environment, from himself, and from other people.

This kind of disconnection is truly a nightmare, and Coleridge uses a fairly standard catalog of Gothic images to reinforce slavery's horror. J. R. Ebbotson traces *The Ancient Mariner*'s use of Gothic imagery—the spectre-bark, the living-dead crew—to Coleridge's reading of M. G. Lewis's play *The Castle Spectre.* For Lewis, the Gothic symbolized various forms of subjection: Each and every character in the play endures the "shame of servitude."[65] The enslaved include the noble Percy, who is imprisoned in a guarded room for just a few hours, and the poor Reginald, who is secretly chained in the castle's subterranean dungeon for years. Even the evil Osmond, who sets himself up as the master, refers to himself as the "slave of wild desires."[66] Lewis's play was so popular not least because it appealed to the early nineteenth-century British audience's own feelings of subjection.

But if British audiences saw in *The Castle Spectre*'s Gothic atmosphere the buried truth of their own slavish condition, Lewis makes it clear that the enslavement of Africans is the real buried secret facing the nation. He does this through two principle characters: a white person and a black one. In contrast to the castle spectre, who appears as a "figure" in "white and flowing garments spotted with blood" stands Hassan, an African slave.[67] Hassan implies that the castle's inhabitants unwittingly find themselves in subjection because of the subjection they impose on Africans: "Vengeance!" he cries, "Oh! How it joys me when the white man suffers!—Yet weak are his pangs, compared to those I felt when torn from thy shores, O native Africa!"[68] Slavery is experienced as both a painful reality and a metaphysical condition. "Oh! When I forget my wrongs, my I forget myself!" wails Hassan. The mammoth irony of all this is, of course, that Lewis later wrote the *Journal of a West Indian Proprietor,* an account of his own slave-labor plantation in Jamaica.

Though Coleridge was influenced by Lewis's long-running play, the aspect of "losing self in another" within a Gothic slave story was solely Coleridge's idea. As "Life-in-Death" begins her work on the ancient Mariner, he tries to reconcile his split identity. His experiences with emblems of the slave trade—the spectre-bark, Life-in-Death, fever victims, diseased ships—results in a psychological disease that takes him to several levels of self-confrontation. His blessing of the slimy water snakes, linked by their "flash of golden fire" to the epidemic waters, is a move to acknowledge what is radically "alter." It is a move to attempt on a material level Coleridge's idea of "losing self in another form by loving the self of another as another." It is also a move to release himself from what the wedding guest comes to recognize as the "plague" of Western seafaring missions (1.80). Who can forget this truly strange moment in the poem when the albatross falls from the mariner's neck:

> O happy living things! No tongue
> Their beauty might declare:
> A spring of love gushed from my heart,
> And I blessed them unaware: . . .
> That self-same moment I could pray;
> And from my neck so free
> The Albatross fell off, and sank
> Like lead into the sea.
>
> (4.271-91)

James McKusick has recently suggested that the mariner's ecological enlightenment involves learning to "cross the boundaries that divide him from the natural world, through unmotivated acts of compassion between 'man and bird and beast.'"[69] But it is more than that. This sudden, uncanny recognition of the water snakes as "self-same" initiates him in a process of ever-deeper questioning of himself and of the assumption underlying his culture.

Coleridge's doubly-identified mariner tells his listener early on about his feverish mission. Through the simple telling of a tale, he feels he must introduce this two-sided sense of individual self into the British national body. The tale that "burns" within him aligns him with the "storyteller" who, as Michael Taussig explains, has the crucial cultural job of bringing alterity home. In his book *Mimesis and Alterity,* Taussig suggests that Coleridge's ancient mariner is the quintessential storyteller. He brings

> The far-away to the here-and-now as metastructure of the tale. Coleridge provides the classic instance, the Ancient Mariner who has spread his wings in the tradewinds of the world, now returned and beginning his desperate tale, "He stoppeth one of three." And the man apprehended responds: "By thy long grey beard and glittering eye, Now wherefore stopp'st thou me?" . . . It is at this point that the freedom and foreboding bringing the traveler home insists on audience and attains voice, and it is here, in this moment of apprehension, that the listening self is plunged forward into and beyond itself.[70]

Readers find the mariner again and again trying to convince the wedding guest of his own need to recognize the "other" as a moral being, trying to plunge the listening self "forward into and beyond itself." The mariner's dramatic and final claim that "He prayeth best, who loveth best / All things both great and small" is more than a simple moral to a seafaring tale (7.614). It is a statement about how to relate to what is outside or other than self.

. . . . .

Yellow fever putrefied or dissolved the body's vital organs and thus confounded definitions of the self and its alterity (or abjection) in a biological and completely empirical sense. The abolition of the slave trade, on a much more complex level, demanded that the British face questions about their national identity with the changing status of slaves to citizens. Like yellow fever, which wiped out fleets and armies by dissolving individual bodies, a realignment of Africans would redefine British identity and thus individual selfhood by dissolving a certain self-construction. *The Rime of the Ancient Mariner* appeared in the midst of these changes. Although Coleridge referred to the poem as a work of "pure imagination," its diseased climate points out just how obsessed he was with questions of contamination and purity.[71] His dream of a Pantisocrasy—a government of self-rule that emphasized the equality of all its members—was the dream of a society based on moral, political, and social purity. Most of all, it was the dream of a society free from "the contagion of European vice," as he called slavery and the political structure that supported it (*W,* 240).

Given Coleridge's interest in the nature of disease and the debate on slavery at the time he wrote *The Ancient Mariner,* it is not at all surprising that the poem is heavy with images of disease and nuances of slavery. For both disease and slavery concerned, at a fundamental level, questions of how foreign matter and foreigners became part of the physical or political body. Coleridge would use these materials to contemplate ways in which the British could dissolve their personal and national borders, yet still maintain their identity. What we do not know is if this double identity, this "loving the self of another as another" really worked for the ancient mariner, since he never finishes telling his story. But we do know that it would be a long time before the rest of the culture would even come close.

Notes

1. Charles Powell, *A Treatise on the Nature, Causes, & Cure, of the Endemic, or Yellow Fever of Tropical Climates, as it occurs in the West Indies* (London: John Callow, 1814), 24; James Clark, *A Treatise on the Yellow Fever as it Appeared in the Island of Dominica, in the years 1793-4-5-6* (London: J. Murray and S. Highley, 1797), 8.

2. Powell, 23.

3. Thomas Trotter, *Medicina Nautica: An Essay on the Diseases of Seamen* (London: T. Cadell, 1797), 184; Robert Southey, *Selections from the letters of Robert Southey,* ed. J. W. Warter, 4 vols. (London, 1856), 1:317. The full quotation from Southey is as follows: "I have a sort of theory about such diseases [smallpox], which I do not understand myself,—but somebody or other will one of these days. They are so far analogous to vegetables, as that they take root, grow, ripen, and decay. Those which are eruptive blossom and seed; for the pustules of the smallpox is, to all intents and purposes, the flower of the disease, or the fructification by which it is perpetuated. Now these diseases, like vegetables, choose their own soil; as some plants like clay, others sand, other chalk, so the yellow fever will not take root in a negro, nor the yaws in a white man."

4. Clark, 63.

5. William Hillary, *Observations on the Changes of the Air and the Concomitant Epidemical Disease, in the Island of Barbadoes,* 2nd. ed., (London: Hawes, W. Clarke and R. Collins, 1766), iii.

6. John Hume, "Letter VII, An Account of the True Bilious, or Yellow Fever; and of the Remitting and Intermitting Fevers of the West Indies," *Letters and Essays on The Small Pox and Inoculation, The Measles, The Dry Belly-Ache, and Yellow, and Remitting and Intermitting Fevers of the West Indies* (London: J. Murray, 1788), 237.

7. Trotter, 322.

8. Philip Curtin, *Death by Migration: Europe's Encounter with the Tropical World in the Nineteenth Century* (Cambridge: Cambridge Univ. Press, 1989), 18. For other contemporary books on the subject, see Francois Delaporte, *Disease and Civilization: The Cholera in Paris* (1832), tr. Arthur Goldhammer (Cambridge: MIT Press, 1986), and Francois Delaporte, *The History of Yellow Fever: An Essay on the Birth of Tropical Medicine,* tr. Arthur Goldhammer (Cambridge: MIT Press, 1991).

9. J. R. Ebbotson, "Coleridge's Mariner and the Rights of Man," *Studies in Romanticism* 11 (1972): 198. A number of writers have interpreted the poem by looking at it alongside Coleridge's writings on the slave trade and slavery. Jonathan Livingston Lowes (*The Road to Xanadu,* [Boston: Houghton Mifflin, 1964]) established Coleridge's use of travel reports and ship logs in many of the tropes and descriptions used in *The Ancient Mariner.* Ebbotson's classic article establishes a logical link between the poem, voyages of discovery, colonialism, slavery, and abolitionist poetry, the most important of which is Robert Southey's 1799 "From a Sailor Who had Served in the Slave Trade."

10. See Patrick Keane, *Coleridge's Submerged Politics:* The Ancient Mariner *and* Robinson Crusoe (Columbia: Univ. of Missouri Press, 1994). Keane uses an approach similar to Ebbotson, arguing that slavery is the hidden politics under *The Ancient Mariner's* surface. Keane's study is especially useful in his rigorous bibliographic unearthing of Coleridge's references to the slave trade and related topics. Coleridge's involvement in the slave trade and its application to *The Ancient Mariner* is also discussed by Joan Baum, *Mind Forg'd Manacles: Slavery and the English Romantic Poets* (New Haven: Archon Books, 1994); Eva Beatrice Dykes, *The Negro in English Romantic Thought* (Washington: Associated Publishers Inc., 1942); James McKusick, "'That Silent Sea': Lee Boo, and the Exploration of the South Pacific," *The Wordsworth Circle* 24 (1993): 102-6; William Empson, "*The Ancient Mariner*: An Answer to Warren," *The Kenyon Review* 15 (1993): 155-77. See also Anthea Morrison, "Samuel Taylor Coleridge's Greek Pride Ode on the Slave Trade," *An*

Infinite Complexity: Essays in Romanticism, ed. J. R. Watson (Edinburgh: Edinburgh Univ. Press, 1993).

11. For critics who see the mariner's experience shaped by Coleridge's concerns with political and historical issues, see Jerome G. McGann, "The Meaning of *The Ancient Mariner,*" *Critical Inquiry* 8 (1981): 63-86; Daniel P. Watkins, "History as Demon in Coleridge's *The Rime of the Ancient Mariner,*" *Papers in Language and Literature* 24 (1988): 23-33; and Joseph C. Sitterson, Jr., "'Unmeaning Miracles' in *The Rime of the Ancient Mariner,*" *South Atlantic Review* 46 (1981): 16-26. Among critics who also offer psychological explanations for the poem's mysteries are Raimonda Modiano, "Words and 'Languageless' Meanings: Limits of Expression in *The Rime of the Ancient Mariner,*" *Modern Language Quarterly* 38 (1977): 40-61; Paul Magnuson, *Coleridge's Nightmare Poetry* (Charlottesville: Univ. Press of Virginia, 1974); and Joseph C. Sitterson, Jr., "*The Rime of the Ancient Mariner* and Freudian Dream Theory," *PLL* [*Papers on Language and Literature*] 18 (1982). Readers who, like Lowes find contextual sources for the poem include Martin Bidney, "Beneficent Birds and Crossbow Crimes: The Nightmare-Confessions of Coleridge and Ludwig Tieck," *PLL* 25 (1989): 44-58; James B. Twitchell, "*The Rime of the Ancient Mariner* as Vampire Poem," *College Literature* 4.2 (1977): 21-39; Bernard Smith, "Coleridge's *Ancient Mariner* and Cook's Second Voyage," *Journal of the Warburg and Courtauld Institutes* 29 (1956): 117-54; Donald P. Kaczvinsky, "Coleridge's Polar Spirit: A Source," *English Language Notes* 24.3 (1987): 25-28; Arnd Bohm, "Georg Forster's *A Voyage Round the World* as a Source for *The Rime of the Ancient Mariner.* A Reconsideration," *ELH* 50 (1983): 363-77. Alan Bewell delivered an unpublished paper on yellow fever called "'Voices of Dead Complaint': Colonial Military Disease Narratives." His paper is part of an unpublished chapter of the same title, which will appear in his forthcoming book *Romanticism, Geography, and Colonial Disease Environments.*

12. For the text of *The Rime of the Ancient Mariner,* I use *Samuel Taylor Coleridge: A Critical Edition of the Major Works,* ed. H. J. Jackson, (Oxford and New York: Oxford Univ. Press), hereafter cited parenthetically in the text by stanza and line number.

13. William Roscoe, *The Wrongs of Africa* (London: R. Faulder, Part 1, 1787; Part 2, 1788). Reprinted in *William Roscoe of Liverpool,* ed. George Chandler, introduction by Sir Alfred Shennan, preface by Vere E. Cotton, (London: B. T. Batsford Ltd., 1953), 378.

14. Hannah More, "Slavery" (1788), *Women Romantic Poets,* ed. Jennifer Breen (London: Everyman, 1992), 11, ll. 37-38.

15. *Marginalia* in *The Collected Works of Samuel Taylor Coleridge* 12, ed. George Whalley, 3 vols. (London: Routledge, 1980), 1:680. *Marginalia* is hereafter cited parenthetically by page number and abbreviated *M.*

16. Although it is difficult to tell exactly what Coleridge means by "alterity," in one place at least, he defines it as "the healthful positiveness of compleat polarity, instanced in that chasm between the Subjective and the Objective" (*The Notebooks of Samuel Taylor Coleridge,* ed. Kathleen Coburn, 4 vols. [New York: Pantheon, 1957], 4:5281 f. 33; hereafter cited parenthetically by page number and abbreviated *CNB*). Tim Fulford has pointed out to me that *The Ancient Mariner* often portrays the physical body as a "slave" to some other force than its own soul (Fulford, personal communication to the author). The zombie-like state of the crew, for instance, parallels a state of slavery, where the body is controlled by some force external to it.

17. Although I do not explore Kristeva's theory of the alterity that stems from the maternal, this is an important component of her philosophy. Coleridge's *Ancient Mariner* has been insightfully interpreted using Kristeva's ideas on the maternal and the symbolic by Diane Lon Hoeveler ("Glossing the Feminine in *The Rime of the Ancient Mariner,*" *European Romantic Review* 2 [1992]: 145-62) and Anne Williams ("And I for an Eye: 'Spectral Persecution' in *The Rime of the Ancient Mariner,*" *PMLA* 108 [1993]: 1114-27). Hoeveler sees the mariner "trapped forever in the realm of the linguistic, in patriarchal language, in contrast to the recognition of the power of the 'good' maternal that he has ostensibly experienced" (158-59). The mariner longs for unity (experienced through the maternal), which he cannot have as a result of being a speaking subject, telling his tale again and again. Williams employs Kristeva to examine how *The Ancient Mariner* "provides a genealogy of Coleridgean Imagination . . . it traces the means by which meaning is constructed out of separation, need, fear, guilt, and the need to repair the primal break" (1117).

18. Julia Kristeva, *The Powers of Horror: An Essay on Abjection,* tr. Leon S. Roudiez (New York: Columbia Univ. Press, 1982), 3.

19. Julia Kristeva, *Nations Without Nationalism,* tr. Leon S. Roudiez (New York: Columbia Univ. Press, 1993), 2-3.

20. Julia Kristeva, *Strangers to Ourselves,* tr. Leon S. Roudiez (New York: Columbia Univ. Press, 1991), 187.

21. For a fascinating account of the cultural meanings of the Black Death, see Philip Ziegler, *The Black Death* (New York: Harper, 1969).

22. Gilbert Blane, *Elements of Medical Logick . . . including a statement of evidence respecting the contagious nature of yellow fever* (London: Thomas and George Underwood, 1819), 158.

23. Trotter, 333.

24. Blane, 205.

25. Robert Renny, *A History of Jamaica with observations on the climate, scenery, trade, productions, negroes, slave trade, diseases of Europeans . . .* (London: J. Cawthorn, 1807), 241.

26. *Shorter Works and Fragments* in *The Collected Works of Samuel Taylor Coleridge* 11, ed. H. J. Jackson and J. R. de J. Jackson, 2 vols. (London: Routledge, 1995), 1409-10. James McKusick (*Coleridge's Philosophy of Language* [New Haven: Yale Univ. Press, 1986]), makes a connection between Coleridge and Lord Monboddo, who first believed the orangutans had the physiological ability to articulate language but could not because of intellectual inferiority. Monboddo implicitly established a link between African man and ape.

27. Empson, 167. Empson states, "The Mariner, at this first magical event in the poem, has a premonition of a Slaver, with its planks rotted off by the insanitary exudations of the dying slaves—that was going to be the final result of his heroic colonial exploration, and well might his heart beat loud."

28. Raimonda Modiano has pointed out to me that Ebbotson inadvertently sees the mariner as doubly-identified as well. Just when Ebbotson states that the mariner represents European culture's involvement with slavery when he kills the albatross and guiltily hangs it around his neck, Ebbotson adds a footnote identifying the mariner as a slave. Ebbotson says, "The act of hanging the albatross round the Mariner's neck, though probably derived from religious allegory, might also be an image of the slave laden with ball and chain; and what has usually been dismissed as an absurdly large crew of 200 becomes less remarkable when one recalls that a slave ship would carry double the crew of a normal vessel" (201, n76).

29. Renny, 192-93.

30. John Redman, *Proceedings of the college of Physicians of Philadelphia relative to the prevention of the introduction and spreading of contagious diseases* (Philadelphia: Thomas Dobson, 1789), 30 ("imported contagion").

31. Henry Clutterbuck, *Observations on the Prevention and Treatment of the Epidemic Fever* (London: Longman, Hurst, Rees, Orme, and Brown, 1819), 39.

32. Thomas Beddoes, *A Lecture Introductory To A Course of Popular Instruction on the Constitution and Management of the Human Body* (Bristol: N. Biggs, 1797), 48.

33. Besides, the search for origins was thus central to understanding the fever's most terrifying feature: uncontrollability. For the British who had been used to controlling the way cultures interacted, yellow fever's uncontrollability was particularly unsettling because it highlighted just how susceptible British physical and political bodies were to the invisible and invidious forces of foreign climates. In 1772, Dr. Charles Blicke (*An Essay on the Bilious of Yellow Fever of Jamaica* [London: T. Becket and Co., 1772]) insisted that the first step toward containing yellow fever was "to know its origin" (11).

34. William Deverell, *Andalusia; or, Notes tending to shew that the yellow fever of the West Indies . . . was a Disease Well Known to the Ancients* (London: S. Gosnell, 1803), 2.

35. Deverell, 71-72,

36. Coleridge, *The Collected Letters of Samuel Taylor Coleridge,* ed. Earl Leslie Griggs, 4 vols. (Oxford: Clarendon, 1956), 2:455.

37. Beddoes, 48; and John Wilson, *Memoirs of the West Indian Fever* (London: Burgess and Hill, 1827), 139. Coleridge's interest in the origin of disease and the notion of "alterity" can be traced to German Romantic philosophy and the medicine of Schelling, Schiller, and Fredreich Schlegel, as Hermione De Almeida (*Romantic Medicine and John Keats* [New York and Oxford: Oxford Univ. Press, 1991], 139) and many other Coleridge scholars have pointed out. Coleridge applied his interest in the philosophical "other" to certain contemporary debates on disease and to the debate on slavery, both of which sought out classifications and origins.

38. Quoted in Keane, 71.

39. Helen Maria Williams, *Poem on the bill lately passed for regulating the slave trade* (London: T. Cadell, 1788), ll. 107-9.

40. Coleridge's Review of Thomas Clarkson's *History of the Abolition of the Slave Trade* in the *Edinburgh Review* 24 (1808): 357. Coleridge actually

wrote that this "evil in the form of guilt" was "evil in its most absolute and most appropriate sense, that sense to which an impression deeper than could have been left by mere agony of body, or even anguish of mind, in proportion as vice is more hateful than pain, eternity more awful than time."

41. Coleridge, "[Lecture] on the Slave Trade," *The Watchman* in *The Collected Works of Samuel Taylor Coleridge* 2, ed. Lewis Patton (London: Routledge, 1979), 130-40; hereafter cited parenthetically by page and abbreviated *W.*

42. McKusick, 106.

43. Erasmus Darwin, *The Botanic Garden; A Poem in Two Parts* (London: J. Johnson, 1791), 7.29-30.

44. Darwin, 7.168-73.

45. James Montgomery, *The West Indies,* in *The Poetical Works of James Montgomery,* 5 vols. (Boston: Little, Brown, and Company), 1:165. In a footnote to this passage, Montgomery writes, "For minute and afflicting details of the origin and progress of the yellow fever in an individual subject, see Dr. Pinkard's *Notes on the West Indies . . .* in which the writer, from experience, describes its horrors and sufferings."

46. Renny, 192-93.

47. Molly Lefebure (*Samuel Taylor Coleridge: A Bondage to Opium* [New York: Stein and Day, 1974], 371-73) explains this passage in the context of Coleridge's guilt-ridden opium dreams.

48. Thomas Pringle, "Sonnet on Slaver," in *The Anti-Slavery Album: Selections in verse from Cowper, Hannah More, Montgomery, Pringle* (London: Howlett & Brummer, 1828), 3, l. 3.

49. Coleridge, of course, would go on to see his dependence on opium as one of these imported addictions that acted not just as relief to the pain of disease, but as disease itself, as Roy and Dorothy Porter point out (*In Sickness and in Health: The British Experience 1650-1850* [New York: Basil Blackwell, 1989], 218-19). See also *The Popularization of Medicine 1650-1850,* ed. Roy Porter (New York: Routledge, 1992).

50. Robert Southey, "A Tale of Paraguay," *Southey's Poetical Works* (London: Longman, 1866), canto I, stanza 1, 487.

51. James Stanfield, *The Guinea Voyage* (London: James Philips, 1789), 18.

52. Clark, 63.

53. Curtin, 69.

54. Thomas Dancer, *The Medical Assistant; or Jamaica Practice of Physic designed chiefly for the use of families and plantations* (Kingston: Alexander Aikman, 1801), 70-71.

55. Redman, 29.

56. Clark, 63.

57. William Hutchenson, *The Princess of Zanfara* (London: B. Law & Son, 1792), 11.

58. Trotter, 323.

59. Robert Jackson, *An Outline of the History and Cure of Fever . . . vulgarly the yellow fever of the West Indies* (Edinburgh: Mundell & Son; London: Longman, 1798), 219.

60. Redman, 28.

61. Williams, ll. 111-14.

62. Montgomery, 1:165-66.

63. William Wordsworth, *The Prelude, William Wordsworth,* ed. Stephen Gill (Oxford: Oxford Univ. Press), Book X: 224-36.

64. Stewart Henderson, *A Letter to the Officers of the Army . . . on the means of preserving health and preventing that fatal disease the Yellow Fever* (London: John Stockdale, 1795), 43.

65. Matthew Gregory Lewis, *The Castle Spectre* (1797), in *Seven Gothic Dramas,* ed. Jeffrey N. Cox (Athens: Ohio Univ. Press, 1992), 186. Coleridge referred to the play in a 1798 letter to Wordsworth.

66. Lewis, 175.

67. Lewis, 163, 206

68. Lewis, 199.

69. James McKusick, "Coleridge and the Economy of Nature," *Studies in Romanticism* 35 (1996): 375-92, 387.

70. Michael Taussig, *Mimesis and Alterity* (New York: Routledge, 1993), 41.

71. *Table Talk* in *The Collected Works of Samuel Taylor Coleridge* 14, ed. Carol Woodring, 2 vols. (London: Princeton Univ. Press, 1990), 1:149.

Eric C. Brown (essay date autumn 1998)

SOURCE: Brown, Eric C. "Boyd's Dante, Coleridge's *Ancient Mariner,* and the Pattern of Infernal Influence." *Studies in English Literature 1500-1900* 38, no. 4 (autumn 1998): 647-67.

[*In the following essay, Brown purports that* The Ancient Mariner *contains numerous parallels with Henry Boyd's 1785 translation of Dante's* Inferno, *emphasizing how both works follow a structure of sin, penance, and redemption, and how Coleridge himself underscored the poem's link with Dante in the revisions he made to the 1817 edition.*]

As a literary critic, Samuel Taylor Coleridge was one of the first in the English language to assess the particularities of Dante's *Divina Commedia*. Indeed, his lecture on Dante in 1818 remains one of the most significant landmarks in the popularizing of the Italian epic. Yet in discussions of Coleridge and his poetry, especially **The Rime of the Ancient Mariner**; his relationship to Dante is usually neglected. Coleridge's first exposure to him came relatively early in his poetic career; he borrowed from the Bristol library the first two volumes of a recent translation by Reverend Henry Boyd from 23 June to 4 July 1796. In *The Road to Xanadu*, John L. Lowes writes further that from 1794 to 1798 Dante was "more or less in the air in Coleridge's circle."[1] Soon after reading Boyd's translation, Coleridge proposed in his notebook a "Poem in [three] Books in the manner of Dante on the excursion of Thor," crossing out "three" and rewriting "one" in the manuscript.[2] *The Ancient Mariner* was subsequently composed between November of 1797, on the famous walk among the Quantock Hills, and March of 1798, when Coleridge went to dine with the Wordsworths and brought along the finished ballad. I contend that **The Ancient Mariner** in many ways fulfills Coleridge's scribbled goal of an excursion in the manner of Dante (with "Thor" transformed into a sort of prototypical Heyerdahl), and that distinct verbal and imagistic parallels exist between the *Inferno,* as translated by Boyd, and Coleridge's poem.[3] Moreover, the *Inferno* unlocks further dimensions of one of the great cruxes in **The Ancient Mariner**: the slaying of the albatross and the penance that ensues. The close connection with Dante's *Inferno* suggests that Coleridge first saw **The Ancient Mariner** as an inherently moral tale, one that might demonstrate the kind of spiritual struggle and progression evident in the first part of the *Divina Commedia*. Boyd himself saw the plan of Dante's epic in remarkable **Ancient Mariner**-like terms: "the conversion of a sinner by a spiritual guide, displaying in a series of terrible visions the secrets of Divine Justice, and whose interposition had been procured by the supplication of a Saint in Paradise."[4] Examining Coleridge's poem in light of this paradigm not only emphasizes the very Dantean morality of the poem—a morality some recent critics have tended, unlike Coleridge, to dismiss too readily—but also clarifies and unites many of the local incidents in the narrative into a coherently infernal pattern.[5] The sin, the terrible visions, and the divine guidance all result in a poetic epic akin to Dante's spiritual allegory.

During Coleridge's trip to Italy in 1804, one of his self-professed hopes was to bring along "Dante & a Dictionary," and this was probably his first prolonged exposure to the original text.[6] Still, Lowes asserts, one can "scarcely . . . assume that Coleridge could have done nothing with Dante in the original in 1798."[7] Whether Coleridge knew Dante in the Italian, his first allusion to him appears in the 25 March 1796 edition of the *Watchman*. Discussing issues of slave trade, he writes, "I will not mangle the feelings of my readers by detailing enormities, which the gloomy Imagination of Dante would scarcely have dared attribute to the Inhabitants of Hell."[8] Lowes himself cites only two stanzas of **The Ancient Mariner** as derived from Dante. And with little exception, subsequent critics have surprisingly looked no further into Boyd's translation of Dante, despite Lowes's initial suggestive findings.[9] (Several have, however, attempted to point out connections between Dante's *Inferno* and Coleridge's **Kubla Khan,** nevertheless leaving **The Ancient Mariner** alone on a wide, wide sea.)[10] Several critics relegate the influence of Dante in general to an abysmal level.[11] What makes the inattention perhaps all the more remarkable is the close proximity in time of Coleridge's 27 February 1818 lecture on Dante, and his 1817 republication (with revisions and glosses) of **The Ancient Mariner.** His addenda to the 1817 edition suggest that Dantean influences were resurfacing, for many of the revisions emphasize those parts of the poem that seem most Dantean. But the reading of Boyd more than suffices for any lack of opportunity on Coleridge's part to gather numerous impressions.

Boyd's translation is not an especially successful one, as he freely embellishes the original with frill and ornamentation. One contemporary review (December 1785) of the translation reads, "We cannot say much in praise of this work, but that the translation of Dante is generally faithful, and renders pretty correctly the sense of a very difficult writer"; while yet another critiques, "Of the translator's abilities and execution, we, on the whole, think highly. He has taken some liberty with the original, but it is principally in softening absurd or offensive images."[12] More recent critics have been somewhat less forgiving. Boyd wrote in six-line stanzas, a stricture that forced him occasionally into awkward rhymes (consider the following, from canto 2: "Shall I presume, tho' great Aeneas dar'd / To meet the terrors of the *Stygian* guard"), either expansive or selective imagery, and diction that one critic has called "stiff and pompous."[13] Thomas L. Cooksey remarks of his opening to canto 1, "Boyd's version ('pathless grove') does little to evoke the terror of Dante's dark forest ('*una selva oscura, / Che la diritta via era smarrita*'). In its place one senses a languid weariness. Dante's greatest danger would seem to be ennui."[14] But such criticisms distort what Boyd does accomplish. The difficulties of rhymed translations of Dante have long been catalogued by virtually every writer who has made the attempt; *terza rima*, or a semblance thereof, does not easily fit into English verse. His translation offers an accurate and often vivid display of the major encounters, particularly in the later cantos, and certainly depicted enough of Dante's imaginative power for Robert Southey. He had the first volume for two days and the second for one month in late 1794, and did not dissuade his friend from encountering Dante, perhaps for the first time, through Boyd's rendition.

Lowes writes that Coleridge "was stirred to emulation by Dante's art," and singles out the voyage of Ulysses as particularly influential. He aptly notes that "Ulysses's last voyage, as his restless shade relates it in the *Inferno,* was into the unknown South."[15] Boyd translates the recounting of Ulysses as follows:

> With measur'd stroke the whit'ning surge they sweep,
> Till ev'ry well-known star beneath the deep
> Declin'd his radiant head; and o'er the sky
> A beamy squadron rose, of name unknown,
> Antarctic glories deck'd the burning zone
> Of night, and southern fires salute the eye.
>
> (26.20)

Forging into the Antarctic, Ulysses and his crew do seem, in Boyd's nearly surreal translation, to be entering a land where "snowy clifts / . . . send a dismal sheen," the shimmering zone of the *aurora australis.*[16] Lowes then compares the final submerging of the Mariner's vessel, in which "The ship went down like lead" (line 549), to the swift and climactic flap-dragoning of Ulysses' ship:

> Trembling I saw the Heav'n-commission'd blast
> The canvas tear, and bend the groaning mast;
> In vain we toil'd the ruin to prevent:
> Thrice round and round the found'ring vessel rides,
> The op'ning plank receiv'd the rushing tides,
> And me and mine to quick perdition sent!
>
> (26.23)

Indeed, Dante's imagery resembles that conjured by Coleridge near the conclusion of his poem:

> And straight a sound was heard.
> Under the water it rumbled on,
> Still louder and more dread:
> . . . . .
> Upon the whirl, where sank the ship,
> The boat spun round and round;
> And all was still, save that the hill
> Was telling of the sound.
>
> (lines 545-59)

The ship nearing land after a long voyage into unknown south seas, the sudden uprising of a tremendous force, and the maelstrom whirling and sinking the ship seem resoundingly to echo one another. Lowes does not delve into perhaps the final association, however, that of the penance itself. Most Dantean critics acknowledge the island-mountain of Ulysses to be Mount Purgatory. Ul-

ysses fails to reach the place of penitence and redemption, but the Mariner, like Dante's Pilgrim at the beginning of the *Purgatorio,* is brought aboard a Pilot's boat and transported to his purgatorial circle, in which "ever and anon throughout his future life an agony constraineth him to travel from land to land . . . And to teach, by his own example, love and reverence to all things that God made and loveth" (Gloss, lines 582, 610) Like Ulysses, the Mariner is enclosed in a tongue of flame, for "at an uncertain hour, / That agony returns: / And till my ghastly tale is told, / *This heart within me burns*" (lines 582-5, my emphasis). He is compelled by those he meets to tell his story and show by example the nature of his crime—like Ulysses, and in fact many shades, in the *Inferno.* The "ancient mariner" in Dante *is* the shade of Ulysses.

In addition to Ulysses, a second ancient sailor plays a prominent role in Coleridge's poem: the boatman Charon. The river Acheron his Pacific, Charon appears in the third canto, the whole of which Coleridge would single out in his lecture as full of a "wonderful sublimity." As "picturesque beyond all, modern or ancient," the appearance of Charon at the close of the canto is proffered by Coleridge.[17] And the image of Charon is a startling one. As Dante and Virgil prepare to cross the waters with a contingent of pale shades, they spot from the shore the wizened pilot (*"Un vecchio bianco per antico pelo"*):

> Far off exclaim'd the grizzly mariner,
> "Hither, ye Denizens of Hell, repair!
> The Stygian barque her wonted load requires;
> For you diurnal stars benignant beam,
> Prepare ye now to feel the fierce extreme
> Of frost corrosive, and outrageous fire."
>
> (3.19)

Boyd's dramatic epithet—"grizzly mariner"—evokes quite closely Coleridge's "ancient Mariner" whose "beard with age is hoar" (line 619). The words of Charon are appropriate for the Mariner as well, as if the Wedding-Guest were preparing "to feel the fierce extreme." The baking sun ("All in a hot and copper sky, / The bloody Sun, at noon, / Right up above the mast did stand, / No bigger than the moon" [lines 111-4]) and bitter frost are both pertinent aspects of the Mariner's tale. The mesmerizing powers of the Mariner—"He holds him with his glittering eye," "the bright-eyed Mariner" (lines 13, 20)—resemble Charon's as well. The Stygian guide forces the souls to obey him: "The Fiend, with lifted oar and eyes of flame, / Compell'd the ling'ring soul to haste on board" (3.23).[18] Further, the "spectre-bark" bears some similarities to the skiff of Charon. After Death and his mate depart, "The stars were dim, and thick the night, / The steersman's face by his lamp gleamed white" (lines 206-7). The Mariner's own ship becomes the skiff of

Charon, leading ever further into a realm where, the Mariner says, "never a saint took pity on / My soul in agony" (lines 234-5), where indeed "diurnal stars benignant beam," and where the gleaming white steersman is a ghastly caricature of a mythical ferryman.

The combination of these two figures—Ulysses and Charon—helps establish that the Mariner bears a recurrent infernal trait: a soul who is at once a prisoner and a guide. Aspects of the Mariner, these same forces operate in the poem as a whole, especially insofar as they are expressed in subsequent Dantean elements of Coleridge's poem. Lowes finds one in the "lonesome road" passage. In one of Coleridge's own copies of *Sibylline Leaves,* a penciled note says simply "From Dante" next to the stanza that reads,

> Like one, that on a lonesome road
> Doth walk in fear and dread,
> And having once turned round walks on,
> And turns no more his head:
> Because he knows, a frightful fiend
> Doth close behind him tread.

> (lines 446-51)

Lowes feels confident that the marginalia was not written in Coleridge's hand, but adds, "there is every reason for assuming . . . that information which it records . . . may have come from Coleridge by word of mouth," as the volume was passed from Coleridge to two friends, James Gillman, with whom he lived for eighteen years, and S. B. Watson, "both a pupil and a friend." Finding Boyd's rendering a somewhat imprecise and unlikely source, Lowes appends Carlyle's prose translation.[19] Coleridge may have recollected this canto because of the extended naval metaphor with which it begins, concerning workers in the Venetian shipyards.[20] This question may be resolved below, in the wake of Dantean elements overlooked by Lowes in Boyd.

If the Mariner's tale begins as a recounting of Ulysses' voyage, it soon plunges into deeper waters. Coleridge writes, "And now the STORM-BLAST came, and he / Was tyrannous and strong; / He struck with his o'ertaking wings, / And chased us south along" (lines 41-4). (In canto 21, that of the naval conceit and "lonesome road," Boyd describes a "storm" as "dark-wing'd" [stanza 3]). Immediately, Coleridge decidedly inverts the connotations one might expect from the popular Romantic metaphor of wind. The conventional attitude toward wind is famously explained by M. H. Abrams, who remarks that "air-in-motion, whether it occurs as a breeze or a breath, wind or respiration . . . is not only a property of the landscape, but also a vehicle for radical changes in the poet's mind . . . [T]he rising wind, usually linked with the outer transition from winter to spring, is correlated with a complex subjective process: the return to a sense of community after isolation, the

renewal of life and emotional vigor after apathy and a deathlike torpor, and an outburst of creative power following a period of imaginative sterility."[21] Coleridge's own contribution to this convention is of course *The Eolian Harp*; however, by the time of *The Ancient Mariner,* the wind that in Coleridge's earlier piece brought "motion" and "joyance every where" metamorphoses into something of an abomination: it petrifies and freezes the Ancient Mariner, much like the Mariner's own "breath" of speech entrances and stuns the Wedding Guest (lines 27, 29). As the ship nears the pole, the wind acts as an antithesis to the divine breath that motivates "all of animated nature"; it is, in effect, Satanic. The storm-blast blows the Mariner and ship not only to the south, but downward into the benthic wastes of an infernal Cocytus, Dante's hellish realm of snow and ice.

In the final canto of the *Inferno,* the tyrannical figure of Satan appears "with six shadowy wings" (34.9). Dante's Pilgrim says,

> He wav'd his sail-broad wings, and woke the storm,
> Cocytus shudder'd thro' her tribes deform
> That felt the freezing pow'r in ev'ry gale:
> Keen, polar blasts around his pinions fleet,
> And o'er the region sift th' eternal sleet,
> And mould, with many a gust, the beating hail.

> (34.10)

The motion of the winds in both the *Inferno* and *The Ancient Mariner* creates, paradoxically, a stasis. For just as Satan generates the winds to perpetuate the frozen souls' icy coffin, so too the Mariner's "stormblast" blows the ship into a realm where "The ice was here, the ice was there, / The ice was all around" (lines 59-60)—the "land of ice, and of fearful sounds where no living thing was to be seen" (Gloss, line 55). Dante's Pilgrim has reached the lowest point on earth, the frozen wastes of hell, and the Mariner has arrived as well in the symbolically abysmal environment of the Antarctic, where "now there came both mist and snow, / And it grew wondrous cold: / And ice, mast-high, came floating by" (lines 51-3).[22] This is the glacial, paralytic domain of souls locked in ice as flies in amber. (It is also the home of the polar spirit, who follows the ship "nine fathoms deep," just as Dante's Satan is solidly locked in the ninth circle of hell.)[23] Indeed, further relating Coleridge's domain to the sphere of Satan, Boyd writes of the ninth circle, "here the morning points a purple ray, / And gilds with light the broad *antarctic* wave" (34.23). The pattern of suspension and paralysis needs to be emphasized here, because the paradox of which they form part—the other being the sense of guidance and motion—is embodied by the punishment that takes place in this terrain of immobility.

If Coleridge recalled the twenty-first canto by virtue of its ship imagery, even more dramatic naval imagery begins immediately upon the arrival in Cocytus. Upon being deposited in the ninth circle by the giant, An-taeus, the Pilgrim remarks: "Reclining breathless on the shore unbless'd, / We saw the Libyan rear his stately crest, / Spring like a mast, and tow'r above the view" (31.23). Similarly, the Mariner describes the initial view of the southern sea, where "there came both mist and snow," as a confrontation with "ice, mast-high" (lines 51, 53). Dante's Pilgrim then recites the "wand'ring o'er the frozen flood, / A dreary polar scene, extending wide!" (32.4). He calls the region that of "everlasting ice," and "eternal frost," anticipating the Mariner's perception of the Antarctic as a place of ubiquitous ice (32.6-14). In *The Ancient Mariner,* following the metaphorical inversion of the usually cathartic wind, and the accordant associations with the ninth circle of hell and frozen wastes of Cocytus, the albatross appears within the diabolical surroundings. With the advent of the bird, "The ice did split with a thunder-fit" and "a good south wind sprung up behind" (lines 69, 71). The wind returns as giver of life, a physical and spiritual mover; it is once again a gentle breeze. The visitation of the albatross, and ensuing crime, has been the subject of much criticism.[24] What critics have overlooked, however, is the very specific depiction of the crime and a Dantean tradition of punishment utterly appropriate for the transgression.[25] The punishment melds perfectly the overriding forces of motion and suspension that form the Dantean hallmarks in Coleridge's poem.

Dante reserves Cocytus, the land of mist and ice, for traitors; he reserves a special portion for those treacher-ous to guests ("Ptolomea"—named after Ptolemy, the captain of Jericho who murdered his father-in-law and two sons while dining at a banquet). There, unlike in the prior zones of Cocytus, the souls seemed "for ever bound in iron sleep" (33.19). Upon entering this region, the "bitter blast, / Relentless breathing o'er the sullen waste" begins (33.20). (Here again appears the "storm-blast," signaling arrival in the depths of hell.) In *The Ancient Mariner,* Coleridge is meticulous (perhaps obsessive) in stressing the communal aspects of the sailors' encounter with the albatross. The Mariner relates that the bird "ate the food it ne'er had eat / . . . / And every day, for food or play, / Came to the mariners' hollo!" (lines 67-74). In the Gloss, Coleridge stresses aspects of guest-friendship: the albatross "was received with great joy and hospitality" (Gloss, line 63) and further "perched for vespers nine" (line 76) in anticipation of conviviality. Even more overtly, in the 1800 edition of *Lyrical Ballads* Coleridge appends a rewritten "Argument," focusing on the nature of the crime: "how the Ancient Mariner cruelly, and in contempt of the laws of hospitality, killed a Sea-bird." When the Mariner shoots the bird with his cross-bow, Coleridge glosses the crime in comparable terms: "the ancient Mariner inhospitably killeth the pious bird of good omen" (Gloss, line 79). In Dante's hell, those who are traitorous to guests suffer a unique punishment;

indeed, the punishment is the penultimate in magnitude in all of the *Inferno.* The very first soul that Virgil and the Pilgrim encounter, in the region of hell in which one might expect the Mariner to be punished, goes by the name "Fra Alberigo." (Although Alberigo was a historical personage of questionable mien, in Italian, *al-bergo* can ironically denote hospitality. The assonant resemblance between "Alberigo" and "Albatross" is also tantalizingly coincidental.) In this Dantean episode, Coleridge may have found not only the crime but the appropriate penance for his Mariner.

Alberigo relates to the Pilgrim that those souls in Pto-lomea are often plunged into eternal ice even while their physical forms reside on earth:

> "For ever exil'd from the bounds of day,
> Oft' the sad Spirit seeks the frozen bay,
> And leaves the limbs, posses'd of life, behind.
> When first the Traitor's soul forsakes its seat,
> A chosen demon finds the soul retreat,
> And ev'ry function of the man renews:
> To all his old allies, the form posses'd,
> Still seems the same, caressing or caress'd,
> 'Till age or sickness sets the pris'ner loose.
> Know, Mortal! with the first felonious deed,
>   . . . . .
> A Demon comes to guide the mortal frame;
> Below, in frozen chains the Spirit pines."

(33.24-6)

Alberigo's crime was signaling, under the pretense of serving a dessert of fruit, for his guards to slay guests he had invited for dinner. The Mariner's crime, verily "a hellish thing" (line 91), is also treachery to guests, second in Dante's Hell only to the sin of Judas Iscariot (those treacherous to benefactors), and the Mariner's punishment is identical to that of Fra Alberigo: Life-in-Death.[26] The Mariner leaves a life behind, still chained to the glacial bergs, and embarks upon a demon-driven existence. Notably, Coleridge's Gloss underscores the images of Life-in-Death: "The Wedding-Guest feareth that a Spirit is talking to him; But the Ancient Mariner assureth him of his bodily health" (Gloss, lines 224, 230) The assurance of bodily health, to the exclusion of Spirit, is also made apparent in the hardly solacing lines, "'fear not, thou Wedding-Guest! / This body dropt not down'" (lines 230-1). As with the Dantean shades treacherous to guests, the body functions perfectly well, while the soul suffers eternal torment in the "frozen bay." And the tremulous words of the Wedding-Guest, "'I fear thee, ancient Mariner! / . . . thou art long, and lank, and brown, / As is the ribbed sea-sand'" (lines 224-7), fuse the Mariner with an earlier image, that of the "strange ship" whose "ribs are seen as bars" (Gloss, line 183), "ribs through which the Sun / Did peer, as through a grate" (lines 185-6). Meanwhile, the "Demon" who "comes to guide the mortal frame," while "in frozen chains the Spirit pines," rides upon that very ship, and is none other than Life-in-Death herself, the perfect avatar for the union of motion and utter immobility (33.26).

In a note, Boyd comments that the Dantean supposition of punishment to those traitorous to guests bears "a striking poetical effect, and includes a very fine moral," in that *"a single act of this kind is equivalent to a conformed habit of some other vices"* (Boyd, 2:345, note; my emphasis). The singular act in **The Ancient Mariner** begins to be punished with a second "freezing" of the Mariner's ship, during which neither "breath nor motion" appears. The marginal Gloss, "And the albatross begins to be avenged," appears next to the well-known stanza,

> Water, water, every where,
> And all the boards did shrink;
> Water, water, every where,
> Nor any drop to drink.

(lines 119-22)

This stanza is arrestingly Tartarean; the image is of Tantalus, a gloomy, tortured shade in the classical Underworld who, surrounded by and immersed to the chin in water, seeks to quench an eternal thirst only to have the liquid ebb from his lips as he bends to drink. While the evocation of this famous image need not derive from Dante to emphasize the link between the penance for killing the albatross and infernal punishment, the *Inferno* does contain an analogous victim who thirsts eternally in the presence of water.[27] It should be further noted that the crime for which Zeus punishes Tantalus is also treachery to guests: in order to test the gods' omniscience, Tantalus served his own son, in a stew, to an assemblage of banqueting deities. (Even in Thor's excursion, mentioned in Coleridge's notebook, guests and dining are interwoven in a dismal underground. The expedition to which he most likely refers involves the god's descent into the Norse underworld, in which a disguised Thor disturbs the wedding feast of his enemy. Such an excursion, if in the manner of Dante, should focus too on guests and feasting.)

At Dante's lowest infernal point, where usually swirling fogs have dispersed, the gargantuan figure of Satan confronts the Pilgrim, who cries, "New palsies seiz'd my agonizing frame, / And glowing now I felt the fever's flame, / While life and death by turns my limbs forsook" (34.6). If the punishment of those treacherous to guests failed to capture Coleridge's imagination, the alarming lines of the Pilgrim—"life and death by turns my limbs forsook"—surely would. And it follows in **The Ancient Mariner** that upon the clearing of the fog, the spectre-bark bearing Life-in-Death and her mate arrives.[28] Coleridge added the "Life-in-Death" epithet after the initial publication, and, as with the marginal Gloss, the addition strengthens the ties to Dante, as

Coleridge's own mind became further steeped in the complete *Divina Commedia*.[29] Dante's shades in Cocytus "feel thro' their veins the icy horrors creep. / Their rigid lips were sealed in dumb despair, / Their stony eyes, unconscious of a tear" (34.4-5). As a harbinger of the demonic, the power of cold, which Thomas Hobbes declared "doth . . . generate fear in those that sleep, and causeth them to dream of ghosts, and to have phantasms of horror and danger," permeates the depths of hell.[30] The internalization of such a realm, in frozen veins, betokens the onset of Life-in-Death as well, who "thicks man's blood with cold" (line 194), and at the time of her appearance, the Mariner reports, "Through utter drought all dumb we stood!" (line 157). The "black lips baked" and "throats unslaked" of the Mariner's crew, like the "rigid lips . . . sealed in dumb despair" of the shades, hint at that horrific aspect of nightmares in which one's power of speech is paralyzed, and slack-jawed screams bear the chilled silence of an Edvard Munch rendering. They represent well the forces of motion and stasis entwined.

During the Mariner's return, a remarkable instance of frozen motion recurs. Just before he falls into a very Dantesque "swoon," the ship again becomes becalmed. The Mariner has reached once more the equator, and as to the ship, "The Sun, right up above the mast, / Had fixed her to the ocean" (lines 383-4). In effect, the sun "fixes" the ship in the same way that the Mariner transfixes the Wedding-Guest with his Charon-like gaze. The Wedding-Guest is suspended at the threshold of the banquet, frozen as if either locked in an ice floe or fixed by the sun, while the ship and its crew are suspended at the threshold of a symbolic return north. The Mariner's initial descent south, over the globe's ever-shrinking latitudinal circles, may be seen as a pattern mimicking Dante's own descent through the concentric circles of hell.[31] When the Mariner begins his ascent, he reaches at the liminal equator a position of Dantean suspended animation. The work of such forces in **The Ancient Mariner**, suspending action at some critical threshold, has been noticed by several readers. Lowes sees the Mariner as "a denizen of the borderland between two worlds," while Harold Bloom calls the Mariner "a lurker at the threshold"; Camille Paglia writes of the Wedding-Guest's suspension before the wedding hall—"This doorway is the obsessive scene"— and Coleridge had his own obsessive predilection for the doorway in Dante. He singled out the inscription *"Per me si va"* on Hell's gate, in his 1818 lecture, as especially profound.[32] Coleridge's concern for the supernatural power of such locales is again evident in **Christabel**, when Geraldine is carried over the threshold, a barrier she is otherwise unable to cross. Utter suspension tends to operate as a recurring dramatic threat in both **The Ancient Mariner** and the *Inferno*, both anticipating and recalling the frozen worlds—Cocytus and Antarctica—of absolute immobility.

Following his second collapse, the Mariner hears two voices belonging to the "invisible inhabitants of the element." The Polar Spirit, apparently sated with the "penance long and heavy" imposed upon the Mariner, returns to the land of mist and snow. The air spirits tellingly converse upon the force impelling the ship; the second voice declares of the Mariner and his motion that

> His great bright eye most silently
> Up to the moon is cast—
> If he may know which way to go;
> For she guides him smooth or grim.
> See, brother, see! how graciously
> She looketh down on him.

(lines 416-21)

Such guiding forces in *The Ancient Mariner* continue to echo Dante, and recall Boyd's emphasis on "the supplication of a Saint in Paradise." (The Mariner himself serves as a sort of guide, leading the Wedding-Guest on a tour of his own personal descent, just as Virgil guides Dante's Pilgrim through the underworld.) The dialogue of the spirits may be compared with Virgil's explanation of his intentions and sources of divine aid to the Pilgrim. He first relates the words of Beatrice, one of the guiding compulsions for the entire *Divina Commedia*:

> "I fear, I fear, my succour comes too late;
> For see! he struggles in the toils of fate,
> Beset by Fiends in terrible array!
> Portentous rumours sadden all the sky!"

(2.13)

The "fiends . . . that plague" (line 80) the Mariner are in part dispelled by the succor of the gracious lady who guides him in part 4: the Polar Spirit finally "returneth southward" only after the Mariner becomes protectively entranced. A close proximity also exists in the poem between the giving of the "holy Mother's" grace and portentous rumors saddening the sky, for the Mariner "heareth sounds and seeth strange sights and commotions in the sky" (Gloss, lines 297, 309). And those Dantean lines addressed to the guardian saint intensify the associations with the Mariner's plight: "Ah! gentle Lucia, haste! thy suppliant save; / See what dire shapes around their victim rave; / And see how sorrow bends his tortur'd frame" (2.20). The dire shapes of the ghastly crew, "For a charnel-dungeon fitter" (line 435), surround the Mariner in just this way. The "blessed troop of angelic spirits, sent down by the invocation of the guardian saint" (Gloss, line 346) compare with the spiritual aid sent by three protective women in the *Inferno*: Mary, St. Lucy, and Beatrice. When the Mariner exclaims, "Sure my kind saint took pity on me, / And I blessed them unaware" (lines 286-7), the sanctuary may well have been provided by any one of that divine trio.

During the ship's return to the harbor, the Mariner is reminded of whence he has come. The Dantesque "lonesome road" passage, as noted earlier, appears here. The Mariner then immediately observes, "soon there breathed a wind on me, / . . . It raised my hair, it fanned my cheek" (line 456), and now Abrams's correspondent breeze of "emotional vigor" and "renewal of life" appears rightly oriented. But the apparent rectitude is as delusive as Satan's fog. When the Mariner continues, "It mingled strangely with my fears, / Yet it felt like a welcoming" (lines 458-9), the mingling of fear and invitation unite his past and present. No sooner does he arrive in his "owne countree" than the imagery returns to hellish Cocytus. "The harbour-bay was clear as glass" (line 472), just as those imprisoned in the lowest and innermost region of Cocytus appear "In silent shoals, beneath the frozen bay, / The lowest tenants of the wint'ry waste!" (34.3). The ghoulish paradox of life in death continues to haunt him. The "skiff-boat" (line 523) reappears in the Mariner's homecoming, just as the glass-like harbor of Cocytus returns. The Pilot, Pilot's Boy, and Hermit make up a conglomerate Charon, this time bearing the Mariner not into but out of the Underworld. Truly, "The Devil knows how to row" (line 569).

That *The Ancient Mariner* comes full-circle is further indicated by the symmetrical relation of the harbor's landmarks: the initial "Merrily did we drop / Below the kirk, below the hill, / Below the lighthouse top" (lines 22-4) becomes upon the return "is this indeed / The light-house top I see? / Is this the hill? is this the kirk?" (lines 464-6). Such countercurrent images stress the ouroboric quality of the trip, and lend to the harbor the feeling not just of glass, but of a mirror. It is also highly significant that the scene of penance occurs at a feast, a wedding banquet, and that the penance appropriately is directed toward a Wedding-Guest.[33] The Mariner avers, "That moment that his face I see, / I know the man that must hear me" (lines 589-90). The Guest is the perfect vehicle of penance for one whose treachery has been to unsuspecting visitants. Like the "Hermit good," who first hears the tale, and who also is noted for his hospitality ("He loves to talk with marineres / That come from a far countree" [lines 514-8]), the Wedding-Guest inherits the projected position of albatross: an unwitting participant in a recurring banquet. Returning, as it were, to the scene of the crime, the Mariner instructs "by his own example" the figure who best embodies those traits that previously perished with the "whizz" of a crossbow.

With the circularity of *The Ancient Mariner* in mind, I would like to return to my earlier discussion of the "lonesome road" passage. Lowes thought canto 21 to have been, perhaps, Coleridge's source; but "the lonesome road" passage might well have originated from a much earlier portion of the *Inferno*. As the narrative begins, Dante's Pilgrim remarks,

> Now fled my fear, that thro' the toilsome night
> The vital current froze, and urg'd my flight,
> When the sad moments of despair I told.
> *Then, like a toil-worn mariner I stood,*
> *Who, newly scap'd the perils of the flood,*
> *Turns him again the danger to behold.*
>
> (1.4, my emphasis)

In Coleridge's poem, the marginal Gloss relates that "the curse is finally expiated," but the toil-worn mariner has yet more danger to behold (Gloss, line 442). *The Ancient Mariner* inverts, in a sense, Dante's pattern of descent, beginning in ice-locked Cocytus and continuing with the Mariner's ascent out of the south seas, rather than the corkscrew effect of the *Inferno*. For when "the curse is finally expiated," and the Mariner claims,

> once more
> I viewed the ocean green,
> And looked far forth, yet little saw
> Of what had else been seen.
>
> (lines 442-5)

we are effectively back in canto 1 of the *Inferno*. However, the Mariner's homecoming is also a constant iteration of an eternal plight, "ever and anon throughout his future life," in which he is forever bound with polar chains to the land of ice, and the Circle of souls traitorous to guests.

The exact extent of Coleridge's debt to Dante is, of course, difficult to assess. Yet there is no doubt that Coleridge read the *Inferno* before beginning his own poem of pilgrimage, and that aspects critical to his poem bear similarities, often overt, to Dante's. The mariner figures of Ulysses and Charon begin the pattern of paralysis and motion that the Antarctic realm of Cocytus emanates so potently in the punishment of Life-in-Death, and the punished souls who only delay and stay the Pilgrim's course contend with those "saintly" ones who offer guidance. *The Rime of the Ancient Mariner* possesses distinctly infernal parallels, but they are not present haphazardly. They maintain a powerful convergence of antagonistic forces upon which Coleridge draped his own art. Especially in light of Coleridge's later fascination with Dante, it does not seem far-reaching to suppose his first impressions to have been powerful enough to find their way into a poem so thematically and imaginatively congruent with the latter's work. A passage by a later writer, Edgar Allan Poe, might serve as a sufficient gloss for the whole of the Ancient Mariner's experience and its relation to Dante. In his "MS. Found in a Bottle," the narrator writes of a tumultuous trip to the Antarctic, where cresting and falling upon titanic breakers, "At times we

gasped for breath at an elevation beyond the albatross—at times became dizzy with the velocity of our descent into some watery hell, where the air grew stagnant, and no sound disturbed the slumbers of some kraken."[34] The Mariner's descent to the south finally both oscillates between poles—an albatross and a watery hell—and magnetizes them—motion and immobility, the dizzying and the stagnant, life and death. Coleridge would later note Dante's poem to be "a system of moral[,] political, and theological Truths with arbitrary personal exemplifications—(the punishments indeed allegorical *perhaps*)."[35] If such truths exist in Coleridge's poem, the punishments for transgression are vertiginous allegories indeed: the Mariner observes that "An orphan's curse would drag to hell / A spirit from on high" (lines 257-8). So too his own "hellish thing" draws many into its infernal depths. There, in the manner of Dante, terrible visions of divine justice both haunt and edify, producing a very Coleridgean *Inferno*.

Notes

1. John L. Lowes, *The Road to Xanadu: A Study in the Ways of the Imagination* (1927; rprt. New York: Vintage Books, 1959), p. 422. For further detail of Samuel Taylor Coleridge's borrowings, see George Whalley, "The Bristol Library Borrowings of Southey and Coleridge, 1793-8," *The Library* 4, 2 (September 1949): 114-31. Although, as Whalley points out, many of Coleridge's borrowings contain annotations and marginalia (mostly unidentified), no definitively Coleridgean markings are recorded in Henry Boyd's translation.

2. Coleridge, *The Notebooks of Samuel Taylor Coleridge,* 4 vols., ed. Kathleen Coburn (New York: Pantheon Books, 1957), 1:170.

3. In *The Circle of Our Vision: Dante's Presence in English Romantic Poetry* (Oxford: Clarendon Press, 1994), Ralph Pite also suggests that "This poem [in the manner of Dante] may be one of the projects realized in *The Rime of the Ancyent Marinere*" (p. 69, n. 1). Yet Pite adds merely that "From Boyd's translation, Coleridge could only have gained a sense of Dante's structure." E. E. Stoll, *From Shakespeare to Joyce: Authors and Critics; Literature and Life* (Garden City NJ: Doubleday, Doran, and Company, 1944), pp. 397-8, offers that Coleridge "is able to use superstition, like Dante and Shakespeare, directly . . . marking the transition by a voyage into an antipodean world," and that in "*The Ancient Mariner,* indeed, it is rather Dante's method than Shakespeare's."

4. Henry Boyd, trans., *A Translation of the "Inferno" of Dante Alighieri in English Verse*, 2 vols. (Dublin, 1785). Subsequent citations will be made parenthetically, and, unless otherwise specified, by canto and stanza number.

5. Cf. Coleridge's infamous remarks, many years after writing the poem (31 March 1832) concerning the moral of his story: "it had too much of a moral . . . [and] ought to have had no more moral than the story of the merchant sitting down to eat dates by the side of a well and throwing the shells aside, and the Genii starting up and saying he must kill the merchant, because a date shell had put out the eye of the Genii's son" (*Table Talk*, ed. Carl Woodring, 2 vols. [Princeton: Princeton Univ. Press, 1990], 1:273.) Some of those critics persuaded, and dissuaded, by this comment are noted below.

6. Coleridge, *Letters of Samuel Taylor Coleridge*, 6 vols., ed. Earl Leslie Griggs (Oxford: Clarendon Press, 1956), 2:1059.

7. Lowes, p. 482, n. 92.

8. Coleridge, *The Watchman*, ed. Lewis Patton, vol. 2 in *The Collected Works of Samuel Taylor Coleridge*, 14- vols., hereafter *CW* (Princeton: Princeton Univ. Press, 1970-), 2:133. Coleridge turns an almost identical phrase in his review of *The Monk*, published in 1797: the "man who had been described as possessing much general humanity . . . degenerates into an uglier fiend than the gloomy Imagination of Danté would have ventured to picture" (Coleridge, *Shorter Works and Fragments*, ed. H. J. Jackson and J. R. de J. Jackson, vol. 11 of *CW*, 11:60.

9. In his "Addenda" to *The Road to Xanadu*, p. 567, Lowes relates the suggestions of Albert R. Chandler, who proposes "that details from the story of Ugolino (*Inferno*, canto 33) are woven into part 3 of *The Ancient Mariner*." By far the most comprehensive attempt is that of A. A. Mendilow, "Symbolism in Coleridge and the Dantesque Element in *The Ancient Mariner*," *Scripta Hierosolymitana* 2 (1955): 25-81. Mendilow makes spare use of Boyd's translation, however, and spends little time actually proposing possible textual links between the *Inferno* and Coleridge's poem. Federico Olivero, "Dante e Coleridge," *Giornale Dantesco* 16 (1908): 190-6, may have been the first critic to note resemblances between Dante's Ulysses and the *Ancient Mariner*, cf. Edoardo Zuccato, "S. T. Coleridge as a Critic of Dante," *ConLett* 9, 18 (November 1992): pp. 377-93. A survey of allusions to Dante in the Coleridgean materials then available can be found in Paget Toynbee's *Dante in English Literature from Chaucer to Cary*, 2 vols. (London: Methuen, 1909), 1:612-30. He does miss Coleridge's earliest references, cited in this essay.

10. See especially Donald P. Haase, "Coleridge and Henry Boyd's Translation of Dante's *Inferno*: Toward a Demonic Interpretation of 'Kubla Khan,'" *ELN* [*English Language Notes*] 17, 4 (June 1980): 259-65; cf. Michael Greer, "Coleridge and Dante: Kinship in Xanadu," *UDR* [*University of Dayton Review*] 10, 3 (Summer 1974): 65-74: G. Wilson Knight. "Coleridge's Divine Comedy," in *The Starlit Dome: Studies in the Poetry of Vision* (London: Oxford Univ. Press, 1941; rprt. 1971), pp. 83-178; Maud Bodkin, *Archetypal Patterns in Poetry: Psychological Studies of Imagination* (London: Oxford Univ. Press, 1934), p. 135.

11. For instance, Charles P. Brand, *Italy and the English Romantics: The Italianate Fashion in Early Nineteenth-Century England* (Cambridge: Cambridge Univ. Press, 1957), p. 59, observes that the "poetry of Wordsworth and Coleridge . . . shows little trace of any direct Dante influence." Similarly, Werner P. Friederich, *Dante's Fame Abroad, 1350-1850* (Chapel Hill: Univ. of North Carolina Press, 1950), p. 243, remarks that "With regard to actual influences of Dante upon Coleridge's poetical works, critics are generally agreed that there are none."

12. As quoted in Toynbee, pp. 421-2.

13. Gilbert Cunningham, *The Divine Comedy in English: A Critical Bibliography, 1782-1900* (Edinburgh and London: Oliver and Boyd, 1965), p. 15.

14. Thomas L. Cooksey, "Dante's England, 1818: The Contribution of Cary, Coleridge, and Foscolo to the British Reception of Dante," *PLL* [*Papers on Language and Literature*] 20, 4 (Fall 1984): 355-81, p. 357, n. 4.

15. Lowes, p. 263.

16. Coleridge, *The Rime of the Ancient Mariner*, in *The Complete Poetical Works of Samuel Taylor Coleridge*, 2 vols., ed. E. H. Coleridge (Oxford: Clarendon Press, 1912), pp. 186-209, lines 55-6. All quotations to Coleridge's poems will hereforth be cited in the text by line number. Unless otherwise noted, references to *The Ancient Mariner* are to the version of 1817.

17. See Coleridge, *Lectures 1808-1819 on Literature*, 2 vols., ed. R. A. Foakes (Princeton: Princeton Univ. Press, 1987), 2:401. On the difficulty in precisely dating Coleridge's notes for his two Dante lectures, one 27 February 1818, the other 11 March 1819, see the *Lectures*, 2:184-5.

18. Lowes notes that the "glittering eyes" of professional hypnotists were in particular vogue at the time of the poem's construction, and that Coleridge's "interest in ocular hypnosis . . . is one of the blending elements in the conception of the

Mariner" (p. 232). In "The Power of the Eye in Coleridge," in *Studies in Language and Literature in Honor of J. M. Hart* (New York: Holt, 1910), pp. 78-121, Lane Cooper writes that the poet was generally fascinated with the supposed influence of eyes in magnetically "fixing" susceptible individuals. Cf. Ronnie H. Terpening, *Charon and the Crossing: Ancient, Medieval, and Renaissance Transformation of a Myth* (Lewisburg: Bucknell Univ. Press, 1985).

19. Lowes, pp. 480-1, n. 92. Cf. R. J. Dingley, "Coleridge and the 'Frightful Fiend,'" *N & Q* [*Notes and Queries*] 28, 4 (August 1981):313-4; Paul Magnuson, *Coleridge's Nightmare Poetry* (Charlottesville: Univ. Press of Virginia, 1974), p. 78.

20. Patricia M. Adair, *The Waking Dream: A Study of Coleridge's Poetry* (New York: Barnes and Noble, 1968), p. 81, suggests that the opening of canto 21, the boiling pitch and Venetian ships (Adair accidentally places this allusion in canto 26), may have combined with Coleridge's Malta trip to produce the "o'ertaking wings" of the storm-blast, as well as the continuance, "With sloping masts and dipping prow, / As who pursued with yell and blow / Still treads the shadow of his foe." She singles out the line *"con l'ali aperte, e sopra il pie leggiero"* (line 33), which follows on the heels of the ship conceit, as the probable source. Boyd translates the line, with little similarity, "As high suspended o'er the floating field, / On dragon wing the black Pursuivant came!" (21.5); however, Coleridge had ample time to have read Dante in Italian by the time of these lines, published in 1817.

21. M. H. Abrams, *The Correspondent Breeze: Essays on English Romanticism* (New York: Norton, 1984), pp. 37-8. For a brief critical summation, see Charles J. Rzepka, *The Self as Mind* (Cambridge MA: Harvard Univ. Press, 1986), p. 119, who states that the correspondent breeze is a pattern "which is now taken for granted in Coleridgean criticism." Cf. Duncan Wu, *"The Ancient Mariner*: A Wordsworthian Source," *N & Q* 38, 3 (September 1991): 301; Hans H. Rudnick, "Concretizations of the Aeolian Metaphor," in *Poetics of the Elements in the Human Condition, Part 2: The Airy Elements in the Human Condition,* ed. Anna Theresa Tymieniecka (The Netherlands: Kluwer Academic Publishers, 1988), pp. 145-58. Interestingly, modern climatological studies describe the Antarctic continent as "'the home of the wind,'" where "winds whirl off the immense south polar ice dome with a ferocity seldom matched on earth" (Willy Ley, *The Poles* [New York: Time, 1962], p. 14.)

22. Lowes (pp. 124-39) catalogues a host of possible sources for Coleridge's "fields of ice," including the travel narratives of Frederick Martens, Captain James, and John Harris. But Lowes runs into a problem; the accounts by which "Coleridge vicariously sailed" all concerned Arctic voyages, while the Mariner's venture traverses the Antarctic. He dismisses the incongruity: "Coleridge . . . has imperturbably reversed the poles. Ice is ice, be it austral or boreal waters in which it floats and howls" (p. 136). Lowes misses Dante's voyage into the polar infernal, an expedition not to the Arctic but to the very bottom of the world, and suitable for Coleridge to have adopted without any bipolar disorder.

23. Extended interpretations of the polar spirit, primarily instructed by Coleridge's Gloss, can be found in Lowes, *The Road to Xanadu*, pp. 213-5; Katherine B. Tave. *The Demon and the Poet: An Interpretation of "The Rime of the Ancient Mariner" According to Coleridge's Demonological Sources* (Salzburg: Universität Salzburg, 1983); and Donald P. Kaczvinsky, "Coleridge's Polar Spirit: A Source," *ELN* 24, 3 (March 1987): 25-8.

24. In one of the most influential essays on the poem, Robert Penn Warren ("A Poem of Pure Imagination: An Experiment in Reading," in *Selected Essays* [New York: Random House, 1951], pp. 198-305) remarks that "the crime is, symbolically, a murder, and a particularly heinous murder, for it involves the violation of hospitality and of gratitude . . . This factor of betrayal in the crime is reemphasized in Part V when one of the Spirits says that the bird had 'loved the man' who killed it" (p. 229). George Whalley, "The Mariner and the Albatross," in *Coleridge: A Collection of Critical Essays,* ed. Kathleen Coburn (Englewood Cliffs: Prentice-Hall, 1967), pp. 32-50, sees the bird as "the symbol of Coleridge's creative imagination, his eagle" (p. 44). Knight claims that the slaying of the albatross "may correspond to the death of Christ in racial history" (p. 85). For the anti-moralist, anti-symbolic view, see Earl Leslie Griggs, ed., *The Best of Coleridge* (New York: Nelson, 1934), p. 687, who follows a long line of critics in asserting that "only the reader who cannot enjoy this journey into the realm of the supernatural finds it necessary to seek out a moral"; Stoll, "Symbolism in Coleridge," *PMLA* 63, 3 (March 1948): 214-33; Edward E. Bostetter, "The Nightmare World of *The Ancient Mariner,"* also in *Critical Essays,* ed. Coburn, pp. 65-77, who regards the albatross as part of an "arbitrary exhibition of supernatural power" (p. 70); and

Camille Paglia, *Sexual Personae: Art and Decadence from Nefertiti to Emily Dickinson* (New York: Vintage, 1991), pp. 321-8, for whom "this albatross is the biggest red herring in poetry. Its only significance is as a vehicle of transgression" (p. 324). Frances Ferguson, "Coleridge and the Deluded Reader: *The Rime of the Ancient Mariner*," in *Post-Structuralist Readings of English Poetry*, ed. Richard Machin and Christopher Norris (Cambridge: Cambridge Univ. Press, 1987), pp. 248-63, raises an astute point concerning the crime. She notes that "the notion of a man's hospitality toward a bird contains a rather anomalous and itself prideful assumption—that the bird is a visitor in the Mariner's domain" (p. 252).

25. The traditional source for the albatross is, of course, William Wordsworth. This is the result almost singularly of Wordsworth himself, who in a prefatory note to "We Are Seven," composed around 1843, relates that "Much the greatest part of the story was Mr. Coleridge's invention; but certain parts I suggested; for example . . . I had been reading in Shelvocke's Voyages, a day or two before, that, while doubling Cape Horn, they frequently saw albatrosses in that latitude . . . 'Suppose,' said I, 'you represent him [the Mariner] as having killed one of these birds on entering the South Sea, and that the tutelary spirits of these regions take upon them to avenge the crime'" (as quoted in Lowes, p. 203). Coleridge, according to Thomas De Quincey, denied any debt to Shelvocke.

26. Harold Bloom, "Introduction," in *Samuel Taylor Coleridge: The Rime of the Ancient Mariner* (New York: Chelsea House, 1986), p. 2, interestingly places the Mariner in the "tradition whose dark ancestors include Cain, the Wandering Jew, and the Judas whose act of betrayal is portrayed as a desperate assertion of freedom." Conversely, Seamus Perry, "The Ancient Mariner Controversy," *ChLB* [*Charles Lamb Bulletin*] 92 (October 1995): 208-23, 218, maintains that the "Mariner's shooting of the albatross is as unpremeditated and spontaneous as is his blessing of the water-snakes: one could not even claim the sin to be . . . Luciferan self-assertion."

27. Mendilow, p. 72, suggests that in canto 30, Maestro Adamo "suffers thirst that cracks the tongue," and that "rivulets of water" tease him into a longing for "a drop of water." Boyd writes of the dropsied Adam, whose "bloated form" is "fill'd with wat'ry load," that with "Intense, eternal thirst his bowels burned." For his crime of fraud, ever is "the cooling drop refus'd" (30.8-10).

28. Mendilow, p. 72, makes note of the Life-in-Death parallels, but his focus and interpretation differ significantly from my own. Arguments do exist for reading the figure Life-in-Death as a benevolent characterization. See, for instance, George Bellis. "The Fixed Crime of *The Ancient Mariner*," *EIC* [*Essays in Criticism*] 24, 3 (July 1974): 243-60, who writes, "whatever the look of the monster, 'Life-in-Death' does mean *resurrection*" (p. 246): Bodkin, pp. 26-88.

29. For a consideration of the revisions that Coleridge undertook, see B. R. McElderry, Jr., "Coleridge's Revision of *The Ancient Mariner*," *SP* [*Studies in Philology*] 29, 1 (January 1932): 68-94; more recently, see Jack Stillinger, "The Multiple Versions of Coleridge's Poems: How Many *Mariners* Did Coleridge Write?," *SIR* [*Studies in Romanticism*] 31, 2 (Summer 1992): 127-46, who claims that at least eighteen different versions of the poem exist; and *Coleridge's Ancient Mariner*, ed. Martin Wallen (New York: Station Hill, 1993), esp. pp. 93-144.

30. As quoted in David S. Miall, "The Meaning of Dreams: Coleridge's Ambivalence," *SIR* 21, 1 (Spring 1982): 57-71, 70.

31. Carl Woodring, "The Mariner's Return," *SIR* 11, 4 (Fall 1972): 375-80, 375, writes insightfully that "*The Ancient Mariner* records a transgression of boundaries, a desecration of nature, a descent into hell." Regarding the spiraling motion of Dante's descent, see John Freccero's "Pilgrim in a Gyre," in *Dante: The Poetics of Conversion* (Cambridge MA: Harvard Univ. Press, 1986), pp. 70-92.

32. See Lowes, p. 232; Bloom, p. 1; Paglia, p. 324; *Lectures*, 2: 401.

33. As recently as 1973, Mario L. D'Avanzo ("Coleridge's Wedding-Guest and Marriage-Feast: The Biblical Context," *University of Windsor Review* 8, 1 [Fall 1972]: 62-6, 62) has asserted that the "reason for Coleridge's choice of a wedding guest as auditor and a wedding feast as a frame to *The Rime of the Ancient Mariner* has never been explained or even probed." Lowes offers barely a suggestion (p. 499), and no critic has expansively linked the Guest with his avian predecessor, the visitant albatross. For the relationship between Guest and Mariner, see Ward Pafford, "Coleridge's Wedding-Guest," *SP* 60, 4 (October 1963): 618-26.

34. Edgar Allan Poe, *The Complete Tales and Poems of Edgar Allan Poe* (New York: Random House, 1975), p. 121.

35. *Lectures*, 2: 400.

J. Robert Barth, S.J. (essay date spring 1999)

SOURCE: Barth, J. Robert., S.J. "'A Spring of Love': Prayer and Blessing in Coleridge's *Rime of the Ancient Mariner.*" *Wordsworth Circle* 30, no. 2 (spring 1999): 75-80.

[*In the following essay, Barth offers a reading of the poem based on Coleridge's religious views and his notions of prayer, using as a guide the spiritual writings of St. Ignatius of Loyola.*]

This essay began as a reflection on the relationship between prayer and blessing in Coleridge's poetry, not only in **The Rime of the Ancient Mariner** but also in the beautiful blessings that bring to closure several of the Conversation Poems. Soon it became clear that the primary locus for such a study was the **Ancient Mariner**—and the *locus classicus,* the familiar lines: "A spring of love gushed from my heart, / And I blessed them unaware."

I begin, however, not with Coleridge's poetry but with a philosopher's commentary on Coleridge. It may be unfashionable to begin with a book published in 1930, but I am happy to acknowledge my admiration and respect for a book on Coleridge almost seventy years old: John Muirhead's *Coleridge as Philosopher.* I found it very useful thirty-five years ago when I was just beginning my exploration into the *arcana* of the Coleridge mysteries, and, returning to it recently, was pleased to find Muirhead still a wise and perceptive commentator. To my immediate purpose, I am thinking of his long chapter on Coleridge's "Philosophy of Religion"; while one can find ideas and judgments to cavil at, it remains a thoughtful and suggestive discussion.

What particularly caught my attention in rereading Muirhead was the emphasis on the need for union with God through prayer in Coleridge's movement from Unitarianism to Trinitarian Christianity. "What drove Coleridge from Unitarian Deism," Muirhead begins, "to Spinoza's 'intellectual love of God', thence to Schelling's 'intellectual vision' of Him, and forward from that again, was the failure of one and all to satisfy the demand of the heart for fellowship with God" (219). There were no doubt other reasons as well, including his own sense of guilt and the consequent need for redemption,[1] but clearly Muirhead has come close to the heart of Coleridge's religious sensibility.

Muirhead is quite right, I believe, in linking this religious development to Coleridge's personal gift and need for friendship. One might have some reservations about the first phrases of what follows, since some of his friends were sorely tested at times, but the rest of the passage rings beautifully true:

He was himself a great, and I believe a faithful friend, and he craved friendship and faithfulness in the Source of the being of all things. Even Kant was of little help to him here. The poet in him was repelled by what seemed to him the Stoical note in a philosophy of religion that left no place for the affections; still more by its conception of God as merely the guarantor of the coincidence between virtue and happiness. He would have echoed Cook Wilson's saying, 'We don't want merely inferred friends: can we possibly be satisfied with an inferred God?' What his heart craved, and what to him was the essence of religion, was Communion with God of which prayer was the medium.

(219)

Prayer is often spoken of in the Christian tradition as in turn prayer of praise, thanksgiving, and petition. Although Coleridge does write at times of the prayer of petition—especially as it raises questions about the relationship between human freedom and divine power—and assumes the existence and validity of the prayer of praise and thanksgiving, he is primarily concerned with prayer on a deeper level: as the means of uniting the creature with the Creator. The very need for this union is bound up with what I referred to a moment ago as Coleridge's sense of guilt and his consequent need for redemption. His need for redemption and his need for God's friendship are, I believe, two facets of the same psychological and spiritual reality. I wrote in *Coleridge and Christian Doctrine*: "As he came to realize more and more the innate weakness of man's finite will, Coleridge came more and more to see prayer as an essential means of achieving the necessary union of the finite will with the Absolute Will" (p. 182). Thus prayer was for Coleridge, in a remarkable phrase from his notes on the Divine Ideas, "the effort to connect the misery of Self with the blessedness of God."[2]

It is important, however, especially in considering **The Rime of the Ancient Mariner,** to be aware that this "effort" of prayer is not the work of the creature alone, but the joint work of creature and Creator. Prayer is a gift, but a gift which must be received in order to come into being. It is a case of what scholastic philosophers used to call "mutual causality": one cannot be a husband unless one has a wife, or a wife without a husband—they confer that state of being mutually upon one another. Nor can there be—Narcissus to the contrary notwithstanding—a friendship of one. In prayer, the Creator reaches out to the creature, the creature to the Creator; when they meet, there is prayer.

Thus prayer is a supernatural act, prompted and enabled by God, and the response to this grace is the human act of putting oneself into God's hands. It is an act both divine and human, as Coleridge insists in a notebook entry of 1827: God's "Gifts, Aids, and Defenses will be bestowed on man in such manner that they shall be the product and consequents of his own Act and Will; but from another no less indispensable Postulate we are compelled to declare them the results of the Divine Act and Will; . . . the Gifts, Aids and interventions of the Divine Power . . . are consequent on an Act and Will of the Recipient, which yet is at the same time the Act and Will of the Divine Spirit . . ."[3] In the same notebook reflection, Coleridge summarizes his view of the nature of prayer: a "state of Being, in which the productive energy is the produce, where the agent is at the same moment and the self-same Act the patient, and wrestling conquers for himself what is yet bestowed on him of free grace" (*ibid*). And what is "produced" is the union of the will of the creature with that of the Creator, the finite with the Absolute.

But note that Coleridge speaks of prayer as "wrestling." Prayer is no easy matter, because it involves a mastery of one's self, a conquering of one's own passions and willfulness. Jacob wrestled with the angel, in one of the sacred scripture's most dramatic encounters between man and God—wrestled through the night and won a blessing through the struggle. But Coleridge's struggle in prayer seems to be as much with himself as with the divine power. Coleridge said to his nephew Henry Nelson Coleridge two years before he died: "Believe me, to pray with all your heart and strength, with the reason and the will, to believe vividly that God will listen to your voice through Christ, and verily do the thing he pleaseth thereupon—that is the last, the greatest achievement of the Christian's warfare upon earth. *Teach* us to pray, O Lord!" Then, his nephew records, he broke into tears and begged his nephew to pray for him.[4] The warfare for him was not against the divine power but against one's own self-will, as it strives to conform itself to the Divine Will. As Coleridge wrote in a late notebook: "No Liberty but by co-incidence with the Divine Will—and hence the doctrines of the Spirit—No faith but by the Father's leading—No effectual Prayer but by the *Spirit*" (Notebook 34 [1827], f. 8).

But for all this "leading" by the Father, Coleridge insists that prayer does not take away responsibility for the reasonable use of one's human faculties, rejecting the belief that human beings should "blind themselves to the light, which [God] had himself given them, as the contra-distinguishing character of their Humanity, without which they could not pray to Him at all."[5] Prayer, as communion between finite and infinite, is of its essence an act of mutuality. God gives not only the grace of his "leading," the supernatural "call" to prayer, but the very human faculties themselves—intellect and will—which enable us to respond to God's leading; and the human responsibility, often exercised only through discipline and self-mastery, is to use these faculties attentively and wisely.

This is, I believe, the view of prayer reflected in *The Rime of the Ancient Mariner*. We shall use the *Sibyl-line Leaves* version of 1817 because it is closer in time to most of the prose reflections I have quoted, but I do not believe there would be any substantial difference in the argument were we to use the version of 1798 (ed. E. H. Coleridge [1912] I 186-209). Coleridge's reflections on prayer may have changed as he moved from his Unitarian years to the years of his adherence to Trinitarian Christianity, but I suggest that his religious sensibility about prayer in *The Rime of the Ancient Mariner*—and the spiritual journey dramatized there—was as fully formed in 1797 as it was in 1817. It was already deep in his soul.

I believe we can discern in the poem the following elements: (1) a growing realization of the need for union of the creature with the Creator, the human with the Divine; (2) the awareness of prayer as a gift; (3) the need for responsiveness to the gift of prayer, not simply in words but in attitude and action; (4) the blessings consequent upon prayer given and accepted; (5) a sense of prayer as struggle; and (6) the life-long nature of the process of prayer as a means of union with God. What follows, however, is by no means meant to be a "complete" reading of the poem, but rather the identification of one strand in the weave of it that I believe contributes significantly to its strength and beauty.

We begin with the opening of the Mariner's narration rather than with the beginning of the poem, since the wedding "frame" is an outcome of his adventure, and so will be seen as a later part of the process. It seems evident that from the very beginning the Mariner is in some ways radically disconnected from the world around him. The journey begins as an ordinary voyage, but very quickly the story turns ominous: storm-blasts, mists and snow, the "dismal sheen" of the threatening ice—followed by a period of good winds and progress—and in the very midst of it the Mariner's gratuitous killing of the albatross.

Part II is characterized above all by uncertainty—was it wrong or right to have slain the bird—and by dreadful foreboding: the bloody Sun, the rotting deep, the death-fires, the thirst that stifles speech. The albatross hung about the Mariner's neck seems a fitting emblem of his violation of creation. Part III deepens the mystery and dread, as the Mariner becomes more alienated not only from the world of nature but from his shipmates, as he encounters the phantom ship with its nightmare crew, and as fear drinks the life-blood from his heart. In Part IV the Mariner's alienation is complete: "Alone, alone, all, all alone, / Alone on a wide wide sea! / And never a saint took pity on / My soul in agony" (232-5). It is at this nadir of hope that the Mariner finally, for the first time, realizes his need for support beyond himself and his shipmates:

> I looked to heaven, and tried to pray;
> But or ever a prayer had gusht,

A wicked whisper came, and made
My heart as dry as dust.

                                                    (244-7)

What was the "wicked whisper" that dried up the springs of his heart even as he tried to pray? Perhaps a whisper that there was no God? Perhaps that he was beyond love or forgiveness?

But the moment does not last, and very shortly he sees and blesses the beauty of the once dreadful water-snakes: "A spring of love gushed from my heart, / And I blessed them unaware" (284-85). What then opened the Mariner's eyes to see the beauty of the water-snakes, and the springs of his heart to bless them? Something he did himself, or a gift gratuitously given? I suggest that it is both. His attempt to pray, itself a gift occasioned by his desperate need, is met by the gift of love from his "kind saint," and out of this mutual causality comes prayer: "The self-same moment I could pray" (288). As Coleridge himself wrote years later (in a notebook entry we saw earlier): "The gifts, aids and interventions of the Divine Power . . . are consequent on the Act and Will of the Recipient, which yet is at the same time the Act and Will of the Divine Spirit."

But prayer is not a gift simply given and received once for all, but an ongoing process. For a time the spirit of prayer clearly stays with the Mariner. His sleep is blessed with refreshing dew, and he is granted a vision of the "troop of spirits blest" (350-72). And prayer is not a permanent state. As the spirit says, not threateningly but in a voice "as soft as honey-dew" (l. 407), the Mariner "hath penance done, / And penance more will do" (ll. 408-9). Confronted by the vision of his dead shipmates, he is once again unable to pray: "I could not draw my eyes from theirs, / Nor turn them up to pray" (440-1). Again, though, the gift of prayer is given: "this spell was snapt" (442)—and a welcome breeze "breathd" on him, "mingled strangely," "felt like a welcoming" (458-9).

In all of this, I think, it is not difficult to see prayer as what Coleridge called "the effort to connect the misery of the self with the blessedness of God." However, I should like to dwell more at length on the "wrestling" of the soul, the struggle, through which prayer—as the medium for union with God in love—is achieved. In order to elucidate the nature of this struggle, I would like to turn to a work with which, as far as I know, Coleridge was not familiar, but which is generally accepted as expressing profound insight into the nature of prayer and spiritual struggle: the Spiritual Exercises of St. Ignatius Loyola.[6] Let me emphasize that I suggest no influence whatever, but only that the insights of Loyola into the nature of spiritual journeying may shed light on this most intriguing of poetic journeys of the spirit.

The Spiritual Exercises of Ignatius Loyola may be seen as guidelines for anyone who is seeking closer union with God. They are divided into four stages, or "weeks," that mark a deepening movement toward that union. The first week, beginning with the realization of the human person's essential relationship as creature to Creator, strives to deepen the awareness of one's sinfulness and ultimate dependence on God. The second week focuses on the life of Christ, as he calls each one to follow him in loving service of others. The third week is the week of the Passion, in which Christ's suffering and death are seen as the ultimate proof of the depth of God's love for humankind. Finally, the fourth week turns to the Risen Christ, as efficacious sign of our own "resurrection" to a new life of union with God and more generous commitment to one another in love and service.

At the heart of this spiritual retreat, from the human side, is what Loyola calls the "discernment of spirits." This is the process by which the director, or spiritual guide, helps the exercitant to determine which of the movements of the heart or spirit in prayer are from God ("the good spirit"), and which from one's own selfish lower nature ("the evil spirit"). Central to this process, as to prayer itself, are the movements of "consolation" and "desolation" that come to one during prayer. By "spiritual consolation" Loyola means (in the words of the Spiritual Exercises) "that which occurs when some interior motion is caused within the soul through which it comes to be inflamed with love of its Creator and Lord," which includes "every increase in hope, faith, and charity, and every interior joy which calls and attracts one to heavenly things and to the salvation of one's soul, by bringing it tranquillity and peace in its Creator and Lord" (316). On the other hand, "spiritual desolation" brings "darkness of soul, turmoil within it, an impulsive motion toward low and earthly things, or disquiet from various agitations and temptations," all of which "move one toward lack of faith and leave one without hope and without love. One is completely listless, tepid, and unhappy, and feels separated from our Creator and Lord" (317).

It is not always easy to know the source of the motions of the soul, Loyola says, because it is "characteristic of the evil angel, who takes on the appearance of an angel of light, to enter by going along with the devout soul and then to come out his own way" (332), by enticing the soul to bad ends. For this reason one must "pay close attention to the whole train of our thoughts" (333). If the train of one's thoughts is diverted to something less good, or if it disquiets or disturbs the soul, this is clearly not from God. "It is characteristic of God and his angels, by the motions they cause, to give genuine happiness and spiritual joy," while "it is characteristic of the enemy to fight against this happiness and spiritual consolation, by using specious reasonings, subtleties, and persistent deceits" (329). Anxiety and sadness cannot be from God, the giver of all good gifts. If, however, one's thoughts lead to consolation, whose characteristics are peace and joy of heart, courage and inspiration, one can be certain that this is from God.

As well as to the movements that take place in the soul—consolation or desolation—the director may also look at the way in which the movement touches the soul. For example, "in the case of those going from good to better, the good angel touches the soul gently, lightly, and sweetly, like a drop of water going into a sponge. The evil spirit touches it sharply, with noise and disturbance, like a drop of water falling on a stone" (335).

The exercitant needs to remember, too, that neither consolation nor desolation is a permanent state. "When we are in desolation," Ignatius says, "we should think that the Lord has left us in order to test us, by leaving us to our own natural power," and we should strive to preserve ourselves in patience, for "after a while consolation will return again" (321-2). On the other hand, "one who is in consolation should consider how he or she will act in future desolation, and store up new strength for that time" (323).

The idea of the spiritual struggle or warfare is hardly new in Ignatius Loyola. It reflects an element of Christianity as old as Christianity itself. One of its earliest expressions is St. Paul's "war of the members," which finds its classic formulation in his Epistle to the Romans (7:14-25). "I do not understand my own actions," Paul writes. "For I do not what I want, but I do the very thing I hate . . . I can will what is right, but I cannot do it. For I do not do the good I want, but the evil I do not want is what I do. . . . I delight in the law of God, in my inmost self, but I see in my members another law at war with the law of my mind and making me captive to the law of sin which dwells in my members." It is only God, through Christ, who can deliver him from "this body of death." This warfare within the self between the spirit of God and the lower self is, I suggest, the struggle Loyola analyzes in the Spiritual Exercises and Coleridge dramatizes in the ***Ancient Mariner.***

In the poem, clearly the struggle is acute and for very high stakes: the Mariner's very soul. At the end of Part I, the interior action is set in motion by the gratuitous slaying of the albatross—"the evil I do not want is what I do"—and from that point on the internal "wrestling" within the Mariner precipitates an alternation of "desolation" and "consolation," with occasional breathing spaces of calm, sometimes hopeful and reassuring, at other times ominous. The killing of the bird is followed in Part II by confusion of mind—was the slaying a good or wicked act?—and then by an ominous stillness:

"nor breath nor motion" (116). The spirit that presides over the vision of the "rotting deep" and the "slimy things" is the "Spirit that plagued us so" (132). This in turn ushers in the period of desolation in Part III ("a weary time," 143), followed by a moment of what turns out to be false hope, as the ship that for a moment promised safety is seen to be a phantom ship, carrying the "Night-mare Life-in-Death" (193). All the signs of desolation are here: darkness of spirit, "fear at my heart," reminders of his sinfulness as "every soul, it past me by, / Like the whizz of my crossbow" (222-3). Then in Part IV the Mariner descends into the very depths of desolation as he is thrust into isolation and alienation: "Alone, alone, all, all alone" (232). Prayer is impossible in such a state, and the "wicked whisper"— perhaps of his own despair—dries his heart to dust (244-7).

The Mariner had been cast dramatically into the state of desolation, but at the end of Part IV he is drawn out of it gradually and gently, as the water-snakes metamorphose for him into a vision of ethereal beauty, culminating in "a flash of golden fire" (281). The consolation comes—in "a spring of love"—as gratuitously as his sin had been committed, and with it comes the gift of prayer. In that moment the sign of his sin, the albatross, falls from his neck. Clearly the "good spirit" has touched the Mariner's heart, but just as clearly he has been opened to the movements of the spirit: he has tried to pray, he has opened his eyes to see the beauty manifested to him. There has been a "leading" of the spirit, for (in Coleridge's words) there is "no faith but by the Father's leading—no effectual prayer but by the Spirit." At the same time, though, the Mariner has not (again in Coleridge's words) "blinded himself to the light, which God himself had given" him.

Part V allows the Mariner to experience even more fully the gift of consolation: gentle sleep (292), the slaking of his thirst (300), the lightness of being: "I was so light—almost / I thought that I had died in sleep, / And was a blessed ghost" (306-8). And then the vision of the "troop of spirits blest" (349) draws him into an ecstatic experience of heavenly sights and sounds (350-72), which takes him quite out of himself, before returning him gently to the silent motion of the ship. This section is notable in that the consolation he experiences is so varied, from the gentleness of sleep to an intense ecstatic experience of joy to the peaceful calm of the moving ship—all within the space of less than a hundred lines (292-376).

The Mariner's journey is not yet over, of course, and another period of desolation is to come, but this one is not only shorter in duration but also less dramatic and intense. It begins with the strange stirring of the ship "with a short uneasy motion" (386), throwing the Mariner into a swoon, from which he recovers to hear the voice of the two spirits talking of his sin and his journey, one of them promising "penance more" for him (409). Their voices lead into Part VI, the final stage of his voyage. Again he sees his dead shipmates, and again momentarily he is unable to pray. But almost at once "there breathed a wind on me"—a welcoming breeze that brings him at last home. The final vision of his shipmates, now blessed by a beautiful "seraph-band" (492), brings "silent music" and joy.

Besides the "discernment of spirits" in the patterns of consolation and desolation, one other dimension of the Spiritual Exercises might also serve to help us understand the nature of the Mariner's experience of prayer. It is the "Contemplation for Obtaining Divine Love," the closing and culminating meditation of the four weeks of the Exercises. The Contemplation begins by insisting on two basic principles: first, that "love ought to manifest itself more by deeds then by words" (230); and secondly, that "love consists in a mutual communication between the two persons," a mutual sharing of self between the lover and the beloved (231). The four stages of the meditation (234-7) then go on to show how God shares himself with his people: first, by the gifts he pours out on humankind—the beauties of creation, the graces of salvation, the particular gifts in the life of each person; next, how God not only gives to his creatures but actually dwells in them—in the elements of the earth, in plants and animals, most of all and most intimately in human beings, made in his image; then, how he acts, even "labors," within all created things, charging them with the energy of their being; and finally, the exercitant is asked to imagine all these gifts—filled with God's presence and energy—descending from heaven, like the rays of light from the sun or water from a fountain. Clearly the movement is into deeper and deeper union between ourselves and God, a deeper intensity of relationship.[7]

If the interior struggle of the Mariner finds a parallel in the Ignatian "discernment of spirits," with its alternations of consolation and desolation, I see a striking parallel between the "Contemplation for Obtaining Divine Love"—especially its closing image of God's gifts, filled with his life and energy, descending like the rays of light from the sun—and the Mariner's vision of the blessed spirits which we have seen already:

> Around, around, flew each sweet sound,
> Then darted to the Sun;
> Slowly the sounds came back again,
> Now mixed, now one by one.
>
> Sometimes a-dropping from the sky
> I heard the sky-lark sing;
> Sometimes all little birds that are,
> How they seemed to fill the sea and air
> With their sweet jargoning!

> And now 'twas like all instruments,
> Now like a lonely flute;
> And now it is an angel's song,
> That makes the heavens be mute.

                                                        (354-66)

For the moment, the Mariner's union with transcendent being seems close and intimate—indeed ecstatic—but, significantly, it is in and through the works of nature that the transcendent is most fully revealed to him. He must return from his visionary state, to the world and to human society, to work out his salvation. He must find God in and through the created world.

Ignatius Loyola warned, you will recall, that we must "pay attention to the whole train of our thoughts," not merely to periods of consolation and desolation or even to moments of ecstatic vision. But if the overall movement is toward good, toward peace and joy, toward "increase in faith, hope, and charity," toward "heavenly things and the salvation of one's soul," then the leading of the journey is from God. And in *The Rime of the Ancient Mariner,* it seems clearly so. The Spiritual Exercises never end; they open out into one's daily life, and the process begun there—the "discernment of spirits," the inevitable waxing and waning of consolation and desolation, the attempts to open oneself to God's leading, the offering of self in service to others—must be played out again and again, drawing one on to deeper union with God through prayer and through our deeper sharing in the human community. The solitude, the time alone with God or in search of God—like that of Jesus when he drew apart from the crowds or of Moses alone on the mountain top—is not for its own sake. It is rather a gift to strengthen the prophetic figure for the people one is called to serve. The solitude is ultimately for the sake of the community: for the people of Israel, for the Apostles, for the wedding-guests—in short, for the building up of the human family. Drawing closer to God in solitude is ultimately a means of drawing us closer to one another. Moses did not remain on the mountain top; he returned to strengthen and lead God's people. Jesus did not remain in a quiet place apart; he always returned to his disciples and to the crowds that eagerly sought him out.

This is, I suggest, the vocation of the whole human family—which may explain why *The Rime of the Ancient Mariner* has such universal appeal. We are all called to share in this same dialectic: the movement into solitude and the return to community. Nor is it that we find God only in solitude; we find God in both solitude and community. We find God in the silence of our hearts, in the movements of our prayer, in the beauties of sea and sky. But we also find God in the heart of the human family, where he perhaps most deeply dwells. We need them both: solitude and human community. Through our communion with God in prayer, God prepares us to meet one another more deeply and lovingly, and to find one another in his loving presence.[8]

And so in Coleridge's great poem. Through his own "Spiritual Exercises," the Mariner has reached not only a new level of awareness but a new state of being; newly touched by the presence of the divine in the world and in himself, he is now awake to beauty and to love. He will still have his moments of consolation and desolation, but in moments of desolation he will remember the vision. His heart will burn within him until he tells his tale, for he is now a prophet who has been granted both the vision and the burden, and he must tell the world of the love he has encountered and of the cost of that love. And nowhere better to tell his tale than at a wedding-feast, a celebration of love, for those who celebrate love must come to know it in its fullness—its mysteries and its visions, its pains and its comforts, its moments of loneliness and its times of consolation. And the Mariner's is indeed a wondrous tale—of God's leading and his own reluctant following, of suffering and joy, of despair and hope—but in the end a tale of comfort, of God's patient, unrelenting and forgiving love.

Notes

1. See J. Robert Barth, S. J., *Coleridge and Christian Doctrine* (1969), pp. 11-12.

2. In slightly fuller context the passage reads: "Prayer is the mediation—or rather the effort to connect the misery of Self with the blessedness of God—& its voice is—Mercy! mercy! for Christ's sake in whom thou hast opened out the fountain of Mercy to sinful Man—. It is a sore evil to be and not in God.—but it is a still more dreadful evil & misery to will to be other than in God." John Beer, who kindly identified this passage for me, notes in a personal letter that it is part of a longer meditation "on his own spiritual state and the miserable physical results of his opium addiction." The passage, dated January 7, 1830, is on f. 74v of the folio notebook on the "Divine Ideas" in the Huntington Library.

3. The lines are from one of Coleridge's later still unpublished notebooks, Notebook 34 (1827), ff. 10-12[v]. For fuller information on the manuscript notebooks, see *Coleridge and Christian Doctrine,* pp. 21-22, note 18. Quotations from the still unpublished notebooks are used with the kind of permission of the late Mr. A. H. B. Coleridge.

4. S. T. Coleridge, *Specimens of the Table Talk . . . ,* in *The Complete Works . . . ,* ed. W. G. T. Shedd, 7 vols. (1856), VI, 327n.

5. *On the Constitution of the Church and State,* ed. John Colmer, in *The Collected Works of Samuel Taylor Coleridge,* ed. Kathleen Coburn, 10 (1976), p. 170.

6. Ignatius of Loyola, *The Spiritual Exercises and Selected Works,* ed. George E. Ganss, S. J. (1991), 113-214; hereafter cited in text.

7. This paragraph is adapted from my essay, "The Sacramental Vision of Gerard Manley Hopkins," in *Seeing into the Life of Things: Essays on Religion and Literature,* ed. John L. Mahoney (1998), 217.

8. The preceding two paragraphs are adapted from my reflections on "Wordsworthian Solitude and the Solitude of Christ," *The Allen Review,* no. 19 (1998), 11.

James Engell (essay date 2002)

SOURCE: Engell, James. "Coleridge (and His Mariner) on the Soul: 'As an exile in a far distant land.'" In *The Fountain Light: Studies in Romanticism and Religion; In Honor of John L. Mahoney,* edited by J. Robert Barth, S.J., pp. 128-51. New York: Fordham University Press, 2002.

[*In the following essay, Engell focuses on Coleridge's thinking on spirituality, tracing the poet's changing ideas regarding the nature and existence of the human soul and how* The Ancient Mariner *embodies many of these beliefs.*]

I

Extending a large intellectual pattern of the modern West, prominent thinkers in the century prior to Coleridge dissect the soul into many faculties. In an impassioned section of *The Excursion* (IV, 951-992), as well as in *The Prelude* and his lyrics, Wordsworth decries this method: "We murder to dissect." He echoes Pope, who in the "Epistle to Cobham" had articulated the problem this way: "Like following life thro' creatures you dissect, / You lose it in the moment you detect." Yet the dissecting method supports new discoveries that transform natural philosophy and give rise to modern empirical science. These changes, and the tensions they create, produce what one critic, Paul Ilie, calls "the key idea that bridges eighteenth-century philosophy and science, namely, the changing notion of a vital force or 'soul.'"[1] Some experiments to locate the soul prove heroic. In an attempt to establish that it actually resides in the chest, the physician and philosopher Jean-Baptiste van Helmont administers wolfsbane to himself. The soul is often no longer regarded in purely theological terms. In common usage, it now potentially includes, and overlaps with, whatever is meant by mind, spirit, life, self, self-consciousness, and identity.

Coleridge recognizes this broader usage throughout his writings and notes it a number of times, for example, when he says, "we use the word 'mind' in this place as nearly equivalent to the soul, as the sum of all our faculties, whether active, passive or spontaneous" (*Logic* 153).[2] The whole, too, is greater than its aggregated parts, for "there is *the idea* of the Soul with its undefined capacity and dignity, that gives the sting to any absorption of it by any one pursuit" (*Lects 1808-1819* [*Lectures 1808-1819: On Literature*], II, 172). To define the capacity of the soul seems inherently to fail to realize its worth and potential. As Samuel Johnson said of any attempt to circumscribe poetry with a definition, it shows only the "narrowness of the definer." Of course, this doesn't stop Coleridge. With a new urgency prompted by modern science, the problem of the soul confronts poets, critics, natural philosophers, psychologists, and theologians. And it fascinates Coleridge, which is to say the same thing.

A few thinkers Coleridge admires in the 1790s, especially Hartley, arrived at the soul and religious concerns by starting with "vibrations" of mental tissues and nerves. But Coleridge soon believes that vibrational Associationism means starting with the material and ending with the spiritual. For him, the process is backward. As an explanation of the human spirit he abhors materialism and hylozoism, the doctrine that the organization of matter alone explains life. Everyone perceives and associates the particulars of the material world. But, Coleridge insists, what explains the existence of that material world in the first place? Isn't there, in human nature, separate from the five outward senses, a moral sense, a type of reason, and a freedom of the will that together determine the worth and dignity of the individual? And isn't such an invisible, supersensuous sense just as real as touch, taste, or sight? It is an "undue degradation of the human soul" to subject "all truth to conceptions formed by the senses, or to the notions which the understanding marks for itself by reflection on its own processes" (*Logic* 197). Coleridge objects to "Voltaire, D'Alembert, Diderot" because he sees in their writings the high tide of an old misconception: "the Human Understanding . . . was tempted to throw off all reverence to the spiritual and even to the moral powers and impulses of the soul" (*SM* [*The Statesman's Manual*] 75). Another method of knowing—and of knowing the self in its relationship to nature—is needed.

As so often, Coleridge finds ultimate authority for his position, this method of the soul, in Scripture. On the immortality of the soul, he claims, "Read the first chapter of Genesis without prejudice, and you will be convinced at once. . . . And in the next chapter," Coleridge goes on, Moses "repeats the narrative:—'And the Lord God formed man of the dust of the ground, and breathed into his nostrils the breath of life;' and then he adds these words,—'*and man became a living soul.*' Materialism will never explain those last words" (*TT* [*Table Talk*], II, 36; see I, 31-32). These words are

so important to Coleridge that he quotes them, too, in the "Theory of Life" (1816) and in *Aids to Reflection* (1825). In philosophy, the starting-point so often matters, and Coleridge does not want that starting-point to be matter or nature. He credits Plato with being "the first who supported the immortality of the Soul upon arguments solid and permanent . . . he felt convinced that the diseases and the death of the body could not injure the principle of life or destroy the soul which of itself was of divine origin and of an uncorrupted and immutable essence" (*Lects 1818-1819* [*Lectures 1818-1819: On the History of Philosophy*] 205). The more we regard Coleridge's idea of the soul, the more we see his Platonism.[3] Later, Coleridge is fond of repeating that the pith of his system, if one could call it so fine a thing, is to make the senses out of the mind—not the mind out of the senses, as Locke did (e.g., *TT*, I, 312).

Coleridge is probably regretting youthful errors. For instance, in the earlier *Notebooks* he speculates on the nature of the soul in terms related to motion, time, space, and resistance. His language assumes a cast of logical deduction and draws on the vocabulary of nascent modern physics and the terminology of Locke: "I believe that what we call *motion* is our consciousness of motion, arising from the interruption of motion = the acting of the Soul resisted" (*CN* [*The Notebooks of Samuel Taylor Coleridge*], I, 1771). Little more than a year later, in January 1805, he continues in a similar vein: "Space <is one of > the Hebrew names for God / & it is the most perfect image of *Soul, pure Soul*—being indeed to us nothing but unresisted action." He then deduces that, "thus all body necessarily presupposes soul, inasmuch as all resistance presupposes action" (*CN,* II, 2402).

If Coleridge's thinking here seems strained, it is because, earlier in his career, he wants to use the language of logic and deduction to elucidate religious belief or conviction. He attempts to bridge the widening fissures between religion, philosophy, and science by setting their realms of discourse together, by using the same realm of discourse—the same method—for each, and then by determining, by way of a kind of syllogism, the primacy of the spiritual world: "and thus all body *necessarily* presupposes soul."

But this sort of attempt, as Coleridge soon recognizes, remains unconvincing. When younger and imitating the methods of empirical science or of logical dissection and deduction, he is drawn onto that battleground and there has difficulty sustaining his spiritual flank. Later, in *Biographia Literaria,* he no longer takes up concepts of space and time with reference to the soul. And in the "Theory of Life," his whole account of the living creation, although anticipatory of Darwin's theory of evolution in some ways, nevertheless consciously refuses a unity or even *continuity* of approach between the natural and the human when it comes to the problem of the soul. That is, the soul cannot be accounted for in nature.[4]

Sometime around 1806 Coleridge begins explicitly to credit "revelation" as convincing him "that I have a rational and responsible soul," and that by virtue of that soul there exists a "wide chasm between man and the noblest animals of the brute creation, which no perceivable or conceivable difference of organization is sufficient to *overbridge*" (*SW & F* [*Shorter Works and Fragments*] 501). He will assert, eventually, on the last day of March 1832, that "All Religion is revealed; revealed religion is in my judgment, a mere pleonasm" (*TT*, I, 276). As early as 1806 he writes to Thomas Clarkson, who inquired about the nature of the soul, that "Reason is therefore most eminently the Revelation of an immortal soul, and it's best Synonime—it is the *forma formans*, which contains in itself the law of it's own conceptions" (*CL* [*The Collected Letters of Samuel Taylor Coleridge*], II, 1198).

Thus, in a real sense, the conception of one completely unified system of nature and God, spirit and matter, science and religion, founders on this very point, the soul. It cannot be demonstrated or verified in any empirical or logical manner. As James Boulger points out, Coleridge's ontological arguments about the soul contain an "open admission of circularity . . . dwelt upon to a surprising extent."[5] It was to become a theme, one reiterated in a later *Notebook* entry of May 1826: "The characteristic Formula of all *Spiritual* Verities or Ideas is an apparent *Circle*—" (*CN,* IV, 5377). For it, there exists no proof. As Anya Taylor comments, Coleridge in the *Opus Maximum* "makes the best of a difficult situation by arguing that the proof must be indemonstrable by definition; for to demonstrate a thing is to find its antecedent, and whatever is prior can have no antecedent; therefore the Idea of God or of Soul is indemonstrable and rightly so."[6] The method of knowing nature and the method of knowing spirit cannot be one, at least not one simple unity. Such an identity would lead to pantheism, which, as Coleridge explicitly recognizes, does not easily accommodate the idea of the soul. In 1817 he sniffs that Spinoza needed to "supply a Soul" to his system (*SW & F* 567). Taken together, the advances of science and the convictions of revelation hardly seem to conform to one unitary system, no matter how much the dream of it—"a total and undivided philosophy" where "philosophy would pass into religion, and religion become inclusive of philosophy" (*BL* [*Biographia Literaria*], I, 282, 283)—haunts Coleridge. Even Joseph Henry Green, admirer, collaborator, and literary executor, would confess about one of Coleridge's unfinished projects, apparently the *Opus Maximum,* that "the main portion of the work is a philosophical *Cosmogony,* which I fear is scarcely adapted for scientific readers, or corresponds to the requirements of modern science."[7] Members of Coleridge's family agreed that his science was out of date. In the *Philosophical Lectures,* Coleridge could make unsatisfactory statements, which, even if their ultimate direction might be grasped sympathetically, in literal application would wreak havoc in the laboratory. For example, in claiming to draw on Bacon, though the source is not apparent, he states: "all science approaches to its perfection in proportion as it immaterializes objects" (*Lects 1818-1819* 489).

The temptation attracting Coleridge, especially in his earlier thinking, entices several other Romantic writers, too. Coleridge accuses the *Naturphilosophen* of this weakness. Yet at times he himself conflates the methods and aims of *Naturwissenschaft,* the study of the natural world and the establishment of universal, ahistorical laws, with the methods and aims of *Geisteswissenschaft,* the knowledge and exploration of the human spirit caught up in history and dependent on will, genius, and moral action.[8] To act, one must yoke together and make co-present in consciousness these two kinds of knowledge. But to gain these two kinds of knowledge by the *same* method is not possible, nor can they be wrestled into one seamless system. To do so, Wilhelm Dilthey would argue, is an intellectual aspiration of the Romantic era already suspect at that time, and soon thereafter impossible.[9]

In his mature thought, Coleridge does refuse that aspiration. He treats the soul as a postulate or belief of distinctly human experience, of *Geisteswissenschaft,* rather than as an empirical observation of the natural world. The soul is a fact of the human spirit, not something the human mind can properly conceive of or analyze. Again, in his 1806 letter to Clarkson, he makes this clear: "What the Spirit of God *is,* and what the Soul *is,* I dare not suppose myself capable of *conceiving*: according to my religious and philosophical creed they are *known* by those, to whom they are revealed. . . . *Datur,* non intelligitur" (*CL,* II, 1193). As Stephen Prickett explains, the mind cannot properly conceive of the soul itself; rather, "Man, made in God's image as a living and creative soul, is at his *proper* activity . . . when acting as a mirror to God's enlightenment."[10]

This approach is not, of course, scientific. Yet it need not oppose science. There are parallels and interdependencies between the method of the soul and the methods of science. In November 1801 Coleridge quotes approvingly Sir Kenelm Digby's translation of Plato's *Phaedrus* (270c): "Do you suppose the nature of the soul can be sufficiently understood without the knowledge of the whole of nature?" (*CN,* I, 1002). As Anthony Harding notes, for Coleridge "the point . . . is that our comprehension of Nature's processes is a progressive thing, just as is our moral and religious being."[11] (We shall consider the idea of the soul's growth and progression momentarily.) But the moral and religious being begins with an act of the soul. In this sense, Coleridge remarks, "Faith is a *total* act of the soul: it is the *whole* state of the mind, or it is not at all!" (*Friend*, II, 314). R. J. White identifies this as "the key" to all of Coleridge's "lay preaching" (*LS* [*A Lay Sermon*], xliii). In *The Statesman's Manual*, Coleridge expresses it this way: "Even so doth Religion finitely express the *unity* of the infinite Spirit by being a total act of the soul" (*SM*, 90). (This is a unity of spirit, not of matter with spirit.) As he explains in *The Friend*, "The aim, the method throughout was, in the first place, to awaken, to cultivate, and to mature the truly *human* in human nature, in and through itself, or as independently as possible of the notices derived from sense, and of the motives that had reference to the sensations; till the time should arrive when the senses themselves might be allowed to present symbols and attestations of truths, learnt previously from deeper and inner sources" (*Friend*, I, 500-501). The soul, he reaffirms in the "Theory of Life," is that "which I believe to constitute the peculiar nature of man" and has no connection with, nor is the cause of, "functions and properties, which man possesses in common with the oyster and the mushroom" (*SW & F*, 501). This spiritual method, then, Coleridge claims, is to start from within and proceed dialectically to the external world. He can ally this sense of the soul's dialectical method with Fichte's *Ich bin weil ich bin* and *nicht-Ich* or with Kant's concept of self-apperception. Evident Platonic sources exist as well, many of them familiar to Schelling and Fichte. Coleridge also appeals for the existence of the soul and its method to Christian doctrine and revelation, to Jehovah's "I AM that I AM" and to the passages he quotes from Genesis. He is aware of all of these, as it were, simultaneously.

Yet, as Coleridge comes to realize that attempts to *identify* the method of the soul with the method of science do not quite square, he moves to *reconcile* advances in the method of science with reflection on the method of spiritual life. We should perhaps more often seek for this reconciliation in his thought than insist on its putative or final unity.[12] Near the end of this essay, in the context of **The Rime of the Ancient Mariner** and Coleridge's comments on the power of the imagination, we shall return to the *activity* of reconciliation as distinguished from unity itself, for this activity is vital in understanding how Coleridge deals with both a natural world subject to science and a specifically human world of spirit, conscience, and the moral life. In the vein of such active connection and reconciliation, he praises Thales as the first thinker to perceive that there is "a relationship between the Soul of Man and the laws of Nature" even though the primacy of knowledge comes from "the mind of Man," from "Reason" (*Lects 1818-1819* 101). For this position, Col-

eridge invokes at least three times, in *Biographia*, the *Philosophical Lectures*, and "On the Prometheus of Aeschylus," Milton's lines from *Paradise Lost* that climb the scale of being from natural to spiritual: ". . . whence the soul / Reason receives, and reason is her being" (V, 486-487). Nature and the soul cannot be left to go their separate ways, for they are not separate. If they become entirely so, the result will be a dehumanized society driven by mechanistic technology, a society in which individuals sacrifice their own souls or, worse, enslave the souls of others for material gain. Whether the result is the Faustian bargain of material control over nature in the first instance, or slavery and exploitation in the second instance, matters little. One leads to the other.

Coleridge's dialectical method thus starts in a way different from the dissecting method that he believes has monopolized human energy and gained the upper hand of knowledge. "In short," as he outlines it, first, "all the organs of sense are framed for a corresponding world of sense; and we have it." Yet in pursuing those senses exclusively we cannot help but become materialists. In contrast, "all the organs of spirit are framed for a correspondent world of spirit; tho' the latter organs are not developed in all alike. But they exist in all, and their first appearance discloses itself in the *moral* being." This moral being presupposes a spiritual ground of human life. In the same chapter of *Biographia Literaria*, Coleridge restates this idea by paraphrasing Schelling: "besides the language of words, there is a language of spirits (sermo interior) and . . . the former is only the vehicle of the latter" (*BL*, I, 242, 290). As early as 1805 Coleridge identifies the soul itself as an organ of spiritual or supersensuous perception (*SW & F* 154). The soul possesses the ability to modify and become one with ideas, connecting itself to the natural, external world through those ideas. In 1816, he conveys this with a strikingly poignant image: "At the annunciation" of supersensuous "*principles*, of *ideas*, the soul of man awakes, and starts up, as an exile in a far distant land at the unexpected sounds of his native language, when after long years of absence, and almost of oblivion, he is suddenly addressed in his own mother-tongue" (*SM* 24). Using the very line from Shakespeare's sonnets that John Livingston Lowes quotes from one of Coleridge's notebooks to launch discussion in *The Road to Xanadu*, Owen Barfield remarks that such a relationship between ideas and the soul is the foundation for what Coleridge "understands by method. Because ideas are the permanence and self-circling energies of reason, they are also in an almost literal sense 'the prophetic soul / of the wide world dreaming on things to come' and it is therefore only *their* presence in the mind that can give rise to a knowledge effective for the future as well as analytical of the past; and (which is much the same thing) only that which can produce any radically *new* knowledge."[13]

II

From such starting-points or postulates concerning the "organs of spirit" and "the language of spirits," as well as from Coleridge's belief in the "peculiar" nature of the human endowed with a soul, several points emerge:

(1) Everyone possesses a soul, which is something different and also something more than the mere sum of material senses and the mental operations we perform on the experiences that those material senses supply. Rather than derive the spiritual from models provided by physics, Lockean philosophy, or science, Coleridge concludes that "whatever originates its own acts, or in any sense contains in itself the cause of its own state, must be *spiritual,* and consequently *super-natural*; yet not on that account necessarily *miraculous*. And such must the responsible WILL in us be, if it be at all" (*AR* [*Aids to Reflection*] 251; see *Friend,* II, 79). If we follow *this* line of Coleridge's thought, we are not caught in the trap of using the soul as a bridge that must satisfy the traffic of science, philosophy, and religion all in the same one lane. Now the soul remains essentially outside the realm of science—science can neither find nor murder to dissect it. Yet the soul is able to subsume the results of science in order to inform human feeling and action, particularly to direct our moral being. Apparently unlike the poetic and philosophic imaginations, and unlike genius, the power of the soul is, at least in potential, in every human being. The soul is potentially democratic, with deep implications, as we shall touch on in a minute, for Coleridge's social and political thought. In his later career he highlights these concerns, bolstered by an emphasis on the will, the free agency of the soul to act.

(2) If we develop our spiritual organs, the soul will grow. This growth is by no means a new idea. It is found in Plato, and in earlier English writers well known to Coleridge,[14] and he stresses it constantly. By developing the spiritual organs, we shall realize our best selves, come to know our selves, and adopt a process, a continuing "method" of spiritual quest and pilgrimage, the all-important, ancient command "Know Thyself" (*BL,* I, 252, 291). This is Coleridge's plea on behalf of an organic vision of the human spirit. Even as he believes that the individual soul is inherently flawed, he also believes that it matures by a process of self-evolution or self-actualization, "a growth of consciousness," "a reflex consciousness of it's own continuousness" (*CL,* II, 1196, 1197).[15] The soul he thus describes "as a self-conscious personal Being" (*SW & F,* 427). Whatever is latent in the soul is what the self *might* become. The soul is "saved" in part by its own self-realization, which requires an act of will.

To foster this growth and realization is, in a significant way, the chief purpose of *Aids to Reflection.* Some of these ideas he seems to have met also in Fichte and Schelling, but the sense of process and growth in the soul marks much Romantic thought. It is clear that in this regard Coleridge influenced Emerson, not only through the Kantian distinction between reason and understanding in *The Friend,* but also through the Essays on Method there, and through *Aids to Reflection.* Coleridge's dialectical method informs the growth of the soul set out in Emerson's *Nature.*[16] Emerson's fourth chapter, "Language," ends by quoting Coleridge's *Aids to Reflection*: "Every object rightly seen, unlocks a new faculty of the soul." Coleridge also is the presiding spirit for passages on the soul in "Self-Reliance."[17] If J. H. Green could worry that readers might find Coleridge's science unacceptable, he also expresses, in his "Introduction to the Philosophical Remains of S. T. Coleridge," that Coleridge's philosophic thought at its best traces "the growth of the soul" (*SW & F* 1533) from its spring tide to the mature vision of the moral philosopher, a growth Green illustrates with quotations from Wordsworth, whose theme of the growth of the soul is his greatest and most original. This adds resonance to the name Wordsworth habitually employed for *The Prelude*: "the poem to Coleridge."

Like other contemporaneous thinkers (Keats, Blake, Wordsworth, Schiller, and Schelling), Coleridge conceives of the soul as organic and growing, not a static entity, nor one predestined for redemption or damnation. The soul registers—it constantly creates from within—the moral worth and fate of the individual. Coleridge seems to have this quality in mind when he refers to the "abidingness of the Soul" (*CM* [*Marginalia*], III, 39). Yet, while retaining this capacity, it is flawed with the potential for sin, for evil. Imagination cannot save the self from that flaw. Salvation comes from God, and to receive it the soul must be simultaneously open to experience and open to an inner realization of its own "moral being." This requires neither genius nor extraordinary imaginative power. This process of spiritual growth exists in humankind as well as in individuals, a topic that intrigues Coleridge (as it intrigues Kant and others) and constitutes one aim of the *Philosophical Lectures.* Again, in that seminal letter to Clarkson of 1806, Coleridge states that the "growth of reflex consciousness" in the individual soul "is not conceivable without the action of kindred souls on each other. . . . Man is truly altered by the co-existence of other men. . . . Therefore the human race not by a bold metaphor, but in a sublime reality, approach to, & might become, one body whose Head is Christ (the Logos)" (*CL,* II, 1197). The individual soul, then, develops in a community, and that community itself develops. In this respect, as Anthony Harding notes, "Coleridge shared with the Enlightenment thinkers their respect for science and scholarship and their trust in the ability of the human race to develop from infancy to maturity."[18]

Coleridge perhaps exerts his greatest influence in the nineteenth century in religious questions. During his lifetime and for decades afterward, his best-selling book is *Aids to Reflection*. His meditations on the soul anticipate many developments in theology of the next century and a half. He joins Schleiermacher, for example, in seeking the ultimate concern of human consciousness; scientific data can neither prove nor disprove its existence. No such proof exists for reason: it requires a personal act of self-constructive free will. Rudolf Bultmann later champions faith as a self-authenticating act of the soul. Coleridge also anticipates some elements of Kierkegaard's existentialism and of experiential approaches to Christianity; he speaks directly of "experimentative faith" (*AR* 9). Human history as bound up with the development of a collective human soul—the Holy Spirit in humankind—preoccupies Coleridge as it will Karl Barth. Another connection links Coleridge with Paul Tillich and the concept of "the ground of being," not surprising given Tillich's deep reading in Schelling. Yet sharp differences exist, too, between Coleridge and each of these thinkers. (For example, Schleiermacher's views on revelation are not the same as Coleridge's; Kierkegaard and Barth see a virtual gulf between the human and the divine, compared with Coleridge's belief in a much more intimate relationship—where the human has its being *in* the divine). While Coleridge's influence on religious thought in Britain is well recognized, a full study of Coleridge's theological work and speculation in light of later European developments waits to be written.[19] Among other sources, the later *Notebooks* would provide considerable material.

(3) Language at its best is more than a vehicle to express direct sensations and mental reflections on the ideas formed by objects of sense. Originally, the language of words is a vehicle of the organs of spirit, of inner spiritual life: it is language that humanizes the universe and connects it to the human spirit. For Coleridge, then, true poetic language does not rest in so-called poetic diction or in wrangles over vocabulary and decorum, as much as in the imagery and music and rhythm capable of expressing the inner drama of the soul as it encounters the world at a particular time and place and in a particular mood. Both a realistic psychological dimension and a spiritual sensibility are at work, a duality pertinent to the original plan for *Lyrical Ballads,* and to *The Rime of the Ancient Mariner* in particular. The poems in *Lyrical Ballads* would deal with the commerce between natural and supernatural. Beyond this, the vehicle of language is, or at least can be, the instrument of free will and the soul's free agency, and hence of spiritual and political freedom. Certain great poets are justifiably linked with ideas of liberty. One of them, Milton, likens a book to the soul. Coleridge states, in his famous definition, that "the poet, described in *ideal* perfection, brings the whole soul of

man into activity." But it is also helpful to recall his claim that the whole of his literary criticism in *Biographia* is tied to principles in "Politics, Religion, and Philosophy" (*BL,* II, 15-16; I, 5).

(4) In *The Statesman's Manual* and *A Lay Sermon,* Coleridge posits that not only individual salvation and liberty but social justice and right government ultimately depend on an understanding of, and a reverence for, the soul. Governments must respect and encourage its intrinsic moral worth and its potential for growth. Those gifted or privileged enough to enjoy the leisure and education necessary to develop the language of the spirit and the growth of the soul are expected to foster and encourage this attitude. They are the clerisy. If everyone cannot exercise creative imagination, everyone does possess a soul and the power of free will. Society and its institutions should protect and awaken these potentials of the spirit.

Coleridge's claim has practical economic and social consequences, ones not properly or purely utilitarian. His principles here are simple and profound. They inform Mill's remark that the two greatest presences of his age are Bentham and Coleridge. Coleridge's claim, fully exemplified in *A Lay Sermon* and *On the Constitution of Church and State,* that his political principles derive from religious principles, is cogent. He argues for it with passion because it is true. His idea of the soul does not lead him to espouse pure democracy, but he insists on genuine safeguards against exploitation and oppression. We can recall his long-standing, vehement opposition to the slave trade (his Greek ode on the subject won a prize at Cambridge). He repeatedly and explicitly connects slavery with slavery of the soul. He harbors a prescient fear that industrialization will treat the modern laborer as a soulless person, a commodity used to produce commodities. As early as 1795, he puts labor exploitation in these terms: "those institutions of society which should condemn me to the necessity of twelve hours daily toil, would make my *soul* a slave, and sink *the rational* being in the mere animal" (*Lects 1795* [*Lectures 1795: On Politics and Religion*] 11). Later, with regard to Napoleon, he protests that the public degrades itself "in an inward prostration of the soul before enormous POWER." The Irish, he notes, could have been "firm and able friends," but were treated so ill that they became "a people, into whose souls the <Iron-> ferocity of slaves had at last entered" (*EOT* [*Essays on His Times*], II, 75; III, 240). He displays acute understanding of the oppressive forces that are identified, blasted, and ridiculed by others from Blake to Charlie Chaplin to Marcuse. In middle age, Coleridge agitates for the passage of child labor laws.

III

The Rime of the Ancient Mariner recounts the Mariner's odyssey and trial of soul. About that the poem is explicit, though very few critics are.[20] Coleridge composes it within a year or so of Wordsworth's "Tintern Abbey" and the Prospectus to *The Excursion,* both of which dramatize the wonder of becoming a "living soul"—"an impulse to herself." The text indicates that the theme of Coleridge's poem centers in the soul. To see this we do not even need to accord crucial importance to the Albatross hailed "as if it had been a Christian soul" (65), or to the bird that "made the breeze to blow" (94). As in the **Eolian Harp,** the opening of *The Prelude,* and other Romantic poems, the soul is associated with a correspondent breeze between the natural world and the interior self: *anima,* breath, inspiration, spirit, soul. The death of two hundred sailors prompts this image: "The souls did from their bodies fly . . . And every soul, it passed me by, / Like the whizz of my cross-bow" (220, 222-223). In these instances, "soul" might seem a stock term, despite the fact that identifying it with the Albatross is significant. But at this very point in the poem, the Mariner is left "Alone, alone, all, all alone"; in this state he says, "never a saint took pity on / My soul in agony" (232, 234-235). By its root sense, agony denotes a struggle, as for a prize. In 1827, Coleridge refers to prayer itself as a "wrestling" (*Notebook* 34, ff. 10-12). The prize in the **Rime** is a soul remade—or trying to remake itself.

This plight of subjective self-enclosure, of remorse, existential agony, and despair, changes, or at least seems to change, precisely when his soul is freed by love. The Mariner watches "God's creatures of the great calm" (gloss at 272) and, in awe of their beauty and happiness, he cannot speak, he has yet *no* power of speech. Then, suddenly, "A spring of love gushed from my heart, / And I blessed them unaware" (284-285). It is at this moment that "Sure my kind saint took pity on me" (286). Even if we find "Sure" less than reassuring, we should note that in *Aids to Reflection,* Coleridge explicitly states, "The best, the most *Christianlike* pity thou canst show, is to take pity on thy own soul" (*AR* 53). And at this moment the Mariner ceases, at least in one sense, to be alone: "The self-same moment I could pray" (288). He can now communicate with God; the Albatross falls from his neck, like lead, into the sea. A gentle sleep, he reports, slid "into my soul" (296), and rain revives his body. If the lines near the beginning of Part V are read with the idea in mind, it will not seem far-fetched that the Mariner's soul experiences rebirth in this sleep: "—almost / I thought that I had died in sleep . . ." (306-307).

Returning, the Mariner meets the "Hermit good," who habitually sings godly hymns in the forest. The Mariner's hope concerning the hermit is simple and direct: "He'll shrieve my soul, he'll wash away / The Albatross's blood" (512-513). The shriving involves a continual repeating of the Mariner's tale; he turns poet, and his soul is shriven not only by a priest but by the

telling of his story. This also means that the Mariner's identity, his self-realization, tortured as it is, can finally be exposed. For, when he says, "'O shrieve me, shrieve me, holy man!'" (574), the hermit asks the question of spiritual identity: "'What manner of man art thou?'" This is, in the profound sense, a *personal* question. It is to our wholeness as persons that Coleridge so often points. Mary Anne Perkins ventures that he "believed immortality belonged to *persons,* rather than to rational souls,"[21] an observation confirmed at least once, in the long, late *Notebook* entry on the nature of the soul. There Coleridge says that what is at stake is not the resuscitation "of a Soul or Spirit but *of the Man*" (*CN,* IV, 5377). Facing the hermit's personal question, the Mariner, the person whose "soul hath been / Alone on a wide wide sea" (597-598), gains strange power of speech. He begins to repeat his tale, communicating to others his story, his own identity, and the lesson of "love and reverence to all things" (gloss at 610).

This love, reminiscent of the love that gushed from his heart unaware when he blessed the water creatures (who presumably do not have souls), indicates a primacy of love above reason, higher even than the conscious will.[22] It is at this moment of love, too, that the kind saint takes pity on him. Despite repeatedly quoting from Milton that the soul "reason receives, and reason is her being," Coleridge revisits this idea and concludes instead "that there is an Antecedent even to the Reason and that his Name is *Love*" (*Notebook* 41, f. 12). This is Christ.

In a marginal note to copy H of *Aids to Reflection,* a note written in or after 1825, Coleridge ventures ideas remarkably and eerily pertinent to the Mariner's love of the snakes and his newfound ability to pray, and to the God who "made and loveth all." Coleridge writes, "I would be satisfied to love the Creator in the Creatures, provided *I* love the creatures . . . *chiefly* in reference to the Creator, and as excitements of gratitude to him. . . . God is a pure Act: and it can only be in the purest Acts of the Soul that the Love of God can have its essential Being. . . . Lastly the answer can only be rightly sought for in prayer." To repeat, before the Mariner loved the snakes, no saint "took pity on / My Soul"; afterward, "Sure my kind saint took pity on me," and the Mariner finds that he can pray, and prayer is reaffirmed at the end of the poem (596, 606). (Whatever one thinks of the stated "moral" of the poem, it is often overlooked that it inextricably links the act of love with the act of prayer, and that prayer is not only an act of individual will but an act enabled by God.) In the same long note to *Aids* just quoted, Coleridge expresses revulsion that, despite being lovers of God, men of the Inquisition, when carried away by zealotry, lacked "all feeling of pity" (*AR* 213n). The question remains, though, does the Mariner ever take pity on his own soul, "the most Christianlike pity thou canst show"? He seems inwardly stuttering to voice spiritual self-knowledge but, despite his power of speech, never fully articulating it.

In a manner, then, that is *not* particularly understandable or reasonable—and perhaps why Coleridge jokingly intimates that the poem is "incomprehensible" (*BL,* I, 28*)—the *Rime* enacts one realization of love, love "Antecedent even to the Reason," love linked to prayer. Elsewhere, Coleridge suggests that original sin itself is an abstract excess of the unbalanced "rational instinct" (*SM* 61) over the affective. As J. Robert Barth remarks in his study of the poet's religious thought, "For Coleridge, as for St. John and for Dante, the last thing of all is love,"[23] meaning, in the context here, that love is also the first thing.

The *Rime* dramatizes several elements of Coleridge's thought about the soul: inner spiritual awareness, love, prayer, and suffering both merited and unmerited. The narrative seems to reveal the power of the soul to grow, to seek its way out of the worst existential loneliness. (Presumably, the Mariner prefers his perpetual wandering and tale-telling to remaining all alone on the ocean, even though, at least briefly, he has the community in the kirk.) As elsewhere in Coleridge's thought, the act of prayer—one version of "a language of spirits"—links the soul to God. The Mariner is enjoined to take up the haunted task of telling his story in order to awaken in others the organs of the spirit and the "language of spirits." Each time his agony returns, he retells the tale and attempts, once again, to remake his own soul. The soul in its agony seeks the prize of atonement, which Coleridge regards, in plausible, though not original, etymological terms, as at+one+ment (*SM* 55; see *CM,* III, 47n).

Yet, ever since Leslie Stephen's comments on the poem, it is hardly news to say that the *Rime* appears to have too easy a moral,[24] one that, paradoxically, the narrative cannot easily justify, and it has become common to cite Coleridge's own dissatisfaction with it (*TT,* I, 272-273). If the Mariner is saved, it is a curious salvation: there is much unjust suffering, others die, and the traumas seem endless. Even granting that love comes before reason, the Mariner's love seems inexplicably spontaneous, not a product of the conscious will but simply of looking at the snakes intently. It is grace, and, if so, what kind of grace?[25] His agony of retelling the tale is forced on him; after horrors mount and subside, the Mariner is doomed to an agonizing, repetitive existence that no one would envy. It is hard to accept the story as fully unified, and there seems no moral or spiritual resolution.[26]

Part of the explanation for the Mariner's repeated agony is frequently put in terms of guilt, and certainly what is called "survivor's guilt" is also at work. To this is often added remorse, "the *implicit* Creed of the Guilty" (*AR* 128). Coleridge himself is, of course, often wracked with guilt, for instance, when he confesses to his brother George how his own behavior led to a desperate enlistment in the army: "my soul sickens at it's own guilt" (*CL,* I, 74; see I, 65). But making the Mariner into Coleridge, although virtually authorized, is too common an interpretive mode.[27] Besides, if the Mariner feels guilty, Coleridge himself could counter that, through Christ, sin is "no longer imputable as *Guilt*" (*AR,* 310*).[28]

Thinking of Cain or the Wandering Jew as a precursor to the Mariner is another option, but no one ploy gives the poem the satisfying unity that many readers find lacking. Many discordant qualities remain. In fact, the idea of poetry as potentially *discordant* is one Coleridge encounters when Wordsworth rejects *Christabel.* Coleridge writes in October 1800 that Wordsworth has recently rejected the poem as "disproportionate both in size & merit, & as discordant in it's character.—" Wordsworth had the same word in mind, too, for he wrote the publisher of the 1800 edition that, regarding *Christabel,* "the Style . . . was so discordant from my own that it could not be printed along with my poems with any propriety" (*CL,* I, 643 and n.). Whether in the *Rime* or in his relations with Wordsworth over the rejection of *Christabel,* "discordant" for Coleridge could harbor significant resonances.

A return to the idea of reconciliation rather than unity may prove fruitful. When Coleridge describes the poet as bringing "the whole soul of man into activity," a remark noted above, he does not then say that the poet unifies every faculty and quality in question. While the poet diffuses a "spirit of unity," the power of imagination does not necessarily reveal itself in final unity, but rather "in the balance or reconciliation of opposite or discordant qualities" (*BL,* II, 16). There is that word discordant again. Now, the *Rime* is a poem Coleridge calls "a work of pure imagination" (*TT,* I, 273n), and so we might expect a balance or reconciling of opposite or discordant qualities. This emerges, too, in the way Coleridge glosses the power of the imagination in the Scriptures: "that reconciling and mediatory power" (*SM* 29). If the Mariner's tale offers one moral that is too neat while any other seems inscrutable, if no clear unity seems to arise from the poem, its deeper imaginative and moral power rests in a constant activity—a compulsion almost as great as the one driving the Mariner—of reconciliation and mediation.[29] For the Mariner, it is a task apparently never completed, as it may also be for the reader. Passing from "land to land," the Mariner is that figure of the soul: "an exile in a far distant land," an image of human agony and hope.

IV

In his consideration of the soul, Coleridge tries to reconcile and mediate, not strictly to unify, natural philosophy, science, psychology, moral philosophy, political economy, and all these together with theology. It is significant that he ends the "Theory of Life" with mention of the soul, and again claims for it a supernatural and primary quality. "Nature did not assist" when "her sovereign Master" finally "made Man in his own image, by superadding self-consciousness and self-government, and breathed into him a living soul." The final words are, literally, "concerning the Soul, as the principle both of Reason and Conscience" (*SW & F* 550, 557). Beginnings and endings are revealing. Coleridge begins *The Friend* with an epigraph, an invocation to the soul (I, 2), and he closes *Biographia* with the image of the "Soul . . . in its pure *Act* of inward Adoration to the great I AM, and to the filial WORD that re-affirmeth it from Eternity to Eternity, whose choral Echo is the Universe" (*BL*, II, 247-248).

Alfred North Whitehead once remarked that we should seek not only to learn what Plato thought, but also to imagine what he would think were he alive today. Since Coleridge's death, the theory of Darwinian evolution has become widely accepted. Though many variations of it exist and scientists disagree about its operation, the mass of evidence securely supports it. What would Coleridge think today if he were to confront this fact? He might continue to hold that the soul was at some time in the creation implanted or breathed into human life by divine fiat. Or, he might view that fiat itself more as a process than as an instant of realization, a process directed and sanctioned by the divine. He might elaborate on his numerous suggestions that not only the individual soul but also the idea of the soul in the human race does evolve. After all, he credits Thales and Plato with realizations about the soul that no previous thinker had entertained. If that is so, then there would be no reason why later realizations might not contribute more. Even as we understand more about the origins of the human in nature, we might also understand better what does seem to separate us from other forms of life, even if that separation arose over time rather than in a flash. Coleridge might employ a more elaborate argument from the "Analogy of Being" and modify his proto-evolutionary thinking about life to include an explicitly Darwinian sense of change in species.[30] Thinking about such evolution might lead to a greater realization of the peculiar nature of the human. It is a tricky proposition, but Coleridge's sense of process and his conviction about organic growth in the soul, in the soul of the individual and of humanity at large, might fairly be applied to an idea of the self-realization of the soul over long periods of biological time. At any event, it is hard to imagine that Coleridge, facing the issue, would become reactionary.

Entering into an agonized contest with the spiritual crises and dehumanizations of his era, as well as with its accompanying fragmentation of knowledge, Coleridge displays such penetration, often in a sentence or phrase, that his struggles, false starts, self-doubt, and contradictions are punctuated with soaring insights and hope. Spiritual life remains for him always a personal struggle uphill, not an Olympian survey. He starts, after all, with some remarkable attitudes. In 1787, only fourteen, he writes in one of his first preserved letters, jocularly but a little dismissively, to his brother Luke, "Heaven would not be large enough to hold all the souls of all men, who have ever liv'd" (*CL*, I, 2). He quips almost a decade later to John Thelwall that "Ferriar believes in a *Soul,* like an orthodox Churchman—So much for Physicians & Surgeons" (*CL*, I, 295). He lives his own odyssey, his own self-realization, his own agony. This experience is at once the strength and the vulnerability of his genius. He is a reconciling and mediatory spiritual thinker, and the spiritual dimension comes to suffuse all his thought. Convincing or not, the position is deeply, personally earned. One reason that Coleridge continues to attract so many readers is that the world and our knowledge of it, as well as our realization of what it means to be human in that world, seem ever to present us with more, rather than less, to reconcile and to mediate.

As with other ideas vital to Coleridge—the mystery of language, the imagination, the nature of idea, image, and symbol—no one passage sets out fully what he means by the soul. From this seminal idea other ideas evolve and are generated. He treats the soul as if it were as real as the marrow of the bones or the translucent lens of the eye. Light, vision, and reflection are metaphors for the soul's being, perception, and exercise (see Beer, *AR* xciv-xcvi). The soul is an organ of spirit, and among all "organs of spirit" it is primary. To learn its method, its "language of spirits," is to acquire a strange power of speech, and to begin a journey in which language leads not only to knowledge of the world but also to knowledge of the self. For Coleridge, then, as Stephen Prickett concludes, "words are living powers *because* they are the tools of self-knowledge."[31] When Coleridge draws up early plans for a "philosophical" dictionary, which would, through the mediation of his grandson Herbert Coleridge, eventually become the *Oxford English Dictionary,* he notes that such a dictionary should treat "words as living growths, offlets, and organs of the human soul" (*Logic* 126). Especially in the study of language, he urges, it is vital to attend to the method of the soul, to the agonies it suffers, and to the story it cannot choose but tell.

Notes

1. Rev. of *Nature's Enigma: The Problem of the Polyp in the Letters of Bonnet, Trembley and Réaumur,* by Virginia P. Dawson, *Eighteenth-Century Studies* 24 (1991): 518.

2. Parenthetical citations are to standard editions of Coleridge's collected works, letters, and notebooks

(see list of Works Cited). Abbreviations are: *Aids to Reflection* (AR); *Biographia Literaria* (BL); *Collected Letters* (CL); *Essays on His Times* (EOT); *A Lay Sermon* (LS); *Lectures 1795: On Politics and Religion* (Lects 1795); *Lectures 1808-1819: On Literature* (Lects 1808-1819); *Lectures 1818-1819: On the History of Philosophy* (Lects 1818-1819); *Marginalia* (CM); *Notebooks* (CN); *Shorter Works and Fragments* (SW & F); *The Statesman's Manual* in *LS* above (SM); *Table Talk* (TT).

3. Douglas Hedley, *Coleridge, Philosophy and Religion: "Aids to Reflection" and the Mirror of the Spirit* (Cambridge, 2000) 97-99, 105-116, 160-161. Hedley throughout pays close attention to the idea of the soul and traces in detail Coleridge's knowledge of it in earlier thinkers.

4. W. J. Bate, *Coleridge* (New York, 1968) 194-195. Bate points out Coleridge's difficulties in accounting for the special nature of the human and ventures that, on that very point, "The essay falls apart" (195).

5. *Coleridge as Religious Thinker* (New Haven, 1961) 163.

6. *Coleridge's Defense of the Human* (Columbus, 1986) 163.

7. H. J. Jackson, "Coleridge's Collaborator, Joseph Henry Green," *Studies in Romanticism* 21 (1982): 178.

8. For general discussion, see Hans Eichner, "The Rise of Modern Science and the Genesis of Romanticism," *PMLA* 97.1 (1982): 8-30.

9. *Selected Writings,* ed. and trans. H. P. Rickman (Cambridge, 1976) 122-130. Dilthey states: "no metaphysics can satisfy the demand for a scientific proof," arguing that while philosophy retains its respective valences in science, in the search for meaning, and in the study of human conduct, it can not unify these: "We can notice, as it were, only one side of our relationship" to the world at a time (123).

10. *Coleridge and Wordsworth: The Poetry of Growth* (Cambridge, 1970) 181.

11. Anthony John Harding, *Coleridge and the Inspired Word* (Kingston and Montreal, 1985) 39.

12. For excellent treatment of the tension inherent in Coleridge's search for unity amidst his recognition of diversity, see Seamus Perry, *Coleridge and the Uses of Division* (Oxford, 1999). Perry emphasizes Coleridge's attempts at reconciliation in his literary criticism (233-274), but the theme is apparent throughout, including on the subject of religion.

13. *What Coleridge Thought* (Middletown, 1971) 119.

14. For example, see Patricia Meyer Spacks, "The Soul's Imaginings: Daniel Defoe, William Cowper," *PMLA* 91 (1976): 420-435. Spacks sees growth and self-realization taking place in Crusoe's soul (429). Connections between Coleridge's Mariner and Crusoe are well established. Coleridge read Defoe's book as a child.

15. Although he does not dwell specifically on the soul, for treatment of moral growth and realization of the self, see Laurence S. Lockridge, *Coleridge the Moralist* (Ithaca, 1977) 146-198.

16. See Barry Wood, "The Growth of the Soul: Coleridge's Dialectical Method and the Strategy of Emerson's *Nature*," *PMLA* 91 (1976): 385-397. Wood credits Coleridge with "most profound" influence (388) and argues that Coleridge's method of the soul "duplicated the process of the mind during its organic assimilation of the universe" (395), a dialectical method that Emerson adopts.

17. See David Vallins, "Self-Reliance: Individualism in Emerson and Coleridge," *Symbiosis* 5 (2001): 51-68, esp 59.

18. *Inspired Word* 38.

19. For suggestive remarks on various connections with later theologians, see J. Robert Barth, S. J., *Coleridge and Christian Doctrine* (1969; New York, 1987) 196-198. Among other things, Barth underscores Coleridge's prescient ability to grapple with "the old radical discontinuity between the natural and the supernatural" (196); see also Claude Welch, *Protestant Thought in the Nineteenth Century,* 2 vols. (New Haven, 1972), I, 108-126. Hedley (291-300) sees chiefly a "surface affinity" among Coleridge, Kierkegaard, and Barth, and stresses key differences. Still, while their answers sometimes differ, the questions are frequently the same.

20. See James Engell, "The Soul, Highest Cast of Consciousness," *The Cast of Consciousness: Concepts of the Mind in British and American Romanticism,* ed. Beverly Taylor and Robert Bain (New York, 1987) 8-9; also J. Robert Barth, S. J., "'A Spring of Love': Prayer and Blessing in Coleridge's *Rime of the Ancient Mariner,*" *The Wordsworth Circle* 30 (1999): 75-80. Barth writes: "In the poem, clearly the struggle is acute and for very high stakes: the Mariner's very soul" (78).

21. *Coleridge's Philosophy: The Logos as Unifying Principle* (Oxford, 1994) 225.

22. See John Beer, *Coleridge's Poetic Intelligence* (London, 1977) 160-161; also J. Robert Barth, S. J., *Coleridge and the Power of Love* (Columbia, Mo., 1988) 61-75.

23. Barth, *Doctrine* 195.

24. The objections heat up with E. E. Bostetter, "The Nightmare World of *The Ancient Mariner*," *Studies in Romanticism* 1 (1962): 241-254. He states that Robert Penn Warren's famous 1946 interpretation of crime, punishment, love, and redemption "entirely ignores the capricious and irrational elements in the universe of *The Ancient Mariner*" (244). George Watson, *Coleridge the Poet* (London, 1966), insists that the moral is the Mariner's, not Coleridge's, and that "The truth of the poem . . . is a dramatic truth" (99).

25. For grace as habitual, actual, or prevenient, see Barth, *Doctrine* 148-149 and note.

26. See Stephen Prickett, *Romanticism and Religion* (Cambridge, 1976) 16-17; also Lockridge 145, and Perry 281-291.

27. I realize, however, that, as most critics do, I am reading the poem through the index and context of an interpretation of Coleridge's thought expressed outside the poem, an interpretation with justifications but also liabilities. See David Perkins, "The *Ancient Mariner* and Its Interpreters: Some Versions of Coleridge," *Modern Language Quarterly* 57 (1996): 425-448.

28. For treatment generally, see David Miall, "Guilt and Death: The Predicament of the Ancient Mariner," *Studies in English Literature, 1500-1900* 24 (1984): 633-653.

29. Although not relying on the characterization of the imagination as a reconciling and mediatory power, David Jasper, "The Two Worlds of Coleridge's *The Rime of the Ancient Mariner*," *An Infinite Complexity: Essays in Romanticism,* ed. J. R. Watson (Edinburgh, 1983) 125-144, sees two worlds in the poem not compatible with each other, and calls upon the imagination to "focus and bring coherence to the different levels of experience" (140).

30. For a related discussion, see Anthony John Harding, "Coleridge, Natural History, and the 'Analogy of Being,'" *History of European Ideas* 26 (2000): 143-158. Harding explores Coleridge's "attempt to show how the findings of contemporary science might support a philosophical account of a rationally ordered universe" (143). While recognizing that Coleridge's view is not "Darwinian," Harding explores how Coleridge regards the unique nature of humanity as analogous to—and therefore connected with—other forms of being (152). Yet human life, the soul, "needs to be actualized" (156) in a manner not shared by other beings.

31. *Poetry of Growth* 197.

Works Cited

Barfield, Owen. *What Coleridge Thought.* Middletown: Wesleyan University Press, 1971.

Barth, J. Robert, S. J. *Coleridge and Christian Doctrine.* 1969. New York: Fordham University Press, 1987.

———. *Coleridge and the Power of Love.* Columbia: University of Missouri Press, 1988.

———. "'A Spring of Love': Prayer and Blessing in Coleridge's *Rime of the Ancient Mariner.*" *The Wordsworth Circle* 30 (1999): 75-80.

Bate, W. J. *Coleridge.* New York: Macmillan, 1968.

Beer, John. *Coleridge's Poetic Intelligence.* London: Macmillan, 1977.

Bostetter, E. E. "The Nightmare World of *The Ancient Mariner.*" *Studies in Romanticism* 1 (1962): 241-254.

Boulger, James D. *Coleridge as Religious Thinker.* New Haven: Yale University Press, 1961.

Coleridge, Samuel Taylor. *Aids to Reflection.* Ed. John Beer. Princeton: Princeton University Press, 1993. *CC* [*The Collected Works of Samuel Taylor Coleridge*] Vol. IX.

———. *Biographia Literaria.* Ed. James Engell and W. J. Bate. 2 vols. Princeton: Princeton University Press, 1983. *CC* Vol. VII.

———. *The Collected Letters of Samuel Taylor Coleridge.* Ed. Earl Leslie Griggs. 6 vols. Oxford: Clarendon Press, 1956-1971.

———. *The Collected Works of Samuel Taylor Coleridge.* Ed. Kathleen Coburn. 16 vols. Bollingen Series 75. Princeton: Princeton University Press, 1969-. Cited as *CC*.

———. *Essays on His Times.* Ed. David V. Erdman. 3 vols. Princeton: Princeton University Press, 1978. *CC* Vol. III.

———. *The Friend.* Ed. Barbara E. Rooke. 2 vols. Princeton: Princeton University Press, 1969. *CC* Vol. IV.

———. *Lay Sermons.* Ed. R. J. White. Princeton: Princeton University Press, 1972. *CC* Vol. VI.

———. *Lectures 1795: On Politics and Religion.* Ed. Lewis Patton and Peter Mann. Princeton: Princeton University Press, 1971. *CC* Vol. I.

———. *Lectures 1808-1819: On Literature.* Ed. Reginald A. Foakes. 2 vols. Princeton: Princeton University Press, 1984. *CC* Vol. V.

———. *Lectures 1818-1819: On the History of Philosophy.* Ed. J. R. de J. Jackson. 2 vols. Princeton: Princeton University Press, 2000. *CC* Vol. VIII.

————. *Logic.* Ed. J. R. de J. Jackson. Princeton: Princeton University Press, 1980. *CC* Vol. XIII.

————. *Marginalia.* Ed. H. J. Jackson and George Whalley. 5 vols. to date. Princeton: Princeton University Press, 1980-. *CC* Vol. XII.

————. *The Notebooks of Samuel Taylor Coleridge.* Ed. Kathleen Coburn. 4 vols. to date. Bollingen Series 50. Princeton: Princeton University Press, 1955-.

————. *Shorter Works and Fragments.* Ed. H. J. Jackson and J. R. de J. Jackson. 2 vols. Princeton: Princeton University Press, 1995. *CC* Vol. XI.

————. *Table Talk.* Ed. Carl Woodring. 2 vols. Princeton: Princeton University Press, 1990. *CC* Vol. XIV.

Dilthey, Wilhelm. *Selected Writings.* Ed. and trans. H. P. Rickman. Cambridge: Cambridge University Press, 1976.

Eichner, Hans. "The Rise of Modern Science and the Genesis of Romanticism." *PMLA* 97.1 (1982): 8-30.

Engell, James. "The Soul, Highest Cast of Consciousness." *The Cast of Consciousness: Concepts of the Mind in British and American Romanticism.* Ed. Beverly Taylor and Robert Bain. New York: Greenwood, 1987. 3-19.

Harding, Anthony John. *Coleridge and the Inspired Word.* Kingston and Montreal: McGill-Queen's University Press, 1985.

————. "Coleridge, Natural History, and the 'Analogy of Being.'" *History of European Ideas* 26 (2000): 143-158.

Hedley, Douglas. *Coleridge, Philosophy and Religion: "Aids to Reflection" and the Mirror of the Spirit.* Cambridge: Cambridge University Press, 2000.

Jackson, H. J. "Coleridge's Collaborator, Joseph Henry Green." *Studies in Romanticism* 21 (1982): 161-179.

Jasper, David. "The Two Worlds of Coleridge's *The Rime of the Ancient Mariner.*" *An Infinite Complexity: Essays in Romanticism.* Ed. J. R. Watson. Edinburgh: Edinburgh University Press for the University of Durham, 1983. 125-144.

Ilie, Paul. Rev. of *Nature's Enigma: The Problem of the Polyp in the Letters of Bonnet, Trembley and Réaumur,* by Virginia P. Dawson. *Eighteenth-Century Studies* 24 (1991): 516-518.

Lockridge, Laurence. *Coleridge the Moralist.* Ithaca: Cornell University Press, 1977.

Miall, David. "Guilt and Death: The Predicament of the Ancient Mariner." *Studies in English Literature, 1500-1900* 24 (1984): 633-653.

Perkins, David. "The *Ancient Mariner* and Its Interpreters: Some Versions of Coleridge." *Modern Language Quarterly* 57 (1996): 425-448.

Perkins, Mary Anne. *Coleridge's Philosophy: The Logos as Unifying Principle.* Oxford: Clarendon Press, 1994.

Perry, Seamus. *Coleridge and the Uses of Division.* Oxford: Clarendon Press, 1999.

Prickett, Stephen. *Coleridge and Wordsworth: The Poetry of Growth.* Cambridge: Cambridge University Press, 1970.

————. *Romanticism and Religion.* Cambridge: Cambridge University Press, 1976.

Spacks, Patricia Meyer. "The Soul's Imaginings: Daniel Defoe, William Cowper." *PMLA* 91 (1976): 420-435.

Taylor, Anya. *Coleridge's Defense of the Human.* Columbus: Ohio State University Press, 1986.

Vallins, David. "Self-Reliance: Individualism in Emerson and Coleridge." *Symbiosis* 5 (2001): 51-68.

Watson, George. *Coleridge the Poet.* London: Routledge & Kegan Paul, 1966.

Welch, Claude. *Protestant Thought in the Nineteenth Century.* 2 vols. New Haven: Yale University Press, 1972.

Wood, Barry. "The Growth of the Soul: Coleridge's Dialectical Method and the Strategy of Emerson's *Nature.*" *PMLA* 91 (1976): 385-397.

Peter Melville (essay date fall 2004)

SOURCE: Melville, Peter. "Coleridge's *The Rime of the Ancient Mariner.*" *Explicator* 63, no. 1 (fall 2004): 15-18.

[*In the following essay, Melville ruminates on the idea of hospitality in* The Ancient Mariner, *specifically discussing the Wedding Guest's decision—whether willed or not—to forego the nuptial festivities in favor of listening to the Mariner's tale.*]

Not unlike the surprise visit of Coleridge's famous Porlockian caller in the preface to **Kubla Khan,** the Mariner's unwelcome arrival at the door of a great wedding banquet in **The Rime of the Ancient Mariner** signals the presence of Coleridge's recurring, yet frequently overlooked, interest in the limits of hospitality. Narratively and chronologically speaking, the first mention of hospitality in **Rime** occurs in the 1800 version of the "Argument," in which Coleridge relates "how the Ancient Mariner cruelly and in contempt of the laws of hospitality killed a Sea-bird" (**PW** [**Coleridge: Poetical Works**] 186n3). Although the main body of the poem does not mention the theme of the hospitable by name, the marginal gloss added in 1815-16 mentions it at least twice more, first with the descriptor "a great sea-bird, called the Albatross, came through the snow-fog, and was received with great joy and hospitality" (*PW* 188), and again in a moment of crisis, "The Ancient Mariner inhospitably killeth the pious bird of good omen" (*PW* 188). It bears mentioning that the initial good will toward the Albatross calls to mind at least one of the limits of hospitality—namely, the tendency of a host to welcome the familiar over and against the strange. As Paul Magnuson argues, in the "nightmarish" landscape of *Rime,* the Albatross "is the one familiar sight," and it is on this account that the "great bird" receives a friendly "Christian" welcome (59). The poem, thus, implicitly raises questions concerning the nature of competing obligations: Where do the Mariner's obligations lie in the end, with the familiar or with the strange and the unknown? Questioning the subtle politics behind a decision to welcome one person or thing over another is, I argue, one of the poem's most crucial, albeit most understated, lines of inquiry.

The Mariner's predilection for the known over the unknown is, interestingly, reversed in the curiously troubled hospitality scene housed by the poem's "Wedding Guest" framework. Faced with conflicting obligations of his own, the Wedding Guest must likewise choose between the strange and the familiar—or, rather, between the strange and the *familial.* As an honored invitee—indeed, as the Bridegroom's "next of kin" (line 6)—the Wedding Guest has a special obligation to join the festivities. It would be rude for him not to arrive. To be sure, he knows this only too well, feeling, as he does, the tremendous pull of his familial duties: "[B]eat-[ing] his breast" (37), he implores the Mariner to "Hold off" and "unhand" him (11). But the Mariner, in a gesture that once more calls to mind the imposition of a certain Porlockian caller, manages to oblige and "detaineth" the Wedding Guest long enough for him to miss the ceremony altogether (5). The Mariner must simply unburden himself by telling his tale, but he can only do so at the expense of another person kind enough to entertain him. Strangely, in this moment, the Wedding Guest transforms from a guest to a host who turns to the peculiar and unfamiliar old Mariner and, "spellbound" by a most commanding obligation, gives this stranger an especially long moment of his time (*PW* 187). More specifically, his will imposed on him by the Mariner's mesmeric "glittering eye" (13), the Wedding Guest is held hostage, as it were, in his *host*age of the Mariner's tale—a predicament that only reinforces the notion that hospitality and *host*ility are often two sides of the same coin.

Anthony Harding, who describes the Wedding Guest scene in the specific terms of "love," understands the scene as a contest between what he calls the "easy

sociability" of the wedding festivities (which, he claims, can become a "prison," trapping love "within an artificially enclosed world") and the more difficult act of love that brings the Mariner and the Wedding Guest together in their precariously sustained communion (65). In essence, the Wedding Guest is obliged to choose one form of hospitality at the expense of another. Should he listen to this Ancient Mariner who is compelled to teach him a lesson—one that will be realized simply in the listening—by choosing to welcome the Mariner's strange tale over the familiar sounds of the wedding feast? (The Mariner is, after all, the Wedding Guest's albatross of sorts. Were he to join his fellow celebrants, he would, in effect, be slaying a great sea bird of his own, thus confirming the tragedy of the Mariner's tale.) Or should he follow his initial instinct to forsake the Mariner and thrash him with his stick: "my staff shall make you skip" (13, 1798)? What looks like a breech of hospitality on the part of the Mariner's detaining the Wedding Guest is, in fact, another form of hospitality that competes with and, as the poem relates, overcomes the hospitality of the wedding festival—albeit not without the hostile mesmerism of the Mariner's glittering eye.

My interest in this competition, however, is not simply to evaluate the merits and shortcomings of either choice as Harding does. The choice that the Wedding Guest does make, or that he is *forced* to make (i.e., to listen to the Mariner's tale), does indeed counterbalance the inhospitable slaying of the Albatross, insofar as he refuses to refuse his would-be interlocutor, his spectral visitor. But the merits of the choice are only relative to the harm it causes. Could it not be argued that the Wedding Guest simply embraces the lesser evil, or that Coleridge's interest in the obligatory nature of the Wedding Guest's choice (i.e., his spellbound inability to refuse) is to question the violence of obligation as such? As "next of kin," the Wedding Guest's presence will surely be missed. His decision will no doubt cause a certain amount of grief. Could it not be suggested (*without* being facetious) that the more difficult decision might have been to choose the banquet, leaving the Mariner to his "agony" (583)? *Tête-à-tête* encounters do, after all, command a significant, even hypnotic, power over a person, obliging that person to respond. It would require an extraordinary repressive apparatus to turn coldly from the stranger's plea. Might it not be more difficult to raise one's stick against a "bright-eyed," greybearded Mariner than to listen (even if impatiently) to his tale? It is difficult to say. And yet Harding seems to say it with some ease. He promptly dismisses the Wedding Guest's duties and the offence that his absence might inflict. More than this, he belittles these duties, characterizing them as part of an "artificially enclosed world" (65). They are of no great concern or consequence. As comprehensive and illuminating as it is, Harding's reading tends to reproduce and confirm what is ostensibly the hospitable ideology of the poem: pity over party.

One need not settle on the idea that the Wedding Guest makes the "right" decision by welcoming and attending the Mariner's tale over and against the wedding feast. Are we not free, as speculative readers, to imagine the insult and impropriety of the Wedding Guest's refusal to attend the wedding, at which, lest we forget, the host has reserved for him a prestigious place as next of kin? Is it so easy and forgivable to refuse such an honor? And why characterize the hospitality of the "garden-bower" as "artificial" or as less authentic or less "real" than other kinds of reception? According to Harding, there is "no wonder" that, in the end, the Wedding Guest is "sadder" and "turn[s] from the bridegroom's door, for his Eden has been shown to be a prison" (65). And yet I do wonder just a little: perhaps it is the case that the Wedding Guest is simply too "stunned" and "forlorn" to join the festivities—which, incidentally, Coleridge's poem never truly characterizes in a negative light and certainly never as a "prison." The dominant "lesson" of the poem might very well be that "He prayeth best, who loveth well / All things both great and small" (614-15)—which is to say, one is better to aid the needy than to pray in a "garden-bower" (593). The poem's scenography, however, suggests that such principles are not executed without consequences. I do not believe that **Rime** means primarily (or, at the very least, *exclusively*) to privilege the decision for pity over party. Rather, the poem compels us to think about the act of choosing itself and of the inevitable inhospitalities that such choices secretly harbor. The "right" choice is always also a wrong choice: something or someone is always wronged. The success of hospitality in **Rime** is accompanied by a failure to realize one's obligations to another. One may decide which decision is more right—whether it is to pity or to party that one will turn—but one cannot forget that suffering is always just around the corner, that it is always the other side of the decision. There are no pure welcomes, the poem seems to suggest, only contending obligations.

Works Cited

Coleridge, Samuel Taylor. *Coleridge: Poetical Works.* Ed. Ernest Hartley Coleridge. London: Oxford UP, 1969.

Harding, Anthony John. *Coleridge and the Idea of Love: Aspects of Relationship in Coleridge's Thought and Writing.* New York: Cambridge UP, 1974.

Magnuson, Paul. *Coleridge's Nightmare Poetry.* Charlottesville: UP of Virginia, 1974.

William A. Ulmer (essay date fall 2004)

SOURCE: Ulmer, William A. "Necessary Evils: Unitarian Theodicy in *The Rime of the Ancyent Marinere.*" *Studies in Romanticism* 43 (fall 2004): 327-56.

[*In the following essay, Ulmer expounds on the connections between Coleridge's Unitarian beliefs, his adherence to the doctrines of Necessity and the One Life, and the multiple allusions to Christianity in the poem, including references to the Crucifixion, Original Sin, and the idea of redemptive suffering.*]

> What we have most to dread, is the almost irrecoverable debasement of our minds by *looking off from God, living without him,* without a due regard to his presence and providence, and *idolizing ourselves and the world,* considering other things as *proper agents and causes*; whereas, strictly speaking, there is but *one cause,* but *one sole agent* in universal nature.
>
> —Joseph Priestley, *Illustrations of Philosophical Necessity*

No question in Coleridge studies has resisted resolution more effectively than the question of the Christianity of **The Rime of the Ancyent Marinere.** Contemporary readers often feel that no theological paradigm survives the nightmarish ironies of Coleridge's tale, of course, but that very feeling requires *some* assumption about the text's theological investments, so the issue of the poem's religious outlook remains a pertinent one. It is an issue that I will reconsider here by invoking Coleridge's Unitarianism. Critics tend to hurry the poet past his Unitarian period, convinced that the glib optimism of Joseph Priestley could accommodate neither Coleridge's "visionary" interests nor his responsiveness to injustice and suffering.[1] What troubles me about that conviction is that it seems so thoroughly at odds with the historical record. For in 1797-1798 Coleridge was still zealously engaged in the Unitarian cause: preaching to Unitarian congregations, corresponding with Unitarian ministers on theological questions, and revising his doctrinaire **Religious Musings.** He renounced his candidacy for the vacant ministry at Shrewsbury not on doctrinal grounds but simply because the Wedgwood legacy allowed him to act on his aversion to ministerial routine.[2] In turning from Coleridge to **The Rime,** moreover, we turn from a devout Unitarian to a conversion narrative organized around Christian motifs from the moment Coleridge introduces Crucifixion imagery into it. Is there no connection between the poet's religious beliefs and the poem's religious speculations? There is indeed, critics reply, but they defend the connection by denying or misrepresenting Coleridge's Unitarianism. For Robert Penn Warren, Coleridge's mythmaking reformulates the orthodox Fall occasioned by Original Sin, in the process ignoring Unitarian and Necessitarian doctrine.[3] For James Boulger, conversely, **The Rime** depends crucially on Necessity, but on a version of Necessity more reminiscent of Hume than Priestley.[4] Jerome McGann advocates reclaiming *The Rime* for historical understanding by looking not to Coleridge's Unitarianism but his interest in Higher Critical hermeneutics.[5] With William Empson, we at last encounter outright insistence on the Unitarianism of *The Rime,* thankfully.[6] Yet we also encounter a reconstruction of Coleridge's Unitarian faith so tendentious as to create more problems than it resolves.

My effort to negotiate these contending positions will appeal to the Unitarian convictions expressed in Coleridge's own letters and prose writings and Priestley's theological treatises. My essay will concede Warren's claim that *The Rime* celebrates the One Life, but then argue that the poem displays a typically Unitarian disinterest in Original Sin and the loss of Eden. I will agree with Boulger, against Warren, that the idea of Necessity shapes Coleridge's narrative profoundly, but I will also argue that Coleridge's conception of Necessity is providential rather than skeptical. While accepting McGann's case for a historicist *Rime,* with the Mariner as a figure of superstition. I will ignore the marginal glosses he privileges and concentrate instead on the 1798 text. My concern with *The Rime* as a Unitarian theodicy, finally, marks the divergence of my argument from Empson's reading. By looking narrowly at the poet's distaste for notions of a hereditary guilt demanding expiation, Empson concludes that Coleridge's Unitarianism disallowed the redemptive rationale of pain and evil—and there I cannot agree. In sum, this essay will present a *Rime of the Ancyent Marinere* in which the theory of the One Life, an inference from Unitarian doctrine, implicates the poem in the related theory of Necessity. I will argue that Coleridge's Unitarian conception of Necessity allows for human moral agency and responsibility while also sanctioning a naturalistic world in which the "supernatural" events of the plot can only be construed as psychological projections. The religious allegory organizing that plot centers not on the Fall but the Crucifixion, a difference important for Coleridge's Unitarian theology, and for our reading of the Mariner's spiritual progress and final situation. In developing these claims, I will not argue that Unitarianism controls, as McGann might say, the Meaning of the poem's meanings. But I do think that the religious vision of *The Rime of the Ancyent Marinere* explores and reaffirms the Unitarian faith that Coleridge himself professed in 1798.

1. NECESSARY EVILS

The months spanning the composition of *The Rime of the Ancyent Marinere* witnessed the full flush of Wordsworth and Coleridge's enthusiasm for the One Life. In early 1798 Wordsworth was recasting his tragic version of *The Ruined Cottage* to give it an optimistic One Life

resolution, and for that purpose describing how the Pedlar "saw one life, and felt that it was joy," even as Coleridge was affirming the One Life in both his poems and letters.[7] For all its pantheist affinities, the idea of the One Life was Coleridge's direct extrapolation from Unitarian theology. When Wordsworth and Coleridge came to believe that "There is an active principle alive in all things" (line 1, Gill Appendix), and from that belief affirmed "a universe of blessedness and love," in Jonathan Wordsworth's phrase ("Wordsworth's Borderers" 176), their affirmation merely reformulated Coleridge's more doctrinaire Unitarian proclamation, "There is one Mind, one omnipresent Mind / Omnific. His most holy name is Love" (*Religious Musings,* lines 105-6). Entangled in Unitarianism, the idea of the One Life became entangled in the theory of Necessity too. Priestley stressed that the doctrines "of that which is commonly called *Socinianism,* and of philosophical *necessity,* are equally parts of *one system.*"[8] It is a mark of Coleridge's dependence on Priestley that his own Unitarianism was bound up integrally with the doctrine of Necessity. Declarations of belief in Necessity toll through Coleridge's early correspondence, and as late as 1817 he was still insisting that Unitarians by definition "believe men's actions necessitated" (*LS* [*Lay Sermons*] 182, n. 2). In Wordsworth and Coleridge's poetry, perhaps the most explicit connection between Necessity and the One Life occurs in the "Not useless do I deem" lines, in which by "deeply drinking in the soul of things," we will progress in virtue "From strict necessity" ("Not useless," Gill appendix, lines 92, 94). But Unitarianism, Necessity, and the One Life were mutually inseparable facets of a single conceptual constellation. The One Life merely named the power of Necessity informing the natural world. As a poem dedicated to the sacramental "theme of the 'One Life'" (Warren 214). *The Rime of the Ancyent Marinere* presupposes not only Unitarian theology but the theory of Necessity as well.

What then was that theory? Necessity was a concept prominent in British philosophical debates about free will from at least the time of Milton and Hobbes. For Coleridge, Necessity had both metaphysical and psychological aspects, designating a causal principle of the universe internalized in human consciousness. For the form of its internalization, he was, like Priestley before him, indebted to Hartley's explanations of cognitive association. Yet Hartley's psychological exposition had also demonstrated that "the Doctrine of Necessity," as Hartley admitted in his Preface, "followed from that of Association" (*OM* [*Observations on Man, His Frame, His Duty, and His Expectations* (1749)] 1.vi). So Necessity emerged as the direct metaphysical corollary of Hartley's theory of the mind. The second part of *Observations on Man* reconciled that metaphysics with traditional Christianity; Priestley's discussions of Necessity, especially *Illustrations of Philosophical Necessity,* then reconciled Hartley's Christian Necessitarianism with Unitarian theology—to the end that Necessity was conceived as an encompassing principle of orderly causation. For defenders of Necessity, the will lacked any power of self-determination and was irresistibly obligated to laws of motivation that, originating ultimately in God, exert their influence from beyond the self. These laws of causality anchored the moral order and intelligibility of the universe, protecting it from incursions of the random and purposeless. For "To suppose, that the Action *A,* or its contrary *a,* can equally follow previous Circumstances, that are exactly the same," observed Hartley, "appears to me the same thing, as affirming that one or both of them might start up into Being without any Cause" (*OM* 1.503). Although atheistic versions of Necessity were available—most notably in Godwin's *Enquiry Concerning Political Justice*—Coleridge deplored naturalistic schemes that rendered man an "outcast of blind Nature ruled by a fatal Necessity" (*CN* [*The Notebooks of Samuel Taylor Coleridge*] 1.Text, 174G.169) and invoked the providential Necessity of Priestleyan theology in denigrating Humean skepticism, that "system of Causation—or rather non-causation" which he denounced in 1798 as "the *sole* pillar of modern Atheism" (*CL* [*The Collected Letters of Samuel Taylor Coleridge*] 1.385-86).

So Coleridge's concept of Necessity provided a theological bulwark against atheism and skepticism, a point deserving a certain emphasis. I noted at the beginning that in our one recent reading of **The Rime** as a Necessitarian poem, Boulger employs the idea of Necessity precisely to assimilate Coleridge's text to the traditions of philosophical skepticism. As an expression of "*ultimate* religious mystery" based on the poet's recognition "that necessitarianism explained nothing in the *ultimate* sense." **The Rime,** for Boulger, discloses "the uneasy Christian skepticism that has been with us since Newton and Kant" (Boulger 444, 451; my emphasis). Now, Christianity traditionally allows the mysteriousness of the Divine Will, but that recognition leaves Christian faith and Humean doubt on opposite sides of a philosophical chasm. It is certainly the case that the providential notions of Necessity familiar to Coleridge subordinated local mystery to foundational conviction, rather than the other way around. So we find Priestley writing, "of the *beginning of motion, or action,* we must sit down with acknowledging, that we have, in reality, no conception at all," only to add that, nevertheless, "we know there must be a *first cause* of all things, because things do actually exist, and could never have existed without a cause, and all *secondary causes* necessarily lead us to a *primary one*" (*MS* [*Disquisitions Relating to Matter and Spirit*] *300).* Priestley recurrently admits that we cannot understand the processes of secondary causation. From such admissions, however, he shifts typically to an emphasis on the ordered reality of causal relations: "as to the *man-*

ner in which the power of perception results from organization and life, I own I have no idea at all; but the *fact* of this connexion does not appear to me to be, on that account, the less certain" (*MS* 303). Priestley's Unitarian notion of Necessity admitted, in short, that several laws of the physical universe had yet to be explained, but that admission circumscribed the unknown within an encompassing assent to Christian truth claims. Deeply respectful of spiritual mystery, Coleridge could occasionally find Priestley's concessions of incomprehension inadequate; he censures Priestley in one letter for seemingly forgetting "that *Incomprehensibility* is as necessary an attribute of the First Cause, as Love, or Power, or Intelligence" (*CL* 1.193). Yet that hardly warrants claims that the Mariner's disordered perceptions testify to the inscrutable cosmos hypothesized by philosophical skepticism. The Christian version of Necessity propounded in Priestley and Hartley insisted on orderly causation that was divinely controlled—and that was the position to which Coleridge subscribed. One cannot summon the poet's understanding of Necessity, then, in contending for a skeptical **Rime.** In its debts to Coleridge's faith in Necessity, **The Rime of the Ancyent Marinere** anchors its mysteries in ultimate spiritual truth: a providential order construed as the benevolent consequence of God's certain existence.

The theory of Necessity grounded the optimism that resounds through Coleridge's early writings, as when he admonishes Southey. "I would ardently, that you were a Necessitarian—and (believing in an all-loving Omnipotence) an Optimist," or jots down the Notebooks entry, "Optimist—by having no will but the will of Heaven, -an- we call in Omnipotence to fight our battles!—" (*CL* 1.145; *CN* 1.Text.22). Yet Necessity worked the will of God only through the secondary agencies of natural law and psychological association. For Coleridge, Necessity represented an effort, itself an exemplary bit of natural supernaturalism, to adapt traditional faith in divine providence to the discoveries of science. The version of Necessity espoused by Hartley and Priestley illustrates what Norman Fiering calls "the depersonalization of providence": the shift, inspired by Newton, from the sovereign will of God to "considerations of structure and intrinsic relations" in explanations of the moral order of the universe.[9] As such, the theory of Necessity underlies Priestley's case against the supernatural interventions presupposed by conventional notions of fate and predestination, and by non-Unitarian belief in unmediated spiritual experience. Suspicious of Wesley's religion of the heart, and confident that Necessity rendered natural law the vehicle of divine causality, Priestley insisted that "the work of conversion and reformation, is something that takes place according to the usual course of nature" (*DI* ["The Doctrine of Divine Influence on the Human Mind"] 85). Just so, he discounted experiences of inspiration and rapture by insisting upon the "doctrine of the exclusion of *all immediate agency of the Deity on the minds of men*" (*DI* 83). While unwilling to rule out the possibility of miracle, Priestley envisioned a world order in which divine purpose was massively displaced through the mediating laws of the physical universe. Akin to Deism in that respect, Priestleyan rational theology insisted on God's providential direction of worldly affairs while widening the gulf between the natural and supernatural.

The world-view implied by Necessity bears crucially on the ostensible "supernaturalism" of *The Rime,* but also on Coleridge's approach to the issue of moral agency. Regrettably, it is as a monochromatic determinism that Coleridge scholarship usually glosses Necessity—although understandably so. For Coleridge's own references to Necessity seem at times to wave off human freedom and ethical responsibility: at moments Coleridge the Unitarian will advocate "the Automatism of Man" (*CL* 1.147); inform John Thelwall, "*Guilt* is out of the Question—I am a Necessarian and of course deny the possibility of it" (*CL* 1.213); or confess to a public audience in Bristol, "Reasoning strictly and with logical Accuracy I should deny the existence of any Evil, inasmuch as the end determines the nature of the means and I have been able to discover nothing of which the end is not good" (*LRR* [*Lectures 1795 on Politics and Religion*] 105). What we must see about such statements is precisely that they all presuppose an unspoken distinction between the ultimate and the existential. "If, as a Necessarian, I cease to blame men for their vices in the *ultimate* sense of the word," Priestley remarked, "in the common and proper sense of it, I continue to do so as much as other persons," for "how necessarily soever they act, they are influenced by a base and mischievous disposition of mind" (*PN* [*The Doctrine of Philosophical Necessity Illustrated*] 508: my emphasis). The enlightened Necessitarian "cannot accuse himself of having done wrong, in the *ultimate* sense of the words," Priestley counseled, and will therefore have "nothing to do with repentance, confession, or pardon"—in theory (*PN* 518: my emphasis). Struggling with the ethical and psychological complexities of human nature, however, even the most disciplined Necessitarian will invariably "feel the sentiments of shame, remorse, and repentance" and, "oppressed with a sense of *guilt,* he will have recourse to that *mercy* of which he will stand in need" (*PN* 518). Coleridge's most explicit recourse to the same organizing distinction occurs in his "you are *lost* to *me*" letter to Southey:

> You quoted likewise the last sentence of my Letter to you as a proof that I approved of your design—you *knew* that sentence to imply no more than the pious confidence of Optimism—however wickedly you might act, God would make it ULTIMATELY the best—. You *knew,* this was the meaning of it. I could find twenty Parallel passages in the Lectures—indeed such expressions applied to bad actions had become a habit of my Conversation—you had named, not unwittily, Dr Pangloss. And Heaven forbid, that I should not now have faith, that however foul your Stream may run here, yet it will filtrate & become pure in its subterraneous Passage to the Ocean of Universal Redemption.

> (*CL* 1.168)

His former friend's foul behavior will be assimilated by God's encompassing benevolence, and turned to the best account—but only "ULTIMATELY," and that eventual dispensation hardly nullifies the reality of Southey's "bad actions." Coleridge can "deny the existence of any Evil" only because, at the moment of denial, he speaks from the perspective of ultimate metaphysical reality.

The theory of Necessity allowed for human guilt and immorality, of course, only because it independently allowed for human freedom. "I would observe," wrote Priestley, "that I allow to man all the liberty or power that is *possible in itself,* and to which the ideas of mankind in general ever go, which is *the power of doing whatever they will, or please*" (*PN* 459); "first then," wrote Hartley, "I nowhere deny practical Free-will, or that voluntary Power over our Affections and Actions, by which we deliberate, suspend, and choose, and which makes an essential Part of our Ideas of Virtue and Vice, Reward and Punishment" (*OM* I.vii-viii). Human choice occurred within a motivational field limited by powers beyond individual consciousness, and remained subject to the ulterior ordinations of the Divine Will, so freedom was not absolute—but it was quite real. Rather than denying volitional freedom, the doctrine of Necessity located it within a dialectical alternation between the human will and cosmic imperative. For me, in fact, *The Rime* brilliantly conveys the economy of freedom and determinism in Coleridgean Necessity in showing the Mariner interacting with his world. On the own hand, his behavior reveals a passivity that struck even the poem's first readers. In his note to the second edition of *Lyrical Ballads,* Wordsworth observed of *The Rime* that "the principal person has no distinct character," and that "he does not act but is continually acted upon"; Lamb described the Mariner, similarly, as someone in whom "all consciousness of personality is *gone*."[10] More recent readers have also noticed an unsettling vacuity in the Mariner's character and conduct. Seamus Perry summarizes this aspect of the text in remarking that

> Coleridge contrives to make the Mariner seem somehow non-volitional while killing the albatross, as he is at the second of the poem's two apparent turning-points, the blessing of the snakes. . . . [there is a] strange inactivity marking the cruces of the allegory; the bird is shot before we know it, with any description of intent or motive or decision quite elided; and the snakes are blessed "unaware," the action recognised for what it was only in retrospect.

> (283)

To this catalogue of passive crises, one can add the Mariner's recitation of his tale, which occurs only when a rhapsodic anguish usurps his vice, compelling him to speech. By rendering the Mariner the secondary vehicle of forces acting through him, Coleridge dramatizes the power of Necessity directing the events of *The Rime.* Of course, the Mariner manages to return home at all only by falling into a trance that leaves him utterly passive while supernatural forces drive his ship to harbor. At the same time, the poem also awards the Mariner a capacity for action: he employs his crossbow, climbs the mast, bites his arm, cries aloud, works the sails and ropes, rows the Pilot's boat, and so on. Coleridge's representation of the Mariner braids voluntary energy together with inert receptiveness because the workings of Necessity incorporate both elements: "though the chain of events is necessary," Priestley advised, "our *own determinations and actions* are necessary links of that chain" (*PN* 503).

In defending the Mariner's powers of agency, one need not stress his physical gestures and acts, however, for the key events of his voyage are themselves the products of his feverishly energetic imagination. By banishing unmediated manifestations of the supernatural from human experience, the doctrine of Necessity set the terms for Coleridge's naturalistic treatment of the Mariner's spectral visions. Due largely to the commentary of the *Biographia Literaria,* **The Rime** enjoys a considerable reputation as a "supernatural" poem markedly dissimilar from Wordsworth's secular and ironic *Peter Bell,* in which the only spirits discernible are "Spirits of the mind" (*Peter Bell,* line 923). Yet recent years have witnessed the emergence of a critical counter-tradition which psychologizes Coleridge's supernaturalism, reading the uncanny encounters of **The Rime** as the hallucinations of a fevered imagination. So Paul Magnuson suggests that in **The Rime** the "supernatural is the product of the seer's own mind"; observing that the "vision of Death and Life-in-Death are interior and singular phantasms rather than a communal hallucination," Richard Matlak similarly interprets the poem's supernaturalism as "the Mariner's solipsistic fabrication"; while Susan Eilenberg finds the Mariner "unable to recognize his fears and desires as his own or distinguish himself from his surroundings," so that he "apprehends the contents of his own psyche as alien and inexplicable, perceptible only in the forms of an unnatural nature, frightened and hostile men, and spirits."[11] De Quincey recalled Coleridge planning a poem "on delirium, confounding its own dream-scenery with external things, and connected with the imagery of high latitudes": *The Rime of the Ancyent Marinere* is that poem, surely, its portrayal of delirium informed by Coleridge's related interest in the affects of the "calenture."[12] **The Rime** was one of a number of studies in the psychology of superstitious projection that Wordsworth and Coleridge composed in early 1798, and we must

approach it as we approach "The Thorn," reading past the distortions of the narrating consciousness to whatever can be inferred of original events. Or we must read **The Rime** as Priestley read Scripture, discounting improbabilities as fallible human testimony, since "the prophets themselves were not exempt from error . . . but were liable to be misled by their imaginations, and especially by their passions, like other men" (*IE* ["Introductory Essays to Hartley's Theory of the Mind"] 327). Above all, we must read the poem in the light of Necessity, with its postulate of a world subject to providence but governed by natural law, for then we must look to the mind of the Mariner in seeking the source of the "supernatural."

If the theory of Necessity in its naturalistic aspect requires us to construe the Mariner's visions as delusory, the providential superintendence ordained by Necessity precludes dismissing those visions as *merely* delusory. Critics have occasionally argued that the Mariner's superstitious projections superimpose nostalgic longing for purpose against an impassively blank natural realm. "The mariner's continuing, futile attempts to rationalise his experience into meaning," Perry remarks, "might indeed be a type of parable, not of theological order, but of the human need to discern order at all, and of the pathos of that need" (289). From this perspective, the visions of supernatural forces reflect an atavistic guilt unallied to any real spiritual teleology: unadulterated delusion. I would suggest, with McGann, that Coleridge employs the Mariner's visionary terrors to unveil the spiritual awakening of the primitive mind, with the poem sketching a historical genealogy of faith along the lines of *The Destiny of Nations*:

> Fancy is the power
> That first unsensualizes the dark mind,
> Giving it new delights; and bids it swell
> With wild activity; and peopling air
> By obscure fears of beings invisible,
> Emancipates it from the grosser thrall
> Of the present impulse, teaching self-control,
> Till Superstition with unconscious hand
> Seat Reason on her throne.
>
> (80-88)

Conceiving of superstitious error as the vehicle of a spiritual teleology, Coleridge can psychologize the supernatural in **The Rime** without ironically reducing it to utter mystification. In *The Prelude,* similarly, Wordsworth's account of a "huge cliff" that punitively pursued his rowboat, leaving its nightmare legacy of "huge and mighty forms," leads immediately to an apostrophe to the "Wisdom and spirit of the universe" in which he thanks God for intertwining "for me / The passions that build up our human soul" (1805 *Prelude* 1.424, 433-34). The incident is retrospectively understood as the boy's projection of the anxious guilt and, at the same time, celebrated as genuine evidence of God working in and through the human mind. Coleridge's understanding of Necessity similarly married divine mandate to the associative orchestrations of human consciousness; for him, as for Hartley and Priestley, "Providence was not an external force: it was God-internalized-within-men."[13] The presupposition of Necessity in the religious organization of *The Rime* helps Coleridge explore the power of superstitious guilt, then, while anchoring his exploration within a supervening moral order, the sacramental order of the One Life.

Taking *The Rime* as a dramatic monologue illustrating the psychology of projection changes the moral stakes of the poem appreciably. If the phantoms dicing for the crew are "Spirits of the mind," for instance, they may disclose the haunting of the Mariner's psyche without indicating the amoral caprice of his world. Edward Bostetter has argued influentially that the dice game "knocks out any attempt to impose a systematic philosophical or religious interpretation, be it necessitarian, Christian, or Platonic, upon the poem."[14] Below I argue conversely that the dicing incident can be read as an element in an allegory both Necessitarian and Christian. What above all prevents enlisting the incident as proof of a "Nightmare World," however, is the fact that it remains a representation not of the poem's world but of the protagonist's psyche. Like critics influenced by him, Bostetter realizes that the Mariner's supernatural encounters may be "a product of his delirium" (68). He simply believes that psychological genealogies of the Mariner's anguish leave the moral issues unaltered: if the Mariner is a madman, God created madmen too, and remains responsible for their delusions. The problem here does not lie with the leap from mental phenomenon to the nature of the cosmos. It lies, more restrictedly, with the assumption that the latter must be the direct reflex of the former—that mind and cosmos must be reflexively congruent. Yet in Priestley's Unitarianism, "every thing is the *Divine power*; but still, strictly speaking, every thing is not *the Deity himself,*" for "every inferior intelligent being has a consciousness distinct from that of the Supreme Intelligence" (*MS* 241). Since it is intent that "constitutes the sinfulness of an action," Priestley contended similarly, Hume was unjustified in claiming that if human actions "can have any moral turpitude, they must involve our Creator in the same guilt, while he is acknowledged to be their ultimate cause and author" (*PN* 510, 511), for God may permit pain for benevolent purposes which the finite mind cannot know. Again, Coleridge's own notion of Necessity never became so comprehensively deterministic as to deny the mind its freedoms, and with them a capacity for perceptual error at odds with divine intent. If Life-in-Death and the Polar Spirit are real, we have powers of the cosmos directly acting to destroy human happiness; if they are psychological projections, the involvement of the

cosmos, or God, in the Mariner's dementia remains at most secondary, and to that extent he becomes the source of his suffering—and understandably so, for sin is fundamentally a condition of self-victimization. By no means do his sufferings, terrors born of his errant perceptions, preclude or disprove the existence of a moral order.

Coleridge's sense of "Superstition" as a form of primitive revelation authorized him to regard the Mariner's visionary terrors as actualizing means of that order. If the human will, in its existential separation from "the Supreme Intelligence," could lapse into error and evil, and experience suffering as a result, Necessity ultimately assimilated those errors and sufferings to God's benevolent purposes. Viewed in Necessitarian terms, all human actions signified doubly: first, in their local motivations and immediate mundane consequences, and second, in their contribution to an emergent providential design. "It was wicked in Joseph's brethren to sell him into Egypt, because they acted from envy, hatred, and covetousness." Priestley explained: at the same time, "it was not wicked in God to ordain it to be so, because, in appointing it, he was not actuated by any such principle," but rather planning the eventual salvation of His chosen people (*PN* 510). If Coleridge eventually felt doubts about motive as an ethical criterion, he believed in 1798, with Priestley, that mundane occurrences took on their meaning at the juncture of two separate moral perspectives. That belief provides a specific theological rationale for the "double character," the "double mood of admiration and fear," that Humphrey House sensed in the acts and images of Coleridge's poem.[15] In *The Rime* events can qualify as existential evils and yet, in their doubleness, help enfranchise a moral harmony-in-progress ordained by Necessity.

Coleridge's Unitarianism conceded not only the existential reality of evil and suffering, then, but the essential contribution of suffering to human redemption. I mentioned above that in his own Unitarian reading of *The Rime,* Empson vigorously refutes such claims, denying that the text stages what he calls "an allegory in favour of redemption by torment, the central tradition of Christianity" (*"Ancient Mariner"* 297). What it stages instead, Empson argues, is an ironic savaging of the Anglican Atonement as a Moloch-like doctrine demanding suffering for salvation. Empson's reading has been praised by accomplished critics, and he deserves enormous credit for insisting that Unitarianism provides the real historical context of the religious vision of *The Rime of the Ancyent Marinere,* but I cannot agree with his reconstruction of Coleridge's Unitarianism. As David Perkins notes, the problems begin when Empson gives "the concept of the Atonement greater prominence than any interpreter had before"—Perkins' polite way of saying that Empson uses the Atonement as a straw man position.[16] The problems grow when Empson ignores both Coleridge's restricted grounds for censuring the orthodox doctrines of Original Sin and Atonement—linked in his mind by the unacceptable postulate of hereditary guilt—and his alternative Unitarian account of the providential purpose of human pain and moral evil. For Coleridge, evil *had* to be divinely purposive because, ultimately, it was divinely controlled. Like others in his Unitarian circle, he accepted a progressive theodicy in which humankind slowly learn to choose virtue for themselves, and in which encountering evil crucially clarified the attractions of goodness, motivating people to seek it. "According to the most fundamental laws of nature, and indeed the very *nature of things*," Priestley wrote, "great virtues in some could not be generated, or exist, but in conjunction with great vices in others; for it is this opposition that not only exhibits them to advantage, but even, properly speaking, *creates* them" (*PN* 513-14). It is consequently necessary, Coleridge wrote, "that Man should run through the Course of Vice & Mischief since by Experience alone his Virtue & happiness can acquire Permanence & Security" (*LRR* 108). In short, Coleridge did think that suffering was good for us, as Empson might bluntly put it, and he thought so on specifically Unitarian grounds. He subscribed to a Unitarian theodicy which envisioned mundane tribulation as an educative precondition for salvation. The Mariner's conversion illustrates the moral logic of that theodicy through the elaborate Crucifixion allegory of Coleridge's narrative.

2. COLERIDGE'S CRUCIFIXION ALLEGORY

The Mariner stops the Wedding Guest, fixes his attention, and begins the story of his voyage and its pivotal act of violence: "With my cross bow / I shot the Albatross" (79-80). If one gives *The Rime* credit for a symbolic agenda, as most Coleridgeans do, accounting for this act means explaining the existence of evil. Critical agreement on that question helps explain the endurance of Warren's analysis as a point of departure. Warren takes the gratuitous killing as a sign of the hereditary and universal perfidy of the human will: Original Sin in action. For him, the Mariner's killing of the Albatross represents a re-enactment of the Fall. Coleridge's protagonist sins from the depths of his humanity—unnecessarily, perversely, and without any specific reason. His motives remain so baffling precisely because Coleridge conceives Original Sin as a foundational postulate of human moral experience, and thus as a ground of explanations that cannot itself be explained. So it would be perverse to suggest that the Mariner's motives can be roughly inferred after the fact, or that his very ability to kill without self-conscious motivation in itself psychologically individuates him. With Original Sin as Coleridge understands it, "there is no previous determination of the will, because the will exists outside the chain of cause and effect, which is of Nature and

not of Spirit" (Warren 227). These claims deserve respect: all Christian explanations of *The Rime* must incorporate the idea of Original Sin, clearly, for Original Sin remains the source and premise of all earthly wrongs.

At the same time, it seems perplexing that Coleridge, as a Unitarian, should organize the religious vision of *The Rime* around the issue of Original Sin. In the late eighteenth century, most Unitarians—Priestley among them—rejected the idea of Original Sin. It is not surprising, consequently, that Warren should discount Coleridge's Unitarianism in constructing *The Rime* as a Fall-and-Redemption parable, preferring to take his bearings from what he describes as the proto-Anglicanism of the poet's March 1798 letter to his brother George:

> Of GUILT I say nothing; but I believe most stedfastly in original Sin; that from our mothers' wombs our understandings are darkened; and even where our understandings are in the Light, that our organization is depraved, & our volitions imperfect; and we sometimes see the good without *wishing* to attain it, and oftener *wish* it without the energy that wills & performs—And for this inherent depravity, I believe, that the *Spirit* of the Gospel is the sole cure.
>
> (*CL* 1.396)

But this letter neither shows Coleridge decisively rejecting Unitarianism, as Warren suggests, nor reveals his subscription to an orthodox version of Original Sin. In disallowing "GUILT," Coleridge confirms the demotion of guiltiness encouraged by philosophical Necessity. "Sin being in its own nature a personal thing, and not transferable," the idea of a specifically hereditary guilt was an affront to reason and justice, Priestley argued (*CC* [*The History of the Corruptions of Christianity*] 158-59), and Coleridge's unwillingness to countenance inherited "GUILT" seems similarly motivated. While darker in tone than ordinary Unitarian rational theology, Coleridge's sense of the human will's alienation from divine plenitude simply rephrases, in the idiom of his brother's orthodoxy, Necessitarian distinctions between ultimate reality and humanity's existential situation: revisiting these issues in a later letter, Coleridge will refer to "an original corruption in our nature" (*CL* 2.807), while here, in deference to George's orthodoxy, he refers instead to "Original Sin." The poet's Necessitarian Optimism certainly survives this nod to "original Sin": earlier in the letter, he describes himself to his brother as "believing that no calamities are permitted but as the means of Good" (*CL* 1.395). In its theological bearing, the March 1798 letter does not grandly announce an Anglican Coleridge or demonstrate the irrelevancy of Unitarianism to *The Rime*.[17]

If we indulge even a modest skepticism about Warren's claims, and then carry that skepticism to the poem itself, problems arise almost immediately. For in several respects the myth of the Fall does not really fit *The Rime* closely. House was justified in pointing to the inconsistencies that ensue when Warren tries to broaden the symbolic pertinence of his Fall analogy to cover the actual incidents of Coleridge's plot. "Mr. Warren is here somewhat confused," wrote House:

> at one point he seems to equate the killing of the bird with the murder of a human being . . . and at another point to say that the killing "symbolises" the Fall. If these two things are to be held together, it is clear that the symbol must be functioning not merely towards different objects but in different ways: for the killing cannot *equate* with both a murder and the Fall, which are very different kinds of things.
>
> (House 59)

House catches Warren trying to shore up the centrality of the Fall by finessing the fact that Coleridge's tale, unlike Genesis, involves an actual killing—and all such efforts implicitly confess that the parallels between the Old Testament story and *The Rime* are significantly inexact. Another problem lies with Warren's notion of the moral will's existence "outside the chain of cause and effect," a notion inimical to Coleridge's 1798 belief in causal law as the Necessary vehicle of God's will. By removing the will from time and nature, Warren elides the experiential matrices of the Mariner's act, its rootedness in existential particularity—and that is the gravest disadvantage of interpretations of Coleridge's poem as a Romantic myth of the Fall. To offer Original Sin as the sufficient cause of the Mariner's killing of the Albatross is, as David Miall complains, "to replace one mystery by another."[18] For by its very universality the idea of the Fall has limited explanatory power. If all men are fallen, not all men kill.

The Fall has proven so central to religious readings of *The Rime* that one can feel a bit churlish in questioning its importance. But surely the imagery of Coleridge's poem implies a re-enactment not of the Fall but of the Crucifixion. These two events are typologically consonant, I realize, with Christ as a second Adam in whose fate the Fall repeats itself. At the same time, the spiritual meanings of the Fall and the Crucifixion are sufficiently dissimilar as to render them antithetical complements. Christ's role as Redeemer realigns fallen human nature with God's redemptive plan, making the Crucifixion stand to the Fall as solution to problem. Ultimately, it is his resistance to an easy symbolic conflation of the Fall and the Crucifixion that prompts House's legitimate objections to having a single incident "hold together" meanings so disparate as Adamic disobedience and human murder. In any event, the symbolic investments of *The Rime* seem nowhere harder to read past than in Coleridge's invocations of the Crucifixion in his account of the killing of the Albatross: in addition to the cross-bow as an instrument of death, there is a homonymic glance at the Resurrection, arguably, in the lines

"Ne dim ne red, like God's own head, / The glorious sun uprist" (93-94), the crew substituting the Albatross for a crucifix, the spirit voice mentioning "him who died on cross," and several other touches. The Albatross has been likened to "the innocent victim, Christ" by readers as shrewd as W. H. Auden.[19] When the Mariner slays the bird with his cross-bow, he figuratively kills God's benevolent messenger just as the centurions killed Christ on the cross: with his poem's opening gambit, Coleridge claims the traditional significance of the Crucifixion for his One Life sense of nature's divinity. That is the point of the cross imagery, even as it explains Coleridge's association of the Mariner with an archetypal sinner, the Wandering Jew, present at the Crucifixion but not at the expulsion from Eden. And the poem offers little incentive, surely, for regarding shipboard conditions as Edenic prior to the Mariner's devastating act. I have no objection to keeping the Fall in the background of *The Rime* as a secondary analogue, in the spirit of Wordsworth's contention that "the fall of Man presents an analogy" to the theme of preexistence in the Immortality Ode (Fenwick Note, Wu 418). But I cannot agree that the theological interests of Coleridge's text should be subordinated to the Fall as an organizing motif.

Why then does the Mariner "crucify" the Albatross? It is a thoughtless, unselfconscious act yet an act possible for the Mariner only because of his individual character. Concerned to create a mood of ballad-like mystery, Coleridge leaves the Mariner's character radically undeveloped, as Wordsworth complained. Yet mystery differs from opacity: we can infer some aspects of the Mariner's spiritual condition, at least, from his actions—or from the fact that certain actions, whatever specific impulse induced them, were existentially and morally possible for him. If the Mariner's confession, "I shot the Albatross" introduces the first person pronoun into the poem, then, that reflects not the representative dependence of identity formation on violence but the egocentrism enabling the Mariner's aberrant will to destroy.[20] Emotionally self-absorbed, he embodies an instinctive pride willing to sacrifice other beings to whatever inclinations arise within him. With his later reference to the water-snakes as "a million million slimy things" (line 230), we get a glimpse of the same contempt for created nature that made the earlier killing of the Albatross morally conceivable for him. When Coleridge identifies the bird with Christ, he attributes the Mariner's casual violence to moral blindness—to a hardened inability to recognize the God around him. Coleridge's protagonist epitomizes what Priestley, in the words of my epigraph, declared the mentality "we have most to dread": an "almost irrecoverable debasement of our minds by *looking off from God, living without him,* without a due regard to his presence and providence, and *idolizing ourselves and the world*" (PN 519). This blindness to spiritual realities, reinforced in Coleridge's later epigraph from Burnet, leaves the Mariner the one man among an entire crew so morally ungenerous as to kill without apparent reason.

In these ways, Coleridge offers his protagonist as personification of modern infidelity. With respect to his conscious religious creed, the Mariner appears to be a superstitious Medieval Catholic, calling in his distress on saints, Christ, and "Mary-queen." But Coleridge stressed the mutual implication of superstition and atheism and, more important, understood atheism itself less as a theological position than an emotional and psychological dysfunction—and *that* is what he dramatizes in his protagonist's act of violence. Following Hartley and Priestley, Coleridge the Unitarian blamed atheism on "great selfwilledness joining with great coldness of Affections" (*LRR* 96). A combination of egocentrism and emotional sterility shrinks the relational capacities of the atheist's mind. So Coleridge could censure Godwinian atheism for a

> Pride which affects to inculcate benevolence while it does away with every home-born Feeling, by which it is produced and nurtured. The filial and paternal affections discipline the heart and prepare it for that blessed state of perfection in which all our Passions are to be absorbed in the Love of God. But if we love not our friends and Parents whom we have seen—how can we love our universal Friend and Almighty parent whom we have not seen. . . . Jesus knew our Nature—and that expands like the circles of a Lake—the Love of our Friends, parents and neighbours, lead[s] us to the love of our Country to the love of all Mankind
>
> (*LRR* 162-63)

As the patriotic sentiments suggest, behind these claims lies Burke's famous declaration "that man is by his constitution a religious animal; that atheism is against, not only our reason, but our instincts; and that it cannot prevail long."[21] Directly behind Coleridge's statement, however, is Hartley's associative grounding of religious faith in humanity's emotional responsiveness to immediate experience—in human contact and relationship, especially family relationships, but in immediate experience of nature too. Possessing a "deadened and petrified Heart," the Coleridgean atheist becomes a "Man who could wander among the fields in a vernal Noon or summer Evening and doubt his [God's] Benevolence!" (*LRR* 94). Unresponsiveness to nature is therefore evidence of "that intellectual Deformity an Atheist" (*LRR* 93). So the Mariner's destruction of a creature redolent of the One Life reflects the negation of divinity organizing his moral sensibility: blasphemy materialized, it is the denial of God rendered as an observable action.

When the Mariner symbolically crucifies the Albatross, he activates those counter measures whereby Necessity accommodates sin to its own providential imperative.

The benevolent purpose *The Rime* awards Necessity is to make the Mariner's violence, through his awakened reinterpretation of it, confirm the reality of a sacramental One Life. So the Mariner must achieve the required enlightenment through a process equally punitive and educational. Since what is at issue is self-understanding, he must be compelled, more specifically, to confront his atheism in its true guise. So he does in encountering Death and Life-in-Death. While Eilenberg observes that "in the *Rime* you become what you meet" (Eilenberg 305), here it is perhaps truer that the Mariner meets what he has become—that this spectral (specular) encounter transfers the state of his soul onto the world he inhabits. That may be why the scene so plainly restages Satan's meeting with Sin and Death in *Paradise Lost*. Several critics have presented Life-in-Death as a maternal figure, but in her whorishness she seems more like a potential or former lover, as Milton's Sin was to Satan—and to her son Death.[22] Recollecting that Sin and Death are equally Satan's progeny, Sin springing to life from his head, we should look at Life-in-Death and Death similarly as the Mariner's creations: they are his psychological progeny, outward projections of an atheistic mind's superstitious terrors. Through the precedent of the Satan/Sin relationship, Coleridge's mythmaking can convey the self-love at the heart of atheism. But the erotic power of Life-in-Death emanates less from her association with the ego than the body, and with bodily pleasure. Since "to a Sensualist and to the Atheist that alone can be beautiful which promises a gratification to the appetite," Coleridge linked atheism with sexual license (*LRR* 158). In pairing Life-in-Death with Death he refashions a Renaissance before-and-after diptych of the temporal fate of the body. The horror that transforms prospective pleasure into sexual threat for the Mariner, giving Life-in-Death her predatory swagger, arises from the carrion repulsiveness of the body when existence lacks an afterlife. The figures the Mariner envisions merely portray mortality in different ways: when human life is naturalistically circumscribed, and we are not incarnated souls, then we are corpses whether or not the charnel rot has actually started.

As an anatomy of atheism, the appearance of Death and Life-in-Death glances back to the "allegoric vision" that initiates the *Lectures on Revealed Religion*. There Coleridge's protagonist enters a "Temple of Superstition"— Superstition is herself a Goddess—in which people averse to orthodox Mystery fly to an "unnaturally cold" cave at the mouth of which "sate two Figures the first, a female whom by her dress & gestures I knew to be Sensuality the second from the fierceness of his Demeanor and the brutal Scornfulness of his Looks declared himself to be the Monster Blasphemy" (*LRR* 91-92). This Monster is a figure of blasphemy in the sense that all atheists are "dim eyed Sons of Blasphemy" (*LRR* 165). The blasphemy in question involves outright dismissal of God, in short, with Coleridge's boasting Monster ("he uttered big words") providing a transition to the naturalistic sage who appears next, and who dismisses God by conceiving of the universe as a succession of physical effects unguided by divine intelligence. Mann explains that

"Superstition" refers both to the Church of England and to atheistic materialism as extremes standing on either side of the true religion of Unitarianism, which is founded equally on reason and revelation. The two extremes meet in their acceptance and worship of "Mystery," the former in religion and the latter in nature. Hence C[oleridge] places the cave of atheism in the precincts of the Temple of Superstition, and the horrified traveler who flees from religious superstition to total disbelief in all religion merely completes a circle that brings him back to "Mystery" in another guise.

(*LRR* 89 n. 1)

The 1798 poem freely regroups the motifs constellated in the 1795 essay. Coleridge's prose allegory establishes the complicity of Superstition and atheism by locating the Cave within the Temple, and uses its male and female porters to suggest a secondary complicity of sensuality and skepticism as components of the atheistic sensibility. In *The Rime* the characters on Coleridge's ghost-ship dissociate atheism into sensuality and superstition, on the one hand, and putrescent corporeality on the other. The two figures play dice, of course, because in Coleridge's eyes all materialistic explanations of the cosmos enthrone Chance, exchanging spiritual guidance for "the accidental play of Atoms."[23] Life-in Death "whistled thrice" because, as with Peter and the crowing cock, she devotes herself to denying Christ.

Although the Mariner's meeting with Death and Life-in-Death marks the moral nadir of his experiences, it also allows his spiritual despair to bottom out, and his penitential recovery to begin. Through all his sufferings—his exposure to a burning seascape, his projections of superstitious awe, the terrors of his solitude—Coleridge hints at providential energies stirring and gathering themselves. Revealing the morally doubled nature of events as they transpose evil into good, these energies subject the Mariner to a dramatic role reversal. Raimonda Modiano remarks that "the Mariner carries a dual identity; he is at once the perpetrator and the victim of a transgression, both guilty and innocent, and in a sacrificial context, both sacrificer and sacrificed."[24] I would simply add that the antithetical identities predominate by turns, with Coleridgean Necessity successively transforming the Mariner from victimizer to victim. The moral logic of this transformation rests on a principle announced in *Religious Musings,* the principle that through God's "vast family no Cain / Injures uninjured (in her best-aimed blow / Victorious murder a

blind suicide)" (119-21). Constrained by divine purpose, violence rebounds on its wielder. So in *The Rime,* the man who restaged the Crucifixion through an unchecked impulse to destroy becomes the object of his own Crucifixion-like violence—which is to say, the Mariner becomes a Christ figure. That is the manifest implication, surely, when he is compelled to bear the cross figuratively by having the Albatross, crucifix-like, draped around his neck. But the text corroborates these implications at other moments. The Mariner's act of biting his arm to moisten his throat—"this is my body . . . this is my blood"—can be taken as a garish re-enactment of the Last Supper. Stationed on "the cross-like mast of the ship," below the spectral figures dicing for him as the centurions diced for Christ's garments, the Mariner is placed symbolically in a crucified position.[25] These Christ analogies mark an unavoidable stage in the Mariner's search for salvation, and should hardly occasion surprise. Christian redemption requires "Taking the Cross and Following Christ," as Priestley entitled a sermon, and as Coleridge reminded the stricken Charles Lamb, "We cannot arrive at any portion of heavenly bliss without in some measure imitating Christ" (*CL* 1.239).

Now, the Christ analogies by no means dominate the Mariner's identity in the poem. Even in his role as Gospel messenger, he ends up more reminiscent of an Apostle than Christ himself. The Mariner becomes an Apostle of the One Life when he awakes, renewed by sleep and rain, to a "roaring wind" approaching the ship and "a hundred fire-flags" flickering above him, for these images recast the original Pentecostal inspiration of Christ's disciples:

When the day of Pentecost had come, they were all together in one place. And suddenly a sound came from heaven like the rush of a mighty wind, and it filled all the house where they were sitting. And there appeared to them tongues as of fire, distributed and resting on each one of them. And they were all filled with the Holy Spirit and began to speak in other tongues, as the Spirit gave them utterance.

(Acts 2:1-4)

The "woeful agony" that later forces the Mariner to tell his tale represents a darker form of this plenary inspiration. As Coleridge turns the Biblical story to his own purposes, naturalizing it, he ignores the Holy Spirit and attributes the Mariner's "strange powers of speech" to a repetition compulsion recalling Dante's infernal re-enactments: here, we might reflect, is Apostolic rhetorical power as the guilt-scarred Wandering Jew would experience it. Yet the references to painful compulsion merely show how the Mariner understands himself—or how Coleridge, recollecting a certain kind of untutored prophet, conceived the Mariner as a dramatic character. In the *Biographia Literaria* Coleridge would profess his admiration for "BEHMEN, DE THROYAS, GEORGE FOX, &c," for such men.

in simplicity of soul, made their words immediate echoes of their feelings. Hence the frequency of those phrases among them, which have been mistaken as pretences to immediate inspiration; as for instance, *"it was delivered unto me,"* *"I strove not to speak,"* *"I said, I will be silent,"* *"but the word was in heart as a burning fire,"* and *"I could not forbear"*. . . . O! it requires deeper feeling, and a stronger imagination, than belong to most of those, to whom reasoning and fluent expression have been as a trade learnt in boyhood, to conceive with what *might,* and with what inward *strivings* and *commotion,* the perception of a new and vital TRUTH takes possession of an uneducated man of genius. . . . Need we be surprised, that under an excitement at once so strong and so unusual, the man's body should sympathize with the struggles of his mind; or that he should at times be so far deluded, as to mistake the tumultuous sensations of his nerves, and the co-existing spectres of his fancy, as parts or symbols of the truths which were opening on him?

(*BL* [*Biographia Literaria*] 1.149, 150-51)

The phrase, "This heart within me burns" was not added to **The Rime** until 1817. Still, the *Biographia* account of an uneducated mind in the throes of spiritual enthusiasm, struggling with a revelation that threatens to master the body, seems like a wonderfully apt gloss on the character of the Mariner even in 1798. He is Coleridge's untutored Romantic Apostle, possessed by residual guilt, but possessed of genuine spiritual inspiration too.

That fact marks the final disadvantage of reading **The Rime of the Ancyent Marinere** as a reenactment of the Fall. The motif of the Fall encourages the expectation of redemption, making the Mariner's "penance more" wanderings a problem so disturbing for some readers as to demonstrate "the Christian universe gone mad" (Bostetter 75). In my view, the poem's concentration on the continuing trials of faith defers the entire issue of an achieved salvation. **The Rime** is a poem of revelation, not redemption, and its revelations never deliver the Mariner from existential contingency. Consider his climactic vision of the angelic chorus. Acting as spirit to letter, angels animate the bodies of the crew and sail the ship, pausing when the sun rises:

> The day-light dawn'd—they dropp'd their arms,
>   And cluster'd round the mast:
> Sweet sounds rose slowly thro' their mouths
>   And from their bodies pass'd.
> Around, around, flew each sweet sound,
>   Then darted to the sun:
> Slowly the sounds came back again
>   Now mix'd, now one by one.

(339-46)

While Milton's angelic choruses may lie behind these lines, they particularly recall the description of Theopathic rapture in **Religious Musings.** There when a man truly accepts the existence of a God of Love,

> He from his small particular orbit flies
> With blest outstarting! From Himself he flies,
> Stands in the sun, and with no partial gaze
> Views all creation; and he loves it all,
> And blesses it, and calls it very good!
> This is indeed to dwell with the most High!
> Cherubs and rapture-trembling Seraphim
> Can press no nearer to the Almighty's Throne.

(109-16)

Each of the bodies has been reanimated by "a seraph-man" (490). Saluting the dawn with their hymn, these Seraphim stand "in the sun" literally, but also figuratively, as their song darts to the sun before circularly returning. As visitants from eternity, Coleridge's angels inhabit the bodies to allegorize humanity's resurrection to eternal life. As a visionary rendering of the Mariner's inner state, the angelic chorus allegorizes a Hartleyan loss of selfhood in assent to God. At the same time, the entire scene retains an almost garish uncanniness. The "resurrected" dead remain estranged *things* to him—"The body and I pull'd at one rope," he reports (335)—and he observes their proceedings with fascinated revulsion, and a measure of fear. So the Mariner's alienation and terror imbue even his experience of spiritual epiphany as they will accompany his later One Life ministry, continuing as the process of progressive illumination itself continues. By the end of the poem, the Mariner has recognized the existence of a sacramental One Life and witnessed a symbolic revelation of the Resurrection, yet he remains a figure of the awed primitive mind, wavering between insight and delusion.

His closing homily reflects his struggle to distill some form of ethical closure from his experience of the religious sublime. "Our understandings being limited," Priestley wrote, "it is best that we, and all finite creatures, should govern our conduct by certain *inviolable rules*" (*PN* 512). The Mariner's praise of creaturely love offers just such a rule of conduct, based on the moral claims of the One Life. Coleridge's "All things both great and small" lines have been regularly bludgeoned for their sing-song piety. The lines can be defended as a dramatic utterance appropriate to the Mariner's character, however, and Coleridge himself, for all his revisions of the text, and despite his avowed unhappiness over obtrusive moral sentiments, never revised them significantly. They seem intended to show a progression from sublimity to beauty, as in his 1796 remark that "the Terrors of the Almighty are the whirlwind, the earthquake, and the Fire that precede the still small voice of his Love" (*CL* 1.267). They certainly convey an attitude that both Wordsworth and Coleridge would have endorsed in 1798. The idea of the One Life moved Wordsworth to avow, "I would not strike a flower / As many a man would strike his horse"—understandably so, since "every flower / Enjoys the air it breathes"—and to observe that "he, who feels contempt / For any living thing, hath faculties / Which he has never used."[26] It is a familiar Romantic attitude: "every thing that lives is Holy," Blake declared. But it enjoyed a specifically Unitarian sanction as well. Unitarian benevolence not only views "the whole [as] but *one family*" of a Deity who *"despises nothing that he has made,"* Priestley believed, but also "makes the lower animals to differ from us in degree only, and not in kind" (*PN* 508, *IE* 182). Similar convictions moved Coleridge to sympathize with trapped mice and tethered asses, to reflect, upon hearing a "creeking" rook, "No sound is dissonant which tells of Life" (*This Lime-Tree Bower,* line 76), and to remark, "Nature has her proper interest; & he will know what it is, who believes & feels, that every Thing has a Life of it's own, & that we are all *one Life*" (*CL* 2.864). For all its unsophisticated simplicity, then, the Mariner's moral expresses a typically Coleridgean reverence.

3. CONCLUSION: THE UNITARIAN *RIME*

Coleridge's Unitarianism informs *The Rime of the Ancyent Marinere* in complex interaction with various other influences, many of conflicting tendency, predictably, and in some ways *The Rime* ramifies beyond Unitarian values and interests. The most important of these influences derives from Coleridge's commercial interest in the ballad vogue, which bequeaths his story a Gothicism most apparent in the Mariner's Wandering Jew associations. Through those associations, *The Rime* accepts the motif of an unexpiated guilt. In my view, it is that motif which disrupts the text's Unitarian moral vision most powerfully. While the deaths of the crew and alienation of the Wedding Guest trouble some critics, the dispensations of those characters have never proven central to my own reading experience of the poem. Far more important, surely, are the Mariner's own shipboard feelings of isolation and anguish, but those experiences Unitarianism can account for. Even Christ's "sufferings were absolutely necessary to qualify him for the work on which he was sent, and, as it were, to *perfect his character*," Priestley wrote, adding that "one of the rewards of Christ's suffering was that "he should be the means, or the instrument, by which the doctrines of true religion . . . should be preached to all the world" ("One Great End" 217-18). Coleridge consistently follows Priestley in defending violence and suffering on moral grounds when they contribute to benevolent ends. He justified the slaughter of the Canaanites in the *Lectures on Revealed Religion* (*LRR* 142-45), and in *Religious Musings* envisioned a Unitarian apocalypse accompanied by tremendous political violence. With respect to individual salvation, Coleridge could reflect similarly, almost as if anticipating the Mariner, that "there is a state of depravity from which it seems impossible to recall mankind except by impressing on them worthy notions of Supreme Being, and other hopes & other fears than what visible objects supply" (*LRR* 111). The case of hardened sinners

required punitive terrors extending into the afterlife. The liberal Christianity that appealed to Coleridge anticipated a Universalist redemption without eternal Damnation. Yet Priestley followed Hartley in accepting "any long Period of Time, short of an absolute Eternity," and speculated on the subjection of the wicked to "actual Fire . . . to burn out the Stains of Sin" (*OM* 2.396, 399). As long as the Mariner's tribulations at sea can be conceived as the corrective vehicles of his spiritual enlightenment, they can be reconciled with Unitarian theology.

So what unsettles the Unitarianism of *The Rime* is not in the disparity between the Mariner's One Life homily and the agonies of his voyage. It is rather the disparity between the homily and the Mariner's agonizing compulsion to tell his tale, a compulsion rooted in an unpurged Gothic guilt. The moral problem of this guilt is not simply that Coleridge invokes it to display a holistic spiritual order constituting itself through exclusionary gestures. Instead, the problem lies with the fact that to all appearances the Mariner has met the requirements for inclusion: he seems to have escaped the state of moral reprobation that, for Priestley, would have alone justified his continuing penance. He has discovered the existence of a sacramental One Life, repented for his self-absorbed violation of it, and accepted an evangelical mission. Does the moral obligation to love all creatures not obligate the "one Mind" whose "most holy name is Love" to love the Mariner (*Religious Musings,* lines 105-6)? Why should his anguish and alienation continue? Why should so intense an irrational guilt periodically prey upon him? How Priestley would answer such questions is difficult to conceive. For him, the truth of Christianity and the process of salvation were matters of reasoned deference to the force of evidence. His theology rarely notices the darker psychological complexities of human spiritual experience. Never regarding conversion as a struggle against intractable inner impulse, Priestley can cheerfully dismiss Original Sin as that "strange doctrine of the utter inability of men to do what God requires of them" (*Appeal* 388). If Coleridge's 1798 letter to his brother George dismisses orthodox notions of "original Sin" by denying hereditary "GUILT," it also acknowledges a slothful, perverse human will unable to do exactly the thing needful for redemption. Moreover, Priestley discounts revelatory experiences of spiritual renewal as confidently as he minimizes the psychological complexities of sinfulness. The "doctrine of the exclusion of *all immediate agency of the Deity on the minds of men,*" he insisted.

> is utterly incompatible with the very principle and
> ground of the doctrine of *sovereign and irresistible
> grace,* the possibility of *instantaneous conversion,* and,

consequently, of any true and availing conversion at the latest hour of life. . . . [the] doctrine of a *new* and *miraculous birth* is altogether unscriptural and deceitful.

(*DI* 83)

With grace unnecessary, men and women could always save themselves—the contrary assumption affronted Priestley's faith in divine benevolence—just by assenting to the truths of the New Testament as established by Unitarian theological exegesis. To all appearances, however, the Mariner cannot simply save himself through gestures of intellectual assent: he must be reborn through an emotional reorientation no moral calculus could predict. Coleridge's respect for the possibilities of sudden revelation explains the interest he took in Methodist conversion narratives for their emotional honesty, an interest that emerges in *The Rime* through his recourse to John Newton's spiritual autobiography.[27] Its debts to Priestley's rational theology notwithstanding, *The Rime of the Ancyent Marinere* remains the characteristic product of the poet who confessed that, at a moment of religious crisis, his "philosophical refinements, & metaphysical Theories lay by me in the hour of anguish, as toys by the bedside of a Child deadly-sick" (*CL* 1.267).

Through its portrayal of the Mariner's residual guilt, *The Rime* displays the moral compassion and sense of human frailty that would finally move Coleridge beyond Necessitarian optimism. Still, *The Rime* ramifies beyond Unitarian paradigms only so far as to qualify those paradigms without undermining or abandoning them. The Unitarianism of *The Rime* explains Coleridge's relative disinterest in the Fall, an event Priestley believed never in fact occurred (*EI* 306-10). In its commitment to a human Christ, and consequent demotion of the Incarnation, Unitarianism also explains Coleridge's concentration on the Crucifixion. When his text refigures the Crucifixion as an allegory of atheism, he draws on the same conception of atheistic psychology analyzed in his Unitarian *Lectures on Revealed Religion.* Then of course there is the poem's presupposition of Necessity. *The Rime* may appear to invoke Necessity most notably by allowing the Mariner active energies while subjecting him, at key moments, to that passivity noticed by so many readers. Yet Coleridge's greatest debts to Necessity in *The Rime* may follow from the theory's privileging of naturalistic and psychological causality. The God of Necessity pursued His providential purposes through the laws of nature and human association, directing events secondarily and declining to meddle in earthly affairs. Necessitarian disbelief in supernatural intervention supported Coleridge's staging of the Mariner's spectral encounters as projections of fearful credulity. As propounded by Hartley and Priestley, then, the idea of Necessity encouraged the internalizations of the text while also linking them to a displaced providential teleology. The natural manifestation of that moral order was of course the One Life, the Romantic motif in which the Unitarian sympathies of *The Rime* emerge most clearly.

In defending the closing moral which celebrates those sympathies, House once wrote that, "coming in context, after the richness and terror of the poem, it is no more a banal moral apothegm, but a moral which has its meaning *because it has been lived*" (House 54). Here I would like to transpose House's emphases. I want to suggest not that the Mariner's suffering legitimizes and enables his sacramental affirmation but, rather, that his latent spiritual sense underlies and enables his sufferings. For contemporary critics of the "Nightmare" school, the devoutly Christian Coleridge was of the devil's party when he wrote *The Rime,* assigning his protagonist experiences of solitude and terror which expose the sentimentality of all claims that a spiritual purpose imbues human life. Extending this viewpoint, Anne Mellor has even assured readers that in *The Rime* Coleridge himself "desperately wanted to believe in the absolute validity of an ordered Christian universe but *could not,* could not because his own acute intelligence perceived the existence of an underlying chaos"— because "his own acute intelligence," that is, prevented him from accepting what she terms "the too-simple certainties of Christian theology."[28] For critics such as Bostetter and Mellor, there can be no affirmation of God in *The Rime* because of the poem's extravagant darkness. My contrary suggestion is that there could be no darkness, not of the sort Coleridge gives us, without the pre-supposition of God. Born of guilt, the hallucinatory horrors of the Mariner's voyage follow from the fact that finally he cannot kill unfeelingly—and in that inability Coleridge finds the touch of God. Atheism, as Burke avowed, "is against . . . our instincts." My final, reiterative suggestion is simply that the theological paradigms at issue in Coleridge's poem come principally from the Unitarian theology he still endorsed in 1798. It is Unitarianism that should be at issue as we continue to grapple with the question of the Christianity of *The Rime of the Ancyent Marinere.*

Notes

1. For the claim that Unitarianism had little impact on Coleridge's native visionary orientation as a poet, see John Beer's influential *Coleridge the Visionary* (1959; New York: Collier Books, 1962) 49, 51, 113. In "Coleridge, Hartley, and the Mystics," *JHI* [*Journal of the History of Ideas*] 20 (1959): 477-94. Richard Haven argues conversely that certain strains of British empiricism—the associationism of David Hartley, but implicitly the Unitarianism of Joseph Priestley as well—effectively accommodated Coleridge's mystical interests, yet Haven's respected argument has had

little influence on readings of *The Rime.* Our one Hartleyan interpretation of the poem dates to 1936: Dorothy Waples, "David Hartley in *The Ancient Mariner,"* JEGP [*Journal of English and Germanic Philology*] 35 (1936): 337-51. Although Hartley was no Unitarian, Coleridge had every reason to associate him with Priestley: Priestley published an edition of Hartley, quotes him with approval over and again, and takes his Christian conception of Necessity largely from the *Observations on Man.*

2. In correspondence about the Shrewsbury position. Coleridge told Josiah Wedgwood that "the *necessary* creed in our sect is but short—it will be necessary for me, in order to my continuance as an Unitarian Minister, to believe that Jesus Christ was the Messiah—in all other points I may play off my intellect *ad libitum,"* in *The Collected Letters of Samuel Taylor Coleridge,* ed. Earl Leslie Griggs, 6. vols. (Oxford: Clarendon, 1956-71) 1.366; hereafter cited parenthetically as *CL.* For Coleridge's prose, I use *The Collected Works of Samuel Taylor Coleridge,* gen. ed., Kathleen Coburn, assoc. ed., Bart Winer, 16 vols., Bollingen Series 75 (Princeton: Princeton UP, 1971-): individual vols. cited include vol. 1, *Lectures 1795 on Politics and Religion,* ed. Lewis Patton and Peter Mann (1971), hereafter cited parenthetically as *LRR*; vol. 6, *Lay Sermons,* ed. R. J. White (1972), hereafter cited parenthetically as *LS*; and vol. 7, *Biographia Literaria,* ed. W. Jackson Bate and James Engell (1983), hereafter cited parenthetically as *BL*). Notebook entries are cited from *The Notebooks of Samuel Taylor Coleridge,* ed. Kathleen Coburn, 2 vols., each subdivided to cover Text and Notes, (Princeton: Princeton UP, 1957), and are identified parenthetically by the abbreviation *CN.* Citations of Coleridge's poetry are not parenthetically identified, but come from *Coleridge: The Complete Poems,* ed. William Keach (Harmondsworth: Penguin, 1997). Although my essay treats the 1798 text of *The Rime of the Ancyent Marinere,* I drop the final e and refer to Coleridge's protagonist simply as the Mariner and, for convenience, to the inhabitants of the ghost ship as Life-in-Death and Death, although the poem avoids those names until the introduction of the 1817 glosses.

3. Warren, "A Poem of Pure Imagination: An Experiment in Reading," in *Selected Essays* (New York: Random House, 1941) 198-305; for Warren's treatment of Original Sin, see 226-33. Warren's emphasis on the motifs of Original Sin, moral agency, and guilt, coming in tandem with an understanding of Necessitarianism as a form of strict determinism, led him to reject the early Necessitarian reading of Coleridge's poem offered by Solomon Gingerich in *Essays in the Romantic Poets* (New York: Macmillan, 1924) 30-31. While Warren's essay has been frequently challenged over the years, its enduring prestige in Coleridge studies lies behind Seamus Perry's recent remark. "I suppose the standard reading [of *The Rime*] to be some kind of One Life allegory," in *Coleridge: The Uses of Division* (Oxford: Clarendon, 1999) 282.

4. "Christian Skepticism in *The Rime of the Ancient Mariner,"* in Frederick W. Hilles and Harold Bloom ed., *From Sensibility to Romanticism: Essays Presented to Frederick A. Pottle* (New York: Oxford UP, 1965) 439-52.

5. Noting Coleridge's familiarity with the Higher Criticism, McGann presented the glossed 1817 text of *The Rime* as an "imitation of a culturally redacted literary work," with the poem's layered testimonies dramatizing the transmission of a historically progressive faith, in "The Meaning of the Ancient Mariner," *Critical Inquiry* 8 (1981-1982): 35-67 (51). For McGann's claim that his reading works for the earlier, unglossed text too, see page 50 of his article. Although I have cited McGann's historicist reading for its presence in Coleridge scholarship, my own sense of the poem's genealogy of faith owes more to Alan Bewell's account of the "Natural History of Religion" in *Wordsworth and the Enlightenment: Nature, Man, and Society in the Experimental Poetry* (New Haven: Yale UP, 1989) 119-41. My subsequent paragraph, let me add, alludes to McGann re-entitling his essay *"The Rime of the Ancient Mariner*: The Meaning of the Meanings" when republishing it in *The Beauty of Inflections: Literary Investigations in Historical Method and Theory* (Oxford: Clarendon, 1985) 135-72.

6. Empson offers Unitarian readings of *The Rime* in *"The Ancient Mariner,"* rpt. in *Argufying: Essays on Literature and Culture,* ed. with an Introduction by John Haffenden (London: Chatto & Windus, 1987) 297-319; in the lengthy Introduction to *Coleridge's Verse: A Selection,* ed. William Empson and David Pirie (London: Faber, 1972); and in "The Ancient Mariner: An Answer to Warren," *Kenyon Review* n.s. 15 (1993): 155-77. These readings have been much praised: Paul Fry, for example, writes that Empson "delivered perhaps the most telling blow" to Warren's Christian interpretation "by pointing out that in 1797 Coleridge was still a Unitarian," in *The Rime of the Ancient Mariner,* ed. Paul H. Fry, Case Studies in Contemporary Criticism (New York: Bedford/ St. Martin's, 1999) 84: hereafter cited as Case Studies. In his eagerness to enlist Unitarianism for Christianity-bashing, however, Empson dismisses

the doctrinal continuities linking Unitarianism and Anglicanism by slighting both the *Lectures on Revealed Religion* and complicating statements in Coleridge's letters. He offers Coleridge's Unitarianism as an attack on traditional Christian defenses of the moral purposefulness of human suffering despite the fact that the *Lectures on Revealed Religion* expressly argue for a progressive theodicy in which suffering not only contributes to redemption but is an unavoidable precondition for it. I return to this point below, but interested readers may also consult Mann's notes in *LRR* (especially 108-111) and the analysis of Empson's Coleridge criticism in David Perkins, "The *Ancient Mariner* and Its Interpreters: Some Versions of Coleridge," *MLQ* [*Modern Language Quarterly*] 57 (1996): 425-48.

7. "The Pedlar," line 218, from the reading text included in Jonathan Wordsworth's *The Music of Humanity: A Critical Study of Wordsworth's "Ruined Cottage" incorporating texts from a manuscript of 1799-1800* (New York: Harper and Row, 1969) 172-83. My understanding of the One Life rests on this book: Jonathan Wordsworth's essay "Wordsworth's Borderers," in M. H. Abrams, ed. *English Romantic Poets: Modern Essays in Criticism,* 2nd edition (New York: Oxford UP, 1975) 170-87; H. W. Piper's *The Active Universe: Pantheism and the Concept of Imagination in the English Romantic Poets* (London: Athlone P, 1962); and the Introduction in James E. Butler, ed. *"The Ruined Cottage" and "The Pedlar,"* The Cornell Wordsworth (Ithaca: Cornell UP, 1979) 3-33. Exposed to Coleridge's One Life advocacy on an almost daily basis in late 1797. "Wordsworth seems to have absorbed a philosophic system," Butler notes, but not "its theological underpinnings" (16): Wordsworth was of course no Unitarian. Unless otherwise indicated, Wordsworth's poetry is cited from Stephen Gill, ed. *Wordsworth: The Major Works,* Oxford World's Classics (Oxford: Oxford UP, 1984).

8. My citations of Priestley come from John Towill Rutt, ed. *The Theological and Miscellaneous Works of Joseph Priestley,* 25 vols. in 26 (London: G. Smallfield, 1817-1832) 3.220; citations appear parenthetically with the following abbreviations; *MS: Disquisitions Relating to Matter and Spirit* (vol. 3); *PN: The Doctrine of Philosophical Necessity Illustrated* (vol. 3); *IE*: "Introductory Essays to Hartley's Theory of the Mind" (vol. 3); *CC: The History of the Corruptions of Christianity* (vol. 5); "Inspiration"; "Observations on the Inspiration of Moses," from *Essays on Inspiration* (vol. 7); "Taking the Cross"; "Taking the Cross and Following Christ"; *DI*: "The Doctrine of Divine Influence on the Human Mind" (vol. 15).

My citations of Hartley come from *Observations on Man, His Frame, His Duty, and His Expectations (1749),* ed. with an Introduction by Theodore L. Huguelet (Gainesville: Scholar's Facsimiles and Reprints, 1966), hereafter abbreviated *OM*.

9. Fiering, *Jonathan Edwards's Moral Thought and Its British Context* (Chapel Hill: U of North Carolina P, for the Institute of Early American History and Culture, 1981) 93.

10. Wordsworth's *Note to "Ancient Mariner,"* from the second edition of *Lyrical Ballads,* rpt. in Duncan Wu, ed. *Romanticism: An Anthology,* 2nd edition (Malden, MA: Blackwell, 1998) 345; Lamb's remark occurs in an 1801 letter to Wordsworth, in *The Letters of Charles and Mary Anne Lamb,* ed., Edwin W. Marrs, Jr., 3 vols. (Ithaca: Cornell UP, 1974-1978) 1.266. Below I cite Wordsworth's Fenwick Note to the Immortality Ode from Wu's volume.

11. Magnuson, *Coleridge and Wordsworth: A Lyrical Dialogue* (Princeton: Princeton UP, 1988) 72; Matlak, *The Poetry of Relationship: The Wordsworth and Coleridge, 1798-1800* (New York: St. Martin's P, 1997) 96-97; Eilenberg, *Strange Power of Speech: Wordsworth, Coleridge, and Literary Possession* (New York: Oxford UP, 1992), rpt. in Case Studies (282-314 [283]). On behalf of this approach, Magnuson cites an 1830 Coleridge Notebook entry on the supernatural in poetry: "the Poet of his free will and judgement does what the Believing Narrator of a Supernatural Incident, Apparition or Charm does from ignorance and weakness of mind, i.e. mistake a *Subjective* product . . . for an objective fact" (Magnuson 72).

12. De Quincey reported Coleridge's interest in writing "a poem on delirium, confounding its own dream-scenery with external things, and connected with the imagery of high latitudes," in "Samuel Taylor Coleridge," in David Masson, ed. *The Collected Works of Thomas De Quincey* (Edinburgh: A. & C. Black, 1889-1890) 2: 145. Beer connects this project to Coleridge's familiarity with the calenture, a fever besetting mariners, in *Coleridge's Poetic Intelligence* (New York: Barnes & Noble, 1977) 152.

13. Jack Fruchtman, Jr., *The Apocalyptic Politics of Richard Price and Joseph Priestley: A Study in Late Eighteenth-Century English Republican Millennialism,* Transactions of the American Philosophical Society, vol. 73, part 4 (Philadelphia: The American Philosophical Society, 1983) 96.

14. "The Nightmare World of The Ancient Mariner," rpt. in Kathleen Coburn, ed. *Coleridge: A Collection of Critical Essays,* Twentieth-Century Views (Englewood Cliffs, N.J.: Prentice-Hall, 1967) 65-77 (68).

15. House stresses the "double character" of symbols and events, and "the double mood of admiration and fear" in the poem, in *"The Ancient Mariner,"* in James D. Boulger, ed. *Twentieth-Century Interpretations of the Rime of the Ancient Mariner* (Englewood Cliffs, N.J.: Prentice-Hall, 1969) 48-72 (52).

16. Perkins 439. Noting Empson's claim that critics "project on the poem the Christian doctrine of the Atonement," Perkins justly adds, "I cannot find many critics who have done it as specifically as Empson leads one to suppose. Of the critics whom Empson is likely to have read, R. L. Brett seems to have gone farthest in this direction; in summary, his view is that 'sin leads to separation from God.' In other words, the Mariner's sufferings are neither inflicted on him by God as a punishment nor offered in a Christlike way to God, but express the state of a soul that has fallen away from God" (439). The allusion to Brett is to his *Reason and Imagination: A Study of Form and Meaning in Four Poems* (London: Oxford UP, 1960) 102. Perkins' well-taken point is that the representations of suffering in *The Ancyent Marinere* cannot be simply taken as references to the Atonement: one would have to *argue* for that equivalency, and do so in the face of alternative explanations compelling enough that no modern academic critic known to me, other than Empson, has even assumed the equivalency.

17. In this regard, J. A. Appleyard contends merely that the often-cited letter of March 1798 *"cautiously* anticipates elements of Coleridge's later religious philosophy" while remaining consistent in other respects with Coleridge's Unitarian rationalism, in *Coleridge's Philosophy of Literature* (Cambridge: Harvard UP, 1965) 60; my emphasis. J. A. Stuart concludes similarly that "it was not necessary . . . that Coleridge completely abandon his Socinianism in 1798 and espouse "Trinitarianism" in order to make the statements in the letter to George, in "The Augustinian 'Cause of Action' in Coleridge's *Rime of the Ancient Mariner,"* *Harvard Theological Review* 60 (1967): 179. For Stuart, Coleridge's understanding of Original Sin was consistently Augustinian, with Coleridge distinguishing between Original Sin and Adam's Fall as early as 1797-1798 (Stuart 180).

18. David S. Miall, "Guilt and Death: The Predicament of *The Ancient Mariner,"* *SEL* [*Studies in English Literature, 1500-1900*] 24 (1984): 633-73 (639).

19. W. H. Auden, *The Enchafed Flood, or the Romantic Iconography of the Sea* (New York: Random House, 1950) 72.

20. The point about the first person pronoun and the argument about identity formation can be found in Anne Williams' brilliant essay, "An I for an Eye: 'Spectral Persecution' in *The Rime of the Ancient Mariner,"* *PMLA* 108 (1993): 1114-27; see 1118.

21. Edmund Burke, *Reflections on the Revolution in France,* ed., with an Introduction and Notes, J. G. A. Pocock (Indianapolis: Hackett, 1987) 80.

22. Coleridge anticipated the Miltonic suggestiveness of this topos in the depiction of Catholic Superstition in *Religious Musings*: "For she hath fallen / On whose black front was written Mystery; / She that reeled heavily, whose wine was blood; / She that worked whoredom with the Demon Power, / And from the dark embrace all evil things / Brought forth and nurtured" (329-34).

23. In the first of the *Lectures on Revealed Religion,* Coleridge wrote that most Atheists "attempt to explain the formation of the Universe from the accidental play of Atoms acting according to mere mechanical Laws, and derived the astonishing aptitude and ineffable Beauty of Things from a lucky hit in the Blind Uproar" (*LRR* 98). One of the attractions of Hartley's system for Coleridge. Mann notes, was that "it removed the element of 'chance' from life, which was the atheist's and materialist's only alternative hypothesis as to the nature and origin of things" (*LRR* lx). So, again, the two spectral figures play dice because they represent not the randomness of events in *The Rime* but the assumption of randomness inherent in atheism as Coleridge understood it.

24. Modiano, "Sameness or Difference? Historicist Readings of *The Rime of the Ancient Mariner,"* in Case Studies, 187-219 (205-6).

25. Daniel Watkins notes the visual resemblance of cross and mast in "History as Demon in Coleridge's *The Rime of the Ancient Mariner,"* *PLL* [*Papers on Language and Literature*] 24 (1988): 23-33 (27).

26. The lines, "I would not strike a flower," from MS. JJ of the 1799 *Prelude,* are most commonly available as reprinted in Jonathan Wordsworth, M. H. Abrams, and Stephen Gill, ed., *The Prelude: 1799, 1805, 1850.* Norton Critical Editions (New York: Norton, 1979) 493. The other quotations in my sentence are from "Lines written in Early Spring" (lines 11-12) and "Lines left upon a Seat in a Yew-tree" (lines 48-50).

27. Coleridge informed Tom Poole, "I never yet read even a Methodist's 'Experience' in the Gospel Magazine without receiving instruction & amusement," in a letter of early 1797 (*CL* 1.302). Bewell discusses Wordsworth's recourse to Method-

ist conversion narratives for *Peter Bell* (110-23); for Coleridge's similar use of Newton, see Bernard Martin, *The Ancient Mariner and the Authentic Narrative* (London: Heinemann, 1949).

28. Mellor, *English Romantic Irony* (Cambridge: Harvard UP, 1980) 137, 141.

John Ower (essay date fall 2006)

SOURCE: Ower, John. "Coleridge's *Rime of the Ancient Mariner.*" *Explicator* 65, no. 1 (fall 2006): 19-21.

[*In the following essay, Ower considers how Coleridge used aspects of the science of alchemy to symbolize the Mariner's painful and hellish experience of spiritual transformation and redemption.*]

In line 111 of the **Rime of the Ancient Mariner,**[1] the poem's protagonist speaks of the "hot and copper sky" of the equatorial Pacific doldrums in which his vessel was becalmed. The adjective "copper" refers primarily to the discoloration of the firmament (which arises from the reddish light of the "bloody Sun" of line 112, a phenomenon that may be produced by a "dry fog" of volcanic ash suspended in the atmosphere).[2] However, the word "copper" in line 111 is most probably "overdetermined"[3] or polysemous, having a variety of implicit referents. To begin with, the "copper" of line 111 is part of a pattern of alchemical imagery through which Coleridge renders the Mariner's gradual redemption by a long and agonizing purgatorial "penance" (**Mariner** 408-09).[4] This occult symbolism involves a progression in parts 2-4 of the **Rime** from the base metals of copper and lead (with which last the heavy, dead albatross of **Mariner** [141-42] is eventually associated in line 291), through mercury or silver (suggested by the moonlit sea of **Mariner,** lines 267-68), to the gold, which is alluded to in line 281. In this regard, the pivotal episode that culminates with the Mariner's blessing of the watersnakes (263-91) is suggestive of the consummation of the alchemist's goal of transmuting the base metals into the precious ones. Such a transformation signifies the completion of the first stage of the Mariner's spiritual renewal, a rebirth that is effected through the sacrifice of Christ[5] (such a meaning being consonant with the way in which, for many of the alchemists, "[t]he achievement of metallic transmutation became symbolic of the religious regeneration of the human soul").[6]

In line 111 of the **Rime,** at the very beginning of the Mariner's regenerative penance, he is being subjected to an extremely harsh purgatorial environment (the severity of which is suggested by its very strong infernal overtones). This stringent purgatory/hell may be rendered in line 111 through an implicit secondary reference by the Mariner to a ship's "copper" (defined by

The Oxford English Dictionary as "A vessel made of copper, particularly a large boiler for cooking or laundry [. . .] the large boilers or cooking vessels on board ship.").[7] If the Mariner is indeed referring to such a container, then his "copper sky" would include an implicit figurative comparison of the reddened heavens to an inverted ship's copper (which is boiling "hot" like such a vessel when it is being used for cooking or for doing laundry). If this "submerged"[8] trope is in fact present in line 111, then the Mariner would be using a familiar item of ship's furniture as the "vehicle" of a figure that suggests the purgatory/hell of **Mariner** (107-262) is at once a torture chamber and a prison (a complex of meanings that is again conveyed by the "grate" of **Mariner** [179], which suggests not only the bars over a dungeon window, but also the "grate" in a fireplace,[9] and the ship's grates, to which sailors were tied for flogging).

Notes

1. All quotations from *Mariner* in the preceding study are uniform with the text in Stillinger (158-84).

2. This meaning could have been suggested conjointly to Coleridge by three very likely sources for the "bloody Sun, at noon" of line 112 of the *Rime.* These are Bishop Thomas Burnet's *The Sacred Theory of the Earth,* Gilbert White's *The Natural History and Antiquities of Selborne* and part 2 of Erasmus Darwin's *The Botanic Garden.* These three works, respectively, mention a "bloudy" "Sun" (297), a "blood-colored" sun (302), and a sun of "dilute red" that "appears [. . .] only about noon" (170), as well as a sun that is "as red as blood" (171). Those phenomena are in turn associated with "exhalations" into the "Atmosphere" (297), a "*haze,* or smokey fog" (301), and a "fog or haze" (170, as well as a "dry fog" 171). The preceding two sets of occurrences are in turn connected with the imminent "Eruption of a fiery mountain" (297), with a "*volcano*" that "sprung out of the sea on the coast of *Norway*" (203), and with "volcanic" outbursts (171), among these a "violent eruption of Mt. Hecla" (171). Because the first of these three sets of natural phenomena appears explicitly in *Mariner* (line 112), it seems reasonable to assume that the second is implied by the "copper sky" of line 111, whereas the third is submerged within the implicit subtext of the two just-mentioned verses. For the possible influence of Burnet and White on line 112 of *Mariner,* see Lowes 158-60.

3. For Freud's definition of "overdetermination," see Freud, *Standard Edition*: "each element in the content of a dream is 'overdetermined' by material in the dream-thoughts; it is not derived from a

single element in the dream-thoughts, but may be traced back to a whole number. These elements need not necessarily be closely related to each other in the dream-thoughts themselves; they may belong to the most widely separated regions of the fabric of those thoughts. A dream-element is, in the strictest sense of the word, the 'representative' of all this disparate material in the content of the dream" (5:652-53). The *Ancient Mariner* is of course in various ways like a dream, lines 107-262 having a nightmarish quality. See Magnuson 60-65.

4. Images that recur in the literature of alchemy are clustered in lines 263-81 of the *Rime*. These include (*a*) the snake (see Read 106-08; the *Ouroboros,* or serpent that bites its own tail, being brought to mind by the coiling of the water-snakes in line 280 of the *Ancient Mariner*), (*b*) the sun and the moon (see Read 88-89; the "golden fire" of line 281 of the *Rime* having obvious solar connotations), and (*c*) the colors black, white, yellow, and red (see Read 145-48; the just-mentioned hues appearing respectively in *Mariner* lines 279, 274, 281, and 271). To the just-mentioned imagery is added in the *Rime* (*a*) the references to lead and gold in lines 291 and 281, and (*b*) the suggestions of the alchemical concepts of "mortification" and of "resurrection" (see Read 95; these implications occurring respectively in *Mariner* lines 236-60 and 263-81). When all of the preceding considerations are taken together, it seems pretty certain that Coleridge is using alchemical ideas and images in lines 236-81 of the *Rime* to help render the Mariner's regeneration.

5. The albatross has, as some previous critics of *Mariner* have already noted, a number of associations with Christ. See, for example, Warren 362. The water-snakes are likewise connected indirectly with Christ through the "golden fire" of their tracks ("Mariner" 281). This image links the water-snakes through (*a*) a double reference to the "fiery serpent" of a golden-colored "brass" that is used by Moses to cure of snakebite the faithless Israelites (Numbers 21.6, 8-9), to (*b*) the employment of the brazen serpent of Moses in the Gospel of John as a symbol of man's regeneration through Christ's sacrifice on His cross (John 3.14-15).

6. Eliade 194. See also Frye 146 and Read 114-15.

7. *The Oxford English Dictionary,* vol. 2, 973.

8. I borrow this useful term from Keane's *Submerged Politics.*

9. Coleridge of course uses the word in this second sense in line 15 of "Frost at Midnight."

Works Cited

Burnet, Thomas. *The Sacred Theory of the Earth.* Carbondale: Southern Illinois UP, 1965.

Darwin, Erasmus. *The Botanic Garden.* Vol. 2. 2nd ed. London: Johnson, 1790.

Eliade, Mircea, ed. *The Encyclopedia of Religion.* Vol. 1. New York: Macmillan, 1987.

Freud, Sigmund. *The Standard Edition of the Complete Psychological Works of Sigmund Freud.* Ed. James Strachey. Vol. 5. London: Hogarth, 1973.

Frye, Northrop. *Anatomy of Criticism.* Princeton: Princeton UP, 1957.

The Interpreter's Bible. Vols. 2 and 8. New York and Nashville: Abingdon-Cokesbury, 1953 and 1952.

Keane, Patrick J. *Coleridge's Submerged Politics.* Columbia: U of Missouri P, 1994.

Lowes, John Livingston. *The Road to Xanadu.* Boston: Houghton, 1927.

Magnuson, Paul. *Coleridge's Nightmare Poetry.* Charlottesville: U of Virginia P, 1974.

The Oxford English Dictionary. Vol. 2. Oxford: Clarendon, 1961.

Read, John. *Prelude to Chemistry.* Cambridge: MIT P, 1965.

Stillinger, Jack. *Coleridge and Textual Instability.* New York: Oxford UP, 1994.

Warren, Robert Penn. *New and Selected Essays.* New York: Random, 1989.

White, Gilbert. *The Natural History and Antiquities of Selborne.* London: White, 1789.

Nicholas Reid (essay date 2006)

SOURCE: Reid, Nicholas. "The Ancient Mariner." In *Coleridge, Form and Symbol, or The Ascertaining Vision,* pp. 43-60. Aldershot, UK: Ashgate, 2006.

[*In the following essay, Reid analyzes* The Ancient Mariner *as part of the Higher Critical movement, focusing on the poem as a self-conscious text that is aware of its status as a fictional construct and examining its symbolic method.*]

In the opening section of this book I outlined a view which places concrete form at the centre of knowledge, and indicated very briefly how such a view fits in with Coleridge's thought.[1] In this section I want to begin looking more closely at Coleridge's views, by starting with the poems in which Coleridge first worked out the basis of his later theories of symbol and form. In this chapter I look at *The Ancient Mariner,* and the mythological and intertextual context of the Coleridgean symbol; in the next chapter I look more closely at the symbol itself, through the conversation poems; and in the fifth chapter I draw together these strands, both conceptual and imaginative, through a reading of Mark Akenside's *The Pleasures of Imagination.*

THE ANCIENT MARINER

We should turn, then, to *The Ancient Mariner.* And I should say here (of a poem which seems able to invite—and indeed to endorse—very different kinds of readings) that I have not in this [essay] pursued the predominant contemporary image of the Mariner as a type of the existential situation, nor as an odyssey of the soul.[2] Clearly much of the poem's emotional energy derives from and is concentrated on that situation. But there is also evidence of a larger framework which 'places' the Mariner's experience, and even if that 'placement' is not to be read as complete (if the poem's emotion continues to resonate beyond its frame) it reveals a ludic element which has its own systematic aspirations.

In this, I accept Humphry House's argument that one of the keynotes of the poem is its particular consciousness of the question of 'method' in its own reading (*Ancient Mariner* 55). But where House describes a poem which resists interpretation, my experience is of a poem which at least in one dimension invites, and indeed demands a method of *contextuality*. This is something which in part I can convey only in the method of my own reading, but it is also something which reflects Coleridge's Higher Critical views, views which, as we shall see, Coleridge had already formulated, though not thoroughly embodied, in his **'Destiny of Nations.'** For where earlier generations of critics were inclined to see a poem notable for its intensely imagined experience (and that is undoubtedly the source of its power), I am also impressed by something which Seamus Perry has remarked on, the poem's curious insistence on it own fictionality (286). This fictional element points to three important aspects of the symbol—its historical and intertextual placement; its transitivity or resistance to reification; and the vital role of the reading imagination as the place wherein it figures.

MORAL AND METHOD

Readers and critics would appear always to have felt an embarrassment in the face of Coleridge's apparent mysticism in *The Ancient Mariner.* Charles Lamb, rebuking Wordsworth for his less than generous comments, wrote that 'I was never so affected with any human tale' (Brett and Jones 270-271). The effusion is genuine, but there is a qualification: 'I dislike all the miraculous part of it.'

The miraculous part has continued as an embarrassment in our own century. The first systematic study, J. Livingston Lowes's *The Road to Xanadu,* sought an escape in treating the poem as 'a work of pure imaginative vision,' by which Lowes, misinterpreting Coleridge's comment to Mrs. Barbauld, meant a poem of pure fancy (Lowes 299-302). And Stoll and Schneider, in respected studies which sought to refute early attempts at a more positive interpretation, followed in Lowes's footsteps by arguing at length the position indicated by Muirhead's unfortunate comment on the daemonic poems—that 'it would be pedantry to look for philosophical doctrines in their magical lines.'[3] More recently, Lawrence Lipking, in an interesting study of the relation between the 1817 gloss and the main body of the text, was able to view the earlier text as an amalgam of barely related parts in which the reader is cast utterly adrift. Apparently the gloss explains and interprets for us where we, and the Mariner, are otherwise lost in a sea of fancy.

Coleridge himself, of course, did not help. Whilst his contemporary, Clement Carlyon, has described Coleridge's exultation in teasing his friends with metaphysical explanations of his poem, only one interpretative comment, if we discount the gloss, has survived (Beer, *Visionary* 140).[4] Few authorial comments can have caused such mayhem as Coleridge's response to Mrs. Barbauld:

> Mrs. Barbauld once told me that she admired the Ancient Mariner very much, but that there were two faults in it,—it was improbable, and had no moral. As for the probability, I owned that that might admit some question; but as to the want of a moral, I told her that in my own judgment the poem had too much; and that the only, or chief fault, if I might say so, was the obtrusion of the moral sentiment so openly on the reader as a principle or cause of action in a work of such pure imagination. It ought to have had no more moral than the Arabian Nights' tale of the merchant's sitting down to eat dates by the side of a well, and throwing the shells aside, and lo! a genie starts up, and says he *must* kill the aforesaid merchant *because* one of the date shells had, it seems, put out the eye of the genie's son.
>
> (*Table Talk,* 31 May 1830, quoted here from House 53)

As Humphry House has pointed out, a tale with no more moral than the Arabian Nights' story, is not a tale with no moral at all. But what is the moral? Leslie Stephen offered the helpful suggestion that the moral 'would apparently be that people who sympathise with a man who shoots an albatross will die in prolonged torture of thirst' (Beer, *Visionary* 135). Stephen noted that such a moral 'is open to obvious objections.'

There have of course been more successful attempts at positive interpretation, for many critics have been motivated by an overwhelming sense of moral concern within the poem. Robert Penn Warren produced his celebrated reading of the one life as the poem's subject, though the performance is a little wooden in places and aspects of the gloss remain unintegrated. The interpretative tone becomes, however, a little strained at times: Humphry House finds himself forced to defend the Mariner's obtruding moral on the grounds that 'coming in context, after the richness and terror of the poem, it is no more a banal moral apothegm, but a moral which has its meaning *because it has been lived*' (House's emphasis, 54). If the moral has truly been lived, then it is surely unnecessary. But one detects a note of special pleading: Coleridge is to be forgiven for the obtrusive moralising (for which he has apologised to Mrs. Barbauld) because of the strength of the performance.

Let us, then, pursue the question of the moral further. The elementary point to make about Coleridge's comment is, as House noted, its implication that the poem does contain a moral, which Mrs. Barbauld has missed—not necessarily 'He prayeth best who loveth best / All things both great and small.' But we should note that Coleridge's interest lies in the effect 'on the reader,' or in an 'obtrusion' which may reflect rather a disappointment with the way the contemporary audience chose to read the poem, than a fundamental flaw in the poem's design. Coleridge may not have wanted his audience to swallow the Mariner's moral quite as readily as they have sometimes done.[5]

There is another strand here. On House's account the obtrusive moral is unfortunate, but the poem as a whole, like the tale of the genie and the merchant, does have a broader moral concern. House takes some pains to point to the way Coleridge's objection is to a moral which *obtrudes*. Coleridge is playing a characteristic game: the first impression, and the impression Mrs. Barbauld was intended to receive, is that a story with 'no more moral than the Arabian Nights' tale' is a story with no moral at all. But House is right to point out that 'one cannot possibly read the [Arabian Nights'] story without being very aware of moral issues in it; aware that its whole development is governed by moral situations, and that without them there wouldn't really be a story' (House 53). *The Ancient Mariner* as a whole, we may take it, is imbued with a similar concern for the moral order.

We need not, however, (as seems to be House's intention) endorse the Mariner's own conclusion, about which the most that can be said is that (on Coleridgean presuppositions) it is true as far as it goes. In support of his argument, House supplies the ending of *The Arabian Nights* tale, which Coleridge omitted. I wish to quote his account of the complete tale because I think Coleridge's omission is, again, characteristic; and because I believe that in general we have not appreciated its significance:

The story of the Merchant and the Genie in *The Arabian Nights* is briefly this. A merchant is travelling in a desert with nothing to eat but some biscuits and dates in a wallet. He sits down to eat dates and throws the stones about: a huge and terrible genie appears, with a great scimitar, and says he will cut off the merchant's head. Why? Because one of the stones was flung into the eye of the genie's son and killed him. The merchant pleads that it was quite accidental: but the genie is relentless. Finally the genie allows the merchant one year's respite. He is free to go home to provide for his wife and children, and to order his affairs. This he does, with great justice and generosity and, after a struggle, he returns to the same spot in the desert, as arranged with the genie, exactly one year later. Here he falls in with three old men, mysterious strangers, to whom he tells his story; the genie then appears again. And each of the strangers in turn makes a bargain with the genie that if he can tell the genie a story more marvellous than he has ever heard before, the genie is to remit one-third of the merchant's punishment. The stories cap each other for marvellousness; the genie is honest to the bargain; the merchant goes free and triumphant home, and the three old men go off mysteriously into the desert as they came.

(House 53)

To read Coleridge's partial account, one would gain the impression that the merchant was doomed, whereas in its broadest sense the tale is a tale of Redemption. But the crucial point, I think, is the mode of Redemption— the telling of tales.[6] The mariner himself suffers the recurrent compulsion to tell his tale, though blind to the larger implications of this process. Fiction making is an activity imbued with special significance—and that, I take it, is one of the points of Coleridge's comment; though we should note in passing that even in its detail the Coleridge version differs from that given by House. In House's version the genie's son actually dies, whereas Coleridge refines the crime by specifying that the merchant had 'put out the eye of the genie.' In the redemptive context we may speculate that story-telling becomes a means of *seeing*. And the metaphor of sight or vision (a metaphor which lies also at the heart of *Lear*) is drawn from John IX:13 ('For judgment I came into this world, that those who do not see may see')— which reinforces the Christian theme within the poem.

Coleridge's comment to Mrs. Barbauld implies, then, that the 'moral' of *The Ancient Mariner* lies in the role it diagnoses for story-telling, or myth. Such an account of the poem clearly demands to be placed in the context of the Higher Critical movement in Biblical interpretation.[7] Coleridge's own contribution to this movement, the posthumously published *Confessions of an Enquiring Spirit,* has long been known—and our understanding of his position (and its conservatism relative to the more extreme elements in Higher Criticism) will be further consolidated once the notebook material from the late 1820s, and onwards, is more widely digested.[8]

However, it is not entirely necessary to refer to this later material in order to establish Coleridge's views—nor indeed could that establish the degree of Higher Critical influence in 1797—for Coleridge makes a number of explicit statements about the status of poetry as myth, and the significance of myth itself, in his poem, **'The Destiny of Nations.'** Here we find, in 1796, an explicit treatment of nature conceived symbolically, and of an epistemological function for myth. It is thus curious that this, the strongest evidence for a Higher Critical influence, is not so far as I am aware quoted by Shaffer, though it was referred to in a different context by R. L. Brett in the early 1950s, and the omission is made good by McGann and, more recently, Harding (Brett 108-109; Harding, *Reception* 43.)[9]

Two passages from **'The Destiny of Nations'** are important for our purposes here. The first runs from lines eighteen to twenty:

> For all that meets the bodily sense I deem
> Symbolical, one mighty alphabet
> For infant minds.

These lines identify the crucial human activity as the confrontation of the divine scheme, making quite explicit a conception of the natural world as symbolic and necessitating a symbolic interpretation.[10] In the second passage (running from line 80) the function of myth, the means of internalising symbol, is developed:

> For Fancy is the power
> That first unsensualises the dark mind,
> Giving it new delights; and bids it swell
> With wild activity; and peopling the air,
> By obscure fears of Beings invisible,
> Emancipates it from the grosser thrall
> Of the present impulse, teaching Self-control,
> Till Superstition with unconscious hand
> Seat reason on her throne. Wherefore not vain,
> Nor yet without permitted power impressed,
> I deem those legends terrible, with which
> The polar ancient thrills his uncouth throng.

Though the 'polar ancient' bears no direct relation to the Mariner himself, the reference does establish a context in Coleridge's later poem.[11] And Coleridge could scarcely have written more direct instructions for a reading of *The Ancient Mariner.* Myth, or fancy (which we may read as imagination, for Coleridge had not formulated his famous distinction in 1796), unsensualises the mind, removing it from the domain of naturalism and materialism. Moreover myth making has an epistemological function, being part of a developmental schema or progress towards Truth: 'Till Superstition with unconscious hand / Seat Reason on her throne.'

But there is another point to be made here. As we have already begun to see, *The Ancient Mariner* has a tendency to accrete other texts which are clearly aware

of their own status as tales (the story of the merchant and the genie) or as myth (**'The Destiny of Nations'**). This tendency points to a particular consciousness of fictionality within *The Ancient Mariner* itself. And this mythic self-reflexiveness, I shall claim, identifies its place within the Higher Critical progress—points indeed to the fact that *The Ancient Mariner* is not what it presents itself as (a tale belonging to the late fifteenth-century border between Catholicism and the Reformation) but, rather, in its self-awareness is a product of late eighteenth-century Higher Criticism. It is to *The Ancient Mariner* that we must now turn.

APPLYING THE MORAL: *THE ANCIENT MARINER*

The outlines of the Christian theme within the poem are fairly clear. The Mariner's voyage begins, for instance, with a strongly repeated image of the Fall:

> The ship was cheered, the harbour cleared
> Merrily did we *drop*
> *Below* the kirk, *below* the hill,
> *Below* the lighthouse top.

> (1.21, my emphases)

The Mariner's voyage, then, is the voyage of human experience: of sin, purgation and a kind of salvation.[12] And the Mariner's salvation introduces the theme of the imagination, for the Mariner's salvation results from the imaginative regeneration which allows his appreciation of the Creation—a growth symbolished in his appreciation of the beauty of the sea snakes.[13]

The problem with such a reading (though it is in general a reading which I would defend) is that it leaves a lot in the poem unexplained. Robert Penn Warren, of course, has clarified much in the poem about the theme of imagination and the business of the sun and the moon. And readings, like that of John Beer, have made us more aware of the breadth of Coleridge's desire to subsume preceding mythologies—more so than had Lowes, whose theoretical conceptions prevented him from advancing a 'reading' at all. But such criticism, while it has traced very fully the origins of Coleridge's images in the writings of a broad range of traditions, does not, I think, provide the kind of integrative motive which would explain the purpose of all this intellectual flotsam and jetsam in the Mariner's wake: the tendency of many readings (where they do not, in the contemporary fashion, eschew all notions of coming to a reading) has been towards an overarching mysticism. But, as we shall see in Coleridge's *Lectures 1795,* mystical readings are improbable. And so the problems remain.

This leads us to the controversial nature of the Mariner's crime, a particular problem for criticism but one which, I think, bears with it a lesson on contextuality and interpretation. One of Wordsworth's complaints was that the Mariner 'does not act, but is continually acted upon' (Brett and Jones 271). Wordsworth's mystification in the face of the Mariner's sin has been shared by more recent critics. For Robert Penn Warren the Mariner's is a motiveless and gratuitous act paralleling the Fall (26). For John Beer, the Mariner's crime 'is existentially right' because it belongs to the world of the imagination (*Visionary* 150). And J. D. Boulger sees the logical world of the Wedding Guest, with its concomitant morality, as a form of spiritual death: the Mariner's purpose is to get the Wedding Guest to see beyond the limits of reason and 'understanding' (*Interpretations* 10-13).

The problem with such readings lies, again, in their incipient mysticism, for they tend to posit a world of imagination which lies beyond reason. Here Wordsworth's remarks seem to help. Even if the killing of the albatross, by virtue of a genuinely akratic[14] nature, does become a mark of freedom, the Mariner's passivity in the rest of the poem provides an inconsonance for which mystical readings find it hard to account—the Mariner is no Don Juan indulging an innocent passion and being persecuted by a tyrannous God.[15] These critical approaches, then, seem to ask the wrong question. It is enough, I think, to assert in line with Coleridge's theory of evil that the Mariner's sin, though it asks questions of freedom, is primarily characterised by ignorance of its consequences; an ignorance reflecting a deeper Imaginative failure which the poem delineates. The Mariner's crime reflects, then, a failure of the imagination. In what follows I wish to propose that this failure is related to *despair*; but also to expose some of the intertextual games Coleridge plays in seeking to render conscious the process of interpretation, the process by which interpretation emerges.

First we should document the themes of imaginative failure and despair at its simplest level. One dimension of the Mariner's act is revealed at line 65, when he says of the albatross:

> As if it had been a Christian soul
> We hailed it in God's name.

The reference is not merely allusive, but reveals the deeper subsuming aspiration of the poem. The killing of the albatross is akin to the killing of a person; and the murder which comes most strongly to mind in the Christian tradition is the murder of Abel. The journey of the Mariner thus suggests the wanderings of Cain in his exile from God, but typically, and as Coleridge's dynamic view of myth would suggest, there is no specificity. The Mariner suggests just as forcibly the Wandering Jew, doomed to wait for Christ's second coming for having mocked Christ (from the standpoint of contemporary Jewish pessimism) for his slowness on the way to Calvary and the enactment of Salvation

(Harvey 1042). And similarly the Mariner subsumes quest figures as diverse as Sinbad, Burger's daemonic hunter (who, 'heeding not the laws of God or man, was forced to hunt eternally'), the heroes of numerous gothic tales, and even Prometheus (Beer, *Visionary* 145-150). Coleridge's more than allusive technique (the poem's conscious accretion of contexts) insists upon the genuine function of his own symbolic construction, for *The Ancient Mariner* views itself not as an act of Christian mimesis but as the Romantic tool of exploration and the Mariner cannot be reduced to Cain or any other traditional figure.

The experience of Cain, however, provides on one level a possible reading of the nature of the Mariner's crime. Indeed it is well known that Coleridge contemplated writing a poem about Cain. The plan for such a poem, entitled 'The Wanderings of Cain,' exists in some detail, but what is perhaps most significant is its curious insistence on its intertextual relation to *The Ancient Mariner*—a relation which is pointed to in yet another text (a 'Prefatory Note') and which, as we shall see, draws in a third, an unpublished fragment which continues on from where the published prose-plan finishes. In a prefatory note Coleridge describes the undertaking as follows:

> The work was to have been written in concert with another [Wordsworth], whose name is too venerable within the precincts of genius to be unnecessarily brought into connection with such a trifle. . . . My partner undertook the first canto: I the second: and which ever had done first, was to set about the third. Almost thirty years have passed by; yet at this moment I cannot without something more than a smile moot the question which of the two things was the more impractical, for a mind so eminently original to compose another man's thoughts and fancies, or for a taste so austerely pure and simple to imitate the Death of Abel? Methinks I see his grand and noble countenance as at the moment when having dispatched my own portion of the task at full finger-speed, I hastened to him with my manuscript—that look of humorous despondency fixed on his almost blank sheet of paper, and then its silent mock-piteous admission of failure struggling with the sense of the exceeding ridiculousness of the whole scheme—which broke up in a laugh: and the Ancient Mariner was written instead.
>
> (*PW* [*Poetical Works*] I.1.359)

The last remark serves to set *The Ancient Mariner* in the context of Cain's deed, but we should note again that the context has asserted its status as con*text* quite explicitly.

In 'The Wanderings of Cain' a 'Shape that was like Abel' appears to Cain who, like the Mariner, suffers torments of thirst. The Shape tells Cain that it is in torment because it sacrificed to the God of the Living, who is insignificant beside the God of the Dead. We are told: 'Then the child Enos [Cain's innocent son] lifted up his eyes and prayed; but Cain rejoiced secretly in his heart.' Why, we may ask, should Cain rejoice at such a terrible notion? And what was going on in the Mariner when

> A wicked whisper came, and made
> My heart as dry as dust

(1.247)?

Cain is not unnaturally anxious to know how to placate this greater God of the dead—and there the published fragment ends. But in an unpublished fragment which continues the story, Cain is about to offer the blood of his innocent son to the God of Death when the archangel Michael arrives and reveals the Shape of Abel as a devil. If we look at *Genesis* IV we find that Cain is quick to assume that he is damned, though God says nothing of the sort and the mark of Cain is in some ways a sign of God's protection for His sinful subject. But Cain is susceptible to one of the deadlier sins, despair,[16] and this seems to be what Coleridge means by the God of the Dead. It also provides a powerful means of reading Life-in-Death. Despair is deadly precisely because it is inimical to faith and therefore to the very possibility of salvation, a point the young Coleridge makes with ultra-protestant zeal in his critique of orthodoxy (both Catholic and Anglican), in the *Lectures 1795.* The later Coleridge, in 1819, quotes Luther to the same effect:

> We are better prepared for, and more inclined to, Despair than Hope: for Hope proceedeth from the Holy Spirit and is his Work; but Despair cometh of our Spirit, and is our Strength, our work and act. Therefore God hath forbidden it under highest penalty.
>
> (*CN* [*The Notebooks of Samuel Taylor Coleridge*] IV.4600)

Leaving aside, then, the intertextual issue, we can see how the theme of despair would work in **The Ancient Mariner.** The crew of the ship display no moral perception in their judgement of the Mariner's action (Beer, *Visionary* 149-150). They first reprove it out of superstition, then lend their approbation when it appears that the killing of the albatross has freed the ship from the mist and snow, and finally curse the Mariner when they think his act has led them into the doldrums. There is no moral dimension to their judgement, nor is there an imaginative one such as would allow them to perceive the presence of God in the natural world. They succumb to despair, and in sign of this remove the cross (a symbol of hope and promise) from the Mariner's neck, replacing it with the albatross. In this substitution the dead albatross becomes a symbol of despair; and the very process of this 'becoming' throws interesting light on the nature of the Coleridgean symbol.

Like the evil spirit in 'The Wanderings of Cain' (and, again, as Satan does in *Paradise Lost*), Life-in-Death

may wish to contaminate the human world with despair. Certainly the Mariner succumbs to a sense of abandonment:

> Alone, alone, all all alone
> Alone on a wide wide sea!
> And never a saint took pity on
> My soul in agony

(1.232)

This of course is merely the Mariner's interpretation: as Beer argues, God's presence is imaged throughout; and this is only one point where we should treat the Mariner's interpretation as little more than that (Beer, *Visionary* 143-145, 161, etc.). The Mariner does, however, possess that 'shaping spirit of Imagination' of which Coleridge wrote in **Dejection,** though the Mariner, unlike Coleridge, does not begin to understand its nature. The albatross unfolds into embodied despair when hung about the Mariner's neck in the place of the cross, but in that reified form it is arguably the symbol only for the other sailors who placed the bird on the Mariner and who are soon to die. For the Mariner himself (I shall present the argument in more detail in the next chapter [of *Coleridge, Form and Symbol*]) the symbol never loses its fluidity, remaining a symbol of the imaginative function in the broader sense but not quite of imagination-denying despair. Under its aegis the Mariner, whose imaginative struggle began the quest, has still to struggle with the images of God and the possibilities of death and despair (or the wicked whisper of his heart (1.246)) before finding a resolution in the vision of beauty which puts the albatross through what in a sense is its penultimate transformation. For the vision is a vision of imaginative affirmation, the moment at which

> . . . from my neck so free
> The Albatross fell off, and sank
> Like lead into the sea.

(1.289)

The cross, which it had replaced, is silently resurrected. And in the following lines (the drinking of the dew) the poem constitutes itself as an gloss on *John* VI.35, the text with which our Victorian ancestors adorned public water fountains: 'he that believeth on me shall never thirst.'[17]

Since the Mariner overcomes despair through his imaginative faculty (in the recognition of the beauty of the sea snakes) we may suggest (and this method of reading—a reading from hindsight or, as it were, a reading back from the 'cure' to the 'disease'—seems the only means of proceeding if we are to come to a 'reading' at all) that the Mariner's original crime was an act of imaginative failure, or failure to see the albatross as part of the natural creation and to be reverenced. Coleridge's comments on idolatry in the *Lectures 1795* (to bring in another context) may, however, help us further to locate this emphasis on imaginative failure, for Coleridge there argues that this sort of imaginative failure demonstrates the lack of faith which undermines comprehension of the divine good, and provides the roots of despair (340). This point constituted the basis of Coleridge's Unitarian objection to Orthodoxy, and makes doubly significant the Mariner's orthodox Catholicism. One might suggest that the Mariner has been predisposed by the teachings of his church to an idolatrous reification (a belief in works) of what should be imaginatively alive and transitive (faith). For his fellow sailors (and especially in their conversion of the albatross into an icon of despair) this becomes more than a predisposition.

MYTHIC CONSCIOUSNESS

In something like this fashion a Christian reading of the poem can be justified—and while I am sure that there are many reasons for wanting to resist such a reading, I am also sure that in some respects at least we cannot deny Coleridge's own allegiance to a Christian world view. But it would be a mistake to see the poem solely as an exemplification of the moral,

> He prayeth best, who loveth best
> All things both great and small

> (l.614)

for what makes the poem peculiarly Romantic is its self-reflexivity, its interest not only in the content of the vision, but in the process by which it is derived. And here we should turn to a closer examination of symbol. For in pointing to the way the poem, with its conscious misdirection and gamesmanship, establishes its own mythic or fictional consciousness, I do not wish to mount the kind of argument which would see the poem engaging in a kind of deconstruction. For me, the poem directs attention to its own function as myth, and to the function of the reader in participating in the interpretation of divine symbols; and thus to the status of the commitments it holds.

The symbolic method begins with the opening line, 'It is an ancient Mariner.' Not only is the present tense curious, establishing the existential contemporaneity of the events described, but the first word itself, and the construction of the line (not 'There was an ancient Mariner,' but 'It is an ancient Mariner') insists peculiarly on the function and status of the character, as symbol. The Mariner, in his symbolic guise, is becoming already the self subsistent entity of Coleridge's later theory,

> the Idea [containing] it's necessity in it's actual presence. The *so it must be . . .* involved in the *So it is.*[18]

Many of the elements of the symbolic construction have been mentioned already, and others will be obvious. The poem is framed within a marriage; and the bride thus comes into opposition with Life-in-Death. If, as I have argued, Life-in-Death is the spirit of despair then the opposition is a productive one. Like the bride, 'Her lips were red, her looks were free;' and Coleridge's emphasis underlies the parallel of true marriage and false. Life-in-Death is described as the mate of death, and their pseudo-marriage contrasts with that of the bride—a symbol (as the Minister reminds the congregation during most weddings) of the true community of the Church in its relation to Christ. Despair, rooted in Imaginative failure, results in the loss of the sense of communion, and alienation. And similarly, much of the iconography of Christian myth is subsumed. When we are told

> Through utter drought all dumb we stood!
> I bit my arm, I sucked the blood,
> And cried, A sail! a sail!

> (l.159)

the grotesque parody of the communion prefigures, again, the vision of despair, just as the Mariner's thirst suggests Christ upon the cross and his 'strange power of speech' (l.587) alludes to the Pentecostal miracle (*Acts* 2).

Such symbols draw on the cultural tradition in its widest sense, and arguably have a positive interpretative function, but others seem to operate less in this way. The image of the glory (a halo representing sanctification) at lines 97 and 98 asserts a much narrower context of reading, though still public to the educated reader of the day: the image of the snake (as a symbol for imagination) draws on a much more private and arcane body of reference, and challenges the more obvious readings from *Genesis* (Beer, *Visionary* 5). Words like 'joy' (which in the Wesleyan context, for instance, refers to the divine experience, the sense of the light that lighteth every person) derive from very specific interpretative vocabularies and seem to delight in the consciousness of their hidden reference, as if again their reflexive qualities are what matter as much as any positive implication (Prickett, *Coleridge* 103-104, and chapter I). And similarly, the typology of the Trinity (which must have aroused Coleridge's curiosity in its appearance through the three strangers in the Muhammadan *Arabian Nights*' Tale) arises in the second line (the Mariner 'stoppeth one of three') and again when Life-in-Death 'whistles thrice:' it too can no doubt be explained[19]—but it is so far from fitting in any immediate way into the poem's image or ideational structure that such explanations seem beside the point. Rather, their very incidentality, like the buried but not expanded paranomism of the *cross*bow, seems to assert the fictional nature of the poem's material, providing more a methodological context than a positive reading. The same could be said of the dice-game which Life-in-Death wins, or thinks she does. The figure invites a Necessitarian reading; and reminds us even of 'The Godwinian System of Pride' in which man is 'an outcast of blind Nature ruled by a fatal Necessity,' which Coleridge had rejected in 1796 (*CN* I.174, f. 25). But though, again, this allows us to interpret the dimensions of Life-in-Death as a symbol, the main function seems to be that of asking questions, of the reader, about reading.

Such moments disrupt the tendency to fall completely into the Mariner's world: we recognise not so much a deeper layer of meaning as the author's presence, teasing us with possibilities—inviting us to think not of particular solutions but to become conscious of the status of the text and what House called the problem of 'method.' I don't wish to describe such moments of resistance as complete (that would be to violate Coleridge's own Higher Critical but conservative hermeneutics). But this is a text which is (and wants its reader to be aware that it is) self-aware.

This quality of resistance (of fictional self-consciousness) can also be seen in the way the text resists mystical readings, something I have so far only talked about in a general way. Yet, read in the light of the *Lectures 1795,* this resistance can be quite spectacular. Any reading of **The Ancient Mariner** must meet the Mariner's declaration, at line 294,

> To Mary Queen the praise be given!
> She sent the gentle sleep from Heaven,

and the Mariner's subsequent request for the hermit to 'shrieve' him or offer confession and absolution. Yet for Coleridge at this time the very 'foundations' of the episcopal church are to be found in the *mystery* to which he repeatedly turns in the lectures, the source not only of the exploitation of the people by the church, but also of the confusion and the repulsion which costs them their faith. In the vision which begins the first lecture, Coleridge adopts the figure of the circle to represent the progress of the disillusioned from the superstition of Orthodoxy to the superstition of Atheism: both are superstition since both promulgate a mystery with no adequate means of explanation. Unitarianism (as the catchcry has it) provides explanation without mystery.

If Anglicanism is mere superstition, then the Mariner's Catholicism is just as bad (the Mariner is a rather uncertain guide to theology at least). Coleridge's language on the subject, as one who comes from the dissenting tradition and is still in some danger from the antidisestablishmentarianism of the time, is scarcely restrained:

> He who sees any real difference between the Church of Rome and the Church of England possesses optics which I do not possess—the mark of antichrist is on both of them.
>
> (*L1795* [*Lectures 1795: On Politics and Religion*] 210)

Coleridge was of course to develop the optics which would justify the distinction later in life.

If this were not enough, the Mariner's cry is to Mary; and yet for Coleridge the cult of the Virgin was pure idolatry—something which asserts the power of the reified idol over that of the divine act, and is thus essentially destructive of true faith. In one of the fragments of theological lectures written in the mid-1790s Coleridge describes the origin of the cult in the established church:

> Pagan rites were transferred to Christian Temples and Images were worshipped as the Virgin Mary and the infant Jesus [which] antiquarians have shewn to be antique . . . Venus & Cupid.
>
> (*L1795* 340)

Read, then, in the light of the specific cultural tradition out of which it grew, the dissenting tradition, the text clearly resists the sorts of interpretations which the Mariner himself draws—and in a manner which, again, seems methodological.

If the Mariner himself is an unreliable and naive guide to his experience then in an even more fundamental sense so is the author of the narrative. Readings of the poem must question the relation between the narrator and the Mariner, and the deeper relation between them both and the created consciousness which has so knowingly assembled the components of the poem.[20] Lawrence Lipking, for instance, believes that the addition of the gloss to the 1817 version of **The Ancient Mariner** amounts to a redefinition of the nature of poetry (614). As it appears in his seminal article, 'The Marginal Gloss,' Lipking's argument depends upon the view that the main text of 1798 is essentially fragmentary and that the purpose of the gloss is to relate the parts to a whole. The 1817 version, he claims, is 'the critical essay on the uses of the Supernatural in poetry' which Coleridge had promised but never written (614). The gloss, 'a kind of secondary imagination' (which, we remember, 'dissolves, diffuses, dissipates, in order to re-create'), 'casts an entirely new light' upon the interpretative process (*BL* [*Biographia Literaria*] I.304; Lipking 613-614). In the 1798 version the reader is cast adrift within a world of incoherent parts, whilst in the 1817 version the gloss explains and interprets for us in a way which reveals the true nature of interpretation:

> The gloss is superbly—some might say smugly—knowing. Not in thrall to the mariner's perspective, it understands the meaning of his experiences . . . as he cannot understand himself. . . . Above all, the author of the gloss knows that the world makes sense.
>
> (616)

Lipking proceeds to quote from Chapter XIV of the *Biographia* on the way the reader should be carried on 'like the motion of a serpent,' and argues that with the gloss the poem completes itself, the eye darting from text to gloss, from experience to interpretation, in a constantly collected movement (620). The gloss has redefined poetry by showing that meaning resides in the dialectic of interpretation and text.

This story can, I think, be expanded a little, for it is in the very knowingness of the main text that the process of redefinition, not only of poetry but also of interpretation of natural and biblical symbol, takes place. The relation between gloss and text which Lipking describes is a figure for the broader relation between the reader and the poem as a whole. And on trial in a broader sense is the voice and consciousness of the gloss, created within us as the ostensible assembler of the whole and locus of meaning. For the gloss too collapses in the face of the broader context which it dictates, revealing the deeper consciousness which, I believe, most nearly represents Coleridge himself.

As Lipking points out, the author of the gloss, and the one who quotes the motto from Burnet (I shall treat these as one and the same), speaks with the voice of scholastic authority. This truly is the voice of one who 'knows that the world makes sense,' and furthermore can explain it—at line 131 the ship's woes are attributed to

> A Spirit [which] had followed them; one of the invisible inhabitants of this planets, neither departed souls nor angels; concerning whom the learned Jew, Josephus, and the Platonic Constantinopolitan, Michael Psellus, may be consulted. They are very numerous, and there is no climate or element without one or more.

(The underlying conception here, as in the image of the star-dogged moon, is of the great chain of being.) But against the voice of the gloss we need to place Coleridge's own comment, in the second of the *Lectures 1795* that

> One of the chief and most influencing Principle[s] of Idolatry was a Persuasion that the temporal Blessings of Life, Health, Length of Days, fruitful Seasons, Victory in Wars, and such advantages were to be expected and sought for as the Gifts of some inferior & subordinate Beings, who were supposed to be the Guardians of Mortal Men.
>
> (140)

Though this predates the gloss by many years Coleridge did not change his views on this matter, and it reveals fairly clearly what we should make of the interpretation put forward by the author of the gloss, and to some extent what we should make of 'all the miraculous part.'

Coleridge plays the same game with Burnet's motto. Burnet tells us that 'I easily believe that there are more invisible than visible beings in the universe.'[21] Col-

eridge's real interest, however, is not in the question Burnet asks: 'But who will tell us the families of all these? And the ranks, affinities, differences, and functions of each?' Rather, if we remember the doctrine of myth propounded in **'The Destiny of Nations,'** Coleridge's attention must have been drawn by the lines,

> The human mind has always circled after knowledge of these things, but has never attained it. But I do not deny that it is good sometimes to contemplate in thought, as in a picture, the image of a greater and better world; otherwise the mind, habituated to the petty matters of daily life, may contract itself too much.

Coleridge put it rather more succinctly: 'Fancy is the power / That first unsensualises the dark mind' (**'Destiny of Nations'** 1.80).[22] But the earlier lines, with Burnet's talk of invisible beings, do have a function as part of Coleridge's conscious misdirection of the reader. As Lipking points out, Coleridge has omitted a line from Burnet's Latin: 'But of what Value are all these Things? Has this Seraphic Philosophy any Thing sincere or solid about it?' Lipking takes the omission as evidence (and his tone is perhaps ironic) that the author of the gloss is 'more knowing' than Burnet himself, but it seems also to point to the way the author of the gloss is more foolhardy (616-617). The omitted lines, it seems, are meant to focus our attention squarely on the question of method.

CONCLUSION

We may begin then to draw some conclusions. One is that the reading I have given here is only *a* reading, for this is a poem which constantly displays new dimensions. Debbie Lee, for instance, has only recently shown us that when the mariner sees, in the spectre ship, the 'bars' and the 'dungeon grate' (ll. 177-179), we should see a slave ship. Another conclusion is that the reading I have offered is the kind of thing criticism predisposed us towards in the early 1980s, albeit with an intentionalist underpinning. But I think that we can also claim, as McGann has shown, that this emphasis on textuality and readership reflects Coleridge's own hermeneutics, hermeneutics which are in some ways remarkably unchanged from the mid-1790s to the late biblical criticism. And we can thus see that in *The Ancient Mariner* Coleridge displays a mythic self-consciousness through the use of a variety of fiction-realising strategies which centre on the symbol, but include the conscious adoption of biblical and poetic languages, overt but misdirecting acts of interpretation within the poem, and the bringing to bear of the cultural and personal traditions within which the poem was written so as to explode prima facie readings and force the reader's attention onto the act of reading itself. And in the 1817 version, the very structure of the poem, with its apposition of preface, motto, text and marginal comment, belies any notion of a meaning located in the words on the page—in what New Criticism and its cognates in earlier twentieth-century aesthetics tended to think of as the serenely autonomous text.

Nor does **The Ancient Mariner,** as a poem, endorse the Mariner's own conclusion, for whilst that, within the context of the poem, is probably true it is also highly reductive. Like all the possible embarrassments in the poem, its function is to challenge its putative status, and, by elevating the presence of the reader into consciousness, to point to the essential transitivity of the symbol and to the textuality of the text. That textuality (that conscious fictionality) points in turn to the status of the poem as part of the Higher Critical progress outlined in **'The Destiny of Nations'** from earlier to later mythic form. But we can draw a slightly broader conclusion than this, for this is a book on the Coleridgean symbol or concrete form. With its implied context the poem presents a picture of the Coleridgean universe. **The Ancient Mariner** presents a role in which the imagination, in a kind of secondary idealism, must grapple with the symbols of the natural world and of received religion, a world in which (as **'The Destiny of Nations'** shows) God speaks symbolically.

Notes

1. An earlier version of this [essay] first appeared in *AUMLA* [*Journal of the Australasian Universities Language and Literature Association*] 84 (Nov. 1995): 21-40.

2. For existential readings, see Buchan, Bostetter, and Whalley; and on the soul, see Engell's 'Coleridge (and His Mariner).' More recent readings are less centred on subjectivity than were existential readings, but also in their more radical critiques of 'meaning,' less likely to find meaning in the Mariner's universe.

3. Muirhead is quoted in Beer's *Coleridge the Visionary* (133). However, the philosophical doctrines Muirhead had in mind were those which appeared in Coleridge's earlier poems, the doctrines of Hartley and radical empiricism (Muirhead 43). Beer discusses the poem's critical history on pages 133 to 137. Schneider's concern in *Coleridge, Opium and Kubla Khan* was of course mainly with *Kubla Khan,* because she felt its indeterminacy offered more scope for critical abuse, but on *The Ancient Mariner* see 14-16.

4. Carlyon unfortunately records nothing of interest on this subject.

5. Jasper also points to the questionable naivety of the concluding moral (130).

6. For Arac the moral found in the wider Arabian Nights' tale is that of fabulation as an attempt to control the arbitrary nature of the trope, and the

tales told by the old men all assert 'transformations between man and beast, magic versions of the theme of "one life"' (269).

7. My reading takes place within the general background documented by Shaffer and adopted by McGann, that of the German Higher Critical Tradition in which scripture was reduced (or otherwise) to myth. But it does not share Shaffer's assumption (pointed to by Prickett) 'that the position of Coleridge, and later of Hare and Maurice, is based on the same premises as their German forerunners' (Prickett, review of *Kubla Khan* 617). Nor do I share the view that Coleridge's scriptural hermeneutic amounts to an argument for the complete historical relativity (as we understand the concept today) of the Bible—that the historical method becomes 'a critique of all "positive" claims for the objectivity of the interpretation of texts, Biblical or poetic' (10), and thus marks a continuity with contemporary practice, structuralist (Shaffer) or post-deconstructionist (McGann). For such a view fails to see the particular direction of Coleridge's interest in myth which, as I seek to show in my discussion of *On Poesy or Art,* lies in his symbolic view of mind and its concomitant implication that only in myth can universal symbols be internalised and comprehended. Coleridge's view of myth belongs fundamentally in the neoplatonic context dismissed by Shaffer (7), and myth arguably represents the a-historic idea of Plato made dynamic, as the form of what Brisman would call the 'kenotic.' This particular crux seems to license a reading which is at once positive and relativised, which recognises the fictionality of any explanation and yet grants it a Popperian orientation towards truth.

8. Haney usefully discusses Coleridge's higher criticism (83-93).

9. McGann interprets 'The Destiny of Nations' from a Marxian perspective, claiming that the poem's presentation of a processive or developmental view of myth amounts to complete historical relativity. Thus he wishes to deconstruct any positive account of *The Ancient Mariner*'s meanings, though he does allow some room for a Coleridgean interpretation in his double-edged claim that '[t]he meaning of the *Rime* emerges through the study of the history of its illusions' (55). Harding places both 'The Destiny of Nations' and *The Ancient Mariner* in the context of sceptical currents within the mythographers Coleridge was reading, arguing that 'if a consistent mythology could be extracted from [*The Ancient Mariner*], it would probably be quite close to the *religion universelle* of Dupuis' (*Reception* 49-50). Engell (in *The Committed Word,* 119-140) and Prickett (in

Words and the Word) both usefully discuss the origins of Higher Criticism in the writings of Robert Lowth.

10. Stephen Prickett once suggested to me that a symbolic *alphabet* is an alphabet of purely conventional (rather than presentational) symbols. However, the parallels with Plato's analogy of the Cave in the passage which follows suggests that the symbolic 'alphabet' shadows the forms of reality itself. See Swiatecka's discussion of the passage (60-63).

11. Harding points to the writings of David Cranz as Coleridge's source for the polar ancient or Greenlander (*Reception* 43).

12. Moreover, in the context of the *Lectures 1795,* and Coleridge's Unitarianism at the time, it is worth noticing the nature of that salvation, as a form of divine beneficence rather than being in any sense Redemption through the Crucifixion.

13. Moreover, as Beer has pointed out, the snake for Coleridge is a symbol of imagination—the image of the snake biting its tail figures imaginative unity (*Visionary* 5).

14. An akratic action is the knowing doing of wrong. Socrates argued in the *Apology* that, rightly understood, akratic actions are an impossibility.

15. Indeed, to look for an act, or to specify sin as an activity, is to misconceive Coleridge's doctrine of the Fall. Ultimately analysed, sin is not an act of pure will but a *failing* of the impure will. See, for instance, *OM* [*Opus Maximum*] 236-247.

16. For Coleridge's comments on despair, see *CN* [*The Notebooks of Samuel Taylor Coleridge*] IV.4600.

17. Coleridge quotes *John* in *CN* IV.5240.

18. *Sic.* Quoted by Prickett, *Romanticism and Religion* 56, from *CN* V.5817.

19. They perhaps serve as clues that a reading through the Unitarian/Trinitarian dichotomy is appropriate, and Life-in-Death's use of the Trinitarian type in particular may be suggestive in the light of Coleridge's vehement Unitarianism at the time.

20. Jasper raises similar issues (130).

21. Bloom and Trilling provide a translation of the Latin.

22. Coleridge made the same point in his letter to Poole on the effect of an early exposure to tales of the supernatural (*CL* I.210 (16 October 1797)).

Works Cited

Arac, Jonathon. 'Repetition and Exclusion: Coleridge and New Criticism Reconsidered' in William V. Spanos et al. (ed.), *The Question of Textuality: Strategies of Reading in Contemporary American Criticism* (261-273). Bloomington: Indiana UP, 1982.

Barth, J. Robert, ed. *The Fountain Light: Studies in Romanticism and Religion, in Honour of John H. Mahoney.* New York: Fordham UP, 2002.

Bate, W. J. *Criticism: The Major Texts.* NY. Harcourt Brace Jovanovich: 1970.

Beer, John B. *Coleridge the Visionary.* London: Chatto and Windus, 1970.

Bloom, Harold and Lionel Trilling (eds). *Romantic Poetry and Prose.* New York: OUP, 1973.

Bostetter, Edward E. 'The Nightmare World of *The Ancient Mariner,*' reprinted in *Coleridge: The Ancient Mariner and Other Poems—A Casebook,* ed. A. R. Jones and W. Tydeman. London: Macmillan, 1973.

Boulger, J. D. (ed.). *Twentieth Century Interpretations of The Rime of the Ancient Mariner.* Englewood Cliffs NJ: Prentice Hall, 1969.

Brett, R. L. *The Third Earl of Shaftesbury: A Study in Eighteenth-Century Literary Theory.* London: Hutchinson, 1951.

Brett, R. L. and A. R. Jones (eds). *Lyrical Ballads.* London: Methuen, 1965 rev. edn.

Brisman, Leslie. 'Coleridge and the Supernatural.' *Studies in Romanticism* 21 (Summer 1982): 123-159.

Buchan, A. M. 'The Sad Wisdom of the Mariner,' reprinted in J. D. Boulger (ed.), *Twentieth Century Interpretations of the Rime of the Ancient Mariner.* Englewood Cliffs NJ: Prentice-Hall, 1969.

Carlyon, Clement. *Early Years and Late Reflections.* London: Whittaker, 1836.

Coleridge, Samuel Taylor. *Biographia Literaria,* 2 Vols, ed. James Engell and W. Jackson Bate. Princeton NJ: Princeton UP/Bollingen, 1983.

————*Biographia Literaria* ed. John Shawcross. London: OUP, 1907.

————*Lectures 1795 On Politics and Religion,* ed. L. Patton and P. Mann. London: Routledge and Kegan Paul/Bollingen, 1971.

————*The Notebooks of Samuel Taylor Coleridge,* ed. Kathleen Coburn *et al* . . . London: Routledge and Kegan Paul, 1957-2002.

————*Opus Maximum,* ed. Thomas McFarland and Nicholas Halmi. Princeton: Princeton UP/Bollingen, 2002.

————*Poetical Works,* ed. J. C. C. Mays. Princeton: Princeton UP/Bollingen, 2001.

————*Table Talk,* ed. Carl Woodring. Princeton: Princeton UP/Bollingen, 1990.

————*Table Talk and Omniana.* London: OUP, 1917.

————*The Table Talk and Omniana of Samuel Taylor Coleridge,* arranged and edited by T. Ashe. London: George Bell, 1905.

————*On Poesy or Art,* reprinted in W. J. Bate, *Criticism: The Major Texts* (393-399). New York: Harcourt Brace Jovanovich, 1970.

Engell, James. *The Committed Word: Literature and Public Values.* University Park, Pennsylvania: Pennsylvania UP, 1999.

————'Coleridge (and His Mariner) on the Soul: "As an exile in a far distant land,"' in J. Robert Barth, *The Fountain Light,* 128-151.

Haney, David P. *The Challenge of Coleridge.* University Park Pennsylvania; Pennslyvania State UP, 2001.

Harding, Anthony John. *The Reception of Myth in English Romanticism.* Columbia: U of Missouri P, 1995.

Harvey, Sir Paul. *The Oxford Companion to English Literature,* 5th edn revised by Margaret Drabble. Oxford: OUP/Clarendon, 1989.

House, Humphry. *The Ancient Mariner,* reprinted in J. D. Boulger (ed.), *Twentieth Century Interpretations of the Rime of the Ancient Mariner.* Englewood Cliffs NJ: Prentice-Hall, 1969.

Jasper, David. 'The Two Worlds of Coleridge's *The Rime of the Ancient Mariner,*' in J. R. Watson, ed., *An Infinite Complexity: Essays in Romanticism.* Edinburgh: Edinburgh UP, 1983: 125-144.

Lee, Debbie. 'Yellow Fever and the Slave Trade: Coleridge's *The Rime of the Ancient Mariner,*' [*ELH: English Literary History*] 65.3 (Fall 1998): 675-700.

Lipking, Lawrence. 'The Marginal Gloss.' *Critical Enquiry* 3 (1977): 609-655.

Lowes, John Livingston. *The Road to Xanadu: A Study in the Ways of the Imagination.* Rev. edn London: Constable, 1930?

McGann, Jerome J. 'The Meaning of *The Ancient Mariner.*' *Critical Enquiry* 8 (1981): 35-67.

Milton, John. *The Poetical Works of John Milton,* ed. L. Valentine. London: Warne, 1896?

Muirhead, John H. *Coleridge as Philosopher.* London: George Allen and Unwin, 1930/1954.

Perry, Seamus. *Coleridge and the Uses of Division.* Oxford: OUP, 1999.

Prickett, Stephen. *Coleridge and Wordsworth: The Poetry of Growth.* Cambridge: CUP, 1970.

————Review of '*Kubla Khan*' and '*The Fall of Jerusalem:*' *The Mythological School in Biblical Criticism and Secular Literature, 1770-1880* by E. S. Shaffer [London and New York: CUP, 1975] in *Modern Language Review* 73 (1978): 616-617.

————*Romanticism and Religion.* Cambridge, CUP, 1976.

————*Words and The Word.* Cambridge: CUP, 1986.

Schneider, Elisabeth. *Coleridge, Opium and Kubla Khan.* New York: Octagon Books, 1966; reprint of Chicago UP edn, 1953.

Shaffer, Elinor S. . . . *Kubla Khan and The Fall of Jerusalem: The Mythological School in British Criticism and Secular Literature 1770-1880.* Cambridge: CUP, 1975.

Stoll, E. E. . . . "Symbolism in Coleridge". *PMLA* lxiii (1948), pp. 214-233.

Swiatecka, M. Jadwiga. *The Idea of the Symbol.* Cambridge: CUP, 1980.

Warren, Robert Penn. 'A Poem of Pure Imagination: An Experiment in Reading' in R. P. Warren, *Selected Essays by Robert Penn Warren.* London: Eyre and Spottiswoode, 1964.—also available in an edited version in J. D. Boulger (ed.), *Twentieth Century Interpretations.*

Whalley, George. 'The Mariner and the Albatross,' reprinted in *Coleridge: The Ancient Mariner and Other Poems—A Casebook,* ed. A. R. Jones and W. Tydeman. London: Macmillan, 1973.

Thomas Dilworth (essay date summer 2007)

SOURCE: Dilworth, Thomas. "Parallel Light Shows in Coleridge's *The Rime of the Ancient Mariner.*" *Explicator* 65, no. 4 (summer 2007): 212-15.

[*In the following essay, Dilworth points out the affinities between the "death-fires" (St. Elmo's fire) and the "fire-flags" (the Southern Lights) in* The Ancient Mariner, *professing that both function as positive signs in the poem.*]

Since first reading **The Rime of the Ancient Mariner** many decades ago, I have wondered about the strong resemblance in it between two natural nocturnal light shows: one is the corposant or St. Elmo's fire (lines 127-30); the other, the Southern Lights or Aurora Australis (313-17).[1] The corposant is blue static-electric light dancing in the rigging and mastheads. Visually and verbally, it corresponds strikingly with the Southern Lights, but this has never been noted in print. It is an omission in criticism explained, I think, not by failure to notice the resemblance, which must be obvious to most readers, but by inability to discern in it any symbolic or thematic implications. This inability is doubtless due to the fact that most scholars are landlubbers and consequently inclined to trust uncritically the Ancient Mariner's negative evaluation of the exclusively maritime corposant. He refers to this phenomenon as "death-fires" (128). As he narrates events, his negative valuation may express anticipatory dread of his own suffering and the fate of his crewmates, but it contradicts nautical tradition in a way that would elicit skepticism if not outright disagreement from any other sailor. Freed from the Mariner's unconventional and, at best, dubious valuation, the corposant can only be seen as symbolically positive in meaning. Its correspondence with the Southern Lights then becomes thematically significant, illuminating the Mariner's pivotal blessing of the water snakes and its fictional setting, the supernaturally inhabited physical universe of the poem.

The correspondence between the light shows is verbally signaled by the association of each light show with fire and dancing and by a shared rhyme. The Mariner sees the corposant after the shooting of the Albatross, during the doldrums (when there is no wind to move the ship): "About, about, in reel and rout / the death-*fires danced* at night" (127-28; emphasis added). Nearly two hundred lines later, he sees the Southern Lights after blessing the water snakes and sleeping and quenching his thirst with rain:

> The upper air burst into life!
> And a hundred *fire*-flags sheen,
> To and fro they were hurried about!
> And to and fro, and in and out,
> the wan stars *danced* between.
>
> (313-17; emphasis added)

The descriptions of these two light shows resemble each other strikingly, calling to each other across much of the length of the poem—or rather, because they are visual images, mirroring each other. Their mirroring is secured by the repeated combination of the words *fire* and *danced*. The word *danced* occurs nowhere else in the poem and therefore exclusively marks the mirroring. The passages are also exclusively linked by the rhymes "about . . . rout" and "about . . . out"—a rhyming that occurs nowhere else in the poem.[2]

The visual mirroring, with its accompanying verbal echoes, has seemed meaningless to critics because we have always merely accepted the Mariner's valuation of the corposant as "death-fires." But in Western symbolic culture, they cannot be death-fires. No mere natural fact, St. Elmo's fire is what Jerome McGann, writing of another matter, calls a "pre-interpreted" phenomenon.[3] As such, moreover, it is universally regarded as a fortunate sign, hence its association with a saint. The fire of St. Elmo, also identified with St. Clare, St. Helen,

and St. Nicholas, was, in the Middle Ages and later, sometimes called by mariners simply Corpo Santo, the saint's body. It was regarded as a certain sign of the saint's presence and protection. In a note to *The Anathemata*, David Jones writes, "This phenomenon has always been regarded by seamen as beneficent, perhaps for the reason cited by William Dampier in the seventeenth century '. . . the height of the storm is commonly over when a Corpus Sant is seen aloft.'"[4] In earlier, Classical times, these fires indicated the presence of the Dioscori (Castor and Pollux), patron gods of sailors, because they were among the Argonauts and because, in response to Orpheus's prayer, they saved Jason's ship during a storm. St. Paul sailed in a ship named after Castor and Pollux (Acts 28.2) because of their saving power, signaled by the static-electric fires. the ancient, continuous, and—in the Western world, at least—universally positive interpretation of these fires in nautical culture contextualizes the Mariner's negative valuation of them and contradicts it. His "death-fires" are everybody else's "life-fires." In the poem, therefore, they probably do not mean what the Mariner says they do.

The emphatically positive meaning of the corposant in nautical tradition aligns it thematically with the Southern Lights, which correspond to it visually and verbally and which seem to dance in celebration of the blessing of the water snakes and the immediate positive effects of that blessing. Seen positively by the reader, the corposant dancing early in the poem implies that the universe has been urging the Mariner toward blessing all along, in this instance by supplying beauty to encourage it—as, later on, "their beauty" (283) leads the Mariner to bless the water snakes. Moreover, the corposant is closely associated with the water snakes because it dances in the rigging immediately after the lines: "Yea, slimy things did crawl with legs / Upon the slimy sea" (125-26). These are, or are very like, the water snakes. The Mariner here "despiseth" them (gloss at 238) but later sees them, or the snakes resembling them, as beautiful (283) and blesses them.[5] Despising the "slimy things" is a metaphysical error akin to shooting the Albatross. Negatively valuing the corposant is a similar mistake. That the corposant actually has positive meaning in the poem (that is, for Coleridge and the knowledgeable reader, although not the Mariner) is emphasized by visual affinity between the corposant's reflection on the water and the appearance of the water snakes just before the Mariner blesses them—an affinity unremarked in criticism and that I also noticed decades ago and have since wondered about. Like nothing else in the poem, this affinity is multicolored. The reflection of the corposant "Burnt green, and blue and white" (130). The water snakes are "Blue, glossy green, and velvet black, / [. . .] and every track / Was a flash of golden fire" (279-81). This is the third and only other occurrence of the word *fire* in the poem—its appearance here emphasizing association with the saint's "fires" in their correspondence with the Auroral "fire-flags."

If, as they seem, both natural lightshows are symbolically positive, then their verbally marked visual correspondence implies that physical nature in the poem is altogether beautiful in a divinely ordered, benign economy, which has metaphysical dimensions. Physical nature in the poem invites love and blessing. If this is so, the corresponding lightshows pose a serious challenge to recent interpreters of **The Ancient Mariner** who see the universe of the poem as morally unintelligible, a cosmic meaninglessness on which the Mariner and the writer of the gloss to the poem unconvincingly impose Christian benignity.[6]

Notes

1. Samuel Taylor Coleridge, *The Rime of the Ancient Mariner,* 1834 version, printed with all the textual variants of previous versions in Jack Stillinger, *Coleridge and Textual Instability: The Multiple Versions of the Major Poems* (New York: Oxford, 1994), 158-84. Subsequent references are to lines in this text.

2. The medievalist Joanna Luft noticed the rhyme in both passages, in conversation with the author.

3. *The Beauty of Inflections, Literary Investigations in Historical Method and Theory* (Oxford: Clarendon, 1985) 162.

4. David Jones, *The Anathemata* (London: Faber, 1952), 142. *The Anathemata* and *The Ancient Mariner* are the two great nautical poems in English.

5. I think that the gloss is accurate here. There is a debate in Coleridge criticism over the authority of the gloss, added to the poem in 1817—to aid bewildered readers, most critics assume. Huntington Brown and Jerome McGann argue that the glossifier is an independent figure, identifiable by late-seventeenth-century vocabulary (Brown, "The Gloss to *The Ancient Mariner, MLQ* [*Modern Language Quarterly*] 6 [1945] 320; McGann, *The Beauty of Inflections* [Oxford: Clarendon, 1985] 142). The evidence for this is inconclusive, however, because his vocabulary is not consistently seventeenth century. Although he seems distinct from the primary narrator, he may be transparent to Coleridge.

6. These metaphysical pessimists (at least insofar as the poem is concerned) include Edward Bostetter, "The Nightmare World of *The Ancient Mariner,*" *Studies in Romanticism* 1.4 (Summer 1962), rpt. in *Coleridge,* ed. Kathleen Coburn (Englewood Cliffs: Prentice-Hall, 1967) 67-77; Norman Fru-

men, *Coleridge the Damaged Angel* (New York: Braziller, 1971); Paul Magnuson, *Coleridge and Wordsworth* (Princeton: Princeton UP, 1988); Raimonda Modiano, "Word and 'Languageless' Meanings: Limits of Expression in *The Rime of the Ancient Mariner,*" *MLQ* 38.1 (1977): 40-61, rpt. in *Romantic Poetry,* ed. Karl Kroeber and Gene Ruoff (New Brunswick: Rutgers UP, 1993) 222-39; Seamus Perry, *Coleridge and the Uses of Division* (Oxford: Clarendon, 1999); and Arden Reed, *Romantic Weather* (Hanover: UP of New England, 1983). The more recent among these appear biased in their interpretation by the Marxist materialism of cultural studies and the nihilism of deconstruction.

Gilles Soubigou (essay date 2007)

SOURCE: Soubigou, Gilles. "The Reception of *The Rime of the Ancient Mariner* through Gustave Doré's Illustrations." In *The Reception of S. T. Coleridge in Europe,* edited by Elinor Shaffer and Edoardo Zuccato, pp. 61-87. London: Continuum, 2007.

[*In the following essay, Soubigou focuses on French illustrator Gustave Doré's artwork for his 1876 edition of the poem, tracing the impetus behind the project, Doré's artistic process, and the financial and critical reception of the volume, particularly its effect on the popularity of Coleridge worldwide.*]

By the beginning of 1876, Gustave Doré's edition of **The Rime of the Ancient Mariner** (**AM**) was available in London; one year later, the French publisher Hachette distributed in Paris a French version of the poem, translated by Auguste Barbier and reusing Doré's plates. Although this edition of **AM** was not the first appearance of Coleridge in French cultural life, it quickly established itself as a major reference. So much so, in fact, that it displaced the previous contributions to his reception and, as a consequence, is often presented today as the first sign of knowledge of Coleridge in nineteenth-century France.[1]

Some previous modern academic works analysed Doré's illustrations for Coleridge. The first study entirely dedicated to this subject was Millicent Rose's preface to the 1970 Dover edition of *AM* (Coleridge 1970, v-xi). Thirteen years later, on the occasion of the celebration of the centenary of Gustave Doré's death, the first important exhibition dedicated to the artist was organized in the Museum of Modern and Contemporary Art in Strasbourg, Doré's Alsatian birthplace; a significant place was dedicated to Doré's Coleridge (Favière 1983, 259-62). In 1985, Renée Riese Hubert examined Doré's illustrations and compared Doré's visual response to the literary text with Lhote's, Prassinos's and Masson's (Hubert 1985, 80-92). In 1989, an article by Renate Brosch synthesized the knowledge on Doré's project and analysed his plates (Brosch 1989). Finally, two recent books focused on the poem and its illustrators, enhancing the importance of Doré's work (Woof and Hebron 1997, 72-81 and 129-30 and Klesse 2001, 60-74). The goal of this [essay] is not to draw up a general overview of the artistic fortune of *AM,* but to focus on Doré's contribution, using these previous works together with new evidences and archive material, in order to understand how and why these plates achieved such a phenomenal reputation, even if Doré's undertaking is commonly described as a financial failure (Leblanc 1931, 74; Poiret 1983, 98; Renonciat 1983, 240-43 and Kaenel 2005, 439). The fact remains that Coleridge's poem was carried along on this wave of approval into a variety of editions in a variety of countries.

It seems obvious that the reception of Doré's book had a direct effect on the reception of Coleridge in the countries where this volume was distributed. As far back as 1932, Edouard Tromp wrote that 'Doré's visions brilliantly contributed to the diffusion of the poem out of his homeland' (Tromp 1932, 38).[2] But we must be aware that two distinct reception problems are linked in the present case. The first is the reception of Coleridge's perhaps most famous poem by one of the greatest French illustrators of his time; the 1877 Hachette edition was not only the first separate-volume French translation entirely dedicated to one of Coleridge's poems, but also the first illustrations for Coleridge's works ever drawn by any French artist. The second is the reception of a *livre d'artiste* by readers on a European scale—and even on a worldwide scale, for volumes also travelled to the United States. The success—or failure—of the reception of Doré's Coleridge must be discussed here. Finally, the reception of this book includes its artistic reception and the potential influence of these plates, characterized by a gothic, dark and dramatic atmosphere, on other French illustrators, particularly those who later illustrated Coleridge's poem.

Coleridge was far from being the most famous British writer in France during the first half of the nineteenth century. His celebrity never matched Walter Scott's or Byron's, particularly among French artists. Compared to the popularity and success of Scott, Byron, Ossian or Shakespeare,[3] Coleridge's works were virtually unknown in France, except by specialists. Moreover, whenever he was known, he was treated with distrust, if not even patronized. For the eighth volume of the *Biographie universelle Michaud* (Michaud's Universal Biography), published in 1854, an article on Coleridge was written by Valentin Parisot (1800-61). Parisot was professor of foreign literatures at the Université de Douai and developed at the same time the activities of

a versatile writer. He was famous for his translations of Greek and Latin authors and for his translation of the *Ramayana* in 1853, the first French translation of the Indian sacred text. About Coleridge, this classical mind wrote that 'although having many of the qualities which make a great poet, Coleridge missed his destiny. There was something incoherent in his mind, in his ideas, in his wishes'.[4] In the same text, Parisot called the British poet 'this whimsical minstrel of the nineteenth century' ('ce fantasque trouvère du XIXe siècle') (Parisot 1854, 8: 572).

Yet despite this lack of understanding, the 'whimsical' Coleridge inspired only ten years later in Gustave Doré a true masterpiece and a major work of late Romanticism in French art.

The Rime of the Ancient Mariner: a challenge for illustrators

French artists were traditionally reluctant to illustrate literary fantasies and dreams. Fantastic stories were generally treated with caution and the success of British gothic novels during the 1790s and early 1800s in France was led by Ann Radcliffe, whose stories always had a logical final explanation, rather than by 'Monk' Lewis. And even if Shakespeare was illustrated by French artists, they generally avoided his fantasy plays, such as *The Tempest* or *A Midsummer Night's Dream.* Moreover, Coleridge was considered at first to be the oddest and most bizarre writer English literature had ever brought forth, and *AM* was regarded as the weirdest poem of this weird author. In 1827, the anonymous editor of *The Living Poets of England* wrote as an introduction to his selection of Coleridge's poems published by Galignani:[5]

> [The ***Ancient Mariner***] is Coleridge's best ballad. It is a whimsical conception; but we cannot, like the author's friends, pronounce it to be at once *astonishing and original.* It is, they affirm, a poem which must be felt, admired, and meditated upon, but which cannot possibly be described, analysed, or criticized. We doubt whether it would, in France, be acknowledged to be the most singular of the creations of genius.[6]

From a French critical point of view, Coleridge was terribly difficult to understand, and had to be linked with the medieval tradition if one wanted to explain his poetry rationally. As Parisot explained about *AM*:

> The medieval beliefs living still in so many hearts, under so many thatched roofs, the remnants of old customs, the legends that are told during the evenings round the fire or in the barn, and which are believed in like the Gospel, these are the subjects a familiar poetical spirit, capable of a flight of enthusiasm but not of a sustained work, should lovingly indulge in. Such subjects were also able to enthral an audience very similar to the poet and like him impressionable and easily upset.[7]

Described by Parisot as 'whimsical', 'impressionable' and 'easily upset', Coleridge was clearly assimilated to the figure of a poet choosing to depict medieval subjects which sent the reader back to a world of legends and ancient terrors, very far from the French classical tradition Parisot championed. Otherwise, it had been stated that Coleridge did not encourage artists to illustrate his poems and that his taste in painting was essentially classical (Woodring 1978, 91-106). Yet it is possible to consider that Coleridge, as an upholder of the sublime in poetry (Shaffer 1969, 213-23), was also interested in Romanticism in art. Some evident connections can be traced between Coleridge's works and the interest in the sublime in British painting, particularly in Turner's work (Twitchell 1983, 85-108). Elinor Shaffer has also described Coleridge's personal interest in the work of Washington Allston, now considered one of the major American Romantic painters. It was Coleridge's attempts to gain attention for Allston's Bristol exhibition that led him to publish several of his shorter aesthetic essays (Shaffer 1993). Even if Coleridge's aesthetic was not an incitement to produce pictures based on his poems, in so far as it rested on the principle that painting was in no way as universal as poetry (Woodring 1978, 99), *AM* could be considered as a call for illustration, with explicit references to painting, such as appear in verses 115-19:

> Day after day, day after day,
> We stuck, nor breath nor motion;
> As idle as a painted ship
> Upon a painted ocean.

This is—paradoxically if we refer to what we previously said of Coleridge's ideas on the matter—a use of the *Ut pictura poesis* principle: the poet, in wishing to evoke a powerful visual image in the reader's mind, uses a reference to painting, a practice that Mario Praz, in his famous essay on *The Parallel between Literature and the Visual Arts,* called 'directions to the painter' (Praz 1974, 7). This visual dimension of Coleridge's poem, this direct call to illustrators, is the reason why, despite Coleridge's reservations about the evocative power of fine arts and pictorial representation, artists will risk a confrontation with the poet's works. As a consequence, Thomas Stothard (1755-1834) was commissioned in 1828 to produce a plate for Coleridge's *Christabel* for *The Bijou; or Annual of Literature and the Arts,* published by William Pickering in 1829 (Bentley 1981, 111-16). He decided to represent Geraldine glancing at Sir Leoline (lines 564-91), a 'scene chosen for its picturesque qualities' (Bentley 1981, 112). It is known that Coleridge saw Stothard's design and commented on it.

But the most frequently illustrated poem remains the most visually complex: *AM.* Before Doré, two British—or, more exactly, Scottish—artists illustrated *AM,* namely David Scott (1806-49) in 1837 and Joseph Noel Paton (1821-1900) in 1863. David Scott's twenty-five etchings (Coleridge 1837) are characteristic of the Victorian romantic style, with a vigorous linear drawing which evokes the legacy of William Blake's late-eighteenth-century illustrations; Paton's plates (Coleridge 1863), however, were clearly linked to the Pre-Raphaelite movement and a certain Victorian revival of medievalism. One of the main interests of David Scott's illustrations is that when the artist wrote to Coleridge in January 1832 to inform him that he was illustrating *AM,* Coleridge responded that he appreciated 'the compliment, paid to me, in having selected a poem of mine for ornamental illustration and alliance of the Sister Arts, Metrical and Graphic Poesy' (Woof and Hebron 1997, 57), a statement which could easily be applied to Doré's work.

Furthermore, the French perception of Coleridge began to change after 1850. The publication of Philarète Chasles's recollections of his early years, *Etudes sur les hommes et les moeurs au XIXe siècle* (Studies on Men and Customs in the Nineteenth Century), containing a whole chapter on Coleridge (Chasles 1850, 93-98), contributed greatly to this evolution. Chasles expressed his admiration for Coleridge, 'poet, philosopher, thinker, artist, critic, man of taste, erudite man' ('poète, philosophe, penseur, artiste, critique, homme de goût, homme érudit') (Chasles 1850, 98), and it is very possible that his book influenced Baudelaire's interest in Coleridge, and perhaps even Doré's. Another book which could have been read by Doré was the republication of Sainte-Beuve's *Portraits contemporains* (Contemporary Portraits). In the first volume, originally published in 1855 and republished in 1870, Sainte-Beuve's portrait of the Romantic poet Alphonse de Lamartine (1790-1869) contained a comparison between the French poet, author of *Les Méditations,* and two British authors: Coleridge and Wordsworth, 'les deux poëtes méditatifs' ('the two meditative poets') (Sainte-Beuve 1870, 1: 337). Sainte-Beuve enhanced Coleridge's contemplative, thoughtful, spiritual and elevated character, quoting *The Aeolian Harp* as the best example of this high-minded poetic style, and stating that 'there is in him, if I dare say, a Buddhist trying to be a Methodist' (Sainte-Beuve 1870, 1: 339).[8]

Now it is precisely three years after the republication of Sainte-Beuve's *Portraits contemporains* that Gustave Doré became involved in the project of illustrating Coleridge's *AM,* that is to say precisely when Coleridge began to be regarded with a greater and deeper interest by French writers and critics. Doré seized on an author who had been largely ignored by the French 1830 Romantic generation—either writers (Hugo, Vigny or Musset never mention him) or artists (Delacroix illustrated Shakespeare, Byron, Walter Scott, and also

Robert Burns's *Tam O'Shanter,* although he had to read this poem directly in the Scottish dialect as it was not available in a French translation at the time, but never developed any interest in Coleridge)—but who was on the verge of a rediscovery. And Doré's illustrations, taking up the difficult challenge *The Rime* threw down to any artist, contributed to a great extent to this rediscovery.

GUSTAVE DORÉ AND BRITISH LITERATURE

If, among all French illustrators of his generation, Gustave Doré (1832-83) remained the only one who illustrated Coleridge, the reason must be found first in Doré's personal ideas on the best way of illustrating books and then in his special relationship with Great Britain and British culture.

The Coleridge volume by Doré must be understood as part of a general plan. Doré had the admitted ambition to complete a gigantic collection of illustrated books. In 1865 he dictated to his mother several lines addressed to one of his biographers and later reproduced by his American friend Blanche Roosevelt[9] explaining his plan to 'produce in a uniform style an edition of all the masterpieces in literature of the best authors, epic, comic, and tragic', taking the form of 'a grand collection of illustrated books in folio' (Roosevelt 1885, 208-10). Doré proposed a list of thirty-seven masterpieces of world literature to illustrate. Six names of British writers appeared in this list: Ossian, Milton, Byron, Shakespeare and Goldsmith, who had been famous in France since the second half of the eighteenth century (except Byron, who belonged to the young Romantics, and published his first book of poems only in 1807), and the contemporary of Shakespeare, Spenser, who had enjoyed a very considerable revival in England in the eighteenth century, but was on the contrary very little known in France, except by specialists. But this initial plan was not to be respected, as the list of Doré's actual contributions to the illustration of British literature shows. His link with Great Britain began when he was a young illustrator and caricaturist and regularly contributed to the British press, notably the *Illustrated London News* in 1855-56, then the *Illustrated Times* and the *Illustrated Travels* (Leblanc 1931, 147-49). At the time, Doré was a true dandy, showing off a perfectly British chic in his clothes, as Blanchard Jerrold noticed in 1869, even calling him a 'gentleman' (Jerrold 1869, 443). But the decisive moment was his 1868 travels in Great Britain (Valmy-Baysse and Dézé 1930, 279-99; Gosling 1973, 24-26), for on this occasion Doré, who had begun the previous year to send paintings to London for exhibition (Coolidge 1994, 21), understood that he was more famous and appreciated in England than in France. Moreover, the British audience accepted him as a painter, although the French critics considered him at the time as an illustrator who wrongly thought he had a gift for painting. In 1869, he opened in London, at 35 New Bond Street, the 'Doré Gallery', run by two British managers with whom Doré had been in contact since 1867, James Liddle Fairless and George Lord Beeforth. The gallery exhibited and sold the paintings that Doré completed in Paris (Roosevelt 1885, 330-56). In the following years, Doré returned regularly to Great Britain, and even travelled in Scotland in 1873 with his friend Colonel Teesdale (Roosevelt 1885, 383). In 1875, the Prince of Wales introduced him to Queen Victoria, which was the apogee of Doré's career in Great Britain.

Nevertheless, Doré did not wait until his first travels in England to begin to illustrate British literature. As early as 1853, he collaborated with Charles Mettais and Etienne Bocourt on the illustrations of Lord Byron's complete works (Byron 1853). This book was in fact his first work as a professional illustrator and the very beginning of his prestigious career. In 1856, Blanchard Jerrold suggested Doré's illustrations for *Le Juif errant* (The Wandering Jew), published in Paris by Michel Lévy (Dupont 1856), should be republished in London by Addey & Co. (Dupont 1857) 'as a Christmas book, the plates being carefully printed in Paris' (Jerrold 1869, 440), a publishing strategy which must be kept in mind in order to understand the Coleridge project, twenty years later. In 1858 Doré illustrated W. F. Peacock's *The Adventures of Saint George* (Peacock 1858), published in London, and drew six plates for Edouard Schefter's French adaptation of Shakespeare's *Macbeth* (Schefter 1858). Then he worked regularly for British editors, providing five plates for *The Tempest* in 1860 (Shakespeare 1860), fifty for *Paradise Lost,* a book specially commissioned by the British firm Cassell, Petter & Galpin in 1866 (Milton, 1866), thirty-six for Tennyson's *Idylls of the King,* published by Edward Moxon in 1867-69 (Tennyson 1867a, 1867b, 1867c, 1868a and 1868b), nine plates for Thomas Hood in 1870 (Hood 1870) and illustrations for his close friend the journalist and playwright Blanchard Jerrold (1826-84), the first for *The Cockaynes in Paris* (Jerrold 1871) and the second for the famous *London, a Pilgrimage* (Jerrold 1872), the plates from which were reused four years later in France to illustrate a book on London by Louis Enault (Enault 1876). The 180 woodcuts realized for this last book remain the best proof of Doré's interest in British life (Woods 1978, 1.3: 341-59; Jouve 1981 and Coolidge 1994).

Doré's illustrations for Coleridge were his last contribution to the illustration of British literature. His ultimate project, the illustration of Shakespeare's complete plays (that is to say about 300 plates), was left uncompleted when he died in 1883 (Leblanc 1931, 324). Thus *AM* is Doré's ultimate legacy as far as British literature is concerned.

DORÉ'S ILLUSTRATIONS FOR *THE RIME*

With the new information provided since the end of the nineteenth century by the artist's first biographers and the exploitation of new documents kept in the collections of the Musée d'Art Moderne et Contemporain in Strasbourg,[10] the chronology of the realization of Doré's illustrations for *AM* can be fully reconstructed.

On 2 October 1874, back from a trip to Brittany, during which he visited Saint-Malo and Mont-Saint-Michel, Doré sent a letter to Fairless & Beeforth, asking for a very precise piece of information. The artist wanted to know 'if the *poet Coleridge's works* are today fallen into the *public domain*; that is, if any person have the right to print and publish [these works]'[11] and asked his British associates to 'consult the exact date of [Coleridge's] death and the law on lapsing [of copyright] for England'.[12] A few days later, Fairless & Beeforth assured Doré they would give him a quick answer,[13] and on 10 October a long letter gave him the pieces of information he was waiting for:

> We have made some enquiries about Coleridge's Poems from what we can learn the Copyright of the principal poems have expired. We send you a non copyright edition [. . .] From this is omitted sixty six short poems which are in the copyright edition. Some of these we know are yet copyright, & the probability is the whole of the sixty six are yet copyright. But these poems are minor ones. His great works are the **Ancient Mariner & Christabel** & they are included in the works the copyright of which have expired. Forty two years is the limit for copyright in England from 1st publication & so late as 1854 one short poem of Coleridge was published for the *first time* in his works. This of course could not be published by any one until *1896*! [. . .] We have enquired at some of the Foreign booksellers for a French translation of Coleridge but cannot hear of one—if such exists you will probably get it in Paris.[14]

Three days later, Doré thanked his London agents and confided for the first time his growing interest in Coleridge's *AM*:

> According to what I see by carefully reading the [copyright] law, it seems certain to me that the poem **The Ancient Mariner** has come into the public domain for it was published during the author's youth.[15]

It is interesting to notice that, from the very beginning, Doré selected this poem out of Coleridge's works and never expressed any intention to pay attention either to the rest of the 1798 *Lyrical Ballads* or to any other poem by Coleridge.

During the year 1875 Doré worked on the illustrations. We do not know if he perused the English edition Fairless & Beeforth sent him—unlikely, as he didn't know English (Jerrold 1891, 194-95)—or if, as is likely, he managed to find one of the French translations which were available at the time.[16] Doré originally planned to realize 'eighteen to twenty plates' ('18 ou 20 planches'),[17] but in total he executed forty, and finally published thirty-eight. His technique for realizing his illustrations is well known through testimonies of friends and biographers, and for *AM* we enjoy a large amount of material. First, Doré drew sketches in a sketchbook which is now kept in Strasbourg.[18] He used the same sketchbook he carried with him in Brittany in 1873, which indicates that this seashore travel might have been the first element which launched Doré's interest in Coleridge's sea tale. The nine first folios of this sketchbook can be directly linked to *AM*: they show drawings of ships, ropes and cables, but also lists of illustrations with the names of the engravers Doré employed and even tests for the written form of the names 'Coleridge' and 'Coleridge-Doré' for the title page of the definitive volume. Three preparatory drawings have now been identified, one for Plate V in the Museum of Strasbourg ('And now there came both mist and snow, and it grew wondrous cold')[19] and two in the Victoria & Albert Museum, for Plate XVI ('And never a saint took pity on my soul in agony')[20] and Plate XXXVIII ('The Mariner, whose eye is bright').[21] The last sketch is particularly interesting for it contains several differences from the final image. Such preparatory drawings are extremely rare in Doré's work; he usually drew directly on the woodblocks (Delorme 1879, 25-26). This phase of preparation of blocks was essential and Doré, who distrusted the engravers raised in the Romantic tradition of the *vignette,* trained his own team of wood-engravers (Blachon 2001, 146-50). For *AM,* he brought together the best engravers who worked with him on Dante's *Divine Comedy* and Milton's *Paradise Lost*. These craftsmen who collaborated on *AM* by cutting the wood blocks Doré prepared for them were Désiré-Mathieu Quesnel (1843-1915), Héliodore Pisan (1822-90), Adolphe Gusman (1821-1905), Paul-Emile Deschamps (1822-93), Albert Bellenger (1846-1914), Firmin Gillot (1820-72), Charles Laplante (d. 1903), Florentin Jonnard-Pacel (1840-1902) and Adolphe-François Pannemaker (1822-1900). Their part was decisive as they had to interpret faithfully Doré's thought. We also know that Doré used to draw the same design—with slight variants—on several blocks of wood and entrusted different engravers with these blocks, choosing at last only the best. For example Plate VI for *AM* had been cut by Jonnard and refused—the original wood is kept in a private collection (Favière 1983, 152)—and also by Bellenger, whose plate was accepted and inserted in the volume. The same thing happened for Plate XIX ('The moving moon went up the sky'). The plate in the volume is signed by Jonnard, while another plate was realized by Pisan and rejected, but later reproduced by Delorme (1879, 7). The one and only original woodcut that has been located among the thirty-eight accepted by Doré and used in the final book is now kept in Strasbourg.[22] It is Plate VIII ('With my cross-bow I shot the albatross') but unfortunately the name of the engraver does not appear.

In October 1875, Doré began to print the folio volumes in Crété's printing office in Corbeil. On 12 October he wrote to the Doré Gallery that the first board-binding copies were to be available by 20 November. These first copies were dated '1875' on the title page, and the publisher's name was indicated as 'The Doré Gallery'. Doré also sent to the London Gallery 'a frame with four drawings [for the Coleridge]' ('un cadre contenant quatre dessins') and asked Beeforth & Fairless to exhibit it in order to give the audience a first glimpse of his work, so they would be ready to buy it for Christmas.[23] On 26 October, he wrote that he had recently amended a misprint in the title on the bookbinding.[24] But in November Doré had to face facts: he wouldn't be ready for Christmas. 'A failure in my few last engravings' ('Un insuccès dans mes quelques dernières gravures') obliged him to defer the sale of his folio until the beginning of 1876. As a consequence, he modified the date on the title page, which generated the false idea that Doré published two editions of his London version of *AM* (Leblanc 1931, 74), the first in 1875 (Coleridge 1875) and the second a year later (Coleridge 1876a). In fact, it is the same edition, with two different title pages. Another change in the title page concerned the publisher. In the new version, to the Doré Gallery was added the name of Hamilton, Adams & Co., a British publisher the Doré Gallery contacted in order to distribute and advertise the book in England. Finally, in this letter Doré mentioned for the first time an estimate of the print run, saying he thought it could grow to 1,200 copies.[25]

On 6 December, he sent 500 leaflets to the Doré Gallery and announced 500 more to arrive in the next few days.[26] Ten days later, he asked Fairless & Beeforth if they needed 100 or 200 copies of the book, to begin with.[27] On 30 December, together with his New Year Greetings, he announced new delays in the printing of the de luxe copies 'on China paper with signature' ('sur Chine signés').[28] Finally, by January 1876, *The Rime of the Ancient Mariner, Illustrated by Gustave Doré* was sold in London. At the same time, Doré sold 240 copies in Paris, principally, as he explained in a letter dated 1 March, to British residents.[29]

Doré's edition of *AM* was a huge folio volume, with red cloth boards and gold-letter title, containing fourteen pages for the frontispiece, the title page illustrated with a vignette and finally the poem, in English, illustrated with two vignettes, one at the beginning of the text, the other at the end. The thirty-eight folio plates came after, grouped together at the end of the volume, with no interconnections with the text. As we will see, Doré expected a great deal from this superb book he had

taken such special care in bringing to fruition; but he was cruelly disappointed in his hopes, at least during the first months of the sale.

The distribution of Doré's book in England and Europe

Doré's edition of *AM* has been commonly described as a financial failure. This derives from Doré himself, who complained about the slow sales of his book, whose success he had never doubted.

It must first be understood that Doré financed the whole project by himself. On 12 October 1875, he wrote to Fairless & Beeforth that he spent almost £3,000 to print *AM*,[30] and on 10 January 1876, in a letter to his friend Canon Hartford, he said that he 'spent about 3500 *l.* [sic] to have this work engraved' (Roosevelt 1885, 422). For this reason, Doré affixed a sale price of four guineas, which was double the original price the Doré Gallery had in mind.[31] The reason why he decided to bear all the expenses for the publishing process is that he wanted to share in the profits and keep absolute control over his work. On 21 October 1875, he sent a long letter to Fairless & Beeforth, who apparently felt very concerned about the whole Coleridge project. In this letter Doré explained his business strategy, from an editor and publisher's point of view, and he asserted that he saw a certain success in this book. His great originality was to attempt to get rid of the traditional distribution and marketing channels of the publishing and bookselling business:

> I perfectly know that, through the very modest system I want to use and which is to make a *mere deposit* in a location which would be known [the Doré Gallery], I deprive myself of the great means of expansion and publicity that all the *professional* booksellers have, like sales representatives, credits, press advertising etc. etc. etc. and that I cannot expect a quick sale. I know the whole of that. But what I also know very well is the fate my property will receive if I place it in the hands of people who have, as you say, the means to distribute quickly a book all over the globe [. . .]; for doing that, they would offer me a kind of association I would be fooled by after a time[32]

Despite his displayed good intentions and his reiterated assurances that he wouldn't worry in the event of a possible slow and uneasy start of his book, Doré lived in anxiety for the first months that *AM* was put up for sale. Several letters prove his increasing concern, verging on panic. In January 1876, he wrote to his friend Canon Hartford:

> the sale of [*AM*] preoccupies me greatly. I cannot engage in any other work until I see some of the money reimbursed that I have spent on this book, a sum which, up to the present time, is something really enormous. I feel that I have the sympathy of the public and the press; but the number of my purchasers is still limited.

I do not know whether I am to attribute this to the laziness of my trustees, or to another drawback which I dare not mention[33]

On 23 January, he asked Fairless & Beeforth about Hamilton, Adams and Co.[34] and, three days later, he confided to the same his concern at not seeing reports of the publication of *AM* in the British press.[35] On 1 March, he finally specifically accused Hamilton of being responsible for what he thought to be an abnormal slump:

I am, just like you, astonished by the sterility of the **Mariner** business. There must be a cause one doesn't let me know about and that the future will bring to light, I hope. For the moment I can only attribute this to the ineptitude of MM. H . . . [Hamilton, Adams & Co.] or at least to the insufficiency of their professional contacts as booksellers.[36]

Nevertheless the situation seemed to normalize afterwards. On 28 June 1876, Doré thanked Fairless & Beeforth for speaking with Hamilton.[37] He also began to receive payments for sold copies of *AM*: £334 on 15 July 1876[38] from Beeforth & Fairless; £160.10 from the same on 12 June 1877;[39] £18 again on 30 July 1880, this time from Hamilton, Adams & Co.[40] This represents a total amount of £512.10,[41] which is considerably less than the £3,500 Doré claimed he had spent. A sum of £512.10 represents the sale of only 121 copies at four guineas each; of course, it is possible that Doré signed other receipts, now lost, and we must add the 240 copies Doré affirmed he sold by himself in Paris. But the fact remains that in 1883, after Doré's death, 450 unbound and unsold copies of *AM* were found in his studio (*Catalogue des tableaux, etc.* 1885, 57).

Clearly Doré's London edition of *AM* cannot be described as a huge success; but if we consider the sales through time, and above all if we take into consideration the foreign editions of this book, this 'failure' must be kept in perspective. For the European and even worldwide distribution of *AM* began almost immediately after the publication of the volume in Great Britain. On this topic, Doré had a long experience and very firm ideas, as he explained to Fairless & Beeforth on December 1875 in a letter by which he declined a collaboration with Kirberger, a Dutch publisher. Doré wrote:

I cannot grant by treaty the monopoly on the sale of my book, neither in Holland, nor in any other country, for I am preparing, as is usual for *typographical* publications, to sell in various countries the *photographs* of this work, including the monopoly on the publications in the *language of the country,* yet without forbidding the importing of British copies.[42]

For *AM,* Doré produced such photographs of the plates with the technique of photography on zinc, or zincography, also called electrotype or *'gillotage'* because it was invented by the engraver Gillot, one of Doré's collaborators on *AM.* This technique allowed the making of a perfect relief copy of the original woodcut on a zinc medium, by photographing the original plate and transferring this photography onto a plate of zinc covered with sensitized emulsion, which was then treated with an acid resist. Such zinc photographs were sent to the editors who paid Doré and the Doré Gallery for the rights to reproduce the plates. An original zincography of Plate XXXII of *AM,* fixed on a wood panel, is kept in Strasbourg.[43] The legend, in French—'Je remuai les lèvres: le pilote poussa un cri / Et tomba en défaillance' ('I moved my lips—the Pilot shrieked / And fell down in a fit')—indicates this plate was made for the French edition of *AM.*

An interesting fact revealed by the previous letter is that Doré was perfectly aware that his plates had to be accompanied by foreign translations to be effectively received in foreign countries. For this reason, Gustave Doré's illustrations carried Coleridge's poem across Europe together with various translations, ancient or new ones, into various languages. Very likely, Doré's illustrations were the true pretext for republishing or translating—in some cases for the very first time—Coleridge's poem. Let us consider also that in each country, Doré's illustrations of its own native author sold best—in Spain, it was Cervantes, in Italy, Dante; but Coleridge's presence was also felt, and here is a list of the republications we have been able to trace.

In December 1876, New York publishers Harper & Brothers published the 'Elephant Folio' edition of *AM* with its famous red cloth hardcover with gilt title and flying albatross (Coleridge 1876b), sold at the price of ten dollars. This American edition was reviewed in *Harper's Weekly* (Malan 1995, 133) and republished by the same company in 1877 (Coleridge 1877c), 1878 (Coleridge 1878), 1881 (Coleridge 1881), 1882 (Coleridge 1882) and, after Doré's death, in 1886 (Coleridge 1886). Another American edition was published in Boston by Estes & Lauriat in 1884 (Coleridge 1884); it mixed Gustave Doré's illustrations with plates by Birket Foster (1825-99) and other artists. A last nineteenth-century American edition appeared in Philadelphia in 1889 (Coleridge 1889c). All these American editions used the English original text and Doré's photographs, probably furnished by Fairless & Beeforth.

In France, the illustrations were published in 1877 by Hachette et Cie, a publisher Doré used to work with (Coleridge 1877a). This edition was again printed by Crété in Corbeil, using zinc photographs. The French translation of Coleridge's poem was provided by the poet Auguste Barbier (1805-82). Barbier became famous after the French Revolution of July 1830, when he published his satiric poems entitled *Iambes* (Iambics).

In the following years, he applied his gift for satire to England, a country he knew very well, by publishing *Lazare* (Lazarus) in 1837, a poem denouncing the importance of commerce and trade business in Great Britain. He also translated Shakespeare's *Julius Caesar* into French verse in 1848. When he published his translation of *AM,* he had been a member of the French Academy since 1869, but was mostly forgotten as a poet. Doré and Barbier's version of *AM* happened to be the first translation in a volume of Coleridge's work ever published in France. Hachette also published a poster to advertise this book (Favière 1983, 261). The *Bibliographie de la France* (Bibliography of France) recorded the publication of *La Chanson du vieux marin* on 24 January 1877,[44] specifying that the book was sold for fifty francs. The date of the publication means that Doré achieved what he was unable to do in 1875, namely publishing a *livre d'étrennes* ('New Year's Day present book').

In Germany, the illustrations had been first published by Amelangs Verlag in Leipzig during the same year, 1877, together with a German translation by Ferdinand Freiligrath (1810-76). This edition of *Der Alte Matrose* (Coleridge 1877b) was republished in 1898 by C. B. Griesbach, a publisher in Gera (Coleridge 1898a), and a third time in 1925 (Coleridge 1925). By then Freiligrath's translation had established itself as a classic, and it was combined with the equally renowned Doré illustrations in a lavish gift book.

In Italy, Doré's plates appeared for the first time in December 1889, as a special edition published and offered by the journal *Il Corriere della sera* to its subscribers for the New Year period (Coleridge 1889a and 1889b). The illustrations, apparently reproduced from the French edition, were accompanied by the first Italian translation of *AM,* signed by Enrico Nencioni (1837-96). Nencioni's translation also established itself as a pre-eminent version of Coleridge's poem, and this book has been recently republished (Coleridge 1994b). It seems that the practice of newspapers publishing Doré's illustrations for *AM* as New Year's present books had originated at an unknown date in France. We identified in the Bibliothèque de Strasbourg a copy of the 1876 French edition[45] with a red cloth hardcover stating: 'Samuel Coleridge / *The Rime of the Ancient Mariner* / Illustrated by Gustave Doré / Offered by the Nineteenth Century Journal / to its subscribers' ('Samuel Coleridge / *La Chanson du Vieux Marin* / Illustrée par Gustave Doré / Offert par le XIXe siècle / à ses abonnés'). In this case, it is very likely that the French journal *Le dix-neuvième siècle* (The Nineteenth Century) bought some of the unsold copies found in Doré's studio after his death.

A Russian edition appeared in 1893 (Coleridge 1893) and was republished in 1897 (Coleridge 1897). These late dates and the poor quality of the reproductions suggest a pirated edition of Gustave Doré's plates, accompanied by a Russian translation of Coleridge's poem by the Russian poet Apollon Apollonovitch Korinfsky (b. 1868).

To complete our list, a first Spanish edition appeared in 1898 in Barcelona (Coleridge 1898b).[46] This pioneer translation of *AM* in Spanish presents three remarkable characteristics. First, it bears witness to Gustave Doré's popularity in Spain (Guigon, Geyer and Reyero 2004, 46-63). If Doré was loved by the British people, it can also be claimed that Spain was very fond of the French artist and that he returned those feelings. As early as 1855 Doré and his friend Théophile Gautier toured the Spanish Pyrenees, which resulted in the illustrations for *Tour through the Pyrenees* by Hippolyte Taine in 1860. Later on, in 1862 and 1871, he travelled all around Spain with Charles Davillier, which led to the engravings for *Don Quichotte* in 1863 and to the travel book *L'Espagne* by Davillier in 1875. These two series of engravings have made Doré extremely popular in Spain ever since, and have been reproduced hundreds of times. In 1868, Doré's illustrations for Tennyson's *The Idylls of the King* inspired a Spanish poet, José Zorrilla, whose original poem, entitled *Los Ecos de las Montañas* (Echoes of the Mountains) was published together with Doré's plates (Zarandona 2004). The second characteristic of the 1898 Spanish Coleridge is the mysterious translator who did not give his full name, B. Archer M., and who seems not to have left any trace. Finally, it provides a prose target text in Spanish which, as stated in the first pages, had been translated 'directly from the English', which is very surprising for nineteenth-century Spain, where most English texts were rendered into Spanish using French as an intermediate language. The Spanish National Library keeps another translation by the same mysterious B. Archer M.: *El judío errante* (The Wandering Jew), from the French original by Eugène Sue, which only proves that he could also translate from French into Spanish and that he was probably very aware of Coleridge's sources of inspiration when devising his *Mariner.* Archer M. Huntington (1870-1955), the wealthy American philanthropist and scholar who founded the Hispanic Society of America in New York in 1904 could have been the translator. He was a writer and a poet both in English and Spanish, and an English-Spanish translator, as his masterpiece, the first full English version of *The Poem of The Cid* (1897-1903) proves. He travelled to the Peninsula in 1892 and in 1898, when the first translation of *AM* was published. Among his many other cultural enterprises, Archer founded the Mariners' Museum in Newport News, Virginia, in 1930. Finally, the Hispanic Society stores many of the original Doré engravings for *Don Quixote,* acquired by the founder himself. Archer's translation departs from the others that followed in being a prose rendering of the original. While the rest struggle, more or less successfully, to produce close metrical renderings of the original, this one chooses the freedom of poetic prose, which provides an opportunity to take Doré's visual additions and interpretations into account in the translation. One early example: where the original says: 'He holds him with his skinny hand' (v. 9), the translator concludes: 'El Viejo marino aprieta cada vez más el brazo del joven con su descarnada mano.' Archer writes names where there were pronouns, and describes what he is seeing in the illustration: that the Mariner is holding a young man's arm, but this is not stated in Coleridge's poem. In other words, he is not only translating a text, but also an image. As usual, Doré's interpretations not only contributed to the reception of the literary works he chose to illustrate, but conditioned the translation work as well due to his powerful talent to enrich the texts and dominate the popular imagination. A second edition of this translation was issued some two years later, around 1900, larger in size since it was a 'de luxe' edition. However, this rare book was not reprinted again, nor did *AM* receive another Spanish translation until 1945, which proved to be the starting point for the great number of them that have been published in Spain since then, no doubt due to the sound development of English Studies during the second half of the twentieth century in Spain. Only one Spanish graphic artist has dared to produce an alternative set of illustrations for this poem: Antonio Jiménez Lara, in 1981, for José Siles Artés's (b. 1930) translation (Coleridge 1981). In other words, Doré's canonical vision of Coleridge's poem has dominated the imagination of Spain in this regard.

We must add, to put an end to this list, that apparently no editions of Gustave Doré's edition of *AM* were published during the nineteenth century in Holland, despite the Doré Gallery's request to the artist to collaborate with Kirberger.

THE RECEPTION OF DORÉ'S ILLUSTRATIONS

The first element we must take into consideration about the critical reception of Doré's edition of *AM* is Doré's own opinion about his work. His correspondence reveals a tremendous attachment to this book.

On 12 October 1875, he wrote to Fairless & Beeforth: 'It is, as you can see, a major, sumptuous book, which could be put at the top of my illustrated works'.[47] On November 1875, he added: 'As you see, this book is *my child* and I would certainly feel grateful towards those who gave him a hand in making his entry into the world.'[48] On 10 January 1876, he wrote to Canon Hartford that he considered this work of his to be 'one of [his] best and more original' (Roosevelt 1885, 422). On 1 March 1876, he wrote to Fairless and Beeforth: 'All my works as an *illustrator* always had an easy and quick launch; and this one is certainly not inferior to the previous ones.'[49]

The pride Doré felt in this book explains why he had been so disappointed by the slowness of the sale, which left him frustrated. He was also very upset by the lack of information and reviews in the British press. But this was only the direct result of his commercial strategy and his refusal to use the traditional commercial channels for bookselling. Moveover, when they came, British reviews of Doré's version of *AM* were disappointing for the artist. Of course, *The Illustrated London News,* a journal to which Doré had been a contributor, published a very enthusiastic review illustrated by a reproduction of Plate XX ('And the rain poured down from one black cloud'), stating that:

> In, however, that unique and wondrous tale of Coleridge, everything seems exactly suited to him; poet and illustrator are equally fortunate in each other.
>
> (1876, 68.1903: 57)

Taking the opposite view, *The Athenaeum* published a very severe criticism comparing the book with the artistic failure of Doré's illustrations for *The Idylls of the King,* stating of Doré and Tennyson that 'it was a misfortune for artist and poet that they were thus brought together' (1876, 271). About *AM,* the anonymous reviewer adds that 'it is sad to find that the spirit of spectacular and spasmodic effort, the melodramatic effulgence of lurid fancy, have prevailed again.' There is a clearly nationalist reading of Doré's work, constantly put down in his attempts to illustrate British authors. It is said, for example, about his illustrations for Milton that 'an artist so essentially French could not be expected to translate into art-language the Puritan epic as felicitously as he had rendered [. . .] the wit of Rabelais, and the quaint sentiment of Balzac.' And about his illustrations for *AM,* it is affirmed that 'only Blake could have done anything like justice to it; our French artist has evolved an idea as prosaic as a quasi-allegory of [James] Barry's, but hardly so graceful as Barry might have made it' (272).

On the other hand, the French critical reception of Doré's edition of *AM* revealed a true effort to understand the personal involvement of the artist in his work which must be linked with the last throes of a certain tradition of Romantic rebellion, often mentioned in connection with this work (Farner 1975, 276-77). In 1877, for his foreword to his translation of Coleridge's poem, Auguste Barbier paid tribute to Doré by saying:

> Let's hope that, helped by Mr. Gustave Doré's amazing and powerful pencil, we will be able to give the audience of our country a complete enough idea of the famous work of the English poet.[50]

On January 1877, an article was published by Charles Buloz in the *Revue des Deux-Mondes* about Doré's illustration for *AM* and for Joseph Michaud's *Histoire des Croisades* (History of the Crusades) published by

Furne the same year (Michaud 1877). After celebrating Doré's 'inexhaustible verve' ('verve intarissable') and 'truly extraordinary fertility' ('fécondité vraiment extraordinaire') (Buloz 1877, 237), he analysed the illustrations by saying that Doré's book made the reader 'leave the world of reality to penetrate into the phantasmagoria of dreams'.[51] About Doré's visual response to Coleridge's poetry, he wrote:

> In this dark legend (which original version is presented facing Auguste Barbier's good translation), the supernatural has a great importance: there are apocalyptic scenes only Doré's pencil could entirely master.[52]

In his 1879 biography of Gustave Doré, René Delorme (1848-90) painted a portrait of Doré which showed him as a kind of poet and a man outside of schools. About *AM,* he added, relating these illustrations with those created for Tennyson:

> After the real travels [London and Spain], here are the imaginary travels. Gustave Doré is departing, together with Coleridge, for the polar seas, where the albatross is soaring in his boundless flight. Here he can give free rein to his imagination.[53]

It is certain, as most of the reviewers were aware, that the illustrations for Coleridge could be in many ways compared to the plates illustrating Tennyson. In both British poets, Doré found a visual dimension which was pre-eminent in his mind—in short, they 'called for the painter'. In his speech for Doré's funeral in 1883, his friend the journalist Paul Dalloz (1829-87) conjured up the ghosts of the writers Doré illustrated, among whom appeared both Coleridge and Tennyson:

> I am appealing to the masters of every time and every country whose thoughts he revived, whose dreams he condensed, whose speech he set in motion and whose visions he crystallised. All of them—Dante, Cervantes, Rabelais, Ariosto, Chateaubriand, Balzac, La Fontaine, Perrault, Tennyson, Coleridge, [. . .]—all are here. Each one is holding a palm, and is putting it down on the coffin of this malcontent with himself who satisfied them all. All of them are thanking their posthumous associate.[54]

Others' enthusiastic analyses can also be quoted. In 1885, Georges Duplessis (1834-99), a specialist on printers and engravers, writing a biographical notice for the catalogue of the Doré sale, wrote:

> For this work of fiction which almost always takes place at sea, between the sky and the water, Gustave Doré seems to have elevated his style. [. . .] Between the poem which tells with a rare talent the physical and moral torments of the deprived mariner and the drawings which express these torments in a gripping way, there is a complete correlation. Here, like every time he interpreted the work of a writer of considerable merit, he managed, with the assistance of his pencil, to increase the interest of the narration.[55]

The same year, Blanche Roosevelt wrote about the American editions of *AM* these words which are traditionally quoted as the ultimate evidence of the popularity of Doré and the success of his Coleridge in the United States:

> Hundreds of thousands of copies have been sold there, and I do not know of any city, from the State of Maine to the Pacific coast, where, in some cultivated household, there would not be found a well-bethumbed copy of this great classic [. . .] Granddames and grandsires, fathers and mothers, youths and maidens, boys and girls, will speak to you of Doré's ***Ancient Mariner.*** [. . .] They will show you all these masterful creations, and with their soft voices will tenderly lisp Doré's name in a way which, could he but have heard it, would have given him more pleasure than many riper and more judicious tributes of admiration.[56]

Many comments on Doré's work insisted on the fact that the plates for *AM* were characteristic of the artist's 'visionary' talent, a term first used about Doré by Théophile Gautier in 1861: 'He has this visionary eye the poet speaks of, which knows how to extract Nature's secret and unique facet.'[57] The word was later reused and interpreted by many modern scholars (Poiret 1983, 6; Foucart 1983; Kaenel 1985, 25-45), often making Doré a precursor of Surrealism (*Gustave Doré illustrateur* 1984, 6-7). The artist's most ardent admirers were even able to sever the relationship between the illustrator and the writer: the illustrator now gives the true greatness to the text he works on. About *AM,* it was said once that 'this superb book's illustrations, where the tragic and the marvellous become intermingled, promote Coleridge's poem to the status of masterpiece'.[58] At the other extreme, this visionary talent could upset certain writers, notably Emile Zola and the brothers Edmond and Jules de Goncourt, the major opponents of the Romantic medievalism promoted by Doré. Zola, (the leader of the Naturalists, dedicated to rooting out the Romantic vision), commenting on Doré's illustration for the Bible, wrote that Doré could only represent dreams and was unable to show reality (Zola 1866, 85-96) and Edmond de Goncourt—who called Doré 'this illustrations layer' ('ce pondeur d'illustrations') (Goncourt, 1989, 1: 764)—reported in his *Journal,* on 4 February 1880, that Doré confided to him:

> The art of illustration is only amusing for an artist with the geniuses of the ancient times, who say: 'He entered a dark wood, where he arrived at a palace whose walls seemed to be made of diamond'.[59]

This was precisely what Doré found in Coleridge. Even the positive reviews of Doré's illustrations for *AM* emphasize essentially the odd nature of Coleridge's poem, which is recurrently described as 'visionary', 'supernatural', 'sinister' or 'frightening'. Nevertheless, we must also observe that the critical reception of

Doré's work concerns relatively few texts. The general perception is that Gustave Doré's illustrations, as they are weird in themselves, match perfectly with Coleridge's work. First, because these illustrations seemed strange—even if beautiful—to French eyes, and secondly because Doré became soon after this publication an artist of the past. The true reception of Doré's Coleridge is probably more an artistic reception than a literary one. Doré's illustrations became a visual model, to be followed or rejected.

ILLUSTRATING *THE RIME* IN FRANCE AFTER DORÉ

The first thing to say is that the art of illustration in France seems to have been marked by Doré's illustrations of Coleridge. Doré dealt with iconographical themes which he powerfully introduced into French art. The visual success of Doré's version of *AM* was rooted in its offer of cross-over themes, that is themes which were used both in art and in literature and operated, like myths, on both levels. Doré's pictures had a strong hold on his contemporaries' imagination, and it is usual to insist on the fact that, in French, *imagerie* ('pictures') and *imaginaire* ('imagination') sound practically the same. The themes Doré used and placed in parallel with Coleridge's poems dealt with both science and imagination, as all Doré's work constantly did. He was persistently striking a balance between the real and the imaginary and in his illustrations for Coleridge the phantasmagoria is intimately mixed with scientific elements; or more exactly the real is always there, twisted by the fantastic. For example, he used the drawings he made in Brittany for representing the Mariner's ship or the harbour-bar—which looks like the Mont-Saint-Michel—and his vision of the bottom of the sea brings to mind a lot of earlier nineteenth-century scientific encyclopedia plates which he probably used as a reference.

If we consider Gustave Doré as a late Romantic artist, as many of his contemporaries did (Kaenel 1985, 25), it is easy to understand how Coleridge offered him some themes very close to his own preoccupations and to several private interests he had developed long ago. Like Coleridge, Doré cultivated the worship of nature, dramatized through raging elements, fantastical landscapes and architectures of a supernatural world. This is what he was looking for when he travelled to Germany or Scotland. This is why he painted huge-scale oil canvases which had little success in France but were acclaimed in Great Britain, because the aesthetic of the sublime prepared the audience to appreciate such images. Doré's interest in medieval time and legends can also be mentioned as an element of understanding. In *AM*, Doré found some elements he had previously encountered in Tennyson's *Idylls of the King*, namely enchantment, a legendary past and mysteries of Nature,

except that the fairy forests of the Arthurian world were replaced with the vastness of the sea and ruined castles with shipwreck. Doré was particularly fascinated by the sea, and in 1867 he illustrated an English translation of Victor Hugo's *The Toilers of the Sea* for a British publisher (Hugo 1867), which was praised by the French author in 1866 in a letter to Doré (Tromp 1932, 31). The first plate shows the broken shell of a stranded vessel upon which stands a tiny human figure, while, in the foreground, flies a seagull which prefigures the albatross of *AM*. The second plate represents the fight between Hugo's hero and the giant octopus. In these two plates, engraved on wood by J. Cooper, are contained the seeds of his illustrations for *AM*: human actions are enacted in front of limitless spaces and divine nature, a theme he found again in Coleridge's poem.

Doré's private life also contributed to his interest in *AM*. He was a deeply religious spirit (Valmy-Baysse and Dézé 1930, 301-14) and, as the Mariner did, he felt like a sort of wanderer after the 1870 war between France and Prussia made his native Alsace a German land. The despair of the survivor which is the Mariner's is a feeling Doré himself knew. Interestingly, Coleridge's poem's dimension as religious parable, which has been abundantly commented on by modern French critics (Ergal 2001, 69), escaped nineteenth-century French analysts but appeared very clearly in Doré's plates. For example, the rescue of the Mariner by the fishermen (Plate XXXII) is depicted as if it were intended to illustrate the *Book of Jonas*.

Many current cultural and visual references can be identified in Doré's version of *AM*, among which are the Ghost Ship, the Wandering Jew and the Polar expedition. The Ghost Ship was known through Richard Wagner's opera *Der fliegende Holländer* (The Flying Dutchman), which the German composer completed in Paris in 1841. But the same theme can be found in Edgar Allan Poe's 1833 *MS Found in a Bottle,* translated by Baudelaire in 1856 (*Manuscrit trouvé dans une bouteille*). Besides, Doré illustrated Poe's *The Raven*, although the plates were not published before his death (Poe 1884). Ghost Ships and cursed vessels were a very common theme, as a poem by Henri de Latouche (1785-1851), *Le Navire inconnu* (The Unknown Ship) (Latouche 1825), bears witness. This poem, reproduced in Taylor and Nodier's *Voyages pittoresques et romantiques* (Picturesque and Romantic Travels), was illustrated with a vignette by Horace Vernet, dated 1822. Latouche's version of the ancient mariner is represented holding the lifeless body of his son, victim of the curse which struck all slave traders, a curse which is embodied by a ghost slave ship wandering in the tempest, 'from Pole to Pole' (Latouche 1825, 9). Of course this lithograph illustrated a derived text, and not the original poem by Coleridge, but some of the elements Doré would exalt were already there. The Wandering Jew was a much more ancient legend—it appeared during the thirteenth century in Roger de Wendover's *Flores historiarum* and in Matthieu Paris's *Chronica maiora*—but was brought back to life in nineteenth-century Romantic France (*Le Juif errant, un témoin du temps,* 2001). Eugène Sue (1804-57) wrote in 1844-45 *Le Juif errant* (The Wandering Jew), a social novel illustrated by Gavarni. Doré himself illustrated in 1856 Pierre Dupont's book *La Légende du Juif errant* (The Legend of the Wandering Jew) with twelve plates (Dupont 1856) which in various ways announced his drawings for the character of the Ancient Mariner and his dark and chaotic world. This book and its plates were known in England through a translation by George W. Thornbury (Dupont 1857). Coleridge's intention was clearly to establish such a parallel with the Wandering Jew (Fulmer 1969, 797-815), and indeed shortly before undertaking *AM* had written the prose poem *The Wanderings of Cain* (1797), which in amplifying the underlying biblical legend (the Old Testament Cain is condemned to wander after his murder of his brother, as the later Wandering Jew is said to have been condemned to wander forever to bear witness to Jesus's crucifixion, at which he, an unbeliever, was present), displays his powerful interest in the theme; and this thematic element was perfectly understood in France (Coleridge 1877a, 1 and Duplessis 1885, 50). Finally, the theme of the ship in the North Pole had become a classic of its kind in literature and art, since the first eighteenth-century polar expeditions. Mary Shelley's *Frankenstein* (translated into French for the first time in 1821) depicts the monster's last appearance in a polar landscape. Paintings, novels—particularly Jules Verne's—and travel books accustomed the French audience to such images.

All these elements explain the richness of the posterity of Doré's pictures. Many illustrators used Doré's plates as a visual reference for works related to sea tales or wanderers' stories. A good example is Léon Benett's (1839-1916) frontispiece to one of Jules Verne's educational books called 'Histoire des grands voyages' (History of Great Travels), the first part of his three-volume *Découverte de la terre* (Discovery of the Earth) (Verne 1870). This engraving shows Christopher Columbus at the prow of the *Santa Maria,* with all his crew behind him, looking at a seabird flying just above water level. The gloomy atmosphere of this picture is very close to the Ancient Mariner's visions. In another surprising development, during the second half of the twentieth century, Doré's plates influenced several French comic-strip authors (Favière 1983, 47). In 1974, two cartoonists, collaborators on the weekly magazine *Pilote,* published comic books containing allusions to Doré's Coleridge. Jacques Tardi (born in 1946) used several images from Doré's book in *Le Démon des glaces* (The demon of the ice) (Tardi 1974), and Philippe

Druillet (born in 1944), in association with the writer Philippe Demuth (born in 1939), drew *Yragaël ou la fin des temps* (Yragaël or the End of Time), in which Coleridge's poem furnished some scenes, particularly the killing of the prophetical bird (Demuth and Druillet 1974 and, in English translation, Demuth and Druillet 1978).

But the most striking influence of Doré's plates was exerted on the other French illustrations for *AM.* It is interesting to see that no other illustrator of the nineteenth century dared risk a confrontation with this text. Only in the twentieth century did French artists illustrate new translations of *AM,* usually accompanying a new translation. Two solutions could be privileged: illustrating the poem as Doré did, with a series of independent, sequential plates, or choosing un-narrative illustrations, condensing several episodes of the poem.

In 1920, André Lhote (1885-1962) illustrated *AM,* translated by Odette and Guy Lavaud (Coleridge 1920). A Cubist artist—he exhibited with the 'Section d'Or' group in the 1910s—Lhote developed a style mixing geometrical deconstruction, rigorous composition and identifiable subjects. In 1921, André Deslignières (1880-1968), a French woodcutter who illustrated several literary works, carried out eight woodcuts for *AM* in a realistic style. This edition, presenting for the first time the translation written in 1893 by Alfred Jarry (1873-1907), and for a long time left unpublished, had a print run of only 374 copies.[60] In 1939, Noël Santon produced illustrations for a new translation by J.-A. Moisan (Coleridge 1939). In 1942, Jean Bruller translated and illustrated *AM* with seven pencil and gouache drawings (Coleridge 1942 and Konstantinovic 1969, 192-93). His contribution must be re-evaluated. Jean Bruller (1902-91) is now better known as Vercors, the pseudonym he used as a writer during the Occupation period in France, 1942 being precisely the year he wrote his best-known book *Le silence de la mer* (The Silence of the Sea). Bruller was also a cartoonist, drawing before 1939 ironical pictures denouncing the world's absurdity. Deeply pessimistic, he probably found in *AM* an echo of his own attitude towards life and solitude. His illustrations for Coleridge have recently been republished (Bruller 2002).

In 1946, Mario Prassinos (1916-85), a French artist with Greek origins, drew twenty-two illustrations for Coleridge's *AM,* translated by the Surrealist poet, typographer and publisher Guy Lévis Mano (1904-80). This edition had a print run of 695 copies (Coleridge 1946). Prassinos was a member of the Surrealist circle, which took a great interest in Coleridge. The Surrealists encouraged the publication of several classic French or foreign texts with new illustrations (Hubert 1988) and Prassinos began to illustrate literary texts in 1934: Coleridge came after Nodier, Apollinaire and Queneau and before Sartre, Edgar Allan Poe and Arthur Rimbaud. In the same period, Guy Lévis Mano translated Lorca, Rafael Alberti and Góngora. Significantly, it is another Surrealist who made the greatest contribution—after Doré—to the French illustrations of *AM*: in 1948, André Masson (1896-1987) drew twelve black-and-white lithographs for *AM,* translated by Henri Parisot (Coleridge 1948). As many as 309 copies of this de luxe edition were published in February 1948 (Passeron 1973, 170) and the twelve lithographs were exhibited in London by the Arts Council of Great Britain (Will-Levaillant 1972a, 2: 143). Masson used a technique based on automatism, the use of incidental stains and unusual visual connections (Klesse 2001, 144-56). Françoise Levaillant even suggested that for Masson the technical aspects of the printing process were more important than the text he illustrated (Will-Levaillant 1972a, 2: 143). Nevertheless, Masson, who travelled in England in the late 1920s (Masson 1956, 1: 23) explained later his special interest in Romantic writers during the late 1940s:

> I got into the habit. As a passionate reader I was look-ing towards the past, searching for illustration subjects which were in accordance with the spirit of the time (after the Second World War) when I was under the spell—the expression isn't too extravagant—of the Romantics from every nation. I do not deny it.[61]

This illustrated edition inspired an essay on Coleridge by the former Surrealist writer Antonin Artaud (1896-1948), who wrote in November 1946 his *Coleridge le traître* (Coleridge the Traitor)—a letter to the translator Henri Parisot (Artaud 1949). In 1951 were posthu-mously published the illustrations Jean-Gabriel Daragnès (1886-1950) drew for Valéry Larbaud's (1881-1957) translation (Coleridge 1951), the last work of this prolific illustrator. In 1963 (Coleridge 1963a) were published illustrations by André Collot (d. 1976), painter and illustrator, for a translation by the Belgian poet (member of André Breton's second Surrealist group) Marianne Van Hirtum (1925-88), prefaced by the French sea novelist Pierre Mac Orlan (1882-1970). In 1969, Roland Cat (b. 1943) illustrated *AM* (Coleridge 1969), very appropriately for an artist who likes to evoke the masters of the past, particularly those who produced fantastic works, like Albrecht Altdorfer and, significantly, Gustave Doré, by creating a dreamlike vi-sion in which the human being remains lost. In 1971, Michel Terrapon (d. 1989) produced illustrations for Coleridge's *AM,* and also for *Kubla Khan* and *Christa-bel* (Coleridge 1971). In 1975, Philippe Mohlitz (b. 1941), a member of the 'Art fantastique' (Fantasy Art) movement, was the most recent French artist to illustrate *AM* (Coleridge 1975a). Very understandably, this artist, fascinated by strangeness, obsession and unreality, felt attracted to Coleridge's poem.

CONCLUSION

The fame of Doré's plates increased considerably dur-ing the second half of the twentieth century. This grow-ing popularity and reach of Doré's illustrations is prob-ably linked to the fact that they came into the public domain in the mid-1960s, so that many editions of *AM* have used them since that time. Apparently, the first at-tempt to republish Doré's woodcuts as inseparable from Coleridge's poem appeared in the Western world in 1963 in Italy (Coleridge 1963b). This edition had been preceded only by a Hungarian edition in 1957: the translation of Coleridge's poem by Szabó Lőrinc was illustrated with pirated low-quality reproductions of thirty-seven of Gustave Doré's thirty-eight prints and one of the three original vignettes (Coleridge 1957). Actually, the most important contribution to this post-war revival, considering its quality in the rendering of the textual and visual relevance, was Martin Gardner's American edition of *The Annotated Ancient Mariner* (Coleridge 1965). He inserted each illustration twice, the first time as vignettes facing the definitive 1834 ver-sion published in Coleridge's *Poetical Works,* the second time as full-page plates, facing the original 1798 text. In his introduction, Gardner explained why he chose to illustrate this annotated edition with Doré's pictures, saying he was conscious it was a 'gamble' in a time of triumphant abstraction in the United States, but explaining that he was also convinced that Coleridge's 'fantasy' poem demanded 'realism' for its illustrations. In another way, he thought that the audience called out for such realistic illustrations, breaking the dictatorship of abstract art and providing what he called 'a refresh-ing visual holiday' (Coleridge 1965, 2-3). Another interesting contribution to this revival of Doré's plates is the 1966 Milanese edition of Coleridge's poem, in English, published by the International Book Society, with an introduction by the British writer Anthony Burgess and a vinyl recording read by Sir Ralph Rich-ardson (Coleridge 1966a).

These editions coupling Doré and Coleridge increased in the following years. The first French edition using Doré's illustrations since the 1877 Hachette edition was published in 1966, to accompany Henri Parisot's translation (Coleridge 1966b). In 1968, Doré's plates for *AM* were inserted in an edition of Victor Hugo's *Les travailleurs de la mer* (The Toilers of the Sea), an interesting, albeit ill-advised example of engravings be-ing re-used to illustrate another text, the only common factor being that each was a sea tale (Hugo 1968). In 1970 the Dover edition of *AM* was published in the United States, with an introduction entitled 'Gustave Doré and *The Rime of the Ancient Mariner*' (Coleridge 1970, v-xi), signed by Millicent Rose, also author of a biography of Doré (Rose 1946). Dover Publications, Inc., was dedicated at the time to republishing the major books illustrated by Gustave Doré, as part of a huge visual encyclopaedia. They usually republished the prints facing abridged extracts from the original texts; but for *AM,* they republished Coleridge's unabridged text as it had been published by Harper & Brothers in 1878. New editions in French (Coleridge 1978, 1985a, 1986, 1988a and 2001a), Italian (Coleridge 1973, 1985b, 1988b, 1994a, 1994b, 1995a, 2000 and 2004), Spanish (Coleridge 1975b, 1993a and 2002), Serbian (Coleridge 2003b), American (Coleridge 1993b and 2003a) and British editions (Coleridge 2001b) contributed to this rediscovery in the following years by using Doré's pictures. Also a Basque translation by Joseba Sarrionandia (b. 1958), published in Pamplona, reproduced Doré's plates (Coleridge 1995b).

The visual power of Doré's illustrations also attracted animation movie makers. In 1977, Larry Jordan (born in 1934) shot a forty-two-minute animated film entitled *Rime of the Ancient Mariner,* produced by Facets Multi-Media, partly with a grant to the film-maker awarded by the National Endowment for the Arts. Orson Welles (1915-85) acted as the reader of Coleridge's poem, with, as visual support, Gustave Doré's plates animated by using a cut-out style, moving the camera, zooming in on details and changing colours (Jordan 1977).

To conclude, we must insist on the fact that despite their huge popular success—or perhaps because of it—Doré's illustrations are still sniped at by the critics and the amateurs, who often prefer Masson's intellectual and nearly abstract compositions. If most of the modern biographers of Doré praised the illustrations for Coleridge, and the 'unearthly story [which] inspired some of his most unforgettable images' (Gosling 1973, 81), some of them attacked violently this 'puzzling world', wondering 'how carefully Doré read the text' (Richardson 1980, 128). In a way, even Doré's strongest defenders lost sight of the true originality of his work. It is interesting to remark that all the new editions of *AM* illustrated by Doré privileged a solution Doré rejected: the presentation of each plate with the corresponding verses on the opposite page. It is strongly opposed to Doré's requirement of separate folio illustrations, which had to be seen individually. For Doré's goal was to publish voluminous editions, certainly awkward for the act of reading but agreeable to view. Doré didn't give to the relationship between text and image the same importance as modern publishers do. This explains why modern aesthetic critics often preferred Masson's illustrations to Doré's, because Doré seemed to fail to respect the inner rhythm of the poem and split the visual from the verbal, while Masson's quasi-abstract lithographs seem to give a visual pendant to Coleridge's poetry and respond better to modern preoccupations with intertextuality by echoing other famous literary texts. Nevertheless, such an interpretation ignored what Doré's contemporaries observed in

his work, namely his capacity to enrich and improve a text; what Blanchard Jerrold meant when he called Doré a 'pictorial-poet', who '*adds* to those poets at whose fires he lights his imagination' (Jerrold 1869, 446).

Despite all the reservations, Doré's wager that his illustrations for *AM* were destined to achieve success seems—even if rather late—to have been fulfilled. Today, Doré's name is strongly and closely allied to Coleridge's, to the greatest mutual enrichment.

Notes

1. For the actual early reception of Coleridge in France see Michael John Kooy's essay in chapter 2 of this volume [*The Reception of S. T. Coleridge in Europe*].

2. 'Les visions de Doré contribuèrent brillamment à la diffusion du poème en dehors de son pays d'origine.'

3. See in the other volumes of this Series the articles of Colin Smethurst on the influence of Ossian on Chateaubriand (Gaskill 2004, 126-42), Joanne Wilkes on Byron's nineteenth-century French readers (Cardwell 2004, 1: 11-31), Peter Cochran on Byron's influence on French nineteenth-century literature (Cardwell 2004, 1: 32-70), Richard Maxwell on the French reception of Walter Scott (Pittock 2007, 11-30) and Paul Barnaby on Scott's most famous French translator, Jean-Baptiste Defauconpret (Pittock 2007, 31-44).

4. 'Avec beaucoup des qualités qui font le grand poëte, Coleridge a manqué sa destinée. Il y avait du décousu dans son esprit, dans ses idées, dans ses désirs.'

5. This introduction is signed 'A. P.' The editor could be in this case Amédée Pichot (1795-1877), French journalist, novelist and translator of many British authors, including Byron, Walter Scott, Bulwer-Lytton, Fielding and Dickens. See M. J. Kooy's essay in chapter 2 of this volume for Amédée Pichot's part in the discovery of Coleridge in France in the early 1820s.

6. *The Living Poets of England* 1827, 1: 415.

7. 'Les croyances du moyen âge vivantes encore dans tant de cœurs, sous tant de toits de chaume, les vestiges de vieilles coutumes, les légendes que l'on se conte à la veillée au coin de l'âtre ou dans la grange, et auxquelles on croit comme à l'Evangile, voilà les sujets auxquels devait se porter avec amour un esprit poétique familier, capable d'essor et incapable d'une longue traite. Ces sujets étaient aussi de nature à captiver un public assez semblable au poëte, impressionnable et superficiel comme lui' (Parisot 1854, 8: 572).

8. 'il y a en lui, si je l'ose dire, du bouddhiste qui tâche d'être méthodiste.'

9. Doré's biography by Blanche Roosevelt is an invaluable account of Doré's life and work. We will refer throughout to the American version of this book (Roosevelt 1885), far more complete and detailed than the French edition translated by Du Seigneux (Roosevelt 1887), who considerably altered the original text.

10. The Musée d'Art Moderne et Contemporain in Strasbourg purchased in 1992 the Samuel Francis Clapp collection dedicated to Gustave Doré (Geyer and Lehni 1993). Among the various pieces in this collection was a set of letters exchanged between Doré and the managers of the Doré Gallery in London ('Documentation des collections, Fonds Gustave Doré, Correspondance', from DOR1992/1-001 to DOR1992/1-118 and from DOR1992/2-001 to DOR1992/2-223).

11. 'si les *œuvres* du *poète Coleridge* sont aujourd'hui tombées dans le *domaine public*; c'est-à-dire, si toute personne à le droit d'imprimer et de publier' (Strasbourg, Musée d'Art Moderne et Contemporain [MAMC], Documentation des Collections, Fonds Gustave Doré, Correspondance, DOR1992/2-079).

12. 'C'est à consulter pour vous la date exacte de sa mort; et le texte de la loi de péremption pour l'Angleterre' (Strasbourg, MAMC, DOR1992/2-079).

13. Strasbourg, MAMC, DOR1992/2-078.

14. Strasbourg, MAMC, DOR1992/2-206.

15. 'D'après ce que je vois en lisant attentivement les textes de la loi [sur le copyright]; il me paraît certain que la poësie *The ancient mariner* est dans le droit public car elle a été publiée dans la jeunesse de l'auteur' (Strasbourg, MAMC, DOR1992/2-080).

16. See chapter 2 of this volume [*The Reception of S. T. Coleridge in Europe*] about the 1837, 1841 and 1859 French translations of *AM*.

17. Strasbourg, MAMC, DOR1992/2-095.

18. Strasbourg, MAMC, Cabinet des Estampes, Inv. 55.992.13 64 (Geyer and Lehni 1993, 87). This sketchbook is labelled 'Sketches (The Ancient Mariner)' ('Croquis (Le vieux marin)').

19. Brown wash drawing and white gouache on paper, Strasbourg, MAMC, Cabinet des Estampes (Favière 1983, 150-51; Guigon, Geyer and Reyero 2004, 131).

20. Pen and wash, grey and black and brown, London, Victoria & Albert Museum (Woof and Hebron 1997, 130).

21. Charcoal, grey, black, brown pen and wash, London, Victoria & Albert Museum (Woof and Hebron 1997, 130).

22. Strasbourg, MAMC, Cabinet des Estampes, Inv. 55.992.13-165 (Geyer and Lehni 1993, 90).

23. Strasbourg, MAMC, Documentation des Collections, Fonds Gustave Doré, Correspondance, DOR1992/2-095.

24. Strasbourg, MAMC, DOR1992/2-097.

25. Strasbourg, MAMC, DOR1992/2-098.

26. Strasbourg, MAMC, DOR1992/2-099.

27. Strasbourg, MAMC, DOR1992/2-100.

28. Strasbourg, MAMC, DOR1992/2-101.

29. Strasbourg, MAMC, DOR1992/2-105.

30. Strasbourg, MAMC, DOR1992/2-095.

31. Strasbourg, MAMC, DOR1992/2-095 and DOR1992/2-096.

32. 'Je sais fort bien qu'avec le système tout à fait modeste que je veux employer et qui est de faire un *simple dépôt* dont on connaîtra la place, je me prive des grands moyens d'expansion et de publicité que connaissent tous les libraires *professionnels,* tels que les voyageurs, les crédits, la presse mise en œuvre etc etc etc et que je ne puis pas compter sur une vente rapide; tout cela je le sais. Mais ce que je sais bien aussi; c'est le sort qu'aura ma propriété; si je la plaçais dans les mains des personnes qui, comme vous le dites, sont en mesure de distribuer rapidement un livre aux quatre coins du globe [. . .] ce pourquoi ils m'offriraient un genre d'association dont je serais la dupe après peu de temps' (Strasbourg, MAMC, DOR1992/2-096).

33. Roosevelt 1885, 422.

34. Strasbourg, MAMC, DOR1992/2-103.

35. Strasbourg, MAMC, DOR1992/2-104.

36. 'Je suis, comme vous, étonné de la stérilité de l'affaire du *Mariner.* Il y a là sans doute une cause que l'on ne me laisse pas connaître et que l'avenir me révèlera je l'espère. Pour le moment je ne puis attribuer cela qu'à l'inhabilité de MM H . . . ou au moins à l'insuffisance de leurs relations comme libraires.' (Strasbourg, MAMC, DOR1992/2-105).

37. Strasbourg, MAMC, DOR1992/2-106.

38. Strasbourg, MAMC, DOR1992/1-043.

39. Strasbourg, MAMC, DOR1992/1-050.

40. Strasbourg, MAMC, DOR1992/1-098.

41. Philippe Kaenel, reading '1,800 £' instead of '18 £' on the 30 July 1880 receipt, affirmed that the Doré Gallery paid Doré £2,200 in all for *AM* (Kaenel 2005, 440). But the sum which appears on the receipt is definitely eighteen pounds ('dixhuit livres sterling').

42. 'Je ne puis accorder par traité le monopole unique de la vente de mon livre en Hollande, ni autre pays, pour la raison que je me dispose, comme il se fait toujours pour les publications *typographiques* de vendre en différents pays les *clichés* de l'ouvrage ce qui comporte le monopole de publications dans la *langue du pays,* mais cependant sans empêcher l'introduction d'exemplaires anglais' (Strasbourg, MAMC, DOR1992/2-100).

43. Strasbourg, MAMC, Cabinet des Estampes, Inv. 55.992.13-166 (Geyer and Lehni 1993, 90).

44. *Bibliographie de la France, journal général de l'imprimerie et de la librairie,* 66ᵉ année, 2ᵉ série, 24 Février 1877, p. 103, no. 1988.

45. Strasbourg, Bibliothèque nationale et universitaire, R 276.

46. The following passage, casting new light on the Spanish reception of Gustave Doré's *AM,* was provided for the present volume [*The Reception of S. T. Coleridge in Europe*] by Juan Zarandona. The author and editors wish to thank him for his contribution to this [essay].

47. 'C'est comme vous voyez un livre capital, somptueux, et que l'on pourra placer au premier rang de mes illustrations' (Strasbourg, MAMC, DOR1992/2-095).

48. 'Comme vous voyez, ce livre est *mon enfant* et j'aurais [assurément] un sentiment de gratitude pour ceux qui lui auront donné la main pour faire son entrée dans le monde' (Strasbourg, MAMC, DOR1992/2-098).

49. 'Toutes mes œuvres en *illustrateur* ont toujours un début aisé et rapide; et celle là n'est certainement pas inférieure aux précédentes' (Strasbourg, MAMC, DOR1992/2-105).

50. 'Espérons qu'aidés par le merveilleux et puissant crayon de M. Gustave Doré, nous pourrons donner au public de notre pays une idée assez complète de l'œuvre célèbre du poëte anglais' (Coleridge 1877a, 2).

51. '[Doré] nous fait quitter le monde de la réalité pour nous introduire dans la fantasmagorie des rêves'.

52. 'Dans cette sombre légende (dont le texte original est donné ici en regard de l'heureuse traduction en prose que l'on doit à Auguste Barbier), le surna-

turel tient une très large place: ce sont des scènes apocalyptiques que seul le crayon de Doré pouvait complètement maîtriser.' (Buloz 1877, 238).

53. 'Après les voyages réels, voici les voyages imaginaires. Gustave Doré part avec Coleridge dans les mers polaires, où l'albatros plane dans son vol immense. Ici sa fantaisie se donne libre carrière.' (Delorme 1879, 22).

54. 'J'en appelle aux maîtres de tous les temps et de tous les pays dont il a ravivé les pensées, condensé les rêves, mis en action les paroles et cristallisé les visions. Je les évoque autour de cette tombe. Tous—le Dante, Cervantes, Rabelais, l'Arioste, Chateaubriand, Balzac, La Fontaine, Perrault, Tennyson, Coleridge, [. . .]—tous sont ici. Chacun d'eux tient une palme, et la dépose sur le cercueil de ce mécontent de lui-même qui les contenta tous. Tous remercient leur collaborateur posthume' (Duplessis 1885, 214).

55. 'Pour cette fiction qui se passe presque toujours en mer, entre le ciel et l'eau, Gustave Doré semble avoir encore agrandi sa manière. [. . .] Entre le poème où sont racontées avec un rare talent les souffrances physiques et morales du marin déshérité et les dessins où ces souffrances sont exprimées d'une façon saisissante, il y a une corrélation complète. Ici, comme toutes les fois où Doré a traduit l'œuvre d'un écrivain de haute valeur, il a trouvé moyen, à l'aide de son crayon, d'accroître l'intérêt du récit.' (Duplessis 1885, 50-52).

56. Roosevelt 1885, 424-25.

57. '[i]l possède cet œil visionnaire dont parle le poète qui sait dégager le côté secret et singulier de la nature' (Théophile Gautier, *Le Moniteur universel,* 30 July 1861, 1163).

58. 'Les illustrations de cet ouvrage superbe, où s'entremêlent le tragique et le merveilleux dans un monde irréel, élèvent le poème de Coleridge au chef-d'œuvre' (*Gustave Doré illustrateur* 1984, 49).

59. 'L'illustration n'est amusante pour un artiste, qu'avec les génies du passé qui disent: 'Il entra dans un bois sombre, où il arriva devant un palais dont les murs semblaient de diamant.' (Goncourt, 1989, 2: 854).

60. The Bibliothèque Nationale de France keeps a de luxe copy of this book (RES P-YN-132) containing, among other documents, Alfred Jarry's original manuscript of the translation of *AM* (dated 18-21 November 1893) together with twelve original drawings and eighteen preparatory sketches by Deslignières.

61. 'Le pli était pris. Liseur passionné j'allais aussi vers le passé chercher matière à illustration conforme à l'état d'esprit de cette époque (après la première Guerre mondiale) où j'étais envoûté—le mot n'est pas trop fort—par les romantiques de tous les pays. Je ne le dénie pas' (Masson 1972, 128).

Bibliography

Artaud, Antonin (1949) *Supplément aux lettres de Rodez, suivi de Coleridge le traître,* Paris: G. L. M. [Guy Lévis Mano].

Bate, Walter Jackson (1950) 'Coleridge on the Function of Art', in *Perspectives of Criticism,* Cambridge, MA: Harvard University Press, pp. 125-59.

Bentley, G. E. (1981) 'Coleridge, Stothard and the First Illustration of *Christabel*', *Studies in Romanticism,* 20: 111-16.

Blachon, Rémi (2001) *La gravure sur bois au XIXe siècle. L'âge du bois debout,* Paris: Les Editions de l'Amateur.

Bostetter, E. E. (1962) 'The Nightmare World of the *Ancient Mariner*', *Studies in Romanticism,* 1: 241-54.

Brosch, Renate (1989) 'Coleridges *The Rime of the Ancient Mariner* von Doré illustriert', *Germanisch-Romanische Monatsschrift,* new series, 39: 41-57.

Bruller, Jean (2002) *Les silences de Vercors, Jean Bruller,* Paris: Création et recherche.

Buloz, Charles (1877) 'Les livres illustrés', *Revue des Deux Mondes,* XLVIIe année. troisième période, 19: 237-38.

Byron, George Gordon, Lord (1853) *Œuvres complètes de Lord Byron,* trans. Louis Barré, illus. Ch. Mettais, Bocourt, Gustave Doré, Paris: J. Bry aîné.

Cardwell, Richard A. (ed.) (2004) *The Reception of Lord Byron in Europe,* 2 vols, Athlone Critical Traditions Series: The Reception of British and Irish Authors in Europe, series ed. Elinor Shaffer, London; New York: Thoemmes Continuum.

Catalogue des tableaux, études et esquisses, aquarelles, dessins et sculptures laissés dans son atelier par feu Gustave Doré (1885) Paris: Imprimerie de l'Art.

Chasles, Philarète (1850), *Etudes sur les hommes et les mœurs au XIXe siècle: portraits contemporains, scènes de voyage, souvenirs de jeunesse,* Paris: Amyot.

Coleridge, S. T. (1837) *The Rime of the Ancient Mariner by Samuel Taylor Coleridge. Illustrated by Twenty-five Poetic and Dramatic Scenes Designed and Etched by David Scott,* Edinburgh: Alexander Hill; London: Ackermann & Co.

Coleridge, S. T. (1863) *Coleridge's Rime of the Ancient Mariner,* illus. J. Noel Paton, London: Art-Union.

Coleridge, S. T. (1875) *The Rime of the Ancient Mariner,* illus. Gustave Doré, London: Doré Gallery.

Coleridge, S. T. (1876a) *The Rime of the Ancient Mariner,* illus. Gustave Doré, London: Doré Gallery; Hamilton, Adams & Co; same edn as 1875, different title page.

Coleridge, S. T. (1876b) *The Rime of the Ancient Mariner,* New York: Harper & Brothers.

Coleridge, S. T. (1877a) *La Chanson du Vieux Marin,* trans. A. Barbier, illus. Gustave Doré, Paris: Librairie Hachette & Cie.

Coleridge, S. T. (1877b) *Der Alte Matrose,* trans. Ferdinand Freiligrath, illus. Gustave Doré, Leipzig: C. F. Amelang's Verlag.

Coleridge, S. T. (1877c) *The Rime of the Ancient Mariner,* New York: Harper & Brothers.

Coleridge, S. T. (1878) *The Rime of the Ancient Mariner,* New York: Harper & Brothers.

Coleridge, S. T. (1881) *The Rime of the Ancient Mariner,* New York: Harper & Brothers.

Coleridge, S. T. (1882) *The Rime of the Ancient Mariner,* New York: Harper & Brothers.

Coleridge, S. T. (1884) *The Rime of the Ancient Mariner, in Seven Parts,* illus. Gustave Doré, Birket Foster and others, Boston: Estes & Lauriat.

Coleridge, S. T. (1886) *The Rime of the Ancient Mariner,* New York: Harper & Brothers.

Coleridge, S. T. (1889a) *La leggenda del vecchio marinaio di Samuele Coleridge,* prose trans. Enrico Nencioni, illus. Gustave Doré, Milan: Tipografia Bernardoni.

Coleridge, S. T. (1889b) *La Leggenda del Vecchio Marinaio,* prose trans. Enrico Nencioni, illus. Gustave Doré, Milan: Tipografia Bernardoni di C. Rebeschini E. C.

Coleridge, S. T. (1889c) *The Rime of the Ancient Mariner,* ed. Henry C. Walsh, illus. Gustave Doré, Philadelphia: H. Altemus.

Coleridge, S. T. ([1890]) *El viejo marino por Samuel Coleridge,* trans. B. Archer M., illus. Gustave Doré, Barcelona: E. Serra Borrell.

Coleridge, S. T. (1893) Старый Моряк (*Staryi moryak*) (*AM*), trans. and intro. Apollon Korinfsky, 37 illus. Gustave Doré, St Petersburg: Brothers D. & M. Fedorov.

Coleridge, S. T. (1897) Кольридж С. Старый Моряк (*AM*); (перевод Аполлона Коринфского. иллюстрации Густава Доре) (trans. Apollon Korinfsky, illus. Gustave Doré), Сиев-Харьков: Южно-русское издательство Ф.А.Йогансона.

Coleridge, S. T. (1898a) *Der alte Matrose*, trans. Ferdinand von Freiligrath, illus. Gustave Doré, Gera: C. B. Griesbach.

Coleridge, S. T. (1898b) *El viejo marino*, trans. B. Archer M., illus. Gustave Doré, Barcelona: E. Serra Borrell

Coleridge, S. T. (1920) *Le Dit de l'Ancien Marinier, en sept parties, par S. T. Coleridge, nouvellement mis en français par Odette & Guy Lavaud & embelli de dessins par André Lhote*, Paris: Emile-Paul Frères.

Coleridge, S. T. (1921) *La ballade du vieux marin*, trans. Alfred Jarry, illus. André Deslignière, Paris: R. Davis.

Coleridge, S. T. (1925) *Der alte Matrose*, trans. Ferdinand Freiligrath, illus. Gustave Doré, Munich: Verlag J. Müller.

Coleridge, S. T. (1939) *Le Vieux marin, poème: Traduction inédite équirythmique de J.-A. Moisan; Gravures originales de Noël Santon*, Paris: Editions Corymbe.

Coleridge, S. T. (1942) *Les stances du vieux matelot, de Coleridge*, trans. and illus. Jean Bruller, Paris: Jean Bruller.

Coleridge, S. T. (1946) *La Ballade du vieux marin, en sept parties, par S. T. Coleridge, contenant le texte anglais, une version française par Guy Lévis Mano et 22 images et lettrines par Mario Prassinos*, Paris: G. L. M. [Guy Lévis Mano].

Coleridge, S. T. (1948) *Le Dit du vieux marin, Christabel et Koubla Khan*, trans. Henri Parisot, illus. André Masson, Paris: Editions Pro-Francia.

Coleridge, S. T. (1951) *La chanson du vieux marin*, trans. Valéry Larbaud, illus. J.-C. Daragnès, Paris: Société des Francs-Bibliophiles.

Coleridge, S. T. (1957) *Rege a vén tengerészről: Hét részben (1798)*, trans. Szabó Lőrinc, illus. Gustave Doré, Budapest: Magvető Könyvkiadó.

Coleridge, S. T. (1963a) *Le Dit du vieux marin de Samuel Taylor Coleridge dans son texte original et traduit en français par Marianne Van Hirtum; Préfacé par Pierre Mac Orlan; Illustré de gravures sur cuivre par André Collot*, Paris: aux dépens de bibliophiles amis de l'artiste.

Coleridge, S. T. (1963b) *La leggenda del vecchio marinaio*, illus. Gustave Doré, Rome: Edizione d'Arte 'Felix'.

Coleridge, S. T. (1965) *The Annotated Ancient Mariner, With an Introduction and Notes by Martin Gardner; The Rime of The Ancient Mariner by Samuel Taylor Coleridge, Illustrated by Gustave Doré*, New York: Clarkson N. Potter.

Coleridge, S. T. (1966a) *The Rime of the Ancient Mariner*, intro. Anthony Burgess, illus. Gustave Doré, Edizione d'Arte 'Felix', ed. Giuseppe Massani, Milan: International Book Society.

Coleridge, S. T. (1966b) *The Rime of the Ancient Mariner / Le Dit du vieux marin*, trans. Henri Parisot, illus. Gustave Doré, Paris: Le Club français du Livre.

Coleridge, S. T. (1969) *Le Dit du vieux marin de Samuel Coleridge*, trans. Auguste Barbier, illus. Roland Cat, Paris: Editions Axium.

Coleridge, S. T. (1970) *The Rime of The Ancient Mariner, with 42 Illustrations by Gustave Doré*, ed. Millicent Rose, New York: Dover Publications.

Coleridge, S. T. (1971) *Le Dit du vieux marin, Christabel, Koubla Khan*, trans. Henri Parisot, illus. Michel Terrapon, Albeuve: Editions Castella.

Coleridge, S. T. (1973) *La ballata del vecchio marinaio*, trans. Mario Luzi, intro. Giampaolo Dossena, 42 illus. Gustave Doré, Milan: Rizzoli.

Coleridge, S. T. (1975a) *La Chanson du vieux marin*, trans. Valéry Larbaud, illus. Philippe Mohlitz, Paris: Le livre contemporain et les Bibliophiles Franco-Suisses.

Coleridge, S. T. (1975b) *La oda del viejo marinero*, trans. Eduardo Chamorro, illus. Gustave Doré, Barcelona: Bocaccio.

Coleridge, S. T. (1978) *Le Dit du vieux marin*, trans. Henri Parisot, illus. Gustave Doré, Paris: Gallimard.

Coleridge, S. T. (1981) *La balada del marinero de antaño*, trans. José Siles Artés, illus. Antonio Jiménez Lara, Madrid: José Siles Artés.

Coleridge, S. T. (1985a) *La Ballade du vieux marin, Illustré par Gustave Doré*, Paris: Kryptogramma.

Coleridge, S. T. (1985b) *La ballata del vecchio marinaio*, trans. Mario Luzi, illus. Gustave Doré, ed. Ginevra Bompiani, Milan: Rizzoli.

Coleridge, S. T. (1986) *La ballade du vieux marin*, trans. Jean-Louis Paul, illus. Gustave Doré, Paris: Editions Ressouvenance.

Coleridge, S. T. (1988a) *La Chanson du vieux marin*, trans. Auguste Barbier, illus. Gustave Doré, Paris: Inter-Livres.

Coleridge, S. T. (1988b) *La ballata del vecchio marinaio*, trans. Mario Luzi, illus. Gustave Doré, ed. Ginevra Bompiani, 2nd edn, Milan: Rizzoli.

Coleridge, S. T. (1993a) *La leggenda del vecchio marinaio di Samuel T. Coleridge*, trans. Enrico Nencioni, illus. Gustave Doré (38 plates, 4 drawings), Milan: Tea.

Coleridge, S. T. (1993b) *The Rime of the Ancient Mariner*, illus. Gustave Doré, Lewisville, TX: School of Tomorrow

Coleridge, S. T. (1994a) *La ballata del vecchio marinaio*, trans. Giuliano Acunzoli, illus. Gustave Doré, Vimercate: La Spiga

Coleridge, S. T. (1994b) *La leggenda del vecchio marinaio,* prose trans. Enrico Nencioni, illus. Gustave Doré, Milan: Tea.

Coleridge, S. T. (1995a) *La ballata del vecchio marinaio e altre poesie,* ed. and trans. Tommaso Pisanti, illus. Gustave Doré, bilingual edn, Rome: Newton & Compton.

Coleridge, S. T. (1995b) *Marinel zaharraren balada,* trans. Joseba Sarrionandia, illus. Gustave Doré, Pamplona: Pamiela.

Coleridge, S. T. (2000) *La balata del vecchio marinaio,* trans. Mario Luzi, illus. Gustave Doré, Milan: Biblioteca universale Rizzoli.

Coleridge, S. T. (2001a) *Le Dit du Vieux Marin,* trans. Henri Parisot, illus. Gustave Doré, ed. John Beer, Paris: Hazan.

Coleridge, S. T. (2001b) *The Rime of the Ancient Mariner,* illus. Gustave Doré, London: Cassell & Co.

Coleridge, S. T. (2002) *La balada del Viejo marinero / The Rime of the Ancient Mariner,* trans. and prologue Jaime Siles, illus. Gustave Doré, Barcelona: Circulo de Lectores.

Coleridge, S. T. (2003a) *The Annotated Ancient Mariner,* intro. and notes Martin Gardner, illus. Gustave Doré, Amherst, NY: Prometheus Books.

Coleridge, S. T. (Samjuel Tejlor Kolridž) (2003b) *Ispovest starog pomorca* (*AM*), illus. Gustave Doré, trans. Ranka Kuić, intro. Žika Bogdanović, epilogue Millicent Rose (Milisent Rouz), Belgrade: Ateneum (Vojna štamparija [military printing office]); 94 pp.; 30 cm (Biblioteka Itaka); circulation 400; intro 'O grehu i ispaśtanju' ('About sin and atonement'), pp. 5-10; epilogue 'Gistav Dore i *Ispovest starog pomorca*' ('Gustave Doré and *AM*'), pp. 89-94.

Coleridge, S. T. (2004) *La ballata del vecchio marinaio e altre poesie,* ed. and trans. Tommaso Pisanti, illus. Gustave Doré, bilingual edn, Rome: Newton & Compton.

Coolidge, John (1994) *Gustave Doré's London: A Study of the City in the Age of Confidence 1848-1873,* Dublin, NH: William L. Bauhan.

Delorme, René (1879) *Gustave Doré, peintre, sculpteur, dessinateur et graveur,* Paris: Ludovic Baschet.

Demuth, Michel and Philippe Druillet (1974), *Yragaël ou la Fin des Temps,* Paris: Dargaud.

Demuth, Michel and Philippe Druillet (1978) *Yragael: Urm,* trans. Pauline Tenant, Paris; London: Dragon's Book.

Duplessis, Georges (1885) *Catalogue des dessins, aquarelles et estampes de Gustave Doré exposés dans les salons du Cercle de la Librairie (mars 1885) avec une notice biographique par M. G. Duplessis, portrait gravé par Lalauze, d'après Carolus Duran,* Paris: Cercle de la Librairie, de l'imprimerie et de la papeterie.

Dupont, Pierre (1856) *La Légende du Juif errant; Compositions et dessins par Gustave Doré, gravés sur bois par F. Rouget, O. Jahyer et J. Gauchard imprimés par J. Best; Poëme avec prologue et épilogue par Pierre Dupont; Préface et notice bibliographique par Paul Lacroix, avec la ballade de Béranger mise en musique par Ernest Doré,* Paris: Michel Lévy frères.

Dupont, Pierre (1857) *The Legend of the Wandering Jew illustrated by Gustave Doré: Poem, with prologue and epilogue; Bibliographical notice by Paul Lacroix; With the Complaint and Béranger's Ballad; Translated, with Critical Remarks, by George W. Thornbury,* London: Addey.

Enault, Louis (1876) *Londres, par Louis Enault,* illus. Gustave Doré, Paris: Librairie Hachette et Cie.

Ergal, Jean-Michel (2001) 'Portrait de l'artiste en *Ancient Mariner*', in Dethurens, Pascal (ed.) *Une amitié européenne: Nouveaux horizons de la littérature, mélanges offerts à Olivier H. Bonnerot,* Paris: Honoré Champion, pp. 67-72.

Farner, Konrad (1975) *Gustave Doré der industrialisierte Romantiker,* Munich: Rogner & Bernhard.

Favière, Jean and others (1983) *Gustave Doré 1832-1883,* exhibition catalogue, Strasbourg: Musée d'Art Moderne—Cabinet des Estampes.

Foucart, Bruno (1983) 'Gustave Doré, un réaliste visionnaire', *Beaux-Arts Magazine,* 5 (September): 32-41.

Fulmer, Bryan O. (1969) 'The *Ancient Mariner* and the Wandering Jew', *Studies in Philology,* 66: 797-815.

Gaskill, Howard (ed.) (2004) *The Reception of Ossian in Europe,* Athlone Critical Traditions Series: The Reception of British and Irish Authors in Europe, series ed. Elinor Shaffer, London; New York: Thoemmes Continuum.

Geyer, Marie-Jeanne and Nadine Lehni (1993) *Gustave Doré, une nouvelle collection,* exhibition catalogue, Strasbourg: Palais Rohan and Galerie Robert Heitz, 5 November 1993-23 January 1994.

Goncourt, Edmond and Jules (1989) *Journal: Mémoires de la vie littéraire 1851-1896,* ed. and notes Robert Ricatte, 3 vols, Paris: Robert Laffont.

Gosling, Nigel (1973) *Gustave Doré,* Newton Abbot: David & Charles.

Guigon, Emmanuel, Marie-Jeanne Geyer and Carlos Reyero (2004) *Gustave Doré, œuvres de la collection du Musée d'Art moderne et contemporain de Stras-*

bourg, exhibition catalogue, Museo de Bellas Artes de Bilbao, 4 October-12 December 2004, Salle d'expositions San Eloy, Caja Duero, Salamanca, 28 January-3 March 2005 and Museo de Bellas Artes de Sevilla, 10 March-1 May 2005.

Gustave Doré 1832-1883 (1982) vol 1: *Gustave Doré: Illustrator—Maler—Bildhauer. Beiträge zu seinem Werk,* vol. 2: *Gustave Doré: Katalog der ausgestellten Werke,* Dortmund: Harenberg.

Gustave Doré illustrateur (1984) exhibition catalogue, Ville du Havre, Bibliothèque Municipale, 28 September-27 October 1984.

Hood, Thomas (1870) *Thomas Hood, illustrated by Gustave Doré,* London: E. Moxon, Son & Co.

Hubert, Renée Riese (1985) 'The Ancient Mariner's Graphic Voyage Through Mimesis and Metaphor', in Rawson, C. J. (ed.) *The Yearbook of English Studies: Anglo-French Literary Relations,* Special Number, 15: 80-92.

Hubert, Renée Riese (1988) *Surrealism and the Book,* Berkeley; Los Angeles; Oxford: University of California Press.

Hugo, Victor (1867) *The Toilers of the Sea: Authorized English Translation, by W. Moy Thomas; Two illustrations by Gustave Doré,* London: Sampson Low & Marston.

Hugo, Victor (1968) *Les Travailleurs de la mer; Illustrations de Gustave Doré tirées de 'The Rime of the Ancient Mariner' de Samuel Taylor Coleridge, Londres, 1876,* Levallois-Perret: Cercle du Bibliophile.

Jerrold, Blanchard (1869) 'Gustave Doré at Home', *The Gentleman's Magazine,* September, 439-49.

Jerrold, Blanchard (1871) *The Cockaynes in Paris or 'Gone Abroad'; With Sketches by Gustave Doré and Other Illustrations of the English Abroad From a French Point of View,* London: John Camden Hotten.

Jerrold, Blanchard (1872) *London, a Pilgrimage, by Gustave Doré and Blanchard Jerrold,* London: Grant & Co.

Jerrold, Blanchard (1891) *Life of Gustave Doré, with one hundred and thirty-eight illustrations from original drawings by Doré,* London: W. H. Allen.

Jordan, Larry (producer, director, animator) (USA, 1977) *Rime of the Ancient Mariner,* narrated Orson Welles, animated engravings Gustave Doré, music Mark Ellinger, colour short (42 mins), distrib. Canyon Cinema; Facets Video.

Jouve, M. (1981) 'Le pèlerinage à Londres de Gustave Doré', *Gazette des Beaux-Arts,* 97: 41-48.

Le Juif errant, un témoin du temps (2001) exhibition catalogue, Musée d'art et d'histoire du Judaïsme, Paris, 26 October 2001-24 February 2002.

Kaenel, Philippe (1985) *Gustave Doré, réaliste et visionnaire, 1832-1883,* exhibition catalogue, Bevaix, Galerie Arts Anciens, Geneva: Editions du Tricorne.

Kaenel, Philippe (2005) *Le métier d'illustrateur, 1830-1880: Rodolphe Töpffer, J.-J. Grandville, Gustave Doré,* Geneva: Droz.

Klesse, Antje (2001) *Illustrationen zu S. T. Coleridges 'The Rime of the Ancient Mariner': Eine Studie zur Illustration von Gedichten,* Memmingen: Curt Visel.

Konstantinovic, Radivoje D. (1969) *Vercors, écrivain et dessinateur, avec des commentaires de Vercors et 18 dessins de Jean Bruller,* Paris: Librairie C. Klincksieck.

Latouche, Henri de (1825) 'Le Navire inconnu', *Voyages pittoresques et romantiques dans l'ancienne France,* eds Charles Nodier, Isidore Taylor and Alphonse de Cailleux, 23 vols, Paris: Gide fils and A.-F. Lemaître, 1820-78, 2: 8-11.

Leblanc, Henri (1931) *Catalogue de l'oeuvre complet de Gustave Doré,* Paris: Ch. Bosse.

Leiris, Michel (1947) *André Masson et son univers,* Lausanne: Les trois collines.

The Living Poets of England: Specimens of the Living British Poets, with Biographical and Critical Notices and an Essay on English Poetry (1827) 2 vols, Paris: Baudry, Bobée et Hingray et A. et W. Galignani.

Malan, Dan (1995) *Gustave Doré: Adrift on Dreams and Splendor (A Comprehensive Biography and Bibliography),* St Louis, MO: Malan Classical Enterprises.

Masson, André (1956) *Métamorphose de l'artiste,* 2 vols, Geneva: Pierre Cailler.

Masson, André (1972) 'Comment j'ai illustré des livres', *Bulletin du Bibliophile,* 2: 127.

Michaud, Joseph (1877) *Histoire des Croisades par Michaud, de l'Académie française,* illus. Gustave Doré, Paris: Furne, Jouvet et Cie.

Milton, John (1866) *Milton's Paradise Lost,* ed. and notes Robert Vaughan, illus. Gustave Doré, London: Cassell, Petter & Galpin.

Paley, Morton D. (1999) *Portraits of Coleridge,* Oxford: Clarendon Press.

Parisot, Valentin (1854) 'Coleridge', *Biographie universelle (Michaud) ancienne et moderne, histoire, par ordre alphabétique, de la vie publique et privée de tous les hommes qui se sont fait remarquer par leurs écrits, leurs actions, leurs talents, leurs vertus ou leurs crimes,* new edn, 44 vols, Paris: Madame C. Desplaces, 8: 569-73.

Passeron, Roger (1973) *André Masson: Gravures 1924-1972,* Fribourg: Office du Livre.

Peacock, William F. (1858) *The Adventures of Saint George: After his Famous Encounter with the Dragon,* London: James Blackwood.

Pittock, Murray (ed.) (2007) *The Reception of Sir Walter Scott in Europe,* Athlone Critical Traditions Series: The Reception of British and Irish Authors in Europe, series ed. Elinor Shaffer, London; New York: Continuum.

Poe, Edgar Allan (1884) *The Raven,* illus. Gustave Doré, comments Edmund C. Stedman, New York: Harper & Brothers.

Poiret, Marie-France (1983) *Gustave Doré dans les collections du musée de Brou,* exhibition catalogue, Musée de Brou, Bourg-en-Bresse, Centre Culturel Albert Camus—Salle Gustave Doré, December 1983-January 1984.

Praz, Mario (1974) *Mnemosyne: The Parallel between Literature and the Visual Arts,* Princeton; London: Princeton University Press.

Renonciat, Annie (1983) *La vie et l'œuvre de Gustave Doré,* Paris: ACR Edition, Bibliothèque des Arts.

Richardson, Joanna (1980) *Gustave Doré: A Biography,* London: Cassell.

'*The Rime of the Ancient Mariner.* Illustrated by Gustave Doré (Doré Gallery)' (1876), *The Athenaeum: Journal of English and Foreign Literature, Science, the Fine Arts, Music and Drama,* 19 February, 271-72.

'*The Rime of the Ancient Mariner.* Illustrated by Gustave Doré' (1876) *The Illustrated London News,* 68.1903 (15 January): 57.

Roosevelt, Blanche (1885) *Life and Reminiscences of Gustave Doré, compiled from Materials Supplied by Doré's Relations and Friends, and From Personal Recollection,* London: Sampson Low, Marston Searle, & Rivington.

Roosevelt, Blanche (1887) *La vie et les œuvres de Gustave Doré, d'après les souvenirs de sa famille, de ses amis et de l'auteur,* trans. Du Seigneux, preface Arsène Houssaye, Paris: Librairie illustrée.

Rose, Millicent (1946) *Gustave Doré,* London: Pleiades Books.

Sainte-Beuve, Charles-Augustin (1870) *Portraits contemporains, Nouvelle édition, revue, corrigée et très-augmentée,* 5 vols, Paris: Michel Lévy frères.

Schefter, Edouard (1858) 'Macbeth', *La Semaine des Enfants,* 26 Nov. and 3 Dec.

Shaffer, Elinor S. (1969) 'Coleridge's Revolution in the Standard of Taste', *Journal of Aesthetics and Art Criticism,* 28: 213-23.

Shaffer, Elinor S. (1993) 'Coleridge and the Object of Art', *The Wordsworth Circle,* 24.2: 117-28.

Shakespeare, William (1860) *The Tempest, by William Shakespeare,* illus. Birket-Foster, Gustave Doré, Frédérik Skill, Alfred Slader and Gustave Janet, London: Bell & Daldy.

Tardi, Jacques (1974) *Le Démon des glaces,* Paris: Dargaud.

Tennyson, Alfred (1867a) *Elaine, by Alfred Tennyson,* illus. Gustave Doré, London: Edward Moxon & Co.

Tennyson, Alfred (1867b) *Vivien, by Alfred Tennyson,* illus. Gustave Doré, London: Edward Moxon & Co.

Tennyson, Alfred (1867c) *Guinevere,* illus. Gustave Doré, London: Edward Moxon & Co.

Tennyson, Alfred (1868a) *Enid,* illus. Gustave Doré, London: Edward Moxon & Co.

Tennyson, Alfred (1868b) *Idylls of the King,* illus. Gustave Doré, London: Edward Moxon & Co.

Tromp, Edouard (1932) *Gustave Doré,* Paris: Editions Rieder.

Twitchell, James B. (1983) *Romantic Horizons: Aspects of the Sublime in English Poetry and Painting, 1770-1850,* Columbia: University of Missouri Press.

Valmy-Baysse, Jean and Louis Dézé (1930) *Gustave Doré par J. Valmy-Baysse: Bibliographie et catalogue complet de l'œuvre, par Louis Dézé,* Paris: Editions Marcel Seheur.

Verne, Jules (1870) *Découverte de la terre: Histoire des grands voyages et des grands voyageurs,* 3 vols, Paris: Jules Hetzel.

Will-Levaillant, Françoise (1972a) 'André Masson et le livre: dessin, gravure, illustration', *Bulletin du Bibliophile,* 2: 129-55.

Will-Levaillant, Françoise (1972b) 'Catalogue des ouvrages illustrés par André Masson, de 1924 à février 1972 (première partie)', *Bulletin du Bibliophile,* 2: 156-80.

Will-Levaillant, Françoise (1985) 'Le prétexte du livre: André Masson graveur et lithographe', in *André Masson: Livres illustrés de gravures originales,* exhibition catalogue, Centre littéraire, Fondation Royaumont.

Woodring, Carl (1978) 'What Coleridge Thought of Pictures', in Kroeber, Karl and William Walling (eds) *Images of Romanticism: Verbal and Visual Affinities,* New Haven; London: Yale University Press, pp. 91-106.

Woods, A. (1978) 'Doré's *London*: Art and Evidence', *Art History,* 1.3: 341-59.

Woof, Robert and Stephen Hebron (1997) *The Rime of the Ancient Mariner: The Poem and its Illustrators,* Grasmere: The Wordsworth Trust.

Zarandona, Juan Miguel (2004) *Los 'Ecos de las Montañas' de José Zorilla y sus Fuentes de inspiración: de Tennyson a Doré,* Valladolid: Secretariado de Publicaciones e Intercambio Editorial.

Zola, Emile (1866) *Mes haines, causeries littéraires et artistiques,* Paris: Achille Faure.

FURTHER READING

Criticism

Goodwin, Sarah Webster. "Domesticity and Uncanny Kitsch in *The Rime of the Ancient Mariner* and *Frankenstein.*" *Tulsa Studies in Women's Literature* 10, no. 1 (spring 1991): 93-108.

Focuses on the central character of the monster in *Frankenstein* and *The Ancient Mariner* (represented by Life-in-Death) in order to analyze the connection between kitsch and feminine domesticity in both works.

Jones, David. "An Introduction to *The Rime of the Ancient Mariner.*" In *The Rime of the Ancient Mariner,* by Samuel Taylor Coleridge, edited by Thomas Dilworth, pp. 13-42. London: Enitharmon Press, 2005.

Reflects on Jones's experience creating copper-plate engravings for a 1929 edition of *The Rime of the Ancient Mariner,* revealing his enthusiasm for the project as well as his reservations about his ability to capture the poem's complexity and depth.

Ower, John B. "Crantz, Martens and the 'Slimy Things' in *The Rime of the Ancient Mariner.*" *Neophilologus* 85 (2001): 477-84.

Investigates the sources for the poem's references to "slimy things" in an attempt to evaluate the techniques employed by John Livingston Lowes in *The Road to Xanadu* (1927), his landmark study of the narrative sources for the poem.

Additional coverage of Coleridge's life and career is contained in the following sources published by Gale: *Authors and Artists for Young Adults,* **Vol. 66;** *Beacham's Guide to Literature for Young Adults,* **Vol. 4;** *British Writers,* **Vol. 4;** *British Writers Retrospective Supplement,* **Vol. 2;** *Concise Dictionary of British Literary Biography, 1789-1832; Dictionary of Literary Biography,* **Vols. 93, 107;** *Discovering Authors; Discovering Authors 3.0; Discovering Authors: British Edition; Discovering Authors: Canadian Edition; Discovering Authors Modules: Most-Studied Authors, Poets; Exploring Poetry; Literary Movements for Students,* **Vol. 1;** *Literature and Its Times Supplement,* **Vol. 1:1;** *Literature Resource Center; Nineteenth-Century Literature Criticism,* **Vols. 9, 54, 99, 111, 177, 197;** *Poetry Criticism,* **Vols. 11, 39, 67;** *Poetry for Students,* **Vols. 4, 5;** *Poets: American and British; Reference Guide to English Literature,* **Ed. 2;** *Twayne's English Authors; World Literature and Its Times,* **Vol. 3;** *World Literature Criticism,* **Ed. 2; and** *World Poets.*

Sydney Dobell
1824-1874

(Also wrote under the pseudonym Sydney Yendys) English poet and critic.

INTRODUCTION

A prominent member of the Spasmodic School of poetry, Dobell is known for his intensely emotional poetic style, a style that was praised for its eloquence at the same time it was criticized for its incoherence and rhythmic inconsistency. His most famous works are *The Roman, Balder,* and *Sonnets on the War* (a collaboration with the Scottish poet Alexander Smith).

BIOGRAPHICAL INFORMATION

One of ten children, Dobell was born on April 5, 1824, in Cranbrook, Kent, to John and Julietta Thompson Dobell. Dobell's parents were devout members of a radical religious sect, the Church of God, founded by Samuel Thompson, Dobell's maternal grandfather. One of the strictest tenets of the faith involved the prohibition of any unnecessary social interaction with those outside the church. Thus, since Dobell was prohibited from attending public school, his education was limited to private tutors at home. An avid reader, he was an intellectually precocious child and began writing poetry as well as essays on theology at an early age. He also suffered several incidents of illness, many of them quite serious, during his childhood. Dobell's father was a wine merchant and Dobell joined the family business in his youth. He married Emily Fordham in 1844, at the age of twenty and at that time became owner of the Gloucester branch of the wine business. After nearly dying from rheumatic fever in 1847, Dobell turned to literary pursuits, publishing *The Roman* in 1850, and the first part of *Balder* four years later. He and his wife traveled to Scotland, hoping to improve his health with a change in location, and to consult with a doctor on Emily's condition, as she also suffered from a number of physical afflictions; they remained there for three years. Dobell produced two more poetry collections, in 1855 and 1856, but published little else afterwards, probably due to his deteriorating physical condition. In their later years the Dobells maintained their primary residence in the Cotswolds, but spent winters in warmer climates such as Spain, southern France, and Italy. Dobell died on August 22, 1874.

MAJOR WORKS

Dobell's first major publication, *The Roman: A Dramatic Poem,* which he published under a pseudonym, was well received by both readers and critics. The work featured an account of the revolutionary activities of its main character, Vittorio Santo, whose eloquent impassioned pleas on behalf of an independent Italy and the restoration of the Roman Republic were much admired by Dobell's contemporaries. Unfortunately, the poet's popularity took a sharp downturn with his next publication, *Balder: Part the First,* a lengthy dramatic work of 7500 verses. The title character is an unprincipled Romantic poet who willingly sacrifices his family to pursue his desire to experience all that the world offers. The work was considered morbid and even shockingly immoral by Dobell's contemporaries and its poor reception, along with the poet's precarious physical condition, prevented him from writing Parts 2 and 3 as he had originally planned.

Dobell's next volume of poetry, *Sonnets on the War* (1855), was written in collaboration with Alexander Smith, and was inspired by the Crimean War. The following year, Dobell produced *England in Time of War,* which included the critically-acclaimed "A Nuptial Eve," more commonly referred to as "Keith of Ravelston." Although Dobell wrote very little after the publication of the two volumes of war poetry, his collection *Poems* was published in 1860, and the two-volume *The Poetical Works of Sydney Dobell* appeared in 1875, a year after the poet's death.

CRITICAL RECEPTION

The contemporary response to Dobell's work was mixed, with his first publication enjoying great popularity and his second effort being almost universally condemned by an outraged public. John Nichol, commenting shortly after Dobell's death, praises *The Roman* for "the intrinsic merit of the work, the flow of the lyrics, the strong sweep of the graver verse, the richness and beauty of the imagery." Nichol reports that, in contrast, *Balder*'s "plot is painful and the thought somewhat monotonous," and he questions "the admissibility of such exhibitions of horror and disgust," as well as "the repulsive egotism of the hero." In addition, the critic complains that the work is "not only incomplete, but confusingly chaotic." Robert Buchanan offers a defense of *Balder*, contending that it "contains passages of unequalled beauty and sublimity," but qualifies his praise by acknowledging that the poem's "general treatment verges on the ridiculous." The subsequent publication in *Blackwood's Magazine* of a satire on *Balder* led to the identification of Dobell with the so-called "Spasmodic School" of poetry, which also included his friend and literary collaborator Alexander Smith. Buchanan reports that "the poets satirised enjoyed the joke as much as anybody, but they little guessed that it was a joke of a very fatal kind." In fact, Dobell's reputation never recovered; the two volumes of war poetry he published—the first in collaboration with Smith—were almost universally dismissed by critics.

The Spasmodic School actually began with the publication of Philip Bailey's *Festus* in 1839, but Dobell became the poet most often considered its main adherent. According to Martha Westwater, when Dobell produced *Balder*—which he considered his master work—his goals were "to de-mythologize a male-dominated culture, to dramatize a divided consciousness, and . . . to invigorate poetry by metaphoric language which followed the untrammelled path of free association." Unfortunately, claims Westwater, "he succeeded only in infuriating critics." But Westwater, who urges a reexamination of Spasmodism, defends both the movement and Dobell, contending that "Spasmodic romanticism attempted to incorporate elements of revolt against patriarchal oppression so as to bring about a new social order wherein the male principle of power would be subverted by the female principle of compassion."

Another common criticism of Spasmodic poetry in general, and of Dobell's poetry in particular, involves the irregularity of rhythm. Jason R. Rudy has studied Dobell's ideas on poetic rhythm and contends that the poet believed that "poetry transmits knowledge and feeling primarily through rhythm, rather than through words or other formal structures." Rudy reports that contemporary critics of Dobell, such as William Edmonstoune Aytoun, who objected to the revolutionary nature of Dobell's ideas on gender, also objected to the irregular rhythms the poet employed, since for Aytoun "metrical regularity enforces cultural stability as much as rhythmic spasms encourage much that is 'wrong' with the times." Emma Mason has examined the details of Dobell's religious beliefs in an effort to determine the extent of his faith's influence on the composition of his poetry. She maintains that Dobell's poetry "is inflected by a fitful rhythmic pace that reflects his frantic and perhaps conflicted desire to both read God and implement what he perceived to be the true Christian message in society." This feature, according to the critic, is not confined to his religious verse, but pervades all of his poetry.

PRINCIPAL WORKS

Poetry

The Roman: A Dramatic Poem [as Sydney Yendys] 1850
Balder: Part the First 1854
Sonnets on the War [with Alexander Smith] 1855
England in Time of War 1856
Poems 1860
The Poetical Works of Sydney Dobell 1875

Other Major Works

Of Parliamentary Reform: A Letter to a Politician (essay) 1865
Thoughts on Art, Philosophy, and Religion: Selected from the Unpublished Papers of Sydney Dobell (prose) 1876

CRITICISM

John Nichol (essay date 1875)

SOURCE: Nichol, John. "In Memoriam." In *The Poetical Works of Sydney Dobell*, pp. ix-xxxvi. London: Smith, Elder, & Co., 1875.

[*In the following essay, Nichol discusses the critical reception of Dobell's work during the poet's lifetime.*]

The poet whose work is for the first time, in a proximately complete form, brought before the public, has been removed from us under circumstances which devolve on those who were privileged with his companionship the duty of endeavouring to supplement the somewhat fragmentary impressions of his career. Mr. Sydney Dobell died on August 22, in his fifty-first year; his literary fame was achieved before his thirtieth; his literary labours may be said to have well nigh closed with his thirty-fifth. Two longer poems and a volume of minor pieces, making the greater bulk of what he has left behind him, are the product of comparative youth, but bear the stamp of an original and singularly subtle mind, and exhibit sufficient power to continue to affect the thoughts and sympathies of his contemporaries. Passing in his prime, he has yet lived through fifteen years of enforced silence—his brilliant promise having been cruelly curtailed by physical disaster—into a new atmosphere of the rapidly shifting cloud-strata of nineteenth century criticism. 'Proterit dies diem.' Every decade has its standards, idols, aversions and neglects. The Preraphaelite has succeeded to the so-called Spasmodic, as the Spasmodic flashed for a season across the Tennysonian, as the Tennysonian superseded the Byronic school. This is not the place to attempt to estimate the import of these changes in the history of Art; but they testify to the shortness of our memories. Our wish is to be permitted briefly to direct attention to some of the attributes of a character which, more steadfast than fashions, stronger than suffering, and superior to the frustration of unselfish ambitions, has left to all within the range of its influence a noble example of an English life.

Sydney Dobell was born on April 5, 1824, at Cranbrook, in Kent, the eldest son of the descendant of an old Sussex family distinguished on the Cavalier side when Charles was king. From both sides of his ancestry he inherited literary and speculative tastes, manifested during his early years, spent at Peckham Rye, near London, by the composition of some precocious juvenile verses. His mother was a daughter of Samuel Thompson, a well-known political reformer in the early part of the century, and advocate of a new union of Christians on a comprehensive basis. His father was John Dobell, author of a pamphlet on Government, who subsequently settled as a wine merchant at Cheltenham. In his twelfth year the family removed to Gloucestershire, and the poet maintained with various degrees of activity till his death his connection with the calling and the district. In practical illustration of a theory like that carried out with results in some respects similar by the elder Mill, he was, with four other sons and five daughters, educated by private tutors, and by his own study, pursued with a zeal already excessive, entirely at home, and was never sent to school or University. To this fact he makes an interesting reference in the course of some frequently humorous verses on Cheltenham College, which date from his eighteenth year. They profess to have been discovered in an ancient manuscript, and copy, with imperfect success, the spelling of Chaucer, but they evince the passion for nature which is one of the most easily appreciable charms of his maturest work:

> 'Little in human schules have I beene;
> My colledge is all carpeted with greene,
> And archèd with a roof of spangled blue,
> My Hippocrene is the early dewe,
> My seate turf-piled is dight with faery sheene,
> My table some old stone no handes did hewe,
> Or twisted roote of oake or classicke beech.
> My servitor, the sweetly spoken breeze,
> Strange unwritte books doth bringe me one by one.
> Well pleased I make and take my own degree,
> Master of many arts no schule can teach;
> My colledge hath no termes. Its doctors are
> Righte eloquent sweet flow'res and whisperinge trees,
> Whereof the winde takes counselle; everie star
> That discourseth all nighte with silent speeche;

> Greye reverende hilles with foreheads bare with age,
> Great stormes that argue sternlie each with each
> When woods chant anthems, and a streame or two
> For work-day musicke.'

Home education undoubtedly fosters the precocious forms of genius; but in absence of social checks it too often permits originality to degenerate into eccentricity. To the circumstances of the poet's early training may be traced many peculiarities of a mind never sufficiently influenced by the contact and friction of its equals. Innate benevolence of nature ($\epsilon\dot{\upsilon}\phi\upsilon\acute{\iota}\alpha$) prevented this isolation in Mr. Dobell's case from manifesting itself as a moral, but it remained an intellectual, defect. He lived more for those around him than *for himself*, but he lived mentally to a great extent *by himself*; for though he gave much he received little, and found it hard to descend from the heights among which, even in boyhood, in solitary night-watches, he loved to lose himself, to the beaten paths of meaner life. He had all the reverence for superior wisdom which belongs to wisdom, but to ordinary criticism he remained singularly unamenable.

In 1844 he married Emily, daughter of George Fordham, of Odsey House, Cambridgeshire—whose family is one of the oldest in that county—a lady to whom in his sixteenth year he had been engaged; for thirty years his constant companion in 'the quiet woodland ways.' The early years of their wedded life were divided between residence at Cheltenham, where Sydney continued to superintend his father's business, and some pleasant country places among the hills, the chief of which were Hucclecote on the Via Arminia and Coxhorne House, their home for five summers in the valley of Charlton Kings. This period, as that which preceded it, was marked by the composition of many minor pieces, in some of which he appeared as a zealous politician and ardent reformer, and by the progress of his first considerable work.

The charm of Mr. Dobell's manner had in his youth at Cheltenham attracted the attention of the most cultivated men in the neighbourhood and some distinguished strangers; among these Thomas Campbell visited him and admired his powers of conversation. A meeting with Mr. Stansfeld and Mr. George Dawson at Coxhorne is said to have originated the society of the 'Friends of Italy.' The poet's enthusiasm for the Italian cause, with the various fluctuations of which he continued to be intimately acquainted, never abated; it remained—as evinced by one of his latest fragments entitled **'Mentana'**—amid many changes of opinion, a link between his earlier and later politics. The outcome of this sentiment, his first published poem **'The Roman,'** written among the Cotswolds, and inspired by the stirring events which have since proved prophetic of the liberation of the Peninsula, appeared in 1850. Its success was rapid and unmistakable. The theme and its treatment, in happy accord with a prevalent vein of popular feeling—in no less degree the intrinsic merit of the work, the flow of the lyrics, the strong sweep of the graver verse, the richness and beauty of the imagery—attracted universal attention, and enlisted the favour alike of the general public and of the most discerning critics. At this distance of time we may be permitted to reproduce a few sentences from the welcome given to **'The Roman'** by the *Athenæum*—from the pen, it is believed, of a highly accomplished and successful author, to whom the identity of the young poet, veiled under the assumed name of Sydney Yendys, was then unknown. After adverting to the opposite and equally fatal defects of the merely florid and the bald style of verse, to one or other of which most minor poets are liable, the reviewer proceeds: 'Any work, therefore, which indicates a return to the completeness of poetic art must have welcome at our hands, and we know of none for years that so thoroughly fulfils the condition as this dramatic poem. . . . It possesses unity of purpose and of conduct. In dealing with emotions the writer touches with equal power the pathetic and the sublime, and to the illustration of these feelings he brings a fancy which can rivet by its boldness and enchain by its beauty. Never shrinking from a conception on account of its daring, he generally seeks to present it in the most lucid form. To a large extent he fulfils both the requirements of the poet: he comprehends his inspiration and renders it comprehensible to others. Throughout his whole volume we can recall but few offences against perspicuity and good taste—the chief faults being an occasional diffusiveness and verbal iteration, and some abruptness in the development of a love-interest at the beginning. It is less a fault than an immaturity that the author's images are sometimes so lavished as rather to display the opulence of his store than to turn it to account.' . . . Then after an outline of the plot and a selection of passages, in which the description of the hero-monk, the exquisite lyric—

'Oh, Lila! round our early love,'

the impassioned appeal to the children, and the account of the brother's death figure conspicuously, the critic adds: 'Should anyone, after the preceding extracts, doubt whether we have a new poet amongst us, we should almost despair of his conversion.' He goes on, however, to adduce Mr. Dobell's 'Coliseum,' the classic grandeur of which justifies the apparent audacity of encountering the comparison which it suggests. He concludes: 'The poet's defects are those of youth, and it might excuse far graver ones. His merits, combining art with impulse and imagination, are such as youth rarely attains, but which are the true pledges of high and lasting excellence.' This critique, as just as cordial, struck the key-note of a general acclaim, in the echo of which the book was read and admired on both sides of the

Atlantic. It had abundance of minor merits, but its presiding charm lay in its novelty and earnestness of noble aim. **'The Roman'** was hailed as the product of a man of refined culture, whose sympathies went beyond the mere love of 'harmony in tones and numbers hit' to the wider movements of his age. In spite of some traces of haste and the excessive preponderance of monologue in the drama, it is marked by a cosmopolitan grasp evidencing catholic interests beyond the 'streak of silver sea,' often wanting in the masterpieces of more consummate artists.

About this time, when the gates of the temple or the mart of literature seemed to open wide to the rising author, he made a hurried visit to London, and was frequently urged by editors and others to write for various periodicals; but circumstances interfered with his availing himself to any considerable extent of their invitations. In the summer of 1851 he made, with Mrs. Dobell, a short tour in Switzerland, which left its natural impress on his subsequent work. On his return to England, during a longer residence in the capital, he gathered round him a circle of literary admirers, and, either by personal intercourse or correspondence, at this or subsequent periods, made the acquaintance of most of the eminent writers of the day, among whom may be mentioned Robert Browning, Coventry Patmore, and Philip Bailey, George Macdonald, Mr. Thomas Hughes, Mr. Deutsch of the Talmud, Mr. Monckton Milnes, now Lord Houghton, and Mr. Westland Marston, with the last of whom he remained through life on terms of cordial friendship. Acknowledgment should also be made to the generous appreciation of his genius effectively expressed by a discerning though sometimes erratic critic, the Rev. George Gilfillan. The poet's appreciation of art, of which he was a fine critic, brought him into pleasant relationship with Mr. Ruskin, Holman Hunt, and Gabriel Rossetti; his zeal for continental liberty was a passport to the affection of Joseph Mazzini; at a later date he met and thoroughly appreciated the greatest orator of our century, Louis Kossuth. Introduced to Mr. Tennyson at Cheltenham, and to Mr. Thomas Carlyle in London, he was brought into closer contact with those leaders of our literature during their common stay at Malvern. They had many walks and talks together, and maintained a considerable degree of intimacy. He had afterwards opportunities of meeting Mr. Tennyson in the Isle of Wight, and it may be conjectured that Mr. Carlyle's influence played its part in weaning Mr. Dobell from the more or less democratic views which marked the early stages of his intellectual career. Among his letters we may refer to those interchanged with Charlotte Brontë was of acknowledged literary interest on both sides. Meanwhile he published his second considerable poem, **'Balder,'** begun at Coxhorne, continued among the Alps, and finished in 1853 at Amberley Hill. This remarkable work, destined to be the first part of a trilogy of the artistic life, is the embodiment of the author's deepest thought and highest poetry. No more exquisite descriptions of external nature in her various phases of glory and of gloom, are to be found in our language than those scattered over its finest pages. The profound psychological analysis which underlies the exuberance of a somewhat recluse imagination, bears witness to the comparative maturity of a powerful mind battling with the problems of a complex age. **'Balder'** was, with the general public and the majority of critics, less fortunate than its predecessor; nor, while demurring to their judgment, can we altogether wonder at the contrast. In the first place, it is harder to read, as it must have been much harder to write, than **'The Roman,'** and the majority of readers are intolerant of poetry that taxes their wits. The plot is painful and the thought somewhat monotonous—for it harps, though with marvellous subtilty, on a few strings—and we are wont to demand from verse above all things pleasure and variety. Its faults of detail are more numerous than in **'The Roman.'** Side by side with passages of Shakespearean grasp we have outrages against taste and sense. The admissibility of such exhibitions of horror and disgust as the picture of Tyranny is at least questionable, though the example of Dante may be pleaded in their behalf. In the second place, the moral purpose of the whole work has been so utterly mistaken that **'Balder'** has, even by friendly critics, been supposed to be the author's ideal character, and even preposterously confounded with a character between which and it there was not one common feature—his own. The repulsive egotism of the hero was probably recognised by no one so much as by Mr. Dobell—himself perhaps the most unselfish literary man of our century—and the object of the whole was to show, in another fashion than that of Lear or Faust, how even such an incarnation of arrogance and pride might be wrenched by trial and suffering 'μαθήματα παθήματα' to a higher life. Even the dénouement of the fragment before us was misunderstood; for Amy, saved from death at the last moment, was to play an important part in the subsequent evolution of the drama. But the plan of the book is unfortunate. It is pitched on too great a scale, and demanded more than the energy of one life for its accomplishment.

Every part of a consummate work of art ought, like the hand or foot of a finished organism, to bear evidence of its purpose. Did the 'Inferno' stand by itself, it would still have a terrible unity. The same holds good of every section of any of the great ancient trilogies, as it does in our own day of Mr. Swinburne's 'Bothwell.' Mr. Dobell's tragedy, on the other hand, is not only incomplete, but confusingly chaotic; the richness of its imagery is like cloth of gold flung over the limbs created by a Frankenstein. But while any criticaster can sneer at those lapses where the poet manifestly crosses the boundary line between the sublime and the ridiculous, it may be doubted if any living English poet has scaled the same heights. There is not a chapter which does not bear witness to the author's indefinite power and almost measureless capacity for noble passion. Its dioramas of scenery are drawn by the eye and pencil of one who from a watch-tower on the hills outgazed the stars, and paid homage to a hundred dawns, and

> 'hung his room with thought
> Morning and noon and eve and night, and all
> The changing seasons.'

His Chamouni rivals that of Coleridge, as his Coliseum rivals that of Byron. His descriptions of Spring have the luxuriance and the truth of Shelley's. The pastoral loveliness of the long summer's day on the hills (Scene XXIV.) recalls the idyll in the Bohemia of the 'Winter's Tale.' The music of Amy's songs ripples alongside of the terror and tumult of the tragedy with 'a dying fall like the sweet south.' 'Genius,' said one of its few appreciative critics, the writer of a review in 'Fraser's Magazine,' 'is so unmistakably present in every page of the strange book before us, that to give examples from one without injustice to the others we find to be beyond possibility in our limits.' **'Balder'** is not likely to become popular in our generation; to most readers it will remain a portent; but, in spite of flagrant defects, it has stamina for permanence, and will keep its place in our literature as a mine for poets.

In 1854 Mr. Dobell left Coxhorne and took up his residence in Edinburgh, having gone there to seek medical advice for his wife, whose health had for some time back caused him great anxiety. In the course of the three subsequent years, the winters of which were spent mainly in Edinburgh, the summers in various parts of the Scotch Highlands, he became associated with another group of literary men, with some of whom he maintained a lifelong friendship. Twenty years ago, though the noon-tide glory of the Northern Athens had waned, a pleasant twilight of culture lingered about her halls and hills. Original force and talent, apart from that which is strictly professional or physical, had not been driven south of the Tweed by 'the Franciscan and Dominican licensers.' Mr. Dobell was soon brought into contact with the brightest and best spirits within his new radius. Foremost among these were Mr. John Hunter, the Mæcenas of Craigcrook, whose genial hospitality resembled that of the poet in delicacy and open-handedness; the lamented Dr. Samuel Brown—our modern Paracelsus, with the keen eye of genius for all its kindred; Dr. John Brown, 'der Einzige,' our prose poet, who happily remains 'the loved of all,' transmitting to ours the spirit of a more magnanimous age; the veteran Dr. George Combe; Hugh Miller, of the Rocks, his strong mind yet undistracted by the clash of irreconcilables; the industrious and intelligent Chamberses; Dr. and Mrs. Hanna; Miss Catherine Sinclair, Mrs. Steuart Menteath, the gifted authoress of 'Lays of the Kirk and

Covenant;' Mrs. Stirling, sister of Mr. Hunter, and authoress of 'Fanny Hervey;' the artists, Sir Noel Paton and James Archer; among Professors, Dr. afterwards Sir James Simpson; Edward Forbes, equally subtle in literature and science; Piazzi Smyth, the Astronomer Royal; the poet Aytoun, a man whom this generation regretfully recalls as one who, himself excelling, had a claim to teach; and the indomitable Blackie with his accomplished wife: with all of these Mr. and Mrs. Dobell maintained, throughout the term of their stay, and with many of them till the close of his life, a more or less intimate intercourse. On occasion of a visit to St. Andrews they were cordially welcomed by the venerable Sir David Brewster, and made the acquaintance of Professor Ferrier. Of eminent or learned men who, belonging to other centres, were introduced to Mr. Dobell in Edinburgh, we may mention Professor Craik of Belfast, Sir William Thomson and the late Professor Nichol of Glasgow, Mr. Spencer Baynes—now Professor Baynes of St. Andrews—Canon Kingsley, Mr. Dallas, the redoubtable critic of the 'Times,' and Mr. Alfred Vaughan, the accomplished author of 'Hours with the Mystics.'

During almost the whole of this period the Poet was united by ties of social intercourse and literary brotherhood with the late Mr. Alexander Smith, a man of imperfect culture, but endowed with a rich native genius, whom it has been a late fashion to depreciate as unduly as it was, during the meteor blaze of his 'Life Drama,' to over-exalt. With this friend he issued in 1855 a series of stirring sonnets on our Crimean struggle; this was followed by a volume inspired by the same theme, *'England in Time of War,'* in which the lyrical genius, patriotic zeal, and 'fair humanities' of the author are variously and amply displayed. The success of this work was intermediate between that of **'The Roman'** and **'Balder.'** The theme was well chosen, and the incisive force of some of the chants, expressive of the hopes and fears that then thrilled through the heart of England, commanded general sympathy and appreciation. Among the most deservedly admired of these are **'The Mother's Lesson,' 'Tommy's Dead,' 'The Little Girl's Song,' 'Home Wounded,' 'An Evening Dream,' 'An Aspiration of the Spirit,'** and **'Grass from the Battle-field.'**

Mr. Dobell was always a patriotic politician, but there is little of politics, in a narrow sense, in these volumes: the author dismisses diplomacy in an angry sonnet, and prefers to bring before us the joys and woes of poor soldiers and their wives, to discussing the debates of courts and cabinets. In other pieces, his rich picturesque power and delicate sense of melody find full scope. The opening lines of **'A Shower in War-Time'** are remarkable for their music, **'Lady Constance'** for its rich dramatic variety, **'The Prayer of the Understanding'** for its subtle under-currents of religious thought; **'He Loves and he Rides Away,'** combines these qualities, and is, with **'Keith of Ravelston,'** a genuine ballad, deservedly a universal favourite. There is room for difference of opinion with regard to the success with which the author has made use of the Scotch dialect, and no room for doubt as to his excessive employment of verbal repetition in such pieces as **'Wind,' 'Farewell,' 'The Recruit's Ball,'** and others. In the last-named, as elsewhere, it is manifest that the Author's forte did not lie in the direction of humorous writing; but the volumes, as a whole, marked by depth of sympathy and vigour of style, are not unworthy his fame.

Mr. Dobell's residence in Edinburgh was distinguished by many of those acts of disinterested kindness towards struggling men of letters which do not always meet with a return of gratitude. During these years more than one of our so-called minor poets was the frequent recipient of bounties remarkable alike for the delicacy of the manner in which they were offered and the comparatively slender resources from which they were drawn. Mr. Dobell's benevolence in proportion to his means was throughout more than munificent. His practice was in accordance with his theory expressed in **'Balder'**—

> 'Charitable they
> Who, be their having more or less, *so* have
> That less is more than need, and more is less
> Than the great heart's goodwill.'

Simple to the verge of austerity in his own life, charity was his one extravagance. His favourite answer to any remonstrance on giving or paying 'too much' was a quotation from Tennyson's 'Enid'

> 'You will be all the wealthier, cried the Prince.'

This benevolence was, as may be supposed, frequently abused, but neither extortion nor ingratitude availed to sour the disposition of the giver. His kindness did not confine itself to pecuniary aid: in the case of all rising aspirants to literary fame, a class the most difficult to deal with, his advice and encouragement were as ready as his substantial aid. Among the worthiest of those who were deeply indebted to this poet's criticism and counsel we may mention the short-lived and precocious David Gray of Merklands. One of Mr. Dobell's happiest acts of benevolence was the generous zeal which resulted in the early sheets of 'The Luggie' being placed in the author's hands shortly before his death. About a year before his own death, he left his room, to which he was confined during the greater part of the day, to revise the manuscript of a literary friend whose obligations to his suggestions are indefinite.

Towards the close of the poet's residence in Edinburgh his health began to give way, his originally strong constitution having been impaired by hard work and anxiety. His chest had suffered by the delivery to the members of the Philosophical Institution of a lecture, remarkable for its comprehensive view of the subject, on the Nature of Poetry. Advised to seek a milder climate, he spent the winters of the four following years at Niton in the Isle of Wight. The house he there occupied was so exposed to the waves that it has since been removed, and the situation may have suggested some of the most striking of the sonnets and other occasional pieces which at this time were his sole contributions to literature. His summer residence was at Cleeve Tower and other 'coignes of vantage' in the Cotswolds. The following notes, condensed from the reminiscences of an intimate and appreciative friend, which we have permission to insert, find here their proper place:—

'At this time, 1858, regular literary work being forbidden by his physicians, Mr. Dobell, with characteristic energy, turned his thoughts into another channel of usefulness; he planned and superintended the organisation of a new and ultimately extensive branch of the business in which, for so many years of his youth, he had actively taken part. In conducting this he was one of the first, if not the first in England, to introduce and apply the system of Co-operation which has since been widely extended. He held that every mercantile firm should be a kind of Commonwealth, in which the advancement of one ensures the advancement of all, and his efforts were always directed towards the realisation of this idea. He wished, moreover, to prove that a poet might be a thoroughly capable "man of affairs," and that the poetic or ideal faculty, rightly cultivated and employed, should assist instead of impeding practical life. It was one of the articles of his creed not merely that a good man of business might be a gentleman, but that in order to be the one in any thorough sense of the word, he *must* be the other. These views, maintained at a time when most people considered them to be visionary, are among the many instances in which the "dreams" of one man in advance of the rest prove the truisms of a later generation. Hence it happened that these years, during which he was withheld from any continuous imaginative or philosophical writing, were fruitful of good work in other ways. All who knew Gloucester were alive to the fact that Sydney Dobell was, in every sense of the word, a good citizen; his name was identified with every movement in the direction of social, literary, or artistic progress, and with every charitable enterprise in the town.

> Increasing delicacy of health rendered it necessary for Mr. Dobell, after the summer of 1862, to spend the winters abroad; in that of '62-'63 his head-quarters were at or near Cannes; in '63-'64 in Spain; in '64-'65, '65-'66, in Italy; the summers of those years were still spent in Gloucestershire. During these journeys, in all of which he was accompanied by his wife, the Poet was constantly gathering fresh historic and imaginative material. His letters of this period show the vivid and warm interest with which he studied the characteristic

life, the social and political aspects, of every country with which he became familiar. He acquired new languages rapidly; he spoke and wrote French and Italian with singular facility; after five months' residence in Spain he could converse easily in the native tongue, to which he had hitherto been a stranger. It is scarcely necessary to say how well the author of **"The Roman"** loved Italy, and he must have exulted in seeing, as achieved facts, the Freedom and Unity of which, in the enthusiasm of youth, he had sung; it is equally needless to say how much he was welcomed by the Italian patriots. The pleasure of his continental sojourns was enhanced by his devotion to music and the fact that he was a student and fine critic of pictorial art. He had a profound admiration for Spain, its noble scenery, its language, certain innate qualities of its people, and he always expressed the strongest faith in a future revival of her ancient glories. But his closest ties were still to his own country, which he loved with an almost excessive patriotism. Though debarred from more massive work, he evinced, by numerous contributions in prose and verse to current literature, his ardent interest in all relating to her welfare. In 1865 he contributed to the discussion concerning Parliamentary Reform a pamphlet written in the spirit of the liberal conservatism to which he latterly adhered. In this striking brochure, the masculine vigour of which commands the admiration even of those who disagree with its conclusions, he advocates a system of graduated Suffrage and Plurality of Votes in proportion to the status and responsibilities of each voter, a view to which the majority of our great thinkers have inclined.[1]

During one of his visits to Italy, in the course of a day's excursion to the ruins of Pozzuoli, near Naples, he met with an accident which had serious results. While trying to realise the scene that St. Paul must have looked on when he landed there, Mr. Dobell stepped on a spot where only a thin crust of earth covered an opening into one of the great ancient underground works, through which he fell to a depth of ten or twelve feet. Though nearly stunned by a blow on the back of the neck, he seemed to recover almost immediately, and all injurious effects appeared to subside; but from that time dates the occasional recurrence of distressing symptoms which culminated in the summer of 1866, while he was again staying at Edinburgh, in a definite seizure of epileptiform disease. From the consequences of this severe and prolonged attack, his naturally sound constitution and the simple English country life to which he returned, enabled him to rally. His physicians especially urged "plenty of fresh air," and to Mr. Dobell, who always delighted in manly sports and keenly enjoyed pursuing the natural sciences in the sun and breeze, this prescription was eminently acceptable. As soon as his strength permitted he took exercise, chiefly on horseback, and by degrees it became habitual to him to be out of doors for many hours of the day. 'Rest from all brain-work' was the other condition insisted on, but this was impossible; the power and sensitiveness which mark the highest order of minds can never have perfect rest in human life. To live without breathing would have been as easy to Sydney Dobell as to live without thinking strenuously.

During this time, with occasional visits to Clifton in the colder season, during which he benefited by the kind care of the late accomplished Dr. Symonds, formed the acquaintance of the Miss Winkworths and contracted a friendship with Dr. Percival of the College, the poet lived at Noke Place—a small house, beautifully situated on the slope of Chosen Hill, near Gloucester. Here, through the ensuing three years, he enjoyed some intervals of comparative health and strength, too brief to enable him to attempt any continuous literary work. But among his papers belonging to this time, there are many eloquent letters to the current journals on various questions of the day, besides the pamphlet, "Consequential Damages," suggested by the American difficulty, and the poem called **"England's Day."**

In the summer of 1869, while residing during the hot weather in a house on Minchinhampton Common, he met with a second accident, from the indirect effects of which he was destined never to recover. He was trying a recently purchased mare, before allowing the lady for whom it was intended to mount, when the animal, suddenly developing viciousness, after exhausting all efforts to throw her rider, reared and fell over with and on him. When he slowly began to regain the use of his limbs, it was found impossible for him to resume the constant exercise in the open air which had hitherto been the chief means towards his restoration. In 1871 the residence of Noke Place was exchanged for one fourteen miles on the other side of Gloucester, in a beautiful district above the Stroud valley. Barton End House, old-fashioned, ample, homelike, with its gardens and plantations, and its outlook on softly-sloping meadows and orchards and the grey roofs of the near hamlet, was an ideal home for the English poet, to whom this kind of English scenery had always been especially attractive. The last three years of his life were spent here, under the almost constant pressure of disabling weakness. But nothing could dull the keenness of his delight in the natural loveliness by which he was surrounded, the various phases of which, when no longer able to go out of doors, he never tired of watching from his windows. Mr. Dobell continued, moreover, to be earnestly concerned about public affairs, and the results of his mature thought often took form in prose or verse, on social, artistic, national or international questions of the day. A mass of material for future work remains among his MS. fragments, many of which are, even in their incomplete form, well worthy of publication. His daily life was such as most men of his tameless energy would have found unbearably monotonous; but he lived in an atmosphere of fresh thought, and his keen perception of humour helped to keep around him the flow and stir of healthy human life. To the last he was the most sunshiny of invalids; nothing could exhaust his cheerfulness, nor wear out the sweetness of his patience; his innate brightness and elasticity of mind was strengthened and elevated by spiritual culture into something holier and nobler than mere temperament. But with the spring of 1874 came a train of circumstances which involved for him more than one shock of peculiar pain, and necessitated mental wear and tear of a kind for which he was now absolutely unfit; so that the constitution which had gallantly struggled through so much was vanquished at last.'

The Poet's friend then contributes some pages of general remark, from which we extract the following:— 'He whom some of his critics persisted in identifying with the morbid and dreamy **"Balder"** was one of the most healthy-minded and sagaciously practical of men; far from being a cynic or misanthrope, he "loved his kind" in no mere theoretic sense; his instincts were pre-eminently social, with nothing of that shy reserve held to be characteristic of his race; he encouraged every opportunity of intercourse with his fellows of whatever class, and whether it was a labourer breaking stones on the highway, or a cultured fellow-passenger on a journey with whom occasion led to some brief converse, he never departed from one of these chance encounters without leaving an impression of brightness and kindliness not soon to be forgotten. He was free from all those vices, as from all those weaknesses, often held to belong to the artistic life; he burned no midnight oil in pursuit of fitting seasons of inspiration: he loved simple fare and the freshness of the morning. Yet he was too genial to be an ascetic, and amid his own "plain living and high thinking" exercised towards others a generous and refined hospitality. He was a most careful critic, keenly perceiving defects of imagination or faults of style; but penetrating at once, wherever it existed, to the essential excellence of book or picture, sketch or poem, political creed or popular enthusiasm. Many dicta of his so-called Toryism are now accepted by acknowledged Liberals; but his philosophy, political as well as religious, started from a loftier basis, and took "an ampler range" than that which is commonly appreciated by most newspaper and magazine readers or writers. A thinker above all things, he was nevertheless not unskilled in active exercises, seldom so valued by one whose resources are so independent of them. He was expert in riding and driving, and was a good shot, taking great pleasure in rifle-practice long before volunteering made it a fashion; he had a loving knowledge of horses and dogs (his name may be familiar to some, less in connection with books than as the owner of a rare and peculiarly beautiful breed of deer-hounds), and was keenly interested in hunting and all country sports.

'Mr. Dobell was loved to enthusiasm by all children and young people with whom he came in contact: he had a rare power not only of amusing but of insensibly arousing and elevating their minds. Few who have been privileged to meet him in this relationship will forget the charm of his talk, the kindness of his sympathy, the gentleness of his counsel. His interests being so wide he was singularly free from the tendency—to which deep thinkers are prone—to let one idea override the rest or to be engrossed by one subject to the neglect of others. He could without effort turn his mind from the great public matters to which we have referred, to some simple village incident or affair of domestic import. There was not a cottager within the range of his daily exercise who had not learnt to know the bright face and kindly voice, and few who had not cause to be grateful to the considerate adviser as well as to his liberal hand. Only those who knew him best could estimate the resources of the intellect that was for so many years mysteriously fettered from its fitting work. It may be hoped that among the papers he has left are some treating of the religious subjects which were ever dominant in his mind, and which may evidence is words as he did in life the living Faith, at once deeply reverent and enlightened, in God and Christ, which was never shaken by temptations of the intellect nor weakened by years of suffering and privation.' The fact of Mr. Dobell's belonging to no one of the recognised denominations suggests the question and the answer of Schiller:

'Welche Religion ich bekenne? Keine von Allen
Die du mir nennst. Und warum Keine? Aus
Religion.'

We may here appropriately quote a sentence, found among his memoranda, which seems to us to bear as striking witness to the width of his views as did his whole 'Art zu seyn' to the reality of his convictions. 'Whatever things are true for Man the Immortal I call religion, and, in this sense, religion is the only worthy object of Human Study.'

A few words are all that, in anticipation of a fuller biography, it seems needful here to add to these notes.

Latterly Mr. Dobell's attacks of illness to some slight extent affected his memory, but he remained till within two or three weeks of his death in the full possession of his other intellectual powers, drawing round him, by the charm of his presence, a small circle of devoted friends, and enlisting the love and gratitude of all with whom he came in contact, by unostentatious but ever active beneficence. At the last, his disease assumed an acuter form and he passed through the cloud-land of delirium to his rest: without a murmur spent on broken hopes and noble ambitions so largely wrecked; in his own words, 'trusting not God the less for an unanswered prayer.' 'Vir pietate egregius, valde deflendus amicus.'

Mr. Dobell's true place among the English Poets of this century seems to us, in spite of manifest faults which critics will variously estimate, to be a high and permanent one. He belonged to the spasmodic school, with which he was, during his residence in Edinburgh, topographically associated, in virtue of defects shared with men indefinitely his inferiors. Of these the chief were, occasional violences and frequent involutions of expression, recalling the conceits of Donne and others of the so-called metaphysical School of the seventeenth century; a tantalizing excess of metaphor, a deficient sense of artistic proportion, and a weakness, latterly outgrown, for outré 'fine things.' But from the graver intellectual and moral offences of the galvanic, finical

and later sentimental schools, from their subordination of sense to sound, their 'bubbles blown from minds incompetent,' their scorn of study and consequent ignorance, their egotistical disregard of all beyond themselves and their art, he was wholly free. Though unequal, his verse at its best is in strength and delicacy seldom surpassed by that of any of his contemporaries: his imagery, though redundant, is remarkably original and incisive. But the great merit of his work is that it is steeped in that higher atmosphere towards which it is the aim of all enduring literature to raise our spirits. His most attractive and in this age most *distinctive* quality as an author is the freshness of thought and depth of sympathy with the nobler aspirations of our nature— only possible to noble souls—and which endeared him to all who were privileged to enjoy his society. The charm of Mr. Dobell's conversation has been often remarked: few brilliant talkers have had at their command a greater variety of unexpected illustrations: few trained metaphysicians have exhibited acuter reasoning power. In close argument—during which he was ready to listen as well as to assert—he found few masters. On the other hand his victories did not always carry conviction; for his love of analysis led him, even when dealing with themes of every-day life, into super-subtle distinctions. His real fascination lay in the incommunicable beauty of a character in which masculine and feminine elements, strength and tenderness, were almost uniquely blended. Manliness in its highest attributes of courage, energy, and independence pervaded his life. It often occurred to us that Mr. Dobell would have made a great general; he was absolutely without fear, and being under all circumstances perfect master of himself, was pre-eminently fit to master and command others. Pure without pedantry, he had the 'scorn of scorn' for every form of falsehood; but the range of his charity was limited only by his love of truth. The sense of humour, comparatively absent from his writings, showed itself in the delicate irony of his rare rebukes. His loyalty to friendship—that half-forgotten virtue of an earlier age—has never been surpassed. He was chivalrous to an extreme, and this sometimes led his judgment astray on behalf of fallen causes, with a touch of lofty yet gracious mannerism which recalled the ideal of a Castilian knight. A radical reformer in some directions, he had little sympathy with the extreme phases of democracy, and held the tyranny of mobs and autocrats in equal aversion. Like those of most poets, his theoretical politics had a visionary side: but he was far from being a mere dreamer. Of practical welldoing towards the poor, of encouragement to the young and all who were struggling for a recognition of their merits, he was never weary: for of the jealousy which is one of the main blots of our literature, he had not a tinge. He could afford to be generous: and to almost all with whom he came in contact, grateful or ungrateful, he had done some kindnesses. His criticisms on men, books and systems, if not always sound, were invariably valuable: everything he said was so suggestive that he awoke in his listeners a consciousness of new capacities as well as of new duties. His hospitality was bestowed under guise of receiving a favour. His house was full of 'sounds and sweet sights that give delight and hurt not.' To live with him a few days was to breathe a serener air. 'To know him was a liberal education.' An old chronicler writes of Sir Philip Sidney: 'It pleased God that he should be born on earth as a sample of ancient virtue.' His friends will be pardoned for venturing to apply these words to Sydney Dobell.

Note

1. 'It is hard in all causes, but especially in matters of Religion, when voices shall be *numbered* and not *weighed*.'—LORD BACON.

    'There being in *number* little virtue, but by *weight* and measure wisdom working all things.'—MILTON.

    This is a point on which MILL and CARLYLE meet: perhaps the only one.

Robert Buchanan (essay date 1887)

SOURCE: Buchanan, Robert. "Sydney Dobell, and The 'Spasmodic School.'" In *A Look Round Literature,* pp. 185-203. London: Ward and Downey, 1887.

[*In the following essay, Buchanan traces Dobell's literary career and discusses the criticism of* Balder *that led to Dobell's association with the Spasmodic School.*]

In the winter of 1860, as I sat alone, writing, in what David Gray described as the "dear old ghastly bankrupt garret at No. 66," Lucinda from the kitchen came panting upstairs with a card, on which was inscribed the name of "Sydney Dobell;" and in less than five minutes afterwards I was conversing eagerly, and face to face, with a man who had been my first friend and truest helper in the great world of letters. It was our first meeting. David Gray, whom Dobell had assisted with a caressing and angelic patience, never knew him at all, but was at that very moment lying sick to death in the little cottage at Merkland, pining and hoping against hope for such a meeting. "How about Dobell?" he wrote a little later, in answer to my announcement of the visit. "Did your mind of itself, or even against itself, recognise through the clothes *a man—a poet?* Has he the modesty and make-himself-at-home manner of Milnes?" What answer I gave to these eager inquiries I do not remember, nor would it be worth recording, for I myself at that time was only a boy, with little or no experience of things and men. But even now, across the space of dull and sorrowful years, comes the vision of

as sweet and shining a face as ever brought joy and comfort this side of the grave; of a voice musical and low, "excellent" in all its tones as the voice of the tenderest woman; of manners at once manly and caressing, bashful and yet bold, with a touch of piteous gentleness which told a sad tale of feeble physical powers and the tortured sense of bodily despair.

I saw him once or twice afterwards, and had a glimpse of that fellow-sufferer, his wife. He was staying with some friends on the hills of Hampstead, and thither I trudged to meet him, and to listen to his sparkling poetic speech. I recall now, with a curious sense of pain, that my strongest feeling concerning him, at that time, was a feeling of wonder at the gossamer-like frailness of his physique and the almost morbid refinement of his conversation. These two characteristics, which would be ill comprehended by a boy in the rude flush of health and hope, and with a certain audacity of physical well-being, struck me strangely then, and came back upon my heart with terrible meaning now. Combined with this feeling of wonder and pity was blended, of necessity, one of fervent gratitude. Some little time previous to our first meeting, I had come, a literary adventurer, to London; with no capital but a sublime self-assurance which it has taken many long years to tame into a certain obedience and acquiescence. About the same time, David Gray had also set foot in the great City. And Sydney Dobell had helped us both, as no other living man could or would. For poor Gray's wild yet gentle dreams, and for my coarser and less conciliatory ambition, he had nothing but words of wisdom and gentle remonstrance. None of our folly daunted him. He wrote, with the heart of an angel, letters which might have tamed the madness in the heart of a devil. He helped, he warned, he watched us, with unwearying care. In the midst of his own solemn sorrows, which we so little understood, he found heart of grace to sympathise with our wild struggles for the unattainable. At a period when writing was a torture to him, he devoted hours of correspondence to the guidance and instruction of two fellow-creatures he had never seen. To receive one of his gracious and elaborate epistles, finished with the painful care which this lordly martyr bestowed on the most trifling thing he did, was to be in communication with a spirit standing on the very heights of life. I, at least, little comprehended the blessing then. But it came, with perfect consecration, on David Gray's dying bed; it made his last days blissful, and it helped to close his eyes in peace.

No one who knew Sydney Dobell, no one who had ever so brief a glimpse of him, can read without tears the simple and beautiful Memorials, now just published, of his gracious, quiet, and uneventful life. Predestined to physical martyrdom, he walked the earth for fifty years, at the bidding of what to our imperfect vision seems a pitiless and inscrutable Destiny. Why this divinely gifted being, whose soul seemed all goodness, and whose highest song would have been an inestimable gain to humanity, should have been struck down again and again by blows so cruel, is a question which pricks the very core of that tormenting conscience which is in us all. Ill-luck dogged his footsteps; sickness encamped wherever he found a home. His very goodness and gentleness seemed at times his bane. At an age when other men are revelling in mere existence he was being taught that mere existence is torture. We have read of Christian martyrs, of all the fires through which they passed; but surely not one of them ever fought with such tormenting flames as did this patient poet, whose hourly cry was of the kindness and goodness of God. From first to last, no word of anger, no utterance of fierce arraignment, passed his lips.

> The best of men
> That e'er wore earth about him was a sufferer—
> The first true Gentleman that ever lived.

And like that "best of men," Sydney Dobell troubled himself to make no complaint, but took the cup of sorrow and drained it to the bitter dregs. Such a record of such a life stops the cry on the very lips of blasphemy, and makes us ask ourselves if that life did not possess, direct from God, some benediction, some comfort unknown to *us*. So it must have been. "Looking up," as a writer[1] on the subject has beautifully put it, "he saw the heavens opened." These pathetic glimpses seemed comfort enough.

Doubtless to some readers of this book the very name of Sydney Dobell is unfamiliar. To all students of modern poetry it is of course more or less known, as that of one of the chief leaders of the school of verse known by its enemies as "the Spasmodic." With Philip James Bailey and Alexander Smith, Dobell reigned for a lustrum, to the great wonder and confusion of honest folk, who pinned their faith on Tennyson's "Gardener's Daughter" and Longfellow's "Psalm of Life." His day of reign was that of Gilfillan's "Literary Portraits" and of the lurid apparition, Stanjan Bigg; of the marvellous monologue, and the invocation without an end; of the resurrection of a Drama which had never lived, to hold high jinks and feasting with a literary Mycerinus who was about to die. It was a period of poetic incandescence; new suns, not yet spherical, whirling out hourly before the public gaze, and vanishing instantly into space, to live on, however, in the dusky chronology of the poetic astronomer, Gilfillan. The day passed, the school vanished. Where is the school now?

> Where are the snows of yester-year?

Yet they who underrate that school know little what real poetry is. It was a chaos, granted; but a chaos capable, under certain conditions, of being shaped into such creations as would put to shame many makers of much of our modern verse. As it is, we may discover in the writings of Sydney Dobell and his circle solid lumps of pure poetic ore, of a quality scarcely discoverable in modern literature this side of the Elizabethan period.

Sydney Dobell was born at Cranbrook, in Kent, on April 5, 1824. Both on the paternal and maternal side he was descended from people remarkable for their Christian virtues and strong religious instincts; and from his earliest years he was regarded by his parents as having "a special and even apostolic mission." The story of his child-life, indeed, is one of those sad records of unnatural precocity, caused by a system of early forcing, which have of late years become tolerably familiar to the public. He seems never to have been strong, and his naturally feeble constitution was undermined by habits of introspection. It is painfully touching now to read the extracts from his father's note-book, full of a quaint Puritan simplicity, and an over-mastering spiritual faith. Here is one:

> I used frequently to talk to him of how delightful and blessed it would be if any child would resolve to live as pure, virtuous, and holy a life, as dedicated to the will and service of God, as Jesus. I used to say to him that if one could ever be found again who was spotless and holy, it was with me a pleasing speculation and hope that such a character might even in this life, be called as a special instrument of our Heavenly Father for some great purpose with His Church, or with the Jews.

The seed thus sown by the zealous parent bore fruit afterwards in a disposition of peculiar sweetness, yet ever conscious of the prerogatives and prejudices of a Christian warrior. Out of the many who are called, Sydney Dobell believed himself specially chosen, if not to fulfil any divine mission "with the Church or with the Jews," at least to preach and sing in the God-given mantle of fire which men call genius. In his leading works, but especially in **"Balder,"** he preached genius-worship; of all forms of hero-worship, devised by students of German folios, the most hopeless and the most hope-destroying. Thenceforward isolation became a habit, introspection an intellectual duty. With all his love for his fellow-men, and all his deep sympathy with modern progress, he lacked to the end a certain literary robustness, which only comes to a man made fully conscious that Art and Literature are not Life itself, but only Life's humble handmaids. He was too constantly overshadowed with his mission. Fortunately, however, that very mission became his only solace and comfort when his days of literary martyrdom came. He went to the stake of criticism with a smile on his face, almost disarming his torturers and executioners.

When Sydney was three years old his father failed in business as a hide merchant, and, removing to London started as a wine merchant. "About this time," says the biographer, "Sydney was described as of very astonishing understanding, as preferring mental diversion to eating and drinking, and very inventive with tales." Strange moods of sorrow and self-pity began to trouble his life at the age of four. At eight, it was recorded of him that he "had never been known to tell an untruth." From seven years of age he imitated the paternal habit, and used "little pocket-books" to note down his ideas, his bits of acquired knowledge, his simple questions on spiritual subjects. For example: "Report of the Controversy of Porter and Bagot. Mr. Porter maintains that Jesus Christ lived in heaven with God before the beginning of the world." At the age of ten, he was an omnivorous reader, and the habit of verse-writing was growing steadily upon him. I know nothing more pitiful in literature than the story of his precocity, in all its cruel and touching details. At twelve years of age he was sufficiently matured to fall in love, the object of his passion being Emily Fordham, the lady who only nine years afterwards became his wife. By this time his father had removed to Cheltenham, and had set up in business *there*. Sydney and the rest of the children still remained at home, and thus missed all the invigorating influences of a public school; for the father belonged to the sect of Separatists which holds as cardinal the doctrine of avoiding those who hold adverse, or different, religious views.

The account of that dreary life of drudgery and overwork at Cheltenham may be sadly passed over; it is a life not good to think of, and its few gleams of sunshine are too faint and feeble to detain the reader long. From the date of his removal to Cheltenham he acted as his father's clerk. The account of the period extending from his twelfth year to the date of his marriage is one of hard, uncongenial toil, varied by scripture-readings of doubtful edification, and a passion morbid and almost pedantic in the old-fashioned quaintness of its moods. The biographer's record may form, as we are told, "a one-sided and painful picture," but we suspect that it is a true one, truer, that is to say, than the idea in its author's memory of "light, buoyant, various, and vigorous activity." The truth is, the parents of the poet blundered in blindness, a blindness chiefly due to their remarkable religious belief. His father especially, despite all his kindness of heart, was strenuous to the verge of bigotry. One can scarcely remark without a smile the inconsistency with which one who was "a publican," and by profession a vendor of convivial and intoxicating liquors, held aloof from the non-elect among his fellow-creatures. "Business is not brisk," he wrote; "I can't account for it, except, as usual, in our retired life and habits." The idea of a sad-eyed Separatist dealing in fiery ports and sherries, shutting out the world and yet lamenting when "business was not brisk," is one of those grim, cruel, heart-breaking jokes, in which Humanity is so rich, and of which the pathetic art of the humourist offers the only bearable solution.

At the age of twenty, Sydney Dobell was married to an invalid like himself, and one like himself of a strong Puritan bias. The humourist must help us again, if we are to escape a certain feeling of nausea at the details of this courtship and union, with its odd glimpses of personal yearning, its fervent sense of the "mission," and its dreary scraps from the Old Testament. The young couple settled down together in a little house at Cheltenham; and though for a time they avoided all society and still adhered to the tenets of the elect, this was the beginning of a broader and a healthier life. All might perhaps have been well, and the poet have cast quite away the cloud of his early training, but for one of those cruel accidents which make life an inscrutable puzzle. Just as Sydney Dobell was beginning to live, just as his mind was growing more robust, and his powers more coherent and peaceful, he was struck by rheumatic fever, caught during a temporary removal to a Devonshire farmhouse. As if that were not enough, his wife, always frail, broke down almost at the same time. From that time forward, the poet and his wife were fellow-sufferers, each watching by turns over the attacks of the other. It may be said without exaggeration, that neither enjoyed one day of thoroughly buoyant physical health. Still, they had a certain pensive happiness, relieved in the husband's case by bursts of hectic excitement.

By this time, when Dobell was four-and-twenty years of age, the great wave of '48 had risen and fallen, and its influence was still felt in the hearts of men. It was a time of revolutions, moral as well as political. Dobell, like many another, felt the earth tremble under him; watched and listened, as if for the signs of a second advent. Then, like others, he looked across France, towards Italy. Thus the **"Roman"** was planned; thus he began to write for the journals of advanced opinion. He had now a wine business of his own, and had a pleasant country house on the Cotswold Hills. Having published a portion of the **"Roman"** in *Tait's Magazine,* he was led to correspond with the then Aristarchus of the poetic firmament, the Rev. George Gilfillan. Gilfillan roundly hailed him as a poetic genius, and he, not ungrateful, wrote: "If in after years I should ever be called 'Poet,' you will know that my success is, in some sort, your work." Shortly after this, he went to London and interviewed Mr. Carlyle. "We had a tough argument," he wrote to Gilfillan, "whether it were better to have learned to make shoes or to have written 'Sartor Resartus.'" At the beginning of 1850 he published the **"Roman."** This was his first great literary performance, and it was tolerably successful: that is to say, it received a good deal of praise from the newspapers, and circulated in small editions among the general public.

The subject of this dramatic poem was Italian liberty, and the work is full of the genius and prophecy of 1848. The leading character is one Vittorio Santo, a missionary of freedom, who (to quote the author's own argument) "has gone out disguised as a monk to preach the cause of Italy, the overthrow of the Austrian domination, and the restoration of a great Roman Republic." Santo, in the course of the poem, delivers a series of splendid and almost prophetic sermons on the heroic life and the great heroic cause. As an example of Dobell's earlier and more rhetorical manner, I will transcribe the following powerful lines:

> I pray you listen how I loved my mother,
> And you will weep with me. She loved me, nurst me,
> And fed my soul with light. Morning and even
> Praying, I sent that soul into her eyes,
> And knew what heaven was, though I was a child.
> I grew in stature, and she grew in goodness.
> I was a grave child; looking on her taught me
> To love the beautiful: and I had thoughts
> Of Paradise, when other men have hardly
> Looked out of doors on earth. (Alas! alas!
> That I have also learned to look on earth
> When other men see heaven.) I toiled, but even
> As I became more holy, she seemed holier;
> Even as when climbing mountain-tops the sky
> Grows ampler, higher, purer as ye rise.
> Let me believe no more. No, do not ask me
> How I repaid my mother. O thou saint,
> That lookest on me day and night from heaven,
> And smilest. I have given thee tears for tears,
> Anguish for anguish, woe for woe. Forgive me
> If in the spirit of ineffable penance
> In words I waken up the guilt that sleeps,
> Let not the sound afflict thine heaven, or colour
> That pale, tear-blotted record which the angels
> Keep of my sins. We left her. I and all
> The brothers that her milk had fed. We left her—
> And strange dark robbers with unwonted names
> Abused her! bound her! pillaged her! profaned her!
> Bound her clasped hands, and gagged the trembling
>   lips
> That prayed for her lost children. And we stood,
> And she knelt to us, and we saw her kneel,
> And looked upon her coldly and denied her.
>   . . . . .
>
> You are my brothers. And my mother was
> Yours. And each man amongst you day by day
> Takes bowing, the same price that sold my mother,
> And does not blush. Her name is Rome. Look around
> And see those features which the sun himself
> Can hardly leave for fondness. Look upon
> Her mountain bosom, where the very sky
> Beholds with passion; and with the last proud
> Imperial sorrow of dejected empire
> She wraps the purple round her outraged breast,
> And even in fetters cannot be a slave.
> Look on the world's best glory and worst shame.

The **"Roman"** is full of this kind of fervour, and is maintained throughout at a fine temperature of poetic eloquence. Its effect on the ardent youth of its generation must have been considerable. Perhaps now, when the stormy sea of Italian politics has settled down, it may be lawful to ask oneself how much reality there

was in the battle-songs and poems that accompanied or preluded the tempest. It is quite conceivable, at least, that a man may sing very wildly about "Italy" and "Rome" and "Freedom" without any definite idea of what he means, and without any particular feeling for human nature in the concrete. This was not the case with Dobell; every syllable of his stately song came right out of his heart. For this Christian warrior, like many another, was just a little too fond of appeals to the sword; just a little too apt to pose as "an Englishman" and a lover of freedom. He who began with sonorous cadence of the **"Roman"** wrote, in his latter moods, the wild piece of gabble called **"England's Day."** The **"Roman,"** however, remains a fine and fervid poem, worthy of thrice the fame it is ever likely to receive. What Mazzini wrote of it in 1851 may fully be remembered at this hour, when it is pretty well forgotten:

> You have written about Rome as I would, had I been
> born a poet. And what you did write flows from the
> soul, the all-loving, the all-embracing, the prophet-soul.
> It is the only true source of real inspiration.

Meantime the air was full of other voices. Carlyle was croaking and prophesying, with a strong Dumfriesshire accent. Bailey had amazed the world with "Festus," a colossal Conversationalist, by the side of whom his quite clerical and feebly genteel "Devil" seemed a pigmy. Gilfillan had opened his wonderful Pie of "Literary Portraits," containing more swarms of poetical blackbirds than the world knew how to listen to. Mazzini was eloquent in reviews, and George Dawson was stumping the provinces and converting the *bourgeoisie.*

> The world was waiting for that trumpet-blast,
> To which Humanity should rise at last
> Out of a thousand graves, and claim its throne.

It was a period of prodigious ideas. Every literary work was macrocosmic and colossal. Every poet, under his own little forcing glass, reared a Great Poem—a sort of prodigious pumpkin which ended in utter unwieldiness and wateriness. No sort of preparation was necessary either for the throne or the laurel. Kings of men, king-hating, sprang to full mental light, like fungi, in a night. Quiet tax-paying people, awaking in bed, heard the Chivalry of Labour passing, with hollow music of fife and drum. But it was a grand time for all the talents. Woman was awaking to a sense of her mission. Charlotte Brontë was ready with the prose-poem of the century, Mrs. Browning was touching notes of human pathos which reached to every factory in the world. Compared with our present dead swoon of Poetry, a swoon scarcely relieved at all by the occasional smelling-salts of strong æsthetics, it was a rich and golden time. It had its Dickens, to make every home happy with the gospel of plum-pudding; its Tennyson, to sing beautiful songs of the middle-class ideal, and the comfortable clerical sentiment; its Thackeray, to relieve the passionate, overcharged human heart with the prick of cynicism and the moisture of self-pity. To be born at such a time was in itself (to parody the familiar expression) a liberal education. We who live now may well bewail the generation which preceded us. Some of the old deities still linger with us, but only "in idiocy of godhead," nodding on their mighty seats. The clamour has died away. The utter sterility of passion and the hopeless stagnation of sentiment nowadays may be guessed when some little clique can set up Gautier in a niche: Gautier, that hairdresser's dummy of a stylist, with his complexion of hectic pink and waxen white, his well-oiled wig, and his incommunicable scent of the barber's shop. What an apotheosis! After the prophecies of '48; after the music of the awakening heart of Man; after Emerson and the newly-risen moon of latter Platonism, shining tenderly on a world of vacant thrones!

Just as the human soul was most expectant, just as the Revolution of '48 had made itself felt wherever the thoughts of men were free, the Sullen Talent, tired of the tame-eagle dodge, perpetrated his *coup d'état,* stabbed France to the heart with his assassin's dagger, and mounted livid to his throne upon her bleeding breast. It is very piteous to read, in Dobell's biography and elsewhere, of the utter folly which recognised in this moody, moping, and graceless ruffian a veritable Saviour of Society. The great woman-poet of the period hailed him holy, and her great husband approved her worship. Dobell had doubts, not many, of Napoleon's consecration. But Robert Browning and Sydney Dobell both lived to recognise in the lesser Napoleon, not only the assassin of France political and social, but the destroyer of literary manhood all over the world. Twenty years of the Second Empire, twenty years of a festering sore which contaminated all the civilisation of the earth, were destined to follow. We reap the result still, in a society given over to luxury and to gold; in a journalism that has lost its manhood, and is supported on a system of indecent exposure and black-mail; in a literature whose first word is flippancy, whose last word is prurience, and whose victory is in the orgies of a naked Dance of Death.

Be all that as it may, those were happy times for Sydney Dobell. In one brief period of literary activity, he wrote nearly all the works which are now associated with his name. To this period belongs his masterly review of "Currer Bell," a model of what such criticism should be. The review led to a correspondence of singular interest between Miss Brontë and Dobell. "You think chiefly of what is to be done and won in life," wrote Charlotte; "I, what is to be suffered . . . If ever we meet, you must regard me as a grave sort of elder sister." By this period the fountain of Charlotte Brontë's genius was dry; she knew it, though the world thought otherwise, and hence her despair. She had lived her life, and put it all into one immortal book. So she sat, a veiled figure, by the side of the urn called "Jane Eyre." The shadow of Death was already upon her face.

Dobell now began to move about the world. He went to Switzerland, and on his return he was very busy with his second poem, **"Balder."** While labouring thus he first heard of Alexander Smith, and having read some of the new poet's passages in *The Eclectic Review,* wrote thus to Gilfillan: "But has he [Smith] not published already, either in newspapers or periodicals? Curiously enough, I have the strongest impression of *seeing the best images before,* and I am seldom mistaken in these remembrances." This was ominous, of course, of what afterwards took place, when the notorious charge of plagiarism was made against Smith in *The Athenæum.* Shortly afterwards he became personally acquainted with Smith, and learned to love him well. He was now himself, however, to reap the bitters of adverse criticism in the publication of his poem of **"Balder."** In this extraordinary work, the leading actors are only a poet and his wife, a doctor, an artist, and a servant. It may be admitted at once that the general treatment verges on the ridiculous, but the work contains passages of unequalled beauty and sublimity. The public reviews were adverse, and even personal friends shook their heads in deprecation. At the time of publication he was in Edinburgh, having gone thither to consult Dr. (afterwards Sir James) Simpson on the illness of his wife, and there he was to remain at bay during all the barking of the journals. A little cold comfort came from Charlotte Brontë.

> "There is power in that character of *Balder,*" she wrote, "and to me, a certain horror. Did you mean it to embody, along with force, many of the special defects of the artistic character? It seems to me that those defects were never thrown out in stronger lines."

Despite the ill-success of his second book, Dobell spent a very happy season in Edinburgh. If not famous, he was at least notorious, and was well enough in health to enjoy a little social friction. Alexander Smith, the secretary to the University, was his bosom friend; and among his other companions were Samuel Brown, Blackie, and Hunter of Craigcrook Castle. "Smith and I," he wrote, "seemed destined to be social twins." Just then there appeared in *Blackwood's Magazine* the somewhat flatulent satire of "Firmilian," written at high jinks by the local Yorick, Professor Aytoun. The style of Dobell and Smith was pretty well mimicked, and the scene in which Gilfillan, entering as Apollodorus, was killed by the friends thrown by Balder from a tower, was really funny. The poets satirised enjoyed the joke as much as anybody, but they little guessed that it was a joke of a very fatal kind. From the moment of the appearance of the "spasmodic" satire, the so-called spasmodic school was ruined in the eyes of the general public. A violent journalistic prejudice arose against its followers. Even Dobell's third book, **"England in Time of War,"** though full of fine lyrics, entirely failed to reinstate the writer in public opinion. He was classed, though in a new sense, among the "illustriously obscure," and he remained in that category until the day he died.

Perhaps the pleasantest of all his days were those days in Edinburgh, when, in conjunction with Smith, he wrote a series of fine sonnets on the war, which won the warm approval of good judges, like Mr. Tennyson. There was something almost rapturous in Smith's opening sonnet to Mrs. Dobell—

> And if we sing, I and that dearer friend,
> Take *thou* our music. He dwells in thy light,
> Summer and spring, blue day and starry night.

A friend wrote that he could love "Alexander" for that sonnet; and, indeed, who could not love him for a thousand reasons? The story of Smith's martyrdom has yet to be told—nay, can never be told this side of the grave. But let this suffice—it *was* a martyrdom and a tragedy. How tranquilly, how beautifully, Smith took the injustice and the cruelty of the world, many of us know. Few know the rest. It was locked up in his great gentle heart.

When I have mentioned that, immediately after the War Sonnets, Sydney Dobell issued independently his volume of prose, **"England in Time of War,"** his literary history is told. Though he lived on for another quarter of a century, he never published another book. Three works, **"The Roman,"** **"Balder,"** and **"England in Time of War,"** formed the sum total of his contributions to literature while alive; and all three were written at one epoch, in what Smith called "the after-swell of the revolutionary impulse of 1848." For the last half of his life he was almost utterly silent, only an occasional sonnet in a magazine, or a letter in a journal on some political subject, reminding the public that he still lived. Of this long silence we at last know the pathetic cause. Sickness pursued him from day to day, from hour to hour, making strenuous literary effort impossible. Never was poet so unlucky. Read the whole heart-rending story in his biography; I at least cannot bear to linger over these tortures. He had to fight for mere breath, and he had little strength left him to reach out hands for the laurel. How meekly he bore *his* martyrdom I have already said.

When I met him he had the look of one who might not live long, a beautiful, far-off, suffering look, wonderfully reproduced in the exquisite picture by his younger brother, an engraving of which faces the title-page of his biography. Many years later, not long indeed before his death, he sent me a photograph with the inscription *"Convalescens convalescenti"*; but all photographs reproduce the man but poorly, compared with the picture of which I have spoken. Even then, in the joyfulness of his eager heart, he thought himself "convalescent," and was looking forward to busy years of life. It was not to be. No sooner was his gentle frame reviving from one luckless accident, than Fate was ready with another. "The pity of it, the pity of it!" It is impossible to think of his sufferings without wondering at the firmness of his faith.

When Death came at last, after years of nameless torture, only a few cold paragraphs in the journals told that a poet had died. The neglect, which had hung like a shadow over his poor ruined life, brooded like a shadow on his grave. But fortunately for his fame, he left relatives behind him who were determined to set him right, once and for ever, with posterity. To such reverent care and industry we owe the two volumes of collected verse, the exquisite volume of prose memoranda, and lastly, the beautiful Life and Letters. Thus, although only a short period has elapsed since Dobell's death, though it seems only yesterday that the poet lay forgotten in some dark limbo of poetic failures, the public is already aware of him as one of the strong men of his generation, strong, too, in the sublimest sense of goodness, courage, and all the old-fashioned Christian virtues. He would have been recognised, perhaps, sooner or later, though I have my doubts; but that he has been recognised so soon is due to such love and duty as are the crown and glory of a good man's life. The public gratitude is due to those who have vindicated him, and made impossible all mistakes as to the strength of his genius and the beauty of his character. His music was not for this generation, his dreams were not of this earth, his final consecration was not to be given here below.

> Vex not his ghost: oh, let him pass! He hates him much
> That would upon the rack of this rough world
> Stretch him out longer.

But henceforth his immortality is secure. He sits by Shelley's side, in the loneliest and least accessible heaven of Mystic Song.

Note

1. Matthew Browne, in the *Contemporary Review*.

Martha Westwater (essay date fall 1989)

SOURCE: Westwater, Martha. "Sydney Dobell: Sunk without Trace." *Dalhousie Review* 69, no. 3 (fall 1989): 357-65.

[In the following essay, Westwater discusses the irreversible damage to Dobell's literary reputation caused

by the publication of Balder *and the poet's subsequent identification with the Spasmodic School.*]

Who can account for the changes in literary tastes? Why is it that what was valued in a former age ceases to be esteemed in a latter one? Conversely, why is it that what at a future date might be hailed as brilliantly insightful, thereto, was totally neglected? These questions certainly arise when one considers the poetic reputation of Sydney Dobell and the Spasmodics. Dobell is now little more than a footnote in the annals of English literature—and the Spasmodics are nothing but a vulgar burp after the glorious intoxication of the Romantics.[1] Yet, Dobell had worked out his own theory on "equivalents" long before Eliot's "objective correlative."[2] And the Spasmodics' influence on nineteenth-century poetics, especially in their unique emphasis on the Poet as living "on the edge of things," is yet to be evaluated.

Victorian literary critics have a lopsided tendency to concentrate on the poets writing after 1850 and to ignore entirely the Spasmodic controversy. First, then—briefly—let me situate Sydney Dobell in the history of Spasmodism, a history which began when Henry Taylor published his anti-Romantic Manifesto in 1824—the year in which Byron died and Sydney Dobell was born. Poetry was undergoing a particularly "flat" time after the death of Byron.[3] In his Preface to *Philip Van Artevelde,* which is now remembered while the play itself is forgotten, Taylor called on young poets to free themselves from the pernicious influences of Byron and Shelley who were condemned for their "unbounded indulgence in the mere luxuries of poetry."[4] They lacked "subject matter," Taylor expostulated as he stirred up his anti-romantic forces; they had "little concern with what [was] rational or wise" (xii). Nor was Taylor alone in his distrust of imagination. One has only to remember Thomas Peacock's *Four Ages of Poetry* in which he deprecated sentiment as "canting egotism in the mask of refined feeling," and passion as "the commotion of a weak and selfish mind."[5] Or of Isaac Taylor's warning to beware the dangerous depiction of "solitary and unsocial indulgence."[6] And Taylor was aided and abetted by John Keble, the inspiring Anglican Divine, who in his *De Poetica Vi Medica Praelectiones Academicae* condemned Byron.[7] No wonder Edmund Gosse in characterizing literature in the reign of William IV, wrote that it formed "a small belt or streak of the most colorless, drawn across our variegated intellectual chronicle."[8] A poetic quietism marked the second quarter of the nineteenth century.

Sydney Dobell's poetic apprenticeship, then, was passed in that lull which was to precede a storm. Henry Taylor had given two new commandments to poets of the second quarter of the nineteenth century: Thou shalt worship reason, thy lord and god, and thou shalt not exhibit extreme passion. The commands held for at least five years. Then, in 1839, Philip Bailey (1816-1902)—a name with which Sydney Dobell's would henceforth be associated—published *Festus.*[9] This poem marked the dawn of Spasmodism which struggled to keep alive the Romantic bequest characterized by consciousness of the subjective, imperial self and birth-marked by passion and riotous, exuberant, imagination.

Bailey was only twenty-three years old when he published his spectacular poem, which was to go through eleven editions in England and thirty in the United States. *Festus* has an extremely simple plot and consists chiefly of long debates between Lucifer and Festus. But what *is* rather extraordinary—Bailey has Lucifer redeemed! The devil turns out to be not a hateful source of corruption and violence, but rather the victimized "hit man" of history.

The 1839 edition of the poem did not at first catch fire.[10] But then Thomas Pickering brought out a second edition of Bailey's *Festus* (1845) in which he advertized every snippet of favorable criticism he could gather.[11] Tennyson had written to Edward Fitzgerald that *Festus* contained "really very grand things."[12] He further avowed that these "grand things" were "grander than anything he had written."[13] Critics saw echoes of Carlyle's "natural supernaturalism" in *Festus* with a generous dose of universalism and a new note of optimism.[14]

Sydney Dobell was fifteen when *Festus* was published. His biographer claimed that he considered reading the poem a "literary banquet"—a banquet which must have been devoured by a child brought up in a strict, even crankish religious tradition.[15] His grandfather, Samuel Thompson, was the founder of a church based on primitive Christianity—a group whose spirit has been immortalized in the opening pages of George Eliot's *Silas Marner.* Dobell appears to have had one of those formidable educations in which Victorians took such pride. At four or five his father would give him a line to which the child would respond in rhyme. At ten Sydney's first poem was privately printed and for the next fifteen years the young Sydney continued working in his father's wine business, marrying when he was barely twenty years of age and writing poetry which was published mostly in religious magazines.[16] Then Sydney Dobell came in contact with George Gilfillan.

In the craze following *Festus,* George Gilfillan (1813-1878), a minister editor from Scotland, called on new poets, the "rising sons of morning" as he called them, to baptize the romanticism anathematized by Henry Taylor.[17] Gilfillan, although little heard of now, had an astonishing critical following in the periodicals of the day. "It may be doubted," wrote W. Robertson Nicoll, in referring to his influence, "whether even Carlyle had more power over young minds than Gilfillan."[18] He looked towards the poets to propagate the new spiritual romanticism.[19] To Gilfillan, more than to any other man, Sydney Dobell owed his rapid rise to literary prominence and his even more rapid demise.

In July of 1848 Gilfillan printed in *Tait's Edinburgh Magazine* extracts from the first scene of **The Roman,** Dobell's first major poem, which Dobell had sent him. A correspondence had already begun between the two men and Gilfillan's support would never desert the young poet. When Dobell went up to London, he went armed with letters of introduction from Gilfillan to Leigh Hunt and, more significantly, to Thomas Carlyle. Within the year after the publication of **The Roman,** Dobell was considered an established poet. There is no doubt that without George Gilfillan's backing, Sydney Dobell might well have been an unknown minister in the Church of Free-thinking Christians rather than a neglected member of the Spasmodic poets.

Dobell then brought out his master work **Balder** toward the end of 1853. He imposed upon himself an almost impossible task in **Balder.** He attempted to de-mythologize a male-dominated culture, to dramatize a divided consciousness and, perhaps most significantly, to invigorate poetry by metaphoric language which followed the untrammelled path of free association. He succeeded only in infuriating critics who entirely misconstrued his aims.

Balder is the victim of an unbridled egoism which led him to think that only by allowing himself complete freedom to plumb the depth of all knowledge and experience—knowing death, possibly even knowing the ultimate power of murder in the killing of his wife—could he transcend the limits of mortality by writing about the unwritable. However, in exploring the dark recesses of his own egoism, Balder comes to a deeper awareness of his own humanity and of the complementarism between the sexes.

Because the action of the poem is internal, chiefly in the mind of Balder, Dobell effectively dramatizes mental progressions by blurring precise limitations of time and space in the elimination of formal act divisions. But Dobell brilliantly structures the play as a symbolic struggle on three, highly complex, concentric levels—the psychological, the social and the personal. Symbolically the struggle is represented in the contrasting characters of Balder and his wife Amy who are imaged by the rocks and flowers of the first scene which, in turn, dramatically presents the incompatibility of the demands made by reason and imagination and also those made by egoism and feminism. Thus the rocks of the tower in which Balder dwells image the forces of reason and experience, the masculine world of the protagonist, while flowers, trees and water delineate the female world of sensitivity and subservience—a subservience which Amy will subsequently reject.

As the poem opens, Balder is in his tower study surrounded by books, manuscripts and statues—all testaments to reason's (and the male's) domination. A window overlooks a country valley and an open door leads to another room, Amy's, which is never seen. The setting underlines Amy's lack of place, of identity and of function. Balder's tower, a male image, signifies power and control. He has the first (and last) words of the play.

> Tomorrow I count thirty years, save one.
> Ye grey stones
> Of this old tower gloomy and ruinous,
> Wherein I make mine eyrie as an eagle
> Among the rocks; stones, valleys, mountains, trees,
> In which I dwell content as in a nest
> Of Beauty,—comprehended less by more—
> Or above which I rise, as a great ghost
> Out of its mortal hull; vale, mountains, trees,
> And stones of home, which, as in some old tale
> O' the East keep interchange of prodigies
> With me, and now contain me and anon
> Are stomached by mine hunger, unappeased
> That sucks Creation down, and o'er the void
> Still gapes for more; ye whom I love and fear
> And worship, or i' the hollow of my hand
> Throw like a grain of incense up to heaven,
> Tell me your secrets! That ye have a heart
> I know; but can it beat for such as I?[20]

Balder's birthday vespers offer nothing of the emotional joys of being a husband and a father. Instead they form a litany of frustrations. Beauty was unattainable: "comprehended less by more." The world of nature—valley, mountains, trees—all "are stomached by mine hunger, unappeased." He, the proud quester, has been thwarted because nature will not reveal its secrets. Balder has a disconcerting sense of nature's exclusiveness. Does nature have consciousness of the poet as the poet has of it? Balder has begun to ask some preposterous questions. He has made natural objects individuals. He speaks to them, prays to them because they have been able to take him out of his common, ordinary world. Ominously, however, he has begun to suspect, even to resent, nature's superiority since he cannot know all her secrets.

From the outset the action of the drama is internal in the minds of the chief actor, Balder, who is aware of his contrarieties and responds with acute sensitivity to the delicate changes in consciousness that take place moment by moment. These contrary moods are reflected in the abrupt changes in his image patterns. For example, the tower's window is first "eyelashed with balmy sprays of honeysuckle," but his own eye next catches the "ivy ever sad," then darts to the "midnight bolt" that "starts like a bloody eyeball" (12). The eye imagery reflects his own diseased sight and mirrors his own vacillating moods: awe at nature's wonder, frustration because he cannot comprehend her secrets, then concern for his wife whom he describes as a "delicate flower / In a deserted garden" wherein he has set her like a "wandering clown," and where she is hemmed in by these "unmannered rocks" (11).

This opening scene is convincing in showing Dobell's power in depicting both the actual process of a scrutinized moment in time, and his remarkable power of manipulating language so that it follows the path of free association. Startling metaphors link "stones" to "mountains" to "nest" for eagles. Balder, eagle among men—powerful, lofty, isolated—is also singularly impervious to the affective needs of his wife, the "flower"—delicate, fragrant but grounded in subservience. Vaguely conscious that there is a rupture in his union with nature as there is in his relationship with his wife, in this opening scene Balder questions why "The sweet light is put out in the long rain, / The flower is withered on the wall" (12). His speech is not the language of an ordinary mind expressing ordinary relations. Deficient in the simple, human interests of wife and family, his soliloquy shows him teetering on the brink of a monstrous curiosity that will lead to the bizarre. The scene also establishes Balder as a serious poet preoccupied with his own destiny and repeating over and over the central question: "have I lived / Not unloved, and shall I pass away / Not all unwept?" (11). In asking these questions Balder's powers are bound to be tempted.

Isolated as Balder is in this first scene, the stage directions indicate that a door in the study communicates with an adjoining room. Immediately after Balder's soliloquy Amy's voice is heard. The physical dissociation of Balder from his wife indicates a deeper separation in their human relationship. Immediately after Balder's soliloquy, Amy's voice, singing of flowers, trees, and defenceless animals, images the female world of emotion and of accommodation. Her first song is a lullaby to her infant daughter.

Amy's is the quiet but disturbed imagination singularly attentive to sounds—detailed sounds of wailing, wild night winds, of rain echoing human tears, of weeping, blighted willows. Hers is a distorted view which is all the more unnatural because of the quiet, soothing, simple rhythm of her lullaby. The very acuteness of her sense of hearing makes her a listener attentive to the voice of despair, while her visual acuity gives her a certain clarity in seeing her husband as he is. But the contrast between the two willows of Amy's song, "one hale, one blighted" (14) is the most unequivocal image of the deep breach between the tenderness of Amy and the demonic hubris of Balder which has led to Amy's neglect. Dobell has endowed Amy with an intuitive insight that balances her husband's arrogant intellectualism. At the outset he allows only Amy's voice to be heard; she is seen on stage only three times in all. In

this way Dobell carefully crafts a structure of emotions shifting alternately between Balder's tediously long, philosophic soliloquies and his wife's brief, tender songs. There is a variation in excitement and mood that makes the opening of the play very successful in establishing the suppressed energy of inner conflict, for from the first scene it is clear that Amy and Balder represent two sides of the same psyche.

Dobell was an intuitive psychologist. Nichol, Dobell's editor, seemed to sense as much when he hailed Dobell as the "Poet of the Future" ("Memoir": *Poetical Works* 1: xix). Another critic maintained that a future study of the poem would "lead to a fuller acknowledgment of its grandeur."[21] It is the psychological dimensions of the poem—the alienation of Balder's affective from his intellectual life, the coupling of egoism and feminism—that are most significant and contribute to the untapped power of Dobell's major work.

None of Dobell's poetic aims was appreciated by William Edmondstoune Aytoun (1813-1865), a rising editor of *Blackwood's Edinburgh Magazine,* who had been chafing at the adulation given to the younger poets, and proceeded to pan all Spasmodists, particularly those endorsed by George Gilfillan. Aytoun, under the guise of an editor, claimed to have received a letter from an earnest, young poet, T. Percy Jones, who submitted excerpts from his recent epic, "Firmilian" for critical evaluation. Aytoun (acting as both the editor who received the poem and the poet who wrote the submitted fragments) proceeded to tear to shreds "Firmilian" and all other Spasmodic poems.

> It is not very easy to comprehend the exact creed and method of the new school of poets, who have set themselves at work upon a principle hitherto unknown, or at all events unproclaimed. This much we know from themselves, that they regard poetry not only as a sacred calling, but as the most sacred of any . . . that they are to the fainting race of Adam, the sole accredited bearers of the Amreeta cup of immortality. . . . But apart from their exaggerated notions of their calling, let us see what is the practice of poets of the Spasmodic School. In the first place, they rarely, if ever, attempt anything like a plot. . . . In the second place, we regret to say that they are often exceedingly profane, not, as we suppose, intentionally but because they have not sense enough to see the limits which decency, as well as duty, prescribes. In the third place, they are occasionally very prurient. And in the fourth place, they are almost always unintelligible.[22]

This is a serious editor writing a sensible critique, but that same editor became a magnificent wit when he pretended to be the adjudicator of T. Percy Jones's *Firmilian,* a full length play published by Aytoun four months after his *Blackwood's* essay.[23]

There is no doubt that "the exaggerated notions of their calling" were given the young Spasmodics by George Gilfillan whom Aytoun disguises in the play as the puffy figure of Appolodorus. One of the zaniest episodes of the play occurs in scene X when Appolodorus, a critic, is walking through a square in the neighborhood of Badajoz, praying for new poetic talent. At that instant, the body of Haverillo, slain by Firmilian who wanted to experience remorse, falls on Appolodorus and crushes him.[24]

Reviewers of *Firmilian* in most journals were quick to see the satire, particularly directed against "Gilfillan with his cognate style of criticism, and ill-judged laudation of every erring son of the Muses."[25] Aytoun wittily but none the less cruelly destroyed Gilfillan who, as a critic, was as dead as Haverillo. None took his criticism seriously after 1854. The effects on Dobell were even more disastrous. His poetic career was over. Thus, effectively squelched, Dobell's influence and the Spasmodic impulse went underground only to reemerge as self-conscious decadence in figures like Swinburne and Wilde.

Dobell wrote two other volumes of poetry after *Balder*: *Sonnets on the War* with Alexander Smith and *England in time of War,* but both met with critical dismissal. He has since been classed among the "basement dwellers of literature."[26] Perhaps his chief merit in literary history was his articulation of a poetic theory that might well serve as a transition point between the Romantic and Victorian periods—even of the Victorians and the Moderns. For his poetry embodies characteristics of the three ages—the subjective, passionate, liberty-loving Romantic who glorifies the ordinary until it becomes extraordinary, the alienated, yet prosperous Victorian who glorifies the triumphs of empire while becoming increasingly fearful of the ghostly demons within, and the complicated, despairing modern who discovers the failure of reason and of patriarchy. Dobell was a seminal poet who took his craft seriously and provided some striking innovations in his layering of meanings onto the associative metaphor. He had his faults of effusiveness and discursiveness, to be sure, but he was given no recuperative space in which to tame his over-exuberant fancy, his voluptuous imagery, his diffuse obscurity. Extreme, even cruel, criticism broke his spirit. He died in 1874, aged fifty-two years. He never finished his *Balder.*

Notes

1. Dobell appears as footnote 12 in *A Literary History of England,* Albert C. Baugh, ed. (London: Routledge & Kegan Paul, 1948) 1387. For the title of this paper I am indebted to Robert Birley's *Sunk without Trace: Some Forgotten Masterpieces Reconsidered* (London: Rupert Hart Davis, 1962).

2. Robert Preyer, who has the distinction of being the first to give Dobell's theory of poetry a scholarly analysis, judged it "an impressive and significant document for the literary historian and theorist" and a work which should have "considerable interest for anyone who concerns himself with the cultural history of the period." See "Sydney Dobell and the Victorian Epic," *University of Toronto Quarterly* 30 (Jan. 1961): 163-78. Isobel Armstrong in her study, "The Role and the Treatment of Emotion in Victorian Criticism of Poetry," (*Victorian Periodicals Newsletter* 10 [1977]: 3-16), judged Dobell's theory as "one of the most sophisticated accounts of metaphor" she had read.

3. Henry Taylor, *Autobiography* vol. 2 (London, 1874): 119.

4. ———. Preface to *Philip Van Artevelde: A Dramatic Romance* vol. 1 (London, 1834): xi.

5. Thomas Love Peacock, *Four Ages of Poetry,* ed. H. F. B. Brett-Smith (Oxford: Blackwell, 1921) 18.

6. Isaac Taylor, *Natural History of Enthusiasm* (London, 1829) 2.

7. John Keble, *De Poetica Vi Medica Praelectiones Academicae* (London, 1844) 222-3; his criticism of Byron, 573, 687.

8. Edmund Gosse, "Philip James Bailey," *The Critic* Nov. 1902: 457.

9. Philip James Bailey, *Festus: A Poem* (London, 1839) 238.

10. For example, see the complaints about the paucity of good poetry in "Reviews," Literature of 1841, *St. James Magazine* Jan. 1842: 127.

11. The poem of 8103 lines in 1839 had grown to 12,795 lines in 1845, and was to grow to 39,159 lines in 1903. See Morse Peckham's, "English Editions of Philip James Bailey's *Festus,*" *Papers of the Bibliographical Society of America*: 55-58; also "American Editions of **Festus**: A Preliminary Survey," *Princeton Library Chronicle* June 1947: 177-84.

12. Hallam Tennyson, *Alfred Lord Tennyson, A Memoir* vol. 1 (London, 1897) 234.

13. Charles Tennyson, *Alfred Tennyson* (New York: MacMillan, 1949) 215.

14. This optimistic note was affirmed when Bailey, introducing the fiftieth anniversary edition of *Festus,* affirmed that the poem was opposed "as far as possible to that of the partialist, pessimist, and despairing sceptic, the belief of the misbeliever, so prevalent in our time." Philip James Bailey, *Festus: A Poem,* Fiftieth Anniversary Edition (London, 1889) 1.

15. Emily Jolly, ed., *The Life and Works of Sydney Dobell* vol. 1 (London: 1878) 108. For Jolly's

discussion of Dobell's precocity and religious background see 1:37, also Appendices A & B, 64-67.

16. "Isabel" (1847), "A Musing on Victory" (1847), Some of his early poems—"A Village Colloquy," "The Dying Girl to Her Mother," "The Massacre at Glencoe," "The French People to Armand Carrell,"—appeared in *The People's Journal* during 1847 and 1848; however, his poetry was appreciated by few beyond the confines of his own family, church friends, and the readership of *The People's Journal*. Jerome Thale discovered that the poems Jolly claimed had been published in *Chamber's Journal* had really been published in *The People's Journal*: 4 (1847): 122; 5 (1848): 151; 5 (1848): 54-56, 59-61; 5 (1848): 192-93 (Thale, 434-35). Jerome Thale, "Sydney Dobell: A Spasmodic Poet," diss. Northwestern U., 1954.

17. George Gilfillan, rev. of "The Roman," *Eclectic Review* 27ns (1850): 672-84.

18. W. Robertson Nicoll ed., *A Gallery of Literary Portraits* (London & New York: Dent, Dutton, 1909) vii.

19. "In Memoriam—The Reverend George Gilfillan," *The Dundee Advertiser* (August 1878): 10.

20. John Nichol, ed., *The Poetical Works of Sydney Dobell* vol. 2 (London: Smith Elder, 1875) 9-10. Dobell did not number his lines, nor did Nichol. All subsequent citations are from Nichol's edition and numbers refer to pages.

21. Rev. Donald MacLeod, ed. "In Memoriam—Sydney Dobell" *Good Words for 1874* (London, 1874) 718.

22. William Aytoun, "Firmilian: A Tragedy," *Blackwood's Edinburgh Magazine* May 1854: 533-555. This essay is cited as "Firmilian."

23. ———. *Firmilian or the student of Badajoz: A Spasmodic Tragedy* (Edinburgh and London: 1854).

24. Aytoun describes Apollodorus (Gilfillan) in raptures over the young, "undiscovered" poet, Sancho, who sings:

> Down in the garden behind the wall,
>   Merrily grows the bright-green leek;
> The old sow grunts as the acorns fall,
>   The winds blow heavy, the little pigs squeak.
> One for the litter, and three for the teat—
>   Hark to their music, Juanna my sweet!

25. Rev. of "Firmilian" *Westminster Review* Oct. 1854: 615.

26. Virginia Woolf, *The Second Common Reader* (London: Faber, 1942) 126.

Martha Westwater (essay date 1992)

SOURCE: Westwater, Martha. "A Footnote in Literary History" and "Mother Church and Child Bride." In *The Spasmodic Career of Sydney Dobell*, pp. 1-32. Lanham, Md.: University Press of America, 1992.

[*In the following excerpts, Westwater discusses Dobell's literary reputation and the influence of his religious upbringing on his poetry.*]

When he was born in 1824, few would suspect that Sydney Dobell would become the unrecognized leader of an unsuccessful anti-patriarchal revolt. Few would dare name patriarchy as an existing institution let alone question the accepted rightness and reasonableness of that system which assigned such unequal roles to the two biological genders—a role which Kate Millett describes as being "the birthright priority whereby males rule females."[1] And yet, in the first half of the nineteenth century, such was the pervasiveness of these socially constructed sex roles that they permeated even the poetic debates between classicism and romanticism. Classicism decreed that the male principle of reason should dominate over the female principle of imagination and feeling. Spasmodism, whose chief poet Dobell was to become, reacted against this principal with a redefined emphasis on feeling. Spasmodic romanticism attempted to incorporate elements of revolt against patriarchal oppression so as to bring about a new social order wherein the male principle of power would be subverted by the female principle of compassion. Because Spasmodism presages elements of modern critical thought, it is necessary to reexamine—in the context of the frequent skirmishes between classicism and romanticism—how solidly entrenched was the male principle of reason and order in the third and fourth decades of the nineteenth century.

Only an aged Wordsworth reached the half-point in the century, for Blake died in 1827; Coleridge, in 1834. And all the younger Romantics had predeceased them: Keats died in 1821; Shelley, in 1822 and Byron, in 1824. These great Romantics who had thrown such tremendous light on the nature of poetry, regarded the great Classicists, Pope and Dryden, as dangerous to their genius. To the average reader labels like "romantic" and "classic" describe irreconcilable opposites like "male" and "female," but they represent two opposing attitudes and two opposing kinds of poetry—attitudes and kinds which existed long before the nineteenth century and perhaps best articulated by Blake's "contraries" in *The Marriage of Heaven and Hell*. These contraries go back to the ancient distinction between the Apollonian and the Dionysian; the orthodox priesthood and the Delphic oracle; divine law and the mystery of human personality. One view recognizes that civilization consists of a central nucleus of religion, science, law, morality, tradition etc., which radiate through the media of the arts; the other views all ideas, official beliefs, institutions as projections of the dreams of individuals, and the conflicts of individual wills. The classic view sees poetry exemplifying values set by orthodox civilization's intellectual and moral consciousness; its emphasis is on reason. The romantic view sees the poet as independent of society; the poet's vision may re-affirm orthodoxy's values but may also condemn them. The emphasis is on imagination. Blake in all his writings, Wordsworth in his Prefaces, and Coleridge in the *Biographia Literaria* all rejected imagination's subservience to reason, tradition and law. The poetic imagination impregnates matter—feeling, subject, form and language—to generate a new creature. Imagination is the maternal, eternal act of creation.

Since Dobell was only ten years old when a fresh onslaught of the old classic/romantic battle broke into print in 1834, he paid scant attention to the ongoing war of words. But by the time he reached adolescence, he was already caught up in a sensitive analysis of individual experience and feelings. An ardent admirer of *Manfred,* Byron's exploration of the tyranny of reason, Dobell memorized whole sections of the poem which, his biographer tells us, he knew "by heart."[2] From his youth Dobell was a committed romantic, convinced that the poet must be the voice of his age. He was determined to articulate the spirit of that age. To a dehumanizing factory system, he would propose a natural landscape valued as humankind's safe refuge in turmoil; to collectivization and a growing capitalism, he offered an individualism that was almost anarchic for his times. And primarily interested in curing a diseased society ruled over by the arrogant male who relies too heavily on reason, he intended in his major poem **Balder** to dramatize the legitimacy of both reason's and feelings' demands. He simply wanted to use his poetic gifts to raise the intellectual and spiritual level of the general public.

Dobell should have paid more attention to classicism's early attack on romanticism in 1834, because in the second battle, erupting twenty years later, he would bear the brunt of classicism's powerful onslaught on the lingering romantic tradition. Henry Taylor's "Preface" to *Philip Van Artevelde* (1834) spearheaded the first attack. Even though he admitted that poetry was undergoing a particularly "flat" time, Taylor (1800-1886) decreed that no reader of "masculine" judgment could be attracted by the poetry of the Romantics. Berating what he considered the emotional excess of the Romantics, he called for restraint in experimentation.[3] Taylor's Preface to *Philip Van Artevelde,* which is now remembered while the play is forgotten, became an anti-romantic war cry, calling for young poets to free themselves from the pernicious influences of Byron and Shelley who were castigated for their exclusive concern with the image and condemned for their "unbounded indulgence in the mere luxuries of poetry."[4] Criticizing the Romantics on moral grounds and on their lack of "subject matter," Taylor appealed for a balancing of poetry's affective power with its appeal to the intellect and will. The Romantics had "little concern with what [was] rational or wise," he wrote (xii). Byron's heroes were "creatures abandoned to their passions, and essentially, therefore, weak of mind" (xviii). Shelley seemed "to have written under the notion that no phenomena [could] be perfectly poetical until they [had] been decomposed from their natural order and coherence as to be brought before the reader in the likeness of a phantasma or a vision" (xxii). In his *Autobiography* Taylor renewed his cry for a return to the decorum and restraint of classicism by showing even the older Romantics the errors of their ways. After Coleridge, he complained, "poetry could never again be content to dance in a court dress with Pope, or to go through a course of gymnastics with Dryden, or to sit by the fireside with Cowper, or to mount the pulpit with Young" (2:117-18). Court, Family, Religion, Prosody— all the old verities and institutions, the "reasonable" aspects of life—seemed to have been abandoned by the Romantics. And although Wordsworth had successfully united reason with passion, he was criticized because he simply "wrote too much" (2:218). Only Southey, now the least esteemed of the Romantics, escaped abuse. Nor was Taylor alone in his distrust of the feminine principle of imagination. One has only to review what Peacock had written in praise of reason in his *Four Ages of Poetry* in which he deprecated sentiment as "canting egotism in the mask of refined feeling," and passion as "the commotion of a weak and selfish mind."[5] In Peacock's view the Romantics belonged to a degenerating age of brass. His essay so provoked Shelley that he responded with his spirited *Defence of Poetry* in which he deliberately made imagination a masculine principle, the "Sun of life." Reason was but "the watery orb which is the Queen of his pale Heaven" (*Defence of Poetry,* 48).

But in the third and fourth decades of the nineteenth century, Shelley had fewer followers than Taylor. People seemed to distrust contemporary poetry, this "unforeseen and unconceived delight" even more than they distrusted science. Both Poetry and Science were threats to Religion which, if it had to take sides, was on the side of reason. In his *Natural History of Enthusiasm,* Isaac Taylor, although never condemning imagination's power, certainly wanted to keep it under reason's control, and he warned that "whoever, instead of repressing the irregularities of the imagination, and forbidding its predominance, would altogether exclude its influence, must either sink far below the common level of humanity, or rise much above it."[6] Beware the dangerous depiction of "solitary and unsocial indulgence," he warned (9). John Keble, the inspiring

Anglican Divine, while dedicating his Latin treatise *Ode Poetica Vi Medica Prelectiones Academicae* to that "true man and philosopher," William Wordsworth, took the same position as Taylor—on the dangers of the imagination—and condemned Byron.[7]

In characterizing the literature of William IV's reign, Edmund Gosse wrote that it formed "a small belt or streak of the most colourless, drawn across our variegated intellectual chronicle."[8] The Romantic impetus had sunk into emotional abeyance. An aged Wordsworth dominated the poetic scene, but, to a great extent, critical control was in the hands of Southey to whom Henry Taylor had dedicated his *Philip Van Artevelde*. In the last line of the dedicatory sonnet, Taylor had affirmed that "Learning still keeps one calm, sequestered seat." And certainly publishers, particularly the editors of *Blackwood's Edinburgh Magazine* were determined that Learning retain dominance so that reason and right order would always rule over feeling.

Blackwood's was in the vanguard of the Romantics' hostile critics. As early as 1830 John Wilson lamented, "In the Poetry of our own age we miss the principle of Intellectual strength." He condemned Byron together with Scott "for the confusion of intellectual processes and the violation of intellectual laws."[9] The age tended to be "effeminate" and by 1839 the romantic bequest, particularly as exemplified by Byron who taught "his pupils to despise the homely expedient of regulating the passions" and of preserving "the wild license of infinite complaint," was still under attack in the pages of *Blackwood's*.[10]

As R. G. Cox has shown, an even more useful context of Taylor's Preface can be seen in the Victorian periodicals of the twenties, thirties and forties which prove that there was a fair body of criticism directed against the poetic tradition coming down from the Romantics.[11] There is also Morris Greenhut's study, "George Henry Lewes and the Classical Tradition in English Criticism" which proves that the Romantics had their critics among Victorian essayists and alludes to Lewes as the progenitor of many of the classic ideals later propounded first by Arnold and then by Eliot.[12] As Cox's essay illustrates, *Blackwood's* would keep up a steady attack on the Romantics with the result that a poetic quietism marked the second quarter of the nineteenth century. Sydney Dobell's poetic apprenticeship, then, was passed in that lull which was to precede a storm. It was a period of practical logic, of cold reason, and of crippling complacency. Henry Taylor's fears that poetry would transfer allegiance from reason to passion should have been allayed when he considered the books that became popular after the publication of his Preface. As Goss, remarked, "there was a great searching of heart in families" (458). Copies of "Childe Harold" and of "Manfred" were burned, and Pollock's

"Course of Time" was substituted. Any poetry of a highly imaginative style was ignored. Robert Browning had published his "Pauline" and "Paracelsus" during this period, and Elizabeth Barrett her "Seraphim." Both were disregarded or condemned by the critics. Tennyson, too, had to bear some brutal attacks on his lovely, lonely ladies.

Then, in 1839, Philip Bailey (a name with which Sydney Dobell would henceforth be associated), published *Festus,* a "literary banquet" for Dobell (*L & L* [*The Life and Works of Sydney Dobell*] 1:108). It was the dawn of Spasmodism which struggled to keep alive the romantic bequest characterized by consciousness of the imperial self and birthmarked by passion and imagination. Born in 1816, Bailey was only twenty-three years old when he published his strange, even spectacular, poem which has an extremely simple plot and consists rather of long debates between Lucifer and Festus. But underneath the simple plot is Bailey's identification with the profound changes taking place in religion and in society. Lucifer is permitted to tempt Festus who falls and commits himself to the Prince of devils. The two then go through the earth discussing contemporary problems of free will, salvation, the conflict between good and evil, the soul, etc. In one scene Festus sums up his understanding of good and evil:

> God fitted it [the Soul] for good; and evil is
> Good in another way we are not skilled in.
> The good we do is of His own good will,—
> The ill of His own letting.[13]

Festus falls in love with several women, one of whom is Lucifer's own beloved, Elissa. In the final scenes Festus gains control of the world and ushers in the millenium after which the world ends and both Festus and Lucifer are saved. The old, unholy creatures of sin, death and Eve are dramatically changed into salvation, new life, and a new woman, Elissa, who ignites Lucifer's stirrings of repentance. The poem did not at first catch fire. Writing in 1841, two years after *Festus* was first published, an anonymous reviewer bewailed "the extraordinary abasement of light reading; poetry has long been defunct, magazines have lost their character and intention, and true vivid romance seems extinct."[14] But then Thomas Pickering brought out a second edition of Bailey's *Festus* (1845) in which he advertised every snippet of favourable criticism he could gather. The poem of 8103 lines in 1839 had grown to 12,795 lines in 1845, and was to grow to 39,159 lines in 1903.[15] The many notices of *Festus* which Pickering amassed attracted both serious men of literature and the evangelical presses of the day. Religious readers were amazed and delighted that the poem combined religion with romantic poetry, while more serious critics of poetry rhapsodized over Bailey's startling imagery. Taylor's stone tablets with his new commandments had been pulverized.

> We are willing for our part to confess . . . we regard it
> [*Festus*] as unsurpassed, perhaps unequalled by any
> creation of genius in the light literature of our age. . . .
> It is the confession in the ear of humanity; a pouring
> out of the soul's most holy secrets as at a judgment
> day; a prayer in the temple of the all-present witness.
> No poem of any time or language has manifested
> greater keenness of sensation.[16]

Tennyson wrote to Edward Fitzgerald that *Festus* contained "really very grand things."[17] He further avowed that these "grand things" were "grander than anything he had written."[18] Critics saw echoes of Carlyle's "natural supernaturalism" in *Festus* with a generous dose of universalism and a new note of optimism. When Bailey came to write a Preface to the fiftieth anniversary edition, he made this optimistic note very clear: "The poem has been taken to be a sketch of world-life, and is a summary of its combined moral and physical conditions, estimated on a theory of spiritual things, opposed as far as possible to that of the partialist, pessimist, and despairing sceptic, the belief of the misbeliever, so prevalent in our time."[19]

It should be noted, however, that Bailey never considered himself a Spasmodic poet. He acknowledged "the bright colouring, pure morality, happy imagery, and exquisite similitudes" manifest in one or two of the Spasmodics' poems; but he had no sympathy "with their works especially or with their ways."[20] (He never elaborated on what precisely were Spasmodic "ways".) But with *Festus* something "new" had occurred in poetry. The poet's sentiments were "masculine" and acceptable. "Mr. Bailey . . . has eschewed, with a manly taste, all that looks like affectation. Following Milton in the general character of his diction, and mostly Shakespeare in the rhythm of his blank verse, he has sought neither to become himself an innovator, nor to follow the innovation of others."[21] But Bailey was an innovator—particularly in his delineation of the unoriginal hero, Faust. The old German pantomines, Marlowe's *Doctor Faustus,* those of Mountfort, of Müller, and pre-eminently of Goethe—had all pre-dated *Festus*. The human mind has always been fascinated by the principle of evil. Part of Bailey's originality, however, resulted from his downplaying the evil element in Lucifer, humanizing him, and in situating the confrontation between Festus and Lucifer at the end of the world. What is even more extraordinary—Bailey has Lucifer redeemed! Through Elissa, the new Eve, Lucifer becomes capable of love. The devil turns out to be not a hateful source of corruption and violence, but rather the victimized "hit man" of history.

Weinstein noted the great popularity the poem had in America. It was introduced by a coterie of English Transcendentalists, spurred on by Westland Marston, who launched the poem on its successful American career.[22] Longfellow recorded in his journal (2 November 1845), "For a youth of twenty to write thus is a miracle."[23] (Actually, the poem was begun when Bailey was twenty; the chief portion of it was written before he was twenty-two, and published when he was twenty-three.)[24] The ordinary, non-religious Victorian reader might not have been so rhapsodic. Walter Bagehot seems to have summarized the views of a practical man of affairs in a letter of 3 (or 10) February 1848. He wrote: "I have just been turning the leaves of the third Edition of a poem called *Festus* recently written by a [man] named Bailey. It is very good to be written by a living poet in these days; only the author seems to be not in his right mind exactly."[25] And certainly not all the reviews were favourable. The powerful *Blackwood's* in a restrained review registered the chief complaint: *Festus* "is the most extraordinary instance which our times, or we think any times have produced, of the union of genuine poetic power with utter recklessness of all the demands of art, or indeed of the requisitions of commonsense."[26] More serious critics of poetry, however, recognized in *Festus* the loosening of the reins which had kept the poetic imagination in check. Bulwer Lytton judged it "a most remarkable and magnificent production," and James Montgomery, on reading it, remarked that "one feels as if one has eaten of the insane root that takes the reason prisoner."[27] Dante Gabriel Rossetti was introduced to the "glories" of Bailey's *Festus* by Charley Ware, an American living in London,[28] and William Rossetti reported that it was "enormously relished" by his brother.[29] Elizabeth Barrett's impressions of it had more far-reaching influences. She wrote to Richard Hengist Horne in 1844:

> Have I read 'Festus'? Certainly I have. . . . Oh, yes! I
> was much struck by 'Festus,' and it was only by accident that I did not ask you whether you would not do
> honour to the author of it. You told me yourself he was
> a man of genius, and of no ordinary genius undoubtedly. Both the 'Festus' and the supplement apologetic
> to it, which appeared in the 'Monthly Repository' (I
> think) filled me with admiration.[30]

Indeed the Brownings themselves might be considered the parents of Spasmodism. Robert Browning, with his publication of *Pauline* (1833), and not Philip Bailey, should be credited with fathering the New Poetry, and Elizabeth Barrett in her nurturing of Hengist Horne proved to be a more than marvelous mother figure. *Pauline* had been cruelly condemned by critics for its extreme Romanticism, but their ostracizing laughter, echoing in *Fraser's Magazine* (December 1833), might have been only a sign that an original genius had appeared. In 1844, when Richard Hengist Horne (1803-1884) took seriously Elizabeth Barrett's request to "do honour" to James Philip Bailey (and in doing so became the principal antagonist of Henry Taylor), he used the exact words his "mother" had taught him.

Horne, publishing his full essay on *Festus* in the *British Quarterly Review* (May 1846), stated categorically that

Bailey's "poem is not a work of promise only—it is one of performance" (388). Nearly two years before this praise, however, he had done "honour" to Bailey in his *A New Spirit of the Age* (1844), when he recommended him, along with Tennyson and Browning, to Henry Taylor as promising new poets.[31] It was in this two-volume work that he launched an attack on Taylor in which he tried to demolish the powerful defences of masculine reason that Taylor had so carefully constructed in his Preface to *Philip Van Artevelde*. Horne began quietly enough by praising the "steady, classical and perspicuous style" of the accomplished author of *Philip Van Artevelde,* but he went on to condemn Taylor for his repressing of the imagination, for the principle enunciated in the Preface that "all splendour of imagery is mere redundancy." Horne claimed Taylor's notion became an "excuse for the pride of natural barrenness" (286). He went on to ask several pertinent questions— questions which reveal Elizabeth Barrett's influence; for the very issues Horne raised had been plucked verbatim from Miss Barrett's letters.[32] What is "a dramatic poem without passion;—what does that amount to?" What is "a contemplative poet without a haven of ideality?" For "there is no such thing as pure reason, pure imagination, pure judgment—but each helps the other and of necessity" (290). Horne called for new poets, men with "creative passion" (304) who are able to give "an incentive to hope, a refuge for sorrow . . . to bring good things to mankind" (305). He felt that the spirit of the age was preparing an "unknown, unlaurelled laborer" (306), and cried for a "new poetry" from "new men with whom abstract power and beauty [were] a passion" (291). These men would be essential in the approaching poetic war "certain to take place" (283).

> The public does not see this [struggle]; . . . the critics do not see the struggle; but let anybody look at the persevering announcements of new poems of some half dozen of the best and then the truth of our assertion will become apparent.
>
> (292)

Philip Bailey could be counted among the best of the new poets. But Horne's message would have more of an impact on Sydney Dobell. In her *Life and Letters* Emily Jolly does not mention Horne, and it is almost certain that Horne never met Dobell since young Dobell's associates were strictly limited to family members and fellow workers at church or business. There is little doubt, as this study hopes to prove, that the Spasmodics would emerge as Horne's new poets, his "unknown, unlaurelled labourer[s]."

Taylor, Bailey and Horne hold centre stage in the romantic-classic war spanning the twenty years from 1834 when Henry Taylor published his Preface to *Philip Van Artevelde* until 1854 when the new poetry, spawned by Bailey, championed by Horne, and epitomized by

Dobell, was assailed by another champion of reason, William Edmondstoune Aytoun. The significance of the period from 1834 to 1854 in England's literary history deserves more careful study, for it has influenced Victorians and Moderns in ways yet to be examined. The three principles introducing the Spasmodic interlude can be disposed of easily enough, but the chief actor in the main part of the tragedy will be the subject of this book.

Bailey's fall was as spectacular as his rise. He never fulfilled the promise of his youth, even though by 1865 seven editions of *Festus* had appeared in England. At least one reviewer pointed out that "no poet of our time, if we perhaps except Mr. Tennyson, . . . has had a larger acceptance. . . . How few readers know Mr. Browning's *Sordello* and *Paracelsus,* which have attained a greater age, and have only reached their third edition."[33] But Bailey's revisions became more "heavily freighted;" and "bulkier" as the years went on.[34] Perhaps Amy Cruse was correct in her summation of Philip Bailey and his *Festus:*

> Another false start [in selecting a poet to represent the age] was made when the Victorians ran after Philip James Bailey, whose *Festus* was published in 1839. It was a long poem, and told, with many variations and digressions, the old story of Dr. Faustus . . . read by the thoughtful, intelligent people who were interested in philosophical and theological subjects.[35]

As for Horne, his *A New Spirit of the Age* has been summarily dismissed by George Saintsbury as containing "some of the most inept criticism in English."[36] It must be admitted that Horne was something of a maverick—soldier, sailor in the Mexican navy, adventurer, gold-digger, patriot, musician, poet, essayist, dramatist, biographer, critic, humanitarian, writer of children's stories etc. For him effort was the principle of vitality.[37] One of his most prophetic accomplishments, especially in the light of Dobell's downfall, was his attack on that bastion of male domination—editorial power. His was a spirited defense against indifference to literary merit on the part of both publishers and the public. He also denounced the preponderance of criticism and analysis to more creative work in the thought of his day.[38] And Horne does seem to have been sensitive to his times; his writings give some indication of the state of literature, particularly of poetry, in the third and fourth decades of the nineteenth century. It was a time of bedlam and upheaval. Horne's works reflect that upheaval. His endorsement of Bailey might have been another "false start" but it represented the need for change. Bailey was important in Horne's estimation not in a philosophical or theological light but in an aesthetic light—in endorsing the unrepressed vigor and vitality of the feelings and of imagination. Horne's work is a most important document in the history of Victorian literature before 1850, and in the recurrent dialectic between classic and romantic tastes. In summary, then, one could say that Horne, in his *A New Spirit of the Age* and in his own poetic drama *Orion,* demanded a freeing of the imagination to explore the ordinary man who worked with his hands; he called for a new ecumenism in poetry, a new attitude towards sex and the body, and a new appreciation of the confessional element in poetry. Horne's writings were to have a profound effect on the Spasmodic movement in English literature—and on Sydney Dobell.

Horne's vision of poetry as expressive of a new ecumenism among all the religions of mankind led to the formation of the Syncretic Society which had among its members Horne himself, J. A. Heraud, Westland Marston and George Stephens. Syncretism has also been defined as a "science of coalition."[39] In their Romantic idealism the Syncretics resemble the American Transcendentalists, particularly in their philosophy of the return to nature. But along with their idealism, the Syncretics possessed a hard-nosed practicality evident in their literary endeavours to have the theatrical patents repealed and to re-establish a poetical English drama (Shackford, 38). They looked forward longingly to the redressing of all injustices and the harmonizing of all religions. Their views found expression in two short-lived magazines, *The Sunbeam* and the *Monthly Magazine.* But Horne and the Syncretics themselves fell victims to changing tastes. So did Henry Taylor who was to be unequivocally eclipsed by Tennyson.[40]

The thirties and forties, then, were times of ever-fluctuating literary fashions. Change was in the air. Although Wordsworth and Byron still dominated the poetic scene, the fire of romanticism would blaze briefly, only to have some cautious classicist extinguish it. By the 1850's, however, Shelley and Keats were to become extremely popular, and a new wave of romanticism flourished. In the celebrated debate between the undergraduates of Oxford and Cambridge on the relative merits of Byron and Shelley, Shelley's poems were still so relatively unfamiliar to the Oxford debaters that some of Tennyson's lyrics had been slipped in among the Shelley poems and had gone undetected by the Oxonians.[41] Keats did not attain much popularity until "discovered" by Rossetti in 1846 (*Family Letters* 1: 100). By 1853 Charles Kingsley wrote that Shelley's influence was outliving that of his compeers, and growing and spreading for good and for evil. He thought it would continue to grow and to spread for years to come, as long as the present great unrest went on smouldering in men's hearts. It was in describing this unrest that Kingsley first used the word "spasmodic" which Aytoun later adopted to describe the "new" poetry. Kingsley, equating "spasmodic" with "effeminate," wrote:

> There was, then, a strength and a truth in all these men [Romantics]; and it was this—that more or less clearly, they all felt that they were standing between two

worlds; amid the ruins of an older age; upon the threshold of a new one. To Byron's mind, the decay and rottenness of the old was, perhaps, the most palpable; to Shelley's, the possible glory of the new

> . . . Byron has the most intense and awful sense of moral law—of law external to himself. Shelley has little or none. . . .

> And thus there arose a spasmodic, vague, extravagant effeminate, school of poetry, which has been too hastily and unfairly fathered upon Byron.[42]

Not Byron but Dobell would later be considered the Father of All Spasmodics.

The Romantics had always been labelled in schools: the Lake School of Wordsworth and Coleridge; the Cockney School of Hunt, Hazlitt, and perhaps Keats; the Satanic School of Byron and Shelley; and finally, the Spasmodic School of Philip Bailey, Alexander Smith and Sydney Dobell. But whereas the first three have attained respectability and have been absorbed into the glorious Romantic movement, the last is still an object of derision. Even though Sydney Dobell imbibed a bit too much of the heady new wine of individualism and might have been overly conscious of the imperial self (which made all would-be poets a bit drunk with a sense of their own importance), he was the most gifted poetically of the Spasmodics and deserved fairer treatment. Pampered and spoiled by an over-enthusiastic George Gilfillan, and ridiculed and destroyed by the Gigadibs of public opinion which William Aytoun so brilliantly manipulated, Sydney Dobell's poetry has been shamefully ignored. As a responsible aesthetician, his poetry calls for a re-examination because it reflects new thinking in a time of change and upheaval.

Although the great expectations of the French Revolution had been dampened by 1824, the year of Dobell's birth, it was still a world of promise. A buoyant belief in social improvement continued past the Reform bill of 1832, past Victoria's accession to the throne in 1837, and remained undimmed until the great depression and the coup d'Etat of Louis Napoleon in 1848. With this belief in progress there would always be an outpouring of energy, experimentation, even of excess. When Keats wrote to his editor, John Taylor (27 February 1818), while *Endymion* was in press, "I think poetry should surprise by a fine excess and not by singularity—it should strike the Reader as a wording of his own highest thoughts," he was defining, in a very real sense, a mood which would control poetry for the next three decades.[43] (Certainly Bailey had dazzled by excess.) A new generation of Romantics would continue to dazzle—by excess.

It should be reiterated here that the poets designated as the Spasmodics—chiefly Philip Bailey, Sydney Dobell, Alexander Smith, but sometimes J. Stanyan Biggs and

Westland Marston—never flourished as a group with well-defined poetic principles. Most of them never met. Only Smith, Dobell and Marston knew one another socially as well as professionally, and only Dobell ever attempted to elucidate his thoughts on poetry. But they were all, in varying degrees, discontented with the *status quo.* Nowhere is Dobell's longing for a new society more evident than in his early defence of Charlotte Brontë.

Dobell was one of the earliest to decide that Currer Bell was a woman—"not feminine, but female." Writing in *The Palladium* for September, 1850, Dobell praised Currer Bell as a missionary "in the reconstruction of society;" he was certain that "in that sure and silent social revolution" her novels would play their part because "she has blown so vigorously before walls that must surely come down (those grim old feudal bastions of prejudice, and those arabesque barriers of fashion)." Into society "she is carrying, unperceived, the elements of infallible disruption and revolution. . . . in the exuberant and multiform vigour of her idiosyncrasy—in her unmistakable hatred of oppression, and determination to be free—in the onward tendencies of a genius so indisputably original" she cannot fail to act strongly (*L & L* 1:178, 183). Charlotte Brontë would effect in the novel what he would attempt in poetry.

As a poet, grandiosely, like the Romantics before him, and more humbly, like his contemporaries, the Syncretics, Dobell sought an ideal society where the social scale would be inverted and where the poet would be harmoniously integrated. Moreover, he felt that the poet must play an active and conscious part in bringing to birth the new, improved society. Perhaps the clearest exposition of Dobell's and of the Spasmodic aim has been given by Jack Lindsay:

> The New Poetry—called in its later phase that of the Spasmodics—set out to advance beyond the points defined by Byron, Shelley and Keats. Byron with his *Cain, Don Juan* and *Manfred,* dominated the epoch still to a considerable extent and determined the lines of movement, the terms in which the struggle was formulated; but there were efforts at the same time to incorporate Shelley's revolt and his pantheist sense of unity with the elements, as well as the Keatsian image of beauty, in which was felt to be distilled the demand for the fullness of life on earth, the right to fullness and the entry into its realm of enjoyment. The New Poets sought one way or another to bring these poetic elements together in a new synthesis which clarified the place and destiny of man on earth, of poetry in society—specifically in the expanding capitalist Industrialism.[44]

Dobell, especially, used the new poetry to bring about changes in religion. As a dissenter, he was well aware that religion in the nineteenth century was beginning to lose its domination over the minds and hearts of men.

Religion, divorced from ordinary life, needed secularization. His was a deliberate effort to concretize religious abstractions, like love and purity, and to have poetry embody states of mind—guilt, fear, anger, ambition, cowardice etc. By means of the confessional element in poetry, he tried to dramatize how divisions, especially those between the sexes, are assimilated into the creation of a new person. He gave the clearest exposition of his aims in ***Balder.*** For it was not until Amy confessed her violent anger at her husband's neglect of her emotional needs, accused him of substituting cerebral activities for legitimate sexual ones, that the hero, Balder, was able to change, to become a new creation.

Seeking a freedom that would enable humans to resist all the efforts to coerce or repress, Dobell was well aware of the necessity of a new revelation of man to woman and woman to man. That is why the confessional element is so relevant in Spasmodic poetry, and why Dobell used the confession as a means of communicating greater freedom between the sexes. So eminent a divine as Dr. Channing was quoted as saying that "the great revelation which man now needs is a revelation of man to himself;" and that "the mystery within ourselves, the mystery of our spiritual, accountable, immortal nature, it behoves us to explore; happy are they who have begun to penetrate it."[45] The confessional element would help alleviate the age-old Christian fear of sex.

Both the Spasmodics and the Syncretics before them opted for a new openness in poetry. Horne condemned the oppressive attitude to sex when he wrote: "Notwithstanding all the knowledge of physiology, and the psychology inextricably involved in our corporeal fabric and conditions, the same dead-set against man's body is constantly made."[46] And Dobell had the same idea. "The Greek," he wrote, "saw in the world and the body the possibilities of ideal perfection," whereas the Christian "saw only the imperfection. . . . the Christian made demons of faculties that should have developed to divine."[47] So when his wife, Amy, exhibits a demonic fury in unburdening a repressed sexuality which Balder has manipulated for his own end, Dobell looked on this confessional aspect as part of the educative process by which the feelings could be analyzed and by which stereotypes associated with women as passive receivers and other outworn conventions imposed by a patriarchal society, could at least be re-presented if not overturned. Dobell shared John Stuart Mill's ideas on the exploration of the feelings. Writing in the *Monthly Repository* which upheld the new "subjective" poetry, Mill, as "Antiquus," lamented that too much of education was made up of "artificialities and conventionalisms" and that the feelings were neglected. Yet, he continued, from the mere fact that: "the human intellect has not yet reached perfection, must necessarily be false; it is not always clear that the poet of acquired ideas has the advantage over him whose feeling has been his sole teacher."[48]

Despite some eloquent defenders like Mill, the New Poetry failed, branded ignominiously as Spasmodic. Dobell's career lasted approximately five years. It began in 1850 with his first long poem, *The Roman,* a work which received instant recognition: "no young poet of this century had received so great and unexpected a success."[49] Three years later his major poem, *Balder,* which contained some of the most delicate nature lyrics in the language, attracted only denigrators. Dobell suffered most at the hands of William Edmondstoune Aytoun (1813-1865), and *Balder* fell victim to one of the cleverest (and cruelest) hoaxes in the annals of English literature.

In May 1854, six months after *Balder* was published, Aytoun issued in *Blackwood's Edinburgh Magazine,* a bogus review of an imaginary, unpublished poem entitled *Firmilian* supposed to have been written by a hypothetical T. Percy Jones.[50] Aytoun had just finished giving a series of lectures on the nature of poetry at the University of Edinburgh where he was Professor of Belles Lettres. In these lectures he was, as would be expected, on the side of Henry Taylor and his anti-romantic theory of poetry.[51] His *Blackwood's* essay on Firmilian began with a parodying of George Gilfillan's discovery of new poets, particularly of Sydney Dobell: "We have great pleasure, in announcing to our readers the fact, that we have at last discovered that long-expected phenomenon, the coming Poet, and we trust that his light will very soon become visible in the literary horizon" (533). Firmilian was a true "spasmodic" hero—an aloof, misunderstood genius who nourished both a guilty secret and some terrible impulses. Readers of Aytoun's review took the burlesque seriously; most of them defended Percy Jones. They begged the besmirched Percy to publish his noble tragedy. Aytoun, ecstatic over the success of his hoax, incorporated all the extracts he had quoted in his fake review and published the completed poem entitled *Firmilian or the Student of Badajoz* in July, 1854.[52]

When reviewers finally caught on to the hoax, some took revenge on Dobell for their own gullibility. One remarked, "The recent poem of *Balder* . . . is the immediate object of the parody; but remembrances of *Festus, A Life Drama* etc. flash before us as we read and laugh and in that laugh condemn."[53] *Balder* came to be looked upon only as a "mine for poets."[54] Lampooned in this way, Dobell's poetic career was finished. His next two volumes, *Sonnets on the War,* written in collaboration with Alexander Smith, (1855) and *England in Time of War* (1856), were never seriously examined. What Aytoun exposed was the ridiculous extremism of the New Poetry. What needs re-examination, however, is the degree to which Aytoun's attack on excess, while

legitimately aiming to destroy one fault, ended by wiping out the career of a sensitive, genuine poet—the "Poet of the Future"[55] who, as even Buckley admits, was of all the Spasmodics the "ablest aesthetician."[56]

Dobell was Aytoun's most tragic victim, but the attack also affected other poets. Arnold withdrew his *Empedocles* from the edition of his *Poems;* eventually he would bury his romantic inheritance, proclaim that the poetry of the first quarter of the century did not "know enough," and surrender to classicism.[57] Tennyson's reputation was seriously threatened. The closest Tennyson ever came to exploring the unconscious self was *Maud* (1855). Perhaps he had been influenced by Dobell, whose *Balder* had been published late in 1853, for the similarities between the two poems did not pass undetected. Like Dobell, Tennyson was pilloried by the critics. Goldwin Smith, in the *Saturday Review* of 3 November 1855, accused Tennyson of writing "bathos."[58] The critic in *Blackwood's Edinburgh Magazine* (Margaret Oliphant) was even more condemnatory:

> Mr. Tennyson may have a private reason of his own for making such a miserable grumble as his last hero. Mr. Dobell may hold himself justified in the heights of self-complacence . . . for his atrocious Balder . . . ; but we would crave to know what right these gentlemen have to seize upon our genial nature and craze her healthful looks and voices by their hysterical and ghastly fancy?[59]

Undoubtedly the hero of *Maud,* broken by a cutthroat, competitive, industrialized society, is "a kinsman" of Balder, "a dispossessed, disconsolate young man."[60] But at the same time, notwithstanding adverse critical reviews, *Maud* is "probably the most original and highly experimental poem that Tennyson ever wrote" (Martin, 383). Browning might also have shared Dobell's fate had he not already left England during those mid-fifty years when Spasmodism was being routed.

And Dobell, more than the other three Victorians, is perhaps a better figure of transition between the Romantics and the Moderns. He seems to have had a deeper psychological grasp of the conflicting demands of Romantic self-consciousness and Victorian social earnestness, of legitimate egoism and an equally legitimate feminism. His poetry provides an exploration of female consciousness which is essential to his narrative. Furthermore, he possesses a broader appreciation of identifying the poet more with the present than with the past, and of legitimizing the present through the denunciation of rulers who tyrannize either in politics—like the Germans in *The Roman* or in society, especially in the family—like the husband and father in *Balder.* Dobell himself fell victim to those literary "fathers," particularly the editors of *Blackwood's Edinburgh Magazine* who pilloried his *Balder.*

Moreover, Dobell lived at a time when poetry was not only esteemed but also very popular. In 1856 Margaret

Oliphant could surely, if a bit arrogantly, substantiate poetry's appeal to the common people: "It is a sad fact," she wrote, "yet we cannot dispute it—poetry is fast becoming an accomplishment, and the number of people in 'polite society' who write verses is appalling" (Oliphant, 128). Dobell wanted to make poetry even more popular.

Had Sydney Dobell's poetry been taken seriously, perhaps the great gulf now existing between poet and public might have been narrowed. For in his major poems Dobell sought to explore the main intellectual, political and social problems of the day. His work would have prepared the twentieth century for Freud, because the obsessive concern of modern poets with the self, the incessant self-analysis and self-absorption, together with the agonizing search for the most intimate word or symbol to reveal the deepest level of the self has lain buried in Dobell's poetry since 1854. And Dobell intended his poetic explorations of the psyche not for an intellectual elite but for the person in the back of the bus. Had his "new" poems received competent literary analysis, the feminist cause might have been advanced by at least three decades; the average reader of his day would have been more accepting of change, and poetry which should reach the general public would not have become limited to a public of poets only. Moderns would have been prepared for a poetry which is audaciously concerned with a craftsmanship reduced to the essential search for the right word, the right symbol. It was this fascination with the search for the most private metaphor, the deepest "equivalent," that most distinguished Dobell's poetry. But he had no champion to explain his craft, to unravel the ambiguities of his "equivalents," and the ordinary reader was left with no alternative but to seek enjoyment and instruction in less demanding literature. Poetry, which once nourished the common reader, now delicately teases the taste of the few.

Two feminine influences shaped Sydney Dobell—his church and his wife—and perhaps the influence of the spiritual bride was more pervasive than that of his bride in the flesh. All his life Sydney Dobell was to bear the deeply graven marks of his parents' unusual, even crankish, religious beliefs; his unique sense of the complementariness of the sexes, however, was nourished by his very early, earthy love affair with Emily Fordham.

Dobell came from a line of religious individualists who rebelled against the imprisonment of the Creator in any one particular person—be that king or pope, in any particular institution or church, in any particular book. The spirit was alive and active and could not be confined. Yet, anomalously, Sydney Dobell became entrapped in the very church that was meant to set him free. A descendant of Daniel Dobell (b. 1700), a Quaker of Cranbrook in Kent who sired twenty-three sons and one daughter, Dobell's ancestors were cavaliers who lost their estates in fighting against Cromwell. But they "maintained in comparative poverty" the intellectual tastes that distinguished the original stock.[61] Because they had to use both brain and brawn to preserve their intellectual and social status, the Dobells had always been rugged democrats. They were even more serious dissenters. They would always be expected to challenge the status quo. According to E. Alston Mott, the Dobells of Cranbrook, the Chatfields and the Motts were all of the Weald. Members of these three families, intense and introspective in their religious views, intermarried. Sydney Dobell's mother, Julietta, was the daughter of Samuel Thompson and the sister of Eliza Mott. Eliza left her own reminiscences in which she described her trip, over mud-gutted roads to Cranbrook in Kent, in order to assist her sister at the birth, on 5 April 1824, of Sydney Thompson Dobell, the first of Julietta's ten children.[62]

The infant's second name honoured Julietta's father, Samuel Thompson, founder of a church based on primitive christianity—a group whose spirit has been immortalized in the opening pages of George Eliot's *Silas Marner*. In addition to Eliot, Robert Southey also registered his fascination with the sect—especially its "strict discipline" and its "strict regularity of conduct."[63] Thompson's church, known first as the church of "The Humble Enquirers after Truth," became popularly called the church of "Free-thinking Christians" and was a group split from Elhanan Winchester's branch of Universalism (*L & L* 1: Appendices A and B, 64-76).

Born in 1766 Samuel Thompson, Dobell's maternal grandfather, had a brief education at the Blue Coat School in London. Later he was apprenticed to a watchmaker, married young, and subsequently entered the wine business. At aged twenty, three years after his wife died, Samuel, "with a body enfeebled by worldly pursuits," became a member of William Vidler's congregation, meeting at Parliament Court, Bishopsgate Street, London. The group appears to have been inadequate for his particular religious needs because he then joined Winchester's church and rose to be a preacher and a deacon before he again seceded to form his own church.[64] It is difficult to understand the core belief of Thompson's church; however, it is known that he rejected the atonement, original sin, the doctrines of election and rejection, baptism, the eucharist etc. He did insist on fearless discussion of all problems and accepted the New Testament, if rationally considered, as the true guide to man's conduct here on earth. One of the eager young men recruited for the church was John Dobell, Sydney's father; but in his idealism, his fierce independence, even exclusiveness, Sydney Dobell bears closer affinity to his maternal grandfather, Samuel Thompson, than to his father, John Dobell.

Emily Jolly, who wrote *The Life and Letters of Sydney Dobell,* tends to be overly-pious in her treatment of biographical material. She presents a thoroughly detailed religious background but a very sketchy literary one. She seems more interested in writing the life of a saint than of a poet.[65] Samuel Thompson's church is thus amply documented, but we know very little about John Dobell's background other than that he was born in 1797, that he was a hide merchant before he married Julietta Thompson in 1823, and that after the marriage he assisted his new father-in-law in his very successful wine business, moving to the London office of the firm in 1828 when Sydney was four. In 1835 John Dobell was transferred to another branch in Cheltenham.

If Samuel Thompson was very eclectic in his choice of doctrines and teachings, there was one principle he stressed, and one which was to have a tragic effect on Sydney Dobell's career as a poet. This was his teaching on Judaic exclusiveness with its insistence on separation from the world. John Dobell seems to have acted more on this principle in bringing up his own ten children than on any other garnered from his father-in-law's religion. The young Dobells were deprived of the ordinary social intercourse of school and playground. Because the only people they knew were family intimates and members of their grandfather's church, they lived too tightly within the closet of family concerns and were smothered socially. John Dobell published at least one tract underscoring the free-thinking church's teaching on exclusiveness, "Man Unfit to Govern Man." If man was unfit to govern man, then man was certainly unfit to teach him. Sydney was educated entirely at home and here he was given a sense of his own brilliance and his own uniqueness. School might have weakened the child's precocity, but being deprived of like minds also deprived the child of effective criticism. Despite all his admissions that he knows his faults, the evidence contained in *Life and Letters* reveals an irritating vein of self-righteousness. Perhaps the most valuable part of school life—whether that be kindergarten or university—is the opportunity it provides for rubbing off rough edges, of refining, moderating, testing ideas and personalities. Sydney Dobell lacked this experience.

But no man was more convinced of his own uniqueness than was Sydney Dobell. His was a striking individuality that had its roots deep within a dissenting tradition wherein each man had to find his own meaning in his own existence. "It may be said," Dobell wrote, "that God designs each soul to find its own creed out of the record" (*Thoughts* 153). The "record" was specifically, but not entirely, scripture, and man's own experience of it. His education, however, by no means neglected other subjects, and Dobell appears to have had one of those formidable educations in which Victorians took such

pride. At four or five his father would give him a line to which the child would respond in rhyme (*L & L* 1:9). From the age of seven Sydney used little pocket books to jot down "acquired bits of knowledge" (*L & L* 1:11). At ten his father could record: Sydney reads all Miss Martineau's books on Political Economy, and devours any other book I give him. He seems to understand all he reads and does, and catches some things sooner than I do (*L & L* 1:12).

That same year (1834) Sydney's first poem is noted, and it is truly a remarkable piece—if totally written by a ten-year-old child.

> Hush gentle streams, within your little rill;
> Ye dead leaves trembling on the breeze be still;
> Quiet, ye boisterous winds that roar on high,
> Let peace reside throughout the earth and sky:
> The brooks replied, with rippling gentle tone,
> God we'll obey, and God alone;
> The leaves replied, in rustling noise,
> And in so soft and sweet a voice,
> The God of Heaven who gave us birth
> Him we'll obey, He rules the earth;
> The winds replied, 'Tis music to the Lord,
> And all our roaring is to praise our God
> Oh! if then nature will obey
> The Lord of Hosts, let no man delay.
>
> (*L & L* 1:13)

Even allowing for the fact that in Dobell's age poetry had a popularity (and a piety) which it has lost in our day, and that a ten-year-old would be learning rhyme and rhythm as he learned a basic vocabulary, still, the child's use of diction, his control of the iambic foot, his sensitivity to nature are truly impressive.

Dobell's Wordsworthian love of nature, his close study of its details and his thorough enjoyment of these observations are faithfully recorded in Jolly's *Life and Letters.* During his French lesson one day, the young Sydney writes of seeing a "largish hawk" which attacked a "small bird that kept flying this way and that in confusion" until it was rescued by "five or six pigeons" who attacked the hawk "in file":

> The hawk made some desperate swoops among the pigeons, which they avoided, and the hawk flew away discomfited. They pursued him as he retreated, and he flew into the town as low as the houses, the pigeons above, below, and on all sides of him, he shooting in front, then wildly diving towards the ground. Thus they pursued him over the town and having gone round nearly to the place where he was first attacked, the discomfited hawk was obliged to seek shelter in some trees, and the pigeons returned triumphant to their homes.
>
> (*L & L* 1:20-21)

At a very early age he demonstrated an imaginative responsiveness to shading and to colour. "Last night about nine o'clock," he recorded,

while it was light, I was witness to a splendid phenomenon. About N.W. from our window there was a large
black cloud, unbroken and deep black, reaching to
about 25 above the horizon. Above the cloud was the
clear blue sky, specked here and there with little white
clouds. Venus was shining brightly, not a breath stirred
. . . suddenly the black cloud was lit up by a stream of
red light . . . making what before seemed a black mass
resemble a mountain of chasms and cliffs.

(*L & L* 1:22)

Sometimes his nature comments are less dramatic and
more scientific, as when he observes that

. . . a stream nearly one cubit broad, minus four inches,
running at the rate of about one cubit in two seconds,
and not more than half an inch deep, would by its force
carry stones (of different shapes), some roundish, others square &c., of the size of a large pea and rather
larger, a considerable distance. Might not then the erratic blocks of granite found at great distances from
their mountains have been carried by a larger stream;
for instance, if half an inch carry a grain, what will ten
feet do?

(*L & L* 1:20)

No less impressive than young Sydney Dobell's
observation of nature is the catalogue of his other
mental accomplishments. At twelve he was reading
Latin and French by himself. At fifteen his father
engaged a tutor so that he might learn Greek. The
amount of Aeschylus he had learned astounded his
master. He was also reading Blackstone and writing
poetry (*L & L* 1:27). There is no mention of his playing
with lads of his own age, but there is a reference to his
forming a new system for the classification of birds (*L
& L* 1:18).

Dobell was nourished on Shakespeare which the father
took upon himself to feed to his children. And not the
father but the son became critical of the poet's "course-
ness": "After tea Papa read Shakespeare aloud for a
couple of hours. Play 'Merchant of Venice'—one of his
most exciting plays in parts for the criticalness of the
situations, but spoiled in others by the low language of
Launcelot and the coarse jests which abound in the low
characters" (*L & L* 1:23).

During this adolescent period he was writing poetry
which appeared in the local papers and in *Chamber's
Magazine*.[66] His first poetic drama, "Napoleon" won his
father's approval—parts of which he pronounced "very
fine" (*L & L* 1:18). John Dobell submitted the drama to
Colburn the publisher. Although Colburn rejected it, the
poet Campbell prophesied that young Dobell would
make his way as a writer and that with care "there is no
doubt of . . . [his] becoming a poet" (*L & L* 1:46).
Unfortunately there is no trace of this first long poem,
but one suspects that some of the later poems collected
in ***England in Time of War*** and ***Sonnets on the War***
might well be remnants from this early work.

Not only his eldest son's poetry but also his religious
zeal impressed the father. John Dobell was amazed at
his son's prodigious memory of the Bible which he
studied, lexicon in hand, every evening, and on which
he preached with such enthusiastic fervor that his father
recognized him as "a beautiful orator" who could "speak
on the spur of the moment really eloquently," and one
capable of assuming one day the leadership of Grandfather Thompson's church (*L & L* 1:61). From the time
he was eight, Sydney had been attending the Sunday
service of the "Freethinking Christians" where discussion, not preaching, was the custom. At sixteen he was
lecturing his brothers and sisters either on the history of
the Reformation or on Prophecy, the latter subject having a peculiar fascination for Dobell. One Sunday

. . . he spoke on till (just, as he used laughingly to
relate, when he found himself well-warmed to his
subject and beginning to master his fast-crowding
ideas), his eldest sister was deputed to enquire whether
he would be much much longer, as he had already been
speaking upwards of two hours!

(*L & L* 1:42)

Along with parental enforcement of Sydney's intellectual precocity, there was also planted in the boy a
belief in his extraordinary destiny. His father saw him
as a special instrument and had "great reason to bless
an All-gracious Father for such a domestic treasure" (*L
& L* 1:18). Without a doubt he would become a leader
in working out the religious and social reforms of the
Church of God. In his mother's eyes Sydney was
"indeed precious," but one of her well-remembered, if
terrible, exclamations was, "I would rather see him die
than neglect his duty" (*L & L* 1:55). Thus confirmed in
his unique sense of self, of his high destiny, the boy
was burdened with an awesome self-consciousness
which could only prove crippling. When reviewing *The
Life and Letters* of Sydney Dobell, Edmund Gosse, who
would have known the dangers of a rigidly religious
upbringing, passed a harsh but fair judgment:

One of the most remarkably sensitive children of the
century was trained in infancy to a constant and precocious self-analysis; one of the most perilously religious
minds was dedicated in the cradle to the apostleship of
a narrow sect; one of the most eager and restless of
spirits was encouraged, nay urged, to outspeed itself
during those very years of early youth when repose and
a judicious division of employment are absolutely
necessary. The result was as disastrous as might have
been expected. Fatigue developed into disease, the
causes of disease were ignored, and the evil became
chronic; an immense vitality struggled against all these
disabilities, and dragged its possessor painfully into a
shattered middle age. With the documents before us
which these volumes present, it is not possible to refrain
from the observation that an education more radically
and obstinately wrong-headed than that inflicted on

Sydney Dobell is scarcely to be conceived, and to this are plainly and almost entirely due the ruin of his constitution and the comparative failure of his glorious poetic promise.[67]

The burden of perfection, a harsh asceticism, and a rigorous middle-class respect for work, imposed by loving but stern parents, began to tax the nervous system of a highly sensitive boy. By the age of twelve he was already employed in the office of his father's wine distribution business. His learning was relegated to the hours before and after work. At fourteen he had his first very serious bout with ill health. His father called Sydney's illness typhus, but his mother, more honestly recognizing the symptoms of an over-taxed mind and body, called it a "nervous fever." The cause was not explored. Rather it was conveniently, if vaguely and inexplicably, attributed to a break-in at the Dobell home which somehow led to Sydney's exposure to cold and resulted in a malady after which there was a "distinct change." Sydney became "broken-spirited, morbid"—so reported his mother who was recovering after the birth of her eighth child. He ate little, Mrs. Dobell added, and all he wanted was his "crack-brained books" (*L & L* 1:25-26).

Thereafter there were frequent references to Sydney's "breakdowns." Towards the end of 1840, when John Dobell had been ill and his eldest son, then sixteen, took his place in the office, the strain which accompanied the extra work, together with his church duties and his studies, brought on another bout with illness. Young Dobell suffered from pain and numbness in the head, afterward with obstinate deafness and irritability—the last malady one which previously had been attributed usually to Dobell senior (*L & L* 1:47). But little was done either to alleviate the strain of overwork or to discover the nature of Sydney's complaints.

John Nichol was to attribute Dobell's "disabling weakness" to a disastrous fall he had when trying to break in a new horse.[68] Perhaps the simplest explanation of Dobell's repeated illnesses is that he suffered from epilepsy.[69]

If the cause of ill health remained undetermined, Dobell himself seems to have understood the effect of the tensions and pressures in his life. His letters supply frequent records of the exasperating frustrations of his exclusively cerebral activities—work, study and business. His emotional life, however, found an early release in love.

> . . . business, business, with only a little slice of Greek. Life is a regular drive. I have not only to act double, but to think for all of them, which bustles me about confoundedly. But I don't care; it is better than having nothing to do, and, however hurried and driven, the thought of _____ hovers like a guardian angel over the turmoil of my brain.
>
> (*L & L* 1:47)

Dobell's "guardian angel" was his future wife, Emily Fordham, with whom he would share a profound intimacy. During the thirty-one years of their married life, they were never to be separated for more than four and twenty consecutive hours (*L & L* 1:110). In a letter to his friend, Dr. Samuel Brown (no date but presumably 1850), Dobell confessed to his unusual attraction: "I fell in love with her at ten, we were engaged at fifteen, and married at twenty" (*L & L* 1:145). John Dobell blamed the intensity of Sydney's adoration of Emily as contributing to his son's physical exhaustion, but it seems more than likely that she weaned him away from the control of mother church and was the predominant female influence in his life. Despite parental opposition they became engaged in 1839. Sydney Dobell was fifteen years old. Emily was seventeen.

The boy had been allowed to visit Emily at her father's house, Sandon Manor, Cambridgeshire, in September of that year in which the engagement took place. Here in the quiet of the countryside which he loved, Sydney built up his strength and escaped from the "distresses and disgusts of business" (*L & L* 1:29). One suspects that the young poet wanted to escape from more than business. The father's authoritarianism and the mother's weary religiosity were taking their toll. Poetry-writing seemed to be gaining ascendancy over church-going. When Dobell returned to Cheltenham, he and his fiancee were restricted to writing to each other once a week. Mr. Fordham, along with Mr. Dobell, objected to "the painful and excessive feelings" noted in the boy's letters. Dobell, in a letter intended to mollify Mr. Fordham, tried to cover up the sexuality in the letters by appealing to religion.

> I am but a young religionist, and, therefore, ought to be careful in hazarding an opinion, but I should think that even the very constant anxiety to do right and the fear of being mistaken as to what is or is not right, which must pervade the mind of one devoted to the Will of God, and possessing the humility of mind towards that God which is so enjoined by Him, would necessarily tend to destroy that calm and tranquility which you say religion teaches. . . .
>
> (*L & L* 1:40)

Our knowledge of Dobell's personal history is fragmentary, uncertain, and biased. It is possible, though, to piece together a basic structure. No doubt he was a deeply intelligent, sensitive child bound to parents who exerted a powerful influence on his mental and moral development. It is fairly clear also that he was precociously awake to sexual love and that his youthful marriage was complicated by parental disapproval. That Dobell sought to escape parental suffocation seems fairly evident. His wife promised to give him the emotional security his parents could not. (She at first promised to provide financial security also—until Mr. Fordham lost most of his money and two estates just prior to the marriage.) Of the years of his engagement, Dobell's biographer writes:

> It is difficult to give any true notion of the stress and tension of this period [1841-1844] . . . without touching things almost too sacred for handling; and yet, without some reference to these inner phases of his mind, no indication can be given of one of the causes of the early and disastrous breakdown of his physical system.
>
> (*L & L* 1:52)

Everything about Dobell at this period was overly "sacred." Emily's love was destined to become "lord of all" (*L & L* 1:15). In her he fused poetry and religion. "The more we loved, the more we prayed" (*L & L* 1:51). At seventeen he was writing poetry for her and to her. One of these was a five hundred line poem dealing with an imaginary legend to account for the place names in the Cambridgeshire neighbourhood where Emily lived. It was written in two "pieces of days" when Emily and Sydney shared the same study table (*L & L* 1:59-60). Emily's house truly was a refuge for Dobell:

> Here at last I am at peace. Here in the scene of my first and only love. . . . To these placid fields, murmurous—I have no other word—with sheep bells; this solitary hamlet, with its church beside the green, where for five years of happiest courtship I was the ever-welcomed hero of village tattle and romance.[70]

His emotional security was reflected in lines of pastoral tranquility.

> 'Tis sorrow in the summer time
> These city walls to see,
> And know the kindred world without
> Is brotherless to me.
> A village home, a village home!
> Oh, what were better joy
> Than just beneath a village cot
> To be a village boy.
> To look on country flowers and know
> That hand-in-hand we grew,
> And feel the breeze that loves the trees
> Was made to love me too.
>
> (*L & L* 1:29-30)

Sydney Dobell and Emily Fordham were married 18 July 1844. They settled in a pleasant little house in a village that looked onto the Cotswold Hills. Idyllic as it sounds, there is something a bit menacing in Sydney's attempts to impose his rarified spirituality on Emily who became a member of the church of "Freethinking Christians" at the time of her marriage. Emily now adopted Sydney's pattern of resolute, rigorous prayer. (He seems to want to compensate for his absence at church discussions.) For years he had a habit of night meditation and prayer (at the cost of his rest) in addi-

tion to his day-time prayer. Dobell himself admitted: "About three or four years before our marriage I adopted an excessive practice of prayer" (*L & L* 1:52). No wonder Emily's health declined after marriage. Faithful to the church's teaching on exclusiveness, and fearing lest they be contaminated by the world, the young couple agreed not to mix with any society, however high or intellectual, however morally superior they might be, if they did not hold the same religious views as they did (*L & L* 1:86).

Dobell idealized his wife into the perfect woman just as he imposed on himself the burden of becoming the perfect man. He saw "in all womanhood the reflection of his own ideal of it—his wife" (*Good Words for 1879*, 315). The same religious zealotry his parents had bequeathed to him, Sydney now bequeathed to his wife who seems to have accepted it readily enough. But so high a degree of other-worldliness and precocity, which Dobell showed at so early an age, contributed to an extremism in life and art for which Dobell was to be soundly condemned. Even Robert Buchanan, a devoted admirer, thought that his search for the ideal had dimmed the glory of his poetic career: "He was too constantly overshadowed with his mission."[71] For the critic who saw too much "flesh" in the poetry of the Pre-Raphaelites, Buchanan saw too much "spirit" both in the life and work of Sydney Dobell who "lacked to the end a certain literary robustness, which only comes to a man made fully conscious that Art and Literature are not life itself, but only Life's humble handmaids" (190).

Dobell's extreme idealism was to be noted by other critics. Garnett spoke of his character as being one of "uniform elevation."[72] John Nichol, in alluding to his solitariness, his living "mentally to a great extent by himself" was quick to note that he did not live for himself (1: xii). Dobell had a habit, wrote another observor, "of spending many hours out of every twenty-four in the effort to abstract himself from all earthly things, and to pass into communion with God and the spiritual world" (*Good Words for 1874*, 719). It has already been noted how easily Dobell slipped from the natural to the spiritual and the moral in his earliest recorded verse, **"Hush Gentle Streams"**. The spiritual, with a tinge of "old morality," took on even more significance after his engagement and marriage to Emily.

Young Dobell had written a poem for his wife entitled **"The Lament of a Husband after the Death of His Wife"** wherein he scolded the husband because to him "this life was all;" he did not trust "in a God who forbids us to mourn as those without hope" (*L & L* 1:49).[73] Sydney had taught his lofty idealism even in the marriage chamber. Emily Jolly summarized their life together:

. . . the increasing persistency and consistency of his petitions for growth, in moral and spiritual beauty, of her whom he had chosen 'not for time but for eternity,' gives a painful monotony to his Diaries, and testifies to the truth of his wife's succinct history of this time: 'the more we loved, the more we prayed.'

(L & L 1:51)

But in their own lives Mr. and Mrs. Dobell seem to have achieved a rare unity of mind and heart. They had no children. Emily's health was even more delicate than Sydney's, but she dedicated her life to her husband as Sydney gave his life to her. She believed in her husband's genius, and there is every indication that she was more of an encouragement to his poetry than his parents were. She had chosen him "for eternity" (*L & L* 1:50-51).

Thus the first five years after his marriage passed quietly enough for Sydney Dobell. He still attended his grandfather's church but with less frequency; he wrote his poetry: **"Isabel"** (1847), **"A Musing on Victory"** (1847); and he earned annually the four hundred pounds necessary to support himself and his wife by managing the Cheltenham branch of his father's wine trade. Some of his early poems—**"A Village Colloquy," "The Dying Girl to Her Mother," "The Massacre at Glencoe," "The French People to Armand Carrell,"**—appeared in *The People's Journal,* a weekly newspaper published from January, 1846 until June, 1849, and whose proprietor, John Saunders, was to remain a lifelong friend. Dobell wrote most of these poems during 1847 and 1848; however, he was appreciated by few beyond the confines of his own family, church friends, and the readership of *The People's Journal.*[74]

All that was soon to change. Tiny blades of rebellion, mere seedlings when Dobell insisted on becoming engaged, soon sprouted into open defiance when he moved away from home after his marriage. Love of his bride gave him a new-found security. Little by little he began to separate himself from parental and institutional control. There was a growing disinterest in church affairs. More and more Dobell was turning to the God within and to poetry for spiritual sustenance, and he found in two contemporary critics, George Gilfillan and Thomas Carlyle, the spiritual, intellectual and aesthetic satisfaction he craved.

Notes

1. Kate Millet, *Sexual Politics* (New York: Doubleday, 1972) 25.

2. Emily Jolly, ed. *The Life and Works of Sydney Dobell* 2 vols. (London: 1878) 1: 37. Henceforth this work will be cited as *L & L.*

3. Henry Taylor, *Autobiography* 2 vols. (London, 1874) 2:119.

4. ———. Preface to *Philip Van Artevelde: A Dramatic Romance* 2 vols. (London, 1834) 1:xi.

5. Thomas Love Peacock, *Four Ages of Poetry* ed. by H. F. B. Brett-Smith (Oxford: Blackwell, 1921) 18. Shelley's *Defence of Poetry* is also found in this volume.

6. Isaac Taylor, *Natural History of Enthusiasm,* London, 1829) 2.

7. John Keble, *De Poetica Vi Medica Praelectiones Academicae* (London, 1844) 222-3; his criticism of Byron, 573, 687.

8. Edmund Gosse, "Philip James Bailey," *The Critic* (Nov. 1902): 457.

9. John Wilson, "The Christian Year" [John Keble] *Blackwood's Edinburgh Magazine* 27 (June 1830): 835.

10. William H. Smith, "A Prosing upon Poetry," *Blackwood's Edinburgh Magazine* 46 (Aug. 1839): 200.

11. R. G. Cox, "Victorian Criticism of Poetry: The Minority Tradition," *Scrutiny* 18 (1951): 2-17.

12. Morris Greenhut, "George Henry Lewes and the Classical Tradition in English Criticism," *Review of English Studies* XXIV (Jan. 1948) 126.

13. Philip James Bailey, *Festus: A Poem* (London, 1839) 238.

14. "Reviews," Literature of 1841, *St. James Magazine* (Jan. 1842): 127.

15. Morse Peckham, "English Editions of Philip James Bailey's *Festus*" *Papers of the Bibliographical Society of America*: 55-58; also "American Editions of *Festus*: A Preliminary Survey" *Princeton Library Chronicle* (June 1947): 177-84.

16. "Festus," *The Christian Examiner* (Nov. 1845): 365-79.

17. Hallam Tennyson, *Alfred Lord Tennyson, A Memoir* 2 vols. (London, 1897) 1: 234.

18. Charles Tennyson, *Alfred Tennyson* (New York: MacMillan, 1949) 215.

19. Philip James Bailey, *Festus: A Poem,* Fiftieth Anniversary Edition (London, 1889) 1.

20. W. Robertson Nicoll and Thomas J. Wise eds., *Literary Anecdotes of the Nineteenth Century*: Contributions towards a Literary History of the Period 2 vols. (London, 1896) 2: 413.

21. Robert A. Vaughan, "Festus, A Poem" *British Quarterly Review* 3 (May 1846): 387.

22. Mark A. Weinstein, *William Edmondstoune Aytoun and the Spasmodic Controversy* (New Haven and London: Yale UP, 1968) 77.

23. Quoted in Alan D. McKillop's, "A Victorian Faust," *PMLA* 40 (1925) 763. Samuel Longfellow, *Life of Henry Wadsworth Longfellow* (Boston, 1891) 2: 24. McKillop's article is the best source of general information on the impact of *Festus* on the Victorians. I am likewise indebted to McKillop's doctoral dissertation "The Spasmodic School in Victorian Poetry," Harvard, 1920.

24. "The First Edition of *Festus*," *Book-Lore* Dec. 1884: 24.

25. Walter Bagehot, "Festus," *The Prospective Review,* (Nov. 1847), in, *The Collected Works of Walter Bagehot* ed. by Norman St John-Stevas, 15 vols. (London: The Economist, 1984) 1: 109.

26. William Henry Smith, "Festus," *Blackwood's Edinburgh Magazine* 67 (April 1850): 416. A random selection of "Festus" reviews shows that all were not favorable. See: "Festus," *The American Review* (Jan. 1847): 43; also (Feb. 1847): 123; "Bailey's Festus," *Dublin University Review* (July 1847): 92; "Festus," *The New Englander* (April 1847): 178.

27. Quoted in Robert Birley's *Sunk without Trace: Some Forgotten Masterpieces Reconsidered* (London: Rupert Hart Davis, 1962) 173.

28. William M. Rossetti ed., *Dante Gabriel Rossetti: His Family Letters with A Memoir* 2 vols. (London, 1895) 1:89.

29. ———. *The Collected Works of Dante Gabriel Rossetti* 2 vols. (London, 1896) 1: xxvi.

30. Elizabeth Barrett Browning, "To Richard Hengist Horne," dated "Wednesday Morning" (1844), *Letters of Elizabeth Barrett Browning Addressed to Richard Hengist Horne* (London, 1872) 2:12-13.

31. Richard Hengist Horne, "Henry Taylor and the Author of 'Festus', *A New Spirit of the Age* 2 vols. (London, 1844), 281-310.

32. Elizabeth Barrett had written to Horne, "Taylor, who is understood . . . by many men . . . to be the great poet of the day, is, to my apprehension, scarcely a poet at all, and stands coldly outside of my sympathies. Consider! a dramatic poet without passion! what does *that* amount to? A contemplative poet without a heaven of ideality above his head! What shall we call *that*? A rhymed writer who denies the distinct element of poetry!" *Letters of EAB to RHH* 2: 8.

33. "The New Edition of Mr. Bailey's 'Festus'," *Eclectic Review* (June 1865): 540.

34. "The Fiftieth Anniversary Edition of 'Festus'," *The Nation* 49 (1889): 216. Also "The Passing of Festus," *The Nation* 75 (1902) 241.

35. Amy Cruse, *The Victorians and Their Books* (London: Allen, Unwin, 1935) 180.

36. George Saintsbury, "Lesser Poets," 1790-1837, *The Cambridge History of English Literature* 15 vols. (Cambridge: Cambridge UP, 1970) 12: 118.

37. Martha Hale Shackford, *E. B. Browning: R. H. Horne: Two Studies* (Wellesley, MA: The Wellesley Press, 1935) 32.

38. Eric Partridge, Introduction to *Orion* by R. H. Horne (London, 1928) xx, xxiii.

39. Fred C. Thompson, "A Crisis in Early Victorian Drama: John Westland Marston and the Syncretics," *Victorian Studies* (June 1966), 378.

40. For Tennyson's and Taylor's pursuit of the laureateship in 1850, see Robert Martin's *The Unquiet Heart* (Oxford: Clarendon, 1980) 351.

41. Edgar Finley Shannon, *Tennyson and the Reviewers* (Cambridge: Harvard UP, 1952) 22. See also *The Unquiet Heart,* 99.

42. Charles Kingsley, "Thoughts on Shelley and Byron," *Fraser's Magazine* (Nov. 1853): 568-576.

43. John Keats, "To John Taylor," 27 Feb. 1818, letter 65 of *The Letters of John Keats 1814-1821,* ed. by Hyder Edward Rollins, 2 vols. (Cambridge: Harvard UP, 1956) 1: 239.

44. Jack Lindsay, *George Meredith* (London: Bodley Head, 1956) 44.

45. "Pauline: A Fragment of a Confession," *Monthly Repository* 7 ns (1833) 253.

46. Richard Hengist Horne, "Brief Commentary," *Orion* (London, 1874) xvi-xvii.

47. Sydney Dobell, *Thoughts on Art, Philosophy and Religion,* ed. by John Nichol (London, 1876) 99-100. Henceforth cited as *Thoughts.*

48. John Stuart Mill, ("Antiquus"), "The Two Kinds of Poetry," *Monthly Repository* ns (1833): 723.

49. William Sharp, ed., Introduction, "The Roman," *The Poems of Sydney Dobell* (London, 1876) x.

50. T. Percy Jones [William Edmondstoune Aytoun], "Firmilian: A Tragedy, "*Blackwood's Edinburgh Magazine* 75 (May 1854): 533-551.

51. ———. Lectures delivered by Aytoun, *National Library of Scotland* Add. Ms. 4908.166f. Also 4897, 4906, 4909, 4912.

52. T. Percy Jones [William Aytoun], *Firmilian or the Student of Badajoz: A Spasmodic Tragedy* (Edinburgh and London, 1854).

53. Jane Sinnett, rev. of "Firmilian," *Westminster Review* 12 ns (Oct. 1854): 614-615.

54. John Nichol ed., "Memoir," *The Poetical Works of Sydney Dobell* 2 vols. (London, 1875), 1: xix. Henceforth cited as *Works.*

55. Donald MacLeod, ed., "In Memoriam—Sydney Dobell," *Good News for 1874* (London: 1874): 718.

56. Jerome H. Buckley, *The Victorian Temper* (London: Allen, Unwin, 1952) 54.

57. Matthew Arnold, "The Function of Criticism at the Present Time," *Lectures and Essays in Criticism,* ed. R. H. Super (Ann Arbor: U of Michigan P, 1973) 262.

58. Goldwin Smith, "Review of Maud," *Saturday Review* (3 Nov. 1855): 14-15.

59. Margaret Oliphant, "Modern Light Literature: Poetry," *Blackwood's Edinburgh Magazine* 79 (Feb. 1856): 128.

60. Jerome H. Buckley, *The Growth of A Poet* (Cambridge and London: Harvard UP, 1960) 141.

61. "Biographical Sketch," *Poems by Sydney Dobell* (Boston, 1860) vii. The Library of Congress lists this as the "author's edition."

62. Information on Dobell's background came chiefly from interviews with, and a letter from, E. Alston Mott (21 September 1984).

63. Robert Southey, "To the Rev. Neville White," 11 Sept. 1823. *Selections from the Letters of Robert Southey,* ed. John Wood Warter, 4 vols (London, 1856) 3:403.

64. See John Dobell, "Samuel Thompson, Esq." (Obituary notice of his father-in-law) *The Christian Reformer,* Jan. 1838: 67-72.

65. Emily Jolly, a minor novelist, lived for a time with the Dobells, married into the family, and became Dobell's literary executress. Perhaps this close proximity caused her to fail in that objectivity so essential to a biographer. She deleted most names from the letters and, what is more exasperating, apparently destroyed what letters had been printed. E. Alston Mott assured me there were no Dobell papers in existence, and Jerome Thale wrote that Eva Dobell reported to him in a letter (2 November 1952) that any of Dobell's unpublished notes and papers "were destroyed in a fire of 1893" ("Sydney Dobell: A Spasmodic Poet," diss., Northwestern U, 1953, v). However, Barbara McPherson, a grandniece of Frederick Mott, wrote me in a letter (11 October 1991) that there were papers, but, she added, "I cannot find the Dobell papers anywhere, although I have seen them. . . ." Thus, the researcher must rely on

Emily Jolly's work. Her lack of objectivity, added to Mrs. Dobell's determination to canonize Dobell's memory, is further exposed in a letter which John Stuart Blackie wrote to his wife. Jolly had asked Blackie to contribute a critical essay on Dobell's work. Blackie, a long-time friend of Dobell's, wrote on May 4 1875 with more than a bit of exasperation: "I have been much occupied with that wretched Dobell business, which I now see will come to nothing. . . . My conclusion is that I must write to Miss Jolly that either I must speak the truth and offend the worshipping widow, or print lies and prostitute my own intellect." On May 7 he confessed that he had "thrown overboard forever" the Dobell business. He would not "be bribed by tears or smiles, or any other female artillery." (*The Letters of John Stuart Blackie to His Wife* ed. A. S. Walker [Edinburgh: Blackwood, 1909] 240-241).

66. Jerome Thale, "Sydney Dobell: A Spasmodic Poet," 435. Thale checked the assertion made in *L & L* that Dobell had published some poems in *Chamber's Magazine.* A search of *Chambers* for 1843 and adjacent years revealed no poems appearing under his name and none that could definitely be assigned to him on the basis of style.

67. Edmund Gosse, rev. of *The Life and Letters of Sydney Dobell, The Academy,* 14 December 1878: 553.

68. John Nichol ed., "Memoir," *The Poetical Works of Sydney Dobell* 2 vols. (London, 1875) 1:xxix.

69. "In Memoriam," *Good Words for 1874,* ed. by Donald McLeod (London, 1874) 719. The article refers to Dobell's 1865 trip to Puteoli near Naples. Trying to visualize the exact scene St. Paul saw when he landed, Dobell fell into a 10-12 ft. hole and suffered a blow on the head and neck which, it was claimed, became "the last provoking cause" of his "epileptiform seizures."

70. E. J. Smith ed., "De Mortuis," rev. of *Life and Letters of Sydney Dobell, Good Words,* 20 (1879): 315.

71. Robert Buchanan, *A Look Round Literature* (London, 1887) 190.

72. Richard Garnett, "Sydney Dobell," *The Poets and Poetry of the Century* (London, 1891) 180.

73. The subject of this poem might have come from a bizarre incident wherein John Dobell, either trying to prepare his son for the rejection of his poem "Napoleon" or to relieve the over-seriousness of his son's love for his wife, once reported, "Sydney, I have sad news for you. . . . You did not know that Emily was dead" (*L & L* 1:45).

74. Thale discovered that the poems Jolly claimed had been published in *Chamber's Journal* had really been published in *The People's Journal*: 4 (1847): 122; (1848): 151; 5 (1848): 54-56, 59-61; 5 (1848): 192-93 (Thale, 434-35).

Works Cited

Arnold, Matthew. *Lectures and Essays in Criticism.* Ed. R. H. Super. Ann Arbor: U of Michigan P, 1973.

Aytoun, William (T. Percy Jones). *Firmilian or the Student of Badajoz: A Spasmodic Tragedy.* Edinburgh and London, 1854.

———. "Review of Alexander Smith's *Poems.*" *Blackwood's Edinburgh Magazine* (March 1854): 345-348.

———. "Firmilian." *Blackwood's Edinburgh Magazine* 75 (May 1854): 533-55

Bailey, Philip James. *Festus: A Poem.* London, 1839.

———. *Festus: A Poem.* Fiftieth Anniversary Edition London, 1889.

Birley, Robert. *Sunk without Trace: Some Forgotten Masterpieces Reconsidered.* London: Rupert Hart Davis, 1962.

Browning, Elizabeth Barrett. *Letters of Elizabeth Barrett Browning Addressed to Richard Hengist Horne.* London, 1872.

Buchanan, Robert. *A Look Round Literature.* London, 1887.

Buckley, Jerome H. *The Victorian Temper.* London: Allen, Unwin, 1952.

———. *The Growth of A Poet.* Cambridge and London: Harvard UP, 1960.

Cox, R. G. "Victorian Criticism of Poetry: The Minority Tradition," *Scrutiny* 18 (1951): 2-17.

Cruse, Amy. *The Victorians and Their Books.* London: Allen, Unwin, 1935.

Dobell, John. "Samuel Thompson, Esq." *The Christian Reformer.* Jan. 1838.

Dobell, Sydney. *Balder.* 2nd ed. London, 1854

———. Smith, Alexander. *Sonnets on the War* London: 1855.

———. *England in Time of War.* London, 1856.

———. *Poems by Sydney Dobell.* Boston, 1860.

———. *The Poetical Works of Sydney Dobell.* 2 vols. Ed. John Nichol. London, 1875.

———. *The Poems of Sydney Dobell.* Ed. William Sharp. London, 1876.

———. *Thoughts on Art, Philosophy and Religion.* Ed. John Nichol. London, 1876.

———. *Life and Letters of Sydney Dobell.* 2 vols. Ed. Emily Jolly. London, 1878.

———. *The Poems of Sydney Dobell.* Ed., Introd. Emily Dobell. London: 1887.

———. Review of "Gilfillan's Galleries," *The Palladium,* (July 1850): 25.

Garnett, Richard. "Sydney Dobell," *The Poets and Poetry of the Century.* London, 1891.

George Gilfillan. *A Gallery of Literary Portraits* 2 vols. Edinburgh, 1856.

———. *George Gilfillan: Letters and Journals with Memoir.* Eds. Robert A. and Elizabeth Watson. London, 1892.

———. "Advertisement." *A Gallery of Literary Portraits.* Edinburgh, 1845.

———. "Gerald Massey." *Hogg's Instructor* ns 3 (1854): 189.

———. "A Third Bundle of Books." *Hogg's Instructor* 3 ns. (1849): 337-41.

———. "A Sixth Bundle of Books." *Hogg's Instructor* 6 ns (1851): 173.

———. "A Tenth Bundle of Books." *Hogg's Instructor* 9 ns (1852): 344.

———. Review of "The Roman." *Eclectic Review* 27ns (1850): 672-84.

———. "The Martyrs, Heroes and Bards of the Scottish Covenant." *The Eclectic Review* 5ns (1853): 335-44.

Gosse, Edmund. "Philip James Bailey." *The Critic* (Nov. 1902): 457.

———. Review of *The Life and Letters of Sydney Dobell. The Academy* (14 Dec. 1878): 553.

Greenhut, Morris. "George Henry Lewes and the Classical Tradition in English Criticism." *Review of English Studies* XXIV (Jan. 1948) 126.

Horne, Richard Hengist. "Henry Taylor and the Author of 'Festus'." *A New Spirit of the Age.* 2 vols. London, 1844.

———. "Brief Commentary." *Orion.* London, 1874.

———. *Orion.* Introd. Eric Partridge. London, 1928.

Jolly, Emily, ed. *The Life and Works of Sydney Dobell.* 2 vols. London, 1878.

Jones, T. Percy (William Aytoun). *Firmilian or the Student of Badajoz: A Spasmodic Tragedy.* Edinburgh and London, 1854.

————. "Firmilian." *Blackwood's Edinburgh Magazine* 75 (May 1854): 533-55

Keats, John. *The Letters of John Keats 1814-1821.* Ed. Hyder Edward Rollins. 2 vols. Cambridge: Harvard UP, 1956.

————. *The Poems of John Keats.* Ed. E. de Selincourt. London: Methuen, 1905.

Keble, John. *De Poetica Vi Medica Praelectiones Academicae.* London, 1844.

Kingsley, Charles. *Literary and Critical Essays.* London, 1880.

————. "Thoughts on Shelley and Byron." *Fraser's Magazine* (Nov. 1853) 568-576.

Lindsay, Jack. *George Meredith.* London: Bodley Head, 1956.

MacLeod, Donald, Rev. "In Memoriam—Sydney Dobell," *Good News for 1874.* London: 1874:

Martin, Robert. *The Unquiet Heart.* Oxford: Clarendon, 1980.

McKillop, Allan D. "The Spasmodic School in Victorian Poetry," Ph.D. diss. Harvard, 1920.

————. "A Victorian Faust." *PMLA* 40: (1925) 763.

Mill, John Stuart ("Antiquus"). "The Two Kinds of Poetry." *Monthly Repository* 1833: 723.

Millet, Kate. *Sexual Politics.* New York: Doubleday, 1972.

Nicoll, W. Robertson and Thomas J. Wise eds. *Literary Anecdotes of the Nineteenth Century: Contributions towards a Literary History of the Period.* 2 vols. London, 1896.

Partridge, Eric, ed. "Introduction" to *Orion.* London, 1928.

Peacock, Thomas Love. *Four Ages of Poetry.* Ed. H. F. B. Brett-Smith. Oxford: Blackwell, 1921.

Peckham, Morse. "English Editions of Philip James Bailey's Festus." *Papers of the Bibliographical Society of America*: 55-58.

Rossetti, William, ed. *Dante Gabriel Rossetti: His Family Letters with A Memoir.* 2 vols. London, 1895.

————. *The Collected Works of Dante Gabriel Rossetti.* 2 vols. London, 1896.

Saintsbury, George. "Lesser Poets 1790-1837." *The Cambridge History of English Literature.* 15 vols. Cambridge: Cambridge UP, 1970.

Shackford, Martha Hale. *E. B. Browning: R. H. Horne: Two Studies.* Wellesley, MA: The Wellesley Press, 1935.

Shannon, Edgar Finley. *Tennyson and the Reviewers.* Cambridge: Harvard UP, 1952.

Sinnett, Jane. "Rev. of 'Firmilian'." *Westminster Review* 12 ns. (Oct. 1854):614-615.

Smith, Alexander. Sydney Dobell. *Sonnets on the War.* London, 1855.

Smith, E. J. ed. "De Mortuis," Review of *Life and Letters of Sydney Dobell." Good Words,* 20: 1879.

Smith, Goldwin. "Review of *Maud*." *Saturday Review* (3 Nov. 1855): 14-15.

Smith, William H. "A Prosing upon Poetry," *Blackwood's Edinburgh Magazine* 46: (Aug. 1839): 200.

————. "Festus." *Blackwood's Edinburgh Magazine* 67: (April 1850) 416.

Southey, Robert. *Selections from the Letters of Robert Southey.* Ed. John Wood Warter. 4 vols. London, 1856.

Taylor, Henry. *Autobiography.* 2 vols. London, 1874.

————. Preface to *Philip Van Artevelde: A Dramatic Romance.* 2 vols. London, 1834.

Taylor, Isaac. *Natural History of Enthusiasm.* London, 1829.

Tennyson, Alfred, Lord. *The Works of Alfred Lord Tennyson.* Ed. Hallam Tennyson. 9 vols. London: Macmillan, 1908.

Tennyson, Charles. *Alfred Tennyson.* New York: MacMillan, 1949.

Tennyson, Hallam. *Alfred Lord Tennyson, A Memoir.* 2 vols. London, 1897.

Thale, Jerome. "Sydney Dobell: A Spasmodic Poet." Ph.D. diss., Northwestern U, 1953.

————. "Browning's 'Popularity' and the Spasmodic Poets." *The Journal of English and Germanic Philology* 54 (1955): 348-54.

Thompson, Fred C. "A Crisis in Early Victorian Drama: John Westland Marston and the Syncretics," *Victorian Studies 9* (June 1966): 378.

Vaughan, Robert A. "Festus, A Poem." *British Quarterly Review* 3: (May 1846): 387.

Weinstein, Mark A. *William Edmondstoune Aytoun and the Spasmodic Controversy.* New Haven and London: Yale UP, 1968.

Wilson, John. "The Christian Year" [John Keble] *Blackwood's Edinburgh Magazine.* 27 (June 1830): 835.

SELECTED REVIEWS

"The Roman." *The Athenaeum* (13 April 1850): 389-90.

"The Roman." *Bentley's Miscellany* 28 (1850) 65-66.

"*The Roman*. Criticism on Books" *The British Quarterly Review,* (August 1850): 295.

"*The Roman.*" *Chamber's Edinburgh Review* (21 September 1850): 187.

"*The Roman.*" *Chamber's Edinburgh Journal* 14 (1850): 187-189.

"*The Roman.*" *The Literary Gazette and Journal of Belle Lettres* (January 1851): 62-63.

"*The Roman.*" *Hogg's Instructor* 18 (1854): 268.

"*Balder Part the First.*" *The Athenaeum* (14 January 1854): 50.

"*Firmilian.*" *New Monthly Review* (Oct. 1854): 147.

"*Arnold's Poems.*" *Eclectic Review* (March 1855): 276-284.

"*Men and Women.*" *Athenaeum* (17 Nov. 1855): 1327-28.

"*Men and Women.*" *Saturday Review* (24 Nov. 1855): 69-70.

"*Browning's Men and Women.*" *Bentley's Miscellany* 39 (1856): 64-70.

"*England in Time of War.*" *The Spectator* (19 July 1856): 775.

"*England in Time of War.*" *The Saturday Review* (26 July 1856): 304-5.

"*England in Time of War.*" *Gentleman's Magazine* (Aug. 1856): 227.

"*England in Time of War.*" *The New Quarterly Review* 20 (1856): 420-423.

"Poems on the War," *The National Review* (6 Oct. 1856): 442-48.

"George Gilfillan's *History of A Man.*" *Fraser's Magazine* (Sept. 1856): 260-69

"*Festus* and Recent Poetry." *The Athenaeum* (1 April 1875): 465.

Jason R. Rudy (essay date winter 2004)

SOURCE: Rudy, Jason R. "Rhythmic Intimacy, Spasmodic Epistemology." *Victorian Poetry* 42, no. 4 (winter 2004): 451-72.

[*In the following essay, Rudy discusses the metrical irregularities of Dobell's poetry and explains Dobell's theories on poetic rhythm.*]

Among the many reasons critics in the 1850s condemned what was called the Spasmodic style, none appears to have perplexed and frustrated readers so much as the poets' seemingly irregular use of rhythm. In response to Sydney Dobell's 1856 volume **England in Time of War,** a critic for the *Saturday Review* complains that the poet "neither sees, feels, nor thinks like ordinary men. . . . Before we are half through the book, we begin to distrust the evidence of our senses."[1] A writer for the *National Review* similarly critiques the apparent disorder of Dobell's poetry: "His thoughts and fancies flow like the sounds from an instrument of music, struck by the hand of a child,—a jumble of sweet and disconnected notes, without order or harmony."[2] But Dobell and his Spasmodic compatriots were not alone in challenging the senses of their readers, and literary critics in the 1850s show increasing indignation and anxiety that any poet should "rel[y] on the sympathy of the interpreter" to intuit a poem's intended rhythmic design.[3] Writing of Robert Browning's *Men and Women,* a reviewer in the *Athenaeum* protests that recent poets

> have expected [the reader] here to lean on a cadence,—there to lend accent to the rhyme, or motion to the languid phrase; in another place, to condense a multitude of syllables, so as to give an effect of concrete strength. . . . Our poets now speak in an unknown tongue,—wear whatever unpoetic garniture it pleases their conceit or their idleness to snatch up; and the end too often is, pain to those who love them best, and who most appreciate their high gifts and real nobleness,—and to the vast world, whom they might assist, they bring only a mystery and receive nothing but wonder and scorn.
>
> (Chorley, p. 1327)

Though concerned with more than formal irregularity, the reviewer identifies his contemporaries' rhythmic waywardness as part and parcel of their poems' "unpoetic garniture," their difficult language, and, here in the case of Browning, the shocking images and figurative language. Many critics simply did not know how to read rhythmically irregular poetry, and they did not trust, or did not want to trust, to their intuition.[4]

The criticism perhaps would not have been as vehement had not Victorian readers associated the Spasmodics' unruly formal styles with Britain's own fragmented and increasingly heterogeneous culture. When a writer for *Putnam's Monthly Magazine,* an American journal, called Alexander Smith "a child of the time," the point was clear enough.[5] As other contributors to this special issue demonstrate, the Spasmodic poets were linked by their critics to cultural crises in gender and sexuality (Blair, Hughes), class and national identity (Tucker, Harrison, Boos), and religious practice (Mason, LaPorte). Perhaps most threatening were not the particular cultural values Spasmodic poetry seemed to defy, but the formal methods poets such as Smith and Dobell used to propagate these challenges to British readers. According to Sydney Dobell, the most sophisticated theorist of Spasmodic poetics, the self-conscious work of poetic interpretation matters little next to the unselfconscious effects of rhythm on the physical bodies of readers. As we shall see, Dobell's poetic theory holds that poetry transmits knowledge and feeling primarily through rhythm, rather than through words or other formal structures. Rhythm for Dobell expresses metonymically the physiological conditions of the human body—its pulses either harmonize with or strain against the throbbing of our physical beings—and poets communicate most readily through a reader's sympathetic and unmediated experience of these stressed and unstressed rhythmic impulses.[6] Physiologically felt rhythm creates an intimacy between poet and reader such that the reader shares in the physical, and sometimes even mental, experiences of the poet. Hence if Spasmodic poetry threatens Victorian cultural values by unseating conventional notions of gender, sexuality, class, nationality, and religion, Spasmodic poetics—and especially Dobell's notion of rhythm—threatens Victorian culture by promulgating these unconventional values, by offering a vehicle for the widespread dispersal of the eccentric. Indeed, for William Edmondstoune Aytoun, a firm Tory and the most vocal critic of the Spasmodic poets, metrical regularity enforces cultural stability as much as rhythmic spasms encourage much that is "wrong" with the times (which for Aytoun included new reform measures and the granting of rights to women).[7]

Dobell was well aware of this sort of critique, and in many ways his theory of poetry solicits such a response. Whereas Edmund Gosse would later dismiss Spasmodic poetry as "blustering blank verse," Dobell values bluster insofar as it enables poets to impress themselves more firmly upon readers' bodies and to forge intimate, affective links between poets and readers.[8] "Depend on it," Dobell writes to an aspiring poet, "whatever is to live on paper, must have lived in flesh and blood."[9] Physiological spasms reflect a "truth" of feeling, which the poet then publicizes for others to experience: "I have lived what I have sung," proclaims the poet Balder, "And it shall live."[10] In a profoundly democratizing gesture, poetry in the Spasmodic model seems no longer limited to an elite few, but directed instead to the human body and universal experiences. Looking beyond the threats to cultural stability that Aytoun would soon make synonymous with Spasmody, Arthur Hugh Clough in 1853 praised the "real flesh-and-blood heart and soul" of Spasmodic poetry insofar as it might speak to more than just those with "refined . . . and highly educated sensibilities." Whereas Matthew Arnold's poetry seems perhaps "too delicate . . . for common service," Smith's *A Life-Drama* radiates outward with language and feelings intelligible to all its readers.[11] George Henry Lewes writes with similar enthusiasm in an 1853 *Westminster Review* essay on Alexander Smith, declaring that the young poet's "eager senses have embraced the world" with "sensuousness of imagery, and directness of fervid expression."[12]

In what follows, I will focus on the work of Sydney Dobell to examine how such a universalized notion of feeling—a physiologically experienced feeling that embraces "the world"—translates into a poetic theory. We will look first to Dobell's poetic theories, then to the passionate rhythms of *Balder,* and finally to Dobell's last volume of poems, *England in Time of War* (1856). Of particular interest will be Dobell's development of poetic theory in response to contemporary advances in the physiological sciences, as well as hypotheses of social structure emerging at the time from theorists such as Comte, Herbert Spencer, and Lewes, all of whom looked regularly to physiology to substantiate their various theoretical claims. Far from being engaged in an isolated and anomalous endeavor, the Spasmodic poets in fact operated very much within the mainstream of mid-Victorian philosophy and social science. Dobell, in other words, had his finger on the pulse of Victorian thought in experimenting with what I will be calling rhythmic epistemology, the communication of knowledge and feeling through physiological pulses. And the initial popularity of his work indicates that, while controversial, his poetry struck a nerve in readers of the mid-Victorian period.

But first we would do well to interrogate more fully the term Victorian critics used to isolate Dobell's poetic theory and to disparage its practice. The word "spasmodic" never had an especially positive connotation. The British witnessed in the 1830s an epidemic known as "Spasmodic Cholera"; the disease was to strike again in 1853-54, the period of the Spasmodic literary crisis, killing 26,000.[13] In 1847 Jane Eyre feels Rochester's "spasmodic movement of fury or despair" when Richard Mason interrupts their marriage ceremony.[14] And Elizabeth Gaskell describes Ruth's "spasmodic effort" to tell the painful story of her son's illegitimate origins: "She at length, holding him away from her, and nerving herself up to tell him all by one spasmodic effort."[15] In her contribution to this volume, Kirstie Blair traces the use of the word through nineteenth-century medical discourse, showing its association with weakness and effeminacy. The OED defines "spasmodic" in terms roughly equivalent to those W. E. Aytoun used to characterize the Spasmodic poets: "Agitated, excited; emotional, highstrung; given to outbursts of excitement; characterized by a disjointed or unequal style of expression." But the OED's definition of "spasm" gets more to the uncontrollable nature to which the word refers, as it is used by Brontë and Gaskell: "Any sudden or convulsive movement of a violent character; a convulsion." This is also the sense of "spasmodic" as it is used by Darwin in *The Descent of Man* (1871):

> Animals of all kinds which habitually use their voices utter various noises under any strong emotion, as when enraged and preparing to fight; but this may merely be

the result of nervous excitement, which leads to the spasmodic contraction of almost all the muscles of the body, as when a man grinds his teeth and clenches his hands in rage or agony.[16]

When in 1854 W. E. Aytoun launched his attack on what he called, borrowing the term from Charles Kingsley, the "Spasmodic" school, he might have been surprised to know how accurately the term reflected Dobell's own theory of poetry. To Dobell, poetry necessarily originates in spasmodic—that is to say, uncontrollable and unpremeditated—vibrations of the human body. Dobell suggests as much in an 1857 lecture on the "Nature of Poetry" that he gave in Edinburgh, wherein he argues that poetry "is actually in tune with our material flesh and blood," that it relies on "certain modes of verbal *motion, . . .* certain *rhythms* and measures [that] are metaphors of ideas and feelings."[17] The most extreme examples of Spasmodic poetry seem to have been written with Dobell's theory in mind, as though conscious, formal analysis were to be cast aside in favor of one's own bodily response to poetry. It is in one's "material flesh and blood" that the reader will properly understand the Spasmodic poem, as the brain intuitively converts rhythmic impulses into knowledge, "ideas and feelings." It is through the spasmodic reaction of the human body to rhythm that the poetry will "live."

As I have already suggested, Dobell's understanding of rhythm develops in part from contemporary advances in the physiological sciences. In *The Senses and the Intellect* (1855), perhaps the most notable among the many physiological studies published in the decade, Alexander Bain argues for the dependence of thought on the physical experiences of the body. Bain, very much a part of the intellectual circle that included G. H. Lewes and Herbert Spencer, was among the first to insist that thought itself results from physical "currents" moving through the brain, a radical departure from the alternate theory of the time which envisioned the brain as "a *sanctum sanctorum,* or inner chamber, where impressions are poured in and stored up."[18] In Bain's model, the human body becomes a living organism that derives knowledge through subjective, physiological experience, rather than an objective container into which knowledge from the surrounding world is "stored." Over several hundred pages, Bain catalogues each of the five senses, and the processes by which encounters with the physical world inspire nerve transmissions, which transmissions ultimately constitute "the very essence of cerebral action" (p. 62). Our knowledge of the world, in other words, comes from the brain's interpretation of nerve impulses, a transformation of physical rhythmic patterns into conscious thought. Bain compares the nervous system to the newly developed technology of the electric telegraph:

> *The function of a nerve is to transmit impressions, influences, or stimuli, from one part of the system to*

another. . . . Hence the term *"conductor"* applies to the lines of nerve passing to and fro throughout the body. These are in their essential function telegraph wires; for although the force conveyed by a nerve differs from the force conveyed by a telegraphic wire, there is an absolute sameness in this, that the influence is generated at one spot and transmitted to another through an intermediate substance, which substance acts the carrier part solely.

(p. 38)

Like a telegraph clerk who comes to understand a message through the experience of long and short electrical impulses, or Morse code, the human brain encounters and comes to understand the surrounding world through the rhythmic impress of sensation on the physical body. Sound waves, for example, "enter the passage of the outer ear, and strike the membrane of the tympanum" (p. 199). The auditory nerve then "propagate[s] to the brain a different form of excitement according as the *beats* [received on the tympanum] are few or many," and according to "extremely minute differences of pitch [that] *impress themselves* discriminatively on the fibres" (p. 206; italics mine). The brain at last interprets these rhythmic variations and determines the nature of the sound. While not entirely a new concept—David Hartley had elaborated on "the vibrations which belong to ideas" as early as 1749—Bain yet establishes for his Victorian audience an epistemology of rhythm, a comprehensive physiology of the human body that locates in rhythmic experience the origin of all knowledge.[19]

Spasmodic poetics emerges out of such an insistently physical understanding of the human body and its experience of the world, an understanding located not only in Bain's study, but in a wide-ranging mid-Victorian discourse on physiology.[20] In this discourse, Spasmodic poets find justification for understanding rhythm—and the human body's physical experience of rhythm—as a foundation for thought: rhythmically inflected sound waves strike the ear, causing vibrations, which the brain converts to forms of knowledge, much as workers at the telegraph convert electric impulses into intelligible language. Sydney Dobell makes these connections explicit in his 1857 lecture, in which he describes poetic rhythm as "vibrations . . . propagated through matter" and concludes that we must expect "a *general* submission" of the human body to these physical principles of sound (*Thoughts,* pp. 23, 24). Dobell makes clear the origins of his rhythmic epistemology in referencing Sir Charles Wheatstone, co-inventor of the electric telegraph in Britain. Along with the German scientist Ernst Chladni and the French-born Felix Savart (both of whom conducted important experiments with sound waves in the early nineteenth century), Wheatstone, Bain writes, had "shown to what a wonderful extent vibrations . . . when once set in motion are repeated by sympathetic and other action in innumerable reflexes, each bearing computable relations to the original impulse" (*Thoughts*, p. 24). Dobell connects Wheatstone's model for rhythmic communication with the work of Bain and other physiological scientists, describing the successive stages of an individual's sensory encounter with the world. In Bain's model, information progresses from the physiological experience of the body to the processes of the mind. So too, argues Dobell, poetry moves through paths of *"rhythmic succession,"* such that the body experiences the "lower data" of poetic rhythm as a physical force, which is converted by the brain into "higher data," thoughts and ideas. The brain, in other words, converts the physical experience of rhythm into an intellectual construction of the poem and its meaning. In a powerfully assertive gesture of secularization, Dobell describes this process as "the word of Man made flesh and dwelling amongst us" (*Thoughts*, pp. 25, 26). Thus, like the telegraph, which seems through patterns of electric impulses to cancel the effects of physical distance among individuals, poetic rhythm conveys across time and space the physical impress of a speaking poet on a community of readers. Poetry comes to "dwell" intimately in the bodies of its readers, individuals who vibrate to the rhythm of stressed and unstressed syllables and who come to forms of knowledge through their rhythmic experiences.

With mixed results, Dobell explores the communicative potential of poetry with physiologically inspired rhythms. Here is an "evensong" from *Balder,* sung during one of the poem's few lighthearted moments, an idyllic interlude that interrupts what is otherwise an oppressive investigation into metaphysics and aesthetics (topics to which we shall turn momentarily). Balder sings, accompanying himself on a harp:

> The mavis sings upon the old oak tree
> Sweet and strong,
> Strong and sweet,
> Soft, sweet, and strong,
> And with his voice interpreteth the silence
> Of the dim vale when Philomel is mute!
> The dew lies like a light upon the grass,
> The cloud is as a swan upon the sky,
> The mist is as a brideweed on the moon.
> The shadows new and sweet
> Like maids unwonted in the dues of joy
> Play with the meadow flowers,
> And give with fearful fancies more and less,
> And come, and go, and flit
> A brief emotion in the moving air,
> And now are stirred to flight, and now are kind,
> Unset, uncertain, as the cheek of Love.

>   (*Balder* XXIII, pp. 123-124)

Dobell's rhythm consistently surprises as it leaps among pentameter, dimeter, and trimeter lines. Echoing Tennyson's "Short swallow-flights of song, that dip / Their wings in tears, and skim away," Balder's song is meant to "come, and go, and flit / A brief emotion in the mov-

ing air."[21] But unlike Tennyson's balanced tetrameter measures, Dobell's poem refuses a regular meter, and in fact seems to rely for its effects precisely on its irregularity. A Pindaric ode, perhaps, Balder's song may more appropriately be considered in light of Tennyson's nearly contemporaneous "Ode on the Death of the Duke of Wellington" (1852), which similarly abstains from strict metrical regularity. Like Dobell's *Balder,* Tennyson's Wellington ode was attacked by some as "disdaining all rules of rhythm and metre": "an intrinsically poor performance."[22] But as Dobell instructs us in his lecture, we are not meant to think consciously about such poems' formal designs, but rather to "submi[t]" to the spasms of the rhythmic "vibrations" and trust that some form of knowledge will come as a result.

We can intuit from Dobell's unpublished writings some of the poet's justification for believing so forcefully in rhythm. In an entry on the "Origin of Rhythm, Sleep, &c.," Dobell emphasizes the centrality of rhythmic experience to human life. Life, writes Dobell, "is a systole and diastole"; be it waking and sleeping, inhaling and exhaling, or any number of other reflexive actions, rhythmic patterns govern the human body (*Thoughts*, p. 128). Dobell hypothesizes that our sense of rhythm, art, and even language originates in our bodies through the various processes of "systole and diastole," through patterned experience, in part because these processes are common to all human beings. Like Bain, whose physiological study implicitly argues for a fundamental universality in human experience (Bain suggests for example that a pattern of "waxing and waning" sound "wakens up [in listening individuals] an intense current of emotion; in general, I believe, of a very solemnising kind" [p. 207]), Dobell believes that all individuals respond in a like manner to patterned phenomena. Bain, we know, takes his inspiration for such thinking from the *System of Logic* (1840) of his friend John Stuart Mill, which surmises that the "thoughts, feelings, and actions of human beings" might eventually be understood within a system of "general laws" from which "predictions [with respect to behavior and emotional response] may be founded"; Mill, that is, believes that scientists might in due time forecast— "though often not with complete accuracy"—the processes of human thought, feeling, and action.[23] If such predictions might be made by the scientist of human nature—or, to use Comte's neologism, by the sociologist—then the poet, in Dobell's view, might accurately predict how readers will respond to rhythmic patterns. Dobell writes in another unpublished essay, "Notes on the Relation of Language and Thought," that the poet uses sound to recreate "sense"

> by producing the same state of mind as the thing represented would produce—and this is done in various ways—by sounds that have essential connection with certain attitudes of mind, or by sounds that, by *suggesting certain acts of the organs of utterance,* influence

the feelings, or by *rhythm* that, through various laws, affects the whole human system.

(Thoughts, p. 138)

The poet, then, is something of a scientist of human nature, crafting verses to elicit through physiological association patterns of universal thought and feeling. We as readers can only intuit the intended effect of Balder's evensong as we read the poem, experience its various rhythmic cadences, and note our unselfconscious passionate responses.

Curiously enough, however, the chief point of **Balder** seems not to experiment with rhythmic variation and physiological association, but rather to suggest the potential dangers of such poetic handiwork. And though large passages of the poem engage with rhythmic experimentation, it must be said that most of **Balder** progresses as lines of regular iambic pentameter. Rather than indulging uncritically in rhythmic hedonism, then, Dobell's poem speculates primarily on the hazards of rhythm understood as a physiological effect. Says Balder, meditating on a poem he hopes to compose,

> This hot breast
> Seems valley deep, and what the wind of Fate
> Strikes on that harp strung there to bursting, I,
> Descending, mean to catch as one unmoved
> In stern notation.

(XVII, p. 70)

Balder here imagines himself an aeolian harp set to vibrate and transmit song originating in his own "hot breast." Balder means to capture his own passionate vibrations and to convert them into "stern notation," language and rhythm, so that he might broadcast them telegraphically to the world at large. He later develops this notion, referring to himself as the "Bard of the future! Master-Prophet! Man / Of Men, at whose strong girdle hang the keys / Of all things!" (XXIV, p. 161). Such exaggerated Carlylean aspirations turn gruesome when one learns that Balder gives his speech immediately after having murdered his own daughter, whom he kills specifically so that in "los[ing] / What nothing can restore" (XVI, p. 66) he might be more intensely moved to feeling, and hence to compose poetry more intensely resonant with passion:

> I rise up childless, but no less
> Than I. There was one bolt in all the heavens
> Which falling on my head had with a touch
> Rent me in twain. This bursting water-spout
> Hath left me whole, but naked.

(XVI, p. 69)

Dobell was sympathetic to Balder's ideal of the poet as a telegraph-like aeolian harp. But his connection of this ideal to infanticide indicates no small degree of uncertainty in the telegraphic process.[24] **Balder** quickly

degenerates into farce if one takes seriously, for example, the electric "bolt" meant to set the poet's composition flowing like a "bursting water-spout" (a parody, no doubt, of Wordsworthian spontaneous overflow). It is thus in the extremes of Balder's aspirations that we can read most clearly Dobell's critique of his own theory of poetry. Balder is self-absorbed, self-pitying, and immoral, and "Balderism," writes Dobell in a defensive preface to the poem's second edition, "is a predominant intellectual misfortune of our day."[25]

Perhaps Balder does not represent the necessary result of rhythmic spasms, but his actions suggest at least one appalling misuse of Dobell's poetic theory. The challenge, it would seem, is to communicate spasmodic rhythm without degenerating into self-absorption and morbidity (terms Victorian critics commonly used to describe Dobell's poem). **Balder** returns consistently to this problem in an anxious inquiry into the physical nature of thought and feeling. Balder speaks for both Dobell and his age when remarking that

> our heart-strings over-strung
> Scare us with strange *involuntary* notes
> Quivering and quaking.

(XIV, p. 61; italics mine)

Or again, in a revelry at once ecstatic and anxiety-ridden,

> I know the wind!
> The utter world doth touch me! I can grasp
> The hands that stretch forth from the mystery
> That passeth! I am crowded with my life!
> It is too much! the vital march doth stop
> To press about me!

(XXIV, p. 134)

And near the end of the poem, as Balder considers murdering his wife (whose grief for her murdered daughter and escalating madness distract Balder from his composition), he laments,

> The dark excess
> That for so many days o'er-loaded all
> My swollen veins, strangled each vital service,
> And pressing hard the incommoded soul
> In its unyielding tenement *convulsed*
> The wholesome work of nature

(XXXIX, pp. 255-256; italics mine)

In each passage, Balder considers the dangers of sensory overload, the intense impress of sensation on his physical and psychological being. He is horrified at the "involuntary" nature of these impulses, feeling "crowded" by sensation that ultimately "convulse[s]" from out of him, an uncontrolled—that is to say, spasmodic—physiological excretion (a metaphor to which we shall return shortly). Physical and metaphysi-

175

cal collapse upon one another in Balder's language, as the boundaries between mind and body, "swollen vein" and "incommoded soul," seem less and less distinct. Balder's whole being, an "unyielding tenement," writhes to convulsions inspired by "dark excess," grief and self-loathing. These convulsions are reflected in the haphazard rhythms of his lines, themselves a seemingly Spasmodic overflow of powerful feeling—feeling clearly not recollected in tranquility, but convulsed from within onto the written page. Rhythm here becomes a metonymic extension of the writing poet at the moment of his tortured composition.

Balder offers its readers little objective distance from its passionate subjectivity. As in dramatic monologues such as **"Porphyria's Lover"** (1836), we intuit a critical attitude toward the poem's speaker only through the speaker's own excesses.[26] And yet there are, upon close examination, moments of critical self-reflection in *Balder,* moments when Balder himself seems to consider the ill effects of his own poetic style. One of the most remarkable of these instances appears early in Balder's musings. He has been thinking in his study, as he is wont to do—indeed, almost the whole of the poem transpires in Balder's study—when a group of sailors pass by below his window, singing a "chant of Freedom" (IX, p. 46). The song inspires Balder to reflect on what he considers freedom's opposite, tyranny. "Lo Tyranny!" he begins, and then envisages the progress of tyranny personified, a figure of excrement making his way across the landscape:

> thro' gurgling weight
> Of seething full corruption night and day
> His craving bowels, famished in his fill,
> Bellowed for more. Which, when the creature heard
> That bore him, dread, like a great shock of life,
> Convulsed it, and the myriad frantic hands,
> Sprang like the dances of a madman's dream.
> And so he came; and o'er his head a sweat
> Hung like a sulphurous vapour, and beneath
> Fetid and thunderous as from belching hell,
> The hot and hideous torrent of his dung
> Roared down explosive, and the earth, befouled
> And blackened by the stercorous pestilence,
> Wasted below him, and where'er he passed
> The people stank.

(IX, pp. 47-48)

Balder's idea of a tyranny that spews its infectious waste upon all those it passes seems in many ways a self-reflexive critique of his own Spasmodic style. Dobell—and Balder himself, it seems—would have agreed with W. E. Aytoun's comparison of his poem to "a beer-bottle voiding its cork, and spontaneously ejecting its contents right and left."[27] Dobell's self-reflexivity seems especially apparent given the preceding sailors' song on Freedom, a tale of naval victory told in a fairly regular metrical style:

> "See yon ugly craft
> With the pennon at her main!
> Hurrah, my merry boys,
> There goes the Betsy Jane!"

(IX, p. 45)

Freedom, associated here with the bravery of the British navy, is also a simple, ballad-like narrative, a tale sung without internal reflection or metaphysical anxiety. Thus the "hot and hideous torrent" of tyranny's progress strikes an image "contrary" (IX, p. 46) to freedom's song both thematically and formally. Tyranny as Balder imagines it convulses in a violently abject projection of rhythmic impulses, whereas freedom performs a rhythmically predictable chorus, a key perhaps to reading *Balder* as a critique of its own Spasmodic style. Dobell's point is not of course that Spasmodic rhythm necessarily resembles a "torrent of . . . dung," but rather that the possibility always exists, that the "corruption" of Spasmodic excess (which, ironically, so much of *Balder* exemplifies) must be carefully avoided.

In direct contrast to tyranny's corrupting torrent, Dobell in a posthumously published essay on "Beauty, Love, Order, Unity" emphasizes the value of "the *harmony* of rhythmic *parts*" (*Thoughts,* p. 113). "Love," Dobell suggests, is a "passion toward unity," an effort to attain rhythmic harmony. Tyranny, on the other hand, might be construed as a passion toward disunity, the making of perpetual chaos. In *Balder,* then, freedom expresses itself with rhythmic predictability, as that which has already achieved formal harmony, whereas tyranny is a cacophony of sound. Dobell had meant *Balder* (subtitled "Part the First") to be a three-part progress "from Doubt to Faith, from Chaos to Order" (*Works,* 2:3-4), but for reasons unknown, though probably connected with the critical sacking of the first part, Dobell never wrote the second two volumes of his poem. Within the overarching project of *Balder,* then, the second and third parts would have realized the order and unity that come of the poet's intense struggles. Balder's spasmodic bellowing would eventually have indicated his personal struggle against tyranny and toward freedom. The negative possibilities in physiological rhythm would have been overcome, and the poet would have reveled in Spasmodic impulses freed from the tyranny of introspection and morbidity.

This of course never happens in *Balder,* but it is I believe one way of reading the trajectory of Dobell's post-*Balder* publications. Dobell published only two volumes of poetry after *Balder.* The first, *Sonnets on the War* (1855), was a collaboration with fellow Spasmodic poet Alexander Smith; the second, *England in Time of War* (1856), features Dobell's personal response to the Crimean struggle. The poems in the second volume indicate more clearly than his earlier efforts Dobell's program for embodying passionate thought and feeling in rhythmic impulses. The poems take the perspective of various individuals touched by the war: a woman awaiting the return of her son; an estranged lover; a sailor returning from battle. Periods of metrical regularity alternate with highly irregular passages that enlist repetition, assonance, and rhythmic stresses to produce in the reader a somatic response resonant with the scene described. In this, his final published volume of poetry, we see Dobell at last employing rhythm as a decisive vehicle for expression. For example, **"An Evening Dream"** recalls a British charge into battle:

> Clarion and clarion defying,
> Sounding, resounding, replying,
> Trumpets braying, pipers playing, chargers neighing,
> Near and far
> The to and fro storm of the never-done hurrahing,
> Thro' the bright weather banner and feather rising and
>   falling, bugle and fife
> Calling, recalling—for death or for life—
> Our host moved on to the war,
> While England, England, England, England, England!
> Was blown from line to line near and far,
> And like the morning sea, our bayonets you might
>   see,
> Come beaming, gleaming, streaming,
> Streaming, gleaming, beaming,
> Beaming, gleaming, streaming, to the war.
>
> (***Works,*** 1:323)

The passage alternates in speed, from the light-footed "Trumpets braying, pipers playing, chargers neighing," to the ponderous repetitions of "England," which seem ultimately not indicative of patriotism but rather only a line of pressing trochees, a leaning in and a retreating "to and fro." We are, indeed, like the lines of British soldiers, "blown . . . near and far" by the poem's rhythmic cadences. We also find ourselves in the midst of a confusing melée of sounds, words difficult to distinguish from one another both in meaning and sound: "Streaming, gleaming, beaming." We feel, through the rhythm and the sound of the words, something physically and conceptually of the rushed confusion of a battle charge, "line to line" (and these words make explicit the congruence between the lines of soldiers and lines of Dobell's poem). The affective experience here comes remarkably not through the literal definitions of the words themselves, but rather through the impress of rhythm and sound on the reader of the poem. These are the "certain modes of verbal *motion*" that Dobell advocates in his 1857 lecture, "certain *rhythms* and measures [that] are metaphors of ideas and feelings."

It is not necessary to call this great poetry to see the daring of its experimentation. Dobell's goal, essentially, is to capture in language the chaotic motions of the human mind, and thus to transmit to his readers the actual, felt experience he describes. To do this requires getting beyond words to the inner ideas and feelings words are

meant to conjure.[28] "We are all irretrievably word-struck," he writes sometime around 1850 (*LL* [*The Life and Letters of Sydney Dobell*] 1:161)

> We are too apt to confound words with language. Are not visible images or the ideas of them the only language in the highest sense? Words are the outward noises by which we recall the inward shape. . . . To reason by ideas, to compare ideas with ideas, to speak from the first-hand idea, to call up in the hearer a picture, not a sentence, should be our great aim.
>
> (*LL* 1:155, 162)

Dobell says much the same in his 1857 lecture: "Words rhythmically combined affect the feelings of the poetic hearer or utterer in the same way as the fact they represent: and thus by a reflex action the fact is reproduced in the imagination" (*Thoughts,* pp. 36-37). This is the governing project of **"An Evening Dream,"** in which rhythmic impulses ultimately supersede the poem's words. Dobell maximizes the rhythmic effects of the concluding battle charge, quoted above, by opening the poem with fairly regulated fourteener couplets:

> I'm leaning where you loved to lean in eventides of
>   old,
> The sun has sunk an hour ago behind the treeless
>   wold,
> In this old oriel that we loved how oft I sit forlorn,
> Gazing, gazing, up the vale of green and waving corn.
>
> (***Works,*** 1:315)

Dobell's image of physical "leaning" underscores the physiological press of rhythm, the measured lines that gradually break apart and become increasingly irregular as the speaker's dream moves from "the treeless wold" to a scene of invasion by the Russian army. It is precisely at the point of the invasion, a "flood that swelled from some embowelled mount of woe" that Dobell most clearly breaks from metrical regularity (and note again in "emboweled" the excremental trope, which Dobell consistently links to rhythmic spasm):

> Waveless, foamless, sure and slow,
> Silent o'er the vale below,
> Till nigher still and nigher comes the seeth [*sic*] of
>   fields on fire,
> And the thrash of falling tress, and the steam of rivers
>   dry,
> And before the burning flood the wild things of the
>   wood
>   Skulk and scream, and fight, and fall, and flee,
>   and fly.
>
> (p. 318)

The confusion climaxes in the British charge, the "to and fro storm . . . blown from line to line," during which the metrical structure modulates freely, in the style of an ode, to maximize the physiological impact of rhythmic play.

One might highlight the effect of Dobell's dissolution of rhythmic consistency by reading **"An Evening Dream"** alongside Tennyson's nearly contemporaneous "Charge of the Light Brigade" (first published December 9, 1854). Even Charles Kingsley, generally a great admirer of the poet laureate, suggests that "the dactyl is surely too smooth and cheerful a foot to form the basis of such a lyric."[29] But perhaps what makes the poem appear disturbingly "smooth and cheerful" is not so much Tennyson's use of dactyls, but rather the unwavering consistency of the rhythm. More than most poets, Dobell understood the psychological and physiological effects of rhythmic inconsistency. In a letter of December 1855, Dobell writes that

> anyone who would wholly understand any of my poetry . . . must read it with the mind of a musician. I don't mean that it is *musical,* in the common sense, but that it is written on the principles of music, *i.e.* as a series of combinations that shall produce certain *states* in the hearer, and not a succession of words which he is separately to "intellectuate" by the dictionary.

(LL, 1:447)

Certainly **"An Evening Dream"** makes the most of this "musical" understanding of poetry, a movement away from words ordered metrically and toward an enactment of rhythmic epistemology, or physiological states of embodied, rhythmic passion. Dobell's poetry attempts to offer not intellectual reflection but unselfconscious, passionate experience.

Many of Dobell's contemporaries shared the poet's interest in physiology and the unselfconscious work of rhythm on the human body. Herbert Spencer's 1857 essay on "The Origin and Function of Music," for example, argues—like Dobell's lecture on poetry from the very same year—that "there is a direct connection between feeling and motion."[30] This connection, Spencer claims, is both "innate" and inexplicable: "Why the actions excited by strong feeling should tend to become rhythmical, is not very obvious; but that they do so there are divers evidences" (pp. 220, 223). If unsure of why rhythm and feeling reflect one another, Spencer is quite clear on the implications of this connection. Along with tonal modulations of voice (and the essay, I should emphasize, is primarily on the effects of music and not specifically poetry), rhythm enables other individuals "not only to *understand* the state of mind" that inspired a composition, "but to *partake* of that state" (p. 235). Such participation, writes Spencer, is "the chief med[ium] of *sympathy*" (p. 236), the glue to hold together an increasingly complex and atomized social structure.[31]

Spencer's essay helps to explain why his close friend George Henry Lewes found Alexander Smith so compelling as a poet: "His eager senses," Lewes had written in 1853, "have embraced the world." Lewes' only criticism for Smith is that he should "deepen and extend the nature of his passion, making it the flaming utterance of his *whole* being, sensuous, moral, and intellectual" ("Poems of Alexander Smith," p. 524). Such a fully corporeal and, simultaneously, intellectual project relies on the spasmodic imbrication of body and mind, rhythm and thought. In his later writings on physiology, Lewes would propose that "all our knowledge *springs from,* and is *limited by,* Feeling."[32] For Lewes, any comprehension of objective nature comes necessarily through the individual human body; "subjective" bodily passions *lead to* "objective" knowledge, and each individual's subjective experience of passionate sensation puts him in touch with, or at least opens the door to, objectivity. This necessarily subjective approach to objective knowledge is, for Lewes, the only way the world may be apprehended. Lewes values Smith because in his view the poet's "embrace . . . [of] the world" demonstrates the potential for both a universal, objective synthesis of subjective knowledge and feeling and, through such a synthesis, the reinvigoration of sympathetic human relations.[33]

George Eliot too had much to say about the consequences of feeling in poetic thought. Through her regular and anonymous contributions to the "Belles Lettres" section of the *Westminster Review,* Eliot was an active and little-acknowledged participant in the poetic debates emerging out of the Spasmodic controversy. Eliot by and large shared Lewes' ideal of knowledge springing from feeling, and in an essay from January 1857, she criticizes the eighteenth-century poet Edward Young precisely for his "disruption of language from genuine thought and feeling."[34] Later in the same issue of the *Westminster,* Eliot praises Elizabeth Barrett Browning's *Aurora Leigh* for accomplishing what Young so miserably fails at, the perfect melding of "what we may call [her poem's] poetical *body*" with "genuine thought and feeling": in *Aurora Leigh* "there is simply a *full mind pouring itself out in song as its natural and easiest medium.*"[35] It should come as no surprise, given this praise for Barrett Browning, that Eliot could not help but be swayed in part by the work of the Spasmodic poets. She insists in a brief review of Dobell's **England in Time of War** that she is "not [an] enthusiastic admirer . . . either of Mr. Dobell or of the school of poetry to which he belongs," and yet she admits her appreciation for his occasional "passage[s] of simple pathos, [and] exquisite rhythmic melody laden with fresh and felicitous thought."[36] Eliot here intuits (before Dobell had publicized his rhythmic theory) that rhythm and thought in the 1856 volume are to be understood as one and the same; it is Dobell's rhythm, she writes, that bears his thought.

What these various reviews gesture at is how, within a particular school of thought, Dobell's views on poetry must be seen as entirely commonplace. Dobell's rhythmic epistemology does not spring *sui generis* out of the poet's rabid imagination, but from an important body of mid-century scientific and philosophical thought. It is in part for its not being anomalous that Dobell's Spasmodism seems dangerous to his critics (the mutterings of a madman might more easily have been dismissed). The forty years between Arthur Hallam's 1831 review of Tennyson's poetry of "sensation" and Robert Buchanan's 1871 attack on Dante Rossetti and the "fleshly" school witnessed a concentrated inquiry into the physiological nature of poetic experience. It is no coincidence that Dobell's poetry, and the Spasmodic movement more broadly considered, falls at the mid-point of this inquiry. Following in the empiricist tradition of Locke, Hartley, and Hume, Hallam argues that "sound conveys . . . meaning where words would not"; Buchanan opens his screed against Rossetti deploring those who "aver that poetic expression is greater than poetic thought."[37] Both critics here address essentially the same point, though from opposite argumentative positions; that is, reading poetry in the mid-Victorian period seems no longer an intellectual endeavor, but a full-bodied, spasmodic experience. Dobell's poetic theory, characterized most often (when characterized at all) as an abnormality, should be seen instead as the epicenter of a widespread literary movement entirely resonant with the mid-Victorian intellectual climate.

And yet it was a movement in which Dobell himself, as we have seen, lacked a certain degree of confidence. Dobell stresses that a poet can never know, really, the effect his rhythmic utterances will have on readers of his poem. He may only surmise, as Mill asserts in his *Logic,* "how the great *majority* of the human race, or of some nation or class of persons, will think, feel, and act" (*Works,* 8:847; italics mine). Insofar as poetry is a "carrying out and efflorescence of a human soul, according *to its own laws*" (*Thoughts,* p. 64), the poet can only hope that those personal laws will translate into universal ones. Thus if poetic rhythms resemble the long and short impulses of Morse code, they form a language only some will be able to read, and that perhaps many will misread and others entirely fail to read, as if readers of poetry were each to hold a unique code book for the incoming patterns of stressed and unstressed syllables. The critics had a point when they grumbled over having "here to lean on a cadence,—there to lend accent to the rhyme." *Balder* repeatedly calls attention to moments when rhythm necessarily fails to communicate, most notably in what has become a signal moment of Spasmodic excess, Balder's thirteen repetitions of "ah!" (*Balder* XXXVIII, p. 250). These lines scan equally well as iambs or trochees, anapests alternating with pyrrhics or solid runs of spondees; any attempt at scansion necessarily resorts to guesswork, and this seems to be Dobell's point precisely. Each

reader will determine his or her own rhythmic pattern for the line, thereby rendering moot the possibility of it bearing a predetermined form of knowledge or feeling. At a certain point, then, the analogy between rhythm and the electric telegraph breaks down, as does the notion of interpersonal intimacy facilitated by poetic rhythm. Much as Dobell wants to align his rhythmic epistemology with the scientific work of Alexander Bain, Sir Charles Wheatstone, Ernst Chladni, and Felix Savart, the play of rhythm on individual human bodies seems in the end too variable for consistent objective analysis.

And it was consistency, of course, that many of the critics writing against Spasmodic poetics most desired. Edmund Gosse, for example, writes in 1877 of the need to make "immortal art out of transient feeling," and to accomplish this by "chisel[ing] material beauty out of passing thoughts and emotions." Gosse assumes here, in language entirely familiar to readers of Dobell, that "transient feeling" might be captured in poetic form. But to do this, Gosse continues, requires "dismiss[ing] . . . purely spontaneous and untutored expression" such as that of the Spasmodics, and focusing instead on universally appreciated feelings and forms (Gosse, p. 53). In a similar vein, Coventry Patmore, whose 1857 *Essay on English Metrical Law* was in large part a response against Spasmodic poetics, writes that poetry "is truth or fact . . . expressed so as to affect the feelings." For Patmore, it is precisely because poets access the realm of feeling that they must so carefully restrain themselves through form: "The free spirit of art, in its noblest developments," he concludes, "has ever been obtained, not by neglect, but by perfection of discipline."[38] These claims are not terribly distinct from Dobell's own insistence that beauty is "the *harmony* of rhythmic *parts*" and that love is a "passion toward unity." The question, as Dobell puts it in a letter to his future father-in-law, is not *whether* to restrain passionate experience, but "*what* is the proper restraint." Though Dobell here is not writing specifically about poetry, his thoughts reflect the complex negotiations of rhythm and form later played out in his poetry: "I must express my perfect agreement with your assertion that the *proper* regulation of the passions is the mark of difference between a wise and a foolish man, or rather as I should more harshly term it, between a wicked and a righteous one" (*LL,* 1:39). Dobell clearly believes in regulating the physiological experience of rhythm, but only in extreme circumstances; even Balder must rage in order that he might (in the unwritten sequels to Dobell's first volume) ultimately achieve "unity" and "harmony." Patmore and Aytoun, on the other hand, could not abide such liberty; their aesthetic, cultural, and political views require the constant maintenance of strict form. And Dobell's notion of restraint in art ultimately rejects any semblance of Patmore and Aytoun's formalism: "All art that is the application of principles," he writes in an essay on Charlotte Brontë, "smacks not of the artist, but the artisan." Dobell praises Brontë for her "*Instinctive* art; for to the imaginative writer, all art that is not instinctive is dangerous" (*LL,* 1:173).

By 1877, Gosse believed Spasmodic poetics to have been rendered impotent. He writes of poets such as William Morris and Dante Gabriel Rossetti reinvigorating formal structures, returning technical dexterity to the fore of poetic composition:

> The actual movement of the time, then, appears certainly to be in the direction of increased variety of richness of rhyme, elasticity of verse, and *strength of form.* The invertebrate rhapsodies of Sydney Dobell, so amazing in their beauty of detail and total absence of style, are now impossible. We may lack his inspiration and his insight, but we understand far better than he the workmanship of the art of verse.
>
> (Gosse, p. 55; italics mine)

To the contrary, however, the return to form that Gosse heralds carries with it unmistakable traces of Dobell's Spasmodic epistemology, the belief that rhythm—when properly composed—transmits knowledge and feeling with even more ease, in many cases, than words on a page. The stressed systems of Hopkins' poetry, for example, would be hard to imagine without the Spasmodic experiments of the 1850s, and the passionate variability of Whitman's rhythms—thought by Gosse and others to embody the Spasmodic sensibility—builds unmistakably on Dobell, Smith, and their compatriots (Whitman in fact was reading Smith's 1853 volume as he prepared the first edition of *Leaves of Grass* [1855]).[39] Poets such as Christina Rossetti, Swinburne, and innumerable others insist for the most part on formal regularity, and yet also admit to and cultivate a belief in the communicative power of rhythmic variability. Their poetry, like so much of the poetry composed in the post-Spasmodic years, negotiates anxiously between the formal regularity of Aytoun and Patmore and what the poet Mathilde Blind, following Dobell, considered the "primal and universal in the fate and feelings of man."[40] Sydney Dobell's "invertebrate rhapsodies" echo persistently and with surprising strength through the late Victorian period, much as in the 1850s they helped determine the foremost poetic questions of the day.

Notes

I am grateful for the many comments and suggestions I have received while working on this project. I thank especially Carolyn Williams, Virginia Jackson, Barry V. Qualls, Yopie Prins, Jonah Siegel, Herbert Tucker, Emma Mason, Linda K. Hughes, and Charles LaPorte.

1. [Anonymous], review of *England in Time of War,* by Sydney Dobell, *Saturday Review* 2 (1856): 304.

2. [Anonymous], "Sydney Dobell's Poems on the War," *National Review* 3 (1856): 442.

3. [Henry Fothergill Chorley], review of Robert Browning, *Men and Women, Athenæum* 1464 (November 17, 1855): 1327.

4. This is not always the case, of course. George Eliot, writing anonymously in the *Westminster Review,* finds in *Men and Women* "freshness, originality," and the feeling that "what we took for obscurity in [Browning] was superficiality in ourselves" ("Belles Lettres," *Westminster Review* 65 [January, 1856]: 290, 291). On Browning's relation to the Spasmodics, see Antony H. Harrison, *Victorian Poets and Romantic Poems: Intertextuality and Ideology* (Charlottesville: Univ. Press of Virginia, 1990), pp. 44-68; and Mark A. Weinstein, *William Edmondstoune Aytoun and the Spasmodic Controversy* (New Haven: Yale Univ. Press, 1968), pp. 183-187.

5. [Anonymous], "The Poems of Alexander Smith," *Putnam's Monthly Magazine* 2 (July 1853): 99.

6. The argument retains its strength, as Derek Attridge recently suggests: "I don't think it's possible to discuss rhythm without relating it to the movements of the human body" ("Rhythm in English Poetry," *NLH* [*New Literary History*] 21 [Autumn 1990]: 1022). See also Richard Cureton, *Rhythmic Phrasing in English Verse* (New York: Longman, 1991).

7. See my discussion of Aytoun and the cultural work of poetic form in "On Cultural Neoformalism, Spasmodic Poetry, and the Victorian Ballad," *VP* [*Victorian Poetry*] 41 (Winter 2003; special issue, ed. Linda K. Hughes, "Whither Victorian Poetry?"): 590-596. For Aytoun's political arguments, see especially "The Reform Measures of 1852" (*Blackwood's* 71 [March 1852]: 369-386), "The New Reform Bill" (*Blackwood's* 75 [March 1854]: 369-380), and "The Rights of Women" (*Blackwood's* 92 [August 1862]: 183-201).

8. Edmund Gosse, "A Plea for Certain Exotic Forms of Verse," *Cornhill Magazine* 36 (1877): 54.

9. Quoted in E[mily] J[olly], ed., *The Life and Letters of Sydney Dobell,* 2 vols. (London, 1878), 1:292. Hereafter cited as *LL.*

10. Sydney Dobell, *Balder Part the First* (London, 1854), Scene 3, p. 19. Hereafter cited by scene and page number.

11. [Arthur Hugh Clough], "Recent English Poetry" *North American Review* 77 (1853): 6, 12.

12. [George Henry Lewes], "Poems of Alexander Smith." *Westminster Review* 59 (April 1853): 523-524; emphases mine.

13. A. N. Wilson, *The Victorians* (New York and London: Norton, 2003), p. 36. For a contemporary history of the disease, see Michael Durey, *The First Spasmodic Cholera Epidemic in York, 1832* (York: St. Anthony's Press, 1974).

14. Charlotte Brontë, *Jane Eyre* (1847; Peterborough, Ontario: Broadview, 2000), p. 378.

15. Elizabeth Gaskell, *Ruth* (1853; New York: Penguin, 1997), p. 281.

16. Charles Darwin, *The Descent of Man, and Selection in Relation to Sex* (1871; Princeton: Princeton Univ. Press, 1981), 2:275.

17. Sydney Dobell, *Thoughts on Art, Philosophy and Religion* (London, 1876), pp. 22, 25.

18. Alexander Bain, *The Senses and the Intellect* (London, 1855), p. 61.

19. David Hartley, *Hartley's Theory of the Human Mind* (London, 1775), p. 25.

20. Physiology figures prominently in several studies of Victorian fiction; poetry, though more central to mid-Victorian thinking on physiological experience, figures less frequently in recent literary accounts of the period. Some examples include Barbara Hardy, *Forms of Feeling in Victorian Fiction* (London: Peter Owen, 1985); Peter Melville Logan, *Nerves and Narratives: A Cultural History of Hysteria in 19th-Century British Prose* (Berkeley: Univ. of California Press, 1997); Gesa Stedman, *Stemming the Torrent: Expression and Control in the Victorian Discourses on Emotions, 1830-1872* (Burlington, Vermont: Ashgate, 2002); Janet Wood, *Passion and Pathology in Victorian Fiction* (New York: Oxford Univ. Press, 1991).

21. Alfred Tennyson, *In Memoriam,* sec. 48, in *The Poems of Tennyson,* 3 vols., ed. Christopher Ricks (Berkeley: Univ. of California Press, 1987), 2:366.

22. See Edgar F. Shannon, Jr., "The History of A Poem: Tennyson's *Ode on the Death of the Duke of Wellington,*" *SB* [*Studies in Bibliography*] 13 (1960): 155-156. My thanks to Herbert Tucker for pointing out the structural parallels between Dobell and Tennyson.

23. John Stuart Mill, *Collected Works,* ed. John M. Robson and Jack Stillinger (Toronto: Univ. of Toronto Press, 1981), 8:846, 845. For the impact of Mill's science of human nature on Victorian thought, see Diana Postlethwaite's section on "Universal Causation" in *Making It Whole: A Victorian Circle and the Shape of Their World* (Columbus: Ohio State Univ. Press, 1984), pp. 25-39.

24. In his contribution to this volume, Herbert Tucker argues that Balder may not, in fact, murder his daughter. Whatever the case, Dobell connects the idea of infanticide—real or imagined—to an extreme poetic sensationalism.

25. Sydney Dobell, *The Poetical Works of Sydney Dobell,* 2 vols. (London, 1876), 2:5.

26. On "unnatural [emotional] intensity" in Victorian dramatic monologues, see Robert Langbaum, *The Poetry of Experience: The Dramatic Monologue in Modern Literary Tradition* (New York: Norton, 1963), esp. pp. 88-89.

27. [W. E. Aytoun], "Firmilian: A Tragedy," *Blackwood's* 75 (May 1854): 534.

28. Dobell himself seems to have experienced the world in much the same Spasmodic fashion his verses attempt to embody. On traveling through the Welsh mountains by train, for example, he "sat speechless the whole way. All my brain made chaos, heaving over and over. Too great for tears or any quick emotions" (letter to his parents, August 7, 1850 [*LL,* 1:120]). Dobell was also ill through much of his life, suffering from what his father described in 1844 as a "spasmodic action of the heart" (*LL,* 1:99).

29. [Charles Kingsley], "Tennyson's Maud," *Fraser's* 52 (September 1855): 272.

30. Herbert Spencer, "The Origin and Function of Music," *Fraser's* (October 1857); repr. in Spencer, *Essays: Scientific, Political, and Speculative* (London, 1868), p. 213.

31. Victorian intellectuals agreed for the most part that passionate experience, though dangerous, was a necessary component of great art. Arthur Hallam, for example, writes glowingly in 1831 of what he calls the "poets of sensation," while yet cautioning of the "danger" in "linger[ing] with fond attachment in the vicinity of sense" ("On Some of the Characteristics of Modern Poetry," *Englishman's Magazine* 1 [August 1831]: 616-628; repr. in *Victorian Scrutinies: Reviews of Poetry 1830-1870,* ed. Isobel Armstrong [London: Athlone Press, 1972], pp. 87, 88). Mill, too, writes that the greatest of poets write "under the overruling influence of some one state of feeling"—and then warns against "stretching and straining; for strength, as Thomas Carlyle says, does not manifest itself in spasms" ("Thoughts on Poetry and Its Varieties" [1833], *Collected Works,* 1:360, 353).

32. George Henry Lewes, *Problems of Life and Mind* II. *The Physical Basis of the Mind* (London, 1877), p. 311.

33. George Levine has recently argued that "the question of how to universalize knowledge, lift it from *mere* contingency and singularity, pervades almost

all nineteenth-century thought about how we know. Raw fact is not knowledge at all" (*Dying to Know: Scientific Epistemology and Narrative in Victorian England* [Chicago: Univ. of Chicago Press, 2002], p. 68). This is most definitely what is at stake for Lewes, who was a key figure in a circle of Victorian thinkers dedicated, to borrow the title of Diana Postlethwaite's excellent book on the subject, to "making it whole"—that is, to finding proof of the universe's manifold unity, and to discerning truth within that unity. Postlethwaite writes that throughout the 1850s, the project for Lewes and his friend Herbert Spencer was to determine "the unity of composition and the multiplicity of adaptation; in man, the animal kingdom, organic creation, and, in a grand progressive synthesis, the cosmos itself" (*Making It Whole,* p. 191). For Lewes' contributions to Victorian thought, see also Peter Allan Dale, *In Pursuit of a Scientific Culture* (Madison: Univ. of Wisconsin Press, 1989), esp. pp. 59-84.

34. [George Eliot], "Worldliness and Other-Worldliness: The Poet Young," *Westminster Review* 67 (January 1857): 27.

35. [Eliot], "Belles Lettres," *Westminster Review* 67 (January 1857): 307; emphasis mine.

36. [Eliot], "Belles Lettres," *Westminster Review* 66 (October 1856): 567, 568. John M. Picker has recently suggested the importance to George Eliot of the German scientist Hermann von Helmholtz, who began work on acoustical physiology in 1856 (see *Victorian Soundscapes* [New York: Oxford Univ. Press, 2003], esp. pp. 84-99). Eliot's essays on poetry in the 1850s pre-date Helmholtz's important publications on the subject, and show Eliot to be thinking on the matter before she could have known of Helmholtz's work. More likely sources for her early thinking on sound, rhythm, and physiology include Alexander Bain, an acquaintance of both Lewes and Eliot, and the discourse on rhythm inspired by the Spasmodic controversy.

37. [Arthur Hallam], "On Some of the Characteristics of Modern Poetry," p. 96; [Robert Buchanan], "The Fleshly School of Poetry: Mr. D. G. Rossetti," *Contemporary Review* 18 (1871): 335. On Hallam's relation to empiricist philosophy, see Donald Hair, *Tennyson's Language* (Toronto: Univ. of Toronto Press, 1991), pp. 41-56.

38. [Coventry Patmore], "New Poets," *Edinburgh Review* 104 (1856): 340, 360.

39. "I hope," writes Gosse, that "I may be dead before the English poets take Walt Whitman for their model in style" (Gosse, p. 71). Whitman records

reading Smith's *A Life-Drama* in his journal of 1854 (Walt Whitman, *Notebooks and Unpublished Prose Manuscripts,* ed. Edward F. Grier [New York: New York Univ. Press, 1984], 5:1771).

40. Mathilde Blind, "Music and Moonlight," *The Examiner* (March 28, 1874): 320.

Emma Mason (essay date winter 2004)

SOURCE: Mason, Emma. "Rhythmic Numinousness: Sydney Dobell and 'The Church.'" *Victorian Poetry* 42, no. 4 (winter 2004): 537-51.

[*In the following essay, Mason examines Dobell's religious beliefs in an effort to determine the influence of his faith on his poetry*]

full of faith, but full of charity—wise in head and large in heart—poet and a priest an "eternal child," as well as a thoroughly furnished man.[1]

When George Gilfillan called for "a tutor to the rising age," he had in mind several 'young, ardent and gifted spirits" who wrote poetry to inspire religious feeling in their readers. Philip Bailey seemed a likely candidate, but lacked forcefulness; Alexander Smith was regarded as a poet in possession of a profound mode of expression but failed to direct it into religious contemplation. Only Sydney Dobell, a poet who had employed to great effect the current trend for spasmodic feeling in poetics, appeared to lay true claim to Gilfillan's "vacant laurel."[2] That this feeling was inherently religious in tone was Gilfillan's view, but modern criticism remains unclear regarding the question of Dobell's religion and how, if at all, it inflects his poetry. This essay aims to clarify the issue first by unravelling the details of his faith, and second by using such detail to work through his religious lyrics. Religious or otherwise, all of his poetry is inflected by a fitful rhythmic pace that reflects his frantic and perhaps conflicted desire to both reach God and implement what he perceived to be the true Christian message in society. Like the "snow-muffled, dim and sweet" snow-drop, Dobell wrote in **"The Snow-drop in the Snow"** (1851), the "Poet" produces a music often misunderstood, being himself lost amidst "drifting snows" and blooming only in "loneliness" (11. 45-47, 59).[3] Yet as a figure "Full of faith," in Dobell's poem, the poet must tread, albeit precariously, a path between the winter of mortality and "Heaven / The dome of a great palace all of ice" (11.1-2). Dutiful behavior on earth to his "fellow men" was certainly as significant to Dobell as his longing for paradise, a tension that sent a shudder through both his verse and his allegiance to a specific form of Christianity known simply as "the Church."

The first part of this discussion turns to "the Church," a religious community based on the Christian Church of the first century and headed by Samuel Thompson.

Thompson, Dobell's grandfather, carefully outlined the philosophy of his "Church" in *Evidences of Revealed Religion* (1814), which he published under the name Christophilus as a series of letters that are everywhere echoed in Dobell's own correspondence and verse. The influence of Evidences also extended to the Birmingham politician-preacher and social reformer George Dawson, who forwarded a radicalized version of Thompson's "Church" philosophy in numerous sermons. As one of Dobell's more intimate friends, Dawson seems to have touched the poet's concept of religion almost as much as Thompson, all three men intent on putting individuals back in touch with their feelings in order to create a national community founded on religious sensibility. Part two thus opens with Dobell's own prose explication of religion and "the Church" in *Thoughts on Art, Philosophy and Religion* (1876), a text usually cited to support Dobell's broad church position. "Broad Church," however, is a rather generalized and inadequate label to describe Dobell's position in light of Thompson's *Evidences* and Dawson's sermons. We might instead wish to regard the poet's religious identity as one characterized by its struggle to articulate the value of religious feeling over religious doctrine. While critics like W. David Shaw have attributed such feeling to a Hegelian model of spirit, it is also worth rendering this feeling as affective, spasmodically issuing from the believer entranced by God.[4] Dobell remains Christian even as he rethinks this tradition through Thompson and Dawson, and the most recognizably religious of his lyrics reinforce his emotive belief, as part two will illustrate by reading **"The Harps of Heaven"** (c. 1851), **"To a Cathedral Tower"** (1850) and **"In War-Time: A Psalm of the Heart"** (c. 1855).

1

Emily Jolly's *The Life and Letters of Sydney Dobell* establishes itself from the fore as a testimony to Dobell's faith, which she traces from his childhood as a product of his parents' rather fervent religious beliefs. His father recorded that he used to talk to his son "of how delightful and blessed it would be if any child would resolve to live as pure, virtuous and holy a life, as dedicated to the will and service of God, as Jesus."[5] Dobell's mother too commented: "In my eyes he was indeed precious, precious in that highest sense in which a highly wrought religious temperament beheld him. . . . Surely never were prayers more devotedly uttered than for him" (Jolly, 1:7). This immediate pressure to commit to some kind of religious or apostolic mission drew Dobell, even as it strained his nerves, and from just eight years old, he was regularly attending the meetings of "the Church." As Jolly iterates, it is apparent that his parents regarded their son as the means for implementing the "religious and social reforms. . . . the Church" was to effect in society, despite his obvious draw to "the inspirations of art" as well as "the fervours

of theology" (Jolly, 1: ix, 8). As we will see later, Dobell connected his interest in art, and specifically poetry, to his religious belief, both expressive of a pulsating and convulsive emotion that put the individual in a correct state of mind to contemplate God. One of Dobell's early letters to his future father-in-law, also a member of "the Church," conveys such a sentiment. On reading Dobell's zealous letters to his daughter, Emily, Mr. Fordham invited the future poet to yield to "calm reasoning," and refrain from writing "at all, if, by so doing, you only excite and encourage painful and excessive feelings." "All the difference between an unhappy and a happy man," wrote Fordham, "lies in the proper government of our passions. . . . Religion, too, which has for its sole object the happiness of man, above all other things teaches us the absolute necessity of self-government, and the cultivation of calm and tranquil feelings" (letter to Dobell, 1838 in Jolly, 1:38). Dobell did not concur. While he agreed that "the proper regulation of the passions" enabled wisdom and righteousness, he could not see the link between faith and tranquillity:

> The simple command "to love the Lord our God with all our hearts and with all our souls," seems to me to imply an intensity which would require some rather more active state of feeling than that calm and tranquil one which you so pleasingly describe. I am but a young religionist, and, therefore, ought to be careful in hazarding an opinion, but I should think that even the very constant anxiety to do right, and the fear of being mistaken as to what is or is not right, which must pervade the mind of one devoted to the Will of God, and possessing the humility of mind towards that God which is so enjoined by Him, would necessarily tend to destroy that calm and tranquillity which you say religion teaches.

(Letter to Fordham, 1838, in Jolly, 1:39)

Finding "the Church" lacking in liberalism and increasingly alienated by the religious intensity to which Dobell calls attention in his letter, the Fordhams withdrew their membership. Certainly Dobell quickly became notorious for his two-hour long improvisations on prophecy and revelation at "Church" meetings, enough to put anyone off, and by the early 1840s the poet was a regular preacher in the sect. So seriously did he take his beliefs at this time that after his marriage to Emily in 1844, Dobell limited their "associations and domestic intercourse" to "Church" members. "I belong," he stated, "the connection is hereditary—to a very small religious sect—'small' for we do not consider it our mission to proselytise—very much resembling the Quakers" (Jolly, 1:87).

Yet "the Church" was very much a religion of its own, also known to its members, the "Humble Enquirers after Truth," as "the Church of God" or "Freethinking Christianity."[6] Initiated by Thompson in 1798, the first meetings proper of the new group were held in 1799, wherein a kind of hierarchy was established to categorize associates. Following the form of organization instituted by the Apostles, "the Church" appointed ordained elders or overseers rather than clerics (the former "brothers among brethren" rather than mediators between believers and God); deacons, who assisted the elders; and messengers, whose role consisted of personally communicating the mission of "the Church" to other parishes (Brief Account, p. 74). Imperative to Thompson was that no one assume the stance of teacher or priest within the association, members taking turns to speak at meetings rather than lead prayer or meditation. Indeed, "the Church" believed public social prayer, Sabbaths, holy days, and all other forms of religious ceremony both pointless and devoid of sanction from their main focus of debate, the New Testament. Moreover, any hint at dogma, doctrine, or creed was entirely at odds with the being of "the Church," which had only two guiding directives: the right to private judgment; and the sufficiency of the scriptures to establish benevolent action in society. Certainly Thomas Paine's *The Age of Reason* (1794-96) seems to have effected a profound impact on Thompson, a text which he quotes in *Evidences of Revealed Religion* as largely accurate in its assumption that "Jesus Christ founded no new system: he called men to the practice of moral virtues and the belief of one God. The great trait in his character is philanthropy."[7]

Thompson centralized the figure of Jesus Christ both as a human exemplar to which members of "the Church" should aspire; and also a guarantee of the genuine benevolence, "goodness" and charity to be ideally found at the heart of faith. As George Dawson echoed in a lecture on Holman Hunt's "The Light of the World" (1853): "Christ, and not Christianity, is to save the world. . . . The only thing that will ever save this world is the passionate dependence on the man Christ Jesus. And a picture like this, overflowing with endless humanity and sweet charity, is worth a whole bundle of dissertations about election and reprobation, fate and free will."[8] Dobell assented, declaring that while as humans we may feel deficient and worn down by worldliness, God "has given one bright example of what" we "might become, one shining proof, that the trials of this world are not, though heavy, too weighty to be overcome" (Jolly, 1:44). Collectively, these statements sound like a denial of the divinity of Christ, but there are two important and connected factors inherent to "Church" philosophy which counter such a suggestion. First, Thompson wished to distance "the Church" as much from any of those systems associated with the denial of Christ's divinity, like Unitarianism, as he did from "supernatural" beliefs like Trinitarianism. Here is Thompson attempting to remove his community from the fraught religious debate of the time:

> I do not, then, mean to defend the articles, creeds or dogmas, of established churches, or of any of those sects and parties who take their religion from the priest;—I do not mean to defend sacraments, pulpit preaching, public social worship, nor an order of men called priests or preachers; as the administrators of religion;—I do not mean to defend the doctrine of the trinity, the miraculous conception, original sin, atonement, predestination, or endless torment;—I do not mean to defend the Bible as the word of God, and as being all written by divine inspiration, because I am fully convinced that the Scriptures do not teach or lay claim to any such things.
>
> (*Brief Account*, p. 17)

Throwing out systems, doctrines, mysteries, and even the divine basis of the Bible, Thompson seems more attuned to his secular contemporaries, Paine and Godwin, than to his Christian peers. Yet Paine and Godwin are valued by Thompson because he regarded them as contributing to a process by which the world is gradually made fit "for the reception of pure religion," one grounded in virtue and compassion (*Brief Account*, p. 33). The Bible might not have been divinely related and recorded, but the messages inherent in its words can only be understood through what he consistently refers to as "revelation."

This brings us to the second reason Thompson was not interested in refuting Christ's divinity: namely, his dependence on the necessity of revelation to any belief in God. In this context, revelation signifies both the "truth" that God imparted through Christ as well as the process or method by which such communication is achieved. Thompson called revelation the "grammar" by which one deciphered the language of the Bible, indicating its primacy to the multiple interpretations that might be forwarded by the "freethinking" members of "the Church." If revelation describes the process of understanding, then it might refer to faith, feeling, insight, sense, or any inner impression of God that the believer experienced. It is worth noting that Thompson's discussion of revelation stretches into a rather convoluted discussion of the historical reality of the Resurrection by which all other mysteries could technically be proven. Briefly stated, he argues that Christ's death, burial, and resurrection were publicly recognized by the Jews and Roman government, two factions who would have been otherwise invested in recording this chain of events differently (*Brief Account*, p. 87). For Thompson, Christ's resurrection is natural, rather than supernatural, because it was enacted by the same God who mobilized "twelve illiterate men and their followers" to establish their belief-system through "the whole civilized world" (*Brief Account*, p. 108). We know the latter task was motivated by something, so it makes sense that the same power might effect equally miraculous happenings. While this makes little logical sense, the core of Thompson's convictions might be rescued, as declared above, in the form of revelation as feeling, instinct, impulse, divination. Dobell called this the "spiritual sense" and it is this that he attempts to beat out in his religious lyrics by invoking a kind of rhythmic numinousness that mimics that revelatory process by which divinity is uncloaked by the believer.

Certainly Dawson believed that religion had to be initially "clothed" in order to be decoded and so make sense to humans, declaring that "all spiritualism must consent to clothe itself in form," poetical or otherwise.⁹ The only real betrayal of "Christian religion" for Dawson was "the Christian Church," an institution which ideally offered a "scaffold by which to erect a nobler building" but so often degenerated into a law of its own (*Demands*, pp. 3, 5). Spirituality and faith of the kind Thompson advocates dwells "in the heart" rather than "any outward temple," Dawson argues, the Bible granting believers a feeling of love rather than "a code or formulae" (*Demands*, pp. 5-6). The preacher calls for a new "idea of a Church" able to "reach our sympathies" and "in nowise whatsoever limit, hinder, or make difficult, full FREEDOM OF THOUGHT," echoing the freethinking philosophy of "the Church" itself (*Demands*, pp. 8, 10). For Dawson, the moderation of the age may permit outward freedom, emancipation, and relief bills liberating Roman Catholics and Jews, but it fails to allow for private autonomy: "Is there no soul-freedom?" he asks (*Demands*, p. 16). The greater Christian community simply made matters worse by instituting priesthoods or leaders, Dissenting communities as much like "a temple of money-changers" as Anglican or Catholic establishments (*Demands*, p. 23). Religion rings with "Mammonic sound" rather than spiritual feeling, rendering the whole arena of faith dry and lethargic (*Demands*, p. 23). As Dawson feared in his essay on Tennyson's "Idylls of the King": "Who can now feel a new affection, or suffer a new emotion?" (*Shakespeare*, p. 472). This was the pressing question that Gilfillan believed Dobell could meet, and while the poet defended Dawson against Gilfillan's accusations that he was a charismatic fraud, he confessed to the critic that Dawson's "idea of a Church seems to me an amiable chimera, a benevolent impossibility, ludicrously unscriptural, and equally at variance with Divine dispensation and human nature." Dobell nevertheless admired and respected Dawson for setting "the middle classes thinking," for denouncing the idea of the Church as institution and club, and for modelling instead a "moral hospitable" which he had no doubt "does unspeakable good" (letter to Gilfillan, May 1850, in Jolly, 1:130).

Dobell's matured religious stance shifts between Thompson and Dawson, although technically he remained a member of "the Church," reconverting his wife Emily despite her worries that they alienated their non "Church" neighbors. Certainly Dobell loosened his

earnest dedication to "the Church," reminiscing on a long-gone youthful and ascetic self in a letter to his eldest sister: "I cannot look back without a melancholy interest to the years when I never thought a thought or said a word but under the very eyes of God" (letter to eldest sister, 1850, in Jolly, 1:113). Yet his mid-twenties was precisely the period wherein he began to express his faith, not in "Church" meetings, but in poetry, which he rendered religious by casting it in spasmodic terms. As he assured his friend, Reverend Paton in 1852: "If, therefore, my next book has less of the Christian and the Scripture, do not infer that I am less Christian or Scriptural" (letter to Paton, April 5, 1852, in Jolly, 1:256). Dobell realized that if religion was to be communicated at all, it had to move the individual, allowing the experience of that new kind of affection Dawson doubted could be sparked. All Dawson's talk of soul-freedom, however, coupled with Thompson's stress on revelation as a package of faith, insight, and feeling, confirmed for Dobell that the only religious mission worth pursuing was emotional. In 1853, he decided to share his premise with "the Church" at their weekly meeting:

> I do hope and trust that we are all beginning to feel more than we did, the very social and personal character of "Church" union; to recognise more and more that "the Church" is not a mere machine for theoretical religious instruction, but an association for purposes. A church, not a congregation; a body, not a crowd; an association, and not only that, but an association for purposes.

> (Jolly, 1: 283)

The emphasis on an association of people who would effect real change in society seems directly to echo Dawson's and Thompson's insistence on moral action here. Yet Dobell's repetition of the idea of "association" itself reveals more than an interest in good works, pointing to his almost Hartleyan fascination in connectedness and association between people and between ideas. Such association was poetry itself when rhythmically conveyed, lyrical chains of words lulling the reader into a higher, benevolent feeling.

All thoughts or feelings, then, however oblique or confusing, became for Dobell signifiers of God's presence which in turn created in his head "lines of thought" which passed "behind the scenes, in my brain." This "mental feeling," as he called it, relaxed and reshaped his mind in such a manner that new trains of thought were able to emerge easily, "larger, warmer, clearer, nobler, better, brighter than anything I can think of in my ordinary hours" (letter to Sam Brown, 1852, in Jolly, 1:193). Association, then, is a word that for Dobell conveyed both the manner by which "words rhythmically combined" on the page as well as the impact such words had on "the feelings of the poetic hearer or utterer." In one sense, the meaning of these words was rather beside the point given that all readers, and believers, were to interpret language as they saw fit, being as they are true "freethinking" individuals. What could be rendered was the feeling behind the rhythm, a feeling that overflows in Dobell's poetry but often in a jerky and convulsive manner that betrays the intensity (rather than, as he wrote to Emily's father, tranquillity) of faith. Before finally looking at this verse, we might want to turn to Dobell's own explicit statements regarding religion in his prose criticism, significant because of the way in which it links, or associates, religion, poetry, and feeling. As Dobell suggested in response to his mother's concern that poetry was "mere vanity" when compared with religious preaching, "She forgets that the nature of poetry is precisely the question that underlies the most difficult and serious questions that concern the human mind, and those human thoughts and feelings with which religion has to do" (letter to eldest sister, 1857, in Jolly, 2:71).

2

Dobell was sure that the nature of poetry and religion were the same, thus satisfying Gilfillan's hope that he might become a tutor to a rising and notably utilitarian age in which Christianity, like poetry, was increasingly interrogated. Dobell's devout mother was not alone in her fear that writing poetry was a vain pursuit, but many secular critics challenged religion for the same reason: what did it do in a period of real material reform and change? The answer resided in the realm of feeling, which while no less strongly experienced by the often sentimental Victorians, was certainly supposed an aspect of the human to be held back and controlled. In his "Lecture on the 'Nature of Poetry'" (1857), Dobell agreed that the "ideal mind weaves order" and restraint, yet asserted too that poetry spoke to something else within us, "our Divinest faculties," he wrote, "our material flesh and blood."[10] As Jason Rudy's work conveys, Dobell believed that because the body beats time like a poem, our experience of reading such poetry is necessarily affective, uniting the "inward" heartbeat with the "outward" sound of rhythmic language (*Thoughts*, p. 53). Moreover, this experience is "religious" for Dobell because it reconciles the "spirit" with "Matter," securing our physical reality in a world we only come to know through the immaterial feelings that give rise to language (*Thoughts*, p. 53). Elsewhere, Dobell intimates that "the universe" is a "Divine Language" and so if poetry formalizes the universe, "clothes it," as Dawson would say, it performs the same function as any religious system that strives to square the spiritual with lived reality. This, I think, is the reasoning behind Dobell's statement that "Poetry should be Religious" (*Thoughts*, p. 66).

One might respond to this argument by claiming that Dobell, like Arnold, wished to replace religion with feeling, and might not be classed as a defender of Christianity in any of its guises. Even Unitarianism was an empty and cold system to the poet who wrote in his notebook: "Religion is philosophy made human" (in Jolly, 1:150). Protestantism was even worse, however, a "narrow, ugly, impudent, unreasonable, inconsistent . . . babel of logomachy and literalism," Dobell wrote, anathema to a believer more interested in feelings than ongoing debates over signifiers. On visiting the South of France in 1864, his aversion to Protestantism was confirmed when he witnessed an evangelical "pasteur" refuse to perform a marriage ceremony between a young Protestant girl and her Catholic beau, unless she promised never to convert. As a freethinker, Dobell was horrified and claimed that while Protestants had no problem with a felony like lying, which they do "morning, noon and night," to "fail in an iota of the creed, that is mortal sin" (letter to father, March 6, 1863, in Jolly, 2:206). Catholicism seemed more favorable to Dobell, who was attracted to the "rhythmic undulation" of its sung prayer, as well as its "great, beautiful, wise powerful" myths and mysteries (letter to father, March 6, 1863 in Jolly, 2:255; Poetical Works, p. 154). Of course, the projected but unwritten second part of **Balder** was intended as an attack on the "Church of Rome" which Dobell considered too emotive, lacking any kind of educative foundation and riddled with corrupt priests. Like Thompson, Dobell despised the idea of the priest, an office which not only led to the hierarchization of faithful communities, but usurped the role of the poet by pronouncing "absolution" and "release" on believers (*Thoughts*, p. 186). If Protestant clerics were mechanical and pompously enlightenment, Catholic priests were corrupt storytellers who enveloped the Scriptures in such dark passions that they were stripped of their use-value in working through the feelings of humankind (*Thoughts*, pp. 187-188).

The problem with organized religion was that it was prescriptive and controlled, leaving no space for soul-freedom, spiritual sense, or developed trains of emotive thought that revealed God's presence in the world. Echoing Thompson, Dobell argued that if Christianity was intended to be a "permanent undevelopable outward system," then the Apostles would have made considerable effort to "engrave the formula on tables of stone." Christianity was not to be thrown out, however, for its representative figure, Jesus Christ, still glowed as the perfected model of human benevolence and charity; instead, Dobell argued Christianity was to be reshaped as feeling:

> Supposing there were no such thing as words what idea should we have of an Invisible God? We should have ideas of His effects and of such of the Attributes producing such effects as we could feel in ourselves by our possession of the same. But of the Total Agent what? I think only a dim Image, the reflection of our consciousness of our own existence: or the result of the

effort of the mind to conceive, which effort may produce the vague figure of its own action; a shape on the corrugating brain; and impression on the soul, like that of the wind on water. Therefore in reality none. A spiritual world, then, could only be directly apprehended in so far as it agreed with our own faculties and experience. Dismissing, therefore, as mere shadows and reflections of ourselves, all intellectual notions of the spiritual world, what, apart from words, remains as testimony to it? This: that from the top and culmen of all perception the mind as it were stretches up arms into vacancy, desires towards—what? The testimony therefore to the unknown is of feeling.

(*Thoughts*, pp. 147-148).

This is Dobell's most important statement regarding religious belief. In it, he claims that religion's current mode of evincing God's reality and the power of spirituality is to express it through human language. Without words, the individual can only conceive of God through thoughts already buried in the mind, producing a spiritual world that mirrors or reproduces the conditions of "our own existence." Such a statement works for Dobell in that he already regarded religion as humanized philosophy. Yet he is at the same time concerned that testifying to God by rendering him a part of the human risks reducing the numinous either to mortal experience, or to something so immaterial ("the wind on water") that it resists all definition. If God is not a reflection of the human, then, he is instead that emotional part of the self that strives toward that which lies beyond it, grounded in the individual but morphing into those "lines of thought" Dobell argued originated in the brain and reached up to reveal God's presence. This seems to be what the narrator of **"To the Same"** implies when he renders the soul as "A god that, for being god, believest in God / The more" (11,12-13). That implicit connection between the believer's immaterial self (the soul) and God is not only affective, however, but spasmodic, convulsive, and a little desperate, grounded in a desire for something unknowable but deeply felt.

"The Harps of Heaven" puts into poetry what Dobell theorized in *Thoughts*, framed by the story of a believer who scrambles up into the highest part of heaven in order to understand those feelings that motivate him in mortal life. Within this empyrean world, the narrator interrogates a seraph (those angels able to dwell with God in the furthermost point of heaven) in an attempt to solve the puzzle of faith as well as its origin. Before dwelling on this part of the poem, it is worth assessing how the narrator enters heaven, a process which is achieved in the same way Dobell intimated he experienced the divine, that is, as a mental feeling that forges a pathway to God. The narrator here declares that he ascends the "bulwark" between earth and heaven by

scaling it with a rope made of his own prayer, an utterance which when articulated explodes ("flecks") across the sky to create a sort of spiritual web on which he steadies himself:

> On a solemn day
> I clomb the shining bulwark of the skies:
> Not by the beaten way,
> But climbing by a prayer,
> That like a golden thread hung by the giddy stair
> Fleck'd on the immemorial blue.

(11, 1-6)

The speaker specifically avoids the "beaten way" by which believers conventionally access God—organized religion—and follows instead a trail only the "brave and few," united by their ability to feel, might endeavor to mount (l. 7). For only those who can emotionally sense God attempt the venture, "stirr'd by echoes of far harmonies," and then so overcome with religious feeling that they "Must either lay . . . down and die of love, / Or dare / Those empyrean walls" (11, 8-11).

As the narrator advances, his footing slips and he becomes suspended "in the swaying air" between Earth and Heaven, a "sheer eternal precipice" on either side of him. This predicament does not induce the pleasurable fear of sublime terror but instead instills an anxiety that God might be forever cut off. Caught in a moment of extreme anguish, the narrator declares:

> Then when I,
> Gigantic with my desperate agony,
> Felt even
> The knotted grasp of bodily despair
> Relaxing to let go,
> A mighty music, like a wind of light,
> Blew from the imminent height,
> And caught me in its splendour; and, as flame
> That flickers and again aspires,
> Rose in a moment thither whence it came;
> And I, that thought me lost,
> Pass'd to the top of all my dear desires,
> And stood among the everlasting host.

(11, 22-34)

The climactic pitch and increasingly dense syntax of this passage reiterates Dobell's sense that the individual is connected to God through feeling: only when the dangling narrator decides to relax his body and let emotion flow through him does God respond by releasing his divinity through music. The sensation of these majestic melodies blows through the narrator in the same manner that Dobell depicted God's presence in Thoughts, "the wind on water" becoming "a wind of light." Now lifted to the heavens and firmly located on a rock of amethyst, the narrator is confronted with a scene of harp-playing seraphs who produce the music that so allured him. Like his own prayer, the notes that the angels strike roll from their harps to form a "sea of choristry" that bursts over the earth giving intimations of divinity. The music,

> like an odorous luminous mist, doth leap the eternal
>   walls,
> And falls
> In wreaths of melody
> Adown the azure mountain of the sky;
> And round its lower slopes bedew'd
> Breathes lost beatitude;
> And far away,
> Low, low, below the last of all its lucent scarps,
> Sprinkles bewildering drops of immortality.

> (11, 72-80)

The beauty of this passage is intensified further when the narrator learns that the angels are deaf to the "sound of harpers harping on their harps," a revelation confessed through the tears his seraph-guide sheds at the mention of these sacred tunes (l. 83). The "rapt celestial auditory" is reserved for the "sweet lower air" and, while the seraph mourns the loss of this harmonious solace, he is given "back his bliss" by the dazzling "glory of immortal light" which makes visible his music. The glittering realms of heaven, then, serve to flesh out God's presence by lighting up his divine refrain, one which emanates from angelic harps and is understood by mortals as lyricism.

Communicating the significance of religious feeling through a spasmodic poetics, Dobell captures the jerky manner by which God casts his light on the world, a light that is absorbed, fragmented, and inclined by the bodily being of believers: standing under a ray or spark only jars its trajectory. Such jarring also points to the kind of relation the freethinker might have with God, individually shaped and sometimes offbeat. For Dobell, God's light only becomes uniform and stagnant when closeted within the institutional church-space, an idea he addresses in "**To a Cathedral Tower,** on the Evening of the Thirty-Fifth Anniversary of Waterloo." When the narrator does look up toward the sun from his cathedral-tower vicinity, it is "As a babe smiles into his murderer's face" to forge a destructive bond from which issues a "palpitat[ing] light" that ushers in the poem's central scene of war and "red Waterloo" (11. 16, 19, 82). It is typical of Dobell to versify on organized or institutional religion through images of war and death, coupling war's empty glory with Old Testament dogmatism and its associated vengeful God. Here is the narrator of "**In War-Time: A Psalm for the Heart**" calling on the "Lord of Thunder" (l. 139) to

> SCOURGE us as Thou wilt, oh Lord God of Hosts;
> Deal with us, Lord, according to our transgressions;
> But give us Victory!

> Victory, victory! oh, Lord, victory!
> Oh, Lord, victory! Lord, Lord, victory!

> (11, 1-5)

The ostensible war-mongering quickly gives way to a tumult of hysteric references to the "sick and crazed," "Strained and cracked" vision of the soldier, "swarmed and foul with creeping shapes of midnight"; "the strings" of wartime life "strung to the twang of torture"; and the "stench" of "Weevils, and rots, and cankers" tormenting those who bear any strength to fight (11, 19-21, 35-36, 41). The plea that God should "fear not to bless" such horror seems darkly ironic, invoking a hypocritical master figure willing to encourage the believer's faith in victory from war.

The same correlation is made by the narrator of "**To a Cathedral Tower,**" but it is notable that he steadily distances himself from the tower; "I am not moved / To frenzy" he claims, thus intimating his rejection of rancorous church-trapped divinity (11, 4-5). The cathedral tower itself also appears dead, its depiction as an "Unchanging Pile," a "Grey Pile," evoking a funereal atmosphere that lingers into the vision of Waterloo. "War" and "Death" are figures directly set against Freedom and Christ ("the genius of his race"), crushing all in their wake and setting their newly dead captives back on those "tyrants" who invoked the conflict (11, 38, 59). Death is even granted the power to resurrect the "bloody dust" of slaughtered warriors, now rising as "obscene shapes" who, "like / A swoop of black thoughts thro' a stormy soul" attack everything around them (11, 51, 56-57). As they "snatch joys" from "the Victor" only to confer it on "all the tyrants of the darkened globe," all forms of rulership and power are gloomily ridiculed to elevate indirectly democratic, peaceful forms of government (11, 58-59). The poem is by no means specific regarding what form this government should take, and instead concerns itself with shifting readers' feelings and perceptions of God in order to root them in a different way of experiencing religion. Even the angels are castigated for gazing upon God with "averted eyes / (As one who feels the wrong he will not see)," and only Dobell's allusion to Christ as a personification of "Freedom" seem to evade the brand of hypocrisy:

> And the genius of his race,
> Pale, leaning on a broken eagle, dies.
> High in the midst departing Freedom stands
> On hills of slain; her wings unfurled, her hands
> Toward heaven, her eyes turned, streaming, on the
>   earth,
> In act to rise.

> (11, 38-43)

Standing between God and the war-torn landscape, Freedom appears to evince real feeling through her tears, but she is nevertheless ready to flee the scene and rise up toward heaven. Christ is almost entirely buried in the poem, shattered but propped up against the already redundant and damaged image of Christianity suggested in the eagle, and then erased from the scene as another "king of men" who might otherwise yield to the "Warmarish, Victory and Glory" (11. 29, 36).

The frenzy initiated here, as in the poems discussed above, is arguably disturbing and unsettling to any reader even without the added dismantling of Christian tradition, and it certainly upset many of Dobell's contemporaries. For not only was Dobell using a spasmodic turn of expression to enact religious experience in poetry, but he was suggesting that the feelings such expression sparked might replace doctrine itself to render religion a matter of convulsive affect. Certainly Edward Knight Everett's sermon, "Spasmodic Christian Zeal" (1883) seems to respond directly, if belatedly, to Dobell's proposition, with a paper that rails against such feeling as a twisted mode of enthusiasm. For Everett, any "excited ephemeral emotion and energy" is "alien to the very spirit of Christianity," attaching itself only to those who focus the soul on the "Unknown."[11] The believer might well pour out a "perfect 'volcano' of zeal," but this inevitably fades to become nothing more than "the petrified lava of a reactionary indifference" (Everett, p. 4). Echoing Dobell's dour father-in-law, Everett claims that Christianity should instead be "a permanent force":

> Its current, a regular current. Its vitality, a sustained vitality. . . . Have your revival meetings, but let your activity then be a fair and honest sample of your regular serving in the Master's course; which is promoted best, not by spurs, and spurts, and spasms, not by the ardour of fine feeling, which bums the soul's energy to ash, but by the more uniform yet no less real devotion, which to many a pastor is the strength of his hands and the joy of his heart.
>
> (Everett, p. 5)

Without such moderation, Everett predicted that religion would literally expire, degenerating gradually into "fever" and "chattering chills" of the kind that inflict Dobell's Christ figure in **"To a Cathedral Tower"** (Everett, p. 5). Dobell's poetry clearly stands on the opposite side of such an argument, breaking its readers from their tranquil restraint to stir them into a re-examination of faith fuelled by fine feeling. Like Wordsworth, who used the lyric form to train the readers' thoughts into the transcendent and beyond the poem, Dobell shaped his verse into a catalyst of emotion so intense that readers are cast up with the angels like the narrator of **"The Harps of Heaven."** How to get back down again was not the most pressing of issues for a poet so passionately attached to God, and yet it is perhaps this very nihilistic desire that troubled the Victorians, even as it has distracted modern readers from Dobell's beliefs.

Notes

1. George Gilfillan, *A Second Gallery of Literary Portraits* (Edinburgh, 1850), p. 393.

2. George Gilfillan, review of *The Roman, Eclectic Review* 91 (1850): 678-679.

3. All quotes from Dobell's poetry from *The Poetical Works of Sydney Dobell*, 2 volumes (London, 1875).

4. W. David Shaw, "Poetry and Religion," in *A Companion to Victorian Poetry*, ed. Richard Cronin, Alison Chapman, and Antony H. Harrison (Oxford: Blackwell, 2002), p. 466.

5. E[mily] J[olly], *The Life and Letters of Sydney Dobell*, 2 volumes (London, 1878), 1:6. Hereafter cited in text as "Jolly" with volume and page number.

6. See Samuel Thompson, *A Brief Account of the Church of God, Known as Freethinking Christians: Also, an Abstract of the Principles which they believe, and the law of church fellowship they have adopted.* Reprinted in Jolly, 1:68-76.

7. Samuel Thompson ("Christophilus"), *Evidences of Revealed Religion on a new and original Plan being an Appeal to Deists on their own Principles of Argument* (London, 1814), p. 17.

8. George Dawson, *Shakespeare and other Lectures*, ed. George St. Clair (London, 1888), p. 457.

9. George Dawson, *The Demands of the Age upon the Church: A Discourse delivered on the Opening of the "Church of the Saviour" Edward Street, Birmingham, on August 8, 1847* (London, 1847), p. 4.

10. Sydney Dobell, *Thoughts on Art, Philosophy, and Religion; Selected from the Unpublished Papers of Sydney Dobell*, intro. John Nichol (London, 1876), pp. 7, 22.

11. Edward Knight Everett, "'Spasmodic Christian Zeal': A Paper Read at the Meeting of the Lancashire and Cheshire Association of the Baptist Churches held at Preston, June 14, 1883" (Burnley, 1883), p. 4.

FURTHER READING

Criticism

Houston, Natalie M. "Reading the Victorian Souvenir: Sonnets and Photographs of the Crimean War." *Yale Journal of Criticism* 14, no. 2 (fall 2001): 353-83.

Exploration of the use of the sonnet form during the Victorian Age, including a discussion of Smith and Dobell's *Sonnets on the War.*

Additional coverage of Dobell's life and career is contained in the following sources published by Gale: *Dictionary of Literary Biography,* **Vol. 32;** *Literature Resource Center*; *Nineteenth-Century Literature Criticism,* **Vol. 43; and** *Reference Guide to English Literature,* **Ed. 2.**

Seamus Heaney
1939-

(Full name Seamus Justin Heaney) Irish poet, critic, essayist, and translator.

For additional discussion of Heaney's career, see *PC,* Volume 18.

INTRODUCTION

The winner of the 1995 Nobel Prize in Literature, Heaney is Ireland's most celebrated living poet. He is extraordinarily versatile, writing on a wide variety of subjects from detailed descriptions of rural life, to Irish political and social issues, to the appropriate role of the poet in society.

BIOGRAPHICAL INFORMATION

The eldest of nine children, Heaney was born on April 13, 1939, in County Derry in Protestant Northern Ireland to Patrick and Margaret McCann Heaney, both Roman Catholics. His father owned and worked Mossbawm, a fifty-acre farm northwest of Belfast and also worked as a cattle dealer. Heaney was educated at a local primary school until the age of twelve when he was awarded a scholarship to St. Columb's College, a Derry boarding school some forty miles from his home. From there he went on to Queen's University in Belfast, where he studied literature as well as Latin and Irish. Using the pen name Incertus, he began writing poems, several of which were published in various literary magazines. Heaney graduated with honors in 1961 and was awarded a teaching certificate the following year from St. Joseph's College of Education. He initially taught at the secondary school level and then as a lecturer at Queen's University. In 1965, Heaney married Marie Devlin; they have three children: Michael, Christopher, and Catherine. The following year Heaney published his first book of poetry, *Death of a Naturalist,* which was an immediate critical and popular success. In 1972 the family moved to Dublin and Heaney devoted himself exclusively to writing until 1975 when he resumed his teaching career, accepting a position at Caryfort College in Dublin. He has also taught at Harvard University, Oxford University, and the University of California, Berkeley, and has traveled extensively in England and America, giving poetry readings and lectures.

Heaney's numerous awards include the Eric Gregory Award (1966), the Somerset Maugham Award (1968), the Irish Academy of Letters Award (1971), the Denis Devlin Award (1973), the E. M. Forster Award (1975), the Bennett Award (1982), the Whitbread Award (1987), the Lannam Foundation Award (1990), and the T. S. Eliot Prize (2006). He has received honorary doctorates from a number of universities, including Queen's University, Harvard, the University of Birmingham, Rhodes University in South Africa, and the University of London. In 1995 he was awarded the Nobel Prize for Literature. Heaney currently makes his home in Dublin.

MAJOR WORKS

Heaney's first major publication was the award-winning *Death of a Naturalist,* published by Oxford University Press, in 1966; this was followed by *Door Into the Dark* three years later. These first two collections were characterized by detailed descriptions of the natural world and rural life, infused with memories of the poet's childhood at Mossbawm. In 1972, with the publication of *Wintering Out,* Heaney began dealing more explicitly with political issues, focusing on the "Troubles" in Northern Ireland and the history of violence and unrest in the region dating back to the Iron Age. The 1975 volume *North* continues the poet's concentration on historical issues and on the colonization of Ireland by the English. Heaney returned in part to more personal subject matter in 1979 with the publication of *Field Work,* but again dealt with Irish history and myth in *Station Island* (1984), one of his most important collections. Its formal structure is modeled on Dante's *Divine Comedy.*

Seeing Things (1991) features a number of images and metaphors associated with sports and children's games in such poems as "Markings," "Nights of '57," and "The Augean Stables." *The Spirit Level* (1996) continues this emphasis on play, much of it based on the poet's idyllic recollections of his youth, but here the memory of children's play constitutes only a pleasant, but temporary, diversion from the more serious concerns of adult life. Heaney's most recent publications are a verse translation of *Beowulf* (1999), the favorably-received *Electric Light* (2001), and *District and Circle* (2006), in which Heaney returns to the nature poetry and reminiscences of boyhood that characterized his early volumes. In 2007, *The Riverbank Field* was published in a limited edition, with illustrations from the drawings and paintings of Martin Gale. In addition to his poetry and translations, Heaney has also produced award-winning collections of critical essays, a drama, and two volumes of his lectures.

CRITICAL RECEPTION

Heaney's poetry has focused on a wide variety of subject matter—from the simple pleasures associated with rural life to the political upheaval associated with Northern Ireland's occupation by British forces—and this versatility has contributed to his wide-ranging popularity with readers as well as with critics. His early work, which concentrates on images of agrarian Ireland, earned him a reputation as a regional poet whose work was infused with local color and detailed descriptions of the rustic chores of agricultural workers. The term was sometimes used dismissively; Elmer Andrews notes that during this period of Heaney's career, his readers in England considered him "harmless." Beginning with the 1972 volume *Wintering Out,* however, Heaney's focus shifted to more social and political themes, or as Andrews puts it, "away from the bucolic world of childhood and engagement with the harsher adult world." This shift was not limited to content but was also characterized by a retreat from traditional forms and "the comforting echo of regular rhyme" in favor of a looser style, resulting in poetry characterized by "a more immediate psychological spontaneity."

Heaney's innovative use of language has been discussed by such critics as Dennis O'Driscoll, who praises the poet's "ability to link evocative words never before found in combination and, indeed, seldom chanced upon in isolation." Calvin Bedient, in his review of the 2006 volume *District and Circle* also admires the language of Heaney's poetry. "Oh, to be a word in one of Heaney's lines," writes Bedient, "loved and sharp as the taste of a raw turnip, knowing its exact worth." Joseph Heininger has studied the "auditory qualities" or the "acoustic" of the language, noting that the influence of Dante's poetics is apparent to audiences at Heaney's readings, particularly in the poems of *Field Work* and *Station Island.* Stephen James has examined Heaney's critical theories on poetry as well as the poetry itself to comment on Heaney's "verbal acrobatics," noting the way he makes use of the ambiguity of certain words, and the way his "delivery is two-toned, swaying between austerity and irony."

Heaney has always been concerned with the proper role of the poet, particularly in relation to violence and injustice. Daniel Tobin has studied *North,* Heaney's first major collection following his move from Belfast to the outskirts of Dublin, and suggested that the book represents the poet's "quest for self-definition within the realm of tragedy," and his realization that "he must use his poetry to reveal the legacy of violence that is a significant part" of the history of Northern Ireland. Eugene O'Brien contends that many of the poems of *North* have been interpreted as a justification of violence, but the critic holds that such a view is an oversimplification. According to O'Brien, Heaney's ideas about the role of poetry insist that "it should not simplify." Rather, "it must be true to the complexities of modern, or postmodern life," and O'Brien believes that Heaney's work "parallels the growing complexity of life, political, social, religious and cultural, in contemporary Ireland." Similarly Michael Parker believes Heaney's work has been misinterpreted because his use of ambiguity and irony have been overlooked by those critics who pejoratively label him a "nationalist" poet, citing as an example the poem "Kinship," which joins the terms "slaughter" and "common good." However, Parker claims that "to miss the irony of the macabre juxtaposition of [the two terms] is a bit like assuming that Swift was serious about breeding babies for consumption."

PRINCIPAL WORKS

Poetry

Eleven Poems 1965
Death of a Naturalist 1966
Door into the Dark 1969
A Lough Neagh Sequence 1969
Boy Driving His Father to Confession 1970
Wintering Out 1972
Bog Poems 1975
North 1975
Stations 1975
After Summer 1978
Field Work 1979
Hedge School: Sonnets from Glanmore 1979
Poems: 1965-1975 1980
Sweeney Praises the Trees 1981
Sweeney Astray: A Version from the Irish [translator and adapter] 1983
Station Island 1984
The Haw Lantern 1987
New and Selected Poems: 1966-1987 1990
The Tree Clock 1990
Seeing Things 1991
The Spirit Level 1996
Opened Ground: Selected Poems, 1966-1996 1998
Beowulf: A New Verse Translation [translator] 1999
Electric Light 2001

District and Circle 2006
The Riverbank Field [paintings and drawings by Martin Gale] 2007

Other Major Works

The Fire i' the Flint: Reflections on the Poetry of Gerard Manley Hopkins (criticism) 1975
Robert Lowell: A Memorial Address and Elegy (nonfiction) 1978
Preoccupations: Selected Prose 1968-1978 (essays) 1980
The Government of the Tongue: Selected Prose, 1978-1987 (essays) 1988
The Cure at Troy: A Version of Sophocles' Philoctetes (play) 1990
The Redress of Poetry (lectures) 1995

CRITICISM

Elmer Andrews (essay date 1988)

SOURCE: Andrews, Elmer. "*Wintering Out.*" In *The Poetry of Seamus Heaney: All the Realms of Whisper,* pp. 48-81. Houndmills, England: Macmillan, 1988.

[*In the following essay, Andrews provides a detailed analysis of the evolving thematic focus, poetic style, language, and imagery displayed in the poems of* Wintering Out.]

The title of Heaney's third volume, *Wintering Out,* indicates a move away from the bucolic world of childhood and engagement with the harsher adult world. It highlights the notions of survival, continuance and durability amid the severities of 'winter'. We anticipate some account of the conditions that give rise to this exacerbated feeling, and some indication of the sustaining and assuaging resources that make continuance possible.

Most of the poems in *Wintering Out* were written between 1969 and 1973, a time when the political situation in Northern Ireland had become suddenly volatile and violent: 'There was an energy and excitement and righteousness in the air at that time, by people like myself who hadn't always been political',[1] said Heaney. Up to then Heaney had made a reputation as a poet of the parish pump, providing local interest and colour, employing a regional voice that tended to be regarded by his English audience as essentially diversionary, harmless and rustic. He wrote of folksy-crafty things like butter-making and thatchers. '*Door into the Dark*

will consolidate him', Christopher Ricks believed, 'as the poet of muddy-booted blackberry picking.'[2] But with the resurgence of the Troubles in the late 1960s, Heaney's notions about what poetry should be changed: 'From that moment the problems of poetry moved from being simply a matter of achieving the satisfactory verbal icon to being a search for images and symbols adequate to our predicament.'[3] the prefatory poem, part of a sequence entitled '**Whatever You Say, Say Nothing**', which originally appeared in *The Listener,* presents a series of nightmarish images of Ulster's Troubles: the internment camp, a bomb crater, machine-gun posts which 'defined a real stockade'. To complete the feeling of unreality, a white mist enshrouds the horrifying scene:

> and it was déjà-vu, some film made
> of Stalag 17, a bad dream with no sound.

The last stanza questions the quality of life that is possible amid such conditions. The rest of the poems in the book have to be read in the context of this numbed despair. In Part I, 'our predicament' is treated in cultural and political terms, but in Part II he presents a series of more personalized dramatic images—often from the point of view of women—in which human loss, hurt, derangement and alienation are absorbed within a timeless, archetypal and cosmic perspective.

'**Fodder**', the first poem in *Wintering Out,* suggests the poet's vulnerability and need, and introduces 'the backward look' as a source of assuagement. He yearns for the prelapsarian, childhood world where nature's providence (imaged in the hay-rick) offered the possibility of 'comfort'. Another source of assuagement for the poet is knowing who you are, and where you come from. There is nurture in belonging to and knowing intimately a certain place and people and life-style. In his first two books Heaney concentrated on natural cycles, the rituals of rural life, the carrying on of family traditions: this emphasis on durability is extended into a preoccupation with his and his people's cultural history. He is looking for roots that go deeper than the purely personal ones of childhood. The title, *Wintering Out,* comes from '**Servant Boy**', where the suggestion of continuity in the use of the present tense ('He is wintering out') and the emblematic power conferred upon this first line through its appropriation as title for the volume, emphasize identity between poet and servant boy: 'how / you draw me into / your trail', writes Heaney. Despite dispossession and hardship, the servant boy, 'old work-whore, slave- / blood', is associated with the life-force, as the croppies had been. He comes 'first-footing' to the Big Houses carrying the 'warm eggs', symbols of regeneration, survival and warmth, even in winter. 'Resentful / and impenitent', the servant boy is neither unaware of his condition nor broken by it. Not far beneath the surface of the poem is 'the slightly aggravated young Catholic male'.

In **'Bog Oak'** the poet takes another 'backward look' into the past to affirm his ancestry amongst 'the moustached / dead, the creel-fillers'. They are also the pathetic dispossessed, wild men of the woods, nosing among the primitive facts: 'geniuses who creep / "out of every corner / of the woodes and glennes" / toward watercress and carrion'. These ancient figures survive as shadowy spirits of place, possessors of 'hopeless wisdom', poised between life and death. The privileged, aristocratic values of imperialist power, represented by Sir Edmund Spenser 'dreaming sunlight', have little relevance to the dark indigenous reality. In a *Guardian* article Heaney explained:

> From his castle in Cork, he (Spenser) watched the effects of a campaign designed to settle the Irish question. "Out of every corner of the woods and glens they came creeping forth upon their hands, for their legs could not carry them; they looked like anatomies of death . . ." At that point I feel closer to the natives, the geniuses of the place.[4]

Another shadowy genius is **'The Last Mummer'** for whose demise the poem is a lament. A sense of loss pervades the poem, achieving repeated and cumulative emphasis from the way each section ends with an image of the mummer's withdrawal and disappearance. Heaney cannot claim the travelling player as a specifically Irish phenomenon (as Hardy's mummers in *The Return of the Native* would serve to remind us), but the mummer's intimacy with his people, his reliance on a sense of community and tradition, and his skill in portraying the mores and manners of the folk, give him a special place in the poet's esteem. A pagan, poetic spirit, he had led the imagination out of the miasma of blood and feuding into the realms of myth and magic:

> The moon's host elevated
>
> in a monstrance of holly trees,
> he makes dark tracks, who had
>
> untousled a first dewy path
> into the summer grazing.

Now, his popularity has been supplanted by the new magic of television. The lack of attention and appreciation he now receives breeds frustration and anger. The traditional values he had embodied with such tact and skill are perverted into violence, as he beats the bars of the gate and throws the stone onto the roof.

All three of these poems dispense with the comforting echo of regular rhyme. This highlights the facility of Heaney's choice of words, sentence structure and individually imposed principles of organization. **'Servant Boy'** and **'Bog Oak'** use a short, four-lined stanza form, **'The Last Mummer'**, the couplet, but despite this kind of punctuation imposed by the line arrangement, the general run of these poems is more like that of blank verse rather than the couplet or any stanza form (even though there are a few sporadic rhymes and a few lines are shorter than the others). This looser, more fluid, fainter and more tenuous kind of versification gives the poems a more immediate psychological spontaneity than rigidly traditional forms would permit. Freedom is attained not by breaking down the form but reshaping it. It is a poetic idiom related to a concern with the living speech of the day and the place, but as well as that it marks a continuing development of technique. The poems are in essence meditative and reminiscent, a half-shy, uncertain snatching at a fleeting vision. Heaney's fondness for the run-on line gives them an insinuating quality, the syntactical movement always tending to diverge from the rhythmical movement provided by the ideal metrical norm. This is why there is an exploratory and tentative feel about the rhythm, for it is out of the play of sense and sound that the penumbra of the past is conjured into time present, with the associative and emotional logic of a dream or day-dream. In **'Bog Oak'** it is out of the 'smoke' and 'mizzling rain' which 'blurs the far end / of the cart track', that the poet dimly discerns his ghostly ancestors. The servant boy is 'a jobber among shadows', the last mummer a dream-figure who 'moves out of the fog'.

This lack of definition is typical of many of the poems in *Wintering Out*. The heavy, thickly-textured idiom which Heaney used to evoke the visible world in his first two books is severely tempered. In *Death of a Naturalist* and *Door into the Dark* there was a sense of the poem's completeness and self-containment because each poem had its own 'action'—Ned Kelly's bull servicing a Friesian cow, a thatcher at work, butter churning, gathering blackberries, digging bait, lifting the catch into the boat—which depended on the concrete particularity of the language for its precise and vivid evocation. By contrast, poems like **'Servant Boy'**, **'Bog Oak'** and **'The Last Mummer'** emerge as extensions of the poet's mind, as the products of dream. They are gestures toward something that remains imprecise and, accordingly, their hold on the physical world relaxes. The external world is still there, but not so emphatically, for Heaney is now setting out to pursue ideas rather than simply recreate objects and processes. Sensory impression is organized and constructed within a probing intellectual purpose. As a result, the poems often strike us as reveries or musings. Sometimes much is left to the reader, if he is to discover from the poem's pulse of feeling, its fractional connections and private images, the implicit order amongst the array of particulars. This is particularly true of the series of poems entitled **'A Northern Hoard'** at the centre of the book, and, to a slightly lesser extent, of **'Gifts of Rain'**.

In **'Gifts of Rain'** Heaney is once again the water diviner. The Moyola's flood-water is the music of the place, the place giving tongue, uttering its secrets like the hidden source in **'The Diviner'** 'suddenly broadcasting through a green aerial its secret stations'. The water cleanses, re-vitalizes, satisfies thirst, creeps into the earth's secret recesses and leaves behind the 'word-hoard' of its singing in the alluvium of language and history. Heaney burrows in that 'word-hoard' to re-create that music. The poem is a version of composition as 'soundings', as a listening, a wise passiveness. The Moyola, like Wordsworth's Derwent, acts as tutor of his poetic ear, and the strength and originality of the poem lie first in the poet's trusting the validity of his intuitions once the normal inhibitions of consciousness are relaxed; then in discovering through the operation of his auditory imagination the sounds and rhythms proper to his sense. He dispenses with the facile continuity of pursuing a train of thought, opting instead for a variety of angles of approach, a restlessness of poetic style, and a somewhat strained metaphysical ingenuity and use of words with double or multiple meanings—all suggestive of a desire to devour a wide range of experience and ensure that the poem is neither attenuated by customary perception or conventional expectation, nor idealized away into a thin and misty abstraction.

It begins by directing our attention outwards, into the countryside, with two strongly visual images—of the animal in the mud, and a farmer wading lost fields—both suggesting the primal bond between inanimate nature and all living things. Animal and flood are one:

> A nimble snout of flood
> licks over stepping stones
> and goes uprooting.

This mysterious unity of being is further emphasized in the image of the farmer's quasi-sexual relationship with the land:

> and sky and ground
>
> are running naturally among his arms
> that grope the cropping land.

The mud water which he disturbs swirls up and mingles with his reflection. The man

> breaks the pane of flood:
>
> a flower of mud-
> water blooms up to his reflection
> like a cut swaying
> its spoors through a basin.

These complicated conceits, so exquisitely and so economically organized, again emphasize the continuity between man and nature. The life-giving water, when it is disturbed, 'blooms up' like a flower, and flows over and into the man. It merges with human life as the homonym of 'pane' suggests; the mud-water becomes

human blood, then both are linked with animal life through the reference to the tracks of a hunted animal.

After this, the poem flows inward. The river-water streams hypnotically in the background, gathering, slabbering, brimming, whispering, spelling itself, chanting, breathing, as it gradually 'deals out its being' (to use Hopkins' phrase) to the poet. He is a still consciousness, a finely attuned instinct, attentively sounding like the 'still mammal' in part I. And, like the farmer in part II, he is involved in a quasi-sexual communion with nature, alert to the 'shared calling of blood', the 'mating call' of sound which rises to pleasure him. In the sound of the rain he can hear ancestral voices calling to him, whispering of the famine and nature's destructive power. **'Waterfall'** was an early version of the same thing: in its 'slabber and spill', the poet heard 'the cries of villains dropped screaming to justice'. In **'Gifts of Rain'** the flood-voices have a distinctly tribal or racial timbre, as the double-meaning implies in the reference to 'the race / slabbering past the gable'. Language itself seems to be conditioned by landscape: the name Moyola strikes the poet as an onomatopaeic re-creation of the river-water itself. The landscape 'breathing its mists / through vowels and history' represents a continuity that is inextricably connected with language and history.

All these perceptions depend on the intimacy and precision of the correspondence which exist between the external landscape as a system of signs and the poet's internal landscape as a system of thinking and feeling. He is 'Dives / hoarder of common ground', and the flood-voices 'arrive' to meet his 'need / for antediluvian lore'. The word 'need' is telling. It points to a concern with establishing relationships—relationships with nature, landscape, history, community. From the beginning of his career—in **'Digging'**—Heaney is troubled by a sense of exclusion, a feeling which continues into much later poems, such as the tormented **'Exposure'** with which his next collection ends. There, he is still a marginal figure whose chosen stance is one of indirection. It is within this framework that we must see his preoccupation with relationships. There is the vital connection between man and nature in the parable of the diviner, the binding force of communal ritual which is motivated by a feeling for the land in **'At a Potato Digging'**, the ancestry the poet seeks in **'Servant Boy'** and **'Bog Oak'**, the 'soundings' he makes in **'Gifts of Rain'**. These are the product of an outsider desperately seeking to assuage his alienation and establish a direction for himself through embracing a communal consciousness and a sense of the mysterious unity of being that breathes through river mists, through vowels and history.

'In Ireland our sense of the past, our sense of the land and even our sense of identity are inextricably interwoven',[5] Heaney has said. When he asks himself who he is he is compelled to make a connection with a history, a landscape, a heritage. The sense of place, the feeling for a place, assuages and steadies him and gives him a point of view. Landscape is hallowed by associations that come from growing up and thinking himself into a place. Anahorish, Moyola, Broagh, Toome, Derrygarve, are names of what is known and loved, cherished because of their tribal, etymological implications. Heaney thinks of himself as a survivor, a repository, a keeper: he is 'Dives / hoarder of common ground'. Names and place-names are precious because they are bearers of history and ancestry, resonant clues to a shared and diminished culture. Unlike Kavanagh, and more like John Montague, Heaney's imagination is historic and mythopaeic. And at the bottom of it is the 'life-force' itself. The 'soft blastings' pronouncing the word 'Toome' are like explosions opening up a valuable find—'loam, flints, musket-balls / fragmented ware / torcs and fish-bones'. From the 'loam' of the recent past to the neckware of the ancient Irish to the 'alluvial mud' and 'bog-water', the poet traces through a 'hundred centuries' to the primeval source of self and race.

In comparing Heaney with the older, Protestant poet, John Hewitt, we can see how Heaney is bound to his place in a way Hewitt is not. For Hewitt the Glens of Antrim constitute 'the world my pulses take for true',[6] but he is always aware that he cannot share 'the enchantments of the old "tree magic"'.[7] In 'The Colony' he asserts attachment and identity by argument and formulated proof, whereas Heaney works on the level of implication, in terms of something that is naturally and automatically received, and can therefore be understated. Heaney is bound to his place though a lineage which he traces back to origins in 'alluvial mud' and through the figure of a mythological goddess. Hewitt's attachment on the other hand, as Heaney has pointed out, originates in rights conferred by Act of Parliament. Hewitt's primeval symbols, as Heaney further remarks, are 'bifocal',[8] including the Rollright Stones of Oxfordshire as well as Ossian's Grave. Hewitt's is the urbane, rational voice of a civilized man, Heaney's the voice of instinct probing the soft mulches of feeling and sensation, articulating 'realms of whisper'.

'Anahorish'—'soft gradient / of consonant, vowel-meadow'—rehearses in sound the landscape it names. In Heaney's place-name poems language is pushed towards a magical relationship with the things it is speaking about. The word 'Anahorish' means 'place of clear water', and the poem begins with an image of pristine beauty cast in the past tense:

> My 'place of clear water',
> the first hill in the world
> where springs washed into
> the shiny grass

This modulates into a darker picture of winter-time, past merges with present, and the feeling of loss and hardship intensifies. At the end the well-water no longer runs freely and cleanly and the 'mound-dwellers', though still in touch with the life-force, are now lost in dreamlike mists.

'Broagh' is another place-name which seems to Heaney to echo the sound of the rain, 'its low tattoo / among the windy boortrees / and rhubarb-blades.' The name (meaning 'riverbank') contains residual sounds of the native Irish language: 'that last / *gh* the strangers found / difficult to manage'. **'Broagh'** is a highly formalised poem, intent and concentrated, each word asking for scrutiny as to how good it is making these 'soundings'. Exploring the relationship between landscape, language and people, it ends by alerting us to the nationalistic implications of all this.

What the place-name poems proved to Heaney was that, while using English, he could still express a sensibility conditioned by belonging to a particular place, an ancestry, a history, a culture, that was not English:

> I had a great sense of release as they (the place-name poems) were being written, a joy and devil-may-careness, and that convinced me that one could be faithful to the nature of the English language—for in some senses these poems are erotic mouth-music by and out of the Anglo-Saxon tongue—and, at the same time be faithful to one's own non-English origin, for me that is County Derry.[9]

Ultimately, it is not even relevant that he should use English for it is a language of nature he aims for. **'Oracle'** gives us the image of a child—the incipient poet—hiding in the hollow trunk of a willow tree, taking in and re-producing the sounds of nature:

> small mouth and ear
> in a woody cleft,
> lobe and larynx
> of the mossy places.

'The Backward Look' recognizes that the Irish language is a thing of the past. Heaney describes its faltering career in terms of the flight of the snipe, the irregular, short-lined stanza-form reinforcing the sense of uncertain, fugitive movement. The snipe flees its nesting ground, just as the language fled its origins into dialects and variants. The etymologist transliterates Irish and English: the snipe's tail-feathers drum an elegy for the language and culture as the bird follows in the slipstream of the vanished wild goose and bittern. By the end of the poem, snipe and language disappear among 'gleanings and leavings / in the combs / of a fieldworker's archive'. The sense of loss is imbued with a vaguely elegiac, romantic feeling, as Heaney follows the snipe 'over twilit earthworks / and wall-steads'. In **'Traditions'** and **'A New Song'** it is more difficult to deduce his attitude.

'Traditions' begins with an image of violation, a brutal sexual metaphor to describe the displacement of the feminine Gaelic vowel by the hard consonantal language of English:

> Our guttural muse
> was bulled long ago
> by the alliterative tradition

The Irish 'are to be proud' of their Elizabethan inheritance, the notion of enforced submission in this phrase leading to ironic self-congratulation at having mastered the colonist's language. There is resentment against the pride of the planter in re-modelling the Ulster dialect, and against the English who do not take the Irish seriously. The third part of the poem begins with a reference to Macmorris in *Henry V*, the first stage Irishman, 'gallivanting' about the Globe, 'whingeing' about his national identity: '"What ish my nation?"' Despite dispossession, despoliation and caricature, the poem resolves itself 'sensibly', in resignation and bathos, with the words of Joyce's Wandering Jew, Leopold Bloom, who answers Macmorris: '"Ireland . . . / I was born here. Ireland."'

'A New Song', like **'Anahorish'**, opens with a nostalgic, soothing vision of an Edenic past. The recreation of the poet's colourful Arcadian childhood in Derrygarve implies acceptance of irrecoverable loss. But that abruptly changes:

> But now our river tongues must rise
> From licking deep in native haunts
> To flood, with vowelling embrace,
> Demesnes staked out in consonants.
>
> And Castledawson we'll enlist
> And Upperlands, each planted bawn—
> Like bleaching-greens resumed by grass—
> A vocable, as rath and bullaun.

He contemplates the possibility of retrieval and advance, but is unsure whether this will be effected through natural evolution or by force, an uncertainty conveyed in the ambiguity of 'must rise'. 'Embrace' suggests an act of love, the military metaphors ('staked out', 'enlist', 'bawn', 'rath') something more ominous. Castledawson and Upperlands are 'planted bawns'—'bawn' being the word, adapted from the Irish *Bábhun* (bulwark, rampart; a fold, enclosure for cattle), which the planters used to refer to their fortified farmhouses. Curiously, it is these he wishes to 'enlist'. The neutral word 'resumed' in the penultimate line does not help to clarify his attitude as it could refer equally to the forceful repossession of the

'bleaching-greens' of the planters' disappearing linen industry by the native Irish, or a peaceable return to origins in which both communities will participate. The linguistic token of the new dispensation is the 'vocable' (the crossing of Irish vowels with English consonants) displayed in survivals like 'rath' (a rath being a prehistoric hill-fort or fairy building) and 'bullaun' (a bullaun being basin stones some of which may have been the bases of small crosses). The poem moves from past tense to future tense, the 'backward look' giving way to a tentatively optimistic, but somewhat confused, forward look.

Other poems like **'The Wool Trade'**, **'Midnight'** and **'Linen Town'** are imbued with a sense of cultural loss that culminates by appropriating an intensely personalized frustration. **'Midnight'** speaks of a native energy that has disappeared from Irish life: 'The wolf has died out,' 'Nothing is panting, lolling, / Vapouring'. A series of images of emasculation dramatizes a psychic condition brought about by a history of dispossession and alienation: 'My tongue's / Leashed in my throat'.

The leashing of the tongue in the throat is directly enacted in **'The Wool Trade'**. The bulk of the poem is a passionate, mellifluous, vowel-based lament over a lost language and a lost way of life, their interrelatedness emphasized by making the spools, waterwheels, looms and spindles the very forms of language: 'Hills and flocks and streams conspired / To a language of waterwheels / A lost syntax of looms and spindles.' The loose and flowing paratactic style, which dissolves those verbal controls whereby reality is normally distanced, classified and subdued, is a version of the 'rambling' and 'unwinding' which characterize the indigenous language; it expresses the romantic notion of Gaelic intractability to the requirements of 'civilization', a notion which fuelled the traditional ideology of Irish cultural nationalism. This is then counterpointed in the last two lines by a harsh, tight-mouthed and heavily consonantal structure reflecting the rational authority of colonial influence:

> And I must talk of tweed,
> A stiff cloth with flecks of blood.

Historically, the poem alludes to the dismantling of the social and political system of Gaelic Ireland following the surrender of Hugh O'Neill in 1603, and to the steady infiltration of colonists, especially of lowland Scots, inaugurated by James I's plantation policy. Heaney takes the wool trade and places it in the context of a highly generalized regime of dispossession: thus, the colonial influence is responsible for replacing a pleasureable, easy-going warmth with authoritarian stiffness, feeling with reason, instinct with efficiency, freedom with coercion, the organic community with violence and alienation. Most conspicuous of all is the much-lamented loss of the Gaelic language. The terms of the various oppositions, however, are ill-defined and so unable to constitute a firm and energetic structure which would save the poem from sentimentality. The root emotion is a nostalgic craving for origins and presence: even more satisfying than Gaelic 'vowels' from the point of view of the mythologist of origins is the pure, unmediated, preliterate expression of looms and spindles into which the Gaelic language metamorphoses half-way through. It is this 'original' language which is then displaced by the planter's 'blood-stained' language, the currency of which is the symbol—the necessarily insufficient word. The contrast is between 'natural' or 'original' language which remains close to its sources in passionate utterance, in feeling, in nature, in the community at large, and 'artificial' or 'foreign' language imposed from outside and governed by the rules and devices of an alien culture. Heaney yields to the Rousseauesque dream of an innocent language and community untouched by the evils of progress, a mythology of presence, which ignores the self-alienating aspect of any language and all social existence.

In **'Linen Town'** political disappointment and failure are linked with linguistic loss. The hanged body of Henry Joy McCracken, the Protestant leader of a small insurrection of United Irishmen in Antrim in 1798, is referred to as 'a swinging tongue'. Heaney is contemplating a civic print of High Street, Belfast, 1786, twelve years before the execution of the Irish rebel. The past becomes vividly alive, recreated in the present tense. As the print 'unfreezes' the poet experiences with equal urgency its sensuous reality and the political excitement of the time:

> Smell the tidal Lagan:
> Take a last turn
> In the tang of possibility.

There is an unmistakable poignancy which manages to avoid sentimentality in the best of these poems in which the poet figures as a survivor probing and commemorating 'native haunts', interrogating the 'tints' of a diminished culture, listening attentively for the echoes of a cherished, vital past from which he has been disinherited, and which exists now as 'gleanings and leavings', no more than a 'realm of whisper', almost a dreamworld—but to which he feels indissolubly bound. Its vestigial life, even though bereft of the last 'tang of possibility' and depending for its re-creation on a foreign language, still remains a potent source of nourishment and imaginative freedom.

The poems of place and place-name, Heaney tells us, 'politicize the terrain and imagery of the first two books'.[10] His relationship with the ground he grew up on is complicated by the fact that it is a country of division—historic social, political and cultural divisions that have had a profound effect on the whole psychic life of himself and his people. While he is, naturally enough, principally concerned with defining his relationship with his own community and his own past, **'The Other Side'** is an exact and subtly evocative expression of the relationship between Catholic and Protestant as experienced by the poet on the farm where he grew up. The neighbouring Protestant farmer impinges as a large, dramatic presence. Standing amid the sedge and marigolds, he reminds the poet of an Old Testament prophet and the description of him, 'white-haired, / swinging his blackthorn', subtly hints at the straightforward, black-and-white morality by which he lives. The Puritan aversion to ornament and ritual, the simplicity, sturdiness and orderliness of the man's life, the way in which his every thought is determined by the precepts of his religion, are emphasized in the hard consonantal music and strong accentual rhythms:

> his brain was a whitewashed kitchen
> hung with texts, swept tidy
> as the body o' the kirk.

Even his speech is Biblical, and while the poet may find the grandiloquent high seriousness of his idiom impressive, it is as divisive as the *gh* in **'Broagh'**. It does not speak for the poet, for it is the self-righteous 'tongue of chosen people' that is inappropriate to the poet's perceptions of himself and his world. From his less privileged perspective, the poet cannot resist deflating the 'patriarchal dictum', comparing its 'magnificence' to loads of hay too big for his small lanes. The Protestant farmer speaks twice—first to dismiss his neighbour's land as hopelessly barren and then his religion as unscriptural—each remark a blunt, unfeeling rejection that increases awareness of the man's sense of superiority. When he moves off towards his 'promised furrows', he disturbs the weed-pollen which drifts in to infect his neighbour's fields—an image of the unwitting damage which he causes.

Section III moves to the poet's 'side of the house', and he is not uncritical of it either. The rosary is 'dragging mournfully' on in the kitchen, the lack of vitality in Catholic practice contrasting with the obsessive vigour of the Protestant's religion. Now it is the Protestant who is the outsider. As the prayers draw to a close, he is like a stranger in the dark outside, intruding on something intensely personal, forever outside his concern. The gestures of friendship are guarded and embarrassed. The Protestant visitor has to make excuses for calling, and whistle casually to maintain a pretence of disinterest while the family finish the litany and answer his knock on the door. The poet's reaction is equally hesitant and unspontaneous:

> Should I slip away, I wonder,
> or go up and touch his shoulder
> and talk about the weather
>
> or the price of grass-seed?

Even if they strike up a conversation, what degree of intimacy can they hope to achieve? What the poem offers is a picture of two worlds which can never fully meet. The poem marks a considerable development beyond **'Docker'** in its balance and emotional complexity.

Faced with the inconceivable horror spawned by Ulster's traditional divisions, the kind of objective dramatization of the relationship between the two communities which we find in **'The Other Side'** cannot be maintained. The pain cannot be supported by such a mannerly style. The five poems which constitute **'A Northern Hoard'** are amongst the few in *Wintering Out* which turn to the subject of the volume's prefatory poem and take us into the immediate horror of the Troubles in Belfast in 1969. The Northern hoard of history and racial consciousness is filled with blood and death. Actuality mingles with nightmare. 'All shifts dreamily', as Heaney says in the first poem, **'Roots'.** Here, the opening stanza's troubled, eerie music introduces the idea of derangement, dissolution and death being deeply embedded in the very geology of the country. It is a quiet, stunned lament over the conditions which make love impossible in the Ulster Gomorrah. Outside are the sounds of gunshot, siren and exploding gas. 'We petrify or uproot now'—the lovers harden to stone, freeze with fear, find themselves cut off from every sustaining thing in their environment. 'Uproot', however, may be active rather than passive, suggesting another alternative—confronting the horror and trying to 'uproot' it. The poet goes on to say he will dream the symbolic release of the evil spirits which plague the lovers:

> I've soaked by moonlight in tidal blood
>
> A mandrake, lodged human fork,
> Earth sac, limb of the dark;
> And I wound its damp smelly loam
> And stop my ears against the scream.

The mandrake-shriek that was supposed to be heard when the plant was uprooted was, according to tradition, the scream of the long-dead murderers buried where the mandrake grew. But there is also the suggestion in these densely enigmatic lines of enwinding oneself with primordial, instinctual forces, returning to the dark, reuniting oneself with the natural world, thereby assuming the magical, healing virtue that was reputedly attached to the mandrake root, itself a human surrogate because of its resemblance to the shape of the human torso. As in **'Oracle',** or in later poems like **'Exposure'** or *Sweeney Astray,* the poet is 'Taking protective colouring / From bole and bark.'[11] The poem expresses an intense desire for exorcism, but the sustained sense of strain in the use of pararhyme and the muted confidence of its exploratory, tentative metres demonstrate that the magical properties of dream and superstitious ritual have not found their aesthetic equivalents in the poetic structure. The poem stands more as a melodramatic expression of need than an imaginative transcendence of it.

In the second poem, **'No Man's Land',** the poet, as the title implies, has cut himself off from community and communal consciousness. He has 'deserted', tried to 'shut out' the horror of the violence. He resents having to confront it, but acknowledges that if he doesn't, he forfeits his humanity. Resentment finally gives way to guilt: 'Why do I unceasingly / arrive late to condone / infected sutures / and ill-knit bone?'

The agony of doubt and dividedness is registered in another rhetorical question in the next poem, **'Stump':** 'What do I say if they wheel out their dead?' This is the question which burdens Heaney from now on. His response here—'I'm cauterized, a black stump of home'—expresses a sense of failure and ineffectuality. The crisis of savagery has obliterated the vitalizing and sustaining influences which he celebrates elsewhere as springing from a sense of place and a sense of community. The title of the fourth poem, **'No Sanctuary',** anticipates the condition he describes in **'Exposure'.** It may be Halloween, the time of harvest celebration and solemn recollection of the Feast of All Souls, but in Ulster 'the turnip-man's lopped head', instead of averting the avenging dead, has an even more sinister meaning—it is the very emblem of the country's horror.

The sequence of poems concludes with **'Tinder'** which presents a dark and savage view of human nature and human history. On one level it is an allegory of the underprivileged tribe who light the tinder of revolution and then wonder what to do with their 'new history'. But the prehistoric imagery makes it clear that Heaney is not just thinking of Ireland. He is describing 'the terror behind all', the 'unproductive fury'[12] in human nature. The use of the first person plural emphasizes the continuum of history, the fundamental similarity between primitive man and modern technological man. His concern is with primal consciousness which seems to Heaney to be inclined ineluctably toward destruction. Reference to the 'flames' soft thunder' and facing into 'the tundra's whistling bush', is the apocalyptic imagery of the nuclear holocaust, which further helps to universalize the poem's application. Destruction, desolation and disappointment inevitably seem to attend human 'progress'. 'Canine', the word with which the poem ends, is the essential predisposition, as Heaney sees it, of the human animal. In the picture of the survivors, stunned and silenced, surrounded by the ashes of their own devastation and having to face into desolate psychic tundras, we recognize the anguish of the poet wondering what his role should be.

The question as ever is, 'How with this rage shall beauty hold a plea?' Heaney's answer now is: 'by offering "befitting emblems of adversity"'.[13] Heaney's search for befitting emblems was greatly helped by his reading of P. V. Glob's book, *The Bog People*. It tells of the discovery in Danish bogs of bodies dating back to the Iron Age who had been sacrificial victims to the Mother Goddess, Nerthus, the goddess of the ground, who required new bridegrooms each winter to bed with her in her sacred place, in the bog, to ensure renewal and spring fertility. Heaney uses this archaic, barbarous rite as an archetypal pattern within which may also be contained the tradition of Irish political martyrdom. It offered a way of understanding, of dealing with, a monstrous violence. By presenting contemporary events in Ulster as elements of a timeless continuum they are rendered smaller, more manageable, bearable. It is a technique of assuagement, an effort to find the grounds for endurance and continuance. The realms of whisper are now located in the sucking mud of the bog, whose ancient messengers raised from darkness excite Heaney, speaking to him of a system of reality beyond and behind the visible world.

'The Tollund Man' opens by describing the Iron Age corpse which now 'reposes' in the museum at Aarhus. The details indicate the absorption of the man's pathetic mortality in the timeless processes of nature, their rhythmic organization possessing a narcotic quality which reinforces the 'gentleness', 'mildness' and 'repose' of his appearance, despite the tell-tale sign of the noose. A quiet, reflective wonderment imbues the lines, as the physical particulars are gradually gathered into the larger pattern of meaning: the man is 'Bridegroom to the goddess', the earth is both mother and lover, both fecund maternal principle and demanding lover. In part II the fate of the ancient victim sacrificed to the goddess is linked with that of contemporary victims of Ireland's Troubles whose lives have been sacrificed in the cause of Mother Ireland. Heaney would like to think that the promise of renewal which motivated the Iron Age sacrifice will apply to the Irish situation. The Tollund Man is more than merely a spiritual ancestor of the Irish dead. His union with the Earth Goddess has initiated a transfiguring process ('Those dark juices working / Him to a saint's kept body') that is paralleled by his imaginative apotheosis effected through the ritual of art. He becomes a possible intercessor to whom the poet would pray to redeem his slaughtered countrymen. The recognition of wishfulness in 'I *could* risk blasphemy, / Consecrate the cauldron bog / Our holy ground . . .' (my italics) imparts a special urgency and tension. The long rambling sentence which follows from the words just quoted occupies the entire second part of the poem, but the auxiliary 'could', in 'could risk blasphemy', while still officially controlling the other verbs 'consecrate' and 'pray', acts with increasingly diminished force. It is as if the poet's need

is being imaginatively fulfilled in the momentum of the poem's writing. That need takes charge of the second part of the poem as Heaney goes on to make germinate in his own imagination the image of the four young brothers who were victims of an ugly sectarian killing in the 1920s. The rituals of art and religion are closely connected in Heaney's mind, and the whole poem may be seen as an enaction of that pilgrimage to which he pledges himself in the first line: 'Some day I will go to Aarhus.' In language and feeling **'The Tollund Man'** is devotional. 'When I wrote that poem', Heaney confirms, 'I had a sense of crossing a line really, that my whole being was involved in the sense of—the root sense—of religion, being bonded to something, being bound to do something. I felt it a vow . . .'.[14] He saw himself quite explicitly as devotee or pilgrim, remarking on 'My sense of occasion and almost awe as I vowed to go to pray to the Tollund Man and assist at his enshrined head.'[15]

The Tollund Man, as well as releasing profoundly religious feelings which for Heaney are connected with his apprehension of the Irish territorial numen and the curious fact of political martyrdom, is also embraced as a kind of ancestor who will perhaps offer the poet a revelation of artistic destiny. The wishfulness of this notion is again acknowledged: 'Something of his sad freedom / As he rode the tumbril / *Should* come to me' (my italics). The poet's bold, leap into a dark, mythic, timeless zone that is also the bog-like depths of self does make available some kind of 'sad freedom' from the contemporary horror. It represents an intellectual distancing of himself from the inchoate pieties that bind him unconditionally to a specific place and past and people. The ancient victim's last journey to his execution merges with the poet's imagined pilgrimage to Aarhus, and as Heaney moves through this psychic territory, chanting the place-names, seeing the people pointing at him but not understanding their tongue, his own complex relationship to the 'man-killing parishes' of Ulster gradually clarifies itself, and the poem reaches toward its climactic, starkly ambivalent recognition:

> Out there in Jutland
> In the old man-killing parishes
> I will feel lost,
> Unhappy and at home.

This tension between allegiance to 'our holy ground' with its sacrificial demands, and the claims of individual values which react against the barbarism of the sacrifice is where Heaney's most intense poetry is located. The discrepancy between communal consciousness and an outsider's sympathy with the victimized individual produces an anguished stance of indirection.

In the poems in Part Two of **Wintering Out** he focuses on personal situations, exploring the tensions which taint marriage, the strange unaccountable forces in life which confuse or pervert love, the hurt and derangement occasioned by social taboo and, beyond that, the cruel imperfections of the human condition itself.

The first poem, **'Wedding Day',** begins with the simple statement: 'I am afraid.' It goes on to present the poet's confused emotions on his wedding day, his experience of an eerie sense of unreality, of grief pervading celebration, and remarks on his bride's demented fears. In the gents he comes across the banal popular emblem of romance, 'a skewered heart / And a legend of love'— even it intimates violence and, in the word 'legend', the unreality of love's promise. But despite the inescapability of taint and vulnerability, the poem ends with an affirmation of simple faith, a gesture of trust and tenderness: 'Let me / Sleep on your breast to the airport.' The use of the quatrain and the reluctance to stretch or distort its metrical rigidities too severely limit the variety of tunes the poet can play and inhibit the intimacy and complexity of his probing of pain. The form enforces the desire to cling to order and propriety in the face of confusion.

A much more accomplished piece of work, **'Summer Home',** appears a few pages further on. Its complex music demonstrates an adventurous expansion of sensibility, an effort to achieve the maximum of individual and personal expression. Using a variety of stanza forms, Heaney stretches the structures and tactics of a rational, orderly conventionalized poetic to reveal intense and fugitive areas of feeling. The freer movement and more 'open' form implies that feeling has not been made to fit into pre-set patterns but that the form has been determined by the dynamics of the subject matter. We are admitted to a terrible privateness in which the movement of the poem is the writhing, anguished movement of consciousness. Discursive and logical language modulates into the invocatory, repetitive and intuitive structures of painful intimacy in which we hear, or rather overhear, the guilt and hurt of marital tension. The source of this pain, we realize, is 'the spirit that plagues us so' in **'A Northern Hoard'**—an evil, unidentifiable force in the world which prevents love and pushes us toward self-destruction. In **'Summer Home'** it is a foul and bestial contagion in the 'possessed air'.

Smitten with knowledge of taint and pain, the poet's probing is conducted in an unconfident, querulous voice embodied in the wavering, meditative rhythms, the irregular rhyme and hovering half-rhymes ('summer'—'sour'—'somewhere'—'wondered'—'inquisitor'—'air'). His discourse, unified by its olfactory and animal imagery, is, in its terms of reference—summer soured, wind off the dumps, 'something' in heat dogging the pair, fouled nest incubating 'somewhere', larval mat—generalized, oblique and deliberately vague. Part I works its way up to an explosive climax as the poet,

proposing a symbolic ritual of self-purgation, vents his desperation in a poetry of the sheer present, a poetry which is, in the words of D. H. Lawrence, 'the insurgent naked throb of the instant moment'.[16]

Part II attempts a more mannerly, fluent movement:

> Bushing the door, my arms full
> of wild cherry and rhododendron,
> I hear her small lost weeping
> through the hall, that bells and hoarsens
> on my name, my name.
>
> O love, here is the blame.

The lines are haunted by a traditional iambic cadence, but their lyricism also depends on an intricately varied, individual and unpredictable musical organization of rhyme (internal as well as end-rhyme), pararhyme and verbal repetition. The long, heavily stressed syllables in the third line intensify pain and desolation, the caesura in the next creating the pause in which the woman's weeping suddenly becomes harsh and ugly, as if for the man's benefit once she is aware of his presence in the hall. Thus the poignancy of 'small lost weeping' becomes quickly inflamed by rancour and revulsion in 'bells and hoarsens'. These heavily-stressed verbs appropriate the emotional focus of the passage, along with the sounds—the forceful *b*, liquid *l*, resonant *r* and the long straining vowels—which had expressed the poet's initial blustering vigour as he approached with a show of confidence, bearing his peace-offering. The isolated last line can direct us forwards to the lesson in love's 'taint' which follows, or backwards—a possibility which is pointed by the 'name'—'blame' end-rhyme—thus suggesting the poet's awareness that it may be some ineradicable thing about himself that is the cause of pain.

The remainder of the second part takes the form of a meditation on the possibility of ritual healing. The poet's exhortation that he and his wife compose a May altar out of the 'loosened flowers' of their relationship is complicated by recognition of nature's evanescence. Instead, the blooms might more appropriately form a 'sweet chrism' containing the holy unction of their own mortality. The poet is looking for a structure of feeling and a code of practice which will, through required ritual observance, magically bring about a harmonious order out of existence and guarantee love's mystery. Part II ends with the ritual summons: 'Attend. Anoint the wound.'

The liturgical afflatus is abraded and overthrown by the harsh, colloquial irony of the first lines of part III: 'O we tented the wound all right.' Further deflating the high style of ritual confidence is the brutal image of the two of them lying as if winded by the flat of a blade. But watching his wife in the shower, the poet's cadences and vocabulary once again attune themselves to a liturgical music: 'as you bend in the shower / water lives down the tilting stoups of your breasts'. This is the poet as postulant, struggling to reassert a sexual piety, longing for benediction to offset human imperfection.

Part IV is composed of short, strong pulsations and an imagery of phallic penetration and natural growth, through which the poet seeks to affirm renewed intimacy. The process is 'unmusical' and violent, but contains the possible engendering moment of more honest confrontation. Once again they 'sap' the worn, 'white' path to the heart, 'white' suggesting purity of motive, 'sap' alluding both to the regenerative sources from which the couple, like the maize and vine, draw strength, and, in its other sense of excavate, to the hard work involved to re-open the submerged, blocked channels of love. The short line, 'we sap', is the critical moment of effort and renewal, and leads to the restoration of movement and direction in the longer, though still rhythmically tense, closing two lines of the section.

The tidal ebb and flow which characterizes the poem's structure returns the poet at the beginning of part V to rancour and unease. But the poem does not end until some source of hope and healing has been found. The natural world 'attends' upon them, proclaiming the promise of nurture and fulfilment. In the dark depths of being there survives the possibility—fragile and unconfident though it may be—of love and harmony:

> Yesterday rocks sang when we tapped
> Stalactites in the cave's old, dripping dark—
> Our love calls tiny as a tuning fork.

The ritual affirmation requires none of the extravagant liturgical diction used earlier. After all the metrical strain and uneasiness of the rest of the poem, the poet ultimately contains his hopeful intuition in a quiet, attentive iambic pentameter. Love and lyric ('rocks sang', 'Our love calls tiny as a tuning fork') are modes of resisting the dark.

In 'Shore Woman' marital tension is explored, as in 'The Wife's Tale', through the form of a Frostian dramatic monologue, from the point of view of the woman, and in such a way that the poem becomes an emblem of the opposition between the masculine and feminine principles in life. The epigraph, 'Man to the hills, women to the shore', grounds the poem in the countryman's stock of proverbial wisdom, as many of Frost's poems are grounded in some piece of local knowledge, some small event or folk tale. But in the work of both poets this sense of community, this primitive level of myth-making, is combined with a subtlety of insight beyond the reach of any crudely populist consciousness. The poetry of 'Shore Woman' results

from a highly disciplined casualness of tone which comes under increasing pressure to accommodate the barely contained panic; a remarkable actuality of detail developed with delicately allusive logic; and a sophisticated blend of observation and reminiscence, realism and fancy, as the poem moves with assurance from mood to mood, image to image, thought to thought. Devotion to both craft and technique produces a rich texture of sound and meaning—not so passionate and exciting perhaps as that of 'Summer Home'—but one that is finely attuned to the working of this particular mind; the complex drama of a single life, continually revealing itself in its concrete quality, never reduced to a mere interplay of ideas, exemplifying and developing Heaney's sexual myth.

The poem begins with the woman walking along the firm margin between the 'riddling' dunes and the far rocks where 'a pale sud comes and goes'. Here is a severely delimited, phantasmal realm, haunted by suffering and death, and bathed in the light of the moon, the deranging influence of which is suggested in the metaphorical extravagance of the description of the moonlit shore.

In the next section the rhythm and diction are more forceful, as the woman remembers a frightening experience at sea when she accompanied her husband on a night's fishing. What remains with her is the memory of the man's absorption, his silence and his skill. She thinks of her own ignorance of potential danger, registers her own giddy insouciance: 'He was all business in the stern. I called / "This is so easy that it's hardly right."' This sense of the drama of the situation co-exists with an oblique and covert expression as the fearful moment approaches: they drift 'out beyond the head'—they have left the safety of the shore and are moving into a symbolic and psychic realm of hidden terror where the tensions between them are most strongly focussed. The woman says she is 'conscious' of what is happening, but her language itself has hidden depths in which we recognize her unwillingness to confront the full implications of the situation: drifting beyond the head is drifting beyond rational control, the drifting apart of their marriage.

In the deep waters they encounter a school of porpoises:

> I saw the porpoises' thick backs
> Cartwheeling like the flywheels of the tide,
> Soapy and shining . . .
> Tight viscous muscle, hooped from tail to snout.

The porpoises are the metaphorical embodiment of a dark, instinctual power lying in the submerged depths. Their relentless physicality, their slimy, secret, absorbing life, like the frogs in the flax-dam or the eels in Lough Neagh, threaten to engulf and destroy. Insofar as she associates them with brute male sexuality, they are a projection of the way the woman perceives her husband. Then comes the critical moment—the memory of the dunt and slither of the porpoises against the bottom of the boat. The poem's formal decorum is pushed to its limit so that we experience at one and the same time the tense effort to contain and control, and the yawing, violent rhythms of terror and nausea.

The woman turns to her husband and asks him to return to shore but he, his 'machismo' awakened, is only interested in pursuing the physical challenge, and disregards the woman's feelings. He enjoys an attitude of superiority for, as in **'The Wife's Tale',** the poem's central incident belongs to the male domain. The woman is an outsider, she has no experience of the routines of fishing; indeed, according to tradition, it is bad luck for a woman to be in the fishing boat at all. By allowing her to be there the man defies superstitious belief. When the woman tells him the porpoises will attack a boat, he scathingly dismisses her pronouncement as a yarn that has fooled her people far too long. The reference to the woman's people further heightens their separateness, implying a basic tribal distinction between them. Brutally, he refuses her the comfort and understanding she needs. The sea which she finds alien and hateful belongs to him, and its intractibility is reflected in the husband's attitude. The last part of the poem returns to the woman walking the shore:

> I sometimes walk this strand for thanksgiving
> Or maybe to get away from him
> Skittering his spit across the stove.

Her hatred and revulsion surface with a sudden and explicit virulence. The man offends her sensitivity and her piety. Solitariness is a price she is glad to pay for peace and safety. The shore is her 'fallow avenue', the phrase suggesting rest and renewal, and also something with definite direction, something civilized and therefore safe. Counterpointing this faith, however, is the haunting, half-acknowledged awareness of the continued presence of death and danger. She remarks on the shelving sand and notices the abandoned relics of what once were living organisms lying like 'debris' along the shore. More gross and threatening tokens of horror— the gasping carcasses of whales—can be managed for they belong to the realm of hear-say and yarn, to which she and her people are said to be too susceptible. On the shore she feels she has 'rights', but the effort to convince herself of safety and direction is undermined by acknowledgement that she is 'Astray upon a debris of scrubbed shells.' She is anxious to maintain a careful distance from those encompassing forces which threaten destruction, and which she perceives in the 'parched dunes' (spiritlessness, exhaustion, deadness) and 'salivating wave' (bestial, voracious appetite). She is 'a membrane between moonlight and my shadow'—an image of the woman's fragile, marginal existence between madness and death.

In the remaining poems of ***Wintering Out*** Heaney continues his meditation on the pain and hurt of life. The poems are based firmly on local, rural incident, but continually gesture toward archetypal significance and a perspective of cosmic emptiness. The first three, **'A Winter's Tale', 'Maighdean Mara'** and **'Limbo'** are about women, **'Bye-Child'** is about a child, and **'First Calf'** uses the imagery of animal life as an emblem of universal, psychic life. In all of them there is a tender regard for the lost, the outsider, for the deranged, the rejected and the alienated. The tone is elegiac, unsentimentally bleak and desolating.

In **'A Winter's Tale'** a young girl, weeping and bloodstained, is suddenly illuminated by a car's headlights on a country road. She is a 'maiden daughter' who roams naked through the countryside at night, often to be found by neighbours, when they return home, lying sleeping by their hearths. The girl's appearance is regarded as good luck, and neighbours are kindly and solicitous towards her. In the course of the poem she accrues larger significance—as an Ulster Perdita, a kind of Vestal Virgin or elemental spirit of the hearth, a female Sweeney fleeing the containments and conventions of civilization, a nature spirit who awakened 'as from a winter / Sleep. Smiled. Uncradled her breasts'. The poem's strength is that these larger implications do not distract from the girl's primary physical actuality which elicits tender concern from family and neighbours and is firmly set amid the realistic detail of 'lanterns, torches / And the searchers' gay babble'.

'Maighdean Mara' is also a subtle blend of realism and symbolism. It opens with a mesmeric, elegiac but realistically detailed image of what appears to be an actual drowned girl. Her cold breasts are 'dandled by undertow', her hair is 'lifted and laid', sea wracks are 'cast about shin and thigh'. Through the slow, dignified sway of the language and the delicate loveliness of the imagery, the horror of death is dispelled, appropriated by the poet's transfiguring, aestheticizing impulse. The real girl merges with the legendary mermaid who had to leave the sea and marry the man who stole her magic garment, suffer love-making and motherhood, before retrieving her garment and returning to the sea. The legend follows the archetypal pattern of entry into the suffering of human existence, which is endured until eventual release and return to the source. The notion of 'homecoming' offers a form of assuagement in the face of death's inevitability. The poem ends by repeating the lines with which it began thus enacting the legend's cyclical pattern.

The very fine **'Limbo'** presents a picture of an unregenerate world. The social order is reductive, authoritarian and responsible for the corruption or denial of natural human feeling; the private life is speculative, repressed and infinitely sad; the natural world and, beyond that, the whole cosmic order, are cold and dead. Consequently, all creation is condemned to a state of inescapable and perpetual limbo.

The poem opens with a precisely defined time and place, announcing with documentary bluntness that last night fishermen at Ballyshannon found the drowned body of an illegitimate infant in their nets. This is the mode of social discourse. It takes the form of a broadcast, its prime function is utilitarian—to inform; it works by assertive statement, it assumes an audience, and above all it is reductively objective.

The pivotal 'But I'm sure / As she stood in the shallows . . .' moves us from objective to subjective, from the anonymous to the personal, from public world to private feeling, and from statement to speculation. Focusing on the mother's action, the speaker's language dispels horror and accusation. We concentrate on the mother's pain which is placed against a natural world that is also 'dead'. Ironically, the infant, with his hooks tearing her open, becomes the instrument of her 'death', an idea implying a level of abstraction and play of mind that take us further from the empiricist kind of truth. 'But I'm sure' points the contrast between the opening section which asks to be taken as disinterested, verifiable truth and what follows, which attempts to penetrate the empirical facts, addressing meanings that can only be imaginatively or intuitively apprehended, and which does not try to hide its status as interpretative gesture, even while laying claims to certainty.

The fourth stanza is a continuation of the imaginative reconstruction, now seeking to understand the mother's action in a broader social context and gathering to itself the authority of definitive statement as the initial acknowledgement of subjectivism ('But I'm sure . . .') loses force. It is less intimate and more abstract, the shift in the speaker's perspective signalled by the retrospect within a retrospect—the doubling back to refocus on the point where the woman first enters the water.

'She waded in under / The sign of her cross' and 'He was hauled in with the fishes' is a conspicuous, localized instance of the poem's ruling structure of parallelism and antithesis. In the first sentence the active voice signifies choice as opposed to the passivity of the second sentence, where the infant is completely in the hands of the fishermen (the social order). But the mother's choice is illusory since social taboo deriving from religious pressure is the main determinant of her action. 'In' has two different points of reference: the child is hauled into the safety of the boat, but the salvation afforded by the social order (and the religious order insofar as the fishermen are associated with Christ's

'fishers of men') is cold comfort indeed since it is helpless in the face of death; the mother leaves the safety of the social world and wades into the sea, performing there an action which, we come to see, confirms a human condition of unalterable and absolute degeneracy. 'Under' in the first sentence suggests both subjection and protection; 'with' in the second indicates a more neutral relationship, an association devoid of the mother's hierarchical structure which demands subjection and affords protection: the infant's situation is starkly primordial—he is now one of the fishes. But, despite the mother's ostensible order of signs and symbols and hierarchical structure, that (social and religious) order is eventually revealed as factitious and invalid: both mother and child are, from the very start, lost souls. That her monstrous crime against Life should still elicit our sympathy is a measure of the pathetic absurdity of human existence.

Acting 'under / The sign of her cross', it is as if her religion initiates and endorses what she does. She is fulfilling a ritual sacrifice at the cost of her own humanity and all natural feeling. In turning to the sea, the eternal mystery, her only framework of address is that provided by her religion. Wading in 'under / The sign of her cross' suggests the extreme delimiting, formalizing operation of the Christian *disciplina* which seeks to codify and control the vast mystery of the sea. 'Her cross' (as opposed to 'the cross') indicates personal appropriation. If 'under' refers to her subjection by her religion, 'her cross' implies her subjection of religion to her own need. The cross loses something of its original and universal meaning, it is subjectivized, and the view is reinforced that religion, far from being a body of inviolate truth, in instead a structure of belief constructed according to human need.

Allusion to the cross sets up the anticipation of salvation and, indeed, in the next line we read of the infant being fished out of the sea. Salvation, however, is of the most minimal kind since the infant is already dead; and, as the poem sweeps on to its climax, its ultimate statement is that there is no redemption for the soul. The mother's action, even though we have been led to view it sympathetically, is what contradicts the possibility of redemption. Her action is causative: 'Now limbo will be / A cold glitter of souls . . .' 'Now' indicates an economy of cause and effect. The Christian myth is rewritten in the light of actual human nature and actual human action. 'Now' also displaces the concept of limbo as a state existing outside time. Heaney goes on to relocate and re-define it within a discourse that at least started off as frankly speculative, but, by shaking itself free of the qualifying 'But I'm sure . . .', strains toward unequivocal certainty. Within this discourse the refurbished concept of limbo itself occupies a 'limbo' position somewhere between self-confessed speculation and incontestible truth. Such relativity, the poem demonstrates, is the inescapable condition of all meaning.

Redemption and transcendence of the Christian kind are refuted in the face of an existence which in every way denies them: they are themselves the conceptual products of that existence, framed in unregeneracy. The eternal is predicted on the temporal, a continuity which is expressed in the description of limbo as 'some far briny zone', figuratively composed of the same element as that in which the mother drowned her child. The denial of transcendence demands that the paraphernalia of the Christian myth are de-spiritualized and de-mystified. Hence, there are fishers of men in the poem, but only in the most literal sense; Christ bears his stigmata, but they have no miraculously healing powers; 'her cross' refers to a debased and commonplace 'Passion'—the woman's suffering—and only ironically alludes to the symbol of Christ's redemptive sacrifice as the 'transcendental signifier'.

The 'transcendental signifier' as the term is used by post-structuralists such as Derrida and Lacan implies the possibility of indivisible identity, unequivocal meaning and final truth. The 'transcendental signifier' is the sign which provides the key to all other signs, the 'transcendental signified' the idea, intention or referent to which all signs are subservient and can be seen to point. The post-structuralist critique (part of the larger intellectual effort sponsored by Marx, Nietzsche and Heidegger to extirpate the last vestiges of idealism from western thought) challenges society's 'logocentric' belief in some ultimate 'word', essence, idea, reality which will constitute the grounds of all our thought, language and experience. The notion of a final truth, it is argued, is illusory since it depends on the system of thought and language it is supposed to legitimize. All signification is merely an insistent, endless chain in which the signs have meaning only by virtue of their difference from other signs. There is no necessary correspondence between mind and world, or even between mind and meaning. Transcendental meaning is a fiction.

Heaney reflects the contemporary scepticism, but resists its most far-reaching and radical conclusions. Limbo is a powerfully suggestive metaphor for the post-structuralist condition of meaning as a constant flickering of presence and absence, continually eluding the grasp of a full, self-present awareness. The poem itself is an ostensibly transgressive kind of writing in which Heaney's discursive practices may be seen to problematize the notion of fixed meaning and representation. At the same time as he conveys meaning, he indicates something of its relative, artificial status as well, thus hoping to persuade us that he is keeping his distance from an authoritarian or ideological view of the world.

Yet, even while acknowledging the arbitrariness and instability of the elements out of which the poem is composed, he does not forgo the will to knowledge and mastery. He is still in quest of the 'transcendental signifier'. The poem as a total structure is in the end what we are asked to take as just that.

Heaney knows, and **'Limbo'** shows, that meaning is the product of a particular system, not something that is neutral and natural. And the system on which Heaney ultimately bases his claims to knowledge is one that belongs to a totalizing order of thought, to the poet's own strong imagining, his own creative vision and will to expression and persuasion. The poem's final truth is the product of the complex interaction of its internal meanings and attitudes which, in themselves, are shown to constitute only partial or limited 'truths'. Heaney forces us to acknowledge the rhetorical basis of all 'truth' and, thus clearing a space for his own imagination, confronts a whole prior system of thought and belief, and subverts it through a reinterpretation of its own figurative structures. This reconstructive 'troping' simultaneously disguises and asserts his Romantic will to be self-begotten (a source of unease with Heaney as far back as **'Digging'** and **'Follower'**). And it is aware of its own liabilities, for it proceeds with sensitivity to the entire range of impulses relevant to the situation (not the suppression of some) and works to integrate all of them—concrete and abstract, subjective and objective, temporal and eternal—so that **'Limbo'** can finally achieve its own kind of transcendence, momentary though it may be. The contradiction here, it might be argued, is that the poem rests on assumptions of a knowledge beyond reason and linked to the ineffable certitudes of faith, even while setting out to proclaim the absence or impossibility of these things in the limbo of life. But for Heaney, Art is, as it is not for many modern thinkers, a special, privileged category, wherein 'the limbo of lost words' (the phrase is from **'The Loaning'** in *Field-Work*) can be at least momentarily redeemed.

'Bye-Child' concerns another illegitimate child, another reject, who has been confined in a henhouse. The poet is deeply touched by this prisoner of darkness, as he was by the Tollund Man. The image of the moon-faced child remains vividly with the poet, palpable proof of an inconceivable cruelty. It stirs dark fears which lie deep in his mind. Re-activating the earlier moon images, the poem concludes with a poignant description of the boy's removal from the centre of life and love and sanity, into a realm which defies words and all natural human feeling.

'First Calf' reworks the conventions of pastoral. A cow is grazing with characteristic bovine serenity, her calf is hard at her udder. But the first thing to catch the poet's attention is the afterbirth:

The afterbirth strung on the hedge
As if the wind smarted
And streamed bloodshot tears.

The description is realistically vivid, but it is also used as an emblem which complicates the more fluent, euphonious image of nurture. 'The afterbirth strung on the hedge' emphasizes a raw brutishness which the harsh music of the next two lines helps to turn into an image of universal suffering. It is the boldness of the conceit which saves it from sentimentality. Only after these observations does the poet's attention shift to the cow and calf. Pain takes precedence over nurture in the poem's emotional priorities, a point further reinforced by the casual way in which the cow is introduced: 'Somewhere about the cow stands . . .'. The poem ends by returning to the afterbirth:

The semaphores of hurt
Swaddle and flap on a bush.

The onomatopaeic ugliness of the last line combines with 'swaddle''s more normal connotations of infant care and its associations with comfort and warmth, to encapsulate the ambivalence of the poet's vision. As always, the natural world is a complex system of signs requiring divination, a 'semaphore' which the poet must articulate.

Wintering Out concludes with a group of poems, mostly based on personal experience, in which Heaney considers the possibility of relief, rediscovery or illumination. **'Good-Night'** is a fine, tightly-wrought little poem that makes its impact with a simple, sharply-rendered image. A door opens, 'an edged den of light / Opens across the yard', the people coming out of the house step into the 'honeyed corridor', then walk off into darkness. The woman on the doorstep remains for a moment in the 'block of brightness', then re-enters the house, closes the door, 'And cancels everything behind her.'

'Fireside' also uses imagery of light and darkness. Around the fireside stories are exchanged about eerie goings-on under the moonlight. One story is about the lamping of fish, and in the atmosphere of heightened imaginative awareness, the poet, imagining himself swinging the moon-like beam of his flashlamp over the stream, suddenly wonders: 'Was that the beam / buckling over an eddy or a gleam / of the fabulous?' The real world permits only a fleeting, uncertain intuition of the fabulous: a voice interrupts his reverie bidding him to come to his senses and say good-night.

The concern to escape from rational confinement and experience the 'fabulous' (which is the essential impulse behind Heaney's use of the Tollund Man to explore the contemporary Ulster situation), the desire to protect the private vision against public pressure, becomes a matter of increasing urgency. For Heaney this involves renew-ing intimacy with nature. 'May' is a quest-poem of this kind, a paen to nature's invigorating, nurturing influence, which the poet longs to re-discover. There is a Hopkinsian lushness in his descriptions:

Wading green stems, lugs of leaf
That untangle and bruise
(Their tiny gushers of juice) . . .

The imagery betrays too great a straining after effect: 'My toecaps sparkle now / Over the soft fontanel / Of Ireland'; the desire for union with nature leads to prosaic and sentimental excess: 'I should wear / Hide shoes, the hair next my skin, / For walking this ground.'

'Dawn' speaks of the need to 'get away out by myself'—the phrase resonating into the line in **'Casualty',** one of the poems in *Field-Work,* where he discovers 'a rhythm / Working you, slow mile by mile, / Into your proper haunt / Somewhere, well out, beyond . . .'. Getting away out, as Heaney explains in the short poem **'Travel',** is a quest for psychic release, an effort to transcend routine responsibility, to discover the means to cope with violence and aftermath. In **'Dawn'** he is motoring through a town in early morning. The physical world reveals itself as hard, nervous, cacophonous. Human reason is reduced to a 'tut-tutting colloquy' of pigeons. Everything is dead and empty. There is a 'pompeian silence'. The poet eventually manages to get 'away out by myself', but once on the beach and walking over the cockles and winkles, is suddenly forced into the paralyzing recognition of his own destructiveness: 'Unable to move without crunching / Acres of their crisp delicate turrets.'

In **'Westering',** the last poem in the collection, we see that though the poet may be 'away out' in California, sitting under Rand McNally's 'Official Map of the Moon', his imagination is still bound to Ireland. In the space of eight lines he is back in Ireland, recalling his last night in Donegal, in particular the moonlight. What he remembers is the ghostly illumination of his own mortality, and an acute feeling of drifting and emptiness. It is as if Ireland endures the empty stillness and 'falling light' of a continual Good Friday, her people 'bent / To the studded crucifix', bowed in a posture of perpetual supplication.

At the end, the moon and Ireland merge in imagination:

Under the moon's stigmata

Six thousand miles away,
I imagine untroubled dust,
A loosening gravity,
Christ weighing by his hands.

The 'untroubled dust' and 'loosening gravity' are obvious lunar characteristics. The former is an image of desolation (lunar dust that has never been troubled); but also, through its association with the stillness of the Irish town the poet passes through on Good Friday, when everyone is at Mass, it suggests a projected fantasy of a redeemed and peaceful world (terrestrial dust that is no longer troubled). 'Loosening gravity' is ambiguous too. It is connected with the congregation's shedding its burden of guilt and sin, intimated earlier in, 'What nails dropped out that hour?'; but it may also refer to a condition of diminished faith, in which case we are given the picture of a society of ritual pretensions but no true centre of spiritual gravity—an ironic image of the communicants' readiness for revelation. All these ambiguities and possibilities are focussed in the last line which brings the poem to its climax by concentrating our attention on the Christian symbol of universal redemption. Significantly, however, the poem refuses to take us beyond Christ Crucified to Christ Risen. We are required to make a connection between Christ's supposedly redemptive stigmata and the dead moon's pitted surface: the whole poem is composed, both literally and metaphorically, 'Under the moon's stigmata'. The earth-bound rituals of deliverance take place within a larger context of cosmic emptiness.

What makes **'Westering'** such a subtly and powerfully compelling poem is the fact that its composition is not simply a matter of local materials being illuminated by cosmic perspectives, but rather of internally consistent local material being used to develop a vision of universal application. The poem is characteristic of Heaney's poetic attitude: he does not argue with or attempt to explain the human situation, nor does he subordinate to any specific doctrine his sad longing for an ideal real enough to encompass and transform his experience. Rather, he relies on the momentum and coherence of the creative act itself. Within the poem, a whole set of conflicts which are felt to be insoluble in ordinary life—between subject and object, the universal and the particular, the sensuous and the conceptual, material and spiritual, order and spontaneity—are magically resolved.

The bleak vision which *Wintering Out* has been working towards is a vision of a world beyond redemption, of 'damnation on this earth',[17] as Laforgue described the Baudelairean vision. We can see why one of Heaney's crucial symbols in later work should be Dante's pictured prisoners in the antechamber of Hell, worthy of neither blame nor praise. In releasing his dark, subversive, inward self and exploring a deranged world which, like Eliot's, is 'held in lunar synthesis',[18] Heaney is still seen to be struggling to keep in touch with the springs of joy and vitality. His vision of emptiness is counterpointed by an effort to establish vital continuities with whatever in the past is myth-making, wonder-contemplating and strength-giving, and to discover widened, fresher meanings that can be brought to us through heightened sense-alertness. To validate these

findings, there is his faith in the creative alchemy whereby general ideas or feelings are taken, transmuted into aspects of the poet's personality and subjected to the determining influence of his artistic sensibility which makes poetic speech normative—something that at once reveals unregeneracy and the vast richness that is available to us, and thus suggests an ideal.

Hopkins, for whom Heaney had such affection and admiration, regarded composition as a compliance with the will of God, an enactment of the beauty of God's creation, an imitation of Christ, a sign of Grace. Unquestioning faith was the premise of his poetry. Without this external, absolute, validating point of reference, Heaney's essentially religious sensibility, his longing for transcendence and assuagement, relies—like Yeats's—on the mediation of art itself. Heaney's faith is in the 'religion of art' allied with a belief in that other great concept of the nineteenth century post-Romantic, the 'life-force'. His poetry is a demonstration of Walter Pater's view that poets desired mainly to bring to life 'a beauty born of unlikely elements, by a profound alchemy, by a difficult initiation, by the charm which wrings it even out of terrible things'.[19] Heaney's fundamental artistic principle is taken from Yeats which Yeats himself had learnt from Blake:

> Argument, theory, erudition, observation, are merely what Blake called "little devils who fought for themselves," illusions of our visible passing life, who must be made to serve the moods, or we have no part in eternity. Everything that can be seen, touched, measured, explained, understood, argued over, is to the imaginative artist nothing more than a means . . .[20]

This aesthetic liberated Heaney, as it liberated Yeats, from the bonds of dogma and agnosticism simultaneously by reducing both to subordinate status in an aesthetically created universe of symbols. It involves placing his art and its motives beyond the reach of literal-minded morality. It allows him to assert the beauty and preciousness of life in the teeth of the worst it has to offer. In the work to follow, however, this is an ideal which Heaney becomes more and more conscious of as being also an ideological enterprise. If the old religious ideologies have lost their force and he, like a kind of Hibernian Arnold, is proposing a more subtle communication of moral values, one which does not argue openly nor relay beliefs directly, but which works by concrete enactment rather than rebarbative abstraction, by sensitive concern with the oblique, nuanced particulars of human experience—then is not the preoccupation with timeless truths not merely a form of distraction from immediate commitments? In time of war, how responsible is it of the poet to cling to the notion of art as a pacifying, assuaging influence, fostering meekness, self-sacrifice and the contemplative inner life?

Notes

1. Heaney, interview, in Monie Begley, *Rambles in Ireland* (Old Greenwich, Conn.: Devin-Adair, 1977) p. 165.

2. Christopher Ricks, 'Lasting Things' in *The Listener* (26 June 1969) p. 900.

3. Heaney; 'Feeling into Words' in *Preoccupations,* p. 56.

4. Heaney, 'The Trade of an Irish Poet' in *The Guardian* (25 May 1972) p. 17.

5. Heaney, 'Landlocked' in *The Irish Press* (1 June 1974) (review of P. V. Glob's *The Mound People*).

6. John Hewitt, 'Conacre' in *Collected Poems 1932-1967* (London: MacGibbon and Kee, 1968).

7. John Hewitt, 'The Colony' in *Collected Poems 1932-1967*.

8. Heaney, 'The Sense of Place' in *Preoccupations,* p. 147.

9. Heaney, interview with Seamus Deane, 'Unhappy and at Home' in *The Crane Bag,* 1, 1 (1977) p. 65.

10. 'An Interview with Seamus Heaney' (James Randall) in *Ploughshares,* 5, 3 (1979) p. 17.

11. The lines are from 'Exposure', in *North,* p. 73.

12. These were phrases used by Heaney at a poetry reading, quoted by Robert Buttel, in *Seamus Heaney* (Lewisburg: Bucknell University Press, 1975) p. 71.

13. Heaney, 'Feeling into Words' in *Preoccupations,* p. 57.

14. Interview with Randall, p. 18.

15. Heaney, 'Feeling into Words' in *Preoccupations,* p. 59.

16. D. H. Lawrence, *Phoenix* (London: Heinemann, 1967) p. 224.

17. *Selected Writings of Jules Laforgue,* ed. and trans., William Jay Smith (New York: Grove Press, 1956) p. 211.

18. T. S. Eliot, 'Rhapsody on a Windy Night' in *Collected Poems 1909-1962* (London: Faber, 1963).

19. Walter Pater, *Appreciations* (New York: Macmillan, 1903) p. 260.

20. W. B. Yeats, *Essays* (London: Macmillan, 1924) p. 239.

Bibliography

Works by Seamus Heaney

Death of a Naturalist (London: Faber, 1966).

Door into the Dark (London: Faber, 1969).

Wintering Out (London: Faber, 1972).

North (London: Faber, 1975).

Field Work (London: Faber, 1979).

Preoccupations: Selected Prose 1968-1978 (London: Faber, 1980).

Sweeney Astray (Derry: Field Day, 1983, London: Faber, 1984).

Interviews

Interview in Monie Begley, *Rambles in Ireland* (Old Greenwich, Conn.: Devin-Adair, 1977) pp. 159-69.

'Unhappy and at Home' (Seamus Deane). *The Crane Bag,* 1, no. 1 (1977) pp. 61-7.

'An Interview with Seamus Heaney' (James Randall), *Ploughshares,* 5, no. 3 (1979) pp. 7-22.

Selected Criticism of Seamus Heaney

Buttel, Robert. *Seamus Heaney* (Lewisburg: Bucknell University Press, 1975).

Ricks, Christopher, 'Lasting Things', *The Listener* (26 June 1969) pp. 900-1.

Daniel Tobin (essay date 1999)

SOURCE: Tobin, Daniel. "Cooped Secrets of Process and Ritual: *North.*" In *Passage to the Center: Imagination and the Sacred in the Poetry of Seamus Heaney,* pp. 103-41. Lexington: University Press of Kentucky, 1999.

[*In the following essay, Tobin focuses on* North, *which he describes as the culmination of Heaney's early work and the start of his efforts to find his own voice.*]

On January 30, 1972, British paratroopers killed thirteen Catholic demonstrators in Derry. They had been protesting the institution of forced internment without trial in Northern Ireland for Republicans suspected of IRA affiliation, as well as practices of torture committed on internees by the British authorities. The Bloody Sunday Massacre only swelled Catholic grassroots support for those who would kill for what Heaney called the Nationalist myth, the idea of an integral Ireland variously personified as Kathleen Ni Houlihan and the Shan Van Vocht: the Old Mother, the native feminine spirit of the land. In Dublin, the British embassy was bombed, and a wave of random sectarian murders began in the north. Meanwhile, Protestants embracing "the Unionist myth" whose "fountainhead . . . springs in the Crown of England,"[1] responded in kind. Random murders of Catholics ensued in Belfast and Derry. Regardless of whether one assents to Heaney's mythologizing, one thing is certain: the fault he envisioned in **"A Northern Hoard"** had opened in earnest.

It was amid this atmosphere of bloody retribution that Heaney left his teaching post at Queen's University and moved with his family to Glanmore, County Wicklow, in the south of Ireland. The move met with a stir of publicity. Many Catholics within the literary community and outside of it felt betrayed. Heaney himself was bothered by the impression that he had seemed to break ranks with his friends there, both Catholics and Protestants.[2] On the other side, Paisleyite extremists hailed the departure of a "well-known Papish propagandist."[3] But Heaney's own reasons for leaving had only marginally to do with the Troubles:

> I left in 1972 not really out of any rejection of Belfast but because. . . . Well, I had written three books, had published two, and one was due to come out. I had the name for being a poet but I was also discovering myself being interviewed as, more or less, a spokesman for the Catholic minority during this early stage of the troubles. I found the whole question of what was the status of art within my own life and the question of what is an artist to do in a political situation very urgent matters. I found that my life, most of the time, was being spent in classrooms, with friends, at various social events, and I didn't feel that my work was sufficiently at the center of my life, so I decided I would resign; and now I realize that my age was the age that is probably crucial in everybody's life—around thirty-three. I was going through a sort of rite of passage, I suppose. I wanted to resign. I wanted to leave Belfast because I wanted to step out of the rhythms I had established; I wanted to be alone with myself.[4]

Elsewhere he confessed, "I didn't leave because of 'the troubles.' It had to do with going into silence and wilderness. It was the first real move I had made that stepped away from the generic life."[5] Heaney's reasons for leaving were artistic and spiritual, and only nominally political. He sensed the journey of his early poetry edging towards some new expression. Yet *North,* the book born of his entry into the wilderness, is more a decisive plunge into the dark of self and history. It is the book in which he follows the historical horizon to its source. More than evincing "a hunger for images of the self in history, of personal identity in relation to the historical process,"[6] *North* locates Heaney's quest for self-definition within the realm of tragedy. By tragedy here I mean the vision of "malevolent transcendence" described by Larry Bouchard in *Tragic Method, Tragic Theology*: a vision of "overweening violence" that comes to have a life of its own seemingly beyond individual human actions, and which finally resists thought.[7] In the tragic world of *North,* the violence of history and the violence of myth merge, and the center itself is stained with the blood of atrocity.

"To quest closely and honestly into the roots of one's own sensibility, into the roots of one's own sense of oneself, into the tribal dirt that lies around the roots of all of us," so Heaney described the Northern Irish writer's task.[8] Indeed, in his first three books Heaney seems to be following this injunction and, at the time of their publication, each largely met with critical praise. But with *North,* criticism of his work became torrid. To be pro-*North* or anti-*North* involved one in a heated political and aesthetic debate, and still does. Edna Longley speaks for many who object to Heaney's treatment of Northern Ireland when she says that in *North* Heaney turns his "instinctive sureties into a philosophy."[9] In *North,* she believes, Heaney's desire to juxtapose present and past becomes an equation. Rather than illuminating the dark, *North* "plunders the past for parallels," thereby embracing historical determinism. David Lloyd echoes this view when he asserts *North* reduces history to myth,[10] and George Watson concurs when he argues that in *North* "Heaney aestheticizes the stark facts of brutality."[11] For these critics Heaney's use of myth is merely "decorative." More severely, Conor Cruise O'Brien accused him of widening the gap between the communities by condoning Republican violence.[12] Still others, such as Elmer Andrews, see him succumbing both to the temptation of too deeply embroiling himself in the fray, and of exploiting "a situation of brutal factionalism for a kind of aestheticism which the poet indulges in for his own sake without committing himself": in "luxurious indolence" he assumes an air of quiet acceptance before the goddess.[13] As such "the original motivation for researching into the past—to find emblems of adversity—" is subordinated "to an aestheticizing compulsion in which emblems themselves count for more than what they can be made to mean."[14] Perhaps most damning was Ciaran Carson's charge that with *North* Heaney had moved "from being a writer with the gift of precision, to become a laureate of violence—a mythmaker, an anthropologist of ritual killing, an apologist for 'the situation,' in the last resort, a mystifier."[15]

Certainly in its ruminations on the tradition, on the brutal milieu of Ulster, on what he takes to be the atavistic roots of the conflict there, and on the poetic process itself, *North* is a self-consciously literary book. Its tone and structure suggest the sweep of epic poetry, or myth.[16] Heaney himself sees *North* as his first book that was "to some extent designed."[17] Composing it, he saw himself for the first time as having the authority to do his own work, "as having *auctoritas.*"[18] That authority arose through the learning experience of his first three books, through resigning his job and committing himself to being a poet, and through his obsession with P. V. Glob's *The Bog People.* This final transforming influence did not so much provide him with crucial subject matter for his most ambitious book as confirm and enlarge his own instinctive energies and poetic intuitions. If in **"Bogland"** Heaney discovered a symbol central to the life of his culture, then the bog poems of *North* attempt to give the symbol its fullest possible expression. Beyond the weight of any single poem, the poems of *North* seek not so much to forge "the uncreated consciousness of the race" as to expose the violent, unconscious proclivities by which that consciousness has been in part created. Nevertheless, like Stephen Daedalus's ambition, Heaney's aspiration puts "daunting pressures and responsibilities on anyone who would risk the name of poet" (P 60). It also leaves him vulnerable to the charges of mystification levied against him by his most ardent critics.

My hope in this chapter is to show how the question of Heaney's success in *North* hinges on his ability to use myth as a method of interrogation into the "tribal" conflict that continues to shape the history of Northern Ireland, and into myth itself as a catalyst for civilized barbarism. Against his critics' charges, he does not substitute a new myth for lost atavisms. Instead, his use of myth is exploratory, not restorative,[19] and suggests that while myth may well serve "an ideological function,"[20] if handled properly it may reveal its own capacity for instigating tribal, nationalistic factionalism and the violence that ensues. More than this, I hope to show how Heaney's achievement in *North* transcends the political and historical circumstances of his own province. In *North*, to borrow a phrase from Mary Douglas, Heaney uncovers "the relation of order to disorder, being to non-being, form to formlessness, life to death."[21] He would expose a process of violence hidden within culture itself. This task requires the poet be highly self-conscious in his art. As such, the dangers to the poetry are equally high. On the one hand, complicity leads to propaganda. On the other, art for art's sake leads to irrelevance, an abdication of the poet's civic responsibility.

In "The Interesting Case of Nero, Chekhov's Cognac and a Knocker," Heaney speculates that in the face of suffering, song may be a "culpable indulgence," a betrayal of such responsibility (GT [*The Government of the Tongue*] xii). Yet pure song, he argues, "however responsible, always has an element of the untrammeled about it." In lyric poetry there is a sense "of liberation and abundance which is the antithesis of every hampered and deprived condition" (GT xviii). In the face of suffering, the poet may be lured to silence, to the truth-telling witness of a Wilfred Owen, or to the deep witness of pure song whose premier spokesman, for Heaney, is Osip Mandelstam (GT xx). Heaney's use of myth in *North* involves each of these three options. When a bomb killed the barman at the end of Heaney's road in Belfast, Heaney found that "words didn't live in the way they have to live in a poem when they were hovering over that kind of horror and pity" (GT 60). Instead, in those victims "made strangely beautiful by the process of lying in the bogs," he found a way to "make offerings or images that were emblems, attempts to be adequate to what was happening" (GT 60-61). In light of this statement, *North* may be seen as an attempt

to let the poetry of what is "secret and natural" come under the influence of a world that is "public and brutal." *North* sets song and suffering in dialogue.

Heaney's urge to juxtapose visions and discourses is apparent in the structure of *North* itself. Like *Wintering Out,* the book is divided into two distinct parts, only now the binary structure has been more self-consciously wrought by Heaney to achieve his artistic ends. As he comments, "the two halves of the book constitute two different types of utterance, each of which arose out of a necessity to shape and give palpable linguistic form to two kinds of urgency—one symbolic, one explicit."[22] He might easily have said "secret" and "public," "mythic" and "historical," "Antaean" and "Herculean," instead of "symbolic" and "explicit," for each of these dichotomies represents a tension explored in the book. Yet while such division is built into *North,* the purpose of its dialogical structure is to see which, if either, is more adequate to the task of exposing the underlying roots of the tragedy. As such, the division between the two parts is not as stable as it might first appear.[23] Nevertheless, for all the oppositions in *North,* the volume opens with two poems that create a sense of peaceful continuity. Dedicated to Heaney's Aunt Mary, **"Mossbawn: Sunlight"** and **"The Seed Cutters"** comprise a prelude to the tragedy that follows. They stand in stark contrast to it, and so quietly judge its world of violence and bloodshed, and thus advocate the hope of another world. Though Heaney finds a metaphor for Ulster's split culture in the name of his family farm, that split is nowhere present in these poems. Where "For David Hammond and Michael Longley" casts *Wintering Out* in the relief of internment camps and bogside graffiti, **"Sunlight"** and **"The Seed Cutters"** place the grim history of *North* within the context of the timeless rhythms of the yard that compose the center of Heaney's other world, the world of the *omphalos.*

While giving a reading at The Blacksmith House in Cambridge, Heaney commented that in **"Mossbawn: Sunlight"** he tried to write from the perspective of a fetus in the womb. The poem is almost a paean to a maternal, nurturing presence. Not surprisingly, the "iron idol" of Heaney's *omphalos*—the "helmeted pump" in the yard—figures prominently. The first line of the poem suggests that light has so filled the yard that everything not present here and now has been thrown into "absence." We have a vision of transcendent clarity, the pure seeing we might expect to involve otherworldliness. On the contrary it is the homeliness of the scene that impresses. The sun is a "griddle," an image that undercuts a presumptive transcendentalism even while it communicates an aura of a mysterious and gracious immanence. This feeling carries over into Heaney's description of his aunt. The repetition of the words "now" and "here" twice as the poem moves towards its climax evokes a sense of time lived in the fullness of the moment, or in the fullness of time, as poem's ending suggests:

> here is a space
> again, the scone rising
> to the tick of two clocks.
>
> And here is love
> like a tinsmith's scoop
> sunk past its gleam
> in the meal-bin.

[*N* [*North*] 9]

As Blake Morrison observes, with this final image, the poem discovers "beneath the transient gleam of sunlit surfaces the deep common substance of love."[24] Beyond this, within the context of a volume given over to exploring the brutal processes of myth and history, the poem reveals Heaney's hope for a time and space that exists apart from the horrors of history and the violent inclinations of the human imagination. **"The Seed Cutters"** takes this hope and places it within the wider customs of the community, though a community raised out of tribal darkness, beyond the sway of the capricious black Mother of **"At a Potato Digging."** A sonnet, the poem's formality underscores its theme of order and continuity. Here, as in **"Sunlight,"** we are given "the ticking of two clocks": chronological time, the time of history, and a more elusive but no less real inner time, the time of the seed cutters as they exist in their "calendar customs." This is time Heaney would capture in his art, a time of personal significance, of a community's shared cultural experience. In Heaney's vision, such sacred time is bestowed in relation to the center, which in this instance manifests itself as a dark watermark inside the halved potato. Like the sacramental absence of **"Sunlight,"** the anonymities of the poem's final line gesture toward a vision of ideal order that transcends the strife of history.

Reading these two poems in isolation, one might have the impression that, like his Northern Irish contemporary, Derek Mahon, Heaney would declare that he is "through with history."[25] Yet, also like Mahon, it is precisely his inability to be through with history that so pervades the poems that follow. **"Mossbawn: Sunlight"** and **"The Seed Cutters"** only convey the promise of peace and protection from historical terror. They are moments of respite that stand apart amid all the tragic scene, and yet they are crucial because they set that scene in relief. When we do enter the scene, the "time to kill" is no longer the time to rest from noble work: it is the time to murder. The "calendar customs" become tribal allegiances that reveal only the "anonymities" of

murderer and victim. Among these, even the earth gives no comfort, having become herself a vengeful goddess for whose love the faithful sink themselves in a cycle of reciprocal violence.

In Part I of **North** we enter fully into the "sterner myth" presaged in Heaney's early poems. The poems of this section ought to be read as a sequence or cycle in which the mythic and symbolic origins of the political tragedy of contemporary Ulster are explored. The cycle opens with the poem **"Antaeus"** and ends with its companion piece **"Hercules and Antaeus."** In Greek myth, Hercules is the son of the sky god, Zeus, while Antaeus is a titanic son of earth. For Antaeus every fall is a renewal, and yet he is usurped by the shrewder Hercules, whose "intelligence / is a spur of light" that eventually lifts the other "out of his element / into a dream of loss / and origins" (*N* 52). Antaeus, the "mould-hugger," and Hercules, the hero "sky-born and royal," are binary oppositions that suggest a range of possible meanings in addition to the obvious mythic allusions. In Heaney's own view, "Hercules represents the balanced rational light while Antaeus represents the pieties of illiterate fidelity."[26] More allegories and oppositions unfold. Antaeus is associated with the native feminine ground. He represents art as a matter of intuition, gift. Hercules, in contrast, is associated with the poet as craftsman and resembles Heaney's masculine mode. Antaeus's strength is cradled in the womb of the dark; Hercules's in the spur of light. The one is instinctual, the other rational. Antaeus is also a figure for the backward nation colonized by the technologically and economically superior one: he is "banked" by the "royal" Hercules. Like Caliban, Enkidu, and Esau, Antaeus may be seen as a figure for the culturally dispossessed.[27]

While the figures of Hercules and Antaeus offer an impressive range of interpretive possibilities, each of these separate allegories points toward a more fundamental structural relationship. The warring heroes are mirror images of each other, doubles bonded together by violence who resemble such enemy brothers as Cain and Abel, Jacob and Esau, or Romulus and Remus. Despite their apparent distinctiveness, Hercules and Antaeus are locked together in a violent symmetry that, as Rene Girard argues in *Violence and the Sacred,* effaces differences.[28] This loss of difference is the product of a terrifying mimesis in which brutality compounds brutality until individual humanity itself is lost to a tragically self-generating process of increasing violence. To follow Girard's lead, the story of Hercules and Antaeus is not only "a parable of imperialism generally," but a parable of the destructive potential that lies within culture itself. With Hercules's defeat of Antaeus the cycle of retribution only seems to end. That very defeat becomes "the pap" that will nurture new cycles of violence in which the dispossessed seek to regain possession. The pap actually breeds allegiance to a violent, essentialist myth of origins that sustains the same brutal mythic struggle of Hercules and Antaeus throughout history. Nor does Hercules, with his seemingly technological and rational advantage, escape delusion. If Paul Ricoeur is right in claiming that the idea of logos ruling over mythos is itself a mythical claim,[29] then Hercules's victory is merely the provisional triumph of one myth over another through superior force. Because history records the rise and fall of such myths, the relation between Hercules and Antaeus suggests an immemorial cycle of violence, a cycle that Rene Girard maintains is the source of all human cultures.

As we have already seen, cycles recur in Heaney's poetry and are central to his artistic vision. The eel of **"A Lough Neagh Sequence"** is only one example, as is the resurrection of the croppies in Heaney's **"Requiem."** As suggested by the latter poem, though it gives the appearance of linear progression, history is in fact self-enwound, a cyclical process in which similar events recur in new manifestations. The process of symbolization through which myths and cultures arise and history is made is also implicated in the process of cyclical recurrence, an idea that resonates with the understanding of culture and history advanced by Mircea Eliade, though unlike Heaney he gives this process of repetition a distinctly positive interpretation. For Eliade, sacred time is cyclical, and reflects the human desire to return to the time of beginnings. Even when time is desacralized by history, the collective memory is still fundamentally ahistorical, that is, "the memory of historical events is modified . . . in such a way that it can enter into the mold of archaic mentality, which cannot accept what is individual and preserves only what is exemplary."[30] What Eliade calls the "terror of history" stems from modern humanity's dissociation from the primal cycles and consequently its doomed effort to "make history" at any cost, even the cost of genocide.

The terror of history, however, presents a problem for Eliade: How does such terror arise if archaic people have no concept of history to begin with? What archaic peoples apparently fear are the terrors of the natural world, which they then personify as gods in order to make disorder intelligible to the imagination. In *North,* historical terror and natural terror conjoin in the figure of Nerthus. The natural cycle of generation and death takes the form of an historical cycle of violence fueled by symbols and myth. Hence, Heaney's vision of history in *North* matches Eliade's, but with a crucial difference: the terror of history arises precisely from the symbolic mechanism that would preserve only the emblem, not the individual, thereby creating a milieu in which the violence sanctioned by myth appears self-justifying. Individuals, in fact, are lost in the unanimous violence of endless reprisals. The view anticipates Jonathan Smith's insight that the "language of the center

is primarily political and only secondarily cosmological."[31] Still, unlike Smith, Heaney's work suggests that the violent origins associated with the center may be exposed, and thereby defeated. *North* is analogous to a self-negating or self-interrogating myth, in Paul Tillich's words, a "broken myth,"[32] for it invites us to be conscious of the brutal cycle in which we are intimately involved, and by making us conscious hopes to break the cycle.

Following **"Antaeus," "Belderg"** begins to expose the cyclic nature of history and the violence that underlies it. Inspired by an archeologist friend who unearthed a Stone Age field system in County Mayo and found it mirrored exactly the modern fields on the facing hillside, **"Belderg"** takes the find as evidence of an ever widening cyclic pattern repeated through centuries and across cultures:

> 'They just kept turning up
> And were thought of as foreign'—
> One-eyed and benign
> They lie about his house,
> Quernstones out of a bog. . . .
>
> A landscape fossilized,
> Its stone-wall patternings
> Repeated before our eyes
> In the stone walls of Mayo.
>
> [*N* 13]

For Heaney, the bog is Jungian ground, a memory bank in which the patterns of centuries are preserved and repeated. Unearthed from this ground, the querns come to symbolize "persistence, / a congruence of lives." As the poem proceeds, the bogland name "Mossbawn" comes to embody similar "growth rings." It reflects both English and Irish origins: *bawn,* meaning an English fort, is pronounced *ban* by the poet, suggesting the Irish word for white (*P* [*Preoccupations*] 35). The music of Heaney's old home thus composes a "forked root" reflecting both the split culture from which it derives and the poet's own "forked tongue." Yet, as Heaney's friend observes, *moss* implies the "older strains of Norse" as well, and so the rings of the poet's ancestral tree widen further, deepening that congruence of lives.

What is the nature of this congruence? In light of the poem's end, the querns can hardly be viewed as benign. Rather, they are Cyclops's eyes that inevitably draw the poet into their terrifying vision. Seeing himself as "grist to an ancient mill," the threat to identity first revealed in an early poem like **"The Barn"** now portends a cosmic horror. The "world-tree" mentioned in the poem is Yggdrasil from Norse mythology, but it is also the skeletal tree of history whose rings accrue through the crushed marrow of individual lives and lost cultures. Crucially, in this dark epiphany, a congruence is implied between the "eye" of the poet (and by association his "I") and the "eye" of the quern. As such, he acknowledges his complicity with the secret, monstrous, shadow side of world-making, whether mythic or historical. The insight carries tremendous gravity, for in it Heaney sees his own poetry bound to the violent origins of culture. Belderg's congruence of lives, a congruence founded on "mimetic desire," leads to "a sacrificial cult based on war," on reciprocal violence that is "not substantially different from . . . nationalistic myths with their concept of an hereditary enemy."[33] Moreover, aware that the very language he employs houses a violent inheritance, Heaney is confronted with two choices. He may, like those writers who after the Holocaust ceased to work in the German tongue out of respect for the dead and a sense that the language itself had been irreparably stained, choose to keep silent.[34] Or he may choose to speak with full knowledge that risking speech he risks affronting the victims. **"North,"** the collection's signature poem, represents Heaney's assent to the latter choice. Famously, in the poem Heaney hears the "ocean-deafened voices" of Vikings. For Edna Longley, the appearance of Vikings here is the stuff of costume drama. In her view, they have no organic relation to Ulster. Though as both **"Belderg"** and **"North"** suggest, their presence *is* integral to a vision of culture that moves beyond the merely provincial. The actual Norse invasions of Ireland give Heaney's insight historical weight, though that weight reaches mythic proportions when the voices of the "fabulous raiders" lift in "violence and epiphany." At this moment the sacred assumes a truly malevolent prospect. Rather than trivializing the division Heaney discerns in his Irish and English roots, the Viking line only intensifies it. Once again, Heaney's intention is to widen and deepen the scope of his exploration beyond the Troubles themselves. Echoing Yeats in **"Viking Dublin: Trial Pieces,"** he entreats:

> Old fathers, be with us.
> Old cunning assessors
> of feuds and of sites
> for ambush or town.

[N 24]

Yet where Yeats sought pardon from the old fathers for not preserving the line, Heaney wants to illuminate the nature of his "being with" them. He wants to understand his place in the line—for a violent congruence of lives connects the Vikings both to Heaney's ancestors, and to the primordial fathers at the dawn of human culture.

Memory incubates spilled blood, Heaney writes in **"North."** If this is so, then perhaps memory also harbors the answer to ending the cycle of violence that not only plagues Heaney's homeland but that has plagued human history across times and cultures. In the poem, when the longship's "swimming tongue," "buoyant with hindsight," speaks to him, it not only warns

him of the revenges endemic to cultures in which peace is realized momentarily and only through exhaustion, it also alerts him to his poetic responsibility. To "lie down in the word-hoard," to "compose in darkness," are entreaties that coincide with the goals of Heaney's first three books. What the longship's swimming tongue encourages him to do is to remain faithful to his quest. This is no mere act of aesthetic indulgence or mystification. Heaney's mythmaking is done in the service of exposing the violent propensity of myth itself; in Henry Hart's words, he uncovers "the shadowy demarcations between story and history and tabulates the consequences of blind devotion to fossilized myths."[35] In taking on such a task, what Heaney most requires of his art is clarity, an eye "clear as / the bleb of the icicle." Heaney associates this image with the exacting spareness of early Irish nature poetry,[36] but more importantly the image suggests that only a poetry of such clarity can adequately describe history's ritual cycles of violence and revenge.

Lawrence K. Langer in his book *The Holocaust and the Literary Imagination* observes that trying to write out of the experience of atrocity many Holocaust authors embraced an aesthetic of "disfigurement."[37] By disfiguring metaphors and disrupting narrative, poetry comes close to expressing the horror for which, in Langer's view, even tragedy is inadequate. One need not claim that the immediate horrors of **North** are of the same magnitude as those of the Holocaust to see a similar aesthetic at work in the poems. In an interview with Harriet Cooke, Heaney stated that in **North** he wanted "to take the English lyric and make it eat stuff that it had never eaten before . . . all the messy and, it would seem, incomprehensible obsessions in the North, and make it still an English lyric."[38] Again, to Frank Kinahan he explained, "I thought that music, the melodious grace of the English iambic line, was some kind of affront, that it needed to be wrecked."[39] As a result, Neil Corcoran is right when he states that "an intense, almost claustrophobic obsessiveness" inheres in the poetry.[40] In trying to embody the wreckage of history, it takes on the character of the "ruminant ground" itself. Enjambments are roughened, lines cut sharply against the grain of syntax. Diction becomes disruptive, technical, philological. Heaney makes ample use of kennings, some of which like "bone-house" (*ban hus*) he adapts from a variety of linguistic sources; others he invents himself: "oak-bone," "brain-firkin." He imports words from his own Northern dialect and from Irish. His intention is to use poems as "drills" to excavate the origins of his culture, and out of the debris to compose a kind of tortured mosaic adequate to revealing the violence he discerns in its depths.

This strategy holds true for the portrayal of the poet's identity in the poem. When asked about the constricted lineation of most of the poems in **North,** Heaney replied that "the line and the life are intimately related; that narrow line, that tight line, came out of a time I was very tight with myself."[41] Certainly the poems are as much about the poet's growth to consciousness as about history and myth. The tightness of the poems reflects that urgency. Yet the "I" we so often encounter would seem to be mythologized, "ruminatively entranced, the hero of its own imaginative constructions and elaborations."[42] In **"Belderg,"** for example, the "I" passes through the eye of a quernstone. In **"North"** Heaney listens to the advice of the longship's swimming tongue. In **"Viking Dublin: Trial Pieces"** he imagines himself Hamlet. As we shall see, in **"Bone Dreams," "Come to the Bower," "Kinship,"** and **"Punishment"** his "I" almost merges with the murdered dead. One way to view identity in these poems, then, might be to see it as "withdrawn in solipsistic meditation."[43] Another would be to see it as fragmented, a trace assuming a plethora of personae. There is a third way, however: "the 'I' of the poem is at the eye of the storm within the 'I' of the poet," so Heaney remarks in **"Place and Displacement."**[44] Paradoxically, within this shifting tempest of self, the mythologized "I" of *North* functions to demythologize any false sense of identity. In exposing the self's hiding places, Heaney risks self-dissolution to gain greater consciousness. One can say that the poetry of *North* self-consciously ruminates both on its own process of composition and its own dramatizations of identity in order to expose any traces of the poet's complicity in the culture's deep-rooted violence. Heaney's method is therefore deeply mimetic. The "disfigurement" of the poems is a measure of the disorder inherent in the culture, as if Heaney's art could mirror the mimetic reciprocity of violence itself. The strategy implies a twofold hope. First, the poems would uncover "the potency of disorder"[45] in culture without succumbing to chaos. Second, by dramatizing the connection between violence and culture, he hopes to expose that process to consciousness.

We can find this process of exposure most obviously revealed in **"Viking Dublin: Trial Pieces." "Viking Dublin"** opens with Heaney gazing at a relic, here a jawbone or rib on which "a small outline / was incised," then follows his imagination's plunge into the *quiddity* of the thing that houses its history. Through Heaney's imaginative flight the poem is transformed into an allegory of the creative process itself, as well as history:

> Like a child's tongue
> following the toils
> of his calligraphy,
> like an eel swallowed
> in a basket of eels,
> the line amazes itself
>
> eluding the hand
> that fed it.

[*N* 21]

The image of the child's tongue recalls Heaney's meditations on the "grafted tongue" of his language in *Wintering Out.* It hints both at the beginnings of the artistic process (Heaney called his own early poems "trial-pieces") and the dispossession of his native tongue from its cultural origins. In the section's penultimate line the snipe of **"The Backward Look"** appears again as a bill in flight, emblematic of the fleeting nature of language. Likewise, in the image of the eel and of the swimming nostril we are once again in the world of *Door into the Dark,* with its natural rhythms and cycles. Heaney's self-inwoven similes enjoin both the things themselves and all the cycles of nature and history drawn into the artistic act.

In the five sections that follow, the line of history and the line of the poem become ever more inwoven. In the second section, Heaney declares the relics "trial pieces." Metaphorically, they are the poems themselves, "the craft's mystery / improvised on bone." Metaphor and metamorphosis dovetail. Magnified on display, as are poems, the eel's swimming nostril becomes "a migrant prow sniffing the Liffey" which in turn dissembles itself in the debris of the lost Viking culture in Ireland. In the third section, the longship's hull is "spined and plosive as *Dublin,*" the word inscribing the history of the Norse invaders. The trial piece is now "a buoyant / migrant line" to inscribe the line of history. That line enters the poet's "longhand" in the fourth section. The inscription of longship into longhand is accomplished though a disruptive segue. Taking up the pattern of the trial piece, the poet's own writing becomes "cursive, unscarfing / a zoomorphic wake, a worm of thought / I follow into the mud." More forcefully than the horrid cable of **"A Vision,"** the worm hints at a malignancy within thought itself as defined by the quintessential human act of writing. Realizing this, Heaney's identity becomes unhinged. In an even more wildly imaginative flight, he declares he is "Hamlet the Dane" who finds himself, like the poet, "infused" in the poisons of the state as he gradually "comes to consciousness"—consciousness of his place in a cycle of revenge.[46] Though hyperbolic, Heaney's portrayal of himself finally inscribes a progressive devolution of language into incomprehensibility, a process that continues in the next section where the poet proclaims in the voice of the mock-bard, "Come fly with me / come sniff the wind / with the expertise of the Vikings." The boastfulness of the lines would be overbearing should we take them as a serious claim by the poet. Yet, it is clear by now that Heaney's voice has yielded to that of the "bill in flight"—to the metamorphosing nature of language itself whose line traces history and delves back into muddy origins.

Such conceit is dangerous, given Heaney's subject, but rather than laud the virtues of the protean imagination *North* would reveal to us a cycle of "civilized" butchery that has its origin in the violent congruence of lives primordially established by the "old fathers." The crescendo reached in the proclamation "Come fly with me"—notably a cliché—is undercut in the last section where the voice of Jimmy Farrell from Synge's "The Playboy of the Western World" intones "Did you ever hear tell . . . of the skulls they have / in the city of Dublin?" Through Farrell's tongue-in-cheek words the "compounded history" of death is given the last word. In that history, Hamlet himself (and as such the poet) becomes merely "an old Dane . . . was drowned / in the Flood." Confronted with the nameless dead, language no longer proclaims the triumph of flight. Instead the worm of thought devolves once again towards the mud of its birth:

> My words lick around
> cobbled quays, go hunting
> lightly as pampooties
> over the skull-capped ground.
>
> [*N* 24]

Here is the circumstance of poetry and language: they are astraddle silence. Heaney acknowledges this, but only after he has dramatized what Wallace Stevens in "Of Modern Poetry" called "the poem of the mind in the act of finding / what will suffice": the poem as a process of coming to consciousness rather than a as static artifact. Heaney's adaptation of Stevens's injunction finds him struggling with his own idea of order while at the same time acknowledging the constitutive powers of disorder that have shaped human culture and history. The awareness of such disorder was nascent at the outset of Heaney's work. As his breakthrough poem **"Digging"** showed, Heaney's quest for self-definition begins in discontinuity. By digging with his pen he hopes to define his identity in relation to his native place and ancestry, though the quest itself never quite permits him to rest easy in that relationship. Now, in **"The Digging Skeleton,"** Heaney adapts Baudelaire's *fleur du mal* to his own experience of evil. The anatomical drawings on which Heaney meditates in the poem are more likely to be found buried along Dublin's "dusty quays" than Paris's. Yet, like Baudelaire's original, **"The Digging Skeleton"** gives us a vision of human horror that persists beyond death. Moreover, their unrelenting task reverberates with the poet's. **"The Digging Skeleton"** thus offers us the infernal version of Heaney's ideal poetry: instead of transcending his fate, he falls prey to it.

In keeping with his conceit of writing as a dig into lost origins, **"Bone Dreams"** marks an advance on Heaney's exploration of his historical, cultural, and linguistic roots. Like a colonial David to England's imperial Goliath, Heaney winds a bone found on the grazing "in the sling of mind / to pitch it at England," as if to act out one possible response to conquest—the response that enacts the mechanism of violent reprisal. Throughout

North such answers to the poet's crisis are neither definitive nor stable. He must go deeper. So in the second section it is as if the poet had reentered the souterraine of **"Toome"** to prospect with even greater attention. Disclosed now is the hoard of lost tongues that compose English, "ivied declensions," "the scop's twang," "the iron flash of consonants cleaving the line." The line languages cleave to is "the migrant line" of history. As such, they are not only bone houses but treasure troves. **"Bone Dreams"** is therefore Heaney's homage to the English language. Rather than imaginatively fueling the feud, Heaney once again explores the linguistic prospects of reconciliation. Such tuning, of course, demands that the "masculine" English consonant embrace the "feminine" Irish vowel. So, in the poem's third section, *ban-hus* is uncovered, the Danish origin of "bone-house." Telling the story of this one word's origin, he retells the story of the language itself. *Banhus* thus becomes a "a cauldron / of generation swung at the center." The union of masculine and feminine in language is generative and approaches the sacred, though elsewhere in *North*—as in **"Ocean's Love to Ireland"**—that union will signify the imperial rape of the colony in another act of cyclic violation.

In **"Bone Dreams,"** however, language itself is still an idealized "love-den," a "dream-bower." As the poem progresses it further mythologizes the linguistic act of union in a dreamlike transformation of the poet into a chalk giant carved upon the downs of England. In this union the binary oppositions masculine/feminine, England/Ireland exist in dynamic and creative equipoise. **"Bone Dreams"** goes still further in its play of oppositions, for in sections IV and V Heaney reverses his mythology. Harkening back to an even earlier history, England is now perceived as the feminine, Ireland as the masculine conquering force. The sections may be read as a fantasy of the embrace of split cultures in which English imperialism is overturned by the poet's mastery of the English lyric. David *has* overthrown Goliath, imaginatively if not historically. Once again, however, Heaney demythologizes his own fantasy. Just as the mock bard of **"Viking Dublin: Trial Pieces"** finds his words licking the skull-capped ground, so at the end of **"Bone Dreams"** his dream of cultural unity suffers a similar reduction. The dead mole he finds one morning in Devon suggests a permanent fault between cultural and political oppositions of his troubled cultural inheritance. The mole, indigenous to England but not to Ireland, was thought by Heaney to be "a big-boned coulter." Blowing back the fur to see the little points of its eyes, he confronts something more kin to the rat of **"An Advancement of Learning"** than to Hercules. In doing so, Heaney once again alerts us to his own self-consciously dramatized misperception of achieving too easy an accord between oppositions.

I have discussed how Heaney's preoccupation with cyclic time influences his vision of history in *North,* and how he must use his poetry to reveal the legacy of violence that is a significant part of that history. A central project in exposing that legacy is Heaney's search for emblems that might reveal the violent origins of culture, a search begun in **"The Tollund Man."** Yet the emblems of ritual violence we find in *North* embody the horror of victimization more drastically than that poem does. The true brutality of human sacrifice inheres in them far more than any religious or artistic repose. The repetition of blood sacrifice by which, according to both Mircea Eliade and Rene Girard, archaic humanity derived its symbols and established order, infuses them with emblematic power, now as at the dawn of culture.[47] Again, the danger of Heaney's project is that he might repeat unconsciously the violent atavisms of the past in a more civilized context. Its strength is that their adequacy as emblems will be questioned, and so the mythic process that underlies the violence will be exposed to consciousness.

As befitting emblems, the ritual victims of **"The Grauballe Man," "Strange Fruit,"** and **"Punishment"** attempt to expose myth's violent roots. Comparing **"The Tollund Man"** to **"The Grauballe Man,"** Edna Longley argues that the earlier poem "summed up profound feelings and wishes about the situation in Northern Ireland," while the latter "almost proclaims the victory of metaphor over actuality."[48] For that reason, she believes **"The Grauballe Man"** implicates itself and the poet in the crime it uncovers: the obscuring of atrocity through myth. For Longley, the repose of the Tollund Man signifies a destination which the Grauballe Man cannot transcend: "The ultimate difference between the two poems is between Christ on the Cross and a holy picture."[49] What Longley fails to recognize, however, is that the figure of Christ also derives its power from its status as an emblem. At a profound level Christ on the cross *is* a holy picture, just as the Tollund Man *is* a poem. They are both symbols, and it is through their status as symbols that they gain the power to move us. That is also the source of their danger, for throughout history the power of symbols has been abused and manipulated to violent ends, including the symbol of Christ. The ambiguous nature of symbols is precisely what Heaney exposes in **"The Grauballe Man."**

Where **"The Tollund Man"** began with an air of indefinite meditation commensurate with the poet's feeling of religious awe, **"The Grauballe Man"** begins with stark immediacy. The tone of the poems could not be more different. Rather than an image of repose—the "mild pods" of the Tollund Man's eyelids—**"The Grauballe Man"** is first characterized by an image of anguish that fills his entire being, even in death. Though the opening simile renders the photograph appearing in Glob's book in stunning precision, its power transcends particular circumstance, once again associating metaphor with metamorphosis. The "black river" of the Grauballe Man's identity is only the beginning of his transformations. The self-consciousness of his metamorphosis through Heaney's sequence of similes is pointed, for, as Neil Corcoran observed, with it the poet exposes the "appropriation of the human victim into the poem's own form and order."[50] Just as the longship's swimming tongue was transformed into the poet's longhand in **"Bone Dreams,"** so here we find the Grauballe Man pouring himself into the imaginative process itself. Like a negative taking shape in a darkroom, he rises into the poem before the reader's eyes, thereby enacting the mimesis so fundamental to the process that fuels reciprocal violence.

If Heaney's concern were solely to exploit the figure for the sake of writing a poem about writing a poem his critics' charges would be justified, but one simply cannot read the poem that way without ignoring both the insistence of the text itself and its context. With the fifth stanza, there is a subtle tonal shift in which the purpose of Heaney's seeming indulgence becomes evident, and the metaphors give way to revelation:

> The head lifts,
> the chin is a visor
> raised above the vent
> of his slashed throat . . .

> [*N* 35]

At this moment, the difference between the Tollund Man and the Grauballe Man is revealed. The former's repose rests in his "sad freedom," his consent to be sacrificed, his willing participation as a scapegoat in a savage rite that perpetuates itself. The Grauballe Man made no such consent. His slashed throat and agonized gaze, the contortion of his kept body, are proof he was an unwilling victim. Each is "bridegroom to the goddess," but only the Tollund Man assumes that responsibility willingly, and so the "cured wound" of the Grauballe Man's slashed throat communicates a different conception of "the befitting emblem" or symbol than does the Tollund Man's equanimity. Heaney's use of the word "cured" is ironic, for the Grauballe Man's wound is anything but cured. It is the fault that opens in the depths of myth and is inscribed violently on the bodies of the victims. Moreover, when one realizes that in Irish lore Christ's cross is made from the wood of the elderberry tree, Heaney's description of the Grauballe Man's wound as "a dark elderberry place" takes on profound implications. The Grauballe Man becomes a type of Christ whom Girard sees as the scapegoat whose sacrifice ends the cycle of violence by revealing the demonic nature of such rites. In Girard's words, "by exposing the secret of the persecutor's representation, it prevents the mechanism of the victim from . . . creating, at the height of mimetic disorder, a new order of ritual expulsion that replaces the old."[51] As such, when the poet asks rhetorically, "Who will say 'corpse' / to his vivid cast? / who will say 'body' / to his opaque repose?" the answer is neither no one, nor is it the poet. It is the Grauballe Man himself who bears witness to the atrocity of sacrifice, the Grauballe Man whose incurable wound opens again in the poem, thereby forcing Heaney to weigh the "perfected memory" of myth against the actual horror the myth would obscure.

As the poem implies, to perfect atrocity in memory is to glorify death for the sake of myth: *Dulce et decorum est pro patria mori.* As Heaney would have it, like Girard, the same process lies behind blood sacrifice and the blood feuds of nationalism. Heaney uncovers the origins of this fallacy in the origins of culture itself, a fallacy underscored by the enjambment "lies / perfected," which is the second time the word "lies" ends a line of the poem. In fact, the Grauballe Man does lie both literally on his pillow of turf and figuratively by superficially suggesting at first that beauty may be separated from atrocity, that all our cultural artifacts are somehow innocent of the violent origins of culture. The birth of the Grauballe Man into the poem recapitulates a process of blindness that inheres in symbolization, in which myth and art may "too strictly compass" that which by its nature cannot be encompassed, only to progressively deconstruct its own emblematic nature. **"The Grauballe Man"** is thus a symbol that desymbolizes itself by exposing its own complicity, and the poet's, in the violence of culture. Atrocity most starkly exposes this blindness for what it is, but only when art holds a mirror up to itself and questions its own claims. What especially needs questioning is the presumption of perfectibility in which "each hooded victim" disappears into the exemplary, into the terrible beauty of an emblem that would perpetuate the vicious cycle of the scapegoat.

The point is made again in **"Strange Fruit,"** in which Heaney meditates on another victim, the Windeby Girl. She too emerges like a fetus out of the bog in which a single phrase, "pash of tallow" (*pash* being the Northern Irish dialect word for head) embodies the connection between the ancient fertility sacrifice and the contemporary victims of ritual violence. In a manner similar to Spenser, who oversaw the mass starvation of the indigenous Irish, the Roman historian Diodorus Siculus witnessed human sacrifice in pre-Christian Britain and Ireland and so could stand as an example of the learned official drawn into the banality of evil. The girl outstares both his gradual ease and the poet's own pretensions to beatify and revere her. In **"Strange Fruit,"** the poet is outstared by the emblem he himself has created.

That stare, like the slashed throat of the Grauballe Man, judges a world in which atrocity is not only possible but acceptable just as it judges the world of the poet's art.

Judgment implies distance, and in both **"The Grauballe Man"** and **"Strange Fruit"** Heaney is a distanced observer. His "I" appears but once, and then only to observe memory in the process of myth-making. His empathy involves no personal risk. He does not offer to go on pilgrimage to see the Grauballe Man, nor does he wish to ride the tumbril in his place. In **"Punishment"** this changes. Having implicated memory's desire to "perfect" history in the process of sacrificial violation, the poet now risks his identity in order to reveal his true relationship to the victim and to determine its bearing on his vocation. The identification at the beginning of the poem is as great as in **"The Tollund Man,"** perhaps more so, since the poet is now with the girl at the moment of sacrifice. The girl was an adulteress, Glob suggests, who had been beaten out of her village and vilified, not unlike the women who refused to abide by the brutal customs of Heaney's own Catholic tribe. The injustice of her murder and its pathos inspire Heaney to direct address, a depth of identification not risked in **"The Tollund Man"**:

> My poor scapegoat,
>
> I almost love you
> but would have cast, I know,
> the stones of silence.
> I am the artful voyeur
>
> of your brain's exposed
> and darkened combs,
> your muscle's webbing
> and all your numbered bones:
> I who have stood dumb
> when your betraying sisters,
> cauled in tar,
> wept by the railings,
>
> who would connive
> in civilized outrage
> yet understand the exact
> and tribal, intimate revenge.
>
> [*N* 38]

Several allusions are submerged here which bear greatly on the meaning of the poem. The first allusion is to the scapegoat of Leviticus onto which the sins of the community are projected. The second is to the adulterous woman of John 8:6-7 who was saved from death through Christ's intercession. The last is to Christ himself, derived from Psalm 22: "They have pierced my hands and feet; they have numbered all my bones."[52] As Neil Corcoran remarks, "the chilling irony of these allusions is that they both judge this act of tribal revenge by the more merciful ethic enshrined in the biblical religion while they implicate that religion in precisely those sacrificial rituals which join Jutland and Irish Republicanism."[53] The scapegoat of **"Punishment"** has both Catholic and Protestant sisters in the tarred and feathered adulteresses of the Troubles—a congruence of lives to be sure. But the poet's more searching moral question involves his own stance toward his art. If **"The Tollund Man"** gives us the victim risen to the status of emblem, then in **"The Grauballe Man," "Strange Fruit,"** and **"Punishment"** we encounter the crucifixion of the emblem on the cross of actual atrocity. Faced with atrocity, poetry may well become artful voyeurism. The apparently civilizing nature of even the most befitting emblem may nonetheless conspire with the violent forces underlying culture. Yet, as the poem's final lines suggest, by seeking to understand those forces, by exposing them to consciousness, art may avoid connivance and so make its emblems truly befitting. The crux of Heaney's problem, then, may be summed up in a single question: How, to use his own words, can he "grant the religious intensity of the violence its deplorable authenticity and complexity" and still "encompass the perspectives of humane reason?" (*P* 56). By "religious" Heaney does not mean sectarian division, but the deeper enmity that "can be viewed as a struggle between the cults and devotees of a god or a goddess" (*P* 57). This view claims that the imaginative parallels between early Iron Age Northern Europe and contemporary Ulster comprise a vision of terrible continuity.[54] That continuity emerges most powerfully in his scapegoats, for they reflect Heaney's awareness of an archaic cultic numen whose power is still operative behind the mask of civilization as an "exact and tribal, intimate revenge."

What, more specifically, is the nature of this revenge? As I have observed already, Heaney's understanding of the violent congruence of lives that binds together the Catholic and Protestant "tribes" of Northern Ireland with the old fathers finds theoretical support in Rene Girard's idea of the origins of myth and symbols in his studies *Violence and the Sacred* and *The Scapegoat*. For Girard, the kinds of sacrifices Heaney portrays represent a congruence between the sacred and the violent acts sanctioned and concealed in religious rituals and, ultimately, in the symbolic process itself. Violence and the sacred are inseparable in Girard's view, and it is the presence of the surrogate victim in the sacrificial act that testifies to this reality across centuries and cultures. Manifesting the sacred, the victim becomes a vessel into which all the violence of the tribe is deflected, "the violence that would otherwise be vented on its own members."[55] For Girard, this act of projection or deflection constitutes a "mechanism" from which symbolic thought exfoliates, and hence all of culture. The cathartic effect of sanctioned violence gives rise to systems of thought and behavior the whole effort of which is to conceal humanity's inherently violent

nature. Both art and the institutions of culture merely mask this final, intensely disturbing truth. All human cultures, like Janus, wear a face of order and disorder, the former often concealing the latter.

As Girard conceives it, then, the surrogate victim mechanism, and thus the sacrificial process, requires misunderstanding, an Oedipal act of self-blinding. Without such misunderstanding vengeance would escalate to the point of destroying the whole social fabric.[56] As such, the sacred becomes indispensable, for humans "can dispose of their violence more efficiently if they regard the process not as something emanating within themselves, but as a necessity imposed from without, a divine decree whose least infraction calls down terrible punishment."[57] What the sacred sanctions is "transcendental violence" which prevents society from lapsing into the dizzying spiral of "reciprocal violence" in which the differences between feuding parties is effaced, their individual identities obliterated like Hercules and Antaeus by the very act of violence they believe will preserve what is most truly their own. When such effacement takes hold, a sacrificial crisis has developed that can only be diffused through a new manifestation of the sacred, that is, of transcendental violence. For Girard, myths themselves are "retrospective transfigurations of sacrificial crises, the reinterpretation of these crises in the light of the cultural order that has arisen from them."[58] With a similar urge to transfigure the past retrospectively, though with a clarity of reason to match Girard's powers of disclosure, the poems of *North* like a Greek tragedy uncover the more brutal habitations of the dark that lie just beyond the civilized.

In light of Girard's vision of the origins of myth and culture, another of his statements is prescient in the context of *North*: "If the tragic poet touches upon the violent reciprocity underlying all myths, it is because he perceives these myths in the context of weakening distinctions and growing violence."[59] Heaney's work in *North* does nothing if not explore the violent outcome of a sacrificial crisis by inquiring into its origin in myths that have shaped the consciousness of his country and himself. In the midst of this crisis, the distinct personae of Hercules and Antaeus are blurred. The apparent superiority of the Herculean mind masks an atavism as brutal as Antaeus's. Just so, the Antaean reliance on the seemingly more primitive mentality of myth becomes enmeshed in its own deadly logic. The result is a spiral of reciprocal violence that matches Girard's analysis almost exactly. Heaney's interrogation of the crisis in his poems likewise shows the Irish poet and the French theorist sharing common ground. For each, humanism alone is inadequate to explain violence.

Yet, is there an antidote to violence if neither demystification nor myth are adequate to reverse the cycle? The one actually increases the violence, the other only quells it. *North* reveals that such cultural blindness is precisely what permits reciprocal violence to maintain its hold on the divided communities until violence serves to justify the brutal logic of the tribal myth. Only by demystifying the myth is the cycle broken. But, again, how is this done if rationality, too, has its origins in the violent birth of culture? Heaney's answer in *North* is that myth is demythologized through a myth that, like **"The Grauballe Man,"** exposes its potential for disorder through the self-conscious interrogation of its own origins. Only by paradoxically representing the self-inwoven nature of this hidden cultural process can symbolization be redeemed from its collusion with atrocity. This does not mean that poetry transcends its origins. Instead, by being conscious of those origins and its own processes poetry can avoid the cultural somnambulism that obscures the realization that "the original potential of any genuine myth will always exceed the limits of a particular community or nation."[60] Myth and art have the power to transcend the brutalities of history, but only insofar as they expose their potential for disorder.

The key figure of Heaney's poetry is the sacred center, the *omphalos,* associated initially at least with the feminine ground of his native place. We have seen how in *Death of a Naturalist* Heaney shaped a textured poetry highly cognizant of this feminine ground, of the fecundity of the natural world, but also of that world's more disturbing qualities, especially its apocalyptic threat to identity. *Door into the Dark* explicitly connected the center to historical and cultural horizons through the symbol of the bog. In *Wintering Out,* the center is associated for the first time with the goddess Nerthus, who personifies the demonic or shadow side of the earth mother, the side that demands blood sacrifices. Now, in *North,* by exposing the terrifying "congruence of lives" that was always just beneath the surface of his poetry, Heaney stares into the violent heart of his home. The feminine *omphalos* is revealed to be insatiable, malevolent, evocative of a primal terror. In the figure of this remorseless goddess the tragic dimensions of *North* gain their fullest expression.

Tragic myth, as Paul Ricoeur observes, "concentrates good and evil at the summit of the divine."[61] Its version of ultimate reality stands in stark contrast to rational religion which, like the humanism to which it gave birth, promotes a beneficent version of divinity "at the expense of primordial brutality." Lost is the archaic sense of the intractable, a "malevolent transcendence" that cannot be fully comprehended by theodicy the whole effort of which is to reconcile a purely rational God's ways to our own.[62] According to Larry Bouchard, in this latter view, culture like religion provides "the source and justification of actions within a framework of unconditioned meaning."[63] Even in a secular world, culture supplies pivotal "norms and values, orders

nature and the cosmos" and so "provides communities with ontological bearings."[64] As such, from Bouchard's perspective, the irreducible nature of evil tests "the limits of a culture's vision and version of the real."[65] What the tragic myth impresses on us, then, is "that evil is a real force, that its negativity and destructiveness are no less an aspect of the human structure than is that structure's potency for good," and that "evil has an ontic reality no less than the good."[66] "Tragedy," in Paul Ricoeur's words, "has never finished dying."[67]

A similar vision of evil's irreducibility is found in the terrible goddess of *North.* She represents the limit of Heaney's "version of the real," as well as the limit of his version of the sacred center. To see her, as he does, "in relation to the tradition of Irish political martyrdom whose icon is Kathleen Ni Houlihan," is to make the fertility sacrifice to the Mother Goddess "more than an archaic barbarous rite." "It is," as Heaney himself observed, "an archetypal pattern" (*P* 57). This pattern is exposed in **"Come to the Bower"** and **"Bog Queen,"** where the allure of the feminine ground is revealed in all its numinous sexuality. In **"Come to the Bower,"** the Mother Goddess manifests herself as "the dark bowered queen" whom Heaney unpins in a necrophilic fantasy. Though she is one of the sacrificed, the bog queen has through the efficacy of the rite essentially become one with the fertility goddess herself. Hence she emerges from "the black maw / of the peat" until Heaney reaches "the bullion / of her Venus bone." Here, once again, Heaney's vivid description associates beauty and atrocity, insatiable desire with a demonic love that would end in the destruction of the lover. In writing this disturbing fantasy, the poet is testing his own imaginative intimacy with the feminine ground, with the goddess of Irish Republicanism. In **"Bog Queen"** the poet's identification is taken further when he assumes the persona of the victim herself, who was discovered on the Moira Estate south of Belfast in 1781. Such intense identification between the victim, the poet, and the act of writing comes very near to indulging in a dangerous kind of bathos that might confer upon the goddess too much power. Rather than bowing down before her, however, both poems demonstrate Heaney's ambivalence toward his art. Heaney intends to draw attention to his indulgence, to have the reader look upon it with suspicion. The title **"Come to the Bower"** itself derives from a traditional Republican song, and so clearly Heaney's embrace of the goddess is self-consciously ironic.[68] Moreover, the corpse of **"Bog Queen"** gradually disappears into the territory, her brain becoming "a jar of spawn / fermenting underground." What also ferments underground, of course, is the archetypal pattern that spawns the atrocities of contemporary Ireland. Her resurrection thus recapitulates the pattern witnessed in **"Requiem for the Croppies"**: the fertility myth becomes an historical myth in which the seeds of primitive sacrifice give birth to a new incarnation.

In **"Kinship,"** the archetypal pattern of reciprocal violence gains its fullest expression. At the same time, the poem is Heaney's most personal rendering of the bog symbol. It is also the one in which the Mother Goddess is revealed as the imaginative limit of Heaney's sacred center. In it, Heaney's intimacy with the territory is transformed into an abiding kinship with the victims. Divided into six sections, the poem opens with a meditation on the word "kinship" itself, one of the few importations from the Irish language into English:[69]

> Kinned by hieroglyphic
> peat on a spreadfield
> to the strangled victim,
> the love-nest in the bracken,
>
> I step through origins
> like a dog turning
> its memories of wilderness
> on the kitchen mat.

> [*N* 40]

These opening lines offer a commentary on the idea of bogland as Jungian ground, a center that houses the hieroglyphs of the culture and delves into its origins. Heaney, for all his seeming indulgences, yet again deflates bardic pretention by portraying himself in the less than grandiose image of a dog no longer game for the hunt. As in **"A Northern Hoard,"** such deflation lets him speak with a straightforwardness eschewed in the mythologizing strain of the earlier poems:

> I love this turf-face,
> its black incisions,
> the cooped secrets
> of process and ritual. . . .

> [*N* 40]

Cooped secrets of process and ritual are to Heaney's poetry what nobility and ceremony were to Yeats's. It is no wonder he acknowledges his love for them. Nonetheless, he does not let that admission blind him to the goddess's violent powers of disorder. The bog-pool with its unstopped mouth is a moon-drinker, a drinker of imagination and of genuine transcendence. As such, he must own that there are some things which are inexpressible, "not to be sounded / by the naked eye." In a marvelous sleight-of-hand this final synaesthesia intentionally confutes the senses and so inscribes the limit of which it tells.

Nevertheless, as the poem continues, it recapitulates Heaney's whole imaginative relationship to the feminine ground. The second section is a Whitmanesque catalogue of the bog's attributes that traces Heaney's path to self-consciousness in which the reader moves through perceptions associated in turn with the worlds of *Death of a Naturalist* to *Door into the Dark* and *Wintering*

Out. Finally, we come to the brutal, sacrificial world of *North,* and so the bog is deemed, among other things, "ruminant ground" and "insatiable bride." The full periodic stop at this point underscores the finality of the revelation. She is in Celtic lore the threefold goddess of birth, life, and death,[70] but more than this she is at once "floe of history" and "outback" of the poet's mind. The goddess reveals the poet's destined complicity in the violent origins of culture and the reciprocal violence of history, his quest for self-definition leading here to an unexpected and chilling end. Nevertheless, by articulating that relationship in no uncertain terms, Heaney also demonstrates his need to raise the outback of his mind to consciousness as the most urgent undertaking of his art.

This process of raising the past to consciousness deepens in the third and fourth sections of the poem, where Heaney explores more fully than is possible in a catalogue his vision of the bog. In the third, he recalls finding a turf-spade covered with moss. That obelisk is "twinned" with the cloven oak-limb symbolic of Nerthus. Once the poet has faced the goddess, in the fourth section he explicitly connects her to the bog, the sacred center:

> This center holds,
> then spreads.
> sump and seedbed,
> a bag of waters
>
> and a melting grave.

> [*N* 43]

"The center cannot hold," Yeats wrote in "The Second Coming." For Heaney, the center is at once immoveable and ecstatic, the origin of human culture and of creation itself. At this moment, the goddess hardly appears insatiable, holding everything in a version of transcendence: the center is "a windfall / composing the floor it rots into." This self-inwoven image would seem merely to give credence to the idea that Heaney's poetry incorporates ritual as "an indomitable, sacred embodiment of the life-force principle,"[71] were it not for the fact that the center is rotting. The association of composition and decomposition in the image prevents Heaney's goddess from being construed as merely a post-Romantic adaptation of D. H. Lawrence's Life-Force. Heaney's image of the center in **"Kinship"** suggests instead that composition and decomposition, like order and disorder, are irrevocably intermingled in the ground of being itself. The Life-Force is also a Death-Force. Heaney's agricultural metaphor is a faintly disguised analogue for the hidden processes of culture, whose mimetic, self-inwoven circularity may well spawn violence and the attribution of that violence to a sacred symbol or myth. The sorrow that comes from opening a door into the outback of the mind is articulated in the reversal on which the section ends:

I grew out of all this
like a weeping willow
inclined to
the appetites of gravity.

[*N* 43]

The double movement inscribed in these lines—an inclination to return to the source and center even as one grows away from it—is a defining moment for Heaney's poetry, for it makes evident the complex process that is seemingly always at work in his imagination.

The grave melts. The center rots. The appetites of gravity are no less devouring than Yeats's center presaging the rough beast. Both mingle order and disorder, though while Yeats's center loses its hold passively at the end of an historical cycle Heaney's appears to be a primal, active, enduring principle of culture. Yet Heaney's goddess reveals herself in a particular territory, and therefore **"Kinship"** mingles the beauty of bogland with the potential fanaticism of the locative vision, the urge to fix the sacred within a particular place. The poem's title hints at the kinds of blood feuds that ensue when place itself becomes blindly steeped in myth. On the other hand, by inquiring more closely into the nature of the center, two insights suggest themselves. First, the principle of disorder is virulent when one's attachment to a place is fixed in a locative vision of order. At that point, disorder assumes the mask of order, becomes idolatrous, even demonic. One need only think of any number of contested "tribal" territories around the globe. Second, it is by raising the element of disorder in culture to the light of consciousness that one escapes the sacrificial mechanism supported by a locative world-view, the blood-lust of the "insatiable bride."

It would seem, having reached the groundswell of his sacred center, Heaney's apocalyptic quest reveals an intolerable truth. If the center is stained with the blood of sacrifice how can the poet's imagination trust its own generative processes? The poetry of *North,* generally speaking, finds its inspiration in a hermeneutic of suspicion in which Heaney questions his own fundamental artistic presuppositions. Yet no poet, regardless of the severity of his sensibility, can write under the shadow of absolute suspicion, in which the efficacy of the word is wholly negated. Therefore, at the nadir of his descent, Heaney discovers grounds for a chastened hermeneutic of trust:

This is the vowel of earth
dreaming its root
in flowers and snow,

mutation of weathers
and seasons,
a windfall composing
the floor it rots into.

[*N* 43]

These lines, like those above, make an analogy between culture and agriculture, only now the very process of decomposition itself is placed in the wider context of a center that encompasses all. As the vowel of earth, a kind of all-pervading *logos,* the center appears as an invisible power that "dreams" into existence its own visible root. Yet, paradoxically, it also mutates, reincarnates itself into weathers and seasons, and finally rots or empties itself into the ground, the ground of being. This self-inwoven image culminating in the center's "windfall" describes the process of *kenosis,* a self-emptying that transfigures everything—sump, seedbed, ferments of husk and leaf, mutation of weathers and seasons—into its momentary, and momentous, incarnations. By virtue of this process, decomposition gives rise to new composition, a stunning negation of the brutal side of mimetic circularity; and one that is necessary unless the poet is willing to commit imaginative suicide.

What this remarkable reversal reveals is Heaney's desire to redeem the symbol of the center itself. Used by Paul in his Letter to the Philippians (2:5-11), the term *kenosis* refers to Christ's choice in the act of incarnation to divest himself of his divinity in order to become human, a supreme sacrifice that finds its ethical equivalent on the cross. The word and its variants have a range of meanings, including references to the emptying of vessels, exhaustion, the breeding of famine, or any empty space. Moreover, the concept finds theological variations in contemplative traditions that emphasize the emptying of the human ego before the divine, as well as the divine's own radical transcendence. I mention this range of associations for as Heaney's work evolves the notion of an empty source becomes more and more central to his vision. "I thought of walking round and round a space / utterly empty, utterly a source, / like the idea of sound," Heaney remarks in *Station Island* (68), an image that appears again in *The Haw Lantern* (32). As a matter of course, Heaney's digging, his door into the dark, lead to this vision of a generative emptiness that appears even in *North,* the book that would on the surface appear to be his most despairing. That generative emptiness, as we shall see in later chapters (where it is more explicitly refined by the works of St. John of the Cross and others) comprises a definitive development of Heaney's sacred center beyond the sense of place alone. As for now, his *via negativa* brings him to the point at which suspicion of the source is transformed into trust through a willingness to empty himself of any illusions about his personal or communal past.

Something of that self-negation is felt in the final sections of **"Kinship"** where, having pictured the center, the poet turns away once again to consider his complicity in the tragedy, and to give us his final grim evocation of its origin. We are now in the world of *Death of a Naturalist.* Heaney as a boy is the "privileged attendant / bearer of bread and drink" behind his great-grandfather in a turf-cart. Like the old fathers before him, Heaney mythologizes him, though with a self-consciousness that simultaneously demythologizes the act:

> I deified the man
> who rode there,
> god of the wagon,
> the hearth feeder.

[*N* 44]

It is impossible to read these lines without seeing the Tollund Man riding the tumbril, as well as hearing the poet's note of self-accusation. Trundling down the road, the old man and his "squire" gain "right-of-way," which gives the young Heaney a false sense of manly pride, the kind of false pride that may give rise to "tribalism" and xenophobia. By demythologizing his childhood, Heaney assumes in his own work the kind of negative capability that allows him to decode dangerous myths of self and community. Such hard-won demythologizing renders the violence of the sacred inoperative even as Heaney inclines his imagination to take critical stock of the entire past out of which he grew. It permits the center once again to become a creative source for his imagination.

Heaney's strategy of invoking and dramatizing the myth of the center in order to demythologize it is given its most direct treatment in the final section of **"Kinship"** where it takes the form of an address to Tacitus who wrote about Ireland in his *Agricola* and described the cult of Nerthus in his *Germania.*[72] The first stanza of the poem bitterly lampoons the poet as *fili*, priestly druid bard. Making his sacred grove on "an old cran-nog," or lake isle, Heaney at once pulls down the vanity of his enterprise and acknowledges the desolation of the solitary poet separated by conscience from his community. Yet what he also witnesses is the desolate peace of **"North"** nominated by the exhaustion of violence that recurs. The Christian faith with its "sacred heart" merely reenacts the brutal sacrifices of an older barbarous one. Instead of being a beneficent presence, the feminine ground "inhumes" the faces of casualty and victim, the choice of word itself drawing their humanity back into the humus of earth. In this final section Heaney envisions an apotheosis of the tragic, what the Jewish writer and theologian Arthur Cohen called the *tremendum,* a malevolent transcendence that opens up an imaginative caesura in which "the raising up and release of a chthonic instinctualism" forebodes the cruelties and murders of cultural holocausts and whose form signifies "an ontic breach"[73]—a "slaughter for the common good." Confronted with such a breach and the violence it breeds across cultures, "nothing will suffice," for such evil exceeds the powers of rational thought and religious theodicy. Heaney's line echoes

Yeats's "Easter 1916" ("Too long a sacrifice / Can make a stone of the heart. / O when may it suffice") and therefore plays on Yeats's own conception of historical cycles and the violent origins of cultures. It likewise questions the efficacy of poetry itself before such a breach, for it also echoes Wallace Stevens's "Of Modern Poetry": "the poem of the mind in the act of finding / what will suffice."[74] By the end of **"Kinship"** both heart and mind appear ineffectual before the powers of the goddess who swallows our humanity along with our love and terror. But if heart and mind are silenced, where does hope lie? As a sustained sequence that exposes the violent nature of history and the sacred, *North* suggests that there is hope in the act of naming the terror. By naming the terror, by exposing the violent origins of culture, the poet orders the disorder that might swell into violence through self-blindness. In Heaney's words, "I think a poet cannot influence events in the North because it is the men of action that are influencing everybody and everything, but I do believe that poetry is its own special action and that having its own mode of consciousness, its own mode of reality, has its own efficacy gradually."[75] That special action makes *North* an apocalyptic work in the root meaning of the term. It reveals or uncovers the cooped processes of violence at work beneath the surface of the culture and exposes its rituals to the light of consciousness. To again borrow from Rene Girard, *North* might be said to "replace myth with a representation,"[76] though it might be more accurate to say that *North* is a myth of place that demythologizes myths of place. In light of this, it is difficult to see how, as Blake Morrison claimed, the lines "how we slaughter / for the common good" grant "sectarian killing in Northern Ireland a respectability which it is not granted in day-to-day journalism,"[77] for it is only by naming the terror and questing after its source that consciousness progresses beyond the somnambulism of inherited myths.

"Archimedes said that he could move the world if he had a point whereon to rest his machine. Who has not felt the same aspiration as regards the world of his own mind?"[78] so Wordsworth observed with respect to the powers of imagination. His question is germane to Heaney's poetry. By *North,* Heaney's desire to gain leverage over his psychic inheritance includes discerning the fulcrum of the mind's outback as well as his own consciousness. Part I of *North* is essentially an attempt to use poetry as a kind of Archimedean machine to reposition the tragic world of Ulster imaginatively so that conscience may become a guiding force within consciousness. Though Heaney ruefully parodies that lever and its effects in **"The Unacknowledged Legislator's Dream,"** the poems of the first part of the volume do enable him to engage the tragedy more explicitly in Part II. If the goal of *North* is revelation, then the poems of the second part risk exposure more through public address and autobiography than through obviously symbolic modes of discourse. Nevertheless, one ought not to make too strong a distinction between Part I and Part II. Just as there are moments of symbolic utterance in the second part of *North* so there are opportunities for explicit utterance in the first part. The effect is to blur the distinction Heaney himself made in describing the structure of his book. More than this, the blending of the two modes of utterance at key moments actually underscores Heaney's desire to at once set myth in dialogue with itself in order to unearth its dangerous proclivities, and at the same time to reveal the presence of myth even in the most explicit language. Hence, set amidst poems in which Heaney's "I" achieves a mythic intensity, **"Funeral Rites"** dramatizes the poet's growth to consciousness as that growth is cast against the backdrop of sectarian violence. Heaney's rendering of his first world in the poem resembles a kind of dream state, and so his feelings of intense confinement within the unexamined customs of his community gradually become evident. That sense of communal or tribal enclosure deepens when, consistent with the hallucinatory world of the poems which surround **"Funeral Rites,"** the funeral procession pushes away like a "black glacier." Heaney's image reveals the cortege to be a mimetic rite that carries into the future the precedent of centuries of violent reprisals.

Elaborating its vision of mimetic, cyclic reprisal, the poem soon evokes the "customary rhythms" that, while assuaging, nevertheless implicate themselves in "each neighborly murder." Ironically, these very ceremonies and rhythms are the cultural vessels that fuel the blood feud. From the time of origins such rites and customs have been implicated in the tribal mentality that leads to reciprocal violence. Thus the homes of Heaney's neighbors are "blinded" by more than window shades. They are blinded by the rhythms that bind them to the shades of the murdered dead. Faced with this blindness, Heaney declares his hope in a return to origins in which the center itself is purged of primordial violence: "I would restore / the great chambers of the Boyne." Here again we find the poet longing to miraculously turn back history, since Newgrange and the other burial mounds of the Boyne Valley are among the world's most ancient. In the context of the poem they hint at the wellsprings of culture. Moreover, the Boyne River is named after the Celtic fertility goddess Badh, another "incarnation" of Nerthus. As if Heaney's allusion were not already suggestive enough, the Boyne Valley was the sight of the final defeat of James II in 1691 by William of Orange. After that defeat, the Irish would be ousted and their lands given to English Planters. Ireland would be dispossessed both politically and culturally.[79] So when Heaney finally imagines the "slow triumph" of the funeral cortege moving "quiet as a serpent" towards the mounds, its tail in the Gap of the North, its head in the megalithic doorway, he is not simply evoking the wrongs of English imperialism but envisioning centuries

of reciprocal violence. **"Funeral Rites"** traces in microcosm the whole history of violence *North* would expose.

As we have seen, for Heaney, myth can only be demythologized through a "broken myth," one that raises consciousness out of tribal custom by dramatizing the process of violence and exposing it to self-awareness. The "black glacier" that pushes away in the first section of **"Funeral Rites"** becomes the serpent that returns to the source in the second, the funeral cortege retracing the archetypal pattern back to its origin at the dawn of civilization. In the third section, however, it is clear that Heaney is not satisfied to retrace the path back without offering an emblem that promises more than a simple disclosure of the tragic cycle. Instead, he would offer the hope that the "arbitration of the feud" may be placated, the "cud of memory" allayed. He now imagines the victims of sectarian violence:

> disposed like Gunnar
> who lay beautiful
> inside his burial mound,
> though dead by violence
>
> and unavenged.

[*N* 17]

Gunnar, murdered in a blood feud in the Norse *Njals Saga,* represents the scapegoat in whose death the cycle of violence is ended rather than renewed because it is unavenged.[80] To use Girard's distinction, Gunnar, like the Grauballe Man, is in fact more martyr than scapegoat for by his death he exposes the cycle for what it is—a brutal sacrificial rite.[81] In his death reciprocal violence is diffused, the archetype having been exposed to the conscious mind. This reading is especially fitting since Heaney alters the story told in the *Saga.* Gunnar is, in fact, avenged. In contrast, **"Funeral Rites"** ends with Gunnar turning "with a joyful face / to look at the moon," an image that conjures the suspended Christ of **"Westering,"** an association underscored by the fact that the cortege makes its way to a sepulchre over whose mouth a stone has been rolled back. The figure of Gunnar thus functions as a kind of dynamic, psychic node in which all of the strains of Heaney's cultural past, as well as the legacy of human violence, come together. Though Gunnar is not a Christ-figure in any doctrinal sense, his association with Christ is intended to compensate imaginatively for the brutal perversion of Christianity embodied in the tribal, sectarian customs of Catholics and Protestants in the North of Ireland.

Like **"The Grauballe Man,"** Heaney placed **"Funeral Rites"** early in Part I, which suggests that while he wanted to offer an image of possible transcendence of the cycle of violence he did not want that image to overshadow the real historical tragedy of sectarian division. As such, the four poems appearing at the end of Part I recount the actual history of Irish and English politics and therefore form a thematic and structural bridge to the more explicit poems of Part II. In doing so, they implicate myth in history, history in myth, and so the historical relationship between Ireland and England is couched in metaphors of sexual violence consistent with the fertility rites of the goddess. In **"Ocean's Love to Ireland,"** Heaney transposes a passage from John Aubrey's life of Raleigh, in which Raleigh rapes a maid, into a metaphor for Ireland's relationship to England, a relationship defined by recurrent violence, "the ground possessed and repossessed." Similarly, **"Aisling"** reveals the historical curse levied on "masculine" England for the ruin it has brought upon "feminine" Ireland. A traditional Irish poem in which a man wandering in a wood has a vision of a woman who reveals herself to be Ireland to whom he must pledge allegiance with his life, this aisling once again dramatizes the historical cycle of reciprocal violence by alluding to myth. Here, Ireland is Diana, England Actaeon, "his high lament / the stag's exhausted belling" as the goddess transforms herself into a pack of hounds. Raleigh's "decadent sweet art" finds as its offspring the terror of Irish Republicanism.

The mythology that links sexuality to the historical rape of cultures finds its fullest expression in **"Act of Union."**[82] The poem discloses its meaning through an imaginative intercourse that connects the parliamentary act of 1800, which created the "United Kingdom of Great Britain and Ireland," to the poet's conjugal act of union with his wife. In its first section, Heaney imagines himself the "tall kingdom" over his wife's shoulder. The sexual act is rendered as a "bog-burst" that occurs after "the rain in bogland" has "gathered head." She, in turn, is the "heaving province" where their past has grown. Making love to her, however, Heaney realizes that "conquest is a lie." Unlike the lurid sexual fantasies of **"Bog Queen," "Bone Dreams,"** and **"Come to the Bower,"** the act of union in marriage is now seen as a state of mutual concession rather than an affair of propitiation before the insatiable bride, or an opportunity for an imperial, masculine show of force. In the poem's second section, however, this promise of mutual respect gives way to internal strife. Heaney's voice modulates into that of England, "imperially male," whose act of union is "a rending process in the colony" that sprouts "an obstinate fifth column": the Protestant descendants of the Planters. In this act of union between colony and empire there is no mutual concession, and what is foreseen by the poet is a continuation of the cycle of violence. This same sense of despair is reiterated in **"The Betrothal of Cavehill"** where shots from a "ritual gun" hint that the bridegroom is betrothed both to his wife and to Ulster's other "goddess," the Queen of England. This betrothal, like the betrothal England to

Ireland, or the bridegrooms of the goddess Nerthus, all recapitulate the same brutal cycle of possession, dispossession, and repossession of violence committed in the name of the sacred.

The ritual gun that sounds at the end of the first part of **North** resounds into the second where Heaney turns to a more explicit treatment of his themes without neglecting or losing the amplitude of his symbols. Such explicit treatment of Heaney's particular historical and cultural milieu is powerfully at work in **"Whatever You Say, Say Nothing."** Written in ballad stanzas, Heaney's stance is obviously public, his voice attempting the passionate utterance found in Yeats's "Meditations in Times of Civil War," which the poem echoes at the beginning of the second section within the context of contemporary Ulster: "Men die at hand. In blasted street and home / The gelignite's a common sound effect." Yet it also throws into doubt the shallow humanism that often governs such speech. Heaney inclines "as much to rosary beads / As to the jottings and analyses / Of politicians and newspapermen," implying the language of common speech has been tainted by the violence it tries, unsuccessfully, to describe. It is not surprising, then, that in another poem, **"Freedman,"** he praises poetry for having set him apart from those who use language uncritically, and who therefore may fall prey to slogans and symbols that condone and reiterate sectarian violence. Despite these overtures at public speech, in the second part of **North** the most intensely sustained exploration of the relationship between sectarianism and Heaney's own quest for self-definition occurs in **"Singing School."** It is appropriate that a book obsessive about the origins of consciousness end with an appeal to autobiography. The sequence, of course, gets its title from "Sailing to Byzantium": "Nor is their singing school but studying / Monuments of its own magnificence."[83] In the poem, Yeats speaks of monuments that comprise the ideal realm of human spirit, a realm that would transcend "whatever is begotten, born and dies." Heaney's "singing school," however, is located in the tragic world of history, and while it champions poetry's place in that world it harbors no illusions of escaping from the temporal. Comprising the sequence are key moments or "stations" in his growth to greater self-awareness. The sequence thus draws both in spirit and subject from the prose poems of **Stations.** As Heaney observed, those pieces attempt to touch "spots of time," "moments on the very edge of consciousness" (S [**Stations**] 3), a few of which appear to be core inspirations for a number of later poems. **"Singing School,"** like **Stations,** renders "points on a psychic *turas*" (S 3) through which Heaney gains a deeper understanding of his origins and his art.

The first poem of the sequence, **"The Ministry of Fear,"** recounts the poet's growth away from home, the inferiority complexes of growing up Catholic in

Northern Ireland, his growing sense of sectarian violence, and lastly his realization that, like Patrick Kavanagh (whose "Epic" he echoes in the poem's opening lines), the Irish poet may indeed claim rights on the English lyric. In turn, **"A Constable Calls"** and **"Orange Drums"** further name the fear suggested by the previous poem. In **"A Constable Calls"** we are made to feel that his father's lie about crop reports could end in his being carted off to jail. Knowing his father lied, the child imagines "the black-hole in the barracks," a fear that is exacerbated by the constable's demeanor, as well as his revolver and the "doomsday book" of tallies. The poem ends with the haunting sound of the constable's bicycle ticking down the road like a bomb about to go off. An air of oppression hovers about the scene, and while we know that neither the father nor the son will respond violently to that oppression, the poem nevertheless suggests that a violent reprisal will someday detonate in this explosive social climate.

That growing sense of a violence brewing just below the surface of tense but cordial relations is reinforced when the ticking of **"A Constable Calls"** explodes into the sectarian display of **"Orange Drums, Tyrone, 1966."** Here, Heaney portrays the brutality of Protestant sectarianism through grotesque caricature. The drummer lodges "thunder / Grossly there between his chin and knees." Raleigh's "superb crest" from Part I has softened to the lewd impotence of sectarian ritual that celebrates the triumph of William of Orange each year on July 12, and therefore celebrates a version of the sacred at once primordial and imperial. In a searing inversion of Herculean masculinity, the drummer "is raised up by what he buckles under." Heaney's own impotence to allay the violence of his home is explored, in turn, in **"Summer 1969."** In the poem, Heaney assumes what will become a familiar stance for him: the poet, faced with tragedy, considers what mode of action he should take. As he does repeatedly in his work, Heaney discovers a model in an artist who faced similar circumstances without relinquishing his art to either political pressure or silence. Here the artist is Goya. Retreating to the Prado, Heaney observes his **"Shootings of the Third of May"** and his **"Nightmares"**:

> Dark cyclones, hosting, breaking; Saturn
> Jewelled in the blood of his own children,
> Gigantic Chaos turning his brute hips
> Over the world.
>
> [*N* 70]

These lines explicitly connect the public and autobiographical discourse of Part II with Part I's symbolic exploration of reciprocal violence. Saturn's malevolent transcendence, his insatiable appetite for his own offspring, inscribes the same acts of violence committed by Heaney's goddess who swallows her victims. As if to underscore further the mimetic nature of the

sacrificial process, Heaney next sees "that holmgang / Where two berserks club each other to death / For honour's sake, greaved in a bog, and sinking." Here, again, we find Hercules and Antaeus, mirroring each other's violence in a blood feud seemingly without end. Both these images bind the violent, disordering potential of myth to sectarianism in Northern Ireland. And yet, as Michael McClaverty reminds him in **"Fosterage,"** "description is revelation." In seeking to master his art it is the poet's vocation to uncover truth, however disturbing, and so to bear witness to a finer human potential than can be encompassed by the pattern of reciprocal violence.

The final poem of **"Singing School," "Exposure"** offers an apt commentary on Heaney's whole project in *North,* within the context of his own artistic quest. In the poem, Heaney's two modes of utterance—symbolic and explicit—conjoin as the poet comes to terms with himself, his past, and his future.[84] Literally, the "exposure" of the title refers to the dramatic circumstance of the poem, in which Heaney walks out of doors under the stars. But its meanings proliferate. Heaney's fame has exposed him and made him a public figure. More deeply, the title suggests the kind of exposure of the darker, tragic vision of life that *North* strived to bring to consciousness. The same self-questioning that fuels the earlier poems governs **"Exposure."** The poem opens with Heaney in his first December in Wicklow, away from Belfast, looking for a comet that in the context of *North* recalls the longship's warning: "Expect aurora borealis / in the long foray / but no cascade of light" (*N* 20). By the poem's end, Heaney in fact will miss "the once in a lifetime portent," though not before he redefines his vision in light of the tragedy struggled with in the poems that came before.

As such, Heaney's choice of **"Exposure"** as the culminating poem of *North* is appropriate in at least two ways. First, its title inscribes the process of demythologizing at work throughout the volume. Second, the poem explicitly pits the figure of the hero who at once recapitulates and sustains the cycle of violence against the figure of the martyr who reveals that cycle for what it is. Walking "the spent flukes of autumn," Heaney imagines "a hero / on some muddy compound, His gift like a slingstone / whirled for the desperate." The image recalls the fanciful "sling of mind" mentioned in **"Bone Dreams,"** and so we are again in the mythic world of a colonial David confronting an imperial Goliath. The muddy compound Heaney mentions now could be an internment camp, Long Kesh, the "hero" an internee willing to starve himself for his cause; or he could be Hercules or Antaeus, or Raleigh, or Heaney himself in one of his mythologized incarnations. Yet the range of the poem's allusiveness also includes a "hero" who was martyred for his refusal to pay homage to any god or goddess and lost his life by exposing a tyrant's brutality through his art—Osip Mandelstam. "David faced Goliath with eight stoney couplets and his sling," Heaney writes of Mandelstam in *The Government of the Tongue,* compounding the allusion. His comment refers to the Russian poet's "Stalin Epigram," for which he was arrested and eventually killed. The muddy compound therefore recalls also the Stalinist death camp in which Mandelstam died, but which was (ironically) powerless against "the free state" of the poet's imagination. "Mandelstam served the people by serving their language," Heaney likewise observes in **"Faith, Hope, and Poetry"** where he quotes one of Mandelstam's poems: "The people need poetry that will be their own secret / to keep them awake forever" (*P* 89). These words could easily serve as Heaney's new poetic credo as *North* comes to its end. Throughout the book Heaney himself has been serving the language of his tribe by exposing its hidden violent origins both symbolically and explicitly; and, like Mandelstam, Heaney sees the highest goal of poetry in the seemingly covert action of keeping people awake, warning them from blind allegiance. **"Exposure"** even draws an analogy between Heaney's "responsible *tristia*" and Mandelstam's *Tristia,* the collection of poems he wrote during his exile in Voronezh. Heaney's exile, of course, was voluntary, not forced, which might make the analogy bathetic were it not for Heaney's ruthless self-questioning. Indeed, his self-questioning in **"Exposure"** is a self-exposure that examines the poet's motive of writing in a time of crisis, questions that also dramatize the poet's willingness to struggle with his own role in that crisis.

Given what we've already seen of *North,* it is appropriate that at the book's end Heaney eschews the obvious sign for a vision of "the diamond absolutes." That revelation and recognition permits him, in the spirit of Mandelstam, to make his own declaration of poetic freedom:

> I am neither internee nor informer;
> An inner emigre, grown long-haired
> And thoughtful; a wood-kerne
>
> Escaped from the massacre,
> Taking protective colouring
> From bole and bark, feeling
> Every wind that blows;
>
> Who, blowing up these sparks
> For their meagre heat, have missed
> The once-in-a-lifetime portent,
> The comet's pulsing rose.

[*N* 73]

The final lines of **"Exposure"** balance a vision of the poet as "inner emigre" and "wood-kerne," a romantic rebel figure who at the time of the plantations preyed on colonists "from woods and mountains."[85] Heaney's

choice of images is once again crucial for the first transposes the official status of Osip and Nadezhda Mandelstam during their exile into a state of consciousness, of awakened imagination. Similarly, the second allusion transposes the "wood-kerne," into a model for the poet who would remain true to his artistic freedom by willingly disappearing into his art. Like the bird-like Sweeney whose voice Heaney will assume in *Station Island* and *Sweeney Astray,* the figure of the wood-kerne privileges the free "man of imagination" over the "internee or informer" who blindly reiterates inherited myths and symbols. That very assumption nevertheless exposes Heaney to the winds of his conscience and of a consciousness of origins that at once binds him to the culture's disturbing past and remains a source of mastering that past through poetry.

In *The Necessary Angel* Wallace Stevens remarks that "a violence from within protects us from a violence without; it is the imagination pressing back against the pressure of reality."[86] This pressure could strip the individual of his powers of contemplation, and so it is the poet's task to expose to the light of consciousness those forces that would bring us to delusion and despair. In *North* the pressure of reality confronted by Heaney's imagination originates in the immediate tragedy of sectarian violence in Ulster, though it quickly uncovers a violence at the heart of culture itself. Heaney's view of history is never mere chronology but always story, the unfolding of a myth that can be both terrifying and redemptive. Yet redemption is never possible where the human mind remains locked in tribal customs, nor where imperial reason forgets its origins in the depths of a reality that eludes its grasp. The hope of redemption and the promise of transcendence always pursue a liminal path, incorporating both the inquiry into origins and the reading of new distances.

It is possible, then, to see Heaney's *North* as embodying Jung's notion "that the trauma of the individual consciousness is likely to be an aspect of the forces at work in the collective life."[87] By bringing that trauma to bear on his imagination, Heaney hopes to raise "the historical record to a different power,"[88] the power of imagination shaped and tempered by critical discernment. As he said to Michael Huey, "a poem begins in delight and ends in self-consciousness."[89] For Heaney, such growth entails both an "obliteration" and a "clarification" of the poet's identity.[90] In this way, in Derek Mahon's words, "a good poem becomes a paradigm of good politics" for it embodies that inward dialogue which seeks to unmask our untried myths and rationalizations. Likewise, *North* brings the present into dialogue with the past, not as a matter of cultural restoration, but under the auspices of the poet's own imaginative inquisition. Finally, in *North,* Heaney does not so much forge the uncreated consciousness of his race as expose the terrors of the consciousness already created. In a profound way, *North* reveals the apocalyptic potential of Heaney's early experience of *akedah*—his sense of being bound to a place—for in *North* the religious intensity of Northern Ireland's history of violence is understood as a product (on either side) of blind obedience to a myth of oneself and one's community. It is, paradoxically, a binding obedience that can break the still deeper bounds of civility. The book therefore constitutes the culmination of Heaney's early work. In it he brought to fruition many of his early obsessions—the numinous landscape with its threat to identity and its promise of continuity; his passion for the dark and the unfolding symbol of the bog; the lure and dangers of tribal customs; the vision of sexual opposition and reconciliation as a constitutive aspect of imagination and culture; his fascination with cycles both natural and historical, and with relics as emblems of individual and communal memory. By exploring these obsessions in *North,* and by exposing the violent proclivities at the root of culture and consciousness, Heaney also reminds us that tragedy is never fully overcome, but "remains a creative challenge . . . a source of possibility and vitality over against, yet inextricably related to, order and the Sacred."[91] Having said that, *North* is more than a culmination. It is the origin in which Heaney's quest finds a new voice.

Notes

1. Heaney, "Place and Displacement," 5.

2. Randall, "An Interview with SH," 8.

3. Ibid.

4. Ibid., 9.

5. David Remnick, "Bard of the Bogs," interview, *Washington Post* (May 3, 1985): c1, c4.

6. Jeremy Hooker, "Seamus Heaney's *North,*" in *The Poetry of Place,* ed. Jeremy Hooker (Manchester: Carcanet, 1982) 71-74.

7. Larry D. Bouchard, *Tragic Method, Tragic Theology* (University Park: Pennsylvania State University Press, 1989) 4.

8. Brian Donnelly, "An Interview with Seamus Heaney," in *Seamus Heaney: Skolaradioen 1977,* ed. Edward Broadbridge (Kobenhavn: Danmarks Radio, 1977) 60.

9. Edna Longley, "*North*: Inner Emigre or Artful Voyeur?" in *The Art of Seamus Heaney,* ed. Tony Curtis (Bridgend: Poetry Wales Press, 1985) 84.

10. Lloyd, "Pap for the Dispossessed," 331.

11. George Watson, "The Narrow Ground: Northern Poets and the Northern Irish Crisis," in *Irish Writers and Society at Large* (Gerrard's Cross: Colin Smythe, 1985) 213.

12. Quoted in Edna Longley, "Inner Emigre," 63.

13. Andrews, *The Poetry of SH,* 80.

14. Ibid., 90.

15. Quoted in Fiona Mullen, "Seamus Heaney: The Poetry of Opinion," *Verse* 1 (1984): 15.

16. Morrison, *Seamus Heaney,* 52.

17. Kinahan, "Artists on Art: An Interview," 410.

18. Ibid.

19. See A. V. C. Schmidt, "Darkness Echoing: Reflections on the Return of Mythopoeia in Some Recent Poems of Geofrey Hill and Seamus Heaney," *Review of English Studies* 33.142 (1985): 208.

20. Richard Kearney, *Transitions,* 274.

21. Mary Douglas, *Purity and Danger* (London: Ark, 1984) 5.

22. Corcoran, *Seamus Heaney,* 98.

23. Morrison, *Seamus Heaney,* 57.

24. Ibid., 22.

25. Derek Mahon, *Selected Poems* (London: Penguin, 1991) 122.

26. Deane, "Unhappy and at Home," interview, 67.

27. See Jolly, "Transformations," 295-330.

28. For another discussion of Heaney's *North* in light of Rene Girard's work see also Charles O'Neill, "Violence and the Sacred in Heaney's *North,*" in *Seamus Heaney: The Shaping Spirit,* eds. Catharine Molloy and Phyllis Casey (Newark: University of Delaware Press, 1996) 91-105; see also Tobin, "Passage to the Center: Imagination and the Sacred in the Poetry of Seamus Heaney," diss., University of Virginia, 1991.

29. Ricoeur, "Myth," 263.

30. Eliade, *Sacred and Profane,* 40.

31. Quoted in Kees W. Bolle, "Imagining Ritual," *History of Religions* 30.2 (1990): 205.

32. Paul Tillich, *Dynamics of Faith* (New York: Harper and Row, 1958) 53.

33. Rene Girard, *Violence and the Sacred,* trans. Patrick Gregory (Baltimore: Johns Hopkins University Press, 1979) 280.

34. George Steiner, *Language and Silence* (New York: Atheneum, 1986) 36.ff.

35. Hart, *Seamus Heaney,* 87.

36. Kinahan, "Artists on Art: An Interview," 417.

37. Lawrence K. Langer, *The Holocaust and the Literary Imagination* (New Haven: Yale University Press, 1975) 1.

38. Quoted in Corcoran, *Seamus Heaney*, 95.

39. Kinahan, "Artists on Art: An Interview," 416.

40. Corcoran, *Seamus Heaney*, 106.

41. Kinahan, "Artists on Art: An Interview," 411.

42. Corcoran, *Seamus Heaney*, 77.

43. Ibid.

44. Heaney, "Place and Displacement," 4.

45. Douglas, *Purity and Danger*, 3.

46. O'Neill, "Violence and Sacred in Heaney's *North*," 96.

47. Eliade, *Sacred and Profane*, 100.

48. Edna Longley, "Inner Emigre," 76-77.

49. Ibid.

50. Corcoran, *Seamus Heaney*, 116.

51. Rene Girard, *The Scapegoat*, trans. Yvonne Freccero (Baltimore: Johns Hopkins University Press, 1986) 190.

52. James A. Lafferty, "Gifts from the Goddess: Heaney's Bog People," *Eire-Ireland* 17.3 (1982) 134.

53. Corcoran, *Seamus Heaney*, 117.

54. Bruce Bidwell, "A Soft Grip on a Sick Place: The Bogland Poetry of Seamus Heaney," *Dublin Magazine* 10.3 (1973/74): 89.

55. Girard, *The Scapegoat*, 4.

56. Ibid.

57. Ibid., 14.

58. Girard, *Violence and the Sacred*, 65.

59. Ibid.

60. Ricoeur, "Myth," 263.

61. Paul Ricoeur, *The Symbolism of Evil*, trans. Emerson Buchanan (Boston: Beacon, 1967) 216.

62. Bouchard, *Tragic Method*, 4.

63. Ibid., 24.

64. Ibid.

65. Ibid.

66. Arthur Cohen, *The Tremendum* (New York: Crossroad, 1981) 33.

67. Ricoeur, *Symbolism of Evil*, 327.

68. See Corcoran, *Seamus Heaney*, 113.

69. Ibid., 118.

70. Sharkey, *Celtic Mysteries*, 7.

71. Andrews, *The Poetry of SH*, 106.

72. Corcoran, *Seamus Heaney*, 118.

73. Cohen, *The Tremendum*, 53.

74. Wallace Stevens, *Collected Poems* (New York: Alfred Knopf, 1978) 229.

75. Caroline Walsh, "The Saturday Interview: Caroline Walsh Talks to Seamus Heaney," *Irish Times* (December 6, 1975): 5.

76. Girard, *The Scapegoat*, 65.

77. Morrison, *Seamus Heaney*, 67.

78. Quoted in Rehder, *Wordsworth*, 278.

79. See J. G. Smith, "The Restoration and the Jacobean Wars," in *The Course of Irish History*, eds. T. W. Moody and F. X. Martin (Cork: Mercier, 1984) 204-16.

80. For a fuller account see Henry Hart, *Seamus Heaney*, 84-85.

81. See Girard, *The Scapegoat*, 1ff.

82. For an excellent discussion of this aspect of Heaney's work see Jonathan Allison, "Acts of Union: Seamus Heaney's Trope of Sex and Marriage," *Eire-Ireland* 27 (winter 1992): 106-121.

83. Yeats, *Collected Poems*, 193.

84. Corcoran, *Seamus Heaney*, 124.

85. R. F. Foster, *Modern Ireland*, 64-65.

86. Wallace Stevens, *The Necessary Angel* (New York: Vintage, 1951) 36.

87. Heaney, "Place and Displacement," 3.

88. Seamus Heaney, "The Pre-Natal Mountain: Vision and Irony in Recent Irish Poetry," *Georgia Review* 42.3 (1988): 465.

89. Michael Huey, "An Interview with Seamus Heaney," *The Christian Science Monitor* (January 3, 1980): 16.

90. Ibid.

91. Smith, *Map Is Not Territory*, 377.

Bibliography

I. Primary Sources

A. Books

Heaney, Seamus. *Death of a Naturalist*. London: Faber and Faber, 1966.

———. *Door into the Dark.* London: Faber and Faber, 1969.

———. *The Government of the Tongue.* London: Faber and Faber, 1988.

———. *The Haw Lantern.* London: Faber and Faber, 1987.

———. *North.* London: Faber and Faber, 1975.

———. *Preoccupations.* New York: Farrar, Straus, and Giroux, 1980.

———. *Station Island.* New York: Farrar, Straus, and Giroux, 1985.

———. *Stations.* Belfast: Ulsterman, 1975.

———. *Sweeney Astray.* New York: Farrar, Straus, and Giroux, 1984.

———. *Wintering Out.* London: Faber and Faber, 1972.

B. UNCOLLECTED ARTICLES

———. *Place and Displacement: Recent Poetry in Northern Ireland.* Grasmere: Dove Cottage, 1985.

———. "The Pre-Natal Mountain: Vision and Irony in Recent Irish Poetry." *Georgia Review* 42.3 (1988): 465-80.

C. INTERVIEWS

Huey, Michael. "An Interview with Seamus Heaney." *The Christian Science Monitor* (January 3, 1980): 16.

Kinahan, Frank. "Artists on Art: An Interview with Seamus Heaney." *Critical Inquiry* 8.3 (1982): 405-14.

Randall, James. "An Interview with Seamus Heaney." *Ploughshares* 5.3 (1979): 7-22.

Remnick, David. "Bard of the Bogs." *Washington Post* (May 3, 1985): c1, c4.

II. SECONDARY SOURCES

A. CRITICISM ABOUT HEANEY AND HIS WORK

Allison, Jonathan. "Acts of Union: Seamus Heaney's Trope of Sex and Marriage." *Eire-Ireland* 27 (winter 1992): 106-21.

Andrews, Elmer. *The Poetry of Seamus Heaney.* New York: St. Martin's Press, 1988.

Bidwell, Bruce. "A Soft Grip on a Sick Place: The Bogland Poetry of Seamus Heaney." *Dublin Magazine* 10.3 (1973/74): 86-90.

Broadbridge, Edward, ed. *Seamus Heaney: Skolaradioen 1977.* Kobenhavn: Danmarks Radio, 1977.

Corcoran, Neil. *Seamus Heaney.* London: Faber and Faber, 1986.

Hart, Henry. *Seamus Heaney: Poet of Contrary Progressions.* Syracuse, N. Y.: Syracuse University Press, 1994.

Hooker, Jeremy. "Seamus Heaney's *North.*" In *The Poetry of Place.* Manchester: Carcanet, 1982.

Jolly, Rosalind. "Transformations of Caliban and Ariel." *World Literature Written in English* 26.2 (1986): 295-330.

Lafferty, James A. "Gifts from the Goddess: Heaney's Bog People." *Eire-Ireland* 17.3 (1982): 127-36.

Lloyd, David. "Pap for the Dispossessed: Seamus Heaney and the Poetics of Identity." *Boundary 2* 13.2-3 (1984/85): 319-42.

Longley, Edna. "*North*: Inner Emigre or Artful Voyeur?" In *The Art of Seamus Heaney.* ed. Tony Curtis (Bridgend: Poetry Wales Press, 1985): 63-96.

Morrison, Blake. *Seamus Heaney.* London: Methuen, 1982.

Mullen, Fiona. "Seamus Heaney: The Poetry of Opinion." *Verse* 1 (1984): 15-22.

O'Neill, Charles. "Violence and the Sacred in Heaney's *North.*" In *Seamus Heaney: The Shaping Spirit,* eds. Catharine Molloy and Phyllis Casey (Newark: University of Delaware Press, 1996): 91-105.

Schmidt, A. V. C. "Darkness Echoing: Reflections on the Return of Mythopoeia in Some Recent Poems of Geoffrey Hill and Seamus Heaney." *Review of English Studies* 33.142 (1985): 199-225.

Watson, George. "The Narrow Ground: Northern Poets and the Northern Irish Crisis." In *Irish Writers and Society at Large,* ed. Masaru Sekine. Gerrard's Cross: Colin Smythe, 1985.

B. LITERATURE AND ART

Langer, Lawrence K. *The Holocaust and the Literary Imagination.* New Haven: Yale, 1975.

Mahon, Derek. *Selected Poems.* London: Penguin, 1991.

Rehder, Robert. *Wordsworth and the Beginnings of Modern Poetry.* London: Croom Helm, 1981.

Steiner, George. *Language and Silence.* New York: Atheneum, 1986.

Stevens, Wallace. *Collected Poems.* New York: Alfred Knopf, 1978.

———. *The Necessary Angel.* New York: Vintage, 1951.

C. IRISH HISTORY AND CULTURE

Foster, R. F. *Modern Ireland: 1600-1972.* London: Penguin, 1988.

Kearney, Richard. *Transitions: Narratives in Modern Irish Culture.* Dublin: Wolfhound Press, 1988.

Moody, T. W., and F. X. Martin, eds. *The Course of Irish History.* Cork: Mercier Press, 1984.

Sharkey, John. *Celtic Mysteries: The Ancient Religion.* London: Thames and Hudson, 1975.

D. THEOLOGY, PHILOSOPHY, HISTORY OF RELIGIONS

Bolle, Kees W. "Imaging Ritual." *History of Religions* 30.2 (1990): 205.

Bouchard, Larry D. *Tragic Method and Tragic Theology.* University Park: Pennsylvania State University Press, 1989.

Cohen, Arthur. *The Tremendum.* New York: Crossroad, 1981.

Douglas, Mary. *Purity and Danger.* London: Ark, 1984.

Eliade, Mircea. *The Sacred and the Profane,* trans. Willard Trask. New York: Harcourt, Brace, Jovanovich, 1959.

Girard, Rene. *The Scapegoat,* trans. Yvonne Freccero. Baltimore: Johns Hopkins, 1986.

————. *Violence and the Sacred,* trans. Patrick Gregory. Baltimore: Johns Hopkins University Press, 1979.

Ricoeur, Paul. "Myth as the Bearer of Possible Worlds." In *The Crane Bag Book of Irish Studies: 1977-1981,* eds. M. P. Hederman and Richard Kearney. Dublin: Blackwater, 1982.

————. *Symbolism of Evil,* trans. Emerson Buchanan. Boston: Beacon, 1967.

Smith, Jonathan Z. *Map Is Not Territory.* Leiden: E. J. Bull, 1978.

Tillich, Paul. *Dynamics of Faith.* New York: Harper and Row, 1958.

Jonathan Bolton (essay date spring 2001)

SOURCE: Bolton, Jonathan. "'Customary Rhythms': Seamus Heaney and the Rite of Poetry." *Papers on Language and Literature* 37, no. 2 (spring 2001): 205-22.

[*In the following essay, Bolton focuses on what he calls Heaney's "station poems," concluding that their structure constitutes Heaney's most direct contribution to modern poetry.*]

> Ceremony's a name for the rich horn
> And custom for the spreading laurel tree.
>
> —W. B. Yeats, "A Prayer for My Daughter"

Near the conclusion of his Nobel Prize address, *Crediting Poetry,* Seamus Heaney speaks of two kinds of "adequacy" ascribable to poetry: "documentary adequacy" and "lyric adequacy." The former has to do with the impact and emotive power of description and is as old as Homer's account of the Fall of Troy. "Even today, three thousand years later," Heaney says, "as we channel surf over so much live coverage of contemporary savagery, highly informed but in danger of growing immune . . . Homer's image can still bring us to our senses. . . . [It] has that documentary adequacy which answers all that we know about the intolerable" (49). The second kind of adequacy has to do with the poetic process itself, what Heaney calls "'the temple inside our hearing' which the passage of the poem calls into being" (49). This interior space is the domain of national conscience and consciousness, a receptacle for personal and racial memory, the etymology of the tribe, the spirit of place, and the ground in which the dead, victims of the Great Hunger, sectarian violence, and the tragic accidents of life are interred. This "temple of our hearing" is exhumed and recovered through the rites or stations of the poem, where truthfulness becomes audible via intonation and cadence. "Lyric adequacy," Heaney adds, is something that he has always "strained towards" (*Crediting Poetry* 49), and this desire is borne out by the form and process of his poetic rites, which may begin with the empirical here and now but ultimately delve beneath the merely documentary, the photographic witness that is not the end but prelude to the rite of poetry.

My chief concern in this essay is with the manner in which Heaney's three to four part station poems have come to serve as the formal equivalent of a liturgical rite—a highly-structured, habitually-observed practice that, for him, enacts the temporal and ritualistic steps required to recover and articulate aspects of national consciousness. Although Heaney does not refer to such divisions as stations, nor to such short sequences as station poems, the idea of stations has, since early in his career, a crucial and resonant place in his work, and I believe that "station poem" should serve as a convenient and apt descriptive and critical term for this signature procedure and the religious, archaeological, and historical concerns it helps to formulate. According to Catholic liturgy, a station refers not only to the stations of the cross but also to a stopping point in a procession for the purpose of song, recitation, or ritual action.[1] This sense of the station as a stopping point or stage in a devotional rite is especially true of the Lough Derg pilgrimage Heaney imaginatively reenacts in **Station Island**. As Heaney describes this three-day vigil, "each unit of the contemporary pilgrim's exercises is called a 'station,' and a large part of each station involves walking barefoot and praying round 'beds,' stone circles which are said to be the remains of early monastic cells" (**Station Island** 122). "Stations," as Heaney would also be aware, refers to the rural Irish custom of celebrating Mass at the houses of parishioners on a rotating basis—a custom that conferred honor on each house and reflects a popular, egalitarian spirit of Irish Catholicism that is also evident in Heaney's work.[2]

In Heaney's work, the ecclesiastical significance of the performance of stations must be enlarged so as to include analogous experiences of discovery and devotion, such as the stages in archaeological excavation, funeral processions, pilgrimages, and other kinds of purposeful walking and doings. The station poem's element of mechanical, psychic action, typically executed in three stages, makes it formally distinct from Heaney's longer sequences, such as **"Clearances"** and the **"Glanmore Sonnets,"** as well as unified thematic sequences, such as **"Sweeney Redevivus"** and *Stations,* both of which tend to deliver Heaney's discoveries without the procedure used to bring them to light. In other words, one gets the find without the excavation. Describing the series of poems in *Stations* (1975), Heaney explains, "I think of the pieces now as points on a psychic *turas,* stations that I have often made unthinkingly in my head. I wrote each of them down with the excitement of coming for the first time to a place I had always known completely" (*Stations* 3). He also likens such poems to Wordsworthian "spots of time" (3) that he seeks to recover or that arise involuntarily, and so differ from the painstaking, requisite procedures in his shorter station poems in order to uncover or achieve such "psychic turas." There are, however, significant parallels between the station poems and the organization of the longer sequences. In **"Glanmore Sonnets,"** for instance, the opening poems follow a procedure similar to the station poems, with acts of verbal digging and plowing early in the sequence serving to open a door to the past in the middle sonnets, then a meditative concentration is attained, and dreams and visions follow. In addition, ritualized forms of action, such as stepping, stirring, and unwinding, open **"Sweeney Redevivus,"** and the sequence describes numerous journeys and wanderings, both temporal and terrestrial, that lead to dream visions and the attainment of knowledge.[3]

As Jacob Korg has noted in *Ritual and Experiment in Modern Poetry,* "ritual communicates through such physical acts as uncovering, uplifting, separating, combining, cutting, and touching . . . the objects involved in these movements and the place in which they are performed" (11), and Heaney's station poems typically involve some form of physical, usually tactile and ambulatory, action. A mainstay in the Heaney canon, the form is also well-suited to his dual religious and nationalistic impulses in that it serves as a mode of verbal action, or of fusing versification and religious devotion. Catherine Bell, for instance, describes two patterns of ritual in *Ritual Theory, Ritual Practice.* One pattern of ritual, according to Bell, is "thoughtless ac-

tion—routinized, obsessive, mimetic—and therefore [is] the purely formal, secondary, and merely physical expression of logically prior ideas" (20). The second pattern, which is closer to Heaney's practice, is "a type of functional or structural mechanism to reintegrate the thought-action dichotomy" (20). In other words, ritual in this second manifestation serves as a means of making thought and idea meaningful in a physical or devotional manner. In addition, the stratified or layered design of Heaney's station poems is particularly useful in his project of recovering aspects of Irish indigenousness, both historical and etymological, and to commemorate the victims of sectarian violence. Moreover, the temporal disjunctions that partition his lyric stations produce startling juxtapositions of a remote Celtic or Viking past and contemporary events, thereby disclosing previously unacknowledged historical continuities. To borrow a phrase from **"Bogland,"** Heaney's station poems "keep striking / Inwards and downwards" (*Selected Poems* 22), descending to strata of submerged memory and ascending to the heights of vision.[4] As Helen Vendler recently observed, "To enter the megalithic doorway is to go underground, working back into what seems a bottomless pre-history, to a 'matter of Ireland'" (38), and to reach such depths of racial consciousness, Heaney has recognized, one must perform the necessary lyric-devotional descent. The epode, or "aftersong," typically involves some form of return, as if from a trance, a resurfacing or unearthing motion that completes the ritual and brings the excavated find or renewed sense of racial consciousness to light.

I

Heaney has remarked that composing poetry is like "building a trellis and training a vine across it" (qtd. in Foster xxx), and his career is marked by a increasing reliance on the station poem as a "trellis" for his "vines." He used it once in his first volume, *Death of a Naturalist* (1966), twice in *Door into the Dark* (1969), nine times in *Wintering Out* (1972), seven in *North* (1975), and so on to the eleven short sequences in *The Spirit Level* (1995). The title poems of *Field Work* and *Seeing Things* are also divided into three stations. The only poem to use this form in *Death of a Naturalist,* **"At a Potato Digging"** establishes certain precedents. In the first station of the poem, the sight of the "processional stooping through turf" of the fieldhands conjures an image of the great hunger. In the second station, Heaney proceeds to inspect the potatoes, the image of which, informed by historical consciousness, comes to resemble in his mind the remains of famine victims, "piled in pits; live skulls, blind-eyed." This recollection of the famine creates a temporal disjunction in station three, transporting him back to "the scoured land in 'forty five." He can smell the "putrefied" crop, see the people "grubbing, like plants, in the bitch earth." The fourth station returns to the present, now considerably altered by an intensified consciousness of the famine, to witness the fieldhands "breaking timeless fasts," "spill-[ing] / Libations of cold tea," and "scatter[ing] crusts" (*DN* [*Death of a Naturalist*] 23).

The ending is, in many ways, a bit too pat, but the procedure is important, and the poem answers Heaney's aesthetic imperative that poetic process be used to develop "a new level of consciousness" and, more ambitiously, to "forge the uncreated conscience of the race" (*Preoccupations* 60). The poem also involves two levels of experience that are crucial to Heaney's sense of Ireland: first, the experience that is "lived, illiterate and unconscious" and, second, the "learned, literate, and conscious" historical and cultural knowledge of place derived from books, both of which contribute vitally to the poem's "lyric adequacy" (*Preoccupations* 131). Although **"At a Potato Digging"** is a crude antecedent of the more elaborate station poems to come, the poem does suggest Heaney had come to realize that consciousness-raising entails stages or stations of excavation and that his promise to dig with his pen perhaps required a formal, liturgical method. One senses this need clearly in his description of the "processional" steps of the fieldhands, which anticipate how such deliberate, ritualistic actions lead to a vision in his later verse.

The more ambitious and increasingly "ungoverned" lyrical rites in *Wintering Out* mark a crucial point of departure in Heaney's career. As poetry critic Blake Morrison notes, Heaney was attempting to devise a form "more suited to archaeology" in order to "draw on previously repressed psychic and mythic material" (45), and the critic Elmer Andrews recognizes in these poems a "move away from the childlike world [of his first two books] into the harsh adult world" (48). In addition, Heaney had also tried to incorporate into his verse "the piety of objects" that he found evident in P. V. Glob's photographs in *The Bog People.*[5] As a result, the station poems of *Wintering Out* exhibit a devotional and ritualistic element missing in his earlier work, particularly the kind of integration of thought and action essential to religious rites. **"Tollund Man,"** for instance, is an archetypal station poem. It involves in the first station a pilgrimage, or in this instance the promise of one, made convincing by the performative, "I will go to Aarhus," that imagines the bog working the corpse into a "saint's kept body" (*SP* [*Selected Poems 1966-1987*] 39). The opening section also involves the same kind of minute inspection used in **"At a Potato Digging,"** but with a more pious, sensuous attention to details, such as the "peat-brown head," the "mild pods of his eye-lids," and the "gruel of winter seeds / Caked in his stomach" (*SP* 39). The second station enacts a devotional rite, consecrates the "cauldron bog / Our holy ground" (*SP* 39-40), fuses past and present, and forges a connection between Jutlander and Celt. The third station involves a similar resurfacing gesture to that found in **"At a Potato Digging,"** but to it Heaney adds an element of incantation, spiritual empathy and vision:

> Saying the names
>
> Tollund, Grauballe, Nebelgard
> Watching the pointing hands
> Of country people,
> Not knowing their tongue.
>
> Out there in Jutland
> In the old man-killing parishes
> I will feel lost,
> Unhappy and at home.

> (*SP* 40)

Heaney scholar Neil Corcoran has argued that *Wintering Out* "'gestures towards' the realities of the [then] present historical moment rather than attempting to address them with any specificity or intimacy" (64). **"Tollund Man"** does in fact respond to the present, but it does so in a manner typical of Heaney's indirection, invoking Irish history, past and present, via a lyrical rite that digs "inwards and downwards" (literally away from Ireland and into the continent) toward a distinctly national concern—the victims of sectarian violence. The liturgical procedure in **"Tollund Man"** invokes the fertility rites of the Jutes in order to sanctify the victims of the current struggle and to offer the hope that single deaths would prevent multiple deaths, that those "Stockinged corpses / Laid out in the farmyards" (*SP* 40) like scarecrows would protect against further acts of violence. As cultural theorist René Girard has noted, the "objective of ritual is the proper reenactment of the surrogate-victim mechanism; its function is . . . to keep violence outside the community" (92), and Heaney is clearly invoking violence in order that it might be curtailed.

The formal procedures observed in *Wintering Out,* in fact, become quite formulaic. Heaney walks, comes to rest, performs some act, is transported back in time, and returns enlightened. This simple formula is highly versatile, however. His steps, like a dowsing rod, can lead in infinite directions, the actions vary, as do the historical moments he revisits, and his epiphanies are never exactly the same. As poetry critic Maurice Harmon has noted, the basis of Heaney's archaeology is "a Jungian concept of the Irish past and of the Irish psyche as richly tapered and opening inwards in a series of endless discoveries" (71). Indeed, many of the station poems in *Wintering Out* may well have been exercises designed to strike such deep wells of personal and racial unconsciousness. Heaney pays homage to **"The Last Mummer,"** who, in station one, roams the land with "a stone in his pocket, / an ashplant under his arm" (*WO* [*Wintering Out*] 18). In station two, Heaney laments the passing of the bardic tradition and canonizes the tramping poet in station three: "The moon's host elevated / in a monstrance of holly trees, / he makes dark tracks . . . / into the summer's grazing" (*WO* 20). In "Land," Heaney ambles across "the outlying fields," builds a cairn, and likens the writing of a poem to footsteps across "blank acres," "ready to go anywhere" (*WO* 21). His ritualistic steps direct him, somewhat magically, to a spot amidst "grass and clover" and "shifting hares" in which he sounds the silence, ear to ground, imagining himself snared and pending in air (*WO* 23). Again, the poem follows the same "inwards and downwards" trajectory and concludes, literally, in an elevated state of mind. **"Gifts of Rain"** traces, in stations one and two, the steps of farmer and animal, wading through flooded terrain, to dig for or root out food. In the third section of the poem, the burgeoning of the river is internalized, a trope for racial continuity (the archetypal river of time) that unites him with ancestral ways of life in which the river was both a means of survival to the community and a potential agent of its destruction. "Cocking [his] ear / at an absence," Heaney hears in the "Soft voices of the dead" (*SP* 31-32) a reproach to his fear and anger at the flood, at the days of rain, ruined crops, and muddy terrain. In the final station, the river rises to "pleasure him" with its music and with the sound of its name:

> Moyola
> is its own score and consort
>
> bedding the locale
> in the utterance,
> reed music, an old chanter
>
> breathing its mists
> through vowels and history.

> (*SP* 32)

Taken as a whole, the station poems in *Wintering Out* constitute a formal and procedural breakthrough in Heaney's career as he discovered that perhaps the most effective means of sounding the depths of racial consciousness, of imagining and revisiting crucial historical moments, and of addressing national political crises lay in the liturgical action of his poetic stations.

II

In "The Poet as Christian," Heaney recalls that, during his formative years, the experience attending wakes and funerals, with their "inner system of courtesy and honour and obligement," had a "definite effect" on him.[6] The ritualistic observances of Catholic burial—the stationary observation at the wake, the rhythmic steps of the funeral procession, and the downward motion of interment (what poetry critic Jonathan Hufstader has referred to as "coming to consciousness by jumping in graves")[7]—appear to be intimately connected with

Heaney's development of the station poem. One of his earliest station poems is **"Elegy for a Still-Born Child,"** and he uses a three part division in all of his major elegies: **"Funeral Rites," "Triptych,"** and **"Casualty."** As the critic Bernard O'Donoghue has noted, Heaney's formal decisions are "never *only* formal, but at once formal and also emotional" (ix), and his station poems reflect emotional as well as liturgical stages of mourning. In **"Funeral Rites,"** for instance, the first station revisits the wakes of dead relatives, recalling in sensuous detail their "glistening" eyelids and "dough-white hands / shackled in rosary beads," and how he "knelt courteously" and "kiss[ed] their igloo brows" (*SP* 65). In station two, Heaney returns to the violence and murder of the present, and pronounces a deep need to revive public ritual, those "customary rhythms." His ideal is to "restore / / the great chambers of the Boyne" (*SP* 66), at New Grange, site of Neolithic burial mounds, for a mass burial that would draw thousands and lay violence to rest for once and all. The second station concludes with a vision of a long, sinuous funeral procession, like a serpent with its tail in Ulster and its head in the South, about to pass through a megalithic doorway—a funeral procession that would unify Ireland by invoking an ancient pagan ritual. Station three returns to the present, but it is a present enlightened and informed by a consciousness of the past and of the unifying potential of ritual. The poem ends, appropriately enough, at the tomb of Gunnar, the epic hero of *Njal's Saga*, whose death at the hands of enemies remains unavenged. Although in the saga Njal's son swears vengeance, for Heaney "arbitration / of the feud [is] placated" (*SP* 67) by the death of Gunnar, and the ritualistic sacrifice of the hero terminates the cycle of violence, just as Heaney's ritual form is designed to heal and placate. **"Triptych,"** from *Field Work,* is Heaney's somewhat belated but nevertheless powerful response to the Bloody Sunday massacre, generated retrospectively following a later, isolated killing. The first station, titled **"After a Killing,"** shrinks from an expansive vision of Ireland, "that neuter original loneliness / From Brandon to Dunseverick" (*SP* 108), to a particular vision of a stone house by a pier where the ancient rural economy of fishing and planting survives. In station two, **"Sybil,"** Heaney asks the oracle: "What will become of us?" The Sibyl predicts a change for the worse "unless forgiveness finds its nerve and voice" (*SP* 109). The oracle goes on to reproach the habitual reticence of the people, who discuss the weather and fail to confront political reality, and who are seduced by the promise of economic gain away from nationalistic imperatives. "My people," says the Sibyl, "think money / And talk weather. Oil rigs lull their future / On single acquisitive stems" (*SP* 109). Station three shifts to the monastic sites at Devenish, Boa, and Horse Island, the silence of which is disturbed by an Army helicopter patrolling. The poem concludes with Heaney being overwhelmed by a ritualistic impulse, a compulsion to act, physically and verbally, in order to disturb the silence:

> Everything in me
> Wanted to bow down, to offer up,
> To go barefoot, foetal and penitential,
>
> And pray at water's edge.
> How we crept before we walked! I remembered
> The helicopter shadowing our march at Newry,
> The scared, irrevocable steps.

(SP 110)

Once again, **"Triptych"** attests to the versatility of the station poem. In this instance, the ritualistic steps occur at the end instead of the beginning of the rite (steps that normally initiate the pilgrimage here serve to end it), and instead of being transported back to a remote past, Heaney returns to a recent event, the march at Newry in protest of the Bloody Sunday massacre. The poem returns to incidents that Heaney had failed to consecrate in verse as they occurred, not in a distant past but during his own lifetime. The line, "How we crept before we walked," is especially revealing about Heaney's poetic response to political crises, as the contemplative, reflective procedure of the station poem redirects the more volatile impulses that instigated the poem.

III

Over the past decade, Heaney's work, in volumes such as *The Haw Lantern* (1987), *Seeing Things* (1991), and *The Spirit Level* (1995), has entered a new phase in which personal recollections, often nostalgic preoccupations with his own past, have supplanted the broader national and historical concerns of his early to mid career. In these volumes, generally, Heaney has tended to focus on the numinous and mnemonic qualities of individual objects, odd ordinary things such as thimbles, hailstones, a sofa, a swing, jackets and footballs, pitchforks and schoolbags—anything with associations potent enough to reconstitute a submerged past. Although Heaney's focus has changed, his exploration of personal memory represents a new form of digging, with the station poem providing a formal demarcation of mnemonic processes. As he writes in **"The Poet's Chair,"** the poem is "a ploughshare that turns time up and over" (*SL* [*The Spirit Level*] 57). Heaney's excavation of personal history, as in his poetic rites, is performed in three stages. First, the sight of a numinous object (i.e. "seeing things") opens a door into the past. This opening into the past prompts a mental pilgrimage—whether it be a journey to the underworld or the proverbial stroll down memory lane—that terminates in a return journey. The cycle is completed as the poet climbs to light or is roused from a trance with a cache of memories and a newfound awareness of personal

history, "a revelation of the self to the self" (*Preoccupations* 54), and of the atemporal existence of objects and people.

Heaney has come to view memory and the space-time continuum in terms of the relation between absence and presence, and he has come to acknowledge that certain things, presences that exist in the here and now, uncover or disclose absences that exist in past time. In this sense, in his later verse, certain phenomenal objects, provided that one really *sees* them and apprehends their numinous potential, serve as passports to an otherwise inaccessible underworld of buried memories. Two poems from *The Haw Lantern* serve to illustrate Heaney's notion of memory as a stockpile of absences that can be retrieved via a presence. In **"Hailstones,"** Heaney confides, "I make this [poem] now / out of the melt of the real thing / smarting into its absence" (*SP* 241). The sting of hailstones in the present involuntarily triggers a sensation not felt for forty years, what Heaney describes as "the truest foretaste of your aftermath" (*SP* 242). A similar idea appears in sonnet 8 from **"Clearances,"** a moving elegy to his mother in which Heaney registers a desire to circle the empty space that used to contain a chestnut tree, planted on his birthday but chopped down when the farm changed hands. The tree's existence, however, is preserved in the poet's memory, its absence "A soul ramifying and forever / Silent, beyond silence listened for" (*SP* 253). For Heaney, then, what is lost is never irretrievable, but rather exists on an immaterial plane, a "spirit level," that can be recovered, reincorporated via a three-part process of remembrance.

In many ways, the personal void created by such absences as the chestnut tree, a symbol of his own life and inevitable absence from it, has led Heaney to use lyric ritual in order to recover an absence through an intense concentration on a presence, to recompose the unseen via the seen. As the critic Catherine Malloy has noted, "his recollections of these things inform his way of seeing and knowing, enhancing his vision as he moves onward" (159). Hence, the act of remembering is often cast figuratively in the form of a miniature epic in three stations that reenact the cycle of journey and return. The translation of the golden bough section from Book VI of *The Aeneid* at the beginning of *Seeing Things* is especially significant and aptly chosen. As the Sibyl tells Aeneas, who is seeking his dead father, the way down is easy and the gateway stands open, but the return journey is perilous for, by entering the underworld, one has gone "beyond the limit" (*ST* [*Seeing Things*] 5). Moreover, the golden bough must be procured in order to gain passage, hence the bard (Heaney) rises to the status of epic hero.[8] Heaney's invocation of Aeneas's journey to the underworld at the opening of *Seeing Things* prefigures his own search for his father in the title poem. Here, once again, the past is visited through careful observation of "things" that serve as his golden bough and the vessel that will carry him across the Stygian Lake to the fields of the blessed.

In **"Seeing Things,"** Heaney repeats Aeneas's journey in three lyric stations. The first station of the poem recounts a pilgrimage to a monastic site off the coast of Donegal, beginning with a sensual composition of place: "Inishbofin on a Sunday morning. / Sunlight, turfsmoke, seagulls, boatslip, diesel" (*ST* 18). As the Sibyl had said, the journey down is easy, and the sea, as Heaney recalls, was calm and the boat skimmed the surface. Yet the journey is not without a sense of foreboding and danger. The craft shifts and sways, "the gunwales sank" beneath the trough of the waves, and Heaney, in a transcendent moment, as if sailing in the air above their craft, notices "How riskily we fared into the morning" (*ST* 18). Throughout the first station, the solemnity of the pilgrims' crossing is apparent, as if Charon himself were the ferryman: heads are bared and bowed; they sit on cross-benches as if in church pews; and silence is reverently observed.

Heaney writes, near the end of station one, of the "seeable-down-into water," which anticipates the *"Claritas"* (*ST* 19), or moment of mnemonic clarity, described in station two. Heaney likens this transparency of past time to a church relief in which carved stone is cut expertly so as to appear liquid, the water John the Baptist pours over Christ's head—a rite of initiation as well as purification. Heaney notes that "The stone's alive with what's invisible" (*ST* 19), an image of memory as something real, extant, though submerged as in water, "a shadowy, unshadowed stream" that constitutes "the zigzag hieroglyph for life itself" (*ST* 19).

Station three of the poem shifts to a vision of his father's ghost emerging "undrowned" from the river, an imagined resurrection authenticated by the *"claritas"* attained through this ritual of remembrance. The resurrected image of his father is divined, magically, through a clairvoyant window of memory. As Heaney writes,

> I was inside the house
> And saw him through the window, scatter-eyed
> And daunted, strange without his hat,
> His step unguided, his ghosthood immanent.
> When he was turning on the riverbank,
> The horse had rusted and reared up and pitched
> Cart and sprayer and everything off balance,
> So the whole rig went over into adeep
> Whirlpool, hoofs, chains, shafts, cartwheels, barrel
> And tackle, all tumbling off the world,
> And the hat already merrily swept along
> The quieter reaches.
>
> (*ST* 20)

This scene is described in such a way as deliberately to confuse the time preceding and succeeding the drowning and "undrowning"—a reversal of time and mortal-

ity. Looking through the window, Heaney is seeing his father's ghost, "immanent" not "imminent," and because he is bareheaded, his death has already occurred—his hat was swept downstream with the current—but because he did not witness the drowning, he does not admit the possibility of his father's death. Likewise, the poem concludes with Heaney meeting his father that afternoon, not of his death but the afternoon of the Inishbofin crossing. As he gazes down into the paradoxically dark yet clear, "shadowy, unshadowed" waters of the North Atlantic, this memory rises up to meet him, face-to-face, "with his damp footprints out of the river" (*ST* 20). This is to say, memory and vision, combined with the ritualistic power of the lyric sequence, enables Heaney to resurrect his father, to replace his absence by recovering his presence, as he emerges through this window of time on a boat off the coast of Donegal.

The station poem has been a crucial component of Heaney's versification almost from the outset of his career, and it constitutes what is arguably his most distinct, though widely unacknowledged, contribution to the modern poetic sequence. And, although Heaney's career has culminated in a set of longer poetic sequences, the early station poems were, I believe, essential to the evolution of lengthier projects, such as **"Glanmore Sonnets,"** which enact similar ritualistic procedures, and **"Station Island,"** which is essentially an epic repetition of the shorter lyric rites in twelve stations. But perhaps most significantly, the kinds of temporal disjunction, ritual action, and cultural and historical excavations facilitated by such a sequential form have enabled Heaney to articulate aspects of Irish historical and racial consciousness, commemorate victims of Ireland's troubled history, mine the darker regions of personal memory, and achieve the formal perfection he modestly calls "lyric adequacy."

Notes

1. See John Harper's *Forms and Orders of Western Liturgy from the Tenth to the Eighteenth Century: A Historical Introduction for Students and Musicians* (New York: Oxford UP, 1991) 128-29.

2. In his notes to J. M. Synge's *The Aran Islands,* Tim Robinson describes stations as "an annual custom—still practiced in many rural western parishes—of hearing confessions and celebrating Mass in a parishioner's house, the honour passing from house to house in rotation within each community" (146).

3. This three-part structure is also evident in the organization of Heaney's books. Gale C. Schricker has identified a tripartite method of organization in *Station Island, The Haw Lantern,* and *Field Work,* particularly a three part temporal division between past, present, and future. See "'Deliber-

ately at the Centre': The Triptych Structure of Seamus Heaney's *Field Work*" (*Eire-Ireland* 26. 3 [Fall 1991]: 107-20).

4. All subsequent quotes of poetry are from *Selected Poems 1966-1987* (*SP*) unless otherwise indicated by *DN* (*Death of a Naturalist*); *WO* (*Wintering Out*); *ST* (*Seeing Things*); and *SL* (*The Spirit Level*).

5. The influence of Glob's book on Heaney is well-documented. As Heaney suggests in his essay "Feelings into Words," Glob's photos merged in his mind with recent atrocities in Northern Ireland (see *Preoccupations* 57).

6. Also, in "The Poet as a Christian," Heaney recalls, "I remember after writing 'Tollund Man' I began to think, if I were to go to an analyst, he would certainly link the outlined and pacified and *rigor mortis* with all that submerged life and memory [of funerals]" (qtd. in Corcoran 15).

7. In his essay "Coming to Consciousness by Jumping in Graves," Hufstader identifies Heaney's "ritual procedure [as being] one of sequence: entrance rite, central action, and the subjects emergence form the ritual in a new state of mind" (61-62).

8. This status has long been crucial to Heaney's ideal of the poet as, in the Latin, *Vates,* someone with "a gift for being in touch with what is there, hidden and real, a gift for mediating between the latent resource and the community" ("Feelings into Words," *Preoccupations* 47-48).

Works Cited

Andrews, Elmer. *Seamus Heaney: All the Realms of Whisper.* London: Macmillan, 1988.

Bell, Catherine. *Ritual Theory, Ritual Practice.* New York: Oxford UP, 1992.

Corcoran, Neil. *Seamus Heaney.* London: Faber and Faber, 1986.

Foster, R. F. *Yeats: A Life.* Oxford: Oxford UP, 1997.

Girard, René. *Violence and the Sacred.* Trans. Patrick Gregory. Baltimore: John Hopkins UP, 1977.

Harmon, Maurice. "'We Pine for Ceremony': Ritual and Reality in the Poetry of Seamus Heaney, 1965-75." *Seamus Heaney: A Collection of Critical Essays.* Ed. Elmer Andrews. New York: St. Martin's Press, 1992. 67-86.

Heaney, Seamus. *Crediting Poetry: The Nobel Lecture.* New York: Farrar, Straus, and Giroux, 1996.

———. *Death of a Naturalist.* London: Faber and Faber, 1966.

———. *Preoccupations: Selected Prose 1968-1978.* New York: Farrar, Straus, and Giroux, 1980.

———. *Seeing Things.* New York: Farrar, Straus, and Giroux, 1991.

———. *Selected Poems 1966-1987.* New York: Farrar, Straus, and Giroux, 1990.

———. *The Spirit Level.* New York: Farrar, Straus, and Giroux, 1997.

———. *Station Island.* New York: Farrar, Straus, and Giroux, 1985.

———. *Stations.* Belfast: Ulsterman Publications, 1975.

———. *Wintering Out.* New York: Oxford UP, 1973.

Hufstader, Jonathan. "Coming to Consciousness by Jumping in Graves." *Irish University Review* 26.1 (Spring/Summer 1996): 61-74.

Korg, Jacob. *Ritual and Experiment in Modern Poetry.* New York: St. Martin's Press, 1995.

Malloy, Catharine. "Seamus Heaney's *Seeing Things*: Retracing the Path Back. . . ." *Seamus Heaney: The Shaping Spirit.* Ed. Catharine Malloy and Phyllis Carey. Newark: U of Delaware P, 1996. 157-73.

Morrison, Blake. *Seamus Heaney.* London: Methuen, 1982.

O'Donoghue, Bernard. *Seamus Heaney and the Language of Poetry.* New York: Harvester, 1994.

Synge, J. M. *The Aran Islands,* with Essay and Notes by Tim Robinson. Harmondsworth, Middlesex: Penguin, 1992.

Vendler, Helen. *Seamus Heaney.* Cambridge: Harvard UP, 1998.

Dennis O'Driscoll (essay date 2002)

SOURCE: O'Driscoll, Dennis. "Steady under Strain and Strong through Tension." *Parnassus: Poetry in Review* 26, no. 2 (2002): 149-67.

[*In the following essay, O'Driscoll gives a glowing review of* Electric Light, *focusing on connections to Heaney's earlier work and to the penultimate poem of 1996,* The Spirit Level.]

In Seamus Heaney's collections, the last shall usually be first. Many critics over the years have observed that the final poem in a Heaney volume will serve advance notice of what may be expected in the following book. Blake Morrison, who in his 1982 study of the poet pioneered this prognostic or divinatory approach to the Heaney canon, wrote of *Field Work* (1979) that it begins "not at the beginning but, as is Heaney's custom, with the last poem of the book that preceded it." The critic is not reproving the poet for repetition but admiring Heaney's orderly transfer of power from book to book, as—in Morrison's words—he "takes up and develops" the theme of the final poem of the previous collection. Thus *Field Work* probed artistic and political dilemmas adumbrated in **"Exposure,"** the closing poem of *North* (1975). In turn, the **"Ugolino"** episode from Dante's *Inferno,* with which *Field Work* ended, pointed the way forward to the penitential *purgatorio* of the title-sequence of *Station Island* (1984). Then the "bare wire" poetry plaited into the **"Sweeney Redivivus"** sequence, the third and final section of *Station Island,* ushered in the plain-speaking parables of *The Haw Lantern* (1987). "And so on," as Heaney himself writes in the final line of **"The Thimble"** in *The Spirit Level* (1996).

But **"The Thimble"** was not the last word in *The Spirit Level.* The collection ended with one of Heaney's most affecting poems, **"Postscript"**, which retraces a drive along Ireland's west coast, during which the light and the foam and the sight of "a flock of swans" (maybe even a Yeatsian "nine-and-fifty" of the birds) left him inwardly as well as outwardly shaken:

> Useless to think you'll park and capture it
> More thoroughly. You are neither here nor there,
> A hurry through which known and strange things pass
> As big soft buffetings come at the car sideways
> And catch the heart off guard and blow it open.

As early as 1979, when he turned forty, Heaney expressed concern that, as one gets older, the "space occupied by the instinctual life" contracts. Nearly twenty years later, **"Postscript"** rejoices not only in the vision that he has been momentarily granted, but also in inspiration itself, the capacity of an aging heart to be caught "off guard" and, in an image used irenically and almost ironically by an Ulster poet, blown open.

I am not sure that **"Postscript"** can be said to offer clues to Heaney's next collection, *Electric Light,* except in the general sense that it affirms his determination to keep his imaginative arteries open for the next hoped-for flush of afflatus. Yet even if **"Postscript"** fails fully to conform to the soothsaying theory of Heaney's work, it does find an exact companion piece in **"Ballynahinch Lake."** Beginning briskly with "so," the much-discussed opening word of Heaney's *Beowulf* translation, a word strongly suggestive of an ongoing narrative, the poem is a postscript to **"Postscript."** The setting again is a lake with "waterbirds" in western Ireland, but it is no longer "useless to think you'll park and capture" the scene: "this time, yes, it had indeed / Been useful to stop." If the swan-bearing lake of **"Postscript"** has its literary antecedent in "The Wild Swans at Coole," **"Ballynahinch Lake"** may owe something to Wordsworth's

"uncertain heaven received / Into the bosom of the steady lake." In neither **"Postscript"** nor **"Ballynahinch Lake,"** however, does Heaney's respect for his literary elders stifle his own voice; pace, phrasing, and imagery all conspire to reveal his authorship:

> So we stopped and parked in the spring-cleaning light
> Of Connemara on a Sunday morning
> As a captivating brightness held and opened
> And the utter mountain mirrored in the lake
> Entered us like a wedge knocked sweetly home
> Into core timber.

Heaney's acknowledgement of his literary peers and forebears, principally confined to his essays and interviews at first, has increasingly spilled over into his poems through citation, homage, dedication, and elegy. If Yeats and Wordsworth are subtly present in the poems just mentioned, a whole cross-section of the pantheon—including Graves, Brodsky, Hopkins, Patrick Kavanagh, Virgil, and many figures from Greek literature and mythology—populates *Electric Light.* Admirers of Heaney's early books, where an occasional cameo appearance by Undine, Venus, or Narcissus was the only barrier between the reader and uncomplicated lyrical bliss, may find this perplexing, and Heaney may seem in danger of reaching reflexively for a quotation or developing an over-dependency on poetical or mythological allusions. While such perils are real, Heaney is sensitive to them, and it is bracing to behold him—especially given that his readership extends far beyond the academy—refusing to pander to lazy populism, instead choosing to make ever-greater demands on his audience. Although he outsells any other living poet in English, he is steadfast and uncompromising in his standards; in the face of the challenges of literary politics and theory, he stoutly defends the canon as a thriving, evolving force.

And yet Heaney never allows his learning to get in the way. Consider the eidetic, single-sentence **"Perch,"** a poem as transparent as the "water-roof" through which he spies on fish:

> Perch on their water-perch hung in the clear Bann
>   River
> Near the clay bank in alder-dapple and waver,
>
> Perch we called 'grunts', little flood-slubs, runty and
>   ready,
> I saw and I see in the river's glorified body
>
> That is passable through, but they're bluntly holding
>   the pass,
> Under the water-roof, over the bottom, adoze,
>
> Guzzling the current, against it, all muscle and slur
> In the finland of perch, the fenland of alder, on air
>
> That is water, on carpets of Bann stream, on hold
> In the everything flows and steady go of the world.

With its fluid syntax and liquid rhythms, its assonance and echoes, its gestures towards end-rhymes, its visual puns and vivid use of dialect words, **"Perch"** will have swept most readers along in its flow before they note that it, too, contains numerous allusions—to the Bible, Heraclitus, and Hopkins' "Pied Beauty," for example. Even readers who miss these will nonetheless be rewarded with a verbally, musically, and imagistically satisfying poem; as with the River Bann itself, they are offered a choice between a wade in the shallows or a dunk in the deeper currents.

Heaney remains, almost uniquely in contemporary poetry, an erudite poet who educates rather than alienates, frequently proffering subtle illustration or annotation of his more arcane references. For instance, **"Out of the Bag"**—one of the "loose-weave" poems with which he has experimented in recent collections—quickly moves from innocent opening stanzas about the doctor's arrival in the Heaney household, where his mother will again give birth ("All of us came in Doctor Kerlin's bag"), to allusions to the hyperboreans and to the sanctuaries of Asclepius. His description of Doctor Kerlin's eyes as "hyperborean" is immediately glossed by "beyond-the-north-wind blue"; and readers hitherto unfamiliar with the term "hyperborean" can almost supply it for themselves later in the book when they sense it hovering behind the opening line of **"To the Shade of Zbigniew Herbert"** ("You were one of those from the back of the north wind"), having en route encountered Heaney himself, on vacation in Greece, becoming pleasantly "hyper, boozed, borean." Similarly, in **"Out of the Bag,"** the uninitiated reader is put at ease when Heaney refers to the sanctuaries of Asclepius. He explains, through consultations with "*poeta doctus* Peter Levi" and "*poeta doctus* (Robert) Graves," that those sanctuaries were "the equivalent of hospitals / In ancient Greece. Or of shrines like Lourdes"; and he memorably chronicles his own visits to Epidaurus, the site of the temple of Asclepius, and Lourdes. Later in the collection, places like Arcadia and the Castalian Spring are lifted out of myth and quickened into life when Heaney's pilgrimages to them are recounted; in **"Sonnets from Hellas,"** an Arcadian goatherd chanced upon "in the forecourt of the filling station" is described as "subsisting beyond eclogue and translation." Heaney's exposure to the poetry of Zbigniew Herbert and Miroslav Holub, two Eastern Europeans who frequently drew on Greek myth and literature, will have helped to convince him of the continued relevance of those ancient sources; these poets, whom he championed in *The Government of the Tongue* (1988), proved their classical allusions to be resilient enough to survive censorship and universal enough to survive translation into English.

In his own practice as a translator—of Old English, Early Irish, and classical works—Seamus Heaney has been scrupulously respectful towards the original texts, having learned from his long labor on *Sweeney Astray* (1983) that an "obedient, literal" approach yields more substantial dividends than the kind of skillful but exploitative asset-stripping undertaken by Robert Lowell in *Imitations*. Heaney's aptitude for resurrecting and revitalizing ancient texts, illustrated on a grand scale in *Beowulf,* can be seen in miniature in **"Moling's Gloss,"** one of the brief poems clustered in *Electric Light* under the title **"Ten Glosses"** (spontaneous Gaelic poems inscribed in the margins of early monastic manuscripts were termed "glosses"). This four-line poem, dating from the tenth century and rhyming *a-a-b-b,* is attributed to Moling (presumably the saint with whom the protagonist reaches an "uneasy reconciliation" in the closing pages of *Sweeney Astray*). In a literal prose rendition by the scholar Gerard Murphy, it reads: "When I am among my seniors I am proof that games are forbidden; when I am among the wild they think I am younger than they." Responding gamely to the humor of the Gaelic text and retaining its terse musicality (though altering the rhyme scheme), Heaney adds a contemporary, colloquial "gloss":

> Among my elders, I know better
>   And frown on any carry-on;
> Among the brat-pack on the batter
>   I'm taken for a younger man.

Colloquial, too, is **"Virgil: Eclogue IX"** ("watch / The boyo with the horns doesn't go for you"). But what lends this translation a modern reverberation is not so much Heaney's diction as Virgil's own political undertones ("An outsider lands and says he has the rights / To our bit of ground") and, above all, the debate—redolent of the quandaries aired in the opening essay of *The Government of the Tongue*—about the efficacy of art in the face of terror ("songs and tunes / Can no more hold out against brute force than doves / When eagles swoop"). In translating Virgil's ninth eclogue, Heaney is again assisting his readers: in this case, by providing, for an age in which classical studies have waned, a context in which his two other poems in eclogue form—neither of which lays claim to the status of a translation—may be read. In addition, he is enlarging the modern eclogue tradition, whose distinguished contributors include Robert Hass, Heaney's fellow-Ulsterman Louis MacNeice, and the doomed Hungarian Miklós Radnóti. Radnóti, in fact, began work on his devastating poems in eclogue form after translating Virgil's ninth eclogue, which served for him—as for Heaney—as a personal and political echo chamber. Heaney himself has tellingly written of Virgil's *Eclogues*: "What these poems prove is that literariness as such is not an abdication from the truth. The literary is one of the methods human beings have devised for getting at reality. . . ."

Besides the Virgil translation, *Electric Light* also contains two original eclogues. The light and playful **"Glanmore Eclogue,"** set in a part of County Wicklow that Heaney has been writing about since *Field Work,* is essentially a tribute to Ann Saddlemyer, called "Augusta" in the poem—after Lady Gregory, whose plays she edited. Saddlemyer, who owned Glanmore Cottage, is termed (in a Yeatsian epigraph to **"Glanmore Sonnets"** that again tacitly acknowledges the parallel with Lady Gregory) the Heaney family's "heartiest welcomer" to Wicklow; but she is best-known as a scholar of J. M. Synge, who had close family ties with Glanmore and who is, in this eclogue, assigned the Virgilian name Meliboeus. The poem also portrays an Irish Republic in which the small farmers who regained their "bit of ground" politically are being "priced out of the market" economically in the Celtic Tiger conditions that prevailed in the 1990s.

But the most impressive of the three is **"Bann Valley Eclogue,"** set in a land of milk and honey-tinted hay. Like Virgil, Heaney has a firsthand knowledge of farming, and the "cows in clover" of **"Virgil: Eclogue IX,"** with "canted teats / And tightening udders," are of the same breed as the County Derry herd that appears in the richly maternal, and indeed mammarial, final stanza of **"Bann Valley Eclogue"**:

> Child on the way, it won't be long until
> You land among us. Your mother's showing signs,
> Out for her sunset walk among big round bales.
> Planet earth like a teething ring suspended
> Hangs by its world-chain. Your pram waits in the corner.
> Cows are let out. They're sluicing the milk-house floor.

The epigraph to **"Bann Valley Eclogue,"** *"Sicelides Musae, paulo maiora canamus"* ("Sicilian Muses, sing we greater things" in Sir John Beaumont's enduring version), is the first line of Virgil's "Golden Age" or "Messianic" eclogue, number IV. Yet the poem is no translation; rather, it is an independent text that is aware of—without being dependent on—the trajectory of Virgil's fourth eclogue. If Heaney yields to hopes of a golden age for the child whose birth is anticipated in the poem, it is because she is being born into a post-ceasefire Ulster; and if the poem predicts an auspicious event, it is certainly not the arrival of a male Messiah. Virgil's expectations of a male birth contrast with Heaney's certainty that the young woman in the poem is bearing a daughter; the baby's father goes unmentioned; and, in fact, the only identifiable male presence—aside from Virgil—is Heaney himself, remembering the shamrock "with its twining, binding, creepery, tough, thin roots" that he picked for his own mother on St. Patrick's Day.

Aside from the obvious bucolic affinities, perhaps part of the reason why Heaney gravitates toward eclogues is

that the form constitutes a kind of miniature drama. He has long shown an interest in pitching voice against line and meter against speech, as in his radio verse-play *Munro,* his version of Sophocles' *Philoctetes* (called *The Cure at Troy*), and the dramatic monologues in *Station Island.* This impulse finds another outlet in one of the most enjoyable poems in *Electric Light,* **"The Real Names"**—a drama in ten short scenes. The setting is St. Columb's College in Derry, circa 1954; the dramatis personae are Heaney and his classmates. Shakespeare, though, is the real hero of the poem: School performances of his plays (in which—true to Elizabethan practice—female parts were played by boys) are fondly and humorously recollected, and his language has engraved itself deeply into Heaney's sensibility. As an Irish poet from the nationalist tradition, Heaney has no wish to speak the Queen's English ("My passport's green. / No glass of ours was ever raised / To toast *The Queen*"), but he is proud to speak Shakespeare's tongue. It takes only the merest whisper from the inner prompter—whether the name of a character from *The Tempest,* a line or two from *The Merchant of Venice,* or an image from *Henry IV, Part I*—to transport him to that oak-beamed corner of his memory, where an instant chain reaction of Shakespearean associations is set in motion. The most virtuosic cadenza in the poem is an offshoot of a line from *Hamlet*:

> *There is a willow grows aslant the brook*
> But in the beginning it was *sally tree.*
> Sallies in hedges and sallies on the bank
> Of the Moyola River and black sallies
> Like a line of daunted stragglers bogging down
> In the sedge and glarry wetness of our meadow.
> The one in the yard was tetter-barked and hollow,
> Two-timing earth and air: corona top
> Of flick-and-shimmer, sprout-and-tremble growth . . .

One of Heaney's favorite poems by Robert Lowell, "Epilogue," pleads for "each figure in the photograph" to be accorded "his living name." **"The Real Names"** not only reveals the identities of those who participated with Heaney in school productions, but also lays considerable stress on local habitations and local names—in this instance, Hamlet's willow at Elsinore is supplanted by Heaney's sally at the Moyola River in County Derry. "Sally" is a regional variant on "sallow" (from the Latin *"salix,"* for "willow"). One is reminded of Heaney's essay "Mossbawn," in which he remarks of Keats's "To Autumn": "I had a vague satisfaction from 'the small gnats mourn / Among the river sallows', which would have been complete if it had been 'midges' mourning among the 'sallies'."

This localizing tendency—already seen in the substitution of Heaney's Glanmore and Bann Valley for Virgil's Arcadia—resurfaces in **"On His Work in the English Tongue,"** a poem in celebration and commemoration of Ted Hughes. As an elegy for a close friend (and a fellow-writer), this is an intensely literary poem. Even here, however, in the surge of a bravura description of the underside of a bridge ("the tremor-drip / And cranial acoustic of the stone"), Heaney specifies that the structure—which the reader might otherwise have assumed to be a generic bridge, or perhaps a bridge in Ted Hughes's Yorkshire—is in fact "the one / Over the railway lines at Anahorish" in County Derry. Similarly, in **"The Little Canticles of Asturias,"** the road to Piedras Blancas in Spain is compared with the "home ground, / The Gaeltacht, say, in the nineteen-fifties" (the Gaelic-speaking districts of Ireland are known as the "Gaeltacht"). And in **"Desfina"** (one of the **"Sonnets from Hellas"**), numerous and humorous Gaelic equivalents for Mount Parnassus spill out over dinner and ouzo:

> Mount Parnassus placid on the skyline:
> *Slieve na mBard, Knock Filiocht, Ben Duan.*
> We gaelicized new names for Poetry Hill
> As we wolfed down horta, tarama and houmos
> At sunset in the farmyard, drinking ouzos . . .

Seamus Deane terms Heaney's insistence on the local a species of "domestication . . . a search for an origin." No wonder Heaney has alluded to Carson McCullers' view that "to know who you are, you have to have a place to come from" and has cited Patrick Kavanagh as illustrative of the fact that "Loved places are important places, and the right names 'snatch out of time the passionate transitory'."

Heaney's habit of drawing comparisons between home and abroad can take a more somber turn, as in **"Known World,"** a crucial poem centered on his recollections of the Struga Poetry Festival in Macedonia in 1978. The Balkans, riven as they are, like Ulster, by sectarian violence, bring out all Heaney's empathy and sense of solidarity. It is as a farmer's son—admittedly one conversant with *Four Quartets*—that he writes of the rural people displaced by the conflict in Kosovo (the poem is dated May 1998), simultaneously viewing them through the "cloud-boil of a camera lens" and the lens of memory:

> At the still centre of the cardinal points
> The flypaper hung from our kitchen ceiling,
> Honey-strip and death-trap, a barley-sugar twist
> Of glut and loathing . . .
>   In a nineteen-fifties
> Of iron stoves and kin groups still in place,
> Congregations blackening the length
> And breadth of summer roads.
>   And now the refugees
> Come loaded on tractor mudguards and farm carts,
> On trailers, ruck-shifters, box-barrows, prams,
> On sticks, on crutches, on each other's shoulders . . .

But the poem incorporates a more upbeat tone as well. Heaney remembers the festival as companionably bibulous—"we hardly ever sobered"—and his vignettes

convey the giddy exuberance of the occasion: the banter, the booze, the camaraderie. In fact, some of the memories of people (Hans Magnus Enzensberger in panama hat and "pressed-to-a-T cream linen suit") and events (including a sensuously sketched Madonna's Day gathering in the mountains) owe part of their freshness to their origins in contemporaneous notes:

> Then, the notebook says,
> 'People on the move, field full of folk,
> Packhorses with panniers, uphill push
> Of families, unending pilgrim stream.
> Today is workers' day in memory
> Of General Strike. Also Greek Orthodox
> Madonna's Day.'

This reliance on raw notes is not a feature unique to **"Known World."** One of the previous high points of Heaney's work, the final section of **"The Flight Path"** in *The Spirit Level,* ends: "Eleven in the morning. I made a note: / 'Rock-lover, loner, sky-sentry, all hail!' / And somewhere the dove rose. And kept on rising." *Field Work,* written when his entrancement with Robert Lowell was at its height, contains a poem, **"High Summer,"** in which lines are quoted from a notebook or letter. But in other ways **"Known World"** breaks new ground: in its daring admixture of registers, in the unprecedented heterogeneity of its component sections, and in Heaney's willingness at last to admit into his work, however self-deprecatingly, the experiences of the international literary traveler (which, at this post-Nobel juncture, it would be dishonest to exclude).

The international literary life also features, if less centrally, in a poem in memory of Joseph Brodsky, **"Audenesque."** This poem, one of a group of elegies in the second part of *Electric Light,* is an instance of what Heaney has termed "the Lycidas syndrome," whereby "one artist's sense of vocation and purpose is sent into crisis by the untimely death of another." We are allowed backstage at a reading in Massachusetts, where Brodsky is decanting pepper vodka, and are taken on board a train in Finland ("Lenin's train-trip in reverse") where Brodsky and Heaney are "swapping manuscripts and quips." Heaney's imitative ingenuity in **"Audenesque"** is both formal and linguistic: formal in its borrowings from "Wystan Auden's metric feet," the trochaic tetrameter employed in the third section of "In Memory of W. B. Yeats"; linguistic in the way it affectionately and accurately captures the clumsiness of Brodsky's English verse. In a *New York Times Book Review* tribute to Brodsky, Heaney commented on Brodsky's "bewilderment at the self-delusion of second raters" in poetry. But for many of us not privileged to have enjoyed the friendship of this courageous and charismatic man, Brodsky's own first-rateness was a matter for conjecture or trust. Here Heaney brilliantly mimics Brodsky's gauche verbosity:

Nevermore that wild speed-read,
Nevermore your tilted head
Like a deck where mind took off
With a mind-flash and a laugh,

Nevermore that rush to pun
Or to hurry through all yon
Jammed enjambements piling up
As you went above the top,

Nose in air, foot to the floor,
Revving English like a car . . .

The appropriateness of "In Memory of W. B. Yeats" as a model for an elegy of Joseph Brodsky lies not only in Brodsky's lifelong obsession with Auden and devotion to his elegy for Yeats (which inspired Brodsky's own "Verses on the Death of T. S. Eliot"), but also in the fact that both Yeats and Brodsky died on the same "double-crossed and death-marched date, / January twenty-eight."

The finest of the literary elegies clustered in the second part of *Electric Light* is **"Would They Had Stay'd,"** a lament for a quartet of recent Scottish poets. In approaching his task, Heaney must have been conscious of the majestic precedent set by William Dunbar's elegy "Lament for the Makaris," which he first encountered as a student and which, having modernized the late medieval Scottish text, he recorded for Harvard University's Poetry Room. The four poets lamented by Heaney are Norman MacCaig, George Mackay Brown, the Gaelic-language Somhairle MacGill-Eain (under his more familiar English name, Sorley MacLean), and the bilingual Iain Crichton Smith (under his less familiar Gaelic name, Iain MacGabhainn). The poem contains heroic and heraldic language worthy of a medieval poem, as well as interlinked images of deer, which help bind the five sections of the poem together:

The colour of meadow hay, with its meadow-sweet
And liver-spotted dock leaves, they were there
Before we noticed them, all eyes and evening,
Up to their necks in the meadow.

Not all of the elegies are for literary figures. The deeply touching **"Seeing the Sick,"** for example, elegizes Heaney's father. Although his father was an unliterary man and (as commemorated in **"The Stone Verdict"**) a taciturn one, Heaney looks to his own literary forebear, Gerard Manley Hopkins, for an elegiac template with which he can feel comfortable—perhaps because it would have been out of character, embarrassing even, for son to address father directly in matters involving the emotions and affections. "Felix Randal," Hopkins' elegy for a "big-boned and hardy-handsome" blacksmith, facilitates Heaney's oblique and clipped, but intense and unfeigned, tribute to his cattle-dealing father. The poem's title, its opening phrase ("anointed and all"), and much of its imagery derive from "Felix

Randal"; both Heaney and Hopkins use the word "tendered" differently (Hopkins in connection with Holy Communion, Heaney with the secular balm of morphine) but with an equal upwelling of *tendresse*.

Just as Heaney's reliance on Hopkins in **"Seeing the Sick"** illuminates rather than occludes his dying father, in the title poem his allusions to Chaucer, Shakespeare, Dante, and Larkin do not overshadow his "desperate" grandmother. **"Electric Light"** also contains a striking example of Heaney's attunement to verbal nuance at the level of the single word:

We were both desperate

The night I was left to stay, when I wept and wept
Under the clothes, under the waste of light
Left turned on in the bedroom. 'What ails you, child,

What ails you, for God's sake?' Urgent, sibilant
Ails, far off and old. Scarcesome cavern waters
Lapping a boatslip. Her helplessness no help.
     . . . . .

Lisp and relapse. Eddy of sybilline English.
Splashes between a ship and dock, to which,
Animula, I would come alive in time

As ferries churned and turned down Belfast Lough
Towards the brow-to-glass transport of a morning
   train,
The very 'there-you-are-and-where-are-you?'

Of poetry itself. Backs of houses
Like the back of hers, meat-safes and mangles
In the railway-facing yards of fleeting England,

An allotment scarecrow among patted rigs,
Then a town-edge soccer pitch, the groin of distance,
Fields of grain like the Field of the Cloth of Gold.

To Southwark too I came,
From tube-mouth into sunlight,
Moyola-breath by Thames's 'straunge stronde'.

His grandmother's use of "ails" deepened the child's sense of home-sickness because it was at variance with the usage in his own house, where, as the prose-poem **"Hedge-School"** reveals, "What are you crying about now, son?" would be more typical. (Early evidence, this, of the future poet's ultra-sensitivity to language!) To Heaney, an enthusiastic exponent of Eliot's "auditory imagination," words are sounds before they are sense, or rather their sounds are inextricably linked to their sense. Just so, the proximity of "ails" to "nails" acts as a mnemonic, since his abiding memory of his grandmother is of her "smashed thumb-nail." Perhaps the further proximity of "nail" to "alien" is not accidental either, in a poem which opens with his alienation from the strange life and light of his grandmother's house. The electric light there, to which he was unaccustomed, is transformed into the *lux perpetua* of poetry as the poem comes to rest on an elegiac note, "among beads and vertebrae in the Derry ground."

While poets should, of course, be linguistic virtuosi, what most of them actually display is a talent for mediocre writing; in attempting to distract the reader from their shortcomings, they rely on a range of diversionary tactics, from vainglorious obscurity to sensational subject-matter. One thing which, by contrast, makes Heaney so deservedly revered is his ability to link evocative words never before found in combination and, indeed, seldom chanced upon in isolation. His ease with words of various provenance, from the Gaelic and Anglo-Saxon to the Scots Ulster and Latin; his rooted sense of language as a living dialect; his brio with metaphor: These are at the heart of his colossal achievement. There is a radiance about his poems that is an attribute not of his optimism (though he is more comfortable with celebration than censure) but of the way in which he revives, refreshes, and refurbishes language. His verse seems so unimpeded, so undaunted, that what it ultimately conveys is a sense of the limitless possibilities of the art in the hands of the truly gifted.

Perhaps nothing in *Electric Light* more amply demonstrates Heaney's mastery than the fourth section of **"The Loose Box."** These lines, which deal with grain-threshing, are themselves like a machine that picks up momentum as it operates. Soon it is generating words "hard as shot" (to borrow a phrase from an earlier threshing poem, **"The Wife's Tale"**), as Heaney recalls—and surpasses—the threshing scene in *Tess of the D'Urbervilles*:

> Raving machinery,
> The thresher bucking sky, rut-shuddery,
> A headless Trojan horse expelling straw
> From where the head should be, the underjaws
> Like staircases set champing—it hummed and slugged
> While the big sag and slew of the canvas belt
> That would cut your head off if you didn't watch
> Flowed from the flywheel. And comes flowing back,
> The whole mote-sweaty havoc and mania
> Of threshing day, the feeders up on top
> Like pyre-high Aztec priests gutting forked sheaves
> And paying them ungirded to the drum.
> Slack of gulped straw, the belly-taut of seedbags.
> And in the stilly night, chaff piled in ridges,
> Earth raw where the four wheels rocked and battled.

This is high-octane writing of a high order, aided by Heaney's verbal compounds ("rut-shuddery," "mote-sweaty," "sag and slew") and abetted by his genius at transmuting observation and experience into language of great physical precision.

Such pyrotechnics are by no means Heaney's only forte. His tonal and emotional range becomes evident when **"The Loose Box"** is contrasted with **"The Clothes Shrine,"** a gentle, transparent poem that also revels in electric light, although this time of a figurative kind. It recalls the "early years" of marriage to his wife, Marie, and is a perfect instance of his contention that, through "poetic technique," an intimate experience can mutate into "an object to be inspected. It calls you close and the intimacy is not embarrassing":

> It was a whole new sweetness
> In the early days to find
> Light white muslin blouses
> On a see-through nylon line
> Drip-drying in the bathroom
> Or a nylon slip in the shine
> Of its own electricity . . .

                    * * *

Having earlier, with some hesitation, applied to **"Postscript"** (the last poem in *The Spirit Level*) Blake Morrison's theory that the final poem of a Heaney collection yields clues to the subsequent volume, I would like to add a postscript of my own. Since **"Postscript"** may, as its title suggests, be considered separately from the preceding poems in *The Spirit Level,* there is a case for contending that it falls to **"Tollund,"** the penultimate poem, to illuminate the reader forward into *Electric Light.* Set in Denmark at the time of the 1994 IRA ceasefire announcement, the poem marks Heaney's first visit to the setting of **"The Tollund Man,"** a "bog poem" recognized as central to Heaney's corpus since its appearance in *Wintering Out.* In **"The Tollund Man,"** the analogy foremost in Heaney's mind is that between the Iron Age man found in a Jutland bog, apparently a sacrificial victim, and the violence of Ulster:

> Out there in Jutland
> In the old man-killing parishes
> I will feel lost,
> Unhappy and at home.

By the time, over twenty years later, that **"Tollund"** came to be written, "things had moved on":

> . . . it was user-friendly outback
> Where we stood footloose, at home beyond the tribe,
>
> More scouts than strangers, ghosts who'd walked abroad
> Unfazed by light, to make a new beginning
> And make a go of it, alive and sinning,
> Ourselves again, free-willed again, not bad.

Although Heaney remains a profoundly responsible poet, incapable of forgetting the overriding fidelity of the artist to the truth he or she experiences, his capacity to "credit marvels" has found a fresh impetus in the fragile peace process celebrated in **"Tollund."** Admittedly, poems such as **"Known World"** and **"The Border Campaign"** show Heaney continuing to engage with political subject-matter; and **"The Augean**

Stables," one of the **"Sonnets from Hellas,"** chillingly records a moment when the "whitewashed light" of Greece was clouded by news of the sectarian murder of a friend in Ulster. Death, whether violent or natural, weighs heavily on parts of *Electric Light.* Yet Heaney has finally begun to heed the exhortations of James Joyce's ghost in **"Station Island"** to "write / for the joy of it," to "let others wear the sackcloth and the ashes. / Let go, let fly, forget." The light of Heaney's title brightens many of these post-ceasefire poems, and there is a **"Tollund"**-like lightness to his poetical gait. Consider, for instance, the mischievous way he plays with the title **"Red, White and Blue."** In previous collections such a title would, in all likelihood, have presaged a politically-tinctured poem. Here, the poem's colors are fondly associated with items of clothing worn by Marie during their courtship and the early years of their marriage. The "hunting-jacket look" of the scarlet coat in the first of the poem's three sections does not prompt references to Yeats's Anglo-Irish world of "hard-riding country gentlemen" any more than the knights and battlements of **"Castle Childbirth"** are used, in the second section, to make a point about foreign conquerors. And when, in the third part, the young couple hitch-hiking through the Irish Republic in 1963 are drawn into a sensitive political discussion, they plead "We're from the north." Heaney clearly relishes the memory of a pre-Troubles halcyon period, when to be from Ulster was to be from a place that, discriminatory though it was toward Catholics, was not yet synonymous with violence.

Another possible parallel between *The Spirit Level* and *Electric Light* lies in their respective opening poems, **"The Rain Stick"** and **"At Toomebridge."** **"The Rain Stick"** is an opening movement that calls for an encore ("Listen now again"); it makes no apology for revisiting familiar Heaney themes: "What happens next / Is undiminished for having happened once, / Twice, ten, a thousand times before." In this spirit, **"At Toome-bridge"** also recalls earlier Heaney poems, including **"A Lough Neagh Sequence"** from *Door Into the Dark,* **"Toome"** from *Wintering Out,* and **"The Toome Road"** from *Field Work.* Acting as a kind of "You Are Here" sign for Heaney, the poem anchors him firmly at the start of this peripatetic collection in a known and loved place—a place at which a troubled history ("Where the checkpoint used to be. / Where the rebel boy was hanged in '98") is counterpointed by the "continuous present" of the Bann River, and where even "negative ions in the open air / Are poetry to me."

Demonstrating his own version of the "continuous present," Heaney breaks old ground in new ways, relating everything he experiences in the wider world to the "known world" of Ulster. Like his exemplar, Patrick Kavanagh, he is aware that to get to know one small field takes a lifetime's exploration. Yet, however distant he may have grown, through time and travel, from the first field—perhaps the "field behind the house" where he was lost among the pea-drills as a child—it remains a real place to which he is imaginatively bound and permanently rooted: a touchstone for authenticity and a fertile source of vision. As he writes in **"The Loose Box,"** in lines which again carry a faint echo of Shakespeare ("Now would I give a thousand furlongs of sea for an acre of barren ground: long heath, broom, furze, anything"):

> On an old recording Patrick Kavanagh states
> That there's health and worth in any talk about
> The properties of land. Sandy, glarry,
> Mossy, heavy, cold, the actual soil
> Almost doesn't matter; the main thing is
> An inner restitution, a purchase come by
> By pacing it in words that make you feel
> You've found your feet in what 'surefooted' means
> And in the ground of your own understanding . . .

A book of present and past, multiple births and deaths, instinctive evocations and intellectual allusions, the lambently local and the urbanely international, *Electric Light* shows Heaney—now in his sixties—still eluding categorization, or what he calls a "last definition." To paraphrase **"A Norman Simile"** (one of the **"Ten Glosses"**), he is marvelously himself; and the poems in this collection—in the punning words which conclude **"The Clothes Shrine"**—are "got through / As usual, brilliantly." It seems fitting to end with yet another of the glosses, **"The Bridge."** Remove the title, and you are left with a riddle; remove the bridge and you see the poet himself:

> Steady under strain and strong through tension,
> Its feet on both sides but in neither camp,
> It stands its ground, a span of pure attention,
> A holding action, the arches and the ramp
> Steady under strain and strong through tension.

Don Johnson (essay date spring 2002)

SOURCE: Johnson, Don. "Heaney at Play." *Southern Review* 38, no. 2 (spring 2002): 358-71.

[*In the following essay, Johnson discusses Heaney's use of images of child's play to explore the serious theme of enduring in the face of continual evidence of human degradation in* Seeing Things *and* The Spirit Level.]

In commenting upon the "geometry" in the poems of Seamus Heaney's *Seeing Things,* Darcy O'Brien "cannot help but think of Bart Giamatti's reminder to us that the proportions of a baseball diamond are perfect and that the word *paradise* comes from the Persian and means *enclosure, park,* or *green.*" Giamatti's link to Heaney through Dante is readily apparent, but O'Brien's connecting of the two through their interest in sport and play is equally relevant. Seamus Deane, in a recent *New Yorker* reminiscence, recalls that at St. Columb's College "Heaney didn't play football, either soccer or Gaelic, except when required," but he would smile from the sidelines. Heaney obviously took a keen interest in what was taking place on the pitch. **"Markings,"** the second poem in *Seeing Things* and the first in a series of four sporting poems, perfectly captures the marking of the field, the choosing of sides, and the transcendent play in which the speaker participated as a young man. Sporting terms and metaphors have appeared with increasing frequency in Heaney's criticism of the past decade, and even in his Nobel Prize address he proposed that a step toward settling the Troubles in a divided Ireland would call for the border dividing the antagonists to "become a bit more like the net on a tennis court, a demarcation allowing for agile give and take, for encounter and contending." Finally, both poems accompanying Deane's *New Yorker* article, **"Nights of '57"** and **"The Augean Stables,"** are clearly dependent upon sport and play.

In his introduction to *The Redress of Poetry,* Heaney cites Robert Frost's description of the children's playhouse in "Directive" as an example of the poet's "imaginative transformation of human life . . . the means by which we can most truly grasp and comprehend it." The cast-off dishes and utensils the children had appropriated for their games anchored their fantasies, which became "a kind of freely invented answer to everything experienced in the 'house in earnest' where (the tone makes this clear) life was lived in sorrow and anger." Frost's evocation of child's play in "Directive" oscillates throughout Heaney's course of lectures as a potent illustration of the "imagination pressing back against the pressure of reality," both as a response to pain and injustice, a balancing argument, and as a countervailing power. In this last role Heaney celebrates poetry

> not only as a matter of proffered argument and edifying content, but as a matter of angelic potential, a motion of the soul. And this is why I have tried to profess the pleasure and surprise of poetry, its rightness and thereness, the way it is at one moment unforeseeable and at the next indispensable, the way it arrives as something unhindered and self-directing, sweeping ahead into its full potential.

The lectures printed in *The Redress of Poetry* were delivered at Oxford between 1989 and 1994 and revised in 1995, overlapping the publication of *Seeing Things* (1991) and preceding *The Spirit Level* (1996) by only a year. All three works, therefore—as well as *Crediting Poetry,* the Nobel acceptance speech (1995)—emerged from the same critical/creative ferment. What is remarkable is not that the poems validate the criticism, or that the lectures add critical weight to individual poems, but

that taken as a whole they confirm Michael Molino's assertion that *Seeing Things* represents a "transition for Heaney as he passes through the frontier of his own writing—the social and political issues, the conflicts of the dialogue of the tribe he explored for years—in favor of a poetry that focuses upon the often-overlooked beauty in the quotidian." (Molino qualifies his argument, however, warning that "it would be excessive to suggest that Heaney has abandoned the Irish question or his heritage in favor of a transcendent or neo-romantic aesthetic.") The transition Molino perceives in *Seeing Things* extends to *The Spirit Level* as well, but the breakdown of the 1994 truce between the IRA and the Protestant paramilitaries darkens the latter volume and underscores Molino's caveat. Both collections elevate "the pleasure and surprise of poetry, its rightness and thereness," but the bloody facts of *The Spirit Level* provide a formidable reality for the imagination to press against.

In *Seeing Things,* Heaney achieves a perspective similar to Wordsworth's at the conclusion of the "Intimations Ode," where the English poet labors to authenticate his vision by recollecting earlier glimpses of the noumenal realm. Though barred by age and experience from direct access to that glorious world, we can travel back through memory and "see the Children sport upon the shore, / And hear the mighty waters rolling evermore." For Wordsworth the children in his metaphor are puppets of the creative intelligence, witnesses to our primal sympathy with the eternal. Their sport is a pantomime, part of the skeletal framework over which his argument is stretched. For Heaney in *Seeing Things,* child's play is not evidence of proximity to the ideal world but a vehicle through which vision can be attained, and recaptured, not merely through the memory of exceeding phenomenal limits, but through reenvisioning those memories from a mature perspective. Heaney works through grief by celebrating the wonder in the ordinary, by reexperiencing childhood games in which an intense physicality led to visionary breakthroughs. Play is also a source of imaginative energy in *The Spirit Level,* but here Heaney evokes memories of play in an effort to restore equilibrium, not so much to transcend reality but to endure it.

Child's play similar to that in Frost's "Directive" flows throughout both *Seeing Things* and *The Spirit Level,* from **"Markings"** in the former through **"The Errand"** in the latter, which recalls Heaney's father sending him to find "a bubble for the spirit level, / And a new knot for this tie." The child's response to this "fool's errand" is a knowing smile that leaves them both "Waiting for the next move in the game." In between **"Markings"** and **"The Errand"** are poems about fishing; marbles; a board game; pure play with an upside-down bicycle in a water hole; a fantasy game in which a sofa became a locomotive; a performance by Heaney's brother mimicking a piper, marching through the house with a chair over his shoulder and a whitewash brush for a sporran; and playing on a swing hung in a shed. Add to these the number of self-reflexive poems—for example **"At the Wellhead"** and **"The Rain Stick"**—in which the speaker makes music by *playing* with a wholly natural instrument, and it becomes apparent that sport and games have been one of Heaney's central preoccupations over the last decade.

In this emphasis Heaney has evidently been influenced by Simone Weil's *Gravity and Grace.* In "The Redress of Poetry" he offers as a "law" Weil's assertion that "If we know in what way society is unbalanced, we must do what we can to add weight to the lighter scale . . . we must have formed a conception of equilibrium and be ever ready to change sides like justice, 'that fugitive from a camp of conquerors,'" thus, paradoxically in this instance, adding gravity to levity. This shifting of weight to the lighter side, with the opportunity to shift back when necessary, says Heaney, "corresponds to deep structures of thought and feeling derived from centuries of Christian teaching." That teaching, primarily from Aquinas, draws heavily upon Aristotle's Nicomachean Ethics, in which he defined the concept of *eutrapelia,* defined by Hugo Rahner as the "nimbleness of mind which allows a man to play."

Play, and the nimbleness of mind to bring it to bear upon the most serious human questions, is critical in Heaney's later works. If, as Helen Vendler declares, the "given" of *Seeing Things* resides in the question "What does the phenomenal world look like contemplated through eyes made intensely perceptive by unignorable annihilation?" then the power to redress the imbalance, the agility required to render that world not only acceptable but beautiful and good, must be considerable. Vendler argues in *Seamus Heaney* that the world of *Seeing Things* looks simultaneously vivid and unrecapturable. Thus the perceiver is repeatedly distanced, blocked from fully participating in the phenomenal world. His memories are concrete but abstracted, so that descriptions become "symbolic and indicative hieroglyphs." The strength of the poems in *Seeing Things* lies in Heaney's "reimagining everything—not representing it mimetically as it happened; nor representing it embalmed in memory; but representing it on an abstract and symbolic plane that presents itself as such."

Vendler's argument is compelling and comprehensive. In the poems dealing with play, however, primary experience is represented in overwhelmingly concrete terms. The poet insists he is seeing *things.* These things, their heft and weight, their measurement and delineation, often their resistance to the child's efforts to deal with them, generate in the child a visceral response, which leads to vision, to *seeing* things. The greater the resistance, the greater the force needed to overcome it,

but that force, once active, carries one along with it. As Henry Hart points out, "[L]imits abet rather than deter the final performance." Just as the children in "Directive" press back against the reality of their parents' house in their imagined domicile, so Heaney's players in their roles and games go beyond their everyday worlds to glimpse at least momentary transcendence. The poems that record this are, obviously, abstract renderings of experiences that circumscribe them with self-consciousness, but generally the interpretation of the phenomenal world emerges after an experience is recorded. Heaney usually signals this movement from the concrete to the abstract with a shift in focus or point of view. Even in **"Seeing Things,"** the triptych that gives the volume its title, and in which the adult speaker reconfigures the wavering air "we stood up in" as a "zigzag hieroglyph for life itself," the child at the poem's center is shown as capable of his own vision. He imagines himself above the group of children being ferried across Inishbofin,

> as if I looked from another boat
> Sailing through air, far up, and could see
> How riskily we fared into the morning,
> And loved in vain our bared, bowed, numbered heads.

The scene interpolates the incident in **"Squarings"** viii, which Vendler designates as the "theory poem of the volume." There, the anchor of an airy ship has become entangled on the altar rail in the chapel at Clonmacnoise, and the sailor who climbs down the rope to free his ship is exposed to what must seem a miraculous place. The abbot, recognizing that the man will "drown" if he remains earthbound, rallies the other monks to his aid. They free the ship, and the man climbs up "Out of the marvelous as he had known it."

The child in **"Seeing Things"** does not so much experience the "marvelous" as he expands his vision well beyond his years to assume the point of view of a watchful spirit of the place. His solicitous "overseeing" of the craft on the lake beneath him exemplifies the way in which the child in these poems often reaches beyond his immediate situation to encounter the experienced (and intensely self-conscious) adult on his way back in. The childhood visions become Heaney's spots of time, his intimations of a noumenal realm that make up what he has referred to as a poet's "instinctual ballast." It is worth noting that the two major passages from *The Prelude* that Heaney uses to illustrate this instinctual ballast are the skating and swimming scenes from Book I.

The notion of instinctual ballast as a stabilizing factor underscores the importance of balance in *Seeing Things* (recall the child's perception of the precariousness of the boat in the title poem), and connects its themes even more explicitly to **The Spirit Level.** As the cover of that volume makes clear, one's perception of leveling derives from the centered bubble, and *Seeing Things* is replete with things squared, reciprocated, centered. There is the basket of chestnuts slung round in play so that centrifugal force seems to make the burden disappear, until it reaches the bottom of the circle, its "Downthrust and comeback ratifying you." **"Wheels within Wheels"** (perhaps recalling Ezekiel's vision) are created when the young Heaney turns his bicycle upside down in a water hole and pedals with his hands so that the back wheel spins out a mare's tail and allows him for weeks to "create a nimbus of old glit." His exhilaration comes to an abrupt end when the bicycle's chain snaps, and is not re-created until later on he sees cowgirls in a circus, "drum-rolled and spotlit," "each one immaculate / At the centre of a lariat." If there is a pivotal image in *Seeing Things* it is the ash plant, the walking stick Heaney has inherited from his father, which will allow him to "face the ice this year" in equanimity, despite "dangerous pavements." The ash plant might well function as a metonym for all the memories recorded in *Seeing Things,* since Heaney says in **"Squarings"** xxxii that "It steadies me to tell these things."

The third poem in *Squarings,* the forty-three-poem sequence Vendler describes as "'airy' rather than 'laden,' static rather than dynamic," describes the elaborate postures, tensings, and alignments undertaken by young boys behind "a drawn line" about to lag marbles toward "three round holes" gouged in the dirt. These squarings represented

> All the ways your arms kept hoping towards
>
> Blind certainties that were going to prevail
> Beyond the one-off moment of the pitch.
> A million million accuracies passed
> Between your muscles' outreach and that space

where the target lay. Squaring up, aligning oneself, anticipating success ("certainties" and "accuracies"), Heaney says, "You squinted out from a skylight of the world."

Though little actual movement is involved in **"Squarings,"** the muscular tension created through "hunkerings," "test outs," and "reenvisagings" is as much a part of the game as the lagging. In *Homo Ludens,* Johan Huizinga stresses tension as a critical element in play. It "means uncertainty, chanciness; a striving to decide the issue and so end it. The player wants something to 'go,' to 'come off'; he wants to 'succeed' by his own exertions. . . . It is this element of tension and solution that governs all solitary games of skill." The poem's squarings, then, combine physical posturing with sympathetic magic in an effort to influence success, which, from the player's point of view, seems assured. But his optimism serves merely to ratchet up the ten-

sion, since "a million million accuracies" admits the possibility of at least an equal number of inaccuracies.

The dual perspective Heaney achieves through the simile that ends the first section of **"Seeing Things"** is established in the "squarings" poem through the use of the second person. The speaker relives the boy's efforts to align himself for success, but also addresses him as another person who "squinted out from a skylight of the world." The line celebrates what Henry Hart calls a "visionary breach," but the child's muscular optimism is tempered by the mature man's knowledge. While squinting often sharpens one's vision, it also narrows it.

The speaker in this poem is twice removed from the game. There is a child who believes that "readiness is all," squaring ensures success, but there also has to be another child who is not new to the game, who knows that loss overshadows any contest. Finally there is the man, who acknowledges, by expanding the realm of the poem to the world, that the game is a metaphor for life, but who simultaneously cautions that this is a child's metaphor. The poem, for which the entire suite of poems is named, is an effort to *square* his experienced view with the youthful vision. It dovetails perfectly with Stephen Sandy's conclusion that *Seeing Things* is "an intricate exercise in knowing how past sensations and experiences can help him to face the totality of self and the prospect of salvation. Each slightest memory, so often here one of sensory response, is planed and fitted into the puzzle set, the game."

In **"Markings,"** the first of four "play" poems that precede **"Seeing Things,"** Heaney provides the fullest expression of the significance of play as well as a template for his method of "reenvisioning" that invigorates the entire volume. The poem begins in first person, with boys marking the pitch with "four jackets for four goalposts," thus satisfying Huizinga's first criterion for true play, the creation of the separate space, the "charmed magic circle" that allows freedom from ordinary reality, but that imposes upon the players "an absolute and peculiar order." The demand for order is manifest in the imaginary lines of the pitch, which would be "Agreed about or disagreed about / When the time came." After the boundaries were determined, teams were made up, with each boy crossing the line "our called names drew between us."

The political implications here are inescapable. Anytime lines are drawn between Irishmen, the specter of political and religious separation appears. In this case, however, the Troubles are enveloped in what sociologist Fred Davis calls "interpretive nostalgia." By definition nostalgia must be personally experienced, not secondhand. It also demands an awareness of the present as a foil to our reconstruction of the past: "[T]he nostalgic evocation of some past state of affairs always occurs in the context of present fears, discontents, anxieties, or uncertainties, even though they may not be in the forefront of awareness." Interpretive nostalgia moves beyond this comparison between precarious present and secure past to question memory itself. In this mode, the individual asks: "Why am I now feeling nostalgic? What may this mean for my past, for my now? Is it that I am likely to feel nostalgia at certain times and not others?" According to Davis, interpretive nostalgia "is one of the means . . . we employ in the never-ending work of constructing, maintaining, and reconstructing our identities," exactly what is happening in the poet's reenvisioning of his past in these poems.

"Markings" becomes more interpretive when Heaney distances himself from personal experience to describe

> Youngsters shouting their heads off in a field
> As the light died and they kept on playing
> Because by then they were playing in their heads
> And the actual kicked ball came to them
> Like a dream heaviness and their own hard
> Breathing in the dark and skids on the grass
> Sounded like effort in another world . . .

These are any youngsters whose surrender to play has allowed them to transcend both the self-imposed boundaries of their game and the harsher ordinances of time. "Some limit had been passed," the poet observes. The players become embodiments of "fleetness, furtherance, untiredness / In time that was extra, unforeseen and free." Heaney moves in two stanzas from "we," to "youngsters," to abstractions of athletic prowess played out beyond time. But transcendence has been accomplished through physical exertion in a compressed space, as a conseqence of physical activity, not a corollary to it. Henry Hart simply has it wrong when he asserts that "Like all good athletes, Heaney's football players are 'playing in their heads,' so assured are they that their bodies will follow what their minds dictate." In sports, the body never follows the mind. Christian Messenger has it right in *Sport and the Spirit of Play in American Fiction* when he says that in games like the one Heaney describes, "we 'play back to' a sense of our physical well-being in a natural drive to mastery and expression. Such a drive is toward our most intimate or 'original' knowledge of our physical selves. Physical sport momentarily 'frees us from the domination of mind and reason.'"

In Part II of "Markings," Heaney reverts to the second person in a transitional movement between the memory of the soccer games and the comprehensive assessment of Part III. Part II records the poet's attraction to other markings, "lines pegged out in the garden," the string tied to corner battens marking a prospective foundation (another "squaring"), the imagined line between headrigs set in a pasture to guide the plow. "All these

things"—setting boundaries for the soccer field and playing beyond them, taking in the real and imagined markings that regulate his physical world—"All these things entered you / As if they were both the door and what came through it." The revelatory trope here is one not of airiness and distance but of entrance and penetration. These *things* entered the young man, "marked time and held it open." These visionary moments, the mature poet implies, came not from "fallings from us, vanishings," Wordsworth's neo-Platonic glimmerings, but from a thorough grounding in things physical.

"The Pitchfork" reiterates the theme of "Markings" and anticipates the muscular tension of "Squarings." Whether the young man in the poem "played the warrior or the athlete" and imagined throwing it like a javelin or simply worked with it tossing grain, the pitchfork was the one tool that "came near to an imagined perfection." Heaney devotes almost a third of "Pitchfork" to describing the implement's physical (largely tactile) qualities, its heft and balance, the satiny texture of the handle's patina, "the springiness, the clip and dart of it." Virtually enthralled by its attributes, the boy then imagines the launched pitchfork surpassing the farthest probes of space, its "prongs starlit and absolutely soundless." In the years following, the man "has learned," however, that the "perfection" of the flight "or the nearness to it—is imagined / Not in the aiming but the opening hand." Perfection, or its approximation, derives not from the dreamy projection but from the physical gesture. The perception of the ideal is determined by the real. All the squarings, the physical tension, the balanced elemental weight of the boy's world represented in the volume fuse in the instant before the hand opens, thus determining the distance and trajectory of the launch, the authority of the vision.

If *Seeing Things* transforms the base metal of existence through the alchemy of play, *The Spirit Level*, darkened by the reemergence of sectarian violence in Ireland after the 1994 truce broke down, looks at play almost exclusively as a counterbalance, a way to "add weight to the lighter side," to use Weil's phrase. If *Seeing Things* is Heaney's "Intimations Ode," *The Spirit Level* is his "Ode to Duty." Play is prominent in several of its poems, most significantly in "A Sofa in the Forties," "Keeping Going," and "The Swing." But though play can momentarily transport the player, it does not transform the world he returns to. Play, or our memory of it, lightens the burden and facilitates our carrying on, Heaney's major concern in this volume.

The visionary poet is not wholly absent from *The Spirit Level*. In "At the Wellhead," for example, the speaker encourages a rural singer (his wife, according to Helen Vendler) whose songs "are like a local road / We've known every turn of in the past" to "Sing yourself to where the singing comes from." The "cut off" singer is then compared to a blind neighbor, a piano player who "'saw' / Whoever or whatever":

> Being with her
> Was intimate and helpful, like a cure
> You didn't notice happening. When I read
> A poem with Keenan's well in it, she said,
> "I can see the sky at the bottom of it now."

Inspired by the poem being read to her, the neighbor woman, blind from birth, *sees* the sky reflected in the well's dark lens. Her vision generates in turn the poet's "glimpsed alternative, a revelation that is denied or constantly threatened by circumstances," where Heaney's "singing comes from," in this instance. Rosie Keenan is one of several admirable stoics in this book who emerge as models of continuity and equanimity, who are level-spirited in the way someone in another context might be praised as being levelheaded.

The contrast between Heaney's handling of play in *Seeing Things* and in *The Spirit Level* is immediately apparent in **"A Sofa in the Forties,"** in which the poet recalls how he and his siblings transformed their parlor sofa into a train: "kneeling / Behind each other, eldest down to youngest / Elbows going like pistons," their "speed and distance were inestimable." Like the boys on the football pitch in **"Markings,"** the children could play beyond their situation and "be transported," but this play was mimetic, not athletic, the sofa a stage for the children's assimilation into the real world, not a vehicle for transcendence. That real world was first brought to them via the radio, which sat on the shelf above the sofa/train and reminded them daily of the "great gulf" between themselves and the broadcast's source. Not surprisingly, that gulf was, for Heaney, bound up in the newscaster's "pronunciation," which "reigned tyrannically."

Seamus Deane makes much of Heaney's being a boarder at St. Columb's College, a boy from "beyond the city" [Londonderry], where in the minds of the day students "all civility ceased." The distinction between rural and city boys was readily apparent in the boarders' accents. They "talked so slowly that sometimes you thought a sentence had been spoken when only a place-name had," and they all had crystal sets in their rooms, through which Deane "imagined that they had a splintered, ethereal vision of the world beyond as it came hissing through those clever and pathetic sets." How much more splintered and ethereal must that world have seemed to Heaney and his siblings, lined up on the sofa of their Mossbawn home. On their train beneath the radio they "entered history and ignorance," a theme that begins and ends the poem's second section. **"History"** obviously refers to World War II and its aftermath, and violence associated with Irish nationalism, condi-

tions for which "ignorance" might function as a synonym for "history." But "ignorance" might also refer to their own naïveté, which would become apparent only by their brushing up against the outside world.

On their make-believe train the Heaney children learned "already" that "constancy was its own reward." As they rumbled through dark fields, their "only job" was to "sit, eyes straight ahead, / And be transported, and make engine noise." Play became a job, a "freely invented answer" to questions the children were as yet unable to frame.

Steadfastness and tenacity are the key themes of **"Keeping Going."** which immediately follows **"Sofa."** There, the "engine noise" in **"Sofa"**'s last line is transmogrified into the steady drone of a bagpipe imitation. The "music" emanates from Heaney's brother Hugh, to whom the poem is dedicated. In a moment of pure exuberance he had thrown a chair over his shoulder, hung a whitewash brush at his waist for a sporran, and led his siblings on a march around the kitchen with "pop-eyes and big cheeks nearly bursting." This incident, though clearly fixed in Heaney's childhood, occurs in this first section in an eternal present. "The piper coming from far away is you," the poem begins, with "is" serving as the eight-line sentence's only verb. The vignette is, therefore, ever accessible, a reservoir of innocence and good humor to be drawn upon in times of stress.

The whitewash brush/sporran links this opening section with the poem's five other parts, all but the last in past tense. Ordinarily it applied the diluted lime with which Heaney and his brother annually restored the appearance of their house and outbuildings. The "greeny burning" and thoughts of brimstone brought on by mixing the whitewash and the manner in which it gradually grew whiter and whiter, "like magic," evoke other memories of witchcraft and rural folklore, introducing a sinister element into the poem. Summing up a childhood fraught with superstition, Heaney recalls that

> We were all together there in a foretime,
> In a knowledge that might not translate beyond
> Those wind-heaved midnights we still cannot be sure
> Happened or not.

Folklore becomes literary when in the next section Heaney compares his mother's warning him against the "bad boys / In that college that you're bound for" to the witches' admonitions to Macbeth. As Vendler points out, the poem at this point has moved from innocence and frivolity through folk ritual and magic to the potential for moral evil.

That potential is fulfilled in the penultimate section, where Heaney describes the assassination of a "part-time reservist, toting his lunch box." The killing occurred in the middle of town on a normal day, and was carried out by a man with an "ordinary face." The victim fed the gutter with "copious blood." Pieces of his brain flecked the wall he leaned against, staining its whitewashed surface.

Juxtaposed with the detailed but understated description of the murder is the poem's final section, a tribute to Hugh Heaney, who, in contrast to the poet, has elected to "stay on where it happens." The brother has "good stamina," and good humor. He drives his tractor into town and "shout[s] and laugh[s] about the revs." Heaney reminds us that Hugh transformed a whitewash brush into a sporran "and dressed up and marched us through the kitchen," but he realizes that Hugh's high-spirited magic is helpless in the face of genuine evil; he "cannot make the dead walk or right wrong." He knows that his older brother sometimes reaches "the end of his tether," and describes a spell of vertigo overtaking him as he goes about his milking. Hugh holds himself up between two cows until his "turn goes past," then comes to "in the smell of dung again" and asks the eternal question, "Is this all?" He undermines any possibility of a religious response to his dilemma by recasting the declarative assurance of the Doxology into the interrogative: "As it was / in the beginning, is now and shall be?" The question suggests that it is not God's glory that persists, but man's inhumanity to man.

The poem ends with Hugh Heaney rubbing his eyes (to ensure that in the aftermath of his turn he is not *just* seeing things) and "seeing our old brush / Up on the byre door, and keeping going." Despite his inability to right wrongs or raise the dead, the dairyman emerges as a paragon, a model of stamina and good humor in the face of violence and abrasive difficulties. A genuine *eutrapelos,* he endures, as does the poet, by balancing the present against the past, drawing on the reservoir of joy that, having been, is now and ever shall be.

Another of Heaney's stoic models in *The Spirit Level* is his mother, who is also presented in the context of play. In **"The Swing,"** the poet recalls how his mother, fresh from scouring the enamel basin in which she regularly steeped her "swollen feet," came out and "sat to please us on the swing." Heaney begins by describing how in the swing he and his playmates "all learned one by one to go sky high." He repeats this forty lines later, nine lines before the poem's end. The repeated line documents the potential for transcendence in play, but its two occurrences frame the mother's brief appearance on the swing, which tips the poem's balance in favor of the "earthbound."

Hanging from a header over the shed-mouth, the swing is "A lure let down to tempt the soul to rise," a fishing metaphor implying that taking the bait could lead to one's undoing. The mother is "tempted by it for a moment only / Half-retrieving something half-confounded," and the children leave her alone in her reverie. Undoubtedly she is recalling similar play from her childhood and the exuberance and optimism that accompanied it. Foot-weary, but dedicated to "the life she would not fail," the mother, steadying the swing at its lowest point, becomes an icon for earthbound endurance. Having once experienced the joys of childhood, she is not "out of place" on the swing. But neither is she "in her element," having set aside childish aspirations. Positioned as it is between the poet's descriptions of the way he and his siblings soared, the mother's appearance underscores the fact that in each full swing the pendulum brushes the earth.

Like the "history and ignorance" of **"A Sofa in the Forties"** and the explicit, personalized violence of **"Keeping Going,"** **"The Swing"** contrasts youthful innocence with degradation and inhumanity. After the poet and his playmates "learned . . . to go sky high,"

> townlands vanished into aerodromes,
> Hiroshima made light of human bones,
> Concorde's neb migrated towards the future.
> So who were we to want to hang back there
> In spite of all?
>   In spite of all, we sailed
> Beyond ourselves and over and above
> The rafters aching in our shoulder-blades,
> The give and take of branches in our arms.

The children could not impede "progress" or forestall mass destruction. Nevertheless, their swinging provided a glimpse of something "beyond ourselves." They experienced the "give and take of branches" in their arms; but trees are firmly anchored, like the mother, to the earth.

The conclusion of **"The Swing"** recalls Richard Wilbur's nuns at the end of "Love Calls Us to the Things of This World," who "walk in a pure floating / Of dark habits, / keeping their delicate balance." Like these nuns, the substantial figures of *The Spirit Level* (and Heaney himself) have achieved a balance that sustains continuity, a spirit level, in Miltonic terminology. In *Seeing Things,* Heaney argues for a muscular equanimity as the basis for childhood vision. In *The Spirit Level,* he credits that childhood vision as an indispensable tool for keeping going.

Irene Gilsenan Nordin (essay date October 2002)

SOURCE: Nordin, Irene Gilsenan. "Nihilism in Seamus Heaney." *Philosophy and Literature* 26, no. 2 (October 2002): 405-14.

[*In the following essay, Nordin describes Heaney's poetry—particularly the poems of* Seeing Things—*as a positive accommodation to the nihilism articulated by Neitzsche and later postmodern philosophers.*]

I wish to begin with the words of Nietzsche's madman as he makes his famous appearance, running into the crowded marketplace in the bright morning with his lit lantern in his hand, crying out his proclamation of the death of God: "'Where has God gone?' he [cries]. 'I shall tell you. We have killed him—you and I. We are all his murderers.'" He calls out in despair to the bemused and indifferent crowd his rhetorical questions:

> How were we able to drink up the sea? Who gave us the sponge to wipe away the entire horizon? What were we doing when we unchained the earth from its sun? Whither is it moving now? Away from all suns? Are we not plunging continually? Backward, sideward, forward, in all directions? Is there still any up or down? Are we not straying as through an infinite nothing?[1]

These words of the madman express the abyss of despair experienced on the realization that God is dead, the state of desolation which articulates what Nietzsche himself understood to be the consequences of the triumph of the Enlightenment. But these words of despair sum up more than that; they sum up the underlying problems of Nietzsche's age, and indeed our age: the basic mistrust of all previously held systems of value; the collapse of all ordering principle; and the erosion of the authority of tradition. In other words, reason has revealed the inadequacy of tradition, and has itself lost the ability to provide us with any reliable means of evaluation—since any such evaluation must be based on the very principles which are themselves under attack.

This stark realization of the absence of all sense of meaning in values previously held to be true leads to the condition that Nietzsche calls "nihilism," (Latin *nihil,* "nothing"), the condition that he considered to be the central problem of Modernity. This condition, Nietzsche believed, is brought about by the realization of three factors: first, the loss of faith in what he calls a "'meaning' in all events," a loss which contributes to an experience of aimlessness; second, the realization that there is no inherent pattern to the world or to history that can lend universal coherence; and third, the loss of faith in the existence of a stable world of being which can be evaluated according to steadfast, enduring principles. The rejection of these three categories, which Nietzsche terms "aim," "unity," and "being," leads to an experience of a world that appears "valueless," in other words, the experience of nihilism.[2]

Nietzsche, whose thought was considered by Heidegger to be the "final thought of Western metaphysics,"[3] is seen as a heralding voice of postmodernism.[4] In this respect, Nietzsche's "death of God" can be seen to be about the death of modernist philosophical presuppositions, the death of the logocentric metaphysics of presence. But, parallel with the notion of crisis that Nietzsche's announcement of the death of God expresses and the ensuing critique of "metanarratives" which his thought has helped to give rise to,[5] Nietzsche's declaration of crisis can also be seen as a statement of faith. His interpretation of the problems of our age, while on the one hand "negatively" proclaiming the death of God and denying the possibility of shared meaning—or in Lyotard's terms "the consensus of a taste which would make it possible to share collectively the nostalgia for the unattainable" (p. 81), can, on the other hand, be viewed in a more "positive" light. The term "nihilism" itself, as Nietzsche has shown us, is ambiguous, comprising both the concepts of what he termed "active nihilism" and "passive nihilism," which involves a complex interplay between the dual forces of affirmation and negation (*WP* [*The Will to Power*], p. 22).

As the Italian philosopher, Gianni Vattimo, points out, the most general distinction between these forces can be seen in terms of "strength of spirit," where nihilism is considered as both "a sign (*Zeichen*) of the strengthened power of the spirit or a sign of the spirit's fall."[6] Viewed in this way, "active nihilism" is equated with the "positive" idea of "the strengthened power of the spirit," while "passive nihilism" is equated with the "negative" concept of the fall; and the whole of Nietzsche's interpretation of the philosophical problems that he wrestled with lies just in the possibility of "the transformation of passive nihilism into active nihilism" ("NRA," ["Nihilism: Reactive and Active] p. 15). Passive, or reactive nihilism, refuses to acknowledge the absence of meanings and values, while active nihilism, on the other hand, in realizing the state of nothingness that is unmasked, sets about creating new interpretations and values. Such an understanding of nothingness, he believes, is suggested by Heidegger in the concepts of what Heidegger calls the "small, marginal, unnoticeable" ("NRA," pp. 19-21).

In line with Vattimo's view of nihilism as an active force which stresses the strengthening power of the spirit, some recent assessments of postmodern thought remind us that Nietzsche himself anticipated the emergence of what he called "a divine way of thinking" from the critical tradition he helped to form.[7] Nietzsche's comment that nihilism is the "uncanniest of all guests" seems to point forward to emerging new ways of thinking the "otherness," broadly termed spiritual, which the more deconstructive elements of poststructuralist literary criticism have tended to turn their back on. The tentative emergence of this changing direction in contemporary thinking can be seen in terms of enduring interest in the spiritual dimension of human existence and in matters that can be termed transcendent. I use the word "transcendent" not in a metaphysical sense but in the sense of an experiential transcendence which is discovered within one's lived experience of what Heidegger calls "being-in-the world," or what G. B. Madison calls a "transcendence within immanence."[8]

I define the term "spiritual" as those experiences which occur beyond our categorical frameworks for understanding the world, in what Geraldine Finn calls "the space-between," the space where the interaction takes place between what she calls "category and reality, text and context, language and being," the space which allows for our meeting with otherness.[9]

Against the background outlined above, this paper will explore this meeting with otherness and the spiritual elements of negativity as a governing metaphor in the poetry of the Irish, Nobel-prize-winning poet, Seamus Heaney, especially in the collection *Seeing Things,*[10] the publication of which marks a turning point in Heaney's writing. In this volume, we see a clear departure from Heaney's earlier preoccupation with the outer physicality of things to a deepened awareness of the inner landscapes of the mind, where world and word are brought together and expressed in language. In this respect the poetic utterance can be seen as bearing witness to an encounter with what Levinas calls "the face of the Other."[11] This encounter with the Other that takes place in language is expressed in what Heidegger calls the "nothing" (*das Nichts*),[12] an encounter, he believed, which is necessary if nihilism is to be overcome.

For Heidegger the problem of the "nothing" is of central interest and in this respect he shows close similarities with the mystical thinking of Meister Eckhart.[13] In the mystical tradition we see examples of a negative theology which attempts to define God, not by what he is, but rather by what he is not, for to arrive at any intellectual definition of the deity is not possible. Poets of the mystical tradition, for instance, the religious mystic, St. John of the Cross, and the modern German Jewish poet, Paul Celan, pay tribute to what can be called the hidden power of Nothingness. In the words of St. John of the Cross, even if the presence of faith "brings certitude to the intellect, it does not produce clarity, but only darkness." Thus, it follows that the soul, in its search for "knowledge" and "truth," must find its journey to God by "unknowing."[14] In the mystical tradition, this journey, or search, is termed the *via negativa,* or "the dark night of the soul," which represents the emptying, or alienation, of the self—the purification of the soul, in order to achieve closer communion with God.[15] Heidegger thinks of nothingness in similar terms to this mystical concept of "detachment." He defines the "nothing" as not any *thing* at all but rather a "fundamental experience," by which we cut ourselves off from beings and allow ourselves to become open to the nothing, or in Heidegger's words, we allow "the total strangeness of beings to overwhelm us." This experience, or encounter, evokes a state of wonder, which calls forth a questioning, and, as Heidegger explains: "Only on the ground of wonder—the revelation of the nothing—does the 'why?' loom before us. Only because the 'why' is possible as such can we in a

definite way inquire into grounds, and ground them" (*BW* [*Basic Writings*], p. 109). Thus, it follows, that only by facing the nothing and asking the question of the nothing—the basic question of the meaning of Being that Heidegger claims has been forgotten (p. 41)—that nihilism can be overcome.

In Heideggerian terms, this experience of openness is called "letting-be" (*Gelassenheit,* or Releasement), an experience, as Caputo puts it, which "shakes us from our preoccupation with 'what is,' which detaches us from the sphere of things" (p. 19). Caputo expresses this state of susceptibility in a spiritual sense as follows: one opens oneself up "to the presence of something which surpasses man, yet from which alone man receives his essence as man . . . [one lets] the thing lie forth as the thing which it is, to break the shell of creatures to find God within" (p. 8).

In the poetry of Seamus Heaney, especially in his later poetry (from the volume, *The Haw Lantern,* 1987),[16] we see similar moments of visionary awareness celebrated, moments which can be said to arise paradoxically from a state of absence or nothingness, where absence is perceived as the source.[17] This whole concept of empty space as a generating source resurrecting new life is a metaphor that informs much of Heaney's poetry.[18] The dialectic that he engages in can be seen as a constant journeying between the dual forces of absence and presence, homelessness and home—between the *via negativa* and the celebration of the word. We see an example of how Heaney conveys this sense of hidden presence in the following poem, "**Hailstones,**" where the power of a particular experience of hailstones lashing against the speaker's face is, in its absence, recalled and celebrated:

> I made a small hard ball
> of burning water running from my hand
>
> just as I make this now
> out of the melt of the real thing
> smarting into its absence.[19]

Here, the speaker marvels at the fact that this particular experience, which—like the hailstones—has melted away, nevertheless can be relived and reexperienced, and "out of the melt of the real thing smarting in its absence," is re-created in the language of the poem as an enactment of poetic creation.

In his essay, "The Placeless Heaven: Another Look at Kavanagh," Heaney reflects on the concept of absence or empty space which he refers to in terms of what he calls "a kind of luminous emptiness,"[20] which carries with it visionary and spiritual connotations, where world becomes word and what he calls "solidly based phenomena are transformed" to become "a visionary presence forever" (p. 10). Thus, what Heaney terms "truly creative writing" arises not as a "reactive response to some sort of stimulus in the world out there" but rather "from a source within and it spills over to irrigate the world beyond the self" (p. 13). This empowering source is only possible through an experience of loss or withdrawal, and, in this respect, Heaney's empty space can be compared to the "nothing" of Heidegger, outlined above, since it involves the idea of detachment, or as Heaney expresses it, "an abandonment of life in order to find more abundant life" (p. 12).

The idea of the "empty centre" as the generating force is paid tribute in the image of the tree at the end of the sonnet sequence, **"Clearances,"** in *The Haw Lantern.* Here, the "utterly empty" space that is left behind by the felled chestnut tree becomes "utterly a source," a "bright nowhere," from which presence emanates:

> I thought of walking round and round a space
> Utterly empty, utterly a source
> Where the decked chestnut tree had lost its place
> In our front hedge above the wallflowers.

> *(NSP [New Selected Poems 1966-1987]*, p. 232)

These lines evoke the image of the chestnut tree, "deep planted . . . / . . . from a jam jar" long ago, which once stood firm and strong in place in the front hedge, and which has now been cut down. The tree no longer physically exists, but, in its very absence, it still manages to radiate a sense of presence in the inner world of the speaker, who remembers the tree of his childhood as it was. And, just as this absence acts as an empowering force in the empty, physical space left behind, the poem itself, in its very articulation, issues forth as textual evidence that bears witness to that absent presence. In an interview given in 1988, Heaney discusses this poem as a favorite example of the image of space in his poetry. He describes space as something "definite," something which is "both empty and full of potential." In this way, space is seen as a dialectic meeting place between two opposite forces, or, as he explains it, as "a node that is completely clear where emptiness and potential stream in opposite directions."[21]

Another example of empty space as source is seen in the poem **"Clearances,"** where the vacant space created by the mother's death[22] becomes a life-force and source of "pure change" for those left gathered round her deathbed:

> . . . Then she was dead,
> The searching for a pulsebeat was abandoned
> And we all knew one thing by being there,
> The space we stood around has been emptied
> Into us to keep, it penetrated
> Clearances that suddenly stood open.
> High cries were felled and a pure change happened.

> *(NSP,* p. 231)

Just as the word "Clearances" here is applied to the absence of the mother, it also embodies the invisible and unspoken presence that her death leaves. As the mother passes away, the space around her deathbed is transformed, and her dying spirit becomes an empowering force for the loved ones left behind. With the death of the mother, a change takes place: physically, she no longer exists, yet something "even more" remains, something intangible, which cannot be seen, but which nevertheless is deeply felt. In the "clearing," the open space which arises from her death, a new force is created which calls forth an experience of "pure change"— pure in the sense of its transformational and creative character; there emerges a hidden presence that is only possible as a result of the original loss or absence.

Thus, the encounter that takes place between the withdrawing, passive force of death, and the active, creative force of life, can be related to our earlier discussion on Vattimo. It is the "disappearance of Being" (p. 21), associated with passive nihilism, that is first necessary in order for active nihilism to call forth a transformative response. The Heideggerian concept of "Letting-be" can also be applied here, and the death of the mother can thus be compared to the "nothing" of Heidegger, which brings with it an experience of "fundamental" change, by which we allow "the total strangeness of beings [to] overwhelm us," an experience which, in turn, is given new life in the language of the poem.

In a similar way, many of the poems in *Seeing Things* have the motif of empty space, or nothingness, as their central theme. Heaney, himself, for instance, in **"Stepping Stones,"** refers to the themes of "lightenings and brightening" which run through the whole collection, and comments on the poems in the subsection **"Lightenings"** as forming a sort of "constellation around an image of an unroofed space."[23] This image of emptiness, as he sees it, is closely associated with the then-recent deaths of both his parents. Many poems indeed throughout the collection echo the cleansing, purifying transformational experience that is a central feature in the sonnets from **"Clearances."** An example of this is seen in the first poem of **"Lightenings,"** where the image of the beggar in a bare, wintry setting, standing "shivering in silhouette" on the doorstep, conjures up images of the soul awaiting its "particular judgement" after death. This cold, naked image is linked in the final lines of the poem with the purifying experience of the emergence of "knowledge-freshening wind," which rises as a transformational image out of the unroofed ruin of the house where the beggar, in his state of emptiness, finds himself (*ST [Seeing Things]*, p. 55). Another example of the nothing as a source is the image of the "good thief" hanging on Christ's side on the cross, where he scans the "empty space." This can be seen as an image of absence, which is answered in the final line of the poem with the promise of the resurrection: *"This day thou shalt be with Me in Paradise"* (p. 66).

There are many such examples of empty space as source throughout the collection. In these poems we see language as a source of renewal or rebirth, by which past phenomena are not only re-called, but also recreated in the empty space, and through the creative energies of the word are "seen" in a new way. A final example of this is seen in the following poem, entitled **"The Settle Bed."** Here, the speaker refers to that which is "given," the Noah's ark of collective memory that is passed down to us and in which we have no say—that which is "willed down" as part of our "inheritance." But, as the poem suggests, no matter how "cart-heavy, painted an ignorant brown" this inherited weight may be, it can always be reshaped and "conquered," and made new by the transformative power of language. That which is

> . . . cargoed with
> Its own dumb, tongue-and-groove worthiness
> And un-get-roundable weight.
>
> . . . . .
>
> Can always be reimagined, however four-square,
> Plant-thick, hull-stupid and out of its time
> It happens to be . . .
>
> *(ST,* p. 28)

To conclude, I have argued that Heaney's retreat into absence and empty space bears witness to the power of the nothing, the spiritual "space-between" where word and world come together and are expressed in language. In the interplay between the dual forces of affirmation and negation, Heaney's poetry crosses the limits of conceptuality between the visible and the invisible; and in the in-between realms of the nothing new meanings are produced which pay tribute to the mystery of the other. As we have seen, Heaney's retreat into nothingness, while it acknowledges an initial experience of absence and loss, is followed by the creation of new meanings. In this way, poetry becomes a celebration of the nothing, or—in Heideggerian terms—a celebration of "being-in-the-world."

Thus, against the philosophical background of the death of God and the aesthetically exhausted expressive tradition that postmodernism gives voice to, Heaney's poetry offers an alternative "positive" view. Against the general state of skepticism, absence of meaning, and "negative" nihilism that is reflected in much of contemporary critical discourse, Heaney offers a poetics that manifests itself by its visionary qualities: he offers a poetry of liberation that shows us a way out of the labyrinth of the text. In the makings of new meanings, loss and absence are overcome in an act of creative celebration, or in the words of Nietzsche, "To redeem the past and to transform every 'it was' into an 'I wanted it thus!'—that alone do I call redemption!"[24]

Notes

1. Friedrich Nietzsche, *The Gay Science,* trans. Walter Kaufmann (New York: Random House, 1974), p. 125.

2. Friedrich Nietzsche, *The Will to Power,* ed. Walter Kaufmann, trans. W. Kaufmann and R. J. Hollingdale (New York: Random House, 1968), p. 12; hereafter abbreviated *WP.*

3. Martin Heidegger, *Nietzsche,* trans. David Farrell Krell (San Francisco: Harper and Row, 1984), p. 232.

4. See Jürgen Habermas, *The Philosophical Discourse of Modernity,* trans. Frederick Lawrence (Cambridge, MA: The MIT Press, 1987), p. 85. See also, for example, Jacques Derrida, *Spurs: Nietzsche's Styles,* trans. Barbara Harlow (Chicago: University of Chicago Press, 1978); Gilles Deleuze, *Nietzsche and Philosophy.* trans. Hugh Tomlinson (New York: Columbia University Press, 1983).

5. Jean-François Lyotard, *The Postmodern Condition. A Report on Knowledge,* trans. Geoff Bennington and Brian Massumi (Manchester: Manchester University Press, 1984), p. xxiv.

6. Gianni Vattimo, "Nihilism: Reactive and Active," *Nietzsche and the Rhetoric of Nihilism: Essays on Interpretation, Language and Politics,* eds. Tom Darby, Béla Egyed, and Ben Jones (Ottawa: Carleton University Press, 1989), p. 15; hereafter abbreviated "NRA."

7. See Philippa Berry and Andrew Wernick, eds., *Shadow of Spirit: Postmodernism and Religion* (London: Routledge, 1992), p. 3.

8. G. B. Madison, "A Critique of Hirsch's Validity," *The Hermeneutics of Postmodernity: Figures and Themes* (Bloomington: Indiana University Press, 1988), pp. 14-15.

9. Geraldine Finn, "The Politics of Spirituality: the Spirituality of Politics," in *Shadow of Spirit,* eds. Berry and Wernick, p. 118.

10. Seamus Heaney, *Seeing Things* (London: Faber, 1991); hereafter abbreviated *ST.*

11. Emmanuel Levinas, *The Levinas Reader,* ed. Séan Hand (Oxford: Blackwell, 1989), p. 82.

12. Martin Heidegger, "What is Metaphysics?" *Basic Writings,* ed. David Farrell Krell (San Francisco: Harper, 1993), pp. 93-110; hereafter abbreviated *BW.*

13. John D. Caputo, *The Mystical Element in Heidegger's Thought* (New York: Fordham University Press, 1986), p. 8.

14. St. John of the Cross, *The Ascent of Mount Carmel. The Collected Works of St. John of the Cross,* trans., Kieran Kavanaugh and Otilio Rodriguez (Washington, DC: ICS, 1979), p. 119.

15. For an interesting discussion on the difference between the religious practice of the *via negativa* and the theological concept of negative theology, see Kevin Hart, *The Trespass of the Sign: Deconstruction, Theology and Philosophy* (Cambridge: Cambridge University Press, 1989), pp. 174-77.

16. Seamus Heaney, *The Haw Lantern* (London: Faber, 1987); hereafter abbreviated *HL.*

17. This sense of hidden presence, radiating from a state of emptiness—found also, for instance, in the work of the Welsh poet R. S. Thomas—can, as Elaine Shepherd has suggested, be related also to Jean-Paul Sartre's words in *Being and Nothingness*: "We see nothingness making the world irridescent [sic], casting a shimmer over things." Jean-Paul Sartre, *Being and Nothingness: An Essay on Phenomenological Ontology,* trans. Hazel E. Barnes (London: Methuen, 1969), pp. 23-24. See Elaine Shepherd, *R. S. Thomas: Conceding an Absence: Image of God Explored* (Basingstoke: Macmillan, 1996), p. 152.

18. Heaney's conception of space can be compared to the "positive nothingness" of Beckett, where Beckett sees space or place (Amiran uses both terms interchangeably) as "agent, as the divine Mind, seat and germ of all." See Eyal Amiran, *Wandering and Home: Beckett's Metaphysical Narrative* (University Park: Pennsylvania State University Press, 1993), p. 184.

19. Seamus Heaney. *New Selected Poems 1966-1987* (London: Faber, 1990), p. 220; hereafter abbreviated *NSP.*

20. Seamus Heaney, *The Government of the Tongue: The 1986 T. S. Eliot Memorial Lectures and Other Critical Writings* (London: Faber, 1989), p. 3.

21. As Heaney points out in this interview, the empty space, or "clearing," also occurs in "The Wishing Tree," in "The Frontier of Writing," and in "The Disappearing Island." And he adds disarmingly: "I'm delighted to find [it] in one of my favourite earlier poems—'Sunlight Mossbawn'—a line (I don't know where it came from)." See "Seamus Heaney: An Interview," Randy Brandes, *Salmagundi* (Fall, 1988): 6.

22. These eight sonnets in "Clearances," which appeared in *The Haw Lantern* (1987), were written in memory of the poet's mother and given the dedication: "In memoriam M. K. H., 1911-1984."

23. Seamus Heaney. "Stepping Stones" (Audio Books, 1995).

24. Friedrich Nietzsche, *Thus Spoke Zarathustra: A Book for Everyone and No One,* trans. R. J. Hollingdale (1961; reprint, Harmondsworth: Penguin, 1969), p. 161.

Howell Chickering (essay date winter 2002)

SOURCE: Chickering, Howell. "Beowulf and 'Heaneywulf.'" *Kenyon Review* 24, no. 1 (winter 2002): 160-78.

[*In the following essay, Chickering—who has himself translated* Beowulf—*presents a mixed review of Heaney's version, arguing that some of the choices made in the act of translation betray an attempt by Heaney to be seen as an author, rather than merely a translator, of the work.*]

Over the last two years Seamus Heaney's long-awaited translation of *Beowulf* has been issued by three separate publishing houses to overwhelming critical acclaim. It won the 1999 Whitbread Book of the Year Award and reached the best-seller lists in both the United States and the United Kingdom. Its reception was quite a phenomenon.

Heaney was initially commissioned by Norton to represent the Old English poem to undergraduates in a free-standing and relatively faithful translation, to appear in their anthology. When the translation was published separately, with a couple of notable exceptions (Tom Shippey in the *Times Literary Supplement,* Nicholas Howe in *New Republic*), the reviewers had little or no knowledge of Old English and responded to it as a new poem by the 1995 Nobel Prize winner. Some even praised his translation for the strength of its narrative design, as if he had invented the final conflict between the hero and the dragon. Heaney's own assessment, as reported by Mel Gussow in an interview in the *New York Times,* is that the translation is "about one-third Heaney, two-thirds 'duty to the text.'" (B4). On the other hand, professional Anglo-Saxonists early on derogated it with the name "Heaneywulf" since to them it was "just not *Beowulf.*" It isn't, of course. No translation follows its exemplar exactly, no matter how "faithful." The nickname stuck, in academic circles anyway, but has now lost its pejorative sense and instead signals Heaney's efforts to mark the translation as his own poem.

Someone is always translating *Beowulf,* it seems. Since 1900, amazingly enough, there has been one new translation every two years on average. In the short time since Heaney's first appeared, three more have been published or promised.[1] This is in marked contrast to English translations of Homer or Dante, where one poetic translation will hold the field for decades before a new attempt appears. Why this steady stream? Perhaps one answer is that many university students on both sides of the Atlantic learn Old English, often painfully, and they wish to turn their pain into pleasure. Another reason is that the poem is mercifully short (3,182 lines) in comparison to Homer, and hence apparently less daunting. A more important factor is the persistent genetic fallacy that mistakes the remote historical continuity between Old English and Modern English as an indication of their essential identity, when in reality a whole millennium separates the two culturally and linguistically.

Yet even if conscientious translators treat Old and Modern English as separate source and target languages, they don't seem to "get it right" in others' eyes. Disagreement over what constitutes fidelity to the original has prevented general acceptance of a standard Modern English *Beowulf*. This is as it should be, whether we mean fidelity to the letter or to the literary qualities of the original. It's not only that it is impossible to bring *any* poem's full literary effect across in translation. There also is a special problem in going from Old to Modern English because we cannot help but see prominent features of Old English poetry—alliteration, parataxis, and nominal compounding—as properties of Modern English poetry, when they actually create very different literary effects in Old English. The unavoidable temptation for the poetic translator is to try to transpose these literary effects by using the same linguistic features in Modern English. The results never satisfy everyone, and so translations continue to appear.

Twentieth-century poetic versions of *Beowulf* have mainly been paraphrases, to use Dryden's term, translating sense for sense rather than word for word. Since the Scottish poet Edwin Morgan's 1952 rendition, based on his eloquent plea for a chastened modern diction instead of archaisms and literal compounds, a kind of stylistic consensus can be seen in the more successful poetic paraphrases. They tend to be literal rather than to introduce new metaphors, and they try to mute the effect of the features shared by Old and Modern English poetry. Thus they use a four-or five-stress poetic line, only light alliteration, and what the translator considers a restrained modern diction. (Dictional equivalents in Modern English for the kenning-heavy compounding of *Beowulf* have remained an area of disagreement.) Those versions that also reproduce the syntactical and rhetorical designs of the original come closest to representing at least a faint ghost of their grand exemplar. They remain honorable failures, since Modern English poetry simply cannot match the clangorous magnificence of the Old English, but they show how the poem's thoughts and images develop. Among them I count Kevin Crossley-Holland's 1968 version, my own in

1977, Marc Hudson's in 1990, and Roy Michael Liuzza's 2000 translation. The successful aspects of Heaney's translation place it in this group of poetic paraphrases, although he frequently departs from the Old English syntax and often mixes dictional registers so as to mar his own literary decorum. For fidelity to both the letter and spirit of the original, it is a resounding but mixed success, with some awkward missteps amid many fine poetic achievements.

The very finest passages in Heaney's rendering are the dramatic speeches, which make up about forty percent of the poem. The speeches are freshly faithful to the point of ventriloquism (Nicholas Howe's term). To a reader who knows the original well, passage after passage delivers the sense and tone of the Old English with effortless grace. It doesn't matter which character is speaking, nor whether with enthusiasm or stoic irony: Heaney captures their verbal gestures just about perfectly. When Unferth, Hrothgar's sour-minded retainer, challenges Beowulf upon his arrival at Heorot, Heaney makes his voice modulate from a sneering reproach into a stately catalogue of verbs implicitly acknowledging heroic action. The original moves exactly this way. Similarly, in the close of Beowulf's thoroughly devastating reply to Unferth, Heaney gets the pulse of feeling exactly right:

> "The fact is, Unferth, if you were truly
> as keen or courageous as you claim to be
> Grendel would never have got away with
> such unchecked atrocity, attacks on your king,
> havoc in Heorot and horrors everywhere.
> But he knows he need never be in dread
> of your blade making a mizzle of his blood
> or of vengeance arriving ever from this quarter—
> from the Victory-Shieldings, the shoulderers of the
>   spear.
> He knows he can trample down you Danes
> to his heart's content, humiliate and murder
> without fear of reprisal. But he will find me different.
> I will show him how Geats shape to kill
> in the heat of battle. Then whoever wants to
> may go bravely to mead, when morning light,
> scarfed in sun-dazzle, shines forth from the south
> and brings another daybreak to the world."
>
> (590-606)

This passage also shows the translator as tactful interpreter. Here "you Danes" are more sharply contrasted with the Geats than in the Old English text, but most critics read Beowulf's boast as thinly veiled aggression and Heaney simply makes it overt. The brilliant image of the morning light "scarfed in sun-dazzle" is Heaney's own, resting on good textual warrant, and lends subtle symbolic force to what gives "another daybreak to the world," namely Beowulf's proposed salvation of the Danes.

Heaney's final verbs here mirror the confident future indicative of the original. However, there are uncertain touches of diction in the passage as well. "Heart's content" and "fear of reprisal" are shopworn phrases. "[S]uch unchecked atrocity" smacks of journalese, and "need never be in dread . . . of vengeance arriving ever from this quarter" sounds like a backbencher in Parliament. American readers are unlikely to know, even from context, that "mizzle" is dialectal for "drizzle." In fact it seems selected not only as a countryman's word but also to alliterate with "making," and therefore feels slightly forced.

That line—"of your blade making a mizzle of his blood"—exhibits one of Heaney's favorite rhetorical enrichments, chiasmus, here played out across the *bl-m-m-bl* alliteration. Generally his poetic form is more lightly alliterated, sometimes on unstressed syllables, sometimes only twice in a line, and on rare occasions not at all. Sometimes we hear a strong medial caesura, sometimes only the lightest pause. He has tried, as he says in his Introduction, for "the sound of sense" (xxix) in Frost's famous phrase, and this flexible form allows him to stay focused on it. His translation can thus keep pace with the original nearly line by line.

Heaney says that he sought to recreate "a kind of four-squareness about the utterance" (xxviii) which he encountered when he first read the Old English poem. He acknowledges that his own prejudice in favor of "forthright delivery" has led him to scant, to some degree, the extended appositions of the poem's syntactical variations and some of its ornate compound-making. This is true: we sorely miss the craggy, bejeweled difficulty of the original in Heaney's flattened-out "directness of utterance." I myself certainly wouldn't call the style of the original Old English "foursquare." It is both restrained and exuberant, often ironic, oblique, ceremonial, sometimes sententious.

Nonetheless, Heaney's mode of translation often works exceptionally well in narrative passages. Here, for instance, is a famous description of nonheroic action, when Beowulf and his men first cross the ocean to Denmark:

> Time went by, the boat was on water,
> in close under the cliffs.
> Men climbed eagerly up the gangplank,
> sand churned in surf, warriors loaded
> a cargo of weapons, shining war-gear
> in the vessel's hold, then heaved out,
> away with a will in their wood-wreathed ship.
> Over the waves, with the wind behind her
> and foam at her neck, she flew like a bird
> until her curved prow had covered the distance
> and on the following day, at the due hours
> those seafarers sighted land,
> sunlit cliffs, sheer crags
> and looming headlands, the landfall they sought.
> It was the end of their voyage and the Geats vaulted
> over the side, out on to the sand,

and moored their ship. There was a clash of mail
and a thresh of gear. They thanked God
for that easy crossing on a calm sea.

(210-28)

This is a brilliant rendering of what is already a brilliant passage in the original. Heaney has successfully spread out the ship-as-bird simile over more lines than it takes in the Old English and he has resegmented some of the sentences, but everything works to create an effect equivalent to the Old English. This kind of clear vigor is typical of his best narrative passages. So is his arrival at the translation "It was the end of their voyage," an adroit negotiation of the crux at line 224a, *ēoletes æt ende,* discussion of which takes up nearly seven inches of small print in Dobbie's variorum edition. To my mind, Heaney has made sensible, or at least defensible, decisions about translating all the major cruces in the poem.

In other passages Heaney is less responsive to the text. When he comes upon the most surprising periodic delay in the entire poem, he does not preserve it in his translation. After Grendel's Dam attacks, the Danes and the Geats track her to the mere, and the sentence at 1417b-21 reads literally (to use Roy Liuzza's very exact translation):

> To all of the Danes
> the men of the Seyldings, many a thane,
> it was a sore pain at heart to suffer,
> a grief to every earl, when on the seacliff
> they came upon the head of Æschere.

In the Old English the "when" clause delays the discovery of the head (*hafelan*) of Hrothgar's beloved counselor until the last half-line: "syðþan Æscheres / on þam holm-clife hafelan melton." This delivers a real narrative shock to the reader as well as to the Danes. However, in Heaney's version Æschere's head is displaced from emphatic final position to the "foot" of the cliff, which isn't even in the original:

> It was a sore blow
> to all of the Danes, friends of the Shieldings,
> a hurt to each and every one
> of that noble company when they came upon
> Æschere's head at the foot of the cliff.

"[A] sore blow" and "a hurt to each and every one" are flaccid phrases compared to the pained literal sense of the Old English. It's notable, too, that Heaney doesn't seek the emphasis of alliteration when he reaches this climax.

Heaney's fidelity to "the sound of sense" may also be tested by his treatment of Grendel's approach to Heorot, much admired by generations of readers. I will cite only lines 710-11, which have a horrifying sound in Old English, like a tolling bell:

Dā cōm of mōre   under mist-hleoþum
Grendel gongan,   Godes yrre bær.

The double *g*'s of "gongan" extend the growl in "Gren-del" and then become more portentous as they contrast with the even heavier weight of the *g* sound that he must bear, "Godes yrre," God's wrath. In my dual-language edition, with this astonishing texture of sounds on view across the page, I could afford to render the lines quite literally:

Then up from the marsh,   under misty cliffs,
Grendel came walking;   he bore God's wrath.

Roy Liuzza, with different nuances in his diction, is also literal:

Then from the moor, in a blanket of mist,
Grendel came stalking—he bore God's anger.

Both of us are careful to mimic the grammar and rhythm of the Old English, and hope against hope that the effect will speak for itself. Heaney, on the other hand, has:

In off the moors, down through the mist-bands
God-cursed Grendel came greedily loping.

By changing the verbal construction, Heaney loses the sound of slow-marching menace and turns Grendel into a sort of hyena. The *gr* alliteration of his second line no longer sets the monster against his Maker but instead links him to animal appetite. That Grendel has aplenty, and he soon gobbles up a sleeping Geat, but the eerie ritual dignity of his horrid visit has vanished. Of course it is also true that neither my nor Liuzza's version recreates the *sound* of that eerieness. In that sense, none of us "gets it right." Whether or not a young reader of "Heaneywulf" will like Grendel as a greedy loper is another matter.

The most daunting literary task facing every translator of *Beowulf* is to find an equivalent for the dominant voice of the poem, which moves back and forth between pell-mell narrative and lingering reflection even at the most exciting moments. The Old English achieves this duality of mode in part through its ornate diction and elaborated syntax, aspects that Heaney means to eschew. His solution is, as he says, to establish a firm, level tone with his "foursquare" line and language. This tone has its gains and its costs. Usually it has clarity and force. It helps Heaney to avoid an overblown and compound-clogged Modern English, but not always. Sometimes it merely leaves us with dull stretches. Furthermore, in his attempt to keep on an even keel, he frequently recasts the shape of sentences in startling and distracting ways. On the whole, the chief virtue of his style—apart from the clarity and force of the dramatic speeches—is that it establishes a *decorum* of language that accords well with the heroic dignity of the Old English.

Such decorum is no mean poetic achievement. I therefore find it ironic that he often unintentionally breaks his own decorum. This happens in three ways: by overwrought images derived from already strong metaphors in the Old English; by clunky over-alliterations not required by his form; and by wildly varying dictional choices. At such moments he becomes so enthusiastic about the sense and sound of the original, and about his command over it, that he has to exercise the full range of his poetic talents. He breaks into florid song, as it were, and it clashes with his own levelness.

For instance, when Beowulf tells Hrothgar he has vanquished Grendel, Heaney has him conclude by say-ing:

And now he won't be long for this world.
He has done his worst but the wound will end him.
He is hasped and trooped and hirpling with pain,
limping and looped in it. Like a man outlawed
for wickedness, he must await
the mighty judgement of God in majesty.

(974-79)

The first line is colloquial to the point of flipness. The *h* alliteration of the "hirpling" line is showy overkill, which is carried over into the internal rhyming of "limp-ing and looped." "Hirpling" is a recondite dialectal word for "hobbling" and was not known to several British friends when I tried it out on them. It might as well be a word from "Jabberwocky." Heaney's exuberant performance is more in evidence here than the subject of the passage itself, Grendel's death-wound.

An example of both over-alliteration and overwrought imagery is Heaney's identification of Yrse, the queen of Swedish king Onela, in an early lineage. In line 64 she is literally called "the neck [hence 'close, dear'] bed-companion of the Battle-Scylfing [i.e., Battle-Swede]," a compound name which suggests both the stately and the intimate, but Heaney renders her as "A balm in bed for the battle-scarred Swede." This seems a thumpingly gratuitous foregrounding of the erotic, even though one can admire it as interpretive translation.

Alliteration by itself, especially on *b* sounds, often distracts the reader from the sense. Lines 81b-84a:

The hall towered,
its gables wide and high and awaiting
a barbarous burning. That doom abided,
but in time it would come: the killer instinct
unleashed among in-laws, the blood-lust rampant.

"Barbarous burning"—is there any other kind? "Abided" might have come from any one of a dozen earlier translations. The over-connection of "and . . . and" (not in the original) also flattens out the sense. When Grendel first attacks Heorot, he rushes back to his lair in lines 124-25,

flushed up and inflamed from the raid,
blundering back with the butchered corpses.

That second line itself seems to blunder. There are a number of other instances of verbal overkill that break decorum, and do not create the "forthright delivery" the poet says he sought. It is worth noting that they are mainly confined, for whatever reason, to the Grendel's Dam episode and the early part of the dragon fight.

One could argue, I suppose, that the overcooked imagery and the bumping alliteration are deliberate adornments that extend, rather than break, Heaney's basic decorum of style. Certainly such imagery has been cited admiringly in various reviews. However, the more serious problem is his extravagant use of disparate registers of diction, since the disparities cause his normally level tone to dip or knot up. I see three different kinds of dictional shifts that break his own decorum. First, part of Heaney's "foursquareness" is a man-to-man informality with flourishes of emphasis of the sort we love to hear in oral storytelling. The gain is a conversational "readable" quality in the translation. But his sudden drops into the chummily colloquial can be unsettling when the rest of the sentence is not informal. Second, there are what I can only call clichés of speech, which you simply don't expect in a poet of Heaney's stature. Third, there are the deliberate Ulsterisms.

All of these can be seen in the opening lines of "Heaneywulf," which is far and away the most frequently cited passage in the sheaf of reviews I've collected.

> So. The Spear-Danes in days gone by
> and the kings who ruled them had courage and greatness.
> We have heard of those princes' heroic campaigns.
>
> There was Shield Sheafson, scourge of many tribes,
> a wrecker of mead-benches, rampaging among foes.
> This terror of the hall-troops had come far.
> A foundling to start with, he would flourish later on
> as his powers waxed and his worth was proved.
> In the end each clan on the outlying coasts
> beyond the whale-road had to yield to him
> and begin to pay tribute. That was one good king.
>
> Afterwards a boy-child was born to Shield,
> a cub in the yard, a comfort sent
> by God to that nation. He knew what they had tholed,
> the long times and troubles they'd come through
> without a leader; so the Lord of Life,
> the glorious Almighty, made this man renowned.
> Shield had fathered a famous son:
> Beow's name was known through the north.
> And a young prince must be prudent like that,
> giving freely while his father lives
> so that afterwards in age when fighting starts
> steadfast companions will stand by him
> and hold the line. Behaviour that's admired
> is the path to power among people everywhere.
>
> (1-25)

In the first three lines Heaney alters the syntax unnecessarily, losing the original shape of the sentence, and ends up with a subdued, rather flat tone. Here are the lines in Old English and a literal gloss:

> Hwæt! Wē Gār-Dena   in geārdagum
> þēodeyninga   þrym gefrūnon,
> hūd ā æpelingas   ellen fremedon
>
> What! We of the Spear-Danes   in the old days
> of the tribal kings   the strength have heard tell,
> how those noblemen   courage performed.

The grammatical relationships can be sorted out thus:

> Listen! We have heard tell   of the strength of the
>   tribal kings
> of the Spear-Danes   in the old days,
> [of] how those noblemen   performed [deeds of] courage!

The first verb in the poem, *gefrignan,* is an epic formula of poetic authority that means "to hear tell of," and its first object is the "þrym" of the ancient Danish kings, a word that means "power" or "military troop," and by extension "glory." I punctuate the sentence with an exclamation point because the verb's second object, the "how" clause expanding upon "þrym," is uttered with great warmth of feeling, with the heavy nouns *æpelingas* ("noblemen") and *ellen* ("courage") receiving full metrical emphasis. Despite his announced commitment to the living voices of tellers, Heaney suppresses the initial indication of oral reception and recitation in "wē . . . gefrūnon" and dilutes the syntactic force of line 2 by introducing the two "ands." Then he makes line 3 a separate sentence, which cools its warmth considerably, as does its oddly high-toned propaganda-like diction: "those princes' heroic campaigns." These are uncertain first steps into the poem.

The last sentence of this opening passage is also askew. Literally it reads "in every tribe a man must prosper by deeds of praise," a maxim of conduct that clinches not only the Anglo-Saxon value of a lord's generosity to his men but also their reciprocal loyalty under duress. Heaney's version suggests nothing so much as a modern political climber's recipe for success: "Behaviour that is admired / is the path to power among people everywhere." Perhaps the excesses of the last American presidential election have given me a tin ear. But consider a different tone, in line 11b: "That was one good king." By simply adding "one" for colloquial emphasis to an otherwise exact translation of "þæt wæs gōd cyning," he has deflected our attention from the object of praise to the sound of the praising voice. Perhaps this deflection is always part of the project of a modern poet, but in this case it trivializes when it should emphasize. The colloquial note in line 20, "And a young prince must be prudent like that," doesn't work either; it loses the dignity and decorum of the Old English in head-wagging sententiousness.

Then there are the clichés, some of which I have already cited. "Hold the line" at the end of this passage was originally "bear the brunt" in a version that circulated prior to publication, so I know it's intended as an improvement. A few lines past this quotation we get "laid down the law" for when Scyld literally "ruled by words." These phrases are legitimate interpretive translations. The problem lies in their jazzy tone, as though the words were too easily found. The sense that they are *ad hoc* affects my response to the choice of "boy-child" (for *eafera*, 'son, offspring') and also "cub" (for the adjective *geong* 'young'); those words seem chosen mainly for alliteration.

But the most controversial single word in this opening passage is its first: "So." The Old English opens with the interjection "Hwæt!" which is literally "What!" but can be translated as "Listen" or "Hear me!" or, as some wags have recently suggested on the Anglo-Saxon electronic network, "Hey!" or "Yo!" Older translations had "Hark!" and one even had "What ho!" While there is some controversy over whether "Hwæt" is part of the first complete sentence or a free-standing call for attention, what really matters, as these modern alternatives suggest, is that the Modern English choice for this first word will boldly declare the tonal landscape of any translation. Probably "Hwæt" functioned the same way in the Old English, but we don't know its precise tone or social occasion.

Heaney slices through this Gordian knot by the confident substitution of his own sensibility as a modern Irish poet. To my ear, "So." sounds either tight-lipped and almost grim, or else like a buddy-to-buddy acknowledgment. To other American ears (Nicholas Howe, the members of ANSAXNET) it has implied a continuation of some prior speech, or has sounded like a Yiddish greeting, or like urban guy talk ("So. What's up with the Danes of yore?") To Heaney, however, it comes out of his rural family history. "So." is the first declaration of his desire to appropriate the act of translation to his own complicated cultural heritage. The second indication in this passage is his use of the Ulsterism "tholed" for "suffered," which derives from the Old English verb *þolian.*

In his Introduction he sketches a history of his personal relationship to the Old English. After the translation was first commissioned in the mid-1980s, Heaney says he bogged down after getting part way through.

> Even so, I had an instinct that it should not be let go. An understanding I had worked out for myself concerning my own linguistic and literary origins made me reluctant to abandon the task. I had noticed, for example, that without any conscious intent on my part certain lines in the first poem in my first book conformed to the requirements of Anglo-Saxon metrics. These lines were made up of two balancing halves,

> each half containing two stressed syllables—"The spade sinks into gravelly ground: / My father digging. I look down . . ."—and in the case of the second line there was alliteration linking "digging" and "down" across the caesura. Part of me, in other words, had been writing Anglo-Saxon from the start. . . . I suppose all I am saying is that I consider *Beowulf* to be part of my voice-right.

> (*New Verse* xxiii)

This goes down very smoothly, and one needs to stop and reflect on how metaphorical it is to say "Part of me . . . had been writing Anglo-Saxon from the start." This claim and the slippery coinage of "voice-right," playing off "birth-right," show his desire to appropriate *Beowulf* for his own poetic voice. Of course Heaney also knew Irish and "For a long time . . . I tended to conceive of English and Irish as adversarial tongues, as either/or conditions rather than both/and." He had inklings of "the possibility of release from this kind of cultural determination early on" during his first year at Queen's University, Belfast, where through a lecture on the Irish etymology of the English word "whiskey" he glimpsed "some unpartitioned linguistic country, a region where one's language would not be simply a badge of ethnicity or a matter of cultural preference or an official imposition, but an entry into further language" (xxv). Then he discovered *þolian* in the Glossary to Wrenn's edition of *Beowulf* and realized it was

> the word that older and less educated people would have used in the country where I grew up. "They'll just have to learn to thole," my aunt would say about some family who had suffered an unforeseen bereavement. And now suddenly here was "thole" in the official textual world, mediated through the apparatus of a scholarly edition, a little bleeper to remind me that my aunt's language was not just a self-enclosed family possession but an historical heritage. . . .

> (xxv)

But if "þolian had opened my right of way," he still had to find "the note and pitch for the overall music of the work." And that he found close to home:

> a familiar local voice, one that had belonged to relatives of my father, people whom I had once described (punning on their surname) as "big-voiced Scullions" [in the poem **"The Strand at Lough Beg"**].

> I called them "big-voiced" because when the men of the family spoke, the words they uttered came across with a weighty distinctness, phonetic units as separate and defined as delph platters displayed on a dresser shelf. A simple sentence such as "We cut the corn today" took on immense dignity when one of the Scullions spoke it . . . when I came to ask myself how I wanted *Beowulf* to sound in my version, I realized I wanted it to be speakable by one of those relatives. I therefore tried to frame the famous opening lines in cadences that would have suited their voices, but that still echoed with the sound and sense of the Anglo-

Saxon . . . in Hiberno-English Scullionspeak, the particle "so" came naturally to the rescue, because in that idiom "so" operated as an expression that obliterates all previous discourse and narrative, and at the same time functions as an exclamation calling for immediate attention. So, "so" it was.

(xxvii)

The way I read this account, Heaney's reasoning for arriving at this choice is emphatically not "a release from cultural determination" but instead a reinstatement of it. He says he used his Ulsterisms sparingly and only when one "presented itself uncontradictably" (the case in point was "keshes" for *frēcne fen-gelād* 1359a). It is true that there are only about a dozen Ulsterisms in "Heaneywulf." In addition to "hirpling," "keshes," and "tholed," they include "wean" (as a noun), "hoked," "stook," "brehon," "session" (from Irish *seissiún*), "reavers," "bothies," "graith," and "bawn" (a word I will return to). To readers who are not speakers of Irish English, which must be the overwhelming majority of Heaney's audience, these Ulsterisms, occurring as they do throughout the translation, are a signal of cultural difference. They act as little bleepers, to use his own term, reminding you that you are not part of the Ulster English-language community. That's if you have read his writing explaining his intentions for "Heaneywulf." Most readers of the *Norton Anthology* will not have done so, since his Introduction is not printed there. For them, these are incomprehensible words that need to be translated into standard English to be understood, and in fact Heaney has had to gloss most of them in explanatory notes in the anthology.

In his 1999 Saint Jerome Lecture, "The Drag of the Golden Chain," he goes out of his way to approve of that peculiar procedure, giving an intensely personal reason:

What keeps the translator in a state of near (but never quite complete) fulfilment is this tension between the impulse to use the work in its first language as a stimulus and the obligations to give it a fair hearing in the second. . . . there could be no better illustration of the fact of the tension itself than the footnotes in the new volume. At certain points, it is the very translation that has to be translated for the benefit of the worldwide audience of English-speakers to whom the anthology is directed.

(16)

One can only sympathize with the poet's desire to be at once original and faithful, but this is also a self-serving apologia that makes no concessions to the target audience of the translation. It seems that once he decided to push on with his translation he found that he was really writing for himself, and not for the audience of the *Norton Anthology*. A poet *should* write for himself, without a doubt, and to do so may make "Heaneywulf"

more his own work. But this strange dictional coloration does not accurately represent the language of *Beowulf*. There are no Irish words in the Old English poem, and it does a disservice to students to make it look like there is an amalgam of Irish and English in the original poem.

There is yet a deeper difficulty in Heaney's deliberate blending of these different Englishes: it is bad cultural and linguistic history. It does not acknowledge that the varieties of English are shaped by social forces. In his other writings Heaney knows this quite well, and has even noted how the name "Seamus" immediately identified him as a Catholic in Ulster. But in the Saint Jerome Lecture, he would like his posited connections between Old English and the Ulster dialect to work so that when successful "the flash of the right word choice should create a tremor that makes readers feel they exist as 'full strength' members of the language-group" (16). The problem for the majority of his audience is, which language-group is it, Irish or English? It can't be both, given the history of Northern Ireland.

Which brings me back to "bawn." At the end of his Introduction, Heaney says

. . . for reasons of historical suggestiveness, I have in several instances used the word "bawn" to refer to Hrothgar's hall. In Elizabethan English, bawn (from the Irish *bó-dhún,* a fort for cattle) referred specifically to the fortified dwellings that the English planters built in Ireland to keep the dispossessed natives at bay, so it seemed the proper term to apply to the embattled keep where Hrothgar waits and watches. Indeed, every time I read the lovely interlude that tells of the minstrel singing in Heorot just before the first attacks of Grendel, I cannot help thinking of Edmund Spenser in Kilcolman Castle, reading the early cantos of *The Faerie Queene* to Sir Walter Raleigh, just before the Irish would burn the castle and drive Spenser out of Munster back to the Elizabethan court. Putting a bawn into *Beowulf* seems one way for an Irish poet to come to terms with that complex history of conquest and colony, absorption and resistance, integrity and antagonism, a history that has to be clearly acknowledged by all concerned in order to render it ever more "willable forward / again and again and again."

(xxx)

(The last lines are from his own poem **"The Settle Bed,"** which he uses as the epigraph to his translation.) This pleasantly fanciful picture of Spenser in his bawn is deeply confused as an analogy to Hrothgar in Heorot. It makes the historical equation read: the oppressed Irish = Grendel, and the colonizing English = Hrothgar. Surely Heaney can't mean that he takes his Elizabethan Irish forebears to have been monsters from the race of Cain, nor the exploitative English planters to have been wise rulers like Hrothgar. Yet that's the way the analogy works. Putting a "bawn" into his translation is *not* a way "to come to terms" with Irish-English history. Ulsterisms like "bawn" operate polemically in "Heaneywulf." They drive home a sense of difference, if not conflict, between Irish English and other varieties of English. Although he doesn't *mean* them to subvert the Englishness of the poem, that is what they must do, as terms coming from a particular history and geography. Heaney can't avoid history, as much as he might wish, in his Christian pacifism, to "will it forward." To use "bawn" in this context is like using the word "intifada" when translating the Old Testament.

How could a poet whose other work is so alive to political and linguistic tensions in the United Kingdom so badly mistake the effect of using his own local dialect in a different cultural context? How, to ask a related question, can his translation often be quite faithful to the sense, and yet at points be so quirky and overheated? I couldn't find an answer to these questions until I realized that before and since publication he has been working hard to induce readers to accept "Heaneywulf" as actually having realized his own personal intentions. He wants it to be seen as a poem by Seamus Heaney—as a poem *said* by Seamus Heaney—more than as a translation from the Old English, despite his assertions to the contrary. This seems confirmed by the availability of audio cassettes and now a CD, and by the many public readings he has given, where the audience not only hears the story of the Introduction once again but also experiences firsthand a seamless continuity of accent and intonation between his poetic art and his talk about it. When he turns to excerpts from his *Beowulf* after an hour of his other work, they sound very like his own poems.

To put it another way, he is now actively engaged in his own canon formation. He wants to be sure, or so it seems to me, that this big hit, his *Beowulf,* has a place in the already well-developed are of his career, a place that will, with only a little more hindsight smartly applied to it, come to seem inevitable. No poet writing mainly for himself, after all, would want a new volume to be seen as a wild side step in mid-career, or merely an exercise for the left hand. Especially not after the 1995 Nobel Prize. His writing about the genesis of "Heaneywulf" is therefore an example of that kind of fictional myth-making we call autobiography.

The myth begins from a premise of fact: Norton approached him, he agreed to the project, and got started. After that, the hero of the story (the poet as translator is always a potentially doomed hero) enters the Dark Wood of Despair, gets stuck, loses interest. He is ready to abandon the project and hence, by implication, to turn his back on tawdry Academic Commercialism. But then he has an epiphany: he encounters the word *þolian* and connects it with "thole," and a newly green hedge-lane of opportunities and connections opens up before

him, or, more accurately, within him. As he writes in the first of his **"Glanmore Sonnets"**:

> Vowels plough the other: opened ground.

> (***Opened Ground*** 156)

Pulling the Ulsterism "thole" from his memory is like pulling the Sword from the Stone (the genre of the myth is ultimately Romance). Now he sees the analogies between Old English poetry and Ulster dialect, and, more important, between heroism and familial manners in these two violent worlds, and he is ready to go onward and upward. The final completion of the translation is the capstone of the narrative. Upon its publication and astounding success, the myth enters the realm of public discourse where it now has an active life as a sanctioned explanation of his intentions. The sanction of the myth is so strong that some readers see the intentions as actual effects.

There is one final segment of the narrative yet to come, like the prediction of Arthur's Return. It is the realization of "an entry into further language." In his Nobel lecture "Crediting Poetry," Heaney sketches out his heartfelt belief that there is a "wholeness" of language which poetry can confer upon "partition." In that essay, in contrast to his remarks about his translation, he acknowledges the pain of division in Northern Ireland, and he looks to "the local" to energize the future. His great example is Yeats's poetry, which "does what the necessary poetry always does, which is to touch the base of our sympathetic nature while taking in at the same time the unsympathetic reality of the world to which that nature is constantly exposed" (***Opened Ground*** 430). In his 1997 *Paris Review* interview, Heaney was asked if he was now trying "to go back to, not a Wordsworthian innocence, but a place pre-language, pre-nationalism, pre-Catholicism." He replied that he had "a definite desire to write a kind of poem that cannot immediately be ensnared in what they call the 'cultural debate.' This has become one of the binds as well as one of the bonuses for poets in Ireland. Every poem is either enlisted or unmasked for its clandestine political affiliations" (106). Thus, if we could only see his ***Beowulf*** as he does, it would provide a vision of the prelapsarian *Urlage,* a place where poetry tells the truth about both the harshness and the sweetness of reality, a place of wholeness beneath and beyond the brutal Irish-English political conflict and its concomitant linguistic division.

This myth of Heaney's is not new. Many elements of it are present in his earlier writing. In his essay "Feeling into Words" (1974), he approvingly connects, through a poem of W. R. Rodgers, the craggy Anglo-Saxonisms of Hopkins, his own first empowering poetic model, with the harsh consonants of the Ulster accent. And in the 1972 essay "Belfast," he places himself symbolically between the two components of the name of his family's farm, Mossbawn. In 1999 he returned to this name in a poem in the *New Yorker* titled **"Mossbawn."** His affection for and idealized conceptualization of the "bawn," as we see it justified in the **Beowulf** Introduction, have been with him for a long time.

If it is his larger project to inscribe upon English literary culture a poem of his own that is newly "willable forward," I do not believe that he has achieved his intention. However, "Heaneywulf" certainly stands up as one of the better poetic paraphrases of the original, even as it calls attention to itself as his own poem. I predict that, after its day in the sun as a publishing phenomenon, future critics of contemporary poetry will treat it as part of his own corpus, just as he hopes. As a translation of *Beowulf,* it will be assigned out of the *Norton Anthology* by foot-soldiering non-specialists teaching required survey courses. At the same time, other translations of *Beowulf* will continue to appear as the 2000s roll along, and among them English teachers will find equally good translations, of mixed success, to choose from. In turn, those translations will annoy students who have learned Old English and have read the poem in the original. Some few of them will always have the chutzpah to think they have enough poetic talent to render the original into Modern English verse. And *Beowulf* will go on being newly translated for the foreseeable future.

Note

1. Roy Michael Liuzza, *Beowulf: A New Verse Translation* (Peterborough, Ontario: Broadview Press, 2000); Alan Sullivan and Timothy Murphy, *Beowulf,* to be published by Story Line Press; and, still in process at this writing, Timothy Romano's online translation of *Beowulf* at members.dca.net/tim/beowulf_trans.htm.

Works Cited

Chickering, Howell D., Jr. *Beowulf: A Dual-Language Edition.* New York: Anchor Books, 1977.

Crossley-Holland, Kevin. *Beowulf.* New York: Farrar, Straus & Giroux, 1968.

Dobbie, Elliot van Kirk, ed. *Beowulf and Judith.* The Anglo-Saxon Poetic Records, vol. iv. New York: Columbia U P, 1953.

Gussow, Mel. "An Anglo-Saxon Chiller (With an Irish Touch): Seamus Heaney Adds His Voice to 'Beowulf,' *New York Times,* Mar. 29, 2000: B4.

Heaney, Seamus. "Feeling into Words" and "Belfast," in *Preoccupations: Selected Prose 1968-1978.* New York: Farrar, Straus & Giroux, 1980.

———. Interview by Henri Cole, "The Art of Poetry LXXV," *Paris Review,* No. 144 (1997): 106.

———. *Opened Ground: Selected Poems 1966-1996.* New York: Farrar, Straus & Giroux, 1998.

———. "The Drag of the Golden Chain," *Times Literary Supplement,* November 12, 1999: 16.

Howe, Nicholas. "Scullionspeak," *New Republic* 222.9 (Feb. 2000): 32-37.

Hudson, Marc. *Beowulf: A Translation and Commentary.* Lewisburg: Bucknell UP, 1990.

Klaeber, Friedrich, ed. *Beowulf and the Fight at Finnsburg.* 3rd ed. Boston: D. C. Heath, 1950.

Leonard, William Ellery. *Beowulf: A New Verse Translation for Fireside and Classroom.* New York: Century, 1923.

Liuzza, Roy Michael. *Beowulf: A New Verse Translation.* Peterborough, Ontario: Broadview Press, 2000.

Morgan, Edwin. *Beowulf: A Verse Translation into Modern English.* Aldington: Hand and Flower Press, 1952.

Shippey, Tom. "*Beowulf* for the Big-voiced Scullions," *Times Literary Supplement,* Oct. 1, 1999: 9-10.

Wrenn, Charles Leslie, ed. *Beowulf, with the Finnesburg Fragment.* 3rd ed., revised W. F. Bolton. London: Harrap, 1973.

Jason David Hall (essay date summer 2004)

SOURCE: Hall, Jason David. "Rhyme in Seamus Heaney's Group Poems." *ANQ* 17, no. 3 (summer 2004): 55-60.

[*In the following essay, Hall analyzes a particular rhyming technique used frequently by Heaney in the poems written during his participation in Philip Hobsbaum's Belfast Group.*]

From 1963 to 1966 Seamus Heaney participated in Philip Hobsbaum's so-called Belfast Group, a writing workshop based on Hobsbaum's own rigorous methods of practical criticism. This period was crucial to the development of Heaney's poetry, and it is in the poems that issued from these workshops that we can perceive Heaney's signature style beginning to emerge. Although some of the poems from this period of creative exchange have found their way into print, there remains a substantial body of verse that exists only in the cyclostyled sheets that were distributed and critiqued at the Group sessions held in Hobsbaum's Belfast flat. An examination of these sheets reveals a number of significant fluctuations in the structure of Heaney's developing poetry, from his handling of the iambic line to his gravitation toward quatrains and sonnets. But it is

Heaney's management of rhyme in these Group poems that is perhaps most noteworthy, not only because it is here that rhyme first pronounces itself in Heaney's oeuvre but also because the rhymes he chooses are distinctive and indicative of his preference to borrow from the various poetic traditions at hand.

Throughout Heaney's Group sheets, his management of rhyme reveals a preference for imprecise echoes. For example, **"Blackberry-Picking"**—which survived what Michael Longley once called the "kitchen heat" of Group discussion and appeared in Heaney's first book, *Death of a Naturalist* (Ormsby et al. 56)—makes liberal use of original rhymes. Although he prefers to concentrate on the poem's themes rather than its "traditionalist forms," Michael Parker does notice the "decasyllabic lines," which he argues are "arranged in half-rhymed couplets" (67). Heaney's use of the couplet form is fluid and effective. But at least one of the pairings Parker casually identifies as an instance of half-rhyme is rather more peculiar than his assessment suggests. Although alongside the poem's two legitimate instances of full rhyme—*clot/knot* and *rot/not* (lines 3-4, 23-24), the latter of which clinches, a little too firmly, the poem's summary statement on the loss of innocence—Heaney does employ some fairly routine half-rhymes, as Parker acknowledges—*lust for/hunger*; *byre/fur, cache/bush, sour/fair* (7-8, 17-18, 19-20, 21-22)—a rhyming pair such as *sun/ripen*, which occurs in the poem's opening lines, suggests another form of rhyme altogether. At first glance, the two words do not appear to rhyme at all, but because the rest of the poem is plainly written in rhyming couplets, these first lines, one imagines, must conform to that pattern. Admittedly, it does not take much work to hear that there is a phonetic similarity between the two words, but the distribution of stresses presents a problem. The first word, *sun*, a monosyllable, rhymes with the second and unaccented syllable of *ripen*. A similar variety of near rhyme occurs in lines 9 and 10, with *jam-pots* and *boots*. In fact, this unusual near rhyme variant can be found in several of the poems from Heaney's Group sheets. In **"Oh Brave New Bull"**—an early version of *Door into the Dark*'s **"The Outlaw"**—he rhymes *there* and *tether* (3-4); in **"Death of a Naturalist,"** *farting* and *kings* are coupled (29-30); *hill* is paired with *wilful* and *deck-rail* with *flail* in **"National Trust"** (1, 3; 13, 15); *sit* and *armpit,* from **"Men's Confessions"** (2, 4), and, more loosely, *bent* and *children,* from **"In Glenelly Valley"** (8-9), and *embarrass* and *past* from **"The Evangelist"** (14-15), exhibit a similar rhyming property. Other instances could be added to this short list.

The particular type of rhyme outlined immediately above is worth noticing because it has inspired a certain amount of hermeneutic disagreement. For example, in his essay on *Death of a Naturalist,* Roland Mathias calls attention to similar rhymes, which he locates in the poem **"Ancestral Photograph"**:

> One becomes aware, too, of the kinds of rhymes which, though in no sense outrageous, are sufficiently unusual to obviate the smallest feeling of rhythmic dullness and predictability. *Cattle/Wall, then/bargain, still/chronicle, stick/attic*—these help to maintain wayward, stumbling movement in the poem, a movement entirely in keeping with cautious farmers and hesitant cattle.
>
> (21)

One could add the rhyming of *turnip* and *lip,* which occurs in the same poem, and certainly these rhymes do help to "obviate," as Mathias suggests, some of the rather formulaic formalism of Heaney's early poetry.

Bernard O'Donoghue sees something more calculated in such phonetic deviations. He has devoted particular attention to the presence of this unusual kind of rhyme in Heaney's early poetry, and he believes that the reading offered by Mathias is, in fact, a "misreading" (39). O'Donoghue posits that several critics of Heaney's early poetry, including Mathias, have been at pains to explain a "roughness" that he believes they have "mistakenly diagnosed" because of their habit of reading Heaney's formal maneuvers within "an essentially smooth quantitative, rather than accentual, metrical context" (36). Essentially, O'Donoghue's assertion derives from his belief that what has been interpreted by other critics as "roughness" (he dismisses the passage from Mathias's article that I have cited as "well-intentioned but uncomprehending" [39]) is, in fact, evidence of Heaney's employment of "the formalities of Irish poetry in Irish" (28). Specifically, the unusual rhymes appear to O'Donoghue to be an example of a particular feature of *deibidhe,* which, according to Brian Ó Cuív, was one of the two main types of meter in Old and Middle Irish poetry, the other being *rannaigheacht* (276).[1] One characteristic of *deibidhe*—or *deibhidhe,* as Ó Cuív spells it—is the use of a seven-syllable line, something one finds infrequently in Heaney's Group poems. Another feature of *deibidhe* verse, however, is apposite to Heaney's choice of rhymes, as O'Donoghue explains: "One other detail of *deibidhe* practice might be noted; it is the favourite detail of poets from Austin Clarke to [Paul] Muldoon [. . .]. This is the elegant, but initially very rough and un-English, rhyming of a monosyllable with a disyllable stressed on a syllable other than the rhyming one" (31). It is this particular stylistic device, argues O'Donoghue, that is used to "decorative" effect by Heaney early in his poetic career, although his "involvement with Irish-derived metrical schemes," he comments, "has become increasingly slight" (35). O'Donoghue attempts to show this progression by plotting the tapering off of these rhymes in Heaney's first five books (30-39).

O'Donoghue's argument concerning Heaney's importation of devices from Irish poetry is lucid and persuasive. To support his claims, he refers to Michael Parker's critical biography of Heaney, demonstrating how Heaney's familiarity with Daniel Corkery's *The Hidden Ireland* (1925), which discusses and provides examples of *deibidhe* rhyme, coincides with these formal innovations (38). O'Donoghue's reading also is sensitive in that it attempts to address what he feels to be honest misunderstandings of Heaney's early formal practices. By identifying formal features borrowed from Irish poetry, O'Donoghue challenges readings that insist on finding something inept or gauche about Heaney's early formalism. But as O'Donoghue himself points out, "[t]he enterprise of writing or interpreting the prosodic effects of one language or dialect in another is a dangerous one" (34). Although it may be possible that Heaney did in fact have *deibidhe* devices in mind, it remains true that some of Heaney's Group poems suggest that his use of *deibidhe* rhyme may not have been as calculated, or possibly as fluent, as O'Donoghue insists. One example is **"Personal Helicon,"** another of Heaney's Group poems to find its way into ***Death of a Naturalist.*** It is dedicated to Michael Longley—possibly an ironic gesture, as Longley and Derek Mahon displayed "a good deal of the jocose" concerning Heaney's "rural elements" (Haffenden 28), which this poem certainly displays. Taken at face value, however, the dedication could be a discreet acknowledgment of the importance of rhyme to both poets (**"Personal Helicon"** is written in alternating quatrains, a form that Longley employs frequently in his Group poetry). Heaney's poem, however, does not exhibit Longley's preference for true rhymes. The true rhymes Heaney does employ (*wells/smells, call/tall, slime/rhyme* [lines 1, 3; 13, 15; 17, 19]) occur alongside instances of slant rhyme, *deibidhe* rhyme (*bucket/it* [6, 8]), and other rhymes that appear to belong to no recognizable tradition—Irish or English. The rhymes *aquarium/bottom* and *one/reflection* (10, 12; 14, 16) are similar to *deibidhe* rhyme in that rhyming syllables are unstressed in one of the rhyming words, but they are certainly not examples of *deibidhe* in its pure form. Here Heaney could be misusing *deibidhe* or simply delighting in the possibilities afforded by imprecise echoes.

Heaney's comments to Karl Miller diminish the security of O'Donoghue's reading. When Miller prompts Heaney concerning the "curiosity about your relation to Gaelic poetry—about certain rhyming practices, for example, which may have been derived from Gaelic literature, but which may also owe something to Irish writers of English like Austin Clarke," he must have O'Donoghue's discussion of *deibidhe* in mind. Heaney responds:

> Nowadays [1999-2000] I'm more conscious of metrical rhyming considerations than I was at the beginning. In the beginning, I was for ever displacing myself from regularity and correctness. [. . .] I always liked a down-turn, a clipping-off rather than a lifting-up, something un-Anglican, if you know what I mean. And that was audible in the Austin Clarke of *Pilgrimage* and in some Irish poems I knew by heart at school, like Sean O'Coilean's "Lament for Timoleague." Still, *I never made a systematic study of Irish language metrics, even though I was responsive to what I took to be a reined-in quality in many of the stanza forms.*

(Miller 39; emphasis added)

Elsewhere, Heaney has discussed a renewed interest in Irish metrics, but he makes clear that in his early verse he resisted introducing these rhythmic patterns: "I do things now metrically that I wouldn't have done twenty-five years ago because in those days I thought some meters were too folksy" (Hass and Heaney 23).

If Heaney did draw on his knowledge of Irish prosody, then he was not alone. The classical refinement of Michael Longley's Group poems admits nearly as many occurrences of what O'Donoghue labels *deibidhe* as one finds in Heaney's sheets. Throughout Longley's Group sheets are scattered rhymes like *survives/ perspectives, brainstorm/home* (**"Dr. Johnson on the Hebrides"** [lines 10, 12; 13-14]); *bay/away/holiday, floor/downpour/shore* (**"Leaving Inishmore"** [6, 8, 10; 11, 13, 15]); *age/advantage/camouflage* (**"Camouflage"** [19, 21, 23]); *numskulled/skilled* (**"Persephone"** [5-6]); *birthmark/dark, lexicon/icon* (**"To Derek Mahon"** [1, 3; 8, 11]); *eccentric/Greek* (**"A Working Holiday"** [9, 11]); *beck/slapstick, trail/camel, be/thirsty* (**"Words for Jazz Perhaps"** [3, 5; 7, 9; 11, 13]); *since/silence* (**"Her Mime of the Lame Seagull"** [9, 12]); and *flotsam/calm* (**"Circe"** [13, 15]). Even Philip Hobsbaum's poems "Derry City" and "Undergraduate Party" employ this species of rhyme: *walls/Guildhall* (1, 3) and *eyes/notices* (9, 11), respectively. The conspicuous abundance of such an unusual kind of rhyme leads me to believe that it is probable that Heaney, although perhaps aware of the existence of Irish rhyming conventions, may simply have been following the lead of more experienced poets. It is even possible that Heaney's affinity for so-called *deibidhe* rhymes results from his familiarity with Hughes's poetry, particularly *Lupercal*, which, as Michael Parker reminds us, he had been reading at the time (44). *Lupercal* is replete with such rhymes: *undone/ abandon* ("Things Present" [lines 1-2]); *something/bring* ("Historian" [18, 20]); *press/darkness, toadstools/souls* and *No/hollow* ("Nicholas Ferrer" [3-4; 13, 16; 14-15]); *cats/inherits* and *bottom/home* ("Of Cats" [1, 3; 17, 19]); *elsewhere/there* ("The Voyage" [6, 8]); and *nowhere/chair* ("An Otter" [38, 40]).[2]

Hughes was fond of rough rhymes, as he was of rough terrain, but there is no reason to believe that he borrowed devices from poetry written in Irish. Furthermore, these unusual rhymes are not, as O'Donoghue suggests, "un-English." It is more likely that they belong firmly to English tradition, however unusual and foreign they might seem. In fact, the editors of the *New Princeton Encyclopedia of Poetry and Poetics* not only acknowledge such a distinctive species of rhyme but also reveal that it has a well-founded history of usage in English verse:

> Rhyming masculine with feminine words, i.e. a stressed monosyllable with a disyllable the rhyming syllable of which is unstressed (e.g. *sing/loving, free/crazy, afraid/decade*) Tatlock called "hermaphrodite" r[hyme . . .]. Others have called it "apocopated" or "stressed-unstressed" r[hyme]; it was popular in the 16th-17th c[enturie]s and is used extensively by Donne and latterly by Pound (*Hugh Selwyn Mauberley*).
>
> (Preminger and Brogan 1055)

Given Heaney's attraction to Hughes and his appreciation for "the rich stratifications of the English language itself" (*Preoccupations* 46), it is likely that he would be familiar with such a rich, and English, tradition of variant rhyme.

Like Heaney's burgeoning metrics, which begin to exert themselves during this period, his rhyme signifies his decision to engage with the mechanics of English verse. Also like his metrics, Heaney's rhyme, as employed in his Group poems, signifies the way in which he will accommodate that convention. Although Heaney demonstrates an inclination toward regular form, both his metrical and his rhyming tendencies reveal an antagonistic relationship with English prosody. Rhyme, although increasingly employed, is frequently corrupted. Often true rhyme is outnumbered by more unorthodox echoes, and the variant rhymes discussed immediately above are extreme examples. For O'Donoghue, the identification of *deibidhe* rhyme is part of his reading of Heaney's antagonism to normative form as part of the complicated process of negotiation between Irish and English poetic discourses, in which stylistic features play a primary role in signifying the preoccupation that Heaney feels about his cultural hybridity. Much of the first chapter of O'Donoghue's book is devoted to just such an analysis. However, O'Donoghue's reading may exaggerate the subversive implications of Heaney's early formal maneuvers, lending the unusual rhymes that are scattered throughout Heaney's Group sheets the political perspicuity one generally associates with the linguistic insurgence found in the place-name poems of Heaney's third book, **Wintering Out** (1972). Poems in that volume do borrow devices from the Irish poetic tradition, specifically the convention of *dinnseanchas*. But although at points throughout his career Heaney uses formal devices to signify insurgence, the politicization of form will tend to take other, more direct, approaches.

Notes

1. Offering a list of certain "rules" that govern *deibidhe*, Ó Cuív calls attention to the rhyme characteristic, which is slightly stricter than what O'Donoghue describes: "the final word in *b* must have one syllable more than the final word in *a*, and the final word in *a* must make perfect rime with the unstressed syllable(s) of the final word in *b*; similarly in the case of *c* and *d* [. . .]" (277).

2. This discussion does not permit an extended look at Hughes's use of such rhymes. It is worth noting, however, that similar rhymes occur with even more frequency in Hughes's first book *The Hawk in the Rain* (1957).

Works Cited

Haffenden, John. "Meeting Seamus Heaney." *London Magazine* 19.3 (1979): 5-28.

Hass, Robert, and Seamus Heaney. *Sounding Lines: The Art of Translating Poetry.* Occasional Papers Ser. 20. Berkeley: The Regents of the University of California and the Doreen B. Townsend Center for the Humanities, 2000.

Heaney, Seamus, Group Sheets 1-6. Belfast Group Papers. Special Collections, Robert W. Woodruff Lib., Emory University, Atlanta.

————. *Preoccupations: Selected Prose 1968-1978.* Boston: Faber, 1980.

Hobsbaum, Philip. Group Sheets. Philip Hobsbaum Papers. Special Collections, Robert W. Woodruff Lib., Emory University, Atlanta.

Hughes, Ted. *Lupercal.* London: Faber, 1960.

Longley, Michael. Group Sheets. Michael Longley Papers. Special Collections, Robert W. Woodruff Lib., Emory University, Atlanta.

Mathias, Roland. "Death of a Naturalist." *The Art of Seamus Heaney.* 2nd ed. Ed. Tony Curtis, Mid Glamorgan: Poetry Wales P, 1985. 11-25.

Miller, Karl. *Seamus Heaney in Conversation with Karl Miller.* London: Between the Lines, 2000.

Ó Cuív, Brian. "Some Developments in Irish Metrics." *Éigse* 12 (1968): 273-90.

O'Donoghue, Bernard. *Seamus Heaney and the Language of Poetry.* Hemel Hempstead: Harvester Wheatsheaf, 1994.

Ormsby, Frank, et al. "The Belfast Group: A Symposium." *Honest Ulsterman* 53 (1976): 53-62.

Parker, Michael. *Seamus Heaney: The Making of the Poet.* London: Macmillan, 1993.

Preminger, Alex, and T. V. F. Brogan, eds. *The New Princeton Encyclopedia of Poetry and Poetics.* Princeton: Princeton UP, 1993.

Jonathan Allison (essay date 2005)

SOURCE: Allison, Jonathan. "'Friendship's Garland' and the Manuscripts of Seamus Heaney's 'Fosterage.'" *Yearbook of English Studies* 35 (2005): 58-71.

[*In the following essay, Allison gives a detailed analysis of unpublished manuscript drafts for the poem "Fosterage," published in the 1975 volume* North.]

1. The Poem as Process

The directors of Special Collections and Archives at Robert W. Woodruff Library (Emory University) have made a number of important acquisitions in recent years in the field of contemporary poetry, including the papers of postwar Irish authors.[1] Anecdotal evidence alone would suggest that Woodruff is becoming a popular destination for research students in the UK and Ireland interested in contemporary Irish writing.[2] This activity is likely to deepen interest generally in contemporary Irish manuscript sources and increase attention on two key areas: writing-as-process, and biography. Authors' drafts show how the finished work emerges from a series of versions; personal papers may throw light on the author's private life, warts and all.

Apparently, biography has eternal appeal, but manuscript study has not invariably been a primary focus for students of contemporary poetry, although central to a particular sort of literary and textual scholarship. There are several reasons for this. In the first place, writing on contemporary poetry tends to focus on exploring the credentials of contemporary authors to be considered interesting or 'major', or on the socio-political 'relevance' of the writing. Commonly, therefore, critical attention will fall on reception, influence, biography, social significance, and political contexts and to a lesser extent on aesthetic form. Therefore, despite successive waves of theoretical 'turns' over the last thirty years, contemporary critics do not invariably leap at the opportunity of studying manuscripts. Partly this is due to the general shifting of attention from the author as the source of meaning towards the reader and reader-based meanings. Having said that, editors continue to seek final authorial intentions in order to establish stable (or at least defensible) primary texts, even if those intentions are elusive or, in some celebrated cases, impossible to determine.[3] Many critics see their work in terms of reading 'definitive' printed texts whose textual stability seems guaranteed by the fact that living authors have authorized (actively or passively) the circulating texts.

Also, manuscripts of contemporary authors tend to be in private hands; in some cases they are available but nevertheless regarded as matter for future generations to examine. There are exceptions to this rule, of course.

It could be argued that creative writing workshops sometimes endorse the study of manuscript drafts to emphasize the idea of writing as a process. This can be a useful lesson to learn and can have the effect of demystifying the aura of solitary genius surrounding highly valued artworks. Furthermore, the study of Modernist authors such as Eliot and Yeats has for many years been enriched by studying manuscript material reproduced in T. S. Eliot's *Waste Land Manuscripts,* for example, Curtis B. Bradford's *Yeats at Work,* or Jon Stallworthy's, *Between the Lines: Yeats's Poetry in the Making.* Volumes in the Cornell Yeats and Cornell Wordsworth series provide reproductions and detailed transcriptions of manuscript material for those inclined to meet the challenge they represent. The *Norton Anthology of Poetry,* a key teaching text in American undergraduate classrooms and elsewhere, has long had an appendix on 'the poem in process', printing well-known poems in juxtaposition with earlier drafts.

The manuscript drafts of Seamus Heaney's poem **'Fosterage'** are held in the Heaney collection (MSS 653, Box 2, Folder 5) at Woodruff Library. Whereas there are other interesting items in MSS 653, there are few drafts of poems, hence the **'Fosterage'** cluster has particular significance. Heaney has made a recent gift of his papers to the Woodruff Library (MSS 960), but it would appear that these are mostly letters, not drafts.[4] Extensive study of Heaney's manuscript drafts therefore must remain a distant prospect, but will surely occur during the next several decades and presumably by 2039, the Heaney centenary year. (Given the pace of technological change in the publishing industry, manuscript collections such as this may eventually be available in an electronic medium.) What I propose to do here is offer a brief overview of the drafts, and to reprint two penultimate drafts, with a view to following the trail of intentions set in motion during final composition, and throwing light on the choices made by the author. As long as authorial intentions are of interest, drafts will be important, as a record of the process by which the finally intended ('definitive') artwork is crafted, an inventory of authorial decisions and excisions, an archive of the author's thoughts during composition.[5]

2. 'Fosterage' and 'Singing School'

'Fosterage', number 5 in the six-part sequence of related lyrics titled **'Singing School',** first appeared in *North* (1975) and is dedicated to Irish novelist Michael McLaverty, who was Headmaster of St Thomas's Intermediate School, Belfast, when Heaney taught there in 1962-63. The poem has not been anthologized (editors favour number 6 in the series, **'Exposure'**) but has been reprinted in *Selected Poems 1965-1975* (1980), *New Selected Poems 1966-1987* (1990), and *Opened Ground: Selected Poems 1966-1996* (2002), suggesting the poet's sense of the significance of this individual lyric and of the sequence.[6] Critics of *North* have traditionally preferred the mythopoeic first part to the more journalistic second part of the volume, and 'Fosterage' has tended to get short shrift in favour of the watershed poem, **'Exposure',** and the opening poem of the sequence, **'The Ministry of Fear'.** Elmer Andrews, for example, dismisses the poem as 'far from being among Heaney's best'.[7]

'Fosterage' consists of sixteen lines, yet the drafts show that it is the result of a longer poem, which at one point was sixty-three lines in length. The drafts are not dated, but were probably composed in 1973 or 1974.[8] The Emory archive includes ten pages (both manuscript and corrected typescript), which constitute Heaney's twelve working drafts, variously titled **'Stylist'** (A4, A5), **'To Michael McLaverty'** (A8, B1, B2), and **'Friendship's Garland'** (B3). Here is a complete list of contents:

A: Untitled. The veins bulge in his very fountain pen [2 stanzas / 11 lines]

A2: Untitled. Your ear was schooled upon your father's pillow [3 stanzas / 16 lines]

A3: Unititled. Too righteous by half: A writer's trick [2 stanzas / 8 lines]

A4: STYLIST [4 stanzas / 19 lines]

A5: STYLIST [1 stanza / 14 lines]. Typescript [TS]

A6: Untitled. We were to go where your uncle slaughtered [1 stanza / 9 lines]

A7: Untitled. Today they'd smash into the lighthouse glass [3 stanzas / 22 lines]

A8: TO MICHAEL McLAVERTY [3 stanzas / 42 lines] TS

A9: Untitled. Try not to end up measuring your spits [1 stanza / 16 lines]

B1: TO MICHAEL McLAVERTY [4 stanzas / 63 lines] TS

B2: TO MICHAEL McLAVERTY [3 stanzas / 43 lines] TS

B3: FRIENDSHIP'S GARLAND [5 stanzas / 40 lines] TS[9]

These drafts indicate the range of images and ideas that underlie **'Fosterage',** constituting a ghostly presence in the poem, a series of intentions revised and suppressed during composition. If there is no doubt that **'Fosterage'** reflects the author's final intentions, these can be more fully appreciated by comparison and contrast with the other intentions set in motion and ultimately rejected during the process.

Each poem in the semi-autobiographical series **'Singing School'** is associated with a particular period in the poet's life; they may be said to constitute a lyric

exploration of the growth of the poet's mind: childhood in the 1940s, school in the 1950s, an influential encounter in 1962, the 'Troubles' in the mid- and late 1960s. The final poem, **'Exposure',** dramatizes a moment of self-reflection in the early 1970s. An allusive poetic sequence, its title refers to Yeats's 'Sailing to Byzantium', in which the poet vows to study the magnificent 'monuments' of literary and artistic tradition, suggesting a Yeatsian commitment to study and meditation as part of the poetic vocation. ('Nor is there singing school but studying | Monuments of its own magnificence', in Yeats's words.) One of the poem's epigraphs is taken from Wordsworth's *The Prelude*: 'Fostered alike by beauty and by fear'. Here is one source of the title of the fifth lyric, but the Burkean sublime—inspiring both beauty and fear—is invoked at various points throughout the sequence, not least in the first poem, **'The Ministry of Fear'.** That poem, set in the 1950s, recalls the experience of boarding school, the onset of puberty and early courtship, and the oppressive sectarianism of an Ulster Catholic childhood. Fear and trepidation are the dominant emotions of **'A Constable Calls',** set in the 1940s, in which the child's perceptions of a policeman's visit are faithfully recalled. The final line, in which the policeman's bicycle sounds 'tick, tick, tick', has suggested to several critics the ominous sound of a time-bomb, building slowly towards explosion. On the other hand, it may suggest the passing of time and the maturation of the subject, reminiscent of the aural imagery at the end of Chapter 1 of Joyce's *Portrait of the Artist as a Young Man*: 'pick, pack, pock, puck: like drops of water in a fountain falling softly in the brimming bowl'.[10]

That image of regular beating is echoed at the end of **'Orange Drums, Tyrone, 1966',** in which the caricatured Orangeman beats a Lambeg drum rhythmically: 'The air is pounding like a stethoscope.' In **'Summer 1969',** the speaker is in Spain, reading the life of Joyce, while the 'battle of the Bogside' rages in Derry. Considering the advice of a friend to go home, to 'try to touch the people', and bearing in mind the examples of Lorca and Goya, he thinks about the role of the artist at times of political upheaval. Should he emulate Goya, who 'painted with his fists and elbows, flourished | The stained cape of his heart as history charged'? The poem implicitly raises questions about the roles of art and the artist which are further explored in **'Fosterage'** and **'Exposure'.** It is unclear whether **'Fosterage'** was written specifically to be placed within **'Singing School',** though we might come closer to an answer by examining all the drafts of each poem in the sequence. It is possible that it was written as a longer poem to stand on its own: the expansiveness of some of the drafts would support this claim. In its final form, however, it is appropriate to the sequence, in terms of its announcement of its own historicity, and in terms of the themes of literary style and artistic labour which it explores.[11]

The central encounter in **'Fosterage'** takes place in Belfast in 1962, a fruitful year for the poet and, as Michael Parker has shown, a watershed moment in his development.[12] Evidently, McLaverty had an influence on the poet at this stage, lending books and recommending authors, including Katherine Mansfield, Hopkins, and Kavanagh. Heaney began to see himself earnestly as a poet in that year: an early poem, **'Tractors',** appeared in the *Belfast Telegraph* in November 1962, followed by **'Turkeys Observed'** in December and **'Mid Term Break'** (in *Kilkenny Magazine*) the following spring. In October 1962 he met Marie Heaney, his future wife and 'reader over his shoulder'. He also enrolled that year for postgraduate studies at Queen's, focusing on Wordsworth's theories of education (he had just completed a thesis at St Joseph's College of Education, on Northern Irish literary journals.) Famously, the first meeting of Philip Hobsbaum's Belfast 'Group' took place in November 1963.

'Description is revelation!': this excited, opening gambit indicates that the relationship between style and insight or visionary possibility will be central to this lyric, and it suggests a response to questions raised in the previous poem about the role of poetry and the proper conduct of the writer.[13] After the questions raised in **'Summer, 1969'**, the poet of **'Fosterage'** casts his mind back seven years, to 1962, though in the next poem (**'Exposure'**) he will shuttle forward again, to the 1970s. He portrays himself in **'Fosterage'** as the youthful writer, 'newly cubbed in language'. McLaverty urges the poet to be intellectually independent ('Go your own way'), persuading him to have trust in himself, much as the voice of the longship in **'North'** urged him to 'keep your eye clear', or as James Joyce in **'Station Island'** persuaded him to go it alone, to 'strike your note'.[14] As such, the poem is one of a small cluster of 'advice' or 'mentor' poems in which the poet takes stock of his direction by dramatizing a situation of receiving wise counsel. Voicing the older man's advice to pay attention to intimate detail and to avoid overstatement ('don't have the veins bulging in your biro') provides a method by which the poet can express his own poetic values, while also showing their provenance. McLaverty was particularly fond of Chekhov, invoked here: the phrase 'note of exile' is Chekhovian, but may be an adaptation by McLaverty.[15] However, the source of the line *I will tell | How the laundry basket squeaked'* is clearly an entry in Katherine Mansfield's journal, 22 January 1916. This was written in Bandol, South of France, where Mansfield and John Middleton Murray had fled the previous October upon hearing that her brother, Leslie Heron Beauchamp ('Chummie'), had been killed in action:

> Ah, the people—the people we loved there—of them, too, I want to write. Another 'debt of love'. Oh, I want for one moment to make our undiscovered country leap

into the eyes of the Old World. It must be mysterious, as though floating. It must take the breath. It must be 'one of those islands . . .' [*sic*] I shall tell everything, even of how the laundry basket squeaked at 75. But all must be told with a sense of mystery, a radiance, an afterglow, because you, my little sun of it, are set. You have dropped over the dazzling brim of the world. Now I must play my part.

> Then I want to write poetry. I feel always trembling on the brink of poetry. The almond tree, the birds, the little wood where you are, the flowers you do not see, the open window out of which I lean and dream that you are against my shoulder, and the times that your photograph 'looks sad'. But especially I want to write a kind of long elegy to you . . . perhaps not in poetry. Nor perhaps in prose. Almost certainly in a kind of *special prose.*[16]

Asking why she wants to write, and how ('Now, really, what is it that I do want to write?'), she determines to be wide-ranging and inclusive—including even the squeak of 'the laundry-basket'—and to offer recollections of her native country which will entail remembrance of her brother and the life they shared there. Partly, she wants to write on behalf of New Zealand—'to make our undiscovered country leap into the eyes of the Old World'—and partly to write a prose elegy for her brother. Primarily, she thinks of writing prose, but what makes it particularly relevant to Heaney's purposes is Mansfield's interest in writing a kind of prose poem ('mysterious, as though floating'), brimming with 'radiance'. Heaney seems in two minds about the visionary potential of such a radiant poetic, as suggested by the warning to avoid vein-bulging overstatement, balanced against the recognition that descriptive writing may lead to 'revelation' and all that entails. In a later poem, **'Fosterling'**, Heaney would contrast a merely descriptive poetic ('the doldrums of what happens') with a more expansive, imaginative mode associated with later middle age ('Me waiting until I was nearly fifty | To credit marvels').[17] In **'Fosterage'**, however, description is seen as the empowering agent of revelation, insight, and poetic truth.

3. Drafts A–A9

During the course of these dozen drafts, Heaney writes seven stanzas of varying lengths, and each draft of the poem offers a different permutation and rewriting of those stanzas. (The following titles are mine, not the author's, and are used for convenience only.) They are: (1) Royal Avenue stanza (meeting McLaverty in Belfast); (2) Street Corner stanza (McLaverty's warning to his pupils); (3) Ballymurphy stanza (violence in West Belfast); (4) Hopkins stanza (McLaverty's admiration for Hopkins); (5) St John's Point stanza (with McLaverty in Donegal); (6) Rosary Beads stanza (prayers for the dying); (7) Cavehill stanza (Cavehill and Tollund Man). **'Fosterage'** comprises elements of only two of these: the Royal Avenue and Hopkins stanzas. The longest version of the poem is B1: 'To Michael McLaverty' (63 lines), which gives some idea of the amount of material dispensed with and (to the best of my knowledge) never recycled.

In A, the earliest version of the Royal Avenue stanza, Heaney introduces a series of images that will recur over the series: the meeting in Royal Avenue, the bulging fountain pen, and McLaverty's father's revolver hidden beneath his pillow (which is cut from **'Fosterage'**). Heaney addresses the older man as 'dear stylist', and introduces the phrase 'Description is revelation', which survives all revisions. A2 opens with the fearful image of the revolver under the pillow: 'Your ear was schooled upon your father's pillow.' This is an early version of the Ballymurphy stanza, which includes images of gunfire in Ballymurphy and burning buses near the Bog Meadows (Falls Road). Both A2 and A3 close with the pronouncement 'Dives rides again', ironically alluding to Max Brand's popular western, *Destry Rides Again,* and to the biblical Dives, the rich man in Hell (Luke 16. 19-31), whom Heaney dubs 'hoarder of common ground' in his poem **'Gifts of Rain'.**[18]

Version A4 brings together the Royal Avenue and Ballymurphy stanzas. The concern with style has been foregrounded, as the new title ('STYLIST') suggests. The poem is now nineteen lines in length (stanza one includes ten lines) and resembles **'Fosterage'**, although there are references to Chekhov and Gorki, later deleted. McLaverty says: 'Don't | Have the veins bulging in your fountain pen', a version of which survives the final cut. The subsequent imagery of gunfire and burning buses in Ballymurphy reflects the contemporary 'Troubles' in Belfast, whereas the images of the father's revolver and other memories of the 1920s echo the setting of McLaverty's novel *Call My Brother Back,* set at the time of Partition. In version A5 (the first typescript draft), the scene-setting line 'a Saturday afternoon' is introduced, which survives the final cut. The words 'dear stylist' have been dropped, and the earlier line 'I caught from you who toed the stylist's line' has been replaced by a simpler rhetorical question: 'How toe the stylist's line?' Version A6 introduces the St John's Point stanza, beginning: 'We were to go where your uncle slaughtered | Trees.' It is used in A8 (stanza 2), and B1 (stanza 3), but finally dropped. It includes references to the 'plainsong of the Irish Sea', to 'vespers in our hearts', and to the daughters of the children of Lir.

Version A7 (which may have been written as a continuation of A6) opens with the earliest version of the Cavehill stanza, including a memorable line which recurs in later drafts (A8, B1, B2, B3): 'The Cavehill's profile is the Tollund Man's.' This clearly links the interests of this poem with two other poems of the period, **'The Betrothal of Cavehill'** and **'The Tollund Man'.** The

title of A8—**'TO MICHAEL McLAVERTY'**—is retained in B1 and B2, and finally becomes the dedication of **'Fosterage'.** A8 is only the second typescript draft, consisting of the Royal Avenue and Ballymurphy stanzas combined (fourteen lines); the St John's Point and Cavehill stanzas combined (fourteen lines); and a combination of the Rosary Beads and Hopkins stanzas (fourteen lines). A9 is a reworking of the Street Corner stanza only, emphasizing the vandalism of the pupils and the use of corporal punishment at the school, in which the Vice-Principal was 'the Wyatt Earp of Ballymurphy'.

4. DRAFTS B1-B3

By the time Heaney writes his most expansive draft, B1 (**'TO MICHAEL McLAVERTY'**) (sixty-three lines— four fourteen-line stanzas in typescript, plus seven manuscript lines), he has already experimented with versions of all seven stanzas, and produced variants of most of them. B1 comprises the Street Corner stanza (st. 1); the Royal Avenue and Ballymurphy stanzas (st. 2); and a long verse paragraph (st. 3) combining the St John's Point, Cave Hill, Rosary Beads, and Hopkins stanzas. The final lines of this version allude to McLaverty's novel, *Call My Brother Back,* with reference to oil lamps on Rathlin Island (scene of Part I of that novel) and the following, from the novel's final sentence: 'A rickle of bones falling dead in York Street.' (These words close McLaverty's novel, but they have appeared earlier, when a street orator satirizes the indifference of the middle classes to the suffering of the poor in riot-torn Belfast in the early 1920s.)[19]

The next version, B2 (**'TO MICHAEL McLAVERTY'**) consists of three fourteen-line stanzas and is twenty lines shorter than B1, since the St John's Point stanza (lines 30-43) has been dropped. I reprint B2 in its entirety below. Please note that material within square brackets was deleted by the author.

"To Michael McLaverty" (B2)

I

"Try not to end up measuring your spits
At a street corner." The class would giggle.
"Mr Heaney, when you see a rugby team
Wouldn't you know to look at them the boys
Who loved poetry?" Then, <u>sotto voce,</u>
"Read them plenty of poems. Read them John Clare.
And listen, you yourself, keep at Shakespeare.
Reading the newspapers will spoil your style."
The boys would rip out phone-boxes, break in
Some evenings to shit on desks and tear
The art-work into ribbons. [We] failed there.
You, at least, played tunes to empty pockets,
A descant on the leather's metronome.
And "Go your own way," you said, "do your own
    work."

II

"Description is revelation": Royal
Avenue, Belfast, 1962,
A Saturday afternoon, [eager] glad to meet
Me, newly cubbed To [lick the] cubs [of] in language,
   you gripped
My elbow: "You should 'tell how the laundry
Basket squeaked at No. 64'."
But always beware exaggeration.
"Don't have the veins bulging in your biro."
I've since heard gunfire in Ballymurphy
And watched across the gulf of the Bog Meadows
The buses burning. Shall beauty hold its plea?
"Oil lamps warming the windows in Rathlin . . .
A rusty tin in the fork of a thorn bush . . .
A rickle of bones falling dead in York Street."

[Rosary beads clicking on the bedhead,
Prayers for the dying in the lower room
And Our Lady of Perpetual Succour,
The Mother of Sorrows and Our Lady
Of the Seven Dolours invoked with love.
Blood in the pigeon-loft, the tenders
Whining into the unlit street, votive
Gules to the Sacred Heart of Jesus:
It is the blight that we were born of.]

III

"Poor Hopkins", you would sigh. I have the Notebooks
You gave me, underlined, your buckled self
Obeisant to his pain. I can find
The lineaments of patience everywhere.
[The Cavehill's profile is the Tollund Man's.]

'To Michael McLaverty'. Copyright © Seamus Heaney.

Stanza 1 (Street Corner stanza) ends by describing the vandalism of the pupils at St Thomas's School. On this issue, the somewhat remorseful speaker admits: 'We failed there.' This was dropped from B3, but McLaverty's advice to be artistically independent ('Go your own way') survives later cuts. Allusions to McLaverty's novel in stanza 2 (Bog Meadows, oil lamps, 'bones in York Street') make it from B1 to B2, but are dropped in B3. The third stanza of B2 (Rosary Beads stanza) invokes the imagery of Roman Catholic prayer for the dying. The focus lies on the pain and pathos of bereavement and Christ's suffering, which is somehow linked to the image of the British Army 'tenders | Whining into the unlit street' (another unsettling image from McLaverty's novel, but with obvious relevance to 1970s West Belfast). Each of these sections (the vandals section of stanza 1; the Ballymurphy section in stanza 2; the Rosary Beads section in stanza 3) was cut from B3, **'Friendship's Garland'.**

The title of B3 alludes to Matthew Arnold's satirical work of that name, a collection of letters to the *Pall Mall Gazette* penned by Arnold and a fictional German professor, the hugely pompous Arminius (Herman) von Thunder-ten-Tronckh.[20] In a major critique of contempo-rary English culture, Arnold and Arminius debate a wide range of issues, including the question of national character, the prevalence of English philistinism, and the compulsory education of children of all classes. In this strange, witty attack on British and German national chauvinism, Arnold castigates the moral, cultural, and intellectual limitations of the English middle classes. Although Heaney and McLaverty make an unlikely Arnold and Arminius, Heaney expresses in his drafts an interest in the relationship between education and social order. Furthermore, as Arminius assails the British press, so McLaverty dismisses the reading of newspapers (which 'will spoil your style'). In Arnold's letters on education, in his discussion of public order, civil society, and education, we find a certain relevance to this poem of culture and anarchy in the schoolroom.

On a more immediate level, the poem is a garland of McLaverty's *bons mots* and a souvenir of their friendship. However, one can see why Heaney dropped this rather over-literary and Arnoldian title, which was perhaps too acutely focused on the idea of friendship, rather than on the aesthetic advice which the friend conveys. The poem as it finally stands ('**Fosterage**'), based as it is on the Royal Avenue stanza, is the poet's tribute to a certain writerly influence, and to a set of aesthetic principles. I reprint B3 in its entirety. Again, material within square brackets was deleted by the author.

"Friendship's Garland" (B3)

i

"Try not to end up measuring your spits
At a street corner." The class would giggle.
"Mr Heaney, when you see a rugby team
Wouldn't you know to look at them the boys
Who loved poetry?" Then, sotto voce,
"Read them plenty of poems. Read them John Clare.
And listen, you yourself, keep at Shakespeare.
Reading the newspapers will spoil your style."

ii

"Description is revelation": Royal
Avenue, Belfast, 1962,
A Saturday afternoon, eager glad to meet
Me, newly cubbed in language [*sic*], you gripped
My elbow. ["You should 'tell how the laundry
Basket squeaked at NO. 64'."]
But always beware exaggeration.
"Don't have the veins bulging in your biro."

iii

When I heard [the] gunfire in Ballymurphy
And watched across the gulf of the Bog Meadows
The buses burning. [I] remembered
Blood in the pigeon-loft, the [tenders] whining tenders,
[Whining into the unlit street, votive
Gules to the Sacred Heart of Jesus,]

Your father coming and going, [the] his gun
Under [Beneath] the pillow that you shared with him.

II

iv

"Poor Hopkins", you would sigh. I have the <u>Notebooks</u>
You gave me, underlined, your buckled self
Obeisant to his pain. You discern[ed]
The lineaments of patience everywhere.
[The Cavehill's profile is the Tollund Man's.]

III

["Read Clare. Read Edward Thomas
"That note of exile". We made a progress]
     Listen, Go your own way.
   Do your own work. Remember
   Katherine Mansfield—I will tell
   How the laundry basket squeaked . . . that note of
   exile."
     [But] to hell with [faking it.] Overstatement.
     "Don't
     And then: "Poor Hopkins.
[Of the strand] at
You talked about your uncle "slaughtering".
Trees—his verb delighted you—that time
We [stepped] the strand at St. J.P.

'Friendship's Garland'. Copyright © Seamus Heaney.

Most of **'Friendship's Garland'** was subsequently deleted by the author, including the Street corner, Ballymurphy and Hopkins stanzas. Elements from the latter were joined to the Royal Avenue stanza to produce **'Fosterage'.** Why Heaney reduced the poem so radically—from sixty-three to sixteen lines—must remain matter for conjecture. We assume there were no drafts written subsequent to B3, but there is always a remote possibility that a number of later drafts were mislaid, withheld, or destroyed. At any rate, the substantial differences between the penultimate draft and the printed poem are striking, and allow the reader to appreciate the overall contrast between the working materials and the final poem.

Stanzas in B3 are numbered i, ii, iii, iv; stanza five is titled 'III.' Each of stanzas i-iii is eight lines in length; the truncated stanza iv has five lines only. The form is now close to the sixteen lines of **'Fosterage',** including two unrhymed eight-line stanzas conjoined. In the first stanza, Heaney recounts the jokey anecdote about McLaverty warning the pupils not to become 'corner boys'; he tells a version of this story elsewhere, in his introduction to McLaverty's short stories (p. xi), as well as in *Finders Keepers.*[21] The title 'Stylist' has been dropped, but style remains the theme of the first, second, and fourth stanzas. The opening lines of the poem suggest something of McLaverty's wry humour, and establish a contrast between the wayward 'corner boys' and the dedicated poet (also at this point a young man

and not much older than the senior pupils of the school). McLaverty's conspiratorial *'sotto voce',* contrasted with the public voice that he uses with his pupils, underlines his friendship with the younger writer, who has now left his boyhood behind; however, in taking advice to 'keep at Shakespeare' he bears traces of the gifted pupil. This opening stanza was dropped from **'Fosterage',** and in so doing, Heaney allows for a more dramatic, direct opening to the poem, with the opening of the Royal Avenue stanza: 'Description is revelation!' This, together with the final remark in this stanza, concerning veins in his 'biro', indicates that the poem's main concern, first and last, is artistic style.

We note the revision between the Royal Avenue stanza of B3 and **'Fosterage',** changing the personal, direct address ('you gripped my elbow') to third-person narrative ('he gripped my elbow'). No specific reference is made in B3 to Mansfield, though the 'laundry basket' passage from her *Journals* is included (albeit cancelled by hand, and Mansfield's '75' has become McLaverty's '64'). There is no instance in stanza 1 (B3) of 'that note of exile' which Heaney associates with Chekhov, but the phrase appears in the final stanza, which is a second, revisionary attempt at the B3 Royal Avenue stanza.

Stanza 3—the Ballymurphy stanza—is dropped, in accordance with the effort to focus on artistic style and friendship. In the Ballymurphy stanza, Heaney comes closest in the drafts to addressing the 'Troubles' of the 1970s ('the buses burning' and so on) By deleting this stanza, he expunges contemporary violence from the poem, as well as its links with McLaverty's fiction, since the 'Bog Meadows', the Sacred Heart of Jesus, and the 'father's gun' are redolent of the world of *Call My Brother Back.* Furthermore, it is the pen, not the gun; which links Heaney to his poetic father (McLaverty) in **'Fosterage',** whereas in the Ballymurphy stanza it is the gun which unites the father and son. In **'Digging',** Heaney described the pen in his hand as 'snug as a gun'; however, in the transition from B3 to **'Fosterage,'** the father's gun is not passed down to the son, and is made to disappear from view.

Stanza 4 of B3 (the Hopkins stanza), closely resembles stanza 3 of B2 and provides the kernel of the second half of **'Fosterage'.** Again, we note in **'Fosterage'** the abandonment of direct address ('you discerned') for third-person narrative ('he discerned'), and the author has dropped the provocative last line in B3 ('The Cavehill's profile is the Tollund Man's'). This can surely be justified by claims of irrelevance (what does the Tollund Man have to do with Hopkins, or with McLaverty's ability to discern 'patience'?). The line appeared early in the drafts, surviving all but the final cut, and explicitly links the poem to **'The Tollund Man',** to the bog poems of *North,* and to **'The Betrothal of Cavehill',** but finally seems distracting from the poem's strict focus.[22]

The final stanza of B3 is an unfinished revision of part of the Royal Avenue stanza, beginning at the point where McLaverty advises Heaney on his reading. References to John Clare and Edward Thomas were subsequently dropped in **'Fosterage',** thus sharpening the focus on Mansfield and Hopkins. It is revealing to study the development of one line in particular: 'But beware exaggeration' (B2, B3), revised to: '[But] to hell with [faking it.] Overstatement' (B3, below), finally revised to: 'But to hell with overstating it' (**'Fosterage'**). A clear progression can be discerned here, from the slightly formal utterance ('beware exaggeration'), to the admonition against 'faking it', to the final version, powerfully and informally conveyed. The poem trails off at the end of B3 with a few lines of the St John's Point stanza, prominent in earlier drafts but now abandoned. The last two lines of **'Fosterage'** witness the word 'fostered' for the first time—as if the idea of fosterage only really became clear somewhere between B3 and the final poem—and also that image, rooted in the Classical world, of 'words | Imposing on my tongue like obols'. In the simile of ancient coinage on the tongue the speaker associates himself with the dead, bearing payment for Charon the ferryman, to cross the river Styx. Here, the poet is placing great significance on the language of poetry—potentially his own language—by virtue of the spiritual, magical value of the currency to which it is compared. It is a remarkable closing image, with nothing comparable in the manuscript drafts, emerging from the creative space in between B3 and **'Fosterage'.**

By comparing B3 with **'Fosterage'** we can see how Heaney has radically narrowed the focus of his poem to the early encounter with McLaverty and that author's advice. A broader description of McLaverty and his anecdote about unwilling school pupils is expunged. All references to the Tollund Man, to contemporary unrest in West Belfast and beyond, and to the 1920s 'Troubles' are cancelled. Finally, the Royal Avenue stanza is joined to lines from the Hopkins stanza, producing a much shorter poem of considerable power. It was to be a poem about style, despite its roots in wider concerns. Of course, the sectarian violence of the province, emerging during the late 1960s, as well as the historical violence adumbrated throughout the poems of *North,* remains implicit in the poem's setting, in that pre-'Troubles' moment on Royal Avenue. However, the poem's potential as an explicit meditation on the roots and effects of violence was forestalled by Heaney's radical excising of many key stanzas in the drafts. To return to the Wordsworthian epigraph concerning fosterage by beauty and by fear, the objects and occasions of fear are cancelled from this particular script, resulting in a sharpening of focus on the aesthetic questions appropriate to fosterage by beauty. However, the atmo-

sphere of foreboding and restriction suggested in the title **'The Ministry of Fear'** remains a theme of **'Singing School'** in general and an undercurrent within **'Fosterage'.**

Notes

Draft poems by Seamus Heaney are reprinted here by permission of the author and of Stephen Ennis, Director, Special Collections & Archives, Robert W. Woodruff Library, Emory University. I thank Seamus Heaney, Stephen Ennis, Ronald Schuchard, and Sarah Stanton for their assistance.

1. These include Peter Fallon. Seamus Heaney, Thomas Kinsella, Michael Longley, Derek Mahon, Paul Muldoon, Tom Paulin, and James Simmons (http://web.library.emory.edu/libraries/speccolls/guides-irishlit.html). There are relevant holdings in the Henry C. Pearson Collection. University of North Carolina Libraries, Chapel Hill, including manuscripts and ALS. A small number of Heaney manuscripts are held at Boston College (Burns Library), and Bellaghy Bawn, Magherafelt.

2. The directors of Woodruff library list nine recipients (1999-2004) of Fellowships to study their Irish Literature collections (http://web.library.emory.edu/libraries/speccolls/pastfellows.html).

3. See Jerome McGann, *A Critique of Modern Textual Criticism* (Charlottesville: University Press of Virginia, 1983; repr. 1992), pp. 37-XX.

4. 'I came to the decision . . . that I should now lodge a substantial portion of my literary archive in Woodruff.' Quoted in M. Terrazas, 'Heaney Honors Chace, Emory with Papers', *Emory Report,* 29 September 2003. See www.emory.edu/EMORY_REPORT.

5. Not much has been written about Heaney's manuscripts, with the exception of Arthur McGuinness, 'The Craft of Diction: Revision in Seamus Heaney's Poems', in *Image and Allusion: Anglo-Irish Literature and Its Contexts,* ed. by M. Harmon (Portmarnock: Wolfhound Press, 1975), pp. 62-91. Tony Curtis published the drafts of 'North' without commentary in 'The Manuscript Drafts of the poem "North"', in *The Art of Seamus Heaney,* ed. by T. Curtis (Bridgend: Poetry Wales Press, 1982), pp. 53-62.

6. 'Singing School' was published in its entirety in *North* (London: Faber, 1975) and *Opened Ground: Selected Poems 1966-1996* (London: Faber, 2002). The third and fourth poems in the sequence ('Orange Drums, Tyrone 1966' and 'Summer

1969') were dropped from *Selected Poems 1965-1975* (London: Faber, 1980). The third poem only was dropped from *New Selected Poems 1966-1987* (London: Faber, 1990).

7. Elmer Andrews, *The Poetry of Seamus Heaney: 'All the Realms of Whisper'* (London: Macmillan, 1988), p. 113. However, he goes on to say: 'What "Fosterage" does importantly represent, though, is a continuation of that troublesome debate about what a poet's role should be, especially in time of war.' See Michael Parker. *Seamus Heaney: The Making of the Poet* (London: Macmillan, 1993), pp. 29, 149; Neil Corcoran, *The Poetry of Seamus Heaney: A Critical Study,* 2nd edn (London: Faber, 1998), p. 243; Bernard O'Donoghue, *Seamus Heaney and the Language of Poetry* (New York and London: Harvester Wheatsheaf, 1994).

8. Seamus Heaney, letter to the present author, 11 May 2001.

9. 'Fosterage' drafts (ten pages; twelve sections); Woodruff, MS 653, Box 2, folder 5.

10. *A Portrait of the Artist as a Young Man* (1916; repr. London: Cape, 1968), p. 60.

11. According to Parker, McLaverty's phrases from 'Fosterage' appear in an unpublished Heaney poem, also dedicated to McLaverty: 'An Evening in Killard' (Parker, p. 256, n. 209). I have been unable to find this poem.

12. 'The winter of 1962 and spring of 1963 marked a major turning point in his career' (Parker, p. 46).

13. The phrase 'Description is revelation' is taken from Wallace Stevens's poem, 'Description Without Place' (*Wallace Stevens: Collected Poems* (New York: Knopf, 1954), pp. 339-46).

14. 'North', *North*; 'Station Island XII', *Station Island* (London: Faber, 1984).

15. Seamus Heaney, letter to the present author, 14 January 2004. Also see Heaney's introduction to Michael McLaverty, *Collected Short Stories,* ed. by Sophia Hillan (Belfast: Blackstaff, 2002): '"Look for the intimate thing," he would say, and go on to praise the "note of exile" in Chekhov' (p. xi).

16. *Letters and Journals of Katherine Mansfield,* ed. by C. K. Stead (London: Allen Lane, 1977), pp. 65-66.

17. 'Fosterling', *Seeing Things* (London: Faber, 1991).

18. 'Gifts of Rain', *Wintering Out* (London: Faber, 1972).

19. 'And maybe at that moment an ould woman—a rickle of bones—is shot dead in York Street. And what's Harold thinking about—Keep them at it! Keep the workers at one another's throats and they'll forget about high rents and low wages' (Michael McLaverty, *Call My Brother Back* (1939; repr. Co. Dublin: Poolbeg, 1979), p. 177).

20. Matthew Arnold, *Friendship's Garland: Being the Conversations, Letters and Opinions of the Late Arminius, Baron von Thunder-ten-Tronckh; Collected and Edited with a Dedicatory Letter to Adolescens Leo. Esq., of 'The Daily Telegraph'* (London, 1871).

21. Seamus Heaney, 'On Poetry and Profession', in *Finders Keepers: Selected Prose 1971-2001* (London: Faber, 2003), pp. 67-73.

22. 'The Tollund Man,' *Wintering Out*; 'The Betrothal of Cavehill,' *North*.

Joseph Heininger (essay date summer 2005)

SOURCE: Heininger, Joseph. "Making a Dantean Poetic: Seamus Heaney's 'Ugolino.'" *New Hibernia Review* 9, no. 2 (summer 2005): 50-64.

[*In the following essay, Heininger analyzes Heaney's engagement with the poetry of Dante, which the critic maintains has informed Heaney's poetry over a period of twenty-five years, beginning with the 1979 volume* Field Work.]

Beginning with *Field Work* (1979), and continuing with *Electric Light* (2001), Seamus Heaney's poetry, translations, and criticism have engaged with the poetic example of Dante. Although he has produced translations from the Irish and Anglo-Saxon, and has explored affinities with poets including Lowell, Frost, Walcott, Larkin, Milosz, Swir, and Herbert, Heaney has consistently returned to Dante during the past twenty-five years of his career. The examples are many: he has translated Cantos I-III of the *Inferno* and published them in Daniel Halpern's *Dante's Inferno: Translations by Twenty Contemporary Poets* (1993). The pilgrimage sequences and encounters with "familiar ghosts" in *Station Island* (1985) are closely modeled on the design of Dante's *Inferno*. Most important, he has created and continues to explore a Dantean poetic in his own work. After writing the poems of *Field Work* and *Station Island,* Heaney has shown his inclination toward Dante's example by working in such forms as the three-line tercets and the occasional terza rima, forms which amplify his earlier reliance on quatrains and sonnets. At Heaney's poetry readings, audiences can hear Dante's formal example in the adaptations of terza rima in his verse as well as in his commentaries, many of which point to Dante's pervasive and philosophically liberating influence in his work.[1]

In two poems from *Field Work,* **"The Strand at Lough Beg"** and **"Ugolino,"** the auditory qualities, or the "acoustic" of Heaney's language, signal his immersion in the poetics and habits of mind cultivated by Dante. The first of the poems in *Field Work* to announce Dante's influence on Heaney's new poetic direction is **"The Strand at Lough Beg,"** a powerful elegy for his murdered cousin, Colm McCartney. The poem's epigraph and its final images of loss, mourning, and poetic reparation are borrowed from the first canto of the *Purgatorio,* in Dorothy Sayers's translation. This poem also signals Heaney's engagement with the visionary and ethical Dante and his fascination with the influence of the poet on other poets. Other *Field Work* poems, especially the elegies and poems that feature addresses to other poets, or such tutelary poems as **"An Afterwards," "Elegy," "Leavings,"** and **"Casualty,"** are marked by Dantean forms, images, and expressions of feeling.[2]

As Seamus Deane and others have shown, the theme of monstrous violence and its personal and cultural costs reaches back to the originary roots of Heaney's imagination. His "touchstone" poems, such as **"Punishment"** from *North* (1975), represent the difficulty of coming to terms with violence and how deeply violence is embedded in the poet's heritage. Although it does not employ three-line stanzas or Dante's speakers, **"Punishment"** sounds a Dantesque note of self-scrutiny as it explores the depths of the poet's misgivings at this ancient ritual killing.[3] At the same time, the figure of the poet, here identifiable with the speaker, explores his perverse pride in his status as "artful voyeur," his moral complicity and tribal implication. Meditating on the duality of a tribal slaying in "the man-killing parishes" of Jutland, Heaney's poem retraces the punishment of the Iron Age girl and allusively speaks to the situation of her contemporary Northern Irish sisters. In a Dantesque manner that points to the ambiguous moral situation of the speaker, Heaney suggestively parallels the speaker's careful observation of the ancient victim and his awareness of how he "would connive / in civilized outrage" in his witness to the modern scapegoating of her "betraying sisters" in 1970s Northern Ireland.

Heaney's extended encounter with the *Divine Comedy* in the Glanmore Cottage years (1972-1976) nourishes his poetry and poetic in fresh ways.[4] The important intellectual and moral turn in Heaney's handling of violent Irish materials develops from Dante's representation of his pilgrims' encounters with sinners in the *Inferno.* Dante proves exemplary on both counts, as Heaney observes in a 1980 review of C. H. Sisson's translation of the *Divine Comedy:*

> The 'big shape' of *The Divine Comedy* is 'the archetypal one of faring forth into the ordeal, going to a nadir and returning to a world that is renewed by the boon won

in that other place. To read it is to go through a refining element, to be steadied and reminded . . . of the immense potential of poetry and its efficacy as a power in the world.'[5]

Writing on Heaney's quarrel with T. S. Eliot over Dante's stature, John Haffenden points out Heaney's declared preference for the colloquial voice and particular energy of the *Divine Comedy:* "Dante is as available to the Irish locality as to the refined voice of international urbanity, his argument runs."[6]

In a ground-breaking essay published in 1985, Seamus Deane observed this enabling of the poet with regard to subject matter and self-confidence by referring to the figure of Sweeney and to the version of Dante's Ugolino as key examples of Heaney's deepened perspectives on the vexed relationship between atrocity and poetry. In "The Timorous and the Bold," Deane writes:

> Atrocity and poetry, in the Irish or in the Italian setting, are being manoeuvred here by Heaney, as he saw Lowell manoeuvre them, into a relationship which could be sustained without breaking the poet down into timorousness, the state in which the two things limply coil. Since *Field Work,* Heaney has begun to consider his literary heritage more carefully, to interrogate it in relation to his Northern and violent experience, to elicit from it a style of survival as poet. In this endeavour he will in effect be attempting to reinvent rather than merely renovate his heritage.[7]

Heaney's version of **"Ugolino"** appears as the final poem in *Field Work,* its placement there speaking intertextually and retrospectively to the violence-marked poems of that volume, especially **"The Strand at Lough Beg"** and **"Casualty."** Its placement at the end of *Field Work* also speaks proleptically to Heaney's future engagements with the violent, treacherous situation in Northern Ireland in *Station Island* and later works, and is the first major indication of his emergent Dantean poetics.

In this light, Dante's Ugolino episode has primary importance for Heaney. Heaney's treatment of the Northern Irish "Troubles" emerging in his version of Dante creates a Dantesque exposure of the monstrosity and self-perpetuating nature of violence. Heaney represents this contemporary parallel by invoking the figure of Ugolino, once again revealing him in his loathsomeness and moral enormity. Heaney's version of Ugolino responds to Dante by re-situating Count Ugolino in Dante's hell and widening the allusive contours and habits of mind of that hell to fit a recognizably Irish context. Specifically, Heaney makes a biblical and classical exemplum of Ugolino's fate, a fate in which the sins of the fathers are visited upon the heads of the children, and the cycles of familial and social violence continue. Heaney responds to Ugolino and to Irish situations by making a version in his proper acoustic: through diction, rhyme, contemporary tonalities, and allusive language, he creates a translation which revisits and allegorizes Dante's scenes of treachery. Similarly, the exemplary qualities of Dante's poetics, specifically the carefully inflected language and political and familial relations of the Ugolino episode, are later redeployed in **"The Flight Path,"** a long poem published in *The Spirit Level* (1996). In the middle section of this journey poem, Heaney again invokes the world of the *Inferno,* and closes the scenes describing his remembered encounter with a partisan accuser by quoting three lines from **"Ugolino"**:

> *When he had said all this, his eyes rolled*
> *And his teeth, like a dog's clamping round a bone,*
> *Bit into the skull and again took hold.*

(OG [Opened Ground: Selected Poems 1966-1996] 386)

By explicitly positioning these lines at the close of the fourth section of **"The Flight Path,"** Heaney connects this recurrence of the violent archetype to his earlier treatment of Ugolino. Indeed, we shall see how this particular interlocutor reveals himself in dream and actuality as a vengeful and hardened monster, a version of an Irish Ugolino.

In appropriating the figure of Ugolino, Heaney articulates a moral and political critique of contemporary acts of violence and the repetitive cycles of hatred and revenge that spawn them. He explicitly positions Ugolino as a self-justifying perpetrator of violence and an unregenerate father—not a pitiable victim of Archbishop Roger's vengeance or Pisa's betrayal. This figure of the self-excusing, self-condemning monster extends from *Field Work* to the shade of Ugolino who inhabits a section of Heaney's light-filled collection *The Spirit Level.* Moreover, Dante's exemplary status in the development of Heaney's poetics reveals itself in what Robert Hollander calls Dante's handling of "the moral situation of the reader" of the *Inferno*:

> Dante, not without risk, decided to entrust to us, his readers, the responsibility for seizing upon the details in the narratives told by sinners, no matter how appealing their words might be, in order to condemn them on the evidence that issues from their own mouths.[8]

In Heaney's translation of the Ugolino episode, one can see this Dantean aesthetic and ethical procedure emerging in the poet's diction, rhymes, allusions, tone and other rhetorical choices, as well as his use of tercets within the unified narrative structure. Examining Heaney's translation in light of some of the most informed commentaries on Dante reveals how Heaney's poetic art invites his readers to distrust Ugolino's professed victimhood and to judge him under the "bestial sign" of his gnawing and his hatred. As John Freccero and Robert Hollander have observed, a non-Romantic reading of Ugolino shows that Dante represents the count misstating his case, misreading his fate, misjudging his claims upon his hearers' sympathy, and finally, as suppressing any acknowledgment of his culpability in his sons' deaths as he returns to his vengeful feeding. He is the archetype of the self-excusing, ravenous hater and, as Freccero notes in his classic essay, "Bestial Sign and Bread of Angels," "there are several indications that Dante intends [the Ugolino episode] to be read, not only as a human and familial horror, but also as political tragedy."[9]

Notably, Freccero identifies the key interpretive sign which must guide the reader's distrust of Ugolino's story when Dante frames the entire encounter under the *bestial segno,* literally, "the bestial sign," of Ugolino's chewing the head of his victim. As will become apparent, this "bestial sign" is a monstrous and un-redemptive sign governing the human fate of Ugolino and his children, as well as an interpretive principle that determines the reader's point of view on Ugolino's account of his sufferings. In the Hollander translation, Dante, the poet-traveler, asks Ugolino:

> 'O you, who by so bestial a sign
> show loathing for the one whom you devour
> tell me why,' I said, 'and let the pact be this:
>
> 'if you can give just cause for your complaint,
> then I, knowing who you are and what his sin is,
> may yet requite you in the world above,
> if that with which I speak does not go dry.'

> (*I* XXXII: 133-39)

Heaney's version of Dante's address to Ugolino is more colloquial and idiosyncratic in its phrasing, and reads as a series of questions:

> 'You,' I shouted, 'you on top, what hate
> Makes you so ravenous and insatiable?
> What keeps you so monstrously at rut?
> Is there any story I can tell
> For you, in the world above, against him?
> If my tongue by then's not withered in my throat
> I will report the truth and clear your name.'

> (*OG* 178)

In Heaney's free yet illuminatingly correct translation, "bestial sign" becomes "monstrously at rut." The monstrousness of the gnawing action is explained by the rhymes, in which Heaney features words that become significant ethical and linguistic concepts in his treatment of Ugolino. "Hate" and "at rut" are Middle English or Anglo-Saxon in origin, while "insatiable" and "ravenous" are Latinate. His choices of diction from both strands of the English linguistic inheritance reinforce each other poetically: the internal vowel rhymes of "hate" and "insatiable," and the strong consonantal end-rhymes of "hate" and "at rut" not only link the idea of monstrous behavior to animality or bestiality but also link the emotion of hatred to its repeated issue in violence.

Heaney's choices of diction also point to a political dimension because his language is charged with particular meaning. If there were any doubt that this Ugolino possesses Irish particularity and resonance, we need only look to Heaney's phrase describing the manner in which Ugolino bites Archbishop's Roger's neck:

> Gnawing at him where the neck and head
> Are grafted to the sweet fruit of the brain,
> Like a famine victim at a loaf of bread.
>
> (*OG* 178)

Whereas Hollander translates the last line thus: "As a famished man will bite into his bread," Heaney's choice of "famine victim" places us immediately within the Irish acoustic and Irish historical circumstances. Further, Heaney's localizing and historicizing phrase is complicated by his next reference to Ugolino's hunger, in which he renders the name of the imprisoning tower as "that jail / Which is called Hunger after me" (*OG* 179). Here he turns away from the explicit choice of rendering the Italian word "fame" as "famine." Interestingly, another Northern Irish poet of the same generation, Ciaran Carson, translates the phrase as "Famine Tower" in his translation of the *Inferno,* published by Granta (2002).[10]

In framing the verbal violence that defines the twin corruptions of Ugolino's fatherhood and his political mentality, Heaney is aware of Dante's careful language, even as he bends it to his purposes. Heaney freely translates Ugolino's phrases, pointedly alluding to the biblical and proverbial admonition that "as you sow, so shall you reap":

> Yet while I weep to say them, I would sow
> My words like curses—that they might increase
> And multiply upon this head I gnaw.
>
> (*OG* 178)

By contrast, Hollander translates Ugolino's words by a more literal rendering of the Italian words and phrases:

> 'But if my words shall be the seeds that bear
> infamous fruit to the traitor I am gnawing,
> then you will see me speak and weep together.'
>
> (*I* XXXIII: 7-9)

By casting Ugolino's death-dealing words as a curse, thus again characterizing his speech under the "bestial sign," Heaney appropriates such biblical phrases as "increase and multiply" from God's blessing of Abraham and creation of the House of Israel (Genesis 22). He also invokes the Greek curse upon Thebes ("I would sow / My words like curses") and links this curse with later self-destructive patriarchies and the tribes and nations that grow from them. These allusions connect the sectarian violence of the Northern Ireland of the 1970s with the fates of Archbishop Roger and Count Ugolino because the everlasting hatred they represent for Dante is replicated morally and emotionally by the Irish betrayers and slayers of children.

Indeed, rather than protecting his children or preserving their lives, Heaney's Ugolino makes the imprisoned children literal and metaphorical famine victims. Their starvation and their deaths occur under the view of their stony-hearted father. According to Dorothy Sayers's notes to her translation of the *Inferno,* a translation which Heaney prizes, the historical Count Ugolino had two sons and two grandsons in the tower with him, and all died. They are imprisoned with their father, starving, and certainly frightened by the sound of the nailing (*chiavar*) of the door, as Sayers suggests. Their greatest emotional deprivation and spiritual starvation, however, comes from the unresponsiveness of their mute father, who by his own account gives no sign of reassurance to them.[11] Heaney's version of this paternal rejection reads:

> They were awake now, it was near the time
> For food to be brought in as usual,
> Each one of them disturbed after his dream,
> When I heard the door being nailed and hammered
> Shut, far down in the nightmare tower.
> I stared in my son's faces and spoke no word
> My eyes were dry and my heart was stony
> They cried and my little Anselm said,
> "What's wrong? Why are you staring, daddy?"
>
> (*OG* 178)

When Ugolino bites his hands "in desperation," we recall that the gesture also accords with his bestial sign and trope of turning away and gnawing at flesh, as he does when Dante first sees him at Roger's nape. Ugolino's children misread his desperation as hunger. Their offer to sacrifice their bodies to his hunger indicates the perversely unnatural position of this family, in which the sons sacrifice themselves for their father, rather than the reverse.

When his children offer to feed him with their flesh, as Freccero points out, "they echo at once the Eucharistic sacrifice and the words of Job: 'The Lord giveth and the Lord taketh away. Blessed be the name of the Lord.'[12] It must not be supposed that the allusions to Christ's passion are merely pietistic embellishments to contrast with the infernal horror story; they are in fact the key to the whole dramatic interpretation. The point of the language here is that the suffering of the children is of a sacred order, carrying with it a redemptive possibility. To accept such suffering with total selflessness and no thought of vengeance is to put an end to the otherwise eternal series of violent acts, making possible a communion that was not possible before. The spirit of their words offers the hope of a shared grief and a reconciliation to their father, but he sees in their death only a spur to his infernal retribution, thereby repeating in hell the pattern set forth in his dream."[13] Yet their suffering continues because their father does not break his silence; Ugolino never speaks to them in response to their cries and suffering:

> But I shed no tears, I made no reply
> All through that day, all through the night that fol-
>   lowed
> Until another sun blushed in the sky
> And sent a small beam probing the distress
> Inside those prison walls. Then when I saw
> The image of my face in their four faces
> I bit on my two hands in desperation
> And they, since they thought hunger drove me to it,
> Rose up suddenly in agitation
> Saying, "Father, it will greatly ease our pain
> If you eat us instead, and you who dressed us
> In this sad flesh undress us here again."
>
> (*OG* 180)

This constitutes the doubly poignant failure of language and feeling. In Freccero's words, Ugolino's "tragedy is a failure of interpretation, as well as an inability to accept the suffering of his children."[14] Heaney's positioning of Ugolino as a damnable slayer of his own children and perpetuator of hatred is magnified and sealed by his failure to speak. Ugolino only cries out only as he gropes over their bodies; he does not cry with them in their suffering or call out to them until it is too late. Instead, "when he had said all this," he returns to his violent "embrace" with Archbishop Roger, a bestial feeding in which Ugolino's anger breeds his greater desire for revenge, and vice versa. This is the "last heart-breaking detail of his failure as a father," as Robert Hollander points out.[15]

As Dante consistently shows in his scenes in the *Inferno*, the sinners' torments are those in which they indulged in life. When telling his story, Count Ugolino must re-live the deaths of his children as well as his own imprisonment and starvation. As Hollander and Freccero demonstrate, the greatest victimhood is the children's, not the self-pitying father's. Ugolino's sons die before his unregenerate eyes, and he does not weep. This is treachery of the first magnitude, a father betraying his sons. It is biblical and Theban, monstrously destructive to family and to the community, as Freccero has suggested.[16]

In closing his version of Ugolino's story, Heaney uses phrases from a well-known passage in Exodus to seal his indictment of Ugolino and the treacheries of Pisa. In this way, Heaney's diction and tone point especially to Ugolino's failures as a father, and his wider betrayal of the responsibilities of the community. His failure to do anything to alleviate his children's suffering is a civic as well as a moral failure because it passes on to later generations:

> Pisa! Pisa, your sounds are like a hiss
> Sizzling in your country's grassy language.

> And since the neighbor states have been remiss
> In your extermination, let a huge
> Dyke of islands bar the Arno's mouth, let
> Capraia and Gorgona dam and deluge
> You and your population. For the sins
> Of Ugolino, who betrayed your forts,
> Should never have been visited on his sons.
>
> (*OG* 180)

In the last three lines, Heaney uses modified terza rima, the half-rhyme of "sins" and "sons." This rhyme perfectly captures the fatal drama of the situation and reinforces, through the reader's auditory sense, a judgment of the moral and political damage done to succeeding generations by the self-indulgent violence of the fathers.

In his version, Heaney chooses once again to translate freely but designedly from Dante: "Che se l'conte Ugolino aveva voce / d'aver tradita te de le castella / No dovei tu i figliuoi porre a tal croce" (*I*). The Hollander translation renders this last line: "You [Pisa] still / should not have put his children to such torture." Freccero, however, reminds us that "tal croce" is literally, "this cross," alluding to the cross of Christ. He argues effectively that Dante's language and vision in this episode are Christological, and that Dante shows the children offering themselves as sacrificial victims to save their sinning father. The children are put to death, nailed by their own father to the cross of sacrifice, as Freccero suggests. He further suggests that Ugolino's hard-hearted refusal to hear and read their "signs," their offering of their bodies to alleviate his starving, is a refusal of a salvific communion and a sign of his turn toward cannibalizing their bodies after their deaths.[17]

The children wish to save him as his life-giving bread, but his refusal and stony silence signal his turn toward cannibalism, an explicit reference to the "bestial sign" of neck-chewing under which his story has been framed and told.[18] So, too, the Exodus language that Heaney uses in his version derives its moral force from its allegorical and historical resonance. Although it is an instance of Heaney "freely translating," it works to locate the atrocity once again in human terms. The poem closes with the conjoined voices of both poets' insistence that these children were innocent:

> Your atrocity was Theban. They were young
> And innocent: Hugh and Brigata
> And the other two whose names are in my song.
>
> (*OG* 180)

Heaney's version of the Ugolino episode and our reception of this translation are powerfully shaped by this closing injunction, and the penultimate echoing of the words of Exodus that "the iniquities of the father will be visited upon the heads of his children unto the third and fourth generations" (Exodus 34: 7). As Robert Hollander comments, "All of Dante's sympathy is lodged with the children, none with Ugolino. And here we are not speaking of the protagonist (who was firm enough himself against Ugolino's entreaties for pity), but of the author."[19]

Consequently, Heaney's representation of Ugolino's death and the deaths of his sons and grandsons reproduces the political and moral condemnations Dante leveled at his Italian original. Significantly, it also suggests an allegory of Irish genocide that proceeds not from the perfidious Saxon oppressors of the 1840s and the famine years, but is perpetrated from within and perpetuated by Irish political self-divisions and sectarian violence. Far removed from the agonized, uncertain stance he took in the last poem of **North** (1974), **"Exposure,"** Heaney is not timorous in the face of this violence, not a retreating figure. Rather, he speaks in the voice of the poet who has found a purchase on his materials, and in an appropriate tone: the prophet and seer who fortifies himself with Dante's vision and foretells the doom unto the third and fourth generations of Irishmen killing sons of Irishmen. This prophetic, biblical stance also coincides with the tragic legendary history of Thebes.

In **Field Work,** Heaney works with the example of Dante as the poet of the *Inferno,* naming the lost souls, the familiar compound ghosts, and the elegized dead. He also writes one of his most admired elegies under the aegis of the *Purgatorio.* Heaney revisits this scene and this subject in his **"Station Island"** sequence, in which the "familiar compound ghost" of Colm McCartney returns to him in an accusatory role. In **"Station Island"** VII, McCartney chastises the poet for being safe, for aestheticizing his death, and for deflecting the violence that caused it into a parallel with wild Sweeney and the poet's ritualized grief (**OG** 239). Yet if the poet's encounter with sectarian violence and death is aestheticized and opened to fault in the Colm McCartney visitation in **"Station Island,"** it acquires a fierce power and gravitas in Heaney's staging of Ugolino's reappearance in **"The Flight Path."**

In **"The Flight Path,"** from **The Spirit Level,** Heaney revisits the journey through physical and metaphysical realms. In the fourth section of the poem, the poet's journey is reimagined in a contemporary fashion as the traveler moves on airplanes and on a train en route to Belfast.[20] We note the particularized and allegorical time sequences in the poem, as the speaker flies back from California to Ireland on "the red-eye special from New York." He sets out the episode: "The following for the record, in the light / Of everything before and since: / One bright May morning, nineteen seventy-nine . . ." (**OG** 385). A dream sequence features Heaney acting at the behest of an IRA man—"Ciaran Nugent"—perhaps one of the Provisional IRA, and carrying out the instructions of his accuser. Heaney frames this vituperative encounter by recounting the speaker's dream sequence

and by his later imagined walk in Virgil's company, "safe as houses and translating freely":

> . . . I'm on the train for Belfast. Plain, simple
> Exhilaration at being back: the sea
> At Skerries, the nuptial hawthorn bloom,
> The trip north taking sweet hold like a chain
> On every bodily sprocket.
>   Enter then—
> As if he were some *film noir* border guard—
> Enter this one I'd last met in a dream,
> More grimfaced now than in the dream itself
> When he'd flagged me down at the side of a mountain
>   road,
> Come up and leant his elbow on the roof
> And explained through the open window of the car
> That all I'd have to do was drive a van
> Carefully in to the next customs post
> At Pettigo, switch off, get out as if
> I were on my way with dockets to the office—
> But then instead I'd walk ten yards more down
> Towards the main street and get in with—here
> Another schoolfriend's name, a wink and smile,
> I'd know him all right, he'd be in a Ford
> And I'd be home in three hours' time, as safe
> As houses . . .
>   So he enters and sits down
> Opposite and goes for me head on.
> 'When, for fuck's sake, are you going to write
> Something for us?' 'If I do write something,
> Whatever it is, I'll be writing for myself.'
> And that was that. Or words to that effect.
> The gaol walls all those months were smeared with
>   shite,
> Out of Long Kesh after his dirty protest
> The red eyes were the eyes of Ciaran Nugent
> Like something out of Dante's scurfy hell,
> Drilling their way through the rhymes and images
> Where I too walked behind the righteous Virgil,
> As safe as houses and translating freely:
> *When he had said all this, his eyes rolled*
> *And his teeth, like a dog's teeth clamping round a*
> *   bone,*
> *Bit into the skull and again took hold.*

                                                     (*OG* 385-86)

Heaney connects the two passages through the similarity of situations: the accosting IRA man and the speaker, the poet, are dramatized as in a scene of accusation and rivalry. This is signaled by the quotation from Ugolino that closes this section of the poem. As Ugolino finishes his speech to Dante and Virgil in *Inferno,* XXXIII, he turns away to gnaw on the neck, to become bestial again, thus invoking the bestial signs of violence, hatred, anger, and cannibalistic feeding on the self. In this case, Heaney foregrounds Ugolino and Roger as emblems of self-starvation, national starvation, false martyrdom, and death. Their reappearance here signals their appositeness to the facts of historical violence in Ireland and to the Dantean poetics of Heaney's response to that violence.

If **"The Flight Path"** deals with modern travel and the poet's illusions of escaping and superseding the old hatreds, it also ironically rehistoricizes them through the speaker's encounter with the IRA man and his naming of the infamous Long Kesh prison. With regard to diction, images, and tone, Heaney brilliantly invokes the inward-turning and outward-turning nature of hatred as he explores the verbal and other violence associated with the poet's interlocutor. The IRA man has the "red eyes" "drilling their way through the rhymes and images" that signal his pathological anger. His words also drill their way into the poet's consciousness: "When, for fuck's sake, are you going to write / Something for us?" Heaney's answer presents a considered alternative: "If I do write something, / Whatever it is, I'll be writing for myself." The verbal violence of these extreme demands for poetry enlisted in a cause is replicated by the iconic images of the writing on the walls of the prison, "smeared with shite." The writing in excrement on the prison walls corresponds to the obscenity of the message delivered to Heaney by the IRA man. Here the debasement of language is matched by the debasement of the means and the places of writing.

Instead of placating the verbal violence of the man's demands, Heaney takes the exemplary and Dantesque position of the classical poet, observing with "the righteous Virgil" how bestially this man gnashes his teeth and gnaws his bone of hatred. Indeed, at Long Kesh "the gaol walls all those months were smeared with / shite," making a new image of a recognizably Dantean hell. Here the colloquialism, "shite," isolated on the page in a line, rhymes darkly with the sounds and tropes of "flight" and "light" and "rising" which elsewhere control the temperament of the poem. Masterfully, Heaney has the excretory and hellish images of Irish dungeons and the self-starvation of the IRA hunger strikes' "dirty protest" recall and rehistoricize the imprisonment and starvation of the sons of Ugolino.

In addition, Heaney uses a word from Old English to align Ciaran Nugent and the Long Kesh hunger strikers with Dante's classic vision of hell in the *Inferno.* Heaney writes: "Like something out of Dante's scurfy hell." "Scurfy hell" is an adjectival usage of the noun "scurf," meaning "scab."[21] It points to the scabs and skin diseases suffered by the Long Kesh hunger strikers, and recalls the sores on the bodies of Count Ugolino's starving children. Yet in face of this scene of suffering, the figure of the poet seems secure; he follows in Virgil's path, "safe as houses." This is a commonly used Hiberno-English locution, but now it is in the poet's hands rather than the promises issuing from the IRA man's mouth. Does this make it somehow smug; does it sound a note of self-righteousness? Or is it rather a form of Heaney's frequent recourse to what Helen Vendler has called "second thoughts," a form of self-indictment, with the poet aware of himself "freely translating," perhaps too privileged in his status with Virgil among the company of poets?

It seems clear that in **"The Flight Path,"** Heaney refigures himself as a privileged and light-seeking pilgrim even as he is repulsed and chastened by the violence of the Irish Ugolinos. To accomplish this contrast, Heaney foregrounds the encounter between the poet and the accosting traveler in a design that imitates Dante's design for presenting the story of Ugolino. Here, Heaney must respond in a self-revealing way, putting into play both himself as actor in the poetic scene and establishing a context for the interpretive situation of the reader who observes the scene. Thus, **"The Flight Path"** records an actual journey as well as a moral and emotional one: Heaney the mental traveler, like Dante the poet traveling through the *Inferno,* encounters not only Ciaran Nugent, but also sees in this dark glass the reflection of his own history, politics, and poetic choices.

The larger narrative structure of the poem reinforces what this section's ending has shown with its quotation of Ugolino's "bestial sign." Although Ciaran Nugent does not die in prison but is released from Long Kesh, he is still seen as a vengeful hater who attempts to enlist the poet's sympathy and thus figuratively turns to gnaw his enemy's neck after recounting his mistreatment and imprisonment. In **"The Flight Path,"** perhaps more powerfully than before, Ugolino and Archbishop Roger, his victim for eternity, figure in the reader's imagination as example of the apparent interminability of the Irish hatreds of the late 1970s and early 1980s. Although they were published seventeen years apart, these poems feature two versions of Ugolino representing Irish familial and political situations. Together, they show Heaney's adaptations of Dante in his middle and later works as a series of aesthetic choices enabling a more open and self-scrutinizing poetic practice and making possible a political stance in which self-acceptance triumphs over rage, timorousness, and guilt. In formal terms, the four-line quatrains of his earlier style remain prominent, as do the sonnets, but in his recent work Heaney often employs three-line stanzas, sometimes explicitly modeled terza rima stanzas, sometimes tercets with off-rhymes.

For Seamus Heaney, poetry must engage the writer in an activity of disobeying the force of gravity, of redressing the balance and "tilting the scales of reality towards some transcendent equilibrium." In the activity of poetry, he continues,

> there is a tendency to place a counter-reality in the scales—a reality which may be only imagined but which nevertheless ha[s] weight because it is imagined within the gravitational pull of the actual and can therefore hold its own and balance out against the historical situation.

> (*FK* [*Finders Keepers: Selected Prose 1971-2001*] 283)

Especially under the pressures of contested political claims, poetry must make room for the government of the tongue, as well as "the idea of counter-weighting, of balancing out the forces, of redress." Through their violations of familial and human rights, and the violence of their utterances, Heaney's Ugolino figures dramatize the endlessness and self-consuming nature of political hatreds. In examining the distance the poet and the reader must journey from those figures in order not to replicate their fates, or to be seduced by their violent words, Heaney shows the Dantean directions of his art.

Notes

1. At a reading at the University of Notre Dame (September 26, 2003) following an International Dante Seminar, Heaney indicated that the poems he read on that occasion were written in response to Dante. He began the reading with the last section of his "Ugolino."

2. According to Helen Vendler, Heaney was stimulated to translate Dante after Robert Lowell's example. Helen Vendler, *Seamus Heaney* (Cambridge: Harvard University Press, 1998), p. 73. Heaney himself has acknowledged Dante's role in his midcareer and later: ". . . the original idea of translating the Ugolino episode came from reading Robert Lowell's version of the Brunetto Lattini canto." Seamus Heaney to Maria Cristina Fumagalli, ref. in Maria Cristina Fumagalli, "Introduction," *The Flight of the Vernacular: Seamus Heaney, Derek Walcott and the Impress of Dante* (Amsterdam: Rodopi, 2001), p. xiii, n. 20. See also "What Dante Means to Me: Seamus Heaney's Translation of the First Three Cantos of Dante's *Inferno*" in Fumagalli, pp. 259-60.

3. Seamus Heaney, *Opened Ground: Selected Poems 1966-1996* (New York: Farrar. Straus and Giroux, 1998), pp. 112-13; hereafter cited parenthetically, thus: (*OG* 112-13).

4. Vendler's account mentions that Heaney was "intensely reading Dante" in the 1970s and working on the "Ugolino" translation. Vendler, p. 73. See also Heaney's letter to Fumagalli, n. 2.

5. Seamus Heaney, "Treely and Rurally," *Quarto* (1980), quoted in John Haffenden, "Seamus Heaney and The Feminine Sensibility," *Yearbook of English Studies,* 17 (1987), 112. See also "Envies and Identifications: Dante and the Modern Poet" (1985) in Seamus Heaney, *Finders Keepers: Selected Prose, 1971-2001* (New York: Farrar, Straus and Giroux, 2002), pp. 184-96; hereafter cited parenthetically, thus: (*FK* 184-96). There, Heaney speaks of the allegorical Dante constructed by T. S. Eliot and then of the more particular and localized powers of the poet identified by Osip

Mandelstam as building a marvelous, multi-chambered "hive of bees" (*FK* 193).

6. Haffenden, 112.

7. Seamus Deane, Celtic Revivals (London: Faber and Faber, 1985), p. 186.

8. Robert Hollander, "Introduction," *The Inferno: a Verse Translation,* trans. Robert Hollander, Jean Hollander (New York: Doubleday, 2000), pp. xxxvi-xxxvii; hereafter cited parenthetically, thus: (*I* xxxvi-xxxvii).

9. John Freccero, *Dante: The Poetics of Conversion* (Cambridge: Harvard University Press, 1986), p. 153.

10. In remarks during his September 26, 2003, reading at Notre Dame, Heaney praised Carson's translation of the *Inferno* in *Granta.*

11. Dante, *The Divine Comedy, I: Hell,* trans. Dorothy L. Sayers (Harmondsworth: Penguin Books, *1949),* p. 283, l. 34, note. See also Sayers's note on the frightening sound of the nailing and on Dante's choice of the verb *chiavar* to express this, p. 283, l. 13.

12. Freccero, p. 156.

13. Freccero, pp. 156-57.

14. Freccero, p. 157.

15. Hollander, "Commentary," *The Inferno,* p. 620.

16. Freccero, pp. 152-53.

17. Freccero, p. 156.

18. Freccero, p. 160.

19. Hollander, "Commentary," p. 621.

20. The complete text of "The Flight Path" appears in *The Spirit Level* (New York: Farrar, Straus and Giroux, 1996), pp. 26-31. *Opened Ground* offers only the Dantesque fourth part of "The Flight Path."

21. *American Heritage College Dictionary,* 4th edition, p. 1625.

Stephen James (essay date fall 2005)

SOURCE: James, Stephen. "Seamus Heaney's Sway." *Twentieth-Century Literature* 51, no. 3 (fall 2005): 263-84.

[*In the following essay, James discusses the political and aesthetic ramifications of Heaney's use of ambiguous words and superfluous language in his poetry and prose.*]

In his essay "The Makings of a Music: Reflections on Wordsworth and Yeats," Seamus Heaney considers Hazlitt's account of a visit to Alfoxden in June 1798, when Wordsworth gave a spirited reading of "Peter Bell." It was "the quality and sway of the poet's speaking voice," as Heaney puts it (*Preoccupations* 64), that moved Hazlitt to record his impressions of the event. The implications of the word *sway* in this formulation are not entirely clear: does Heaney have in mind only the authority of the poet's performance, or does he also mean to suggest that the delivery captured the sweeping rhythmic motions of the verse? The word itself sways a little, fluctuating between possibilities. Heaney develops its ambiguities a few lines later in the essay by positing a connection between the nature of Wordsworth's hold over an audience and his habit of composing aloud to himself on the hoof: "And I imagine that the swing of the poet's body contributed as well to the sway of the voice" (65). This correlation between bodily movement and authority of utterance appears also in Heaney's **"Elegy"** for Robert Lowell in **Field Work,** when he recalls how his American friend would rock on his feet while controlling the flow of conversation: "you swayed the talk / and rode on the swaying tiller / of yourself" (31).[1] Lowell is imagined in **"Elegy"** as a dangerously unstable craft, a "night ferry / thudding in a big sea," as if a living embodiment of the tempestuous energies in his poem "The Quaker Graveyard in Nantucket" (14). "The Quaker Graveyard," in turn, prompts Heaney to exploit further the implications of the word *sway* in his essay on Lowell in *The Government of the Tongue*: noting how "the oceanic symphonies" of the poem "swayed and thundered" (144), Heaney insinuates a link between the turbulent music of the verse and Lowell's air of thundering cultural judgment. Similar associations prevail in his translation of **Beowulf** when he has the Danish queen Wealhtheow say to the eponymous hero, "Your sway is wide as the wind's home, / as the sea around cliffs" (41): the warrior's command, like Lowell's, is naturalized, a manifestation of the turbulent environment.[2] Together, these various instances establish a set of imaginative correspondences between personality, physical presence, and power of utterance; as such, they raise highly suggestive implications regarding Heaney's sense of poetic authority.

In the essay "Sounding Auden" in *The Government of the Tongue,* Heaney proposes to chart "the shifting relation between the kind of authority W. H. Auden sought and achieved and what might be described as his poetic music" (109), but the distinction he proposes between "poetic authority" and "poetic music" is not sharp:

> By poetic authority I mean the rights and weight which accrue to a voice not only because of a sustained history of truth-telling but by virtue also of its tonality, the sway it gains over the deep ear and, through that, over other parts of our mind and nature. By poetic music I mean the technical means, the more or less

describable effects of language and form, by which a certain tonality is effected and maintained.

The case is presented in the terms of an ostensibly clarifying distinction: between, on the one hand, the properties of a poem that are open to summary and analysis and, on the other, the ineffable, influential effects resulting from the combination of those properties. Yet the logic of Heaney's argument is unsettled, firstly by the attempted distinction within the distinction that sets objective "truth-telling" (Auden's engagement with political realities) apart from the inevitably subjective nature of that telling (the inimitable tone of Auden's voice), and secondly by a reluctance to make explicit the mutable implications of the word *sway*; again, there is a suggestive double sense of the poetic voice as both authoritative utterance and, as it extends "over the deep ear and, through that, over other parts of our mind and nature," as a force in sweeping motion. Heaney's prose conspires in the ineffability it describes, wants to go beyond the ear that hears in rational terms and to speak instead to the reader's mysterious and mystery-loving (unlocatable) "deep ear." In one sense, this is what makes Heaney's conception of "poetic authority" compelling: its persuasive air is dependent on the poetic licenses it grants itself and asks to be granted. In another sense, the giddy veerings of implication encourage a less positive reading of the "sway" of Heaney's language.

The authoritative sway of his opinions on poetry is both dependent on and challenged by the swaying and swerving, the semantic shiftiness, of Heaney's chosen vocabulary. His recurrent, seemingly instinctive improvisations on what it means to sway are illustrative of his abiding preoccupation with the serendipities and self-generating processes of poetic composition; as with these processes, his manoeuverings of the possibilities of the word *sway* are neither stable nor open to rational analysis. Indeed, the plasticity of the word (in both its noun and verb forms) is precisely what attracts Heaney to it. In its susceptibility to both physical and metaphysical applications, and to contrasting ideas of immutable control and uncontrolled mutability, of carrying weight and shifting weight, *sway* is a word of peculiar amenability to his creative temperament. One of the great strengths of Heaney's prose is its recognition of the conflicting impulses that cause the writer to lean in different directions. His making words sway between alternative meanings—as when he considers the tension between poet as legislator and poet as subject in the phrase *the government of the tongue*—offers Heaney effective, memorable ways of registering the necessary ambivalence of the creative artist in the face of moral and political complexities. By the same token, he sometimes risks destabilizing the elaboration of an idea through over-reliance on the shifting possibilities of his critical idiom.

This risk is courted throughout *The Redress of Poetry* when the recurrent metaphor of a set of swaying scales suggests his desire to balance out opposing impulses. Voicing objection to the pressures of the politically partisan, those who "will always want the redress of poetry to be an exercise of leverage on behalf of *their* point of view," who "will require the entire weight of the thing to come down on their side of the scales" (2), Heaney invokes Simone Weil's *Gravity and Grace,* in which she writes of the need of those living in an "unbalanced" society to "add weight to the lighter scale" (Weil 151). Her work, Heaney claims,

> is informed by the idea of counterweighting, of balancing out the forces, of redress—tilting the scales of reality towards some transcendent equilibrium. And in the activity of poetry too, there is a tendency to place a counter-reality in the scales—a reality which may be only imagined but which nevertheless has weight because it is imagined within the gravitational pull of the actual and can therefore hold its own and balance out against the historical situation.

> (*Redress* 3-4)

With its implicit reference to the proverbial scales of justice, the familiar symbol of legal "redress," Heaney's metaphor offers him a potentially neat visual aid for his argument, but its figurative possibilities are overdeveloped. The conceptual strain of his insistence that poetry is validated by both its responsiveness and its resistance to "the historical situation" is compounded by a visual strain: in his talk of "tilting the scales of reality towards some transcendent equilibrium," Heaney effects a misalliance between leveling out and lifting off. Unwittingly, he almost converts his metaphorical machinery from a set of scales into a catapult that would propel his argument into the void. The difficulty recurs in similar terms later in *The Redress of Poetry* when Heaney writes that a successful poem "justifies its readers' trust and vindicates itself by setting its [Keatsian] 'fine excess' in the balance against all of life's inadequacies, desolations, and atrocities" (83).[3] A dilemma running through Heaney's prose is the difficulty of reconciling his frequently reiterated ideals of equilibrium and excess; in the words of Neil Corcoran, "his theory of the function of poetry as excess demands that it exceed historical contingency rather than be merely collusive with or subject to it" (214). Heaney has repeatedly insisted that "poetry is born out of the superfluity of language's own resources and energy," that "it's a kind of overdoing it" (Ratiner 99)—or, as he declares in *The Redress of Poetry,* "when language does more than enough, as it does in all achieved poetry, it opts for the condition of over-life, and rebels at limit" (158)—but such claims do not consort easily with any notion of the demands of the world and of the poem holding each other in check. By participating in the figurative excess it advocates for

poetry, Heaney's prose is susceptible to its own "kind of overdoing it," a tendency that both underwrites and unbalances its guiding ideas.

It might be granted that while metaphorical instability imperils the elaboration of an argument in an essay or lecture, the same danger does not prevail in poetry, where multiplicity of implication tends to be regarded as a virtue, and logical development of an analogy is not necessarily the goal. Yet the distinction between ideals of critical consistency and poetic license is complicated in Heaney's case by his tendency to employ the same metaphors in his poems as in his prose. The image of a set of scales, for instance, is employed several times in his verse to describe a weighing up of impulses or perceived imperatives; dwelling on the connections between the poetry and the prose makes it hard to assess Heaney's handling of the image in isolation from a sense of how it operates in his critical writing.

At the end of **"The Grauballe Man"** in *North* (35-36), for example, the scales metaphor is loaded with complex figurative possibilities, but it is difficult to distinguish between felicitous and infelicitous ambiguities.[4] Heaney concludes his meditation on the partially preserved body of an Iron Age murder victim, exhumed from Danish bogland, by considering how its image "lies / perfected" in his memory,

> hung in the scales
> with beauty and atrocity:
> with the Dying Gaul
> too strictly compassed
>
> on his shield,
> with the actual weight
> of each hooded victim,
> slashed and dumped.

The "Dying Gaul" is the noble Celtic warrior who lies vanquished on his shield, an emblem of heroic defeat, in the famous Roman marble statue of that name: the sculptor's achievement has stylized the victim's tragic fate, rendering it beautiful. Wary of too strictly compassing in his own art the violence he contemplates, Heaney contrasts the statue with a description of killing that refuses aesthetic transformation: the anonymous "slashed and dumped" body. (Read in the wider context of the volume, this body clearly figures as an emblematic victim of the Irish "Troubles.") The scales metaphor here anticipates its function in *The Redress of Poetry,* holding in tension as it does the impulse to report the world's suffering directly and the lure of aestheticization.

Yet the neatness of the antithesis is unsettled by the difficulty of establishing precisely how the body of the Grauballe Man is intended to relate to the "Dying Gaul" and the nameless victim. The problem stems in part from the preposition *with,* which sways between implications of reciprocity and opposition. Read from one angle, the ancient bog body can be taken as representative first of "beauty" and then of "atrocity." (In this interpretation, it is as if there is a silent "on the one hand" before the phrase "with the Dying Gaul" and a silent "on the other" before "with the actual weight.") Alternatively, *with* can be read according to its first definition in the *OED:* "in a position opposite to; over against." This reading depends on imagining the Grauballe Man suspended in the opposite scale to the emblems of "beauty" and "atrocity" in turn—which presupposes that there are two sets of scales, not one. Martin Dodsworth interprets Heaney's lines according to this second reading, but deems the problems of visualization and conceptualization appropriate to the poem's ethical difficulties:

> These lines are peculiarly uncomfortable because the idea of suspense is compromised by the logical necessity of there being two sets of scales in question—one in which the Grauballe man is balanced against the beauty of the "Dying Gaul" and another in which a contemporary "hooded victim" occupies the other pan. And indeed the poem ends more effectively for this, its air of irresolution enhanced by the subliminal and "impossible" image of the Grauballe man swinging in two sets of scales simultaneously.

(150)

The point is well made, but a sense of apt complexity is nonetheless hard to disentangle from confusion caused by overworked metaphorical language. This confusion derives from other factors than the ambiguity of the preposition *with.* For instance, a problematic readjustment of interpretation is required as the description shifts from the "Dying Gaul" to the "hooded victim." By the time one has read only the first five lines of the two closing stanzas, the implication seems to be that the sculpture epitomizes both "beauty and atrocity," or atrocity refashioned as beauty.[5] Yet by the end of the poem, one must revise this first reading: artistry and suffering need to be teased apart retrospectively, with the artistry apportioned solely to the statue and the suffering solely to the "hooded victim"; otherwise, the intended antithesis founders. A further problem resides in the phrase "each hooded victim," which conflates ideas of singular and plural, thus raising the possibility of multiple bodies being weighed on one side of the scales. Finally, the efficacy of Heaney's metaphorical contraption is also challenged by the available but clumsy image of the Grauballe Man's body being slung across two scale-pans, weighing in with both art object and real human victim at once. This is not, presumably, an intended implication of the imagery, but the sway of Heaney's language and the strain of visualizing a body (or bodies) and a sculpture hanging in a giant set (or giant sets) of scales allow the implication nonetheless.

The ending of Heaney's poem seems designed to reflect on the processes by which he has hitherto described the Grauballe Man, but the awkwardness of the scales imagery complicates this self-questioning in a not altogether effective way. In the preceding stanzas, the exhumed body is naturalized by a series of graphic comparisons that liken its grainy wrists to "bog oak," the ball of its heel to "a basalt egg," its spine to "an eel arrested / under a glisten of mud," and so forth, with the result that the body is at once presented with sharp physical exactitude and metamorphosed into a set of artistically satisfying correlates for itself. The aesthetic impulse is further complicated by Heaney's insistence on the violent nature of the man's death: his "slashed" throat connects his fate to that of the "slashed and dumped" body at the poem's end, thus signaling Heaney's resistance to his own artistry. At the last, Heaney abandons visual precision and tactile figuration as if to summarize his predicament: the effectiveness of these methods has involved a reprehensible translation of human suffering into "perfected" art. But the problem that had been exemplified with winning clarity in those earlier stanzas—of physical realization leading, paradoxically, to metaphysical falsification—is dwelt upon in the final two stanzas in more cumbersome ways. Here also Heaney both deploys and distrusts metaphorical language, but by "overdoing it" is less successful in articulating the tension; hovering uncertainly between visualization and abstraction—between, that is, a pictorial illustration and an intellectual extrapolation of the paradox his poem has constructed—these stanzas ultimately obscure the terms of the poem's anxious self-interrogation.

To ask hard questions of writing that asks hard questions of itself might seem to bespeak a lack of sympathetic engagement, which might in turn be construed as a covert questioning of the poet's considerable reputation or as disenchantment with the implied politics of his work, or both. Yet circumspection based on one's sense of the relative successes and shortcomings of Heaney's metaphorical language need not (and in my case does not) derive from such reservations or from a lack of overall admiration for his literary achievement. With regard to the end of **"The Grauballe Man,"** where the political implications of Heaney's meditation on victimage are potentially provocative, this circumspection might be considered an essential safeguard against either too easy a vindication or too decisive a condemnation. A temptation to condemn might reflect the supposition that Heaney is contentiously conflating bog victim and heroic Celtic warrior (they are both thought to have been killed in the third century BC) and, by extension, these two figures and "each" anonymous target of contemporary violence. Furthermore, given the connection Henry Hart has posited between "each hooded victim" and those Irish Catholics forced to wear hoods before being assassinated by members of the Ulster Defence Association in the early 1970s (91), it might be argued that Heaney is seeking here to mythologize the specifics of atrocity, to confer members of his "tribe" with the status of heroic victim, and to convey a deterministic sense of the timelessness of such violence—all accusations that have been leveled at him for other metaphorical procedures and turns of phrase in *North*.[6] In such a reading, the word *each* would take on a fatalistic force, as if insinuating that every time someone from the nationalist side is murdered, a timeless paradigm is repeated. A defense of Heaney here would stress the ambiguous relationship between the different victims achieved through the complex operations of the scales imagery; both the fact that Heaney's imagined figures are held in opposition rather than union and the consideration that the poem as a whole explores the risks of subjecting the dead to interpretive distortion would counter readings that see the poem as an expression of ideological affiliations or atavistic impulses. However, either a critique or a defense of Heaney's methods is liable to be founded—but also to founder—on the assumption that the metaphorical machinery of the final stanzas is functioning effectively and according to the author's design. The implications of potential misprision on this score cut both ways: the difficulty of distinguishing suggestive ambiguity from inadvertent obliquity in the scales imagery is continuous with the difficulty of ascribing or denying fixed political alignments to the work.

Such considerations should warn one against being too ready either to suspect or to sanction Heaney's writing when it touches on contentious subject matter. What renders judgment here problematic is the dilemma of disentangling one's sense of how his language operates in terms of semantic or formal control from more ineffable questions of tone, intention, and readerly trust. One of Heaney's most distrustful critics, David Lloyd, has argued that Heaney's poems at times mask their own violent implications by means of a disarming note of "warm and humanising morality" (20). Christopher Ricks, in a review of *Field Work,* maintains that there is something "consciously innocent" in Heaney's handling of verbal ambiguities, that the volume is "alive with trust" in its own language—though trust of a self-conscious, "ungullible" kind—and that this "trust" warrants reciprocal indulgence from the reader. The "uncomplacent wisdom" of the poems, the way in which Heaney practices his art "secure in the grounded trust that he is trusted" by his readers as a good-hearted, square-dealing, scrupulously undeceived sort of poet is, for Ricks, the expression—and the encouragement—of a benign political perspective:

> Ungullible trust will always be of value but especially so in Ireland torn by reasonable and unreasonable distrust and mistrust. [. . .] A great deal of mistrust is misconstruction, and like the acrobat half-feigning a faltering Heaney's poems often tremble with the pos-

sibilities of misconstruing and misconstruction which they openly provide but which only a predator would pounce upon.

The reluctance to acknowledge that Heaney's verbal acrobatics might on occasion falter (although the equivocation of "half-feigning" goes halfway toward granting this possibility) is striking as a manifestation of trust; so too is the characterization of any doubting impulse as predatory. Ricks's sentiments on this point might be read as a rebuke to those critics who called into question the political ramifications of Heaney's preceding volume, *North.* That the manner of Heaney's poetry is taken to be an expression of political optimism says something about the problem of distinguishing recognition of poetic accomplishment per se from whatever cultural authority such recognition implies.

As a high-profile, justly popular ambassador from the republic of letters—a position strengthened by his tenure as Oxford Professor of Poetry from 1989 to 1994 and by his winning the Nobel Prize for Literature in 1995—Heaney has come to occupy a peculiarly trusted position. This has increasingly rendered problematic anything but praise, as Peter McDonald observed in "Levelling Out," noting how, "in attempting to identify certain limits to a writer's achievement, critical response of a less than rapturous cast is exposed instantly to charges of carping and resentment" (39). This predicament is also, as McDonald observed in "Appreciating Assets," attributable to Heaney's genial sensibility, to his "gift for the humane and life-affirming," a gift that "makes critical disagreement with him both difficult and distasteful" (77). Such reflections on the relationship between a poet's artistic temperament and the critical reception of the poet's writing (to which the writing is often alert) open up for consideration the grounds and nature of Heaney's authority as a celebrated poet-critic. As regards his critical reflections on poetry, the authoritative air Heaney commands is of a peculiar kind. The language of his prose characteristically sways between hesitance and exuberance, self-deprecation and self-affirmation, a diffident sense of audience and a forthright insistence that poetry is, as he puts it in *The Redress of Poetry,* a "wilful and unabashed activity" (163); in part, the sway Heaney exerts as a critic is founded on this balancing of accommodative and assertive impulses. The appeal of the prose also derives, as David Trotter has argued, from Heaney's desire to win the reader's sympathetic indulgence through inventive metaphor, to avoid discursiveness by bringing his prose toward the condition of poetry.[7] In effecting this move, Heaney establishes continuities of manner and metaphor between his reflections on poetry and his practice of the art; as Corcoran puts it, "essays and poems form part of a single, even systematic effort of consciousness, an interior meditation which issues at once in acts of the imagination and constructions of the critical intelligence" (139). As the example of the scales imagery has already illustrated, the implications of this are double-edged: while the two modes of writing might be regarded as in certain respects mutually fortified by correspondences between them, reservations about Heaney's powers of control in one mode might well condition responses to aspects of the other.

There is a poem in *The Spirit Level* that provides a striking example of how Heaney's verse works together with his prose in partly fruitful, partly questionable alliance. **"A Sofa in the Forties"** (7-9) is closely linked in its preoccupations and narrative content to autobiographical reflections offered in Heaney's 1995 Nobel lecture, *Crediting Poetry*; beyond this it recalls many other details in his essays and poems. Heaney begins the poem by recollecting a childhood game of make-believe in which he and his siblings transformed the family sofa into a pretend railway train; as the memory of this activity expands, the harmless fantasy is set against intimations of cultural conflict and historical upheaval beyond the secure homestead. These intimations intensify in the third of the poem's four twelve-line sections:

> We entered history and ignorance
> Under the wireless shelf. *Yippee-i-ay,*
> Sang "The Riders of the Range." HERE IS THE
>   NEWS,
>
> Said the absolute speaker. Between him and us
> A great gulf was fixed where pronunciation
> Reigned tyrannically. The aerial wire
>
> Swept from a treetop down in through a hole
> Bored in the windowframe. When it moved in wind,
> The sway of language and its furtherings
>
> Swept and swayed in us like nets in water
> Or the abstract, lonely curve of distant trains
> As we entered history and ignorance.

Heaney's notion of "the sway of language" plays off against each other ideas of externally imposed rhetorical coercion and internally rooted inclination. In an interview with me, he identified the crux of this poem as the dual signification of the word *sway,* noting that it is in part

> an image of command [. . .] and then there is one's swaying in sympathy or of necessity. [. . .] It has that double sense, that double possibility, of active or passive engagement.

The "command" of the newscaster's voice, whose "pronunciation" is presumably that of BBC "Queen's English," is presented in the poem as a form of cultural imperialism in a 1940s County Derry Catholic home. Broadcast across "a great gulf" from the supposed center to the provinces, this voice communicates an ostensibly definitive version ("THE NEWS") of

momentous events going on elsewhere; its tone and concerns are so at odds with the dialect and day-to-day experiences of the rural household as to seem a tyrannical imposition.

Heaney exploits the ambiguity of *sway* to suggest how this influence was nonetheless tacitly resisted: the sway—or controlling power—exercised by the "absolute speaker" was tested, he implies, by the swaying—or fluctuating—nature of the response it received. (The light-hearted pun on "speaker" might itself be said to collude in such resistance, subverting with a touch of whimsy the grave implications of absolutism.) That "The sway of language and its furtherings / Swept and swayed in us like nets in water" conveys, on the one hand, an impression of Northern Ireland trawled by the nets of empire—in this reading "furtherings" are extensions of cultural infiltration—and, on the other, an impression of people simply swaying back and forth, bending as much to their own inclinations as in accommodation of alien influences: water cannot be held by any net. The "sway" of the radio broadcast might also be read as the product of interference, since it is caused by the aerial moving in wind; here the "furtherings" might be glossed as the effects of one radio voice merging with another (this gloss might be overdoing it, but it is prompted—as with certain responses to the scales imagery in **"The Grauballe Man"**—by the wide range of implications that Heaney's metaphorical language generates). In this reading, the local environment controls the broadcast as much as the broadcast controls the environment: the wind and the swaying of the tree arbitrarily determine what is and is not received from the larger world. Complicating these interpretive possibilities further is Heaney's interview remark about one's "swaying in sympathy or of necessity": if necessity denotes the begrudged imposition of a culturally "other" voice bringing news of distant events to the farmstead, then those events themselves, grim tidings perhaps from Europe in the first half of the forties, would nonetheless be liable to evince sympathy; the language "swept and swayed" through its listeners not merely like nets designed to capture something but also, more poignantly, like "the abstract, lonely curve of distant trains." The latter image conjures a mood of far-off unreality and ineffable pathos, stirring thoughts of deportation that can be neither fully imagined nor banished from the mind. To be "swayed" by such promptings is to be "swept" by the strong currents of emotion they are liable to provoke.

"A Sofa in the Forties" hovers uncertainly between an inclination to defend the impulses of creative fancy, as represented by the make-believe train, and a recognition that imaginative processes are always at some level subject to cultural and historical forces. This tension is implicit in the poem's abrupt transition from the "The Riders of the Range" to the sober announcement of the news program. Heaney's unwillingness to value one above the other is reflected in the beguiling phrase that frames this third section—"we entered history and ignorance"—in which conditions of knowing and unknowing are blurred. In the context of the poem as a whole, this paradoxical phrase suggests that the train game is a means of approaching history. As the poem progresses, the sofa takes on a funereal air. It is compared to a "ghost-train" and "death-gondola," and in the closing lines this vehicle of imaginative transport evokes the saddest, most forbidding instances of historical transportation and suffering:

> we sensed
> A tunnel coming up where we'd pour through
> Like unlit carriages through fields at night,
> Our only job to sit, eyes straight ahead,
> And be transported and make engine-noise.

The tunnel that the children enter in their imaginative game represents both the darkness of their historical ignorance and, evoking the Holocaust, the dark phase of history that shadows their activities.[8] These considerations do not, however, condemn the child's play. The game of make-believe on the sofa is continuous with the protected world of the family home life more generally. Heaney's representation of his own personal history is an act of cultural retrieval: he memorializes a vanished time and place, setting it against the "tyrannical" claims of alien media. The imaginative freedom of the children at play is an affirmative aspect of what, in the *Stations* prose poem **"England's Difficulty,"** he terms "that opaque security, that autonomous ignorance" of his childhood life (16).

"A Sofa in the Forties" participates in a larger narrative (some might say a mythology) of rootedness in Heaney's work, an authenticating of cultural identity through remembered childhood experience. Most notably, the contours of the poem's world are faithfully reinscribed in *Crediting Poetry*. Though the children's train game is not mentioned in that lecture, there is a striking degree of continuity between **"A Sofa in the Forties"** and the poet's reminiscences about the secure "den-life" of his family farmhouse, a home world both receptive to and immured from the concerns of the wider world:

> We took in everything that was going on, of course—rain in the trees, mice on the ceiling, a steam train rumbling along the railway line one field back from the house—but we took it in as if we were in the doze of hibernation. Ahistorical, pre-sexual, in suspension between the archaic and the modern, we were as susceptible and impressionable as the drinking water that stood in a bucket in our scullery: every time a passing train made the earth shake, the surface of that water used to ripple delicately, concentrically, and in utter silence.
>
> But it was not only the earth that shook for us: the air around and above us was alive and signalling too.

> When a wind stirred in the beeches, it also stirred an aerial wire attached to the topmost branch of the chestnut tree. Down it swept, in through a hole bored in the corner of the kitchen window, right on into the innards of our wireless set where a little pandemonium of burbles and squeaks would suddenly give way to the voice of a BBC newsreader speaking out of the unexpected like a *deus ex machina*. [. . .]

> We could pick up [. . .] in the resonant English tones of the newsreader the names of bombers and of cities bombed, of war fronts and army divisions, the numbers of planes lost and of prisoners taken, of casualties suffered and advances made; and always, of course, we would pick up too those other, solemn and oddly bracing words, "the enemy" and "the allies." But even so, none of the news of these world-spasms entered me as terror. If there was something ominous in the newscaster's tones, there was something torpid about our understanding of what was at stake; and if there was something culpable about such political ignorance in that time and place, there was something positive about the security I inhabited as a result of it.

(9-10)

"A Sofa in the Forties" and these opening reflections of *Crediting Poetry* both clarify and confuse each other. On one level, the essay reads as a gloss on the poem: it secures Heaney's hitherto location-free image of rippling water by setting it in a bucket in the family scullery, and it reveals that the "abstract, lonely curve of distant trains" is prompted by real activity in the local environment. Yet to read the poem in the light of the lecture, resolving abstract into concrete images, might also be to limit, even to distort, how the poem operates, especially since the lecture establishes a causal link between moving train and swaying water that does not exist in the poem. Moreover, *Crediting Poetry* undoes the chain of associations pursued by Heaney in the third section of **"A Sofa in the Forties."** The poem moves from the commanding tones of the newscaster's voice to the natural movements of rippling water that partly disperse this authority, and thence to the further dissolve of specificity in the realm of the "distant" trains. In the lecture, this movement is reversed: the images of passing train and moving water precede, and explain by analogy, the impact of the newsreader's voice. The householders' susceptibility to his authority is presented as a natural extension of their susceptibility to events in the environment. Nor does this "resonant English" voice invite resistance: in the lecture, it does not preside "tyrannically" by casting nets of British cultural dominance, but is "ominous" only for the news it reports from a world where the menace of actual tyranny is a pressing concern. Although this fearful world is also in the imaginative offing of **"A Sofa in the Forties,"** there is no explicit focus in the poem on the realities of bombs and victims; if there had been, the idea of British pronunciation as a shadow form of tyranny might have faltered against the larger political considerations.

For these reasons, it would be simplistic to claim that the poem and the lecture are mutually supportive. While each could be thought to amplify the authority of the other—the lecture deriving its command from the same imaginative provenance as the poetry, and the poem claiming for itself a significant place in the Heaney canon by being intimately linked to a career-capping speech—one could also maintain that the two works unsettle each other. It is hard to say whether the interrelations of content and image result in an accumulation or a displacement of significance; there is an enhanced authoritative sway but also a swaying instability of reference that calls into question the self-sufficiency of each individual text. This authority and instability are intensified by detailed correspondences with a number of other works of Heaney's. For instance, the poem's idea of the BBC newscaster's voice as culturally invasive is shadowed by a recollection in an essay in *The Government of the Tongue* on radio programs delivered by the poet Patrick Kavanagh from the Irish Republic: "Over the border, into a Northern Ireland dominated by the noticeably English accents of the local BBC, he broadcast a voice that would not be cowed into accents other than its own" (9). More significantly, Heaney's concern with the interfering purchase of British on Irish culture through the medium of radio is considered at length in the essay "The Regional Forecast," which recalls the experience of local households listening to the BBC weather forecaster speaking "in a tone so authoritative it verged upon the tyrannical" (10). The gulf between the tone of certainty with which the forecast was issued from afar and the listeners' own weather-instincts is read by Heaney as a reflection of "the overall cultural situation in which the centre is privileged and the province is debilitated" (16); it suggests to him how the forecaster had "begun to interpose between ourselves and the evidence of our senses a version of the meteorological reality which weakened the sureness of our grip on our own experience" (11). Heaney interprets the eventual distrust of these weather forecasts as a small signal of cultural self-determination. Such reflections lead him to assert that the writer from the cultural margins "must re-envisage the region as the original point" (13) and to observe that

> anywhere where the English language and an imposed anglicised culture have radically altered the original social and linguistic conditions, there is likely to be a literary task [. . .] of subversion and redefinition.
>
> (19).⁹

In certain ways, **"A Sofa in the Forties"** might be said to undertake precisely this task, challenging the tyranny of received cultural judgments by showing the Heaney householders at the center of their own world, swaying to their own impulses.¹⁰

The swayings in **"A Sofa in the Forties"** reflect the preoccupations of the volume in which the poem appears: ***The Spirit Level,*** as its title suggests, is concerned with the precarious equipoise made literal in **"Weighing In,"** which describes how loads were balanced on a weighbridge so that "everything trembled, flowed with give and take" (17).¹¹ Heaney's phrase "the sway of language and its furtherings" can thus be read as an observation on the linguistic carryover from one poem to another. Indeed, the idea of "furtherings" marks an extension of his abiding concern in the previous collection, ***Seeing Things,*** with moments of imaginative dilation—as when, in **"Markings,"** a children's football match acquires in the minds of its players a sense of "fleetness, furtherance, untiredness / In time that was extra, unforeseen and free" (8), or when, in poem 32 of **"Squarings,"** Heaney recalls how "Running water never disappointed. / Crossing water always furthered something" (90). Nor do the ripple effects stop there: the Nobel lecture and **"A Sofa in the Forties"** look back also to the fourth of the **"Glanmore Sonnets"** in ***Field Work,*** where Heaney recalls the time when the local train went past and "in the house, small ripples shook / Silently across our drinking water" (36) and beyond that to the reminiscence in the ***Stations*** prose poem **"Waterbabies"** about playing in muddy water with a childhood companion, while "sometimes a bomber warbled far beyond us, sometimes a train ran through the fields and small ripples quivered silently across our delta" (9). This memory in turn anticipates the "Mossbawn" essay in *Preoccupations,* where Heaney recalls that the "great historical action" of American troops and bomber planes near the family farm did not "disturb the rhythms of the yard," the rhythms by which water was drawn from the family pump (17). Each of these instances serves as a "furthering" of the others, and such furthering might be read as an allegory for Heaney's poetics of transcendence: the ramifications of phrase and image that carry poems beyond their own borders function as tokens of Heaney's belief that poetic language transports consciousness into an "extra" dimension.

In "The Fire i' the Flint: Reflections on the Poetry of Gerard Manley Hopkins," also in *Preoccupations,* Heaney conceives of poetic composition as a mysterious process that builds up "a texture of echo and implication"; a poem achieves indefinable yet irresistible effects, he maintains, by "trawling the pool of the ear with a net of associations" (83). The metaphor anticipates his assertion in "Sounding Auden" that a poem's authority derives from "the sway gained over the deep ear and, through that, over other parts of our mind and nature." The sway of these figurations themselves makes them apt as analogies for considering how the "furtherings" of "echo and implication" in Heaney's writings work on the reader partly in ways that elude description: the ear is trawled with a net of associations; these sweep and sway in consciousness as one moves through and between texts, influencing how one hears and interprets. To say this may be to court the danger of critical impressionism or to risk falling in too easily with the poet's own figurations for poetic process and response, yet any consideration of the shifts and instabilities in Heaney's poetry must acknowledge the subtle, at times ineffable modulations of phrase and rhythm: the sway of the poetic line.

In the title poem of *Seeing Things* (16-17), for instance, swaying and balancing register not merely as motifs but also as musical effects. The following extract makes this clear:

> The sea was very calm but even so,
> When the engine kicked and our ferryman
> Swayed for balance, reaching for the tiller,
> I panicked at the shiftiness and heft
> Of the craft itself. What guaranteed us—
> That quick response and buoyancy and swim—
> Kept me in agony.

It would be insufficient merely to note that the imagery here points toward related metaphors in Heaney's work, such as the portrayal of Lowell riding "on the swaying tiller" of himself in **"Elegy,"** or, more generally, toward Heaney's preoccupation with precarious equipoise, or toward his descriptions of mutable impulses in terms of shifting water. One needs also to recognize how the ideas of swaying and balancing are played out in the movements of the verse—in "undulant cadences" of the kind Heaney commends, in *Finders Keepers,* in the poetry of T. S. Eliot (34). The poem registers both the physical tremors and the psychological trepidation of a remembered family boat trip by engineering metrical turbulence in the swing of the line turn from "ferry-man" to "Swayed" and in such rocking phrases as "When the engine kicked," "reaching for the tiller" and "shiftiness and heft." The ear responds to these volatile fluctuations in rhythm precisely because of the steadiness of surrounding lines: the sure, level iambic pentameter of "The sea was very calm but even so" and "That quick response and buoyancy and swim" is what guarantees Heaney's handling of his own "craft." The authoritative sway he achieves in the medium of poetic language is intimately bound up with his assured control of the swaying meter, its fluid "give and take."

Heaney has repeatedly conceived of poetic accomplishment in terms of nautical metaphors, though these have not all been equally fit for voyage. In the introduction to his *Beowulf,* for example, he offers a fanciful description of "moments of lyric intensity" in the Anglo-Saxon poem, when

> the keel of the poetry is deeply set in the element of sensation while the mind's lookout sways metrically and far-sightedly in the element of pure comprehension—which is to say that the elevation of *Beowulf* is always, paradoxically, buoyantly down-to-earth.
>
> (xxi)

He also goes overboard in *Crediting Poetry* with his claim that "poetic form is both the ship and the anchor," that "it is at once a buoyancy and a holding, allowing for the simultaneous gratification of whatever is centrifugal and centripetal in mind and body" (29).[12] Although Heaney's precipitous "furtherings" of implication sometimes cause the metaphorical language to capsize, his terms do usefully identify a guiding impulse in his work: the desire to balance the physical and the metaphysical, the importunities of the world and the imperatives of the imagination. In terms of poetic form and language, this desire registers as an audible negotiation between weightiness and wavering. The tension between these alternative modes is explored directly in poem 2 of the **"Squarings"** sequence in *Seeing Things* (56), which ends with self-commands at once firm and fluxional:

> Sink every impulse like a bolt. Secure
> The bastion of sensation. Do not waver
> Into language. Do not waver in it.

As so often in Heaney's poetry, the delivery is two-toned, swaying between austerity and irony. The irony derives from the fact that Heaney insists on the pressure and precision of poetic language with a verbal fluidity that itself represents a form of wavering. Swaying between contrary imperatives, searching for moments of balance and surety yet registering every cross-current of thought that frustrates this aim, Heaney's work vindicates the large claims of his Nobel lecture:

> poetry can make an order as true to the impact of external reality and as sensitive to the inner laws of the poet's being as the ripples that rippled in and rippled out across the water in that scullery bucket fifty years ago.
>
> (11)

Notes

1. In "Robert Lowell: A Memorial Address," Heaney recalls the poet's habit of approaching people in a manner "half buoyant, half somnambulant, on the balls of his feet, his voice at once sharp and sidling" (23). The swaying of Lowell's body is also implicitly linked in "Elegy" to alcohol consumption: "You drank America / like the heart's / iron vodka" (31). Lowell himself records his inebriated rocking motions in the poem "Seventh Year": "I stand swaying at the end of the party, / a half-filled glass in each hand—/ I too swayed / by the hard infatuate wind of love" (812). A different kind of swaying, induced by an attack of mental illness, is recorded in "For Ann Adden 4. Coda": "I have to brace my hand against a wall / to keep myself from swaying—swaying wall, / straitjacket, hypodermic, helmeted / doctors" (536).

2. Heaney has spoken of his attraction to a

> phrase which was still used in the country, about people who were famous or in control. It was said that "they held sway." I thought that was good for a warrior culture, so I began the [*Beowulf*] poem, "So, the Spear-Danes held sway once."
>
> (Hass and Heaney 10)

He subsequently changed this draft line.

3. See also *Redress* 36. The phrase *fine excess* derives from Keats's letter to John Taylor of 27 February 1818: "I think Poetry should surprise by a fine excess and not by Singularity—it should strike the Reader as a wording of his own highest thoughts, and appear almost a Remembrance" (238).

4. Other Heaney poems that use scales imagery in arguably problematic ways are "Terminus" in *The Haw Lantern* (5); poem 40 of "Squarings" in *Seeing Things* (100); "Weighing In" (17), "Mycenae Lookout" (30), and "The Poplar" (50) in *The Spirit Level*; and the *Electric Light* poem "Ten Glosses: 4. A Suit" (54).

5. A Yeatsian sense of "terrible beauty" is in the air here: see "Easter 1916" (Yeats 287-89).

6. The oft-cited criticisms, by Ciaran Carson, Conor Cruise O'Brien, David Lloyd, Edna Longley, Blake Morrison, and others, of *North*'s politicized mythologies are usefully summarized, along with alternative critical readings, in Andrews (80-119).

7. "Heaney's essays [. . .] constantly aspire to a lyric action which would absolve their most important insights from discursiveness" (Trotter 12).

8. In a personal interview, Heaney remarked to me that in these lines he "was thinking, of course, of the Holocaust, and the atrocious callousness of that operation."

9. Heaney's own radio broadcasts for the BBC and Radio Telefis Eireann, especially frequent in the 1970s, could be viewed as part of the project of cultural redress he envisages in "The Regional Forecast."

10. "A Sofa in the Forties" and *Crediting Poetry* also implicitly connect to the *Stations* prose poem "England's Difficulty" (16), with its recollection of the infamous "Haw Haw" radio broadcasts that "called to lamplit kitchens" during the Second World War. Childhood memories of radio voices feature more positively in the *Preoccupations* essay "Feeling into Words" (45) and the seventh of the "Glanmore Sonnets" in *Field Work* (39); both the essay and the poem recall the alluring rhythms of the shipping forecast. In the title poem of *Electric Light* Heaney remembers nostalgically how, as a child listening to the wireless, he "roamed at will the stations of the world" (81) while in "The Real Names," in the same volume, Heaney recalls a "terrible night" of stormy weather and political violence when the chestnut tree was rocked by wind and "the aerial rod like a mast / Whiplashed in tempest" (48).

11. Compare, for example, "The Swing," another poem in which the action of swaying is figured as imaginative liberation: "In spite of all, we sailed / Beyond ourselves" (49).

12. Poems that employ nautical imagery to describe poetic impulse include the title poem of *North* (19-20); the final section of "Casualty" in *Field Work* (23-24); two poems in *The Haw Lantern*, "From the Republic of Conscience" (12) and "From the Canton of Expectation" (47); and poem 8 of the "Squarings" sequence in *Seeing Things* (62).

Works Cited

Andrews, Elmer, ed. *The Poetry of Seamus Heaney.* Cambridge: Icon, 1998.

Corcoran, Neil. *The Poetry of Seamus Heaney: A Critical Study.* London: Faber, 1998.

Dodsworth, Martin. "Edward Thomas, Seamus Heaney, and Modernity: A Reply to Antony Easthope." *English* 49 (2000): 143-54.

Hart, Henry. *Seamus Heaney: Poet of Contrary Progressions.* Syracuse: Syracuse UP, 1992.

Hass, Robert, and Seamus Heaney. *Sounding Lines: The Art of Translating Poetry.* Berkeley: Doreen B. Townsend Center for the Humanities, 2000.

Heaney, Seamus, trans. *Beowulf.* London: Faber, 1999.

———. *Crediting Poetry: The Nobel Lecture 1995.* Loughcrew: Gallery, 1995.

———. *Electric Light.* London: Faber, 2001.

———. *Field Work.* London: Faber, 1979.

———. *Finders Keepers: Selected Prose 1971-2001.* London: Faber, 2002.

———. *The Government of the Tongue: The 1986 T. S. Eliot Memorial Lectures and Other Critical Writings.* London: Faber, 1988.

———. *The Haw Lantern.* London: Faber, 1987.

———. *North.* London: Faber, 1975.

———. Personal interview. 24 May 1994.

———. *Preoccupations: Selected Prose 1968-1978.* London: Faber, 1980.

————. *The Redress of Poetry: Oxford Lectures.* London: Faber, 1995.

————. "The Regional Forecast." *The Literature of Region and Nation.* Ed. R. P. Draper. Basingstoke: Macmillan, 1989. 10-23.

————. "Robert Lowell: A Memorial Address." *Agenda* 18.3 (1980): 23-28.

————. *Seeing Things.* London: Faber, 1991.

————. *The Spirit Level.* London: Faber, 1996.

————. *Stations.* Belfast: Ulsterman, 1975.

Keats, John. *The Letters of John Keats 1814-1821.* Ed. Edward Rollins Hyder. Vol. 1. Cambridge: Harvard UP, 1958.

Lloyd, David. "'Pap for the Dispossessed': Seamus Heaney and the Poetics of Identity." *Anomalous States: Irish Writing and the Post-Colonial Moment.* Dublin: Lilliput, 1993. 13-40.

Lowell, Robert. *Collected Poems.* Ed. Frank Bidart and David Gewanter. London: Faber, 2003.

McDonald, Peter. "Appreciating Assets." Rev. of *Finders Keepers,* by Seamus Heaney. *Poetry Review* 92.2 (2002): 76-79.

————. "Levelling Out." Rev. of *The Spirit Level,* by Seamus Heaney. *Thumbscrew* 5 (1996): 39-48.

Ratiner, Steven. "Seamus Heaney: The Words Worth Saying." Interview. *Giving Their Word: Conversations with Contemporary Poets.* U of Massachusetts P, 2002. 95-107.

Ricks, Christopher. "The Mouth, the Meal, and the Book." Rev. of *Field Work,* by Seamus Heaney. *London Review of Books* 8 Nov. 1979: 4-5.

Trotter, David. "Troubles." Rev. of *The Government of the Tongue,* by Seamus Heaney. *London Review of Books* 23 June 1988: 11-12.

Weil, Simone. *Gravity and Grace.* Trans. Emma Craufurd. London: Routledge, 1952.

Yeats, W. B. *Yeats's Poems.* Ed. Norman A. Jeffares. London: Macmillan, 1989.

Michael Parker (essay date 2006)

SOURCE: Parker, Michael. "Woven Figures: Seamus Heaney and Nationalist Tradition." In *Back to the Present, Forward to the Past: Irish Writing and History since 1798, Volume I,* edited by Patricia A. Lynch, Joachim Fischer and Brian Coates, pp. 27-41. Amsterdam: Rodopi, 2006.

[In the following essay, Parker raises questions about the appellation "nationalist" as it is applied to Heaney by some critics, arguing that they have missed the ambiguity and irony in many of Heaney's more political poems.]

I cannot deny my past to which my self is wed
The woven figure cannot undo its thread.

The speaking voice in Louis MacNeice's poem, "Valediction"[1] seeks to escape the historical, political and cultural patterns that constrain him, but despite his best efforts to extricate himself from its complex weave he cannot. The self is married to the past, and the very language with which he engages the legacy of his Irish past stitches him up. And yet the poet's aim, both in and beyond this single piece of material, is to work at those seams and stitches, to transform the original material and inherited ideological attitudes into something different, less sure, more complex.

Certain critics working in the 1980s and 1990s have discerned and sought to expose a consistent, underlying, coherent design within Seamus Heaney's work over the past thirty plus years, but have at times tended to do so in an over-deterministic way.[2] One of the terms frequently used, or rather ill-used in this context is "nationalist", a political term which I would regard as highly problematical.[3] Frequently it is deployed as a pejorative term, and employed to mean "atavistic", "reactionary", prone to outdated political and religious pieties. One thinks, for example, of the opening section of David Lloyd's critique, "Pap for the Dispossessed: Seamus Heaney and the Poetics of Identity",[4] which constructs a seamless continuum between mid-nineteenth-century nationalism and northern nationalism from the 1940s onward, regardless of historical and political differences between the Ireland of 1843 and Northern Ireland in 1923, 1939 (the date of Heaney's birth), 1969 or 1972.

In an essay entitled "Varieties of Nationalism: Post Revisionist Irish Studies", Willy Maley has taken to task the way "revisionist criticism of nationalism has chosen to represent it as a flat homogeneous whole".[5] "Nationalism", he asserts, "is a complex range of discourses, often contradictory and confused".[6] In a subsequent edition of the same journal,[7] Eugene O'Brien responds to this analysis, querying Maley's omission of "physical force nationalism", and questioning whether nationalism was really as plural and diverse as Maley implied. The origins of nationalism, O'Brien argues, lie in "racial homogeneity, a homogeneity expressed and solidified by linguistic, cultural and religious practices, and by exclusion of any other racial input". His article stresses the doubleness of nationalism, how its inclusiveness—its promoting "of socio-cultural identification and self-definition"[8]—inevitably involves a degree of exclusivity. Nationalism, he goes on to say, involves "a belief in an optative future", and is sanctioned by a monological reading of history and driven by aesthetic totalizations combining, in an Irish context, ideas of mother ground, four green fields blood sacrifice, the necessity for violence, the necessity for a purging of those who are not part of the organic community.[9]

Like a great many other commentators in the Irish Republic in the wake of the conflict in the North, he avers that Nationalism is "a dangerous ideology with a huge potential for violence", and, not surprisingly, "events in the former Yugoslavia" are cited as a prelude to this contention.[10] For O'Brien, as for so many Europeans writing and living through the twentieth century's last years, "Nationalism" has become a heavily guilt-laden term, tainted by association with ethnic cleansing carried out by imperialists, racists, Bolsheviks, Nazis, and most recently Bosnian Serbs and Croats.

O'Brien's comments on Irish Nationalism, however, describe more accurately the militant Republican tradi-tion with its belief in physical force as a legitimate means of securing freedom. To support his argument, O'Brien cites some of the closing lines from Seamus Heaney's **"Kinship"**. Like Elizabeth Butler Cullingford before him,[11] he hears in the lines referring to "how we slaughter / for the common good"[12] the unmediated voice of the poet, and fails to recognize in them a bit-terly ironic indictment of militant *Republican* ideology and its perverse logic. What Heaney's persona is react-ing against here is the glamourized version of the struggle current during his childhood and retained by supporters of the Provisionals. To miss the irony in the macabre juxtaposition of "common good" and "slaugh-ter", is a bit like assuming that Swift was serious about breeding babies for consumption.

Too often in some recent and indeed some earlier critiques of Heaney's work, its indeterminacies and ironies have been missed or ignored, and his poems reduced to a tapestry of traditional Nationalist—for Nationalist read "republican"—tropes. What strikes me about Heaney's writing, particularly from the early 1970s onwards, however, is its "contradictory aware-nesses",[13] the way in which it frequently voices original impulses in order to challenge them, to suggest that they represent positions which may no longer be ten-able. It is unwise to construct from Heaney's poems—or the work of any poet for that matter—a consistent, homogeneous political narrative. Though his writing is clearly deeply watermarked by attitudes and values derived from his *Northern* Nationalist upbringing, even his earliest work can be seen as articulating a longing beyond belonging. There are early poems which are nervous and anxious about charges of betrayal, and which voice guilt at breaking with or seeming to break with tradition and the community, but these also speak out of a desire for individuation, for authority.

This essay will focus on some of Seamus Heaney's changing responses to a changing political climate from the mid-1960s onwards, and the extent to which he was a "woven figure", working with "woven figures". Liter-ary criticism can never be ideologically neutral, and

there is much to be said for setting both literary texts and critical texts within their chronological contexts so that one does not become too strongly swayed by "the prevailing political climate",[14] by what J. C. D. Clark and subsequently D. George Boyce have referred to as "present-mindedness".[15]

EARLY POLITICAL INTERVENTIONS[16]

The year 1966 marked a turning point both in Seamus Heaney's literary career and in the history of the province. His critically-acclaimed first book, *Death of a Naturalist,* appeared in the spring of that year, at the very time when the political situation began to worsen. That year saw two intensely emotive anniversaries, fuel-ling recalcitrance north and south of the border. In his highly polemical account of the present *States of Ireland* (1972), Conor Cruise O'Brien stresses the significance of these commemorations in the subsequent narrative of violence, and how in the Nationalism and unionist com-munities in the North they reinforced entrenched, passionately-held beliefs in the separateness of their histories:

> In 1966, the Republic—and also many of the Northern Catholics—solemnly commemorated the Easter Rising of 1916. These celebrations had to include the reminder that the object for which the men of 1916 sacrificed their lives—a free and united Ireland—had still not been achieved. The general calls for rededication to the ideals of 1916 were bound to suggest to some young men and women not only that these ideals were in practice being abandoned but that the way to return to them was through the method of 1916: violence ap-plied by a determined minority . . .

> Ulster Protestants, in the summer of 1916, com-memorated not only their usual seventeenth century topics but also the fiftieth anniversary of the Battle of the Somme, when the Ulster Division was cut to pieces at Thiepval Wood. From the perspective of those who commemorated these events, the commemorations in Dublin seemed a celebration of treachery, and at the same time a threat to "Ulster" . . . the spirit and character of the Dublin celebrations showed that the leopard had not changed his spots.[17]

Seamus Heaney's contemporaneous poetic response to the first of these anniversaries, the Easter Rising, was the poem, **"Requiem for the Croppies".**[18] Following Yeats' precedent in *Cathleen Ni Houlihan,* Heaney recalls an earlier period in the complex narrative of Ireland and Britain, a time when history was simple and the "truth" of the Nationalist version self-evident. The drama and immediacy of the poem owes much to its insistent first person plurals—"We moved quick", "We found", "We'd cut", "our great coats", "our own country". Eventually, as the poem's closure acknowl-edges, tricksy, energetic, active subjects—all those "we"s—become stricken objects ("our broken wave", "they buried us"). At the barbarousness meted out on

Vinegar Hill, the reader is told, "the hillside blushed", an image of intimate embarrassment which does not sit easily alongside the images of cannon, broken waves and the slaughter of "terraced thousands". With its final image of resurrection, resurgence and insurgency, the poem discovers Heaney perhaps at his most Pearsean.

In attempting to construct an analogy between Easter 1916 "heroes" and Catholic rebels killed in the Wexford rising of 1798, Heaney might be seen as proffering a version of the 1798 Rebellion that in effect writes the Nonconformist Protestant contribution—and the United Irishmen—out of Ireland's history.[19] There are always dangers, however, in passing judgements on the basis of reading single poems, and indeed **"Linen Town"** from *Wintering Out* redresses any perceived imbalance by acknowledging the role of Irish Protestants in the events of '98.[20] The poem speaks of the "swinging tongue" of Henry Joy McCracken, the hanged leader of the Antrim rebellion against English rule, and reflects Heaney's later view of 1798 as "the last turn / In the tang of possibility", a time when Northern Presbyterians and Catholics fought alongside each other and temporarily found "common ground" in the cause of independence.

Considerable insight into Seamus Heaney's political thinking in the pre-Troubles period may be found in an important prose article from 1 July 1966, "Out of London: Ulster's Troubles",[21] coincidentally published on the fiftieth anniversary of the beginning of the Battle of the Somme, and shortly before a visit to Belfast by Queen Elizabeth II. Here Heaney constructs and contrasts two Northern Irelands: one, the political state, tainted, jaded and backward-looking; the other, the cultural entity, energetic, exciting and thriving, where artists of indeterminate religious origin add their individual enterprise to a common endeavour. For much of the piece, certainly a traditional Nationalism antagonism towards Unionist Ulster and Britain is apparent. Though he had been Prime Minister for three years and had made some gestures towards *rapprochement* with the South and with Northern Catholics, significantly O'Neill is an absence from Heaney's text. One hesitates to suggest that the title itself might contain a coded reference to the prime minister, who spoke with a patrician English accent. Heaney might have been thinking of this when he suggests that to Unionist ears an English accent is a sound signifier, a guarantor of loyalty to the Crown and support for the Border, signalling the recognition that "gerrymandering is a necessary evil in order to maintain a loyalist government". Certainly the title itself implies an external, metropolitan source for "Ulster's Troubles". Its opening sentence refers slightingly to Belfast as the "*official* capital of the *partitioned* state of Northern Ireland" (my italics). Later Heaney goes on to voice his disapproval

of its "country town" provincialism, its cultural and economic dependency on England, that "state of mind that looks to England for approbation".

In a section which anticipates the place-name poems of *Wintering Out*—and Friel's *Translations*—Heaney draws attention to the lost, rural, "Irish" reality beneath the urban, "bourgeois", anglicized veneer, by pointing out the etymological origins of the Falls Road and Malone Road—"the road of the hedges" and "the plain of the lambs". Heaney's language is, as always, revealing, as is his choice of oppositions. The Falls, the soon-to-be English lecturer at Queen's informs us, is "the preserve of the Nationalism mass", where "mass" implies not only a Catholic area, but also serves to remind his readers that Nationalisms are a majority on the island as a whole. By contrast, the Malone Road is cited as a preserve of the "bourgeois ascendancy", which clearly positions its largely Protestant inhabitants as relics and hangers-on from a colonial era, and adds the class factor to the inequitable equation.

The article treats the annual preparations for the Twelfth of July, "something of a cross between religious and folk festival", with a mixture of awe and amusement. They are seen as constituting little threat to "the papist minority", who apparently console themselves with the thought that, "We'll outbreed them in the end". Having emphasized that belligerence and triumphalism also lie behind this "folk festival", the writer taunts Unionists here with one of their greatest long-standing anxieties, that Northern Catholics' higher birthrate would eventually bring them majority status.

Far more serious in the long term for the stability of both communities, Heaney realized, was the danger posed by Paisleyism, a movement

> directed at the breaking down of any bridges that might exist between Catholic and Protestant; it would create its own Troubles and set the political and religious question back 40 years. The atmosphere of the Troubles has been growing: there have been stabbings, shootings and bomb-throwings. . . . Life goes on, yet people are reluctant to dismiss the possibility of an explosion. A kind of doublethink operates: something is rotten, but maybe if we wait it will fester to death.

The final image of a festering wound within the state of Ulster, harks back to **"At a Potato Digging"** from *Death of a Naturalist,* and looks forward to **"Summer Home"**,[22] encouraging one perhaps to see in that poem an analogy between private and public disorders. The allusion to *Hamlet* implies that rottenness has been endemic since the creation of the state itself; it is uncertain whether he means to apply it to the festering resentment within his own community, since the passage quoted identifies Paisleyism as the destabilizing factor. Frequently in his poems, Heaney provides alternative readings of the same phenomenon, yet here both readings originate in and conclude in dismay and trepidation. One possibility is that Paisley's current prominence may signal "*the death throes* of the ignorant and ugly bigotry that has numbed the social life of the community for years". There is an interesting verbal slippage here, a suggestion that there is really only one community in Northern Ireland. The other, more alarming hypothesis sees Paisley as "*a phoenix figure,* stirring the embers of old feuds into a new conflagration".[23]

Roy Foster claims that Heaney's article exhibits "a poet's prescience",[24] but events such as the formation early in 1966 of the loyalist paramilitary group, the Ulster Protestant Volunteers, the emergence in May of another group ominously styling themselves the Ulster Volunteer Force, and a number of individual sectarian incidents gave pointers towards the way ahead. During May and June 1966 two people had been killed in sectarian attacks. The first was an elderly Protestant lady, Mrs Martha Gould, who died of injuries following a UVF petrol bomb attack on a Catholic-owned Belfast pub. Late in May, John Scullion, a Catholic, was stabbed on the Falls Road by a group who later escaped in a car. The worst incident, one referred to in "Out of Ulster", was the shooting on 26 June of four Catholic barmen walking home from work. Two were injured, and one, an eighteen-year-old, Peter Ward, died. Five Protestants, including Gusty Spence, the leader of the UVF, were soon after charged and convicted of the murder. One of them, Hugh McClean, allegedly told police, "I am terribly sorry I ever heard of that man Paisley or decided to follow him".[25] In J. Bowyer Bell's study, *The Irish Troubles,* we are informed that "in Stormont, O'Neill attacked Paisley for thanking the UVF for their support and called the organization 'this evil thing in our midst'". O'Neill labelled the Reverend and his supporters as "self-appointed defenders who 'see moderation as treason and decency as weakness'".[26]

Heaney's much later, stated conviction that poetry, like the other arts, could become "a force, almost a mode of power, certainly a mode of resistance"[27] within the public sphere is implicit within the closure of the article, which contrasts the Reverend Paisley's divisive rhetoric with the "urgent tracts" of the playwright, Sam Thompson who had died the previous year. Known best as the author of *Over the Bridge,* whose bravely antisectarian stance caused its initial production to be axed, Thompson is clearly presented by Heaney as an exemplary figure, a man with a "passion for justice", with "an anger at hypocrisy in high places"—in short the antithesis of Paisley and O'Neill. Interestingly, the reader is never informed as to which community Thompson springs from, and indeed when Heaney's discussion focuses upon the arts all sectarian labels

disappear, as if to suggest that Belfast's artistic community can fly by the nets of "ignorant and ugly bigotry"[28] elsewhere in the province.

THE POLITICIZATION OF HEANEY'S POETRY
1969-1970

That Seamus Heaney's poetry underwent fundamental changes at the close of the 1960s and the beginning of the 1970s has been widely acknowledged, though some of the key literary and political factors behind these changes have not yet received the attention they deserve. Undoubtedly the most telling factor in the politicization of Heaney's poetry was the local political narrative—events such as the Burntollet march in January 1969, the street killings in Derry and Belfast in August 1969, the Falls curfew of July 1970, and the introduction of internment without trial in August 1971.

Elsewhere, I have discussed the importance of Heaney's political, cultural and literary encounters in America between 1970 and the autumn of 1971 as sources for analogues with which to address the painful native text.[29] However, even before his sojourn in the States, Heaney had been opening up to a widening range of cultural influences, and to the politics of myth. Heaney's "discovery" in 1969 of P. V. Glob's *The Bog People* presented him with a series of startling images and potential narratives, opening up new possibilities for his art, which in the coming years would increasingly concern itself with questions of moral, artistic and political responsibilities. The book supplied him not only with analogues with which to view contemporary violence, both close-up and at a distance, but also with a mythology with which to interpret it. In one interview, Heaney went so far as to claim kinship with the Tollund Man, who "seemed to me like an ancestor almost, one of my old uncles, one of those moustachioed faces you used to meet all over the Irish countryside".[30] And, yet as Neil Corcoran points out, the face in the photograph is "not very obviously moustached" and not particularly avuncular. What Heaney is endeavouring to do is to translate this "much younger and more elegant"[31] figure into an archetype central to Nationalist ideology, that of the Victim. The figure admits and exhibits violence, but also transcends it, as Heaney hoped his poetry might do.

Heaney in the spring and summer of 1969 would have been much preoccupied by the violence being inflicted upon his community. This is evident in **"Summer 1969"**, from Part Two of *North,* where the first person narrator, who is on holiday in Spain, repeatedly encounters images which serve as bitter reminders of home. Although the poem opens asserting distance, identifying difference:

> While the Constabulary covered the mob
> Firing into the Falls, I was suffering
> Only the bullying sun of Madrid . . .[32]

—quickly the new context in which he finds himself is made familiar, and similarly afflicted. Despite being, or rather *because* he is cut off by an alien language like the persona at the end of **"The Tollund Man"**—"The air a canyon rivering in Spanish"[33]—the speaker assimilates the smells and sights before him into his own cultural and spiritual landscape. Not surprisingly, given that he is under the influence of "the life of Joyce", his journey back is prompted by a pungent odour, "stinks from the fish-market / Rose like the reek off a flaxdam". Heaney's reference to his reading-matter, "the life of Joyce", may seem at first pretentious, self-regarding even, but in fact is particularly apposite; it emphasizes that though the narrator is abroad, he is immersed in his culture of origin, and already reflecting upon an iconic presence. Yet, there is also an obvious irony in his talk of sweating over a literary biography, which hardly ranks as comparable to the experience of being fired upon. The allusion also, of course, draws attention to the narrator's role as an artist/communicator, and Heaney's own ambivalence towards that role.

As Spain reasserts itself, other, increasingly sombre and / or sinister images accrue—"A sense of children in dark corners", "Old women in black shawls", the deadly gleam of the Guardia Civil and their leather-wear—compelling the narrator to abandon the streets for the "safer" world of art-objects. Instead of the hoped-for, cool, aesthetic encounter, he walks into a wall and an accusing image, Goya's *Shootings of the Third of May*. The painting, depicting a rebel, arms outstretched in a Christ-like pose, about to be shot by the representatives of an occupying power, contains an obvious charge for a traditional Irish Nationalism. However, rather than confining himself to that one confirmatory likeness, the poem's numbed "I" moves on to even more disturbing texts, which, by analogy, implicate both Northern communities in a grotesque failure to rise above sectarian "stupidity and reaction, cruelty and oppression":[34]

Saturn

Jewelled in the blood of his own children,
Gigantic Chaos turning his brute hips
Over the world. Also, that holmgang
Where two berserks club each other to death
For honour's sake, greaved in a bog, and sinking.[35]

Clearly here we are far removed from the repose of the preserved head at Aarhus, and very much again in Yeatsian territory, as Heaney anticipates the second coming of civil war, envisaged as a war without prospect of liberation.

The presence of "foreign" narratives is indicative of a conscious effort on Heaney's part to enlarge the scope and scale of his poetic programme. Although Patrick Kavanagh had proved and would continue to be a valuable exemplar, undoubtedly Heaney recognized that if

his artistic project were to develop a translation must occur; his attention to the parish and to traditional forms was a strength, but one that was in danger of becoming a shortcoming. Heaney's strategy for extending his range was necessarily a complex one, and involved not only the cross-cultural "imports" already referred to, but also a close scrutiny of shifts in the body poetic and politic of the North and South of Ireland.

The year 1969 saw the publication of Thomas Kinsella's translation of *The Táin*. In his review of *The Táin*, Heaney is at pains to stress the political and cultural ramifications of this artistic act, which revealingly he links with Yeats' project and that of the earlier literary revival. According to Heaney's reading of literary history, the Ireland of the late 1960s and early 1970s—like the Ireland of the last decade of the nineteenth century and the first two decades of the twentieth—seems once more at a crossroads. Again its artists' energies, he implies, may prove a decisive force, enabling the peoples of Ireland to choose a new direction, and to renew themselves in the "common ground" of a shared, imagined Gaelic past. Heaney does not dwell on the fact that the Ireland(s) that emerged after the earlier national struggle was (were) far removed from the state envisaged by Yeats and his Anglo-Irish collaborators, nor on how previous attempts to enlist *linguistic* and *aesthetic* means to heal the "divided consciousness" and deep rifts within Irish culture and society emanating in large part from the long colonial encounter, had not enjoyed conspicuous success.[36]

At a time of violence which served to heighten an already acute sense of their cultural particularity as northern Catholics, it is hardly surprising that writers from the Nationalist tradition like Heaney and Montague should credit Kinsella's act of retrieval with political value, and hail it as "a landmark in Anglo-Irish poetry's repossession of its past".[37] Evidence of its impact may perhaps be seen in the place-name poems of **Wintering Out,** in which Heaney revives the ancient Irish tradition of *dinnseanchas*. In his Introduction, Kinsella had placed great weight on the importance of topography within *The Táin* and followed up this point within the book's preliminaries by supplying three maps "restoring" ancient Gaelic place-names to Ireland, and a guide to pronouncing Irish words and the names of persons and places:

Place names and their frequently fanciful meanings and origins occupy a remarkable place by modern standards. It is often enough justification for the inclusion of an incident that it ends in the naming of some physical feature; certain incidents, indeed, seem to have been invented merely to account for a place-name. . . . This phenomenon is not confined to the Táin, or the Ulster cycle; it is a continuing preoccupation of early and medieval Irish Literature, which contains a whole class of topographical works.[38]

Another key factor affecting Heaney at this juncture, however, may well have been changes in the poetry of John Montague. Montague's re-emphasis on place-names as loci of cultural history, and his perception of the residual and potential poetry locked within etymology, no doubt made a considerable impression on Seamus Heaney and Brian Friel. Particularly significant was a prose piece published in the *Irish Times* on 30 July 1970, "A Primal Gaeltacht".[39] Heaney would later quote a substantial section from Montague's essay, in "The Sense of Place", a lecture which was delivered in 1977 at the Ulster Museum and later published in *Preoccupations*.[40] "A Primal Gaeltacht" presented an extremely attractive strategy to Heaney, the possibilities of suffusing the lyrical and political. The potent set of myths, images, and cultural allusions it contained opened up the tempting illusion of a renewed "contact with the oldest and most pre-colonial springs of life of their people",[41] sources of "authenticity" like those the poets at Berkeley sought. Repeatedly Heaney engineers such contacts in *Wintering Out* and *North,* increasingly in the full and bitter knowledge that at this particular phase in Irish history, 1969-75, any dreams of reconciliation between past and present, "natives" and "strangers", may only be effected in the rarefied spheres of the imagination.

And yet some gleanings of hope remain, as they must if the poet is to continue. Like Friel's *Translations,* **"The Backward Look"** in Heaney's *Wintering Out*[42] deals in language lost, but also in "language rediscovered". It is a poem which affirms its kinship with the devastated place from which it emerged, signals its own fragile, riven state. From the outset it acknowledges the irreversibility of the displacements that have occurred, literal and psychic, linguistic and demographic.[43] Snipe, wild geese and yellow bittern—like the signs denoting them, and like those who had transmuted them into signs—have been forced to leave their "nesting ground", to make themselves scarce in "vaults" and archives. Each of the birds named by Heaney has a resonance within Irish cultural and literary tradition, and thus the poet's choice of referents includes, and in so doing excludes. Only someone familiar with Gaelic would be aware that the poem's italicized phrases, "little goat of the evening" and "little goat of the frost" are renderings into English of Irish kennings, *gabhairín oidhche* and *gabhairín reo,* denoting the "snipe". Encoded within the references to "wild goose" and "yellow bittern" in stanza five are allusions to those Jacobites who left Ireland for exile in France following William III's triumph and to a Gaelic lament, "An Bonnán Buí" / "The Yellow Bittern", by Cathal Buí Mac Giolla Ghunna (*c.*1680-1756).[44] Now, in the hour of death, the narrator aligns himself even more closely with the

Northern Nationalism reading of history, which looks back keenly to a past of loss as a source for present verification. The closure of this "drumming" elegy imagines survival in the face of contemporary threat ("the sniper's eyrie"), posits the possibility of successfully transcending ancient borders ("earthworks / and wall-steads"). Touch-down comes with an ambivalence typical of Heaney, and sees the lyric-native-snipe:

> disappearing among
> gleanings and leavings
> in the combs
> of a fieldworker's archive.

These "combs" resemble other underground recesses featured in *Wintering Out*—the "sunken drills" of **"Gifts of Rain"**, the "souterrain" of **"Toome"**, "the hollow trunk" and "woody cleft" in **"Oracle"**—but are also suggestive of fertile industry and anticipate the "honeyed" water of **"Mossbawn: Sunlight"**. Penned-in in a broken state, the poet inscribes a breathing-space for himself and others, marks a field where a sustainable rhythm and some measure of continuity might be found. Like the snipe, the yellow bittern, the translated sounds of a lost tongue, his text appears only to disappear, or only appears to disappear, leaving gleanings.[45]

Notes

1. Louis MacNeice, "Valediction", in Louis MacNeice, *Collected Poems,* London, 1969, 53.

2. This is the subject of two of my essays, written for the *Honest Ulsterman*: see Michael Parker, "Levelling with Heaney", in *Honest Ulsterman,* 103 (Spring 1997), 101-105 and 105 (Spring 1998), 47-55.

3. In his book, *Interpreting Northern Ireland* (Oxford, 1991), John Whyte argues that there are two propositions that characterize traditional nationalist thinking: firstly that the people of Ireland constitute one nation; secondly that it is Britain that is primarily responsible for keeping Ireland divided (117). Interestingly, however, the words Fionnuala O'Connor deploys to head her chapter on political allegiances within the nationalist community are "shifting, complex and ambiguous" (see Fionnuala O'Connor, *In Search of a State: Catholics in Northern Ireland,* Belfast, 1993, 44).

4. David Lloyd, *Anomalous States: Irish Writing and the Postcolonial Moment,* Dublin, 1993.

5. Willy Maley, "Varieties of Nationalism: Post Revisionist Irish Studies", *Irish Studies Review,* 15 (Summer 1996), 34-37.

6. *Ibid.,* 35.

7. Eugene O'Brien, "The Epistemology of Nationalism", *Irish Studies Review,* 17 (Winter 1996/7), 15-20.

8. *Ibid.,* 16.

9. *Ibid.,* 19.

10. Not so long ago, during the 1980s, struggles for national self-determination in Poland and Czechoslovakia were warmly applauded by western liberals. Like the vast majority of nationalists in Northern Ireland in 1968, Poles, Czechs and Slovaks did not support the violent overthrow of the regime.

11. Elizabeth Butler Cullingford, "Thinking of her . . . as . . . Ireland", *Textual Practice,* IV/1, (Spring 1990), 1-21.

12. Seamus Heaney, *North,* London, 1975, 45.

13. Seamus Heaney, *Poetry Book Society Bulletin,* 123 (Winter 1984).

14. Seamus Deane, "Wherever Green is Read", in *Interpreting Irish History: The Debate on Historical Revisionism,* ed. Ciaran Brady, Dublin, 1994, 234.

15. D. George Boyce, "Past and Present Revisionism and the Northern Ireland Troubles", in *The Making of Modern Irish History: Revisionism and the Revisionist Controversy,* eds D. George Boyce and Alan O'Day, London, 1996, 216-17.

16. A much expanded version of this section can be found in my essay "Reckonings: The Political Contexts for Northern Irish Literature", *Irish Studies Review,* X/2 (2002), 133-58.

17. Conor Cruise O'Brien, *States of Ireland,* London, 1972, 150.

18. Seamus Heaney, *Door into the Dark,* London, 1969, 24.

19. In his 1974 lecture, "Feeling into Words", published two years after Bloody Sunday—an event which seemed to offer confirmation of traditional nationalist readings of Ireland/England—he constructs a dubious parallel between the situation in 1798 and the summer of 1969. The Year of Liberty becomes replayed as another "murderous encounter" between "Protestant yeoman and Catholic rebel". The lecture is reprinted in *Preoccupations: Selected Prose 1968-1978,* London, 1980, 41-60.

20. Seamus Heaney, "Linen Town", in Seamus Heaney, *Wintering Out,* London, 1972, 38.

21. Seamus Heaney, "Out of London: Ulster's Troubles", *New Statesman,* 1 July 1966, 23-24.

22. Seamus Heaney, *Death of a Naturalist,* London, 1965, 32-33, and *Wintering Out,* 59-61.

23. Heaney, "Out of London: Ulster's Troubles", 23. In *States of Ireland,* perhaps in the light of PIRA violence at the time of writing, Conor Cruise O'Brien foregrounds the threat from recalcitrant Nationalism, and has relatively little to say about the Reverend Ian Paisley or the responsibility of his supporters in raising sectarian tensions and inciting violence. Indeed O'Brien talks almost approvingly of "Mr Paisley's huge, rocky face, with small, shrewd, watchful eyes . . . a symbol of the besieged Ulster fortress for which he stood" (151).

24. R. F. Foster, *Modern Ireland 1600-1972,* Harmondsworth, 1989, 585.

25. Michael Farrell, *Northern Ireland: The Orange State,* London, 1976, 236.

26. Quoted in J. Bowyer Bell, *The Irish Troubles,* Dublin, 1993, 54.

27. Seamus Heaney, interviewed by James Randall, printed in *Ploughshares,* V/3 (1979), 18.

28. Heaney, "Out of London: Ulster's Troubles", 24.

29. Michael Parker, "Gleanings, Leavings: Irish and American Influences on Seamus Heaney's *Wintering Out*", *New Hibernia Review,* II/3 (Autumn 1998), 16-35.

30. Randall interview, 18.

31. Neil Corcoran, *Seamus Heaney,* London, 1986, 45.

32. Heaney, *North,* 69.

33. In some of its images and anxieties, the poem reminds one of Louis MacNeice's representation of Spain in *Autumn Journal,* VI; see *Collected Poems,* 110-12.

34. E. H. Gombrich, *The Story of Art,* London, 1972, 384.

35. Heaney, *North,* 70.

36. See Terence Brown, *Ireland: A Social and Cultural History,* London, 1981, 47-67, 188-96.

37. John Montague, *The Figure in the Cave and Other Essays,* ed. Antoinette Quinn, Syracuse: NY, 1989, 125.

38. Thomas Kinsella, Introduction to *The Tain,* ed. Thomas Kinsella, London, 1969, xiii-xiv.

39. For a detailed analysis of this essay, see my "Gleanings, Leavings", 30-33.

40. Heaney, *Preoccupations,* 131-49. One suspects that Kinsella's translation, Montague's essay and Heaney's own place-name poems in *Wintering Out* may well have had some influence on Brian Friel's acclaimed play, *Translations.*

41. Franz Fanon, *Wretched of the Earth,* Harmondsworth, 1967, 169.

42. Heaney, *Wintering Out,* 29-30.

43. Heaney is undoubtedly alluding to displacements affecting the Catholic population since the Plantation, but also more specifically to those of the summer of 1969, when 1,505 Catholic families were burnt out of their homes. According to the *Scarman Report,* this constituted 3% of all Catholic households in Belfast.

44. John Montague, in "A Primal Gaeltacht", 45, states that for Heaney "The Yellow Bittern / *'An Bonnán Buí'*" constituted "his touchstone for the (Gaelic) tradition". Montague's translation of the poem is included in *The Faber Book of Irish Verse,* London, 1974, 183-84.

45. This image from "The Backward Look" resurfaces in "The Harvest Bow", *Field Work,* 1978, 58, which finds its narrator "Gleaning the unsaid off the palpable". "The Harvest Bow" similarly acknowledges that art, like language, is "a frail device", but one that can survive the passing of time, and connect one generation to another.

Joanny Moulin (essay date 2006)

SOURCE: Moulin, Joanny. "Seamus Heaney's *Versus,* or Poetry as Still Revolution." In *Back to the Present, Forward to the Past: Irish Writing and History since 1798, Volume II,* edited by Patricia A. Lynch, Joachim Fischer, and Brian Coates, pp. 243-50. Amsterdam: Rodopi, 2006.

[*In the following essay, Moulin focuses on the tilling metaphors in* Opened Ground *and* Field Work *and argues that Heaney has attempted to create a poetic mode that exists above the realm of discourse and ideology, rendering himself—in the words of Terry Eagleton—an "end-of-ideologies" writer.*]

In a lecture Seamus Heaney gave in May 1998 in Rennes (France), he announced that the title of his new book of selected poems would be *Opened Ground.* That was also the title of his lecture, and, of course, it looked back to a now well-known metaphor of his, according to which poetry is more or less of the same order and nature as tillage. The first poem in the reading was, rather expectedly, **"Digging"**:

> But I've no spade to follow men like them.
>
> Between my finger and my thumb
> The squat pen rests.
> I'll dig with it.[1]

Then he pushed the simile to include a Greek word, *boustrophedon,* which is made of *bous,* "the ox" and *strophe,* "the turning", or literally "the revolution".

Boustrophedon is a form of writing used in ancient Greek manuscripts, which consists of writing from left to right then from right to left, and so on, just in the same way as a team of oxen pulls the plough in a field, coming and going from one sillion to the next.

This is an old image with Heaney, and already in *Preoccupations* he compared the poet to a ploughman, noting that "'Verse' comes from the Latin *versus* which could mean a line of poetry but could also mean the turn that a ploughman made at the head of a field as he finished the furrow and faced back into another".[2] And again in **Field Work,** poetry is seen as "Vowels ploughed into other, opened ground, / Each verse returning like the plough turned round".[3] Heaney never seems to be tired of dwelling on this homely agricultural grounding of literature, as in **"Alphabets"**, where the scholar learns to write, and "He is the scribe / Who drove a team of quills on his white field".[4]

Now, looking at any kind of *boustrophedon* long enough, one may come to think that it is also reminiscent of the winding pipes of a still, where vapours go a long way while really covering little ground, but finally to come out as something different from what they were when they went in. One reason why this apparently simple-minded metaphor is so often reiterated is that it tells something rather essential about one of the things poetry means for Heaney. I have a notion that this is what Helen Vendler calls "Heaney's historical revisionism",[5] his turning over of the plough or the quill, and that this "turning time up and over" is a patient commitment to the ideological field of our time, with a mind to change it in the long run, or at least to cultivate it and render it more habitable and tame.

I want to look at a few poems from that angle, and examine how they operate, if at all, from an ideological point of view. For, generally speaking, Heaney is not at first perceived as a very strongly committed poet, and some people like Anthony Easthope consider him at best what in the 1930s would have been called an "escapist" poet, and at worst someone whose pastoralism is reactionary, at least in terms of aesthetics. This is perhaps equally true of collections like **Death of a Naturalist** or **Field Work.** Yet, in between, the poems of **Wintering Out** have the roughly-hewn political bias one could rightly expect from an Ulster poet in the 1970s, with a vision of a world clearly split up into two apparently irreconcilable camps; witness poems like **"A Constable Calls", "The Other Side",** or **"Servant Boy",** although a text like **"No Man's Land"** sounds like an early realization of some inadequacy in that particular use of poetry:

> Why do I unceasingly
> arrive too late to condone
> infected sutures
> and ill-knit bone?[6]

It is nothing much, but merely the honest voicing of restless misgivings about the comfortable adoption of an axiology, in which *we* are right and *they* are wrong, and which seems to have been what his Northern-Catholic community more or less explicitly expected from him in those days.

What I am driving at, trying to show and explain, happens first quite clearly in *North.* The collection, and especially its title poem, is an effort to forge the uncreated conscience of the race, and to graft contemporary history to a distant past and half-forgotten mythology. This is no longer or not yet poetry as ploughing and tillage, but rather as haulage and the excavating of obscure subconscious motivations and blueprints, of "memory incubating the spilled blood". The poet presents himself as a seer, or rather hearer, of those "ocean-deafened voices", "buoyant with hindsight".[7] It is a highly seductive kind of discourse, yet one that has been greeted with birchwood and raisings of critical shields since the book came out. Ciaran Carson ("Escaped from the Massacre?")[8] or Edna Longley ("*North*: 'Inner Emigré' or 'Artful Voyeur?'")[9] have been among the most articulate to wage disparaging questioning of Heaney's ideological attitude in *North.* And in a sense, Seamus Heaney has backed out of that position in the poetry that he has written afterwards.

Yet I would like to argue that perhaps there was something that both the poet and his critics have overlooked at the time, and that is closely related to the *versus, boustrophedon* and poetical revisionism. In "Trial Pieces", for instance, there is a fascination with the calligraphic toil of a child's engraving on a piece of bone, where

> like an eel swallowed
> in a basket of eels,
> the line amazes itself.[10]

And this triggers off the day-dream of a quasi-Joycean invocation of the barbarity of the Vikings:

> Old fathers, be with us.
> Old cunning assessors
> of feuds and or sites
> for ambush or town.[11]

This kind of claim for violent instincts is far from being politically correct. But, remarkably, what is happening here is that the poem is, as it were, overturning its ideological position, from culture to barbarity, from the innocence of a child to the apologia for murder, from building to destroying. In a case of literary *enantiodromia,* the poem is a soaring reverie that is pushed to the limit and topples into its nightmarish opposite.

The full title of this poem is "Viking Dublin: Trial Pieces", and its four parts are successive attempts by the poet to try his voice at that kind of cathartic reversal, which willy-nilly succeeds in bringing readers and critics to pass judgement on some apparently innocuous fantasies. The same effect of axiological reversal is paramount in *North,* and that is how I read these much debated stanzas of "Punishment", a poem about the preserved body of a young woman fallen victim to ritual murder in Jutland:

> I almost love you
> but would have cast, I know,
> the stones of silence.
> I am the artful voyeur.
>
> . . . . .
>
> who would connive
> in civilized outrage
> yet understand the exact
> and tribal, intimate revenge.[12]

For this is a recognition of barbarity, that is to say foreign abjection, as an intimate truth about oneself.

One remark to prove my point, which may be seen as particularly apposite, is that some Protestant critics came up saying substantially, see, there is Catholic ritualism for you. But more seriously, this is an application of what Geoffrey Hill calls "Poetry as 'Menace' and 'Atonement'" which he also writes "at-one-ment",[13] considering poetry as a dangerous but necessary flirting with suppressed ideological positions, with a view to purging their emotional potential, or defusing their societal charge. This radical change which was silently taking place in *North* is graphically expressed in the translation from "Antaeus" to "Hercules and Antaeus".

In the classical legend of Antaeus, the titan regained his strength by contact with his mother Gaia every time he touched ground, and Hercules vanquished him by holding him up in the air. Heaney says it is a post-colonial poem: "the more you push them down the more they rear up their heads, so the best way to quiet them down is to educate them."[14] But here again, we have an instance of poetry as still revolution in the form of a paradox, for as Antaeus says:

> He may well throw me and renew my birth
> But let him not plan lifting me off the earth,
>   My elevation, my fall.[15]

The still revolution of poetry may be a way out of a deadlock fight, and a movement towards something other than a perpetual battle between two camps, a future for which those sleeping giants are discarded as "pap for the dispossessed".[16]

What I have been trying to describe here is something that Heaney has considered from a theoretical point of view in *The Redress of Poetry,* as for instance when he compares his own poem "Squarings" with Zbigniew Herbert's "The Pulley", saying that "[b]oth poems are about the way consciousness can be alive to two different and contradictory dimensions of reality and still find a way of negotiating between them".[17] Of course, this brings water to the mill of a definition of the poet as a go-between, which is Helen Vendler's position in *The Breaking of Style,* where she says he is "a Mr Facing-Both-Ways". But I would like to give a slight inflexion to this interpretation of Heaney's poetry, via a detour by the theory of Mikhail Bakhtin and the notion of *double-voicedness.* In "Discourse in the Novel", Bakhtin wrote:

> The double-voiced prose word has a double meaning. But the poetic word in the narrow sense also has a double, even a multiple, meaning. It is this that basically distinguishes it from the word as concept, or the word as term. The poetic word is a trope, requiring a precise feeling for the two meanings contained in it.[18]

"Double-voicedness", which leads to "double-languagedness", is a form of "dialogization" that in Heaney's poetry is the early stage of a development that was to reach the stage of "polyglossia" in *Station Island,* where more than two discursive voices are at work. Very famously, now, it is what is exemplified in the very title of *The Redress of Poetry,* which means both how poetry can be *redressed,* and how it can *redress* things. This is an instance of Heaney's forked tongue, or how his discourse can be diffracted and say two things at the same time. Being simultaneously both active and passive, this is a case of what Greek grammar called "middle voice", as Heaney calls it in *The Government of the Tongue,* with the example of W. H. Auden's poem "The Watershed",[19] identifying this writing technique as "a sleight of semantic hand which unnerves and suspends the reader above a valley of uncertainty".

The point is not so much for the poet to intercede between two or more constructions of meaning, but to exalt his poetic speech on to a plane situated above discourse and any too easily constructed vision or reality, or any form of too ready-made doxa. The title of *The Redress of Poetry* is a minimalist exemplum of a poetic voice that revolves around its own semantic axis, much as Roland Barthes said that myth operates like a "sort of constantly moving turnstile".[20] It is an exemplum of *versus,* a language which is travailed, like kneaded dough or ploughed earth, and which therefore is no longer rigid, but opened to new becomings. To borrow an idea from yet another French philosopher of the 1960s, it may be worth noting that Althusser used to say that ideology, like philosophy for Hegel, is a still revolution, a motionless movement, which means that ideology does change, while remaining in the same place and keeping the same form.[21] In that sense, Heaney's poetry is fighting ideology with its own weapons and on its own ground, as if taking an active part in its necessary change. And this particular use of

language was theorized first in *The Government of the Tongue,* yet another book with an iconic title. For, it has often been noted too, the government of the tongue is both the effort to govern the tongue or to exert control over one's words, and the expected consequence of this, that is, to place the tongue in a governing position, which is the peculiar power of poets.

In a review of **Field Work** (the collection that came immediately after **North**), Terry Eagleton wrote that Seamus Heaney is an "end-of-ideologies" writer,[22] which in fact amounts to the same thing as that which I am trying to demonstrate at much greater length. For the main thesis that both *The Redress of Poetry,* and *The Government of the Tongue* before that are striving to maintain, in a de facto *ars poetica* of Heaney's, is that poetry is a mode of literature which uplifts itself to operate above discourse as the ideologically constructed order of language. In the theory of Jean-François Lyotard, this would indeed make him a post-modern poet, if the post-modern condition is agreed to be posterior to all constructed narratives.[23] In a sense, this would tend to qualify the kind of radical judgement that someone like Anthony Easthope has passed on Heaney in his article "How Good is Seamus Heaney?", which still rests on the assumption that "what makes poetry poetry is what makes poetry ideological".[24] For Heaney's poetry is demonstrably using narratives and discourses as raw material or fuel to soar with its readers to another order of language and another mode of thinking.

To try and end up more than half-facetiously, in a poem in **The Spirit Level** (which has got something to do with both spirituality and bricklaying), there is a double poem entitled **"Two Lorries",**[25] where the "engine-revs" of the diesel engine are the objective correlative of the factor that sets going the performative action of writing. Heaney's poetry is a mode of revisionist writing, and it revises discourses both from the outside and from the inside. The Derridaean notions of *iterability* and *trace* would be more apposite tools for a further evaluation of these poems, as, for instance, the very deconstructionist conviction that concepts are not to be trusted in the absolute, but may be used provisionally as necessary props of writing, and therefore of thinking, but bound from the start to be revised later on. In "Heaneyspeak", as Philip Hobsbaum would have it, this is called "mud pies".[26] Constructed narratives and ideological positions are poetically processed or used as temporary scaffoldings towards future horizons.

Notes

1. Seamus Heaney, *Death of a Naturalist,* London, 1966, 1-2.

2. Seamus Heaney, *Preoccupations: Selected Prose 1968-1978,* London, 1980, 65.

3. *Ibid.,* 34.

4. Seamus Heaney, *The Haw Lantern,* London, 1987, 2.

5. Helen Vendler, *The Breaking of Style: Hopkins, Heaney, Graham,* Cambridge: MA, 1995, 66.

6. Seamus Heaney, *Wintering Out,* London, 1972, 40.

7. Seamus Heaney, *North,* London, 1975, 19-20.

8. Ciaran Carson, "Escaped from the Massacre?", *Honest Ulsterman,* 50 (Winter 1975).

9. Edna Longley, "*North*: 'Inner Emigré' or 'Artful Voyeur?'", in *The Art of Seamus Heaney,* ed. Tony Curtis, Bridgend, 1982.

10. Heaney, *North,* 21.

11. *Ibid.,* 24.

12. *Ibid.,* 38.

13. Geoffrey Hill, *The Lords of Limit: Essays on Literature and Ideas,* London, 1984, 1-19.

14. Seamus Heaney, "Address", Monaco, March, 1998.

15. Heaney, *North,* 12.

16. *Ibid.,* 53.

17. Seamus Heaney, *The Redress of Poetry: Oxford Lectures,* London, 1995, xiii.

18. Mikhail Bakhtin, *The Dialogic Imagination: Four Essays by M. M. Bakhtin,* ed. Michael Holquist, Austin: TX, 1981, 327.

19. Seamus Heaney, *The Government of the Tongue: The 1986 T. S. Eliot Memorial Lectures and Other Critical Writings,* London, 1988, 123: "Similarly, the grammatical peace of the present participle is disturbed by lurking middle voice: the grass is chafing, active, but in so far as the only thing being chafed is itself, it is passive. Then, too, the participle occupies a middle state between being transitive and intransitive, and altogether functions like a pass made swiftly, a sleight of semantic hand which unnerves and suspends the reader above a valley of uncertainty."

20. Roland Barthes, *Mythologies,* London, 1993, 123: "To keep a spatial metaphor, the approximative character of which I have already stressed, I shall say that the signification of the myth is constituted by a sort of constantly moving turnstile which presents alternately the meaning of the signifier and its form, language object and a metalanguage a purely signifying and a purely imagining consciousness."

21. Louis Althusser, *Lire le Capital,* Paris, 1975, 182: "L'idéologie change donc, mais insensiblement, en conservant sa forme d'idéologie; elle se meut, mais d'un mouvement immmobile, qui la maintient *sur place,* en son lieu et son rôle d'idéologie."

22. Terry Eagleton, "Review of *Field Work*", *Stand,* XXI/3 (1980), 77-78: "Heaney, whatever evidence of global imperialist crisis he may find on his doorstep, handles that evidence in the style of an 'end-of-ideologies' writer."

23. Jean-François Lyotard, *La Condition Postmoderne,* Paris, 1979, 63: "Dans la société et la culture contemporaine, société postindustrinelle, culture postmoderne, la question de la légitimation du savoir se pose en d'autres termes. Le grand récit a perdu sa crédibilité, quel que soit le mode d'unification qui lui est assigné: récit spéculatif, récit de l'émancipation."

24. Anthony Easthope, *Poetry as Discourse,* London, 1983, 22.

25. Seamus Heaney, *The Spirit Level,* London, 1983, 13-14.

26. Philip Hobsbaum, "Craft and Technique in *Wintering Out*", in *The Art of Seamus Heaney,* ed. Tony Curtis, 3rd edn, Swansea, 1994.

Nicholas Meihuizen (essay date 2006)

SOURCE: Meihuizen, Nicholas. "The Poetics of Violence: The Parallel Case of Seamus Heaney and Mongane Wally Serote." In *Back to the Present, Forward to the Past: Irish Writing and History since 1798, Volume II,* edited by Patricia A. Lynch, Joachim Fischer, and Brian Coates, pp. 361-76. Amsterdam: Rodopi, 2006.

[*In the following essay, Meihuizen elucidates the similarities between Heaney's work and that of the South African poet Mongane Wally Serote, focusing on the power of literature to engender hope in the face of postcolonial strife and political violence.*]

> We can forgive a man for making a useful thing as long as he does not admire it. The only excuse for making a useless thing is that one admires it intensely. All art is quite useless.[1]

In addressing the work of Irish poet Seamus Heaney and South African poet Mongane Wally Serote under a single umbrella, I hope to reconcile to an extent my natural interest in my motherland with my interest in Irish letters. From one perspective the task is not that difficult, for as political entities South Africa and Ireland have both been subjected to histories of violence based on colonial ethnic discrimination and its variations, including the binaries inherent in colonialism: Master and Slave, First World and Third World, Settler and Indigene. What are the responses of Heaney and Serote to this violence? Leading from this initial broad-based question is another more specific and more contentious one (though certainly not a new one), which has to do with the social reverberations of art.

Can Serote's and Heaney's poetic responses to violence have any value for the individual who is continually subject to the brutality of the times? This is the question I need to consider as a person living in one of the most violent countries in the world today, who nevertheless devotes all his time to the study of literature rather than, say, the abolition of hand guns. I suppose I am especially sensitive to the unqualified certainty of Oscar Wilde's "All art is quite useless" because of the growing admiration in South African educational institutions merely for what are considered useful skills, at the expense of art, music and literature. Educational bureaucrats are not particularly receptive to Wildean irony.

Mongane Wally Serote will need some introduction for most international readers. He was born in Sophiatown near Johannesburg in 1944, four years before the assumption of power by the Nationalist Party. Because he is always conscious of himself in relation to his society, his life and writing afford a chronicle of and commentary on the apartheid era. His writing also provides a means for moving beyond the apartheid mind-set, and so is socially constructive in orientation (though never blandly didactic).

An avid reader from childhood, Serote became aware of the Great Tradition of English Literature at an early age, consuming the works of writers such as Shakespeare, Dickens, Lawrence, Hardy, Wordsworth and Keats. But while imbibing it, he also reacted against this exotic tradition, and, at the age of fourteen, started writing his own work in response to the dearth of subject matter directly pertaining to the life he experienced.

His first volume of poetry was published in 1972. It was entitled *Yakhal' inkomo* (which translates from the Zulu tongue into "the cattle are crying"; the expression is shorthand for the symbolically pregnant notion, "the cattle are crying because of their slaughter at the hands of human beings"). This was followed by *Tsetlo* in 1974, *No Baby Must Weep* in 1975, and *Behold Mama, Flowers* in 1978. He wrote several more works in the 1980s and 1990s, including *Third World Express* (1992), and *Come and Hope with Me* (1994). In this essay I dwell principally on *Behold Mama, Flowers* but also turn briefly to these more recent works.

Dedicated to Steve Biko, *Behold Mama, Flowers* was actually written while Serote was in America, and reflects, to an extent, the tension and despondency of the exile isolated from the coalface. In his Foreword Serote refers to an Osiric myth he learned from Skunder Boghossian, the Ethiopian painter resident in America:

a man chopped a body many, many times—he chopped this body into many, many small pieces and threw them into the flowing river. When the pieces, floating and flowing, began to dance with the rhythm of the river, a child, seeing this, said, "Mama, look at the flowers!"[2]

The title reflects a shift in emphasis—from the slaughtering of helpless cattle, as encoded in the title of his first book, we move to redemptive vision within an implicitly violent context. Begun one year before the Soweto uprising, the book encapsulates, to an extent, the new optimism and strength of resistance that accompanied what are known as the Power days, but also the strenuous trials and tribulations along the road to freedom. This bivalence is exemplified in the manner in which the experiencing self is at once devalued, and enshrined in a communal egalitarianism, through the lower-case "i", which is used as personal pronoun throughout. What we gather from the implied semantics of the case is that, despite its divisive nature, oppression promotes unity among those oppressed, although Serote's extended vision in this respect, which incorporates his other works, notably the novel *To Every Birth Its Blood*[3] has been criticized as being too simplistic in the way it presents black unity in purely socialist terms.

Following a complex trajectory, the self of the present poem seems to float down a river of experience, like a piece of body from the myth of Boghossian, which has the potential to be transformed into a flower, if only in the imagination of the perceiver. But near the beginning of the poem, rather than the beautiful flowers of imaginative transformation, we find the parched sunflowers of a late capitalist landscape: these flowers are "neon", like the "rivers", which are flanked by "tall cement trees". Soon after follow images of the bones of slaves, who died in transportation, "screaming bones still chained and bloodstained", and these are juxtaposed with images of men "digging gold beneath the earth", and references to "the chains of the rand" and "the chains of the dollar". In other words, as the juxtapositions make clear, implicated in Serote's critique are both local and metropolitan elements of exploitation, along with recent and ancient examples of imperialist brutality. The poem, then, is a lament for Africa and her exploited peoples, but also a commentary on current universal dehumanizing and destructive trends. A section on blood and tears follows, the first of repeated references to the formulaic trinity of "blood, sweat and tears", which Serote invests with new life. For example, "blood" modulates into "pus", which makes its diseased mark on the women the speaker holds. Then women and blood are closely linked through childbirth, as in earlier poems, and though Serote empathizes with the agonies of childbirth and bereavement, he chooses to underscore the resilience of women: "after mothers weep, they still make love, and bear other / children."[4] However bleak the present may be, this resilience betokens hope for the future.

In a new section the river is displaced by a road along which we find nightmare tableaux from the apartheid years, incorporate inhuman jail sentences and their impact on wives and children, and the plight of an old man whose home has been bulldozed down for the sake of separate "development". In the midst of this landscape the perceiving consciousness does not simply remain passive. Here and throughout the poem it interrogates its relationship with the world and history. The speaker, for instance, now examines the possibility of forgiveness and the need for the simple rewards of a normal existence, again conflating the South African situation with disturbing global trends:

> what does a man want
> to put his life down for a car
> to go to the moon
> i want to walk with ease, laugh and kiss . . .[5]

The speaker continues on his visionary journey, hearing footsteps, seeing "sidewalks" where other journeys have reached their close in "pools of blood", or "paths" which "seem to vanish into dark passages". Cognate with the endless flux and reflux of life on the rivers, roads and paths, is a sense of longing for a distant "home", which underlines Serote's being in America at the time of writing, but also suggests the more consuming and fundamental existential displacement of the non-person as encoded in the poet's lower-case "i".[6] An apostrophe to Africa at this stage incorporates family figures—brother, sister, child, grandfather, father. But in present times the family is the site of pain and disaster, not comfort, and mother Africa is dogged by nightmare:

> ah, africa, it does matter that you take a look
> and begin to believe that the sahara owns you
> that you own nothing
> behold
> your nightmare grows and grows like waves of the
>   sea.

The image is puissant and terrifying, undercutting the very basis of existence in Africa. As a consequence, her children leave. Serote refers to some of her most gifted absentee children: Coltrane, Eric Dolphy, Miles Davis, Nina Simone, and Miriam Makeba.[7]

Near the conclusion of the poem we find a visionary section on the macabre beginning of Africa, which drops from God's "back pocket" while the Creation is taking place, and is closely scrutinized by the devil, who appears to claim it as his own. But this plunge into the abyss is followed by the section on Skunder Boghossian, exiled from Africa, like Serote, though with his conception of "the continent" intact, along with its implications of a redemptive wholeness.[8] But again, this vision offers no easy end to the quest for liberation, and the conclusion of the poem, which returns to the image of flowers (though now no longer dying), for all its optimism, bears the traces of a continuing journey:

> i can say there is nothing that we know in the end
> i can say, ah
> behold the flowers
> i can say
> your dignity is locked tight in the resting places
> in the places where you shall drink water
> around the fire where you shall laugh with your
>   children
> i can say otherwise
> your dignity is held tight in the sweating cold hands
>   of death
> the village where everything is silent about dignities
> i will say again
> behold the flowers, they begin to bloom![9]

Indeed, the journey over the next twelve years was yet to prove long and dangerous, and close friends would die on the way. After the hardships and the grief, how bizarre, yet how typically South African, that Serote's path should take him to the urbane precincts of the University of Natal, a traditionally "white" university, which awarded him an honorary doctorate in April 1991. But he was pleased by this fact, seeing in the occasion not an Establishment flourish incommensurate with raw human experience, and certainly not the end of a journey. For him the event attested to a communal "searching for a way forward" on the part of all South Africans.[10]

This searching is evident in his own recent writing. In *Third World Express* the experiencing self has been restored, through the personal pronoun, to its own rightful and proud uppercase position. (Unforeseen forces and events at work in the country will make of this a temporary gesture, as will be discussed presently.) Serote's search is extended to incorporate others with shared values:

> I know
> there are good men and women—
> in this place
> and in this time the good are there!
> they look you in the eye
> in search
> their faces are like still trees
> and their shoulders are wide open
> they wear tired eyes
> they search and look
> for what we can share
> or for that moment which can make life magic
> for that simple thing
> for that, which can make us us!
> they are black they are white
> they share this earth with us
> and their hearts are not steel
> or gold
> or stone
> but are simple—flesh!
> they are boers and blacks
> women or men . . .[11]

Considering his involvement in the struggle (and the losses he suffered because of it), the moderateness of his views is indeed salutary. His verse embodies reconciliation. But the process of searching in the book is (once more) universal in its concerns, having to do with finding solutions to the continuing violence and poverty not only in South Africa, but the world at large.

He also anticipates, in a visionary manner akin to the Shelley of *Prometheus Unbound,* a change in the consciousness of suffering humanity, where the poor will seek to change themselves, rather than remain the butt of society, where the rich will stop their self-destructive exploitation. The Third World Express would appear to be the medium of change, the means to reaching a new era, whether in Africa, Asia, or Latin America:

> ah my friends
> sometimes I wonder
> when's the express coming
> with its speedy wind it must come
> at night
> in the morning
> it must come
> the Third World Express must come
> at dawn
> in the twilight
> like the wind
> like a river
> like a mad dam.[12]

At once destroyer and preserver (as suggested in the mirror-image of "mad dam"), the Third World Express will exert a pervasive influence—the references to the different elements and times of the day suggest this fact.

Come and Hope with Me is more brooding and disturbed than *Third World Express.* The lower-case personal pronoun is again deployed by Serote, but not as a sign of obliteration or community, rather as a sign of mourning in the face of threats of civil war and the murder of Chris Hani. It is as if unexpected bars to the process of liberation are suddenly erected, and the occasion is cause for further lament. The struggle of self with self in the personal realm, broached in his novel *To Every Birth Its Blood,*[13] now becomes more externalized, as conflict shifts from a unitary common enemy to power games and destructive situations where inner strengths and resources are necessary, such as the ability to "hope". "Hope", then, becomes a type of transformative tool, a means for achieving a general humanitarian end, rather than a specific, sectarian political end:

> come
> if the truth does stalk us
> we will befriend wisdom
> you and I
> come
> let us return
> come
> come and be with me
> come and hope and dream with me when the dream
> dawns.[14]

If hope is a tool, language is its implement, and, again, Serote would effect transformation through language. His war against apartheid has been a war of words, in the most literal sense, and the world has witnessed that such a war can influence hearts and minds. Serote's words (buttressed—it is true—by his position as British and European cultural attaché for the ANC) spoke to people all around the world, and helped increase the intensity of international pressure on South Africa, pressure so instrumental in local political transformation. Language can help transform the present, and it can also look to the future in order to encapsulate proper responses to that future, as through the word "hope". Serote's is not a shallow hope, but one conditioned by years of struggle, and the successful outcome of that struggle. This hope is contextualized by poetry; put, in other words, into a proper and potent frame, where past and present give impetus to the future, and where the informing power of rejuvenating words (where flowers might displace bloody body pieces) corroborates the fact that history can be cajoled into redemptive directions.

That the whole matter of linguistic intervention in the world of action is more complex and subtle than I have thus far indicated is evidenced in a poem by another South African exile, C. J. Driver. Driver's relation to the political struggle in South Africa, though certainly evident in his writing, does not wholly absorb him as does Serote's, and yet various manifestations of a type of alienation come to the fore in his writing, as if corroborating at some inherent level the distinctive perception of an exile. For example, in his "Wilderness: Written on Water", from *In the Water-margins,* he views the difficult relationship between poet and language from a perspective which interrogates the individual input or agency involved in the act of naming, given the autonomous propensities of language:

> We think of something lost
> In writing down
> The flux of time:
> But what completes our thought?
> (The language knows so much beyond oneself)
>
> The thread of meaning lost
> In noting down
> That fleeting time:
> Precise the moment caught
> (The language knows so much beyond oneself)[15]

If the "moment" is "caught", our own understanding plays but a small part in the matter, we "lose" the "thread of meaning" in our act of naming. "Language"—existing apart, never subject to closure (as the brackets help indicate)—"completes our thought" independently of our conscious ability, as if it is a type of universal knowing which transcends our own individual acts of knowing.

But while individual control is questioned by such a perception (where, in effect, the creative "I" becomes exiled from its own utterances), what also emerges from this perception is the positive sense that the capabilities of the self are extended by language. In another South African poet, Lionel Abrahams (who was actually an early and committed champion of Serote), the association between the self and language is less explicit and less troubled, but again linguistic engagement through the shaping lines of poetry has a positive effect on the self's experience of life. In Abrahams' poem "A Dead Tree Full of Live Birds", for example, "moments" are held by the shaping lines "out of time",[16] implying an aesthetic redemption of such moments, which takes us back, at least, to Shakespeare's sonnet 65:

> Since brass, nor stone, nor earth, nor boundless sea,
> But sad mortality o'ersways their power,
> How with this rage shall beauty hold a plea,
> Whose action is no stronger than a flower?
> O how shall summer's honey breath hold out
> Against the wrackful siege of batt'ring days,
> When rocks impregnable are not so stout,
> Nor gates of steel so strong, but Time decays?
> O fearful meditation: Where, alack,
> Shall Time's best jewel from Time's chest lie hid?
> Or what strong hand can hold his swift foot back,
> Or who his spoil of beauty can forbid?
>   O none, unless this miracle have might,
>   That in black ink my love may still shine bright.[17]

The lines I am particularly interested in here, as anyone familiar with Heaney's *Preoccupations* will appreciate,[18] are lines 3 and 4:

> How with this rage shall beauty hold a plea,
> Whose action is no stronger than a flower?

The question concerns the devouring "rage" of Time, to which all existence is subject, and against which art (metonymically incorporated in the notion of "beauty") must pit itself. Heaney extends the resonance of "rage", to make it refer to any brutal force in life. In order to "hold a plea" against the "rage" of his place and time, he finds his own "befitting emblems of adversity" (Heaney quotes from Yeats' "Meditations in Time of Civil War"), and in doing so embodies the complex meshwork of demands of his public and private visions, which poets at social cutting edges need to do (but often ignore). Heaney's aesthetic strategy incorporates, it hardly needs mentioning, the reflection of a literal preservation—centuries-old human bodies embalmed by bog juices—of the otherwise momentary flux of history. The significance of this preservation is that these figures relate to the current violence in Ireland, and bring into juxtaposition the earth goddess of the original human sacrifices two thousand years ago, and the nationalist feminization of Ireland (as expressed in the populist images of "Mother Ireland" and "Kathleen Ni Houlihan").

Heaney has since sought other means of "holding a plea" against rage. I think, for example, of the crucial organizing image of "Frontiers of Writing", in *The Redress of Poetry*. It is that of five towers—a quincunx of literary towers—by means of which Heaney would "bring the frontiers of the country into alignment with the frontiers of writing", and "attempt to sketch the shape of an integrated literary tradition".[19] The five towers consist of, at the centre, "the tower of prior Irelandness", or the round aboriginal dwelling of the ancients. On the southern point is Kilcolman Castle, Spenser's tower of Anglicization; on the western point is Thoor Ballylee, Yeats' tower of spiritual and magical restoration in the face of English phlegmaticness; on the eastern point we find, of course, Joyce's Martello tower, representing "his attempt to marginalize the imperium which had marginalized him by replacing the Anglocentric Protestant tradition with a newly forged apparatus of Homeric correspondences". Heaney imagines Louis MacNeice's tower at Carrickfergus Castle in the north, and it in a sense subsumes the forces inherent in the other four towers. MacNeice "can be regarded as an Irish Protestant writer with Anglocentric attitudes who managed to be faithful to his Ulster inheritance, his Irish affections and his English predilections". Heaney's sense of political responsibility, his healing vision, his tolerance, his deep humanity, merge in the quincunx, and leave one with an impression of the confluence of life and art, the hope inherent in art, and the fact that poetry really and indisputably matters. Indeed, such is the poet's human canniness and aesthetic strength, that it is almost as if he deploys the rage of political violence to test the credibility of his poetry.

Violence in Heaney's *The Spirit Level,* spills over into public and private spheres, as in **"Two Lorries".**[20] The poem juxtaposes a remembered scene between the poet's mother and a flirtatious coalman in the 1940s who delivers his load in an old lorry, and the bomb-packed lorry of modern times which shatters a bus station in "Magherafelt". The location was an innocent enough one in the time of the first lorry, but is now made terrible and terrifying by the mayhem. The name "Magherafelt" pulses throughout the poem, like an incantation, or the ticking of an explosive device. But consider the conclusion to the poem, where a dream-image combines the tenderness and terror of past and present, and leaves us with something peculiarly beautiful:

>   but which lorry
> Was it now? Young Agnew's or that other,
> Heavier, deadlier one, set to explode
> In a time beyond her time in Magherafelt . . .
> So tally bags and sweet-talk darkness, coalman.
> Listen to the rain spit in new ashes

As you heft a load of dust that was Magherafelt,
Then reappear from your lorry as my mother's
Dreamboat coalman filmed in silk-white ashes.

Political violence is apparent too in a poem dedicated to the poet's brother, **"Keeping Going",**[21] where it is a means for testing human spirit and endurance. The brother's humorous resilience, for example, is evident in his good-natured parody of a military and populist icon of the conflict in the North—an Orangeman piper:

The piper coming from far away is you
With a whitewash brush for a sporran
Wobbling round you, a kitchen chair
Upside down on your shoulder, your right arm
Pretending to tuck the bag beneath your elbow,
Your pop-eyes and big cheeks nearly bursting
With laughter, but keeping the drone going on
Interminably, between catches of breath.

The "brush" itself becomes one of those Heaneyesque objects that offers a perspective on to something else, in this case a family past, when the Heaney farmhouse used to be regularly whitewashed. The brush in those days performed something of a miracle, and so encapsulates Heaney's preoccupation with the transformative power of small things, as the "watery grey" it "lashes" onto the walls, dries out "whiter and whiter".

Another modulation takes us to one of the repeated images in this book, the Homeric blood trench, from which the souls of the dead drink fresh blood and are given human voice. The tar border to the house on which the whitewashing is being done is this "freshly opened, pungent, reeking trench", and the ghosts are memories of a past that Heaney shared with his brother, and which include (in a type of surrealist setting from *Macbeth*) a mother's warning to her wet-behind-the-ears under-graduate son about the danger of "bad boys" at college. This embarrassing warning (a humorous encapsulation of parental naïvety) modulates shockingly into the scene of contemporary violence which follows, and which involves bad boys indeed. The casual, relaxed pose of the victim underscores the everyday nature of the brutal-ity of the vicinity in which Heaney's brother lives. The tar of the street and the gutter conflate with the tar-strip of the whitewashing and the blood trench, and the murdered man becomes a sacrificial victim whose blood (it is implied) only gives voice to the unquiet ghosts of the struggle, and so perpetuates violence:

A car came slow down Castle Street, made the halt,
Crossed the Diamond, slowed again and stopped
Level with him, although it was not his lift.
And then he saw an ordinary face
For what it was and a gun in his own face.
His right leg was hooked back, his sole and heel
Against the wall, his right knee propped up steady,
So he never moved, just pushed with all his might
Against himself, then fell past the tarred strip,
Feeding the gutter with his copious blood.

Set against such scenes, his brother's resilience seems all the more remarkable, but of conclusive redemptive significance in the poem is the functional object, the brush, which takes within its wholesome ambit the goodness of utility and the potency of the magic of transformation:

I see you at the end of your tether sometimes,
In the milking parlour, holding yourself up
Between two cows until your turn goes past,
Then coming to in the smell of dung again
And wondering, is this all? As it was
In the beginning, is now and shall be?
Then rubbing your eyes and seeing our old brush
Up on the byre door, and keeping going.

Another "trench" poem is **"Damson",** which also relies on breathtakingly bold imagistic modulation.[22] The first image of a wound, described with Heaney's usual fresh exactitude, is conflated, disturbingly, with a "packed lunch":

Gules and cement dust. A matte tacky blood
On the bricklayer's knuckles, like the damson stain
That seeped through his packed lunch.

This blood, however, is the result of an honest wound, not of deadening political violence, and the trench scene with its ghosts only serves to underscore the difference between Odysseus, the "sacker", and the present wounded "builder". The stain of his "packed lunch" anticipates the final image of the poem, though it takes this very mundane source of nourishment to the next power. Confronted by the ghosts the builder will:

Drive them back to the wine-dark taste of home,
The smell of damsons simmering in a pot,
Jam ladled thick and steaming down the sunlight.

The imagination picks up on a colour, links it to vari-ous things and senses, and displaces the images and materials of violence with those of domestic creation, nutritious, restorative.

The principal focus of **"The Swing"** is also domestic.[23] Here, a state of grace stems from the sanctuary offered by remembered childhood. The measure of the complex pressures of past, present, and future are recognized and acknowledged by the poem, which chooses to privilege the experiences and sensations of the past, the ana-logue—it may be—of even a socially responsible art's imperative to suspend the multitudinous tide of experi-ence (including the indescribable violence of Hiroshima) and offer (in a way reminiscent of Shakespeare's "miracle" of "black ink") the glimpse of a tension-free and enduring realm of "beauty":

To start up by yourself, you hitched the rope
Against your backside and backed on into it
Until it tautened, then tiptoed and drove off

As hard as possible. You hurled a gathered thing
From the small of your own back into the air.
Your head swept low, you heard the whole shed creak.

We all learned one by one to go sky high.
Then townlands vanished into aerodromes,
Hiroshima made light of human bones,
Concorde's neb migrated towards the future.
So who were we to want to hang back there
In spite of all?
In spite of all, we sailed
Beyond ourselves and over and above
The rafters aching in our shoulder-blades,
The give and take of branches in our arms.

Nevertheless, while the spirit of the past has its own particular merit, Heaney has also captured in powerfully felt terms the spirit of the act of swinging, the spirit, in other words, of continuing process, which implies a moving "beyond" that past. This movement carries the refreshing aspects of that past, and so proclaims Heaney's own involvement with a type of "hope" regarding the future.

As in Serote, the aesthetic bodying forth of the past fuels an enriched engagement with the future. In fact, each type of spirit portrayed in this book has its own resonance, its own level, and Heaney seems able to take the exact measure of all of them, rendering the title **The Spirit Level** linguistically functional, and not just a verbal shadow of the actual spirit level. This sense of the functional worth of language impresses us most in the presence of Heaney, and makes us value the substantial force of his words. To return to the image of the quincunx of towers, it is as if verbal artefacts have the solidity of towers, and can take their stand in the lived world in a similar manner. The towers, in turn, have a significatory function inasmuch as they suggest psychological attitudes, and ways of ordering and confronting lived experience. Heaney's towers are distinctively verbal, just as his words are distinctively substantial. This is the "frontier of writing" of which he is so aware, presided over by towers that blur the edges between words and things. Further, it is from this level of molten potential that he acts. From here he assumes the profound responsibility to reconcile the forces inherent in each of the towers, an act which we might see, again, as a supreme act of hope for the future of Ireland. He thus helps us to appreciate that Serote's encoding of "hope" (the product of a related "frontier of writing", if we consider the close relation it bears to already-achieved humanitarian ends) is more than just a literary gesture, is closer akin to a similar social responsibility, a responsibility shared by all those who work with, or come under the impact of, language.

Notes

1. Oscar Wilde, *The Picture of Dorian Gray,* New York, 1931, 10.

2. Mongane Wally Serote, *Behold Mama, Flowers,* Johannesburg, 1978, 8.

3. Mongane Wally Serote, *To Every Birth Its Blood,* Johannesburg, 1981.

4. Serote, *Behold Mama,* 12-15.

5. *Ibid.,* 19-20.

6. *Ibid.,* 24-25.

7. *Ibid.,* 34.

8. *Ibid.,* 53.

9. *Ibid.,* 60-61.

10. Duncan Brown, "Interview with Mongane Wally Serote", *Theoria,* 80 (1992), 143.

11. Mongane Wally Serote, *Third World Express,* Cape Town, 1992, 4-5.

12. *Ibid.,* 31-32.

13. Serote, *To Every Birth,* 281.

14. Mongane Wally Serote, *Come and Hope with Me,* Cape Town, 1994, 28.

15. C. J. Driver, *In the Water-margins,* Plumstead, 1994, 47.

16. Lionel Abrahams, *A Dead Tree Full of Live Birds,* Plumstead, 1995, 8.

17. Helen Vendler, *The Art of Shakespeare's Sonnets,* Cambridge: MA, 1997, 303.

18. Seamus Heaney, *Preoccupations: Selected Poems 1968-1978,* London, 1980, 41-60.

19. Seamus Heaney, *The Redress of Poetry,* London and Boston, 1995, 199.

20. Seamus Heaney, *The Spirit Level,* New York, 1996, 17.

21. *Ibid.,* 13.

22. *Ibid.,* 19.

23. *Ibid.,* 58.

Eugene O'Brien (essay date 2006)

SOURCE: O'Brien, Eugene. "The Body as Ethical Synecdoche in the Writing of Seamus Heaney." In *The Body and Desire in Contemporary Irish Poetry,* edited by Irene Gilsenan Nordin, pp. 79-100. Dublin: Irish Academic Press, 2006.

[*In the following essay, O'Brien focuses on images of the body—in Heaney's original poems as well as in his translations of Sophocles—as a means by which Heaney uses the aesthetics of poetry to inject politics with an ethical sense of the value of individual human life.*]

This chapter will focus on images of the body in the work of Seamus Heaney as a synecdoche of the ethical imperative that drives the aesthetic in his work. In terms of treading the liminal state between poetry as an autotelic aesthetic discourse and poetry as a site of ideological and socio-political struggle, the bodies that are signified in Heaney's writing serve as a Derridean *brisure*,[1] through which both discourses can mutually enforce each other. By focusing on the materiality of the body, in some of the Bog Poems, the wounded body in *The Cure at Troy* in tandem with his prose musings on the hunger strikes, and the discourse of the dead body in *The Burial at Thebes,* this chapter will examine the images of the body in Heaney's writing, and will trace an ethical line of enquiry from these particular bodies into the singularity and uniqueness of each life, a discourse which he sees poetry as eminently qualified to profess.

Writing at the conclusion of the title essay of *The Government of the Tongue,* Heaney is discussing the 'paradox of poetry and of the imaginative arts in general' in terms of politics,[2] and muses on the efficacy of poetry. He says in one sense, the efficacy is 'nil—no lyric has ever stopped a tank'. However, in another sense he sees its efficacy as 'unlimited' and goes on, quoting from Chapter 8 of St John's Gospel, to cite the metaphor of Jesus' writing in the sand in the face of the scribes and Pharisees who were accusing the woman caught in adultery as an example. He sees this writing 'in the face of which accusers and accused are left speechless and renewed' as analogous to the force of poetry, a 'break with the usual life but not an absconding from it'. In terms redolent of Derrida's notions of différance and the trace, Heaney speaks of the epistemology of poetry as paralleling the writing in the sand, which is ephemeral in the extreme. As he puts it, poetry does not promise a solution to either the 'accusing crowd' or the 'helpless accused':

> Instead, in the rift between what is going to happen and whatever we would wish to happen, poetry holds attention for a space, functions not as distraction but as pure concentration, a focus where our power to concentrate is concentrated back on ourselves. This is what gives poetry its governing power. At its greatest moments it would attempt, in Yeats's phrase, to hold in a single thought reality and justice.[3]

Poetry can be the space through which reality and justice can operate, not overtly in the political sphere, but in terms of influencing the writer and the reader, in other words, in terms of creating more complex forms of individual identity. He goes on to describe poetry as 'more a threshold than a path' and sees it as one that is 'constantly approached and constantly departed from', and affects reader and writer by the experience of being 'at the same time summoned and released'.[4] The oscillatory nature of this dialectical movement demonstrates the complexity of the forces acting on both reader and writer. The fluidity and multi-perspectival nature of these positions are seminal to his notions of the value of poetry in the shaping of ethical attitudes.

In his 'writing in the sand' metaphor, Heaney probes these very notions of efficacy and inefficacy: on the one hand, he sees that poetry does not stop tanks; on the other, however, it may alter the mindset that is sending in those tanks. Ironically, it is the very ephemerality of poetry, the writing in the sand, that gives it any sense of lasting force; it is 'the imagination pressing back against the pressure of reality'.[5] However, the force is microcosmic as opposed to macrocosmic; it has no direct effect on the political, but it has the effect of altering the individual consciousness of both writer and reader. In terms of the relationship between writing and politics, he sees the 'purely poetic force of words' as 'the guarantee of a commitment which need not apologize for not taking up the cudgels since it is raising a baton to attune discords which the cudgels are creating'.[6] And, of course, the core of his 'writing in the sand' metaphor is the wounded female body, the body as victim, faced by hands holding stones but saved by a hand writing in the sand. This focus on the frailty of the body is developed in his Nobel lecture, *Crediting Poetry.*

Here, Heaney exemplifies this point by recalling how, in 1976, a minibus full of workers was stopped at Kingsmills, near Bessbrook in County Armagh at a bogus checkpoint. The occupants were lined up at the side of the road, and were told, 'Any Catholics among you, step out here.' Heaney notes that, since the majority of the group were Protestants, with a single exception, the presumption must have been that 'the masked men were Protestant para-militaries about to carry out a tit-for-tat sectarian killing'.[7] He goes on:

> It was a terrible moment for him, caught between dread and witness, but he did make a motion to step forward. Then, the story goes, in that split second of decision, and in the relative cover of the winter evening darkness, he felt the hand of the Protestant worker next to him take his hand and squeeze it in a signal that said no, don't move, we'll not betray you, nobody need know what faith or party you belong to.[8]

The man did step forward, but was thrown aside to watch the execution of the ten Protestant workers, murdered by 'presumably, the Provisional IRA'.[9] Heaney notes that, in the face of such atrocity, we are 'rightly suspicious of that which gives too much consolation in these circumstances'.[10] However, if art is to be of 'present use', then its redress must take account of both the hand that gripped its other, as well as those which murdered their others. Heaney's field of force hopes to credit the 'marvellous' as well as the 'murderous',[11] but always within a context that respects our responsibility to the other. Derrida has made the point that literature is that genre wherein 'license is given to the writer to say everything he wants to or everything he can'.[12] For Heaney, and his notion of poetry, we could perhaps add to this: licence is given to the writer to say everything he wants to or everything he can, and everything he should to help to attune the discords at work in society. This ethical component of the aesthetic has a transforming function in terms of how one sense of identity views another.

The focus of his attention in the retelling of the Kingsmills massacre is on the materiality of the bodies as individuals, of hands reaching out for each other, of hands reaching for triggers, and of bullets being fired. If poetry is in any way to become a threshold between the two poles of which we spoke at the beginning, then its effect, as Heaney notes, can only be on the individual and it is through the trope of the body that such an effect can be enunciated. Heaney has, throughout his writings, foregrounded the materiality of the *Lebenswelt* about which he is writing. Images of concrete reality characterised his earlier work, and nowhere was this seen more clearly than in his descriptions of bodies in his **'Bog Poems'**. There is a strand that weaves its way through Heaney's poetry which is connected with the body as a symbolic index of identity. It can be traced through the Bog Poems, and their embodiment of racial and psychic memory in images of corporeality which have transcended, in ways, death and time, and yet irrupt within history as harbingers of an essentialist form of identity. Here, desire is enunciated as some form of racial revenge which functions as a means of validating the selfhood of the nationalist consciousness.

As Heaney has noted, there was a sense in which the writers in Northern Ireland were expected to respond to the conflict in their work: 'a simple minded pressure also to speak up for their own side,[13] and clearly this pressure was felt by Heaney, who said that it would 'wrench the rhythms' of his writing procedures to 'start squaring up to contemporary events with more will than ways to deal with them'.[14] He referred to the Yeatsean example of writing in the context of a political and social crisis:

> I think that what he learned there was that you deal with public crisis not by accepting the terms of the public's crisis, but by making your own imagery and your own terrain take the colour of it, take the impressions of it.[15]

This is precisely what Heaney does in his Bog Poems. Heaney told Edward Broadbridge that he was always aware that his own inspiration sprang from 'remembering' and he went on to extrapolate this into a national fixation, seeing it as typical of Irish people that they 'looked back at their own history' rather than forward towards the future. He went on to explore the ramifications of this: 'The word "remember" is a potent word in Irish politics . . . Remember 1690 if you're an Orangeman . . . Remember 1916 . . . if you are a republican'.[16]

His seminal Bog Poem, **'The Tollund Man'**, stemming from pictures in P. V. Glob's book *The Bog People*, focuses on the body as icon. The first stanza is a complete sentence, describing how the poet 'will go to Aarhus' to see the Tollund Man's 'peat-brown head', while the second describes the actual unearthing of the bog figure, as 'they dug him out'.[17] He goes on to describe both the exact physical state of the Tollund Man—his last meal of 'winter seeds' still in his stomach—and the mythic and natural processes which have kept the corpse whole, like 'saint's body'—'She tightened her torc on him' and opened 'her fen'.[18] It is as if his sacrifice for his people to the mother goddess has been rewarded with a kind of immortality. He has almost become like the bog itself, with his 'peat-brown head', his eye-lids looking like 'mild pods' and his skin coloured by the bog's 'dark juices'.[19] While in this poem, there is clearly a sense that his sacrifice may well have been worth while for his people, in later poems, the focus is less on the body as sacrificial icon, and more on the marks of violence that have been inflicted on that body.

This act of unearthing the past is the subject of **'Come to the Bower'**, itself the title of an Irish folk song, which recounts the act of uncovering 'the dark-bowered queen' by 'hand', an image which, as Patricia Coughlin, who has provided a seminal feminist critique of Heaney's work, notes: 'combines the traditional topos of disrobing with the richly sensuous apprehension of the landscape which is one of Heaney's most characteristic features'.[20] The imagery and narrative are suffused with a strong sexual subtext, as the sensory aspects of the act, the hand being 'touched' by sweetbriar before going on to 'unpin' the queen, and to 'unwrap skins' are dwelt upon. This chain is reinforced by the phallic imagery of 'sharpened willow', which 'Withdraws gently' out of 'black maw / Of the peat', and the added image of spring water which starts 'to rise around her'. The culmination of this sexual image chain is the final reaching of the 'bullion' of her 'Venus bone'.[21] Here the female body is very much at the mercy of male phallic and penetrative power.

In the next poem, **'Bog Queen'**, the thematic process is similar but the perspective is completely altered as it is the body itself which speaks. The repeated 'I lay waiting' stresses the fact that, though dead, there is some form of sentience still at work in the consciousness of the bog queen; she remains conscious of all of the processes of decay even as she undergoes them: the 'seeps of winter / digested me'. Her brain is seen as 'darkening', and compared to a 'jar of spawn' which is 'fermenting underground'.[22] The constant use of the pronoun 'my' to explain the processes of nature underlines the consciousness of the speaker, and the fact that she retains some form of life. The length of time she has been 'waiting' is beautifully caught by the use of the unusual verb which describes how the 'Phoenician stitchwork / retted on my breasts' // soft moraines'.[23] This verb, which derives from the Middle English *roten,* meaning 'to soften by soaking in water or by exposure to moisture to encourage partial rotting', captures the gradual rotting of both the body and the clothing which covered that body. The sheer length of time involved in this process is indicated by the use of 'moraines' to describe the queen's breasts, as this word refers to an area or bank of debris that a glacier or ice sheet has carried down and deposited.

The almost complete transformation from human to natural object that is undergone by the bog queen seems to indicate a direction in the poem which will see her totally subsumed by the land: 'the seeps of winter / digested me'.[24] However, in the closing stanza and a half, the imagery of decomposition is inverted, and death becomes metamorphosised into a rebirth:

> The plait of my hair,
> A slimy birth-chord
> Of bog, had been cut
>
> And I rose from the dark,
> Hacked bone, skull-ware.[25]

Here, the sentience of memory is symbolised in this image of death being transformed into rebirth. This is possibly his most graphic figuring of the idea of memory as having a life of its own, and it compliments the previous poem, **'Come to the Bower'.** There, the 'I' of the poem went searching for 'the dark-bowered queen' while here, it is the self-same queen who speaks: she is sentient, aware and 'waiting' for this very moment when she can be unveiled and reborn. It is this latent power of memory to incubate the wrongs of the past and to keep them alive in the minds of a community that is the subject of these poems. The levels of violence and pain that are part of the somatic experience are writ large here, and in **'The Grauballe Man',** the tension between seeing a dead body as an icon, or as a dead body is made very clear:

> Who will say 'corpse'
> to his vivid cast?
> Who will say 'body'
> to his opaque repose?[26]

Thomas Docherty sees this stanza as asking: 'is history dead, a thing of the past; or is it alive, vivid, a presence of the past?'[27] These were the very questions that Irish people, North and South, were asking as sectarian violence flared in the streets of Northern Ireland. The unquestioned assumptions of nationalist Ireland, that

the 1916 Rising was a good thing, that the IRA had the right to bear arms in the name of the Irish people, and that there was a historical imperative that saw a 'United Ireland' as its *telos* were coming into question, though very gradually. Having called the status of the bog figure into question, he goes on to repeat the same death-resurrection trope that we saw in **'Bog Queen'** as the Grauballe Man's hair is compared, again in simile, to a 'foetus', and later, to a 'forceps baby'. The idea that this man's death, a death caused by a 'slashed throat', has somehow been arrested, and that he now becomes the ultimate image of a rebirth is a classic example of the power of the aesthetic to persuade an audience that death for the tribe can have a salvific purpose. This is how much of *North* has been read, as justifying, or glorifying such violence.

However, Heaney also creates a counter-movement, a movement in this case which occurs over the long sentence that is the final four stanzas of the poem. He tells of how he first saw the Grauballe Man's 'twisted face' in a photograph, but says that now he is 'perfected in my memory'. The movement from the external to the internal that structurally underpinned so much of Heaney's artesian imagery is evident here again, as this ancient figure, dug 'out of the peat' is balanced in the poet's memory: 'hung in the scales / with beauty and atrocity'. On one side of this particular scale is the Dying Gaul (a sculpture from the third century BC depicting a dying Celtic warrior, with matted hair, lying on his shield, wounded, and awaiting death, now to be found in the Capitoline museum in Rome), and on the other:

> the actual weight
> of each hooded victim,
> slashed and dumped.[28]

Here, the poem, which seemed to be endorsing an aesthetic approach to this figure, now suddenly broaches the contrast between an actual piece of art, the Dying Gaul, an imaginative creation, and the Grauballe Man, a victim of tribal sacrifice, killed in a most unpleasant manner. Factually, Glob noted that the 'cut ran . . . practically from ear to ear, so deep that the gullet was completely severed'.[29]

The word that tips the balance here is the adjective 'actual', which stresses the reality of lifting the dead weight of hooded victims, after they were 'slashed'. Whether these victims are Iron Age figures or contemporary victims of Northern Irish violence is not specified but I would suggest that he is referring to contemporary figures, and I also feel that he is, once again, foregrounding the victim and the reality of death, as opposed to some form of mythic religious dimension. Again, there was a societal parallel as the images of the victims of the Provisional IRA and Loyalist bombings and shootings began to register with television audiences, and people began to wonder whether political ideology of either sort was worth such suffering. The image of a mutilated body is a synecdoche through which such points can be made. Bodies can be images, symbols, icons and relics, but first and foremost, they are bodies, whose mortality and vulnerability are central to their signification. For a group, or for political expediency, a body may be a sacrifice, or an icon; for the particular body, there is pain, suffering and death, and Heaney's poetry, by stressing the materiality of bodies, makes this abundantly clear. Ethically, these bodies, the woman in adultery, the victims of the massacre in Kingsmills and the long-dead Bog people, remind us of the frailty of life, and the ease with which it can be destroyed. These images are like the writing in the sand with which we began, a break from the usual but not in any way a form of escape from it.

In his translation of Sophocles's *Philoctetes, The Cure at Troy,* the notion of a bodily wound is again seen in terms of being an index of desire, with the somatic wound of Philoctetes functioning synecdochically by symbolising the ongoing wounds of the polarised positions in Northern Ireland. However, at the same time it is the wounded body qua wounded body that is the central signifier of the play. Written for Field Day in 1990, and first produced in October of that year in the Guildhall in Derry, *The Cure at Troy* foregrounds the conflicts between politics and ethics, between loyalty to one's tribe and loyalty to a higher sense of humanity and truth, between values which are the products of a particular ideology, and those which aspire to some form of transcendent position in terms of that ideology, are set out.

In this play, Philoctetes has been left by the Greeks on the island of Lemnos, due to a foul-smelling suppurating wound, which left him 'rotting like a leper' caused by a 'snakebite he got at a shrine'.[30] A Trojan soothsayer, Helenus, one of King Priam's sons, had prophesied that Troy would be captured only if Philoctetes and his bow were present, so Odysseus and the hero of the play, Neoptolemus (the son of Achilles), are sent to obtain the bow. From the beginning, the stage is set in terms of a conflict between tribal loyalty and some transcendental notion of ethical value and responsibility.

Here, the loyalties of Greeks and Trojans are superimposed on to the contemporary situation of Northern Ireland. This becomes unequivocal near the end of the play when the chorus sums up the developments with an interpolation that speaks of a 'hunger-striker's father' standing in a graveyard, and a 'police widow in veils' fainting at 'the funeral home'.[31] Hence, the dilemma of the Greeks obeying orders, and taking the bow of Philoctetes against his wishes, can set up resonances with contemporary Irish communal and sectarian loyal-

ties, but can also avoid succumbing to any gravitational entrapment through the creative use of translation.

Consequently, the chorus can see that a loyalty to the tribe which is not counterweighted by some sense of personal ethics causes people who are convinced that they are 'in the right' to 'repeat themselves . . . no matter what.' This parallel of the Freudian repetition complex (*Wiederholungszwang*), can also be seen as a constitutive factor in the replication of the violence in Northern Ireland, as generation after generation becomes involved (or is interpellated, in Althusserian terms), in sectarian violence in the defence of the ideological certainties of a particular community, be that nationalist or unionist. The modal cause of this repetitive, trans-generational involvement is a sense of communal grievance, the 'self-pity' that 'buoys them up',' which is developed and fed by pondering upon past injustices.

Philoctetes, as symbolic of this tendency, identifies again and again with his wound: 'I managed to come through / but I never healed';[32] 'this ruins everything. / I'm being cut open';[33] 'has the bad smell left me?';[34] 'Some animals in a trap / Eat off their own legs';[35] 'All I've left is a wound'.[36] His subjectivity is intrinsically bound up with his wound; symbolically, he is unable to face the future because of his adhesion to the past; his wound interpellates him as a particular type of ideological subject. The chorus sums up this perspective, and having already spoken of 'self-pity,' it goes on to point out the self-fulfilling prophecy that such an attitude can bring about:

> And their whole life spent admiring themselves
> For their own long-suffering.
> Licking their wounds
> And flashing them around like decorations.[37]

This veneration of the wounds of the past is exactly how sectarian ideology seduces new subjectivities into existing moulds, and this is why the survivor of Kingsmills is such a potent ethical symbol—he has survived to tell how awful such killing is. In this play, Philoctetes embodies the siege mentality that is rife in Northern Ireland in his cry: 'No matter how I'm besieged. / I'll be my own Troy. The Greeks will never take me.'[38]

Another aspect of such entrapment is the sense of immanence within a culture, which sees value only in those areas wherein the tribal imperatives are validated. In *The Cure at Troy,* it is Odysseus who symbolises this voice of political pragmatism. He defines himself and Neoptolemus as 'Greeks with a job to do',[39] and makes similar matter of fact pronouncements as the play proceeds, informing the younger man that 'you're here to serve our cause'.[40] In the service of his cause, Odysseus can rationalise almost anything, telling Philoctetes that his 'aim has always been to get things done / By being adaptable',[41] and this adaptability is grounded in his tribal loyalty. He can gloss over the sufferings of Philoctetes by invoking his own ideological position: 'We were Greeks with a job to do, and we did it', and in answer to the ethical question about the lies that have been told, he gives the classic response of political pragmatism: 'But it worked! It worked, so what about it?'[42] Here is the political overriding the ethical—the voice of *Realpolitik,* the end justifying the means. What is the importance of a single wounded body compared to the general weal of the Polis?

In the climactic confrontation of the play, Neoptolemus, who had shared this perspective earlier in the play: 'I'm under orders',[43] and who had lied to Philoctetes in order to obtain his bow, realises the error of his ways and becomes a more complex character through the introduction of an ethical strand to his *persona*. In a colloquy with Odysseus, the gradual opposition between pragmatic tribal politics and a more open humanistic ethics is unveiled. In response to Neoptolemus's statement that 'I did a wrong thing and I have to right it',[44] and to his further remark that he is going to 'redress the balance' and cause the 'scales to even out'[45] by handing back the bow, Odysseus replies in clichés: 'Act your age. Be reasonable. Use your head.' The reply of Neoptolemus demonstrates the gulf that exists between the two: 'Since when did the use of reason rule out truth?'[46]

For Odysseus, 'rightness' and 'justice' are values that are immanent in the ideological perspective of the tribe or community. There is to be no critical distance between his notions of myth and history. He tells Neoptolemus that there is one last 'barrier' that will stop him handing back the bow, and that is the 'will of the Greek people, / And me here as their representative'.[47] He sees no sense of any transcendental or intersubjective form of justice in what Neoptolemus is attempting. When Neoptolemus speaks of 'doing the right thing,' he is answered by the voice of the tribe: 'What's so right about / Reneging on your Greek commission?' Their subsequent interchange deserves to be quoted in full as it is a *locus classicus* of the conflict between ethics and nationalistic politics; between a view of self and other as connected and mutually responsible, and that of self and other as disparate and in conflict:

ODYSSEUS

>   You're under my command here. Don't you forget it.

NEOPTOLEMUS

>   The commands that I am hearing overrule
>   You and all you stand for.

ODYSSEUS

>   And what about The Greeks? Have they no jurisdiction left?

NEOPTOLEMUS

>   The jurisdiction I am under here
>   Is justice herself. She isn't only Greek.

ODYSSEUS

>   You've turned yourself into a Trojan, lad.[48]

In this exchange, the critical distance already spoken of is evident in the value-ethic of Neoptolemus. He has moved beyond the inter-tribal epistemology of Odysseus, where not to be Greek necessitates one's being Trojan. Such a perspective severely limits one's range of choices: one is either Greek or Trojan—a parallel with the population of Northern Ireland being divided into the adversarial binarisms of Catholicism or Protestantism; nationalism or unionism; republicanism or loyalism. That such identifications exist is beyond question; what is open to question, however, is whether it is wise to see them as all-encompassing, as this can cause the 'entrapment' which has mired Odysseus, and from which Neoptolemus is determined to escape. His notion of justice is intersubjective, a higher ethical command to do right by another human being, regardless of political imperative.

In a ringing assertion earlier in the play, as he begins to have some form of sympathy with Philoctetes, Neoptolemus says 'I'm all throughother. This isn't me. I'm sorry.'[49] Here the beginnings of an ethics of identity, of a view that the self is not defined in simplistic contradistinction to the other, but rather is shot through with traces of that other, is seen as a painful and self-alienating experience. One is reminded of Emannuel Levinas's statement that language is 'born in responsibility', implying that the responsibility involved is to the other, to other traditions, other ideas, but most essentially, to other people.[50] A comparison can be made between the doubt and questioning of Neoptolemus, and Odysseus's conviction that 'he's in the right'.[51] For Heaney, poetry can aid in the creation of such an ethics of selfhood, functioning as 'a source of truth and at the same time a vehicle of harmony,' while at the same time being 'both socially responsible and creatively free'.[52]

For Odysseus, the borderline between self and other is clear and finite; it encompasses all lines of vision. For him, 'justice' is either Greek or Trojan; where Greek jurisdiction ends, he can only imagine Trojan jurisdiction beginning. His binary logic is exactly that of many groupings in contemporary culture, if you are not for *'us'* then you must be for *'them'*. Heaney's view of the relationship between self and other, as voiced by Neoptolemus, is profoundly at odds with this; he feels a sense of ethical responsibility for the other as well as the self. Derrida has made the point, in *Of Spirit,* that the origin of language is responsibility, and it is this sense of responsibility to the other that drives the transformation in Neoptolemus.[53] Speaking of the binary opposition between Ireland and England, as an origin of that between Catholic and Protestant, Heaney sees poetry as a constellation wherein both can be set in dialectical and transformative interchange: 'I think of the personal and Irish pieties as vowels, and the literary awarenesses nourished on English as consonants. My hope is that the poems will be vocables adequate to my whole experience.'[54]

Hence Heaney's view of the line that separates one community from another is similar to what Derrida envisages when he speaks of the irrepressible desire for a 'community' to form but also for it to know its limit: 'and for its limit to be its *opening*'.[55] For Derrida, cultural identity is not the 'self-identity of a thing': he sees cultural identity as 'a way of being different from itself', adding that a 'culture is different from itself' and that 'language is different from itself'.[56] This idea of a limit as an opening to alterity is one which has strong echoes in Heaney's work. Writing about George Herbert's 'The Pulley', and one of his own poems from **'Squarings',** Heaney notes that both works are about 'the way consciousness can be alive to two different and contradictory dimensions of reality and still find a way of negotiating between them'.[57] This concept of negotiation is precisely what is meant by his comment that rhyme 'surprises and extends' the fixed relationships between words, and, by extension, between individuals and communities. One of his methods of achieving this negotiation is the already discussed 'field of force', from *Preoccupations.* In such structures of thought, the border between self and other is very much a Derridean opening, and this is symbolised, in *The Cure at Troy,* by the role of the chorus:

> For my part is the chorus, and the chorus
> Is more or less a borderline between
> The you and the me and the it of it.
>
>   Between
> The gods' and human beings' sense of things.
> And that's the borderline that poetry
> Operates on too, always in between
> What you would like to happen and what will—
> Whether you like it or not.
>
>   Poetry
> Allowed the god to speak. It was the voice
> Of reality and justice.[58]

This borderline will be very much in line with Heaney's notion of a frontier of writing, which allows some form of passage across that border which separates different groups. Borders, says Heaney, are made to be crossed, and poetry may provide the mode of such a crossing. In political terms, Heaney has expressed the hope that the frontier which partitions Ireland into north and south could become 'a little bit more like the net on a tennis court, a demarcation allowing for agile give-and-take'.[59] Yet again there are echoes of Derrida, who says that we 'have to cross the border but not to destroy the border';[60] instead, the border, as a limit point of one community, becomes an opening to the other community. In Heaney's terms, the voice of the chorus, a poetic voice, is a point of opening between the 'you' and the 'me'; it is an intersubjective point of mediation between the gods' and human beings' 'sense of things.' He goes on to make the ethical role of poetry *qua* poetry explicit by extending the connection between the voices which enunciate this poetic vision, and poetry itself: 'And that's the borderline that poetry / Operates on too.'[61]

It is poetry (in this case poetry as translation) as genre that facilitates this ethical interaction between self and other, this sense that borders are not points of closure but instead, points of opening. Hence Neoptolemus can say: 'I'm all throughother', meaning that he is becoming aware that there are not just two essential identities at work here; he realises that there are alternatives to the essentialist ethnocentrisms of Odysseus; he realises that 'reality and justice' are values which can have a transformative effect on notions of being Greek or Trojan. As Philoctetes puts it, in a moment of *anagnorisis*: 'the wheel is turning, the scales are tilting back. Justice is going to be woken up at last.'[62] Neoptolemus, speaking of 'justice herself', makes the point that 'she isn't only Greek',[63] and this is perhaps the crucial message of this play.

While admitting that no 'poem or play or song / Can fully right a wrong',[64] this translation attempts to stake out the ground for poetry to have some effect in a world where people 'suffer', 'torture one another' and get 'hurt and get hard'. Realising the lesson of history, which says: *'Don't hope / On this side of the grave'* (original italics), the chorus concludes the play by suggesting that the:

> once in a lifetime
> The longed-for tidal wave
> Of justice can rise up,
> And hope and history rhyme.[65]

The conditions required for such a tidal wave are the awareness of the necessary relationship between self and other, and of the transformative effects of this relationship in terms of future definitions of selfhood and alterity. As Derrida has put it, in a broadly similar context, the relation to alterity as the responsibility to the other is also a 'responsibility toward the *future,* since it involves the struggle to create openings within which the other can appear' and can hence 'come to transform what we know or think we know'.[66]

Translation, as has become clear, is the vehicle which allows us to achieve this putative transformation, becoming a way not of erasing the original, but of keeping the original alive. It is a way of 'translating oneself into the other language without giving up one's own language.' In political terms, the act of translating is a way of 'welcoming the other's traditions'.[67] It is also a way of transforming the temporal orientation of a culture from the past to the present, as the old tongue becomes transformed into the new tongue which points towards a politics of the future:

> Your wound is what you feed on, Philoctetes.
> I say it again in friendship and say this:
> Stop eating yourself up with hate and come with us.[68]

To see such an exhortation as politically naive would be to forget that, at the end of the play, Philoctetes still has his wound, and the chorus, while certainly hopeful, nevertheless retains an adjectival sense of doubt and uncertainty regarding the future that is set out before the characters in the play, and by analogy, before the communities in Northern Ireland:

> I leave
> *Half-ready* to believe
> That a *crippled* trust might walk
>
> And the *half-true* rhyme is love.[69] [my italics]

The uncertainties that are enunciated in these adjectives certainly undercut any untoward optimism. The parallel with the ongoing peace process, with its analogous uncertainties and half-steps forward, is clearly implied, but it would be incorrect to see this parallel as all-consuming. Heaney's notion of the role of poetry is very much focused on transforming the individual, as opposed to the group or tribe. Tribal loyalty may still be present, but a personal ethic can act as a counter-balance, whether in mythical ancient Ireland where Sweeney's wings gave him this Daedalan perspective, or in ancient Greece, where Philoctetes can become 'all throughother' and see beyond Odysseus's identificatory position which is composed of the Greek-Trojan exclusive binarism, or in the actual space of Northern Ireland.

The metaphor of the wound, which can either cripple any movement beyond itself or else become the catalyst for some form of future which is focused on a form of healing, is seminal in this translation. The treatment of a human being, *in extremis* of suffering, is a standard through which ethical behaviour can be adjudged. Indeed, the wounded or maimed body becomes in both this translation and the Bog Poems already discussed, the structural and symbolic agency for poetry to work on the individual consciousness. The human body, stoned, with its throat slit, or riddled with bullets, becomes the metaphor of an ethical demand on the body politic, it becomes the demand of the other on the writer to seek a horizon that is beyond that of group or tribal loyalty.

In *The Redress of Poetry*, Heaney has made this very point about the role of the writer when faced with a situation of group loyalty versus a sense of humanistic ethics. Taking three examples, an English poet in the First World War One, an Irish poet in the wake of the 1916 Rising and an American poet during the Vietnam war, he notes that the cultural expectations on each would be broadly similar: the First World War: to contribute to the war effort by 'dehumanizing the face of the enemy';[70] 1916: to 'revile the tyranny of the executing power' and Vietnam: to 'wave the flag rhetorically'.[71] These are very much the pressures felt by the early Heaney, and discussed in his poetry. His answer underlines his notion of one of the redresses of poetry: as it can see the German soldier 'as a friend'; the British government as a body 'which might keep faith' and Vietnam as an 'Imperial betrayal':

> In these cases, to see the German soldier as a friend and secret sharer, to see the British government as a body who might keep faith, to see the South-East Asian expedition as an imperial betrayal, to do any of these things is to add a complication where the general desire is for a simplification.[72]

In the above quotation, he crosses the political border by means of the ethical; intersubjective notions of justice are a higher demand than tribal loyalty. It is this need to go beyond simplification that is so important in Heaney's writing. His thoughts on the value of poetry can be brought to this conclusion: it has to be 'a working model of inclusive consciousness. It should not simplify.'[73] It must be true to the complexities of modern, or postmodern life, and as such, Heaney's work parallels the growing complexity of life, political, social, religious and cultural, in contemporary Ireland.

As Heaney puts it in *The Government of the Tongue,* a poem 'floats adjacent to, parallel to, the historical moment'.[74] The poet's role is not to use his gift as a slingstone for the desperate or for any other group. Instead it is, in the words of Zbigniew Herbert, concerned with salvaging 'out of the catastrophe of history at least two words, without which all poetry is an empty play of meanings and appearances, namely: justice and truth'.[75] And it is in the vexed liminal space of the intersection of these two that he speaks in his translation of Sophocles' *Antigone: The Burial at Thebes,* where the notion of non-simplification is at the core of the play and this version of it.

This translation is part of a developing trend in the work of Seamus Heaney. One can trace a line of translations from within individual books of poetry, since **Field Work,** through to individual works themselves: **Sweeney Astray, Beowulf,** *The Cure at Troy* and now *The Burial at Thebes.* As is increasingly the case in Heaney's writing, he tends to view the mater of Ireland best through the lens of another language and culture, imitating the desire of Stephen Dedalus to fly by those nets of language, nationality and religion. In a piece published in the first edition of the *Irish Book Review,* 'Thebes via Toombridge: Retitling Antigone', Heaney sets out the connections between local and universal that motivated the title of this translation. Speaking of Francis Hughes, the dead hunger striker and neighbour of his in county Derry, Heaney stresses the body of Hughes as a site of struggle between the security forces and the nationalist crowd who came to take possession of it. Ownership of the body becomes a seminal metaphor here, as it becomes a potent signifier of the contest between the 'instinctive powers of feeling, love and kinship' and the 'daylight gods of free and self-conscious, social and political life',[76] to quote Hegel. Heaney sees the motivation behind the 'surge of rage in the crowd as they faced the police' as an index of what he terms *dúchas,* and it is here that we come to Antigone's retitling. For her sense of propriety and integrity come from that feeling of kinship with the other as a fellow human, regardless of the political differences that separate us. This sense of kinship with the other is what he spoke of in *Crediting Poetry* about the Kingsmills massacre, in *The Cure at Troy* about Philoctetes, in *The Government of the Tongue* about the woman caught in adultery and in the Bog Poems about the long-dead Iron Age figures.

The play is set after an invading army from Argos has been defeated by the Thebans under their new king, Creon. Two of the sons of Oedipus, brothers to Antigone and Ismene, died in this battle. Eteocles perished defending Thebes but his brother, Polyneices, was part of the attacking army and hence a traitor:

> Their banners flew, the battle raged
> They fell together, their father's sons.[77]

King Creon, outraged by this treachery from one of the royal family, decrees that Polyneices shall not receive the normal purifying burial rites and places under interdict of death anyone who will attempt to provide these rites to the corpse. He decrees that Polyneices that 'Anti-Theban Theban' will not be accorded burial but will be left to rot in the open. We could be listening to the voice of Odysseus in *The Cure at Troy* again, as value is placed on loyalty to the group as opposed to some higher criterion. The results are that 'the dogs and birds are at it day and night, spreading reek and rot'. Creon justifies this, in a manner similar to the British authorities and their treatment of the corpse of Francis Hughes:

> This is where I stand where it comes to Thebes
> Never to grant traitors and subversives
> Equal footing with loyal citizens.[78]

Once again, we are in the territory of the political sense of justice, the betterment of the group or *Polis,* in contradistinction with a higher sense of the value of the individual. For Antigone, the duty she has to her brother as human far surpasses her duty to the Theban notion of patriotism as laid down by Creon, and interestingly, she cites a higher law than that of Creon or Thebes itself:

> I disobeyed the law because the law was not
> The law of Zeus nor the law ordained
> By Justice. Justice dwelling deep
> Among the gods of the dead.[79]

By positing a higher order of the treatment of the other than that of the polis, or group, Antigone is voicing the perennial debate between ethics and patriotism or nationalism. To treat the dead correctly and with honour, she implies, is very much an index of our own humanity. The treatment of people as less than human, as often demanded by the voice of the tribe, is the antithesis of her own actions. Hers is an evocation of a higher, intersubjective sense of ethics:

> This proclamation had your force behind it
> But it was mortal force, and I, also a mortal,
> I chose to disregard it. I abide
> By statutes utter and immutable—
> Unwritten, original, god-given laws.[80]

One of the strongest points about this translation is the degree of moral complexity involved. From his own perspective, and indeed, from that of the chorus, Creon is to be admired:

> Creon saved us
> Saved the country, and there he was, strong king,
> Strong head of family, the man in charge.[81]

However, so is Antigone, as in death she teaches Creon that: 'until we breathe our last breath / we should keep the established law', and in this line we see the credo of both original and translation: our common humanity should transcend our differences. It is the treatment of the dead, themselves no longer part of politics as agents, that is seen as wrong in the dramatic logic of the play and the translation. As Heaney calls it in his prose piece 'it is a matter of burial refused', as Polyneices is being made a 'non-person' and this is what Antigone cannot countenance, and it is this disrespect for the human in death that is the cause of the metaphorical contagion outlined by Tiresias:

> spreading reek and rot
> On every altar stone and temple step, and the gods
> Are revolted. That's why we have this plague,
> This vile pollution.[82]

The result is that tapestry of the power structure that Creon is attempting to consolidate unravels in a litany of dead bodies: Antigone, Haemon, Eurydice all lie dead by the end of the play.

However, as his discussion of the Kingsmills massacre demonstrated, Heaney is not just concerned with bodies long dead, or wounded in biblical or classical drama.

Those dead Protestant workers are very real indices of the need for an ethical warrant to over-ride political imperatives. Similarly, the voices of women demanding justice for their dead brother have a potent contemporary resonance in Irish political life. On 30 January 2005, Robert McCartney was murdered outside Magennis' pub in the Short Strand area of Belfast. Reputedly, the murderers were members of Sinn Fein and the Provisional IRA and, in the aftermath of the murder, the pub was cleaned of fingerprints, CCTV evidence was removed and threats were issued to the witnesses of the act as to the consequences of reporting any of this to the Police Service of Northern Ireland.

The sisters of Robert McCartney—Catherine, Paula, Claire, Donna and Gemma—and his partner Bridgeen have spoken out in a campaign to see justice done to their brother in death, and this is eerily resonant of the voice of Antigone in defence of her own dead brother. Their demand is for justice to be done for their brother, a demand that echoes across the centuries, and that could be spoken in the words of Antigone: 'Justice dwelling deep / Among the gods of the dead.'[83] It is significant that Heaney, in describing the genesis of this text, compares the treatment of the body of Polyneices with that of Francis Hughes, the hunger striker; it is even more significant that this play deals with the voice of women, then, as now, seen as not quite part of the public sphere, women who are totally focused on obtaining justice for the dead:

> I never did a nobler thing than bury
> My brother Polyneices. And if these men
> Weren't so afraid to sound unpatriotic
> They'd say the same.[84]

The partner and sisters of Robert McCartney have suffered the same fate as that of Antigone, they are seen as unusual voices in the public sphere: 'women were never meant for this assembly,'[85] says Creon, words that have a chilling echo in the warning for the sisters by Martin McGuiness about being used by other political forces. Here, the ethical has engaged with the political, and the political is found wanting in the face of that imperative towards justice that has become symbolised by the name and body of Robert McCartney.

The bodies of Francis Hughes, the woman in adultery, the ten Protestant workers, the Bog people and the body of Polyneices are answered, in the contemporary moment, by the body of Robert McCartney, someone who was killed within his Polis, but who, metaphorically, is a revenant, unable to rest. The women who spoke out for their brothers, both in classical drama and in the contemporary world of the political, are ethical voices who demand justice, and common human decency that goes beyond narrow loyalty to the Polis, the tribe or any ideology that seeks to dehumanise those who are on the other side.

One can do no better then wish that those who killed him can take the advice of Tiresias, the blind prophet:

> Yield to the dead. Don't stab a ghost.
> What can you win when you only wound a corpse?[86]

These words, uttered in the present context attest the lasting value of this translation by Seamus Heaney of Sophocles' *Antigone*. This venerable text still speaks to us across the centuries, and the language of this translation, lucid, crisp and intelligent, makes that voice seem ever more relevant. The images of the human body that we have discussed, frail, wounded, vulnerable or ultimately deceased are potent signifiers of the power of the aesthetic to imbricate the ethical into the political in a way that can only benefit those who read it. The efficacy of poetry is precisely this sense of the importance of the individual life, the individual body, in the face of any group or societal imperative to dehumanise it.

Notes

1. J. Derrida, *Of Grammatology,* trans. G. Chakravorty Spivak (London: Johns Hopkins University Press, 1976), pp. 65-73.

2. S. Heaney, *The Government of the Tongue: The 1986 T. S. Eliot Memorial Lectures and Other Critical Writings* (London: Faber 1988), p. 107.

3. Heaney, *Government of the Tongue,* p. 108.

4. Ibid.

5. S. Heaney, *The Redress of Poetry: Oxford Lectures* (London: Faber, 1995), p. 1.

6. S. Heaney, *Place and Displacement* (Grasmere: Trustees of Dove Cottage, 1985), p. 7.

7. S. Heaney, *Crediting Poetry* (Oldcastle: Gallery Press, 1995), p. 18.

8. Ibid.

9. Ibid.

10. Heaney, *Crediting Poetry,* p. 19.

11. Heaney, *Crediting Poetry,* p. 20.

12. J. Derrida, *Acts of Literature,* ed. D. Attridge (London: Routledge, 1992), p. 37.

13. B. Donnelly, interview with Seamus Heaney, in E. Broadbridge (ed.), *Seamus Heaney Skoleradioen* (Copenhagen: Danmarks Radio, 1977), pp. 59-61, p. 60.

14. S. Heaney, *Preoccupations: Selected Prose 1968-1978* (London: Faber, 1980), p. 34.

15. J. Randall, 'An Interview with Seamus Heaney', *Ploughshares,* 5, 3, (1979), pp. 7-22, p. 13.

16. Broadbridge, E. Radio Interview with Seamus Heaney, published in *Seamus Heaney Skoleradioen* (Copenhagen: Danmarks Radio, 1977), pp. 5-16, p. 9.

17. S. Heaney, *Wintering Out* (London: Faber, 1972), p. 47.

18. Ibid.

19. Ibid.

20. P. Coughlin, '"Bog Queens": The Representation of Women in the Poetry of John Montague and Seamus Heaney', in M. Allen (ed.), *Seamus Heaney: New Casebook Series* (London: Macmillan, 1997, pp. 185-205), p. 194.

21. Heaney, Seamus, *North* (London: Faber, 1975), p. 31.

22. Heaney, *North*, p. 32.

23. Ibid., p. 33.

24. Ibid., p. 32.

25. Ibid., p. 34.

26. Ibid., p. 36.

27. T. Docherty, 'Ana-; or Postmodernism, Landscape, Seamus Heaney', in A. Easthope and J. O. Thompson (eds), *Contemporary Poetry Meets Modern Theory* (Hemel Hempstead: Harvester Wheatsheaf, 1991), pp. 68-80, p. 70.

28. Heaney, *North*, p. 36.

29. P. V. Glob, *The Bog People* (London: Faber, 1969), p. 48.

30. S. Heaney, *The Cure at Troy* (London: Faber, 1990), p. 17.

31. Ibid., p. 77.

32. Ibid., p. 18.

33. Ibid., p. 40.

34. Ibid., p. 57.

35. Ibid., p. 53.

36. Ibid., p. 61.

37. Ibid., p. 2.

38. Ibid., p. 63.

39. Ibid., p. 3.

40. Ibid., p. 6.

41. Ibid., p. 57.

42. Ibid., p. 65.

43. Ibid., p. 51.

44. Ibid., p. 52.

45. Ibid., p. 65.

46. Ibid., p. 66.

47. Ibid.

48. Ibid., p. 67.

49. Ibid., p. 48.

50. E. Levinas, *The Levinas Reader,* ed. S. Hand (Oxford: Basil Blackwell, 1989), p. 82.

51. Heaney, *Cure at Troy,* p. 1.

52. Heaney, *Redress of Poetry,* p. 193.

53. J. Derrida, *Of Spirit: Heidegger and the Question,* trans. G. Bennington and R. Bowlby (Chicago: Chicago University Press, 1989), p. 132.

54. Heaney, *Preoccupations,* p. 37.

55. J. Derrida, *Points . . . Interviews, 1974-1994,* ed. E. Weber, trans. P. Kamuf and others (Stanford, CA: Stanford University Press, 1995), p. 355.

56. J. Derrida, *Deconstruction in a Nutshell: A Conversation with Jacques Derrida,* ed. with a commentary by J. D. Caputo (New York: Fordham University Press, 1997), p. 13.

57. Heaney, *Redress of Poetry,* p. xiii.

58. Heaney, *Cure at Troy,* p. 2.

59. Heaney, *Crediting Poetry,* p. 23.

60. J. Derrida, 'On Responsibility', interview with J. Dronsfield, N. Midgley and A. Wilding, *Responsibilities of Deconstruction: PLI—Warwick Journal of Philosophy,* Eds J. Dronsfield and N. Midgley (Summer 1997), pp. 19-36, p. 33.

61. Heaney, *Cure at Troy,* p. 2.

62. Ibid., p. 57.

63. Ibid., p. 67.

64. Ibid., p. 77.

65. Ibid.

66. Derrida, *Acts of Literature,* p. 5.

67. Derrida, 'On Responsibility', p. 32.

68. Heaney, *Cure at Troy,* p. 61.

69. Ibid., p. 81.

70. Heaney, *Redress of Poetry,* p. 2.

71. Ibid., p. 3.

72. Ibid.

73. Heaney, *Redress of Poetry,* p. 8.

74. Heaney, *Government of the Tongue*, p. 121.

75. Ibid., p. xviii.

76. E. O'Brien, '"Burial Refused": A Review Essay of The Burial at Thebes: Sophocles' Antigone', trans. Seamus Heaney, *Irish Book Review,* 1, 1 (Summer 2005), pp. 10-11.

77. S. Heaney, *The Burial at Thebes: Sophocles' Antigone* (London Faber, 2004), p. 8.

78. Ibid., p. 11.

79. Heaney, *The Burial at Thebes,* pp. 20-1.

80. Ibid., p. 21.

81. Ibid., p. 49.

82. Ibid., p. 44.

83. Ibid., pp. 20-1.

84. Ibid., p. 23.

85. Ibid., p. 27.

86. Ibid., p. 44.

References

Broadbridge, E., Radio Interview with Seamus Heaney, in E. Broadbridge (ed.) *Seamus Heaney Skoleradioen* (Copenhagen: Danmarks Radio, 1977), pp. 5-16.

Coughlin, P., '"Bog Queens": The Representation of Women in the Poetry of John Montague and Seamus Heaney', in M. Allen (ed.), *Seamus Heaney: New Casebook Series* (London: Macmillan, 1997), pp. 185-205.

Derrida, J., *Of Grammatology,* trans. G. Chakravorty Spivak (London: Johns Hopkins University Press, 1976).

————*Of Spirit: Heidegger and the Question,* trans. G. Bennington and R. Bowlby (Chicago: Chicago University Press, 1989).

————*Deconstruction in a Nutshell: A Conversation with Jacques Derrida,* ed. with a commentary by J. D. Caputo (New York: Fordham University Press, 1997).

————'On Responsibility', interview with J. Dronsfield, N. Midgley and A. Wilding, *Responsibilities of Deconstruction: PLI—Warwick Journal of Philosophy,* 6, eds J. Dronsfield and N. Midgley (Summer 1997), pp. 19-36.

————*Points . . . Interviews, 1974-1994,* ed. E. Weber, trans. P. Kamuf and others (Stanford, CA: Stanford University Press, 1995).

————*Acts of Literature,* ed. D. Attridge (London: Routledge, 1992).

Docherty, T., 'Ana-; or Postmodernism, Landscape, Seamus Heaney', in A. Easthope and J. O. Thompson (eds), *Contemporary Poetry Meets Modern Theory* (Hemel Hempstead: Harvester Wheatsheaf, 1991), pp. 68-80.

Donnelly, B., Interview with Seamus Heaney, in E. Broadbridge (ed.), *Seamus Heaney Skoleradioen* (Copenhagen: Danmarks Radio, 1977), pp. 59-61.

Glob, P. V., *The Bog People* (London: Faber, 1969).

Heaney, S., *The Government of the Tongue: The 1986 T. S. Eliot Memorial Lectures and Other Critical Writings* (London: Faber, 1988).

————*The Redress of Poetry: Oxford Lectures* (London: Faber, 1995).

————*Place and Displacement* (Grasmere: Trustees of Dove Cottage, 1985).

————*Crediting Poetry* (Oldcastle: Gallery Press, 1995).

————*Preoccupations: Selected Prose 1968-1978* (London: Faber, 1980).

————*Wintering Out* (London: Faber, 1972).

————*North* (London: Faber, 1975).

————*The Burial at Thebes: Sophocles' Antigone* (London: Faber, 2004),

————*The Cure at Troy* (London: Faber, 1990).

Levinas, E., *The Levinas Reader,* ed. S. Hand (Oxford: Basil Blackwell, 1989).

O'Brien, E., '"Burial Refused": A Review Essay of The Burial at Thebes: Sophocles' Antigone', trans. Seamus Heaney, *Irish Book Review,* 1, 1 (2005), pp. 10-11.

Randall, J., 'An Interview with Seamus Heaney', *Ploughshares,* 5, 3 (1979), pp. 7-22.

Charles I. Armstrong (essay date 2006)

SOURCE: Armstrong, Charles I. "Touch and Go: Seamus Heaney and the Transcendence of the Aesthetic." In *The Body and Desire in Contemporary Irish Poetry,* edited by Irene Gilsenan Nordin, pp. 213-25. Dublin: Irish Academic Press, 2006.

[*In the following essay, Armstrong discusses Heaney's departure from traditional aesthetics and the problems and possibilities this raises.*]

Not only is Seamus Heaney an unremittingly personal and sensuously immediate poet, but he is also an unabashedly imaginative one. The coexistence of these characteristics is not always pain-free or without compromises, and it is certainly not to everyone's taste—but it is does contribute to the singularity of his poetry. This combination also makes for a very complex relation to *aesthetics,* which goes to the very heart of Heaney's poetic venture. Using French post-structuralist thought as a backdrop, I would like to argue that the body of Heaney's verse has an ambivalent relation to traditional aesthetics.

Heaney's poetry frequently presents the prototypical aesthetical situation: an individual realises an experience of sensuous harmony, where the factual or contextual characteristics of the sensed object(s) are bracketed out in one manner or another. Yet Heaney often departs from the aesthetic scheme by only partially bracketing out the agency at the other end of the aesthetic equation: the sensing subject is not fully removed from the 'frame', as it were, of what is presented. The title of Heaney's most unreservedly aesthetic collection just about sums it up: in this poetry one encounters not seen things, or a pure act of seeing, but a poet *seeing things*. It is touch and go whether the inclusion of the poet represents a way of going beyond aestheticism, or whether it appropriates aesthetics as a power of the poet's own subjectivity. Heaney is a poet who revels in the feeling of 'being king of infinite space',[1] and whose critical work often affirms a strictly formalist position. At the same time, his poems set to work a sensuous manifold which tends towards overflowing the bounds of his own aesthetic, and the fact that his image of the poet is of someone who is *not untouchable* also contributes to a very complex situation. In what follows, I shall first scrutinise the role of the senses and the self in some chosen instances of his critical prose, before going on to more broadly inspect the role of bodily relations in his poetry.

FINGERPRINTS OF OTHERNESS

From the very first, Heaney has insisted that poetry is characterised by an essential relation to human individuality. Unlike for instance photography, the poem is intimately connected with the person of its begetter: verse differs from this pictorial art not only by virtue of being 'time-stretching', but also because of its fundamentally 'personal' character.[2] At the same time, the essence of a poem is not simply identical to its authorial intention. Heaney's understanding of poetry is, paradoxically, both more ideal and more material than this. The 1974 lecture 'Feeling into Words' makes this clear by denying that 'the subject-matter [of a poem] has any particular virtue in itself' when it is 'an example of what we call "finding a voice"'.[3] This latter kind of poem enacts something like a transubstantiation of the poet's personality:

> Finding a voice means that you can get your own feeling into your own words and that your words have the feel of you about them; and I believe that it may not

even be a metaphor, for a poetic voice is probably very intimately connected with the poet's natural voice, the voice that he hears as the ideal speaker of the lines he is making up.[4]

As a carrier of the poet's essence, the poem represents a secularised version of the vessels embodying divine presence in Communion. The body of the poem is identical, in an essential fashion, to the body of its originator. Like the cup with the inscription '*Remember the Giver* fading off the lip', in **'A Drink of Water'**,[5] Heaney's poem will not relinquish its initial link to its originator. This claim is, however, complicated by the peculiar conflation of the 'natural' with the 'ideal' which accompanies it. The words of the poem are linked with the poet's 'natural voice', but this voice is not identical to an everyday, speaking voice. For the poet's true voice, his 'linguistic hard-core',[6] transcends any practical exertions he might make with his tongue, lips or larynx.

Heaney uses the term 'auditory imagination', a term gleaned from T. S. Eliot, to designate the active workings of this transcendentalised acoustics.[7] In the lecture 'Learning from Eliot' of 1988, a narrative of conversion is sketched where he, at a certain point in time, suddenly attained an understanding of Eliot's transcendentalism. His ear had to be 'pulled outside in' in order to respond to elevated plane of Eliot's lines.[8] He had to become tuned in to 'their music, their nerve-end tremulousness, their treble in the helix of the ear'.[9] Despite the physicality of such references, the experience discussed supersedes any pure materialism. The body of the poetic experience is a virtualised one, one which concerns the 'inner ear' of the poet and which ultimately is of a strictly formal nature.

The natural voice of the poet comes from the outside, from what he hears as its 'ideal speaker'. At the same time, there is some doubt whether such a spectral phenomenon can be straightforwardly classified as a *voice*. This is more evident in 'Feeling into Words' than in the later Eliot lecture. Heaney implicitly points towards this in his use of the word 'feeling' in the passage cited earlier. There is a sudden and peculiar shift from 'feeling' to 'voice', which does not become any less odd when we are told that this transition involves a relation which 'may not even be a metaphor.' Could this mean that Heaney believes that the word 'feeling' *literally* refers to the auditory sense? It is perhaps more fruitful to read this as a suggestion that the poem's sense is not strictly auditory, that it is in part also tactile. Heaney's next paragraph gives some support to such a thesis: a paraphrase of a novel by Solzhenitzyn ends up with the idea 'that a voice is like a fingerprint, possessing a constant and unique signature that can, like a fingerprint, be recorded and employed for identification'.[10] Even if the voice is a unique stylistic marker, its idiosyncrasy can best be grasped through a comparison with the sense of touch. It is as if the senses naturally submit to a process of blurring and reciprocal contamination, making poetry a kind of synaesthesia.

As the senses blur together in 'Feeling into Words', it becomes evident that the sense of a poem is not of an order that easily yields to conceptual explanation. The free play of the aesthetic (a mainstay of aestheticism since Kant and Schiller) also takes place between the senses, making it impossible to univocally determine the essence of the experience of the poem. In a statement which is both the most elliptical and the most sophisticated of his criticism, Heaney stresses that the 'crucial action [of poetry] is pre-verbal, to be able to allow the first alertness or come-hither, sensed in a blurred or incomplete way, to dilate and approach as a thought or a theme or a phrase'.[11] A similar effect of blurring is evident in Frost's definition of the poem's origin, approvingly cited by Heaney, as a 'lump in the throat'. Here not only the auditory sense is involved, but apparently the tactile one too. A similar doubling is evident in his many metonymic references to the poetic *tongue*. Poetry is not only heard, seen or spoken, but also felt—even if what is felt is often only a sense of resistance or absence.

Some of Heaney's unwillingness to engage in the extensive political criticism of his poetry has its roots in this scheme. Poetry has its basis in personal sensations rather than public generality. It cannot be fully determined by theory, either. Although Heaney undoubtedly proffers his own theory in the process, he is unwilling to subordinate the individual's immediate, sensual response to any overarching system:

> in practice, you proceed by your own experience of what it is to write what you consider a successful poem. You survive in your own esteem not by the corroboration of theory but by the trust in certain moments of satisfaction which you know intuitively to be moments of extension. You are confirmed by the visitation of the last poem and threatened by the elusiveness of the next one, and the best moments are those when your mind seems to implode and words and images rush of their own accord into the vortex.[12]

Although Helen Vendler's criticism has gone on to interpret the resulting poetic *oeuvre* as exclusively consisting in solitary symbolic acts of 'the private mind',[13] Heaney's verse consistently escapes such prison-houses even while his prose tends to nudge it towards them. The poetic act is indeed practical, self-pleasuring and non-theoretical. It involves a narcissistic self-indulgence—which can be imaged as the ear of the poet hearing his or her own voice—and leaves itself open for the charge of being an instance of a conservative, aesthetic ideology.[14] Yet there is also a need for transcendence—for the 'trust' in that 'satisfaction' is

not only intensive but also involves 'moments of extension'. Without such an extension, there would be no need for Heaney's 'search for images and symbols adequate to our predicament'.[15] Yet the impetus for such a search does not come as an *addition* to the sensuous realm, but from within it. This is arguably where touch comes in: Heaney is not solely a visionary, but also a feeling poet. Although it has no overarching privilege or rule over the other senses, tactility is what provides the most palpable, manifest contact with other bodies. It is a form of space, openness and 'extension' which comes from within the aesthetic, a self-transcendence of the aesthetic as it were. Thus Jean-Luc Nancy calls touch 'the proximity of the distant', and its activity '*forms one body* with sensing, or it makes of the sensing faculties a body—it is but the *corpus* of the senses'.[16]

A NEW SENSE OF POETRY

Nancy has made the self-transcendence of the aesthetic into an imperative: 'It is a duty', he claims, 'for art to put an end to "art".'[17] Yet he is unwilling to link this duty to ethics. In this respect, Heaney is closer to the thought of Immanuel Kant. The latter has been extremely influential in articulating the argument of that art is, first and foremost, a sensuous experience, embodying a form of freedom that is irreducible to theoretical or conceptual modes of understanding. Similarly, Heaney tends to root artistic experience in non-cognitive feelings of sensuous harmony. He also shares with Kant, though, a desire to reach out to a wider compass: art may be a personal matter, but it is never a private one. Both argue that art places general claims upon us, even if it is not law-bound: whereas Kant speaks of the art work's finality without end, Heaney invokes the 'authority without dogma' of poets.[18] Furthermore, both would like to defend 'the idea that there is an essential connection between the good and the beautiful',[19] between aesthetics and ethics, yet both present this link as something tenuous and roundabout.

While Kant favours an analogous relation, where art's freedom is understood as a symbol for ethical freedom,[20] Heaney is less easy to pin down. The latter not only enacts, but also tries to reformulate the 'elusiveness' of the 'come-hither' of the aesthetic. His poetry includes a form of aesthetic thought, where new theories and images of art are playfully propounded and retracted, in a constant dialogue with ethical and political questions. This is tied to Heaney's personalist emphasis: we are given new images of the poet, new sensings of a vocation that is transformed through its continual exposure to a diversity of exemplars. In this respect, Heaney's verse responds to a post-Kantian exigency. As Nancy and Philippe Lacoue-Labarthe have shown,[21] Kantian formalism effectively leaves us bereft of any way of substantially experiencing the subject. Romanticism subsequently tries to fill the need for subjective self-reflection by the means of art. Art takes upon itself the presentation of the self in a process that is both endless and ultimately impossible.

For Heaney, poetry is a form of verification where the poet rhymes in order to sense himself. **'Digging'** is important as a first of many efforts in this vein, many of which hone in on the physicality of work in a rural context.[22] Although the pen might seem puny beside the heft of the farmer's spade, it too can attain an actively sensuous, harmonious relation to its material. Through the invocation of 'cold smell of potato mould, the squelch and slap / Of soggy peat' and the like in this poem, there is recognition that poetry must deal with the senses: that it must be alive to the materiality of the world, just as a farmer is. Yet at the same time, the poet does not dissemble his own remove from his farming forefathers. Although still insistent, his relations to nature are virtualised. For not only does a window separate him from his father in the opening vignette, but it is also intimated, towards the end of the poem, that the sensory experiences are only indirectly sensed: they 'awaken in my head'. This autobiographical remove, and its subsequent double bind where the son both confirms and surpasses his earthy ancestors, is closely linked with Heaney's aesthetic as I sketched it earlier.

Close to Heidegger's understanding of art as presenting the truth of the everyday, Heaney's poetry seeks to bring out both the lasting, vital core of the quotidian as well as to enrich his own vocation by gaining self-knowledge through the activities of others. The poem **'Cairn Maker'**, from *Wintering Out*,[23] is a characteristic celebration of the accord shared by poetry and other forms of labour. The man who 'robbed the stones' nests' (l. 1), and 'piled up small cairn after cairn' (l. 8), tells of his deeds 'with almost fear' (l. 10). Yet this is not the typically Wordsworthian fear, often evoked by Heaney, resulting from a transgression of nature. Rather, this fear seems to stem from nature's uncanny *willingness* to submit to the cairn-maker's control. Despite his 'unaccustomed hand' (l. 3), he discovers a 'strange affiliation / To what was touched and handled there' (ll. 11-12).

Underlying this poem, and similar descriptions of water-diviners, thatchers and the like, is a commemorative nostalgia for the values of a rapidly disappearing rural lifestyle. Yet these poems also explore the responsibilities and freedoms of art, through the reflecting mirror of related bodily experiences. Heaney's many explorations of the aesthetic common ground between the arts do the same thing, albeit in a more traditional vein. As words relate to touch, the second of the Glanmore sonnets tells us, the tactile implement of the sculptor communicates with its matter:

Sensings, mountings from the hiding places,
Words entering almost sense of touch
Ferreting themselves out of their dark hutch—
'These things are not secrets but mysteries,'
Oisin Kelly told me years ago
In Belfast, hankering after stone
That connived with the chisel, as if the grain
Remembered what the mallet tapped to know.[24]

Art is not merely a sensual encounter between poet and the outside world: it displays a particularly immediate kind of sensuousness. This is also the rationale for Heaney's masterful deployment of onomatopoeic effects, as bodily relations make for a more immediate transcendence of linguistic autonomy than mere representation. As for Deleuze and Guattari, an understanding of language in terms of bodies provides a means for the Irish poet of sidestepping the aporias of mimeticism: writing 'is not representing or referring but *intervening* in a way'.[25] A neglected sense of immediacy becomes approachable, at least as an ideal, through this alternative approach.

Heaney's understanding of immediacy and bodily relations is, however, far more old-fashioned than that of Deleuze, Guattari and their post-structuralist cohorts. Particularly in the teleology which supports his understanding of maturation and memory—the idea that experience represents the fulfilment of an origin—he never seriously questions the organicism which lies at the basis of traditional aesthetics.[26] Writing of Kavanagh, for instance, Heaney presents the process of poetic creativity as akin to the ripening of a fruit: 'the real value of the moment lies in its potential flowering, its blooming, in the imagination'.[27] While post-structuralist thought dismisses organicism because of its latent totalitarianism and ontological equation of the human and the natural, Heaney seems tied to it out of deference to his agricultural roots and a desire to transcend the sectarian divisions of Northern Ireland.

As a result, depictions of non-holistic or fragmentary bodies are consistently shock-laden and negative. The scars of time may be worn like medals, but otherwise the body is to be hale, whole and untainted by violence. The responsibility of the poet makes him an instrument of healing, as he follows the example of Doctor Kerlin (in **'Out of the Bag'**) who assembles in his 'soapy big hygienic hands' the vital elements of a living body.[28] Much of Heaney's verse rehearses various healing processes, either of personal bodies or of the traumatised body politic of the Irish. This does not mean that the body is a completely closed or finite affair. The immediacy of touch occasionally creates unities so intense that an enlarged and extended body is the upshot: this is for instance true of 'Jim of the Hanging Jaw' who, in **'Two Stick Drawings'**, becomes so enamoured of a stick belonging to the speaker's father that it ends up becoming the 'true extension of himself'.[29] In **'The Ash Plant'** it is the father himself who finds a 'phantom limb' in one of these sticks.[30] As Medbh McGuckian has pointed out, Heaney's penchant for depicting himself at the steering-wheel of cars has similar effects: 'his artistic/sexual drive itself may be seen in places to fuel and animate a car-body which is a physical extension of his own'.[31]

Heaney's is a mobile, transportable body, both celebrating and lamenting the spatial displacement of travel. McGuckian has noted how the 'driving metaphor, if it can be called that, allows the necessary stance of objectivity and distance to be fair, rational and yet compassionate, to be in the mess but not of it'.[32] The same can be said of the image of the worldly wise and often slightly inebriated Nobel Prize winner on tour, which is projected in recent efforts such as **'Sonnets of Hellas'** and **'The Little Canticles of Asturias'** (both from *Electric Light*). Both driving and touring facilitate an aesthetic stance: the world is made stranger and more sensuously immediate by its unfamiliarity, yet concomitantly the poet's distance enables him to lift the experience on to a more abstract, decontextualised plane.

A similar remove is evident in Heaney's recent depictions of sexuality. If the Bog Poems tapped into the *necrophilia* and *amour fou* of Surrealism and Symbolism, the ensuing controversy seems to have forced Heaney to withdraw from further exploration of such borderline terrain. Although he has gained well-deserved praise for his rare ability to portray a happy marriage with both tenderness and down-to-earth bluntness, there has been less and less of such discreet eroticism of marriage since *Field Work* provided such *tours de force* as **'The Otter'** and **'The Skunk'**. Heightened sensual receptivity and unconsummated desire only appear in the rare poems where Heaney evokes pre-marital bliss or very early relations with his wife, as a desire to always identify the speaker with the biographical self has lead to a rather limited thematic scope. Rather than being too private, Heaney's poetic persona frequently comes across as inhabiting a too public body, where relations are generally those of an artistic fraternity (as is evident in the steadily increasing number of dedications, elegies, and homages). In so far as this oeuvre enacts what Heaney, in **'The Gravel Walks'**, calls an 'absolution of the body',[33] it is an absolution that frequently comes all too easily, since there is nothing very transgressive about the bodily life of this eminently respectable public figure in the first place.

THE PREGNANCY OF NOTHINGNESS

Yet there are also ample rewards for the way in which Heaney's poems ask to be read in connection with the person of the poet. The poems are episodes in an ongoing lyrical autobiography, life studies where the speaker's personal accountability proffers itself as a guarantee of authenticity. If there are *tableaux vivants* of episodes or walks of life relatively distant from Heaney, he is quick to put himself in the picture. A nostalgic description of teenage libido, for instance, is (in **'The Guttural Muse'**) broached only after first placing the poet on the scene:

> Late summer, and at midnight
> I smelt the heat of the day:
> At my window over the hotel car park
> I breathed the muddied night airs off the lake
> And watched a young crowd leave the discotheque.[34]

Whenever Heaney makes a rare excursion into negative capability, the bracketing of his own self is clearly indicated and usually only temporary. Whether the experiences are purportedly his own or belong to others, there is always a strong propensity to dwell upon the materiality and look of things, or upon the significant gesture.

Heaney's ability to create a performative space where 'utterance and being are synonymous' is linked to this.[35] In *Wintering Out* he started to explore the possibilities of directing his reader around a sensuous, everyday space, where active verbs create movement and directive vectors while mapping a topography. The most advanced early example of this is in **'Line Town'**, which sketches an experience of the High Street of Belfast in 1786, twelve years before the hanging of Henry Joy McCracken and the rebellion of 1798. Having started with a combined reference to time and place ('twenty to four / By the public clock'), the poem returns to the hour of day in an ending that suggests both confinement and the possibility of historical change, both enlightenment and the imminence of sectarian bigotry:

> Pen and ink, water tint
>
> Fence and fetch us in
> Under bracketed tavern signs,
> The edged gloom of arcades.
>
> It's twenty to four
> On one of the last afternoon
> Of reasonable light.
>
> Smell the tidal Langan:
> Take a last turn
> In the tang of possibility.[36]

The 'tang of possibility' is opened up by the imaginative play of the senses, which frees alternative histories and parallel worlds. As so often in Heaney, being fit and ready for whatever comes involves a form of sensory responsiveness, a coming to one's senses.

This kind of aestheticism has been important for Heaney's recent poetry, as a particular relation to objects has facilitated an escape route from political stalemate. Many recent poems are poetic snapshots, as it were, where objects are renovated and relocated by the poet's roaming eye. This process is particularly explicit in **'The Settle Bed',** where Heaney's fancy is seized by an object that has a history transcending any particular faction:

> Yet I hear an old sombre tide awash in the headboard:
> Unpathetic *och ochs* and *och hohs,* the log bedtime
> Anthems of Ulster, unwilling, unbeaten,
>
> Protestant, Catholic, the Bible, the beads,
> Long talks at gables by moonlight, boots on the hearth,
> The small hours chimed sweetly away so next thing it
>   was
>
> The cock on the ridge-tiles.[37]

In this poem Heaney decidedly privileges the ear over the sense of touch, finding only infantile limitation in the imagined feeling of lying down in the settle bed. **'A Basket of Chestnuts'** extends this denigration of touch in the direction of the ideality of Neo-Platonism, as it praises the art of painting for its ability to 'see beyond' the materiality of its object and thereby attain 'what the reach / Of sense despairs of as it fails to reach it, / Especially the thwarted sense of touch'.[38] In another poem in the same collection, though, a form of transcendence is imagined to take place within the bounds of the tactile: children running on the ice go 'from grip to give' as their physical abandon gives them a 'free passage' releasing them of their self-control.[39] Similarly, **'The Pitchfork'** contrasts an 'aiming' hand with the generosity of 'the opening hand'.[40]

Such a varying appraisal of the senses underlines the fact that Heaney's poetry does not give simple answers to philosophical questions. It is rescued from dogmatism by its aestheticism, as every poem becomes a one-off response to an immediately given situation. While this makes for sensuousness and generosity, there is a price to pay that is seldom confronted by Heaney: as Adorno repeatedly pointed out, there is an unavoidable violence in the way art transcends the factual world.[41] When Heaney asks 'Who ever saw / The limit in the given anyhow?',[42] the obvious answer is: certainly not the artist, to be sure. The apology for such violence must either find some underlying affirmation that contradicts art's annihilating gesture, separating its monuments of civilisation from the barbarity that surrounds them, or alleviates it by somehow searching out a non-violent way of keeping in touch with the gifts of sense.

In Heaney's case the key volume with regard to this problem remains *Station Island,* where the poet struggles to free himself from the fetters of tradition and the expectations of his public. Thanks to a new-found independence, the poet can identify with Sweeney's cocky pronouncement: 'my emptiness reigns

at its whim'.[43] Sometimes, Heaney seems to unreservedly celebrate the resulting free play, and rather hastily claim it to the powers of the spiritual self. Thus in a recent speech, he identifies 'the boundlessness of inner as well as outer space' and ascribes it to 'the everlasting self'.[44] Yet at the same time, in a precarious balancing act, much of Heaney's poetry attempts to rein in this reign: to prevent his sense of artistic liberty from becoming a form of subjective nihilism or dilettantish Neo-Platonism.

In order to do this, the grounds and obligations of poetic 'emptiness' must be laid bare, and a more finite sense of belonging must be affirmed. In the *Station Island* volume, there are some hints that the power of that emptiness still partially rests upon an occluded connection with eroticism. In **'A Snowshoe'** the poet's experience of sonority is linked to sensuality rather than the purity of Eliot's auditory imagination: 'I sat there writing, imagining in silence / sounds like love sounds after long abstinence.'[45] More centrally to the volume as a whole, the end of the title sequence features Joyce advocating an eroticism of writing: 'Cultivate a worklust / that imagines its haven like your hands at night // dreaming the sun in the sunspot of a breast.'[46] Originally coupled with the site where a dead dog was discovered, the 'space utterly empty, / utterly a source, like the idea of sound' glimpsed earlier, in the third section of the poem,[47] is now given a positive bodily extension. Whereas the Bog Poems conflated sensuality and the corpse into one ambivalent image of the transgressive beyond of the poet's desire, here the two different avenues of desire are clearly discriminated. In both, though, artistic transcendence arguably goes beyond emptiness to attain a true sense of finitude. To keep in touch with either of these routes may entail the risk of letting sensuousness become a form of sensationalism, but their rewards—primarily in the form of a resistance to a facile aestheticism—should not be underestimated.

Notes

1. S. Heaney, *Finders Keepers: Selected Prose 1971-2001* (London: Faber, 2001), p. 48.

2. S. Heaney, *Sweeney's Flight: Based on the Revised Text of 'Sweeney Astray'* (London: Faber, 1992), p. vii.

3. S. Heaney, *Preoccupations: Selected Prose 1968-1978* (London: Faber, 1980), p. 43.

4. Ibid.

5. S. Heaney, *Field Work* (London: Faber, 1979), p. 8.

6. Heaney, *Preoccupations,* p. 45.

7. Ibid., p. 52.

8. Heaney, *Finders Keepers,* p. 29.

9. Ibid., p. 28.

10. Heaney, *Preoccupations,* p. 43.

11. Ibid., p. 49.

12. Ibid., p. 54.

13. H. Vendler, *Seamus Heaney* (London: Fontana Press, 1998), p. 12.

14. See, for instance, D. Lloyd, "Pap for the Dispossessed': Seamus Heaney and the Poetics of Identity', *Seamus Heaney,* ed. M. Allen (London: Macmillan, 1997), pp. 155-84.

15. Heaney, *Preoccupations,* p. 56.

16. J.-L. Nancy, *The Muses,* trans. P. Kamuf (Stanford, CA: Stanford University Press, 1996), p. 17. Original emphasis.

17. Ibid., p. 38.

18. Heaney, *Preoccupations,* p. 210.

19. Heaney, *Finders Keepers,* p. 69.

20. I. Kant, *Critique of Judgement,* Part I, trans. J. Creed Meredith (Oxford: Clarendon Press, 1952), paragraph 59.

21. See P. Lacoue-Labarthe and Jean-Luc Nancy, *The Literary Absolute: The Theory of Literature in German Romanticism,* trans. P. Barnard and C. Lester (New York: State University of New York Press, 1988).

22. S. Heaney, *Death of a Naturalist* (London: Faber, 1966), pp. 1-2.

23. S. Heaney, *Wintering Out* (London: Faber, 1972), p. 39.

24. Heaney, *Field Work,* p. 29.

25. G. Deleuze and F. Guattari, *A Thousand Plateaus: Capitalism and Schizophrenia,* trans. B. Massumi (London: Athlone Press, 1988), p. 86.

26. According to Andrew Bowie, 'organicism is vital to sustaining the aesthetic as a sphere whose value lies in itself': (*Aesthetics and Subjectivity from Kant to Nietzsche* (Manchester: Manchester University Press, 1990) p. 99.

27. Heaney, *Preoccupations,* p. 117.

28. S. Heaney, *Electric Light* (London: Faber, 2001), p. 8.

29. S. Heaney, *The Spirit Level* (London: Faber, 1996), p. 51.

30. S. Heaney, *Seeing Things* (London: Faber, 1991), p. 19.

31. M. McGuckian, *Horsepower pass by! A Study of the Car in the Poetry of Seamus Heaney* (Coleraine: Cranagh Press, 1999), p. 3.

32. Ibid., p. 22.

33. Heaney, *The Spirit Level,* p. 40.

34. Heaney, *Field Work,* p. 22.

35. Heaney, *Finders Keepers,* p. 235.

36. Heaney, *Wintering Out,* p. 28.

37. Heaney, *Seeing Things,* pp. 28-9.

38. Ibid., p. 24.

39. 'Squarings' xxviii, in ibid., p. 86.

40. Ibid., 19.

41. See for instance T. W. Adorno, *Ästhetische Theorie* (Frankfurt am Main: Suhrkamp, 1970), p. 80.

42. 'Wheels within Wheels', in Heaney, *Seeing Things,* p. 46.

43. 'The Cleric', in S. Heaney, *Station Island* (London: Faber, 1984), p. 108.

44. Heaney, *Finders Keepers,* p. 53.

45. Heaney, *Station Island,* p. 24.

46. 'Station Island' xii, in ibid., p. 93.

47. Ibid., p. 68.

References

Bowie, A., *Aesthetics and Subjectivity from Kant to Nietzsche* (Manchester: Manchester University Press, 1990).

Deleuze, G. and F. Guattari, *A Thousand Plateaus: Capitalism and Schizophrenia,* trans. B. Massumi (London: Athlone Press, 1988).

Heaney, S., *Death of a Naturalist* (London: Faber, 1966).

———*Wintering Out* (London: Faber, 1972).

———*Field Work* (London: Faber, 1979).

———*Preoccupations: Selected Prose 1968-1978* (London: Faber, 1980).

———*Station Island* (London: Faber, 1984).

———*Seeing Things* (London: Faber, 1991).

———*Sweeney's Flight: Based on the Revised Text of Sweeney Astray* (London: Faber, 1992).

———*The Spirit Level* (London: Faber, 1996).

———*Electric Light* (London: Faber, 2001).

————Finders Keepers: Selected Prose 1971-2001 (London: Faber, 2001).

Kant, I., Critique of Judgement, Part I, trans. J. Creed Meredith (Oxford: Clarendon Press, 1952).

Lacoue-Labarthe, P. and J.-L. Nancy, The Literary Absolute: The Theory of Literature in German Romanticism, trans. P. Barnard and C. Lester (New York: State University of New York Press, 1988).

McGuckian, M., Horsepower pass by! A Study of the Car in the Poetry of Seamus Heaney (Coleraine: Cranagh Press, 1999).

Nancy. J.-L., The Muses, trans. P. Kamuf (Stanford, CA: Stanford University Press, 1996).

Vendler, H., Seamus Heaney (London: Fontana Press, 1998).

Wes Davis (essay date 2007)

SOURCE: Davis, Wes. "From Mossbawn to Meliboeus: Seamus Heaney's Ambivalent Pastoralism." Southwest Review 92, no. 1 (2007): 100-15.

[In the following essay, Davis focuses on Heaney's use of agricultural metaphors, as well as on his translations of Virgil, in order to illuminate Heaney's relationship with—and revision of—traditional pastoral motifs.]

> The ageless relationship between poetry and farming has always been sentimental and ironic; the two disciplines would seem to have mostly accidental requirements in common: patience, fatalism, renunciation, awe of nature, reverence for the earth.

It is not Seamus Heaney but his American contemporary Fred Chappell who provides my epigraph, but the misgiving Chappell voices, in an essay entitled "The Poet and the Plowman," is one readers of Heaney's poetry are likely to find familiar. Chappell's suspicion that—however much the tradition of rural poetry might emphasize its practical roots—the poet's digging is at best an ornamental cousin of the sustaining work of the plowman echoes an anxiety audible in Heaney's work from **"Digging"** onward. The practical result of such reservations is that while Heaney has embraced traditional poetic forms ranging from Anglo-Saxon epic to the Petrarchan sonnet and heroic couplet, he has kept up a more or less constant thematic resistance to the pastoral as a genre that discloses the merely literary nature of the rural poem's relationship to agricultural life.

But if this passage from "The Poet and the Plowman" articulates the rural poet's fear that he is laboring for a tangible significance his craft can never quite achieve, it is when Chappell goes on to wonder what we might make of the fact that "our word verse came originally from versus, turning the plow at the end of the furrow," that he offers a way of understanding the détente Heaney seems to have struck with the tradition of pastoral sentimentality in the 2001 volume **Electric Light.** Chappell is noticing a serendipity in language that is, in a sense, as accidental as the conditions he says poetry shares with farming. At the same time, however, his turn from farming to language, in the etymology linking verse to versus, serves as a reminder that agrarian language is the field on which the facts of rural life and the poetry of the pastoral tradition converge with the enterprise of a contemporary poet like Heaney who maintains a deep interest in rural matters.

Like Chappell, Heaney has noticed the historical connection between the English word for a line of poetry and the Latin word for a plow's turning. The link is just under the surface of his second Glanmore sonnet. In that poem from **Field Work** (1979), Heaney describes the years he spent in the rural seclusion of County Wicklow, where he had retreated in 1972 after the outbreak of sectarian strife in the North. What Heaney imagined finding in the "hedge-school" he made for himself at Glanmore was a poetic voice that, he writes, "might continue, hold, dispel, appease," that might offer some reasonable response to the violence in the North while remaining poetic above all else. In a later poem in the series Heaney would ask "What is my apology for poetry?" But in the second sonnet no apology is necessary so long as poetry remains embedded in the rural landscape, its voice the sound of "Vowels ploughed into other, opened ground, / Each verse returning like the plough turned round."

It hardly needs stating that Heaney has drawn on the language of rural work throughout his career, finding in the vocabulary of the farm an unsentimental, if not always un-ironic way of borrowing for poetry some of the force of actual labor, or a "purchase" in the actual world, as he puts it in **"The Loose Box,"** the poem that serves as a kind of program piece in **Electric Light.** Such a purchase depends, however, on the poet's maintaining a sense of the actual in his use of rural language. Pastoral poetry relies, in contrast, on the literary resonance of its language, a quality that both derives from and emphasizes its distance from the actual world. In **Electric Light** Heaney seems determined to reconcile the two modes.

"The Loose Box," for example, takes a retrospective glance at the vocabulary of previous Heaney poems, even as the poet begins to loosen his linguistic hold on the actual world by conceding that the source of his poetic language is not to be found in the landscape it describes, or even simply in a poem about that landscape, but in a recording of a poem:

On an old recording Patrick Kavanagh states
That there's health and worth in any talk about
The properties of land. Sandy, glarry,
Mossy, heavy, cold, the actual soil
Almost doesn't matter; the main thing is
An inner restitution, a purchase come by
By pacing it in words that make you feel
You've found your feet in what "surefooted" means
And in the ground of your own understanding—
Like Heracles stepping in and standing under
Atlas's sky-lintel, as earthed and heady
As I am when I talk about the loose box.

The loose box Heaney refers to is a hayrack or hay box in a barn, an object and setting that could comfortably have appeared in any poem in his first book, *Death of a Naturalist.* But **"The Loose Box"** marks the consummation of a thematic evolution by which Heaney, whose early poetry sometimes struggled in its effort to arrogate for verse an importance as real as that of work like agriculture, has managed to find significance precisely in releasing his poetic hold on the actual.

While there are certainly precedents in Heaney's career for this kind of departure from the solidity of Irish soil and Irish life, his earlier glances away from Ireland have traveled across a more literal distance, while focusing on the gritty, particular details that remind him of home. In *North,* for example, the 1975 volume in which he looked to the bogs of Denmark in order to get a firmer grip on the political drama unfolding on his own immediate landscape, Heaney never let his attention stray from the kind of northern terrain that stands for home, wherever it actually lies. The explicit image he drew of himself in that volume was as a kind of poet-Antaeus, a figure whose strength would drain away if he lost contact with his native soil. The image, because it was a classical figure for rootedness with an established history of use in Irish poetry, was doubly appropriate as a link between the broader world Heaney was beginning to explore and the immediate local setting in which those explorations would need to have their significance. Antaeus is the same figure Yeats pressed into service when, in "The Municipal Gallery Revisited," he wanted to emphasize the local authenticity of the work he did in building an Irish national theater with John Synge and Lady Gregory. "All that we did, all that we said or sang," Yeats wrote, "Must come from contact with the soil, from that / Contact everything Antaeus-like grew strong." Throughout his career Heaney has emphasized this metaphoric contact with the ground of local reality. In *Electric Light,* however, he appears comfortable with the idea that a poem may be both grounded *and* heady, in touch as much with native soul as native soil.

The two poles of Heaney's move from simply grounded to "earthed and heady" are evident in **"The Loose Box,"** where the confident, grounded parochialism epitomized by Patrick Kavanagh gives way to the "inner restitution" of language itself. Kavanagh's presence in Heaney's idea of his own poetry is not new, but there is something surprising in the swing he makes in this poem from Kavanagh's talk of soil to the sense that "the actual soil almost doesn't matter." Heaney's willingness here to let go of the actuality of the thing and to relish the words themselves is indicative of the way his later work has carried out a subtle adjustment in his orientation toward literary tradition and literary language.

In *Electric Light,* this revision shows up as a changing of the guard in Heaney's troop of poetic mentors. While it is an old Kavanagh recording that launches the meditation on the sound of soil in **"The Loose Box,"** the real presiding spirit in the volume is not Kavanagh but Virgil. And while Kavanagh and Virgil are both poets who can provide Heaney with links between poetry and the "inner restitution" of agricultural language, they find their way to that language through very different routes: one local and particular, from Heaney's perspective, the other literary and formal.

It was Kavanagh's local, parochial agrarianism that governed Heaney's early poetry, and you would expect, given the evidence of that poetry's obsession with the textures of agricultural work, that when Heaney came to translate from Virgil's rural corpus it would be the more practical agricultural instructions of the *Georgics* that would attract his attention. Instead, what Heaney translates in *Electric Light* is a series of stylized passages from the *Eclogues,* and it is worth looking back to the double-mindedness of Heaney's early encounter with the pastoral tradition to sort out the roots of this unexpected turn, his new *versus,* on the rural poetic tradition.

Heaney articulates this dual vision of the modern pastoral most clearly in his writing on Robert Frost. He finds, for example, an emblem for the competing interests of his own rural sensibility in the interplay of fact and dream in Frost's "Mowing": "The fact is the sweetest dream that labor knows." What Heaney likes about the line is the way it links the documentary function of poetry—the fact—with its imaginative expansion—the dream.

His early interest in Frost was focused on the fact rather than the dream. "In the beginning," Heaney recalls in an essay in *Homage to Robert Frost* called "Above the Brim,"

> I did love coming upon the inner evidence of Frost's credentials as a farmer poet. I admired, for example, the way he could describe (in "The Code") how forkfulls of hay were built upon a wagonload for easy unloading later, when they would have to be tossed down from underfoot. And sometimes the evidence

was more general but still completely credible, such as that fiercely direct account of a child's hand being cut off by a circular saw and the child's sudden simple death. Coming as I did from a world of farmyard stories about men crushed in quarry machinery or pulled into the drums of threshing mills, I recognized the note of grim accuracy in a poem called "'Out, Out—.'" I was immediately susceptible to its documentary weight and did not mistake the wintry report of what happened at the end for the poet's own callousness.

Heaney's view of Frost's poetry is certainly sensitive to what Frost wrote, but this description may say more about Heaney's own poetic needs than it says about Frost.

Heaney's vision of Frost, that is, focuses first on the way Frost relates the two central elements of Heaney's own sense of poetic responsibility: the real work of rural life and the real facts of atrocity. It's true that in Frost's poetry the victims of atrocity are political victims only insofar as the social circumstances that surround the workers in his poems require them to run certain risks in laboring a living from the earth. But early poems in Heaney's corpus—take, as an example, **"The Early Purges,"** which begins with the shock of watching unwanted animals exterminated and ends with the conclusion that "pests have to be kept down"— show that for the later poet language makes all too passable a bridge between the violence of the well-run farm and that of a poorly run state. What is most significant in Heaney's attention to Frost, however, is that it is *not* Frost's documentary impulse, but his lyrical transfiguring of fact that holds Heaney's interest beyond the initial attraction. Having gestured toward the authenticity of Frost's rural images, Heaney ultimately draws attention to what he calls "the counterweight, the oversound, the sweetest dream within the fact—these things are poetically more rewarding than a record, however faithful, of the data."

It was the data, the record of local experience, that Frost's early readers focused on. "It is a sinister thing that so American, I might even say so parochial, a talent as Robert Frost should have to be exported before it can find due encouragement and recognition," Ezra Pound wrote in his 1914 review of *North of Boston.* But Pound lacked Heaney's sympathy for the parochial, and his interest in Frost was developed on formal, dictional grounds, and in spite of the local focus of his subject matter:

> A book about a dull, stupid, hemmed-in sort of life, by a person who has lived it, will never be as interesting as the work of some author who has comprehended many men's manners and seen many grades and conditions of existence. But Mr. Frost's people are distinctly real. Their speech is real. . . . I don't want much to meet them, but I know that they exist, and what is more, that they exist as he has portrayed them.

Pound's review, which appeared in *Poetry* magazine, called Frost's new poems "Modern Georgics," and the virtues he found in them were those he had been propounding in a series of essays on what he called the "prose virtues" in poetry—clarity, precision. What was significant to Pound was the escape Frost made from traditionally poetic language, an escape, it should be said, that succeeds in *North of Boston* where it had often failed in Frost's previous collection, *A Boy's Will.* But Pound's review misses Heaney's sweet dream when it rather begrudgingly praises the poet's documentary eye for labor, or for the *fact* alone: Frost's people are real people, Pound says. "He is quite consciously and definitely putting New England rural life into verse. He is not using themes anybody could have cribbed out of Ovid." Or, for that matter, out of Virgil.

As Heaney's interest in Frost developed it came to focus on the way Frost's poems form a connection between the facts of a life of rural labor and the dream that a poet like Virgil cultivates above and around those facts. In Frost's *New Hampshire,* the second volume to appear after *North of Boston,* this connection is mapped in a poem called "To Earthward" that moves from life lived in a rarified poetic air "That crossed me," Frost says, "from sweet things," to a craving for the rough excoriation of lived experience. The poem ends like this:

> When stiff and sore and scarred
> I take away my hand
> From leaning on it hard
> In grass and sand,
>
> The hurt is not enough:
> I long for weight and strength
> To feel the earth as rough
> To all my length.

Heaney quotes these stanzas in "Above the Brim," and then goes on to describe the poem's effects in a way that reflects his own poetic evolution from **"Digging"** to the translations of Virgil in **Electric Light**; "we are offered an image of the body hugging the earth," Heaney writes, "seeking to penetrate to the very *humus* in humility, wishing the ground were a penitential bed. But the paradoxical result of this drive toward abasement is a marvel of levitation: in spite of the physical push to earthward, the psychic direction is skyward."

Notice that as Heaney is working here to call our attention to the skyward movement in Frost's earthy ruralism, his own employment of etymology turns in the other direction, paralleling Chappell's move from *verse* to *versus.* Finding the *humus* in humility, Heaney again discovers the fact of agrarian life in the dream of language. Through the first half of his career, Heaney's poems followed a similar course, exalting themselves in that "physical push to earthward."

He recalls the emergence of this tendency in the middle section of **"The Loose Box,"** in which he describes growing "stabler," more himself, when as a child he read Thomas Hardy. What Heaney was moved by in Hardy was the documentary eye of his prose. It wasn't Hardy's poetry, but "the threshing scene in *Tess of the D'Urbervilles*," Heaney writes, "That magnified my soul." Like Frost in Heaney's first encounter with him, Hardy impressed Heaney with the realistic brutality in his descriptions of rural work. Hardy's images of "Raving machinery, / The thresher bucking sky, rut-shuddery" were particularly striking for a reader who, like Heaney, knew that "the big sag and slew of the canvas belt / . . . would cut your head off if you didn't watch." *Tess* struck Heaney because Hardy had put his rural credentials on display and Heaney recognized the book's grim accuracy.

In the same way, Heaney's critical prose has tended to approve those poets whose own direction is earthward, and Heaney has on occasion excluded Virgil from this company. In a review of *The Penguin Book of English Pastoral Verse* that appeared in 1975 and has been reprinted in *Preoccupations*, Heaney registered his disappointment at two omissions brought about by the philosophy that shaped the collection. One is that the English focus of the book put Irish writing outside its field of reference, so that Kavanagh's *The Great Hunger*, which Heaney here labels "anti-pastoral," is not included to supplement the sense created by the editors that pastoral poetry had simply lost its validity and force sometime in the nineteenth century.

Heaney also regretted that the editors chose not to include English translations from the classical pastoral poets, and he went on to imagine a modern version of pastoral that might translate that aristocratic classical tradition into what he calls "a more equable and bourgeois mode, where the Virgilian shepherd disappears to have his place taken by the Horatian farmer."

This, again, might be a good description of Heaney's own poetry, and his vision of a kind of practical proletarian pastoral makes the reappearance of the Virgilian shepherd in **Electric Light** a key event for understanding Heaney's late poetics. The poem that opens the volume, **"At Toomebridge,"** dramatizes the course that brings Heaney to Virgil, a movement from the gritty actuality of his early work to a later concession that the seen world is not the limit of the actual. Heaney first locates himself in the Irish landscape by reference to the landmarks of history—"Where the checkpoint used to be. / Where the rebel boy was hanged in '98."—but that revolutionary locale becomes the setting of his own poetic evolution:

> Where negative ions in the open air
> Are poetry to me. As once before
> The slime and silver of the fattened eel.

The implication here is that Heaney's sense of what makes the poetry of place has broadened from his early focus on the concrete reality of its landscape to include something that might be called the feeling of the place, the sensations of place that exist in but also around and beyond its thingly details. **"Perch,"** the poem that follows this one, performs the same kind of expansion. Its title and opening lines resonate with the grainy language of Heaney's early work: "Perch we called 'grunts,' little flood-slubs, runty and ready, / I saw and I see in the river's glorified body." But where once the river would be glorified only by its present, local reality, now the glory comes in the way that actuality channels an ephemeral flood, a kind of universal Heraclitan flux: "In the finland of perch, the fenland of alder, on air // That is water, on carpets of Bann stream, on hold / In the everything flows and steady go of the world."

It turns out to be that "everything flows and steady go" of the Bann stream that hollows out the geographical space for Heaney's meditation on Virgil's fourth *Eclogue*, which comes into the volume as **"Bann Valley Eclogue,"** accompanied by an epigraph—*Sicelides Musae, paulo maiora canamus* (. . . let us sing of somewhat greater matters)—that preserves the invocation of the original. Heaney's version of the *Eclogue* starts with a kind of double translation of that invocation, moving the poem into a new language, but also moving its action onto a new landscape, a move marked in Heaney's rendering of Virgil's *Sicelides musae* (literally, muses of Sicily, because Virgil's own poetic predecessor, Theocritus, came from Syracuse on the southeastern coast of Sicily) as "Bann Valley muses."

While Virgil's fourth *Eclogue* carries out its mediation on a new, revitalized age in direct address, without the give and take of dialogue that is the trademark of the eclogue form, Heaney's response to the poem picks up Virgil's oracular vision and teases out its implications for poetry in a dialogue between characters he calls "Poet" and "Virgil" that begins with the Poet's invocation of these local muses. As in the fourth *Eclogue* itself, Heaney's invocation here hopes for a song worth singing, one that in this case might please Virgil as Virgil had hoped to please those who demanded from poetry a loftier work than mere description of what Virgil (in translation) calls the "orchards or lowly tamarisk." Both poems are in a sense occasional pieces, written to herald a coming birth. But while Virgil is able to compose a poem that links the birth of the child he is celebrating to the advent of a new golden age, Heaney gets stuck in the gap he perceives between the reality of a child's birth and the difficult work of imagining that child's life unfolding in a better world.

In the course of this dialogue Heaney's Virgil takes on a double role as visionary poetic predecessor and Irish hedge-schoolmaster, setting the Poet's task of translation from his own corpus: "Here are my words you'll have to find a place for: / *Carmen, ordo, nascitur, saeculum, gens.*" The song of poetry itself, the order ushered in by the sacred birth, the new age, the nation: the poet needs to find a place for these words in the poem itself, suggesting that the work of poetry, then, is to imagine a world in which these Virgilian values might again find a central, organizing role, or be put, as Heaney would say, to present use. But the implications of this language start to overwhelm the poem. *"Pacatum orbem,"* the Poet quotes, "your words are too much nearly." The Poet is thinking of a line in Virgil's *Eclogue* that imagines a world to which the old Roman virtues have brought peace: "pacatumque reget patriis virtutibus orbem" ("And he shall rule a world made peaceful by his father's virtues," as it's translated in the Loeb edition). The idea of a peaceful planet is perhaps itself too much for a Northern Irish poet to encompass, but the Poet's "too much" is more generally a problem of language and the bad fit between poetic language and the real material of life. "Even 'orb' by itself," Heaney asks. "What on earth could match it?"

It is not that Virgil wrote in a less turbulent time—his fourth *Eclogue* reflects the period of the civil wars—but rather that for him lyric form provided a less permeable stay against political anxieties than it does for Heaney, who has the slipperiness of a modern idea of language to contend with. Nonetheless, Heaney's imagined Virgil, like the ghostly Joyce who advises the poet in **"Station Island,"** comes through with effective advice that picks up the tendency toward self-reflection already built into the pastoral mode and uses it to throw Heaney back on the resources of his own experience and vernacular. Don't worry about the millennial work of the poem, Virgil implies, focus on the richness of present reality:

> Eclipses won't be for this child. The cool she'll know
> Will be the pram hood over her vestal head.
> Big dog daisies will get fanked up in the spokes.
> She'll like on summer evenings listening to
> A chug and slug going on in the milking parlor.

Fanked, chug, slug. What is happening here is that Heaney's imagined Virgil is adopting Heaney's own customary vernacular. It's as if being given permission to turn from the millennial vision toward the mundane stuff of lived experience—a license, also, to drop from the register of *pacatum orbem* to the old familiar particularity of words like *fanked* and *chug* and *slug*— frees the Poet to drift into the atmospherics of his own experience where memory doesn't take along to make an appropriately Irish symbol from the local landscape: "the shamrock / With its twining, binding, creepery, tough, thin roots / All over the place, in the stones between the sleepers. / Dew-scales shook off the leaves. Tear-ducts asperging."

All a poem can do, Heaney implies, looking eathward at that shamrock, is to recall the *tears* of things, but that memorial function becomes what Heaney elsewhere calls a "responsible *tristia*" that now launches the poem skyward at its close. In an apostrophe to the unborn child, the baby's pregnant mother is described as walking "among big round bales" of an actual landscape suddenly in accord with her own state, "showing signs" that are at once signs of the colloquial "showing" of pregnancy and *words* as signs that nothing on earth can match. The stuff of practical reality is here—"Your pram waits in the corner"—and grounded in that reality the poem finally can imagine the "orb" that was previously unthinkable, but is now suddenly visible in the material facts of the child's life: "Planet earth like a teething ring suspended / Hangs by its world-chain."

Virgil's fourth *Eclogue,* a poem in which the advent of a golden age is signaled by the hearty ploughman freeing his oxen from the yoke ("robustus quoque iam tauris iuga solvet arator"), is unavoidably pressured in the process of translation by Heaney, who in the early poem **"Follower"** had wanted nothing more than to "grow up and plough." But Heaney's wrestling with the poem works to transport the Virgilian pastoral idiom into a sphere of reality Heaney's own poetry imagines as the authentically rural, at the same time that it revitalizes Heaney's rural imagination by attaching his own persuasive but remote rural vocabulary to things as ordinary as prams and teething rings.

The dialogue **"Bann Valley Eclogue"** initiates with Virgil is then carried on through two further poems in *Electric Light.* One is a fairly literal translation of *Eclogue* IX, the other a freer response to Virgil's pastoral poetics. The latter of those two poems, **"Glanmore Eclogue"** gives a contemporary inflection to the disenfranchisement that permeates Virgil's ninth *Eclogue* while rehearsing the situation and phrasing of *Eclogue* I, but like Virgil's riffs on Theocritus, Heaney's poem is not an exact refiguring of any particular Virgilian poem. In a dialogue between the Poet and Myles (the latter's name resonates with both the stock soldier of Roman literature, *miles,* and a stock figure of the Irish stage, "Myles-na-Coppaleen," the roguish hero of Dion Boucicault's play "The Colleen Bawn," a character who also inspired the pseudonym Flann O'Brien used for his most satirical writing on Irish life and culture), Heaney starts from an odd self-reflexive moment lifted from the opening of Virgil's first *Eclogue,* which meditates on the situation of a now-successful poet:

> A house and ground. And your own bay tree as well
> And time to yourself. You've landed on your feet.
> If you can't write now, when will you ever write?

In Heaney's version, the Poet attributes his change of status to a muse he calls Augusta, "Because we arrived in August." Readers of W. B. Yeats may associate the name with that of Yeats's Anglo-Irish patron Augusta Gregory, and Myles certainly takes the name to be something other than native Irish. He responds with a comment that registers this poem's version of the various displacements Virgil himself depicts in *Eclogue* IX: "Outsiders own / the country nowadays, but even so / I don't begrudge you."

Myles may not begrudge the poet the foreign source of his inspiration and comfort, but he does make his own political sympathies clear in his nostalgia for an era of reform. "Those were the days—/" he recalls, "Land Commissions making tenants owners, / Empire taking note at last too late . . ." The situation as Myles describes it is one that links the turmoil of Virgil's period to the dispossession of Irish Catholics, and at the same time makes the link between poetry and farming that Chappell's essay is uneasy about. "First it was Meliboeus's people / Went to the wall" Myles says, invoking the poet who appears in several of Virgil's *Eclogues,* "now it will be us. / Small farmers here are priced out of the market." Myles is suggesting that poets and farmers, whatever their differences, are nonetheless similarly imperiled, though the Poet in his present condition of ease appears to have lost touch with that reality.

The Poet's initial reaction to the statement of crisis is a lapse into nostalgia for his own poverty-ridden days, but Myles is not buying that line. Instead he calls attention to the poet's distance from the economic hardships of farm life: "Book-learning is the thing. You're a lucky man. / No stock to feed, no milking times, no tillage . . ." Here is the key moment in *Electric Light.* That the poet has no tillage is, of course, just the problem with which Heaney's career began. (Again remember the early poem **"Follower"** in which the young poet yearns to "grow up and plough," or the lament in **"Digging"** that the young poet, thinking of the work of his farmer father and grandfather, has "no spade to follow men like them.") Myles's attention to the deficiency of labor in the poet's life leads to a call for some kind of balancing poetic effort, which he imagines, as Chappell did in "The Poet and the Plowman," taking place on the field of language:

> Our old language that Meliboeus learnt
> Has lovely songs. What about putting words
> On one of them, words that the rest of us
> Can understand, and singing it here and now?

Meliboeus's songs are, of course, poems; they are words already, and what Myles is asking for is a kind of poetic language that responds to what he calls the "here and now." The song the Poet sings in response is set in the bog that housed so many of Heaney's early poems, but in this version the gritty reality of the landscape has been stylized out of existence. The poem ends in a flight of lyrical excess:

> Bogbanks shine like ravens' wings.
> The cuckoo keeps on calling *Welcome.*
> The speckled fish jumps; and the strong
> Warrior is up and running.
>
> A little nippy chirpy fellow
> Hits the highest note there is;
> The lark sings out his clear tidings.
> Summer, shimmer, perfect days.

On the one hand Heaney is giving us a model of a poet who has reneged on his responsibility to the here and now, and what his Poet offers is almost a parody of the pastoral tradition. The bogbank, though Irish in origin, is now shining. The landscape has lost the mucky suck and slip it would customarily have in a Heaney poem. The birds—ravens and cuckoos and larks—are the birds of poetry, and the speckled fish is a cartoon alongside the slubs and grunts of **"Perch."** Even the warrior, a stylized vision of the soldierly Myles himself, has become a kind of cut-out figure whose vague outlines blur into the "little chirpy fellow" of the last stanza.

Heaney's own corrections to this kind of pastoral misstep are woven throughout the volume in lines that elevate the immediate landscape over the literary one. The displacement of asphodel in **"Bodies and Souls,"** for example, makes the shift from Arcadia to Ulster explicit: "It wasn't asphodel but mown grass / We practiced on." On the one hand, lines like these register a retreat from the pastoral, but at the same time they bring pastoral imagery, the asphodel, into the rural poem while pruning it to the poet's purposes. Heaney's dialogue with Virgil, that is, has found both the uses and abuses to which the pastoral tradition is subject, and even the failings of the tradition are here put to use in a way that dramatizes the risks of abjuring a poem's responsibility to present reality.

At the same time it is difficult not to feel Heaney's delight in the concluding lines of the **"Glanmore Eclogue."** Playing up the sweet dream that lives alongside the fact, he is clearly taking pleasure in orchestrating the stylized literary images of the pastoral mode itself. Having opened the ground in his own poetry for what he called "a more equable and bourgeois mode, where the Virgilian shepherd disappears to have his place taken by the Horatian farmer," Heaney has gained the kind of purchase on the actual that allows him to bring the formerly exiled Virgilian shepherd back into the poem and let him sing. His revision of the pastoral tradition in *Electric Light* opens up a new pastoral dialogue that resounds with the various interests that have invigorated his rural poetry from the start. It is a dialogue in which Kavanagh and Virgil, the Frost of the fact and the Frost of the sweet dream, the Virgilian shepherd and the Horatian farmer all make themselves heard in a voice that is distinctly Heaney's own, creating a new pastoral colloquy in which the turning of the plow leads credibly to verse and the humus is rich with humility.

With the appearance of *District and Circle* this year it is possible to see more clearly what Heaney accomplished in *Electric Light.* The new collection's confident forays into subjects as unexpected but seemingly inevitable for Heaney as his catabasis into the newly imperiled London Underground and the Tollund man's afterlife escape from the confines of his native bog represent in many respects the fruition of the less obviously successful grafting of styles in the earlier volume. As if to emphasize that lineage, Heaney takes the epigraph for the new book—*"Call her Augusta / Because we arrived in August . . ."*—from his own **"Glanmore Eclogue."**

District and Circle certainly doesn't read, poem by poem, like a sequel to *Electric Light.* Heaney might, for example, have written a work like **"The Turnip Snedder,"** the book's characteristic keynote poem, at any point in his career. Modeling its imagined God's-eye view of existence on the life-cycle of the turnip, that poem finds images for the thick reality of work and war without ever averting its gaze from "the raw sliced mess" dropping "bucketful by glistering bucketful" beneath the farm implement that evokes the poet's ruminations. It is a poem that realizes the promises—the artistic one and the literal one—of **"Digging."** But without the backdrop of Heaney's negotiations with Virgil in *Electric Light* it is hard to imagine that poem and the equally characteristic underground journey of **"District and Circle"** taking their places alongside **"Anything Can Happen,"** in which Heaney, adapting one of Horace's *Odes* as a response to the 9/11 bombings, brings the Horation farmer onstage and lets him sing, much as he had let his imagined pastoral poet sing at the close of the **"Glanmore Eclogue."** The resulting poem does in reality what Heaney had pulled off only as a kind of poetic joke in the earlier poem. Horace's eerily appropriate ode—"Anything can happen, the tallest towers // Be overturned, those in high places daunted, / Those overlooked regarded"—is framed by Heaney in a way that makes the ode less a kind of Nostradamian premonition than a proof that even the most lyrical poetry has already taken stock, as Blackmur might say, of every available reality.

In a speech given in Santa Fe between the publication of the two books, Heaney said of **"Anything Can Happen"** (then a work in progress called "Horace and Thunder") that the "smoke furl and boiling ashes" that give the poem its final image "have been familiar in Northern Ireland for—well they had been—for thirty years, thirty-five years." History, it might be said, has confirmed over the course of those years, which cover

the bulk of Heaney's working life, that his focus on local reality has a broader value. At the same time the expansion of sectarian unrest into a global problem has necessitated a wider scope of attention from all of us. In a world in which anything can happen, the Troubles are no longer a specifically Irish issue, and the local landscape is more than ever the terrain on which history collides with the lived experience of the lyrical self. In this "age of anxiety" as he called it in a recent interview, Heaney's conversations with the Virgilian shepherd and the Horatian farmer emphasize the utility of a poetry that can recognize outside itself versions of its own inwardness, its lyricism as well as its perplexity in the face of catastrophe.

Calvin Bedient (essay date spring 2007)

SOURCE: Bedient, Calvin. Review of Heaney's *District and Circle* and Tomlinson's *Cracks in the Universe. Chicago Review* 53, no. 1 (spring 2007): 160-65.

[*In the following essay, Bedient reviews Heaney's* District and Circle *alongside* Cracks in the Universe *by Charles Tomlinson.*]

"The poet's only hope," Ted Hughes said, "is to be infinitely sensitive to what his gift is, and this in itself seems to be another gift that few poets possess." Seamus Heaney is truest to his gift when he is praising, and his new collection, *District and Circle,* is largely about what can be fondly remembered. Well, so be it, seeing that it's Seamus Heaney doing the remembering. Heaney plops back into childhood with instinctive accuracy, like a frog into a stream, and breathes happily in the sensuous mud. The book might have been called *There Was a Child Went Forth*; it takes back Heaney's childhood and youth from marauding time. The same spirit is in him now as then, the desire to be thigh-wader-deep in the "give and take" of life's "deepest, draggiest purchase."

Heaney can reverse time as few other writers have done because he has a genius for inhabiting his own life—he makes you glad that a life *can* be so lived, so loved, so known, so rich in observation and feeling—and because his other genius, his ear, jumps in the dark of sound and lands, you'd swear it, precisely on that unforeseeable mark where experience is—was—is again. In this book he once again compacts accents and compounds ("clamp-on meat-mincer") with coughing assonance, consonance, and alliteration ("troughs of slops, / hotter than body heat"). His ear is so earthy it allows no empty gaps. Adroitly he varies the "snub and clot" of monosyllables with "the splitter-splatter" of slightly bigger words, all of them harking faithfully to the circle of life in rural Co. Derry. Oh, to be a word in one of Heaney's lines, loved and sharp as the taste of a raw turnip, know-ing its exact worth. Such wholesome virtuosity. Take as an example the following section of **"Moyulla"**:

> Milk-fevered river,
> Froth at the mouth
> of the discharge pipe,
> gidsome flotsam . . .
>
> Barefooted on the bank,
> glad-eyed, ankle-grassed,
> I saw it all
> and loved it at the time—
>
> blettings, beestings,
> creamery spillage
> on her cleanly, comely
> sally trees and alders.

The "gidsome" river is virtually a wet nurse. To the boy, her frothy milk and mouth are not lost objects, in the Lacanian sense, so long as, "ankle-grassed" (lovely invention), the boy can view her with a giddiness of his own.

Together with Robert Graves and Ted Hughes, Heaney broke the crust of the centuries' old snow that had been covering the Green Goddess. In *District and Circle,* there's little left of his self-quickening quickening of the myth. But **"Moyulla"** is happily complemented by the stunning short poem **"A Hagging Match,"** which presents the goddess in her most formidable guise, namely, as hag. Domestic, this particular hag (while still and always an archetype) chops wood outside the house, and the thumps rock the speaker's psyche "like wave-hits through / a night ferry." Simply by virtue of being a woman, his wife incorporates every aspect of the goddess, including her power to drown the frail, floating, ferried male psyche. Ah, but there's nothing, no one, else for the speaker to cling to: "you / whom I cleave to, hew to, / splitting firewood." The speaker takes up the words "cleave" and "hew" on the clinging-child side, leaving the violent side to the axe-wielding hag. He can afford to: after all she's splitting firewood; she's taking care of the two of them.

The new collection is otherwise an assortment of poems in which boys and men dominate. Poems on childhood anxieties (e.g., getting your hair clipped in "Harry Boyle's one-room, one-chimney house," "the plain mysteriousness / Of your sheeted self inside the neck-tied cope— / Half sleeveless surplice, half hoodless Ku Klux cape") are answered by poems on adult male ac-complishments, for instance **"To Mick Joyce in Heaven"**:

> The weight of the trowel,
> That's what surprised me.
> You'd lift its lozenge-shaped
> Blade in the air

> To sever a brick
> In a flash, and then twirl it
> Fondly and lightly.

Joining these last are several elegies on male poets, dead, but still mighty—indeed, all but alive. In **"Stern,"** the powerful short elegy on Ted Hughes, for instance, Heaney cleaves to a stern master of the end-stop, an altogether different prepotency from the chop-chop rhythm of the warming and destroying goddess.

>   Now it seems
> I'm standing on a pierhead watching him
> All the while watching me as he rows out
> And a wooden end-stopped stern
> Labours and shimmers and dips,
> Making no real headway.

Even the Tolland Man, the exhumed Danish bog body celebrated in Heaney's third book, *Wintering Out* (1972), as a sad figure of sacrifice to the goddess, returns here as a strengthener, sacrifice-free. He has spring's spunk (the poem is called **"The Tolland Man in Springtime"**); his re-emergence from the bog is a resurrection. In the earlier poem the speaker thinks that, were he to visit "the old man-killing parishes" of Jut-land, he'd feel "lost, / Unhappy and at home." But in the new poem (an over-extended, six-sonnet sequence), he identifies with the liberated body: "I . . . felt benefit / And spirited myself into the street."

In sum, then, a book seeking and finding reassurance in male strength—as typified by the father who praises the "forged fang" of the harrow-pin, "a true dead ringer // Out of a harder time." In it, Father Craftsman replaces Mother Bounty. The Creator Goddess gives way to Man the Maker. With the exceptions noted, Heaney has covered over again the deep-psyche universality of the goddess myth in favor of on-the-surface poems with a local pop-up vigor and isolation, celebrating the competent, social, stoical male spirit.

The title *District and Circle* is thus accurate as to the book's loving provinciality. For Heaney all but writes as a vocational shut-in: the satisfaction he takes in promoting the image of the talented, disciplined male, the type of himself as poet, is patent—though Heaney wouldn't be Heaney without his exquisite tact. The great Circle of the goddess isn't answered, in this book, by the great, broken Circle of Humanity. As it might have been? Despite the root-seeking nature of Heaney's "gift"? Heaney's earlier, Northern Ireland-based involvement in questions of adversity and atrocity (which sent him in quest of the goddess), at least provoked the gift into tension and anguish, and forced it to be resourceful. Heaney has no doubt written the book he needed to; but though the writing in *District and Circle* has real distinction, the book itself lacks importance. To put it another way: the world has changed, but Heaney's art has not, except to ask somewhat less of itself than before, in all but the golden craft.

The English poet Charles Tomlinson writes with much the same sense of implicit rebuke to our everyday heartlessness toward the earth, but he shifts the theme into present-tense gear. He is more discursive and a good deal less in the language—lacking, as he does, as everyone does, Heaney's creamery and grain-golden ear.

Like Heaney's, Tomlinson's work isn't what it used to be. It never had any fury, but its meditations on spatial happenings were more arresting than they are now; they had written all over them the necessity of discovery. Tomlinson pored over nature's processes as if searching for the microbes of meaning. And his descriptions were often lovely—for example, the rose in "Frondes Agrestes," in *Seeing is Believing,* seen

> Gathered up into its own translucence
> Where there is no shade save colour

or, in "Prometheus," in *The Way of a World,* the trees that

> Continue raining though the rain has ceased
> In a cooled world of incessant codas

At his best he wrote with a breath-held intensity. Now, he seems to practice a somewhat easy observation for its own sake, trusting it to be virtue's path.

Cracks in the Universe could not be a less apt title for this new collection: its violent ontology is betrayed by the shock-proof sphere in which Tomlinson moves, where placid poems track nature's gradual changes. The phrase comes from "A View from the Shore," which trumps up a "crisis in the environment" out of the "aquatic ivy" that has suddenly "festooned" Brooklyn Bridge. My guess is ice, or frost, or snow—any of which would qualify "aquatic ivy" as old-fashioned poetic diction. In any case, the crisis is already pouring "itself back / through this crack in the universe," a crack located, by way of a sudden, asymmetrical wrench, "on this outflanked riverbank." Which all seems to mean: no crisis, really. Like Heaney's, Tomlinson's imaginative sphere is short on catastrophes. When he does go after one, as here, he can only do so deliberately, and even then only figuratively.

As "A View from the Shore" illustrates, Tomlinson no longer *thinks* well in his poems; his verse has softened into gesture and sentiment. Keenly sensible it's not. For instance, in "New Jersey—New York," he writes of

> a million cars, each one
> A travelling eye

> Letting things occur, letting them appear
> As they will, the city itself another nature

There are so many things wrong with this statement—the exaggeration of "a million cars" pouring into one darkened "thoroughfare," the poet-mirroring personification of each car as "A traveling eye," the fantasy that cars have a choice as to letting things "appear / As they will," the potentially disastrous mistake of seeing the city itself as "another nature"—so many things that it gives Tomlinson's brand of aesthetic impressionism a bad name. It's writing as a dreamy maundering. In "In the Mirror" Tomlinson congratulates himself on not being a Narcissus—he knows the mirror's "margins are where true happenings are." But effectively he writes in a folded-in triptych of mirrors. He describes objects as if they were virtuous, harmless, sentient, observant—in other words, as if they were so many Tomlinsons.

Consider the "rose, reader / of the book / of light" in "A Rose from Fronteira": after the exotic title, Tomlinson domesticates the rose to a fault, until there isn't anything "rose is a rose is a rose" about it:

> Head of a rose:
> above the vase
> a gaze widening—
> hardly a face, and yet
> the warmth has brought it forth
> out of itself,
> with all its folds, flakes, layers
> gathered towards the world
> beyond the window,
> as bright as features,
> as directed as a look

Here, personification injects its ichor into a natural object. "Head" destines the rose to have a face, even if "hardly a face," thence a "gaze." Features, as a generic item, are levered up as "bright," but to no good end, since "layers" can't really be seen as features or "gathered towards the world." In all, the labyrinthine rose is more or less flattened out so as to have an intelligent face, in mutuality with the observer. Hasn't humanity had a sickening amount of itself by now? Why is the rose enlisted in its ranks?

At the pen-tip of a Rilke, personification trembles and sings; of a Tomlinson, it cozies up to the universe. Nature, for Tomlinson, is an excellently-designed system of reciprocities. On the one hand, the earth exists to be seen by us; our eyes are its providence. On the other, its purpose is to excite our reflective activity and trigger comparisons, not least to ourselves. In the opening poem, the poet uncharacteristically finds pathos in our being earthbound, saying of pigeons that burst "into dowdy flower" (a tellingly de-energizing metaphor) that they become "in feathery mid-air . . . all that we shall never be, condemned to sit," etc. But he's actually the least Faustian of poets; his is a physics of the near. He specializes in small jobs of observation governed by the law of classical Greek aesthetics: the actual is what one sees. (Fernando Pessoa in *The Book of Disquiet*: "The sufficiency of things fills my weightless, translucent heart, and just to look is a sweet satisfaction. I've never been more than a bodiless gaze.")

In Tomlinson's dialectic, "letting things occur" stands over against the corresponding occurrence in himself, qua poet, of a "second creation, / as intricately unforeseen / as the first" ("Fantasia in Limestone"). Seeing and making—it's Heaney's dialectic, too, but in Heaney's work it benefits from greater passion. Tomlinson, however, is quicker than Heaney to introduce layers of sentiment, and he is even more impelled to dedicate his art to peace. (To which one may object, *pace* Heaney's superb earlier poem, **"The Harvest Bow,"** that peace is the end of vegetables, not of art.) Tomlinson doesn't write of pain with real power: "a lament of all you lose / in life's constrictions / like a wounded violin" doesn't touch it. He can't help it. He was born to be a beautiful soul. "My weightless, translucent heart," etc.

The theme that "nothing is king / in this weather-swept world" prompts his style to meet its subject on equal terms. Thus it can't enjoy salience, has no beehives in its yard, doesn't cascade toward the stupid far end of the world. The language is innocent of Anglo-Saxon grunts, tangy sensations, defamiliarization. To say that "the year is repeating itself afresh," a not untypical statement, fails to make the year *feel* fresh; it's all excess of polite communication. And the rhythms (sometimes metrical, sometimes free) never pass with a tingle into the body.

District and Circle and *Cracks in the Universe,* especially when placed together, suggest that nature poetry and her sister, the poetry of reminiscence, can't be contemporary. They want to rest their chin on a country wall and gaze; they want everything to be agreeable. In the words of Gertrude Stein's Saint Chavez, "The envelopes are all on the fruit of the fruit trees." Meanwhile, all around, catastrophe is picking up speed.

Michael Parker (essay date summer 2007)

SOURCE: Parker, Michael. "From *Winter Seeds* to *Wintering Out*: The Evolution of Heaney's Third Collection." *New Hibernia Review* 11, no. 2 (summer 2007): 130-41.

[*In the following essay, Parker traces the changes made by Heaney to the manuscript for* Winter Seeds, *which was published in 1972 as* Wintering Out. *Parker*

concentrates on how the changes represent Heaney's attempts to deal poetically with the "Troubles" then occurring in Northern Ireland.]

Winter Seeds is the title that Seamus Heaney originally gave to his third collection, which comprises poems written between 1969 and late September, 1971, and which was published as **Wintering Out** (1972) In September, 1971, Heaney had returned to Belfast from a year's sabbatical leave at the University of California, Berkeley. On October 14, 1971, he dispatched a typescript to Faber with the title **Wintering Out.**[1] As he endeavored to get to grips with the rapidly deteriorating situation on the ground in Northern Ireland, over the following six months he modified the collection he had submitted in October. A letter dated April 14, 1972, from Faber and Faber states, "I am pleased to return to you the Mss now incorporating the additional poems. We shall work this at 80 pages instead of 72."[2] On May 15, 1972, Heaney sent on to Faber two copies of his proofs as well as the typescript of **Wintering Out.**[3]

Heaney borrowed the typescript's original title—*Winter Seeds*—from his poem **"The Tollund Man."** A decade later, in the course of introducing a reading of **"The Tollund Man,"** Heaney states that he intended the poem to voice a hope that the "destructive old passions" manifest in Northern Ireland in 1970 "might in some way be . . . transmuted into some kind of benign future."[4] His choice of title suggests a belief that a time of renewal—whether national, political, or cultural—might be at hand.[5] For Heaney at this time, as for his contemporaries Ted Hughes, John Montague, and the American poets whose work he had absorbed in Berkeley (Gary Snyder, Robert Bly, and Robert Duncan), the idea of myth held major attractions. Myth ratified both poet and poems by seeming to embody "timeless" values; it gave access to "universal" narratives, which could then be employed to interrogate—or, more commonly, to castigate—the present. Most importantly, as Clair Wills has suggested, myth opened a door into "the primitive" regions of the human psyche, thereby enabling poets and their readers to re-establish contact with some deeper originary human "essence."[6]

Yet, myth is only one of the routes that Heaney was exploring at this point, as both *Winter Seeds* and the final version of **Wintering Out** testify. The poet is clearly casting around, like his fellow Northern Irish poets, in search of appropriate strategies for addressing the political crisis. Like John Hewitt, Roy McFadden, Michael Longley, Derek Mahon, and John Montague, Heaney turned both to family biography and to other cultures and other histories in a search for analogues to confront what he and the other poets believed were the historical, cultural, and linguistic origins of the province's divisions and sectarian hostilities. A few poets, most notably Padraic Fiacc, attempted to address directly in their work such events in the street as the Falls curfew and the bombing of the Springfield Barracks.[7] Between August, 1969, and December, 1971, Heaney only intermittently opted for the more immediate road taken by Fiacc.

Only one part of a four-part sequence called **"Offerings"**—which appeared in *The Honest Ulsterman* in November, 1969—made its way into *Winter Seeds* and *Wintering Out.* **"Offerings"** contains a dedication to the dead nine-year-old Patrick Rooney, one of the earliest casualties in the violence of the "Troubles" in August, 1969. In the fourth poem in the sequence, **"September Song,"** Heaney alludes to Rooney's "half-filled jotter . . . hidden in the store-room" and how a "thick line" through the school register "blanks his name."[8] Heaney replicates its subject's erasure, a decision that flaws the elegy more than clumsy rhetoric and rhythm. By stressing the way "normal" life in Belfast proceeds despite the killing (*"Tele early! Curse the pope and fire away!"*), he diverts emotion from the victim, giving no insight into who Patrick Rooney was. The poet's touch seems far surer in the sequence's second poem, **"High Street, 1786"** (placed fifth in *Winter Seeds*). As Heaney himself later observed, his poetic energies[9] seemed to be more galvanized by the narratives locked in an eighteenth-century "civic print"[10] or an archaeologist's photograph than by the all-too-immediate brutalities of the present.

Heaney published three more poems set in present-day Belfast in May, 1970, and January, 1971, **"Tinder," "Intimidation,"** and "Nocturne" (poems 10, 11, 7 in *Winter Seeds*).[11] The first of these begins innocently enough with boys collecting pieces of flint. Within the space of a few lines, however, the shards become transformed into "Cold beads of history and home," a painful, disabling rosary; in trying to raise a spark, the boys inflict wounds upon themselves. As the poem shifts into the present, the narrator reads the legacy of fifty years of "shrunken hope" on the burnt-out streets, and imagines a new Ice Age in which survivors "squat"[12] like animals, "red-eyed" from insomnia, grief, guilt, and blood-lust. **"Intimidation"** depicts a Catholic householder sitting "long after bedtime / with the lights out" after loyalists set a bonfire beside his home. Moonlight figures twice in this and its companion piece—though what it illuminates is ash, soot, and "tidal blood,"—the issue of sectarian hatred.

Subsequently retitled **"Roots"** and revised for *Wintering Out,* "Nocturne" is a composition of missed harmonies and rhymes ("struck" / "rock," "dawn" / "down," "loam" / "scream"), in which another wakeful figure attunes himself to the dissonance that intrudes on his privacy nightly. Though drawn to the delicate, intimate, and aesthetic, as in the erotic landscape evoked in lines five through nine—"Leaf membranes lid the

window"—the narrator soon admits disquieting images into the frame. His beloved's body, responsive only moments ago to "the touch of love," eerily transmutes into "drifted barrow, sunk glacial rock." Prepared to acknowledge the prevalence of violence—he refers to "*each* slated terrace"—he seeks to minimize its proximity—"Gunshot and siren *dwindle* towards us"—and, indeed, misrepresents violence by comparing it to a theatrical device: "*Like* well-timed *noises off.*" Further jarring relocations in place and time follow, as a Montague-like "fault"[13] opens "at last" in "our old Gomorrah,"[14] before the poem reaches its bewildering close, which sees the narrator marinating a mandrake in tidal blood.[15] with its flailing analogies and its ill-matched juxtapositions, "Nocturne" well illustrates the disorientating effects of political collapse on the poetic imagination.

Interestingly, several of the poems that Heaney originally chose to start *Winter Seeds* were never published. In **"Museum Pieces,"** inspired by a visit to Madrid's Prado, we find the germ of **"Summer 1969,"** published three years later in *North.* The images Heaney presents in the first section of **"Museum Pieces"**—grafting, cyclone, history charging like a bull, gored linings, a veronica—do not cohere and, again, indicate a fracturing and fragmentation in the poet's consciousness and the culture. Like the head of the Tollund Man, the works of art that Heaney describes are strange, estranging, and yet oddly familiar. The powerful physicality of the painter's technique is conveyed, however. Stanza two's opening—"The fluid wrist is struck / is earthed, conducts"—echoes the description of **"The Diviner"** in *Death of A Naturalist* (1965) and its mythic idea of the artist as a conductor of a natural, earthly, primal energy.[16] Something of that energy dissipates when the anonymous first-person narrator appears finally and switches our attention from Goya to a hellish "sulphurous Van Gogh." The concluding section begins with a grammatical and artistic imperative. Heaney once again depicts art as agency, capable of achieving magical, healing effects. He sets up an opposition between the medicinal "phial" and the phallically aggressive "bayonets" and martial "phalanxes." An interesting correction to the final couplet in the *Winter Seeds* typescript comes in its change of verb, in which the somewhat despairing gesture "*smash* your phial / on the phalanxes" is abandoned, in favor of a more resolute abstract verb, "oppose."[17]

"Hawthorns," the third poem in *Winter Seeds,* takes us away from the artistic and European focus in the preceding poems and back to the house and parish in which Heaney grew up. Unlike the later **"Fodder,"** the home it imagines initially is neither mythologized nor associated with security and fecundity. It is, rather, a beleaguered, tense place, though one in which the children enjoy a solidarity within the collective "we." They are instructed by their father to count their blessings ("Think of the gypsies") and get to sleep, despite the fact that rats are scuttling across the ceiling boards above their heads. The stanza with which part one ends is beautifully executed, combining images that evoke extinct heat ("sputter," "smutch," "ashes") with images of illumination and energy which have passed into the poem itself. "The thousand drops, travelling / along the thorns" return in the later poem **"The Railway Children,"** where the "each one seeded full with the light" travels along the telegraph wires rather than the thorns, and suggest the links between the children's world and a wider world.[18]

The second section of **"Hawthorns,"** which it is clear Heaney intended to cut, centers on gypsies and the disappearing culture they embodied.[19] Their world is bleak and impoverished, not idealized; there is no question of young Heaney and his siblings running off to live with them. They are an absence, signified by the old clouts and rags, and "an old boot cupping rain." Remembering these "frayed," fragmentary relics, the poet reflects on his own relationship with his own originary spaces: "How can I unburden / My love of that small tundra, / Thistle spiking the heath." As in *North*'s **"Strange Fruit,"** the narrator resists his own impulses toward reverence and aestheticization. How, he asks himself, can I "Call the water in the boot / A holy well," or the rags "insignia of our pieties"? The backward look offers Heaney little consolation in this wintry period of his life.

That there is no way back to the Kavanaghan pieties of the parish can be seen in the third section of **"Hawthorns."** There, his focus switches to politics and the unheroic present. Heaney's narrator conceives of civil war in almost filmic terms. He imagines a young man "tensed in a drenching hedge / watching drops web the tiny crook / between thorn and twig." Unable to confront directly the actual carnage that the current civil war leaves, he imagines the would-be assassin picking and palping a haw, which in turn leaves a bloody trail of pustules "between small farm / and small farm." This rural scene is obviously a far cry from the fighting going on in working-class Belfast and Derry.

And it was that actuality which Heaney encountered on his return to Belfast, not long after the imposition of internment in August, 1971, and which compelled him to reassess the content and the shape of this new collection. Peppering Heaney's **"Christmas, 1971"** are allusions to searches, vigilantes, reprisals, the lights at Long Kesh. He speaks wearily of the "continuous adjudication" to be made, "swung at one moment by the long tail of race and resentment, at another by the more acceptable feelings of pity and terror."[20] It quickly became apparent that internment had failed to curb the Provi-

sional IRA: August, 1971, witnessed 131 bombings; September, 196; and October, 117.

Sectarian violence reached a new ferocity during the final months of 1971, the period after Heaney first submitted *Wintering Out* to Faber. On September 29, a massive bomb went off in the packed bar of the Four Step Inn on the Shankill Road, reducing the building to dust and rubble. Two men died in the explosion and twenty-seven were injured: "Belfast had never witnessed anything like it before."[21] Although no organization claimed responsibility, most commentators believe it to have been the work of the Provisionals, who had recently extended their campaign to include nonmilitary and noneconomic targets. The attack exacerbated outrage, embitterment, and frustration within working-class Protestant communities and contributed to the growing polarization in Northern Irish society.

A little more than a month later, on November 2, an explosion in another Belfast pub cost the lives of three Protestants and left more than thirty injured, including thirteen women. Its customers were given a ten-second warning to clear the bar, but before many could do so, the bomb went off, demolishing the building. In a devastating act of reprisal, on Saturday, December 4, loyalist paramilitaries struck back. That evening a fifty-pound bomb was deposited in the doorway of Patrick McGurk's Bar in Belfast's city center, killing fifteen Catholics including the owner's wife and fourteen-year-old daughter. Security sources, including Stormont's minister for home affairs, John Taylor, immediately attributed the bombing to the Provisionals. This claim—disputed at the time by the Catholic community—fueled nationalist alienation from the authorities, who had argued that no loyalist paramilitaries were dangerous enough to be interned.[22]

This, then, formed the conclusion to the bad year in which Heaney found himself "wintering out."[23] The early weeks of the new year 1972 witnessed intense activity. The poems produced in mid-January, 1972, find Heaney homing in on the role of language as a signifier of Irish cultural identity, moving into the kind of terrain marked out by Montague in "A Primal Gaeltacht."[24] In contrast to the accumulation of individual poems in *Winter Seeds, Wintering Out* is a highly structured collection, whose energy initially derives from language lyrics, all of which come out of a compact, sustained period of composition. Heaney held back one of the collection's breakthrough poems, **"Tollund Man,"** until the midway point. By creating a Part Two to *Wintering Out,* Heaney is able to cluster together a collection of lyrics that at first seem to have a primarily private, domestic focus, but which resonate beyond those spheres. The gendered oppositions in **"Summer Home"** are surely on some level political. Summers have regularly "gone sour" in Ulster. And the use of the word "home" in the title might well encourage the reader to draw parallels between guilts and recriminations, hauntings and catharses, in domestic and public spheres.

The maneuver with which Heaney opens **"Fodder"**—"Or, as we said, / *fother*" (*WO* [*Wintering Out*] 13)—is designed, like Doalty's gesture in *Translations,* "to indicate . . . a presence."[25] There is an obvious political dimension to such an intervention at this juncture in Northern Ireland's history. The poem is not merely, as Neil Corcoran suggests, a means of reminding his readers of the existence of "a lexicon and register of pronunciation distinct from 'received' or Standard English."[26] An assertion of autonomy, particularity, familial, local, cultural, and perhaps ethnic difference, **"Fodder"** counters the inclusivist, regionalist emphasis of Hewitt's poem "Gloss: On the Difficulties of Translation," and shifts ground from the linguistic pluralism of the opening of **"Broagh"** (*WO* 27).[27] After employing standard English in the title, the poem's speaker immediately disclaims it and its authority, tendering an alternative voiced in a "grafted tongue."[28] The word's reclamation releases a spill of images, and generates a tumble of enjambed line and alliterated sounds ("swathes of grass / and meadowsweet"), as the narrator revels in a past characterized by solidarity ("the tight vise," "bundle") and miraculous natural and spiritual riches ("multiple as loaves / and fishes"). The final stanza acknowledges that "mucky gaps" exist within this idealized narrative. The unspecific threat posed by "These long nights" to "comfort," "bed," and "stall," is reinforced by the rhythm, as those three stressed syllables press against the last line's iambic dimeter. The intensity of desperation in Ulster at the beginning of 1972 can be sensed in the "anything" which hangs over the final line.

Contemporaneous with **"Fodder"** are the topographical poems of *Wintering Out,* in which Heaney revives and re-energizes the *dinnseanchas* tradition.[29] Each an assertion of cultural difference, most of these poems bear equally traces of anxiety. For the narrator of **"Anahorish,"** however, as for Friel's cartographers, the act of naming gives a satisfying illusion of power and control. Enunciating the name seems to resolve oppositions—light/dark, fluid/solid, vowel/consonant, Gaelic/English—and closes the gap separating the speaker from an earlier, imagined Ireland as past and putative Eden, "a place of clear water" and unobstructed movement. The poet performs again the role of diviner, summoning not only "the subconscious and semantic energies of words," but also cultural energies, and perhaps political expectations of the minority.[30] In endeavoring to resist the poem's celebratory rush and cast **"Anahorish"** as an elegy, Henry Hart misreads it; the "dunghills" of the final line do not "suggest decay,"[31] but rather, as O'Donoghue recognizes, link back to "the fertilising

water"[32] of the opening, and anticipate replenishment, not "the eclipse of a once vibrant life."[33] The ice to be broken is, significantly, "light."

"Broagh" constitutes a further example of Heaney's binding of the lyric with the political, language with landscape. Neil Corcoran's conclusion that the poem constructs "a linguistic paradigm of a reconciliation beyond sectarian division" is undoubtedly sound, verified by the opening lines which bring together three linguistic strands in Northern Ireland.[34] The contiguity of the Gaelic for a riverbank (*bruach*), the Scots for a riverside field (*rigs*), and the Anglo-Saxon plural for the dock-plant (*docken*) points to the poet's desire to ford internal differences, and "to create an inextricable whole."[35] At the same time, however, the poem recognizes in its images of bruising and marking, the "black O" and "low tattoo"[36] sounds and signs of a pain that may not so easily be eased politically or textually. At its close, blame for the "gathering" tensions seems to be attributed to "the strangers," which might be seen as an attempt on the narrator's part to absolve both communities in the North for failing to manage a political accommodation during the previous half-century. While one may applaud—as Tom Paulin does—Heaney's aspiration to find a "language in which everybody from the North of Ireland could feel at home," at the same time one recognizes how **"Broagh"** demonstrates the difficulties of translation, of outgrowing the Irish-British binary, particularly at a juncture when so many encounters in the present appeared to confirm its "authority" and "reality."[37]

The final poem Heaney added in *Wintering Out* was **"The Backward Look."** This poem similarly and simultaneously admits and resists narratives of linguistic and political defeats, as one might expect from its ambivalent title. The phrase and the poem can be read as affirming the importance of the Gaelic past and the Gaelic language in sustaining a sense of "Irish" identity. Heaney's title also admits a contrary reading, however, in which the idea that Gaelic tradition can be revived is judged to be a delusion, and the project judged as regressive, atavistic, and backward. From the outset, irregular stresses make the poem labor to get off the ground, to find a rhythm. Out of this aural and grammatical unease, bird images emerge, allegorized images that are both originary and the products of translation.[38]

Heaney's use of the simple present and present continuous positions the reader as a witness to "an eviction of sorts,"[39] to use Friel's term from *Translations*—a displacement which is literal and psychic, linguistic and demographic. Snipe, wild geese, and yellow bittern, like the signs denoting them—and like those who had transmuted them into signs—are forced to leave their "nesting ground" to make themselves scarce in "vaults" and archives. Each of these named birds has a resonance within Irish cultural tradition, and, thus, the poet's choice of referents again both includes and excludes. Only someone familiar with Gaelic would be aware that the poem's italicized phrases, "little goat of the evening" and "little goat of the frost" are renderings into English of Irish kennings, *gabhairín oidhche* and *gabhairín reo,* denoting the "snipe." Encoded within the references to "wild goose" and "yellow bittern" in stanza five are allusions to the Wild Geese, those Jacobites who left Ireland for exile in France following William III's triumph, and to a Gaelic lament by Cathal Buí Mac Giolla Ghunna (c. 1680-1756). Writing in 1970, John Montague claimed that, for Heaney, "The Yellow Bittern / *An Bonnán Buí*" constituted "his touchstone for the [Gaelic] tradition."[40]

Puzzlingly, Henry Hart mistakenly identifies the snipe as "British." Its function within the allegory is, in fact, to represent the dispossessed "Irish" in general. Perhaps it also alludes to those presently suffering political oppression but capable of retributive violence, the Northern nationalist minority. The deliberately ambiguous imagery Heaney utilizes points toward such a reading; such phrases as "drumming elegies" may suggest a mingling of music and militarism, poetry and defiance, celebration and loss; the "vaults / that we live off" might well be vinous, and, thus, may imply both distilled wisdom or an alcohol-induced obliviousness[41]—but equally could be discerning a necrophiliac element within nationalist and Catholic tradition, and thus reading its pieties toward the dead and martyred as distinctly unhealthy.

The poem's close rehearses a survival in the face of contemporary threat ("the sniper's eyrie"), and a successful transgression of ancient borders ("earth-works / and wall-steads"), before a dramatic touchdown "in the combs of a fieldworker's archive." Although in one respect the "combs" may be connected to other underground recesses—the "sunken drills" of **"Gifts of Rain,"** the souterrain of **"Toome,"** "the hollow trunk" in **"Oracle"**—as an image suggestive of fertile industry, the combs also anticipate the "honeyed" water of **"Mossbawn: Sunlight."** Heaney's presentation of himself as a fieldworker—a Wordsworthian celebrant of rural living, as an academic undertaking practical research, and thus a cultivator of the cultural ground— looks forward to later phases in his literary and artistic career, including ***Field Work*** and Field Day.

Notes

1. The original typescript is noted as "accepted" on October 14, 1971, in the Book of Register at Faber. A later production file refers to an expanded ts. The Faber Archive, Book of Register 55 and Production File 667. Faber and Faber, 3 Queen Square, London. Although I have chosen to present the title *Winter Seeds* in italics throughout this article, no book was ever published under this name.

2. Faber and Faber to David Wood, Latimer Trent Ltd, 13 April 1972.

3. See also Michael Parker, *Seamus Heaney: The Making of the Poet* (Iowa City: University of Iowa Press, 1993), pp. 93-94.

4. Seamus Heaney, *Heaney/Paulin,* Faber Poetry Cassette, 1982, ISBN 0571130917.

5. Seamus Heaney, interview with author, 15 January 2004, Dublin.

6. Clair Wills, *Improprieties: Politics and Sexuality in Northern Irish Poetry* (London: Clarendon, 1993), p. 28.

7. Padraic Fiacc, "Kids at War," *Ruined Pages* (Belfast: Blackstaff, 1997), p. 121.

8. Seamus Heaney, *Honest Ulsterman,* 19 (November, 1969), 6.

9. Seamus Heaney, interviewed by Brian Donnelly, in *Seamus Heaney,* ed. Edward Broadbridge (Copenhagen: Danmarks Radio, 1977), p. 60.

10. "Linen Town," *Wintering Out* (London: Faber, 1972), p. 38; hereafter cited parenthetically, thus: (*WO* 38).

11. "Tinder," *New Statesman,* 15 May 1970, p. 704; "Intimidation," "Nocturne," *The Malahat Review* (January, 1971), 34-35.

12. Compare Derek Mahon's "Entropy," *Lives* (Oxford: Oxford University Press, 1972), p. 31: "We have pared life to the bone / And squat now / In the firelight reading / Gibbon and old comics."

13. "The Fault," the fifth section of *The Rough Field,* first appeared in *Honest Ulsterman* 23 (May-June, 1970), 3-7.

14. According to Genesis 19: 24, the city of Gomorrah was destroyed by "brimstone and fire . . . out of heaven," rather than as a result of an earthquake.

15. See, of course, W. B. Yeats, "The Second Coming," *Collected Poems* (London: Macmillan, 1967), p. 211.

16. Seamus Heaney, *Death of a Naturalist* (London: Faber, 1965), p. 36.

17. These textual alterations appear in the *Winter Seeds* typescript, which remains with Heaney's papers in his Dublin home.

18. Seamus, Heaney, *Station Island* (London; Faber, 1984) p. 45.

19. Heaney struck a line through the second part of "Hawthorns" in the typescript.

20. *The Listener,* December, 1971, rptd. in *Preoccupations* (London: Faber, 1980), pp. 30-33.

21. Peter Taylor, *Loyalists* (London: Bloomsbury, 1999), p. 87.

22. It was not until 1978 that a member of the UVF finally confessed to involvement in the crime. Taylor, *Loyalists,* p. 89.

23. The new title of October 14, 1971, is drawn from "Servant Boy," which constructs lines linking the contemporary Catholic population in the North with their subjugated, alienated predecessors. It harks back to the eighteenth century, to a time when, according to Froude, nine-tenths of the land was occupied by Protestants of English or Scottish extraction.

24. John Montague, "A Primal Gaeltacht," *Irish Times,* 30 July 1970, rptd. in *The Figure in the Cave,* ed. Antoinette Quinn (Dublin: Lilliput, 1989), pp. 42-45.

25. Brian Friel, *Translations,* in *Selected Plays,* ed. Seamus Deane (London: Faber, 1984), p. 391.

26. Neil Corcoran, *English Poetry Since 1940* (London: Longman, 1993), p. 196.

27. For an invaluable and illuminating discussion of the complex linguistic issues addressed in "Fodder" and "Broagh," see Bernard O'Donoghue, *Seamus Heaney and The Language of Poetry* (Brighton: Harvester Wheatsheaf, 1994), pp. 62-65.

28. John Montague, "A Severed Head," *The Rough Field* (Dublin: Dolmen 1972), p. 31.

29. According to Heaney's notebook, the sequence of composition of these early language-poems was "Anahorish," 11 January, "Broagh," 12 January; "Fodder," 15 January, 1972.

30. "The Trade of an Irish Poet," *Guardian,* 25 May 1972, 17.

31. Henry Hart, *Seamus Heaney: Poet of Contrary Progressions* (Syracuse: Syracuse University Press, 1992), p. 62.

32. O'Donoghue, p. 58.

33. Hart, p. 62.

34. Corcoran, p. 90.

35. O'Donoghue, p. 65. With characteristic tact, O'Donoghue avoids spelling out the political implications of Heaney's linguistic maneuvers.

36. See also the "small drumming" picked up in "Land" (*WO* 22).

37. Tom Paulin, in a television documentary, *Poetry, Language and History,* Open University, 1986.

38. These bird images undoubtedly derive from Heaney's contemporaneous work on *Sweeney Astray* (1983), which Heaney had begun translating at this juncture.

39. Friel, *Translations,* p. 420.

40. Montague, p. 45.

41. Taken with the allusion to "An Bunnán Buí," in which the narrator identifies himself with the "yellow bittern" who died of thirst, the "corkscrew" metaphor translates the vaults into wine-cellars.

Elizabeth Lunday (essay date spring 2008)

SOURCE: Lunday, Elizabeth. "Violence and Silence in Seamus Heaney's 'Mycenae Lookout.'" *New Hibernia Review* 12, no. 1 (spring 2008): 111-27.

[*In the following essay, Lunday gives a detailed reading of "Mycenae Lookout"—written shortly after the beginning of the 1994 ceasefire in Northern Ireland—focusing on the themes of silence in the face of atrocities, the resultant guilt, and the possibility of poetry to "open up a space" for healing.*]

Seamus Heaney declares, in **"Mycenae Lookout,"** that there is "No such thing / as innocent / bystanding."[1] The poem appears at the center of *The Spirit Level* (1996) and comprises a sequence of five poems. It is a work that interrogates both how the violence of society affects the individual, and how violence compels connivance in a conspiracy of silence. Heaney suggests that only by returning to a personal mythology can one be purged of one's crimes and yet acknowledges purgation is not enough. To move forward, one must also declare the truth of the sins of the individual and the society.

Heaney wrote **"Mycenae Lookout"** in direct reaction to the politics of Northern Ireland—in particular, the IRA ceasefire that began on August 31, 1994; he began the poem the following October.[2] The ceasefire, he wrote, "was a genuine visitation, the lark sang and the light ascended." Heaney says, in describing that time, that

Everything got a little better and yet instead of being able to bask in the turn of events, I found myself getting angrier and angrier at the waste of lives and friendships and possibilities in the years that had preceded it.[3]

The ceasefire changed the political landscape of Northern Ireland and resulted in profound changes in day-to-day life. The level of violence dropped dramatically: in 1993, 84 persons died of sectarian violence; 476 shootings occurred, and 289 bombs were planted. In contrast, in 1995, nine died, 50 shootings occurred, and only two bombs were planted.[4] The IRA ended the ceasefire in February, 1996, with the bombing at Canary Wharf in London that killed two; however, the 1994 ceasefire did point the way to the 1998 Good Friday Agreement.[5]

Sensing that he was freed from the constraints of what he commonly calls "the tribe," Heaney describes himself in **"Tollund"** (written in September, 1994) as "alive and sinning, / Ourselves again, free-willed again, not bad."[6] Heaney had proven remarkably circumspect when writing about the political realities of his homeland, refusing to write anything that could be considered inflammatory or even remotely propagandistic—a decision castigated by such critics as Ciaran Carson and David Lloyd. Neil Corcoran describes Heaney as a poet who has "been drawn to commentary on, and has withdrawn from propagandistic involvement in, a lengthy, ongoing, local internecine war."[7] However, in *The Spirit Level,* Heaney felt not just the freedom to express himself, but also a compulsion to make himself heard. Such poems such as **"Weighing In"** and **"The Flight Path"** speak out about the need to speak out. **"The Flight Path"** includes a confrontation between Heaney and a nationalist acquaintance:

> 'When, for fuck's sake, are you going to write
> Something for us?' 'If I do write something,
> Whatever it is, I'll be writing for myself.'

(*SL* [*The Spirit Level*] 29)

In **"Mycenae Lookout,"** Heaney also chooses to write for himself, with a meditation that weighs in on Ireland and its violence.

Heaney is not a political poet except in the ancient Greek meaning of "politics"—one who is "interested in the polis," as Heaney says of Yeats. Heaney notes, "Yeats isn't a factional political poet, even if he does represent a definite sector of Irish society and culture. . . . But the whole effort of the imagining is toward inclusiveness. Prefiguring a future."[8] Heaney disclaims any political message in the **"Mycenae Lookout"**:

> I suppose what I want to emphasize is that there was no real communiqué factor at work in the poems, there was the excitement of utterance, the writing was after and into something other than commentary. It was a surge-up through language. I was buoyed by the doing rather than relaying any message.[9]

Sarah Broom records that at a reading of the poem in 1998, Heaney stated the poem reflected "his sudden recognition, after the 1994 ceasefire, of the degree to which the prolonged state of political tension had taken its toll on each individual."[10] In *The Redress of Poetry* (1995), Heaney describes himself as searching for "an adequate response to the conditions in the world at a moment when the world [is] in crisis."[11] **"Mycenae Lookout"** addresses a world polluted by violence at the moment after the violence stops.

After the IRA ceasefire, Heaney found himself drawn to *The Oresteia,* fascinated by the parallels of Mycenae at the end of the Trojan War and Ireland at the end—he hoped—of the "Troubles." He originally considered retelling the entire trilogy: "The three Aeschylus plays could be a kind of rite envisaging the possibility of a shift from a culture of revenge to a belief in a future based upon something more disinterested."[12] However, even as he read the plays, he began to "lose heart in the whole project. It began to seem too trite." But the character of the Watchman haunted Heaney:

> The Watchman . . . began to keep coming back to me with his in-between situation and his responsibilities and inner conflicts, his silence and his knowledge, and all this kept building until I very deliberately began a monologue for him using a rhymed couplet like a pneumatic drill, just trying to bite and shudder in toward whatever was there.[13]

In *Agamemnon,* the Watchman is easy to ignore. He appears in the first scene, gives his forty or so lines and then disappears. Heaney, who has never studied Greek, read *The Oresteia* in several different translations while working on **"Mycenae Lookout"**; none of these translations give the Watchman a distinctive voice.[14] In the Richmond Lattimore translation, for instance, the Watchman speaks in clear, elegant hexameters:

>   The rest
> I leave to silence: for an ox stands huge upon
> my tongue. The house itself, could it take voice, might speak
>   aloud and plain. I speak to those who understand,
> but if they fail, I have forgotten everything.[15]

Louis MacNeice's Watchman reveals the proverbial origins of "The ox is on my tongue," Heaney's epigraph for **"Mycenae Lookout"**:

> As to the rest, I am silent. A great ox, as they say, stands on my tongue. The house itself, if it took voice, could tell the case most clearly. But I will only speak to those who know. For the others I remember nothing.[16]

In the Loeb Classical Library translation by Herbert Weir Smyth, the Watchman seems almost Shakespearean:

> For the rest I'm dumb; a great ox stands on upon my tongue—yet the house itself, could it but speak, might tell a tale full plain; since, for my part, of mine own choice I have words for such as know, and to those who know not I've lost my memory.[17]

Robert Lowell's dramatic translation has the Watchman speaking in terse triand tetrameters:

> Agamemnon is returning. I shall grasp his hand,
> but I've nothing to say to him.
> A black ox stands on my tongue.
> I have a story I can only tell
> someone who knows already. Say nothing—
> this house would speak if it had a tongue![18]

In all of these translations, the Watchman character exists primarily as a device to introduce the setting and start the plot, heralding the beacon announcing the fall of Troy. However, the Watchman's monologue also sets an ominous tone of fear and insinuation, hidden violence, and forced silence. John Herington describes the Watchman as "both more and less than an ordinary human being: less, because he is given no individual traits whatever; more, because out of mere words he can create an overpowering vision of vast landscapes and events."[19] Heaney's insight was to allow the Watchman to function as more than a literary device; he becomes a fully realized individual torn by loyalty and wracked with dread. Heaney observes, through the Watchman, a society contaminated by violence and offers a voice that breaks the silence.

In his review of Joyce's *Ulysses,* T. S. Eliot defined "the mythical method" as using a myth as the framework for a new literary work, thereby "manipulating a continuous parallel between contemporaneity and antiquity."[20] Heaney uses his own "mythical method" in **"Mycenae Lookout."** In an essay on Eliot, he describes this method as "the art of holding a classical safety net under the tottering data of the contemporary, of paralleling, shadowing, archetyping."[21] Heaney parallels past, present, and future; his raped and beaten Cassandra evokes every concentration camp victim, every political prisoner, every internee. He foreshadows the future with the mythic past; by prophesying Romulus' murder of Remus in the last two stanzas of the poem's fourth section, "His Dawn Vision," he presents violence as cyclical and inescapable.[22] And Heaney both uses and refines archetypes: Cassandra is the archetypal female victim of male violence, while the Watchman becomes the archetype of the well-meaning but ineffectual bystander.[23]

Heaney's interest in Classical myth extends to translation and interpretation, seen in his versions of ***Beowulf,*** Dante's *Inferno,* and Virgil's Ninth Eclogue. In considering the act of translation, Heaney differentiates between approaches that he calls the "settlement" and the "raid."[24] With settlement translations, the translator comes to inhabit the text, living within it, adapting to it as it adapts to the translator; Heaney describes his translation of ***Beowulf*** as a settlement. A raid, in contrast, involves a looser approach: the translator or interpreter goes in for what he or she wants and then

leaves. Heaney's approach to *Inferno* was a raid resulting in **"Ugolino."** *Agamemnon* is both mythical and canonical; Heaney's adaptation is perhaps an extreme raid on Aeschylus's material.[25] For **"Mycenae Lookout,"** only a raid approach is appropriate, or even possible:

> No element that should have carried weight
> Out of the grievous distance would translate.
> Our war stalled in the pre-articulate.
>
> (*SL* 40)

In freely adapting the Classical text, Heaney articulates what violence had silenced. The result translates Aeschylus's emotions, not his words.

* * *

The violence that dominates **"Mycenae Lookout"** starts with its language. **"Mycenae Lookout"** frequently employs obscenity, which is unusual for Heaney. Commenting on the poem's aggressive language, particularly in the section titled **"Cassandra,"** Helen Vendler remarks on the text's "unexampled linguistic violence." "Heaney," she notes, "has never before permitted himself such brutal strokes."[26] Broom agrees: "The language of sexual aggression . . . could be seen as offensive in itself."[27] Heaney himself claims the "vehemence" of the language arises in part out of "the wilfulness of the couplet." He continues,

> At that early stage in the writing I was driving hard, forcing it, as if the rhyme were a bit and the two pentameters were directed to it and through it like the handle/shafts of a pneumatic drill. Then too there's the bloodbath element in the Aeschylus play—the butcher-shop aspect of Clytemnestra's welcome probably induced a more brutal approach to the northern Irish killings.[28]

The text's aggressive tone echoes the story's own aggression. Further, the violent language reflects the society in which the Watchman lives; violence contaminates the Watchman's voice as it pollutes his soul. When his violent impulses threaten to overwhelm him, the language rises to its most violent pitch.

Violence stains all it touches, haunting even the Watchman's dreams: "I'd dream of blood in bright webs in a ford, / Of bodies raining down like tattered meat / On top of me asleep" (*SL* 34). The pervasive influence of aggression is like "the beating of the huge time-wound / We lived inside" (*SL* 40). Violence pollutes the entire community, from Agamemnon to the Chorus to the Argive soldiers. The Watchman declares, "The war put all men mad." In Aeschylus' *Agamemnon,* violence equally infects the house of Atreus and the surrounding community. Cassandra sings of the Furies who haunt the palace:

There is a choir that sings as one, that shall not again
leave this house ever; the song thereof breaks harsh
  with menace.
And drugged to double fury on the wine of men's
blood shed, there lurks forever here a drunken rout
of ingrown vengeful spirits never to be cast forth.
Hanging above the hall they chant their song of hate
and the old sin. . . .[29]

In **"Mycenae Lookout,"** sexuality intensifies the violent impulse. From the beginning, "the agony of Clytemnestra's love-shout" echoes "like the yell of troops / Hurled by King Agamemnon from the ships;" (*SL* 35) orgasm and war-lust are one and the same. The link between sexuality and violence is further developed in the description of Cassandra, who looks "camp-fucked // and simple" (*SL* 36). Heaney shoves the reader into the perspective of Cassandra's bystanders, aroused to fantasies of rape upon merely seeing her:

the result-

ant shock desire
in bystanders
to do it to her

there and then.

                     (*SL* 38)

Heaney forces us to recall Cassandra's violations, first by Ajax at the fall of Troy and then repeatedly by Agamemnon. Heaney uses the rape of all of Troy's women to demonstrate how sexuality and violence are linked for the Argive soldiers:

When the captains in the horse
felt Helen's hand caress
its wooden boards and belly
they nearly rode each other.
But in the end Troy's mothers
bore their brunt in alley,
bloodied cot and bed.

                     (*SL* 43)

The fever of aggressive sexuality had risen so high that the rape of Troy was inevitable.[30]

The violence of **"Mycenae Lookout"** has a consistent effect on the individuals within it: violence compels connivance and silences the individual. **"Cassandra"** best emphasizes this connivance and conspiracy. According to Heaney, the section "was written very quickly. It came out like a molten rill from a spot I hit when I drilled down into the *Oresteia* bedrock that's under '**Mycenae Lookout.**'"[31] **"Cassandra"** begins with the Watchman's declaration, "No such thing / as innocent / bystanding" (*SL* 36). The Watchman pities Cassandra, describing her as "a lamb / at lambing time," and he intends only to stand by, innocently, as well as to condemn those who terrorize her. But violence infects

him, and his sexual gaze is itself terrorizing—a violation of the eye and the mind. The Watchman does not rape Cassandra, but his lust implicates him. Nor does he kill her; but he is almost as responsible for her death as the net- and axe-wielding Clytemnestra.

Within this section, prosody reinforces the violence, both real and fantasized, that is inflicted on Cassandra. Written in tight monometer or dimeter tercets, the lines are as clipped as Cassandra's hair; enjambment across stanzas raises tension and creates suspense:

her little breasts,
her clipped, devast-

ated, scabbed
punk head . . .

                     (*SL* 36)

In that stanza break and the long build-up to the line "punk head," we wonder what about Cassandra has been "clipped." Similarly, in describing the "shock desire / to do it to her // there and then," (*SL* 38) the stanza break allows time for the rape fantasy to play itself out in the bystander's mind.

A present-day analogy is clear: Cassandra's poetic image recalls the tarred-and-feathered, shaven-haired Irish girls tortured for "consorting" with British soldiers, as well as the nationalist prisoners in British jails naked and filthy in "dirty protests" and starving in hunger-strikes.[32] A Cassandra-like victim appears in Heaney's **"Punishment"** from *North,* another poem that examines violence forcing connivance and imposing silence. The parallels begin with the descriptions of the two women:
               "Punishment"

the halter at the nape of her neck, the wind on her naked front.

It blows her nipples to amber beads.

her shaved head like a stubble of black corn

you were flaxen-haired, undernourished. . . .
               "Cassandra"

Her soiled vest, her little breasts,

her clipped, devastated, scabbed punk head,

the char-eyed famine gawk.. . .

Heaney wrote both poems in a long and thin style; the lines of **"Cassandra"** are even shorter than those of **"Punishment."** The two works focus on women who both have been objects of a sexual gaze, and have been murdered for their sexuality. In **"Punishment"** as in **"Mycenae Lookout,"** the speaker also acts as watchman, bystander, and "artful voyeur"; he knows, looking back across the centuries, that he would have complied in and with the execution of the young Stone Age adulteress. He connives "in civilized outrage" against the violence, thereby equally conniving in the murder. Caught up in the violent impulse of the community, he "understand[s] the exact / and tribal, intimate revenge" the murder represents—for, in his own day, he:

> stood dumb
> when your betraying sisters,
> cauled in tar,
> wept by the railings. . . .
>
> (*OG* 113)

That is, the speaker did not protest when the IRA tarred the young Catholic women. Communal violence forces the individual into silence—the speaker would and does "cast, I know, / the stones of silence" (*OG* 113). The Watchman casts those stones at Cassandra as she goes in "to the knife, / to the killer wife." (*SL* 38) In the strongest parallel between the two poems, the guilt of silence haunts the speakers of **"Punishment"** and **"Mycenae Lookout."**

For connivance requires silence. The Watchman perceives what is wrong around him, hearing "like struck sound in a gong / That killing-fest, the life-warp and world-wrong"—but this sound is silenced, for

> the ox would lurch against the gong
> And deaden it and I would feel my tongue
> Like the dropped gangplank of a cattle truck,
> Trampled and rattled, running piss and muck. . . .
>
> (*SL* 34)

These lines point back to **"Stone from Delphi,"** when the speaker prays that he may *"escape the miasma of spilled blood"* until the god *"speaks in my untrammelled mouth"* (*OG* 207).

The Watchman keeps silent before Cassandra, neither speaking up in her defense nor offering comfort. Nor does he protest as she goes to her murder. The Watchman also holds his tongue about the affair between Clytemnestra and Aegisthus. "The king should have been told, / but who was there to tell him / if not myself?" (*SL* 42) The queen and her lover treat the Watchman as a confidante for their sexual secrets, giving him the opportunity to urge them to stop, but he holds his tongue: "I willed them / to cease and break the hold / of my cross-purposed silence" (*SL* 42). He is paid to watch, but that is all he does, weighed down as he is by "The ox's tons of dumb / inertia" (*SL* 42). Ultimately this "cross-purposed silence" results in Agamemnon's death:

> it was the king I sold.
> I moved beyond bad faith:
> for his bullion bars, his bonus
> was a rope-net and a bloodbath.
>
> (*SL* 44)

The Watchman's guilt and self-disgust over the deaths of Cassandra and Agamemnon infuse the poem. Agamemnon might have been saved, Cassandra might not have died—but in any case, now he will never know. In *Agamemnon,* the Watchman's silence has no lasting implications and therefore, no guilt ensues. In contrast, the deliberate silence of the **"Mycenae Lookout"** Watchman has as many consequences as his speech; the Watchman fears its implications.

The Watchman is not the only silent figure in **"Mycenae Lookout."** The entire palace—and particularly Aeschylus' Chorus—is "dumbstruck." The Chorus is never named, but its presence is felt—and its silence condemned—in the third section of the poem. Heaney presents Aeschylus' group of anxious old men as "claques," always "Quoting the oracle and quoting dates, / Petitioning, accusing, taking votes" (*SL* 40). They, too, stand before Cassandra and feel the desire "to do it to her // there and then" (*SL* 38); they, too, say nothing as she goes to her death. The Watchman ridicules them; they are merely "mouth athletes." They say nothing active or constructive. With his portrayal of the Chorus, Heaney indicts those in Northern Ireland "who always needed to be seen / And heard as the true Argives" (*SL* 40)—that is, as the true Irish. As in most sectarian disputes, the loyalty question in Northern Ireland, who is the "true" patriot, is a bitter and divisive one.[33] The Watchman describes himself as "isolated in my old disdain" and, as a result, "far, far less // Focused on victory than I should have been" (*SL* 40) However, he condemns the focus on victory as destructive, as arising out of the pervasive atmosphere of violence. The Chorus remains silent when it should speak—when confronting the imminent death of Cassandra. By not speaking out, the "war stalled in the pre-articulate."

* * *

The tone of **"Mycenae Lookout"** shifts dramatically in its fifth and final section, **"His Reverie of Water."** There, the Watchman turns from violence and aggressive sexuality to dreams of glistening water—water that promises baptism to remove contamination, of washing away the stain of blood. The section echoes the concluding speech of the Chorus in *The Cure at Troy*: "Believe in miracles / And cures and healing wells."[34]

Heaney offers three visions of water. The first is of a bath, "still unentered / and unstained" as the battle rages on Troy's plains:

> the hero comes
> surging in incomprehensibly
> to be attended to and be alone,
>
> stripped to the skin, blood-plastered, moaning
> and rocking, splashing, dozing off. . . .
>
> (*SL* 45)

Heaney traces the "blood-plastered" hero image to a documentary film that he saw Heaney saw about the Birmingham Pub Bombs of 1974, in which 21 civilians were killed and 182 injured.[35] Heaney recollects that this documentary left him with "a fierce readiness to go physical":

> A fireman or ambulanceman was recalling what it was like and came out with the shocking information that when he got home and went to bathe, he took off the clothes he had worn in the haulage and carnage and found his whole body was red with blood. It struck me that that's how the killer-heroes would have come in off the battlefield, if they came in.[36]

Perhaps the image of a blood-stained hand, central to Ulster mythology, has been used so long that it has lost its visceral impact, but the sight of an entire body red with gore can still shock and horrify. Of course, Clytemnestra slaughters Agamemnon in his bath, making Heaney's use of the image ironic. Nevertheless, Heaney offers an alternative to the bath as a place of sacrifice; it becomes a place of solace instead, where blood-drenched skin can be cleansed.

The second water vision is a well in the Acropolis, "a set of timber steps / slatted in between the sheer cliff face / and a free-standing, covering spur of rock." The well and its staircase were built in time of war and invasion:

> secret staircase the defenders knew
> and the invaders found, where what was to be
> Greek met Greek,
>
> the ladder of the future
> and the past. . . .
>
> (*SL* 45-46)

Heaney describes a real staircase (built sometime after the Trojan War) that provided an emergency water supply to the Acropolis. Greeks of the Mycenaean era, known to Homer as Achaians, used the Acropolis as a fortress during the invasion of the Greek peninsula by people known as Dorians. The Classicist A. R. Burn asserts that "the Acropolis held out, with access to water by a secret stair, ingeniously fitted between the north face of the rock and a huge, split-off flake."[37] Heaney learned about this well in Burn's *Penguin History of Greece,* noting that it was "A very brief reference, but it was most suggestive."[38] Some archaeologists hold that the Dorian invasion heralded the end of Mycenaean civilization, though the point is disputed. The invasion was however, a settlement and not a raid; the invaders eventually adopted and adapted the existing language, myths, and gods. This is the cultural exchange that Heaney refers to when he states that on that staircase "what was to be / Greek met Greek"—Dorians, the future Greeks, met Achaians, current Greeks.

The third vision is of a well in Mycenae. Such a well actually existed as an "underground stair that gave access to a water supply," although Heaney did not know this when he wrote the poem.[39] Heaney's Watchman describes the digging of the well as "a well-shaft being sunk / in broad daylight, men puddling at the source." The well diggers, coated in "tawny mud," are renewed by their descent:

> coming back up
> deeper in themselves for having been there,
> like discharged soldiers testing the safe ground,
>
> finders, keepers, seers of fresh water
> in the bountiful round mouths of iron pumps
> and gushing taps.
>
> (*SL* 46)

In these last two stanzas, Heaney returns to the depths of his own experience, revisiting images that resonate throughout his writing. He returns to his own personal mythology; the "bountiful round mouths of iron pumps" recall the center of Heaney's childhood world, the iron pump of Mossbawn:

> I would begin with the Greek word, *omphalos,* meaning the navel, and hence the stone that marked the centre of the world, and repeat it, *omphalos, omphalos, omphalos,* until its blunt and falling music become the music of somebody pumping water at the pump outside our back door.[40]

The pump, "a slender, iron idol, snouted, helmeted, dressed down with a sweeping handle, painted a dark green and set on a concrete plinth," (*P* [*Preoccupations: Selected Prose 1968-1978*] 17) recurs in such poems as **"A Drink of Water"** from *Field Work,* where the speaker recalls, "The pump's whooping cough, the bucket's clatter / And slow diminuendo as it filled" (*OG* 144). The image evokes a more healthy, more generative sexuality than the rape fantasies of **"Cassandra;"** the pump is both phallic and feminine, a slender idol that gushes healing water. Further, Heaney consistently associates the pump with his mother and aunt, who are nurturing, maternal figures.

Just as the Watchman observes the well-shaft being dug in Mycenae, Heaney recalls the digging of the pump at Mossbawn: "I remember, too, men coming to sink the shaft of the pump and digging through that seam of sand down into the bronze riches of the gravel, that soon began to puddle with the springwater" (*P* 20). Not only the scene, but also the language—in words like shaft and puddle—are similar. Further, the digging men covered with "tawny mud" evoke a childhood adventure, when

> another boy and myself stripped to the white country skin and bathed in a moss-hole, treading the liver-thick mud, unsettling a smoky muck off the bottom and com-

ing out smeared and weedy and darkened. We dressed
again and went home in our wet clothes, smelling of
the ground and the standing pool, somehow initiated.

(*P* 19)

Digging initiates the Mycenae well-diggers into a new,
uncertain peacefulness. They are reborn, and cauled this
time not with tar, but with the earth itself. Heaney's
digging images, of digging into the depths of things,
reaching downward for the truth, persist throughout his
oeuvre, from *Death of a Naturalist* (1966), through the
bog poems of *North* (1975), with their excavated bodies, to **"Mycenae Lookout."** Heaney associates digging
with both searching out the depths and with speaking
out about what is found there.

Further, Heaney extends **"Mycenae Lookout"** beyond
Agamemnon to the rest of *The Oresteia* and its healing
conclusion, *The Eumenides.* Heaney claims in his *Paris
Review* interview that he chose not to write a version of
the entire *Oresteia.*[41] But **"Mycenae Lookout"** does not
end at the blood-splattered walls of Mycenae: as does
the *omphalos,* but at the iron pump that recalls the Navelstone or *omphalos* of Delphi, seat of the Oracle. Orestes journeys to Delphi as "a suppliant bound for the
Navelstone of Earth"[42] after killing Clytemnestra seeking to be purged of blood by Apollo. Heaney's pump
symbolizes the cleansing waters at the *omphalos,* the
center of the earth, the home of the god.

Heaney's poem suggests that digging inward, returning
to inner sources and personal mythology, results in
cleansing and healing; mouths are no longer bull pens,
cattle trucks, bloody abattoirs. Heaney describes instead
"the beautiful round mouths," mouths that are open,
flowing, gushing with healing, cleansing water. In his
1997 letter to Belfast's *Irish News,* Heaney writes of
his search for "purification, a release from what the
Greeks called the 'miasma,' the stain of spilled blood."[43]

Redemption, in **"Mycenae Lookout,"** finally occurs by
breaking the silence. Although the Watchman's
violence-enforced silence holds through **"Mycenae
Lookout,"** he speaks out in the poem itself. In other
words, the poem is about the Watchman's silence, but
his silence is explained in his own words. Similarly,
Henry Hart, in his assessment of **"Punishment,"**
concludes that "What exculpates Heaney and allays his
guilt, at least partially, however, is the confessional
poem itself."[44]

Heaney again draws upon his source, *The Oresteia.* At
the end of *The Eumenides,* Orestes stands before Athena and a council of judges and pleads his case. He has
been purged of blood by Apollo at the Navelstone, but
still the Furies torment him. Orestes does not claim innocence; he knows his guilt, but he also knows the
blood (the *miasma*) has been washed from his hands.
He has been transformed by his suffering:

I have been beaten and been taught, I understand
the many rules of absolution, where it is right
to speak and where be silent. In this action now
speech has been ordered by my teacher, who is wise.[45]

Fagles and Stanford point out in their introduction to
the *Oresteia* that Athena's judgment "reveal[s] that,
despite Orestes' innocence, Orestes' guilt remains;"[46]
nevertheless, Orestes goes free and The Furies are
transformed into The Kindly Ones. Orestes is guilty, yet
cleansed, in the final act of healing in *The Eumenides*:
the purgation of speech.

Similarly, the Watchman reaches his own *omphalos,* is
cleansed, and yet acknowledges his own guilt; he is
compelled to speak and be purged of the stain of blood:
the Watchman's speech is **"Mycenae Lookout."**[47]
Heaney, in the persona of the Watchman, weighs in,
speaks out, breaks the "cross-purposed silence." Heaney
says, referring to **"Mycenae Lookout,"** "There's a
sense of 'weighing in' / 'no more mr niceguy' in the
poems. I can see the rightness of adducing that
'prophesy, give scandal' line."[48] Heaney, who is the
Watchman, who is Orestes, has "suffered into truth" and
now is compelled to speak. The final act of redemption
in **"Mycenae Lookout"** is the act of the poem itself.
Cassandra's are the only quotation marks in the entire
poem, the only person who "speaks":

> saying, 'A wipe
> of the sponge,
> that's it.
>
> The shadow-hinge
> swings unpredict-
> ably and the light's
>
> blanked out.'

(*SL* 39)

Heaney here freely adapts Aeschylus' words, when Cassandra cries:

> Alas, poor men, their destiny. When all
> goes well,
> a shadow will overthrow it. If it be unkind
> one stroke of a wet sponge wipes all the picture out;
> and that is far the most unhappy thing of all.[49]

Cassandra has nothing to lose, not even her life; a
prophet, she knew as soon as she reached Mycenae she
would die there. Cassandra's speech changes nothing.
Heaney often wrestles with the power of poetry—thinking perhaps of Auden's "poetry makes nothing happen":

> In one sense the efficacy of poetry is nil—no lyric has
> ever stopped a tank. In another sense it is unlimited. It
> is like the writing in the sand in the face of which ac-
> cusers and accused are left speechless and renewed.

(*GT* [*The Government of the Tongue*] 107)

Cassandra leaves the Watchman speechless, shaming him into the realization he should have spoken out, should have helped her. She is not afraid to weigh in—she demonstrates the final act of speech required to cleanse himself of *miasma* and experience renewal.

In his introduction to *The Odyssey,* Heaney wrote that Homer's tale "brings trauma and restoration, and the poem is mercilessly clear about the price of the repose which it finally allows."[50] **"Mycenae Lookout"** is equally clear about the price of repose after trauma, the cost of contamination, and the consequences of bystanding. Heaney is not proud of the conspiracy, the silence, the sexual impulses—but he is not afraid to testify, to prophesy to the truth of his experience and intuition. Four days after the 1994 IRA ceasefire began, he wrote, "The cessation of violence is an opportunity to open a space—. . . in the first level of each person's consciousness—a space where hope can grow."[51] This space compares to the one Heaney claims is created by poetry: "in the rift between what is going to happen and whatever we would wish to happen, poetry holds attention for a space" (*GT* 108). By speaking out in the aftermath of violence in that space opened by history, Heaney and his Watchman stand in a new world, "Ourselves again, free-willed again, not bad" (*SL* 81).

Notes

1. Seamus Heaney, *The Spirit Level* (New York: Farrar, Straus and Giroux, 1996), p. 36; hereafter cited parenthetically, thus: (*SL* 36).

2. Seamus Heaney to author, 1 August 2002; original correspondence in the possession of the author.

3. Seamus Heaney, interview with Henri Cole, "Seamus Heaney: The Art of Poetry LXXV," *Paris Review,* 144 (Fall, 1997), 137.

4. Paul Bew and Gordon Gillespie, *The Northern Ireland Peace Process 1993-1996: A Chronology* (London: Serif, 1996), p. 143.

5. David McKittrick, *The Nervous Peace* (Belfast: Blackstaff Press, 1996), p. 171.

6. Seamus Heaney, "Tollund," in *Opened Ground: Selected Poems 1966-1996* (New York: Farrar, Straus and Giroux, 1998), p. 410; hereafter cited parenthetically, thus: (*OG* 410).

7. Neil Corcoran, *The Poetry of Seamus Heaney: A Critical Study* (London: Faber, 1998), p. 200.

8. Heaney, "Art of Poetry," 104.

9. Heaney to author, 1 August 2002.

10. Sarah Broom, "Returning to Myth: From *North* to 'Mycenae Lookout,'" *Canadian Journal of Irish Studies,* 24, 1 (July, 1998), 72.

11. Seamus Heaney, *The Redress of Poetry* (New York: Farrar, 1995), p. 191.

12. Heaney, "Art of Poetry," 137.

13. Heaney, "Art of Poetry," 137.

14. Heaney to author, 1 August 2002. Heaney states: "Lots of different *Agamemnons*—MacNeice, Lowell, Grene (is it?). I even looked at the Loeb when I was considering a full translation." The Grene translation he is unsure of is the Richmond Lattimore version, part of *The Complete Greek Tragedies* series edited by Grene and Lattimore.

15. *Aeschylus,* transl. Richmond Lattimore, ed. David Grene and Richmond Lattimore, *The Complete Greek Tragedies,* vol. 1 (Chicago: University of Chicago Press, 1953), p. 36.

16. Aeschylus, *The Agamemnon,* transl. Louis MacNeice, *Four Greek Plays,* ed. Dudley Fitts (San Diego: Harvest/HBJ, 1960), p. 12.

17. *Aeschylus,* transl. Herbert Weir Smyth, ed. T. E. Page, et al., Loeb Classical Library, vol. 2 (London: William Heinemann, 1926), p. 9.

18. Aeschylus, *The Oresteia,* trans. Robert Lowell (New York: Farrar, 1978), p. 4.

19. John Herington, *Aeschylus* (New Haven: Yale University Press, 1986), p. 69.

20. T. S. Eliot, *Selected Prose,* ed. John Hayward (London: Penguin Books, 1953), p. 177.

21. Heaney, *The Government of the Tongue* (London: Faber, 1988), p. 116; hereafter cited parenthetically, thus: (*GT* 116).

22. The Watchman has a vision of "Small crowds of people watching as a man / Jumped a fresh earthwall and another man / Amorously, it seemed to strike him down" (*SL* 41). The allusion to the Romulus and Remus myth can be easily missed in these lines. Helen Vendler points out the connection, noting that "In this moil of tradition, Heaney feels a poem stirring, a poem of hitherto pent-up historical anger." Helen Vendler, "Seamus Heaney and the *Oresteia*: 'Mycenae Lookout' and the Usefulness of Tradition," *Proceedings of the American Philosophical Society,* 143, 1 (March, 1999), 116.

23. Heaney has employed a "mythical method" throughout his career. He made use of Irish myths and legends in such poems as "Nerthus." His interpretation of Classical myth goes back as far as the poems "Antaeus" and "Hercules and Antaeus," which treat this Classical myth from two different perspectives, both times paralleling the relationship of the colonizer and the colonized.

Other poems such as "Personal Helicon," "Undine," and "Stone from Delphi" (from "Shelf Life")
touch on themes from Classical mythology;
"Damson" in *The Spirit Level* recalls Odysseus'
encounter with the blood-thirsty ghosts of the
Underworld. Heaney's *Electric Light* contains
extended references to myth, including the sequence "Sonnets from Hellas," where recollections of traveling in Greece are mixed with evocations of related myths. Heaney's two
interpretations of Greek tragedies for the Abbey
Theatre both consider contemporary themes within
Classical contexts. Heaney's 1990 interpretation
of Sophocles' *Philoctetes* as *The Cure at Troy* addresses colonization as well as revenge, hatred,
and political violence, while his 2004 version of
Antigone, The Burial at Thebes, was inspired in
part by the rhetoric of the Bush administration in
the build-up to war in Iraq.

24. Seamus Heaney and Robert Hass, *Sounding Lines: The Art of Translating Poetry,* ed. Christina M. Gillis, Occasional Papers Series, vol. 20 (Berkeley: Doreen B. Townsend Center, 2000), pp. 1-2.

25. Neil Corcoran describes "Mycenae Lookout" as a "meditative version-translation, a literary gloss" on *Agamemnon.* He continues, "its self-intrication makes it the clearest instance yet in Heaney's works of the way literary texts, and notably classi-cal literary texts, operate for this poet as analogue and figurative projection, where the measuring of present and past brings emotions, impressions and attitudes into new clarity." Corcoran, p. 200.

26. Helen Vendler, *Seamus Heaney* (Cambridge: Har-vard University Press, 1998), p. 170.

27. Broom, 65.

28. Heaney to author, 1 August 2002.

29. *Aeschylus,* transl. Richmond Lattimore, p. 72.

30. Surely Heaney is also thinking here of the anguish of Euripides' *The Trojan Women,* the Greek tragedy most concerned with the consequences of violence.

31. Heaney, "Art of Poetry," 136.

32. Tim Pat Coogan, *The Troubles: Ireland's Ordeal 1966-1995 and the Search for Peace* (London: Hutchinson, 1995), pp. 225-26. In the "dirty protests," British prisoners (often IRA members convicted of murder, robbery, or other terrorism-related charges) insisted on the status of political prisoners rather than common criminals. They refused to wear prison-issued clothes and smeared food and excrement on the walls of their cells. Many began the hunger-strikes in which ten ultimately died. Heaney refers to the dirty protests in "The Flight Path."

33. A deadly expression of this impulse is found in the terrorist organization the Real IRA, which claimed responsibility for the 1998 Omagh bomb, which claimed 29 lives and injured hundreds in the single worst incident of violence in Northern Ireland. The Real IRA differentiated itself from the IRA proper, which it claimed had betrayed its cause by participating in the Good Friday Agree-ment.

34. Seamus Heaney, *The Cure at Troy: A Version of Sophocles'* Philoctetes (New York: Noonday Press, 1991), p. 77.

35. The IRA planted two bombs in pubs in Birming-ham on November 21, 1974, as part of a campaign to bring violence to England. The bombings resulted in widespread outrage and pressure on the British government to stamp out terrorism—with long-lasting implications. Eight days later, the government passed the Prevention of Terrorism Act, which has since been widely criticized as undemocratic and excessive. Further, six Irish men, known as the "Birmingham Six," were ar-rested and convicted of the bombing; their convic-tions were apparently based on false forensic evidence and forced confessions. They were freed on appeal in 1991. See *CAIN (Conflict Archive on the Internet) Web Service,* ed. Martin Melaugh, August, 2002, University of Ulster, http://cain.ulst.ac.uk/, September 14, 2002.

36. Heaney to author, 1 August 2002.

37. Andrew Robert Burn, *The Pelican History of Greece* (Hammondsworth: Penguin, 1982), p. 59.

38. Heaney to author, 1 August 2002.

39. Paul MacKendrick, *The Greek Stones Speak: The Story of Archaeology in Greek Lands* (New York: Norton, 1981), p. 133. Heaney discovered the well in October, 1995, when he visited Mycenae—"naturally," he says, "that was a great thrill." Heaney to author, 1 August 2002.

40. Heaney, *Preoccupations: Selected Prose 1968-1978* (New York: Farrar, 1980), p. 17; hereafter cited parenthetically, thus: (*P* 17).

41. Heaney, "Art of Poetry."

42. Aeschylus, *The Libation Bearers, The Oresteia,* transl. Robert Fagles (New York: Penguin, 1977), line 1033.

43. "Seamus Heaney's personal tribute to a man of integrity," *Irish News Online,* 15 May 1997, www.irishnews.com/k_archive/150597/news1.html/, July, 2001. Heaney's letter was writ-ten in horrified and despairing reaction to the sectarian murder of his friend Sean Brown in Bel-laghy. Heaney writes of learning about this murder

while traveling in Olympia in the poem "The Augean Stables" in the "Sonnets from Hellas" sequence in *Electric Light* (2001).

44. Henry Hart, "History, Myth and Apocalypse in Seamus Heaney's *North*," *Contemporary Literature*, 30, 3 (1989), 408.

45. *Aeschylus*, transl. Lattimore, 145.

46. Robert Fagles and W. B. Stanford, introduction, "A Reading of the *Oresteia*: The Serpent and the Eagle," *The Oresteia*, transl. Robert Fagles (New York: Penguin, 1977), p. 82.

47. Throughout *The Spirit Level*, Heaney seems compelled to speak out. In "Weighing In," he writes:

> for Jesus' sake,
> Do me a favor, would you, just this once?
> Prophesy, give scandal, cast the stone.
> Two sides to every question, yes, yes, yes . . .
> But every now and then, just weighing in
> Is what it must come down to, and without
>
> Any self-exculpation or self-pity.
>
> (*SL* 22-23)

These lines make sense only in the context of the restraint Heaney has shown throughout his career, the silence that has gripped him as surely as it gripped his Watchman. It is a silence tormented by guilt. In "Flight Path," Heaney mocks himself as staying "safe as houses" translating Dante while Ciaran Nugent began the dirty protests that would ultimately lead to the deaths of ten hunger-strikers. The guilt resounds throughout Heaney's work, in other poems, among them "Station Island," "Whatever You Say Say Nothing," and "Punishment." In "Punishment," Heaney knows he, too, would have cast "the stones of silence"; in "Weighing In," the stones to be cast are those of truth—the truth of what violence does to the individual.

48. Heaney to author, 1 August 2002.

49. *Aeschylus*, transl. Lattimore, p. 78.

50. Seamus Heaney, "Introduction," *The Odyssey*, transl. Robert Fitzgerald (London: Everyman's Library, 1992), p. xx.

51. Seamus Heaney, *Finders Keepers: Selected Prose 1971-2001* (New York: Farrar, 2002), p. 50.

Richard Rankin Russell (essay date spring 2008)

SOURCE: Russell, Richard Rankin. "Seamus Heaney's Regionalism." *Twentieth-Century Literature* 54, no. 1 (spring 2008): 47-74.

[*In the following essay, Russell discusses Heaney's status—and sense of himself—as a regional poet, primarily focusing on Heaney's prose criticism of other regional poets, Irish and otherwise.*]

> Each person in Ulster lives first in the Ulster of the actual present, and then in one or other Ulster of the mind.
>
> —Heaney (*Place and Displacement* 4)

> [W]hile a literary scene in which the provinces revolve around the centre is demonstrably a Copernican one, the task of talent is to reverse things to a Ptolemaic condition. The writer must reenvisage the region as the original point.
>
> —Heaney ("The Regional Forecast" 13)

In ways that are only just now beginning to be realized, the best writers from Philip Hobsbaum's Belfast Group (1963-66), such as Seamus Heaney, Michael Longley, Stewart Parker, and Bernard MacLaverty, have articulated a regional literature that interacted fruitfully with regional literatures all over the British and Irish archipelago, including Scottish, Welsh, and regional English, and with regional writers from America, such as Robert Frost. The literary devolution that comprises the largely untold story of twentieth-century "English" literature suggests the viability of regionalism generally and a decline in the dominance of London-centered literature. The imaginative efforts of a series of Northern Irish writers beginning in the early twentieth century have led to the establishment of a regional, bicultural, and finally trans-cultural literature that has devolved aesthetically, albeit as a special case, from British and Irish literature.

This regional literature can be placed alongside that developing in Scotland, Wales, and parts of England outside the Home Counties, such as northern England. R. P. Draper has recently discussed how, during the course of the twentieth century,

> places like Liverpool, Manchester, Newcastle and Hull became much more the regional capitals of a still urban, but no longer [solely a] London-based literary activity. Many of the best English poets came from the regions and maintained a non-metropolitan, or even anti-metropolitan outlook.
>
> ("Regional" 161)

We can easily add Belfast to this catalog of regional literary activity in the United Kingdom, although it is an anomaly, geographically detached from the British mainland and profoundly bicultural in a way that no other major British city is, including Glasgow. Although not identified as a specific region in T. S. Eliot's argument about the importance of maintaining regional culture in the United Kingdom, Northern Ireland nonetheless accords with his description of the region or the satellite culture: "the satellite exercises a considerable influence upon the stronger culture; and so plays a larger part in the world at large than it could in isolation" (128). As evidence of this influence of Northern Irish culture on English culture, Neil Corcoran argues that "the Troubles beginning in 1968" have been "the single most influential factor on the subsequent history [. . .] of contemporary 'English' poetry" (qtd. in Stevenson 255). Far from being provincial, Northern Irish literature is actually regional in an expansive sense of the term, astonishingly plural and cosmopolitan in ways that far surpass some Irish and British literature. Only time will tell if the province will be incorporated into the Republic of Ireland, but for now, its literature exists in a fragile and fascinating moment, redolent with hope for its future.[1]

Beginning in the 1960s, the Northern Irish poet Seamus Heaney began developing a regionally based poetry by analyzing his literary predecessors in the province, elsewhere in the United Kingdom, and even in the United States, through a series of book reviews and essays. Although Heaney is a powerful literary critic, his criticism has been either largely neglected in favor of his poetry or read primarily to explain his poetry. Thankfully, a countervailing trajectory has recently emerged. For example, Eugene O'Brien has argued that the poet's prose is "central to his developing project" (*Searches* 10) and should be considered as such, rather than following the usual procedure, which is to see it as "a meta-commentary on his poetry." And in the most recent collection of essays on Heaney's work, two of the contributors specifically defend Heaney's prose criticism as upholding Virginia Woolf's theory of the radical, individual reader and as inscribing a space for poetry's authority while nevertheless interacting with major social and ethical questions.[2]

Through his prose and other work, such as his broadcasts on BBC Northern Ireland, Heaney began conceiving of Northern Ireland as a viable region in which to ground his poetry and anchor his attempts to unify the province's divided inhabitants.[3] The current state of Northern Ireland, however, only retains six of the original nine counties from the traditional Irish province of Ulster because of successful Protestant efforts before partition to exclude the other three counties for fear of their Catholic majority population. Thus, counties Donegal, Monaghan, and Cavan became part of the Irish Republic in 1922, while only counties Fermanagh, Antrim, Tyrone, Londonderry, Armagh, and Down formed the new province of Northern Ireland. Heaney has often recognized the contribution of writers from these excluded counties to literature from the North, such as the Donegal poet Cathal Bui Mac Giolla Ghunna (died c. 1756), who wrote in Irish, and the twentieth-century poet Patrick Kavanagh, who grew up in and devoted his early poetry to writing about County Monaghan. Heaney has also drawn on the work of significant regional writers from contemporary Northern

Ireland, such as John Hewitt and John Montague, along with authors from Wales, Scotland, England, and America, including R. S. Thomas, Edwin Muir, George Mackay Brown, Norman MacCaig, Hugh MacDiarmid, Sorley Maclean, William Wordsworth, Philip Larkin, Ted Hughes, Thomas Hardy, and Robert Frost. Thus his regionalist project bursts the bounds of the six counties of contemporary Northern Ireland, conceiving of Northern Irish regionalism as transhistorical, transcultural, and transterritorial, inherently fluid and receptive—an implicit riposte to monolithic notions of identity inscribed by religion, culture, and politics in Northern Ireland.

In the early twentieth century, partly because of nostalgia for rapidly dwindling rural areas of England and the continued population shift to cities, the concept of regionalism was invoked in theories about rural English literature, while writers in Northern Ireland began articulating versions of Northern Irish regionalism by the 1940s, as we will see. F. W. Morgan's seminal 1939 article, "Three Aspects of Regional Consciousness," for instance, holds that regionalism is marked by "a developing consciousness of the smaller units of the earth" (qtd. in Keith 4). W. J. Keith argues further, quoting the rural English writer H. J. Massingham, that regionalism attains a specificity in the completeness of its presentation analogous to a work of art and, moreover, that the region so presented actually is art.[4] Heaney's artful prose rendering of Northern Ireland as a region, then, deserves critical recognition in its own right. This essay seeks to redress the relative neglect of this important project and to suggest how Heaney's real and imagined region of the North functions as a model for unifying the province's diverse inhabitants.

NORTHERN IRISH REGIONAL EXEMPLARS

In the 1960s, as Heaney was learning to write poetry thoroughly grounded in the actual conditions of Northern Ireland, he interacted not only with other Belfast Group poets but also turned naturally to older literary exemplars from the province. That he was engaged in promoting Northern Irish literature is evident from the influence of "Ulster" writing on him generally, through the Northern Irish literary journals he contributed to in the 1960s and 1970s, and in his recognition of the emergence of other regional literatures across the British and Irish archipelago and even in America. By 1989 he could look back and proclaim, in his suggestively titled essay "The Regional Forecast," that "I have a sense that nowadays the writers on the outskirts know more about one another than ever before and have begun to take cognizance of each other in ways that are fortifying and illuminating" (22).

Michael Parker notes that only a few years after the beginning of the Ulster regionalist movement, Heaney "wrote an extended essay on 'Ulster literary magazines'" in 1962 that brought him into contact with writers such as W. R. Rodgers and John Hewitt, who had "created a poetry out of their local and native background" (36). Four influential Northern writers for Heaney in this regard were Patrick Kavanagh, from Monaghan, part of the historic province of Ulster; John Montague, born in New York but raised in rural County Tyrone, part of present-day Northern Ireland; John Hewitt, born in Belfast; and the novelist and short story writer Michael McLaverty, from Monaghan.

Hobsbaum had so stressed Kavanagh's emphasis on the parochial to the Belfast Group writers that Heaney even recalls Hobsbaum in terms usually associated with the elder Ulster poet: Hobsbaum "emanated energy, generosity, belief in the community, trust in the parochial, the inept, the unprinted" ("Belfast" 29). Heaney would enact Kavanagh's fondness for the parochial by meditating lovingly and intensely on the particularized objects and landscape of his rural Derry childhood. When asked in the 1960s why he dedicated no early poems to Kavanagh, Heaney replied, "I had no need to write a poem to Patrick Kavanagh; I wrote *Death of a Naturalist*" (qtd. in Parker 32). If those poems testify to the Monaghan poet's influence on Heaney, so do two of his early essays.

In the first of these, "From Monaghan to the Grand Canal: The Poetry of Patrick Kavanagh" (1975), Heaney praises the public quality of Kavanagh's work in articulating a rural Catholic consciousness in aquatic terms he had previously reserved for his own poetry's focus on the imagination in poems such as **"The Diviner"** and **"Personal Helicon"** from *Death of a Naturalist* (1966) and **"A Lough Neagh Sequence"** and **"Bogland"** from *Door into the Dark* (1969):[5]

> There is what I would call an artesian quality about his best work because for the first time since Brian Merriman's poetry in Irish at the end of the eighteenth century and William Carleton's novels in the nineteenth, a hard buried life that subsisted beyond the feel of middle-class novelists and romantic nationalist poets, a life denuded of "folk" and picturesque elements, found its expression. [. . .] Kavanagh forged not so much a conscience as a consciousness for the great majority of his countrymen, crossing the pieties of a rural Catholic sensibility with the *non serviam* of his original personality, raising the inhibited energies of a subculture to the power of a cultural resource.
>
> (116)

Thus Kavanagh's poetry brought submerged Northern Catholicism into public literature and culture, an instructive move for the young Catholic poet from rural Derry, and one he would emulate often in his own verse (though while Kavanagh's poetry often laments the brutality and weariness of rural life, Heaney's generally lauds its life-affirming and renewing aspects, with some important exceptions).

Perhaps more important for Heaney was Kavanagh's elevation of "technique" over "craft":

> There is, we might say, more technique than craft in his work, real technique which is, in his own words, "a spiritual quality, a condition of mind, or an ability to invoke a particular condition of mind . . . a method of getting at life."
>
> ("From Monaghan to the Grand Canal" 116)

Kavanagh enabled Heaney to dwell on local landscapes to such a degree that they became mental states as well. Indeed, he sees here the poems of Kavanagh's *Tarry Flynn* as "matter-of-fact landscapes, literally presented, but contemplated from such a point of view and with such intensity that they become 'a prospect of the mind'" (120). While Heaney's early landscape poems, with some notable exceptions such as **"Bogland,"** dwell more on the actual than the abstract, Kavanagh's supple linkage of outer and inner terrain would influence Heaney's later career, especially the poetry that followed *North.*

In 1977, two years after the essay devoted to Kavanagh, Heaney praised him more specifically for his articulation of "parochialism." In "The Sense of Place" he argues that Kavanagh's work was closer to the lives of the majority of Irish people than was Yeats's because of "Kavanagh's fidelity to the unpromising, unspectacular countryside of Monaghan and his rendering of the authentic speech of those parts" (137). Citing Kavanagh's seminal poem "Epic" and his essay "The Parish and the Universe," Heaney argues that he "cherished the ordinary, the actual, the known, the unimportant" (139). For all his intense scrutiny of the local, however, Kavanagh remains on the landscape's surface, and his place names "are denuded of tribal or etymological implications" (140).[6]

John Montague's poetry, on the other hand, is rife with such implications, and Heaney praises his work for this quality immediately after his discussion of Kavanagh's poetry in "The Sense of Place." Employing the aquatic terminology he typically uses to laud poetry of the highest order, Heaney argues that Montague's place names are "sounding lines, rods to plumb the depths of a shared and diminished culture. They are redolent not just of his personal life but of the history of his people, disinherited and dispossessed" (141). Like Kavanagh, Montague evokes a buried culture in the province, but his exploration goes much deeper, suggesting the acute loss of pagan and Gaelic civilization:

> Both Kavanagh and Montague explore a hidden Ulster, to alter Daniel Corkery's suggestive phrase, and Montague's exploration follows Corkery's tracks in a way that Kavanagh's does not. There is an element of cultural and political resistance and retrieval in Montague's work that is absent from Kavanagh's. What is

hidden at the bottom of Montague's region is first of all a pagan civilization centred on the dolmen; then a Gaelic civilization centred on the O'Neill inauguration stone at Tullyhogue.[7]

(141)

Heaney's reading of Montague's sense of place has been critiqued by John Lucas as reductive and as reverting to a rural idyll that rejects the city:

[S]uch a culture is heavily dependent on stock images and attitudes and [. . .] it thus conspires with the sense of diminishment it wishes to discover. [. . .] The trap is sprung by what can fairly be regarded as a dangerous myth of dwelling, where that affirms a commitment to "roots" and "stability" and "history" against those who shift about, "Like some poor Arab tribesman and his tent." [. . .] For this dream of contact with the soil turns into a regressive ruralism which must necessarily regard the city as the antitype of true civilization.

(124)

This is a difficult charge to refute. One is tempted to say that Heaney's immersion in the Belfast of the late 1960s and early 1970s, which was rapidly descending into violence, justified his view of the city as "the antitype of true civilization," but of course many sectarian murders were committed in rural parts of the province as well, most notably by the loyalist Protestant gang called the Shankill Butchers in the mid to late 1970s.

Heaney's supposedly "regressive ruralism," however, is grounded in his religious understanding of his native countryside, which forms an essential component of his rural regionalism. This landscape recalls that of the playwright John Synge's Aran Islands, where both in real life and in Synge's plays such as *Riders to the Sea* (1904), islanders easily moved from belief in Catholic rituals to belief in local spirits such as witches. Heaney recalls this syncretistic terrain in his essay "The Poet as a Christian":

There, if you like, was the foundation for a marvelous or magical view of the world, a foundation that sustained a diminished structure of lore and superstition and half-pagan, half-Christian thought and practice. Much of the flora of the place had a religious force, especially if we think of the root of the word religious in *religare*, to bind fast.

(604-05)

The allure of the countryside, then, both for Heaney and for Montague as read by Heaney, is its evocation of this syncretistic, half-buried world signified by its very plants and trees.[8] This blend of pagan and Christian rootedness confounds binary attempts to categorize Heaney's regionalism, including those marked by sophisticated theoretical forays into his work.[9]

Not content with registering the influence of two fellow Catholic poets on his own developing sense of regionalism, Heaney concludes "The Sense of Place" with a discussion of the Protestant John Hewitt's poetry, lauding Hewitt for his "bifocal" (147) regionalism in contrast to Montague's "monocular" outlook. To exemplify, Heaney details the significance of their archaeological symbols:

When Montague's vision founds itself on the archaeological, it is on Knockmany Dolmen, on the insular tradition. When Hewitt searches for his primeval symbol, it is also megalithic; "a broken circle of stones on a rough hillside, somewhere," is the destination of his search for a "somewhere," and his note tells us that that somewhere is a refraction of two places. "'Circle of stones': for me the archetype of this is the Rollright Stones on the border of Oxfordshire, mingled with the recollection of 'Ossian's Grave,' Glenaan, Co. Antrim." Oxfordshire and Antrim, two fidelities, two spirits that in John Donne's original and active verb, interanimate each other.

(147)

Despite Hewitt's cultural Protestantism, his bicultural regionalism was salutary for Heaney as a stateless, Northern Irish writer influenced by both British and Irish cultures.

While Kavanagh advocated the intense local study of a given writer's immediate milieu in a generally Irish context, Hewitt attempted to articulate a viable Ulster regionalism while acknowledging the particular intractability of his province to a vibrant literary culture. For example, in his 1945 essay "The Bitter Gourd," first published in the third issue of *Lagan*, a short-lived journal of Northern Irish writing that appeared briefly toward the end of World War II, he discusses the regionalism of Wales and Scotland, contrasting their status as "geographical and national entities" (93) with the regions of the West of England and Ulster, which are not as clearly defined. Besides the vexed question of the geographic makeup of the province,

Ulster's position in this island involves us in problems and cleavages for which we can find no counterpart elsewhere in the British archipelago. Scotland has its Lowlands and its Highlands still with shreds and vestiges of historical, linguistic and even religious divergences, but on nothing approaching the scale with which we are faced here.[10]

(94)

The solution for the current crop of writers in the province, as Hewitt saw it, was to draw on their local surroundings for their art; the Ulster writer "must be a rooted man, must carry the native tang of his idiom like the native dust on his sleeve; otherwise he is an airy internationalist, thistledown, a twig in a stream" (99).

Finally, Hewitt argues that Queen's University in Belfast has a significant role to play in promoting Northern Irish writing. Citing various British university literary

groups from the past, including "Marlowe and his fellow pioneers" and "the Auden group" (102), Hewitt
notes that these groups constitute a haven for the
thoughtful safe from the rampant materialism of society:

> The importance of these groups resides, of course, in
> the bringing together of young keen contemporary
> minds enjoying for a period some measure of social
> security and not yet involved in and conditioned by
> openly economic demands and their superstructure of
> material ideals.

No notable coteries of this sort have arisen at Queen's,
he concludes, which "at various times had its groups,
but they have been infrequent, drawing only a tiny
membership and producing little work of significance."
Within 20 years, the emergence of Philip Hobsbaum's
Belfast Group at Queen's would prove the literary
potential of Hewitt's call for Queen's to support "the
bringing together of young keen contemporary minds."
In the meantime, Northern Irish writing would flourish
largely based on the work of its professional writers
such as Hewitt, who would later review Heaney's first
volume, **Death of a Naturalist,** and praise it extensively.[11]

Peter McDonald asks a question pertinent to the corresponding emergence of Northern Irish literature and
Heaney's role in developing his particular concept of
regionalism: "Does regionalism give birth to the
individual artist, or does the artist create for his community the viable concept of regionalism?" (24). To be
sure, Hewitt's regionalism would not have been given
nearly the credence it eventually gained had not the
province of Northern Ireland been created in 1922. For
instance, it took several decades for Hewitt and his
coterie of Sam Hanna Bell, John Boyd, Roy McFadden,
and other writers to consciously define the parameters
of Northern Irish literature, beginning somewhat
formally in 1950, with the founding of the New Literary Dinner Club. As Gillian McIntosh has shown, the
forums of the BBC and PEN (Playwrights, Poets, Editors, Essayists, and Novelists) enabled these writers to
formally and informally begin articulating their view of
Northern Irish literature at least as early as the late
1940s (182).

As Hewitt points out in "The Progress of a Poet," his
review of **Death of a Naturalist,** the final Ulster
regionalist influence on Heaney is Michael McLaverty.
In McLaverty, who supervised Heaney's teacher training at St. Thomas's Intermediate School, Belfast, in
1962, Heaney found another example of a rooted
Catholic Northern Irish writer who, like Kavanagh, also
gazed intensely on his parish. Heaney dedicated **"Fosterage,"** the fifth poem in the sequence **Singing School**
from **North,** to McLaverty, who, the speaker recalls,
"fostered me and sent me out, with words / Imposing
on my tongue like obols" (**Opened Ground** 134). In his

introduction to McLaverty's *Collected Short Stories,*
Heaney praises him for his "fidelity to the intimate and
the local" and "his sense of the great tradition that he
works in, his contempt for the flashy and the topical,
his love of the universal, the worn grain of unspectacular
experience, the well-turned grain of language itself"
(7). Like Kavanagh, McLaverty taught Heaney disdain
for the ephemeral and respect for the lasting, values
that would stand him in good stead as he mostly withheld immediate comment on the violence in the
province beginning in the late 1960s. And like Kavanagh's, McLaverty's deep affection for local landscape gave Heaney another example of a Northern Irish
writer who successfully developed a rich country of the
mind out of a geographic one. Heaney thus concludes
his introduction to McLaverty's stories by observing
how McLaverty's physical region becomes internalized
through loving observation, using the same phrase, "a
prospect of the mind," with which he described Kavanagh's contemplation of his landscape in "From Monaghan to the Grand Canal":

> There is, of course, a regional basis to McLaverty's
> world and a documentary solidity to his observation,
> yet the region is contemplated with a gaze more loving
> and more lingering than any fieldworker or folklorist
> could ever manage. Those streets and shores and fields
> have been weathered in his affections and patient
> understanding until the contours of each landscape have
> become a moulded language, a prospect of the mind.
>
> (8)

REGIONAL INFLUENCES BEYOND NORTHERN IRELAND

Heaney also perceived Northern Irish literature as
participating in a dialogue with other regional literature
of the period. Michael Parker cites a little-known review
of R. S. Thomas's first volume of poetry, *The Bread of
Truth* (1963), published in *Trench* in June 1964, in
which, for example, Heaney enthusiastically praises the
Welshness of the elder poet's work:

> Welsh religion, Welsh landscape, Welsh characters are
> the thongs tightening his imagination and intelligence.
> [. . .] The physical features of the Welsh hill country
> and its inhabitants are presented in pungent detail, so
> that a self-contained world gradually evolves in the
> imagination. [. . .] The sensibility that informs this
> work is instinctive, fermented in the dank valleys of a
> country imagination. [. . .] To regard this poet as
> regional [. . .] is to blind oneself to the blush of the
> universal on his gaunt Welsh features.
>
> (42)

Heaney is concerned to not diminish Thomas's considerable achievement by describing it negatively as
regionalist, which often connotes provincialism and narrowness. That he saw Thomas's distinctive Welsh poetic
project as having both particular and universal qualities
confirmed his own regionalist program to render specific
aspects of Northern Ireland universal.[12]

Norman MacCaig's and Hugh MacDiarmid's Scottish regionalism further confirmed the young poet. Employing "parochial" in a manner reminiscent of Kavanagh's use of the term in "The Parish and the Universe," Parker argues that "No doubt MacCaig's world with its epiphanies spilling easily from local, parochial experience, gave confidence to Heaney as he allowed his bucket to plummet into the well" (44). Heaney also recognized in MacCaig's work the connection between poetry and fishing central to his own (as in **"Casualty"** from *Field Work*):

> He was a great fisherman, master of the cast, of the line that is a lure. And the angler's art—the art of coming in at an angle—is there in his poetry too. He could always get a rise out of the subject. He made it jump beyond itself.[13]

("Norman MacCaig" 433).

More important than MacCaig, though, in developing Heaney's concept of regionalism was the Scottish poet Hugh MacDiarmid, the subject of two different Heaney essays. In a review of *The Hugh MacDiarmid Anthology*, originally published in *Hibernia* in 1972, Heaney explicitly links Wordsworth and MacDiarmid through their common regionalist projects based on everyday language: "both professed a diction that was deliberately at variance with prevalent modes" ("Tradition and an Individual Talent" 195). MacDiarmid incorporates Lallans into his poetry, he stresses, just as Wordsworth incorporated the language of the Cumbrian peasants who lived around him in the Lake District:

> Again like the young Wordsworth, MacDiarmid has a sense of an enervating cultural situation—he saw Scottish civilization as damned and doomed by influences from south of the Border—that is intimately linked with his linguistic obsessions. [. . .] Lallans, his poetic Scots language, is based on the language of men, specifically on the dialect of his home district around Langholm in Dumfrieshire, but its attractive gaudiness is qualified by the not infrequent inanities of his English, for he occasionally speaks a language that the ones in Langholm do not know.

(195-96)

Praising MacDiarmid's "Water Music" in specifically regional terms for the way in which "the Scots and the Latinate English furl together in a downpour of energy," he argues that in this poem, "the local and the indigenous, which were Joyce's obsession also, are affiliated to oral and instinctive characteristics of the region and the intensity and volubility of the regional diction" (196-97). MacDiarmid's successful fusing of Scots and Latinate English in "Water Music" undoubtedly confirmed in Heaney the validity of the mixed dialects of Northern Irish and Irish English he incorporated in—even made the subject of—several important poems in *Wintering Out* such as **"Broagh," "Nerthus,"** and **"Traditions."**[14]

In his Oxford lecture on MacDiarmid some two decades later, Heaney again praised the Scottish poet's linguistic contribution to his home country:

> he effected a reorientation of attitudes to the country's two indigenous languages, the Scots Gaelic of the Highlands and Islands and the vernacular Scots of the Borders and Lowlands. [. . .] MacDiarmid also more or less singlehandedly created a literature in one of those languages.

("A Torchlight Procession" 103)

Despite realizing the excessive output of MacDiarmid's poetry and its unevenness, Heaney clearly recognizes him as laying the groundwork for the great outpouring of Scottish literature in the closing decades of the century:

> There is a demonstrable link between MacDiarmid's act of cultural resistance in the Scotland of the 1920s and the literary self-possession of writers such as Alasdair Gray, Tom Leonard, Liz Lochhead and James Kelman in the 1980s and 1990s.

(104)

Once again Heaney is implicitly reading his own regionalist work as part of a continuum of devolved literatures expressed in varying languages and dialects throughout the twentieth century in the British and Atlantic archipelago. In 2001, he would look back to his coediting of the poetic anthology *The School Bag* with Ted Hughes in the early 1980s and realize that their approach to collecting poetry from different regions and nations in the archipelago was consistent with the thrust of historian Hugh Kearney's landmark work *The British Isles: A History of Four Nations*.[15]

Just as important for Heaney in developing his Ulster regionalist poetry grounded in the particular dialects of his region were the Orcadian Scottish authors George Mackay Brown and Edwin Muir, whose work in *An Orkney Tapestry* Heaney reviewed in *The Listener* on 21 August 1969. Michael Parker reads this review as expressing a type of retreat into the recesses of Heaney's mind from the burgeoning violence in the province (78-79), but Heaney's comparisons of the poetry of Brown and Muir to that of the regional English writers William Barnes and Thomas Hardy suggests that he views Scottish, Northern Irish writing, and English literature from outside London as constituting a matrix of regional literature. Additionally, as he attempted to keep his own poetry and Northern Irish poetry generally from being seen as too narrow and negative, especially in light of the accelerating conflict in the province, Heaney may well have identified with what John Holloway has called the "almost visionary hopefulness and exploratory imagination" of Muir's writing from the 1950s (110). If Muir's late verse gave Heaney hope and a widening imaginative compass,

Mackay Brown's own anthropological impulse must have confirmed Heaney's continued documentation of traditional crafts in rural Ulster.[16]

Heaney recognized that the work of Muir and other regional writers in the British and Irish archipelago suggested a viable third way between the neoromanticism of Dylan Thomas and the "tight formation-flying of the Empson/Auden division," as he argued in his later essay, "The Impact of Translation" (40). In that essay he favorably reviews the young British poet Christopher Reid's volume *Katerina Brac,* "written in the voice of an apocryphal Eastern European poet." For Heaney, Reid's volume signifies "the delayed promise, though not the complete fulfillment, of a native British modernism" (41). He bewails the direction English poetry took with the verse of the Movement poets such as "Larkin, Davie, Enright and others, the inheritors in the Empson/Auden line" and argues:

> Yet it could be thought a matter of regret that Edwin Muir—the poet who translated Kafka in the 1920s and who witnessed the Communist takeover in Czechoslovakia after the war [. . .] did not succeed better in bringing the insular/vernacular/British imagination into more traumatic contact with a reality of which *Katerina Brac* is the wistful and literary after-image.

He concludes:

> there was a road not taken in poetry in English in this century, a road traveled once by the young Auden and the middle-aged Muir. Further, because we have not lived the tragic scenario which such imaginations presented to us as the life appropriate to our times, our capacity to make a complete act of faith in our vernacular poetic possessions has been undermined.
>
> (44)

Heaney is being too hard on himself. For it is precisely in his poetry that we see an "act of faith in our vernacular poetic possessions" through his incorporation of the varying rich dialects of his native province.[17]

In a response to the Good Friday Agreement of 1998, which established the conditions for power sharing between Catholics and Protestants in Northern Ireland, Heaney would reflect again on the interpenetrations of dialect and culture—this time in the work of regional Scottish writer Sorley Maclean. Speculating on the implications of the phrase "totality of relations" in the Agreement, Heaney suggests the inextricability of the cultures throughout the archipelago:

> I thought, for example, of the complexities, religious and cultural, that might be recognised and the extensions that might be suggested if the achievement of Sorley Maclean, a Gaelic-speaking, free Presbyterian, socialist, ex-British soldier poet of the Western Scottish Isles, were to be studied in Ulster schools.
>
> ("Unheard Melodies")

Maclean is a perfect example of the intertwining of religious practice, politics, and language in the Hebridean Islands; moreover, his language and religious affiliation as Free Presbyterian would be anomalous but salutary for Northern Ireland, where Ian Paisley's Free Presbyterian Church typically rejects all things associated with "Irishness," such as speaking Gaelic. Heaney has been drawn to Maclean's example for a number of years, and wrote the introduction to a volume of critical essays on him in 1986.[18]

A final Scottish influence on Heaney's regionalism is Robert Burns. In a 1997 essay, "Burns's Art Speech," Heaney recalls the beneficial effect of Burns's "To a Mouse" on him as a student. The opening line, "Wee, sleeket, cowran, tim'rous beastie," affirmed Heaney's own vernacular speech:

> the word "wee" put its stressed foot down and in one pre-emptive vocative strike took over the emotional and cultural ground, dispossessing the rights of written standard English and offering asylum to all vernacular comers. To all, at least, who hailed from north of a line drawn between Berwick and Bundoran.
>
> (378)

Heaney's equation of the province of historic Ulster (Bundoran is a County Donegal village in Ireland close to the border of Northern Ireland) with Scotland is effected through a common vernacular heritage and is one of his clearest expressions of the cultural and literary affinities he sees between Scotland and Ulster. He approvingly recalls the linguistic rightness of Burns's opening line, its

> truth to the life of the language I spoke while growing up in mid-Ulster, a language where trace elements of Elizabethan English and Lowland Scots are still to be heard and to be reckoned with as a matter of pronunciation and even, indeed, of politics.
>
> (379)

Far from resistant to celebrating the Scottishness of the province, as some of his critics have charged, Heaney has inscribed it occasionally in his poetry, as **"The Other Side"** from ***Wintering Out*** attests.[19]

His approval of "To a Mouse" is paired with his delighted reading of the Donegal Irish poet Cathal Bui Mac Giolla Ghunna's "An Bunnan Bui." Heaney's yoking of these two poems further indicates his perception of himself as a regional poet and displays the kind of linguistic reconciliation he finds rife in literature from the province. Mac Giolla Ghunna, he says, was important for him because he wrote using the Ulster Irish Heaney had learned in school:

> [He was] [s]ignificant because he was a Northern voice and part of a group of Ulster poets [including Seamus Dall Mac Cuarta and Art MacCumhaigh] whose work,

like Burns's, was sustained out of the past by a long and learned literary tradition. [. . .] Their words and intonations belonged to an Ulster Irish in which I felt completely at home, since it was the Ulster version of the language that had been taught in Derry.

("Burns's Art Speech" 384)

He compares his experience reading these Ulster Irish poets to Hewitt's when the elder poet read the Rhyming Weavers, "those local bards of the late eighteenth and early nineteenth centuries who wrote in the Ulster Scots vernacular and who produced in Hewitt 'some feeling that, for better or worse, they were my own people'" (384). Finally, after translating from the Irish of "An Bunnan Bui," Heaney notes that "it's another source of satisfaction to me that *och* reappears at the phonetic centre of this poem in the word *loch* and the word *deoch*—which happens to mean 'drink' in Irish" (386). This reappearance points

> toward a future that is implicit in the mutually pronounceable elements of the speech of Planter and Gael. Even if we grant the deeply binary nature of Ulster thinking about language and culture, we can still try to establish a plane of regard from which to inspect the recalcitrant elements of the situation and reposition ourselves in relation to them. And that plane, I believe, can be reliably projected from poems and poetry.

Despite his unfortunate recourse to the binary terms "Planter and Gael," which reinforces the pervasive view of a province torn between competing cultures, Heaney is to be commended for his artistic regionalist urging of a transcultural linguistic and literary unity across the historic province of Ulster, which has always been the essential ground of any larger cultural and political reconciliation for him.[20]

Two other and somewhat surprising poets who confirmed Heaney in his regionalist aesthetic were Wordsworth and Hughes—English poets whose work Heaney convincingly reappropriates as regionalist because of their geographic locations far from the Home Counties and their commitment to local dialect.[21] We have seen above in his first essay on MacDiarmid how favorably Heaney looked upon Wordsworth for employing the language of the common man to ward off the pernicious cultural influence of English verse far south of the Lake District.[22] But Hughes's example would prove even more powerful for Heaney. He lauds Hughes's incorporation of his heavy native West Yorkshire dialect into his poetry in his lecture "Englands of the Mind." This talk concerns how Hughes, Geoffrey Hill, and Philip Larkin "treat England as a region—or rather treat their region as England—in different and complementary ways" (151).[23] The "desire to preserve indigenous traditions, to keep open the imagination's supply line to the past [. . .] to perceive in these a continuity of communal ways, and a confirmation of an identity which is

threatened—all this is signified by language." Heaney particularly seems to approve of Hughes's language, whose

> sensuous fetch, its redolence of blood and gland and grass and water, recalled English poetry in the fifties from a too suburban aversion of the attention from the elemental; and the poems beat the bounds of a hidden England in streams and trees, on moors and in byres.

(153)

His articulation of Hughes's evocation of a "hidden England" in this May 1976 lecture anticipates his articulation of Kavanagh's and Montague's exploration of a "hidden Ulster" in his January 1977 lecture "The Sense of Place," already discussed. These talks reflect Heaney's concern with the subterranean in this period, often expressed through his desire to burrow into the depths of his mind in poems such as **"North,"** the title poem of his 1975 collection, or through his fascination with the "bog bodies" found in northern Europe in poems such as **"The Tollund Man"** from *Wintering Out* and **"Punishment"** and other bog poems in *North*.[24] Heaney's recognition of a "hidden England" and a "hidden Ulster" signals the subversive nature of his regionalist ethos and his growing awareness of how the regional poetry in the British and Irish archipelago represented a powerful direction for poetry in the English language. As he notes in his conclusion to "Englands of the Mind," "The loss of imperial power, the failure of economic nerve, the diminished influence of Britain inside Europe, all this has led to a new sense of the shires, a new valuing of the native English experience" (169).[25]

Finally, a major transatlantic regionalist influence on Heaney's developing regional aesthetic has been the American poet Robert Frost. Rachel Buxton's recent study of Frost's influence on Heaney and Paul Muldoon carefully traces Heaney's reading of Frost's poetry, starting at Queen's University under Laurence Lerner.[26] Heaney's interest in Frost was confirmed by Hewitt, whose essays Heaney read as a graduate student at Queen's when he was writing his extended essay on Ulster literary magazines in 1962, mentioned at the beginning of this article. In "The Bitter Gourd" Hewitt notices the historic similarities between Northern Ireland and New England but then argues that each region's cultural conditions have changed so much that comparisons are not fruitful. And yet, in the conclusion of "The Bitter Gourd," he cites Frost, in particular his "rural portraits," "his avoidance of ornament and rhetoric," and his "unhurried and sinewy wisdom" (103). After suggesting the applicability of Frost's "The Gift Outright" to the situation in Northern Ireland, Hewitt concludes:

> some of us [. . .] are endeavouring to recreate that story, that art, that enchantment, drawn from and firmly

rooted in what Ulster was and is, and playing our parts in helping to make her, what first in fitful glimpses but now more and more by a steady light, we realize she should and can become.

(104)

Heaney has also recalled how Frost's "credentials as a farmer poet" showed in his poetry: "how forkfuls of hay were built upon a wagonload for easy unloading later, when they have to be tossed down from underfoot" ("Above the Brim" 86). Surely Heaney's own portrayals of rural life in poems such as **"Digging"** obtain something of their documentary immediacy from his immersion in Frost's clear-eyed farming poems (as well as his own immersion in the life of his family's farm). As he says in "Above the Brim" about the "grim accuracy" of Frost's poem "Out, Out—," "I was immediately susceptible to its documentary weight and did not mistake the wintry report of what happened at the end for the poet's own callousness." In her brief discussion of Heaney's terming Frost a "farmer poet" in "Above the Brim," Edna Longley argues that this phrase "places Frost between Kavanagh, more genuinely a farmer, and Hughes, then more exclusively a poet. This fits Heaney's own inside/outside relation to the environment he evokes or constructs" ("'Atlantic's Premises'" 270-71). This construction of Heaney as insider/outsider captures the spirit of such early poems as **"Digging"** and suggests the way he has drawn on his regional influences yet reconfigured them for his own poetic and cultural purposes to offer an imagined Northern Ireland where disparate religious and cultural groups might meet and engage in productive encounters.

THE ETHICS OF HEANEY'S REGIONALISM

Heaney's ongoing regionalist project retrieves unifying cultural elements, particularly dialects and languages, from the landscapes of his long-divided province and other regions. His "descriptions of place," as Eugene O'Brien argues, thus become "gestures towards an ethical revelation or unveiling" (*Place of Writing* 159). Heaney's artful geographic explorations, that is, carry an implicit ethical charge: landscape functions as a repository of cultural and religious signifiers that must be read closely to determine how regionalism has powerful and potentially liberating effects on cultural consciousness.

As a relatively recent and largely artificial political entity, Northern Ireland's region status has been questioned but ably defended. For example, as evidence of the province's uniqueness as a region, John Wilson Foster argues that "Ulster is distinguished by its inability to decide whether it is primarily a region of Ireland or a region of Britain. It is of course both, a fact that has yet to assume unique cultural form" (291). Edna Longley compellingly argues that "Northern

Ireland is potentially a diversified European region where you can live in three places at once (Ireland/Britain/'Ulster')—a liberating condition—not a place that fails to be two other places" ("Multi-Culturalism" 43). Because of Heaney's rendering of an actual yet imagined province steeped in English, Scottish, Irish, and Northern Irish culture, his prose explorations of regionalism offer an important paradigm of rapprochement for a place that is still beset with cultural and political conflict.

Notes

1. Scholars of Irish literature have been considerably reluctant to discuss the existence of something called Northern Irish literature, by and large for very good reasons. Primary among these is probably the desire to assert Irish literature as a distinct entity over against British literature, a natural desire given the centuries of British domination over Irish colonists and given the past tendency by British and American scholars to call such authors as Yeats and Joyce British. Northern Irish literature, with its plurality of styles and cultural implications, complicates the picture of Irish literature fruitfully, but this possibility is seldom admitted. It is treated as a special, disturbing center of literary activity: many Irish literary scholars tend to suspect that literature from the political province of Northern Ireland is linked inextricably with the conflict there and that once the conflict peters out, so will the literature. But as this essay demonstrates, Northern Irish literature has a deep-rooted existence that easily antedates the current conflict and should eclipse it.

2. See Sidney Burris and Michael Baron, respectively.

3. See my essay "Imagining a New Province" for an extended exploration of Heaney's forays into radio in this regard.

4. Massingham writes: "a specific quality manifests itself in the complete presentation of a region, in precisely the same way as it does in a work of art. A region thus presented *is* a work of art" (81; qtd. in Keith 5).

5. See *Opened Ground* 12, 14, 29-35, and 41 for the texts of these poems.

6. See too Heaney's essay "The Placeless Heaven: Another Look at Kavanagh," where he argues that Kavanagh's "early Monaghan poetry gives the place credit for existing, assists at its real topographical presence, dwells upon it and accepts it as the definitive locus of the given world" (4).

7. But Kavanagh's influence is much stronger on Heaney than it has been on Montague. Michael Allen persuasively argues that Kavanagh has been

largely rejected by Montague in favor of a sup-posedly larger cosmopolitanism, but Heaney has stayed faithful to Kavanagh's parochial vision: "Heaney, on the other hand, has never shown any doubt about the social and artistic validity of his parish" (36).

8. See Proinsias MacCana for an explanation of the origins of this syncretism. He argues that the remarkable conservatism of Irish tradition and literature was able to continue after the introduc-tion of Christianity because of this assimilative aspect of Irish ideology: "The subtle *modus viv-endi* which had evolved during the first century and a half of the Christian mission [. . .] permit-ted the complementary coexistence of two ideolo-gies, one explicitly Christian, the other implicitly and essentially pagan" (58).

9. One recent example is Andrew Auge's attempt to import the distinction between arborescent and rhizomatic structures drawn by the theorists Gilles Deleuze and Felix Guattari into a discussion of Heaney's regional ethos. Auge, citing Deleuze and Guattari's *A Thousand Plateaus,* notes that "the aborescent signifies centralized hierarchical systems that privilege continuity and filiation," while the rhizomatic "constitutes an a-centered, non-hierarchical, proliferating multiplicity" (272). Auge argues that Heaney's "aspiration toward an arborescent state of organic connectedness is repeatedly frustrated by disruptive encounters with the rhizomatic." As evidence he cites the uncon-trollable, ambiguous, and unsettling qualities of poems from *Death of a Naturalist,* such as the title poem and "Personal Helicon," which threaten the fixity and hierarchy of poems such as "Dig-ging" (272-74). But as Heaney's own prose and poetry make clear, he moves easily between the "arborescent" and the "rhizomatic" and actually obtains a certain groundedness from the profusion and variety of lore, myth, and religion attached to his local landscape. His work collapses the distinc-tion between these two theoretical terms, which thus do not shed much light on his holistic regional worldview, an outlook that anchors him all the more firmly in his particularized landscape precisely through its multiplicity of meanings, which he adroitly negotiates and variously claims in several passages from "The Poet as Christian."

10. Hewitt did, however, perceive correspondences to Ulster's anomalous political situation with other situations worldwide—for example, French Que-bec's position within Canada. See John Wilson Foster's thoughtful assessment of Hewitt's region-alism and its implications for current consider-ations of Northern Irish identity. Foster draws a fascinating comparison not between Northern

Ireland and French Quebec as Hewitt does, but between Northern Ireland and the Canadian West, following George Melnyk's 1981 book *Radical Regionalism.* Foster argues that just as the Cana-dian West has been oppressed by "the official Anglo-French Canadian cultures," so too has Ulster been penalized by "the twin psychological colonialisms of Irish nationalism and British nationality that have falsified their consciousness and diverted them from the true task of self-realization" (294).

11. See Hewitt's "The Progress of a Poet" for a lengthy encomium on Heaney's early poetry in terms that recall Hewitt's own conception of regionalism. In my essay "Imagining a New Province" I discuss the contours of Hewitt's review (140). Heather Clark points out that Hewitt's poetry anticipates Heaney's in its "set-tings, moods, and poetic language," but notes "readers have come to associate [these aspects] almost exclusively with Heaney" (123).

12. For a helpful discussion of Thomas's regionalism, see Barbara Hardy 93-100.

13. See too Heaney's approval in "The Regional Forecast" of how MacCaig's regionally particular poems attain universality:

> His deceptively simple late poems are testing the echo of the universe as authentically as even a persecuted poet could manage to. [. . .] But his skill in pretend-ing—even to himself—to be a modest inscriber of glosses should not blind his native audience or any other audience to the modernity of his achievement in these lyrics which sing with the constancy and high nervousness of barbed wire on a moorland.
>
> (23)

14. See *Opened Ground* 55 and 64 for the text of "Broagh" and "Nerthus." See *Wintering Out* 31-32 for the text of "Traditions."

15. Heaney points out that Kearney's "Britannic," not "British" approach to history is salutary and inclusive, since it appropriately decenters British history and articulates it as a devolving process:

> "Britannic" works like a cultural wake-up call and gestures not only towards the past but also towards an imaginable future. Without insistence or contention, "Britannic" is a reminder of much that the term "Brit-ish" manages to occlude. "Britannic" allows equal status on the island of Britain to Celt and Saxon, to Scoti and Cymri, to Maldon and Tintagel, to Beowulf and the Gododdin, and so it begins to repair some of the damage done by the imperial, othering power of "British." In fact, one way of describing the era of devolution is to think of it as the moment when Britain went Britannic.
>
> ("Through-Other Places" 411-12).

16. Holloway specifically notes this quality in the Orcadian author's work:

> Brown is clearly thinking in terms of *documenting* the
> distinctive society of which he writes. His vivid
> individualization is in part a kind of social study or
> very superior kind of literary reportage, with analogues
> in the fields of journalism, the TV or radio feature, and
> the documentary film.

(111)

17. "The Impact of Translation" suggests a major
reason why Heaney has been so drawn to the work
of Eastern European poets such as Osip Mandelstam, Miroslav Holub, and Leos Janacek—because
he finds in them the same sort of poetic regionalist ethos that he does in Northern Irish, Scottish,
English regionalist, and Welsh poetry. As one brief
example, see his two-page introduction to his
translation of Janacek's *Diary of One Who Vanished,* where he notes his replacement of "fledg-
lings" with "scaldies" and the "tree in the hedge"
with "boor tree"—an Ulster Scots term. Additionally, as Alan Robinson has ably pointed out in his
discussion of Heaney's "increasing affinity with
East European writers in exile," the poet "admires
them" not so much for "their refusal to succumb
to the pressures of a totalitarian regime, but instead
[. . .] [for] champion[ing] the illusion of individual autonomy enshrined in art's 'free state of
image and allusion'" (123).

18. In his introduction Heaney notes that he drew on
Maclean as an early example of a poet uneasy
about his role as author and citizen. As evidence
of this dilemma he cites a Maclean quatrain
reflecting on his decision finally not to fight in the
Spanish Civil War:

> "I who avoided the sore cross / and agony of Spain, /
> what should I expect or hope, / what splendid prize to
> win?" Such lines were both sustenance and example to
> somebody hugging his own secret uneases about the
> way a poet should conduct himself at a moment of
> public crisis—for I first read them in the days of the
> heavy bombing campaign in Belfast, a town I had left
> in order to make some more deliberate commitment to
> the life of poetry.

(2)

19. In "The Other Side" Heaney recalls the family's
Presbyterian neighbor in a memorable group of
lines that evoke his cultural and religious Scottishness: "His brain was a whitewashed kitchen / hung
with texts, swept tidy / as the body o' the kirk"
(*Opened Ground* 60).

20. Helpful treatments of the development and devolution of twentieth-century Scottish literature are
available in David Hewitt's "Scoticisms and
Cultural Conflict," Ursula Kimpel's "Beyond the
Caledonian Antisyzygy," R. P. Draper's "Regional,

National, and Post-Colonial (1)," and Robert
Crawford's enormously far-ranging and thoughtful
Devolving English Literature, which focuses on
Scottish literature as his case study. Kimpel is
especially helpful for obtaining an overview of the
contributions to Scottish literature by Muir, Mac-
Diarmid, Sorley MacLean, MacCaig, and Edwin
Morgan.

21. Additionally, the influence of Thomas Hardy as an
exemplary regionalist for Heaney cannot be
underestimated. In recalling his early reading in
poetry, Heaney has noted the sterility and removed
quality of much of the literature he explored at
that time: "somehow the world of print was like
the world of proper and official behavior among
strangers. [. . .] There was no dirt on your boots
and you had washed your hands" (Preface xvii).
As he thankfully recalls, "It was not until I read
the novels of Thomas Hardy in my teens that what
was actual at home and what was actually in print
encountered [each other] inside my head." See
also Heaney's Richard Ellmann lecture, "The
Place of Writing," where he briefly discusses
Hardy country and the way "the Hardy birthplace
embodies the feel of a way of life native to the
place. It suggests a common heritage, an adherence to the hearth world of Wessex" (21).

22. See also J. H. Alexander's short but suggestive essay "Wordsworth, Regional or Provincial?" in
which he argues that Wordsworth abhorred provinciality and instead achieved a "profound regionalism which breaks free of spatial and temporal
restrictions to offer a radical challenge to *metropolitan* complacencies, snobberies, and denials of
true life" (25).

23. Larkin is increasingly perceived as a regional or
provincial writer in the most enabling sense of
those terms. See for example Draper's "Philip Larkin: Provincial Poet" and Robert Crawford's
discussion of Larkin in *Devolving English Literature* (271-82). Crawford argues that Larkin's
"provincialism" (not in Kavanagh's negative sense
of the term) was influential in Heaney's development as a regional writer:

> Hull gave Larkin a valued provincial status as a place
> that can only be reached, in the language of his poem
> "Here," by "Swerving" aside from the main flow of the
> traffic, and this provincial status of Larkin's was to be
> of use to such writers as Seamus Heaney, able to see
> Larkin as one of the modern English poets "now pos-
> sessed of that defensive love of their territory which
> was once shared only by those poets whom we might
> call colonial—Yeats, MacDiarmid, Carlos Williams."
> By seeing Larkin as, in some sense, a "colonial" writer,
> Heaney is able both to identify and compete with Lar-
> kin, the poet of "English nationalism" (Heaney, "En-
> glands of the Mind" 150-51, 167). If Larkin's "English

nationalism" is really very much of a provincial variety, that makes him all the closer to the Northern Ireland-born Heaney.

(Crawford 276-77)

24. For the text of "North," see *Opened Ground* 98-99; for the text of "The Tollund Man," see *Opened Ground* 62-63; for the text of "Punishment" and other bog poems from *North* such as "Bog Queen," "The Grauballe Man," "Strange Fruit," and "Kinship," see *Opened Ground* 112-13, 108-09, 110-11, 114, and 115-19, respectively.

25. Edna Longley, arguing that Heaney's *North,* published the year before, reifies and mystifies the rituals of Irish republicanism, reads this lecture as a manifestation of Heaney's hidden nationalism. She sees that Heaney's remark about Hughes's "hidden England" recalls Daniel Corkery's nationalistic study *The Hidden Ireland,* but she infers from that reference that Heaney

> encourages in Hughes ideas of cultural recovery similar to those associated with a particular form of Irish nationalism. [. . .] Heaney [. . .] restores to England, via Northern Ireland, nineteenth-century ethno-critical concepts. In particular, his response to Hughes as Saxon/Protestant Other disregards the historical contingencies (post-war, post-religious, post-industrial) that engender and inform Hughes's myth. This reproduces the Jacobite a-historicity that conditions Heaney's own thinking about Northern Ireland.

("Poetics of Celt and Saxon" 82, 83)

This reading of Heaney's lecture does not recognize its place in the context of his clear approval of other regional literatures. This approval may well be because "Heaney is as alert as Hewitt (for complementary reasons) to those aspects of postwar England that bespeak imperial decline and the dismantling of Protestant Britishness" (83), but Heaney's regionalist ethos, while it may celebrate Britain's imperial decline, is more oriented toward unifying the disparate communities in the province and often recognizes "Protestant Britishness" as an aspect of his Ulster inheritance.

26. See Buxton 39-110 for her thoughtful and persuasive account of Frost's influence on Heaney.

Works Cited

Alexander, J. H. "Wordsworth, Regional or Provincial? The Epistolary Context." Draper, ed. 24-33.

Allen, Michael. "Provincialism and Recent Irish Poetry: The Importance of Patrick Kavanagh." *Two Decades of Irish Writing: A Critical Survey.* Ed. Douglas Dunn. Chester Springs: Dufour, 1975. 23-36.

Auge, Andrew J. "'A Bouyant Migrant Line': Seamus Heaney's Deterritorialized Poetics." *Literature Interpretation Theory* 14.4 (Oct.-Dec. 2003): 269-89.

Baron, Michael. "Heaney and the Functions of Prose." *Seamus Heaney: Poet, Critic, Translator.* Ed. Ashby Bland Crowder and Jason Hall. Houndmills: Palgrave, 2007. 74-91.

Burris, Sidney. "Reading Heaney Reading." *Seamus Heaney: Poet, Critic, Translator.* Ed. Ashby Bland Crowder and Jason Hall. Houndmills: Palgrave, 2007. 59-73.

Buxton, Rachel. *Robert Frost and Northern Irish Poetry.* Oxford: Oxford UP, 2004.

Clark, Heather. *The Ulster Renaissance: Poetry in Belfast, 1962-1972.* Oxford: Oxford UP, 2006.

Crawford, Robert. *Devolving English Literature.* 2nd ed. Edinburgh: Edinburgh UP, 2001.

Draper, R. P., ed. *The Literature of Region and Nation.* New York: St. Martin's, 1989.

———. "Philip Larkin: Provincial Poet." Draper, ed. 81-92.

———. "Regional, National, and Post-Colonial (1)." *An Introduction to Twentieth-Century Poetry in English.* New York: St. Martin's, 1999. 161-86.

Eliot, T. S. *Christianity and Culture: The Idea of a Christian Society* and *Notes towards the Definition of Culture.* San Diego: Harcourt, 1988.

Foster, John Wilson. "Radical Regionalism." *Colonial Consequences: Essays in Irish Literature and Culture.* Dublin: Lilliput, 1991. 278-95.

Hardy, Barbara. "Region and Nation: R. S. Thomas and Dylan Thomas." Draper, ed. 93-107.

Heaney, Seamus. "Above the Brim." *Homage to Robert Frost.* New York: Farrar, 1996. 61-88.

———. "Belfast." *Preoccupations* 28-37.

———. "Burns's Art Speech." *Finders, Keepers* 378-95.

———. "Edwin Muir." *Finders, Keepers* 269-80.

———. "Englands of the Mind." *Preoccupations* 150-69.

———. "Feeling into Words." *Preoccupations* 41-60.

———. *Finders, Keepers: Selected Prose 1971-2001.* New York: Farrar, 2002.

———. "From Monaghan to the Grand Canal: The Poetry of Patrick Kavanagh." *Preoccupations* 115-30.

———. "The Impact of Translation." *The Government of the Tongue: Selected Prose 1978-1987.* New York: Noonday, 1988. 36-44.

———. Introduction. *Diary of One Who Vanished: A Song Cycle by Leos Janacek in a New Version by Seamus Heaney.* London: Faber, 1999. N. pag.

————. Introduction. *Michael McLaverty: Collected Short Stories*. Dublin: Poolbeg, 1978. 7-9.

————. Introduction. *Sorley Maclean: Critical Essays*. Ed. Raymond J. Ross and Joy Hendry. Edinburgh: Scottish Academic P, 1986. 1-7.

————. "Norman MacCaig, 1910-1996." *Finders, Keepers* 433-36.

————. *Opened Ground: Selected Poems 1966-1996*. New York: Farrar, 1998.

————. *Place and Displacement: Recent Poetry of Northern Ireland*. Peter Laver Memorial Lecture. Grasmere: Trustees of Dove Cottage, 2 Aug. 1984.

————. "The Place of Writing: W. B. Yeats and Thoor Ballylee." *The Place of Writing*. Atlanta: Scholar's Press, 1989. 18-35.

————. "The Placeless Heaven: Another Look at Kavanagh." *The Government of the Tongue: Selected Prose 1978-1987*. New York: Noonday, 1988. 3-14.

————. "The Poet as a Christian." *The Furrow* 29.10 (Oct. 1978): 603-06.

————. "The Poetry of John Hewitt." *Preoccupations* 207-10.

————. Preface. *Seamus Heaney: Poems and a Memoir*. New York: Limited Editions Club, 1982. xvii-xviii.

————. *Preoccupations: Selected Prose 1968-1978*. London: Faber, 1980.

————. "The Regional Forecast." Draper, ed. 10-23.

————. "The Sense of Place." *Preoccupations* 131-49.

————. "Through-Other Places, Through-Other Times: The Irish Poet and Britain." *Finders, Keepers* 396-415.

————. "A Torchlight Procession of One: On Hugh MacDiarmid." *The Redress of Poetry*. London: Faber, 103-23.

————. "Tradition and an Individual Talent: Hugh Mac-Diarmid." *Preoccupations* 195-98.

————. "Unheard Melodies." *Irish Times Supplement* 11 Apr. 1998. 1.

————. *Wintering Out*. London: Faber, 1972.

Hewitt, David. "Scoticisms and Cultural Conflict." Draper, ed. 125-35.

Hewitt, John. "The Bitter Gourd: Some Problems of the Ulster Writer." *Lagan* 3 (1945): 93-105.

————. "The Progress of a Poet." *Belfast Telegraph* 19 May 1966. N. pag.

Holloway, John. "The Literary Scene." *The Present*. Vol. 8 of *The New Pelican Guide to English Literature*. Ed. Boris Ford. New York: Penguin, 1983. 65-125.

Kavanagh, Patrick. "The Parish and the Universe." *Collected Prose*. London: Macgibbon, 1967. 281-83.

Keith, W. J. Introduction. *Regions of the Imagination: The Development of British Rural Fiction*. Toronto: U of Toronto P, 1988. 3-20.

Kimpel, Ursula. "Beyond the Caledonian Antisyzygy: Contemporary Scottish Poetry in Between Cultures." *Poetry in the British Isles: Non-Metropolitan Perspectives*. Ed. Hans-Werner Ludwig and Lothar Fietz. Cardiff: U of Wales P, 1995. 135-56.

Longley, Edna. "'Atlantic's Premises': American Influences on Northern Irish Poetry in the 1960s." *Poetry and Posterity*. Newcastle: Bloodaxe, 2000. 259-79.

————. "Multi-Culturalism and Northern Ireland: Making Differences Fruitful." *Multi-Culturalism: The View from the Two Irelands*. Cork: Cork UP, 2001. 1-44.

————. "The Poetics of Celt and Saxon." *Poetry and Posterity*. Newcastle: Bloodaxe, 2000. 52-89.

Lucas, John. "Seamus Heaney and the Possibilities of Poetry." *Seamus Heaney: A Collection of Critical Essays*. Ed. Elmer Andrews. New York: St. Martin's, 1992. 117-38.

MacCana, Proinsias. "Early Irish Ideology and the Concept of Unity." *The Irish Mind: Exploring Intellectual Traditions*. Ed. Richard Kearney. Dublin: Wolfhound, 1985. 56-78.

Massingham, H. J. *Remembrance: An Autobiography*. London: Batsford, 1942.

McDonald, Peter. *Mistaken Identities: Poetry and Northern Ireland*. Oxford: Oxford UP, 1997.

McIntosh, Gillian. *The Force of Culture: Unionist Identities in Twentieth-Century Ireland*. Cork: Cork UP, 1999.

O'Brien, Eugene. *Seamus Heaney and the Place of Writing*. Gainesville: UP of Florida, 2002.

————. *Seamus Heaney: Searches for Answers*. London: Pluto, 2003.

Parker, Michael. *Seamus Heaney: The Making of the Poet*. Iowa City: U of Iowa P, 1993.

Robinson, Alan. *Instabilities in Contemporary British Poetry*. London: Macmillan, 1988.

Russell, Richard Rankin. "Imagining a New Province: Seamus Heaney's Creative Work for BBC Northern Ireland Radio, 1968-1971." *Irish Studies Review* 15.2 (Spring 2007): 137-62.

Stevenson, Randall. *The Last of England?* Oxford: Oxford UP, 2004. Vol. 12 of *The Oxford English Literary History*.

FURTHER READING

Criticism

Bloomer, W. Martin. "Marble Latin: Encounters with the Timeless Language." In *The Contest of Language: Before and Beyond Nationalism,* edited by W. Martin Bloomer, pp. 207-26. Notre Dame, Ind.: University of Notre Dame Press, 2005.

> Discusses Heaney's use and representation of the Latin language in his poetry.

Christie, Tara. "'Something To Write Home About': Seamus Heaney." *Thomas Hardy Journal* 20, no. 2 (June 2004): 35-45.

> Discusses Heaney's "fifty-year engagement with the works of Thomas Hardy," and the profound influence those works have had on Heaney's own poetry.

Cuda, Anthony J. "The Use of Memory: Seamus Heaney, T. S. Eliot, and the Unpublished Epigraph to *North.*" *Journal of Modern Literature* 28, no. 4 (summer 2005): 152-75.

> Studies the influence of T. S. Eliot on Heaney's poetry, notwithstanding Heaney's repeated contention that he consciously strove to resist Eliot's influence rather than to embrace it.

O'Sullivan, Michael. "'Bare Life' and the Garden Politics of Roethke and Heaney." *Mosaic* 38, no. 4 (December 2005): 17-34.

> Examines Heaney's treatment of the relationship between humans and plant and animal life, and compares it to Theodor Roethke's handling of that same relationship.

Rotella, Guy. "Seamus Heaney: 'The Grauballe Man,' 'In Memoriam Francis Ledwidge,' and Others." In *Castings: Monuments and Monumentality in Poems by Elizabeth Bishop, Robert Lowell, James Merrill, Derek Walcott, and Seamus Heaney,* pp. 167-98. Nashville, Tenn.: Vanderbilt University Press, 2004.

> Considers Heaney's attitude toward monuments in cultural and historical terms—primarily through a detailed examination of "The Grauballe Man" and "In Memoriam Francis Ledwidge."

Wheatley, David. "'That Blank Mouth': Secrecy, Shibboleths, and Silence in Northern Irish Poetry." *Journal of Modern Literature* 25, no. 1 (fall 2001): 1-16.

> Examines the secret, largely inaccessible allusions and references in much contemporary Northern Irish poetry, including the work of Seamus Heaney.

Additional coverage of Heaney's life and career is contained in the following sources published by Gale: *Authors and Artists for Young Adults,* **Vol. 61;** *British Writers Retrospective Supplement,* **Vol. 1;** *British Writers Supplement,* **Vol. 2;** *Concise Dictionary of British Literary Biography, 1960 to Present; Concise Major 21st-Century Writers,* **Ed. 1;** *Contemporary Authors,* **Vols. 85-88;** *Contemporary Authors New Revision Series,* **Vols. 25, 48, 75, 91, 128, 184;** *Contemporary Literary Criticism,* **Vols. 5, 7, 14, 25, 37, 74, 91, 171, 225;** *Contemporary Poets,* **Eds. 1, 2, 3, 4, 5, 6, 7;** *Dictionary of Literary Biography,* **Vols. 40, 330;** *Dictionary of Literary Biography Yearbook, 1995; Discovering Authors 3.0; Discovering Authors: British; Discovering Authors Modules: Poet; Encyclopedia of World Literature in the 20th Century,* **Ed. 3;** *Exploring Poetry; Literature Resource Center; Major 20th-Century Writers,* **Eds. 1, 2;** *Major 21st-Century Writers,* **(ebook) 2005;** *Modern British Literature,* **Ed. 2;** *Poetry Criticism,* **Vol. 18;** *Poetry for Students,* **Vols. 2, 5, 8, 17, 30;** *Poets: American and British; Reference Guide to English Literature,* **Ed. 2;** *Twayne's English Authors; World Literature and Its Times,* **Vol. 4; and** *World Literature Criticism Supplement.*

How to Use This Index

The main references

Calvino, Italo
1923-1985 .... CLC 5, 8, 11, 22, 33, 39,
73; SSC 3, 48

list all author entries in the following Gale Literary Criticism series:

AAL = Asian American Literature
BG = The Beat Generation: A Gale Critical Companion
BLC = Black Literature Criticism
BLCS = Black Literature Criticism Supplement
CLC = Contemporary Literary Criticism
CLR = Children's Literature Review
CMLC = Classical and Medieval Literature Criticism
DC = Drama Criticism
FL = Feminism in Literature: A Gale Critical Companion
GL = Gothic Literature: A Gale Critical Companion
HLC = Hispanic Literature Criticism
HLCS = Hispanic Literature Criticism Supplement
HR = Harlem Renaissance: A Gale Critical Companion
LC = Literature Criticism from 1400 to 1800
NCLC = Nineteenth-Century Literature Criticism
NNAL = Native North American Literature
PC = Poetry Criticism
SSC = Short Story Criticism
TCLC = Twentieth-Century Literary Criticism
WLC = World Literature Criticism, 1500 to the Present
WLCS = World Literature Criticism Supplement

The cross-references

See also CA 85-88, 116; CANR 23, 61;
DAM NOV; DLB 196; EW 13; MTCW 1, 2;
RGSF 2; RGWL 2; SFW 4; SSFS 12

list all author entries in the following Gale biographical and literary sources:

AAYA = Authors & Artists for Young Adults
AFAW = African American Writers
AFW = African Writers
AITN = Authors in the News
AMW = American Writers
AMWR = American Writers Retrospective Supplement
AMWS = American Writers Supplement
ANW = American Nature Writers
AW = Ancient Writers
BEST = Bestsellers
BPFB = Beacham's Encyclopedia of Popular Fiction: Biography and Resources
BRW = British Writers
BRWS = British Writers Supplement
BW = Black Writers
BYA = Beacham's Guide to Literature for Young Adults
CA = Contemporary Authors
CAAS = Contemporary Authors Autobiography Series
CABS = Contemporary Authors Bibliographical Series
CAD = Contemporary American Dramatists
CANR = Contemporary Authors New Revision Series
CAP = Contemporary Authors Permanent Series
CBD = Contemporary British Dramatists
CCA = Contemporary Canadian Authors
CD = Contemporary Dramatists
CDALB = Concise Dictionary of American Literary Biography

CDALBS = *Concise Dictionary of American Literary Biography Supplement*

CDBLB = *Concise Dictionary of British Literary Biography*

CMW = *St. James Guide to Crime & Mystery Writers*

CN = *Contemporary Novelists*

CP = *Contemporary Poets*

CPW = *Contemporary Popular Writers*

CSW = *Contemporary Southern Writers*

CWD = *Contemporary Women Dramatists*

CWP = *Contemporary Women Poets*

CWRI = *St. James Guide to Children's Writers*

CWW = *Contemporary World Writers*

DA = *DISCovering Authors*

DA3 = *DISCovering Authors 3.0*

DAB = *DISCovering Authors: British Edition*

DAC = *DISCovering Authors: Canadian Edition*

DAM = *DISCovering Authors: Modules*

    DRAM: *Dramatists Module;* **MST**: *Most-studied Authors Module;*

    MULT: *Multicultural Authors Module;* **NOV**: *Novelists Module;*

    POET: *Poets Module;* **POP**: *Popular Fiction and Genre Authors Module*

DFS = *Drama for Students*

DLB = *Dictionary of Literary Biography*

DLBD = *Dictionary of Literary Biography Documentary Series*

DLBY = *Dictionary of Literary Biography Yearbook*

DNFS = *Literature of Developing Nations for Students*

EFS = *Epics for Students*

EW = *European Writers*

EWL = *Encyclopedia of World Literature in the 20th Century*

EXPN = *Exploring Novels*

EXPP = *Exploring Poetry*

EXPS = *Exploring Short Stories*

FANT = *St. James Guide to Fantasy Writers*

FW = *Feminist Writers*

GFL = *Guide to French Literature,* Beginnings to 1789, 1798 to the Present

GLL = *Gay and Lesbian Literature*

HGG = *St. James Guide to Horror, Ghost & Gothic Writers*

HW = *Hispanic Writers*

IDFW = *International Dictionary of Films and Filmmakers: Writers and Production Artists*

IDTP = *International Dictionary of Theatre: Playwrights*

LAIT = *Literature and Its Times*

LAW = *Latin American Writers*

JRDA = *Junior DISCovering Authors*

MAICYA = *Major Authors and Illustrators for Children and Young Adults*

MAICYAS = *Major Authors and Illustrators for Children and Young Adults Supplement*

MAWW = *Modern American Women Writers*

MJW = *Modern Japanese Writers*

MTCW = *Major 20th-Century Writers*

NCFS = *Nonfiction Classics for Students*

NFS = *Novels for Students*

PAB = *Poets: American and British*

PFS = *Poetry for Students*

RGAL = *Reference Guide to American Literature*

RGEL = *Reference Guide to English Literature*

RGSF = *Reference Guide to Short Fiction*

RGWL = *Reference Guide to World Literature*

RHW = *Twentieth-Century Romance and Historical Writers*

SAAS = *Something about the Author Autobiography Series*

SATA = *Something about the Author*

SFW = *St. James Guide to Science Fiction Writers*

SSFS = *Short Stories for Students*

TCWW = *Twentieth-Century Western Writers*

WLIT = *World Literature and Its Times*

WP = *World Poets*

YABC = *Yesterday's Authors of Books for Children*

YAW = *St. James Guide to Young Adult Writers*

Literary Criticism Series
Cumulative Author Index

20/1631
See Upward, Allen

A/C Cross
See Lawrence, T. E.

A. M.
See Megged, Aharon

Aaron, Sidney
See Chayefsky, Paddy

Abasiyanik, Sait Faik 1906-1954 ... **TCLC 23**
See also CA 123; 231

Abbey, Edward 1927-1989 .... **CLC 36, 59; TCLC 160**
See also AAYA 75; AMWS 13; ANW; CA 45-48; 128; CANR 2, 41, 131; DA3; DLB 256, 275; LATS 1:2; MTCW 2; MTFW 2005; TCWW 1, 2

Abbott, Edwin A. 1838-1926 .... **TCLC 139**
See also DLB 178

Abbott, Lee K(ittredge) 1947- .... **CLC 48**
See also CA 124; CANR 51, 101; DLB 130

Abe, Kobo 1924-1993 ...... **CLC 8, 22, 53, 81; SSC 61; TCLC 131**
See also CA 65-68; 140; CANR 24, 60; DAM NOV; DFS 14; DLB 182; EWL 3; MJW; MTCW 1, 2; MTFW 2005; NFS 22; RGWL 3; SFW 4

Abe Kobo
See Abe, Kobo

Abelard, Peter c. 1079-c. 1142 ..... **CMLC 11, 77**
See also DLB 115, 208

Abell, Kjeld 1901-1961 .... **CLC 15**
See also CA 191; 111; DLB 214; EWL 3

Abercrombie, Lascelles
1881-1938 .... **TCLC 141**
See also CA 112; DLB 19; RGEL 2

Abhavananda
See Crowley, Edward Alexander

Abish, Walter 1931- ... **CLC 22, 246; SSC 44**
See also CA 101; CANR 37, 114, 153; CN 3, 4, 5, 6; DLB 130, 227; MAL 5; RGHL

Abrahams, Peter (Henry) 1919- .... **CLC 4**
See also AFW; BW 1; CA 57-60; CANR 26, 125; CDWLB 3; CN 1, 2, 3, 4, 5, 6; DLB 117, 225; EWL 3; MTCW 1, 2; RGEL 2; WLIT 2

Abrams, M(eyer) H(oward) 1912- ... **CLC 24**
See also CA 57-60; CANR 13, 33; DLB 67

Abse, Dannie 1923- .. **CLC 7, 29, 266; PC 41**
See also CA 53-56; CAAS 1; CANR 4, 46, 74, 124; CBD; CN 1, 2, 3; CP 1, 2, 3, 4, 5, 6, 7; DAB; DAM POET; DLB 27, 245; MTCW 2

Abutsu 1222(?)-1283 .... **CMLC 46**
See also DLB 203

Abutsu-ni
See Abutsu

Achebe, Albert Chinualumogu
See Achebe, Chinua

Achebe, Chinua 1930- .... **BLC 1:1, 2:1; CLC 1, 3, 5, 7, 11, 26, 51, 75, 127, 152, 272, 278; SSC 105; WLC 1**
See also AAYA 15; AFW; BPFB 1; BRWC 2; BW 2, 3; CA 1-4R; CANR 6, 26, 47, 124; CDWLB 3; CLR 20; CN 1, 2, 3, 4, 5, 6, 7; CP 2, 3, 4, 5, 6, 7; CWRI 5; DA; DA3; DAB; DAC; DAM MST, MULT, NOV; DLB 117; DNFS 1; EWL 3; EXPN; EXPS; LAIT 2; LATS 1:2; MAICYA 1, 2; MTCW 1, 2; MTFW 2005; NFS 2; RGEL 2; RGSF 2; SATA 38, 40; SATA-Brief 38; SSFS 3, 13; TWA; WLIT 2; WWE 1

Acker, Kathy 1948-1997 .... **CLC 45, 111; TCLC 191**
See also AMWS 12; CA 117; 122; 162; CANR 55; CN 5, 6; MAL 5

Ackroyd, Peter 1949- .. **CLC 34, 52, 140, 256**
See also BRWS 6; CA 123; 127; CANR 51, 74, 99, 132, 175; CN 4, 5, 6, 7; DLB 155, 231; HGG; INT CA-127; MTCW 2; MTFW 2005; RHW; SATA 153; SUFW 2

Acorn, Milton 1923-1986 .... **CLC 15**
See also CA 103; CCA 1; CP 1, 2, 3, 4; DAC; DLB 53; INT CA-103

Adam de la Halle c. 1250-c.
1285 .... **CMLC 80**

Adamov, Arthur 1908-1970 .... **CLC 4, 25; TCLC 189**
See also CA 17-18; 25-28R; CAP 2; DAM DRAM; DLB 321; EWL 3; GFL 1789 to the Present; MTCW 1; RGWL 2, 3

Adams, Alice 1926-1999 .... **CLC 6, 13, 46; SSC 24**
See also CA 81-84; 179; CANR 26, 53, 75, 88, 136; CN 4, 5, 6; CSW; DLB 234; DLBY 1986; INT CANR-26; MTCW 1, 2; MTFW 2005; SSFS 14, 21

Adams, Andy 1859-1935 .... **TCLC 56**
See also TCWW 1, 2; YABC 1

Adams, (Henry) Brooks
1848-1927 .... **TCLC 80**
See also CA 123; 193

Adams, Douglas 1952-2001 .... **CLC 27, 60**
See also AAYA 4, 33; BEST 89:3; BYA 14; CA 106; 197; CANR 34, 64, 124; CPW; DA3; DAM POP; DLB 261; DLBY 1983; JRDA; MTCW 2; MTFW 2005; NFS 7; SATA 116; SATA-Obit 128; SFW 4

Adams, Francis 1862-1893 .... **NCLC 33**

Adams, Henry (Brooks)
1838-1918 .... **TCLC 4, 52**
See also AMW; CA 104; 133; CANR 77; DA; DAB; DAC; DAM MST; DLB 12, 47, 189, 284; EWL 3; MAL 5; MTCW 2; NCFS 1; RGAL 4; TUS

Adams, John 1735-1826 .... **NCLC 106**
See also DLB 31, 183

Adams, John Quincy 1767-1848 .. **NCLC 175**
See also DLB 37

Adams, Mary
See Phelps, Elizabeth Stuart

Adams, Richard (George) 1920- ... **CLC 4, 5, 18**
See also AAYA 16; AITN 1, 2; BPFB 1; BYA 5; CA 49-52; CANR 3, 35, 128; CLR 20, 121; CN 4, 5, 6, 7; DAM NOV; DLB 261; FANT; JRDA; LAIT 5; MAICYA 1, 2; MTCW 1, 2; NFS 11; SATA 7, 69; YAW

Adamson, Joy(-Friederike Victoria)
1910-1980 .... **CLC 17**
See also CA 69-72; 93-96; CANR 22; MTCW 1; SATA 11; SATA-Obit 22

Adcock, Fleur 1934- .... **CLC 41**
See also BRWS 12; CA 25-28R, 182; CAAE 182; CAAS 23; CANR 11, 34, 69, 101; CP 1, 2, 3, 4, 5, 6, 7; CWP; DLB 40; FW; WWE 1

Addams, Charles 1912-1988 .... **CLC 30**
See also CA 61-64; 126; CANR 12, 79

Addams, Charles Samuel
See Addams, Charles

Addams, (Laura) Jane 1860-1935 . **TCLC 76**
See also AMWS 1; CA 194; DLB 303; FW

Addison, Joseph 1672-1719 .... **LC 18, 146**
See also BRW 3; CDBLB 1660-1789; DLB 101; RGEL 2; WLIT 3

Adichie, Chimamanda Ngozi
1977- .... **BLC 2:1**
See also CA 231

Adiga, Aravind 1974- .... **CLC 280**
See also CA 282

Adler, Alfred (F.) 1870-1937 .... **TCLC 61**
See also CA 119; 159

Adler, C(arole) S(chwerdtfeger)
1932- .... **CLC 35**
See also AAYA 4, 41; CA 89-92; CANR 19, 40, 101; CLR 78; JRDA; MAICYA 1, 2; SAAS 15; SATA 26, 63, 102, 126; YAW

Adler, Renata 1938- .... **CLC 8, 31**
See also CA 49-52; CANR 95; CN 4, 5, 6; MTCW 1

Adorno, Theodor W(iesengrund)
1903-1969 .... **TCLC 111**
See also CA 89-92; 25-28R; CANR 89; DLB 242; EWL 3

Ady, Endre 1877-1919 .... **TCLC 11**
See also CA 107; CDWLB 4; DLB 215; EW 9; EWL 3

A.E.
See Russell, George William

Apollonius of Rhodes
See Apollonius Rhodius
Apollonius Rhodius c. 300B.C.-c.
220B.C. .... **CMLC 28**
See also AW 1; DLB 176; RGWL 2, 3
Appelfeld, Aharon 1932- ... **CLC 23, 47; SSC 42**
See also CA 112; 133; CANR 86, 160;
CWW 2; DLB 299; EWL 3; RGHL;
RGSF 2; WLIT 6
Appelfeld, Aron
See Appelfeld, Aharon
Apple, Max (Isaac) 1941- .... **CLC 9, 33; SSC 50**
See also AMWS 17; CA 81-84; CANR 19,
54; DLB 130
Appleman, Philip (Dean) 1926- .... **CLC 51**
See also CA 13-16R; CAAS 18; CANR 6,
29, 56
Appleton, Lawrence
See Lovecraft, H. P.
Apteryx
See Eliot, T(homas) S(tearns)
Apuleius, (Lucius Madaurensis) c. 125-c.
164 .... **CMLC 1, 84**
See also AW 2; CDWLB 1; DLB 211;
RGWL 2, 3; SUFW; WLIT 8
Aquin, Hubert 1929-1977 .... **CLC 15**
See also CA 105; DLB 53; EWL 3
Aquinas, Thomas 1224(?)-1274 ..... **CMLC 33**
See also DLB 115; EW 1; TWA
Aragon, Louis 1897-1982 .... **CLC 3, 22; TCLC 123**
See also CA 69-72; 108; CANR 28, 71;
DAM NOV, POET; DLB 72, 258; EW 11;
EWL 3; GFL 1789 to the Present; GLL 2;
LMFS 2; MTCW 1, 2; RGWL 2, 3
Arany, Janos 1817-1882 .... **NCLC 34**
Aranyos, Kakay 1847-1910
See Mikszath, Kalman
Aratus of Soli c. 315B.C.-c.
240B.C. .... **CMLC 64, 114**
See also DLB 176
Arbuthnot, John 1667-1735 .... **LC 1**
See also DLB 101
Archer, Herbert Winslow
See Mencken, H. L.
Archer, Jeffrey 1940- .... **CLC 28**
See also AAYA 16; BEST 89:3; BPFB 1;
CA 77-80; CANR 22, 52, 95, 136; CPW;
DA3; DAM POP; INT CANR-22; MTFW
2005
Archer, Jeffrey Howard
See Archer, Jeffrey
Archer, Jules 1915- .... **CLC 12**
See also CA 9-12R; CANR 6, 69; SAAS 5;
SATA 4, 85
Archer, Lee
See Ellison, Harlan
Archilochus c. 7th cent. B.C.- .... **CMLC 44**
See also DLB 176
Ard, William
See Jakes, John
Arden, John 1930- .... **CLC 6, 13, 15**
See also BRWS 2; CA 13-16R; CAAS 4;
CANR 31, 65, 67, 124; CBD; CD 5, 6;
DAM DRAM; DFS 9; DLB 13, 245;
EWL 3; MTCW 1
Arenas, Reinaldo 1943-1990 .. **CLC 41; HLC 1; TCLC 191**
See also CA 124; 128; 133; CANR 73, 106;
DAM MULT; DLB 145; EWL 3; GLL 2;
HW 1; LAW; LAWS 1; MTCW 2; MTFW
2005; RGSF 2; RGWL 3; WLIT 1
Arendt, Hannah 1906-1975 .... **CLC 66, 98; TCLC 193**
See also CA 17-20R; 61-64; CANR 26, 60,
172; DLB 242; MTCW 1, 2

Aretino, Pietro 1492-1556 .... **LC 12, 165**
See also RGWL 2, 3
Arghezi, Tudor
See Theodorescu, Ion N.
Arguedas, Jose Maria 1911-1969 .... **CLC 10, 18; HLCS 1; TCLC 147**
See also CA 89-92; CANR 73; DLB 113;
EWL 3; HW 1; LAW; RGWL 2, 3; WLIT 1
Argueta, Manlio 1936- .... **CLC 31**
See also CA 131; CANR 73; CWW 2; DLB
145; EWL 3; HW 1; RGWL 3
Arias, Ron 1941- .... **HLC 1**
See also CA 131; CANR 81, 136; DAM
MULT; DLB 82; HW 1, 2; MTCW 2;
MTFW 2005
Ariosto, Lodovico
See Ariosto, Ludovico
Ariosto, Ludovico 1474-1533 ... **LC 6, 87; PC 42**
See also EW 2; RGWL 2, 3; WLIT 7
Aristides
See Epstein, Joseph
Aristophanes 450B.C.-385B.C. .... **CMLC 4, 51; DC 2; WLCS**
See also AW 1; CDWLB 1; DA; DA3;
DAB; DAC; DAM DRAM, MST; DFS
10; DLB 176; LMFS 1; RGWL 2, 3;
TWA; WLIT 8
Aristotle 384B.C.-322B.C. .... **CMLC 31; WLCS**
See also AW 1; CDWLB 1; DA; DA3;
DAB; DAC; DAM MST; DLB 176;
RGWL 2, 3; TWA; WLIT 8
Arlt, Roberto (Godofredo Christophersen)
1900-1942 .... **HLC 1; TCLC 29**
See also CA 123; 131; CANR 67; DAM
MULT; DLB 305; EWL 3; HW 1, 2;
IDTP; LAW
Armah, Ayi Kwei 1939- . **BLC 1:1, 2:1; CLC 5, 33, 136**
See also AFW; BRWS 10; BW 1; CA 61-
64; CANR 21, 64; CDWLB 3; CN 1, 2,
3, 4, 5, 6, 7; DAM MULT, POET; DLB
117; EWL 3; MTCW 1; WLIT 2
Armatrading, Joan 1950- .... **CLC 17**
See also CA 114; 186
Armin, Robert 1568(?)-1615(?) .... **LC 120**
Armitage, Frank
See Carpenter, John (Howard)
Armstrong, Jeannette (C.) 1948- .... **NNAL**
See also CA 149; CCA 1; CN 6, 7; DAC;
DLB 334; SATA 102
Arnauld, Antoine 1612-1694 .... **LC 169**
See also DLB 268
Arnette, Robert
See Silverberg, Robert
Arnim, Achim von (Ludwig Joachim von Arnim) 1781-1831 .. **NCLC 5, 159; SSC 29**
See also DLB 90
Arnim, Bettina von 1785-1859 ...... **NCLC 38, 123**
See also DLB 90; RGWL 2, 3
Arnold, Matthew 1822-1888 ..... **NCLC 6, 29, 89, 126, 218; PC 5, 94; WLC 1**
See also BRW 5; CDBLB 1832-1890; DA;
DAB; DAC; DAM MST, POET; DLB 32,
57; EXPP; PAB; PFS 2; TEA; WP
Arnold, Thomas 1795-1842 .... **NCLC 18**
See also DLB 55
Arnow, Harriette (Louisa) Simpson
1908-1986 .... **CLC 2, 7, 18; TCLC 196**
See also BPFB 1; CA 9-12R; 118; CANR
14; CN 2, 3, 4; DLB 6; FW; MTCW 1, 2;
RHW; SATA 42; SATA-Obit 47
Arouet, Francois-Marie
See Voltaire

Arp, Hans
See Arp, Jean
Arp, Jean 1887-1966 .... **CLC 5; TCLC 115**
See also CA 81-84; 25-28R; CANR 42, 77;
EW 10
Arrabal
See Arrabal, Fernando
Arrabal, Fernando 1932- .. **CLC 2, 9, 18, 58; DC 35**
See also CA 9-12R; CANR 15; CWW 2;
DLB 321; EWL 3; LMFS 2
Arrabal Teran, Fernando
See Arrabal, Fernando
Arreola, Juan Jose 1918-2001 .... **CLC 147; HLC 1; SSC 38**
See also CA 113; 131; 200; CANR 81;
CWW 2; DAM MULT; DNFS 2; EWL 3; HW 1, 2; LAW; RGSF 2
Arrian c. 89(?)-c. 155(?) .... **CMLC 43**
See also DLB 176
Arrick, Fran
See Angell, Judie
Arrley, Richmond
See Delany, Samuel R., Jr.
Artaud, Antonin (Marie Joseph)
1896-1948 .... **DC 14; TCLC 3, 36**
See also CA 104; 149; DA3; DAM DRAM;
DFS 22; DLB 258, 321; EW 11; EWL 3;
GFL 1789 to the Present; MTCW 2;
MTFW 2005; RGWL 2, 3
Arthur, Ruth M(abel) 1905-1979 ..... **CLC 12**
See also CA 9-12R; 85-88; CANR 4; CWRI
5; SATA 7, 26
Artsybashev, Mikhail (Petrovich)
1878-1927 .... **TCLC 31**
See also CA 170; DLB 295
Arundel, Honor (Morfydd)
1919-1973 .... **CLC 17**
See also CA 21-22; 41-44R; CAP 2; CLR
35; CWRI 5; SATA 4; SATA-Obit 24
Arzner, Dorothy 1900-1979 .... **CLC 98**
Asch, Sholem 1880-1957 .... **TCLC 3**
See also CA 105; DLB 333; EWL 3; GLL
2; RGHL
Ascham, Roger 1516(?)-1568 .... **LC 101**
See also DLB 236
Ash, Shalom
See Asch, Sholem
Ashbery, John 1927- ... **CLC 2, 3, 4, 6, 9, 13, 15, 25, 41, 77, 125, 221; PC 26**
See also AMWS 3; CA 5-8R; CANR 9, 37,
66, 102, 132, 170; CP 1, 2, 3, 4, 5, 6, 7;
DA3; DAM POET; DLB 5, 165; DLBY
1981; EWL 3; GLL 1; INT CANR-9;
MAL 5; MTCW 1, 2; MTFW 2005; PAB;
PFS 11, 28; RGAL 4; TCLE 1:1; WP
Ashbery, John Lawrence
See Ashbery, John
Ashbridge, Elizabeth 1713-1755 .... **LC 147**
See also DLB 200
Ashdown, Clifford
See Freeman, R(ichard) Austin
Ashe, Gordon
See Creasey, John
Ashton-Warner, Sylvia (Constance)
1908-1984 .... **CLC 19**
See also CA 69-72; 112; CANR 29; CN 1,
2, 3; MTCW 1, 2
Asimov, Isaac 1920-1992 ..... **CLC 1, 3, 9, 19, 26, 76, 92**
See also AAYA 13; BEST 90:2; BPFB 1;
BYA 4, 6, 7, 9; CA 1-4R; CANR 2,
19, 36, 60, 125; CLR 12, 79; CMW 4;
CN 1, 2, 3, 4, 5; CPW; DA3; DAM POP;
DLB 8; DLBY 1992; INT CANR-19;
JRDA; LAIT 5; LMFS 2; MAICYA 1, 2;
MAL 5; MTCW 1, 2; MTFW 2005; NFS
29; RGAL 4; SATA 1, 26, 74; SCFW 1,
2; SFW 4; SSFS 17; TUS; YAW

Bachmann, Ingeborg 1926-1973 ..... **CLC 69;**
  TCLC 192
    See also CA 93-96; 45-48; CANR 69; DLB
    85; EWL 3; RGHL; RGWL 2, 3
Bacon, Francis 1561-1626 ..... **LC 18, 32, 131**
    See also BRW 1; CDBLB Before 1660;
    DLB 151, 236, 252; RGEL 2; TEA
Bacon, Roger 1214(?)-1294 ... **CMLC 14, 108**
    See also DLB 115
Bacovia, G.
    See Bacovia, George
Bacovia, George 1881-1957 .... **TCLC 24**
    See Bacovia, George
    See also CA 123; 189; CDWLB 4; DLB
    220; EWL 3
Badanes, Jerome 1937-1995 .... **CLC 59**
    See also CA 234
Bage, Robert 1728-1801 .... **NCLC 182**
    See also DLB 39; RGEL 2
Bagehot, Walter 1826-1877 .... **NCLC 10**
    See also DLB 55
Bagnold, Enid 1889-1981 .... **CLC 25**
    See also AAYA 75; BYA 2; CA 5-8R; 103;
    CANR 5, 40; CBD; CN 2; CWD; CWRI
    5; DAM DRAM; DLB 13, 160, 191, 245;
    FW; MAICYA 1, 2; RGEL 2; SATA 1, 25
Bagritsky, Eduard
    See Dzyubin, Eduard Georgievich
Bagritsky, Edvard
    See Dzyubin, Eduard Georgievich
Bagrjana, Elisaveta
    See Belcheva, Elisaveta Lyubomirova
Bagryana, Elisaveta
    See Belcheva, Elisaveta Lyubomirova
Bailey, Paul 1937- .... **CLC 45**
    See also CA 21-24R; CANR 16, 62, 124;
    CN 1, 2, 3, 4, 5, 6, 7; DLB 14, 271; GLL
    2
Baillie, Joanna 1762-1851 ...... **NCLC 71, 151**
    See also DLB 93, 344; GL 2; RGEL 2
Bainbridge, Beryl 1934- ...... **CLC 4, 5, 8, 10,**
  14, 18, 22, 62, 130
    See also BRWS 6; CA 21-24R; CANR 24,
    55, 75, 88, 128; CN 2, 3, 4, 5, 6, 7; DAM
    NOV; DLB 14, 231; EWL 3; MTCW 1,
    2; MTFW 2005
Baker, Carlos (Heard)
  1909-1987 .... **TCLC 119**
    See also CA 5-8R; 122; CANR 3, 63; DLB
    103
Baker, Elliott 1922-2007 .... **CLC 8**
    See also CA 45-48; 257; CANR 2, 63; CN
    1, 2, 3, 4, 5, 6, 7
Baker, Elliott Joseph
    See Baker, Elliott
Baker, Jean H.
    See Russell, George William
Baker, Nicholson 1957- .... **CLC 61, 165**
    See also AMWS 13; CA 135; CANR 63,
    120, 138, 190; CN 6; CPW; DA3; DAM
    POP; DLB 227; MTFW 2005
Baker, Ray Stannard 1870-1946 .... **TCLC 47**
    See also CA 118; DLB 345
Baker, Russell 1925- .... **CLC 31**
    See also BEST 89:4; CA 57-60; CANR 11,
    41, 59, 137; MTCW 1, 2; MTFW 2005
Bakhtin, M.
    See Bakhtin, Mikhail Mikhailovich
Bakhtin, M. M.
    See Bakhtin, Mikhail Mikhailovich
Bakhtin, Mikhail
    See Bakhtin, Mikhail Mikhailovich
Bakhtin, Mikhail Mikhailovich
  1895-1975 .... **CLC 83; TCLC 160**
    See also CA 128; 113; DLB 242; EWL 3
Bakshi, Ralph 1938(?)- .... **CLC 26**
    See also CA 112; 138; IDFW 3

Bakunin, Mikhail (Alexandrovich)
  1814-1876 .... **NCLC 25, 58**
    See also DLB 277
Bal, Mieke (Maria Gertrudis)
  1946- .... **CLC 252**
    See also CA 156; CANR 99
Baldwin, James 1924-1987 ...... **BLC 1:1, 2:1;**
  CLC 1, 2, 3, 4, 5, 8, 13, 15, 17, 42, 50,
  67, 90, 127; DC 1; SSC 10, 33, 98;
  WLC 1
    See also AAYA 4, 34; AFAW 1, 2; AMWR
    2; AMWS 1; BPFB 1; BW 1; CA 1-4R;
    124; CABS 1; CAD; CANR 3, 24;
    CDALB 1941-1968; CN 1, 2, 3, 4; CPW;
    DA; DA3; DAB; DAC; DAM MST,
    MULT, NOV, POP; DFS 11, 15; DLB 2,
    7, 33, 249, 278; DLBY 1987; EWL 3;
    EXPS; LAIT 5; MAL 5; MTCW 1, 2;
    MTFW 2005; NCFS 4; NFS 4; RGAL 4;
    RGSF 2; SATA 9; SATA-Obit 54; SSFS
    2, 18; TUS
Baldwin, William c. 1515-1563 .... **LC 113**
    See also DLB 132
Bale, John 1495-1563 .... **LC 62**
    See also DLB 132; RGEL 2; TEA
Ball, Hugo 1886-1927 .... **TCLC 104**
Ballard, James G.
    See Ballard, J.G.
Ballard, James Graham
    See Ballard, J.G.
Ballard, J.G. 1930-2009 ..... **CLC 3, 6, 14, 36,**
  137; SSC 1, 53
    See also AAYA 3, 52; BRWS 5; CA 5-8R;
    285; CANR 15, 39, 65, 107, 133; CN 1,
    2, 3, 4, 5, 6, 7; DA3; DAM NOV, POP;
    DLB 14, 207, 261, 319; EWL 3; HGG;
    MTCW 1, 2; MTFW 2005; NFS 8; RGEL
    2; RGSF 2; SATA 93; SATA-Obit 203;
    SCFW 1, 2; SFW 4
Ballard, Jim G.
    See Ballard, J.G.
Balmont, Konstantin (Dmitriyevich)
  1867-1943 .... **TCLC 11**
    See also CA 109; 155; DLB 295; EWL 3
Baltausis, Vincas 1847-1910
    See Mikszath, Kalman
Balzac, Guez de (?)-
    See Balzac, Jean-Louis Guez de
Balzac, Honore de 1799-1850 ... **NCLC 5, 35,**
  53, 153; SSC 5, 59, 102; WLC 1
    See also DA; DA3; DAB; DAC; DAM
    MST, NOV; DLB 119; EW 5; GFL 1789
    to the Present; LMFS 1; RGSF 2; RGWL
    2, 3; SSFS 10; SUFW; TWA
Balzac, Jean-Louis Guez de
  1597-1654 .... **LC 162**
    See also DLB 268; GFL Beginnings to 1789
Bambara, Toni Cade 1939-1995 ..... **BLC 1:1,**
  2:1; CLC 19, 88; SSC 35, 107; TCLC
  116; WLCS
    See also AAYA 5, 49; AFAW 2; AMWS 11;
    BW 2, 3; BYA 12, 14; CA 29-32R; 150;
    CANR 24, 49, 81; CDALBS; DA; DA3;
    DAC; DAM MST, MULT; DLB 38, 218;
    EXPS; MAL 5; MTCW 1, 2; MTFW
    2005; RGAL 4; RGSF 2; SATA 112; SSFS
    4, 7, 12, 21
Bamdad, A.
    See Shamlu, Ahmad
Bamdad, Alef
    See Shamlu, Ahmad
Banat, D. R.
    See Bradbury, Ray
Bancroft, Laura
    See Baum, L(yman) Frank
Banim, John 1798-1842 .... **NCLC 13**
    See also DLB 116, 158, 159; RGEL 2
Banim, Michael 1796-1874 .... **NCLC 13**
    See also DLB 158, 159

Banjo, The
    See Paterson, A(ndrew) B(arton)
Banks, Iain 1954- .... **CLC 34**
    See also BRWS 11; CA 123; 128; CANR
    61, 106, 180; DLB 194, 261; EWL 3;
    HGG; INT CA-128; MTFW 2005; SFW 4
Banks, Iain M.
    See Banks, Iain
Banks, Iain Menzies
    See Banks, Iain
Banks, Lynne Reid
    See Reid Banks, Lynne
Banks, Russell 1940- . **CLC 37, 72, 187; SSC**
  42
    See also AAYA 45; AMWS 5; CA 65-68;
    CAAS 15; CANR 19, 52, 73, 118; CN 4,
    5, 6, 7; DLB 130, 278; EWL 3; MAL 5;
    MTCW 2; MTFW 2005; NFS 13
Banks, Russell Earl
    See Banks, Russell
Banville, John 1945- .... **CLC 46, 118, 224**
    See also CA 117; 128; CANR 104, 150,
    176; CN 4, 5, 6, 7; DLB 14, 271, 326;
    INT CA-128
Banville, Theodore (Faullain) de
  1832-1891 .... **NCLC 9**
    See also DLB 217; GFL 1789 to the Present
Baraka, Amiri 1934- .. **BLC 1:1, 2:1; CLC 1,**
  2, 3, 5, 10, 14, 33, 115, 213; DC 6; PC
  4; WLCS
    See also AAYA 63; AFAW 1, 2; AMWS 2;
    BW 2, 3; CA 21-24R; CABS 3; CAD;
    CANR 27, 38, 61, 133, 172; CD 3, 5, 6;
    CDALB 1941-1968; CN 1, 2; CP 1, 2, 3,
    4, 5, 6, 7; CPW; DA; DA3; DAC; DAM
    MST, MULT, POET, POP; DFS 3, 11, 16;
    DLB 5, 7, 16, 38; DLBD 8; EWL 3; MAL
    5; MTCW 1, 2; MTFW 2005; PFS 9;
    RGAL 4; TCLE 1:1; TUS; WP
Baratynsky, Evgenii Abramovich
  1800-1844 .... **NCLC 103**
    See also DLB 205
Barbauld, Anna Laetitia
  1743-1825 .... **NCLC 50, 185**
    See also DLB 107, 109, 142, 158, 336;
    RGEL 2
Barbellion, W. N. P.
    See Cummings, Bruce F.
Barber, Benjamin R. 1939- .... **CLC 141**
    See also CA 29-32R; CANR 12, 32, 64, 119
Barbera, Jack (Vincent) 1945- .... **CLC 44**
    See also CA 110; CANR 45
Barbey d'Aurevilly, Jules-Amedee
  1808-1889 .... **NCLC 1, 213; SSC 17**
    See also DLB 119; GFL 1789 to the Present
Barbour, John c. 1316-1395 .... **CMLC 33**
    See also DLB 146
Barbusse, Henri 1873-1935 .... **TCLC 5**
    See also CA 105; 154; DLB 65; EWL 3;
    RGWL 2, 3
Barclay, Alexander c. 1475-1552 .... **LC 109**
    See also DLB 132
Barclay, Bill
    See Moorcock, Michael
Barclay, William Ewert
    See Moorcock, Michael
Barea, Arturo 1897-1957 .... **TCLC 14**
    See also CA 111; 201
Barfoot, Joan 1946- .... **CLC 18**
    See also CA 105; CANR 141, 179
Barham, Richard Harris
  1788-1845 .... **NCLC 77**
    See also DLB 159
Baring, Maurice 1874-1945 .... **TCLC 8**
    See also CA 105; 168; DLB 34; HGG
Baring-Gould, Sabine 1834-1924 ... **TCLC 88**
    See also DLB 156, 190

Beagle, Peter S. 1939- .... **CLC 7, 104**
See also AAYA 47; BPFB 1; BYA 9, 10, 16; CA 9-12R; CANR 4, 51, 73, 110; DA3; DLBY 1980; FANT; INT CANR-4; MTCW 2; MTFW 2005; SATA 60, 130; SUFW 1, 2; YAW

Beagle, Peter Soyer
See Beagle, Peter S.

Bean, Normal
See Burroughs, Edgar Rice

Beard, Charles A(ustin)
1874-1948 .... **TCLC 15**
See also CA 115; 189; DLB 17; SATA 18

Beardsley, Aubrey 1872-1898 .... **NCLC 6**

Beatrice of Nazareth 1200-1268 .. **CMLC 114**

Beattie, Ann 1947- ..... **CLC 8, 13, 18, 40, 63, 146; SSC 11**
See also AMWS 5; BEST 90:2; BPFB 1; CA 81-84; CANR 53, 73, 128; CN 4, 5, 6, 7; CPW; DA3; DAM NOV, POP; DLB 218, 278; DLBY 1982; EWL 3; MAL 5; MTCW 1, 2; MTFW 2005; RGAL 4; RGSF 2; SSFS 9; TUS

Beattie, James 1735-1803 .... **NCLC 25**
See also DLB 109

Beauchamp, Kathleen Mansfield
1888-1923 . **SSC 9, 23, 38, 81; TCLC 2, 8, 39, 164; WLC 4**
See also BPFB 2; BRW 7; CA 104; 134; DA; DA3; DAB; DAC; DAM MST; DLB 162; EWL 3; EXPS; FW; GLL 1; MTCW 2; RGEL 2; RGSF 2; SSFS 2, 8, 10, 11; TEA; WWE 1

Beaumarchais, Pierre-Augustin Caron de
1732-1799 .... **DC 4; LC 61**
See also DAM DRAM; DFS 14, 16; DLB 313; EW 4; GFL Beginnings to 1789; RGWL 2, 3

Beaumont, Francis 1584(?)-1616 .. **DC 6; LC 33**
See also BRW 2; CDBLB Before 1660; DLB 58; TEA

Beauvoir, Simone de 1908-1986 .... **CLC 1, 2, 4, 8, 14, 31, 44, 50, 71, 124; SSC 35; TCLC 221; WLC 1**
See also BPFB 1; CA 9-12R; 118; CANR 28, 61; DA; DA3; DAB; DAC; DAM MST, NOV; DLB 72; DLBY 1986; EW 12; EWL 3; FL 1:5; FW; GFL 1789 to the Present; LMFS 2; MTCW 1, 2; MTFW 2005; RGSF 2; RGWL 2, 3; TWA

Beauvoir, Simone Lucie Ernestine Marie Bertrand de
See Beauvoir, Simone de

Becker, Carl (Lotus) 1873-1945 ..... **TCLC 63**
See also CA 157; DLB 17

Becker, Jurek 1937-1997 .... **CLC 7, 19**
See also CA 85-88; 157; CANR 60, 117; CWW 2; DLB 75, 299; EWL 3; RGHL

Becker, Walter 1950- .... **CLC 26**

Becket, Thomas a 1118(?)-1170 .... **CMLC 83**

Beckett, Samuel 1906-1989 ... **CLC 1, 2, 3, 4, 6, 9, 10, 11, 14, 18, 29, 57, 59, 83; DC 22; SSC 16, 74; TCLC 145; WLC 1**
See also BRWC 2; BRWR 1; BRWS 1; CA 5-8R; 130; CANR 33, 61; CBD; CDBLB 1945-1960; CN 1, 2, 3, 4; DA; DA3; DAB; DAC; DAM DRAM, MST, NOV; DFS 2, 7, 18; DLB 13, 15, 233, 319, 321, 329; DLBY 1990; EWL 3; GFL 1789 to the Present; LATS 1:2; LMFS 2; MTCW 1, 2; MTFW 2005; RGSF 2; RGWL 2, 3; SSFS 15; TEA; WLIT 4

Beckford, William 1760-1844 .... **NCLC 16, 214**
See also BRW 3; DLB 39, 213; GL 2; HGG; LMFS 1; SUFW

Beckham, Barry (Earl) 1944- .... **BLC 1:1**
See also BW 1; CA 29-32R; CANR 26, 62; CN 1, 2, 3, 4, 5, 6; DAM MULT; DLB 33

Beckman, Gunnel 1910- .... **CLC 26**
See also CA 33-36R; CANR 15, 114; CLR 25; MAICYA 1, 2; SAAS 9; SATA 6

Becque, Henri 1837-1899 .... **DC 21; NCLC 3**
See also DLB 192; GFL 1789 to the Present

Becquer, Gustavo Adolfo
1836-1870 .... **HLCS 1; NCLC 106**
See also DAM MULT

Beddoes, Thomas Lovell 1803-1849 .. **DC 15; NCLC 3, 154**
See also BRWS 11; DLB 96

Bede c. 673-735 .... **CMLC 20**
See also DLB 146; TEA

Bedford, Denton R. 1907-(?) .... **NNAL**

Bedford, Donald F.
See Fearing, Kenneth (Flexner)

Beecher, Catharine Esther
1800-1878 .... **NCLC 30**
See also DLB 1, 243

Beecher, John 1904-1980 .... **CLC 6**
See also AITN 1; CA 5-8R; 105; CANR 8; CP 1, 2, 3

Beer, Johann 1655-1700 .... **LC 5**
See also DLB 168

Beer, Patricia 1924- .... **CLC 58**
See also BRWS 14; CA 61-64; 183; CANR 13, 46; CP 1, 2, 3, 4, 5, 6; CWP; DLB 40; FW

Beerbohm, Max
See Beerbohm, (Henry) Max(imilian)

Beerbohm, (Henry) Max(imilian)
1872-1956 .... **TCLC 1, 24**
See also BRWS 2; CA 104; 154; CANR 79; DLB 34, 100; FANT; MTCW 2

Beer-Hofmann, Richard
1866-1945 .... **TCLC 60**
See also CA 160; DLB 81

Beg, Shemus
See Stephens, James

Begiebing, Robert J(ohn) 1946- .... **CLC 70**
See also CA 122; CANR 40, 88

Begley, Louis 1933- .... **CLC 197**
See also CA 140; CANR 98, 176; DLB 299; RGHL; TCLE 1:1

Behan, Brendan (Francis)
1923-1964 .... **CLC 1, 8, 11, 15, 79**
See also BRWS 2; CA 73-76; CANR 33, 121; CBD; CDBLB 1945-1960; DAM DRAM; DFS 7; DLB 13, 233; EWL 3; MTCW 1, 2

Behn, Aphra 1640(?)-1689 .. **DC 4; LC 1, 30, 42, 135; PC 13, 88; WLC 1**
See also BRWS 3; DA; DA3; DAB; DAC; DAM DRAM, MST, NOV, POET; DFS 16, 24; DLB 39, 80, 131; FW; TEA; WLIT 3

Behrman, S(amuel) N(athaniel)
1893-1973 .... **CLC 40**
See also CA 13-16; 45-48; CAD; CAP 1; DLB 7, 44; IDFW 3; MAL 5; RGAL 4

Bekederemo, J. P. Clark
See Clark Bekederemo, J.P.

Belasco, David 1853-1931 .... **TCLC 3**
See also CA 104; 168; DLB 7; MAL 5; RGAL 4

Belben, Rosalind 1941- .... **CLC 280**

Belcheva, Elisaveta Lyubomirova
1893-1991 .... **CLC 10**
See also CA 178; CDWLB 4; DLB 147; EWL 3

Beldone, Phil "Cheech"
See Ellison, Harlan

Beleno
See Azuela, Mariano

Belinski, Vissarion Grigoryevich
1811-1848 .... **NCLC 5**
See also DLB 198

Belitt, Ben 1911- .... **CLC 22**
See also CA 13-16R; CAAS 4; CANR 7, 77; CP 1, 2, 3, 4, 5, 6; DLB 5

Belknap, Jeremy 1744-1798 .... **LC 115**
See also DLB 30, 37

Bell, Gertrude (Margaret Lowthian)
1868-1926 .... **TCLC 67**
See also CA 167; CANR 110; DLB 174

Bell, J. Freeman
See Zangwill, Israel

Bell, James Madison 1826-1902 ..... **BLC 1:1; TCLC 43**
See also BW 1; CA 122; 124; DAM MULT; DLB 50

Bell, Madison Smartt 1957- ..... **CLC 41, 102, 223**
See also AMWS 10; BPFB 1; CA 111, 183; CAAE 183; CANR 28, 54, 73, 134, 176; CN 5, 6, 7; CSW; DLB 218, 278; MTCW 2; MTFW 2005

Bell, Marvin (Hartley) 1937- ...... **CLC 8, 31; PC 79**
See also CA 21-24R; CAAS 14; CANR 59, 102; CP 1, 2, 3, 4, 5, 6, 7; DAM POET; DLB 5; MAL 5; MTCW 1; PFS 25

Bell, W. L. D.
See Mencken, H. L.

Bellamy, Atwood C.
See Mencken, H. L.

Bellamy, Edward 1850-1898 ..... **NCLC 4, 86, 147**
See also DLB 12; NFS 15; RGAL 4; SFW 4

Belli, Gioconda 1948- .... **HLCS 1**
See also CA 152; CANR 143; CWW 2; DLB 290; EWL 3; RGWL 3

Bellin, Edward J.
See Kuttner, Henry

Bello, Andres 1781-1865 .... **NCLC 131**
See also LAW

Belloc, (Joseph) Hilaire (Pierre Sebastien Rene Swanton) 1870-1953 .... **PC 24; TCLC 7, 18**
See also CA 106; 152; CLR 102; CWRI 5; DAM POET; DLB 19, 100, 141, 174; EWL 3; MTCW 2; MTFW 2005; SATA 112; WCH; YABC 1

Belloc, Joseph Peter Rene Hilaire
See Belloc, (Joseph) Hilaire (Pierre Sebastien Rene Swanton)

Belloc, Joseph Pierre Hilaire
See Belloc, (Joseph) Hilaire (Pierre Sebastien Rene Swanton)

Belloc, M. A.
See Lowndes, Marie Adelaide (Belloc)

Belloc-Lowndes, Mrs.
See Lowndes, Marie Adelaide (Belloc)

Bellow, Saul 1915-2005 ...... **CLC 1, 2, 3, 6, 8, 10, 13, 15, 25, 33, 34, 63, 79, 190, 200; SSC 14, 101; WLC 1**
See also AITN 2; AMW; AMWC 2; AMWR 2; BEST 89:3; BPFB 1; CA 5-8R; 238; CABS 1; CANR 29, 53, 95, 132; CDALB 1941-1968; CN 1, 2, 3, 4, 5, 6, 7; DA; DA3; DAB; DAC; DAM MST, NOV, POP; DLB 2, 28, 299, 329; DLBD 3; DLBY 1982; EWL 3; MAL 5; MTCW 1, 2; MTFW 2005; NFS 4, 14, 26; RGAL 4; RGHL; RGSF 2; SSFS 12, 22; TUS

Belser, Reimond Karel Maria de
1929- .... **CLC 14**
See also CA 152

Bely, Andrey
See Bugayev, Boris Nikolayevich

Belyi, Andrei
See Bugayev, Boris Nikolayevich

Berrigan, Daniel 1921- .... **CLC 4**
    See also CA 33-36R, 187; CAAE 187;
    CAAS 1; CANR 11, 43, 78; CP 1, 2, 3, 4,
    5, 6, 7; DLB 5
Berrigan, Edmund Joseph Michael, Jr.
    1934-1983 .... **CLC 37**
    See also CA 61-64; 110; CANR 14, 102;
    CP 1, 2, 3; DLB 5, 169; WP
Berrigan, Ted
    See Berrigan, Edmund Joseph Michael, Jr.
Berry, Charles Edward Anderson
    1931- .... **CLC 17**
    See also CA 115
Berry, Chuck
    See Berry, Charles Edward Anderson
Berry, Jonas
    See Ashbery, John
Berry, Wendell 1934- ..... **CLC 4, 6, 8, 27, 46,**
    279; PC 28
    See also AITN 1; AMWS 10; ANW; CA
    73-76; CANR 50, 73, 101, 132, 174; CP
    1, 2, 3, 4, 5, 6, 7; CSW; DAM POET;
    DLB 5, 6, 234, 275, 342; MTCW 2;
    MTFW 2005; PFS 30; TCLE 1:1
Berryman, John 1914-1972 ... **CLC 1, 2, 3, 4,**
    6, 8, 10, 13, 25, 62; PC 64
    See also AMW; CA 13-16; 33-36R; CABS
    2; CANR 35; CAP 1; CDALB 1941-1968;
    CP 1; DAM POET; DLB 48; EWL 3;
    MAL 5; MTCW 1, 2; MTFW 2005; PAB;
    PFS 27; RGAL 4; WP
Bertolucci, Bernardo 1940- ...... **CLC 16, 157**
    See also CA 106; CANR 125
Berton, Pierre (Francis de Marigny)
    1920-2004 .... **CLC 104**
    See also CA 1-4R; 233; CANR 2, 56, 144;
    CPW; DLB 68; SATA 99; SATA-Obit 158
Bertrand, Aloysius 1807-1841 .... **NCLC 31**
    See also DLB 217
Bertrand, Louis oAloysiusc
    See Bertrand, Aloysius
Bertran de Born c. 1140-1215 .... **CMLC 5**
Besant, Annie (Wood) 1847-1933 ..... **TCLC 9**
    See also CA 105; 185
Bessie, Alvah 1904-1985 .... **CLC 23**
    See also CA 5-8R; 116; CANR 2, 80; DLB
    26
Bestuzhev, Aleksandr Aleksandrovich
    1797-1837 .... **NCLC 131**
    See also DLB 198
Bethlen, T.D.
    See Silverberg, Robert
Beti, Mongo
    See Biyidi, Alexandre
Betjeman, John 1906-1984 ...... **CLC 2, 6, 10,**
    34, 43; PC 75
    See also BRW 7; CA 9-12R; 112; CANR
    33, 56; CDBLB 1945-1960; CP 1, 2, 3;
    DA3; DAB; DAM MST, POET; DLB 20;
    DLBY 1984; EWL 3; MTCW 1, 2
Bettelheim, Bruno 1903-1990 .... **CLC 79;**
    TCLC 143
    See also CA 81-84; 131; CANR 23, 61;
    DA3; MTCW 1, 2; RGHL
Betti, Ugo 1892-1953 .... **TCLC 5**
    See also CA 104; 155; EWL 3; RGWL 2, 3
Betts, Doris (Waugh) 1932- ..... **CLC 3, 6, 28,**
    275; SSC 45
    See also CA 13-16R; CANR 9, 66, 77; CN
    6, 7; CSW; DLB 218; DLBY 1982; INT
    CANR-9; RGAL 4
Bevan, Alistair
    See Roberts, Keith (John Kingston)
Bey, Pilaff
    See Douglas, (George) Norman
Beyala, Calixthe 1961- .... **BLC 2:1**
    See also EWL 3

Beynon, John
    See Harris, John (Wyndham Parkes Lucas)
    Beynon
Bialik, Chaim Nachman
    1873-1934 .... **TCLC 25, 201**
    See also CA 170; EWL 3; WLIT 6
Bialik, Hayyim Nahman
    See Bialik, Chaim Nachman
Bickerstaff, Isaac
    See Swift, Jonathan
Bidart, Frank 1939- .... **CLC 33**
    See also AMWS 15; CA 140; CANR 106;
    CP 5, 6, 7; PFS 26
Bienek, Horst 1930- .... **CLC 7, 11**
    See also CA 73-76; DLB 75
Bierce, Ambrose (Gwinett)
    1842-1914(?) . **SSC 9, 72, 124; TCLC 1,**
    7, 44; WLC 1
    See also AAYA 55; AMW; BYA 11; CA
    104; 139; CANR 78; CDALB 1865-1917;
    DA; DA3; DAC; DAM MST; DLB 11,
    12, 23, 71, 74, 186; EWL 3; EXPS; HGG;
    LAIT 2; MAL 5; RGAL 4; RGSF 2; SSFS
    9, 27; SUFW 1
Biggers, Earl Derr 1884-1933 .... **TCLC 65**
    See also CA 108; 153; DLB 306
Billiken, Bud
    See Motley, Willard (Francis)
Billings, Josh
    See Shaw, Henry Wheeler
Billington, (Lady) Rachel (Mary)
    1942- .... **CLC 43**
    See also AITN 2; CA 33-36R; CANR 44;
    CN 4, 5, 6, 7
Binchy, Maeve 1940- .... **CLC 153**
    See also BEST 90:1; BPFB 1; CA 127; 134;
    CANR 50, 96, 134; CN 5, 6, 7; CPW;
    DA3; DAM POP; DLB 319; INT CA-134;
    MTCW 2; MTFW 2005; RHW
Binyon, T(imothy) J(ohn)
    1936-2004 .... **CLC 34**
    See also CA 111; 232; CANR 28, 140
Bion 335B.C.-245B.C. .... **CMLC 39**
Bioy Casares, Adolfo 1914-1999 ... **CLC 4, 8,**
    13, 88; HLC 1; SSC 17, 102
    See also CA 29-32R; 177; CANR 19, 43,
    66; CWW 2; DAM MULT; DLB 113;
    EWL 3; HW 1, 2; LAW; MTCW 1, 2;
    MTFW 2005; RGSF 2
Birch, Allison CLC 65
Bird, Cordwainer
    See Ellison, Harlan
Bird, Robert Montgomery
    1806-1854 .... **NCLC 1, 197**
    See also DLB 202; RGAL 4
Birdwell, Cleo
    See DeLillo, Don
Birkerts, Sven 1951- .... **CLC 116**
    See also CA 128; 133, 176; CAAE 176;
    CAAS 29; CANR 151; INT CA-133
Birney, (Alfred) Earle 1904-1995 .. **CLC 1, 4,**
    6, 11; PC 52
    See also CA 1-4R; CANR 5, 20; CN 1, 2,
    3, 4; CP 1, 2, 3, 4, 5, 6; DAC; DAM MST,
    POET; DLB 88; MTCW 1; PFS 8; RGEL
    2
Biruni, al 973-1048(?) .... **CMLC 28**
Bishop, Elizabeth 1911-1979 ..... **CLC 1, 4, 9,**
    13, 15, 32; PC 3, 34; TCLC 121
    See also AMWR 2; AMWS 1; CA 5-8R;
    89-92; CABS 2; CANR 26, 61, 108;
    CDALB 1968-1988; CP 1, 2, 3; DA;
    DA3; DAC; DAM MST, POET; DLB 5,
    169; EWL 3; GLL 2; MAL 5; MBL;
    MTCW 1, 2; PAB; PFS 6, 12, 27, 31;
    RGAL 4; SATA-Obit 24; TUS; WP
Bishop, George Archibald
    See Crowley, Edward Alexander

Bishop, John 1935- .... **CLC 10**
    See also CA 105
Bishop, John Peale 1892-1944 ..... **TCLC 103**
    See also CA 107; 155; DLB 4, 9, 45; MAL
    5; RGAL 4
Bissett, Bill 1939- .... **CLC 18; PC 14**
    See also CA 69-72; CAAS 19; CANR 15;
    CCA 1; CP 1, 2, 3, 4, 5, 6, 7; DLB 53;
    MTCW 1
Bissoondath, Neil 1955- .... **CLC 120**
    See also CA 136; CANR 123, 165; CN 6,
    7; DAC
Bissoondath, Neil Devindra
    See Bissoondath, Neil
Bitov, Andrei (Georgievich) 1937- ... **CLC 57**
    See also CA 142; DLB 302
Biyidi, Alexandre 1932- ... **BLC 1:1; CLC 27**
    See also AFW; BW 1, 3; CA 114; 124;
    CANR 81; DA3; DAM MULT; EWL 3;
    MTCW 1, 2
Bjarme, Brynjolf
    See Ibsen, Henrik (Johan)
Bjoernson, Bjoernstjerne (Martinius)
    1832-1910 .... **TCLC 7, 37**
    See also CA 104
Black, Benjamin
    See Banville, John
Black, Robert
    See Holdstock, Robert
Blackburn, Paul 1926-1971 .... **CLC 9, 43**
    See also BG 1:2; CA 81-84; 33-36R; CANR
    34; CP 1; DLB 16; DLBY 1981
Black Elk 1863-1950 .... **NNAL; TCLC 33**
    See also CA 144; DAM MULT; MTCW 2;
    MTFW 2005; WP
Black Hawk 1767-1838 .... **NNAL**
Black Hobart
    See Sanders, Ed
Blacklin, Malcolm
    See Chambers, Aidan
Blackmore, R(ichard) D(oddridge)
    1825-1900 .... **TCLC 27**
    See also CA 120; DLB 18; RGEL 2
Blackmur, R(ichard) P(almer)
    1904-1965 .... **CLC 2, 24**
    See also AMWS 2; CA 11-12; 25-28R;
    CANR 71; CAP 1; DLB 63; EWL 3;
    MAL 5
Black Tarantula
    See Acker, Kathy
Blackwood, Algernon 1869-1951 .... **SSC 107;**
    TCLC 5
    See also AAYA 78; CA 105; 150; CANR
    169; DLB 153, 156, 178; HGG; SUFW 1
Blackwood, Algernon Henry
    See Blackwood, Algernon
Blackwood, Caroline (Maureen)
    1931-1996 .... **CLC 6, 9, 100**
    See also BRWS 9; CA 85-88; 151; CANR
    32, 61, 65; CN 3, 4, 5, 6; DLB 14, 207;
    HGG; MTCW 1
Blade, Alexander
    See Hamilton, Edmond; Silverberg, Robert
Blaga, Lucian 1895-1961 .... **CLC 75**
    See also CA 157; DLB 220; EWL 3
Blair, Eric 1903-1950 .... **SSC 68; TCLC 2, 6,**
    15, 31, 51, 123, 128, 129; WLC 4
    See also BPFB 3; BRW 7; BYA 5; CA 104;
    132; CDBLB 1945-1960; CLR 68; DA;
    DA3; DAB; DAC; DAM MST, NOV;
    DLB 15, 98, 195, 255; EWL 3; EXPN;
    LAIT 4, 5; LATS 1:1; MTCW 1, 2;
    MTFW 2005; NFS 3, 7; RGEL 2; SATA
    29; SCFW 1, 2; SFW 4; SSFS 4; TEA;
    WLIT 4; YAW X
Blair, Eric Arthur
    See Blair, Eric

Blair, Hugh 1718-1800 .... **NCLC 75**

Blais, Marie-Claire 1939- .... **CLC 2, 4, 6, 13, 22**
See also CA 21-24R; CAAS 4; CANR 38, 75, 93; CWW 2; DAC; DAM MST; DLB 53; EWL 3; FW; MTCW 1, 2; MTFW 2005; TWA

Blaise, Clark 1940- .... **CLC 29, 261**
See also AITN 2; CA 53-56, 231; CAAE 231; CAAS 3; CANR 5, 66, 106; CN 4, 5, 6, 7; DLB 53; RGSF 2

Blake, Fairley
See De Voto, Bernard (Augustine)

Blake, Nicholas
See Day Lewis, C.

Blake, Sterling
See Benford, Gregory

Blake, William 1757-1827 . **NCLC 13, 37, 57, 127, 173, 190, 201; PC 12, 63; WLC 1**
See also AAYA 47; BRW 3; BRWR 1; CD-BLB 1789-1832; CLR 52; DA; DA3; DAB; DAC; DAM MST, POET; DLB 93, 163; EXPP; LATS 1:1; LMFS 1; MAICYA 1, 2; PAB; PFS 2, 12, 24; SATA 30; TEA; WCH; WLIT 3; WP

Blanchot, Maurice 1907-2003 .... **CLC 135**
See also CA 117; 144; 213; CANR 138; DLB 72, 296; EWL 3

Blasco Ibanez, Vicente 1867-1928 . **TCLC 12**
See also BPFB 1; CA 110; 131; CANR 81; DA3; DAM NOV; DLB 322; EW 8; EWL 3; HW 1, 2; MTCW 1

Blatty, William Peter 1928- .... **CLC 2**
See also CA 5-8R; CANR 9, 124; DAM POP; HGG

Bleeck, Oliver
See Thomas, Ross (Elmore)

Bleecker, Ann Eliza 1752-1783 .... **LC 161**
See also DLB 200

Blessing, Lee (Knowlton) 1949- .... **CLC 54**
See also CA 236; CAD; CD 5, 6; DFS 23, 26

Blight, Rose
See Greer, Germaine

Blind, Mathilde 1841-1896 .... **NCLC 202**
See also DLB 199

Blish, James (Benjamin) 1921-1975 . **CLC 14**
See also BPFB 1; CA 1-4R; 57-60; CANR 3; CN 2; DLB 8; MTCW 1; SATA 66; SCFW 1, 2; SFW 4

Bliss, Frederick
See Card, Orson Scott

Bliss, Gillian
See Paton Walsh, Jill

Bliss, Reginald
See Wells, H(erbert) G(eorge)

Blixen, Karen 1885-1962 ..... **CLC 10, 29, 95; SSC 7, 75**
See also CA 25-28; CANR 22, 50; CAP 2; DA3; DLB 214; EW 10; EWL 3; EXPS; FW; GL 2; HGG; LAIT 3; LMFS 1; MTCW 1; NCFS 2; NFS 9; RGSF 2; RGWL 2, 3; SATA 44; SSFS 3, 6, 13; WLIT 2

Blixen, Karen Christentze Dinesen
See Blixen, Karen

Bloch, Robert (Albert) 1917-1994 .... **CLC 33**
See also AAYA 29; CA 5-8R, 179; 146; CAAS 20; CANR 5, 78; DA3; DLB 44; HGG; INT CANR-5; MTCW 2; SATA 12; SATA-Obit 82; SFW 4; SUFW 1, 2

Blok, Alexander (Alexandrovich) 1880-1921 .... **PC 21; TCLC 5**
See also CA 104; 183; DLB 295; EW 9; EWL 3; LMFS 2; RGWL 2, 3

Blom, Jan
See Breytenbach, Breyten

Bloom, Harold 1930- .... **CLC 24, 103, 221**
See also CA 13-16R; CANR 39, 75, 92, 133, 181; DLB 67; EWL 3; MTCW 2; MTFW 2005; RGAL 4

Bloomfield, Aurelius
See Bourne, Randolph S(illiman)

Bloomfield, Robert 1766-1823 ..... **NCLC 145**
See also DLB 93

Blount, Roy, Jr. 1941- .... **CLC 38**
See also CA 53-56; CANR 10, 28, 61, 125, 176; CSW; INT CANR-28; MTCW 1, 2; MTFW 2005

Blount, Roy Alton
See Blount, Roy, Jr.

Blowsnake, Sam 1875-(?) .... **NNAL**

Bloy, Leon 1846-1917 .... **TCLC 22**
See also CA 121; 183; DLB 123; GFL 1789 to the Present

Blue Cloud, Peter (Aroniawenrate) 1933- .... **NNAL**
See also CA 117; CANR 40; DAM MULT; DLB 342

Bluggage, Oranthy
See Alcott, Louisa May

Blume, Judy 1938- .... **CLC 12, 30**
See also AAYA 3, 26; BYA 1, 8, 12; CA 29-32R; CANR 13, 37, 66, 124, 186; CLR 2, 15, 69; CPW; DA3; DAM NOV, POP; DLB 52; JRDA; MAICYA 1, 2; MAIC-YAS 1; MTCW 1, 2; MTFW 2005; NFS 24; SATA 2, 31, 79, 142, 195; WYA; YAW

Blume, Judy Sussman
See Blume, Judy

Blunden, Edmund (Charles) 1896-1974 .... **CLC 2, 56; PC 66**
See also BRW 6; BRWS 11; CA 17-18; 45-48; CANR 54; CAP 2; CP 1, 2; DLB 20, 100, 155; MTCW 1; PAB

Bly, Robert (Elwood) 1926- .... **CLC 1, 2, 5, 10, 15, 38, 128; PC 39**
See also AMWS 4; CA 5-8R; CANR 41, 73, 125; CP 1, 2, 3, 4, 5, 6, 7; DA3; DAM POET; DLB 5, 342; EWL 3; MAL 5; MTCW 1, 2; MTFW 2005; PFS 6, 17; RGAL 4

Boas, Franz 1858-1942 .... **TCLC 56**
See also CA 115; 181

Bobette
See Simenon, Georges (Jacques Christian)

Boccaccio, Giovanni 1313-1375 ... **CMLC 13, 57; SSC 10, 87**
See also EW 2; RGSF 2; RGWL 2, 3; TWA; WLIT 7

Bochco, Steven 1943- .... **CLC 35**
See also AAYA 11, 71; CA 124; 138

Bode, Sigmund
See O'Doherty, Brian

Bodel, Jean 1167(?)-1210 .... **CMLC 28**

Bodenheim, Maxwell 1892-1954 .... **TCLC 44**
See also CA 110; 187; DLB 9, 45; MAL 5; RGAL 4

Bodenheimer, Maxwell
See Bodenheim, Maxwell

Bodker, Cecil 1927-
See Bodker, Cecil

Bodker, Cecil 1927- .... **CLC 21**
See also CA 73-76; CANR 13, 44, 111; CLR 23; MAICYA 1, 2; SATA 14, 133

Boell, Heinrich 1917-1985 ..... **CLC 2, 3, 6, 9, 11, 15, 27, 32, 72; SSC 23; TCLC 185; WLC 1**
See also BPFB 1; CA 21-24R; 116; CANR 24; CDWLB 2; DA; DA3; DAB; DAC; DAM MST, NOV; DLB 69, 329; DLBY 1985; EW 13; EWL 3; MTCW 1, 2; MTFW 2005; RGHL; RGSF 2; RGWL 2, 3; SSFS 20; TWA

Boell, Heinrich Theodor
See Boell, Heinrich

Boerne, Alfred
See Doeblin, Alfred

Boethius c. 480-c. 524 .... **CMLC 15**
See also DLB 115; RGWL 2, 3; WLIT 8

Boff, Leonardo (Genezio Darci) 1938- .... **CLC 70; HLC 1**
See also CA 150; DAM MULT; HW 2

Bogan, Louise 1897-1970 .... **CLC 4, 39, 46, 93; PC 12**
See also AMWS 3; CA 73-76; 25-28R; CANR 33, 82; CP 1; DAM POET; DLB 45, 169; EWL 3; MAL 5; MBL; MTCW 1, 2; PFS 21; RGAL 4

Bogarde, Dirk
See Van Den Bogarde, Derek Jules Gaspard Ulric Niven

Bogat, Shatan
See Kacew, Romain

Bogomolny, Robert L. 1938- .... **SSC 41; TCLC 11**
See also CA 121, 164; DLB 182; EWL 3; MJW; RGSF 2; RGWL 2, 3; TWA

Bogomolny, Robert Lee
See Bogomolny, Robert L.

Bogosian, Eric 1953- .... **CLC 45, 141**
See also CA 138; CAD; CANR 102, 148; CD 5, 6; DLB 341

Bograd, Larry 1953- .... **CLC 35**
See also CA 93-96; CANR 57; SAAS 21; SATA 33, 89; WYA

Boiardo, Matteo Maria 1441-1494 .... **LC 6, 168**

Boileau-Despreaux, Nicolas 1636-1711 .... **LC 3, 164**
See also DLB 268; EW 3; GFL Beginnings to 1789; RGWL 2, 3

Boissard, Maurice
See Leautaud, Paul

Bojer, Johan 1872-1959 .... **TCLC 64**
See also CA 189; EWL 3

Bok, Edward W(illiam) 1863-1930 .... **TCLC 101**
See also CA 217; DLB 91; DLBD 16

Boker, George Henry 1823-1890 . **NCLC 125**
See also RGAL 4

Boland, Eavan 1944- ... **CLC 40, 67, 113; PC 58**
See also BRWS 5; CA 143, 207; CAAE 207; CANR 61, 180; CP 1, 6, 7; CWP; DAM POET; DLB 40; FW; MTCW 2; MTFW 2005; PFS 12, 22, 31

Boland, Eavan Aisling
See Boland, Eavan

Boll, Heinrich
See Boell, Heinrich

Bolt, Lee
See Faust, Frederick

Bolt, Robert (Oxton) 1924-1995 ...... **CLC 14; TCLC 175**
See also CA 17-20R; 147; CANR 35, 67; CBD; DAM DRAM; DFS 2; DLB 13, 233; EWL 3; LAIT 1; MTCW 1

Bombal, Maria Luisa 1910-1980 .... **HLCS 1; SSC 37**
See also CA 127; CANR 72; EWL 3; HW 1; LAW; RGSF 2

Bombet, Louis-Alexandre-Cesar
See Stendhal

Bomkauf
See Kaufman, Bob (Garnell)

Bonaventura **NCLC 35**
See also DLB 90

Bonaventure 1217(?)-1274 .... **CMLC 79**
See also DLB 115; LMFS 1

Bond, Edward 1934- .... **CLC 4, 6, 13, 23**
See also AAYA 50; BRWS 1; CA 25-28R; CANR 38, 67, 106; CBD; CD 5, 6; DAM DRAM; DFS 3, 8; DLB 13, 310; EWL 3; MTCW 1

Bonham, Frank 1914-1989 .... **CLC 12**
    See also AAYA 1, 70; BYA 1, 3; CA 9-12R;
    CANR 4, 36; JRDA; MAICYA 1, 2;
    SAAS 3; SATA 1, 49; SATA-Obit 62;
    TCWW 1, 2; YAW
Bonnefoy, Yves 1923- . **CLC 9, 15, 58; PC 58**
    See also CA 85-88; CANR 33, 75, 97, 136;
    CWW 2; DAM MST, POET; DLB 258;
    EWL 3; GFL 1789 to the Present; MTCW
    1, 2; MTFW 2005
Bonner, Marita
    See Occomy, Marita (Odette) Bonner
Bonnin, Gertrude 1876-1938 .... **NNAL**
    See also CA 150; DAM MULT; DLB 175
Bontemps, Arna(ud Wendell)
    1902-1973 ..... **BLC 1:1; CLC 1, 18; HR
    1:2**
    See also BW 1; CA 1-4R; 41-44R; CANR
    4, 35; CLR 6; CP 1; CWRI 5; DAM
    MULT, NOV, POET; DLB 48, 51; JRDA;
    MAICYA 1, 2; MAL 5; MTCW 1, 2;
    SATA 2, 44; SATA-Obit 24; WCH; WP
Boot, William
    See Stoppard, Tom
Booth, Irwin
    See Hoch, Edward D.
Booth, Martin 1944-2004 .... **CLC 13**
    See also CA 93-96, 188; 223; CAAE 188;
    CAAS 2; CANR 92; CP 1, 2, 3, 4
Booth, Philip 1925-2007 .... **CLC 23**
    See also CA 5-8R; 262; CANR 5, 88; CP 1,
    2, 3, 4, 5, 6, 7; DLBY 1982
Booth, Philip Edmund
    See Booth, Philip
Booth, Wayne C. 1921-2005 .... **CLC 24**
    See also CA 1-4R; 244; CAAS 5; CANR 3,
    43, 117; DLB 67
Booth, Wayne Clayson
    See Booth, Wayne C.
Borchert, Wolfgang 1921-1947 .... **TCLC 5**
    See also CA 104; 188; DLB 69, 124; EWL
    3
Borel, Petrus 1809-1859 .... **NCLC 41**
    See also DLB 119; GFL 1789 to the Present
Borges, Jorge Luis 1899-1986 ... **CLC 1, 2, 3,
    4, 6, 8, 9, 10, 13, 19, 44, 48, 83; HLC 1;
    PC 22, 32; SSC 4, 41, 100; TCLC 109;
    WLC 1**
    See also AAYA 26; BPFB 1; CA 21-24R;
    CANR 19, 33, 75, 105, 133; CDWLB 3;
    DA; DA3; DAB; DAC; DAM MST,
    MULT; DLB 113, 283; DLBY 1986;
    DNFS 1, 2; EWL 3; HW 1, 2; LAW;
    LMFS 2; MSW; MTCW 1, 2; MTFW
    2005; PFS 27; RGHL; RGSF 2; RGWL
    2, 3; SFW 4; SSFS 17; TWA; WLIT 1
Borne, Ludwig 1786-1837 .... **NCLC 193**
    See also DLB 90
Borowski, Tadeusz 1922-1951 .... **SSC 48;
    TCLC 9**
    See also CA 106; 154; CDWLB 4; DLB
    215; EWL 3; RGHL; RGSF 2; RGWL 3;
    SSFS 13
Borrow, George (Henry)
    1803-1881 .... **NCLC 9**
    See also BRWS 12; DLB 21, 55, 166
Bosch (Gavino), Juan 1909-2001 ..... **HLCS 1**
    See also CA 151; 204; DAM MST, MULT;
    DLB 145; HW 1, 2
Bosman, Herman Charles
    1905-1951 .... **TCLC 49**
    See also CA 160; DLB 225; RGSF 2
Bosschere, Jean de 1878(?)-1953 ... **TCLC 19**
    See also CA 115; 186
Boswell, James 1740-1795 ... **LC 4, 50; WLC
    1**
    See also BRW 3; CDBLB 1660-1789; DA;
    DAB; DAC; DAM MST; DLB 104, 142;
    TEA; WLIT 3

Boto, Eza
    See Biyidi, Alexandre
Bottomley, Gordon 1874-1948 ..... **TCLC 107**
    See also CA 120; 192; DLB 10
Bottoms, David 1949- .... **CLC 53**
    See also CA 105; CANR 22; CSW; DLB
    120; DLBY 1983
Boucicault, Dion 1820-1890 .... **NCLC 41**
    See also DLB 344
Boucolon, Maryse
    See Conde, Maryse
Bourcicault, Dion
    See Boucicault, Dion
Bourdieu, Pierre 1930-2002 .... **CLC 198**
    See also CA 130; 204
Bourget, Paul (Charles Joseph)
    1852-1935 .... **TCLC 12**
    See also CA 107; 196; DLB 123; GFL 1789
    to the Present
Bourjaily, Vance (Nye) 1922- .... **CLC 8, 62**
    See also CA 1-4R; CAAS 1; CANR 2, 72;
    CN 1, 2, 3, 4, 5, 6, 7; DLB 2, 143; MAL
    5
Bourne, Randolph S(illiman)
    1886-1918 .... **TCLC 16**
    See also AMW; CA 117; 155; DLB 63;
    MAL 5
Boursiquot, Dionysius
    See Boucicault, Dion
Bova, Ben 1932- .... **CLC 45**
    See also AAYA 16; CA 5-8R; CAAS 18;
    CANR 11, 56, 94, 111, 157; CLR 3, 96;
    DLBY 1981; INT CANR-11; MAICYA 1,
    2; MTCW 1; SATA 6, 68, 133; SFW 4
Bova, Benjamin William
    See Bova, Ben
Bowen, Elizabeth (Dorothea Cole)
    1899-1973 . **CLC 1, 3, 6, 11, 15, 22, 118;
    SSC 3, 28, 66; TCLC 148**
    See also BRWS 2; CA 17-18; 41-44R;
    CANR 35, 105; CAP 2; CDBLB 1945-
    1960; CN 1; DA3; DAM NOV; DLB 15,
    162; EWL 3; EXPS; FW; HGG; MTCW
    1, 2; MTFW 2005; NFS 13; RGSF 2;
    SSFS 5, 22; SUFW 1; TEA; WLIT 4
Bowering, George 1935- .... **CLC 15, 47**
    See also CA 21-24R; CAAS 16; CANR 10;
    CN 7; CP 1, 2, 3, 4, 5, 6, 7; DLB 53
Bowering, Marilyn R(uthe) 1949- .... **CLC 32**
    See also CA 101; CANR 49; CP 4, 5, 6, 7;
    CWP; DLB 334
Bowers, Edgar 1924-2000 .... **CLC 9**
    See also CA 5-8R; 188; CANR 24; CP 1, 2,
    3, 4, 5, 6, 7; CSW; DLB 5
Bowers, Mrs. J. Milton 1842-1914
    See Bierce, Ambrose (Gwinett)
Bowie, David
    See Jones, David Robert
Bowles, Jane (Sydney) 1917-1973 ..... **CLC 3,
    68**
    See also CA 19-20; 41-44R; CAP 2; CN 1;
    EWL 3; MAL 5
Bowles, Jane Auer
    See Bowles, Jane (Sydney)
Bowles, Paul 1910-1999 ..... **CLC 1, 2, 19, 53;
    SSC 3, 98; TCLC 209**
    See also AMWS 4; CA 1-4R; 186; CAAS
    1; CANR 1, 19, 50, 75; CN 1, 2, 3, 4, 5,
    6; DA3; DLB 5, 6, 218; EWL 3; MAL 5;
    MTCW 1, 2; MTFW 2005; RGAL 4;
    SSFS 17
Bowles, William Lisle 1762-1850 . **NCLC 103**
    See also DLB 93
Box, Edgar
    See Vidal, Gore
Boyd, James 1888-1944 .... **TCLC 115**
    See also CA 186; DLB 9; DLBD 16; RGAL
    4; RHW

Boyd, Nancy
    See Millay, Edna St. Vincent
Boyd, Thomas (Alexander)
    1898-1935 .... **TCLC 111**
    See also CA 111; 183; DLB 9; DLBD 16,
    316
Boyd, William 1952- .... **CLC 28, 53, 70**
    See also CA 114; 120; CANR 51, 71, 131,
    174; CN 4, 5, 6, 7; DLB 231
Boyesen, Hjalmar Hjorth
    1848-1895 .... **NCLC 135**
    See also DLB 12, 71; DLBD 13; RGAL 4
Boyle, Kay 1902-1992 .... **CLC 1, 5, 19, 58,
    121; SSC 5, 102**
    See also CA 13-16R; 140; CAAS 1; CANR
    29, 61, 110; CN 1, 2, 3, 4, 5; CP 1, 2, 3,
    4, 5; DLB 4, 9, 48, 86; DLBY 1993; EWL
    3; MAL 5; MTCW 1, 2; MTFW 2005;
    RGAL 4; RGSF 2; SSFS 10, 13, 14
Boyle, Mark
    See Kienzle, William X.
Boyle, Patrick 1905-1982 .... **CLC 19**
    See also CA 127
Boyle, T. C.
    See Boyle, T. Coraghessan
Boyle, T. Coraghessan 1948- ..... **CLC 36, 55,
    90; SSC 16**
    See also AAYA 47; AMWS 8; BEST 90:4;
    BPFB 1; CA 120; CANR 44, 76, 89, 132;
    CN 6, 7; CPW; DA3; DAM POP; DLB
    218, 278; DLBY 1986; EWL 3; MAL 5;
    MTCW 2; MTFW 2005; SSFS 13, 19
Boz
    See Dickens, Charles (John Huffam)
Brackenridge, Hugh Henry
    1748-1816 .... **NCLC 7**
    See also DLB 11, 37; RGAL 4
Bradbury, Edward P.
    See Moorcock, Michael
Bradbury, Malcolm (Stanley)
    1932-2000 .... **CLC 32, 61**
    See also CA 1-4R; CANR 1, 33, 91, 98,
    137; CN 1, 2, 3, 4, 5, 6, 7; CP 1; DA3;
    DAM NOV; DLB 14, 207; EWL 3;
    MTCW 1, 2; MTFW 2005
Bradbury, Ray 1920- ... **CLC 1, 3, 10, 15, 42,
    98, 235; SSC 29, 53; WLC 1**
    See also AAYA 15; AITN 1, 2; AMWS 4;
    BPFB 1; BYA 5, 11; CA 1-4R; CANR
    2, 30, 75, 125, 186; CDALB 1968-1988;
    CN 1, 2, 3, 4, 5, 6, 7; CPW; DA; DA3;
    DAB; DAC; DAM MST, NOV, POP;
    DLB 2, 8; EXPN; EXPS; HGG; LAIT 3,
    5; LATS 1:2; LMFS 2; MAL 5; MTCW
    1, 2; MTFW 2005; NFS 1, 22, 29; RGAL
    4; RGSF 2; SATA 11, 64, 123; SCFW 1,
    2; SFW 4; SSFS 1, 20; SUFW 1, 2; TUS;
    YAW
Bradbury, Ray Douglas
    See Bradbury, Ray
Braddon, Mary Elizabeth
    1837-1915 .... **TCLC 111**
    See also BRWS 8; CA 108; 179; CMW 4;
    DLB 18, 70, 156; HGG
Bradfield, Scott 1955- .... **SSC 65**
    See also CA 147; CANR 90; HGG; SUFW
    2
Bradfield, Scott Michael
    See Bradfield, Scott
Bradford, Gamaliel 1863-1932 .... **TCLC 36**
    See also CA 160; DLB 17
Bradford, William 1590-1657 .... **LC 64**
    See also DLB 24, 30; RGAL 4
Bradley, David, Jr. 1950- ...... **BLC 1:1; CLC
    23, 118**
    See also BW 1, 3; CA 104; CANR 26, 81;
    CN 4, 5, 6, 7; DAM MULT; DLB 33
Bradley, David Henry, Jr.
    See Bradley, David, Jr.

Butler, Octavia E. 1947-2006 .... **BLC 2:1; BLCS; CLC 38, 121, 230, 240**
See also AAYA 18, 48; AFAW 2; AMWS 13; BPFB 1; BW 2, 3; CA 73-76; 248; CANR 12, 24, 38, 73, 145, 240; CLR 65; CN 7; CPW; DA3; DAM MULT, POP; DLB 33; LATS 1:2; MTCW 1, 2; MTFW 2005; NFS 8, 21; SATA 84; SCFW 2; SFW 4; SSFS 6; TCLE 1:1; YAW

Butler, Octavia Estelle
See Butler, Octavia E.

Butler, Robert Olen, Jr.
See Butler, Robert Olen

Butler, Robert Olen 1945- .... **CLC 81, 162; SSC 117**
See also AMWS 12; BPFB 1; CA 112; CANR 66, 138, 194; CN 7; CSW; DAM POP; DLB 173, 335; INT CA-112; MAL 5; MTCW 2; MTFW 2005; SSFS 11, 22

Butler, Samuel 1612-1680 . **LC 16, 43; PC 94**
See also DLB 101, 126; RGEL 2

Butler, Samuel 1835-1902 .... **TCLC 1, 33; WLC 1**
See also BRWS 2; CA 143; CDBLB 1890-1914; DA; DA3; DAB; DAC; DAM MST, NOV; DLB 18, 57, 174; RGEL 2; SFW 4; TEA

Butler, Walter C.
See Faust, Frederick

Butor, Michel (Marie Francois) 1926- .... **CLC 1, 3, 8, 11, 15, 161**
See also CA 9-12R; CANR 33, 66; CWW 2; DLB 83; EW 13; EWL 3; GFL 1789 to the Present; MTCW 1, 2; MTFW 2005

Butts, Mary 1890(?)-1937 ... **SSC 124; TCLC 77**
See also CA 148; DLB 240

Buxton, Ralph
See Silverstein, Alvin; Silverstein, Virginia B(arbara Opshelor)

Buzo, Alex
See Buzo, Alexander (John)

Buzo, Alexander (John) 1944- .... **CLC 61**
See also CA 97-100; CANR 17, 39, 69; CD 5, 6; DLB 289

Buzzati, Dino 1906-1972 .... **CLC 36**
See also CA 160; 33-36R; DLB 177; RGWL 2, 3; SFW 4

Byars, Betsy 1928- .... **CLC 35**
See also AAYA 19; BYA 3; CA 33-36R, 183; CAAE 183; CANR 18, 36, 57, 102, 148; CLR 1, 16, 72; DLB 52; INT CANR-18; JRDA; MAICYA 1, 2; MAICYAS 1; MTCW 1; SAAS 1; SATA 4, 46, 80, 163; SATA-Essay 108; WYA; YAW

Byars, Betsy Cromer
See Byars, Betsy

Byatt, Antonia Susan Drabble
See Byatt, A.S.

Byatt, A.S. 1936- .... **CLC 19, 65, 136, 223; SSC 91**
See also BPFB 1; BRWC 2; BRWS 4; CA 13-16R; CANR 13, 33, 50, 75, 96, 133; CN 1, 2, 3, 4, 5, 6; DA3; DAM NOV, POP; DLB 14, 194, 319, 326; EWL 3; MTCW 1, 2; MTFW 2005; RGSF 2; RHW; SSFS 26; TEA

Byrd, William II 1674-1744 .... **LC 112**
See also DLB 24, 140; RGAL 4

Byrne, David 1952- .... **CLC 26**
See also CA 127

Byrne, John Joseph
See Leonard, Hugh

Byrne, John Keyes
See Leonard, Hugh

Byron, George Gordon (Noel) 1788-1824 ..... **DC 24; NCLC 2, 12, 109, 149; PC 16, 95; WLC 1**
See also AAYA 64; BRW 4; BRWC 2; CD-BLB 1789-1832; DA; DA3; DAB; DAC; DAM MST, POET; DLB 96, 110; EXPP; LMFS 1; PAB; PFS 1, 14, 29; RGEL 2; TEA; WLIT 3; WP

Byron, Robert 1905-1941 .... **TCLC 67**
See also CA 160; DLB 195

C. 3. 3.
See Wilde, Oscar

Caballero, Fernan 1796-1877 .... **NCLC 10**

Cabell, Branch
See Cabell, James Branch

Cabell, James Branch 1879-1958 .... **TCLC 6**
See also CA 105; 152; DLB 9, 78; FANT; MAL 5; MTCW 2; RGAL 4; SUFW 1

Cabeza de Vaca, Alvar Nunez 1490-1557(?) .... **LC 61**

Cable, George Washington 1844-1925 .... **SSC 4; TCLC 4**
See also CA 104; 155; DLB 12, 74; DLBD 13; RGAL 4; TUS

Cabral de Melo Neto, Joao 1920-1999 .... **CLC 76**
See also CA 151; CWW 2; DAM MULT; DLB 307; EWL 3; LAW; LAWS 1

Cabrera, Lydia 1900-1991 .... **TCLC 223**
See also CA 178; DLB 145; EWL 3; HW 1; LAWS 1

Cabrera Infante, G. 1929-2005 ... **CLC 5, 25, 45, 120; HLC 1; SSC 39**
See also CA 85-88; 236; CANR 29, 65, 110; CDWLB 3; CWW 2; DA3; DAM MULT; DLB 113; EWL 3; HW 1, 2; LAW; LAWS 1; MTCW 1, 2; MTFW 2005; RGSF 2; WLIT 1

Cabrera Infante, Guillermo
See Cabrera Infante, G.

Cade, Toni
See Bambara, Toni Cade

Cadmus and Harmonia
See Buchan, John

Caedmon fl. 658-680 .... **CMLC 7**
See also DLB 146

Caeiro, Alberto
See Pessoa, Fernando

Caesar, Julius
See Julius Caesar

Cage, John (Milton), (Jr.) 1912-1992 .... **CLC 41; PC 58**
See also CA 13-16R; 169; CANR 9, 78; DLB 193; INT CANR-9; TCLE 1:1

Cahan, Abraham 1860-1951 .... **TCLC 71**
See also CA 108; 154; DLB 9, 25, 28; MAL 5; RGAL 4

Cain, Christopher
See Fleming, Thomas

Cain, G.
See Cabrera Infante, G.

Cain, Guillermo
See Cabrera Infante, G.

Cain, James M(allahan) 1892-1977 .. **CLC 3, 11, 28**
See also AITN 1; BPFB 1; CA 17-20R; 73-76; CANR 8, 34, 61; CMW 4; CN 1, 2; DLB 226; EWL 3; MAL 5; MSW; MTCW 1; RGAL 4

Caine, Hall 1853-1931 .... **TCLC 97**
See also RHW

Caine, Mark
See Raphael, Frederic (Michael)

Calasso, Roberto 1941- .... **CLC 81**
See also CA 143; CANR 89

Calderon de la Barca, Pedro 1600-1681 . **DC 3; HLCS 1; LC 23, 136**
See also DFS 23; EW 2; RGWL 2, 3; TWA

Caldwell, Erskine 1903-1987 ... **CLC 1, 8, 14, 50, 60; SSC 19; TCLC 117**
See also AITN 1; AMW; BPFB 1; CA 1-4R; 121; CAAS 1; CANR 2, 33; CN 1, 2, 3, 4; DA3; DAM NOV; DLB 9, 86; EWL 3; MAL 5; MTCW 1, 2; MTFW 2005; RGAL 4; RGSF 2; TUS

Caldwell, (Janet Miriam) Taylor (Holland) 1900-1985 .... **CLC 2, 28, 39**
See also BPFB 1; CA 5-8R; 116; CANR 5; DA3; DAM NOV, POP; DLBD 17; MTCW 2; RHW

Calhoun, John Caldwell 1782-1850 .... **NCLC 15**
See also DLB 3, 248

Calisher, Hortense 1911-2009 .... **CLC 2, 4, 8, 38, 134; SSC 15**
See also CA 1-4R; 282; CANR 1, 22, 117; CN 1, 2, 3, 4, 5, 6, 7; DA3; DAM NOV; DLB 2, 218; INT CANR-22; MAL 5; MTCW 1, 2; MTFW 2005; RGAL 4; RGSF 2

Callaghan, Morley Edward 1903-1990 ..... **CLC 3, 14, 41, 65; TCLC 145**
See also CA 9-12R; 132; CANR 33, 73; CN 1, 2, 3, 4; DAC; DAM MST; DLB 68; EWL 3; MTCW 1, 2; MTFW 2005; RGEL 2; RGSF 2; SSFS 19

Callimachus c. 305B.C.-c. 240B.C. .... **CMLC 18**
See also AW 1; DLB 176; RGWL 2, 3

Calvin, Jean
See Calvin, John

Calvin, John 1509-1564 .... **LC 37**
See also DLB 327; GFL Beginnings to 1789

Calvino, Italo 1923-1985 .... **CLC 5, 8, 11, 22, 33, 39, 73; SSC 3, 48; TCLC 183**
See also AAYA 58; CA 85-88; 116; CANR 23, 61, 132; DAM NOV; DLB 196; EW 13; EWL 3; MTCW 1, 2; MTFW 2005; RGHL; RGSF 2; RGWL 2, 3; SFW 4; SSFS 12; WLIT 7

Camara Laye
See Laye, Camara

Cambridge, A Gentleman of the University of
See Crowley, Edward Alexander

Camden, William 1551-1623 .... **LC 77**
See also DLB 172

Cameron, Carey 1952- .... **CLC 59**
See also CA 135

Cameron, Peter 1959- .... **CLC 44**
See also AMWS 12; CA 125; CANR 50, 117, 188; DLB 234; GLL 2

Camoens, Luis Vaz de 1524(?)-1580
See Camoes, Luis de

Camoes, Luis de 1524(?)-1580 . **HLCS 1; LC 62; PC 31**
See also DLB 287; EW 2; RGWL 2, 3

Camp, Madeleine L'Engle
See L'Engle, Madeleine

Campana, Dino 1885-1932 .... **TCLC 20**
See also CA 117; 246; DLB 114; EWL 3

Campanella, Tommaso 1568-1639 .... **LC 32**
See also RGWL 2, 3

Campbell, Bebe Moore 1950-2006 . **BLC 2:1; CLC 246**
See also AAYA 26; BW 2, 3; CA 139; 254; CANR 81, 134; DLB 227; MTCW 2; MTFW 2005

Campbell, John Ramsey
See Campbell, Ramsey

Campbell, John W(ood, Jr.) 1910-1971 .... **CLC 32**
See also CA 21-22; 29-32R; CANR 34; CAP 2; DLB 8; MTCW 1; SCFW 1, 2; SFW 4

Chesnutt, Charles W(addell)
1858-1932 .... **BLC 1; SSC 7, 54; TCLC 5, 39**
See also AFAW 1, 2; AMWS 14; BW 1, 3; CA 106; 125; CANR 76; DAM MULT; DLB 12, 50, 78; EWL 3; MAL 5; MTCW 1, 2; MTFW 2005; RGAL 4; RGSF 2; SSFS 11, 26

Chester, Alfred 1929(?)-1971 .... **CLC 49**
See also CA 196; 33-36R; DLB 130; MAL 5

Chesterton, G(ilbert) K(eith)
1874-1936 . **PC 28; SSC 1, 46; TCLC 1, 6, 64**
See also AAYA 57; BRW 6; CA 104; 132; CANR 73, 131; CDBLB 1914-1945; CMW 4; DAM NOV, POET; DLB 10, 19, 34, 70, 98, 149, 178; EWL 3; FANT; MSW; MTCW 1, 2; MTFW 2005; RGEL 2; RGSF 2; SATA 27; SUFW 1

Chettle, Henry 1560-1607(?) .... **LC 112**
See also DLB 136; RGEL 2

Chiang, Pin-chin 1904-1986 .... **CLC 68**
See also CA 118; DLB 328; EWL 3; RGWL 3

Chiang Ping-chih
See Chiang, Pin-chin

Chief Joseph 1840-1904 .... **NNAL**
See also CA 152; DA3; DAM MULT

Chief Seattle 1786(?)-1866 .... **NNAL**
See also DA3; DAM MULT

Ch'ien, Chung-shu 1910-1998 .... **CLC 22**
See also CA 130; CANR 73; CWW 2; DLB 328; MTCW 1, 2

Chikamatsu Monzaemon 1653-1724 ... **LC 66**
See also RGWL 2, 3

Child, Francis James 1825-1896 . **NCLC 173**
See also DLB 1, 64, 235

Child, L. Maria
See Child, Lydia Maria

Child, Lydia Maria 1802-1880 .. **NCLC 6, 73**
See also DLB 1, 74, 243; RGAL 4; SATA 67

Child, Mrs.
See Child, Lydia Maria

Child, Philip 1898-1978 .... **CLC 19, 68**
See also CA 13-14; CAP 1; CP 1; DLB 68; RHW; SATA 47

Childers, (Robert) Erskine
1870-1922 .... **TCLC 65**
See also CA 113; 153; DLB 70

Childress, Alice 1920-1994 .... **BLC 1:1; CLC 12, 15, 86, 96; DC 4; TCLC 116**
See also AAYA 8; BW 2, 3; BYA 2; CA 45-48; 146; CAD; CANR 3, 27, 50, 74; CLR 14; CWD; DA3; DAM DRAM, MULT, NOV; DFS 2, 8, 14, 26; DLB 7, 38, 249; JRDA; LAIT 5; MAICYA 1, 2; MAIC-YAS 1; MAL 5; MTCW 1, 2; MTFW 2005; RGAL 4; SATA 7, 48, 81; TUS; WYA; YAW

Chin, Frank (Chew, Jr.) 1940- .... **AAL; CLC 135; DC 7**
See also CA 33-36R; CAD; CANR 71; CD 5, 6; DAM MULT; DLB 206, 312; LAIT 5; RGAL 4

Chin, Marilyn (Mei Ling) 1955- .... **PC 40**
See also CA 129; CANR 70, 113; CWP; DLB 312; PFS 28

Chislett, (Margaret) Anne 1943- ...... **CLC 34**
See also CA 151

Chitty, Thomas Willes 1926- .... **CLC 6, 11**
See also CA 5-8R; CN 1, 2, 3, 4, 5, 6; EWL 3

Chivers, Thomas Holley
1809-1858 .... **NCLC 49**
See also DLB 3, 248; RGAL 4

Chlamyda, Jehudil
See Peshkov, Alexei Maximovich

Ch'o, Chou
See Shu-Jen, Chou

Choi, Susan 1969- .... **CLC 119**
See also CA 223; CANR 188

Chomette, Rene Lucien 1898-1981 .. **CLC 20**
See also CA 103

Chomsky, Avram Noam
See Chomsky, Noam

Chomsky, Noam 1928- .... **CLC 132**
See also CA 17-20R; CANR 28, 62, 110, 132, 179; DA3; DLB 246; MTCW 1, 2; MTFW 2005

Chona, Maria 1845(?)-1936 .... **NNAL**
See also CA 144

Chopin, Kate
See Chopin, Katherine

Chopin, Katherine 1851-1904 .... **SSC 8, 68, 110; TCLC 127; WLCS**
See also AAYA 33; AMWR 2; BYA 11, 15; CA 104; 122; CDALB 1865-1917; DA3; DAB; DAC; DAM MST, NOV; DLB 12, 78; EXPN; EXPS; FL 1:3; FW; LAIT 3; MAL 5; MBL; NFS 3; RGAL 4; RGSF 2; SSFS 2, 13, 17, 26; TUS

Chretien de Troyes c. 12th cent. - . **CMLC 10**
See also DLB 208; EW 1; RGWL 2, 3; TWA

Christie
See Ichikawa, Kon

Christie, Agatha (Mary Clarissa)
1890-1976 .. **CLC 1, 6, 8, 12, 39, 48, 110**
See also AAYA 9; AITN 1, 2; BPFB 1; BRWS 2; CA 17-20R; 61-64; CANR 10, 37, 108; CBD; CDBLB 1914-1945; CMW 4; CN 1, 2; CPW; CWD; DA3; DAB; DAC; DAM NOV; DFS 2; DLB 13, 77, 245; MSW; MTCW 1, 2; MTFW 2005; NFS 8, 30; RGEL 2; RHW; SATA 36; TEA; YAW

Christie, Ann Philippa
See Pearce, Philippa

Christie, Philippa
See Pearce, Philippa

Christine de Pisan
See Christine de Pizan

Christine de Pizan 1365(?)-1431(?) ...... **LC 9, 130; PC 68**
See also DLB 208; FL 1:1; FW; RGWL 2, 3

Chuang-Tzu c. 369B.C.-c.
286B.C. .... **CMLC 57**

Chubb, Elmer
See Masters, Edgar Lee

Chulkov, Mikhail Dmitrievich
1743-1792 .... **LC 2**
See also DLB 150

Churchill, Caryl 1938- .... **CLC 31, 55, 157; DC 5**
See also BRWS 4; CA 102; CANR 22, 46, 108; CBD; CD 5, 6; CWD; DFS 25; DLB 13, 310; EWL 3; FW; MTCW 1; RGEL 2

Churchill, Charles 1731-1764 .... **LC 3**
See also DLB 109; RGEL 2

Churchill, Chick
See Churchill, Caryl

Churchill, Sir Winston (Leonard Spencer)
1874-1965 .... **TCLC 113**
See also BRW 6; CA 97-100; CDBLB 1890-1914; DA3; DLB 100, 329; DLBD 16; LAIT 4; MTCW 1, 2

Chute, Carolyn 1947- .... **CLC 39**
See also CA 123; CANR 135; CN 7; DLB 350

Ciardi, John (Anthony) 1916-1986 . **CLC 10, 40, 44, 129; PC 69**
See also CA 5-8R; 118; CAAS 2; CANR 5, 33; CLR 19; CP 1, 2, 3, 4; CWRI 5; DAM POET; DLB 5; DLBY 1986; INT

CANR-5; MAICYA 1, 2; MAL 5; MTCW 1, 2; MTFW 2005; RGAL 4; SAAS 26; SATA 1, 65; SATA-Obit 46

Cibber, Colley 1671-1757 .... **LC 66**
See also DLB 84; RGEL 2

Cicero, Marcus Tullius
106B.C.-43B.C. .... **CMLC 3, 81**
See also AW 1; CDWLB 1; DLB 211; RGWL 2, 3; WLIT 8

Cimino, Michael 1943- .... **CLC 16**
See also CA 105

Cioran, E(mil) M. 1911-1995 .... **CLC 64**
See also CA 25-28R; 149; CANR 91; DLB 220; EWL 3

Circus, Anthony
See Hoch, Edward D.

Cisneros, Sandra 1954- .... **CLC 69, 118, 193; HLC 1; PC 52; SSC 32, 72**
See also AAYA 9, 53; AMWS 7; CA 131; CANR 64, 118; CLR 123; CN 7; CWP; DA3; DAM MULT; DLB 122, 152; EWL 3; EXPN; FL 1:5; FW; HW 1, 2; LAIT 5; LATS 1:2; LLW; MAICYA 2; MAL 5; MTCW 2; MTFW 2005; NFS 2; PFS 19; RGAL 4; RGSF 2; SSFS 3, 13, 27; WLIT 1; YAW

Cixous, Helene 1937- .... **CLC 92, 253**
See also CA 126; CANR 55, 123; CWW 2; DLB 83, 242; EWL 3; FL 1:5; FW; GLL 2; MTCW 1, 2; MTFW 2005; TWA

Clair, Rene
See Chomette, Rene Lucien

Clampitt, Amy 1920-1994 .... **CLC 32; PC 19**
See also AMWS 9; CA 110; 146; CANR 29, 79; CP 4, 5; DLB 105; MAL 5; PFS 27

Clancy, Thomas L., Jr. 1947- ... **CLC 45, 112**
See also AAYA 9, 51; BEST 89:1, 90:1; BPFB 1; BYA 10, 11; CA 125; 131; CANR 62, 105, 132; CMW 4; CPW; DA3; DAM NOV, POP; DLB 227; INT CA-131; MTCW 1, 2; MTFW 2005

Clancy, Tom
See Clancy, Thomas L., Jr.

Clare, John 1793-1864 .. **NCLC 9, 86; PC 23**
See also BRWS 11; DAB; DAM POET; DLB 55, 96; RGEL 2

Clarin
See Alas (y Urena), Leopoldo (Enrique Garcia)

Clark, Al C.
See Goines, Donald

Clark, Brian (Robert)
See Clark, (Robert) Brian

Clark, (Robert) Brian 1932- .... **CLC 29**
See also CA 41-44R; CANR 67; CBD; CD 5, 6

Clark, Curt
See Westlake, Donald E.

Clark, Eleanor 1913-1996 .... **CLC 5, 19**
See also CA 9-12R; 151; CANR 41; CN 1, 2, 3, 4, 5, 6; DLB 6

Clark, J. P.
See Clark Bekederemo, J.P.

Clark, John Pepper
See Clark Bekederemo, J.P.
See also AFW; CD 5; CP 1, 2, 3, 4, 5, 6, 7; RGEL 2

Clark, Kenneth (Mackenzie)
1903-1983 .... **TCLC 147**
See also CA 93-96; 109; CANR 36; MTCW 1, 2; MTFW 2005

Clark, M. R.
See Clark, Mavis Thorpe

Clark, Mavis Thorpe 1909-1999 ...... **CLC 12**
See also CA 57-60; CANR 8, 37, 107; CLR 30; CWRI 5; MAICYA 1, 2; SAAS 5; SATA 8, 74

Dunbar, William 1460(?)-1520(?) .... **LC 20; PC 67**
See also BRWS 8; DLB 132, 146; RGEL 2

Duncan, Dora Angela
See Duncan, Isadora

Duncan, Isadora 1877(?)-1927 .... **TCLC 68**
See also CA 118; 149

Duncan, Lois 1934- .... **CLC 26**
See also AAYA 4, 34; BYA 6, 8; CA 1-4R; CANR 2, 23, 36, 111; CLR 29, 129; JRDA; MAICYA 1, 2; MAICYAS 1; MTFW 2005; SAAS 2; SATA 1, 36, 75, 133, 141; SATA-Essay 141; WYA; YAW

Duncan, Robert 1919-1988 ... **CLC 1, 2, 4, 7, 15, 41, 55; PC 2, 75**
See also BG 1:2; CA 9-12R; 124; CANR 28, 62; CP 1, 2, 3, 4; DAM POET; DLB 5, 16, 193; EWL 3; MAL 5; MTCW 1, 2; MTFW 2005; PFS 13; RGAL 4; WP

Duncan, Sara Jeannette
1861-1922 .... **TCLC 60**
See also CA 157; DLB 92

Dunlap, William 1766-1839 .... **NCLC 2**
See also DLB 30, 37, 59; RGAL 4

Dunn, Douglas (Eaglesham) 1942- .... **CLC 6, 40**
See also BRWS 10; CA 45-48; CANR 2, 33, 126; CP 1, 2, 3, 4, 5, 6, 7; DLB 40; MTCW 1

Dunn, Katherine 1945- .... **CLC 71**
See also CA 33-36R; CANR 72; HGG; MTCW 2; MTFW 2005

Dunn, Stephen 1939- .... **CLC 36, 206**
See also AMWS 11; CA 33-36R; CANR 12, 48, 53, 105; CP 3, 4, 5, 6, 7; DLB 105; PFS 21

Dunn, Stephen Elliott
See Dunn, Stephen

Dunne, Finley Peter 1867-1936 ...... **TCLC 28**
See also CA 108; 178; DLB 11, 23; RGAL 4

Dunne, John Gregory 1932-2003 ..... **CLC 28**
See also CA 25-28R; 222; CANR 14, 50; CN 5, 6, 7; DLBY 1980

Dunsany, Lord
See Dunsany, Edward John Moreton Drax Plunkett

Dunsany, Edward John Moreton Drax Plunkett 1878-1957 .... **TCLC 2, 59**
See also CA 104; 148; DLB 10, 77, 153, 156, 255; FANT; MTCW 2; RGEL 2; SFW 4; SUFW 1

Duns Scotus, John 1266(?)-1308 ... **CMLC 59**
See also DLB 115

Duong, Thu Huong 1947- .... **CLC 273**
See also CA 152; CANR 106, 166; DLB 348; NFS 23

Duong Thu Huong
See Duong, Thu Huong

du Perry, Jean
See Simenon, Georges (Jacques Christian)

Durang, Christopher 1949- .... **CLC 27, 38**
See also CA 105; CAD; CANR 50, 76, 130; CD 5, 6; MTCW 2; MTFW 2005

Durang, Christopher Ferdinand
See Durang, Christopher

Duras, Claire de 1777-1832 .... **NCLC 154**

Duras, Marguerite 1914-1996 . **CLC 3, 6, 11, 20, 34, 40, 68, 100; SSC 40**
See also BPFB 1; CA 25-28R; 151; CANR 50; CWW 2; DFS 21; DLB 83, 321; EWL 3; FL 1:5; GFL 1789 to the Present; IDFW 4; MTCW 1, 2; RGWL 2, 3; TWA

Durban, (Rosa) Pam 1947- .... **CLC 39**
See also CA 123; CANR 98; CSW

Durcan, Paul 1944- .... **CLC 43, 70**
See also CA 134; CANR 123; CP 1, 5, 6, 7; DAM POET; EWL 3

d'Urfe, Honore
See Urfe, Honore d'

Durfey, Thomas 1653-1723 .... **LC 94**
See also DLB 80; RGEL 2

Durkheim, Emile 1858-1917 .... **TCLC 55**
See also CA 249

Durrell, Lawrence (George)
1912-1990 ..... **CLC 1, 4, 6, 8, 13, 27, 41**
See also BPFB 1; BRWS 1; CA 9-12R; 132; CANR 40, 77; CDBLB 1945-1960; CN 1, 2, 3, 4; CP 1, 2, 3, 4, 5; DAM NOV; DLB 15, 27, 204; DLBY 1990; EWL 3; MTCW 1, 2; RGEL 2; SFW 4; TEA

Durrenmatt, Friedrich
See Duerrenmatt, Friedrich

Dutt, Michael Madhusudan
1824-1873 .... **NCLC 118**

Dutt, Toru 1856-1877 .... **NCLC 29**
See also DLB 240

Dwight, Timothy 1752-1817 .... **NCLC 13**
See also DLB 37; RGAL 4

Dworkin, Andrea 1946-2005 ..... **CLC 43, 123**
See also CA 77-80; 238; CAAS 21; CANR 16, 39, 76, 96; FL 1:5; FW; GLL 1; INT CANR-16; MTCW 1, 2; MTFW 2005

Dwyer, Deanna
See Koontz, Dean R.

Dwyer, K.R.
See Koontz, Dean R.

Dybek, Stuart 1942- .... **CLC 114; SSC 55**
See also CA 97-100; CANR 39; DLB 130; SSFS 23

Dye, Richard
See De Voto, Bernard (Augustine)

Dyer, Geoff 1958- .... **CLC 149**
See also CA 125; CANR 88

Dyer, George 1755-1841 .... **NCLC 129**
See also DLB 93

Dylan, Bob 1941- .... **CLC 3, 4, 6, 12, 77; PC 37**
See also AMWS 18; CA 41-44R; CANR 108; CP 1, 2, 3, 4, 5, 6, 7; DLB 16

Dyson, John 1943- .... **CLC 70**
See also CA 144

Dzyubin, Eduard Georgievich
1895-1934 .... **TCLC 60**
See also CA 170; EWL 3

E. V. L.
See Lucas, E(dward) V(errall)

Eagleton, Terence (Francis) 1943- .. **CLC 63, 132**
See also CA 57-60; CANR 7, 23, 68, 115; DLB 242; LMFS 2; MTCW 1, 2; MTFW 2005

Eagleton, Terry
See Eagleton, Terence (Francis)

Early, Jack
See Scoppettone, Sandra

East, Michael
See West, Morris L(anglo)

Eastaway, Edward
See Thomas, (Philip) Edward

Eastlake, William (Derry)
1917-1997 .... **CLC 8**
See also CA 5-8R; 158; CAAS 1; CANR 5, 63; CN 1, 2, 3, 4, 5, 6; DLB 6, 206; INT CANR-5; MAL 5; TCWW 1, 2

Eastman, Charles A(lexander)
1858-1939 .... **NNAL; TCLC 55**
See also CA 179; CANR 91; DAM MULT; DLB 175; YABC 1

Eaton, Edith Maude 1865-1914 .... **AAL**
See also CA 154; DLB 221, 312; FW

Eaton, (Lillie) Winnifred 1875-1954 .... **AAL**
See also CA 217; DLB 221, 312; RGAL 4

Eberhart, Richard 1904-2005 ...... **CLC 3, 11, 19, 56; PC 76**
See also AMW; CA 1-4R; 240; CANR 2, 125; CDALB 1941-1968; CP 1, 2, 3, 4, 5, 6, 7; DAM POET; DLB 48; MAL 5; MTCW 1; RGAL 4

Eberhart, Richard Ghormley
See Eberhart, Richard

Eberstadt, Fernanda 1960- .... **CLC 39**
See also CA 136; CANR 69, 128

Ebner, Margaret c. 1291-1351 ...... **CMLC 98**

Echegaray (y Eizaguirre), Jose (Maria Waldo) 1832-1916 .... **HLCS 1; TCLC 4**
See also CA 104; CANR 32; DLB 329; EWL 3; HW 1; MTCW 1

Echeverria, (Jose) Esteban (Antonino)
1805-1851 .... **NCLC 18**
See also LAW

Echo
See Proust, (Valentin-Louis-George-Eugene) Marcel

Eckert, Allan W. 1931- .... **CLC 17**
See also AAYA 18; BYA 2; CA 13-16R; CANR 14, 45; INT CANR-14; MAICYA 2; MAICYAS 1; SAAS 21; SATA 29, 91; SATA-Brief 27

Eckhart, Meister 1260(?)-1327(?) .. **CMLC 9, 80**
See also DLB 115; LMFS 1

Eckmar, F. R.
See de Hartog, Jan

Eco, Umberto 1932- .... **CLC 28, 60, 142, 248**
See also BEST 90:1; BPFB 1; CA 77-80; CANR 12, 33, 55, 110, 131; CPW; CWW 2; DA3; DAM NOV, POP; DLB 196, 242; EWL 3; MSW; MTCW 1, 2; MTFW 2005; NFS 22; RGWL 3; WLIT 7

Eddison, E(ric) R(ucker)
1882-1945 .... **TCLC 15**
See also CA 109; 156; DLB 255; FANT; SFW 4; SUFW 1

Eddy, Mary (Ann Morse) Baker
1821-1910 .... **TCLC 71**
See also CA 113; 174

Edel, (Joseph) Leon 1907-1997 .. **CLC 29, 34**
See also CA 1-4R; 161; CANR 1, 22, 112; DLB 103; INT CANR-22

Eden, Emily 1797-1869 .... **NCLC 10**

Edgar, David 1948- .... **CLC 42**
See also CA 57-60; CANR 12, 61, 112; CBD; CD 5, 6; DAM DRAM; DFS 15; DLB 13, 233; MTCW 1

Edgerton, Clyde (Carlyle) 1944- ...... **CLC 39**
See also AAYA 17; CA 118; 134; CANR 64, 125; CN 7; CSW; DLB 278; INT CA-134; TCLE 1:1; YAW

Edgeworth, Maria 1768-1849 ... **NCLC 1, 51, 158; SSC 86**
See also BRWS 3; DLB 116, 159, 163; FL 1:3; FW; RGEL 2; SATA 21; TEA; WLIT 3

Edmonds, Paul
See Kuttner, Henry

Edmonds, Walter D(umaux)
1903-1998 .... **CLC 35**
See also BYA 2; CA 5-8R; CANR 2; CWRI 5; DLB 9; LAIT 1; MAICYA 1, 2; MAL 5; RHW; SAAS 4; SATA 1, 27; SATA-Obit 99

Edmondson, Wallace
See Ellison, Harlan

Edson, Margaret 1961- ...... **CLC 199; DC 24**
See also AMWS 18; CA 190; DFS 13; DLB 266

Edson, Russell 1935- .... **CLC 13**
See also CA 33-36R; CANR 115; CP 2, 3, 4, 5, 6, 7; DLB 244; WP

Edwards, Bronwen Elizabeth
See Rose, Wendy

El Saadawi, Nawal 1931- ...... **BLC 2:2; CLC 196**
See also AFW; CA 118; CAAS 11; CANR 44, 92; CWW 2; DLB 346; EWL 3; FW; WLIT 2

El-Shabazz, El-Hajj Malik
See Little, Malcolm

Eluard, Paul
See Grindel, Eugene

Eluard, Paul
See Grindel, Eugene

Elyot, Thomas 1490(?)-1546 .... **LC 11, 139**
See also DLB 136; RGEL 2

Elytis, Odysseus 1911-1996 .... **CLC 15, 49, 100; PC 21**
See also CA 102; 151; CANR 94; CWW 2; DAM POET; DLB 329; EW 13; EWL 3; MTCW 1, 2; RGWL 2, 3

Emecheta, Buchi 1944- ... **BLC 1:2; CLC 14, 48, 128, 214**
See also AAYA 67; AFW; BW 2, 3; CA 81-84; CANR 27, 81, 126; CDWLB 3; CN 4, 5, 6, 7; CWRI 5; DA3; DAM MULT; DLB 117; EWL 3; FL 1:5; FW; MTCW 1, 2; MTFW 2005; NFS 12, 14; SATA 66; WLIT 2

Emerson, Mary Moody 1774-1863 .... **NCLC 66**

Emerson, Ralph Waldo 1803-1882 . **NCLC 1, 38, 98; PC 18; WLC 2**
See also AAYA 60; AMW; ANW; CDALB 1640-1865; DA; DA3; DAB; DAC; DAM MST, POET; DLB 1, 59, 73, 183, 223, 270, 351; EXPP; LAIT 2; LMFS 1; NCFS 3; PFS 4, 17; RGAL 4; TUS; WP

Eminem 1972- .... **CLC 226**
See also CA 245

Eminescu, Mihail 1850-1889 .. **NCLC 33, 131**

Empedocles 5th cent. B.C.- .... **CMLC 50**
See also DLB 176

Empson, William 1906-1984 ... **CLC 3, 8, 19, 33, 34**
See also BRWS 2; CA 17-20R; 112; CANR 31, 61; CP 1, 2, 3; DLB 20; EWL 3; MTCW 1, 2; RGEL 2

Enchi, Fumiko 1905-1986 .... **CLC 31**
See also CA 129; 121; DLB 182; EWL 3; FW; MJW

Enchi, Fumiko Ueda
See Enchi, Fumiko

Enchi Fumiko
See Enchi, Fumiko

Ende, Michael (Andreas Helmuth) 1929-1995 .... **CLC 31**
See also BYA 5; CA 118; 124; 149; CANR 36, 110; CLR 14, 138; DLB 75; MAICYA 1, 2; MAICYAS 1; SATA 61, 130; SATA-Brief 42; SATA-Obit 86

Endo, Shusaku 1923-1996 ..... **CLC 7, 14, 19, 54, 99; SSC 48; TCLC 152**
See also CA 29-32R; 153; CANR 21, 54, 131; CWW 2; DA3; DAM NOV; DLB 182; EWL 3; MTCW 1, 2; MTFW 2005; RGSF 2; RGWL 2, 3

Endo Shusaku
See Endo, Shusaku

Engel, Marian 1933-1985 .... **CLC 36; TCLC 137**
See also CA 25-28R; CANR 12; CN 2, 3; DLB 53; FW; INT CANR-12

Engelhardt, Frederick
See Hubbard, L. Ron

Engels, Friedrich 1820-1895 .. **NCLC 85, 114**
See also DLB 129; LATS 1:1

Enquist, Per Olov 1934- .... **CLC 257**
See also CA 109; 193; CANR 155; CWW 2; DLB 257; EWL 3

Enright, D(ennis) J(oseph) 1920-2002 .... **CLC 4, 8, 31; PC 93**
See also CA 1-4R; 211; CANR 1, 42, 83; CN 1, 2; CP 1, 2, 3, 4, 5, 6, 7; DLB 27; EWL 3; SATA 25; SATA-Obit 140

Ensler, Eve 1953- .... **CLC 212**
See also CA 172; CANR 126, 163; DFS 23

Enzensberger, Hans Magnus 1929- .... **CLC 43; PC 28**
See also CA 116; 119; CANR 103; CWW 2; EWL 3

Ephron, Nora 1941- .... **CLC 17, 31**
See also AAYA 35; AITN 2; CA 65-68; CANR 12, 39, 83, 161; DFS 22

Epicurus 341B.C.-270B.C. .... **CMLC 21**
See also DLB 176

Epinay, Louise d' 1726-1783 .... **LC 138**
See also DLB 313

Epsilon
See Betjeman, John

Epstein, Daniel Mark 1948- .... **CLC 7**
See also CA 49-52; CANR 2, 53, 90, 193

Epstein, Jacob 1956- .... **CLC 19**
See also CA 114

Epstein, Jean 1897-1953 .... **TCLC 92**

Epstein, Joseph 1937- .... **CLC 39, 204**
See also AMWS 14; CA 112; 119; CANR 50, 65, 117, 164, 190

Epstein, Leslie 1938- .... **CLC 27**
See also AMWS 12; CA 73-76, 215; CAAE 215; CAAS 12; CANR 23, 69, 162; DLB 299; RGHL

Equiano, Olaudah 1745(?)-1797 ..... **BLC 1:2; LC 16, 143**
See also AFAW 1, 2; CDWLB 3; DAM MULT; DLB 37, 50; WLIT 2

Erasmus, Desiderius 1469(?)-1536 ..... **LC 16, 93**
See also DLB 136; EW 2; LMFS 1; RGWL 2, 3; TWA

Erdman, Paul E. 1932-2007 .... **CLC 25**
See also AITN 1; CA 61-64; 259; CANR 13, 43, 84

Erdman, Paul Emil
See Erdman, Paul E.

Erdrich, Karen Louise
See Erdrich, Louise

Erdrich, Louise 1954- .... **CLC 39, 54, 120, 176; NNAL; PC 52; SSC 121**
See also AAYA 10, 47; AMWS 4; BEST 89:1; BPFB 1; CA 114; CANR 41, 62, 118, 138, 190; CDALBS; CN 5, 6, 7; CP 6, 7; CPW; CWP; DA3; DAM MULT, NOV, POP; DLB 152, 175, 206; EWL 3; EXPP; FL 1:5; LAIT 5; LATS 1:2; MAL 5; MTCW 1, 2; MTFW 2005; NFS 5; PFS 14; RGAL 4; SATA 94, 141; SSFS 14, 22; TCWW 2

Erenburg, Ilya (Grigoryevich)
See Ehrenburg, Ilya (Grigoryevich)
See also DLB 272

Erickson, Stephen Michael
See Erickson, Steve

Erickson, Steve 1950- .... **CLC 64**
See also CA 129; CANR 60, 68, 136; MTFW 2005; SFW 4; SUFW 2

Erickson, Walter
See Fast, Howard

Ericson, Walter
See Fast, Howard

Eriksson, Buntel
See Bergman, Ingmar

Eriugena, John Scottus c. 810-877 .... **CMLC 65**
See also DLB 115

Ernaux, Annie 1940- .... **CLC 88, 184**
See also CA 147; CANR 93; MTFW 2005; NCFS 3, 5

Erskine, John 1879-1951 .... **TCLC 84**
See also CA 112; 159; DLB 9, 102; FANT

Erwin, Will
See Eisner, Will

Eschenbach, Wolfram von
See von Eschenbach, Wolfram

Eseki, Bruno
See Mphahlele, Es'kia

Esekie, Bruno
See Mphahlele, Es'kia

Esenin, S.A.
See Esenin, Sergei

Esenin, Sergei 1895-1925 .... **TCLC 4**
See also CA 104; EWL 3; RGWL 2, 3

Esenin, Sergei Aleksandrovich
See Esenin, Sergei

Eshleman, Clayton 1935- .... **CLC 7**
See also CA 33-36R, 212; CAAE 212; CAAS 6; CANR 93; CP 1, 2, 3, 4, 5, 6, 7; DLB 5

Espada, Martin 1957- .... **PC 74**
See also CA 159; CANR 80; CP 7; EXPP; LLW; MAL 5; PFS 13, 16

Espriella, Don Manuel Alvarez
See Southey, Robert

Espriu, Salvador 1913-1985 .... **CLC 9**
See also CA 154; 115; DLB 134; EWL 3

Espronceda, Jose de 1808-1842 ..... **NCLC 39**

Esquivel, Laura 1950(?)- ... **CLC 141; HLCS 1**
See also AAYA 29; CA 143; CANR 68, 113, 161; DA3; DNFS 2; LAIT 3; LMFS 2; MTCW 2; MTFW 2005; NFS 5; WLIT 1

Esse, James
See Stephens, James

Esterbrook, Tom
See Hubbard, L. Ron

Esterhazy, Peter 1950- .... **CLC 251**
See also CA 140; CANR 137; CDWLB 4; CWW 2; DLB 232; EWL 3; RGWL 3

Estleman, Loren D. 1952- .... **CLC 48**
See also AAYA 27; CA 85-88; CANR 27, 74, 139, 177; CMW 4; CPW; DA3; DAM NOV, POP; DLB 226; INT CANR-27; MTCW 1, 2; MTFW 2005; TCWW 1, 2

Etherege, Sir George 1636-1692 . **DC 23; LC 78**
See also BRW 2; DAM DRAM; DLB 80; PAB; RGEL 2

Euclid 306B.C.-283B.C. .... **CMLC 25**

Eugenides, Jeffrey 1960- .... **CLC 81, 212**
See also AAYA 51; CA 144; CANR 120; DLB 350; MTFW 2005; NFS 24

Euripides c. 484B.C.-406B.C. .... **CMLC 23, 51; DC 4; WLCS**
See also AW 1; CDWLB 1; DA; DA3; DAB; DAC; DAM DRAM, MST; DFS 1, 4, 6, 25; DLB 176; LAIT 1; LMFS 1; RGWL 2, 3; WLIT 8

Eusebius c. 263-c. 339 .... **CMLC 103**

Evan, Evin
See Faust, Frederick

Evans, Caradoc 1878-1945 ... **SSC 43; TCLC 85**
See also DLB 162

Evans, Evan
See Faust, Frederick

Evans, Marian
See Eliot, George

Evans, Mary Ann
See Eliot, George

Evarts, Esther
See Benson, Sally

Evelyn, John 1620-1706 .... **LC 144**
See also BRW 2; RGEL 2

Fenelon, Francois de Pons de Salignac de la
   Mothe- 1651-1715 .... **LC 134**
   See also DLB 268; EW 3; GFL Beginnings
   to 1789

Fenno, Jack
   See Calisher, Hortense

Fenollosa, Ernest (Francisco)
   1853-1908 .... **TCLC 91**

Fenton, James 1949- .... **CLC 32, 209**
   See also CA 102; CANR 108, 160; CP 2, 3,
   4, 5, 6, 7; DLB 40; PFS 11

Fenton, James Martin
   See Fenton, James

Ferber, Edna 1887-1968 .... **CLC 18, 93**
   See also AITN 1; CA 5-8R; 25-28R; CANR
   68, 105; DLB 9, 28, 86, 266; MAL 5;
   MTCW 1, 2; MTFW 2005; RGAL 4;
   RHW; SATA 7; TCWW 1, 2

Ferdousi
   See Ferdowsi, Abu'l Qasem

Ferdovsi
   See Ferdowsi, Abu'l Qasem

Ferdowsi
   See Ferdowsi, Abu'l Qasem

Ferdowsi, Abolghasem Mansour
   See Ferdowsi, Abu'l Qasem

Ferdowsi, Abolqasem
   See Ferdowsi, Abu'l Qasem

Ferdowsi, Abol-Qasem
   See Ferdowsi, Abu'l Qasem

Ferdowsi, Abu'l Qasem
   940-1020(?) .... **CMLC 43**
   See also CA 276; RGWL 2, 3; WLIT 6

Ferdowsi, A.M.
   See Ferdowsi, Abu'l Qasem

Ferdowsi, Hakim Abolghasem
   See Ferdowsi, Abu'l Qasem

Ferguson, Helen
   See Kavan, Anna

Ferguson, Niall 1964- .... **CLC 134, 250**
   See also CA 190; CANR 154

Ferguson, Niall Campbell
   See Ferguson, Niall

Ferguson, Samuel 1810-1886 .... **NCLC 33**
   See also DLB 32; RGEL 2

Fergusson, Robert 1750-1774 .... **LC 29**
   See also DLB 109; RGEL 2

Ferling, Lawrence
   See Ferlinghetti, Lawrence

Ferlinghetti, Lawrence 1919(?)- .... **CLC 2, 6,
   10, 27, 111; PC 1**
   See also AAYA 74; BG 1:2; CA 5-8R; CAD;
   CANR 3, 41, 73, 125, 172; CDALB 1941-
   1968; CP 1, 2, 3, 4, 5, 6, 7; DA3; DAM
   POET; DLB 5, 16; MAL 5; MTCW 1, 2;
   MTFW 2005; PFS 28; RGAL 4; WP

Ferlinghetti, Lawrence Monsanto
   See Ferlinghetti, Lawrence

Fern, Fanny
   See Parton, Sara Payson Willis

Fernandez, Vicente Garcia Huidobro
   See Huidobro Fernandez, Vicente Garcia

Fernandez-Armesto, Felipe 1950- .... **CLC 70**
   See also CA 142; CANR 93, 153, 189

Fernandez-Armesto, Felipe Fermin Ricardo
   See Fernandez-Armesto, Felipe

Fernandez de Lizardi, Jose Joaquin
   See Lizardi, Jose Joaquin Fernandez de

Ferre, Rosario 1938- ...... **CLC 139; HLCS 1;
   SSC 36, 106**
   See also CA 131; CANR 55, 81, 134; CWW
   2; DLB 145; EWL 3; HW 1, 2; LAWS 1;
   MTCW 2; MTFW 2005; WLIT 1

Ferrer, Gabriel (Francisco Victor) Miro
   See Miro (Ferrer), Gabriel (Francisco
   Victor)

Ferrier, Susan (Edmonstone)
   1782-1854 .... **NCLC 8**
   See also DLB 116; RGEL 2

Ferrigno, Robert 1947- .... **CLC 65**
   See also CA 140; CANR 125, 161

Ferris, Joshua 1974- .... **CLC 280**
   See also CA 262

Ferron, Jacques 1921-1985 .... **CLC 94**
   See also CA 117; 129; CCA 1; DAC; DLB
   60; EWL 3

Feuchtwanger, Lion 1884-1958 .... **TCLC 3**
   See also CA 104; 187; DLB 66; EWL 3;
   RGHL

Feuerbach, Ludwig 1804-1872 ..... **NCLC 139**
   See also DLB 133

Feuillet, Octave 1821-1890 .... **NCLC 45**
   See also DLB 192

Feydeau, Georges (Leon Jules Marie)
   1862-1921 .... **TCLC 22**
   See also CA 113; 152; CANR 84; DAM
   DRAM; DLB 192; EWL 3; GFL 1789 to
   the Present; RGWL 2, 3

Fichte, Johann Gottlieb
   1762-1814 .... **NCLC 62**
   See also DLB 90

Ficino, Marsilio 1433-1499 .... **LC 12, 152**
   See also LMFS 1

Fiedeler, Hans
   See Doeblin, Alfred

Fiedler, Leslie A(aron) 1917-2003 ..... **CLC 4,
   13, 24**
   See also AMWS 13; CA 9-12R; 212; CANR
   7, 63; CN 1, 2, 3, 4, 5, 6; DLB 28, 67;
   EWL 3; MAL 5; MTCW 1, 2; RGAL 4;
   TUS

Field, Andrew 1938- .... **CLC 44**
   See also CA 97-100; CANR 25

Field, Eugene 1850-1895 .... **NCLC 3**
   See also DLB 23, 42, 140; DLBD 13; MAI-
   CYA 1, 2; RGAL 4; SATA 16

Field, Gans T.
   See Wellman, Manly Wade

Field, Michael 1915-1971 .... **TCLC 43**
   See also CA 29-32R

Fielding, Helen 1958- .... **CLC 146, 217**
   See also AAYA 65; CA 172; CANR 127;
   DLB 231; MTFW 2005

Fielding, Henry 1707-1754 .... **LC 1, 46, 85,
   151, 154; WLC 2**
   See also BRW 3; BRWR 1; CDBLB 1660-
   1789; DA; DA3; DAB; DAC; DAM
   DRAM, MST, NOV; DLB 39, 84, 101;
   NFS 18; RGEL 2; TEA; WLIT 3

Fielding, Sarah 1710-1768 .... **LC 1, 44**
   See also DLB 39; RGEL 2; TEA

Fields, W. C. 1880-1946 .... **TCLC 80**
   See also DLB 44

Fierstein, Harvey (Forbes) 1954- ..... **CLC 33**
   See also CA 123; 129; CAD; CD 5, 6;
   CPW; DA3; DAM DRAM, POP; DFS 6;
   DLB 266; GLL; MAL 5

Figes, Eva 1932- .... **CLC 31**
   See also CA 53-56; CANR 4, 44, 83; CN 2,
   3, 4, 5, 6, 7; DLB 14, 271; FW; RGHL

Filippo, Eduardo de
   See de Filippo, Eduardo

Finch, Anne 1661-1720 ..... **LC 3, 137; PC 21**
   See also BRWS 9; DLB 95; PFS 30

Finch, Robert (Duer Claydon)
   1900-1995 .... **CLC 18**
   See also CA 57-60; CANR 9, 24, 49; CP 1,
   2, 3, 4, 5, 6; DLB 88

Findley, Timothy (Irving Frederick)
   1930-2002 .... **CLC 27, 102**
   See also CA 25-28R; 206; CANR 12, 42,
   69, 109; CCA 1; CN 4, 5, 6, 7; DAC;
   DAM MST; DLB 53; FANT; RHW

Fink, William
   See Mencken, H. L.

Firbank, Louis 1942- .... **CLC 21**
   See also CA 117

Firbank, (Arthur Annesley) Ronald
   1886-1926 .... **TCLC 1**
   See also BRWS 2; CA 104; 177; DLB 36;
   EWL 3; RGEL 2

Firdaosi
   See Ferdowsi, Abu'l Qasem

Firdausi
   See Ferdowsi, Abu'l Qasem

Firdavsi, Abulqosimi
   See Ferdowsi, Abu'l Qasem

Firdavsii, Abulqosim
   See Ferdowsi, Abu'l Qasem

Firdawsi, Abu al-Qasim
   See Ferdowsi, Abu'l Qasem

Firdosi
   See Ferdowsi, Abu'l Qasem

Firdousi
   See Ferdowsi, Abu'l Qasem

Firdousi, Abu'l-Qasim
   See Ferdowsi, Abu'l Qasem

Firdovsi, A.
   See Ferdowsi, Abu'l Qasem

Firdovsi, Abulgasim
   See Ferdowsi, Abu'l Qasem

Firdusi
   See Ferdowsi, Abu'l Qasem

Fish, Stanley
   See Fish, Stanley Eugene

Fish, Stanley E.
   See Fish, Stanley Eugene

Fish, Stanley Eugene 1938- .... **CLC 142**
   See also CA 112; 132; CANR 90; DLB 67

Fisher, Dorothy (Frances) Canfield
   1879-1958 .... **TCLC 87**
   See also CA 114; 136; CANR 80; CLR 71;
   CWRI 5; DLB 9, 102, 284; MAICYA 1,
   2; MAL 5; YABC 1

Fisher, M(ary) F(rances) K(ennedy)
   1908-1992 .... **CLC 76, 87**
   See also AMWS 17; CA 77-80; 138; CANR
   44; MTCW 2

Fisher, Roy 1930- .... **CLC 25**
   See also CA 81-84; CAAS 10; CANR 16;
   CP 1, 2, 3, 4, 5, 6, 7; DLB 40

Fisher, Rudolph 1897-1934 ...... **BLC 1:2; HR
   1:2; SSC 25; TCLC 11**
   See also BW 1, 3; CA 107; 124; CANR 80;
   DAM MULT; DLB 51, 102

Fisher, Vardis (Alvero) 1895-1968 .... **CLC 7;
   TCLC 140**
   See also CA 5-8R; 25-28R; CANR 68; DLB
   9, 206; MAL 5; RGAL 4; TCWW 1, 2

Fiske, Tarleton
   See Bloch, Robert (Albert)

Fitch, Clarke
   See Sinclair, Upton

Fitch, John IV
   See Cormier, Robert

Fitzgerald, Captain Hugh
   See Baum, L(yman) Frank

FitzGerald, Edward 1809-1883 ...... **NCLC 9,
   153; PC 79**
   See also BRW 4; DLB 32; RGEL 2

Fitzgerald, F(rancis) Scott (Key)
   1896-1940 ... **SSC 6, 31, 75; TCLC 1, 6,
   14, 28, 55, 157; WLC 2**
   See also AAYA 24; AITN 1; AMW; AMWC
   2; AMWR 1; BPFB 1; CA 110; 123;
   CDALB 1917-1929; DA; DA3; DAB;
   DAC; DAM MST, NOV; DLB 4, 9, 86,
   219, 273; DLBD 1, 15, 16; DLBY 1981,
   1996; EWL 3; EXPN; EXPS; LAIT 3;
   MAL 5; MTCW 1, 2; MTFW 2005; NFS
   2, 19, 20; RGAL 4; RGSF 2; SSFS 4, 15,
   21, 25; TUS

Fouque, Friedrich (Heinrich Karl) de la Motte 1777-1843 .... **NCLC 2**
See also DLB 90; RGWL 2, 3; SUFW 1

Fourier, Charles 1772-1837 .... **NCLC 51**

Fournier, Henri-Alban 1886-1914 ... **TCLC 6**
See also CA 104; 179; DLB 65; EWL 3; GFL 1789 to the Present; RGWL 2, 3

Fournier, Pierre 1916-1997 .... **CLC 11**
See also CA 89-92; CANR 16, 40; EWL 3; RGHL

Fowles, John 1926-2005 .... **CLC 1, 2, 3, 4, 6, 9, 10, 15, 33, 87; SSC 33**
See also BPFB 1; BRWS 1; CA 5-8R; 245; CANR 25, 71, 103; CDBLB 1960 to Present; CN 1, 2, 3, 4, 5, 6, 7; DA3; DAB; DAC; DAM MST; DLB 14, 139, 207; EWL 3; HGG; MTCW 1, 2; MTFW 2005; NFS 21; RGEL 2; RHW; SATA 22; SATA-Obit 171; TEA; WLIT 4

Fowles, John Robert
See Fowles, John

Fox, Paula 1923- .... **CLC 2, 8, 121**
See also AAYA 3, 37; BYA 3, 8; CA 73-76; CANR 20, 36, 62, 105; CLR 1, 44, 96; DLB 52; JRDA; MAICYA 1, 2; MTCW 1; NFS 12; SATA 17, 60, 120, 167; WYA; YAW

Fox, William Price, Jr.
See Fox, William Price

Fox, William Price 1926- .... **CLC 22**
See also CA 17-20R; CAAS 19; CANR 11, 142, 189; CSW; DLB 2; DLBY 1981

Foxe, John 1517(?)-1587 .... **LC 14, 166**
See also DLB 132

Frame, Janet 1924-2004 ...... **CLC 2, 3, 6, 22, 66, 96, 237; SSC 29**
See also CA 1-4R; 224; CANR 2, 36, 76, 135; CN 1, 2, 3, 4, 5, 6, 7; CP 2, 3, 4; CWP; EWL 3; MTCW 1,2; RGEL 2; RGSF 2; SATA 119; TWA

France, Anatole
See Thibault, Jacques Anatole Francois

Francis, Claude .... **CLC 50**
See also CA 192

Francis, Dick 1920- .... **CLC 2, 22, 42, 102**
See also AAYA 5, 21; BEST 89:3; BPFB 1; CA 5-8R; CANR 9, 42, 68, 100, 141, 179; CDBLB 1960 to Present; CMW 4; CN 2, 3, 4, 5, 6; DA3; DAM POP; DLB 87; INT CANR-9; MSW; MTCW 1, 2; MTFW 2005

Francis, Paula Marie
See Allen, Paula Gunn

Francis, Richard Stanley
See Francis, Dick

Francis, Robert (Churchill) 1901-1987 .... **CLC 15; PC 34**
See also AMWS 9; CA 1-4R; 123; CANR 1; CP 1, 2, 3, 4; EXPP; PFS 12; TCLE 1:1

Francis, Lord Jeffrey
See Jeffrey, Francis

Franco, Veronica 1546-1591 .... **LC 171**
See also WLIT 7

Frank, Anne(lies Marie) 1929-1945 .... **TCLC 17; WLC 2**
See also AAYA 12; BYA 1; CA 113; 133; CANR 68; CLR 101; DA; DA3; DAB; DAC; DAM MST; LAIT 4; MAICYA 2; MAICYAS 1; MTCW 1, 2; MTFW 2005; NCFS 2; RGHL; SATA 87; SATA-Brief 42; WYA; YAW

Frank, Bruno 1887-1945 .... **TCLC 81**
See also CA 189; DLB 118; EWL 3

Frank, Elizabeth 1945- .... **CLC 39**
See also CA 121; 126; CANR 78, 150; INT CA-126

Frankl, Viktor E(mil) 1905-1997 ...... **CLC 93**
See also CA 65-68; 161; RGHL

Franklin, Benjamin
See Hasek, Jaroslav (Matej Frantisek)

Franklin, Benjamin 1706-1790 .. **LC 25, 134; WLCS**
See also AMW; CDALB 1640-1865; DA; DA3; DAB; DAC; DAM MST; DLB 24, 43, 73, 183; LAIT 1; RGAL 4; TUS

Franklin, Madeleine
See L'Engle, Madeleine

Franklin, Madeleine L'Engle
See L'Engle, Madeleine

Franklin, Madeleine L'Engle Camp
See L'Engle, Madeleine

Franklin, (Stella Maria Sarah) Miles (Lampe) 1879-1954 .... **TCLC 7**
See also CA 104; 164; DLB 230; FW; MTCW 2; RGEL 2; TWA

Franzen, Jonathan 1959- .... **CLC 202**
See also AAYA 65; CA 129; CANR 105, 166

Fraser, Antonia 1932- .... **CLC 32, 107**
See also AAYA 57; CA 85-88; CANR 44, 65, 119, 164; CMW; DLB 276; MTCW 1, 2; MTFW 2005; SATA-Brief 32

Fraser, George MacDonald 1925-2008 .... **CLC 7**
See also AAYA 48; CA 45-48; 180; 268; CAAE 180; CANR 2, 48, 74, 192; DLB 352; MTCW 2; RHW

Fraser, Sylvia 1935- .... **CLC 64**
See also CA 45-48; CANR 1, 16, 60; CCA 1

Frater Perdurabo
See Crowley, Edward Alexander

Frayn, Michael 1933- .... **CLC 3, 7, 31, 47, 176; DC 27**
See also AAYA 69; BRWC 2; BRWS 7; CA 5-8R; CANR 30, 69, 114, 133, 166; CBD; CD 5, 6; CN 1, 2, 3, 4, 5, 6, 7; DAM DRAM, NOV; DFS 22; DLB 13, 14, 194, 245; FANT; MTCW 1, 2; MTFW 2005; SFW 4

Fraze, Candida (Merrill) 1945- .... **CLC 50**
See also CA 126

Frazer, Andrew
See Marlowe, Stephen

Frazer, J(ames) G(eorge) 1854-1941 .... **TCLC 32**
See also BRWS 3; CA 118; NCFS 5

Frazer, Robert Caine
See Creasey, John

Frazer, Sir James George
See Frazer, J(ames) G(eorge)

Frazier, Charles 1950- .... **CLC 109, 224**
See also AAYA 34; CA 161; CANR 126, 170; CSW; DLB 292; MTFW 2005; NFS 25

Frazier, Charles R.
See Frazier, Charles

Frazier, Charles Robinson
See Frazier, Charles

Frazier, Ian 1951- .... **CLC 46**
See also CA 130; CANR 54, 93, 193

Frederic, Harold 1856-1898 ... **NCLC 10, 175**
See also AMW; DLB 12, 23; DLBD 13; MAL 5; NFS 22; RGAL 4

Frederick, John
See Faust, Frederick

Frederick the Great 1712-1786 .... **LC 14**

Fredro, Aleksander 1793-1876 .... **NCLC 8**

Freeling, Nicolas 1927-2003 .... **CLC 38**
See also CA 49-52; 218; CAAS 12; CANR 1, 17, 50, 84; CMW 4; CN 1, 2, 3, 4, 5, 6; DLB 87

Freeman, Douglas Southall 1886-1953 .... **TCLC 11**
See also CA 109; 195; DLB 17; DLBD 17

Freeman, Judith 1946- .... **CLC 55**
See also CA 148; CANR 120, 179; DLB 256

Freeman, Mary E(leanor) Wilkins 1852-1930 .... **SSC 1, 47, 113; TCLC 9**
See also CA 106; 177; DLB 12, 78, 221; EXPS; FW; HGG; MBL; RGAL 4; RGSF 2; SSFS 4, 8, 26; SUFW 1; TUS

Freeman, R(ichard) Austin 1862-1943 .... **TCLC 21**
See also CA 113; CANR 84; CMW 4; DLB 70

French, Albert 1943- .... **CLC 86**
See also BW 3; CA 167

French, Antonia
See Kureishi, Hanif

French, Marilyn 1929-2009 . **CLC 10, 18, 60, 177**
See also BPFB 1; CA 69-72; 286; CANR 3, 31, 134, 163; CN 5, 6, 7; CPW; DAM DRAM, NOV, POP; FL 1:5; FW; INT CANR-31; MTCW 1, 2; MTFW 2005

French, Paul
See Asimov, Isaac

Freneau, Philip Morin 1752-1832 .. **NCLC 1, 111**
See also AMWS 2; DLB 37, 43; RGAL 4

Freud, Sigmund 1856-1939 .... **TCLC 52**
See also CA 115; 133; CANR 69; DLB 296; EW 8; EWL 3; LATS 1:1; MTCW 1, 2; MTFW 2005; NCFS 3; TWA

Freytag, Gustav 1816-1895 .... **NCLC 109**
See also DLB 129

Friedan, Betty 1921-2006 .... **CLC 74**
See also CA 65-68; 248; CANR 18, 45, 74; DLB 246; FW; MTCW 1, 2; MTFW 2005; NCFS 5

Friedan, Betty Naomi
See Friedan, Betty

Friedlander, Saul 1932- .... **CLC 90**
See also CA 117; 130; CANR 72; RGHL

Friedman, B(ernard) H(arper) 1926- .... **CLC 7**
See also CA 1-4R; CANR 3, 48

Friedman, Bruce Jay 1930- ...... **CLC 3, 5, 56**
See also CA 9-12R; CAD; CANR 25, 52, 101; CD 5, 6; CN 1, 2, 3, 4, 5, 6, 7; DLB 2, 28, 244; INT CANR-25; MAL 5; SSFS 18

Friel, Brian 1929- ... **CLC 5, 42, 59, 115, 253; DC 8; SSC 76**
See also BRWS 5; CA 21-24R; CANR 33, 69, 131; CBD; CD 5, 6; DFS 11; DLB 13, 319; EWL 3; MTCW 1; RGEL 2; TEA

Friis-Baastad, Babbis Ellinor 1921-1970 .... **CLC 12**
See also CA 17-20R; 134; SATA 7

Frisch, Max 1911-1991 ...... **CLC 3, 9, 14, 18, 32, 44; TCLC 121**
See also CA 85-88; 134; CANR 32, 74; CD-WLB 2; DAM DRAM, NOV; DFS 25; DLB 69, 124; EW 13; EWL 3; MTCW 1, 2; MTFW 2005; RGHL; RGWL 2, 3

Fromentin, Eugene (Samuel Auguste) 1820-1876 .... **NCLC 10, 125**
See also DLB 123; GFL 1789 to the Present

Frost, Frederick
See Faust, Frederick

Frost, Robert 1874-1963 . **CLC 1, 3, 4, 9, 10, 13, 15, 26, 34, 44; PC 1, 39, 71; WLC 2**
See also AAYA 21; AMW; AMWR 1; CA 89-92; CANR 33; CDALB 1917-1929; CLR 67; DA; DA3; DAB; DAC; DAM MST, POET; DLB 54, 284, 342; DLBD 7; EWL 3; EXPP; MAL 5; MTCW 1, 2; MTFW 2005; PAB; PFS 1, 2, 3, 4, 5, 6, 7, 10, 13; RGAL 4; SATA 14; TUS; WP; WYA

LMFS 2; MTCW 1, 2; MTFW 2005;
NCFS 3; NFS 1, 5, 10; RGSF 2; RGWL
2, 3; SSFS 1, 6, 16, 21; TWA; WLIT 1

Garcia Marquez, Gabriel Jose
See Garcia Marquez, Gabriel

Garcilaso de la Vega, El Inca
1539-1616 .... **HLCS 1; LC 127**
See also DLB 318; LAW

Gard, Janice
See Latham, Jean Lee

Gard, Roger Martin du
See Martin du Gard, Roger

Gardam, Jane 1928- .... **CLC 43**
See also CA 49-52; CANR 2, 18, 33, 54,
106, 167; CLR 12; DLB 14, 161, 231;
MAICYA 1, 2; MTCW 1; SAAS 9; SATA
39, 76, 130; SATA-Brief 28; YAW

Gardam, Jane Mary
See Gardam, Jane

Gardens, S. S.
See Snodgrass, W. D.

Gardner, Herb(ert George)
1934-2003 .... **CLC 44**
See also CA 149; 220; CAD; CANR 119;
CD 5, 6; DFS 18, 20

Gardner, John, Jr. 1933-1982 ... **CLC 2, 3, 5,
7, 8, 10, 18, 28, 34; SSC 7; TCLC 195**
See also AAYA 45; AITN 1; AMWS 6;
BPFB 2; CA 65-68; 107; CANR 33, 73;
CDALBS; CN 2, 3; CPW; DA3; DAM
NOV, POP; DLB 2; DLBY 1982; EWL 3;
FANT; LATS 1:2; MAL 5; MTCW 1, 2;
MTFW 2005; NFS 3; RGAL 4; RGSF 2;
SATA 40; SATA-Obit 31; SSFS 8

Gardner, John 1926-2007 .... **CLC 30**
See also CA 103; 263; CANR 15, 69, 127,
183; CMW 4; CPW; DAM POP; MTCW
1

Gardner, John Edmund
See Gardner, John

Gardner, Miriam
See Bradley, Marion Zimmer

Gardner, Noel
See Kuttner, Henry

Gardons, S.S.
See Snodgrass, W. D.

Garfield, Leon 1921-1996 .... **CLC 12**
See also AAYA 8, 69; BYA 1, 3; CA 17-
20R; 152; CANR 38, 41, 78; CLR 21;
DLB 161; JRDA; MAICYA 1, 2; MAIC-
YAS 1; SATA 1, 32, 76; SATA-Obit 90;
TEA; WYA; YAW

Garland, (Hannibal) Hamlin
1860-1940 .... **SSC 18, 117; TCLC 3**
See also CA 104; DLB 12, 71, 78, 186;
MAL 5; RGAL 4; RGSF 2; TCWW 1, 2

Garneau, (Hector de) Saint-Denys
1912-1943 .... **TCLC 13**
See also CA 111; DLB 88

Garner, Alan 1934- .... **CLC 17**
See also AAYA 18; BYA 3, 5; CA 73-76,
178; CAAE 178; CANR 15, 64, 134; CLR
20, 130; CPW; DAB; DAM POP; DLB
161, 261; FANT; MAICYA 1, 2; MTCW
1, 2; MTFW 2005; SATA 18, 69; SATA-
Essay 108; SUFW 1, 2; YAW

Garner, Hugh 1913-1979 .... **CLC 13**
See also CA 69-72; CANR 31; CCA 1; CN
1, 2; DLB 68

Garnett, David 1892-1981 .... **CLC 3**
See also CA 5-8R; 103; CANR 17, 79; CN
1, 2; DLB 34; FANT; MTCW 2; RGEL 2;
SFW 4; SUFW 1

Garnier, Robert c. 1545-1590 .... **LC 119**
See also DLB 327; GFL Beginnings to 1789

Garrett, George 1929-2008 ... **CLC 3, 11, 51;
SSC 30**
See also AMWS 7; BPFB 2; CA 1-4R, 202;
272; CAAE 202; CAAS 5; CANR 1, 42,
67, 109; CN 1, 2, 3, 4, 5, 6, 7; CP 1, 2, 3,
4, 5, 6, 7; CSW; DLB 2, 5, 130, 152;
DLBY 1983

Garrett, George P.
See Garrett, George

Garrett, George Palmer
See Garrett, George

Garrett, George Palmer, Jr.
See Garrett, George

Garrick, David 1717-1779 .... **LC 15, 156**
See also DAM DRAM; DLB 84, 213;
RGEL 2

Garrigue, Jean 1914-1972 .... **CLC 2, 8**
See also CA 5-8R; 37-40R; CANR 20; CP
1; MAL 5

Garrison, Frederick
See Sinclair, Upton

Garrison, William Lloyd
1805-1879 .... **NCLC 149**
See also CDALB 1640-1865; DLB 1, 43,
235

Garro, Elena 1920(?)-1998 .. **HLCS 1; TCLC
153**
See also CA 131; 169; CWW 2; DLB 145;
EWL 3; HW 1; LAWS 1; WLIT 1

Garth, Will
See Hamilton, Edmond; Kuttner, Henry

Garvey, Marcus (Moziah, Jr.)
1887-1940 ..... **BLC 1:2; HR 1:2; TCLC
41**
See also BW 1; CA 120; 124; CANR 79;
DAM MULT; DLB 345

Gary, Romain
See Kacew, Romain

Gascar, Pierre
See Fournier, Pierre

Gascoigne, George 1539-1577 .... **LC 108**
See also DLB 136; RGEL 2

Gascoyne, David (Emery)
1916-2001 .... **CLC 45**
See also CA 65-68; 200; CANR 10, 28, 54;
CP 1, 2, 3, 4, 5, 6, 7; DLB 20; MTCW 1;
RGEL 2

Gaskell, Elizabeth Cleghorn
1810-1865 .... **NCLC 5, 70, 97, 137, 214;
SSC 25, 97**
See also BRW 5; CDBLB 1832-1890; DAB;
DAM MST; DLB 21, 144, 159; RGEL 2;
RGSF 2; TEA

Gass, William H. 1924- . **CLC 1, 2, 8, 11, 15,
39, 132; SSC 12**
See also AMWS 6; CA 17-20R; CANR 30,
71, 100; CN 1, 2, 3, 4, 5, 6, 7; DLB 2,
227; EWL 3; MAL 5; MTCW 1, 2;
MTFW 2005; RGAL 4

Gassendi, Pierre 1592-1655 .... **LC 54**
See also GFL Beginnings to 1789

Gasset, Jose Ortega y
See Ortega y Gasset, Jose

Gates, Henry Louis, Jr. 1950- ... **BLCS; CLC
65**
See also BW 2, 3; CA 109; CANR 25, 53,
75, 125; CSW; DA3; DAM MULT; DLB
67; EWL 3; MAL 5; MTCW 2; MTFW
2005; RGAL 4

Gatos, Stephanie
See Katz, Steve

Gautier, Theophile 1811-1872 .. **NCLC 1, 59;
PC 18; SSC 20**
See also DAM POET; DLB 119; EW 6;
GFL 1789 to the Present; RGWL 2, 3;
SUFW; TWA

Gautreaux, Tim 1947- .... **CLC 270; SSC 125**
See also CA 187; CSW; DLB 292

Gay, John 1685-1732 .... **LC 49**
See also BRW 3; DAM DRAM; DLB 84,
95; RGEL 2; WLIT 3

Gay, Oliver
See Gogarty, Oliver St. John

Gay, Peter 1923- .... **CLC 158**
See also CA 13-16R; CANR 18, 41, 77,
147; INT CANR-18; RGHL

Gay, Peter Jack
See Gay, Peter

Gaye, Marvin (Pentz, Jr.)
1939-1984 .... **CLC 26**
See also CA 195; 112

Gebler, Carlo 1954- .... **CLC 39**
See also CA 119; 133; CANR 96, 186; DLB
271

Gebler, Carlo Ernest
See Gebler, Carlo

Gee, Maggie 1948- .... **CLC 57**
See also CA 130; CANR 125; CN 4, 5, 6,
7; DLB 207; MTFW 2005

Gee, Maurice 1931- .... **CLC 29**
See also AAYA 42; CA 97-100; CANR 67,
123; CLR 56; CN 2, 3, 4, 5, 6, 7; CWRI
5; EWL 3; MAICYA 2; RGSF 2; SATA
46, 101

Gee, Maurice Gough
See Gee, Maurice

Geiogamah, Hanay 1945- .... **NNAL**
See also CA 153; DAM MULT; DLB 175

Gelbart, Larry 1928- .... **CLC 21, 61**
See also CA 73-76; CAD; CANR 45, 94;
CD 5, 6

Gelbart, Larry Simon
See Gelbart, Larry

Gelber, Jack 1932-2003 ...... **CLC 1, 6, 14, 79**
See also CA 1-4R; 216; CAD; CANR 2;
DLB 7, 228; MAL 5

Gellhorn, Martha (Ellis)
1908-1998 .... **CLC 14, 60**
See also CA 77-80; 164; CANR 44; CN 1,
2, 3, 4, 5, 6 7; DLBY 1982, 1998

Genet, Jean 1910-1986 .. **CLC 1, 2, 5, 10, 14,
44, 46; DC 25; TCLC 128**
See also CA 13-16R; CANR 18; DA3;
DAM DRAM; DFS 10; DLB 72, 321;
DLBY 1986; EW 13; EWL 3; GFL 1789
to the Present; GLL 1; LMFS 2; MTCW
1, 2; MTFW 2005; RGWL 2, 3; TWA

Genlis, Stephanie-Felicite Ducrest
1746-1830 .... **NCLC 166**
See also DLB 313

Gent, Peter 1942- .... **CLC 29**
See also AITN 1; CA 89-92; DLBY 1982

Gentile, Giovanni 1875-1944 .... **TCLC 96**
See also CA 119

Geoffrey of Monmouth c.
1100-1155 .... **CMLC 44**
See also DLB 146; TEA

George, Jean
See George, Jean Craighead

George, Jean Craighead 1919- .... **CLC 35**
See also AAYA 8, 69; BYA 2, 4; CA 5-8R;
CANR 25; CLR 1, 80, 136; DLB 52;
JRDA; MAICYA 1, 2; SATA 2, 68, 124,
170; WYA; YAW

George, Stefan (Anton) 1868-1933 . **TCLC 2,
14**
See also CA 104; 193; EW 8; EWL 3

Georges, Georges Martin
See Simenon, Georges (Jacques Christian)

Gerald of Wales c. 1146-c. 1223 ... **CMLC 60**

Gerhardi, William Alexander
See Gerhardie, William Alexander

Gerhardie, William Alexander
1895-1977 .... **CLC 5**
See also CA 25-28R; 73-76; CANR 18; CN
1, 2; DLB 36; RGEL 2

Glasgow, Ellen (Anderson Gholson)
1873-1945 .... **SSC 34; TCLC 2, 7**
See also AMW; CA 104; 164; DLB 9, 12;
MAL 5; MBL; MTCW 2; MTFW 2005;
RGAL 4; RHW; SSFS 9; TUS

Glaspell, Susan 1882(?)-1948 ..... **DC 10; SSC 41; TCLC 55, 175**
See also AMWS 3; CA 110; 154; DFS 8,
18, 24; DLB 7, 9, 78, 228; MBL; RGAL
4; SSFS 3; TCWW 2; TUS; YABC 2

Glassco, John 1909-1981 .... **CLC 9**
See also CA 13-16R; 102; CANR 15; CN
1, 2; CP 1, 2, 3; DLB 68

Glasscock, Amnesia
See Steinbeck, John (Ernst)

Glasser, Ronald J. 1940(?)- .... **CLC 37**
See also CA 209

Glassman, Joyce
See Johnson, Joyce

Gleick, James (W.) 1954- .... **CLC 147**
See also CA 131; 137; CANR 97; INT CA-137

Glendinning, Victoria 1937- .... **CLC 50**
See also CA 120; 127; CANR 59, 89, 166;
DLB 155

Glissant, Edouard (Mathieu)
1928- .... **CLC 10, 68**
See also CA 153; CANR 111; CWW 2;
DAM MULT; EWL 3; RGWL 3

Gloag, Julian 1930- .... **CLC 40**
See also AITN 1; CA 65-68; CANR 10, 70;
CN 1, 2, 3, 4, 5, 6

Glowacki, Aleksander
See Prus, Boleslaw

Gluck, Louise 1943- . **CLC 7, 22, 44, 81, 160, 280; PC 16**
See also AMWS 5; CA 33-36R; CANR 40,
69, 108, 133, 182; CP 1, 2, 3, 4, 5, 6, 7;
CWP; DA3; DAM POET; DLB 5; MAL
5; MTCW 2; MTFW 2005; PFS 5, 15;
RGAL 4; TCLE 1:1

Gluck, Louise Elisabeth
See Gluck, Louise

Glyn, Elinor 1864-1943 .... **TCLC 72**
See also DLB 153; RHW

Gobineau, Joseph-Arthur
1816-1882 .... **NCLC 17**
See also DLB 123; GFL 1789 to the Present

Godard, Jean-Luc 1930- .... **CLC 20**
See also CA 93-96

Godden, (Margaret) Rumer
1907-1998 .... **CLC 53**
See also AAYA 6; BPFB 2; BYA 2, 5; CA
5-8R; 172; CANR 4, 27, 36, 55, 80; CLR
20; CN 1, 2, 3, 4, 5, 6; CWRI 5; DLB
161; MAICYA 1, 2; RHW; SAAS 12;
SATA 3, 36; SATA-Obit 109; TEA

Godoy Alcayaga, Lucila 1899-1957 .. **HLC 2; PC 32; TCLC 2**
See also BW 2; CA 104; 131; CANR 81;
DAM MULT; DLB 283, 331; DNFS;
EWL 3; HW 1, 2; LAW; MTCW 1, 2;
MTFW 2005; RGWL 2, 3; WP

Godwin, Gail 1937- ...... **CLC 5, 8, 22, 31, 69, 125**
See also BPFB 2; CA 29-32R; CANR 15,
43, 69, 132; CN 3, 4, 5, 6, 7; CPW; CSW;
DA3; DAM POP; DLB 6, 234, 350; INT
CANR-15; MAL 5; MTCW 1, 2; MTFW
2005

Godwin, Gail Kathleen
See Godwin, Gail

Godwin, William 1756-1836 .. **NCLC 14, 130**
See also CDBLB 1789-1832; CMW 4; DLB
39, 104, 142, 158, 163, 262, 336; GL 2;
HGG; RGEL 2

Goebbels, Josef
See Goebbels, (Paul) Joseph

Goebbels, (Paul) Joseph
1897-1945 .... **TCLC 68**
See also CA 115; 148

Goebbels, Joseph Paul
See Goebbels, (Paul) Joseph

Goethe, Johann Wolfgang von
1749-1832 . **DC 20; NCLC 4, 22, 34, 90, 154; PC 5; SSC 38; WLC 3**
See also CDWLB 2; DA; DA3; DAB;
DAC; DAM DRAM, MST, POET; DLB
94; EW 5; GL 2; LATS 1; LMFS 1:1;
RGWL 2, 3; TWA

Gogarty, Oliver St. John
1878-1957 .... **TCLC 15**
See also CA 109; 150; DLB 15, 19; RGEL
2

Gogol, Nikolai (Vasilyevich)
1809-1852 .... **DC 1; NCLC 5, 15, 31, 162; SSC 4, 29, 52; WLC 3**
See also DA; DAB; DAC; DAM DRAM,
MST; DFS 12; DLB 198; EW 6; EXPS;
RGSF 2; RGWL 2, 3; SSFS 7; TWA

Goines, Donald 1937(?)-1974 .... **BLC 1:2; CLC 80**
See also AITN 1; BW 1, 3; CA 124; 114;
CANR 82; CMW 4; DA3; DAM MULT,
POP; DLB 33

Gold, Herbert 1924- ... **CLC 4, 7, 14, 42, 152**
See also CA 9-12R; CANR 17, 45, 125,
194; CN 1, 2, 3, 4, 5, 6, 7; DLB 2; DLBY
1981; MAL 5

Goldbarth, Albert 1948- .... **CLC 5, 38**
See also AMWS 12; CA 53-56; CANR 6,
40; CP 3, 4, 5, 6, 7; DLB 120

Goldberg, Anatol 1910-1982 .... **CLC 34**
See also CA 131; 117

Goldemberg, Isaac 1945- .... **CLC 52**
See also CA 69-72; CAAS 12; CANR 11,
32; EWL 3; HW 1; WLIT 1

Golding, Arthur 1536-1606 .... **LC 101**
See also DLB 136

Golding, William 1911-1993 . **CLC 1, 2, 3, 8, 10, 17, 27, 58, 81; WLC 3**
See also AAYA 5, 44; BPFB 2; BRWR 1;
BRWS 1; BYA 2; CA 5-8R; 141; CANR
13, 33, 54; CD 5; CDBLB 1945-1960;
CLR 94, 130; CN 1, 2, 3, 4; DA; DA3;
DAB; DAC; DAM MST, NOV; DLB 15,
100, 255, 326, 330; EWL 3; EXPN; HGG;
LAIT 4; MTCW 1, 2; MTFW 2005; NFS
2; RGEL 2; RHW; SFW 4; TEA; WLIT
4; YAW

Golding, William Gerald
See Golding, William

Goldman, Emma 1869-1940 .... **TCLC 13**
See also CA 110; 150; DLB 221; FW;
RGAL 4; TUS

Goldman, Francisco 1954- .... **CLC 76**
See also CA 162; CANR 185

Goldman, William 1931- .... **CLC 1, 48**
See also BPFB 2; CA 9-12R; CANR 29,
69, 106; CN 1, 2, 3, 4, 5, 6, 7; DLB 44;
FANT; IDFW 3, 4

Goldman, William W.
See Goldman, William

Goldmann, Lucien 1913-1970 .... **CLC 24**
See also CA 25-28; CAP 2

Goldoni, Carlo 1707-1793 .... **LC 4, 152**
See also DAM DRAM; EW 4; RGWL 2, 3;
WLIT 7

Goldsberry, Steven 1949- .... **CLC 34**
See also CA 131

Goldsmith, Oliver 1730(?)-1774 .... **DC 8; LC 2, 48, 122; PC 77; WLC 3**
See also BRW 3; CDBLB 1660-1789; DA;
DAB; DAC; DAM DRAM, MST, NOV,
POET; DFS 1; DLB 39, 89, 104, 109, 142,
336; IDTP; RGEL 2; SATA 26; TEA;
WLIT 3

Goldsmith, Peter
See Priestley, J(ohn) B(oynton)

Goldstein, Rebecca 1950- .... **CLC 239**
See also CA 144; CANR 99, 165; TCLE
1:1

Goldstein, Rebecca Newberger
See Goldstein, Rebecca

Gombrowicz, Witold 1904-1969 .... **CLC 4, 7, 11, 49**
See also CA 19-20; 25-28R; CANR 105;
CAP 2; CDWLB 4; DAM DRAM; DLB
215; EW 12; EWL 3; RGWL 2, 3; TWA

Gomez de Avellaneda, Gertrudis
1814-1873 .... **NCLC 111**
See also LAW

Gomez de la Serna, Ramon
1888-1963 .... **CLC 9**
See also CA 153; 116; CANR 79; EWL 3;
HW 1, 2

Goncharov, Ivan Alexandrovich
1812-1891 .... **NCLC 1, 63**
See also DLB 238; EW 6; RGWL 2, 3

Goncourt, Edmond (Louis Antoine Huot) de
1822-1896 .... **NCLC 7**
See also DLB 123; EW 7; GFL 1789 to the
Present; RGWL 2, 3

Goncourt, Jules (Alfred Huot) de
1830-1870 .... **NCLC 7**
See also DLB 123; EW 7; GFL 1789 to the
Present; RGWL 2, 3

Gongora (y Argote), Luis de
1561-1627 .... **LC 72**
See also RGWL 2, 3

Gontier, Fernande 19(?)- .... **CLC 50**

Gonzalez Martinez, Enrique
See Gonzalez Martinez, Enrique

Gonzalez Martinez, Enrique
1871-1952 .... **TCLC 72**
See also CA 166; CANR 81; DLB 290;
EWL 3; HW 1, 2

Goodison, Lorna 1947- .... **BLC 2:2; PC 36**
See also CA 142; CANR 88, 189; CP 5, 6,
7; CWP; DLB 157; EWL 3; PFS 25

Goodman, Allegra 1967- .... **CLC 241**
See also CA 204; CANR 162; DLB 244,
350

Goodman, Paul 1911-1972 ..... **CLC 1, 2, 4, 7**
See also CA 19-20; 37-40R; CAD; CANR
34; CAP 2; CN 1; DLB 130, 246; MAL
5; MTCW 1; RGAL 4

Goodweather, Hartley
See King, Thomas

GoodWeather, Hartley
See King, Thomas

Googe, Barnabe 1540-1594 .... **LC 94**
See also DLB 132; RGEL 2

Gordimer, Nadine 1923- ...... **CLC 3, 5, 7, 10, 18, 33, 51, 70, 123, 160, 161, 263; SSC 17, 80; WLCS**
See also AAYA 39; AFW; BRWS 2; CA
5-8R; CANR 3, 28, 56, 88, 131; CN 1, 2,
3, 4, 5, 6, 7; DA; DA3; DAB; DAC; DAM
MST, NOV; DLB 225, 326, 330; EWL 3;
EXPS; INT CANR-28; LATS 1:2; MTCW
1, 2; MTFW 2005; NFS 4; RGEL 2;
RGSF 2; SSFS 2, 14, 19; TWA; WLIT 2;
YAW

Gordon, Adam Lindsay
1833-1870 .... **NCLC 21**
See also DLB 230

Gordon, Caroline 1895-1981 . **CLC 6, 13, 29, 83; SSC 15**
See also AMW; CA 11-12; 103; CANR 36;
CAP 1; CN 1, 2; DLB 4, 9, 102; DLBD
17; DLBY 1981; EWL 3; MAL 5; MTCW
1, 2; MTFW 2005; RGAL 4; RGSF 2

Gordon, Charles William
1860-1937 .... **TCLC 31**
See also CA 109; DLB 92; TCWW 1, 2

Green, Anna Katharine
1846-1935 .... **TCLC 63**
See also CA 112; 159; CMW 4; DLB 202, 221; MSW

Green, Brian
See Card, Orson Scott

Green, Hannah
See Greenberg, Joanne (Goldenberg)

Green, Hannah 1927(?)-1996 .... **CLC 3**
See also CA 73-76; CANR 59, 93; NFS 10

Green, Henry
See Yorke, Henry Vincent

Green, Julian
See Green, Julien

Green, Julien 1900-1998 .... **CLC 3, 11, 77**
See also CA 21-24R; 169; CANR 33, 87; CWW 2; DLB 4, 72; EWL 3; GFL 1789 to the Present; MTCW 2; MTFW 2005

Green, Julien Hartridge
See Green, Julien

Green, Paul (Eliot) 1894-1981 .... **CLC 25**
See also AITN 1; CA 5-8R; 103; CAD; CANR 3; DAM DRAM; DLB 7, 9, 249; DLBY 1981; MAL 5; RGAL 4

Greenaway, Peter 1942- .... **CLC 159**
See also CA 127

Greenberg, Ivan 1908-1973 .... **CLC 24**
See also CA 85-88; DLB 137; MAL 5

Greenberg, Joanne (Goldenberg)
1932- .... **CLC 7, 30**
See also AAYA 12, 67; CA 5-8R; CANR 14, 32, 69; CN 6, 7; DLB 335; NFS 23; SATA 25; YAW

Greenberg, Richard 1959(?)- .... **CLC 57**
See also CA 138; CAD; CD 5, 6; DFS 24

Greenblatt, Stephen J(ay) 1943- ...... **CLC 70**
See also CA 49-52; CANR 115

Greene, Bette 1934- .... **CLC 30**
See also AAYA 7, 69; BYA 3; CA 53-56; CANR 4, 146; CLR 2, 140; CWRI 5; JRDA; LAIT 4; MAICYA 1, 2; NFS 10; SAAS 16; SATA 8, 102, 161; WYA; YAW

Greene, Gael **CLC 8**
See also CA 13-16R; CANR 10, 166

Greene, Graham 1904-1991 .. **CLC 1, 3, 6, 9, 14, 18, 27, 37, 70, 72, 125; SSC 29, 121; WLC 3**
See also AAYA 61; AITN 2; BPFB 2; BRWR 2; BRWS 1; BYA 3; CA 13-16R; 133; CANR 35, 61, 131; CBD; CDBLB 1945-1960; CMW 4; CN 1, 2, 3, 4; DA; DA3; DAB; DAC; DAM MST, NOV; DLB 13, 15, 77, 100, 162, 201, 204; DLBY 1991; EWL 3; MSW; MTCW 1, 2; MTFW 2005; NFS 16; RGEL 2; SATA 20; SSFS 14; TEA; WLIT 4

Greene, Robert 1558-1592 .... **LC 41**
See also BRWS 8; DLB 62, 167; IDTP; RGEL 2; TEA

Greer, Germaine 1939- .... **CLC 131**
See also AITN 1; CA 81-84; CANR 33, 70, 115, 133, 190; FW; MTCW 1, 2; MTFW 2005

Greer, Richard
See Silverberg, Robert

Gregor, Arthur 1923- .... **CLC 9**
See also CA 25-28R; CAAS 10; CANR 11; CP 1, 2, 3, 4, 5, 6, 7; SATA 36

Gregor, Lee
See Pohl, Frederik

Gregory, Lady Isabella Augusta (Persse)
1852-1932 .... **TCLC 1, 176**
See also BRW 6; CA 104; 184; DLB 10; IDTP; RGEL 2

Gregory, J. Dennis
See Williams, John A(lfred)

Gregory of Nazianzus, St.
329-389 .... **CMLC 82**

Gregory of Rimini 1300(?)-1358 . **CMLC 109**
See also DLB 115

Grekova, I.
See Ventsel, Elena Sergeevna

Grekova, Irina
See Ventsel, Elena Sergeevna

Grendon, Stephen
See Derleth, August (William)

Grenville, Kate 1950- .... **CLC 61**
See also CA 118; CANR 53, 93, 156; CN 7; DLB 325

Grenville, Pelham
See Wodehouse, P(elham) G(renville)

Greve, Felix Paul (Berthold Friedrich)
1879-1948 .... **TCLC 4**
See also CA 104; 141, 175; CANR 79; DAC; DAM MST; DLB 92; RGEL 2; TCWW 1, 2

Greville, Fulke 1554-1628 .... **LC 79**
See also BRWS 11; DLB 62, 172; RGEL 2

Grey, Lady Jane 1537-1554 .... **LC 93**
See also DLB 132

Grey, Zane 1872-1939 .... **TCLC 6**
See also BPFB 2; CA 104; 132; DA3; DAM POP; DLB 9, 212; MTCW 1, 2; MTFW 2005; RGAL 4; TCWW 1, 2; TUS

Griboedov, Aleksandr Sergeevich
1795(?)-1829 .... **NCLC 129**
See also DLB 205; RGWL 2, 3

Grieg, (Johan) Nordahl (Brun)
1902-1943 .... **TCLC 10**
See also CA 107; 189; EWL 3

Grieve, C. M. 1892-1978 ... **CLC 2, 4, 11, 19, 63; PC 9**
See also BRWS 12; CA 5-8R; 85-88; CANR 33, 107; CDBLB 1945-1960; CP 1, 2; DAM POET; DLB 20; EWL 3; MTCW 1; RGEL 2

Grieve, Christopher Murray
See Grieve, C. M.

Griffin, Gerald 1803-1840 .... **NCLC 7**
See also DLB 159; RGEL 2

Griffin, John Howard 1920-1980 ..... **CLC 68**
See also AITN 1; CA 1-4R; 101; CANR 2

Griffin, Peter 1942- .... **CLC 39**
See also CA 136

Griffith, David Lewelyn Wark
See Griffith, D.W.

Griffith, D.W. 1875(?)-1948 .... **TCLC 68**
See also AAYA 78; CA 119; 150; CANR 80

Griffith, Lawrence
See Griffith, D.W.

Griffiths, Trevor 1935- .... **CLC 13, 52**
See also CA 97-100; CANR 45; CBD; CD 5, 6; DLB 13, 245

Griggs, Sutton (Elbert)
1872-1930 .... **TCLC 77**
See also CA 123; 186; DLB 50

Grigson, Geoffrey (Edward Harvey)
1905-1985 .... **CLC 7, 39**
See also CA 25-28R; 118; CANR 20, 33; CP 1, 2, 3, 4; DLB 27; MTCW 1, 2

Grile, Dod
See Bierce, Ambrose (Gwinett)

Grillparzer, Franz 1791-1872 .... **DC 14; NCLC 1, 102; SSC 37**
See also CDWLB 2; DLB 133; EW 5; RGWL 2, 3; TWA

Grimble, Reverend Charles James
See Eliot, T(homas) S(tearns)

Grimke, Angelina Weld 1880-1958 ... **HR 1:2**
See also BW 1; CA 124; DAM POET; DLB 50, 54; FW

Grimke, Charlotte L. Forten
1837(?)-1914 .... **BLC 1:2; TCLC 16**
See also BW 1; CA 117; 124; DAM MULT, POET; DLB 50, 239

Grimke, Charlotte Lottie Forten
See Grimke, Charlotte L. Forten

Grimm, Jacob Ludwig Karl
1785-1863 .... **NCLC 3, 77; SSC 36, 88**
See also CLR 112; DLB 90; MAICYA 1, 2; RGSF 2; RGWL 2, 3; SATA 22; WCH

Grimm, Wilhelm Karl 1786-1859 .. **NCLC 3, 77; SSC 36**
See also CDWLB 2; CLR 112; DLB 90; MAICYA 1, 2; RGSF 2; RGWL 2, 3; SATA 22; WCH

Grimm and Grim
See Grimm, Jacob Ludwig Karl; Grimm, Wilhelm Karl

Grimm Brothers
See Grimm, Jacob Ludwig Karl; Grimm, Wilhelm Karl

Grimmelshausen, Hans Jakob Christoffel von
See Grimmelshausen, Johann Jakob Christoffel von

Grimmelshausen, Johann Jakob Christoffel von 1621-1676 .... **LC 6**
See also CDWLB 2; DLB 168; RGWL 2, 3

Grindel, Eugene 1895-1952 .... **PC 38; TCLC 7, 41**
See also CA 104; 193; EWL 3; GFL 1789 to the Present; LMFS 2; RGWL 2, 3

Grisham, John 1955- .... **CLC 84, 273**
See also AAYA 14, 47; BPFB 2; CA 138; CANR 47, 69, 114, 133; CMW 4; CN 6, 7; CPW; CSW; DA3; DAM POP; MSW; MTCW 2; MTFW 2005

Grosseteste, Robert 1175(?)-1253 . **CMLC 62**
See also DLB 115

Grossman, David 1954- .... **CLC 67, 231**
See also CA 138; CANR 114, 175; CWW 2; DLB 299; EWL 3; RGHL; WLIT 6

Grossman, Vasilii Semenovich
See Grossman, Vasily (Semenovich)

Grossman, Vasily (Semenovich)
1905-1964 .... **CLC 41**
See also CA 124; 130; DLB 272; MTCW 1; RGHL

Grove, Frederick Philip
See Greve, Felix Paul (Berthold Friedrich)

Grubb
See Crumb, R.

Grumbach, Doris 1918- .... **CLC 13, 22, 64**
See also CA 5-8R; CAAS 2; CANR 9, 42, 70, 127; CN 6, 7; INT CANR-9; MTCW 2; MTFW 2005

Grundtvig, Nikolai Frederik Severin
1783-1872 .... **NCLC 1, 158**
See also DLB 300

Grunge
See Crumb, R.

Grunwald, Lisa 1959- .... **CLC 44**
See also CA 120; CANR 148

Gryphius, Andreas 1616-1664 .... **LC 89**
See also CDWLB 2; DLB 164; RGWL 2, 3

Guare, John 1938- .... **CLC 8, 14, 29, 67; DC 20**
See also CA 73-76; CAD; CANR 21, 69, 118; CD 5, 6; DAM DRAM; DFS 8, 13; DLB 7, 249; EWL 3; MAL 5; MTCW 1, 2; RGAL 4

Guarini, Battista 1538-1612 .... **LC 102**
See also DLB 339

Gubar, Susan 1944- .... **CLC 145**
See also CA 108; CANR 45, 70, 139, 179; FW; MTCW 1; RGAL 4

Gubar, Susan David
See Gubar, Susan

Gudjonsson, Halldor Kiljan
1902-1998 .... **CLC 25**
See also CA 103; 164; CWW 2; DLB 293, 331; EW 12; EWL 3; RGWL 2, 3

Haliburton, Thomas Chandler
1796-1865 .... **NCLC 15, 149**
See also DLB 11, 99; RGEL 2; RGSF 2

Hall, Donald 1928- ... **CLC 1, 13, 37, 59, 151,**
240; PC 70
See also AAYA 63; CA 5-8R; CAAS 7;
CANR 2, 44, 64, 106, 133; CP 1, 2, 3, 4,
5, 6, 7; DAM POET; DLB 5, 342; MAL
5; MTCW 2; MTFW 2005; RGAL 4;
SATA 23, 97

Hall, Donald Andrew, Jr.
See Hall, Donald

Hall, Frederic Sauser
See Sauser-Hall, Frederic

Hall, James
See Kuttner, Henry

Hall, James Norman 1887-1951 ..... **TCLC 23**
See also CA 123; 173; LAIT 1; RHW 1;
SATA 21

Hall, Joseph 1574-1656 .... **LC 91**
See also DLB 121, 151; RGEL 2

Hall, Marguerite Radclyffe
See Hall, Radclyffe

Hall, Radclyffe 1880-1943 ...... **TCLC 12, 215**
See also BRWS 6; CA 110; 150; CANR 83;
DLB 191; MTCW 2; MTFW 2005; RGEL
2; RHW

Hall, Rodney 1935- .... **CLC 51**
See also CA 109; CANR 69; CN 6, 7; CP
1, 2, 3, 4, 5, 6, 7; DLB 289

Hallam, Arthur Henry
1811-1833 .... **NCLC 110**
See also DLB 32

Halldor Laxness
See Gudjonsson, Halldor Kiljan

Halleck, Fitz-Greene 1790-1867 .... **NCLC 47**
See also DLB 3, 250; RGAL 4

Halliday, Michael
See Creasey, John

Halpern, Daniel 1945- .... **CLC 14**
See also CA 33-36R; CANR 93, 174; CP 3,
4, 5, 6, 7

Hamburger, Michael 1924-2007 ... **CLC 5, 14**
See also CA 5-8R, 196; 261; CAAE 196;
CAAS 4; CANR 2, 47; CP 1, 2, 3, 4, 5, 6,
7; DLB 27

Hamburger, Michael Peter Leopold
See Hamburger, Michael

Hamill, Pete 1935- .... **CLC 10, 261**
See also CA 25-28R; CANR 18, 71, 127,
180

Hamill, William Peter
See Hamill, Pete

Hamilton, Alexander 1712-1756 .... **LC 150**
See also DLB 31

Hamilton, Alexander
1755(?)-1804 .... **NCLC 49**
See also DLB 37

Hamilton, Clive
See Lewis, C.S.

Hamilton, Edmond 1904-1977 .... **CLC 1**
See also CA 1-4R; CANR 3, 84; DLB 8;
SATA 118; SFW 4

Hamilton, Elizabeth 1758-1816 ... **NCLC 153**
See also DLB 116, 158

Hamilton, Eugene (Jacob) Lee
See Lee-Hamilton, Eugene (Jacob)

Hamilton, Franklin
See Silverberg, Robert

Hamilton, Gail
See Corcoran, Barbara (Asenath)

Hamilton, (Robert) Ian 1938-2001 . **CLC 191**
See also CA 106; 203; CANR 41, 67; CP 1,
2, 3, 4, 5, 6, 7; DLB 40, 155

Hamilton, Jane 1957- .... **CLC 179**
See also CA 147; CANR 85, 128; CN 7;
DLB 350; MTFW 2005

Hamilton, Mollie
See Kaye, M.M.

Hamilton, (Anthony Walter) Patrick
1904-1962 .... **CLC 51**
See also CA 176; 113; DLB 10, 191

Hamilton, Virginia 1936-2002 .... **CLC 26**
See also AAYA 2, 21; BW 2, 3; BYA 1, 2,
8; CA 25-28R; 206; CANR 20, 37, 73,
126; CLR 1, 11, 40, 127; DAM MULT;
DLB 33, 52; DLBY 2001; INT CANR-
20; JRDA; LAIT 5; MAICYA 1, 2; MAI-
CYAS 1; MTCW 1, 2; MTFW 2005;
SATA 4, 56, 79, 123; SATA-Obit 132;
WYA; YAW

Hammett, (Samuel) Dashiell
1894-1961 .... **CLC 3, 5, 10, 19, 47; SSC**
17; TCLC 187
See also AAYA 59; AITN 1; AMWS 4;
BPFB 2; CA 81-84; CANR 42; CDALB
1929-1941; CMW 4; DA3; DLB 226, 280;
DLBD 6; DLBY 1996; EWL 3; LAIT 3;
MAL 5; MSW; MTCW 1, 2; MTFW
2005; NFS 21; RGAL 4; RGSF 2; TUS

Hammon, Jupiter 1720(?)-1800(?) . **BLC 1:2;**
NCLC 5; PC 16
See also DAM MULT, POET; DLB 31, 50

Hammond, Keith
See Kuttner, Henry

Hamner, Earl (Henry), Jr. 1923- ...... **CLC 12**
See also AITN 2; CA 73-76; DLB 6

Hampton, Christopher 1946- .... **CLC 4**
See also CA 25-28R; CD 5, 6; DLB 13;
MTCW 1

Hampton, Christopher James
See Hampton, Christopher

Hamsun, Knut
See Pedersen, Knut

Hamsund, Knut Pedersen
See Pedersen, Knut

Handke, Peter 1942- .... **CLC 5, 8, 10, 15, 38,**
134; DC 17
See also CA 77-80; CANR 33, 75, 104, 133,
180; CWW 2; DAM DRAM, NOV; DLB
85, 124; EWL 3; MTCW 1, 2; MTFW
2005; TWA

Handler, Chelsea 1976(?)- .... **CLC 269**
See also CA 243

Handy, W(illiam) C(hristopher)
1873-1958 .... **TCLC 97**
See also BW 3; CA 121; 167

Hanley, James 1901-1985 ..... **CLC 3, 5, 8, 13**
See also CA 73-76; 117; CANR 36; CBD;
CN 1, 2, 3; DLB 191; EWL 3; MTCW 1;
RGEL 2

Hannah, Barry 1942- .. **CLC 23, 38, 90, 270;**
SSC 94
See also BPFB 2; CA 108; 110; CANR 43,
68, 113; CN 4, 5, 6, 7; CSW; DLB 6, 234;
INT CA-110; MTCW 1; RGSF 2

Hannon, Ezra
See Hunter, Evan

Hanrahan, Barbara 1939-1991 .... **TCLC 219**
See also CA 121; 127; CN 4, 5; DLB 289

Hansberry, Lorraine (Vivian)
1930-1965 ... **BLC 1:2, 2:2; CLC 17, 62;**
DC 2; TCLC 192
See also AAYA 25; AFAW 1, 2; AMWS 4;
BW 1, 3; CA 109; 25-28R; CABS 3;
CAD; CANR 58; CDALB 1941-1968;
CWD; DA; DA3; DAB; DAC; DAM
DRAM, MST, MULT; DFS 2; DLB 7, 38;
EWL 3; FL 1:6; FW; LAIT 4; MAL 5;
MTCW 1, 2; MTFW 2005; RGAL 4; TUS

Hansen, Joseph 1923-2004 .... **CLC 38**
See also BPFB 2; CA 29-32R; 233; CAAS
17; CANR 16, 44, 66, 125; CMW 4; DLB
226; GLL 1; INT CANR-16

Hansen, Karen V. 1955- .... **CLC 65**
See also CA 149; CANR 102

Hansen, Martin A(lfred)
1909-1955 .... **TCLC 32**
See also CA 167; DLB 214; EWL 3

Hanson, Kenneth O(stlin) 1922- .... **CLC 13**
See also CA 53-56; CANR 7; CP 1, 2, 3, 4,
5

Hardwick, Elizabeth 1916-2007 .... **CLC 13**
See also AMWS 3; CA 5-8R; 267; CANR
3, 32, 70, 100, 139; CN 4, 5, 6; CSW;
DA3; DAM NOV; DLB 6; MBL; MTCW
1, 2; MTFW 2005; TCLE 1:1

Hardwick, Elizabeth Bruce
See Hardwick, Elizabeth

Hardwick, Elizabeth Bruce
See Hardwick, Elizabeth

Hardy, Thomas 1840-1928 . **PC 8, 92; SSC 2,**
60, 113; TCLC 4, 10, 18, 32, 48, 53, 72,
143, 153; WLC 3
See also AAYA 69; BRW 6; BRWC 1, 2;
BRWR 1; CA 104; 123; CDBLB 1890-
1914; DA; DA3; DAB; DAC; DAM MST,
NOV, POET; DLB 18, 19, 135, 284; EWL
3; EXPN; EXPP; LAIT 2; MTCW 1, 2;
MTFW 2005; NFS 3, 11, 15, 19, 30; PFS
3, 4, 18; RGEL 2; RGSF 2; TEA; WLIT
4

Hare, David 1947- . **CLC 29, 58, 136; DC 26**
See also BRWS 4; CA 97-100; CANR 39,
91; CBD; CD 5, 6; DFS 4, 7, 16; DLB
13, 310; MTCW 1; TEA

Harewood, John
See Van Druten, John (William)

Harford, Henry
See Hudson, W(illiam) H(enry)

Hargrave, Leonie
See Disch, Thomas M.

Hariri, Al- al-Qasim ibn 'Ali Abu
Muhammad al-Basri
See al-Hariri, al-Qasim ibn 'Ali Abu Mu-
hammad al-Basri

Harjo, Joy 1951- ..... **CLC 83; NNAL; PC 27**
See also AMWS 12; CA 114; CANR 35,
67, 91, 129; CP 6, 7; CWP; DAM MULT;
DLB 120, 175, 342; EWL 3; MTCW 2;
MTFW 2005; PFS 15; RGAL 4

Harlan, Louis R(udolph) 1922- .... **CLC 34**
See also CA 21-24R; CANR 25, 55, 80

Harling, Robert 1951(?)- .... **CLC 53**
See also CA 147

Harmon, William (Ruth) 1938- .... **CLC 38**
See also CA 33-36R; CANR 14, 32, 35;
SATA 65

Harper, F. E. W.
See Harper, Frances Ellen Watkins

Harper, Frances E. W.
See Harper, Frances Ellen Watkins

Harper, Frances E. Watkins
See Harper, Frances Ellen Watkins

Harper, Frances Ellen
See Harper, Frances Ellen Watkins

Harper, Frances Ellen Watkins
1825-1911 . **BLC 1:2; PC 21; TCLC 14,**
217
See also AFAW 1, 2; BW 1, 3; CA 111; 125;
CANR 79; DAM MULT, POET; DLB 50,
221; MBL; RGAL 4

Harper, Michael S(teven) 1938- ..... **BLC 2:2;**
CLC 7, 22
See also AFAW 2; BW 1; CA 33-36R; 224;
CAAE 224; CANR 24, 108; CP 2, 3, 4, 5,
6, 7; DLB 41; RGAL 4; TCLE 1:1

Harper, Mrs. F. E. W.
See Harper, Frances Ellen Watkins

Harpur, Charles 1813-1868 .... **NCLC 114**
See also DLB 230; RGEL 2

Harris, Christie
See Harris, Christie (Lucy) Irwin

Hazlitt, William 1778-1830 ...... **NCLC 29, 82**
See also BRW 4; DLB 110, 158; RGEL 2; TEA

Hazzard, Shirley 1931- .... **CLC 18, 218**
See also CA 9-12R; CANR 4, 70, 127; CN 1, 2, 3, 4, 5, 6, 7; DLB 289; DLBY 1982; MTCW 1

Head, Bessie 1937-1986 . **BLC 1:2, 2:2; CLC 25, 67; SSC 52**
See also AFW; BW 2, 3; CA 29-32R; 119; CANR 25, 82; CDWLB 3; CN 1, 2, 3, 4; DA3; DAM MULT; DLB 117, 225; EWL 3; EXPS; FL 1:6; FW; MTCW 1, 2; MTFW 2005; RGSF 2; SSFS 5, 13; WLIT 2; WWE 1

Headley, Elizabeth
See Harrison, Elizabeth (Allen) Cavanna

Headon, (Nicky) Topper 1956(?)- ..... **CLC 30**

Heaney, Seamus 1939- . **CLC 5, 7, 14, 25, 37, 74, 91, 171, 225; PC 18, 100; WLCS**
See also AAYA 61; BRWR 1; BRWS 2; CA 85-88; CANR 25, 48, 75, 91, 128, 184; CDBLB 1960 to Present; CP 1, 2, 3, 4, 5, 6, 7; DA3; DAB; DAM POET; DLB 40, 330; DLBY 1995; EWL 3; EXPP; MTCW 1, 2; MTFW 2005; PAB; PFS 2, 5, 8, 17, 30; RGEL 2; TEA; WLIT 4

Hearn, (Patricio) Lafcadio (Tessima Carlos) 1850-1904 .... **TCLC 9**
See also CA 105; 166; DLB 12, 78, 189; HGG; MAL 5; RGAL 4

Hearne, Samuel 1745-1792 .... **LC 95**
See also DLB 99

Hearne, Vicki 1946-2001 .... **CLC 56**
See also CA 139; 201

Hearon, Shelby 1931- .... **CLC 63**
See also AITN 2; AMWS 8; CA 25-28R; CAAS 11; CANR 18, 48, 103, 146; CSW

Heat-Moon, William Least
See Trogdon, William

Hebbel, Friedrich 1813-1863 . **DC 21; NCLC 43**
See also CDWLB 2; DAM DRAM; DLB 129; EW 6; RGWL 2, 3

Hebert, Anne 1916-2000 . **CLC 4, 13, 29, 246**
See also CA 85-88; 187; CANR 69, 126; CCA 1; CWP; CWW 2; DA3; DAC; DAM MST, POET; DLB 68; EWL 3; GFL 1789 to the Present; MTCW 1, 2; MTFW 2005; PFS 20

Hecht, Anthony (Evan) 1923-2004 .... **CLC 8, 13, 19; PC 70**
See also AMWS 10; CA 9-12R; 232; CANR 6, 108; CP 1, 2, 3, 4, 5, 6, 7; DAM POET; DLB 5, 169; EWL 3; PFS 6; WP

Hecht, Ben 1894-1964 ..... **CLC 8; TCLC 101**
See also CA 85-88; DFS 2; DLB 7, 9, 25, 26, 28, 86; FANT; IDFW 3, 4; RGAL 4

Hedayat, Sadeq 1903-1951 .... **TCLC 21**
See also CA 120; EWL 3; RGSF 2

Hegel, Georg Wilhelm Friedrich 1770-1831 .... **NCLC 46, 151**
See also DLB 90; TWA

Heidegger, Martin 1889-1976 .... **CLC 24**
See also CA 81-84; 65-68; CANR 34; DLB 296; MTCW 1, 2; MTFW 2005

Heidenstam, (Carl Gustaf) Verner von 1859-1940 .... **TCLC 5**
See also CA 104; DLB 330

Heidi Louise
See Erdrich, Louise

Heifner, Jack 1946- .... **CLC 11**
See also CA 105; CANR 47

Heijermans, Herman 1864-1924 .... **TCLC 24**
See also CA 123; EWL 3

Heilbrun, Carolyn G. 1926-2003 ..... **CLC 25, 173**
See also BPFB 1; CA 45-48; 220; CANR 1, 28, 58, 94; CMW; CPW; DLB 306; FW; MSW

Heilbrun, Carolyn Gold
See Heilbrun, Carolyn G.

Hein, Christoph 1944- .... **CLC 154**
See also CA 158; CANR 108; CDWLB 2; CWW 2; DLB 124

Heine, Heinrich 1797-1856 .... **NCLC 4, 54, 147; PC 25**
See also CDWLB 2; DLB 90; EW 5; RGWL 2, 3; TWA

Heinemann, Larry 1944- .... **CLC 50**
See also CA 110; CAAS 21; CANR 31, 81, 156; DLBD 9; INT CANR-31

Heinemann, Larry Curtiss
See Heinemann, Larry

Heiney, Donald (William) 1921-1993 . **CLC 9**
See also CA 1-4R; 142; CANR 3, 58; FANT

Heinlein, Robert A. 1907-1988 .. **CLC 1, 3, 8, 14, 26, 55; SSC 55**
See also AAYA 17; BPFB 2; BYA 4, 13; CA 1-4R; 125; CANR 1, 20, 53; CLR 75; CN 1, 2, 3, 4; CPW; DA3; DAM POP; DLB 8; EXPS; JRDA; LAIT 5; LMFS 2; MAICYA 1, 2; MTCW 1, 2; MTFW 2005; RGAL 4; SATA 9, 69; SATA-Obit 56; SCFW 1, 2; SFW 4; SSFS 7; YAW

Held, Peter
See Vance, Jack

Heldris of Cornwall fl. 13th cent.
- .... **CMLC 97**

Helforth, John
See Doolittle, Hilda

Heliodorus fl. 3rd cent. - .... **CMLC 52**
See also WLIT 8

Hellenhofferu, Vojtech Kapristian z
See Hasek, Jaroslav (Matej Frantisek)

Heller, Joseph 1923-1999 . **CLC 1, 3, 5, 8, 11, 36, 63; TCLC 131, 151; WLC 3**
See also AAYA 24; AITN 1; AMWS 4; BPFB 2; BYA 1; CA 5-8R; 187; CABS 1; CANR 8, 42, 66, 126; CN 1, 2, 3, 4, 5, 6; CPW; DA; DA3; DAB; DAC; DAM MST, NOV, POP; DLB 2, 28, 227; DLBY 1980, 2002; EWL 3; EXPN; INT CANR-8; LAIT 4; MAL 5; MTCW 1, 2; MTFW 2005; NFS 1; RGAL 4; TUS; YAW

Hellman, Lillian 1905-1984 . **CLC 2, 4, 8, 14, 18, 34, 44, 52; DC 1; TCLC 119**
See also AAYA 47; AITN 1, 2; AMWS 1; CA 13-16R; 112; CAD; CANR 33; CWD; DA3; DAM DRAM; DFS 1, 3, 14; DLB 7, 228; DLBY 1984; EWL 3; FL 1:6; FW; LAIT 3; MAL 5; MBL; MTCW 1, 2; MTFW 2005; RGAL 4; TUS

Helprin, Mark 1947- .... **CLC 7, 10, 22, 32**
See also CA 81-84; CANR 47, 64, 124; CDALBS; CN 7; CPW; DA3; DAM NOV, POP; DLB 335; DLBY 1985; FANT; MAL 5; MTCW 1, 2; MTFW 2005; SSFS 25; SUFW 2

Helvetius, Claude-Adrien 1715-1771 .. **LC 26**
See also DLB 313

Helyar, Jane Penelope Josephine 1933- .... **CLC 17**
See also CA 21-24R; CANR 10, 26; CWRI 5; SAAS 2; SATA 5; SATA-Essay 138

Hemans, Felicia 1793-1835 ...... **NCLC 29, 71**
See also DLB 96; RGEL 2

Hemingway, Ernest (Miller) 1899-1961 .... **CLC 1, 3, 6, 8, 10, 13, 19, 30, 34, 39, 41, 44, 50, 61, 80; SSC 1, 25, 36, 40, 63, 117; TCLC 115, 203; WLC 3**
See also AAYA 19; AMW; AMWC 1; AMWR 1; BPFB 2; BYA 2, 3, 13, 15; CA 77-80; CANR 34; CDALB 1917-1929;

DA; DA3; DAB; DAC; DAM MST, NOV; DLB 4, 9, 102, 210, 308, 316, 330; DLBD 1, 15, 16; DLBY 1981, 1987, 1996, 1998; EWL 3; EXPN; EXPS; LAIT 3, 4; LATS 1:1; MAL 5; MTCW 1, 2; MTFW 2005; NFS 1, 5, 6, 14; RGAL 4; RGSF 2; SSFS 17; TUS; WYA

Hempel, Amy 1951- .... **CLC 39**
See also CA 118; 137; CANR 70, 166; DA3; DLB 218; EXPS; MTCW 2; MTFW 2005; SSFS 2

Henderson, F. C.
See Mencken, H. L.

Henderson, Mary
See Mavor, Osborne Henry

Henderson, Sylvia
See Ashton-Warner, Sylvia (Constance)

Henderson, Zenna (Chlarson) 1917-1983 .... **SSC 29**
See also CA 1-4R; 133; CANR 1, 84; DLB 8; SATA 5; SFW 4

Henkin, Joshua 1964- .... **CLC 119**
See also CA 161; CANR 186; DLB 350

Henley, Beth **CLC 23, 255; DC 6, 14**
See Henley, Elizabeth Becker
See also CABS 3; CAD; CD 5, 6; CSW; CWD; DFS 2, 21, 26; DLBY 1986; FW

Henley, Elizabeth Becker 1952- ...... **CLC 23, 255; DC 6, 14**
See Henley, Beth
See also AAYA 70; CA 107; CABS 3; CAD; CANR 32, 73, 140; CD 5, 6; CSW; DA3; DAM DRAM, MST; DFS 2, 21; DLBY 1986; FW; MTCW 1, 2; MTFW 2005

Henley, William Ernest 1849-1903 .. **TCLC 8**
See also CA 105; 234; DLB 19; RGEL 2

Hennissart, Martha 1929- .... **CLC 2**
See also BPFB 2; CA 85-88; CANR 64; CMW 4; DLB 306

Henry VIII 1491-1547 .... **LC 10**
See also DLB 132

Henry, O. 1862-1910 . **SSC 5, 49, 117; TCLC 1, 19; WLC 3**
See also AAYA 41; AMWS 2; CA 104; 131; CDALB 1865-1917; DA; DA3; DAB; DAC; DAM MST; DLB 12, 78, 79; EXPS; MAL 5; MTCW 1, 2; MTFW 2005; RGAL 4; RGSF 2; SSFS 2, 18, 27; TCWW 1, 2; TUS; YABC 2

Henry, Oliver
See Henry, O.

Henry, Patrick 1736-1799 .... **LC 25**
See also LAIT 1

Henryson, Robert 1430(?)-1506(?) ..... **LC 20, 110; PC 65**
See also BRWS 7; DLB 146; RGEL 2

Henschke, Alfred
See Klabund

Henson, Lance 1944- .... **NNAL**
See also CA 146; DLB 175

Hentoff, Nat(han Irving) 1925- .... **CLC 26**
See also AAYA 4, 42; BYA 6; CA 1-4R; CAAS 6; CANR 5, 25, 77, 114; CLR 1, 52; INT CANR-25; JRDA; MAICYA 1, 2; SATA 42, 69, 133; SATA-Brief 27; WYA; YAW

Heppenstall, (John) Rayner 1911-1981 .... **CLC 10**
See also CA 1-4R; 103; CANR 29; CN 1, 2; CP 1, 2, 3; EWL 3

Heraclitus c. 540B.C.-c. 450B.C. ... **CMLC 22**
See also DLB 176

Herbert, Frank 1920-1986 ... **CLC 12, 23, 35, 44, 85**
See also AAYA 21; BPFB 2; BYA 4, 14; CA 53-56; 118; CANR 5, 43; CDALBS; CPW; DAM POP; DLB 8; INT CANR-5; LAIT 5; MTCW 1, 2; MTFW 2005; NFS 17; SATA 9, 37; SATA-Obit 47; SCFW 1, 2; SFW 4; YAW

Hinton, S.E. 1950- .... **CLC 30, 111**
See also AAYA 2, 33; BPFB 2; BYA 2, 3; CA 81-84; CANR 32, 62, 92, 133; CDALBS; CLR 3, 23; CPW; DA; DA3; DAB; DAC; DAM MST, NOV; JRDA; LAIT 5; MAICYA 1, 2; MTCW 1, 2; MTFW 2005; NFS 5, 9, 15, 16; SATA 19, 58, 115, 160; WYA; YAW

Hippius, Zinaida
See Gippius, Zinaida

Hiraoka, Kimitake 1925-1970 ... **CLC 2, 4, 6, 9, 27; DC 1; SSC 4; TCLC 161; WLC 4**
See also AAYA 50; BPFB 2; CA 97-100; 29-32R; DA3; DAM DRAM; DLB 182; EWL 3; GLL 1; MJW; MTCW 1, 2; RGSF 2; RGWL 2, 3; SSFS 5, 12

Hirsch, E.D., Jr. 1928- .... **CLC 79**
See also CA 25-28R; CANR 27, 51, 146, 181; DLB 67; INT CANR-27; MTCW 1

Hirsch, Edward 1950- .... **CLC 31, 50**
See also CA 104; CANR 20, 42, 102, 167; CP 6, 7; DLB 120; PFS 22

Hirsch, Eric Donald, Jr.
See Hirsch, E.D., Jr.

Hitchcock, Alfred (Joseph)
1899-1980 .... **CLC 16**
See also AAYA 22; CA 159; 97-100; SATA 27; SATA-Obit 24

Hitchens, Christopher 1949- .... **CLC 157**
See also CA 152; CANR 89, 155, 191

Hitchens, Christopher Eric
See Hitchens, Christopher

Hitler, Adolf 1889-1945 .... **TCLC 53**
See also CA 117; 147

Hoagland, Edward (Morley) 1932- .. **CLC 28**
See also ANW; CA 1-4R; CANR 2, 31, 57, 107; CN 1, 2, 3, 4, 5, 6, 7; DLB 6; SATA 51; TCWW 2

Hoban, Russell 1925- .... **CLC 7, 25**
See also BPFB 2; CA 5-8R; CANR 23, 37, 66, 114, 138; CLR 3, 69, 139; CN 4, 5, 6, 7; CWRI 5; DAM NOV; DLB 52; FANT; MAICYA 1, 2; MTCW 1, 2; MTFW 2005; SATA 1, 40, 78, 136; SFW 4; SUFW 2; TCLE 1:1

Hobbes, Thomas 1588-1679 .... **LC 36, 142**
See also DLB 151, 252, 281; RGEL 2

Hobbs, Perry
See Blackmur, R(ichard) P(almer)

Hobson, Laura Z(ametkin)
1900-1986 .... **CLC 7, 25**
See also BPFB 2; CA 17-20R; 118; CANR 55; CN 1, 2, 3, 4; DLB 28; SATA 52

Hoccleve, Thomas c. 1368-c. 1437 ...... **LC 75**
See also DLB 146; RGEL 2

Hoch, Edward D. 1930-2008 .... **SSC 119**
See also CA 29-32R; CANR 11, 27, 51, 97; CMW 4; DLB 306; SFW 4

Hoch, Edward Dentinger
See Hoch, Edward D.

Hochhuth, Rolf 1931- .... **CLC 4, 11, 18**
See also CA 5-8R; CANR 33, 75, 136; CWW 2; DAM DRAM; DLB 124; EWL 3; MTCW 1, 2; MTFW 2005; RGHL

Hochman, Sandra 1936- .... **CLC 3, 8**
See also CA 5-8R; CP 1, 2, 3, 4, 5; DLB 5

Hochwaelder, Fritz 1911-1986 .... **CLC 36**
See also CA 29-32R; 120; CANR 42; DAM DRAM; EWL 3; MTCW 1; RGWL 2, 3

Hochwalder, Fritz
See Hochwaelder, Fritz

Hocking, Mary (Eunice) 1921- .... **CLC 13**
See also CA 101; CANR 18, 40

Hodge, Merle 1944- .... **BLC 2:2**
See also EWL 3

Hodgins, Jack 1938- .... **CLC 23**
See also CA 93-96; CN 4, 5, 6, 7; DLB 60

Hodgson, William Hope
1877(?)-1918 .... **TCLC 13**
See also CA 111; 164; CMW 4; DLB 70, 153, 156, 178; HGG; MTCW 2; SFW 4; SUFW 1

Hoeg, Peter 1957- .... **CLC 95, 156**
See also CA 151; CANR 75; CMW 4; DA3; DLB 214; EWL 3; MTCW 2; MTFW 2005; NFS 17; RGWL 3; SSFS 18

Hoffman, Alice 1952- .... **CLC 51**
See also AAYA 37; AMWS 10; CA 77-80; CANR 34, 66, 100, 138, 170; CN 4, 5, 6, 7; CPW; DAM NOV; DLB 292; MAL 5; MTCW 1, 2; MTFW 2005; TCLE 1:1

Hoffman, Daniel (Gerard) 1923- . **CLC 6, 13, 23**
See also CA 1-4R; CANR 4, 142; CP 1, 2, 3, 4, 5, 6, 7; DLB 5; TCLE 1:1

Hoffman, Eva 1945- .... **CLC 182**
See also AMWS 16; CA 132; CANR 146

Hoffman, Stanley 1944- .... **CLC 5**
See also CA 77-80

Hoffman, William 1925- .... **CLC 141**
See also AMWS 18; CA 21-24R; CANR 9, 103; CSW; DLB 234; TCLE 1:1

Hoffman, William M.
See Hoffman, William M(oses)

Hoffman, William M(oses) 1939- ..... **CLC 40**
See also CA 57-60; CAD; CANR 11, 71; CD 5, 6

Hoffmann, E(rnst) T(heodor) A(madeus)
1776-1822 ..... **NCLC 2, 183; SSC 13, 92**
See also CDWLB 2; CLR 133; DLB 90; EW 5; GL 2; RGSF 2; RGWL 2, 3; SATA 27; SUFW 1; WCH

Hofmann, Gert 1931-1993 .... **CLC 54**
See also CA 128; CANR 145; EWL 3; RGHL

Hofmannsthal, Hugo von 1874-1929 ... **DC 4; TCLC 11**
See also CA 106; 153; CDWLB 2; DAM DRAM; DFS 17; DLB 81, 118; EW 9; EWL 3; RGWL 2, 3

Hogan, Linda 1947- ..... **CLC 73; NNAL; PC 35**
See also AMWS 4; ANW; BYA 12; CA 120, 226; CAAE 226; CANR 45, 73, 129; CWP; DAM MULT; DLB 175; SATA 132; TCWW 2

Hogarth, Charles
See Creasey, John

Hogarth, Emmett
See Polonsky, Abraham (Lincoln)

Hogarth, William 1697-1764 .... **LC 112**
See also AAYA 56

Hogg, James 1770-1835 .... **NCLC 4, 109**
See also BRWS 10; DLB 93, 116, 159; GL 2; HGG; RGEL 2; SUFW 1

Holbach, Paul-Henri Thiry
1723-1789 .... **LC 14**
See also DLB 313

Holberg, Ludvig 1684-1754 .... **LC 6**
See also DLB 300; RGWL 2, 3

Holbrook, John
See Vance, Jack

Holcroft, Thomas 1745-1809 .... **NCLC 85**
See also DLB 39, 89, 158; RGEL 2

Holden, Ursula 1921- .... **CLC 18**
See also CA 101; CAAS 8; CANR 22

Holderlin, (Johann Christian) Friedrich
1770-1843 .... **NCLC 16, 187; PC 4**
See also CDWLB 2; DLB 90; EW 5; RGWL 2, 3

Holdstock, Robert 1948- .... **CLC 39**
See also CA 131; CANR 81; DLB 261; FANT; HGG; SFW 4; SUFW 2

Holdstock, Robert P.
See Holdstock, Robert

Holinshed, Raphael fl. 1580- .... **LC 69**
See also DLB 167; RGEL 2

Holland, Isabelle (Christian)
1920-2002 .... **CLC 21**
See also AAYA 11, 64; CA 21-24R; 205; CAAE 181; CANR 10, 25, 47; CLR 57; CWRI 5; JRDA; LAIT 4; MAICYA 1, 2; SATA 8, 70; SATA-Essay 103; SATA-Obit 132; WYA

Holland, Marcus
See Caldwell, (Janet Miriam) Taylor (Holland)

Hollander, John 1929- .... **CLC 2, 5, 8, 14**
See also CA 1-4R; CANR 1, 52, 136; CP 1, 2, 3, 4, 5, 6, 7; DLB 5; MAL 5; SATA 13

Hollander, Paul
See Silverberg, Robert

Holleran, Andrew
See Garber, Eric

Holley, Marietta 1836(?)-1926 .... **TCLC 99**
See also CA 118; DLB 11; FL 1:3

Hollinghurst, Alan 1954- .... **CLC 55, 91**
See also BRWS 10; CA 114; CN 5, 6, 7; DLB 207, 326; GLL 1

Hollis, Jim
See Summers, Hollis (Spurgeon, Jr.)

Holly, Buddy 1936-1959 .... **TCLC 65**
See also CA 213

Holmes, Gordon
See Shiel, M. P.

Holmes, John
See Souster, (Holmes) Raymond

Holmes, John Clellon 1926-1988 ...... **CLC 56**
See also BG 1:2; CA 9-12R; 125; CANR 4; CN 1, 2, 3, 4; DLB 16, 237

Holmes, Oliver Wendell, Jr.
1841-1935 .... **TCLC 77**
See also CA 114; 186

Holmes, Oliver Wendell
1809-1894 .... **NCLC 14, 81; PC 71**
See also AMWS 1; CDALB 1640-1865; DLB 1, 189, 235; EXPP; PFS 24; RGAL 4; SATA 34

Holmes, Raymond
See Souster, (Holmes) Raymond

Holt, Samuel
See Westlake, Donald E.

Holt, Victoria
See Hibbert, Eleanor Alice Burford

Holub, Miroslav 1923-1998 .... **CLC 4**
See also CA 21-24R; 169; CANR 10; CDWLB 4; CWW 2; DLB 232; EWL 3; RGWL 3

Holz, Detlev
See Benjamin, Walter

Homer c. 8th cent. B.C.- .... **CMLC 1, 16, 61; PC 23; WLCS**
See also AW 1; CDWLB 1; DA; DA3; DAB; DAC; DAM MST, POET; DLB 176; EFS 1; LAIT 1; LMFS 1; RGWL 2, 3; TWA; WLIT 8; WP

Hong, Maxine Ting Ting
See Kingston, Maxine Hong

Hongo, Garrett Kaoru 1951- .... **PC 23**
See also CA 133; CAAS 22; CP 5, 6, 7; DLB 120, 312; EWL 3; EXPP; PFS 25; RGAL 4

Honig, Edwin 1919- .... **CLC 33**
See also CA 5-8R; CAAS 8; CANR 4, 45, 144; CP 1, 2, 3, 4, 5, 6, 7; DLB 5

Hood, Hugh (John Blagdon) 1928- . **CLC 15, 28, 273; SSC 42**
See also CA 49-52; CAAS 17; CANR 1, 33, 87; CN 1, 2, 3, 4, 5, 6, 7; DLB 53; RGSF 2

Hood, Thomas 1799-1845 . **NCLC 16; PC 93**
See also BRW 4; DLB 96; RGEL 2

DAM NOV, POP; DLB 278; DLBY 1983; FANT; INT CANR-10; MTCW 1, 2; MTFW 2005; RHW; SATA 62; SFW 4; TCWW 1, 2

Jakes, John William
See Jakes, John

James I 1394-1437 .... **LC 20**
See also RGEL 2

James, Alice 1848-1892 .... **NCLC 206**
See also DLB 221

James, Andrew
See Kirkup, James

James, C(yril) L(ionel) R(obert)
1901-1989 .... **BLCS; CLC 33**
See also BW 2; CA 117; 125; 128; CANR 62; CN 1, 2, 3, 4; DLB 125; MTCW 1

James, Daniel (Lewis) 1911-1988 ..... **CLC 33**
See also CA 174; 125; DLB 122

James, Dynely
See Mayne, William (James Carter)

James, Henry Sr. 1811-1882 .... **NCLC 53**

James, Henry 1843-1916 .... **SSC 8, 32, 47, 108; TCLC 2, 11, 24, 40, 47, 64, 171; WLC 3**
See also AMW; AMWC 1; AMWR 1; BPFB 2; BRW 6; CA 104; 132; CDALB 1865-1917; DA; DA3; DAB; DAC; DAM MST, NOV; DLB 12, 71, 74, 189; DLBD 13; EWL 3; EXPS; GL 2; HGG; LAIT 2; MAL 5; MTCW 1, 2; MTFW 2005; NFS 12, 16, 19; RGAL 4; RGEL 2; RGSF 2; SSFS 9; SUFW 1; TUS

James, M. R.
See James, Montague (Rhodes)

James, Mary
See Meaker, Marijane

James, Montague (Rhodes)
1862-1936 .... **SSC 16, 93; TCLC 6**
See also CA 104; 203; DLB 156, 201; HGG; RGEL 2; RGSF 2; SUFW 1

James, P. D.
See White, Phyllis Dorothy James

James, Philip
See Moorcock, Michael

James, Samuel
See Stephens, James

James, Seumas
See Stephens, James

James, Stephen
See Stephens, James

James, T.F.
See Fleming, Thomas

James, William 1842-1910 .... **TCLC 15, 32**
See also AMW; CA 109; 193; DLB 270, 284; MAL 5; NCFS 5; RGAL 4

Jameson, Anna 1794-1860 .... **NCLC 43**
See also DLB 99, 166

Jameson, Fredric 1934- .... **CLC 142**
See also CA 196; CANR 169; DLB 67; LMFS 2

Jameson, Fredric R.
See Jameson, Fredric

James VI of Scotland 1566-1625 .... **LC 109**
See also DLB 151, 172

Jami, Nur al-Din 'Abd al-Rahman
1414-1492 .... **LC 9**

Jammes, Francis 1868-1938 .... **TCLC 75**
See also CA 198; EWL 3; GFL 1789 to the Present

Jandl, Ernst 1925-2000 .... **CLC 34**
See also CA 200; EWL 3

Janowitz, Tama 1957- .... **CLC 43, 145**
See also CA 106; CANR 52, 89, 129; CN 5, 6, 7; CPW; DAM POP; DLB 292; MTFW 2005

Jansson, Tove (Marika) 1914-2001 ... **SSC 96**
See also CA 17-20R; 196; CANR 38, 118; CLR 2, 125; CWW 2; DLB 257; EWL 3; MAICYA 1, 2; RGSF 2; SATA 3, 41

Japrisot, Sebastien 1931-
See Rossi, Jean-Baptiste

Jarrell, Randall 1914-1965 .... **CLC 1, 2, 6, 9, 13, 49; PC 41; TCLC 177**
See also AMW; BYA 5; CA 5-8R; 25-28R; CABS 2; CANR 6, 34; CDALB 1941-1968; CLR 6, 111; CWRI 5; DAM POET; DLB 48, 52; EWL 3; EXPP; MAICYA 1, 2; MAL 5; MTCW 1, 2; PAB; PFS 2, 31; RGAL 4; SATA 7

Jarry, Alfred 1873-1907 .... **SSC 20; TCLC 2, 14, 147**
See also CA 104; 153; DA3; DAM DRAM; DFS 8; DLB 192, 258; EW 9; EWL 3; GFL 1789 to the Present; RGWL 2, 3; TWA

Jarvis, E.K.
See Ellison, Harlan; Silverberg, Robert

Jawien, Andrzej
See John Paul II, Pope

Jaynes, Roderick
See Coen, Ethan

Jeake, Samuel, Jr.
See Aiken, Conrad (Potter)

Jean-Louis
See Kerouac, Jack

Jean Paul 1763-1825 .... **NCLC 7**

Jefferies, (John) Richard
1848-1887 .... **NCLC 47**
See also DLB 98, 141; RGEL 2; SATA 16; SFW 4

Jeffers, John Robinson
See Jeffers, Robinson

Jeffers, Robinson 1887-1962 .... **CLC 2, 3, 11, 15, 54; PC 17; WLC 3**
See also AMWS 2; CA 85-88; CANR 35; CDALB 1917-1929; DA; DAC; DAM MST, POET; DLB 45, 212, 342; EWL 3; MAL 5; MTCW 1, 2; MTFW 2005; PAB; PFS 3, 4; RGAL 4

Jefferson, Janet
See Mencken, H. L.

Jefferson, Thomas 1743-1826 . **NCLC 11, 103**
See also AAYA 54; ANW; CDALB 1640-1865; DA3; DLB 31, 183; LAIT 1; RGAL 4

Jeffrey, Francis 1773-1850 .... **NCLC 33**
See also DLB 107

Jelakowitch, Ivan
See Heijermans, Herman

Jelinek, Elfriede 1946- .... **CLC 169**
See also AAYA 68; CA 154; CANR 169; DLB 85, 330; FW

Jellicoe, (Patricia) Ann 1927- .... **CLC 27**
See also CA 85-88; CBD; CD 5, 6; CWD; CWRI 5; DLB 13, 233; FW

Jelloun, Tahar ben
See Ben Jelloun, Tahar

Jemyma
See Holley, Marietta

Jen, Gish
See Jen, Lillian

Jen, Lillian 1955- .... **AAL; CLC 70, 198, 260**
See also AMWC 2; CA 135; CANR 89, 130; CN 7; DLB 312; NFS 30

Jenkins, (John) Robin 1912- .... **CLC 52**
See also CA 1-4R; CANR 1, 135; CN 1, 2, 3, 4, 5, 6, 7; DLB 14, 271

Jennings, Elizabeth (Joan)
1926-2001 .... **CLC 5, 14, 131**
See also BRWS 5; CA 61-64; 200; CAAS 5; CANR 8, 39, 66, 127; CP 1, 2, 3, 4, 5, 6, 7; CWP; DLB 27; EWL 3; MTCW 1; SATA 66

Jennings, Waylon 1937-2002 .... **CLC 21**

Jensen, Johannes V(ilhelm)
1873-1950 .... **TCLC 41**
See also CA 170; DLB 214, 330; EWL 3; RGWL 3

Jensen, Laura (Linnea) 1948- .... **CLC 37**
See also CA 103

Jerome, Saint 345-420 .... **CMLC 30**
See also RGWL 3

Jerome, Jerome K(lapka)
1859-1927 .... **TCLC 23**
See also CA 119; 177; DLB 10, 34, 135; RGEL 2

Jerrold, Douglas William
1803-1857 .... **NCLC 2**
See also DLB 158, 159, 344; RGEL 2

Jewett, (Theodora) Sarah Orne
1849-1909 . **SSC 6, 44, 110; TCLC 1, 22**
See also AAYA 76; AMW; AMWC 2; AMWR 2; CA 108; 127; CANR 71; DLB 12, 74, 221; EXPS; FL 1:3; FW; MAL 5; MBL; NFS 15; RGAL 4; RGSF 2; SATA 15; SSFS 4

Jewsbury, Geraldine (Endsor)
1812-1880 .... **NCLC 22**
See also DLB 21

Jhabvala, Ruth Prawer 1927- . **CLC 4, 8, 29, 94, 138; SSC 91**
See also BRWS 5; CA 1-4R; CANR 2, 29, 51, 74, 91, 128; CN 1, 2, 3, 4, 5, 6, 7; DAB; DAM NOV; DLB 139, 194, 323, 326; EWL 3; IDFW 3, 4; INT CANR-29; MTCW 1, 2; MTFW 2005; RGSF 2; RGWL 2; RHW; TEA

Jibran, Kahlil
See Gibran, Kahlil

Jibran, Khalil
See Gibran, Kahlil

Jiles, Paulette 1943- .... **CLC 13, 58**
See also CA 101; CANR 70, 124, 170; CP 5; CWP

Jimenez (Mantecon), Juan Ramon
1881-1958 .... **HLC 1; PC 7; TCLC 4, 183**
See also CA 104; 131; CANR 74; DAM MULT, POET; DLB 134, 330; EW 9; EWL 3; HW 1; MTCW 1, 2; MTFW 2005; RGWL 2, 3

Jimenez, Ramon
See Jimenez (Mantecon), Juan Ramon

Jimenez Mantecon, Juan
See Jimenez (Mantecon), Juan Ramon

Jin, Ba 1904-2005 .... **CLC 18**
See Cantu, Robert Clark
See also CA 244; CWW 2; DLB 328; EWL 3

Jin, Xuefei 1956- .... **CLC 109, 262**
See also CA 152; CANR 91, 130, 184; DLB 244, 292; MTFW 2005; NFS 25; SSFS 17

Jin Ha
See Jin, Xuefei

Jodelle, Etienne 1532-1573 .... **LC 119**
See also DLB 327; GFL Beginnings to 1789

Joel, Billy
See Joel, William Martin

Joel, William Martin 1949- .... **CLC 26**
See also CA 108

John, St.
See John of Damascus, St.

John of Damascus, St. c.
675-749 .... **CMLC 27, 95**

John of Salisbury c. 1115-1180 ..... **CMLC 63**

John of the Cross, St. 1542-1591 .... **LC 18, 146**
See also RGWL 2, 3

John Paul II, Pope 1920-2005 .... **CLC 128**
See also CA 106; 133; 238

Johnson, B(ryan) S(tanley William)
1933-1973 .... **CLC 6, 9**
See also CA 9-12R; 53-56; CANR 9; CN 1; CP 1, 2; DLB 14, 40; EWL 3; RGEL 2

Johnson, Benjamin F., of Boone
See Riley, James Whitcomb

Jovine, Francesco 1902-1950 .... **TCLC 79**
See also DLB 264; EWL 3

Joyaux, Julia
See Kristeva, Julia

Joyce, James (Augustine Aloysius)
1882-1941 .... **DC 16; PC 22; SSC 3, 26, 44, 64, 118, 122; TCLC 3, 8, 16, 35, 52, 159; WLC 3**
See also AAYA 42; BRW 7; BRWC 1; BRWR 1; BYA 11, 13; CA 104; 126; CDBLB 1914-1945; DA; DA3; DAB; DAM MST, NOV, POET; DLB 10, 19, 36, 162, 247; EWL 3; EXPN; EXPS; LAIT 3; LMFS 1, 2; MTCW 1, 2; MTFW 2005; NFS 7, 26; RGSF 2; SSFS 1, 19; TEA; WLIT 4

Jozsef, Attila 1905-1937 .... **TCLC 22**
See also CA 116; 230; CDWLB 4; DLB 215; EWL 3

Juana Ines de la Cruz, Sor
1651(?)-1695 ... **HLCS 1; LC 5, 136; PC 24**
See also DLB 305; FW; LAW; RGWL 2, 3; WLIT 1

Juana Inez de La Cruz, Sor
See Juana Ines de la Cruz, Sor

Juan Manuel, Don 1282-1348 .... **CMLC 88**

Judd, Cyril
See Kornbluth, C(yril) M.; Pohl, Frederik

Juenger, Ernst 1895-1998 .... **CLC 125**
See also CA 101; 167; CANR 21, 47, 106; CDWLB 2; DLB 56; EWL 3; RGWL 2, 3

Julian of Norwich 1342(?)-1416(?) . **LC 6, 52**
See also BRWS 12; DLB 146; LMFS 1

Julius Caesar 100B.C.-44B.C. .... **CMLC 47**
See also AW 1; CDWLB 1; DLB 211; RGWL 2, 3; WLIT 8

Jung, Patricia B.
See Hope, Christopher

Junger, Ernst
See Juenger, Ernst

Junger, Sebastian 1962- .... **CLC 109**
See also AAYA 28; CA 165; CANR 130, 171; MTFW 2005

Juniper, Alex
See Hospital, Janette Turner

Junius
See Luxemburg, Rosa

Junzaburo, Nishiwaki
See Nishiwaki, Junzaburo

Just, Ward 1935- .... **CLC 4, 27**
See also CA 25-28R; CANR 32, 87; CN 6, 7; DLB 335; INT CANR-32

Just, Ward Swift
See Just, Ward

Justice, Donald 1925-2004 ... **CLC 6, 19, 102; PC 64**
See also AMWS 7; CA 5-8R; 230; CANR 26, 54, 74, 121, 122, 169; CP 1, 2, 3, 4, 5, 6, 7; CSW; DAM POET; DLBY 1983; EWL 3; INT CANR-26; MAL 5; MTCW 2; PFS 14; TCLE 1:1

Justice, Donald Rodney
See Justice, Donald

Juvenal c. 55-c. 127 .... **CMLC 8, 115**
See also AW 2; CDWLB 1; DLB 211; RGWL 2, 3; WLIT 8

Juvenis
See Bourne, Randolph S(illiman)

K., Alice
See Knapp, Caroline

Kabakov, Sasha CLC 59

Kabir 1398(?)-1448(?) .... **LC 109; PC 56**
See also RGWL 2, 3

Kacew, Romain 1914-1980 .... **CLC 25**
See also CA 108; 102; DLB 83, 299; RGHL

Kacew, Roman
See Kacew, Romain

Kadare, Ismail 1936- .... **CLC 52, 190**
See also CA 161; CANR 165; EWL 3; RGWL 3

Kadohata, Cynthia 1956(?)- ..... **CLC 59, 122**
See also AAYA 71; CA 140; CANR 124; CLR 121; SATA 155, 180

Kafka, Franz 1883-1924 ... **SSC 5, 29, 35, 60; TCLC 2, 6, 13, 29, 47, 53, 112, 179; WLC 3**
See also AAYA 31; BPFB 2; CA 105; 126; CDWLB 2; DA; DA3; DAB; DAC; DAM MST, NOV; DLB 81; EW 9; EWL 3; EXPS; LATS 1:1; LMFS 2; MTCW 1, 2; MTFW 2005; NFS 7; RGSF 2; RGWL 2, 3; SFW 4; SSFS 3, 7, 12; TWA

Kafu
See Nagai, Kafu

Kahanovitch, Pinchas
See Der Nister

Kahanovitsch, Pinkhes
See Der Nister

Kahanovitsh, Pinkhes
See Der Nister

Kahn, Roger 1927- .... **CLC 30**
See also CA 25-28R; CANR 44, 69, 152; DLB 171; SATA 37

Kain, Saul
See Sassoon, Siegfried (Lorraine)

Kaiser, Georg 1878-1945 .... **TCLC 9, 220**
See also CA 106; 190; CDWLB 2; DLB 124; EWL 3; LMFS 2; RGWL 2, 3

Kaledin, Sergei CLC 59

Kaletski, Alexander 1946- .... **CLC 39**
See also CA 118; 143

Kalidasa fl. c. 400-455 .... **CMLC 9; PC 22**
See also RGWL 2, 3

Kallman, Chester (Simon)
1921-1975 .... **CLC 2**
See also CA 45-48; 53-56; CANR 3; CP 1, 2

Kaminsky, Melvin CLC 12, 217
See Brooks, Mel
See also AAYA 13, 48; DLB 26

Kaminsky, Stuart M. 1934- .... **CLC 59**
See also CA 73-76; CANR 29, 53, 89, 161, 190; CMW 4

Kaminsky, Stuart Melvin
See Kaminsky, Stuart M.

Kamo no Chomei 1153(?)-1216 .... **CMLC 66**
See also DLB 203

Kamo no Nagaakira
See Kamo no Chomei

Kandinsky, Wassily 1866-1944 .... **TCLC 92**
See also AAYA 64; CA 118; 155

Kane, Francis
See Robbins, Harold

Kane, Paul
See Simon, Paul

Kane, Sarah 1971-1999 .... **DC 31**
See also BRWS 8; CA 190; CD 5, 6; DLB 310

Kanin, Garson 1912-1999 .... **CLC 22**
See also AITN 1; CA 5-8R; 177; CAD; CANR 7, 78; DLB 7; IDFW 3, 4

Kaniuk, Yoram 1930- .... **CLC 19**
See also CA 134; DLB 299; RGHL

Kant, Immanuel 1724-1804 ..... **NCLC 27, 67**
See also DLB 94

Kantor, MacKinlay 1904-1977 .... **CLC 7**
See also CA 61-64; 73-76; CANR 60, 63; CN 1, 2; DLB 9, 102; MAL 5; MTCW 2; RHW; TCWW 1, 2

Kanze Motokiyo
See Zeami

Kaplan, David Michael 1946- .... **CLC 50**
See also CA 187

Kaplan, James 1951- .... **CLC 59**
See also CA 135; CANR 121

Karadzic, Vuk Stefanovic
1787-1864 .... **NCLC 115**
See also CDWLB 4; DLB 147

Karageorge, Michael
See Anderson, Poul

Karamzin, Nikolai Mikhailovich
1766-1826 .... **NCLC 3, 173**
See also DLB 150; RGSF 2

Karapanou, Margarita 1946- .... **CLC 13**
See also CA 101

Karinthy, Frigyes 1887-1938 .... **TCLC 47**
See also CA 170; DLB 215; EWL 3

Karl, Frederick R(obert)
1927-2004 .... **CLC 34**
See also CA 5-8R; 226; CANR 3, 44, 143

Karr, Mary 1955- .... **CLC 188**
See also AMWS 11; CA 151; CANR 100, 191; MTFW 2005; NCFS 5

Kastel, Warren
See Silverberg, Robert

Kataev, Evgeny Petrovich
1903-1942 .... **TCLC 21**
See also CA 120; DLB 272

Kataphusin
See Ruskin, John

Katz, Steve 1935- .... **CLC 47**
See also CA 25-28R; CAAS 14, 64; CANR 12; CN 4, 5, 6, 7; DLBY 1983

Kauffman, Janet 1945- .... **CLC 42**
See also CA 117; CANR 43, 84; DLB 218; DLBY 1986

Kaufman, Bob (Garnell)
1925-1986 .... **CLC 49; PC 74**
See also BG 1:3; BW 1; CA 41-44R; 118; CANR 22; CP 1; DLB 16, 41

Kaufman, George S. 1889-1961 ...... **CLC 38; DC 17**
See also CA 108; 93-96; DAM DRAM; DFS 1, 10; DLB 7; INT CA-108; MTCW 2; MTFW 2005; RGAL 4; TUS

Kaufman, Moises 1964- .... **DC 26**
See also CA 211; DFS 22; MTFW 2005

Kaufman, Sue
See Barondess, Sue K.

Kavafis, Konstantinos Petrou
1863-1933 .... **PC 36; TCLC 2, 7**
See also CA 104; 148; DA3; DAM POET; EW 8; EWL 3; MTCW 2; PFS 19; RGWL 2, 3; WP

Kavan, Anna 1901-1968 .... **CLC 5, 13, 82**
See also BRWS 7; CA 5-8R; CANR 6, 57; DLB 255; MTCW 1; RGEL 2; SFW 4

Kavanagh, Dan
See Barnes, Julian

Kavanagh, Julie 1952- .... **CLC 119**
See also CA 163; CANR 186

Kavanagh, Patrick (Joseph)
1904-1967 .... **CLC 22; PC 33**
See also BRWS 7; CA 123; 25-28R; DLB 15, 20; EWL 3; MTCW 1; RGEL 2

Kawabata, Yasunari 1899-1972 ..... **CLC 2, 5, 9, 18, 107; SSC 17**
See also CA 93-96; 33-36R; CANR 88; DAM MULT; DLB 180, 330; EWL 3; MJW; MTCW 2; MTFW 2005; RGSF 2; RGWL 2, 3

Kawabata Yasunari
See Kawabata, Yasunari

Kaye, Mary Margaret
See Kaye, M.M.

Kaye, M.M. 1908-2004 .... **CLC 28**
See also CA 89-92; 223; CANR 24, 60, 102, 142; MTCW 1, 2; MTFW 2005; RHW; SATA 62; SATA-Obit 152

Kaye, Mollie
See Kaye, M.M.

Kaye-Smith, Sheila 1887-1956 .... **TCLC 20**
See also CA 118; 203; DLB 36

Kherdian, David 1931- .... **CLC 6, 9**
    See also AAYA 42; CA 21-24R, 192; CAAE 192; CAAS 2; CANR 39, 78; CLR 24; JRDA; LAIT 3; MAICYA 1, 2; SATA 16, 74; SATA-Essay 125

Khlebnikov, Velimir TCLC 20
    See Khlebnikov, Viktor Vladimirovich
    See also DLB 295; EW 10; EWL 3; RGWL 2, 3

Khlebnikov, Viktor Vladimirovich 1885-1922
    See Khlebnikov, Velimir
    See also CA 117; 217

Khodasevich, V.F.
    See Khodasevich, Vladislav

Khodasevich, Vladislav
    1886-1939 .... **TCLC 15**
    See also CA 115; DLB 317; EWL 3

Khodasevich, Vladislav Felitsianovich
    See Khodasevich, Vladislav

Kidd, Sue Monk 1948- .... **CLC 267**
    See also AAYA 72; CA 202; MTFW 2005; NFS 27

Kielland, Alexander Lange
    1849-1906 .... **TCLC 5**
    See also CA 104

Kiely, Benedict 1919-2007 . **CLC 23, 43; SSC 58**
    See also CA 1-4R; 257; CANR 2, 84; CN 1, 2, 3, 4, 5, 6, 7; DLB 15, 319; TCLE 1:1

Kienzle, William X. 1928-2001 .... **CLC 25**
    See also CA 93-96; 203; CAAS 1; CANR 9, 31, 59, 111; CMW 4; DA3; DAM POP; INT CANR-31; MSW; MTCW 1, 2; MTFW 2005

Kierkegaard, Soren 1813-1855 ..... **NCLC 34, 78, 125**
    See also DLB 300; EW 6; LMFS 2; RGWL 3; TWA

Kieslowski, Krzysztof 1941-1996 .... **CLC 120**
    See also CA 147; 151

Killens, John Oliver 1916-1987 ...... **BLC 2:2; CLC 10**
    See also BW 2; CA 77-80; 123; CAAS 2; CANR 26; CN 1, 2, 3, 4; DLB 33; EWL 3

Killigrew, Anne 1660-1685 .... **LC 4, 73**
    See also DLB 131

Killigrew, Thomas 1612-1683 .... **LC 57**
    See also DLB 58; RGEL 2

Kim
    See Simenon, Georges (Jacques Christian)

Kincaid, Jamaica 1949- . **BLC 1:2, 2:2; CLC 43, 68, 137, 234; SSC 72**
    See also AAYA 13, 56; AFAW 2; AMWS 7; BRWS 7; BW 2, 3; CA 125; CANR 47, 59, 95, 133; CDALBS; CLR 63; CN 4, 5, 6, 7; DA3; DAM MULT, NOV; DLB 157, 227; DNFS 1; EWL 3; EXPS; FW; LATS 1:2; LMFS 2; MAL 5; MTCW 2; MTFW 2005; NCFS 1; NFS 3; SSFS 5, 7; TUS; WWE 1; YAW

King, Francis (Henry) 1923- .... **CLC 8, 53, 145**
    See also CA 1-4R; CANR 1, 33, 86; CN 1, 2, 3, 4, 5, 6, 7; DAM NOV; DLB 15, 139; MTCW 1

King, Kennedy
    See Brown, George Douglas

King, Martin Luther, Jr.
    1929-1968 ... **BLC 1:2; CLC 83; WLCS**
    See also BW 2, 3; CA 25-28; CANR 27, 44; CAP 2; DA; DA3; DAB; DAC; DAM MST, MULT; LAIT 5; LATS 1:2; MTCW 1, 2; MTFW 2005; SATA 14

King, Stephen 1947- .... **CLC 12, 26, 37, 61, 113, 228, 244; SSC 17, 55**
    See also AAYA 1, 17; AMWS 5; BEST 90:1; BPFB 2; CA 61-64; CANR 1, 30, 52, 76, 119, 134, 168; CLR 124; CN 7;

CPW; DA3; DAM NOV, POP; DLB 143, 350; DLBY 1980; HGG; JRDA; LAIT 5; MTCW 1, 2; MTFW 2005; RGAL 4; SATA 9, 55, 161; SUFW 1, 2; WYAS 1; YAW

King, Stephen Edwin
    See King, Stephen

King, Steve
    See King, Stephen

King, Thomas 1943- .... **CLC 89, 171, 276; NNAL**
    See also CA 144; CANR 95, 175; CCA 1; CN 6, 7; DAC; DAM MULT; DLB 175, 334; SATA 96

King, Thomas Hunt
    See King, Thomas

Kingman, Lee
    See Natti, Lee

Kingsley, Charles 1819-1875 .... **NCLC 35**
    See also CLR 77; DLB 21, 32, 163, 178, 190; FANT; MAICYA 2; MAICYAS 1; RGEL 2; WCH; YABC 2

Kingsley, Henry 1830-1876 .... **NCLC 107**
    See also DLB 21, 230; RGEL 2

Kingsley, Sidney 1906-1995 .... **CLC 44**
    See also CA 85-88; 147; CAD; DFS 14, 19; DLB 7; MAL 5; RGAL 4

Kingsolver, Barbara 1955- .... **CLC 55, 81, 130, 216, 269**
    See also AAYA 15; AMWS 7; CA 129; 134; CANR 60, 96, 133, 179; CDALBS; CN 7; CPW; CSW; DA3; DAM POP; DLB 206; INT CA-134; LAIT 5; MTCW 2; MTFW 2005; NFS 5, 10, 12, 24; RGAL 4; TCLE 1:1

Kingston, Maxine Hong 1940- .... **AAL; CLC 12, 19, 58, 121, 271; WLCS**
    See also AAYA 8, 55; AMWS 5; BPFB 2; CA 69-72; CANR 13, 38, 74, 87, 128; CDALBS; CN 6, 7; DA3; DAM MULT, NOV; DLB 173, 212, 312; DLBY 1980; EWL 3; FL 1:6; FW; INT CANR-13; LAIT 5; MAL 5; MBL; MTCW 1, 2; MTFW 2005; NFS 6; RGAL 4; SATA 53; SSFS 3; TCWW 2

Kingston, Maxine Ting Ting Hong
    See Kingston, Maxine Hong

Kinnell, Galway 1927- ..... **CLC 1, 2, 3, 5, 13, 29, 129; PC 26**
    See also AMWS 3; CA 9-12R; CANR 10, 34, 66, 116, 138, 175; CP 1, 2, 3, 4, 5, 6, 7; DLB 5, 342; DLBY 1987; EWL 3; INT CANR-34; MAL 5; MTCW 1, 2; MTFW 2005; PAB; PFS 9, 26; RGAL 4; TCLE 1:1; WP

Kinsella, Thomas 1928- .... **CLC 4, 19, 138, 274; PC 69**
    See also BRWS 5; CA 17-20R; CANR 15, 122; CP 1, 2, 3, 4, 5, 6, 7; DLB 27; EWL 3; MTCW 1, 2; MTFW 2005; RGEL 2; TEA

Kinsella, W.P. 1935- .... **CLC 27, 43, 166**
    See also AAYA 7, 60; BPFB 2; CA 97-100, 222; CAAE 222; CAAS 7; CANR 21, 35, 66, 75, 129; CN 4, 5, 6, 7; CPW; DAC; DAM NOV, POP; FANT; INT CANR-21; LAIT 5; MTCW 1, 2; MTFW 2005; NFS 15; RGSF 2

Kinsey, Alfred C(harles)
    1894-1956 .... **TCLC 91**
    See also CA 115; 170; MTCW 2

Kipling, (Joseph) Rudyard 1865-1936 . **PC 3, 91; SSC 5, 54, 110; TCLC 8, 17, 167; WLC 3**
    See also AAYA 32; BRW 6; BRWC 1, 2; BYA 4; CA 105; 120; CANR 33; CDBLB 1890-1914; CLR 39, 65; CWRI 5; DA; DA3; DAB; DAC; DAM MST, POET; DLB 19, 34, 141, 156, 330; EWL 3; EXPS; FANT; LAIT 3; LMFS 1; MAI-

CYA 1, 2; MTCW 1, 2; MTFW 2005; NFS 21; PFS 22; RGEL 2; RGSF 2; SATA 100; SFW 4; SSFS 8, 21, 22; SUFW 1; TEA; WCH; WLIT 4; YABC 2

Kircher, Athanasius 1602-1680 .... **LC 121**
    See also DLB 164

Kirk, Russell (Amos) 1918-1994 .. **TCLC 119**
    See also AITN 1; CA 1-4R; 145; CAAS 9; CANR 1, 20, 60; HGG; INT CANR-20; MTCW 1, 2

Kirkham, Dinah
    See Card, Orson Scott

Kirkland, Caroline M. 1801-1864 . **NCLC 85**
    See also DLB 3, 73, 74, 250, 254; DLBD 13

Kirkup, James 1918-2009 .... **CLC 1**
    See also CA 1-4R; CAAS 4; CANR 2; CP 1, 2, 3, 4, 5, 6, 7; DLB 27; SATA 12

Kirkwood, James 1930(?)-1989 .... **CLC 9**
    See also AITN 2; CA 1-4R; 128; CANR 6, 40; GLL 2

Kirsch, Sarah 1935- .... **CLC 176**
    See also CA 178; CWW 2; DLB 75; EWL 3

Kirshner, Sidney
    See Kingsley, Sidney

Kis, Danilo 1935-1989 .... **CLC 57**
    See also CA 109; 118; 129; CANR 61; CD-WLB 4; DLB 181; EWL 3; MTCW 1; RGSF 2; RGWL 2, 3

Kissinger, Henry A(lfred) 1923- ..... **CLC 137**
    See also CA 1-4R; CANR 2, 33, 66, 109; MTCW 1

Kittel, Frederick August
    See Wilson, August

Kivi, Aleksis 1834-1872 .... **NCLC 30**

Kizer, Carolyn 1925- ..... **CLC 15, 39, 80; PC 66**
    See also CA 65-68; CAAS 5; CANR 24, 70, 134; CP 1, 2, 3, 4, 5, 6, 7; CWP; DAM POET; DLB 5, 169; EWL 3; MAL 5; MTCW 2; MTFW 2005; PFS 18; TCLE 1:1

Klabund 1890-1928 .... **TCLC 44**
    See also CA 162; DLB 66

Klappert, Peter 1942- .... **CLC 57**
    See also CA 33-36R; CSW; DLB 5

Klausner, Amos
    See Oz, Amos

Klein, A(braham) M(oses)
    1909-1972 .... **CLC 19**
    See also CA 101; 37-40R; CP 1; DAB; DAC; DAM MST; DLB 68; EWL 3; RGEL 2; RGHL

Klein, Joe
    See Klein, Joseph

Klein, Joseph 1946- .... **CLC 154**
    See also CA 85-88; CANR 55, 164

Klein, Norma 1938-1989 .... **CLC 30**
    See also AAYA 2, 35; BPFB 2; BYA 6, 7, 8; CA 41-44R; 128; CANR 15, 37; CLR 2, 19; INT CANR-15; JRDA; MAICYA 1, 2; SAAS 1; SATA 7, 57; WYA; YAW

Klein, T.E.D. 1947- .... **CLC 34**
    See also CA 119; CANR 44, 75, 167; HGG

Klein, Theodore Eibon Donald
    See Klein, T.E.D.

Kleist, Heinrich von 1777-1811 .... **DC 29; NCLC 2, 37; SSC 22**
    See also CDWLB 2; DAM DRAM; DLB 90; EW 5; RGSF 2; RGWL 2, 3

Klima, Ivan 1931- .... **CLC 56, 172**
    See also CA 25-28R; CANR 17, 50, 91; CDWLB 4; CWW 2; DAM NOV; DLB 232; EWL 3; RGWL 3

Klimentev, Andrei Platonovich
    See Klimentov, Andrei Platonovich

Krylov, Ivan Andreevich
  1768(?)-1844 .... **NCLC 1**
  See also DLB 150
Kubin, Alfred (Leopold Isidor)
  1877-1959 .... **TCLC 23**
  See also CA 112; 149; CANR 104; DLB 81
Kubrick, Stanley 1928-1999 .... **CLC 16;**
  TCLC 112
  See also AAYA 30; CA 81-84; 177; CANR
  33; DLB 26
Kueng, Hans
  See Kung, Hans
Kumin, Maxine 1925- .... **CLC 5, 13, 28, 164;**
  PC 15
  See also AITN 2; AMWS 4; ANW; CA
  1-4R, 271; CAAE 271; CAAS 8; CANR
  1, 21, 69, 115, 140; CP 2, 3, 4, 5, 6, 7;
  CWP; DA3; DAM POET; DLB 5; EWL
  3; EXPP; MTCW 1, 2; MTFW 2005;
  PAB; PFS 18; SATA 12
Kundera, Milan 1929- . **CLC 4, 9, 19, 32, 68,**
  115, 135, 234; SSC 24
  See also AAYA 2, 62; BPFB 2; CA 85-88;
  CANR 19, 52, 74, 144; CDWLB 4; CWW
  2; DA3; DAM NOV; DLB 232; EW 13;
  EWL 3; MTCW 1, 2; MTFW 2005; NFS
  18, 27; RGSF 2; RGWL 3; SSFS 10
Kunene, Mazisi 1930-2006 .... **CLC 85**
  See also BW 1, 3; CA 125; 252; CANR 81;
  CP 1, 6, 7; DLB 117
Kunene, Mazisi Raymond
  See Kunene, Mazisi
Kunene, Mazisi Raymond Fakazi Mngoni
  See Kunene, Mazisi
Kung, Hans
  See Kung, Hans
Kung, Hans 1928- .... **CLC 130**
  See also CA 53-56; CANR 66, 134; MTCW
  1, 2; MTFW 2005
Kunikida, Tetsuo
  See Kunikida Doppo
Kunikida Doppo 1869(?)-1908 .... **TCLC 99**
  See also DLB 180; EWL 3
Kunikida Tetsuo
  See Kunikida Doppo
Kunitz, Stanley 1905-2006 ..... **CLC 6, 11, 14,**
  148; PC 19
  See also AMWS 3; CA 41-44R; 250; CANR
  26, 57, 98; CP 1, 2, 3, 4, 5, 6, 7; DA3;
  DLB 48; INT CANR-26; MAL 5; MTCW
  1, 2; MTFW 2005; PFS 11; RGAL 4
Kunitz, Stanley Jasspon
  See Kunitz, Stanley
Kunze, Reiner 1933- .... **CLC 10**
  See also CA 93-96; CWW 2; DLB 75; EWL
  3
Kuprin, Aleksander Ivanovich
  1870-1938 .... **TCLC 5**
  See also CA 104; 182; DLB 295; EWL 3
Kuprin, Aleksandr Ivanovich
  See Kuprin, Aleksander Ivanovich
Kuprin, Alexandr Ivanovich
  See Kuprin, Aleksander Ivanovich
Kureishi, Hanif 1954- .. **CLC 64, 135; DC 26**
  See also BRWS 11; CA 139; CANR 113;
  CBD; CD 5, 6; CN 6, 7; DLB 194, 245,
  352; GLL 2; IDFW 4; WLIT 4; WWE 1
Kurosawa, Akira 1910-1998 ..... **CLC 16, 119**
  See also AAYA 11, 64; CA 101; 170; CANR
  46; DAM MULT
Kushner, Tony 1956- .... **CLC 81, 203; DC 10**
  See also AAYA 61; AMWS 9; CA 144;
  CAD; CANR 74, 130; CD 5, 6; DA3;
  DAM DRAM; DFS 5; DLB 228; EWL 3;
  GLL 1; LAIT 5; MAL 5; MTCW 2;
  MTFW 2005; RGAL 4; RGHL; SATA 160
Kuttner, Henry 1915-1958 .... **TCLC 10**
  See also CA 107; 157; DLB 8; FANT;
  SCFW 1, 2; SFW 4

Kutty, Madhavi
  See Das, Kamala
Kuzma, Greg 1944- .... **CLC 7**
  See also CA 33-36R; CANR 70
Kuzmin, Mikhail (Alekseevich)
  1872(?)-1936 .... **TCLC 40**
  See also CA 170; DLB 295; EWL 3
Kyd, Thomas 1558-1594 .. **DC 3; LC 22, 125**
  See also BRW 1; DAM DRAM; DFS 21;
  DLB 62; IDTP; LMFS 1; RGEL 2; TEA;
  WLIT 3
Kyprianos, Iossif
  See Samarakis, Antonis
L. S.
  See Stephen, Sir Leslie
Labe, Louise 1521-1566 .... **LC 120**
  See also DLB 327
Labrunie, Gerard
  See Nerval, Gerard de
La Bruyere, Jean de 1645-1696 .. **LC 17, 168**
  See also DLB 268; EW 3; GFL Beginnings
  to 1789
LaBute, Neil 1963- .... **CLC 225**
  See also CA 240
Lacan, Jacques (Marie Emile)
  1901-1981 .... **CLC 75**
  See also CA 121; 104; DLB 296; EWL 3;
  TWA
Laclos, Pierre-Ambroise Francois
  1741-1803 .... **NCLC 4, 87**
  See also DLB 313; EW 4; GFL Beginnings
  to 1789; RGWL 2, 3
Lacolere, Francois
  See Aragon, Louis
La Colere, Francois
  See Aragon, Louis
La Deshabilleuse
  See Simenon, Georges (Jacques Christian)
Lady Gregory
  See Gregory, Lady Isabella Augusta (Persse)
Lady of Quality, A
  See Bagnold, Enid
La Fayette, Marie-(Madelaine Pioche de la
  Vergne) 1634-1693 .... **LC 2, 144**
  See also DLB 268; GFL Beginnings to
  1789; RGWL 2, 3
Lafayette, Marie-Madeleine
  See La Fayette, Marie-(Madelaine Pioche
  de la Vergne)
Lafayette, Rene
  See Hubbard, L. Ron
La Flesche, Francis 1857(?)-1932 ...... **NNAL**
  See also CA 144; CANR 83; DLB 175
La Fontaine, Jean de 1621-1695 .... **LC 50**
  See also DLB 268; EW 3; GFL Beginnings
  to 1789; MAICYA 1, 2; RGWL 2, 3;
  SATA 18
LaForet, Carmen 1921-2004 .... **CLC 219**
  See also CA 246; CWW 2; DLB 322; EWL
  3
LaForet Diaz, Carmen
  See LaForet, Carmen
Laforgue, Jules 1860-1887 . **NCLC 5, 53; PC**
  14; SSC 20
  See also DLB 217; EW 7; GFL 1789 to the
  Present; RGWL 2, 3
Lagerkvist, Paer 1891-1974 ... **CLC 7, 10, 13,**
  54; SSC 12; TCLC 144
  See also CA 85-88; 49-52; DA3; DAM
  DRAM, NOV; DLB 259, 331; EW 10;
  EWL 3; MTCW 1, 2; MTFW 2005; RGSF
  2; RGWL 2, 3; TWA
Lagerkvist, Paer Fabian
  See Lagerkvist, Paer
Lagerkvist, Par
  See Lagerkvist, Paer
Lagerloef, Selma
  See Lagerlof, Selma

Lagerloef, Selma Ottiliana Lovisa
  See Lagerlof, Selma
Lagerlof, Selma 1858-1940 .... **TCLC 4, 36**
  See also CA 108; 188; CLR 7; DLB 259,
  331; MTCW 2; RGWL 2, 3; SATA 15;
  SSFS 18
Lagerlof, Selma Ottiliana Lovisa
  See Lagerlof, Selma
La Guma, Alex 1925-1985 .. **BLCS; CLC 19;**
  TCLC 140
  See also AFW; BW 1, 3; CA 49-52; 118;
  CANR 25, 81; CDWLB 3; CN 1, 2, 3;
  CP 1; DAM NOV; DLB 117, 225; EWL
  3; MTCW 1, 2; MTFW 2005; WLIT 2;
  WWE 1
Lahiri, Jhumpa 1967- .... **SSC 96**
  See also AAYA 56; CA 193; CANR 134,
  184; DLB 323; MTFW 2005; SSFS 19,
  27
Laidlaw, A. K.
  See Grieve, C. M.
Lainez, Manuel Mujica
  See Mujica Lainez, Manuel
Laing, R(onald) D(avid) 1927-1989 . **CLC 95**
  See also CA 107; 129; CANR 34; MTCW 1
Laishley, Alex
  See Booth, Martin
Lamartine, Alphonse (Marie Louis Prat) de
  1790-1869 .... **NCLC 11, 190; PC 16**
  See also DAM POET; DLB 217; GFL 1789
  to the Present; RGWL 2, 3
Lamb, Charles 1775-1834 ..... **NCLC 10, 113;**
  SSC 112; WLC 3
  See also BRW 4; CDBLB 1789-1832; DA;
  DAB; DAC; DAM MST; DLB 93, 107,
  163; RGEL 2; SATA 17; TEA
Lamb, Lady Caroline 1785-1828 ... **NCLC 38**
  See also DLB 116
Lamb, Mary Ann 1764-1847 ...... **NCLC 125;**
  SSC 112
  See also DLB 163; SATA 17
Lame Deer 1903(?)-1976 .... **NNAL**
  See also CA 69-72
Lamming, George (William)
  1927- . **BLC 1:2, 2:2; CLC 2, 4, 66, 144**
  See also BW 2, 3; CA 85-88; CANR 26,
  76; CDWLB 3; CN 1, 2, 3, 4, 5, 6, 7; CP
  1; DAM MULT; DLB 125; EWL 3;
  MTCW 1, 2; MTFW 2005; NFS 15;
  RGEL 2
L'Amour, Louis 1908-1988 .... **CLC 25, 55**
  See also AAYA 16; AITN 2; BEST 89:2;
  BPFB 2; CA 1-4R; 125; CANR 3, 25, 40;
  CPW; DA3; DAM NOV, POP; DLB 206;
  DLBY 1980; MTCW 1, 2; MTFW 2005;
  RGAL 4; TCWW 1, 2
Lampedusa, Giuseppe di
  See Tomasi di Lampedusa, Giuseppe
Lampedusa, Giuseppe Tomasi di
  See Tomasi di Lampedusa, Giuseppe
Lampman, Archibald 1861-1899 .. **NCLC 25,**
  194
  See also DLB 92; RGEL 2; TWA
Lancaster, Bruce 1896-1963 .... **CLC 36**
  See also CA 9-10; CANR 70; CAP 1; SATA
  9
Lanchester, John 1962- .... **CLC 99, 280**
  See also CA 194; DLB 267
Landau, Mark Alexandrovich
  See Aldanov, Mark (Alexandrovich)
Landau-Aldanov, Mark Alexandrovich
  See Aldanov, Mark (Alexandrovich)
Landis, Jerry
  See Simon, Paul
Landis, John 1950- .... **CLC 26**
  See also CA 112; 122; CANR 128
Landolfi, Tommaso 1908-1979 .... **CLC 11, 49**
  See also CA 127; 117; DLB 177; EWL 3

Lear, Edward 1812-1888 ..... **NCLC 3; PC 65**
See also AAYA 48; BRW 5; CLR 1, 75;
DLB 32, 163, 166; MAICYA 1, 2; RGEL
2; SATA 18, 100; WCH; WP

Lear, Norman (Milton) 1922- .... **CLC 12**
See also CA 73-76

Least Heat-Moon, William
See Trogdon, William

Leautaud, Paul 1872-1956 .... **TCLC 83**
See also CA 203; DLB 65; GFL 1789 to the
Present

Leavis, F(rank) R(aymond)
1895-1978 .... **CLC 24**
See also BRW 7; CA 21-24R; 77-80; CANR
44; DLB 242; EWL 3; MTCW 1, 2;
RGEL 2

Leavitt, David 1961- .... **CLC 34**
See also CA 116; 122; CANR 50, 62, 101,
134, 177; CPW; DA3; DAM POP; DLB
130, 350; GLL 1; INT CA-122; MAL 5;
MTCW 2; MTFW 2005

Leblanc, Maurice (Marie Emile)
1864-1941 .... **TCLC 49**
See also CA 110; CMW 4

Lebowitz, Fran(ces Ann) 1951(?)- ... **CLC 11,
36**
See also CA 81-84; CANR 14, 60, 70; INT
CANR-14; MTCW 1

Lebrecht, Peter
See Tieck, (Johann) Ludwig

le Cagat, Benat
See Whitaker, Rod

le Carre, John
See le Carre, John

le Carre, John 1931- .... **CLC 9, 15**
See also AAYA 42; BEST 89:4; BPFB 2;
BRWS 2; CA 5-8R; CANR 13, 33, 59,
107, 132, 172; CDBLB 1960 to Present;
CMW 4; CN 1, 2, 3, 4, 5, 6, 7; CPW;
DA3; DAM POP; DLB 87; EWL 3; MSW;
MTCW 1, 2; MTFW 2005; RGEL 2; TEA

Le Clezio, J. M.G. 1940- . **CLC 31, 155, 280;
SSC 122**
See also CA 116; 128; CANR 147; CWW
2; DLB 83; EWL 3; GFL 1789 to the
Present; RGSF 2

Le Clezio, Jean Marie Gustave
See Le Clezio, J. M.G.

Leconte de Lisle, Charles-Marie-Rene
1818-1894 .... **NCLC 29**
See also DLB 217; EW 6; GFL 1789 to the
Present

Le Coq, Monsieur
See Simenon, Georges (Jacques Christian)

Leduc, Violette 1907-1972 .... **CLC 22**
See also CA 13-14; 33-36R; CANR 69;
CAP 1; EWL 3; GFL 1789 to the Present;
GLL 1

Ledwidge, Francis 1887(?)-1917 .... **TCLC 23**
See also CA 123; 203; DLB 20

Lee, Andrea 1953- .... **BLC 1:2; CLC 36**
See also BW 1, 3; CA 125; CANR 82, 190;
DAM MULT

Lee, Andrew
See Auchincloss, Louis

Lee, Chang-rae 1965- .... **CLC 91, 268, 274**
See also CA 148; CANR 89; CN 7; DLB
312; LATS 1:2

Lee, Don L.
See Madhubuti, Haki R.

Lee, George W(ashington)
1894-1976 .... **BLC 1:2; CLC 52**
See also BW 1; CA 125; CANR 83; DAM
MULT; DLB 51

Lee, Harper 1926- ... **CLC 12, 60, 194; WLC
4**
See also AAYA 13; AMWS 8; BPFB 2;
BYA 3; CA 13-16R; CANR 51, 128;
CDALB 1941-1968; CSW; DA; DA3;

DAB; DAC; DAM MST, NOV; DLB 6;
EXPN; LAIT 3; MAL 5; MTCW 1, 2;
MTFW 2005; NFS 2; SATA 11; WYA;
YAW

Lee, Helen Elaine 1959(?)- .... **CLC 86**
See also CA 148

Lee, John CLC 70

Lee, Julian
See Latham, Jean Lee

Lee, Larry
See Lee, Lawrence

Lee, Laurie 1914-1997 .... **CLC 90**
See also CA 77-80; 158; CANR 33, 73; CP
1, 2, 3, 4, 5, 6; CPW; DAB; DAM POP;
DLB 27; MTCW 1; RGEL 2

Lee, Lawrence 1941-1990 .... **CLC 34**
See also CA 131; CANR 43

Lee, Li-Young 1957- .... **CLC 164; PC 24**
See also AMWS 15; CA 153; CANR 118;
CP 6, 7; DLB 165, 312; LMFS 2; PFS 11,
15, 17

Lee, Manfred B. 1905-1971 .... **CLC 11**
See also CA 1-4R; 29-32R; CANR 2, 150;
CMW 4; DLB 137

Lee, Manfred Bennington
See Lee, Manfred B.

Lee, Nathaniel 1645(?)-1692 .... **LC 103**
See also DLB 80; RGEL 2

Lee, Nelle Harper
See Lee, Harper

Lee, Shelton Jackson
See Lee, Spike

Lee, Sophia 1750-1824 .... **NCLC 191**
See also DLB 39

Lee, Spike 1957(?)- .... **BLCS; CLC 105**
See also AAYA 4, 29; BW 2, 3; CA 125;
CANR 42, 164; DAM MULT

Lee, Stan 1922- .... **CLC 17**
See also AAYA 5, 49; CA 108; 111; CANR
129; INT CA-111; MTFW 2005

Lee, Tanith 1947- .... **CLC 46**
See also AAYA 15; CA 37-40R; CANR 53,
102, 145, 170; DLB 261; FANT; SATA 8,
88, 134, 185; SFW 4; SUFW 1, 2; YAW

Lee, Vernon
See Paget, Violet

Lee, William
See Burroughs, William S.

Lee, Willy
See Burroughs, William S.

Lee-Hamilton, Eugene (Jacob)
1845-1907 .... **TCLC 22**
See also CA 117; 234

Leet, Judith 1935- .... **CLC 11**
See also CA 187

Le Fanu, Joseph Sheridan
1814-1873 .... **NCLC 9, 58; SSC 14, 84**
See also CMW 4; DA3; DAM POP; DLB
21, 70, 159, 178; GL 3; HGG; RGEL 2;
RGSF 2; SUFW 1

Leffland, Ella 1931- .... **CLC 19**
See also CA 29-32R; CANR 35, 78, 82;
DLBY 1984; INT CANR-35; SATA 65;
SSFS 24

Leger, Alexis
See Leger, Alexis Saint-Leger

Leger, Alexis Saint-Leger
1887-1975 .... **CLC 4, 11, 46; PC 23**
See also CA 13-16R; 61-64; CANR 43;
DAM POET; DLB 258, 331; EW 10;
EWL 3; GFL 1789 to the Present; MTCW
1; RGWL 2, 3

**Leger, Marie-Rene Auguste Alexis
Saint-Leger**
See Leger, Alexis Saint-Leger

Leger, Saintleger
See Leger, Alexis Saint-Leger

Le Guin, Ursula K. 1929- ...... **CLC 8, 13, 22,
45, 71, 136; SSC 12, 69**
See also AAYA 9, 27; AITN 1; BPFB 2;
BYA 5, 8, 11, 14; CA 21-24R; CANR 9,
32, 52, 74, 132, 192; CDALB 1968-1988;
CLR 3, 28, 91; CN 2, 3, 4, 5, 6, 7; CPW;
DA3; DAB; DAC; DAM MST, POP;
DLB 8, 52, 256, 275; EXPS; FANT; FW;
INT CANR-32; JRDA; LAIT 5; MAICYA
1, 2; MAL 5; MTCW 1, 2; MTFW 2005;
NFS 6, 9; SATA 4, 52, 99, 149, 194;
SCFW 1, 2; SFW 4; SSFS 2; SUFW 1, 2;
WYA; YAW

Lehmann, Rosamond (Nina)
1901-1990 .... **CLC 5**
See also CA 77-80; 131; CANR 8, 73; CN
1, 2, 3, 4; DLB 15; MTCW 2; RGEL 2;
RHW

Leiber, Fritz (Reuter, Jr.)
1910-1992 .... **CLC 25**
See also AAYA 65; BPFB 2; CA 45-48; 139;
CANR 2, 40, 86; CN 2, 3, 4, 5; DLB 8;
FANT; HGG; MTCW 1, 2; MTFW 2005;
SATA 45; SATA-Obit 73; SCFW 1, 2;
SFW 4; SUFW 1, 2

Leibniz, Gottfried Wilhelm von
1646-1716 .... **LC 35**
See also DLB 168

Leino, Eino
See Lonnbohm, Armas Eino Leopold

Leiris, Michel (Julien) 1901-1990 ..... **CLC 61**
See also CA 119; 128; 132; EWL 3; GFL
1789 to the Present

Leithauser, Brad 1953- .... **CLC 27**
See also CA 107; CANR 27, 81, 171; CP 5,
6, 7; DLB 120, 282

le Jars de Gournay, Marie
See de Gournay, Marie le Jars

Lelchuk, Alan 1938- .... **CLC 5**
See also CA 45-48; CAAS 20; CANR 1,
70, 152; CN 3, 4, 5, 6, 7

Lem, Stanislaw 1921-2006 ..... **CLC 8, 15, 40,
149**
See also AAYA 75; CA 105; 249; CAAS 1;
CANR 32; CWW 2; MTCW 1; SCFW 1,
2; SFW 4

Lemann, Nancy (Elise) 1956- .... **CLC 39**
See also CA 118; 136; CANR 121

Lemonnier, (Antoine Louis) Camille
1844-1913 .... **TCLC 22**
See also CA 121

Lenau, Nikolaus 1802-1850 .... **NCLC 16**

L'Engle, Madeleine 1918-2007 .... **CLC 12**
See also AAYA 28; AITN 2; BPFB 2; BYA
2, 4, 5, 7; CA 1-4R; 264; CANR 3, 21,
39, 66, 107; CLR 1, 14, 57; CPW; CWRI
5; DA3; DAM POP; DLB 52; JRDA;
MAICYA 1, 2; MTCW 1, 2; MTFW 2005;
SAAS 15; SATA 1, 27, 75, 128; SATA-
Obit 186; SFW 4; WYA; YAW

L'Engle, Madeleine Camp Franklin
See L'Engle, Madeleine

Lengyel, Jozsef 1896-1975 .... **CLC 7**
See also CA 85-88; 57-60; CANR 71;
RGSF 2

Lenin 1870-1924 .... **TCLC 67**
See also CA 121; 168

Lenin, N.
See Lenin

Lenin, Nikolai
See Lenin

Lenin, V. I.
See Lenin

Lenin, Vladimir I.
See Lenin

Lenin, Vladimir Ilyich
See Lenin

Lennon, John (Ono) 1940-1980 .. **CLC 12, 35**
See also CA 102; SATA 114

Luke, Peter (Ambrose Cyprian)
 1919-1995 .... **CLC 38**
 See also CA 81-84; 147; CANR 72; CBD;
 CD 5, 6; DLB 13
Lunar, Dennis
 See Mungo, Raymond
Lurie, Alison 1926- ..... **CLC 4, 5, 18, 39, 175**
 See also BPFB 2; CA 1-4R; CANR 2, 17,
 50, 88; CN 1, 2, 3, 4, 5, 6, 7; DLB 2, 350;
 MAL 5; MTCW 1; NFS 24; SATA 46,
 112; TCLE 1:1
Lustig, Arnost 1926- .... **CLC 56**
 See also AAYA 3; CA 69-72; CANR 47,
 102; CWW 2; DLB 232, 299; EWL 3;
 RGHL; SATA 56
Luther, Martin 1483-1546 .... **LC 9, 37, 150**
 See also CDWLB 2; DLB 179; EW 2;
 RGWL 2, 3
Luxemburg, Rosa 1870(?)-1919 ..... **TCLC 63**
 See also CA 118
Luzi, Mario (Egidio Vincenzo)
 1914-2005 .... **CLC 13**
 See also CA 61-64; 236; CANR 9, 70;
 CWW 2; DLB 128; EWL 3
L'vov, Arkady **CLC 59**
Lydgate, John c. 1370-1450(?) .... **LC 81**
 See also BRW 1; DLB 146; RGEL 2
Lyly, John 1554(?)-1606 .... **DC 7; LC 41**
 See also BRW 1; DAM DRAM; DLB 62,
 167; RGEL 2
L'Ymagier
 See Gourmont, Remy(-Marie-Charles) de
Lynch, B. Suarez
 See Borges, Jorge Luis
Lynch, David 1946- .... **CLC 66, 162**
 See also AAYA 55; CA 124; 129; CANR
 111
Lynch, David Keith
 See Lynch, David
Lynch, James
 See Andreyev, Leonid
Lyndsay, Sir David 1485-1555 .... **LC 20**
 See also RGEL 2
Lynn, Kenneth S(chuyler)
 1923-2001 .... **CLC 50**
 See also CA 1-4R; 196; CANR 3, 27, 65
Lynx
 See West, Rebecca
Lyons, Marcus
 See Blish, James (Benjamin)
Lyotard, Jean-Francois
 1924-1998 .... **TCLC 103**
 See also DLB 242; EWL 3
Lyre, Pinchbeck
 See Sassoon, Siegfried (Lorraine)
Lytle, Andrew (Nelson) 1902-1995 ... **CLC 22**
 See also CA 9-12R; 150; CANR 70; CN 1,
 2, 3, 4, 5, 6; CSW; DLB 6; DLBY 1995;
 RGAL 4; RHW
Lyttelton, George 1709-1773 .... **LC 10**
 See also RGEL 2
Lytton of Knebworth, Baron
 See Bulwer-Lytton, Edward (George Earle
 Lytton)
Maalouf, Amin 1949- .... **CLC 248**
 See also CA 212; CANR 194; DLB 346
Maas, Peter 1929-2001 .... **CLC 29**
 See also CA 93-96; 201; INT CA-93-96;
 MTCW 2; MTFW 2005
Mac A'Ghobhainn, Iain
 See Smith, Iain Crichton
Macaulay, Catherine 1731-1791 .... **LC 64**
 See also DLB 104, 336
Macaulay, (Emilie) Rose
 1881(?)-1958 .... **TCLC 7, 44**
 See also CA 104; DLB 36; EWL 3; RGEL
 2; RHW

Macaulay, Thomas Babington
 1800-1859 .... **NCLC 42**
 See also BRW 4; CDBLB 1832-1890; DLB
 32, 55; RGEL 2
MacBeth, George (Mann)
 1932-1992 .... **CLC 2, 5, 9**
 See also CA 25-28R; 136; CANR 61, 66;
 CP 1, 2, 3, 4, 5; DLB 40; MTCW 1; PFS
 8; SATA 4; SATA-Obit 70
MacCaig, Norman (Alexander)
 1910-1996 .... **CLC 36**
 See also BRWS 6; CA 9-12R; CANR 3, 34;
 CP 1, 2, 3, 4, 5, 6; DAB; DAM POET;
 DLB 27; EWL 3; RGEL 2
MacCarthy, Sir (Charles Otto) Desmond
 1877-1952 .... **TCLC 36**
 See also CA 167
MacDiarmid, Hugh
 See Grieve, C. M.
MacDonald, Anson
 See Heinlein, Robert A.
Macdonald, Cynthia 1928- .... **CLC 13, 19**
 See also CA 49-52; CANR 4, 44, 146; DLB
 105
MacDonald, George 1824-1905 .... **TCLC 9,
 113, 207**
 See also AAYA 57; BYA 5; CA 106; 137;
 CANR 80; CLR 67; DLB 18, 163, 178;
 FANT; MAICYA 1, 2; RGEL 2; SATA 33,
 100; SFW 4; SUFW; WCH
Macdonald, John
 See Millar, Kenneth
MacDonald, John D. 1916-1986 .. **CLC 3, 27,
 44**
 See also BPFB 2; CA 1-4R; 121; CANR 1,
 19, 60; CMW 4; CPW; DAM NOV, POP;
 DLB 8, 306; DLBY 1986; MSW; MTCW
 1, 2; MTFW 2005; SFW 4
Macdonald, John Ross
 See Millar, Kenneth
Macdonald, Ross
 See Millar, Kenneth
MacDonald Fraser, George
 See Fraser, George MacDonald
MacDougal, John
 See Blish, James (Benjamin)
MacDowell, John
 See Parks, Tim(othy Harold)
MacEwen, Gwendolyn (Margaret)
 1941-1987 .... **CLC 13, 55**
 See also CA 9-12R; 124; CANR 7, 22; CP
 1, 2, 3, 4; DLB 53, 251; SATA 50; SATA-
 Obit 55
MacGreevy, Thomas 1893-1967 .... **PC 82**
 See also CA 262
Macha, Karel Hynek 1810-1846 .... **NCLC 46**
Machado (y Ruiz), Antonio
 1875-1939 .... **TCLC 3**
 See also CA 104; 174; DLB 108; EW 9;
 EWL 3; HW 2; PFS 23; RGWL 2, 3
Machado de Assis, Joaquim Maria
 1839-1908 . **BLC 1:2; HLCS 2; SSC 24,
 118; TCLC 10**
 See also CA 107; 153; CANR 91; DLB 307;
 LAW; RGSF 2; RGWL 2, 3; TWA; WLIT
 1
Machaut, Guillaume de c.
 1300-1377 .... **CMLC 64**
 See also DLB 208
Machen, Arthur **SSC 20; TCLC 4**
 See Jones, Arthur Llewellyn
 See also CA 179; DLB 156, 178; RGEL 2
Machen, Arthur Llewelyn Jones
 See Jones, Arthur Llewellyn
Machiavelli, Niccolo 1469-1527 .. **DC 16; LC
 8, 36, 140; WLCS**
 See also AAYA 58; DA; DAB; DAC; DAM
 MST; EW 2; LAIT 1; LMFS 1; NFS 9;
 RGWL 2, 3; TWA; WLIT 7

MacInnes, Colin 1914-1976 .... **CLC 4, 23**
 See also CA 69-72; 65-68; CANR 21; CN
 1, 2; DLB 14; MTCW 1, 2; RGEL 2;
 RHW
MacInnes, Helen (Clark)
 1907-1985 .... **CLC 27, 39**
 See also BPFB 2; CA 1-4R; 117; CANR 1,
 28, 58; CMW 4; CN 1, 2; CPW; DAM
 POP; DLB 87; MSW; MTCW 1, 2;
 MTFW 2005; SATA 22; SATA-Obit 44
Mackay, Mary 1855-1924 .... **TCLC 51**
 See also CA 118; 177; DLB 34, 156; FANT;
 RGEL 2; RHW; SUFW 1
Mackay, Shena 1944- .... **CLC 195**
 See also CA 104; CANR 88, 139; DLB 231,
 319; MTFW 2005
Mackenzie, Compton (Edward Montague)
 1883-1972 .... **CLC 18; TCLC 116**
 See also CA 21-22; 37-40R; CAP 2; CN 1;
 DLB 34, 100; RGEL 2
Mackenzie, Henry 1745-1831 .... **NCLC 41**
 See also DLB 39; RGEL 2
Mackey, Nathaniel 1947- .... **BLC 2:3; PC 49**
 See also CA 153; CANR 114; CP 6, 7; DLB
 169
Mackey, Nathaniel Ernest
 See Mackey, Nathaniel
MacKinnon, Catharine
 See MacKinnon, Catharine A.
MacKinnon, Catharine A. 1946- .... **CLC 181**
 See also CA 128; 132; CANR 73, 140, 189;
 FW; MTCW 2; MTFW 2005
Mackintosh, Elizabeth
 1896(?)-1952 .... **TCLC 14**
 See also CA 110; CMW 4; DLB 10, 77;
 MSW
Macklin, Charles 1699-1797 .... **LC 132**
 See also DLB 89; RGEL 2
MacLaren, James
 See Grieve, C. M.
MacLaverty, Bernard 1942- ..... **CLC 31, 243**
 See also CA 116; 118; CANR 43, 88, 168;
 CN 5, 6, 7; DLB 267; INT CA-118; RGSF
 2
MacLean, Alistair (Stuart)
 1922(?)-1987 .... **CLC 3, 13, 50, 63**
 See also CA 57-60; 121; CANR 28, 61;
 CMW 4; CP 2, 3, 4, 5, 6, 7; CPW; DAM
 POP; DLB 276; MTCW 1; SATA 23;
 SATA-Obit 50; TCWW 2
Maclean, Norman (Fitzroy)
 1902-1990 .... **CLC 78; SSC 13**
 See also AMWS 14; CA 102; 132; CANR
 49; CPW; DAM POP; DLB 206; TCWW
 2
MacLeish, Archibald 1892-1982 ... **CLC 3, 8,
 14, 68; PC 47**
 See also AMW; CA 9-12R; 106; CAD;
 CANR 33, 63; CDALBS; CP 1, 2; DAM
 POET; DFS 15; DLB 4, 7, 45; DLBY
 1982; EWL 3; EXPP; MAL 5; MTCW 1,
 2; MTFW 2005; PAB; PFS 5; RGAL 4;
 TUS
MacLennan, (John) Hugh
 1907-1990 .... **CLC 2, 14, 92**
 See also CA 5-8R; 142; CANR 33; CN 1,
 2, 3, 4; DAC; DAM MST; DLB 68; EWL
 3; MTCW 1, 2; MTFW 2005; RGEL 2;
 TWA
MacLeod, Alistair 1936- .. **CLC 56, 165; SSC
 90**
 See also CA 123; CCA 1; DAC; DAM
 MST; DLB 60; MTCW 2; MTFW 2005;
 RGSF 2; TCLE 1:2
Macleod, Fiona
 See Sharp, William

MacNeice, (Frederick) Louis
1907-1963 .... **CLC 1, 4, 10, 53; PC 61**
See also BRW 7; CA 85-88; CANR 61;
DAB; DAM POET; DLB 10, 20; EWL 3;
MTCW 1, 2; MTFW 2005; RGEL 2

MacNeill, Dand
See Fraser, George MacDonald

Macpherson, James 1736-1796 .... **CMLC 28;
LC 29; PC 97**
See also BRWS 8; DLB 109, 336; RGEL 2

Macpherson, (Jean) Jay 1931- .... **CLC 14**
See also CA 5-8R; CANR 90; CP 1, 2, 3, 4,
6, 7; CWP; DLB 53

Macrobius fl. 430- .... **CMLC 48**

MacShane, Frank 1927-1999 .... **CLC 39**
See also CA 9-12R; 186; CANR 3, 33; DLB
111

Macumber, Mari
See Sandoz, Mari(e Susette)

Madach, Imre 1823-1864 .... **NCLC 19**

Madden, (Jerry) David 1933- .... **CLC 5, 15**
See also CA 1-4R; CAAS 3; CANR 4, 45;
CN 3, 4, 5, 6, 7; CSW; DLB 6; MTCW 1

Maddern, Al(an)
See Ellison, Harlan

Madhubuti, Haki R. 1942- .... **BLC 1:2; CLC
2; PC 5**
See also BW 2, 3; CA 73-76; CANR 24,
51, 73, 139; CP 2, 3, 4, 5, 6, 7; CSW;
DAM MULT, POET; DLB 5, 41; DLBD
8; EWL 3; MAL 5; MTCW 2; MTFW
2005; RGAL 4

Madison, James 1751-1836 .... **NCLC 126**
See also DLB 37

Maepenn, Hugh
See Kuttner, Henry

Maepenn, K. H.
See Kuttner, Henry

Maeterlinck, Maurice 1862-1949 .... **DC 32;
TCLC 3**
See also CA 104; 136; CANR 80; DAM
DRAM; DLB 192, 331; EW 8; EWL 3;
GFL 1789 to the Present; LMFS 2; RGWL
2, 3; SATA 66; TWA

Maginn, William 1794-1842 .... **NCLC 8**
See also DLB 110, 159

Mahapatra, Jayanta 1928- .... **CLC 33**
See also CA 73-76; CAAS 9; CANR 15,
33, 66, 87; CP 4, 5, 6, 7; DAM MULT;
DLB 323

Mahfouz, Nagib
See Mahfouz, Naguib

Mahfouz, Naguib 1911(?)-2006 . **CLC 52, 55,
153; SSC 66**
See also AAYA 49; AFW; BEST 89:2; CA
128; 253; CANR 55, 101; DA3; DAM
NOV; DLB 346; DLBY 1988; MTCW 1,
2; MTFW 2005; RGSF 2; RGWL 2, 3;
SSFS 9; WLIT 2

Mahfouz, Naguib Abdel Aziz Al-Sabilgi
See Mahfouz, Naguib

Mahfouz, Najib
See Mahfouz, Naguib

Mahfuz, Najib
See Mahfouz, Naguib

Mahon, Derek 1941- .... **CLC 27; PC 60**
See also BRWS 6; CA 113; 128; CANR 88;
CP 1, 2, 3, 4, 5, 6, 7; DLB 40; EWL 3

Maiakovskii, Vladimir
See Mayakovski, Vladimir (Vladimirovich)

Mailer, Norman 1923-2007 ... **CLC 1, 2, 3, 4,
5, 8, 11, 14, 28, 39, 74, 111, 234**
See also AAYA 31; AITN 2; AMW; AMWC
2; AMWR 2; BPFB 2; CA 9-12R; 266;
CABS 1; CANR 28, 74, 77, 130; CDALB
1968-1988; CN 1, 2, 3, 4, 5, 6, 7; CPW;
DA; DA3; DAB; DAC; DAM MST, NOV,

POP; DLB 2, 16, 28, 185, 278; DLBD 3;
DLBY 1980, 1983; EWL 3; MAL 5;
MTCW 1, 2; MTFW 2005; NFS 10;
RGAL 4; TUS

Mailer, Norman Kingsley
See Mailer, Norman

Maillet, Antonine 1929- .... **CLC 54, 118**
See also CA 115; 120; CANR 46, 74, 77,
134; CCA 1; CWW 2; DAC; DLB 60;
INT CA-120; MTCW 2; MTFW 2005

Maimonides, Moses 1135-1204 ..... **CMLC 76**
See also DLB 115

Mais, Roger 1905-1955 .... **TCLC 8**
See also BW 1, 3; CA 105; 124; CANR 82;
CDWLB 3; DLB 125; EWL 3; MTCW 1;
RGEL 2

Maistre, Joseph 1753-1821 .... **NCLC 37**
See also GFL 1789 to the Present

Maitland, Frederic William
1850-1906 .... **TCLC 65**

Maitland, Sara (Louise) 1950- .... **CLC 49**
See also BRWS 11; CA 69-72; CANR 13,
59; DLB 271; FW

Major, Clarence 1936- ...... **BLC 1:2; CLC 3,
19, 48**
See also AFAW 2; BW 2, 3; CA 21-24R;
CAAS 6; CANR 13, 25, 53, 82; CN 3, 4,
5, 6, 7; CP 2, 3, 4, 5, 6, 7; CSW; DAM
MULT; DLB 33; EWL 3; MAL 5; MSW

Major, Kevin (Gerald) 1949- .... **CLC 26**
See also AAYA 16; CA 97-100; CANR 21,
38, 112; CLR 11; DAC; DLB 60; INT
CANR-21; JRDA; MAICYA 1, 2; MAIC-
YAS 1; SATA 32, 82, 134; WYA; YAW

Maki, James
See Ozu, Yasujiro

Makin, Bathsua 1600-1675(?) .... **LC 137**

Makine, Andrei 1957-
See Makine, Andrei

Makine, Andrei 1957- .... **CLC 198**
See also CA 176; CANR 103, 162; MTFW
2005

Malabaila, Damiano
See Levi, Primo

Malamud, Bernard 1914-1986 .. **CLC 1, 2, 3,
5, 8, 9, 11, 18, 27, 44, 78, 85; SSC 15;
TCLC 129, 184; WLC 4**
See also AAYA 16; AMWS 1; BPFB 2;
BYA 15; CA 5-8R; 118; CABS 1; CANR
28, 62, 114; CDALB 1941-1968; CN 1, 2,
3, 4; CPW; DA; DA3; DAB; DAC; DAM
MST, NOV, POP; DLB 2, 28, 152; DLBY
1980, 1986; EWL 3; EXPS; LAIT 4;
LATS 1:1; MAL 5; MTCW 1, 2; MTFW
2005; NFS 27; RGAL 4; RGHL; RGSF 2;
SSFS 8, 13, 16; TUS

Malan, Herman
See Bosman, Herman Charles; Bosman,
Herman Charles

Malaparte, Curzio 1898-1957 .... **TCLC 52**
See also DLB 264

Malcolm, Dan
See Silverberg, Robert

Malcolm, Janet 1934- .... **CLC 201**
See also CA 123; CANR 89; NCFS 1

Malcolm X
See Little, Malcolm

Malebranche, Nicolas 1638-1715 .... **LC 133**
See also GFL Beginnings to 1789

Malherbe, Francois de 1555-1628 .... **LC 5**
See also DLB 327; GFL Beginnings to 1789

Mallarme, Stephane 1842-1898 ...... **NCLC 4,
41, 210; PC 4**
See also DAM POET; DLB 217; EW 7;
GFL 1789 to the Present; LMFS 2; RGWL
2, 3; TWA

Mallet-Joris, Francoise 1930- .... **CLC 11**
See also CA 65-68; CANR 17; CWW 2;
DLB 83; EWL 3; GFL 1789 to the Present

Malley, Ern
See McAuley, James Phillip

Mallon, Thomas 1951- .... **CLC 172**
See also CA 110; CANR 29, 57, 92; DLB
350

Mallowan, Agatha Christie
See Christie, Agatha (Mary Clarissa)

Maloff, Saul 1922- .... **CLC 5**
See also CA 33-36R

Malone, Louis
See MacNeice, (Frederick) Louis

Malone, Michael (Christopher)
1942- .... **CLC 43**
See also CA 77-80; CANR 14, 32, 57, 114

Malory, Sir Thomas 1410(?)-1471(?) . **LC 11,
88; WLCS**
See also BRW 1; BRWR 2; CDBLB Before
1660; DA; DAB; DAC; DAM MST; DLB
146; EFS 2; RGEL 2; SATA 59; SATA-
Brief 33; TEA; WLIT 3

Malouf, David 1934- .... **CLC 28, 86, 245**
See also BRWS 12; CA 124; CANR 50, 76,
180; CN 3, 4, 5, 6, 7; CP 1, 3, 4, 5, 6, 7;
DLB 289; EWL 3; MTCW 2; MTFW
2005; SSFS 24

Malouf, George Joseph David
See Malouf, David

Malraux, (Georges-)Andre
1901-1976 .... **CLC 1, 4, 9, 13, 15, 57;
TCLC 209**
See also BPFB 2; CA 21-22; 69-72; CANR
34, 58; CAP 2; DA3; DAM NOV; DLB
72; EW 12; EWL 3; GFL 1789 to the
Present; MTCW 1, 2; MTFW 2005;
RGWL 2, 3; TWA

Malthus, Thomas Robert
1766-1834 .... **NCLC 145**
See also DLB 107, 158; RGEL 2

Malzberg, Barry N(athaniel) 1939- ... **CLC 7**
See also CA 61-64; CAAS 4; CANR 16;
CMW 4; DLB 8; SFW 4

Mamet, David 1947- .. **CLC 9, 15, 34, 46, 91,
166; DC 4, 24**
See also AAYA 3, 60; AMWS 14; CA 81-
84; CABS 3; CAD; CANR 15, 41, 67, 72,
129, 172; CD 5, 6; DA3; DAM DRAM;
DFS 2, 3, 6, 12, 15; DLB 7; EWL 3;
IDFW 4; MAL 5; MTCW 1, 2; MTFW
2005; RGAL 4

Mamet, David Alan
See Mamet, David

Mamoulian, Rouben (Zachary)
1897-1987 .... **CLC 16**
See also CA 25-28R; 124; CANR 85

Mandelshtam, Osip
See Mandelstam, Osip (Emilievich)
See also DLB 295

Mandelstam, Osip (Emilievich)
1891(?)-1943(?) .... **PC 14; TCLC 2, 6**
See Mandelshtam, Osip
See also CA 104; 150; EW 10; EWL 3;
MTCW 2; RGWL 2, 3; TWA

Mander, (Mary) Jane 1877-1949 ... **TCLC 31**
See also CA 162; RGEL 2

Mandeville, Bernard 1670-1733 .... **LC 82**
See also DLB 101

Mandeville, Sir John fl. 1350- ...... **CMLC 19**
See also DLB 146

Mandiargues, Andre Pieyre de
See Pieyre de Mandiargues, Andre

Mandrake, Ethel Belle
See Thurman, Wallace (Henry)

Mangan, James Clarence
1803-1849 .... **NCLC 27**
See also BRWS 13; RGEL 2

Maniere, J.-E.
See Giraudoux, Jean(-Hippolyte)

Mankiewicz, Herman (Jacob)
1897-1953 .... **TCLC 85**
See also CA 120; 169; DLB 26; IDFW 3, 4

Manley, (Mary) Delariviere
1672(?)-1724 .... **LC 1, 42**
See also DLB 39, 80; RGEL 2

Mann, Abel
See Creasey, John

Mann, Emily 1952- .... **DC 7**
See also CA 130; CAD; CANR 55; CD 5,
6; CWD; DLB 266

Mann, (Luiz) Heinrich 1871-1950 ... **TCLC 9**
See also CA 106; 164, 181; DLB 66, 118;
EW 8; EWL 3; RGWL 2, 3

Mann, (Paul) Thomas 1875-1955 . **SSC 5, 80,**
82; TCLC 2, 8, 14, 21, 35, 44, 60, 168;
WLC 4
See also BPFB 2; CA 104; 128; CANR 133;
CDWLB 2; DA; DA3; DAB; DAC; DAM
MST, NOV; DLB 66, 331; EW 9; EWL 3;
GLL 1; LATS 1:1; LMFS 1; MTCW 1, 2;
MTFW 2005; NFS 17; RGSF 2; RGWL
2, 3; SSFS 4, 9; TWA

Mannheim, Karl 1893-1947 .... **TCLC 65**
See also CA 204

Manning, David
See Faust, Frederick

Manning, Frederic 1882-1935 .... **TCLC 25**
See also CA 124; 216; DLB 260

Manning, Olivia 1915-1980 .... **CLC 5, 19**
See also CA 5-8R; 101; CANR 29; CN 1,
2; EWL 3; FW; MTCW 1; RGEL 2

Mannyng, Robert c. 1264-c.
1340 .... **CMLC 83**
See also DLB 146

Mano, D. Keith 1942- .... **CLC 2, 10**
See also CA 25-28R; CAAS 6; CANR 26,
57; DLB 6

Mansfield, Katherine
See Beauchamp, Kathleen Mansfield

Manso, Peter 1940- .... **CLC 39**
See also CA 29-32R; CANR 44, 156

Mantecon, Juan Jimenez
See Jimenez (Mantecon), Juan Ramon

Mantel, Hilary 1952- .... **CLC 144**
See also CA 125; CANR 54, 101, 161; CN
5, 6, 7; DLB 271; RHW

Mantel, Hilary Mary
See Mantel, Hilary

Manton, Peter
See Creasey, John

Man Without a Spleen, A
See Chekhov, Anton (Pavlovich)

Manzano, Juan Franciso
1797(?)-1854 .... **NCLC 155**

Manzoni, Alessandro 1785-1873 ... **NCLC 29,**
98
See also EW 5; RGWL 2, 3; TWA; WLIT 7

Map, Walter 1140-1209 .... **CMLC 32**

Mapu, Abraham (ben Jekutiel)
1808-1867 .... **NCLC 18**

Mara, Sally
See Queneau, Raymond

Maracle, Lee 1950- .... **NNAL**
See also CA 149

Marat, Jean Paul 1743-1793 .... **LC 10**

Marcel, Gabriel Honore 1889-1973 . **CLC 15**
See also CA 102; 45-48; EWL 3; MTCW 1,
2

March, William
See Campbell, William Edward March

Marchbanks, Samuel
See Davies, Robertson

Marchi, Giacomo
See Bassani, Giorgio

Marcus Aurelius
See Aurelius, Marcus

Marcuse, Herbert 1898-1979 .... **TCLC 207**
See also CA 188; 89-92; DLB 242

Marguerite
See de Navarre, Marguerite

Marguerite d'Angouleme
See de Navarre, Marguerite

Marguerite de Navarre
See de Navarre, Marguerite

Margulies, Donald 1954- .... **CLC 76**
See also AAYA 57; CA 200; CD 6; DFS 13;
DLB 228

Marias, Javier 1951- .... **CLC 239**
See also CA 167; CANR 109, 139; DLB
322; HW 2; MTFW 2005

Marie de France c. 12th cent. - ...... **CMLC 8,**
111; PC 22
See also DLB 208; FW; RGWL 2, 3

Marie de l'Incarnation 1599-1672 ..... **LC 10,**
168

Marier, Captain Victor
See Griffith, D.W.

Mariner, Scott
See Pohl, Frederik

Marinetti, Filippo Tommaso
1876-1944 .... **TCLC 10**
See also CA 107; DLB 114, 264; EW 9;
EWL 3; WLIT 7

Marivaux, Pierre Carlet de Chamblain de
1688-1763 .... **DC 7; LC 4, 123**
See also DLB 314; GFL Beginnings to
1789; RGWL 2, 3; TWA

Markandaya, Kamala
See Taylor, Kamala

Markfield, Wallace (Arthur)
1926-2002 .... **CLC 8**
See also CA 69-72; 208; CAAS 3; CN 1, 2,
3, 4, 5, 6, 7; DLB 2, 28; DLBY 2002

Markham, Edwin 1852-1940 .... **TCLC 47**
See also CA 160; DLB 54, 186; MAL 5;
RGAL 4

Markham, Robert
See Amis, Kingsley

Marks, J.
See Highwater, Jamake (Mamake)

Marks-Highwater, J.
See Highwater, Jamake (Mamake)

Markson, David M. 1927- .... **CLC 67**
See also AMWS 17; CA 49-52; CANR 1,
91, 158; CN 5, 6

Markson, David Merrill
See Markson, David M.

Marlatt, Daphne (Buckle) 1942- .... **CLC 168**
See also CA 25-28R; CANR 17, 39; CN 6,
7; CP 4, 5, 6, 7; CWP; DLB 60; FW

Marley, Bob
See Marley, Robert Nesta

Marley, Robert Nesta 1945-1981 ...... **CLC 17**
See also CA 107; 103

Marlowe, Christopher 1564-1593 . **DC 1; LC**
22, 47, 117; PC 57; WLC 4
See also BRW 1; BRWR 1; CDBLB Before
1660; DA; DA3; DAB; DAC; DAM
DRAM, MST; DFS 1, 5, 13, 21; DLB 62;
EXPP; LMFS 1; PFS 22; RGEL 2; TEA;
WLIT 3

Marlowe, Stephen 1928-2008 .... **CLC 70**
See also CA 13-16R; 269; CANR 6, 55;
CMW 4; SFW 4

Marmion, Shakerley 1603-1639 .... **LC 89**
See also DLB 58; RGEL 2

Marmontel, Jean-Francois 1723-1799 .. **LC 2**
See also DLB 314

Maron, Monika 1941- .... **CLC 165**
See also CA 201

Marot, Clement c. 1496-1544 .... **LC 133**
See also DLB 327; GFL Beginnings to 1789

Marquand, John P(hillips)
1893-1960 .... **CLC 2, 10**
See also AMW; BPFB 2; CA 85-88; CANR
73; CMW 4; DLB 9, 102; EWL 3; MAL
5; MTCW 2; RGAL 4

Marques, Rene 1919-1979 .. **CLC 96; HLC 2**
See also CA 97-100; 85-88; CANR 78;
DAM MULT; DLB 305; EWL 3; HW 1,
2; LAW; RGSF 2

Marquez, Gabriel Garcia
See Garcia Marquez, Gabriel

Marquis, Don(ald Robert Perry)
1878-1937 .... **TCLC 7**
See also CA 104; 166; DLB 11, 25; MAL
5; RGAL 4

Marquis de Sade
See Sade, Donatien Alphonse Francois

Marric, J. J.
See Creasey, John

Marryat, Frederick 1792-1848 .... **NCLC 3**
See also DLB 21, 163; RGEL 2; WCH

Marsden, James
See Creasey, John

Marsh, Edward 1872-1953 .... **TCLC 99**

Marsh, (Edith) Ngaio 1895-1982 .. **CLC 7, 53**
See also CA 9-12R; CANR 6, 58; CMW 4;
CN 1, 2, 3; CPW; DAM POP; DLB 77;
MSW; MTCW 1, 2; RGEL 2; TEA

Marshall, Alan
See Westlake, Donald E.

Marshall, Allen
See Westlake, Donald E.

Marshall, Garry 1934- .... **CLC 17**
See also AAYA 3; CA 111; SATA 60

Marshall, Paule 1929- .... **BLC 1:3, 2:3; CLC**
27, 72, 253; SSC 3
See also AFAW 1, 2; AMWS 11; BPFB 2;
BW 2, 3; CA 77-80; CANR 25, 73, 129;
CN 1, 2, 3, 4, 5, 6, 7; DA3; DAM MULT;
DLB 33, 157, 227; EWL 3; LATS 1:2;
MAL 5; MTCW 1, 2; MTFW 2005;
RGAL 4; SSFS 15

Marshallik
See Zangwill, Israel

Marsilius of Inghen c.
1340-1396 .... **CMLC 106**

Marsten, Richard
See Hunter, Evan

Marston, John 1576-1634 .... **LC 33**
See also BRW 2; DAM DRAM; DLB 58,
172; RGEL 2

Martel, Yann 1963- .... **CLC 192**
See also AAYA 67; CA 146; CANR 114;
DLB 326, 334; MTFW 2005; NFS 27

Martens, Adolphe-Adhemar
See Ghelderode, Michel de

Martha, Henry
See Harris, Mark

Marti, Jose 1853-1895 ..... **HLC 2; NCLC 63;**
PC 76
See also DAM MULT; DLB 290; HW 2;
LAW; RGWL 2, 3; WLIT 1

Martial c. 40-c. 104 .... **CMLC 35; PC 10**
See also AW 2; CDWLB 1; DLB 211;
RGWL 2, 3

Martin, Ken
See Hubbard, L. Ron

Martin, Richard
See Creasey, John

Martin, Steve 1945- .... **CLC 30, 217**
See also AAYA 53; CA 97-100; CANR 30,
100, 140; DFS 19; MTCW 1; MTFW
2005

Martin, Valerie 1948- .... **CLC 89**
See also BEST 90:2; CA 85-88; CANR 49,
89, 165

May, Elaine 1932- .... **CLC 16**
See also CA 124; 142; CAD; CWD; DLB 44
Mayakovski, Vladimir (Vladimirovich) 1893-1930 .... **TCLC 4, 18**
See also CA 104; 158; EW 11; EWL 3; IDTP; MTCW 2; MTFW 2005; RGWL 2, 3; SFW 4; TWA; WP
Mayakovsky, Vladimir
See Mayakovski, Vladimir (Vladimirovich)
Mayhew, Henry 1812-1887 .... **NCLC 31**
See also DLB 18, 55, 190
Mayle, Peter 1939(?)- .... **CLC 89**
See also CA 139; CANR 64, 109, 168
Maynard, Joyce 1953- .... **CLC 23**
See also CA 111; 129; CANR 64, 169
Mayne, William (James Carter) 1928- .... **CLC 12**
See also AAYA 20; CA 9-12R; CANR 37, 80, 100; CLR 25, 123; FANT; JRDA; MAICYA 1, 2; MAICYAS 1; SAAS 11; SATA 6, 68, 122; SUFW 2; YAW
Mayo, Jim
See L'Amour, Louis
Maysles, Albert 1926- .... **CLC 16**
See also CA 29-32R
Maysles, David 1932-1987 .... **CLC 16**
See also CA 191
Mazer, Norma Fox 1931- .... **CLC 26**
See also AAYA 5, 36; BYA 1, 8; CA 69-72; CANR 12, 32, 66, 129, 189; CLR 23; JRDA; MAICYA 1, 2; SAAS 1; SATA 24, 67, 105, 168, 198; WYA; YAW
Mazzini, Guiseppe 1805-1872 .... **NCLC 34**
McAlmon, Robert (Menzies) 1895-1956 .... **TCLC 97**
See also CA 107; 168; DLB 4, 45; DLBD 15; GLL 1
McAuley, James Phillip 1917-1976 .. **CLC 45**
See also CA 97-100; CP 1, 2; DLB 260; RGEL 2
McBain, Ed
See Hunter, Evan
McBrien, William (Augustine) 1930- .... **CLC 44**
See also CA 107; CANR 90
McCabe, Patrick 1955- .... **CLC 133**
See also BRWS 9; CA 130; CANR 50, 90, 168; CN 6, 7; DLB 194
McCaffrey, Anne 1926- .... **CLC 17**
See also AAYA 6, 34; AITN 2; BEST 89:2; BPFB 2; BYA 5; CA 25-28R, 227; CAAE 227; CANR 15, 35, 55, 96, 169; CLR 49, 130; CPW; DA3; DAM NOV, POP; DLB 8; JRDA; MAICYA 1, 2; MTCW 1, 2; MTFW 2005; SAAS 11; SATA 8, 70, 116, 152; SATA-Essay 152; SFW 4; SUFW 2; WYA; YAW
McCaffrey, Anne Inez
See McCaffrey, Anne
McCall, Nathan 1955(?)- .... **CLC 86**
See also AAYA 59; BW 3; CA 146; CANR 88, 186
McCann, Arthur
See Campbell, John W(ood, Jr.)
McCann, Edson
See Pohl, Frederik
McCarthy, Charles
See McCarthy, Cormac
McCarthy, Charles, Jr.
See McCarthy, Cormac
McCarthy, Cormac 1933- .... **CLC 4, 57, 101, 204**
See also AAYA 41; AMWS 8; BPFB 2; CA 13-16R; CANR 10, 42, 69, 101, 161, 171; CN 6, 7; CPW; CSW; DA3; DAM POP; DLB 6, 143, 256; EWL 3; LATS 1:2; MAL 5; MTCW 2; MTFW 2005; TCLE 1:2; TCWW 2

McCarthy, Mary (Therese) 1912-1989 .. **CLC 1, 3, 5, 14, 24, 39, 59; SSC 24**
See also AMW; BPFB 2; CA 5-8R; 129; CANR 16, 50, 64; CN 1, 2, 3, 4; DA3; DLB 2; DLBY 1981; EWL 3; FW; INT CANR-16; MAL 5; MBL; MTCW 1, 2; MTFW 2005; RGAL 4; TUS
McCartney, James Paul
See McCartney, Paul
McCartney, Paul 1942- .... **CLC 12, 35**
See also CA 146; CANR 111
McCauley, Stephen (D.) 1955- .... **CLC 50**
See also CA 141
McClaren, Peter CLC 70
McClure, Michael (Thomas) 1932- ... **CLC 6, 10**
See also BG 1:3; CA 21-24R; CAD; CANR 17, 46, 77, 131; CD 5, 6; CP 1, 2, 3, 4, 5, 6, 7; DLB 16; WP
McCorkle, Jill (Collins) 1958- .... **CLC 51**
See also CA 121; CANR 113; CSW; DLB 234; DLBY 1987; SSFS 24
McCourt, Frank 1930-2009 .... **CLC 109**
See also AAYA 61; AMWS 12; CA 157; CANR 97, 138; MTFW 2005; NCFS 1
McCourt, James 1941- .... **CLC 5**
See also CA 57-60; CANR 98, 152, 186
McCourt, Malachy 1931- .... **CLC 119**
See also SATA 126
McCoy, Edmund
See Gardner, John
McCoy, Horace (Stanley) 1897-1955 .... **TCLC 28**
See also AMWS 13; CA 108; 155; CMW 4; DLB 9
McCrae, John 1872-1918 .... **TCLC 12**
See also CA 109; DLB 92; PFS 5
McCreigh, James
See Pohl, Frederik
McCullers, (Lula) Carson (Smith) 1917-1967 .... **CLC 1, 4, 10, 12, 48, 100; DC 35; SSC 9, 24, 99; TCLC 155; WLC 4**
See also AAYA 21; AMW; AMWC 2; BPFB 2; CA 5-8R; 25-28R; CABS 1, 3; CANR 18, 132; CDALB 1941-1968; DA; DA3; DAB; DAC; DAM MST, NOV; DFS 5, 18; DLB 2, 7, 173, 228; EWL 3; EXPS; FW; GLL 1; LAIT 3, 4; MAL 5; MBL; MTCW 1, 2; MTFW 2005; NFS 6, 13; RGAL 4; RGSF 2; SATA 27; SSFS 5; TUS; YAW
McCulloch, John Tyler
See Burroughs, Edgar Rice
McCullough, Colleen 1937- ...... **CLC 27, 107**
See also AAYA 36; BPFB 2; CA 81-84; CANR 17, 46, 67, 98, 139; CPW; DA3; DAM NOV, POP; MTCW 1, 2; MTFW 2005; RHW
McCunn, Ruthanne Lum 1946- .... **AAL**
See also CA 119; CANR 43, 96; DLB 312; LAIT 2; SATA 63
McDermott, Alice 1953- .... **CLC 90**
See also AMWS 18; CA 109; CANR 40, 90, 126, 181; CN 7; DLB 292; MTFW 2005; NFS 23
McElroy, Joseph 1930- .... **CLC 5, 47**
See also CA 17-20R; CANR 149; CN 3, 4, 5, 6, 7
McElroy, Joseph Prince
See McElroy, Joseph
McEwan, Ian 1948- ... **CLC 13, 66, 169, 269; SSC 106**
See also BEST 90:4; BRWS 4; CA 61-64; CANR 14, 41, 69, 87, 132, 179; CN 3, 4, 5, 6, 7; DAM NOV; DLB 14, 194, 319, 326; HGG; MTCW 1, 2; MTFW 2005; RGSF 2; SUFW 2; TEA

McEwan, Ian Russell
See McEwan, Ian
McFadden, David 1940- .... **CLC 48**
See also CA 104; CP 1, 2, 3, 4, 5, 6, 7; DLB 60; INT CA-104
McFarland, Dennis 1950- .... **CLC 65**
See also CA 165; CANR 110, 179
McGahern, John 1934-2006 .... **CLC 5, 9, 48, 156; SSC 17**
See also CA 17-20R; 249; CANR 29, 68, 113; CN 1, 2, 3, 4, 5, 6, 7; DLB 14, 231, 319; MTCW 1
McGinley, Patrick (Anthony) 1937- . **CLC 41**
See also CA 120; 127; CANR 56; INT CA-127
McGinley, Phyllis 1905-1978 .... **CLC 14**
See also CA 9-12R; 77-80; CANR 19; CP 1, 2; CWRI 5; DLB 11, 48; MAL 5; PFS 9, 13; SATA 2, 44; SATA-Obit 24
McGinniss, Joe 1942- .... **CLC 32**
See also AITN 2; BEST 89:2; CA 25-28R; CANR 26, 70, 152; CPW; DLB 185; INT CANR-26
McGivern, Maureen Daly
See Daly, Maureen
McGivern, Maureen Patricia Daly
See Daly, Maureen
McGrath, Patrick 1950- .... **CLC 55**
See also CA 136; CANR 65, 148, 190; CN 5, 6, 7; DLB 231; HGG; SUFW 2
McGrath, Thomas (Matthew) 1916-1990 .... **CLC 28, 59**
See also AMWS 10; CA 9-12R; CANR 6, 33, 95; CP 1, 2, 3, 4, 5; DAM POET; MAL 5; MTCW 1; SATA 41; SATA-Obit 66
McGuane, Thomas 1939- .. **CLC 3, 7, 18, 45, 127**
See also AITN 2; BPFB 2; CA 49-52; CANR 5, 24, 49, 94, 164; CN 2, 3, 4, 5, 6, 7; DLB 2, 212; DLBY 1980; EWL 3; INT CANR-24; MAL 5; MTCW 1; MTFW 2005; TCWW 1, 2
McGuane, Thomas Francis III
See McGuane, Thomas
McGuckian, Medbh 1950- .... **CLC 48, 174; PC 27**
See also BRWS 5; CA 143; CP 4, 5, 6, 7; CWP; DAM POET; DLB 40
McHale, Tom 1942(?)-1982 .... **CLC 3, 5**
See also AITN 1; CA 77-80; 106; CN 1, 2, 3
McHugh, Heather 1948- .... **PC 61**
See also CA 69-72; CANR 11, 28, 55, 92; CP 4, 5, 6, 7; CWP; PFS 24
McIlvanney, William 1936- .... **CLC 42**
See also CA 25-28R; CANR 61; CMW 4; DLB 14, 207
McIlwraith, Maureen Mollie Hunter
See Hunter, Mollie
McInerney, Jay 1955- .... **CLC 34, 112**
See also AAYA 18; BPFB 2; CA 116; 123; CANR 45, 68, 116, 176; CN 5, 6, 7; CPW; DA3; DAM POP; DLB 292; INT CA-123; MAL 5; MTCW 2; MTFW 2005
McIntyre, Vonda N. 1948- .... **CLC 18**
See also CA 81-84; CANR 17, 34, 69; MTCW 1; SFW 4; YAW
McIntyre, Vonda Neel
See McIntyre, Vonda N.
McKay, Claude
See McKay, Festus Claudius
McKay, Festus Claudius 1889-1948 ...... **BLC 1:3; HR 1:3; PC 2; TCLC 7, 41; WLC 4**
See also AFAW 1, 2; AMWS 10; BW 1, 3; CA 104; 124; CANR 73; DA; DAB; DAC; DAM MST, MULT, NOV, POET;

DLB 4, 45, 51, 117; EWL 3; EXPP; GLL
2; LAIT 3; LMFS 2; MAL 5; MTCW 1,
2; MTFW 2005; PAB; PFS 4; RGAL 4;
TUS; WP

McKuen, Rod 1933- .... CLC 1, 3
See also AITN 1; CA 41-44R; CANR 40;
CP 1

McLoughlin, R. B.
See Mencken, H. L.

McLuhan, (Herbert) Marshall
1911-1980 .... CLC 37, 83
See also CA 9-12R; 102; CANR 12, 34, 61;
DLB 88; INT CANR-12; MTCW 1, 2;
MTFW 2005

McMahon, Pat
See Hoch, Edward D.

McManus, Declan Patrick Aloysius
See Costello, Elvis

McMillan, Terry 1951- .. BLCS; CLC 50, 61,
112
See also AAYA 21; AMWS 13; BPFB 2;
BW 2, 3; CA 140; CANR 60, 104, 131;
CN 7; CPW; DA3; DAM MULT, NOV,
POP; MAL 5; MTCW 2; MTFW 2005;
RGAL 4; YAW

McMurtry, Larry 1936- .... CLC 2, 3, 7, 11,
27, 44, 127, 250
See also AAYA 15; AITN 2; AMWS 5;
BEST 89:2; BPFB 2; CA 5-8R; CANR
19, 43, 64, 103, 170; CDALB 1968-1988;
CN 2, 3, 4, 5, 6, 7; CPW; CSW; DA3;
DAM NOV, POP; DLB 2, 143, 256;
DLBY 1980, 1987; EWL 3; MAL 5;
MTCW 1, 2; MTFW 2005; RGAL 4;
TCWW 1, 2

McMurtry, Larry Jeff
See McMurtry, Larry

McNally, Terrence 1939- ... CLC 4, 7, 41, 91,
252; DC 27
See also AAYA 62; AMWS 13; CA 45-48;
CAD; CANR 2, 56, 116; CD 5, 6; DA3;
DAM DRAM; DFS 16, 19; DLB 7, 249;
EWL 3; GLL 1; MTCW 2; MTFW 2005

McNally, Thomas Michael
See McNally, T.M.

McNally, T.M. 1961- .... CLC 82
See also CA 246

McNamer, Deirdre 1950- .... CLC 70
See also CA 188; CANR 163

McNeal, Tom CLC 119
See also CA 252; CANR 185; SATA 194

McNeile, Herman Cyril
1888-1937 .... TCLC 44
See also CA 184; CMW 4; DLB 77

McNickle, (William) D'Arcy
1904-1977 .... CLC 89; NNAL
See also CA 9-12R; 85-88; CANR 5, 45;
DAM MULT; DLB 175, 212; RGAL 4;
SATA-Obit 22; TCWW 1, 2

McPhee, John 1931- .... CLC 36
See also AAYA 61; AMWS 3; ANW; BEST
90:1; CA 65-68; CANR 20, 46, 64, 69,
121, 165; CPW; DLB 185, 275; MTCW
1, 2; MTFW 2005; TUS

McPhee, John Angus
See McPhee, John

McPherson, James Alan, Jr.
See McPherson, James Alan

McPherson, James Alan 1943- . BLCS; CLC
19, 77; SSC 95
See also BW 1, 3; CA 25-28R, 273; CAAE
273; CAAS 17; CANR 24, 74, 140; CN
3, 4, 5, 6; CSW; DLB 38, 244; EWL 3;
MTCW 1, 2; MTFW 2005; RGAL 4;
RGSF 2; SSFS 23

McPherson, William (Alexander)
1933- .... CLC 34
See also CA 69-72; CANR 28; INT
CANR-28

McTaggart, J. McT. Ellis
See McTaggart, John McTaggart Ellis

McTaggart, John McTaggart Ellis
1866-1925 .... TCLC 105
See also CA 120; DLB 262

Mda, Zakes 1948- .... BLC 2:3; CLC 262
See also CA 205; CANR 151, 185; CD 5,
6; DLB 225

Mda, Zanemvula
See Mda, Zakes

Mda, Zanemvula Kizito Gatyeni
See Mda, Zakes

Mead, George Herbert 1863-1931 . TCLC 89
See also CA 212; DLB 270

Mead, Margaret 1901-1978 .... CLC 37
See also AITN 1; CA 1-4R; 81-84; CANR
4; DA3; FW; MTCW 1, 2; SATA-Obit 20

Meaker, M. J.
See Meaker, Marijane

Meaker, Marijane 1927- .... CLC 12, 35
See also AAYA 2, 23; BYA 1, 7, 8; CA 107;
CANR 37, 63, 145, 180; CLR 29; GLL 2;
INT CA-107; JRDA; MAICYA 1, 2; MAI-
CYAS 1; MTCW 1; SAAS 1; SATA 20,
61, 99, 160; SATA-Essay 111; WYA;
YAW

Meaker, Marijane Agnes
See Meaker, Marijane

Mechthild von Magdeburg c. 1207-c.
1282 .... CMLC 91
See also DLB 138

Medoff, Mark (Howard) 1940- .... CLC 6, 23
See also AITN 1; CA 53-56; CAD; CANR
5; CD 5, 6; DAM DRAM; DFS 4; DLB
7; INT CANR-5

Medvedev, P. N.
See Bakhtin, Mikhail Mikhailovich

Meged, Aharon
See Megged, Aharon

Meged, Aron
See Megged, Aharon

Megged, Aharon 1920- .... CLC 9
See also CA 49-52; CAAS 13; CANR 1,
140; EWL 3; RGHL

Mehta, Deepa 1950- .... CLC 208

Mehta, Gita 1943- .... CLC 179
See also CA 225; CN 7; DNFS 2

Mehta, Ved 1934- .... CLC 37
See also CA 1-4R, 212; CAAE 212; CANR
2, 23, 69; DLB 323; MTCW 1; MTFW
2005

Melanchthon, Philipp 1497-1560 .... LC 90
See also DLB 179

Melanter
See Blackmore, R(ichard) D(oddridge)

Meleager c. 140B.C.-c. 70B.C. ...... CMLC 53

Melies, Georges 1861-1938 .... TCLC 81

Melikow, Loris
See Hofmannsthal, Hugo von

Melmoth, Sebastian
See Wilde, Oscar

Melo Neto, Joao Cabral de
See Cabral de Melo Neto, Joao

Meltzer, Milton 1915- .... CLC 26
See also AAYA 8, 45; BYA 2, 6; CA 13-
16R; CANR 38, 92, 107, 192; CLR 13;
DLB 61; JRDA; MAICYA 1, 2; SAAS 1;
SATA 1, 50, 80, 128, 201; SATA-Essay
124; WYA; YAW

Melville, Herman 1819-1891 ..... NCLC 3, 12,
29, 45, 49, 91, 93, 123, 157, 181, 193;
PC 82; SSC 1, 17, 46, 95; WLC 4
See also AAYA 25; AMW; AMWR 1;
CDALB 1640-1865; DA; DA3; DAB;
DAC; DAM MST, NOV; DLB 3, 74, 250,
254, 349; EXPN; EXPS; GL 3; LAIT 1,
2; NFS 7, 9; RGAL 4; RGSF 2; SATA 59;
SSFS 3; TUS

Members, Mark
See Powell, Anthony

Membreno, Alejandro CLC 59

Menand, Louis 1952- .... CLC 208
See also CA 200

Menander c. 342B.C.-c. 293B.C. .... CMLC 9,
51, 101; DC 3
See also AW 1; CDWLB 1; DAM DRAM;
DLB 176; LMFS 1; RGWL 2, 3

Menchu, Rigoberta 1959- .. CLC 160; HLCS
2
See also CA 175; CANR 135; DNFS 1;
WLIT 1

Mencken, H. L. 1880-1956 .... TCLC 13, 18
See also AMW; CA 105; 125; CDALB
1917-1929; DLB 11, 29, 63, 137, 222;
EWL 3; MAL 5; MTCW 1, 2; MTFW
2005; NCFS 4; RGAL 4; TUS

Mencken, Henry Louis
See Mencken, H. L.

Mendelsohn, Jane 1965- .... CLC 99
See also CA 154; CANR 94

Mendelssohn, Moses 1729-1786 .... LC 142
See also DLB 97

Mendoza, Inigo Lopez de
See Santillana, Inigo Lopez de Mendoza,
Marques de

Menton, Francisco de
See Chin, Frank (Chew, Jr.)

Mercer, David 1928-1980 .... CLC 5
See also CA 9-12R; 102; CANR 23; CBD;
DAM DRAM; DLB 13, 310; MTCW 1;
RGEL 2

Merchant, Paul
See Ellison, Harlan

Meredith, George 1828-1909 .. PC 60; TCLC
17, 43
See also CA 117; 153; CANR 80; CDBLB
1832-1890; DAM POET; DLB 18, 35, 57,
159; RGEL 2; TEA

Meredith, William 1919-2007 ...... CLC 4, 13,
22, 55; PC 28
See also CA 9-12R; 260; CAAS 14; CANR
6, 40, 129; CP 1, 2, 3, 4, 5, 6, 7; DAM
POET; DLB 5; MAL 5

Meredith, William Morris
See Meredith, William

Merezhkovsky, Dmitrii Sergeevich
See Merezhkovsky, Dmitry Sergeyevich

Merezhkovsky, Dmitry Sergeevich
See Merezhkovsky, Dmitry Sergeyevich

Merezhkovsky, Dmitry Sergeyevich
1865-1941 .... TCLC 29
See also CA 169; DLB 295; EWL 3

Merezhkovsky, Zinaida
See Gippius, Zinaida

Merimee, Prosper 1803-1870 . DC 33; NCLC
6, 65; SSC 7, 77
See also DLB 119, 192; EW 6; EXPS; GFL
1789 to the Present; RGSF 2; RGWL 2,
3; SSFS 8; SUFW

Merkin, Daphne 1954- .... CLC 44
See also CA 123

Merleau-Ponty, Maurice
1908-1961 .... TCLC 156
See also CA 114; 89-92; DLB 296; GFL
1789 to the Present

Merlin, Arthur
See Blish, James (Benjamin)

Mernissi, Fatima 1940- .... CLC 171
See also CA 152; DLB 346; FW

Merrill, James 1926-1995 ...... CLC 2, 3, 6, 8,
13, 18, 34, 91; PC 28; TCLC 173
See also AMWS 3; CA 13-16R; 147; CANR
10, 49, 63, 108; CP 1, 2, 3, 4; DA3; DAM
POET; DLB 5, 165; DLBY 1985; EWL 3;
INT CANR-10; MAL 5; MTCW 1, 2;
MTFW 2005; PAB; PFS 23; RGAL 4

Merrill, James Ingram
See Merrill, James
Merriman, Alex
See Silverberg, Robert
Merriman, Brian 1747-1805 .... **NCLC 70**
Merritt, E. B.
See Waddington, Miriam
Merton, Thomas (James)
1915-1968 . **CLC 1, 3, 11, 34, 83; PC 10**
See also AAYA 61; AMWS 8; CA 5-8R;
25-28R; CANR 22, 53, 111, 131; DA3;
DLB 48; DLBY 1981; MAL 5; MTCW 1,
2; MTFW 2005
Merwin, W.S. 1927- ..... **CLC 1, 2, 3, 5, 8, 13,
18, 45, 88; PC 45**
See also AMWS 3; CA 13-16R; CANR 15,
51, 112, 140; CP 1, 2, 3, 4, 5, 6, 7; DA3;
DAM POET; DLB 5, 169, 342; EWL 3;
INT CANR-15; MAL 5; MTCW 1, 2;
MTFW 2005; PAB; PFS 5, 15; RGAL 4
Metastasio, Pietro 1698-1782 .... **LC 115**
See also RGWL 2, 3
Metcalf, John 1938- .... **CLC 37; SSC 43**
See also CA 113; CN 4, 5, 6, 7; DLB 60;
RGSF 2; TWA
Metcalf, Suzanne
See Baum, L(yman) Frank
Mew, Charlotte (Mary) 1870-1928 .. **TCLC 8**
See also CA 105; 189; DLB 19, 135; RGEL
2
Mewshaw, Michael 1943- .... **CLC 9**
See also CA 53-56; CANR 7, 47, 147;
DLBY 1980
Meyer, Conrad Ferdinand
1825-1898 .... **NCLC 81; SSC 30**
See also DLB 129; EW; RGWL 2, 3
Meyer, Gustav 1868-1932 .... **TCLC 21**
See also CA 117; 190; DLB 81; EWL 3
Meyer, June
See Jordan, June
Meyer, Lynn
See Slavitt, David R.
Meyer, Stephenie 1973- .... **CLC 280**
See also AAYA 77; CA 253; CANR 192;
CLR 142; SATA 193
Meyer-Meyrink, Gustav
See Meyer, Gustav
Meyers, Jeffrey 1939- .... **CLC 39**
See also CA 73-76, 186; CAAE 186; CANR
54, 102, 159; DLB 111
**Meynell, Alice (Christina Gertrude
Thompson)** 1847-1922 .... **TCLC 6**
See also CA 104; 177; DLB 19, 98; RGEL
2
Meyrink, Gustav
See Meyer, Gustav
Mhlophe, Gcina 1960- .... **BLC 2:3**
Michaels, Leonard 1933-2003 ..... **CLC 6, 25;
SSC 16**
See also AMWS 16; CA 61-64; 216; CANR
21, 62, 119, 179; CN 3, 45, 6, 7; DLB
130; MTCW 1; TCLE 1:2
Michaux, Henri 1899-1984 .... **CLC 8, 19**
See also CA 85-88; 114; DLB 258; EWL 3;
GFL 1789 to the Present; RGWL 2, 3
Micheaux, Oscar (Devereaux)
1884-1951 .... **TCLC 76**
See also BW 3; CA 174; DLB 50; TCWW
2
Michelangelo 1475-1564 .... **LC 12**
See also AAYA 43
Michelet, Jules 1798-1874 ...... **NCLC 31, 218**
See also EW 5; GFL 1789 to the Present
Michels, Robert 1876-1936 .... **TCLC 88**
See also CA 212

Michener, James A. 1907(?)-1997 . **CLC 1, 5,
11, 29, 60, 109**
See also AAYA 27; AITN 1; BEST 90:1;
BPFB 2; CA 5-8R; 161; CANR 21, 45,
68; CN 1, 2, 3, 4, 5, 6; CPW; DA3; DAM
NOV, POP; DLB 6; MAL 5; MTCW 1, 2;
MTFW 2005; RHW; TCWW 1, 2
Mickiewicz, Adam 1798-1855 . **NCLC 3, 101;
PC 38**
See also EW 5; RGWL 2, 3
Middleton, (John) Christopher
1926- .... **CLC 13**
See also CA 13-16R; CANR 29, 54, 117;
CP 1, 2, 3, 4, 5, 6, 7; DLB 40
Middleton, Richard (Barham)
1882-1911 .... **TCLC 56**
See also CA 187; DLB 156; HGG
Middleton, Stanley 1919-2009 ...... **CLC 7, 38**
See also CA 25-28R; CAAS 23; CANR 21,
46, 81, 157; CN 1, 2, 3, 4, 5, 6, 7; DLB
14, 326
Middleton, Thomas 1580-1627 ...... **DC 5; LC
33, 123**
See also BRW 2; DAM DRAM, MST; DFS
18, 22; DLB 58; RGEL 2
Mieville, China 1972(?)- .... **CLC 235**
See also AAYA 52; CA 196; CANR 138;
MTFW 2005
Migueis, Jose Rodrigues 1901-1980 . **CLC 10**
See also DLB 287
Mihura, Miguel 1905-1977 .... **DC 34**
See also CA 214
Mikszath, Kalman 1847-1910 .... **TCLC 31**
See also CA 170
Miles, Jack CLC 100
See also CA 200
Miles, John Russiano
See Miles, Jack
Miles, Josephine (Louise)
1911-1985 .... **CLC 1, 2, 14, 34, 39**
See also CA 1-4R; 116; CANR 2, 55; CP 1,
2, 3, 4; DAM POET; DLB 48; MAL 5;
TCLE 1:2
Militant
See Sandburg, Carl (August)
Mill, Harriet (Hardy) Taylor
1807-1858 .... **NCLC 102**
See also FW
Mill, John Stuart 1806-1873 ... **NCLC 11, 58,
179**
See also CDBLB 1832-1890; DLB 55, 190,
262; FW 1; RGEL 2; TEA
Millar, Kenneth 1915-1983 .. **CLC 1, 2, 3, 14,
34, 41**
See also AMWS 4; BPFB 2; CA 9-12R;
110; CANR 16, 63, 107; CMW 4; CN 1,
2, 3; CPW; DA3; DAM POP; DLB 2,
226; DLBD 6; DLBY 1983; MAL 5;
MSW; MTCW 1, 2; MTFW 2005; RGAL
4
Millay, E. Vincent
See Millay, Edna St. Vincent
Millay, Edna St. Vincent 1892-1950 ..... **PC 6,
61; TCLC 4, 49, 169; WLCS**
See also AMW; CA 104; 130; CDALB
1917-1929; DA; DA3; DAB; DAC; DAM
MST, POET; DLB 45, 249; EWL 3;
EXPP; FL 1:6; GLL 1; MAL 5; MBL;
MTCW 1, 2; MTFW 2005; PAB; PFS 3,
17, 31; RGAL 4; TUS; WP
Miller, Arthur 1915-2005 ..... **CLC 1, 2, 6, 10,
15, 26, 47, 78, 179; DC 1, 31; WLC 4**
See also AAYA 15; AITN 1; AMW; AMWC
1; CA 1-4R; 236; CABS 3; CAD; CANR
2, 30, 54, 76, 132; CD 5, 6; CDALB
1941-1968; DA; DA3; DAB; DAC; DAM
DRAM, MST; DFS 1, 3, 8; DLB 7, 266;
EWL 3; LAIT 1, 4; LATS 1:2; MAL 5;
MTCW 1, 2; MTFW 2005; RGAL 4;
RGHL; TUS; WYAS 1

Miller, Frank 1957- .... **CLC 278**
See also AAYA 45; CA 224
Miller, Henry (Valentine)
1891-1980 .... **CLC 1, 2, 4, 9, 14, 43, 84;
TCLC 213; WLC 4**
See also AMW; BPFB 2; CA 9-12R; 97-
100; CANR 33, 64; CDALB 1929-1941;
CN 1, 2; DA; DA3; DAB; DAC; DAM
MST, NOV; DLB 4, 9; DLBY 1980; EWL
3; MAL 5; MTCW 1, 2; MTFW 2005;
RGAL 4; TUS
Miller, Hugh 1802-1856 .... **NCLC 143**
See also DLB 190
Miller, Jason 1939(?)-2001 .... **CLC 2**
See also AITN 1; CA 73-76; 197; CAD;
CANR 130; DFS 12; DLB 7
Miller, Sue 1943- .... **CLC 44**
See also AMWS 12; BEST 90:3; CA 139;
CANR 59, 91, 128, 194; DA3; DAM
POP; DLB 143
Miller, Walter M(ichael, Jr.)
1923-1996 .... **CLC 4, 30**
See also BPFB 2; CA 85-88; CANR 108;
DLB 8; SCFW 1, 2; SFW 4
Millett, Kate 1934- .... **CLC 67**
See also AITN 1; CA 73-76; CANR 32, 53,
76, 110; DA3; DLB 246; FW; GLL 1;
MTCW 1, 2; MTFW 2005
Millhauser, Steven 1943- ... **CLC 21, 54, 109;
SSC 57**
See also AAYA 76; CA 110; 111; CANR
63, 114, 133, 189; CN 6, 7; DA3; DLB 2,
350; FANT; INT CA-111; MAL 5; MTCW
2; MTFW 2005
Millhauser, Steven Lewis
See Millhauser, Steven
Millin, Sarah Gertrude 1889-1968 ... **CLC 49**
See also CA 102; 93-96; DLB 225; EWL 3
Milne, A. A. 1882-1956 .... **TCLC 6, 88**
See also BRWS 5; CA 104; 133; CLR 1,
26, 108; CMW 4; CWRI 5; DA3; DAB;
DAC; DAM MST; DLB 10, 77, 100, 160,
352; FANT; MAICYA 1, 2; MTCW 1, 2;
MTFW 2005; RGEL 2; SATA 100; WCH;
YABC 1
Milne, Alan Alexander
See Milne, A. A.
Milner, Ron(ald) 1938-2004 .. **BLC 1:3; CLC
56**
See also AITN 1; BW 1; CA 73-76; 230;
CAD; CANR 24, 81; CD 5, 6; DAM
MULT; DLB 38; MAL 5; MTCW 1
Milnes, Richard Monckton
1809-1885 .... **NCLC 61**
See also DLB 32, 184
Milosz, Czeslaw 1911-2004 .... **CLC 5, 11, 22,
31, 56, 82, 253; PC 8; WLCS**
See also AAYA 62; CA 81-84; 230; CANR
23, 51, 91, 126; CDWLB 4; CWW 2;
DA3; DAM MST, POET; DLB 215, 331;
EW 13; EWL 3; MTCW 1, 2; MTFW
2005; PFS 16, 29; RGHL; RGWL 2, 3
Milton, John 1608-1674 ..... **LC 9, 43, 92; PC
19, 29; WLC 4**
See also AAYA 65; BRW 2; BRWR 2; CD-
BLB 1660-1789; DA; DA3; DAB; DAC;
DAM MST, POET; DLB 131, 151, 281;
EFS 1; EXPP; LAIT 1; PAB; PFS 3, 17;
RGEL 2; TEA; WLIT 3; WP
Min, Anchee 1957- .... **CLC 86**
See also CA 146; CANR 94, 137; MTFW
2005
Minehaha, Cornelius
See Wedekind, Frank
Miner, Valerie 1947- .... **CLC 40**
See also CA 97-100; CANR 59, 177; FW;
GLL 2
Minimo, Duca
See D'Annunzio, Gabriele

Moorcock, Michael 1939- ...... **CLC 5, 27, 58, 236**
See also AAYA 26; CA 45-48; CAAS 5; CANR 2, 17, 38, 64, 122; CN 5, 6, 7; DLB 14, 231, 261, 319; FANT; MTCW 1, 2; MTFW 2005; SATA 93, 166; SCFW 1, 2; SFW 4; SUFW 1, 2

Moorcock, Michael John
See Moorcock, Michael

Moorcock, Michael John
See Moorcock, Michael

Moore, Al
See Moore, Alan

Moore, Alan 1953- .... **CLC 230**
See also AAYA 51; CA 204; CANR 138, 184; DLB 261; MTFW 2005; SFW 4

Moore, Brian 1921-1999 ... **CLC 1, 3, 5, 7, 8, 19, 32, 90**
See also BRWS 9; CA 1-4R; 174; CANR 1, 25, 42, 63; CN 1, 2, 3, 4, 5, 6; DAB; DAC; DAM MST; DLB 251; EWL 3; FANT; MTCW 1, 2; MTFW 2005; RGEL 2

Moore, Edward
See Muir, Edwin

Moore, G. E. 1873-1958 .... **TCLC 89**
See also DLB 262

Moore, George Augustus
1852-1933 .... **SSC 19; TCLC 7**
See also BRW 6; CA 104; 177; DLB 10, 18, 57, 135; EWL 3; RGEL 2; RGSF 2

Moore, Lorrie
See Moore, Marie Lorena

Moore, Marianne (Craig)
1887-1972 ... **CLC 1, 2, 4, 8, 10, 13, 19, 47; PC 4, 49; WLCS**
See also AMW; CA 1-4R; 33-36R; CANR 3, 61; CDALB 1929-1941; CP 1; DA; DA3; DAB; DAC; DAM MST, POET; DLB 45; DLBD 7; EWL 3; EXPP; FL 1:6; MAL 5; MBL; MTCW 1, 2; MTFW 2005; PAB; PFS 14, 17; RGAL 4; SATA 20; TUS; WP

Moore, Marie Lorena 1957- ...... **CLC 39, 45, 68, 165**
See also AMWS 10; CA 116; CANR 39, 83, 139; CN 5, 6, 7; DLB 234; MTFW 2005; SSFS 19

Moore, Michael 1954- .... **CLC 218**
See also AAYA 53; CA 166; CANR 150

Moore, Thomas 1779-1852 .... **NCLC 6, 110**
See also DLB 96, 144; RGEL 2

Moorhouse, Frank 1938- .... **SSC 40**
See also CA 118; CANR 92; CN 3, 4, 5, 6, 7; DLB 289; RGSF 2

Mora, Pat 1942- .... **HLC 2**
See also AMWS 13; CA 129; CANR 57, 81, 112, 171; CLR 58; DAM MULT; DLB 209; HW 1, 2; LLW; MAICYA 2; MTFW 2005; SATA 92, 134, 186

Moraga, Cherrie 1952- ... **CLC 126, 250; DC 22**
See also CA 131; CANR 66, 154; DAM MULT; DLB 82, 249; FW; GLL 1; HW 1, 2; LLW

Moran, J.L.
See Whitaker, Rod

Morand, Paul 1888-1976 .... **CLC 41; SSC 22**
See also CA 184; 69-72; DLB 65; EWL 3

Morante, Elsa 1918-1985 .... **CLC 8, 47**
See also CA 85-88; 117; CANR 35; DLB 177; EWL 3; MTCW 1, 2; MTFW 2005; RGHL; RGWL 2, 3; WLIT 7

Moravia, Alberto
See Pincherle, Alberto

Morck, Paul
See Rolvaag, O.E.

More, Hannah 1745-1833 ...... **NCLC 27, 141**
See also DLB 107, 109, 116, 158; RGEL 2

More, Henry 1614-1687 .... **LC 9**
See also DLB 126, 252

More, Sir Thomas 1478(?)-1535 ... **LC 10, 32, 140**
See also BRWC 1; BRWS 7; DLB 136, 281; LMFS 1; NFS 29; RGEL 2; TEA

Moreas, Jean
See Papadiamantopoulos, Johannes

Moreton, Andrew Esq.
See Defoe, Daniel

Moreton, Lee
See Boucicault, Dion

Morgan, Berry 1919-2002 .... **CLC 6**
See also CA 49-52; 208; DLB 6

Morgan, Claire
See Highsmith, Patricia

Morgan, Edwin 1920- .... **CLC 31**
See also BRWS 9; CA 5-8R; CANR 3, 43, 90; CP 1, 2, 3, 4, 5, 6, 7; DLB 27

Morgan, Edwin George
See Morgan, Edwin

Morgan, (George) Frederick
1922-2004 .... **CLC 23**
See also CA 17-20R; 224; CANR 21, 144; CP 2, 3, 4, 5, 6, 7

Morgan, Harriet
See Mencken, H. L.

Morgan, Jane
See Cooper, James Fenimore

Morgan, Janet 1945- .... **CLC 39**
See also CA 65-68

Morgan, Lady 1776(?)-1859 .... **NCLC 29**
See also DLB 116, 158; RGEL 2

Morgan, Robin (Evonne) 1941- .... **CLC 2**
See also CA 69-72; CANR 29, 68; FW; GLL 2; MTCW 1; SATA 80

Morgan, Scott
See Kuttner, Henry

Morgan, Seth 1949(?)-1990 .... **CLC 65**
See also CA 185; 132

Morgenstern, Christian (Otto Josef Wolfgang) 1871-1914 .... **TCLC 8**
See also CA 105; 191; EWL 3

Morgenstern, S.
See Goldman, William

Mori, Rintaro
See Mori Ogai

Mori, Toshio 1910-1980 ... **AAL; SSC 83, 123**
See also CA 116; 244; DLB 312; RGSF 2

Moricz, Zsigmond 1879-1942 .... **TCLC 33**
See also CA 165; DLB 215; EWL 3

Morike, Eduard (Friedrich)
1804-1875 .... **NCLC 10, 201**
See also DLB 133; RGWL 2, 3

Morin, Jean-Paul
See Whitaker, Rod

Mori Ogai 1862-1922 .... **TCLC 14**
See also CA 110; 164; DLB 180; EWL 3; MJW; RGWL 3; TWA

Moritz, Karl Philipp 1756-1793 .... **LC 2, 162**
See also DLB 94

Morland, Peter Henry
See Faust, Frederick

Morley, Christopher (Darlington)
1890-1957 .... **TCLC 87**
See also CA 112; 213; DLB 9; MAL 5; RGAL 4

Morren, Theophil
See Hofmannsthal, Hugo von

Morris, Bill 1952- .... **CLC 76**
See also CA 225

Morris, Julian
See West, Morris L(anglo)

Morris, Steveland Judkins (?)-
See Wonder, Stevie

Morris, William 1834-1896 . **NCLC 4; PC 55**
See also BRW 5; CDBLB 1832-1890; DLB 18, 35, 57, 156, 178, 184; FANT; RGEL 2; SFW 4; SUFW

Morris, Wright (Marion) 1910-1998 . **CLC 1, 3, 7, 18, 37; TCLC 107**
See also AMW; CA 9-12R; 167; CANR 21, 81; CN 1, 2, 3, 4, 5, 6; DLB 2, 206, 218; DLBY 1981; EWL 3; MAL 5; MTCW 1, 2; MTFW 2005; RGAL 4; TCWW 1, 2

Morrison, Arthur 1863-1945 .... **SSC 40; TCLC 72**
See also CA 120; 157; CMW 4; DLB 70, 135, 197; RGEL 2

Morrison, Chloe Anthony Wofford
See Morrison, Toni

Morrison, James Douglas
1943-1971 .... **CLC 17**
See also CA 73-76; CANR 40

Morrison, Jim
See Morrison, James Douglas

Morrison, John Gordon 1904-1998 ... **SSC 93**
See also CA 103; CANR 92; DLB 260

Morrison, Toni 1931- . **BLC 1:3, 2:3; CLC 4, 10, 22, 55, 81, 87, 173, 194; SSC 126; WLC 4**
See also AAYA 1, 22, 61; AFAW 1, 2; AMWC 1; AMWS 3; BPFB 2; BW 2, 3; CA 29-32R; CANR 27, 42, 67, 113, 124; CDALB 1968-1988; CLR 99; CN 3, 4, 5, 6, 7; CPW; DA; DA3; DAB; DAC; DAM MST, MULT, NOV, POP; DLB 6, 33, 143, 331; DLBY 1981; EWL 3; EXPN; FL 1:6; FW; GL 3; LAIT 2, 4; LATS 1:2; LMFS 2; MAL 5; MBL; MTCW 1, 2; MTFW 2005; NFS 1, 6, 8, 14; RGAL 4; RHW; SATA 57, 144; SSFS 5; TCLE 1:2; TUS; YAW

Morrison, Van 1945- .... **CLC 21**
See also CA 116; 168

Morrissy, Mary 1957- .... **CLC 99**
See also CA 205; DLB 267

Mortimer, John 1923-2009 .... **CLC 28, 43**
See Morton, Kate
See also CA 13-16R; 282; CANR 21, 69, 109, 172; CBD; CD 5, 6; CDBLB 1960 to Present; CMW 4; CN 5, 6, 7; CPW; DA3; DAM DRAM, POP; DLB 13, 245, 271; INT CANR-21; MSW; MTCW 1, 2; MTFW 2005; RGEL 2

Mortimer, John C.
See Mortimer, John

Mortimer, John Clifford
See Mortimer, John

Mortimer, Penelope (Ruth)
1918-1999 .... **CLC 5**
See also CA 57-60; 187; CANR 45, 88; CN 1, 2, 3, 4, 5, 6

Mortimer, Sir John
See Mortimer, John

Morton, Anthony
See Creasey, John

Morton, Thomas 1579(?)-1647(?) .... **LC 72**
See also DLB 24; RGEL 2

Mosca, Gaetano 1858-1941 .... **TCLC 75**

Moses, Daniel David 1952- .... **NNAL**
See also CA 186; CANR 160; DLB 334

Mosher, Howard Frank 1943- .... **CLC 62**
See also CA 139; CANR 65, 115, 181

Mosley, Nicholas 1923- .... **CLC 43, 70**
See also CA 69-72; CANR 41, 60, 108, 158; CN 1, 2, 3, 4, 5, 6, 7; DLB 14, 207

Mosley, Walter 1952- ... **BLCS; CLC 97, 184, 278**
See also AAYA 57; AMWS 13; BPFB 2; BW 2; CA 142; CANR 57, 92, 136, 172; CMW 4; CN 7; CPW; DA3; DAM MULT, POP; DLB 306; MSW; MTCW 2; MTFW 2005

Myers, L(eopold) H(amilton)
1881-1944 .... **TCLC 59**
See also CA 157; DLB 15; EWL 3; RGEL 2

Myers, Walter Dean 1937- ...... **BLC 1:3, 2:3; CLC 35**
See also AAYA 4, 23; BW 2; BYA 6, 8, 11; CA 33-36R; CANR 20, 42, 67, 108, 184; CLR 4, 16, 35, 110; DAM MULT, NOV; DLB 33; INT CANR-20; JRDA; LAIT 5; MAICYA 1, 2; MAICYAS 1; MTCW 2; MTFW 2005; NFS 30; SAAS 2; SATA 41, 71, 109, 157, 193; SATA-Brief 27; WYA; YAW

Myers, Walter M.
See Myers, Walter Dean

Myles, Symon
See Follett, Ken

Nabokov, Vladimir (Vladimirovich)
1899-1977 .... **CLC 1, 2, 3, 6, 8, 11, 15, 23, 44, 46, 64; SSC 11, 86; TCLC 108, 189; WLC 4**
See also AAYA 45; AMW; AMWC 1; AMWR 1; BPFB 1; CA 5-8R; 69-72; CANR 20, 102; CDALB 1941-1968; CN 1, 2; CP 2; DA; DA3; DAB; DAC; DAM MST, NOV; DLB 2, 244, 278, 317; DLBD 3; DLBY 1980, 1991; EWL 3; EXPS; LATS 1:2; MAL 5; MTCW 1, 2; MTFW 2005; NCFS 4; NFS 9; RGAL 4; RGSF 2; SSFS 6, 15; TUS

Naevius c. 265B.C.-201B.C. .... **CMLC 37**
See also DLB 211

Nagai, Kafu 1879-1959 .... **TCLC 51**
See also CA 117; 276; DLB 180; EWL 3; MJW

Nagai, Sokichi
See Nagai, Kafu

Nagai Kafu
See Nagai, Kafu

na gCopaleen, Myles
See O Nuallain, Brian

na Gopaleen, Myles
See O Nuallain, Brian

Nagy, Laszlo 1925-1978 .... **CLC 7**
See also CA 129; 112

Naidu, Sarojini 1879-1949 .... **TCLC 80**
See also EWL 3; RGEL 2

Naipaul, Shiva 1945-1985 .... **CLC 32, 39; TCLC 153**
See also CA 110; 112; 116; CANR 33; CN 2, 3; DA3; DAM NOV; DLB 157; DLBY 1985; EWL 3; MTCW 1, 2; MTFW 2005

Naipaul, Shivadhar Srinivasa
See Naipaul, Shiva

Naipaul, V. S. 1932- . **CLC 4, 7, 9, 13, 18, 37, 105, 199; SSC 38, 121**
See also BPFB 2; BRWS 1; CA 1-4R; CANR 1, 33, 51, 91, 126, 191; CDBLB 1960 to Present; CDWLB 3; CN 1, 2, 3, 4, 5, 6, 7; DA3; DAB; DAC; DAM MST, NOV; DLB 125, 204, 207, 326, 331; DLBY 1985, 2001; EWL 3; LATS 1:2; MTCW 1, 2; MTFW 2005; RGEL 2; RGSF 2; TWA; WLIT 4; WWE 1

Naipaul, Vidiahar Surajprasad
See Naipaul, V. S.

Nakos, Lilika 1903(?)-1989 .... **CLC 29**

Napoleon
See Yamamoto, Hisaye

Narayan, R.K. 1906-2001 ...... **CLC 7, 28, 47, 121, 211; SSC 25**
See also BPFB 2; CA 81-84; 196; CANR 33, 61, 112; CN 1, 2, 3, 4, 5, 6, 7; DA3; DAM NOV; DLB 323; DNFS 1; EWL 3; MTCW 1, 2; MTFW 2005; RGEL 2; RGSF 2; SATA 62; SSFS 5; WWE 1

Nash, Frediric Ogden
See Nash, Ogden

Nash, Ogden 1902-1971 ...... **CLC 23; PC 21; TCLC 109**
See also CA 13-14; 29-32R; CANR 34, 61, 185; CAP 1; CP 1; DAM POET; DLB 11; MAICYA 1, 2; MAL 5; MTCW 1, 2; PFS 31; RGAL 4; SATA 2, 46; WP

Nashe, Thomas 1567-1601(?) . **LC 41, 89; PC 82**
See also DLB 167; RGEL 2

Nathan, Daniel
See Dannay, Frederic

Nathan, George Jean 1882-1958 .... **TCLC 18**
See also CA 114; 169; DLB 137; MAL 5

Natsume, Kinnosuke
See Natsume, Soseki

Natsume, Soseki 1867-1916 .... **TCLC 2, 10**
See also CA 104; 195; DLB 180; EWL 3; MJW; RGWL 2, 3; TWA

Natsume Soseki
See Natsume, Soseki

Natti, Lee 1919- .... **CLC 17**
See also CA 5-8R; CANR 2; CWRI 5; SAAS 3; SATA 1, 67

Natti, Mary Lee
See Natti, Lee

Navarre, Marguerite de
See de Navarre, Marguerite

Naylor, Gloria 1950- . **BLC 1:3; CLC 28, 52, 156, 261; WLCS**
See also AAYA 6, 39; AFAW 1, 2; AMWS 8; BW 2, 3; CA 107; CANR 27, 51, 74, 130; CN 4, 5, 6, 7; CPW; DA; DA3; DAC; DAM MST, MULT, NOV, POP; DLB 173; EWL 3; FW; MAL 5; MTCW 1, 2; MTFW 2005; NFS 4, 7; RGAL 4; TCLE 1:2; TUS

Neal, John 1793-1876 .... **NCLC 161**
See also DLB 1, 59, 243; FW; RGAL 4

Neff, Debra CLC 59

Neihardt, John Gneisenau
1881-1973 .... **CLC 32**
See also CA 13-14; CANR 65; CAP 1; DLB 9, 54, 256; LAIT 2; TCWW 1, 2

Nekrasov, Nikolai Alekseevich
1821-1878 .... **NCLC 11**
See also DLB 277

Nelligan, Emile 1879-1941 .... **TCLC 14**
See also CA 114; 204; DLB 92; EWL 3

Nelson, Alice Ruth Moore Dunbar
1875-1935 .... **HR 1:2**
See also BW 1, 3; CA 122; 124; CANR 82; DLB 50; FW; MTCW 1

Nelson, Willie 1933- .... **CLC 17**
See also CA 107; CANR 114, 178

Nemerov, Howard 1920-1991 .... **CLC 2, 6, 9, 36; PC 24; TCLC 124**
See also AMW; CA 1-4R; 134; CABS 2; CANR 1, 27, 53; CN 1, 2, 3; CP 1, 2, 3, 4, 5; DAM POET; DLB 5, 6; DLBY 1983; EWL 3; INT CANR-27; MAL 5; MTCW 1, 2; MTFW 2005; PFS 10, 14; RGAL 4

Nepos, Cornelius c. 99B.C.-c. 24B.C. .... **CMLC 89**
See also DLB 211

Neruda, Pablo 1904-1973 .. **CLC 1, 2, 5, 7, 9, 28, 62; HLC 2; PC 4, 64; WLC 4**
See also CA 19-20; 45-48; CANR 131; CAP 2; DA; DA3; DAB; DAC; DAM MST, MULT, POET; DLB 283, 331; DNFS 2; EWL 3; HW 1; LAW; MTCW 1, 2; MTFW 2005; PFS 11, 28; RGWL 2, 3; TWA; WLIT 1; WP

Nerval, Gerard de 1808-1855 ... **NCLC 1, 67; PC 13; SSC 18**
See also DLB 217; EW 6; GFL 1789 to the Present; RGSF 2; RGWL 2, 3

Nervo, (Jose) Amado (Ruiz de)
1870-1919 .... **HLCS 2; TCLC 11**
See also CA 109; 131; DLB 290; EWL 3; HW 1; LAW

Nesbit, Malcolm
See Chester, Alfred

Nessi, Pio Baroja y
See Baroja, Pio

Nestroy, Johann 1801-1862 .... **NCLC 42**
See also DLB 133; RGWL 2, 3

Netterville, Luke
See O'Grady, Standish (James)

Neufeld, John (Arthur) 1938- .... **CLC 17**
See also AAYA 11; CA 25-28R; CANR 11, 37, 56; CLR 52; MAICYA 1, 2; SAAS 3; SATA 6, 81, 131; SATA-Essay 131; YAW

Neumann, Alfred 1895-1952 .... **TCLC 100**
See also CA 183; DLB 56

Neumann, Ferenc
See Molnar, Ferenc

Neville, Emily Cheney 1919- .... **CLC 12**
See also BYA 2; CA 5-8R; CANR 3, 37, 85; JRDA; MAICYA 1, 2; SAAS 2; SATA 1; YAW

Newbound, Bernard Slade 1930- .... **CLC 11, 46**
See also CA 81-84; CAAS 9; CANR 49; CCA 1; CD 5, 6; DAM DRAM; DLB 53

Newby, P(ercy) H(oward)
1918-1997 .... **CLC 2, 13**
See also CA 5-8R; 161; CANR 32, 67; CN 1, 2, 3, 4, 5, 6; DAM NOV; DLB 15, 326; MTCW 1; RGEL 2

Newcastle
See Cavendish, Margaret Lucas

Newlove, Donald 1928- .... **CLC 6**
See also CA 29-32R; CANR 25

Newlove, John (Herbert) 1938- .... **CLC 14**
See also CA 21-24R; CANR 9, 25; CP 1, 2, 3, 4, 5, 6, 7

Newman, Charles 1938-2006 .... **CLC 2, 8**
See also CA 21-24R; 249; CANR 84; CN 3, 4, 5, 6

Newman, Charles Hamilton
See Newman, Charles

Newman, Edwin (Harold) 1919- ...... **CLC 14**
See also AITN 1; CA 69-72; CANR 5

Newman, John Henry 1801-1890 . **NCLC 38, 99**
See also BRWS 7; DLB 18, 32, 55; RGEL 2

Newton, (Sir) Isaac 1642-1727 ...... **LC 35, 53**
See also DLB 252

Newton, Suzanne 1936- .... **CLC 35**
See also BYA 7; CA 41-44R; CANR 14; JRDA; SATA 5, 77

New York Dept. of Ed. CLC 70

Nexo, Martin Andersen
1869-1954 .... **TCLC 43**
See also CA 202; DLB 214; EWL 3

Nezval, Vitezslav 1900-1958 .... **TCLC 44**
See also CA 123; CDWLB 4; DLB 215; EWL 3

Ng, Fae Myenne 1956- .... **CLC 81**
See also BYA 11; CA 146; CANR 191

Ngcobo, Lauretta 1931- .... **BLC 2:3**
See also CA 165

Ngema, Mbongeni 1955- .... **CLC 57**
See also BW 2; CA 143; CANR 84; CD 5, 6

Ngugi, James T.
See Ngugi wa Thiong'o

Ngugi, James Thiong'o
See Ngugi wa Thiong'o

Ngugi wa Thiong'o 1938- .... BLC 1:3, 2:3;
    CLC 3, 7, 13, 36, 182, 275
    See also AFW; BRWS 8; BW 2; CA 81-84;
    CANR 27, 58, 164; CD 3, 4, 5, 6, 7; CD-
    WLB 3; CN 1, 2; DAM MULT, NOV;
    DLB 125; DNFS 2; EWL 1, 2;
    MTFW 2005; RGEL 2; WWE 1
Niatum, Duane 1938- .... NNAL
    See also CA 41-44R; CANR 21, 45, 83;
    DLB 175
Nichol, B(arrie) P(hillip) 1944-1988 . CLC 18
    See also CA 53-56; CP 1, 2, 3, 4; DLB 53;
    SATA 66
Nicholas of Autrecourt c.
    1298-1369 .... CMLC 108
Nicholas of Cusa 1401-1464 .... LC 80
    See also DLB 115
Nichols, John 1940- .... CLC 38
    See also AMWS 13; CA 9-12R, 190; CAAE
    190; CAAS 2; CANR 6, 70, 121, 185;
    DLBY 1982; LATS 1:2; MTFW 2005;
    TCWW 1, 2
Nichols, Leigh
    See Koontz, Dean R.
Nichols, Peter (Richard) 1927- .... CLC 5, 36,
    65
    See also CA 104; CANR 33, 86; CBD; CD
    5, 6; DLB 13, 245; MTCW 1
Nicholson, Linda CLC 65
Ni Chuilleanain, Eilean 1942- .... PC 34
    See also CA 126; CANR 53, 83; CP 5, 6, 7;
    CWP; DLB 40
Nicolas, F. R. E.
    See Freeling, Nicolas
Niedecker, Lorine 1903-1970 ..... CLC 10, 42;
    PC 42
    See also CA 25-28; CAP 2; DAM POET;
    DLB 48
Nietzsche, Friedrich (Wilhelm)
    1844-1900 .... TCLC 10, 18, 55
    See also CA 107; 121; CDWLB 2; DLB
    129; EW 7; RGWL 2, 3; TWA
Nievo, Ippolito 1831-1861 .... NCLC 22
Nightingale, Anne Redmon 1943- .... CLC 22
    See also CA 103; DLBY 1986
Nightingale, Florence 1820-1910 ... TCLC 85
    See also CA 188; DLB 166
Nijo Yoshimoto 1320-1388 .... CMLC 49
    See also DLB 203
Nik. T. O.
    See Annensky, Innokenty (Fyodorovich)
Nin, Anais 1903-1977 ..... CLC 1, 4, 8, 11, 14,
    60, 127; SSC 10; TCLC 224
    See also AITN 2; AMWS 10; BPFB 2; CA
    13-16R; 69-72; CANR 22, 53; CN 1, 2;
    DAM NOV, POP; DLB 2, 4, 152; EWL
    3; GLL 2; MAL 5; MBL; MTCW 1, 2;
    MTFW 2005; RGAL 4; RGSF 2
Nisbet, Robert A(lexander)
    1913-1996 .... TCLC 117
    See also CA 25-28R; 153; CANR 17; INT
    CANR-17
Nishida, Kitaro 1870-1945 .... TCLC 83
Nishiwaki, Junzaburo 1894-1982 .... PC 15
    See also CA 194; 107; EWL 3; MJW;
    RGWL 3
Nissenson, Hugh 1933- .... CLC 4, 9
    See also CA 17-20R; CANR 27, 108, 151;
    CN 5, 6; DLB 28, 335
Nister, Der
    See Der Nister
Niven, Larry 1938- .... CLC 8
    See also AAYA 27; BPFB 2; BYA 10; CA
    21-24R, 207; CAAE 207; CAAS 12;
    CANR 14, 44, 66, 113, 155; CPW; DAM
    POP; DLB 8; MTCW 1, 2; SATA 95, 171;
    SCFW 1, 2; SFW 4
Niven, Laurence VanCott
    See Niven, Larry

Nixon, Agnes Eckhardt 1927- .... CLC 21
    See also CA 110
Nizan, Paul 1905-1940 .... TCLC 40
    See also CA 161; DLB 72; EWL 3; GFL
    1789 to the Present
Nkosi, Lewis 1936- .... BLC 1:3; CLC 45
    See also BW 1, 3; CA 65-68; CANR 27,
    81; CBD; CD 5, 6; DAM MULT; DLB
    157, 225; WWE 1
Nodier, (Jean) Charles (Emmanuel)
    1780-1844 .... NCLC 19
    See also DLB 119; GFL 1789 to the Present
Noguchi, Yone 1875-1947 .... TCLC 80
Nolan, Brian
    See O Nuallain, Brian
Nolan, Christopher 1965-2009 .... CLC 58
    See also CA 111; 283; CANR 88
Nolan, Christopher John
    See Nolan, Christopher
Noon, Jeff 1957- .... CLC 91
    See also CA 148; CANR 83; DLB 267;
    SFW 4
Norden, Charles
    See Durrell, Lawrence (George)
Nordhoff, Charles Bernard
    1887-1947 .... TCLC 23
    See also CA 108; 211; DLB 9; LAIT 1;
    RHW 1; SATA 23
Norfolk, Lawrence 1963- .... CLC 76
    See also CA 144; CANR 85; CN 6, 7; DLB
    267
Norman, Marsha (Williams) 1947- . CLC 28,
    186; DC 8
    See also CA 105; CABS 3; CAD; CANR
    41, 131; CD 5, 6; CSW; CWD; DAM
    DRAM; DFS 2; DLB 266; DLBY 1984;
    FW; MAL 5
Normyx
    See Douglas, (George) Norman
Norris, (Benjamin) Frank(lin, Jr.)
    1870-1902 . SSC 28; TCLC 24, 155, 211
    See also AAYA 57; AMW; AMWC 2; BPFB
    2; CA 110; 160; CDALB 1865-1917; DLB
    12, 71, 186; LMFS 2; MAL 5; NFS 12;
    RGAL 4; TCWW 1, 2; TUS
Norris, Kathleen 1947- .... CLC 248
    See also CA 160; CANR 113
Norris, Leslie 1921-2006 .... CLC 14
    See also CA 11-12; 251; CANR 14, 117;
    CAP 1; CP 1, 2, 3, 4, 5, 6, 7; DLB 27,
    256
North, Andrew
    See Norton, Andre
North, Anthony
    See Koontz, Dean R.
North, Captain George
    See Stevenson, Robert Louis (Balfour)
North, Captain George
    See Stevenson, Robert Louis (Balfour)
North, Milou
    See Erdrich, Louise
Northrup, B. A.
    See Hubbard, L. Ron
North Staffs
    See Hulme, T(homas) E(rnest)
Northup, Solomon 1808-1863 ...... NCLC 105
Norton, Alice Mary
    See Norton, Andre
Norton, Andre 1912-2005 .... CLC 12
    See also AAYA 14; BPFB 2; BYA 4, 10,
    12; CA 1-4R; 237; CANR 2, 31, 68, 108,
    149; CLR 50; DLB 8, 52; JRDA; MAI-
    CYA 1, 2; MTCW 1; SATA 1, 43, 91;
    SUFW 1, 2; YAW
Norton, Caroline 1808-1877 .. NCLC 47, 205
    See also DLB 21, 159, 199

Norway, Nevil Shute 1899-1960 .... CLC 30
    See also BPFB 3; CA 102; 93-96; CANR
    85; DLB 255; MTCW 2; NFS 9; RHW 4;
    SFW 4
Norwid, Cyprian Kamil
    1821-1883 .... NCLC 17
    See also RGWL 3
Nosille, Nabrah
    See Ellison, Harlan
Nossack, Hans Erich 1901-1977 .... CLC 6
    See also CA 93-96; 85-88; CANR 156;
    DLB 69; EWL 3
Nostradamus 1503-1566 .... LC 27
Nosu, Chuji
    See Ozu, Yasujiro
Notenburg, Eleanora (Genrikhovna) von
    See Guro, Elena (Genrikhovna)
Nova, Craig 1945- .... CLC 7, 31
    See also CA 45-48; CANR 2, 53, 127
Novak, Joseph
    See Kosinski, Jerzy
Novalis 1772-1801 .... NCLC 13, 178
    See also CDWLB 2; DLB 90; EW 5; RGWL
    2, 3
Novick, Peter 1934- .... CLC 164
    See also CA 188
Novis, Emile
    See Weil, Simone (Adolphine)
Nowlan, Alden (Albert) 1933-1983 ... CLC 15
    See also CA 9-12R; CANR 5; CP 1, 2, 3;
    DAC; DAM MST; DLB 53; PFS 12
Noyes, Alfred 1880-1958 ...... PC 27; TCLC 7
    See also CA 104; 188; DLB 20; EXPP;
    FANT; PFS 4; RGEL 2
Nugent, Richard Bruce
    1906(?)-1987 .... HR 1:3
    See also BW 1; CA 125; DLB 51; GLL 2
Nunez, Elizabeth 1944- .... BLC 2:3
    See also CA 223
Nunn, Kem CLC 34
    See also CA 159
Nussbaum, Martha Craven 1947- .. CLC 203
    See also CA 134; CANR 102, 176
Nwapa, Flora (Nwanzuruaha)
    1931-1993 .... BLCS; CLC 133
    See also BW 2; CA 143; CANR 83; CD-
    WLB 3; CWRI 5; DLB 125; EWL 3;
    WLIT 2
Nye, Robert 1939- .... CLC 13, 42
    See also BRWS 10; CA 33-36R; CANR 29,
    67, 107; CN 1, 2, 3, 4, 5, 6, 7; CP 1, 2, 3,
    4, 5, 6, 7; CWRI 5; DAM NOV; DLB 14,
    271; FANT; HGG; MTCW 1; RHW;
    SATA 6
Nyro, Laura 1947-1997 .... CLC 17
    See also CA 194
Oates, Joyce Carol 1938- .. CLC 1, 2, 3, 6, 9,
    11, 15, 19, 33, 52, 108, 134, 228; SSC 6,
    70, 121; WLC 4
    See also AAYA 15, 52; AITN 1; AMWS 2;
    BEST 89:2; BPFB 2; BYA 11; CA 5-8R;
    CANR 25, 45, 74, 113, 129, 165; CDALB
    1968-1988; CN 1, 2, 3, 4, 5, 6, 7; CP 5,
    6, 7; CPW; CWP; DA; DA3; DAB; DAC;
    DAM MST, NOV, POP; DLB 2, 5, 130;
    DLBY 1981; EWL 3; EXPS; FL 1:6; FW;
    GL 3; HGG; INT CANR-25; LAIT 4;
    MAL 5; MBL; MTCW 1, 2; MTFW 2005;
    NFS 8, 24; RGAL 4; RGSF 2; SATA 159;
    SSFS 1, 8, 17; SUFW 2; TUS
O'Brian, E.G.
    See Clarke, Arthur C.
O'Brian, Patrick 1914-2000 .... CLC 152
    See also AAYA 55; BRWS 12; CA 144; 187;
    CANR 74; CPW; MTCW 2; MTFW 2005;
    RHW
O'Brien, Darcy 1939-1998 .... CLC 11
    See also CA 21-24R; 167; CANR 8, 59

O'Brien, Edna 1932- ..... **CLC 3, 5, 8, 13, 36, 65, 116, 237; SSC 10, 77**
See also BRWS 5; CA 1-4R; CANR 6, 41, 65, 102, 169; CDBLB 1960 to Present; CN 1, 2, 3, 4, 5, 6, 7; DA3; DAM NOV; DLB 14, 231, 319; EWL 3; FW; MTCW 1, 2; MTFW 2005; RGSF 2; WLIT 4

O'Brien, E.G.
See Clarke, Arthur C.

O'Brien, Fitz-James 1828-1862 ..... **NCLC 21**
See also DLB 74; RGAL 4; SUFW

O'Brien, Flann
See O Nuallain, Brian

O'Brien, Richard 1942- .... **CLC 17**
See also CA 124

O'Brien, Tim 1946- .... **CLC 7, 19, 40, 103, 211; SSC 74, 123**
See also AAYA 16; AMWS 5; CA 85-88; CANR 40, 58, 133; CDALBS; CN 5, 6, 7; CPW; DA3; DAM POP; DLB 152; DLBD 9; DLBY 1980; LATS 1:2; MAL 5; MTCW 2; MTFW 2005; RGAL 4; SSFS 5, 15; TCLE 1:2

Obstfelder, Sigbjoern 1866-1900 .... **TCLC 23**
See also CA 123

O'Casey, Brenda
See Haycraft, Anna

O'Casey, Sean 1880-1964 .... **CLC 1, 5, 9, 11, 15, 88; DC 12; WLCS**
See also BRW 7; CA 89-92; CANR 62; CBD; CDBLB 1914-1945; DA3; DAB; DAC; DAM DRAM, MST; DFS 19; DLB 10; EWL 3; MTCW 1, 2; MTFW 2005; RGEL 2; TEA; WLIT 4

O'Cathasaigh, Sean
See O'Casey, Sean

Occom, Samson 1723-1792 .... **LC 60; NNAL**
See also DLB 175

Occomy, Marita (Odette) Bonner 1899(?)-1971 ..... **HR 1:2; PC 72; TCLC 179**
See also BW 2; CA 142; DFS 13; DLB 51, 228

Ochs, Phil(ip David) 1940-1976 .... **CLC 17**
See also CA 185; 65-68

O'Connor, Edwin (Greene) 1918-1968 .... **CLC 14**
See also CA 93-96; 25-28R; MAL 5

O'Connor, (Mary) Flannery 1925-1964 .... **CLC 1, 2, 3, 6, 10, 13, 15, 21, 66, 104; SSC 1, 23, 61, 82, 111; TCLC 132; WLC 4**
See also AAYA 7; AMW; AMWR 2; BPFB 3; BYA 16; CA 1-4R; CANR 3, 41; CDALB 1941-1968; DA; DA3; DAB; DAC; DAM MST, NOV; DLB 2, 152; DLBD 12; DLBY 1980; EWL 3; EXPS; LAIT 5; MBL; MTCW 1, 2; MTFW 2005; NFS 3, 21; RGAL 4; RGSF 2; SSFS 2, 7, 10, 19; TUS

O'Connor, Frank 1903-1966
See O'Donovan, Michael Francis

O'Dell, Scott 1898-1989 .... **CLC 30**
See also AAYA 3, 44; BPFB 3; BYA 1, 2, 3, 5; CA 61-64; 129; CANR 12, 30, 112; CLR 1, 16, 126; DLB 52; JRDA; MAICYA 1, 2; SATA 12, 60, 134; WYA; YAW

Odets, Clifford 1906-1963 ..... **CLC 2, 28, 98; DC 6**
See also AMWS 2; CA 85-88; CAD; CANR 62; DAM DRAM; DFS 3, 17, 20; DLB 7, 26, 341; EWL 3; MAL 5; MTCW 1, 2; MTFW 2005; RGAL 4; TUS

O'Doherty, Brian 1928- .... **CLC 76**
See also CA 105; CANR 108

O'Donnell, K. M.
See Malzberg, Barry N(athaniel)

O'Donnell, Lawrence
See Kuttner, Henry

O'Donovan, Michael Francis 1903-1966 .... **CLC 14, 23; SSC 5, 109**
See also BRWS 14; CA 93-96; CANR 84; DLB 162; EWL 3; RGSF 2; SSFS 5

Oe, Kenzaburo 1935- .. **CLC 10, 36, 86, 187; SSC 20**
See also CA 97-100; CANR 36, 50, 74, 126; CWW 2; DA3; DAM NOV; DLB 182, 331; DLBY 1994; EWL 3; LATS 1:2; MJW; MTCW 1, 2; MTFW 2005; RGSF 2; RGWL 2, 3

Oe Kenzaburo
See Oe, Kenzaburo

O'Faolain, Julia 1932- .... **CLC 6, 19, 47, 108**
See also CA 81-84; CAAS 2; CANR 12, 61; CN 2, 3, 4, 5, 6, 7; DLB 14, 231, 319; FW; MTCW 1; RHW

O'Faolain, Sean 1900-1991 ...... **CLC 1, 7, 14, 32, 70; SSC 13; TCLC 143**
See also CA 61-64; 134; CANR 12, 66; CN 1, 2, 3, 4; DLB 15, 162; MTCW 1, 2; MTFW 2005; RGEL 2; RGSF 2

O'Flaherty, Liam 1896-1984 .... **CLC 5, 34; SSC 6, 116**
See also CA 101; 113; CANR 35; CN 1, 2, 3; DLB 36, 162; DLBY 1984; MTCW 1, 2; MTFW 2005; RGEL 2; RGSF 2; SSFS 5, 20

Ogai
See Mori Ogai

Ogilvy, Gavin
See Barrie, J(ames) M(atthew)

O'Grady, Standish (James) 1846-1928 .... **TCLC 5**
See also CA 104; 157

O'Grady, Timothy 1951- .... **CLC 59**
See also CA 138

O'Hara, Frank 1926-1966 .... **CLC 2, 5, 13, 78; PC 45**
See also CA 9-12R; 25-28R; CANR 33; DA3; DAM POET; DLB 5, 16, 193; EWL 3; MAL 5; MTCW 1, 2; MTFW 2005; PFS 8, 12; RGAL 4; WP

O'Hara, John (Henry) 1905-1970 . **CLC 1, 2, 3, 6, 11, 42; SSC 15**
See also AMW; BPFB 3; CA 5-8R; 25-28R; CANR 31, 60; CDALB 1929-1941; DAM NOV; DLB 9, 86, 324; DLBD 2; EWL 3; MAL 5; MTCW 1, 2; MTFW 2005; NFS 11; RGAL 4; RGSF 2

O'Hehir, Diana 1929- .... **CLC 41**
See also CA 245; CANR 177

O'Hehir, Diana F.
See O'Hehir, Diana

Ohiyesa
See Eastman, Charles A(lexander)

Okada, John 1923-1971 .... **AAL**
See also BYA 14; CA 212; DLB 312; NFS 25

Okigbo, Christopher 1930-1967 ..... **BLC 1:3; CLC 25, 84; PC 7; TCLC 171**
See also AFW; BW 1, 3; CA 77-80; CANR 74; CDWLB 3; DAM MULT, POET; DLB 125; EWL 3; MTCW 1, 2; MTFW 2005; RGEL 2

Okigbo, Christopher Ifenayichukwu
See Okigbo, Christopher

Okri, Ben 1959- .... **BLC 2:3; CLC 87, 223**
See also AFW; BRWS 5; BW 2, 3; CA 130; 138; CANR 65, 128; CN 5, 6, 7; DLB 157, 231, 319, 326; EWL 3; INT CA-138; MTCW 2; MTFW 2005; RGSF 2; SSFS 20; WLIT 2; WWE 1

Old Boy
See Hughes, Thomas

Olds, Sharon 1942- .. **CLC 32, 39, 85; PC 22**
See also AMWS 10; CA 101; CANR 18, 41, 66, 98, 135; CP 5, 6, 7; CPW; CWP; DAM POET; DLB 120; MAL 5; MTCW 2; MTFW 2005; PFS 17

Oldstyle, Jonathan
See Irving, Washington

Olesha, Iurii
See Olesha, Yuri (Karlovich)

Olesha, Iurii Karlovich
See Olesha, Yuri (Karlovich)

Olesha, Yuri (Karlovich) 1899-1960 . **CLC 8; SSC 69; TCLC 136**
See also CA 85-88; DLB 272; EW 11; EWL 3; RGWL 2, 3

Olesha, Yury Karlovich
See Olesha, Yuri (Karlovich)

Oliphant, Mrs.
See Oliphant, Margaret (Oliphant Wilson)

Oliphant, Laurence 1829(?)-1888 .. **NCLC 47**
See also DLB 18, 166

Oliphant, Margaret (Oliphant Wilson) 1828-1897 .... **NCLC 11, 61; SSC 25**
See also BRWS 10; DLB 18, 159, 190; HGG; RGEL 2; RGSF 2; SUFW

Oliver, Mary 1935- ... **CLC 19, 34, 98; PC 75**
See also AMWS 7; CA 21-24R; CANR 9, 43, 84, 92, 138; CP 4, 5, 6, 7; CWP; DLB 5, 193, 342; EWL 3; MTFW 2005; PFS 15, 31

Olivi, Peter 1248-1298 .... **CMLC 114**

Olivier, Laurence (Kerr) 1907-1989 . **CLC 20**
See also CA 111; 150; 129

O.L.S.
See Russell, George William

Olsen, Tillie 1912-2007 .... **CLC 4, 13, 114; SSC 11, 103**
See also AAYA 51; AMWS 13; BYA 11; CA 1-4R; 256; CANR 1, 43, 74, 132; CDALBS; CN 2, 3, 4, 5, 6, 7; DA; DA3; DAB; DAC; DAM MST; DLB 28, 206; DLBY 1980; EWL 3; EXPS; FW; MAL 5; MTCW 1, 2; MTFW 2005; RGAL 4; RGSF 2; SSFS 1; TCLE 1:2; TCWW 2; TUS

Olson, Charles (John) 1910-1970 .. **CLC 1, 2, 5, 6, 9, 11, 29; PC 19**
See also AMWS 2; CA 13-16; 25-28R; CABS 2; CANR 35, 61; CAP 1; CP 1; DAM POET; DLB 5, 16, 193; EWL 3; MAL 5; MTCW 1, 2; RGAL 4; WP

Olson, Merle Theodore
See Olson, Toby

Olson, Toby 1937- .... **CLC 28**
See also CA 65-68; CAAS 11; CANR 9, 31, 84, 175; CP 3, 4, 5, 6, 7

Olyesha, Yuri
See Olesha, Yuri (Karlovich)

Olympiodorus of Thebes c. 375-c. 430 .... **CMLC 59**

Omar Khayyam
See Khayyam, Omar

Ondaatje, Michael 1943- ..... **CLC 14, 29, 51, 76, 180, 258; PC 28**
See also AAYA 66; CA 77-80; CANR 42, 74, 109, 133, 172; CN 5, 6, 7; CP 1, 2, 3, 4, 5, 6, 7; DA3; DAB; DAC; DAM MST; DLB 60, 323, 326; EWL 3; LATS 1:2; LMFS 2; MTCW 2; MTFW 2005; NFS 23; PFS 8, 19; TCLE 1:2; TWA; WWE 1

Ondaatje, Philip Michael
See Ondaatje, Michael

Oneal, Elizabeth 1934- .... **CLC 30**
See also AAYA 5, 41; BYA 13; CA 106; CANR 28, 84; CLR 13; JRDA; MAICYA 1, 2; SATA 30, 82; WYA; YAW

Oneal, Zibby
See Oneal, Elizabeth

O'Neill, Eugene (Gladstone) 1888-1953 ... **DC 20; TCLC 1, 6, 27, 49; WLC 4**
See also AAYA 54; AITN 1; AMW; AMWC 1; CA 110; 132; CAD; CANR 131; CDALB 1929-1941; DA; DA3; DAB;

Pagnol, Marcel (Paul)
1895-1974 .... **TCLC 208**
See also CA 128; 49-52; DLB 321; EWL 3;
GFL 1789 to the Present; MTCW 1;
RGWL 2, 3

Paige, Richard
See Koontz, Dean R.

Paine, Thomas 1737-1809 .... **NCLC 62**
See also AMWS 1; CDALB 1640-1865;
DLB 31, 43, 73, 158; LAIT 1; RGAL 4;
RGEL 2; TUS

Pakenham, Antonia
See Fraser, Antonia

Palamas, Costis
See Palamas, Kostes

Palamas, Kostes 1859-1943 .... **TCLC 5**
See also CA 105; 190; EWL 3; RGWL 2, 3

Palamas, Kostis
See Palamas, Kostes

Palazzeschi, Aldo 1885-1974 .... **CLC 11**
See also CA 89-92; 53-56; DLB 114, 264;
EWL 3

Pales Matos, Luis 1898-1959 .... **HLCS 2**
See Pales Matos, Luis
See also DLB 290; HW 1; LAW

Paley, Grace 1922-2007 ... **CLC 4, 6, 37, 140, 272; SSC 8**
See also AMWS 6; CA 25-28R; 263; CANR
13, 46, 74, 118; CN 2, 3, 4, 5, 6, 7; CPW;
DA3; DAM POP; DLB 28, 218; EWL 3;
EXPS; FW; INT CANR-13; MAL 5;
MBL; MTCW 1, 2; MTFW 2005; RGAL
4; RGSF 2; SSFS 3, 20, 27

Paley, Grace Goodside
See Paley, Grace

Palin, Michael 1943- .... **CLC 21**
See also CA 107; CANR 35, 109, 179; DLB
352; SATA 67

Palin, Michael Edward
See Palin, Michael

Palliser, Charles 1947- .... **CLC 65**
See also CA 136; CANR 76; CN 5, 6, 7

Palma, Ricardo 1833-1919 .... **TCLC 29**
See also CA 168; LAW

Pamuk, Orhan 1952- .... **CLC 185**
See also CA 142; CANR 75, 127, 172;
CWW 2; NFS 27; WLIT 6

Pancake, Breece Dexter 1952-1979 . **CLC 29; SSC 61**
See also CA 123; 109; DLB 130

Pancake, Breece D'J
See Pancake, Breece Dexter

Panchenko, Nikolai CLC 59

Pankhurst, Emmeline (Goulden)
1858-1928 .... **TCLC 100**
See also CA 116; FW

Panko, Rudy
See Gogol, Nikolai (Vasilyevich)

Papadiamantis, Alexandros
1851-1911 .... **TCLC 29**
See also CA 168; EWL 3

Papadiamantopoulos, Johannes
1856-1910 .... **TCLC 18**
See also CA 117; 242; GFL 1789 to the
Present

Papadiamantopoulos, Yannis
See Papadiamantopoulos, Johannes

Papini, Giovanni 1881-1956 .... **TCLC 22**
See also CA 121; 180; DLB 264

Paracelsus 1493-1541 .... **LC 14**
See also DLB 179

Parasol, Peter
See Stevens, Wallace

Pardo Bazan, Emilia 1851-1921 .... **SSC 30; TCLC 189**
See also EWL 3; FW; RGSF 2; RGWL 2, 3

Paredes, Americo 1915-1999 .... **PC 83**
See also CA 37-40R; 179; DLB 209; EXPP;
HW 1

Pareto, Vilfredo 1848-1923 .... **TCLC 69**
See also CA 175

Paretsky, Sara 1947- .... **CLC 135**
See also AAYA 30; BEST 90:3; CA 125;
129; CANR 59, 95, 184; CMW 4; CPW;
DA3; DAM POP; DLB 306; INT CA-129;
MSW; RGAL 4

Paretsky, Sara N.
See Paretsky, Sara

Parfenie, Maria
See Codrescu, Andrei

Parini, Jay (Lee) 1948- .... **CLC 54, 133**
See also CA 97-100; 229; CAAE 229;
CAAS 16; CANR 32, 87

Park, Jordan
See Kornbluth, C(yril) M.; Pohl, Frederik

Park, Robert E(zra) 1864-1944 ..... **TCLC 73**
See also CA 122; 165

Parker, Bert
See Ellison, Harlan

Parker, Dorothy (Rothschild)
1893-1967 . **CLC 15, 68; PC 28; SSC 2, 101; TCLC 143**
See also AMWS 9; CA 19-20; 25-28R; CAP
2; DA3; DAM POET; DLB 11, 45, 86;
EXPP; FW; MAL 5; MBL; MTCW 1, 2;
MTFW 2005; PFS 18; RGAL 4; RGSF 2;
TUS

Parker, Robert B. 1932- .... **CLC 27**
See also AAYA 28; BEST 89:4; BPFB 3;
CA 49-52; CANR 1, 26, 52, 89, 128, 165;
CMW 4; CPW; DAM NOV, POP; DLB
306; INT CANR-26; MSW; MTCW 1;
MTFW 2005

Parker, Robert Brown
See Parker, Robert B.

Parker, Theodore 1810-1860 .... **NCLC 186**
See also DLB 1, 235

Parkes, Lucas
See Harris, John (Wyndham Parkes Lucas)
Beynon

Parkin, Frank 1940- .... **CLC 43**
See also CA 147

Parkman, Francis, Jr. 1823-1893 .. **NCLC 12**
See also AMWS 2; DLB 1, 30, 183, 186,
235; RGAL 4

Parks, Gordon 1912-2006 . **BLC 1:3; CLC 1, 16**
See also AAYA 36; AITN 2; BW 2, 3; CA
41-44R; 249; CANR 26, 66, 145; DA3;
DAM MULT; DLB 33; MTCW 2; MTFW
2005; SATA 8, 108; SATA-Obit 175

Parks, Suzan-Lori 1964(?)- ..... **BLC 2:3; DC 23**
See also AAYA 55; CA 201; CAD; CD 5,
6; CWD; DFS 22; DLB 341; RGAL 4

Parks, Tim(othy Harold) 1954- ...... **CLC 147**
See also CA 126; 131; CANR 77, 144; CN
7; DLB 231; INT CA-131

Parmenides c. 515B.C.-c.
450B.C. .... **CMLC 22**
See also DLB 176

Parnell, Thomas 1679-1718 .... **LC 3**
See also DLB 95; RGEL 2

Parr, Catherine c. 1513(?)-1548 .... **LC 86**
See also DLB 136

Parra, Nicanor 1914- ... **CLC 2, 102; HLC 2; PC 39**
See also CA 85-88; CANR 32; CWW 2;
DAM MULT; DLB 283; EWL 3; HW 1;
LAW; MTCW 1

Parra Sanojo, Ana Teresa de la 1890-1936
See de la Parra, Teresa

Parrish, Mary Frances
See Fisher, M(ary) F(rances) K(ennedy)

Parshchikov, Aleksei 1954- .... **CLC 59**
See also DLB 285

Parshchikov, Aleksei Maksimovich
See Parshchikov, Aleksei

Parson, Professor
See Coleridge, Samuel Taylor

Parson Lot
See Kingsley, Charles

Parton, Sara Payson Willis
1811-1872 .... **NCLC 86**
See also DLB 43, 74, 239

Partridge, Anthony
See Oppenheim, E(dward) Phillips

Pascal, Blaise 1623-1662 .... **LC 35**
See also DLB 268; EW 3; GFL Beginnings
to 1789; RGWL 2, 3; TWA

Pascoli, Giovanni 1855-1912 .... **TCLC 45**
See also CA 170; EW 7; EWL 3

Pasolini, Pier Paolo 1922-1975 .. **CLC 20, 37, 106; PC 17**
See also CA 93-96; 61-64; CANR 63; DLB
128, 177; EWL 3; MTCW 1; RGWL 2, 3

Pasquini
See Silone, Ignazio

Pastan, Linda (Olenik) 1932- .... **CLC 27**
See also CA 61-64; CANR 18, 40, 61, 113;
CP 3, 4, 5, 6, 7; CSW; CWP; DAM
POET; DLB 5; PFS 8, 25

Pasternak, Boris 1890-1960 ... **CLC 7, 10, 18, 63; PC 6; SSC 31; TCLC 188; WLC 4**
See also BPFB 3; CA 127; 116; DA; DA3;
DAB; DAC; DAM MST, NOV, POET;
DLB 302, 331; EW 10; MTCW 1, 2;
MTFW 2005; NFS 26; RGSF 2; RGWL
2, 3; TWA; WP

Patchen, Kenneth 1911-1972 .... **CLC 1, 2, 18**
See also BG 1:3; CA 1-4R; 33-36R; CANR
3, 35; CN 1; CP 1; DAM POET; DLB 16,
48; EWL 3; MAL 5; MTCW 1; RGAL 4

Patchett, Ann 1963- .... **CLC 244**
See also AAYA 69; AMWS 12; CA 139;
CANR 64, 110, 167; DLB 350; MTFW
2005; NFS 30

Pater, Walter (Horatio) 1839-1894 . **NCLC 7, 90, 159**
See also BRW 5; CDBLB 1832-1890; DLB
57, 156; RGEL 2; TEA

Paterson, A(ndrew) B(arton)
1864-1941 .... **TCLC 32**
See also CA 155; DLB 230; RGEL 2; SATA
97

Paterson, Banjo
See Paterson, A(ndrew) B(arton)

Paterson, Katherine 1932- .... **CLC 12, 30**
See also AAYA 1, 31; BYA 1, 2, 7; CA 21-
24R; CANR 28, 59, 111, 173; CLR 7, 50,
127; CWRI 5; DLB 52; JRDA; LAIT 4;
MAICYA 1, 2; MAICYAS 1; MTCW 1;
SATA 13, 53, 92, 133; WYA; YAW

Paterson, Katherine Womeldorf
See Paterson, Katherine

Patmore, Coventry Kersey Dighton
1823-1896 .... **NCLC 9; PC 59**
See also DLB 35, 98; RGEL 2; TEA

Paton, Alan 1903-1988 ..... **CLC 4, 10, 25, 55, 106; TCLC 165; WLC 4**
See also AAYA 26; AFW; BPFB 3; BRWS
2; BYA 1; CA 13-16; 125; CANR 22;
CAP 1; CN 1, 2, 3, 4; DA; DA3; DAB;
DAC; DAM MST, NOV; DLB 225;
DLBD 17; EWL 3; EXPN; LAIT 4;
MTCW 1, 2; MTFW 2005; NFS 3, 12;
RGEL 2; SATA 11; SATA-Obit 56; TWA;
WLIT 2; WWE 1

Paton Walsh, Gillian
See Paton Walsh, Jill

Paton Walsh, Jill 1937- .... **CLC 35**
See also AAYA 11, 47; BYA 1, 8; CA 262;
CAAE 262; CANR 38, 83, 158; CLR 2,
6, 128; DLB 161; MAICYA 1, 2; SAAS
3; SATA 4, 72, 109, 190; SATA-
Essay 190; WYA; YAW

Patsauq, Markoosie 1942- .... **NNAL**
See also CA 101; CLR 23; CWRI 5; DAM
MULT

Patterson, (Horace) Orlando (Lloyd)
1940- .... **BLCS**
See also BW 1; CA 65-68; CANR 27, 84;
CN 1, 2, 3, 4, 5, 6

Patton, George S(mith), Jr.
1885-1945 .... **TCLC 79**
See also CA 189

Paulding, James Kirke 1778-1860 ... **NCLC 2**
See also DLB 3, 59, 74, 250; RGAL 4

Paulin, Thomas Neilson
See Paulin, Tom

Paulin, Tom 1949- .... **CLC 37, 177**
See also CA 123; 128; CANR 98; CP 3, 4,
5, 6, 7; DLB 40

Pausanias c. 1st cent. - .... **CMLC 36**

Paustovsky, Konstantin (Georgievich)
1892-1968 .... **CLC 40**
See also CA 93-96; 25-28R; DLB 272;
EWL 3

Pavese, Cesare 1908-1950 .... **PC 13; SSC 19;
TCLC 3**
See also CA 104; 169; DLB 128, 177; EW
12; EWL 3; PFS 20; RGSF 2; RGWL 2,
3; TWA; WLIT 7

Pavic, Milorad 1929- .... **CLC 60**
See also CA 136; CDWLB 4; CWW 2; DLB
181; EWL 3; RGWL 3

Pavlov, Ivan Petrovich 1849-1936 . **TCLC 91**
See also CA 118; 180

Pavlova, Karolina Karlovna
1807-1893 .... **NCLC 138**
See also DLB 205

Payne, Alan
See Jakes, John

Payne, Rachel Ann
See Jakes, John

Paz, Gil
See Lugones, Leopoldo

Paz, Octavio 1914-1998 . **CLC 3, 4, 6, 10, 19,
51, 65, 119; HLC 2; PC 1, 48; TCLC
211; WLC 4**
See also AAYA 50; CA 73-76; 165; CANR
32, 65, 104; CWW 2; DA; DA3; DAB;
DAC; DAM MST, MULT, POET; DLB
290, 331; DLBY 1990, 1998; DNFS 1;
EWL 3; HW 1, 2; LAW; LAWS 1; MTCW
1, 2; MTFW 2005; PFS 18, 30; RGWL 2,
3; SSFS 13; TWA; WLIT 1

p'Bitek, Okot 1931-1982 . **BLC 1:3; CLC 96;
TCLC 149**
See also AFW; BW 2, 3; CA 124; 107;
CANR 82; CP 1, 2, 3; DAM MULT; DLB
125; EWL 3; MTCW 1, 2; MTFW 2005;
RGEL 2; WLIT 2

Peabody, Elizabeth Palmer
1804-1894 .... **NCLC 169**
See also DLB 1, 223

Peacham, Henry 1578-1644(?) .... **LC 119**
See also DLB 151

Peacock, Molly 1947- .... **CLC 60**
See also CA 103, 262; CAAE 262; CAAS
21; CANR 52, 84; CP 5, 6, 7; CWP; DLB
120, 282

Peacock, Thomas Love
1785-1866 .... **NCLC 22; PC 87**
See also BRW 4; DLB 96, 116; RGEL 2;
RGSF 2

Peake, Mervyn 1911-1968 .... **CLC 7, 54**
See also CA 5-8R; 25-28R; CANR 3; DLB
15, 160, 255; FANT; MTCW 1; RGEL 2;
SATA 23; SFW 4

Pearce, Ann Philippa
See Pearce, Philippa

Pearce, Philippa 1920-2006 .... **CLC 21**
See also BYA 5; CA 5-8R; 255; CANR 4,
109; CLR 9; CWRI 5; DLB 161; FANT;
MAICYA 1; SATA 1, 67, 129; SATA-Obit
179

Pearl, Eric
See Elman, Richard (Martin)

Pearson, Jean Mary
See Gardam, Jane

Pearson, Thomas Reid
See Pearson, T.R.

Pearson, T.R. 1956- .... **CLC 39**
See also CA 120; 130; CANR 97, 147, 185;
CSW; INT CA-130

Peck, Dale 1967- .... **CLC 81**
See also CA 146; CANR 72, 127, 180; GLL
2

Peck, John (Frederick) 1941- .... **CLC 3**
See also CA 49-52; CANR 3, 100; CP 4, 5,
6, 7

Peck, Richard 1934- .... **CLC 21**
See also AAYA 1, 24; BYA 1, 6, 8, 11; CA
85-88; CANR 19, 38, 129, 178; CLR 15,
142; INT CANR-19; JRDA; MAICYA 1,
2; SAAS 2; SATA 18, 55, 97, 110, 158,
190; SATA-Essay 110; WYA; YAW

Peck, Richard Wayne
See Peck, Richard

Peck, Robert Newton 1928- .... **CLC 17**
See also AAYA 3, 43; BYA 1, 6; CA 81-84,
182; CAAE 182; CANR 31, 63, 127; CLR
45; DA; DAC; DAM MST; JRDA; LAIT
3; MAICYA 1, 2; NFS 29; SAAS 1; SATA
21, 62, 111, 156; SATA-Essay 108; WYA;
YAW

Peckinpah, David Samuel
See Peckinpah, Sam

Peckinpah, Sam 1925-1984 .... **CLC 20**
See also CA 109; 114; CANR 82

Pedersen, Knut 1859-1952 .. **TCLC 2, 14, 49,
151, 203**
See also AAYA 79; CA 104; 119; CANR
63; DLB 297, 330; EW 8; EWL 8; MTCW
1, 2; RGWL 2, 3

Peele, George 1556-1596 .... **DC 27; LC 115**
See also BRW 1; DLB 62, 167; RGEL 2

Peeslake, Gaffer
See Durrell, Lawrence (George)

Peguy, Charles (Pierre)
1873-1914 .... **TCLC 10**
See also CA 107; 193; DLB 258; EWL 3;
GFL 1789 to the Present

Peirce, Charles Sanders
1839-1914 .... **TCLC 81**
See also CA 194; DLB 270

Pelagius c. 350-c. 418 .... **CMLC 112**

Pelecanos, George P. 1957- .... **CLC 236**
See also CA 138; CANR 122, 165, 194;
DLB 306

Pelevin, Victor 1962- .... **CLC 238**
See also CA 154; CANR 88, 159; DLB 285

Pelevin, Viktor Olegovich
See Pelevin, Victor

Pellicer, Carlos 1897(?)-1977 .... **HLCS 2**
See also CA 153; 69-72; DLB 290; EWL 3;
HW 1

Pena, Ramon del Valle y
See Valle-Inclan, Ramon (Maria) del

Pendennis, Arthur Esquir
See Thackeray, William Makepeace

Penn, Arthur
See Matthews, (James) Brander

Penn, William 1644-1718 .... **LC 25**
See also DLB 24

PEPECE
See Prado (Calvo), Pedro

Pepys, Samuel 1633-1703 ... **LC 11, 58; WLC
4**
See also BRW 2; CDBLB 1660-1789; DA;
DA3; DAB; DAC; DAM MST; DLB 101,
213; NCFS 4; RGEL 2; TEA; WLIT 3

Percy, Thomas 1729-1811 .... **NCLC 95**
See also DLB 104

Percy, Walker 1916-1990 .... **CLC 2, 3, 6, 8,
14, 18, 47, 65**
See also AMWS 3; BPFB 3; CA 1-4R; 131;
CANR 1, 23, 64; CN 1, 2, 3, 4; CPW;
CSW; DA3; DAM NOV, POP; DLB 2;
DLBY 1980, 1990; EWL 3; MAL 5;
MTCW 1, 2; MTFW 2005; RGAL 4; TUS

Percy, William Alexander
1885-1942 .... **TCLC 84**
See also CA 163; MTCW 2

Perdurabo, Frater
See Crowley, Edward Alexander

Perec, Georges 1936-1982 .... **CLC 56, 116**
See also CA 141; DLB 83, 299; EWL 3;
GFL 1789 to the Present; RGHL; RGWL
3

**Pereda (y Sanchez de Porrua), Jose Maria
de** 1833-1906 .... **TCLC 16**
See also CA 117

Pereda y Porrua, Jose Maria de
See Pereda (y Sanchez de Porrua), Jose
Maria de

Peregoy, George Weems
See Mencken, H. L.

Perelman, S(idney) J(oseph)
1904-1979 .. **CLC 3, 5, 9, 15, 23, 44, 49;
SSC 32**
See also AAYA 79; AITN 1, 2; BPFB 3;
CA 73-76; 89-92; CANR 18; DAM
DRAM; DLB 11, 44; MTCW 1, 2; MTFW
2005; RGAL 4

Peret, Benjamin 1899-1959 .... **PC 33; TCLC
20**
See also CA 117; 186; GFL 1789 to the
Present

Perets, Yitskhok Leybush
See Peretz, Isaac Loeb

Peretz, Isaac Leib (?)-
See Peretz, Isaac Loeb

Peretz, Isaac Loeb 1851-1915 .... **SSC 26;
TCLC 16**
See Peretz, Isaac Leib
See also CA 109; 201; DLB 333

Peretz, Yitzkhok Leibush
See Peretz, Isaac Loeb

Perez Galdos, Benito 1843-1920 ..... **HLCS 2;
TCLC 27**
See also CA 125; 153; EW 7; EWL 3; HW
1; RGWL 2, 3

Peri Rossi, Cristina 1941- .. **CLC 156; HLCS
2**
See also CA 131; CANR 59, 81; CWW 2;
DLB 145, 290; EWL 3; HW 1, 2

Perlata
See Peret, Benjamin

Perloff, Marjorie G(abrielle)
1931- .... **CLC 137**
See also CA 57-60; CANR 7, 22, 49, 104

Perrault, Charles 1628-1703 .... **LC 2, 56**
See also BYA 4; CLR 79, 134; DLB 268;
GFL Beginnings to 1789; MAICYA 1, 2;
RGWL 2, 3; SATA 25; WCH

Perrotta, Tom 1961- .... **CLC 266**
See also CA 162; CANR 99, 155

Perry, Anne 1938- .... **CLC 126**
See also CA 101; CANR 22, 50, 84, 150,
177; CMW 4; CN 6, 7; CPW; DLB 276

Perry, Brighton
See Sherwood, Robert E(mmet)

Perse, St.-John
See Leger, Alexis Saint-Leger

Perse, Saint-John
See Leger, Alexis Saint-Leger
Persius 34-62 .... **CMLC 74**
See also AW 2; DLB 211; RGWL 2, 3
Perutz, Leo(pold) 1882-1957 .... **TCLC 60**
See also CA 147; DLB 81
Peseenz, Tulio F.
See Lopez y Fuentes, Gregorio
Pesetsky, Bette 1932- .... **CLC 28**
See also CA 133; DLB 130
Peshkov, Alexei Maximovich
1868-1936 .... **SSC 28; TCLC 8; WLC 3**
See also CA 105; 141; CANR 83; DA;
DAB; DAC; DAM DRAM; MST; NOV;
DFS 9; DLB 295; EW 8; EWL 3; MTCW
2; MTFW 2005; RGSF 2; RGWL 2, 3;
TWA
Pessoa, Fernando 1888-1935 .... **HLC 2; PC
20; TCLC 27**
See also CA 125; 183; CANR 182; DAM
MULT; DLB 287; EW 10; EWL 3; RGWL
2, 3; WP
Pessoa, Fernando Antonio Nogueira
See Pessoa, Fernando
Peterkin, Julia Mood 1880-1961 ...... **CLC 31**
See also CA 102; DLB 9
Peters, Joan K(aren) 1945- .... **CLC 39**
See also CA 158; CANR 109
Peters, Robert L(ouis) 1924- .... **CLC 7**
See also CA 13-16R; CAAS 8; CP 1, 5, 6,
7; DLB 105
Peters, S. H.
See Henry, O.
Petofi, Sandor 1823-1849 .... **NCLC 21**
See also RGWL 2, 3
Petrakis, Harry Mark 1923- .... **CLC 3**
See also CA 9-12R; CANR 4, 30, 85, 155;
CN 1, 2, 3, 4, 5, 6, 7
Petrarch 1304-1374 .... **CMLC 20; PC 8**
See also DA3; DAM POET; EW 2; LMFS
1; RGWL 2, 3; WLIT 7
Petronius c. 20-66 .... **CMLC 34**
See also AW 2; CDWLB 1; DLB 211;
RGWL 2, 3; WLIT 8
Petrov, Eugene
See Kataev, Evgeny Petrovich
Petrov, Evgenii
See Kataev, Evgeny Petrovich
Petrov, Evgeny
See Kataev, Evgeny Petrovich
Petrovsky, Boris
See Beauchamp, Kathleen Mansfield
Petry, Ann (Lane) 1908-1997 .. **CLC 1, 7, 18;
TCLC 112**
See also AFAW 1, 2; BPFB 3; BW 1, 3;
BYA 2; CA 5-8R; 157; CAAS 6; CANR
4, 46; CLR 12; CN 1, 2, 3, 4, 5, 6; DLB
76; EWL 3; JRDA; LAIT 1; MAICYA 1,
2; MAICYAS 1; MTCW 1; RGAL 4;
SATA 5; SATA-Obit 94; TUS
Petursson, Halligrimur 1614-1674 .... **LC 8**
Peychinovich
See Vazov, Ivan (Minchov)
Phaedrus c. 15B.C.-c. 50 .... **CMLC 25**
See also DLB 211
Phelge, Nanker
See Richards, Keith
Phelps (Ward), Elizabeth Stuart
See Phelps, Elizabeth Stuart
Phelps, Elizabeth Stuart
1844-1911 .... **TCLC 113**
See also CA 242; DLB 74; FW
Pheradausi
See Ferdowsi, Abu'l Qasem
Philippe de Remi c. 1247-1296 ... **CMLC 102**
Philips, Katherine 1632-1664 ..... **LC 30, 145;
PC 40**
See also DLB 131; RGEL 2

Philipson, Ilene J. 1950- .... **CLC 65**
See also CA 219
Philipson, Morris H. 1926- .... **CLC 53**
See also CA 1-4R; CANR 4
Phillips, Caryl 1958- ..... **BLCS; CLC 96, 224**
See also BRWS 5; BW 2; CA 141; CANR
63, 104, 140; CBD; CD 5, 6; CN 5, 6, 7;
DA3; DAM MULT; DLB 157; EWL 3;
MTCW 2; MTFW 2005; WLIT 4; WWE
1
Phillips, David Graham
1867-1911 .... **TCLC 44**
See also CA 108; 176; DLB 9, 12, 303;
RGAL 4
Phillips, Jack
See Sandburg, Carl (August)
Phillips, Jayne Anne 1952- .... **CLC 15, 33,
139; SSC 16**
See also AAYA 57; BPFB 3; CA 101;
CANR 24, 50, 96; CN 4, 5, 6, 7; CSW;
DLBY 1980; INT CANR-24; MTCW 1,
2; MTFW 2005; RGAL 4; RGSF 2; SSFS
4
Phillips, Richard
See Dick, Philip K.
Phillips, Robert (Schaeffer) 1938- .... **CLC 28**
See also CA 17-20R; CAAS 13; CANR 8;
DLB 105
Phillips, Ward
See Lovecraft, H. P.
Philo c. 20B.C.-c. 50 .... **CMLC 100**
See also DLB 176
Philostratus, Flavius c. 179-c.
244 .... **CMLC 62**
Phiradausi
See Ferdowsi, Abu'l Qasem
Piccolo, Lucio 1901-1969 .... **CLC 13**
See also CA 97-100; DLB 114; EWL 3
Pickthall, Marjorie L(owry) C(hristie)
1883-1922 .... **TCLC 21**
See also CA 107; DLB 92
Pico della Mirandola, Giovanni
1463-1494 .... **LC 15**
See also LMFS 1
Piercy, Marge 1936- .... **CLC 3, 6, 14, 18, 27,
62, 128; PC 29**
See also BPFB 3; CA 21-24R; 187; CAAE
187; CAAS 1; CANR 13, 43, 66, 111; CN
3, 4, 5, 6, 7; CP 1, 2, 3, 4, 5, 6, 7; CWP;
DLB 120, 227; EXPP; FW; MAL 5;
MTCW 1, 2; MTFW 2005; PFS 9, 22;
SFW 4
Piers, Robert
See Anthony, Piers
Pieyre de Mandiargues, Andre
1909-1991 .... **CLC 41**
See also CA 103; 136; CANR 22, 82; DLB
83; EWL 3; GFL 1789 to the Present
Pil'niak, Boris
See Vogau, Boris Andreyevich
Pil'niak, Boris Andreevich
See Vogau, Boris Andreyevich
Pilnyak, Boris 1894-1938
See Vogau, Boris Andreyevich
Pinchback, Eugene
See Toomer, Jean
Pincherle, Alberto 1907-1990 .. **CLC 2, 7, 11,
27, 46; SSC 26**
See also CA 25-28R; 132; CANR 33, 63,
142; DAM NOV; DLB 127; EW 12; EWL
3; MTCW 2; MTFW 2005; RGSF 2;
RGWL 2, 3; WLIT 7
Pinckney, Darryl 1953- .... **CLC 76**
See also BW 2, 3; CA 143; CANR 79
Pindar 518(?)B.C.-438(?)B.C. .... **CMLC 12;
PC 19**
See also AW 1; CDWLB 1; DLB 176;
RGWL 2

Pineda, Cecile 1942- .... **CLC 39**
See also CA 118; DLB 209
Pinero, Arthur Wing 1855-1934 .... **TCLC 32**
See also CA 110; 153; DAM DRAM; DLB
10, 344; RGEL 2
Pinero, Miguel (Antonio Gomez)
1946-1988 .... **CLC 4, 55**
See also CA 61-64; 125; CAD; CANR 29,
90; DLB 266; HW 1; LLW
Pinget, Robert 1919-1997 .... **CLC 7, 13, 37**
See also CA 85-88; 160; CWW 2; DLB 83;
EWL 3; GFL 1789 to the Present
Pink Floyd
See Barrett, (Roger) Syd; Gilmour, David;
Mason, Nick; Waters, Roger; Wright, Rick
Pinkney, Edward 1802-1828 .... **NCLC 31**
See also DLB 248
Pinkwater, D. Manus
See Pinkwater, Daniel
Pinkwater, Daniel 1941- .... **CLC 35**
See also AAYA 1, 46; BYA 9; CA 29-32R;
CANR 12, 38, 89, 143; CLR 4; CSW;
FANT; JRDA; MAICYA 1, 2; SAAS 3;
SATA 8, 46, 76, 114, 158; SFW 4; YAW
Pinkwater, Daniel M.
See Pinkwater, Daniel
Pinkwater, Daniel Manus
See Pinkwater, Daniel
Pinkwater, Manus
See Pinkwater, Daniel
Pinsky, Robert 1940- .... **CLC 9, 19, 38, 94,
121, 216; PC 27**
See also AMWS 6; CA 29-32R; CAAS 4;
CANR 58, 97, 138, 177; CP 3, 4, 5, 6, 7;
DA3; DAM POET; DLBY 1982, 1998;
MAL 5; MTCW 2; MTFW 2005; PFS 18;
RGAL 4; TCLE 1:2
Pinta, Harold
See Pinter, Harold
Pinter, Harold 1930-2008 ...... **CLC 1, 3, 6, 9,
11, 15, 27, 58, 73, 199; DC 15; WLC 4**
See also BRWR 1; BRWS 1; CA 5-8R; 280;
CANR 33, 65, 112, 145; CBD; CD 5, 6;
CDBLB 1960 to Present; CP 1; DA; DA3;
DAB; DAC; DAM DRAM, MST; DFS 3,
5, 7, 14, 25; DLB 13, 310, 331; EWL 3;
IDFW 3, 4; LMFS 2; MTCW 1, 2; MTFW
2005; RGEL 2; RGHL; TEA
Piozzi, Hester Lynch (Thrale)
1741-1821 .... **NCLC 57**
See also DLB 104, 142
Pirandello, Luigi 1867-1936 .. **DC 5; SSC 22;
TCLC 4, 29, 172; WLC 4**
See also CA 104; 153; CANR 103; DA;
DA3; DAB; DAC; DAM DRAM, MST;
DFS 4, 9; DLB 264, 331; EW 8; EWL 3;
MTCW 2; MTFW 2005; RGSF 2; RGWL
2, 3; WLIT 7
Pirdousi
See Ferdowsi, Abu'l Qasem
Pirdousi, Abu-l-Qasim
See Ferdowsi, Abu'l Qasem
Pirsig, Robert M(aynard) 1928- ... **CLC 4, 6,
73**
See also CA 53-56; CANR 42, 74; CPW 1;
DA3; DAM POP; MTCW 1, 2; MTFW
2005; SATA 39
Pisan, Christine de
See Christine de Pizan
Pisarev, Dmitrii Ivanovich
See Pisarev, Dmitry Ivanovich
Pisarev, Dmitry Ivanovich
1840-1868 .... **NCLC 25**
See also DLB 277
Pix, Mary (Griffith) 1666-1709 ..... **LC 8, 149**
See also DLB 80
Pixerecourt, (Rene Charles) Guilbert de
1773-1844 .... **NCLC 39**
See also DLB 192; GFL 1789 to the Present

Puig, Manuel 1932-1990 .... **CLC 3, 5, 10, 28, 65, 133; HLC 2**
See also BPFB 3; CA 45-48; CANR 2, 32, 63; CDWLB 3; DA3; DAM MULT; DLB 113; DNFS 1; EWL 3; GLL 1; HW 1, 2; LAW; MTCW 1, 2; MTFW 2005; RGWL 2, 3; TWA; WLIT 1

Pulitzer, Joseph 1847-1911 .... **TCLC 76**
See also CA 114; DLB 23

Pullman, Philip 1946- .... **CLC 245**
See also AAYA 15, 41; BRWS 13; BYA 8, 13; CA 127; CANR 50, 77, 105, 134, 190; CLR 20, 62, 84; JRDA; MAICYA 1, 2; MAICYAS 1; MTFW 2005; SAAS 17; SATA 65, 103, 150, 198; SUFW 2; WYAS 1; YAW

Purchas, Samuel 1577(?)-1626 .... **LC 70**
See also DLB 151

Purdy, A(lfred) W(ellington)
1918-2000 .... **CLC 3, 6, 14, 50**
See also CA 81-84; 189; CAAS 17; CANR 42, 66; CP 1, 2, 3, 4, 5, 6, 7; DAC; DAM MST, POET; DLB 88; PFS 5; RGEL 2

Purdy, James 1914-2009 .... **CLC 2, 4, 10, 28, 52**
See also AMWS 7; CA 33-36R; 284; CAAS 1; CANR 19, 51, 132; CN 1, 2, 3, 4, 5, 6, 7; DLB 2, 218; EWL 3; INT CANR-19; MAL 5; MTCW 1; RGAL 4

Purdy, James Amos
See Purdy, James

Purdy, James Otis
See Purdy, James

Pure, Simon
See Swinnerton, Frank Arthur

Pushkin, Aleksandr Sergeevich
See Pushkin, Alexander

Pushkin, Alexander 1799-1837 . **NCLC 3, 27, 83; PC 10; SSC 27, 55, 99; WLC 5**
See also DA; DA3; DAB; DAC; DAM DRAM, MST, POET; DLB 205; EW 5; EXPS; PFS 28; RGSF 2; RGWL 2, 3; SATA 61; SSFS 9; TWA

Pushkin, Alexander Sergeyevich
See Pushkin, Alexander

P'u Sung-ling 1640-1715 .... **LC 49; SSC 31**

Putnam, Arthur Lee
See Alger, Horatio, Jr.

Puttenham, George 1529(?)-1590 ...... **LC 116**
See also DLB 281

Puzo, Mario 1920-1999 .... **CLC 1, 2, 6, 36, 107**
See also BPFB 3; CA 65-68; 185; CANR 4, 42, 65, 99, 131; CN 1, 2, 3, 4, 5, 6; CPW; DA3; DAM NOV, POP; DLB 6; MTCW 1, 2; MTFW 2005; NFS 16; RGAL 4

Pygge, Edward
See Barnes, Julian

Pyle, Ernest Taylor 1900-1945 .... **TCLC 75**
See also CA 115; 160; DLB 29; MTCW 2

Pyle, Ernie
See Pyle, Ernest Taylor

Pyle, Howard 1853-1911 .... **TCLC 81**
See also AAYA 57; BYA 2, 4; CA 109; 137; CLR 22, 117; DLB 42, 188; DLBD 13; LAIT 1; MAICYA 1, 2; SATA 16, 100; WCH; YAW

Pym, Barbara (Mary Crampton)
1913-1980 .... **CLC 13, 19, 37, 111**
See also BPFB 3; BRWS 2; CA 13-14; 97-100; CANR 13, 34; CAP 1; DLB 14, 207; DLBY 1987; EWL 3; MTCW 1, 2; MTFW 2005; RGEL 2; TEA

Pynchon, Thomas 1937- .. **CLC 2, 3, 6, 9, 11, 18, 33, 62, 72, 123, 192, 213; SSC 14, 84; WLC 5**
See also AMWS 2; BEST 90:2; BPFB 3; CA 17-20R; CANR 22, 46, 73, 142; CN 1, 2, 3, 4, 5, 6, 7; CPW 1; DA; DA3;

DAB; DAC; DAM MST, NOV, POP; DLB 2, 173; EWL 3; MAL 5; MTCW 1, 2; MTFW 2005; NFS 23; RGAL 4; SFW 4; TCLE 1:2; TUS

Pythagoras c. 582B.C.-c. 507B.C. . **CMLC 22**
See also DLB 176

Q
See Quiller-Couch, Sir Arthur (Thomas)

Qian, Chongzhu
See Ch'ien, Chung-shu

Qian, Sima 145B.C.-c. 89B.C. .... **CMLC 72**

Qian Zhongshu
See Ch'ien, Chung-shu

Qroll
See Dagerman, Stig (Halvard)

Quarles, Francis 1592-1644 .... **LC 117**
See also DLB 126; RGEL 2

Quarrington, Paul 1953- .... **CLC 65**
See also CA 129; CANR 62, 95

Quarrington, Paul Lewis
See Quarrington, Paul

Quasimodo, Salvatore 1901-1968 .... **CLC 10; PC 47**
See also CA 13-16; 25-28R; CAP 1; DLB 114, 332; EW 12; EWL 3; MTCW 1; RGWL 2, 3

Quatermass, Martin
See Carpenter, John (Howard)

Quay, Stephen 1947- .... **CLC 95**
See also CA 189

Quay, Timothy 1947- .... **CLC 95**
See also CA 189

Queen, Ellery
See Dannay, Frederic; Hoch, Edward D.; Lee, Manfred B.; Marlowe, Stephen; Sturgeon, Theodore (Hamilton); Vance, Jack

Queneau, Raymond 1903-1976 ..... **CLC 2, 5, 10, 42**
See also CA 77-80; 69-72; CANR 32; DLB 72, 258; EW 12; EWL 3; GFL 1789 to the Present; MTCW 1, 2; RGWL 2, 3

Quevedo, Francisco de 1580-1645 ...... **LC 23, 160**

Quiller-Couch, Sir Arthur (Thomas)
1863-1944 .... **TCLC 53**
See also CA 118; 166; DLB 135, 153, 190; HGG; RGEL 2; SUFW 1

Quin, Ann 1936-1973 .... **CLC 6**
See also CA 9-12R; 45-48; CANR 148; CN 1; DLB 14, 231

Quin, Ann Marie
See Quin, Ann

Quincey, Thomas de
See De Quincey, Thomas

Quindlen, Anna 1953- .... **CLC 191**
See also AAYA 35; AMWS 17; CA 138; CANR 73, 126; DA3; DLB 292; MTCW 2; MTFW 2005

Quinn, Martin
See Smith, Martin Cruz

Quinn, Peter 1947- .... **CLC 91**
See also CA 197; CANR 147

Quinn, Peter A.
See Quinn, Peter

Quinn, Simon
See Smith, Martin Cruz

Quintana, Leroy V. 1944- ...... **HLC 2; PC 36**
See also CA 131; CANR 65, 139; DAM MULT; DLB 82; HW 1, 2

Quintilian c. 40-c. 100 .... **CMLC 77**
See also AW 2; DLB 211; RGWL 2, 3

Quiroga, Horacio (Sylvestre)
1878-1937 ... **HLC 2; SSC 89; TCLC 20**
See also CA 117; 131; DAM MULT; EWL 3; HW 1; LAW; MTCW 1; RGSF 2; WLIT 1

Quoirez, Francoise 1935-2004 ... **CLC 3, 6, 9, 17, 36**
See also CA 49-52; 231; CANR 6, 39, 73; CWW 2; DLB 83; EWL 3; GFL 1789 to the Present; MTCW 1, 2; MTFW 2005; TWA

Raabe, Wilhelm (Karl) 1831-1910 . **TCLC 45**
See also CA 167; DLB 129

Rabe, David (William) 1940- .. **CLC 4, 8, 33, 200; DC 16**
See also CA 85-88; CABS 3; CAD; CANR 59, 129; CD 5, 6; DAM DRAM; DFS 3, 8, 13; DLB 7, 228; EWL 3; MAL 5

Rabelais, Francois 1494-1553 .... **LC 5, 60; WLC 5**
See also DA; DAB; DAC; DAM MST; DLB 327; EW 2; GFL Beginnings to 1789; LMFS 1; RGWL 2, 3; TWA

Rabi'a al-'Adawiyya c. 717-c. 801 .... **CMLC 83**
See also DLB 311

Rabinovitch, Sholem 1859-1916 .... **SSC 33, 125; TCLC 1, 35**
See also CA 104; DLB 333; TWA

Rabinovitsh, Sholem Yankev
See Rabinovitch, Sholem

Rabinowitz, Sholem Yakov
See Rabinovitch, Sholem

Rabinowitz, Solomon
See Rabinovitch, Sholem

Rabinyan, Dorit 1972- .... **CLC 119**
See also CA 170; CANR 147

Rachilde
See Vallette, Marguerite Eymery; Vallette, Marguerite Eymery

Racine, Jean 1639-1699 .. **DC 32; LC 28, 113**
See also DA3; DAB; DAM MST; DLB 268; EW 3; GFL Beginnings to 1789; LMFS 1; RGWL 2, 3; TWA

Radcliffe, Ann (Ward) 1764-1823 ... **NCLC 6, 55, 106**
See also DLB 39, 178; GL 3; HGG; LMFS 1; RGEL 2; SUFW; WLIT 3

Radclyffe-Hall, Marguerite
See Hall, Radclyffe

Radiguet, Raymond 1903-1923 ...... **TCLC 29**
See also CA 162; DLB 65; EWL 3; GFL 1789 to the Present; RGWL 2, 3

Radishchev, Aleksandr Nikolaevich
1749-1802 .... **NCLC 190**
See also DLB 150

Radishchev, Alexander
See Radishchev, Aleksandr Nikolaevich

Radnoti, Miklos 1909-1944 .... **TCLC 16**
See also CA 118; 212; CDWLB 4; DLB 215; EWL 3; RGHL; RGWL 2, 3

Rado, James 1939- .... **CLC 17**
See also CA 105

Radvanyi, Netty 1900-1983 .... **CLC 7**
See also CA 85-88; 110; CANR 82; CDWLB 2; DLB 69; EWL 3

Rae, Ben
See Griffiths, Trevor

Raeburn, John (Hay) 1941- .... **CLC 34**
See also CA 57-60

Ragni, Gerome 1942-1991 .... **CLC 17**
See also CA 105; 134

Rahv, Philip
See Greenberg, Ivan

Rai, Navab
See Srivastava, Dhanpat Rai

Raimund, Ferdinand Jakob
1790-1836 .... **NCLC 69**
See also DLB 90

Raine, Craig 1944- .... **CLC 32, 103**
See also BRWS 13; CA 108; CANR 29, 51, 103, 171; CP 3, 4, 5, 6, 7; DLB 40; PFS 7

Raine, Craig Anthony
See Raine, Craig

Raine, Kathleen (Jessie) 1908-2003 .. **CLC 7, 45**
See also CA 85-88; 218; CANR 46, 109; CP 1, 2, 3, 4, 5, 6, 7; DLB 20; EWL 3; MTCW 1; RGEL 2

Rainis, Janis 1865-1929 .... **TCLC 29**
See also CA 170; CDWLB 4; DLB 220; EWL 3

Rakosi, Carl
See Rawley, Callman

Ralegh, Sir Walter
See Raleigh, Sir Walter

Raleigh, Richard
See Lovecraft, H. P.

Raleigh, Sir Walter 1554(?)-1618 .... **LC 31, 39; PC 31**
See also BRW 1; CDBLB Before 1660; DLB 172; EXPP; PFS 14; RGEL 2; TEA; WP

Rallentando, H. P.
See Sayers, Dorothy L(eigh)

Ramal, Walter
See de la Mare, Walter (John)

Ramana Maharshi 1879-1950 .... **TCLC 84**

Ramoacn y Cajal, Santiago 1852-1934 .... **TCLC 93**

Ramon, Juan
See Jimenez (Mantecon), Juan Ramon

Ramos, Graciliano 1892-1953 .... **TCLC 32**
See also CA 167; DLB 307; EWL 3; HW 2; LAW; WLIT 1

Rampersad, Arnold 1941- .... **CLC 44**
See also BW 2, 3; CA 127; 133; CANR 81; DLB 111; INT CA-133

Rampling, Anne
See Rice, Anne

Ramsay, Allan 1686(?)-1758 .... **LC 29**
See also DLB 95; RGEL 2

Ramsay, Jay
See Campbell, Ramsey

Ramuz, Charles-Ferdinand 1878-1947 .... **TCLC 33**
See also CA 165; EWL 3

Rand, Ayn 1905-1982 ...... **CLC 3, 30, 44, 79; SSC 116; WLC 5**
See also AAYA 10; AMWS 4; BPFB 3; BYA 12; CA 13-16R; 105; CANR 27, 73; CDALBS; CN 1, 2, 3; CPW; DA; DA3; DAC; DAM MST, NOV, POP; DLB 227, 279; MTCW 1, 2; MTFW 2005; NFS 10, 16, 29; RGAL 4; SFW 4; TUS; YAW

Randall, Dudley (Felker) 1914-2000 .... **BLC 1:3; CLC 1, 135; PC 86**
See also BW 1, 3; CA 25-28R; 189; CANR 23, 82; CP 1, 2, 3, 4, 5; DAM MULT; DLB 41; PFS 5

Randall, Robert
See Silverberg, Robert

Ranger, Ken
See Creasey, John

Rank, Otto 1884-1939 .... **TCLC 115**

Rankin, Ian 1960- .... **CLC 257**
See also BRWS 10; CA 148; CANR 81, 137, 171; DLB 267; MTFW 2005

Rankin, Ian James
See Rankin, Ian

Ransom, John Crowe 1888-1974 .. **CLC 2, 4, 5, 11, 24; PC 61**
See also AMW; CA 5-8R; 49-52; CANR 6, 34; CDALBS; CP 1; DA3; DAM POET; DLB 45, 63; EWL 3; EXPP; MAL 5; MTCW 1, 2; MTFW 2005; RGAL 4; TUS

Rao, Raja 1908-2006 . **CLC 25, 56, 255; SSC 99**
See also CA 73-76; 252; CANR 51; CN 1, 2, 3, 4, 5, 6; DAM NOV; DLB 323; EWL 3; MTCW 1, 2; MTFW 2005; RGEL 2; RGSF 2

Raphael, Frederic (Michael) 1931- ... **CLC 2, 14**
See also CA 1-4R; CANR 1, 86; CN 1, 2, 3, 4, 5, 6, 7; DLB 14, 319; TCLE 1:2

Raphael, Lev 1954- .... **CLC 232**
See also CA 134; CANR 72, 145; GLL 1

Ratcliffe, James P.
See Mencken, H. L.

Rathbone, Julian 1935-2008 .... **CLC 41**
See also CA 101; 269; CANR 34, 73, 152

Rathbone, Julian Christopher
See Rathbone, Julian

Rattigan, Terence (Mervyn) 1911-1977 .... **CLC 7; DC 18**
See also BRWS 7; CA 85-88; 73-76; CBD; CDBLB 1945-1960; DAM DRAM; DFS 8; DLB 13; IDFW 3, 4; MTCW 1, 2; MTFW 2005; RGEL 2

Ratushinskaya, Irina 1954- .... **CLC 54**
See also CA 129; CANR 68; CWW 2

Raven, Simon (Arthur Noel) 1927-2001 .... **CLC 14**
See also CA 81-84; 197; CANR 86; CN 1, 2, 3, 4, 5, 6; DLB 271

Ravenna, Michael
See Welty, Eudora

Rawley, Callman 1903-2004 .... **CLC 47**
See also CA 21-24R; 228; CAAS 5; CANR 12, 32, 91; CP 1, 2, 3, 4, 5, 6, 7; DLB 193

Rawlings, Marjorie Kinnan 1896-1953 .... **TCLC 4**
See also AAYA 20; AMWS 10; ANW; BPFB 3; BYA 3; CA 104; 137; CANR 74; CLR 63; DLB 9, 22, 102; DLBD 17; JRDA; MAICYA 1, 2; MAL 5; MTCW 2; MTFW 2005; RGAL 4; SATA 100; WCH; YABC 1; YAW

Ray, Satyajit 1921-1992 .... **CLC 16, 76**
See also CA 114; 137; DAM MULT

Read, Herbert Edward 1893-1968 ..... **CLC 4**
See also BRW 6; CA 85-88; 25-28R; DLB 20, 149; EWL 3; PAB; RGEL 2

Read, Piers Paul 1941- .... **CLC 4, 10, 25**
See also CA 21-24R; CANR 38, 86, 150; CN 2, 3, 4, 5, 6, 7; DLB 14; SATA 21

Reade, Charles 1814-1884 .... **NCLC 2, 74**
See also DLB 21; RGEL 2

Reade, Hamish
See Gray, Simon

Reading, Peter 1946- .... **CLC 47**
See also BRWS 8; CA 103; CANR 46, 96; CP 5, 6, 7; DLB 40

Reaney, James 1926-2008 .... **CLC 13**
See also CA 41-44R; CAAS 15; CANR 42; CD 5, 6; CP 1, 2, 3, 4, 5, 6, 7; DAC; DAM MST; DLB 68; RGEL 2; SATA 43

Reaney, James Crerar
See Reaney, James

Rebreanu, Liviu 1885-1944 .... **TCLC 28**
See also CA 165; DLB 220; EWL 3

Rechy, John 1934- ..... **CLC 1, 7, 14, 18, 107; HLC 2**
See also CA 5-8R, 195; CAAE 195; CAAS 4; CANR 6, 32, 64, 152, 188; CN 1, 2, 3, 4, 5, 6, 7; DAM MULT; DLB 122, 278; DLBY 1982; HW 1, 2; INT CANR-6; LLW; MAL 5; RGAL 4

Rechy, John Francisco
See Rechy, John

Redcam, Tom 1870-1933 .... **TCLC 25**

Reddin, Keith 1956- .... **CLC 67**
See also CAD; CD 6

Redgrove, Peter (William) 1932-2003 .... **CLC 6, 41**
See also BRWS 6; CA 1-4R; 217; CANR 3, 39, 77; CP 1, 2, 3, 4, 5, 6, 7; DLB 40; TCLE 1:2

Redmon, Anne
See Nightingale, Anne Redmon

Reed, Eliot
See Ambler, Eric

Reed, Ishmael 1938- . **BLC 1:3; CLC 2, 3, 5, 6, 13, 32, 60, 174; PC 68**
See also AFAW 1, 2; AMWS 10; BPFB 3; BW 2, 3; CA 21-24R; CANR 25, 48, 74, 128; CN 1, 2, 3, 4, 5, 6, 7; CP 1, 2, 3, 4, 5, 6, 7; CSW; DA3; DAM MULT; DLB 2, 5, 33, 169, 227; DLBD 8; EWL 3; LMFS 2; MAL 5; MSW; MTCW 1, 2; MTFW 2005; PFS 6; RGAL 4; TCWW 2

Reed, John (Silas) 1887-1920 .... **TCLC 9**
See also CA 106; 195; MAL 5; TUS

Reed, Lou
See Firbank, Louis

Reese, Lizette Woodworth 1856-1935 .... **PC 29; TCLC 181**
See also CA 180; DLB 54

Reeve, Clara 1729-1807 .... **NCLC 19**
See also DLB 39; RGEL 2

Reich, Wilhelm 1897-1957 .... **TCLC 57**
See also CA 199

Reid, Christopher (John) 1949- .... **CLC 33**
See also CA 140; CANR 89; CP 4, 5, 6, 7; DLB 40; EWL 3

Reid, Desmond
See Moorcock, Michael

Reid Banks, Lynne 1929- .... **CLC 23**
See also AAYA 6; BYA 7; CA 1-4R; CANR 6, 22, 38, 87; CLR 24, 86; CN 4, 5, 6; JRDA; MAICYA 1, 2; SATA 22, 75, 111, 165; YAW

Reilly, William K.
See Creasey, John

Reiner, Max
See Caldwell, (Janet Miriam) Taylor (Holland)

Reis, Ricardo
See Pessoa, Fernando

Reizenstein, Elmer Leopold
See Rice, Elmer (Leopold)

Remarque, Erich Maria 1898-1970 . **CLC 21**
See also AAYA 27; BPFB 3; CA 77-80; 29-32R; CDWLB 2; DA; DA3; DAB; DAC; DAM MST, NOV; DLB 56; EWL 3; EXPN; LAIT 3; MTCW 1, 2; MTFW 2005; NFS 4; RGHL; RGWL 2, 3

Remington, Frederic S(ackrider) 1861-1909 .... **TCLC 89**
See also CA 108; 169; DLB 12, 186, 188; SATA 41; TCWW 2

Remizov, A.
See Remizov, Aleksei (Mikhailovich)

Remizov, A. M.
See Remizov, Aleksei (Mikhailovich)

Remizov, Aleksei (Mikhailovich) 1877-1957 .... **TCLC 27**
See also CA 125; 133; DLB 295; EWL 3

Remizov, Alexey Mikhaylovich
See Remizov, Aleksei (Mikhailovich)

Renan, Joseph Ernest 1823-1892 . **NCLC 26, 145**
See also GFL 1789 to the Present

Renard, Jules(-Pierre) 1864-1910 .. **TCLC 17**
See also CA 117; 202; GFL 1789 to the Present

Renart, Jean fl. 13th cent. - .... **CMLC 83**

Renault, Mary
See Challans, Mary

Rendell, Ruth 1930- .... **CLC 28, 48, 50**
See also BEST 90:4; BPFB 3; BRWS 9; CA 109; CANR 32, 52, 74, 127, 162, 190; CN 5, 6, 7; CPW; DAM POP; DLB 87, 276; INT CANR-32; MSW; MTCW 1, 2; MTFW 2005

Rivers, Conrad Kent 1933-1968 .... **CLC 1**
See also BW 1; CA 85-88; DLB 41

Rivers, Elfrida
See Bradley, Marion Zimmer

Riverside, John
See Heinlein, Robert A.

Rizal, Jose 1861-1896 .... **NCLC 27**
See also DLB 348

Roa Bastos, Augusto 1917-2005 ...... **CLC 45; HLC 2**
See also CA 131; 238; CWW 2; DAM MULT; DLB 113; EWL 3; HW 1; LAW; RGSF 2; WLIT 1

Roa Bastos, Augusto Jose Antonio
See Roa Bastos, Augusto

Robbe-Grillet, Alain 1922-2008 ..... **CLC 1, 2, 4, 6, 8, 10, 14, 43, 128**
See also BPFB 3; CA 9-12R; 269; CANR 33, 65, 115; CWW 2; DLB 83; EW 13; EWL 3; GFL 1789 to the Present; IDFW 3, 4; MTCW 1, 2; MTFW 2005; RGWL 2, 3; SSFS 15

Robbins, Harold 1916-1997 .... **CLC 5**
See also BPFB 3; CA 73-76; 162; CANR 26, 54, 112, 156; DA3; DAM NOV; MTCW 1, 2

Robbins, Thomas Eugene 1936- . **CLC 9, 32, 64**
See also AAYA 32; AMWS 10; BEST 90:3; BPFB 3; CA 81-84; CANR 29, 59, 95, 139; CN 3, 4, 5, 6, 7; CPW; CSW; DA3; DAM NOV, POP; DLBY 1980; MTCW 1, 2; MTFW 2005

Robbins, Tom
See Robbins, Thomas Eugene

Robbins, Trina 1938- .... **CLC 21**
See also AAYA 61; CA 128; CANR 152

Robert de Boron fl. 12th cent. - .... **CMLC 94**

Roberts, Charles G(eorge) D(ouglas)
1860-1943 .... **SSC 91; TCLC 8**
See also CA 105; 188; CLR 33; CWRI 5; DLB 92; RGEL 2; RGSF 2; SATA 88; SATA-Brief 29

Roberts, Elizabeth Madox
1886-1941 .... **TCLC 68**
See also CA 111; 166; CLR 100; CWRI 5; DLB 9, 54, 102; RGAL 4; RHW; SATA 33; SATA-Brief 27; TCWW 2; WCH

Roberts, Kate 1891-1985 .... **CLC 15**
See also CA 107; 116; DLB 319

Roberts, Keith (John Kingston)
1935-2000 .... **CLC 14**
See also BRWS 10; CA 25-28R; CANR 46; DLB 261; SFW 4

Roberts, Kenneth (Lewis)
1885-1957 .... **TCLC 23**
See also CA 109; 199; DLB 9; MAL 5; RGAL 4; RHW

Roberts, Michele 1949- .... **CLC 48, 178**
See also CA 115; CANR 58, 120, 164; CN 6, 7; DLB 231; FW

Roberts, Michele Brigitte
See Roberts, Michele

Robertson, Ellis
See Ellison, Harlan; Silverberg, Robert

Robertson, Thomas William
1829-1871 .... **NCLC 35**
See also DAM DRAM; DLB 344; RGEL 2

Robertson, Tom
See Robertson, Thomas William

Robeson, Kenneth
See Dent, Lester

Robinson, Edwin Arlington
1869-1935 .... **PC 1, 35; TCLC 5, 101**
See also AAYA 72; AMW; CA 104; 133; CDALB 1865-1917; DA; DAC; DAM MST, POET; DLB 54; EWL 3; EXPP; MAL 5; MTCW 1, 2; MTFW 2005; PAB; PFS 4; RGAL 4; WP

Robinson, Henry Crabb
1775-1867 .... **NCLC 15**
See also DLB 107

Robinson, Jill 1936- .... **CLC 10**
See also CA 102; CANR 120; INT CA-102

Robinson, Kim Stanley 1952- ... **CLC 34, 248**
See also AAYA 26; CA 126; CANR 113, 139, 173; CN 6, 7; MTFW 2005; SATA 109; SCFW 2; SFW 4

Robinson, Lloyd
See Silverberg, Robert

Robinson, Marilynne 1943- ..... **CLC 25, 180, 276**
See also AAYA 69; CA 116; CANR 80, 140, 192; CN 4, 5, 6, 7; DLB 206, 350; MTFW 2005; NFS 24

Robinson, Mary 1758-1800 .... **NCLC 142**
See also BRWS 13; DLB 158; FW

Robinson, Smokey
See Robinson, William, Jr.

Robinson, William, Jr. 1940- .... **CLC 21**
See also CA 116

Robison, Mary 1949- .... **CLC 42, 98**
See also CA 113; 116; CANR 87; CN 4, 5, 6, 7; DLB 130; INT CA-116; RGSF 2

Roches, Catherine des 1542-1587 ...... **LC 117**
See also DLB 327

Rochester
See Wilmot, John

Rod, Edouard 1857-1910 .... **TCLC 52**

Roddenberry, Eugene Wesley
1921-1991 .... **CLC 17**
See also AAYA 5; CA 110; 135; CANR 37; SATA 45; SATA-Obit 69

Roddenberry, Gene
See Roddenberry, Eugene Wesley

Rodgers, Mary 1931- .... **CLC 12**
See also BYA 5; CA 49-52; CANR 8, 55, 90; CLR 20; CWRI 5; INT CANR-8; JRDA; MAICYA 1, 2; SATA 8, 130

Rodgers, W(illiam) R(obert)
1909-1969 .... **CLC 7**
See also CA 85-88; DLB 20; RGEL 2

Rodman, Eric
See Silverberg, Robert

Rodman, Howard 1920(?)-1985 .... **CLC 65**
See also CA 118

Rodman, Maia
See Wojciechowska, Maia (Teresa)

Rodo, Jose Enrique 1871(?)-1917 .... **HLCS 2**
See also CA 178; EWL 3; HW 2; LAW

Rodolph, Utto
See Ouologuem, Yambo

Rodriguez, Claudio 1934-1999 .... **CLC 10**
See also CA 188; DLB 134

Rodriguez, Richard 1944- .... **CLC 155; HLC 2**
See also AMWS 14; CA 110; CANR 66, 116; DAM MULT; DLB 82, 256; HW 1, 2; LAIT 5; LLW; MTFW 2005; NCFS 3; WLIT 1

Roethke, Theodore 1908-1963 ... **CLC 1, 3, 8, 11, 19, 46, 101; PC 15**
See also AMW; CA 81-84; CABS 2; CDALB 1941-1968; DA3; DAM POET; DLB 5, 206; EWL 3; EXPP; MAL 5; MTCW 1, 2; PAB; PFS 3; RGAL 4; WP

Roethke, Theodore Huebner
See Roethke, Theodore

Rogers, Carl R(ansom)
1902-1987 .... **TCLC 125**
See also CA 1-4R; 121; CANR 1, 18; MTCW 1

Rogers, Samuel 1763-1855 .... **NCLC 69**
See also DLB 93; RGEL 2

Rogers, Thomas 1927-2007 .... **CLC 57**
See also CA 89-92; 259; CANR 163; INT CA-89-92

Rogers, Thomas Hunton
See Rogers, Thomas

Rogers, Will(iam Penn Adair)
1879-1935 .... **NNAL; TCLC 8, 71**
See also CA 105; 144; DA3; DAM MULT; DLB 11; MTCW 2

Rogin, Gilbert 1929- .... **CLC 18**
See also CA 65-68; CANR 15

Rohan, Koda
See Koda Shigeyuki

Rohlfs, Anna Katharine Green
See Green, Anna Katharine

Rohmer, Eric
See Scherer, Jean-Marie Maurice

Rohmer, Sax
See Ward, Arthur Henry Sarsfield

Roiphe, Anne 1935- .... **CLC 3, 9**
See also CA 89-92; CANR 45, 73, 138, 170; DLBY 1980; INT CA-89-92

Roiphe, Anne Richardson
See Roiphe, Anne

Rojas, Fernando de 1475-1541 ... **HLCS 1, 2; LC 23, 169**
See also DLB 286; RGWL 2, 3

Rojas, Gonzalo 1917- .... **HLCS 2**
See also CA 178; HW 2; LAWS 1

Rolaag, Ole Edvart
See Rolvaag, O.E.

Roland (de la Platiere), Marie-Jeanne
1754-1793 .... **LC 98**
See also DLB 314

Rolfe, Frederick (William Serafino Austin Lewis Mary) 1860-1913 .... **TCLC 12**
See also CA 107; 210; DLB 34, 156; GLL 1; RGEL 2

Rolland, Romain 1866-1944 .... **TCLC 23**
See also CA 118; 197; DLB 65, 284, 332; EWL 3; GFL 1789 to the Present; RGWL 2, 3

Rolle, Richard c. 1300-c. 1349 ...... **CMLC 21**
See also DLB 146; LMFS 1; RGEL 2

Rolvaag, O.E.
See Rolvaag, O.E.

Rolvaag, O.E.
See Rolvaag, O.E.

Rolvaag, O.E. 1876-1931 .... **TCLC 17, 207**
See also AAYA 75; CA 117; 171; DLB 9, 212; MAL 5; NFS 5; RGAL 4; TCWW 1, 2

Romain Arnaud, Saint
See Aragon, Louis

Romains, Jules 1885-1972 .... **CLC 7**
See also CA 85-88; CANR 34; DLB 65, 321; EWL 3; GFL 1789 to the Present; MTCW 1

Romero, Jose Ruben 1890-1952 .... **TCLC 14**
See also CA 114; 131; EWL 3; HW 1; LAW

Ronsard, Pierre de 1524-1585 . **LC 6, 54; PC 11**
See also DLB 327; EW 2; GFL Beginnings to 1789; RGWL 2, 3; TWA

Rooke, Leon 1934- .... **CLC 25, 34**
See also CA 25-28R; CANR 23, 53; CCA 1; CPW; DAM POP

Roosevelt, Franklin Delano
1882-1945 .... **TCLC 93**
See also CA 116; 173; LAIT 3

Roosevelt, Theodore 1858-1919 ..... **TCLC 69**
See also CA 115; 170; DLB 47, 186, 275

Roper, Margaret c. 1505-1544 .... **LC 147**

Roper, William 1498-1578 .... **LC 10**

Roquelaure, A. N.
See Rice, Anne

Rosa, Joao Guimaraes 1908-1967
See Guimaraes Rosa, Joao

Scannell, Vernon 1922-2007 .... **CLC 49**
See also CA 5-8R; 266; CANR 8, 24, 57, 143; CN 1, 2; CP 1, 2, 3, 4, 5, 6, 7; CWRI 5; DLB 27; SATA 59; SATA-Obit 188

Scarlett, Susan
See Streatfeild, Noel

Scarron 1847-1910
See Mikszath, Kalman

Scarron, Paul 1610-1660 .... **LC 116**
See also GFL Beginnings to 1789; RGWL 2, 3

Schaeffer, Susan Fromberg 1941- ..... **CLC 6, 11, 22**
See also CA 49-52; CANR 18, 65, 160; CN 4, 5, 6, 7; DLB 28, 299; MTCW 1, 2; MTFW 2005; SATA 22

Schama, Simon 1945- .... **CLC 150**
See also BEST 89:4; CA 105; CANR 39, 91, 168

Schama, Simon Michael
See Schama, Simon

Schary, Jill
See Robinson, Jill

Schell, Jonathan 1943- .... **CLC 35**
See also CA 73-76; CANR 12, 117, 187

Schelling, Friedrich Wilhelm Joseph von 1775-1854 .... **NCLC 30**
See also DLB 90

Scherer, Jean-Marie Maurice 1920- .... **CLC 16**
See also CA 110

Schevill, James (Erwin) 1920- .... **CLC 7**
See also CA 5-8R; CAAS 12; CAD; CD 5, 6; CP 1, 2, 3, 4, 5

Schiller, Friedrich von 1759-1805 ...... **DC 12; NCLC 39, 69, 166**
See also CDWLB 2; DAM DRAM; DLB 94; EW 5; RGWL 2, 3; TWA

Schisgal, Murray (Joseph) 1926- .... **CLC 6**
See also CA 21-24R; CAD; CANR 48, 86; CD 5, 6; MAL 5

Schlee, Ann 1934- .... **CLC 35**
See also CA 101; CANR 29, 88; SATA 44; SATA-Brief 36

Schlegel, August Wilhelm von 1767-1845 .... **NCLC 15, 142**
See also DLB 94; RGWL 2, 3

Schlegel, Friedrich 1772-1829 .... **NCLC 45**
See also DLB 90; EW 5; RGWL 2, 3; TWA

Schlegel, Johann Elias (von) 1719(?)-1749 .... **LC 5**

Schleiermacher, Friedrich 1768-1834 .... **NCLC 107**
See also DLB 90

Schlesinger, Arthur M., Jr. 1917-2007 .... **CLC 84**
See Schlesinger, Arthur Meier
See also AITN 1; CA 1-4R; 257; CANR 1, 28, 58, 105, 187; DLB 17; INT CANR-28; MTCW 1, 2; SATA 61; SATA-Obit 181

Schlink, Bernhard 1944- .... **CLC 174**
See also CA 163; CANR 116, 175; RGHL

Schmidt, Arno (Otto) 1914-1979 ...... **CLC 56**
See also CA 128; 109; DLB 69; EWL 3

Schmitz, Aron Hector 1861-1928 ..... **SSC 25; TCLC 2, 35**
See also CA 104; 122; DLB 264; EW 8; EWL 3; MTCW 1; RGWL 2, 3; WLIT 7

Schnackenberg, Gjertrud 1953- ...... **CLC 40; PC 45**
See also AMWS 15; CA 116; CANR 100; CP 5, 6, 7; CWP; DLB 120, 282; PFS 13, 25

Schnackenberg, Gjertrud Cecelia
See Schnackenberg, Gjertrud

Schneider, Leonard Alfred 1925-1966 .... **CLC 21**
See also CA 89-92

Schnitzler, Arthur 1862-1931 ..... **DC 17; SSC 15, 61; TCLC 4**
See also CA 104; CDWLB 2; DLB 81, 118; EW 8; EWL 3; RGSF 2; RGWL 2, 3

Schoenberg, Arnold Franz Walter 1874-1951 .... **TCLC 75**
See also CA 109; 188

Schonberg, Arnold
See Schoenberg, Arnold Franz Walter

Schopenhauer, Arthur 1788-1860 . **NCLC 51, 157**
See also DLB 90; EW 5

Schor, Sandra (M.) 1932(?)-1990 ..... **CLC 65**
See also CA 132

Schorer, Mark 1908-1977 .... **CLC 9**
See also CA 5-8R; 73-76; CANR 7; CN 1, 2; DLB 103

Schrader, Paul (Joseph) 1946- . **CLC 26, 212**
See also CA 37-40R; CANR 41; DLB 44

Schreber, Daniel 1842-1911 .... **TCLC 123**

Schreiner, Olive (Emilie Albertina) 1855-1920 .... **TCLC 9**
See also AFW; BRWS 2; CA 105; 154; DLB 18, 156, 190, 225; EWL 3; FW; RGEL 2; TWA; WLIT 2; WWE 1

Schulberg, Budd 1914-2009 .... **CLC 7, 48**
See also AMWS 18; BPFB 3; CA 25-28R; CANR 19, 87, 178; CN 1, 2, 3, 4, 5, 6, 7; DLB 6, 26, 28; DLBY 1981, 2001; MAL 5

Schulberg, Budd Wilson
See Schulberg, Budd

Schulman, Arnold
See Trumbo, Dalton

Schulz, Bruno 1892-1942 .. **SSC 13; TCLC 5, 51**
See also CA 115; 123; CANR 86; CDWLB 4; DLB 215; EWL 3; MTCW 2; MTFW 2005; RGSF 2; RGWL 2, 3

Schulz, Charles M. 1922-2000 .... **CLC 12**
See also AAYA 39; CA 9-12R; 187; CANR 6, 132; INT CANR-6; MTFW 2005; SATA 10; SATA-Obit 118

Schulz, Charles Monroe
See Schulz, Charles M.

Schumacher, E(rnst) F(riedrich) 1911-1977 .... **CLC 80**
See also CA 81-84; 73-76; CANR 34, 85

Schumann, Robert 1810-1856 ...... **NCLC 143**

Schuyler, George Samuel 1895-1977 . **HR 1:3**
See also BW 2; CA 81-84; 73-76; CANR 42; DLB 29, 51

Schuyler, James Marcus 1923-1991 .. **CLC 5, 23; PC 88**
See also CA 101; 134; CP 1, 2, 3, 4, 5; DAM POET; DLB 5, 169; EWL 3; INT CA-101; MAL 5; WP

Schwartz, Delmore (David) 1913-1966 . **CLC 2, 4, 10, 45, 87; PC 8; SSC 105**
See also AMWS 2; CA 17-18; 25-28R; CANR 35; CAP 2; DLB 28, 48; EWL 3; MAL 5; MTCW 1, 2; MTFW 2005; PAB; RGAL 4; TUS

Schwartz, Ernst
See Ozu, Yasujiro

Schwartz, John Burnham 1965- .... **CLC 59**
See also CA 132; CANR 116, 188

Schwartz, Lynne Sharon 1939- .... **CLC 31**
See also CA 103; CANR 44, 89, 160; DLB 218; MTCW 2; MTFW 2005

Schwartz, Muriel A.
See Eliot, T(homas) S(tearns)

Schwarz-Bart, Andre 1928-2006 .... **CLC 2, 4**
See also CA 89-92; 253; CANR 109; DLB 299; RGHL

Schwarz-Bart, Simone 1938- . **BLCS; CLC 7**
See also BW 2; CA 97-100; CANR 117; EWL 3

Schwerner, Armand 1927-1999 .... **PC 42**
See also CA 9-12R; 179; CANR 50, 85; CP 2, 3, 4, 5, 6; DLB 165

Schwitters, Kurt (Hermann Edward Karl Julius) 1887-1948 .... **TCLC 95**
See also CA 158

Schwob, Marcel (Mayer Andre) 1867-1905 .... **TCLC 20**
See also CA 117; 168; DLB 123; GFL 1789 to the Present

Sciascia, Leonardo 1921-1989 .. **CLC 8, 9, 41**
See also CA 85-88; 130; CANR 35; DLB 177; EWL 3; MTCW 1; RGWL 2, 3

Scoppettone, Sandra 1936- .... **CLC 26**
See also AAYA 11, 65; BYA 8; CA 5-8R; CANR 41, 73, 157; GLL 1; MAICYA 2; MAICYAS 1; SATA 9, 92; WYA; YAW

Scorsese, Martin 1942- .... **CLC 20, 89, 207**
See also AAYA 38; CA 110; 114; CANR 46, 85

Scotland, Jay
See Jakes, John

Scott, Duncan Campbell 1862-1947 .... **TCLC 6**
See also CA 104; 153; DAC; DLB 92; RGEL 2

Scott, Evelyn 1893-1963 .... **CLC 43**
See also CA 104; 112; CANR 64; DLB 9, 48; RHW

Scott, F(rancis) R(eginald) 1899-1985 .... **CLC 22**
See also CA 101; 114; CANR 87; CP 1, 2, 3, 4; DLB 88; INT CA-101; RGEL 2

Scott, Frank
See Scott, F(rancis) R(eginald)

Scott, Joan .... **CLC 65**

Scott, Joanna 1960- .... **CLC 50**
See also AMWS 17; CA 126; CANR 53, 92, 168

Scott, Joanna Jeanne
See Scott, Joanna

Scott, Paul (Mark) 1920-1978 ...... **CLC 9, 60**
See also BRWS 1; CA 81-84; 77-80; CANR 33; CN 1, 2; DLB 14, 207, 326; EWL 3; MTCW 1; RGEL 2; RHW; WWE 1

Scott, Ridley 1937- .... **CLC 183**
See also AAYA 13, 43

Scott, Sarah 1723-1795 .... **LC 44**
See also DLB 39

Scott, Sir Walter 1771-1832 .... **NCLC 15, 69, 110, 209; PC 13; SSC 32; WLC 5**
See also AAYA 22; BRW 4; BYA 2; CD-BLB 1789-1832; DA; DAB; DAC; DAM MST, NOV, POET; DLB 93, 107, 116, 144, 159; GL 3; HGG; LAIT 1; RGEL 2; RGSF 2; SSFS 10; SUFW 1; TEA; WLIT 3; YABC 2

Scribe, (Augustin) Eugene 1791-1861 . **DC 5; NCLC 16**
See also DAM DRAM; DLB 192; GFL 1789 to the Present; RGWL 2, 3

Scrum, R.
See Crumb, R.

Scudery, Georges de 1601-1667 .... **LC 75**
See also GFL Beginnings to 1789

Scudery, Madeleine de 1607-1701 .. **LC 2, 58**
See also DLB 268; GFL Beginnings to 1789

Scum
See Crumb, R.

Scumbag, Little Bobby
See Crumb, R.

Seabrook, John
See Hubbard, L. Ron

Seacole, Mary Jane Grant 1805-1881 .... **NCLC 147**
See also DLB 166

Sealy, I(rwin) Allan 1951- .... **CLC 55**
See also CA 136; CN 6, 7

Shapiro, Karl 1913-2000 ... **CLC 4, 8, 15, 53; PC 25**
See also AMWS 2; CA 1-4R; 188; CAAS 6; CANR 1, 36, 66; CP 1, 2, 3, 4, 5, 6; DLB 48; EWL 3; EXPP; MAL 5; MTCW 1, 2; MTFW 2005; PFS 3; RGAL 4

Sharp, William 1855-1905 .... **TCLC 39**
See also CA 160; DLB 156; RGEL 2; SUFW

Sharpe, Thomas Ridley 1928- .... **CLC 36**
See also CA 114; 122; CANR 85; CN 4, 5, 6, 7; DLB 14, 231; INT CA-122

Sharpe, Tom
See Sharpe, Thomas Ridley

Shatrov, Mikhail CLC 59

Shaw, Bernard
See Shaw, George Bernard

Shaw, G. Bernard
See Shaw, George Bernard

Shaw, George Bernard 1856-1950 ..... **DC 23; TCLC 3, 9, 21, 45, 205; WLC 5**
See also AAYA 61; BRW 6; BRWC 1; BRWR 2; CA 104; 128; CDBLB 1914-1945; DA; DA3; DAB; DAC; DAM DRAM, MST; DFS 1, 3, 6, 11, 19, 22; DLB 10, 57, 190, 332; EWL 3; LAIT 3; LATS 1:1; MTCW 1, 2; MTFW 2005; RGEL 2; TEA; WLIT 4

Shaw, Henry Wheeler 1818-1885 .. **NCLC 15**
See also DLB 11; RGAL 4

Shaw, Irwin 1913-1984 .... **CLC 7, 23, 34**
See also AITN 1; BPFB 3; CA 13-16R; 112; CANR 21; CDALB 1941-1968; CN 1, 2, 3; CPW; DAM DRAM, POP; DLB 6, 102; DLBY 1984; MAL 5; MTCW 1, 21; MTFW 2005

Shaw, Robert (Archibald)
1927-1978 .... **CLC 5**
See also AITN 1; CA 1-4R; 81-84; CANR 4; CN 1, 2; DLB 13, 14

Shaw, T. E.
See Lawrence, T. E.

Shawn, Wallace 1943- .... **CLC 41**
See also CA 112; CAD; CD 5, 6; DLB 266

Shaykh, al- Hanan
See al-Shaykh, Hanan

Shchedrin, N.
See Saltykov, Mikhail Evgrafovich

Shea, Lisa 1953- .... **CLC 86**
See also CA 147

Sheed, Wilfrid 1930- .... **CLC 2, 4, 10, 53**
See also CA 65-68; CANR 30, 66, 181; CN 1, 2, 3, 4, 5, 6, 7; DLB 6; MAL 5; MTCW 1, 2; MTFW 2005

Sheed, Wilfrid John Joseph
See Sheed, Wilfrid

Sheehy, Gail 1937- .... **CLC 171**
See also CA 49-52; CANR 1, 33, 55, 92; CPW; MTCW 1

Sheldon, Alice Hastings Bradley
1915(?)-1987 .... **CLC 48, 50**
See also CA 108; 122; CANR 34; DLB 8; INT CA-108; MTCW 1; SCFW 1, 2; SFW 4

Sheldon, John
See Bloch, Robert (Albert)

Sheldon, Raccoona
See Sheldon, Alice Hastings Bradley

Shelley, Mary Wollstonecraft (Godwin)
1797-1851 .... **NCLC 14, 59, 103, 170; SSC 92; WLC 5**
See also AAYA 20; BPFB 3; BRW 3; BRWC 2; BRWS 3; BYA 5; CDBLB 1789-1832; CLR 133; DA; DA3; DAB; DAC; DAM MST, NOV; DLB 110, 116, 159, 178; EXPN; FL 1:3; GL 3; HGG; LAIT 1; LMFS 1, 2; NFS 1; RGEL 2; SATA 29; SCFW 1; SFW 4; TEA; WLIT 3

Shelley, Percy Bysshe 1792-1822 .. **NCLC 18, 93, 143, 175; PC 14, 67; WLC 5**
See also AAYA 61; BRW 4; BRWR 1; CDBLB 1789-1832; DA; DA3; DAB; DAC; DAM MST, POET; DLB 96, 110, 158; EXPP; LMFS 1; PAB; PFS 2, 27; RGEL 2; TEA; WLIT 3; WP

Shepard, James R.
See Shepard, Jim

Shepard, Jim 1956- .... **CLC 36**
See also AAYA 73; CA 137; CANR 59, 104, 160; SATA 90, 164

Shepard, Lucius 1947- .... **CLC 34**
See also CA 128; 141; CANR 81, 124, 178; HGG; SCFW 2; SFW 4; SUFW 2

Shepard, Sam 1943- .... **CLC 4, 6, 17, 34, 41, 44, 169; DC 5**
See also AAYA 1, 58; AMWS 3; CA 69-72; CABS 3; CAD; CANR 22, 120, 140; CD 5, 6; DA3; DAM DRAM; DFS 3, 6, 7, 14; DLB 7, 212, 341; EWL 3; IDFW 3, 4; MAL 5; MTCW 1, 2; MTFW 2005; RGAL 4

Shepherd, Jean (Parker)
1921-1999 .... **TCLC 177**
See also AAYA 69; AITN 2; CA 77-80; 187

Shepherd, Michael
See Ludlum, Robert

Sherburne, Zoa (Lillian Morin)
1912-1995 .... **CLC 30**
See also AAYA 13; CA 1-4R; 176; CANR 3, 37; MAICYA 1, 2; SAAS 18; SATA 3; YAW

Sheridan, Frances 1724-1766 .... **LC 7**
See also DLB 39, 84

Sheridan, Richard Brinsley
1751-1816 . **DC 1; NCLC 5, 91; WLC 5**
See also BRW 3; CDBLB 1660-1789; DA; DAB; DAC; DAM DRAM, MST; DFS 15; DLB 89; WLIT 3

Sherman, Jonathan Marc 1968- .... **CLC 55**
See also CA 230

Sherman, Martin 1941(?)- .... **CLC 19**
See also CA 116; 123; CAD; CANR 86; CD 5, 6; DFS 20; DLB 228; GLL 1; IDTP; RGHL

Sherwin, Judith Johnson
See Johnson, Judith

Sherwood, Frances 1940- .... **CLC 81**
See also CA 146; 220; CAAE 220; CANR 158

Sherwood, Robert E(mmet)
1896-1955 .... **DC 36; TCLC 3**
See also CA 104; 153; CANR 86; DAM DRAM; DFS 11, 15, 17; DLB 7, 26, 249; IDFW 3, 4; MAL 5; RGAL 4

Shestov, Lev 1866-1938 .... **TCLC 56**

Shevchenko, Taras 1814-1861 .... **NCLC 54**

Shiel, M. P. 1865-1947 .... **TCLC 8**
See also CA 106; 160; DLB 153; HGG; MTCW 2; MTFW 2005; SCFW 1, 2; SFW 4; SUFW

Shiel, Matthew Phipps
See Shiel, M. P.

Shields, Carol 1935-2003 . **CLC 91, 113, 193; SSC 126**
See also AMWS 7; CA 81-84; 218; CANR 51, 74, 98, 133; CCA 1; CN 6, 7; CPW; DA3; DAC; DLB 334, 350; MTCW 2; MTFW 2005; NFS 23

Shields, David 1956- .... **CLC 97**
See also CA 124; CANR 48, 99, 112, 157

Shields, David Jonathan
See Shields, David

Shiga, Naoya 1883-1971 .... **CLC 33; SSC 23; TCLC 172**
See also CA 101; 33-36R; DLB 180; EWL 3; MJW; RGWL 3

Shiga Naoya
See Shiga, Naoya

Shilts, Randy 1951-1994 .... **CLC 85**
See also AAYA 19; CA 115; 127; 144; CANR 45; DA3; GLL 1; INT CA-127; MTCW 2; MTFW 2005

Shimazaki, Haruki 1872-1943 .... **TCLC 5**
See also CA 105; 134; CANR 84; DLB 180; EWL 3; MJW; RGWL 3

Shimazaki Toson
See Shimazaki, Haruki

Shirley, James 1596-1666 .... **DC 25; LC 96**
See also DLB 58; RGEL 2

Shirley Hastings, Selina
See Hastings, Selina

Sholem Aleykhem
See Rabinovitch, Sholem

Sholokhov, Mikhail (Aleksandrovich)
1905-1984 .... **CLC 7, 15**
See also CA 101; 112; DLB 272, 332; EWL 3; MTCW 1, 2; MTFW 2005; RGWL 2, 3; SATA-Obit 36

Sholom Aleichem 1859-1916
See Rabinovitch, Sholem

Shone, Patric
See Hanley, James

Showalter, Elaine 1941- .... **CLC 169**
See also CA 57-60; CANR 58, 106; DLB 67; FW; GLL 2

Shreve, Susan
See Shreve, Susan Richards

Shreve, Susan Richards 1939- .... **CLC 23**
See also CA 49-52; CAAS 5; CANR 5, 38, 69, 100, 159; MAICYA 1, 2; SATA 46, 95, 152; SATA-Brief 41

Shue, Larry 1946-1985 .... **CLC 52**
See also CA 145; 117; DAM DRAM; DFS 7

Shu-Jen, Chou 1881-1936 . **SSC 20; TCLC 3**
See also CA 104; EWL 3

Shulman, Alix Kates 1932- .... **CLC 2, 10**
See also CA 29-32R; CANR 43; FW; SATA 7

Shuster, Joe 1914-1992 .... **CLC 21**
See also AAYA 50

Shute, Nevil
See Norway, Nevil Shute

Shuttle, Penelope (Diane) 1947- .... **CLC 7**
See also CA 93-96; CANR 39, 84, 92, 108; CP 3, 4, 5, 6, 7; CWP; DLB 14, 40

Shvarts, Elena 1948- .... **PC 50**
See also CA 147

Sidhwa, Bapsi 1939-
See Sidhwa, Bapsy (N.)

Sidhwa, Bapsy (N.) 1938- .... **CLC 168**
See also CA 108; CANR 25, 57; CN 6, 7; DLB 323; FW

Sidney, Mary 1561-1621 .... **LC 19, 39**
See also DLB 167

Sidney, Sir Philip 1554-1586 .... **LC 19, 39, 131; PC 32**
See also BRW 1; BRWR 2; CDBLB Before 1660; DA; DA3; DAB; DAC; DAM MST, POET; DLB 167; EXPP; PAB; PFS 30; RGEL 2; TEA; WP

Sidney Herbert, Mary
See Sidney, Mary

Siegel, Jerome 1914-1996 .... **CLC 21**
See also AAYA 50; CA 116; 169; 151

Siegel, Jerry
See Siegel, Jerome

Sienkiewicz, Henryk (Adam Alexander Pius)
1846-1916 .... **TCLC 3**
See also CA 104; 134; CANR 84; DLB 332; EWL 3; RGSF 2; RGWL 2, 3

Sierra, Gregorio Martinez
See Martinez Sierra, Gregorio

Sinibaldi, Fosco
See Kacew, Romain
Sinjohn, John
See Galsworthy, John
Sinyavsky, Andrei (Donatevich)
1925-1997 .... **CLC 8**
See also CA 85-88; 159; CWW 2; EWL 3;
RGSF 2
Sinyavsky, Andrey Donatovich
See Sinyavsky, Andrei (Donatevich)
Sirin, V.
See Nabokov, Vladimir (Vladimirovich)
Sissman, L(ouis) E(dward)
1928-1976 .... **CLC 9, 18**
See also CA 21-24R; 65-68; CANR 13; CP
2; DLB 5
Sisson, C(harles) H(ubert)
1914-2003 .... **CLC 8**
See also BRWS 11; CA 1-4R; 220; CAAS
3; CANR 3, 48, 84; CP 1, 2, 3, 4, 5, 6, 7;
DLB 27
Sitting Bull 1831(?)-1890 .... **NNAL**
See also DA3; DAM MULT
Sitwell, Dame Edith 1887-1964 ..... **CLC 2, 9,
67; PC 3**
See also BRW 7; CA 9-12R; CANR 35;
CDBLB 1945-1960; DAM POET; DLB
20; EWL 3; MTCW 1, 2; MTFW 2005;
RGEL 2; TEA
Siwaarmill, H. P.
See Sharp, William
Sjoewall, Maj 1935- .... **CLC 7**
See also BPFB 3; CA 65-68; CANR 73;
CMW 4; MSW
Sjowall, Maj
See Sjoewall, Maj
Skelton, John 1460(?)-1529 ..... **LC 71; PC 25**
See also BRW 1; DLB 136; RGEL 2
Skelton, Robin 1925-1997 .... **CLC 13**
See also AITN 2; CA 5-8R; 160; CAAS 5;
CANR 28, 89; CCA 1; CP 1, 2, 3, 4, 5, 6;
DLB 27, 53
Skolimowski, Jerzy 1938- .... **CLC 20**
See also CA 128
Skram, Amalie (Bertha)
1847-1905 .... **TCLC 25**
See also CA 165
Skvorecky, Josef 1924- . **CLC 15, 39, 69, 152**
See also CA 61-64; CAAS 1; CANR 10,
34, 63, 108; CDWLB 4; CWW 2; DA3;
DAC; DAM NOV; DLB 232; EWL 3;
MTCW 1, 2; MTFW 2005
Slade, Bernard 1930-
See Newbound, Bernard Slade
Slaughter, Carolyn 1946- .... **CLC 56**
See also CA 85-88; CANR 85, 169; CN 5,
6, 7
Slaughter, Frank G(ill) 1908-2001 ... **CLC 29**
See also AITN 2; CA 5-8R; 197; CANR 5,
85; INT CANR-5; RHW
Slavitt, David R. 1935- .... **CLC 5, 14**
See also CA 21-24R; CAAS 3; CANR 41,
83, 166; CN 1, 2; CP 1, 2, 3, 4, 5, 6, 7;
DLB 5, 6
Slavitt, David Rytman
See Slavitt, David R.
Slesinger, Tess 1905-1945 .... **TCLC 10**
See also CA 107; 199; DLB 102
Slessor, Kenneth 1901-1971 .... **CLC 14**
See also CA 102; 89-92; DLB 260; RGEL
2
Slowacki, Juliusz 1809-1849 .... **NCLC 15**
See also RGWL 3
Smart, Christopher 1722-1771 .... **LC 3, 134;
PC 13**
See also DAM POET; DLB 109; RGEL 2
Smart, Elizabeth 1913-1986 .... **CLC 54**
See also CA 81-84; 118; CN 4; DLB 88

Smiley, Jane 1949- ...... **CLC 53, 76, 144, 236**
See also AAYA 66; AMWS 6; BPFB 3; CA
104; CANR 30, 50, 74, 96, 158; CN 6, 7;
CPW 1; DA3; DAM POP; DLB 227, 234;
EWL 3; INT CANR-30; MAL 5; MTFW
2005; SSFS 19
Smiley, Jane Graves
See Smiley, Jane
Smith, A(rthur) J(ames) M(arshall)
1902-1980 .... **CLC 15**
See also CA 1-4R; 102; CANR 4; CP 1, 2,
3; DAC; DLB 88; RGEL 2
Smith, Adam 1723(?)-1790 .... **LC 36**
See also DLB 104, 252, 336; RGEL 2
Smith, Alexander 1829-1867 .... **NCLC 59**
See also DLB 32, 55
Smith, Alexander McCall 1948- ..... **CLC 268**
See also CA 215; CANR 154; SATA 73,
179
Smith, Anna Deavere 1950- ...... **CLC 86, 241**
See also CA 133; CANR 103; CD 5, 6; DFS
2, 22; DLB 341
Smith, Betty (Wehner) 1904-1972 .... **CLC 19**
See also AAYA 72; BPFB 3; BYA 3; CA
5-8R; 33-36R; DLBY 1982; LAIT 3;
RGAL 4; SATA 6
Smith, Charlotte (Turner)
1749-1806 .... **NCLC 23, 115**
See also DLB 39, 109; RGEL 2; TEA
Smith, Clark Ashton 1893-1961 .... **CLC 43**
See also AAYA 76; CA 143; CANR 81;
FANT; HGG; MTCW 2; SCFW 1, 2; SFW
4; SUFW
Smith, Dave
See Smith, David (Jeddie)
Smith, David (Jeddie) 1942- .... **CLC 22, 42**
See also CA 49-52; CAAS 7; CANR 1, 59,
120; CP 3, 4, 5, 6, 7; CSW; DAM POET;
DLB 5
Smith, Iain Crichton 1928-1998 .... **CLC 64**
See also BRWS 9; CA 21-24R; 171; CN 1,
2, 3, 4, 5, 6; CP 1, 2, 3, 4, 5, 6; DLB 40,
139, 319, 352; RGSF 2
Smith, John 1580(?)-1631 .... **LC 9**
See also DLB 24, 30; TUS
Smith, Johnston
See Crane, Stephen (Townley)
Smith, Joseph, Jr. 1805-1844 .... **NCLC 53**
Smith, Kevin 1970- .... **CLC 223**
See also AAYA 37; CA 166; CANR 131
Smith, Lee 1944- .... **CLC 25, 73, 258**
See also CA 114; 119; CANR 46, 118, 173;
CN 7; CSW; DLB 143; DLBY 1983;
EWL 3; INT CA-119; RGAL 4
Smith, Martin
See Smith, Martin Cruz
Smith, Martin Cruz 1942- .. **CLC 25; NNAL**
See Smith, Martin Cruz
See also BEST 89:4; BPFB 3; CA 85-88;
CANR 6, 23, 43, 65, 119, 184; CMW 4;
CPW; DAM MULT, POP; HGG; INT
CANR-23; MTCW 2; MTFW 2005;
RGAL 4
Smith, Patti 1946- .... **CLC 12**
See also CA 93-96; CANR 63, 168
Smith, Pauline (Urmson)
1882-1959 .... **TCLC 25**
See also DLB 225; EWL 3
Smith, R. Alexander McCall
See Smith, Alexander McCall
Smith, Rosamond
See Oates, Joyce Carol
Smith, Seba 1792-1868 .... **NCLC 187**
See also DLB 1, 11, 243
Smith, Sheila Kaye
See Kaye-Smith, Sheila

Smith, Stevie 1902-1971 .... **CLC 3, 8, 25, 44;
PC 12**
See also BRWS 2; CA 17-18; 29-32R;
CANR 35; CAP 2; CP 1; DAM POET;
DLB 20; EWL 3; MTCW 1, 2; PAB; PFS
3; RGEL 2; TEA
Smith, Wilbur 1933- .... **CLC 33**
See also CA 13-16R; CANR 7, 46, 66, 134,
180; CPW; MTCW 1, 2; MTFW 2005
Smith, Wilbur Addison
See Smith, Wilbur
Smith, William Jay 1918- .... **CLC 6**
See also AMWS 13; CA 5-8R; CANR 44,
106; CP 1, 2, 3, 4, 5, 6, 7; CSW; CWRI
5; DLB 5; MAICYA 1, 2; SAAS 22;
SATA 2, 68, 154; SATA-Essay 154; TCLE
1:2
Smith, Woodrow Wilson
See Kuttner, Henry
Smith, Zadie 1975- .... **CLC 158**
See also AAYA 50; CA 193; DLB 347;
MTFW 2005
Smolenskin, Peretz 1842-1885 .... **NCLC 30**
Smollett, Tobias (George) 1721-1771 ... **LC 2,
46**
See also BRW 3; CDBLB 1660-1789; DLB
39, 104; RGEL 2; TEA
Snodgrass, Quentin Curtius
See Twain, Mark
Snodgrass, Thomas Jefferson
See Twain, Mark
Snodgrass, W. D. 1926-2009 .... **CLC 2, 6, 10,
18, 68; PC 74**
See also AMWS 6; CA 1-4R; 282; CANR
6, 36, 65, 85, 185; CP 1, 2, 3, 4, 5, 6, 7;
DAM POET; DLB 5; MAL 5; MTCW 1,
2; MTFW 2005; PFS 29; RGAL 4; TCLE
1:2
Snodgrass, W. de Witt
See Snodgrass, W. D.
Snodgrass, William de Witt
See Snodgrass, W. D.
Snodgrass, William De Witt
See Snodgrass, W. D.
Snorri Sturluson 1179-1241 .... **CMLC 56**
See also RGWL 2, 3
Snow, C(harles) P(ercy) 1905-1980 ... **CLC 1,
4, 6, 9, 13, 19**
See also BRW 7; CA 5-8R; 101; CANR 28;
CDBLB 1945-1960; CN 1, 2; DAM NOV;
DLB 15, 77; DLBD 17; EWL 3; MTCW
1, 2; MTFW 2005; RGEL 2; TEA
Snow, Frances Compton
See Adams, Henry (Brooks)
Snyder, Gary 1930- . **CLC 1, 2, 5, 9, 32, 120;
PC 21**
See also AAYA 72; AMWS 8; ANW; BG
1:3; CA 17-20R; CANR 30, 60, 125; CP
1, 2, 3, 4, 5, 6, 7; DA3; DAM POET; DLB
5, 16, 165, 212, 237, 275, 342; EWL 3;
MAL 5; MTCW 2; MTFW 2005; PFS 9,
19; RGAL 4; WP
Snyder, Zilpha Keatley 1927- .... **CLC 17**
See also AAYA 15; BYA 1; CA 9-12R; 252;
CAAE 252; CANR 38; CLR 31, 121;
JRDA; MAICYA 1, 2; SAAS 2; SATA 1,
28, 75, 110, 163; SATA-Essay 112, 163;
YAW
Soares, Bernardo
See Pessoa, Fernando
Sobh, A.
See Shamlu, Ahmad
Sobh, Alef
See Shamlu, Ahmad
Sobol, Joshua 1939- .... **CLC 60**
See also CA 200; CWW 2; RGHL
Sobol, Yehoshua 1939-
See Sobol, Joshua

Spivack, Kathleen (Romola Drucker)
  1938- .... **CLC 6**
  See also CA 49-52
Spivak, Gayatri Chakravorty
  1942- .... **CLC 233**
  See also CA 110; 154; CANR 91; FW;
  LMFS 2
Spofford, Harriet (Elizabeth) Prescott
  1835-1921 .... **SSC 87**
  See also CA 201; DLB 74, 221
Spoto, Donald 1941- .... **CLC 39**
  See also CA 65-68; CANR 11, 57, 93, 173
Springsteen, Bruce 1949- .... **CLC 17**
  See also CA 111
Springsteen, Bruce F.
  See Springsteen, Bruce
Spurling, Hilary 1940- .... **CLC 34**
  See also CA 104; CANR 25, 52, 94, 157
Spurling, Susan Hilary
  See Spurling, Hilary
Spyker, John Howland
  See Elman, Richard (Martin)
Squared, A.
  See Abbott, Edwin A.
Squires, (James) Radcliffe
  1917-1993 .... **CLC 51**
  See also CA 1-4R; 140; CANR 6, 21; CP 1,
  2, 3, 4, 5
Srivastav, Dhanpat Ray
  See Srivastava, Dhanpat Rai
Srivastav, Dheanpatrai
  See Srivastava, Dhanpat Rai
Srivastava, Dhanpat Rai
  1880(?)-1936 .... **TCLC 21**
  See also CA 118; 197; EWL 3
Ssu-ma Ch'ien c. 145B.C.-c.
  86B.C. .... **CMLC 96**
Ssu-ma T'an (?)-c. 110B.C. .... **CMLC 96**
Stacy, Donald
  See Pohl, Frederik
Stael
  See Stael-Holstein, Anne Louise Germaine
  Necker
Stael, Germaine de
  See Stael-Holstein, Anne Louise Germaine
  Necker
Stael-Holstein, Anne Louise Germaine
  Necker 1766-1817 .... **NCLC 3, 91**
  See also DLB 119, 192; EW 5; FL 1:3; FW;
  GFL 1789 to the Present; RGWL 2, 3;
  TWA
Stafford, Jean 1915-1979 .. **CLC 4, 7, 19, 68;**
  SSC 26, 86
  See also CA 1-4R; 85-88; CANR 3, 65; CN
  1, 2; DLB 2, 173; MAL 5; MTCW 1, 2;
  MTFW 2005; RGAL 4; RGSF 2; SATA-
  Obit 22; SSFS 21; TCWW 1, 2; TUS
Stafford, William (Edgar)
  1914-1993 .... **CLC 4, 7, 29; PC 71**
  See also AMWS 11; CA 5-8R; 142; CAAS
  3; CANR 5, 22; CP 1, 2, 3, 4, 5; DAM
  POET; DLB 5, 206; EXPP; INT CANR-
  22; MAL 5; PFS 2, 8, 16; RGAL 4; WP
Stagnelius, Eric Johan 1793-1823 . **NCLC 61**
Staines, Trevor
  See Brunner, John (Kilian Houston)
Stairs, Gordon
  See Austin, Mary (Hunter)
Stalin, Joseph 1879-1953 .... **TCLC 92**
Stampa, Gaspara c. 1524-1554 .. **LC 114; PC**
  43
  See also RGWL 2, 3; WLIT 7
Stampflinger, K.A.
  See Benjamin, Walter
Stancykowna
  See Szymborska, Wislawa

Standing Bear, Luther
  1868(?)-1939(?) .... **NNAL**
  See also CA 113; 144; DAM MULT
Stanislavsky, Constantin
  1863(?)-1938 .... **TCLC 167**
  See also CA 118
Stanislavsky, Konstantin
  See Stanislavsky, Constantin
Stanislavsky, Konstantin Sergeievich
  See Stanislavsky, Constantin
Stanislavsky, Konstantin Sergeivich
  See Stanislavsky, Constantin
Stanislavsky, Konstantin Sergeyevich
  See Stanislavsky, Constantin
Stannard, Martin 1947- .... **CLC 44**
  See also CA 142; DLB 155
Stanton, Elizabeth Cady
  1815-1902 .... **TCLC 73**
  See also CA 171; DLB 79; FL 1:3; FW
Stanton, Maura 1946- .... **CLC 9**
  See also CA 89-92; CANR 15, 123; DLB
  120
Stanton, Schuyler
  See Baum, L(yman) Frank
Stapledon, (William) Olaf
  1886-1950 .... **TCLC 22**
  See also CA 111; 162; DLB 15, 255; SCFW
  1, 2; SFW 4
Starbuck, George (Edwin)
  1931-1996 .... **CLC 53**
  See also CA 21-24R; 153; CANR 23; CP 1,
  2, 3, 4, 5, 6; DAM POET
Stark, Richard
  See Westlake, Donald E.
Statius c. 45-c. 96 .... **CMLC 91**
  See also AW 2; DLB 211
Staunton, Schuyler
  See Baum, L(yman) Frank
Stead, Christina (Ellen) 1902-1983 ... **CLC 2,**
  5, 8, 32, 80
  See also BRWS 4; CA 13-16R; 109; CANR
  33, 40; CN 1, 2, 3; DLB 260; EWL 3;
  FW; MTCW 1, 2; MTFW 2005; NFS 27;
  RGEL 2; RGSF 2; WWE 1
Stead, William Thomas
  1849-1912 .... **TCLC 48**
  See also BRWS 13; CA 167
Stebnitsky, M.
  See Leskov, Nikolai (Semyonovich)
Steele, Richard 1672-1729 .. **LC 18, 156, 159**
  See also BRW 3; CDBLB 1660-1789; DLB
  84, 101; RGEL 2; WLIT 3
Steele, Timothy (Reid) 1948- .... **CLC 45**
  See also CA 93-96; CANR 16, 50, 92; CP
  5, 6, 7; DLB 120, 282
Steffens, (Joseph) Lincoln
  1866-1936 .... **TCLC 20**
  See also CA 117; 198; DLB 303; MAL 5
Stegner, Wallace (Earle) 1909-1993 .. **CLC 9,**
  49, 81; SSC 27
  See also AITN 1; AMWS 4; ANW; BEST
  90:3; BPFB 3; CA 1-4R; 141; CAAS 9;
  CANR 1, 21, 46; CN 1, 2, 3, 4, 5; DAM
  NOV; DLB 9, 206, 275; DLBY 1993;
  EWL 3; MAL 5; MTCW 1, 2; MTFW
  2005; RGAL 4; TCWW 1, 2; TUS
Stein, Gertrude 1874-1946 .... **DC 19; PC 18;**
  SSC 42, 105; TCLC 1, 6, 28, 48; WLC
  5
  See also AAYA 64; AMW; AMWC 2; CA
  104; 132; CANR 108; CDALB 1917-
  1929; DA; DA3; DAB; DAC; DAM MST,
  NOV, POET; DLB 4, 54, 86, 228; DLBD
  15; EWL 3; EXPS; FL 1:6; GLL 1; MAL
  5; MBL; MTCW 1, 2; MTFW 2005;
  NCFS 4; NFS 27; RGAL 4; RGSF 2;
  SSFS 5; TUS; WP

Steinbeck, John (Ernst) 1902-1968 ... **CLC 1,**
  5, 9, 13, 21, 34, 45, 75, 124; SSC 11, 37,
  77; TCLC 135; WLC 5
  See also AAYA 12; AMW; BPFB 3; BYA 2,
  3, 13; CA 1-4R; 25-28R; CANR 1, 35;
  CDALB 1929-1941; DA; DA3; DAB;
  DAC; DAM DRAM, MST, NOV; DLB 7,
  9, 212, 275, 309, 332; DLBD 2; EWL 3;
  EXPS; LAIT 3; MAL 5; MTCW 1, 2;
  MTFW 2005; NFS 1, 5, 7, 17, 19, 28;
  RGAL 4; RGSF 2; RHW; SATA 9; SSFS
  3, 6, 22; TCWW 1, 2; TUS; WYA; YAW
Steinem, Gloria 1934- .... **CLC 63**
  See also CA 53-56; CANR 28, 51, 139;
  DLB 246; FL 1:1; FW; MTCW 1, 2;
  MTFW 2005
Steiner, George 1929- .... **CLC 24, 221**
  See also CA 73-76; CANR 31, 67, 108;
  DAM NOV; DLB 67, 299; EWL 3;
  MTCW 1, 2; MTFW 2005; RGHL; SATA
  62
Steiner, K. Leslie
  See Delany, Samuel R., Jr.
Steiner, Rudolf 1861-1925 .... **TCLC 13**
  See also CA 107
Stendhal 1783-1842 .... **NCLC 23, 46, 178;**
  SSC 27; WLC 5
  See also DA; DA3; DAB; DAC; DAM
  MST, NOV; DLB 119; EW 5; GFL 1789
  to the Present; RGWL 2, 3; TWA
Stephen, Adeline Virginia
  See Woolf, (Adeline) Virginia
Stephen, Sir Leslie 1832-1904 .... **TCLC 23**
  See also BRW 5; CA 123; DLB 57, 144,
  190
Stephen, Sir Leslie
  See Stephen, Sir Leslie
Stephen, Virginia
  See Woolf, (Adeline) Virginia
Stephens, James 1882(?)-1950 .... **SSC 50;**
  TCLC 4
  See also CA 104; 192; DLB 19, 153, 162;
  EWL 3; FANT; RGEL 2; SUFW
Stephens, Reed
  See Donaldson, Stephen R.
Stephenson, Neal 1959- .... **CLC 220**
  See also AAYA 38; CA 122; CANR 88, 138;
  CN 7; MTFW 2005; SFW 4
Steptoe, Lydia
  See Barnes, Djuna
Sterchi, Beat 1949- .... **CLC 65**
  See also CA 203
Sterling, Brett
  See Bradbury, Ray; Hamilton, Edmond
Sterling, Bruce 1954- .... **CLC 72**
  See also AAYA 78; CA 119; CANR 44, 135,
  184; CN 7; MTFW 2005; SCFW 2; SFW
  4
Sterling, George 1869-1926 .... **TCLC 20**
  See also CA 117; 165; DLB 54
Stern, Gerald 1925- .... **CLC 40, 100**
  See also AMWS 9; CA 81-84; CANR 28,
  94; CP 3, 4, 5, 6, 7; DLB 105; PFS 26;
  RGAL 4
Stern, Richard (Gustave) 1928- ... **CLC 4, 39**
  See also CA 1-4R; CANR 1, 25, 52, 120;
  CN 1, 2, 3, 4, 5, 6, 7; DLB 218; DLBY
  1987; INT CANR-25
Sternberg, Josef von 1894-1969 .... **CLC 20**
  See also CA 81-84
Sterne, Laurence 1713-1768 .. **LC 2, 48, 156;**
  WLC 5
  See also BRW 3; BRWC 1; CDBLB 1660-
  1789; DA; DAB; DAC; DAM MST, NOV;
  DLB 39; RGEL 2; TEA
Sternheim, (William Adolf) Carl
  1878-1942 .... **TCLC 8, 223**
  See also CA 105; 193; DLB 56, 118; EWL
  3; IDTP; RGWL 2, 3

Tey, Josephine
   See Mackintosh, Elizabeth
Thackeray, William Makepeace
    1811-1863 ...... **NCLC 5, 14, 22, 43, 169, 213; WLC 6**
   See also BRW 5; BRWC 2; CDBLB 1832-1890; DA; DA3; DAB; DAC; DAM MST, NOV; DLB 21, 55, 159, 163; NFS 13; RGEL 2; SATA 23; TEA; WLIT 3
Thakura, Ravindranatha
   See Tagore, Rabindranath
Thames, C. H.
   See Marlowe, Stephen
Tharoor, Shashi 1956- .... **CLC 70**
   See also CA 141; CANR 91; CN 6, 7
Thelwall, John 1764-1834 .... **NCLC 162**
   See also DLB 93, 158
Thelwell, Michael Miles 1939- .... **CLC 22**
   See also BW 2; CA 101
Theo, Ion
   See Theodorescu, Ion N.
Theobald, Lewis, Jr.
   See Lovecraft, H. P.
Theocritus c. 310B.C.- .... **CMLC 45**
   See also AW 1; DLB 176; RGWL 2, 3
Theodorescu, Ion N. 1880-1967 .... **CLC 80**
   See also CA 167; 116; CDWLB 4; DLB 220; EWL 3
Theriault, Yves 1915-1983 .... **CLC 79**
   See also CA 102; CANR 150; CCA 1; DAC; DAM MST; DLB 88; EWL 3
Therion, Master
   See Crowley, Edward Alexander
Theroux, Alexander 1939- .... **CLC 2, 25**
   See also CA 85-88; CANR 20, 63, 190; CN 4, 5, 6, 7
Theroux, Alexander Louis
   See Theroux, Alexander
Theroux, Paul 1941- .... **CLC 5, 8, 11, 15, 28, 46, 159**
   See also AAYA 28; AMWS 8; BEST 89:4; BPFB 3; CA 33-36R; CANR 20, 45, 74, 133, 179; CDALBS; CN 1, 2, 3, 4, 5, 6, 7; CP 1; CPW 1; DA3; DAM POP; DLB 2, 218; EWL 3; HGG; MAL 5; MTCW 1, 2; MTFW 2005; RGAL 4; SATA 44, 109; TUS
Theroux, Paul Edward
   See Theroux, Paul
Thesen, Sharon 1946- .... **CLC 56**
   See also CA 163; CANR 125; CP 5, 6, 7; CWP
Thespis fl. 6th cent. B.C.- .... **CMLC 51**
   See also LMFS 1
Thevenin, Denis
   See Duhamel, Georges
Thibault, Jacques Anatole Francois
    1844-1924 .... **TCLC 9**
   See also CA 106; 127; DA3; DAM NOV; DLB 123, 330; EWL 3; GFL 1789 to the Present; MTCW 1, 2; RGWL 2, 3; SUFW 1; TWA
Thiele, Colin 1920-2006 .... **CLC 17**
   See also CA 29-32R; CANR 12, 28, 53, 105; CLR 27; CP 1, 2; DLB 289; MAI-CYA 1, 2; SAAS 2; SATA 14, 72, 125; YAW
Thiong'o, Ngugi Wa
   See Ngugi wa Thiong'o
Thistlethwaite, Bel
   See Wetherald, Agnes Ethelwyn
Thomas, Audrey (Callahan) 1935- .... **CLC 7, 13, 37, 107; SSC 20**
   See also AITN 2; CA 21-24R; 237; CAAE 237; CAAS 19; CANR 36, 58; CN 2, 3, 4, 5, 6, 7; DLB 60; MTCW 1; RGSF 2
Thomas, Augustus 1857-1934 .... **TCLC 97**
   See also MAL 5

Thomas, D.M. 1935- ..... **CLC 13, 22, 31, 132**
   See also BPFB 3; BRWS 4; CA 61-64; CAAS 11; CANR 17, 45, 75; CDBLB 1960 to Present; CN 4, 5, 6, 7; CP 1, 2, 3, 4, 5, 6, 7; DA3; DLB 40, 207, 299; HGG; INT CANR-17; MTCW 1, 2; MTFW 2005; RGHL; SFW 4
Thomas, Dylan (Marlais) 1914-1953 .... **PC 2, 52; SSC 3, 44; TCLC 1, 8, 45, 105; WLC 6**
   See also AAYA 45; BRWS 1; CA 104; 120; CANR 65; CDBLB 1945-1960; DA; DA3; DAB; DAC; DAM DRAM, MST, POET; DLB 13, 20, 139; EWL 3; EXPP; LAIT 3; MTCW 1, 2; MTFW 2005; PAB; PFS 1, 3, 8; RGEL 2; RGSF 2; SATA 60; TEA; WLIT 4; WP
Thomas, (Philip) Edward 1878-1917 . **PC 53; TCLC 10**
   See also BRW 6; BRWS 3; CA 106; 153; DAM POET; DLB 19, 98, 156, 216; EWL 3; PAB; RGEL 2
Thomas, J.F.
   See Fleming, Thomas
Thomas, Joyce Carol 1938- .... **CLC 35**
   See also AAYA 12, 54; BW 2, 3; CA 113; 116; CANR 48, 114, 135; CLR 19; DLB 33; INT CA-116; JRDA; MAICYA 1, 2; MTCW 1, 2; MTFW 2005; SAAS 7; SATA 40, 78, 123, 137; SATA-Essay 137; WYA; YAW
Thomas, Lewis 1913-1993 .... **CLC 35**
   See also ANW; CA 85-88; 143; CANR 38, 60; DLB 275; MTCW 1, 2
Thomas, M. Carey 1857-1935 .... **TCLC 89**
   See also FW
Thomas, Paul
   See Mann, (Paul) Thomas
Thomas, Piri 1928- .... **CLC 17; HLCS 2**
   See also CA 73-76; HW 1; LLW
Thomas, R(onald) S(tuart)
    1913-2000 .... **CLC 6, 13, 48; PC 99**
   See also BRWS 12; CA 89-92; 189; CAAS 4; CANR 30; CDBLB 1960 to Present; CP 1, 2, 3, 4, 5, 6, 7; DAB; DAM POET; DLB 27; EWL 3; MTCW 1; RGEL 2
Thomas, Ross (Elmore) 1926-1995 .. **CLC 39**
   See also CA 33-36R; 150; CANR 22, 63; CMW 4
Thompson, Francis (Joseph)
    1859-1907 .... **TCLC 4**
   See also BRW 5; CA 104; 189; CDBLB 1890-1914; DLB 19; RGEL 2; TEA
Thompson, Francis Clegg
   See Mencken, H. L.
Thompson, Hunter S. 1937(?)-2005 .. **CLC 9, 17, 40, 104, 229**
   See also AAYA 45; BEST 89:1; BPFB 3; CA 17-20R; 236; CANR 23, 46, 74, 77, 111, 133; CPW; CSW; DA3; DAM POP; DLB 185; MTCW 1, 2; MTFW 2005; TUS
Thompson, James Myers
   See Thompson, Jim
Thompson, Jim 1906-1977 .... **CLC 69**
   See also BPFB 3; CA 140; CMW 4; CPW; DLB 226; MSW
Thompson, Judith (Clare Francesca)
    1954- .... **CLC 39**
   See also CA 143; CD 5, 6; CWD; DFS 22; DLB 334
Thomson, James 1700-1748 .... **LC 16, 29, 40**
   See also BRWS 3; DAM POET; DLB 95; RGEL 2
Thomson, James 1834-1882 .... **NCLC 18**
   See also DAM POET; DLB 35; RGEL 2

Thoreau, Henry David 1817-1862 .. **NCLC 7, 21, 61, 138, 207; PC 30; WLC 6**
   See also AAYA 42; AMW; ANW; BYA 3; CDALB 1640-1865; DA; DA3; DAB; DAC; DAM MST; DLB 1, 183, 223, 270, 298; LAIT 2; LMFS 1; NCFS 3; RGAL 4; TUS
Thorndike, E. L.
   See Thorndike, Edward L(ee)
Thorndike, Edward L(ee)
    1874-1949 .... **TCLC 107**
   See also CA 121
Thornton, Hall
   See Silverberg, Robert
Thorpe, Adam 1956- .... **CLC 176**
   See also CA 129; CANR 92, 160; DLB 231
Thorpe, Thomas Bangs
    1815-1878 .... **NCLC 183**
   See also DLB 3, 11, 248; RGAL 4
Thubron, Colin 1939- .... **CLC 163**
   See also CA 25-28R; CANR 12, 29, 59, 95, 171; CN 5, 6, 7; DLB 204, 231
Thubron, Colin Gerald Dryden
   See Thubron, Colin
Thucydides c. 455B.C.-c. 395B.C. .. **CMLC 17**
   See also AW 1; DLB 176; RGWL 2, 3; WLIT 8
Thumboo, Edwin Nadason 1933- .... **PC 30**
   See also CA 194; CP 1
Thurber, James (Grover)
    1894-1961 .. **CLC 5, 11, 25, 125; SSC 1, 47**
   See also AAYA 56; AMWS 1; BPFB 3; BYA 5; CA 73-76; CANR 17, 39; CDALB 1929-1941; CWRI 5; DA; DA3; DAB; DAC; DAM DRAM, MST, NOV; DLB 4, 11, 22, 102; EWL 3; EXPS; FANT; LAIT 3; MAICYA 1, 2; MAL 5; MTCW 1, 2; MTFW 2005; RGAL 4; RGSF 2; SATA 13; SSFS 1, 10, 19; SUFW; TUS
Thurman, Wallace (Henry)
    1902-1934 .. **BLC 1:3; HR 1:3; TCLC 6**
   See also BW 1, 3; CA 104; 124; CANR 81; DAM MULT; DLB 51
Tibullus c. 54B.C.-c. 18B.C. .... **CMLC 36**
   See also AW 2; DLB 211; RGWL 2, 3; WLIT 8
Ticheburn, Cheviot
   See Ainsworth, William Harrison
Tieck, (Johann) Ludwig
    1773-1853 ..... **NCLC 5, 46; SSC 31, 100**
   See also CDWLB 2; DLB 90; EW 5; IDTP; RGSF 2; RGWL 2, 3; SUFW
Tiger, Derry
   See Ellison, Harlan
Tilghman, Christopher 1946- .... **CLC 65**
   See also CA 159; CANR 135, 151; CSW; DLB 244
Tillich, Paul (Johannes)
    1886-1965 .... **CLC 131**
   See also CA 5-8R; 25-28R; CANR 33; MTCW 1, 2
Tillinghast, Richard (Williford)
    1940- .... **CLC 29**
   See also CA 29-32R; CAAS 23; CANR 26, 51, 96; CP 2, 3, 4, 5, 6, 7; CSW
Tillman, Lynne (?)- .... **CLC 231**
   See also CA 173; CANR 144, 172
Timrod, Henry 1828-1867 .... **NCLC 25**
   See also DLB 3, 248; RGAL 4
Tindall, Gillian (Elizabeth) 1938- ...... **CLC 7**
   See also CA 21-24R; CANR 11, 65, 107; CN 1, 2, 3, 4, 5, 6, 7
Ting Ling
   See Chiang, Pin-chin
Tiptree, James, Jr.
   See Sheldon, Alice Hastings Bradley

Ungaretti, Giuseppe 1888-1970 ... **CLC 7, 11, 15; PC 57; TCLC 200**
See also CA 19-20; 25-28R; CAP 2; DLB 114; EW 10; EWL 3; PFS 20; RGWL 2, 3; WLIT 7

Unger, Douglas 1952- .... **CLC 34**
See also CA 130; CANR 94, 155

Unsworth, Barry 1930- .... **CLC 76, 127**
See also BRWS 7; CA 25-28R; CANR 30, 54, 125, 171; CN 6, 7; DLB 194, 326

Unsworth, Barry Forster
See Unsworth, Barry

Updike, John 1932-2009 .... **CLC 1, 2, 3, 5, 7, 9, 13, 15, 23, 34, 43, 70, 139, 214, 278; PC 90; SSC 13, 27, 103; WLC 6**
See also AAYA 36; AMW; AMWC 1; AMWR 1; BPFB 3; BYA 12; CA 1-4R; 282; CABS 1; CANR 4, 33, 51, 94, 133; CDALB 1968-1988; CN 1, 2, 3, 4, 5, 6, 7; CP 1, 2, 3, 4, 5, 6, 7; CPW 1; DA; DA3; DAB; DAC; DAM MST, NOV, POET, POP; DLB 2, 5, 143, 218, 227; DLBD 3; DLBY 1980, 1982, 1997; EWL 3; EXPP; HGG; MAL 5; MTCW 1, 2; MTFW 2005; NFS 12, 24; RGAL 4; RGSF 2; SSFS 3, 19; TUS

Updike, John Hoyer
See Updike, John

Upshaw, Margaret Mitchell
See Mitchell, Margaret (Munnerlyn)

Upton, Mark
See Sanders, Lawrence

Upward, Allen 1863-1926 .... **TCLC 85**
See also CA 117; 187; DLB 36

Urdang, Constance (Henriette)
1922-1996 .... **CLC 47**
See also CA 21-24R; CANR 9, 24; CP 1, 2, 3, 4, 5, 6; CWP

Urfe, Honore d' 1567(?)-1625 .... **LC 132**
See also DLB 268; GFL Beginnings to 1789; RGWL 2, 3

Uriel, Henry
See Faust, Frederick

Uris, Leon 1924-2003 .... **CLC 7, 32**
See also AITN 1, 2; BEST 89:2; BPFB 3; CA 1-4R; 217; CANR 1, 40, 65, 123; CN 1, 2, 3, 4, 5, 6; CPW 1; DA3; DAM NOV, POP; MTCW 1, 2; MTFW 2005; RGHL; SATA 49; SATA-Obit 146

Urista, Alberto 1947- .... **HLCS 1; PC 34**
See also CA 45-48R; CANR 2, 32; DLB 82; HW 1; LLW

Urista Heredia, Alberto Baltazar
See Urista, Alberto

Urmuz
See Codrescu, Andrei

Urquhart, Guy
See McAlmon, Robert (Menzies)

Urquhart, Jane 1949- .... **CLC 90, 242**
See also CA 113; CANR 32, 68, 116, 157; CCA 1; DAC; DLB 334

Usigli, Rodolfo 1905-1979 .... **HLCS 1**
See also CA 131; DLB 305; EWL 3; HW 1; LAW

Usk, Thomas (?)-1388 .... **CMLC 76**
See also DLB 146

Ustinov, Peter (Alexander)
1921-2004 .... **CLC 1**
See also AITN 1; CA 13-16R; 225; CANR 25, 51; CBD; CD 5, 6; DLB 13; MTCW 2

U Tam'si, Gerald Felix Tchicaya
See Tchicaya, Gerald Felix

U Tam'si, Tchicaya
See Tchicaya, Gerald Felix

Vachss, Andrew 1942- .... **CLC 106**
See also CA 118, 214; CAAE 214; CANR 44, 95, 153; CMW 4

Vachss, Andrew H.
See Vachss, Andrew

Vachss, Andrew Henry
See Vachss, Andrew

Vaculik, Ludvik 1926- .... **CLC 7**
See also CA 53-56; CANR 72; CWW 2; DLB 232; EWL 3

Vaihinger, Hans 1852-1933 .... **TCLC 71**
See also CA 116; 166

Valdez, Luis (Miguel) 1940- ..... **CLC 84; DC 10; HLC 2**
See also CA 101; CAD; CANR 32, 81; CD 5, 6; DAM MULT; DFS 5; DLB 122; EWL 3; HW 1; LAIT 4; LLW

Valenzuela, Luisa 1938- .... **CLC 31, 104; HLCS 2; SSC 14, 82**
See also CA 101; CANR 32, 65, 123; CDWLB 3; CWW 2; DAM MULT; DLB 113; EWL 3; FW; HW 1, 2; LAW; RGSF 2; RGWL 3

Valera y Alcala-Galiano, Juan
1824-1905 .... **TCLC 10**
See also CA 106

Valerius Maximus **CMLC 64**
See also DLB 211

Valery, (Ambroise) Paul (Toussaint Jules)
1871-1945 .... **PC 9; TCLC 4, 15**
See also CA 104; 122; DA3; DAM POET; DLB 258; EW 8; EWL 3; GFL 1789 to the Present; MTCW 1, 2; MTFW 2005; RGWL 2, 3; TWA

Valle-Inclan, Ramon (Maria) del
1866-1936 .... **HLC 2; TCLC 5**
See also CA 106; 153; CANR 80; DAM MULT; DLB 134, 322; EW 8; EWL 3; HW 2; RGSF 2; RGWL 2, 3

Vallejo, Antonio Buero
See Buero Vallejo, Antonio

Vallejo, Cesar (Abraham)
1892-1938 .... **HLC 2; TCLC 3, 56**
See also CA 105; 153; DAM MULT; DLB 290; EWL 3; HW 1; LAW; PFS 26; RGWL 2, 3

Valles, Jules 1832-1885 .... **NCLC 71**
See also DLB 123; GFL 1789 to the Present

Vallette, Marguerite Eymery
1860-1953 .... **TCLC 67**
See also CA 182; DLB 123, 192; EWL 3

Valle Y Pena, Ramon del
See Valle-Inclan, Ramon (Maria) del

Van Ash, Cay 1918-1994 .... **CLC 34**
See also CA 220

Vanbrugh, Sir John 1664-1726 .... **LC 21**
See also BRW 2; DAM DRAM; DLB 80; IDTP; RGEL 2

Van Campen, Karl
See Campbell, John W(ood, Jr.)

Vance, Gerald
See Silverberg, Robert

Vance, Jack 1916- .... **CLC 35**
See also CA 29-32R; CANR 17, 65, 154; CMW 4; DLB 8; FANT; MTCW 1; SCFW 1, 2; SFW 4; SUFW 1, 2

Vance, John Holbrook
See Vance, Jack

Van Den Bogarde, Derek Jules Gaspard
Ulric Niven 1921-1999 .... **CLC 14**
See also CA 77-80; 179; DLB 14

Vandenburgh, Jane **CLC 59**
See also CA 168

Vanderhaeghe, Guy 1951- .... **CLC 41**
See also BPFB 3; CA 113; CANR 72, 145; CN 7; DLB 334

van der Post, Laurens (Jan)
1906-1996 .... **CLC 5**
See also AFW; CA 5-8R; 155; CANR 35; CN 1, 2, 3, 4, 5, 6; DLB 204; RGEL 2

van de Wetering, Janwillem
1931-2008 .... **CLC 47**
See also CA 49-52; 274; CANR 4, 62, 90; CMW 4

Van Dine, S. S.
See Wright, Willard Huntington

Van Doren, Carl (Clinton)
1885-1950 .... **TCLC 18**
See also CA 111; 168

Van Doren, Mark 1894-1972 .... **CLC 6, 10**
See also CA 1-4R; 37-40R; CANR 3; CN 1; CP 1; DLB 45, 284, 335; MAL 5; MTCW 1, 2; RGAL 4

Van Druten, John (William)
1901-1957 .... **TCLC 2**
See also CA 104; 161; DLB 10; MAL 5; RGAL 4

Van Duyn, Mona 1921-2004 .... **CLC 3, 7, 63, 116**
See also CA 9-12R; 234; CANR 7, 38, 60, 116; CP 1, 2, 3, 4, 5, 6, 7; CWP; DAM POET; DLB 5; MAL 5; MTFW 2005; PFS 20

Van Dyne, Edith
See Baum, L(yman) Frank

van Herk, Aritha 1954- .... **CLC 249**
See also CA 101; CANR 94; DLB 334

van Itallie, Jean-Claude 1936- .... **CLC 3**
See also CA 45-48; CAAS 2; CAD; CANR 1, 48; CD 5, 6; DLB 7

Van Loot, Cornelius Obenchain
See Roberts, Kenneth (Lewis)

van Ostaijen, Paul 1896-1928 .... **TCLC 33**
See also CA 163

Van Peebles, Melvin 1932- .... **CLC 2, 20**
See also BW 2, 3; CA 85-88; CANR 27, 67, 82; DAM MULT

van Schendel, Arthur(-Francois-Emile)
1874-1946 .... **TCLC 56**
See also EWL 3

Van See, John
See Vance, Jack

Vansittart, Peter 1920-2008 .... **CLC 42**
See also CA 1-4R; 278; CANR 3, 49, 90; CN 4, 5, 6, 7; RHW

Van Vechten, Carl 1880-1964 ... **CLC 33; HR 1:3**
See also AMWS 2; CA 183; 89-92; DLB 4, 9, 51; RGAL 4

van Vogt, A(lfred) E(lton) 1912-2000 . **CLC 1**
See also BPFB 3; BYA 13, 14; CA 21-24R; 190; CANR 28; DLB 8, 251; SATA 14; SATA-Obit 124; SCFW 1, 2; SFW 4

Vara, Madeleine
See Jackson, Laura

Varda, Agnes 1928- .... **CLC 16**
See also CA 116; 122

Vargas Llosa, Jorge Mario Pedro
See Vargas Llosa, Mario

Vargas Llosa, Mario 1936- .. **CLC 3, 6, 9, 10, 15, 31, 42, 85, 181; HLC 2**
See also BPFB 3; CA 73-76; CANR 18, 32, 42, 67, 116, 140, 173; CDWLB 3; CWW 2; DA; DA3; DAB; DAC; DAM MST, MULT, NOV; DLB 145; DNFS 2; EWL 3; HW 1, 2; LAIT 5; LATS 1:2; LAW; LAWS 1; MTCW 1, 2; MTFW 2005; RGWL 2, 3; SSFS 14; TWA; WLIT 1

Varnhagen von Ense, Rahel
1771-1833 .... **NCLC 130**
See also DLB 90

Vasari, Giorgio 1511-1574 .... **LC 114**

Vasilikos, Vasiles
See Vassilikos, Vassilis

Vasiliu, Gheorghe
See Bacovia, George

Vassa, Gustavus
See Equiano, Olaudah

Vassilikos, Vassilis 1933- .... **CLC 4, 8**
    See also CA 81-84; CANR 75, 149; EWL 3
Vaughan, Henry 1621-1695 .... **LC 27; PC 81**
    See also BRW 2; DLB 131; PAB; RGEL 2
Vaughn, Stephanie CLC 62
Vazov, Ivan (Minchov) 1850-1921 . **TCLC 25**
    See also CA 121; 167; CDWLB 4; DLB
    147
Veblen, Thorstein B(unde)
    1857-1929 .... **TCLC 31**
    See also AMWS 1; CA 115; 165; DLB 246;
    MAL 5
Vega, Lope de 1562-1635 ... **HLCS 2; LC 23,
119**
    See also EW 2; RGWL 2, 3
Veldeke, Heinrich von c. 1145-c.
    1190 .... **CMLC 85**
Vendler, Helen 1933- .... **CLC 138**
    See also CA 41-44R; CANR 25, 72, 136,
    190; MTCW 1, 2; MTFW 2005
Vendler, Helen Hennessy
    See Vendler, Helen
Venison, Alfred
    See Pound, Ezra (Weston Loomis)
Ventsel, Elena Sergeevna
    1907-2002 .... **CLC 59**
    See also CA 154; CWW 2; DLB 302
Venttsel', Elena Sergeevna
    See Ventsel, Elena Sergeevna
Verdi, Marie de
    See Mencken, H. L.
Verdu, Matilde
    See Cela, Camilo Jose
Verga, Giovanni (Carmelo)
    1840-1922 .... **SSC 21, 87; TCLC 3**
    See also CA 104; 123; CANR 101; EW 7;
    EWL 3; RGSF 2; RGWL 2, 3; WLIT 7
Vergil 70B.C.-19B.C. .. **CMLC 9, 40, 101; PC
12; WLCS**
    See also AW 2; CDWLB 1; DA; DA3;
    DAB; DAC; DAM MST, POET; DLB
    211; EFS 1; LAIT 1; LMFS 1; RGWL 2,
    3; WLIT 8; WP
Vergil, Polydore c. 1470-1555 .... **LC 108**
    See also DLB 132
Verhaeren, Emile (Adolphe Gustave)
    1855-1916 .... **TCLC 12**
    See also CA 109; EWL 3; GFL 1789 to the
    Present
Verlaine, Paul (Marie) 1844-1896 .. **NCLC 2,
51; PC 2, 32**
    See also DAM POET; DLB 217; EW 7;
    GFL 1789 to the Present; LMFS 2; RGWL
    2, 3; TWA
Verne, Jules (Gabriel) 1828-1905 ... **TCLC 6,
52**
    See also AAYA 16; BYA 4; CA 110; 131;
    CLR 88; DA3; DLB 123; GFL 1789 to
    the Present; JRDA; LAIT 2; LMFS 2;
    MAICYA 1, 2; MTFW 2005; NFS 30;
    RGWL 2, 3; SATA 21; SCFW 1, 2; SFW
    4; TWA; WCH
Verus, Marcus Annius
    See Aurelius, Marcus
Very, Jones 1813-1880 .... **NCLC 9; PC 86**
    See also DLB 1, 243; RGAL 4
Very, Rev. C.
    See Crowley, Edward Alexander
Vesaas, Tarjei 1897-1970 .... **CLC 48**
    See also CA 190; 29-32R; DLB 297; EW
    11; EWL 3; RGWL 3
Vialis, Gaston
    See Simenon, Georges (Jacques Christian)
Vian, Boris 1920-1959(?) .... **TCLC 9**
    See also CA 106; 164; CANR 111; DLB
    72, 321; EWL 3; GFL 1789 to the Present;
    MTCW 2; RGWL 2, 3
Viator, Vacuus
    See Hughes, Thomas

Viaud, Julien 1850-1923 .... **TCLC 11**
    See also CA 107; DLB 123; GFL 1789 to
    the Present
Viaud, Louis Marie Julien
    See Viaud, Julien
Vicar, Henry
    See Felsen, Henry Gregor
Vicente, Gil 1465-c. 1536 .... **LC 99**
    See also DLB 318; IDTP; RGWL 2, 3
Vicker, Angus
    See Felsen, Henry Gregor
Vico, Giambattista
    See Vico, Giovanni Battista
Vico, Giovanni Battista 1668-1744 .... **LC 138**
    See also EW 3; WLIT 7
Vidal, Eugene Luther Gore
    See Vidal, Gore
Vidal, Gore 1925- .... **CLC 2, 4, 6, 8, 10, 22,
33, 72, 142**
    See also AAYA 64; AITN 1; AMWS 4;
    BEST 90:2; BPFB 3; CA 5-8R; CAD;
    CANR 13, 45, 65, 100, 132, 167; CD 5,
    6; CDALBS; CN 1, 2, 3, 4, 5, 6, 7; CPW;
    DA3; DAM NOV, POP; DFS 2; DLB 6,
    152; EWL 3; GLL 1; INT CANR-13;
    MAL 5; MTCW 1, 2; MTFW 2005;
    RGAL 4; RHW; TUS
Viereck, Peter 1916-2006 .... **CLC 4; PC 27**
    See also CA 1-4R; 250; CANR 1, 47; CP 1,
    2, 3, 4, 5, 6, 7; DLB 5; MAL 5; PFS 9,
    14
Viereck, Peter Robert Edwin
    See Viereck, Peter
Vigny, Alfred (Victor) de
    1797-1863 .... **NCLC 7, 102; PC 26**
    See also DAM POET; DLB 119, 192, 217;
    EW 5; GFL 1789 to the Present; RGWL
    2, 3
Vilakazi, Benedict Wallet
    1906-1947 .... **TCLC 37**
    See also CA 168
Vile, Curt
    See Moore, Alan
Villa, Jose Garcia 1914-1997 ... **AAL; PC 22;
TCLC 176**
    See also CA 25-28R; CANR 12, 118; CP 1,
    2, 3, 4; DLB 312; EWL 3; EXPP
Villard, Oswald Garrison
    1872-1949 .... **TCLC 160**
    See also CA 113; 162; DLB 25, 91
Villarreal, Jose Antonio 1924- .... **HLC 2**
    See also CA 133; CANR 93; DAM MULT;
    DLB 82; HW 1; LAIT 4; RGAL 4
Villaurrutia, Xavier 1903-1950 ...... **TCLC 80**
    See also CA 192; EWL 3; HW 1; LAW
Villaverde, Cirilo 1812-1894 .... **NCLC 121**
    See also LAW
Villehardouin, Geoffroi de
    1150(?)-1218(?) .... **CMLC 38**
Villiers, George 1628-1687 .... **LC 107**
    See also DLB 80; RGEL 2
**Villiers de l'Isle Adam, Jean Marie Mathias
    Philippe Auguste** 1838-1889 ... **NCLC 3;
SSC 14**
    See also DLB 123, 192; GFL 1789 to the
    Present; RGSF 2
Villon, Francois 1431-1463(?) .... **LC 62, 166;
PC 13**
    See also DLB 208; EW 2; RGWL 2, 3;
    TWA
Vine, Barbara
    See Rendell, Ruth
Vinge, Joan (Carol) D(ennison)
    1948- .... **CLC 30; SSC 24**
    See also AAYA 32; BPFB 3; CA 93-96;
    CANR 72; SATA 36, 113; SFW 4; YAW
Viola, Herman J(oseph) 1938- .... **CLC 70**
    See also CA 61-64; CANR 8, 23, 48, 91;
    SATA 126

Violis, G.
    See Simenon, Georges (Jacques Christian)
Viramontes, Helena Maria 1954- .... **HLCS 2**
    See also CA 159; CANR 182; DLB 122,
    350; HW 2; LLW
Virgil
    See Vergil
Visconti, Luchino 1906-1976 .... **CLC 16**
    See also CA 81-84; 65-68; CANR 39
Vitry, Jacques de
    See Jacques de Vitry
Vittorini, Elio 1908-1966 .... **CLC 6, 9, 14**
    See also CA 133; 25-28R; DLB 264; EW
    12; EWL 3; RGWL 2, 3
Vivekananda, Swami 1863-1902 .... **TCLC 88**
Vives, Juan Luis 1493-1540 .... **LC 170**
    See also DLB 318
Vizenor, Gerald Robert 1934- .... **CLC 103,
263; NNAL**
    See also CA 13-16R, 205; CAAE 205;
    CAAS 22; CANR 5, 21, 44, 67; DAM
    MULT; DLB 175, 227; MTCW 2; MTFW
    2005; TCWW 2
Vizinczey, Stephen 1933- .... **CLC 40**
    See also CA 128; CCA 1; INT CA-128
Vliet, R(ussell) G(ordon)
    1929-1984 .... **CLC 22**
    See also CA 37-40R; 112; CANR 18; CP 2,
    3
Vogau, Boris Andreevich
    See Vogau, Boris Andreyevich
Vogau, Boris Andreyevich
    1894-1938 .... **SSC 48; TCLC 23**
    See also CA 123; 218; DLB 272; EWL 3;
    RGSF 2; RGWL 2, 3
Vogel, Paula A. 1951- .... **CLC 76; DC 19**
    See also CA 108; CAD; CANR 119, 140;
    CD 5, 6; CWD; DFS 14; DLB 341;
    MTFW 2005; RGAL 4
Voigt, Cynthia 1942- .... **CLC 30**
    See also AAYA 3, 30; BYA 1, 3, 6, 7, 8;
    CA 106; CANR 18, 37, 40, 94, 145; CLR
    13, 48, 141; INT CANR-18; JRDA; LAIT
    5; MAICYA 1, 2; MAICYAS 1; MTFW
    2005; SATA 48, 79, 116, 160; SATA-Brief
    33; WYA; YAW
Voigt, Ellen Bryant 1943- .... **CLC 54**
    See also CA 69-72; CANR 11, 29, 55, 115,
    171; CP 5, 6, 7; CSW; CWP; DLB 120;
    PFS 23
Voinovich, Vladimir 1932- .. **CLC 10, 49, 147**
    See also CA 81-84; CAAS 12; CANR 33,
    67, 150; CWW 2; DLB 302; MTCW 1
Voinovich, Vladimir Nikolaevich
    See Voinovich, Vladimir
Vollmann, William T. 1959- ...... **CLC 89, 227**
    See also AMWS 17; CA 134; CANR 67,
    116, 185; CN 7; CPW; DA3; DAM NOV,
    POP; DLB 350; MTCW 2; MTFW 2005
Voloshinov, V. N.
    See Bakhtin, Mikhail Mikhailovich
Voltaire 1694-1778 .. **LC 14, 79, 110; SSC 12,
112; WLC 6**
    See also BYA 13; DA; DA3; DAB; DAC;
    DAM DRAM, MST; DLB 314; EW 4;
    GFL Beginnings to 1789; LATS 1:1;
    LMFS 1; NFS 7; RGWL 2, 3; TWA
von Aschendrof, Baron Ignatz
    See Ford, Ford Madox
von Chamisso, Adelbert
    See Chamisso, Adelbert von
von Daeniken, Erich 1935- .... **CLC 30**
    See also AITN 1; CA 37-40R; CANR 17,
    44
von Daniken, Erich
    See von Daeniken, Erich

Wang Wei 699(?)-761(?) . **CMLC 100; PC 18**
See also TWA

Warburton, William 1698-1779 .... **LC 97**
See also DLB 104

Ward, Arthur Henry Sarsfield
1883-1959 .... **TCLC 28**
See also CA 108; 173; CMW 4; DLB 70;
HGG; MSW; SUFW

Ward, Douglas Turner 1930- .... **CLC 19**
See also BW 1; CA 81-84; CAD; CANR
27; CD 5, 6; DLB 7, 38

Ward, E. D.
See Lucas, E(dward) V(errall)

Ward, Mrs. Humphry 1851-1920
See Ward, Mary Augusta
See also RGEL 2

Ward, Mary Augusta 1851-1920 ... **TCLC 55**
See Ward, Mrs. Humphry
See also DLB 18

Ward, Nathaniel 1578(?)-1652 .... **LC 114**
See also DLB 24

Ward, Peter
See Faust, Frederick

Warhol, Andy 1928(?)-1987 .... **CLC 20**
See also AAYA 12; BEST 89:4; CA 89-92;
121; CANR 34

Warner, Francis (Robert Le Plastrier)
1937- .... **CLC 14**
See also CA 53-56; CANR 11; CP 1, 2, 3, 4

Warner, Marina 1946- .... **CLC 59, 231**
See also CA 65-68; CANR 21, 55, 118; CN
5, 6, 7; DLB 194; MTFW 2005

Warner, Rex (Ernest) 1905-1986 ...... **CLC 45**
See also CA 89-92; 119; CN 1, 2, 3, 4; CP
1, 2, 3, 4; DLB 15; RGEL 2; RHW

Warner, Susan (Bogert)
1819-1885 .... **NCLC 31, 146**
See also AMWS 18; DLB 3, 42, 239, 250,
254

Warner, Sylvia (Constance) Ashton
See Ashton-Warner, Sylvia (Constance)

Warner, Sylvia Townsend
1893-1978 .. **CLC 7, 19; SSC 23; TCLC
131**
See also BRWS 7; CA 61-64; 77-80; CANR
16, 60, 104; CN 1, 2; DLB 34, 139; EWL
3; FANT; FW; MTCW 1, 2; RGEL 2;
RGSF 2; RHW

Warren, Mercy Otis 1728-1814 ..... **NCLC 13**
See also DLB 31, 200; RGAL 4; TUS

Warren, Robert Penn 1905-1989 .. **CLC 1, 4,
6, 8, 10, 13, 18, 39, 53, 59; PC 37; SSC
4, 58, 126; WLC 6**
See also AITN 1; AMW; AMWC 2; BPFB
3; BYA 1; CA 13-16R; 129; CANR 10,
47; CDALB 1968-1988; CN 1, 2, 3, 4;
CP 1, 2, 3, 4; DA; DA3; DAB; DAC;
DAM MST, NOV, POET; DLB 2, 48, 152,
320; DLBY 1980, 1989; EWL 3; INT
CANR-10; MAL 5; MTCW 1, 2; MTFW
2005; NFS 13; RGAL 4; RGSF 2; RHW;
SATA 46; SATA-Obit 63; SSFS 8; TUS

Warrigal, Jack
See Furphy, Joseph

Warshofsky, Isaac
See Singer, Isaac Bashevis

Warton, Joseph 1722-1800 ... **LC 128; NCLC
118**
See also DLB 104, 109; RGEL 2

Warton, Thomas 1728-1790 .... **LC 15, 82**
See also DAM POET; DLB 104, 109, 336;
RGEL 2

Waruk, Kona
See Harris, (Theodore) Wilson

Warung, Price
See Astley, William

Warwick, Jarvis
See Garner, Hugh

Washington, Alex
See Harris, Mark

Washington, Booker T(aliaferro)
1856-1915 .... **BLC 1:3; TCLC 10**
See also BW 1; CA 114; 125; DA3; DAM
MULT; DLB 345; LAIT 2; RGAL 4;
SATA 28

Washington, George 1732-1799 .... **LC 25**
See also DLB 31

Wassermann, (Karl) Jakob
1873-1934 .... **TCLC 6**
See also CA 104; 163; DLB 66; EWL 3

Wasserstein, Wendy 1950-2006 . **CLC 32, 59,
90, 183; DC 4**
See also AAYA 73; AMWS 15; CA 121;
129; 247; CABS 3; CAD; CANR 53, 75,
128; CD 5, 6; CWD; DA3; DAM DRAM;
DFS 5, 17; DLB 228; EWL 3; FW; INT
CA-129; MAL 5; MTCW 2; MTFW 2005;
SATA 94; SATA-Obit 174

Waterhouse, Keith (Spencer) 1929- . **CLC 47**
See also BRWS 13; CA 5-8R; CANR 38,
67, 109; CBD; CD 6; CN 1, 2, 3, 4, 5, 6,
7; DLB 13, 15; MTCW 1, 2; MTFW 2005

Waters, Frank (Joseph) 1902-1995 .. **CLC 88**
See also CA 5-8R; 149; CAAS 13; CANR
3, 18, 63, 121; DLB 212; DLBY 1986;
RGAL 4; TCWW 1, 2

Waters, Mary C. CLC 70

Waters, Roger 1944- .... **CLC 35**

Watkins, Frances Ellen
See Harper, Frances Ellen Watkins

Watkins, Gerrold
See Malzberg, Barry N(athaniel)

Watkins, Gloria Jean
See hooks, bell

Watkins, Paul 1964- .... **CLC 55**
See also CA 132; CANR 62, 98

Watkins, Vernon Phillips
1906-1967 .... **CLC 43**
See also CA 9-10; 25-28R; CAP 1; DLB
20; EWL 3; RGEL 2

Watson, Irving S.
See Mencken, H. L.

Watson, John H.
See Farmer, Philip Jose

Watson, Richard F.
See Silverberg, Robert

Watts, Ephraim
See Horne, Richard Henry Hengist

Watts, Isaac 1674-1748 .... **LC 98**
See also DLB 95; RGEL 2; SATA 52

Waugh, Auberon (Alexander)
1939-2001 .... **CLC 7**
See also CA 45-48; 192; CANR 6, 22, 92;
CN 1, 2, 3; DLB 14, 194

Waugh, Evelyn 1903-1966 ... **CLC 1, 3, 8, 13,
19, 27, 44, 107; SSC 41; WLC 6**
See also AAYA 78; BPFB 3; BRW 7; CA
85-88; 25-28R; CANR 22; CDBLB 1914-
1945; DA; DA3; DAB; DAC; DAM MST,
NOV, POP; DLB 15, 162, 195, 352; EWL
3; MTCW 1, 2; MTFW 2005; NFS 13,
17; RGEL 2; RGSF 2; TEA; WLIT 4

Waugh, Evelyn Arthur St. John
See Waugh, Evelyn

Waugh, Harriet 1944- .... **CLC 6**
See also CA 85-88; CANR 22

Ways, C.R.
See Blount, Roy, Jr.

Waystaff, Simon
See Swift, Jonathan

Webb, Beatrice (Martha Potter)
1858-1943 .... **TCLC 22**
See also CA 117; 162; DLB 190; FW

Webb, Charles 1939- .... **CLC 7**
See also CA 25-28R; CANR 114, 188

Webb, Charles Richard
See Webb, Charles

Webb, Frank J. NCLC 143
See also DLB 50

Webb, James, Jr.
See Webb, James

Webb, James 1946- .... **CLC 22**
See also CA 81-84; CANR 156

Webb, James H.
See Webb, James

Webb, James Henry
See Webb, James

Webb, Mary Gladys (Meredith)
1881-1927 .... **TCLC 24**
See also CA 182; 123; DLB 34; FW; RGEL
2

Webb, Mrs. Sidney
See Webb, Beatrice (Martha Potter)

Webb, Phyllis 1927- .... **CLC 18**
See also CA 104; CANR 23; CCA 1; CP 1,
2, 3, 4, 5, 6, 7; CWP; DLB 53

Webb, Sidney (James) 1859-1947 .. **TCLC 22**
See also CA 117; 163; DLB 190

Webber, Andrew Lloyd
See Lloyd Webber, Andrew

Weber, Lenora Mattingly
1895-1971 .... **CLC 12**
See also CA 19-20; 29-32R; CAP 1; SATA
2; SATA-Obit 26

Weber, Max 1864-1920 .... **TCLC 69**
See also CA 109; 189; DLB 296

Webster, John 1580(?)-1634(?) ...... **DC 2; LC
33, 84, 124; WLC 6**
See also BRW 2; CDBLB Before 1660; DA;
DAB; DAC; DAM DRAM, MST; DFS
17, 19; DLB 58; IDTP; RGEL 2; WLIT 3

Webster, Noah 1758-1843 .... **NCLC 30**
See also DLB 1, 37, 42, 43, 73, 243

Wedekind, Benjamin Franklin
See Wedekind, Frank

Wedekind, Frank 1864-1918 .... **TCLC 7**
See also CA 104; 153; CANR 121, 122;
CDWLB 2; DAM DRAM; DLB 118; EW
8; EWL 3; LMFS 2; RGWL 2, 3

Wehr, Demaris CLC 65

Weidman, Jerome 1913-1998 .... **CLC 7**
See also AITN 2; CA 1-4R; 171; CAD;
CANR 1; CD 1, 2, 3, 4, 5; DLB 28

Weil, Simone (Adolphine)
1909-1943 .... **TCLC 23**
See also CA 117; 159; EW 12; EWL 3; FW;
GFL 1789 to the Present; MTCW 2

Weininger, Otto 1880-1903 .... **TCLC 84**

Weinstein, Nathan
See West, Nathanael

Weinstein, Nathan von Wallenstein
See West, Nathanael

Weir, Peter (Lindsay) 1944- .... **CLC 20**
See also CA 113; 123

Weiss, Peter (Ulrich) 1916-1982 .. **CLC 3, 15,
51; DC 36; TCLC 152**
See also CA 45-48; 106; CANR 3; DAM
DRAM; DFS 3; DLB 69, 124; EWL 3;
RGHL; RGWL 2, 3

Weiss, Theodore (Russell)
1916-2003 .... **CLC 3, 8, 14**
See also CA 9-12R; 189; 216; CAAE 189;
CAAS 2; CANR 46, 94; CP 1, 2, 3, 4, 5,
6, 7; DLB 5; TCLE 1:2

Welch, (Maurice) Denton
1915-1948 .... **TCLC 22**
See also BRWS 8, 9; CA 121; 148; RGEL
2

Welch, James (Phillip) 1940-2003 ..... **CLC 6,
14, 52, 249; NNAL; PC 62**
See also CA 85-88; 219; CANR 42, 66, 107;
CN 5, 6, 7; CP 2, 3, 4, 5, 6, 7; CPW;
DAM MULT, POP; DLB 175, 256; LATS
1:1; NFS 23; RGAL 4; TCWW 1, 2

Whitaker, Rodney William
See Whitaker, Rod

White, Babington
See Braddon, Mary Elizabeth

White, E. B. 1899-1985 .... **CLC 10, 34, 39**
See also AAYA 62; AITN 2; AMWS 1; CA 13-16R; 116; CANR 16, 37; CDALBS; CLR 1, 21, 107; CPW; DA3; DAM POP; DLB 11, 22; EWL 3; FANT; MAICYA 1, 2; MAL 5; MTCW 1, 2; MTFW 2005; NCFS 5; RGAL 4; SATA 2, 29, 100; SATA-Obit 44; TUS

White, Edmund 1940- .... **CLC 27, 110**
See also AAYA 7; CA 45-48; CANR 3, 19, 36, 62, 107, 133, 172; DA3; DAM POP; DLB 227; MTCW 1, 2; MTFW 2005

White, Edmund Valentine III
See White, Edmund

White, Elwyn Brooks
See White, E. B.

White, Hayden V. 1928- .... **CLC 148**
See also CA 128; CANR 135; DLB 246

White, Patrick (Victor Martindale)
1912-1990 ...... **CLC 3, 4, 5, 7, 9, 18, 65, 69; SSC 39; TCLC 176**
See also BRWS 1; CA 81-84; 132; CANR 43; CN 1, 2, 3, 4; DLB 260, 332; EWL 3; MTCW 1; RGEL 2; RGSF 2; RHW; TWA; WWE 1

White, Phyllis Dorothy James
1920- .... **CLC 18, 46, 122, 226**
See also BEST 90:2; BPFB 2; BRWS 4; CA 21-24R; CANR 17, 43, 65, 112; CDBLB 1960 to Present; CMW 4; CN 4, 5, 6; CPW; DA3; DAM POP; DLB 87, 276; DLBD 17; MSW; MTCW 1, 2; MTFW 2005; TEA

White, T(erence) H(anbury)
1906-1964 .... **CLC 30**
See also AAYA 22; BPFB 3; BYA 4, 5; CA 73-76; CANR 37; CLR 139; DLB 160; FANT; JRDA; LAIT 1; MAICYA 1, 2; NFS 30; RGEL 2; SATA 12; SUFW 1; YAW

White, Terence de Vere 1912-1994 ... **CLC 49**
See also CA 49-52; 145; CANR 3

White, Walter
See White, Walter F(rancis)

White, Walter F(rancis)
1893-1955 ..... **BLC 1:3; HR 1:3; TCLC 15**
See also BW 1; CA 115; 124; DAM MULT; DLB 51

White, William Hale 1831-1913 ..... **TCLC 25**
See also CA 121; 189; DLB 18; RGEL 2

Whitehead, Alfred North
1861-1947 .... **TCLC 97**
See also CA 117; 165; DLB 100, 262

Whitehead, Colson 1969- ...... **BLC 2:3; CLC 232**
See also CA 202; CANR 162

Whitehead, E(dward) A(nthony)
1933- .... **CLC 5**
See also CA 65-68; CANR 58, 118; CBD; CD 5, 6; DLB 310

Whitehead, Ted
See Whitehead, E(dward) A(nthony)

Whiteman, Roberta J. Hill 1947- ...... **NNAL**
See also CA 146

Whitemore, Hugh (John) 1936- .... **CLC 37**
See also CA 132; CANR 77; CBD; CD 5, 6; INT CA-132

Whitman, Sarah Helen (Power)
1803-1878 .... **NCLC 19**
See also DLB 1, 243

Whitman, Walt(er) 1819-1892 .. **NCLC 4, 31, 81, 205; PC 3, 91; WLC 6**
See also AAYA 42; AMW; AMWR 1; CDALB 1640-1865; DA; DA3; DAB; DAC; DAM MST, POET; DLB 3, 64, 224, 250; EXPP; LAIT 2; LMFS 1; PAB; PFS 2, 3, 13, 22, 31; RGAL 4; SATA 20; TUS; WP; WYAS 1

Whitney, Isabella fl. 1565-fl. 1575 ..... **LC 130**
See also DLB 136

Whitney, Phyllis A. 1903-2008 .... **CLC 42**
See also AAYA 36; AITN 2; BEST 90:3; CA 1-4R; 269; CANR 3, 25, 38, 60; CLR 59; CMW 4; CPW; DA3; DAM POP; JRDA; MAICYA 1, 2; MTCW 2; RHW; SATA 1, 30; SATA-Obit 189; YAW

Whitney, Phyllis Ayame
See Whitney, Phyllis A.

Whitney, Phyllis Ayame
See Whitney, Phyllis A.

Whittemore, (Edward) Reed, Jr.
1919- .... **CLC 4**
See also CA 9-12R, 219; CAAE 219; CAAS 8; CANR 4, 119; CP 1, 2, 3, 4, 5, 6, 7; DLB 5; MAL 5

Whittier, John Greenleaf
1807-1892 .... **NCLC 8, 59; PC 93**
See also AMWS 1; DLB 1, 243; RGAL 4

Whittlebot, Hernia
See Coward, Noel

Wicker, Thomas Grey
See Wicker, Tom

Wicker, Tom 1926- .... **CLC 7**
See also CA 65-68; CANR 21, 46, 141, 179

Wicomb, Zoe 1948- .... **BLC 2:3**
See also CA 127; CANR 106, 167; DLB 225

Wideman, John Edgar 1941- .. **BLC 1:3, 2:3; CLC 5, 34, 36, 67, 122; SSC 62**
See also AFAW 1, 2; AMWS 10; BPFB 4; BW 2, 3; CA 85-88; CANR 14, 42, 67, 109, 140, 187; CN 4, 5, 6, 7; DAM MULT; DLB 33, 143; MAL 5; MTCW 2; MTFW 2005; RGAL 4; RGSF 2; SSFS 6, 12, 24; TCLE 1:2

Wiebe, Rudy 1934- . **CLC 6, 11, 14, 138, 263**
See also CA 37-40R; CANR 42, 67, 123; CN 1, 2, 3, 4, 5, 6, 7; DAC; DAM MST; DLB 60; RHW; SATA 156

Wiebe, Rudy Henry
See Wiebe, Rudy

Wieland, Christoph Martin
1733-1813 .... **NCLC 17, 177**
See also DLB 97; EW 4; LMFS 1; RGWL 2, 3

Wiene, Robert 1881-1938 .... **TCLC 56**

Wieners, John 1934- .... **CLC 7**
See also BG 1:3; CA 13-16R; CP 1, 2, 3, 4, 5, 6, 7; DLB 16; WP

Wiesel, Elie 1928- ...... **CLC 3, 5, 11, 37, 165; WLCS**
See also AAYA 7, 54; AITN 1; CA 5-8R; CAAS 4; CANR 8, 40, 65, 125; CDALBS; CWW 2; DA; DA3; DAB; DAC; DAM MST, NOV; DLB 83, 299; DLBY 1987; EWL 3; INT CANR-8; LAIT 4; MTCW 1, 2; MTFW 2005; NCFS 4; NFS 4; RGHL; RGWL 3; SATA 56; YAW

Wiesel, Eliezer
See Wiesel, Elie

Wiggins, Marianne 1947- .... **CLC 57**
See also AAYA 70; BEST 89:3; CA 130; CANR 60, 139, 180; CN 7; DLB 335

Wigglesworth, Michael 1631-1705 .... **LC 106**
See also DLB 24; RGAL 4

Wiggs, Susan CLC 70
See also CA 201; CANR 173

Wight, James Alfred 1916-1995 .... **CLC 12**
See also AAYA 1, 54; BPFB 2; CA 77-80; 148; CANR 40; CLR 80; CPW; DAM POP; LAIT 3; MAICYA 2; MAICYAS 1; MTCW 2; SATA 86, 135; SATA-Brief 44; TEA; YAW

Wilbur, Richard 1921- .. **CLC 3, 6, 9, 14, 53, 110; PC 51**
See also AAYA 72; AMWS 3; CA 1-4R; CABS 2; CANR 2, 29, 76, 93, 139; CDALBS; CP 1, 2, 3, 4, 5, 6, 7; DA; DAB; DAC; DAM MST, POET; DLB 5, 169; EWL 3; EXPP; INT CANR-29; MAL 5; MTCW 1, 2; MTFW 2005; PAB; PFS 11, 12, 16, 29; RGAL 4; SATA 9, 108; WP

Wilbur, Richard Purdy
See Wilbur, Richard

Wild, Peter 1940- .... **CLC 14**
See also CA 37-40R; CP 1, 2, 3, 4, 5, 6, 7; DLB 5

Wilde, Oscar 1854(?)-1900 ... **DC 17; SSC 11, 77; TCLC 1, 8, 23, 41, 175; WLC 6**
See also AAYA 49; BRW 5; BRWC 1, 2; BRWR 2; BYA 15; CA 104; 119; CANR 112; CDBLB 1890-1914; CLR 114; DA; DA3; DAB; DAC; DAM DRAM, MST, NOV; DFS 4, 8, 9, 21; DLB 10, 19, 34, 57, 141, 156, 190, 344; EXPS; FANT; GL 3; LATS 1:1; NFS 20; RGEL 2; RGSF 2; SATA 24; SSFS 7; SUFW; TEA; WCH; WLIT 4

Wilde, Oscar Fingal O'Flahertie Willis
See Wilde, Oscar

Wilder, Billy
See Wilder, Samuel

Wilder, Samuel 1906-2002 .... **CLC 20**
See also AAYA 66; CA 89-92; 205; DLB 26

Wilder, Stephen
See Marlowe, Stephen

Wilder, Thornton (Niven)
1897-1975 .. **CLC 1, 5, 6, 10, 15, 35, 82; DC 1, 24; WLC 6**
See also AAYA 29; AITN 2; AMW; CA 13-16R; 61-64; CAD; CANR 40, 132; CDALBS; CN 1, 2; DA; DA3; DAB; DAC; DAM DRAM, MST, NOV; DFS 1, 4, 16; DLB 4, 7, 9, 228; DLBY 1997; EWL 3; LAIT 3; MAL 5; MTCW 1, 2; MTFW 2005; NFS 24; RGAL 4; RHW; WYAS 1

Wilding, Michael 1942- ...... **CLC 73; SSC 50**
See also CA 104; CANR 24, 49, 106; CN 4, 5, 6, 7; DLB 325; RGSF 2

Wiley, Richard 1944- .... **CLC 44**
See also CA 121; 129; CANR 71

Wilhelm, Kate
See Wilhelm, Katie

Wilhelm, Katie 1928- .... **CLC 7**
See also AAYA 20; BYA 16; CA 37-40R; CAAS 5; CANR 17, 36, 60, 94; DLB 8; INT CANR-17; MTCW 1; SCFW 2; SFW 4

Wilhelm, Katie Gertrude
See Wilhelm, Katie

Wilkins, Mary
See Freeman, Mary E(leanor) Wilkins

Willard, Nancy 1936- .... **CLC 7, 37**
See also BYA 5; CA 89-92; CANR 10, 39, 68, 107, 152, 186; CLR 5; CP 2, 3, 4, 5; CWP; CWRI 5; DLB 5, 52; FANT; MAICYA 1, 2; MTCW 1; SATA 37, 71, 127, 191; SATA-Brief 30; SUFW 2; TCLE 1:2

William of Malmesbury c. 1090B.C.-c. 1140B.C. .... **CMLC 57**

William of Moerbeke c. 1215-c. 1286 .... **CMLC 91**

William of Ockham 1290-1349 ..... **CMLC 32**

Williams, Ben Ames 1889-1953 ..... **TCLC 89**
See also CA 183; DLB 102

Witkacy
See Witkiewicz, Stanislaw Ignacy
Witkiewicz, Stanislaw Ignacy
1885-1939 .... **TCLC 8**
See also CA 105; 162; CDWLB 4; DLB
215; EW 10; EWL 3; RGWL 2, 3; SFW 4
Wittgenstein, Ludwig (Josef Johann)
1889-1951 .... **TCLC 59**
See also CA 113; 164; DLB 262; MTCW 2
Wittig, Monique 1935-2003 .... **CLC 22**
See also CA 116; 135; 212; CANR 143;
CWW 2; DLB 83; EWL 3; FW; GLL 1
Wittlin, Jozef 1896-1976 .... **CLC 25**
See also CA 49-52; 65-68; CANR 3; EWL
3
Wodehouse, P(elham) G(renville)
1881-1975 .. **CLC 1, 2, 5, 10, 22; SSC 2,
115; TCLC 108**
See also AAYA 65; AITN 2; BRWS 3; CA
45-48; 57-60; CANR 3, 33; CDBLB
1914-1945; CN 1, 2; CPW; DA3; DAB;
DAC; DAM NOV; DLB 34, 162, 352;
EWL 3; MTCW 1, 2; MTFW 2005; RGEL
2; RGSF 2; SATA 22; SSFS 10
Woiwode, L.
See Woiwode, Larry
Woiwode, Larry 1941- .... **CLC 6, 10**
See also CA 73-76; CANR 16, 94, 192; CN
3, 4, 5, 6, 7; DLB 6; INT CANR-16
Woiwode, Larry Alfred
See Woiwode, Larry
Wojciechowska, Maia (Teresa)
1927-2002 .... **CLC 26**
See also AAYA 8, 46; BYA 3; CA 9-12R;
183; 209; CAAE 183; CANR 4, 41; CLR
1; JRDA; MAICYA 1, 2; SAAS 1; SATA
1, 28, 83; SATA-Essay 104; SATA-Obit
134; YAW
Wojtyla, Karol (Josef)
See John Paul II, Pope
Wojtyla, Karol (Jozef)
See John Paul II, Pope
Wolf, Christa 1929- ...... **CLC 14, 29, 58, 150,
261**
See also CA 85-88; CANR 45, 123; CD-
WLB 2; CWW 2; DLB 75; EWL 3; FW;
MTCW 1; RGWL 2, 3; SSFS 14
Wolf, Naomi 1962- .... **CLC 157**
See also CA 141; CANR 110; FW; MTFW
2005
Wolfe, Gene 1931- .... **CLC 25**
See also AAYA 35; CA 57-60; CAAS 9;
CANR 6, 32, 60, 152; CPW; DAM POP;
DLB 8; FANT; MTCW 2; MTFW 2005;
SATA 118, 165; SCFW 2; SFW 4; SUFW
2
Wolfe, Gene Rodman
See Wolfe, Gene
Wolfe, George C. 1954- .... **BLCS; CLC 49**
See also CA 149; CAD; CD 5, 6
Wolfe, Thomas (Clayton)
1900-1938 .... **SSC 33, 113; TCLC 4, 13,
29, 61; WLC 6**
See also AMW; BPFB 3; CA 104; 132;
CANR 102; CDALB 1929-1941; DA;
DA3; DAB; DAC; DAM MST, NOV;
DLB 9, 102, 229; DLBD 2, 16; DLBY
1985, 1997; EWL 3; MAL 5; MTCW 1,
2; NFS 18; RGAL 4; SSFS 18; TUS
Wolfe, Thomas Kennerly, Jr. 1931- .. **CLC 1,
2, 9, 15, 35, 51, 147**
See also AAYA 8, 67; AITN 2; AMWS 3;
BEST 89:1; BPFB 3; CA 13-16R; CANR
9, 33, 70, 104; CN 5, 6, 7; CPW; CSW;
DA3; DAM POP; DLB 152, 185 185;
EWL 3; INT CANR-9; LAIT 5; MTCW
1, 2; MTFW 2005; RGAL 4; TUS
Wolfe, Tom
See Wolfe, Thomas Kennerly, Jr.

Wolff, Geoffrey 1937- .... **CLC 41**
See also CA 29-32R; CANR 29, 43, 78, 154
Wolff, Geoffrey Ansell
See Wolff, Geoffrey
Wolff, Sonia
See Levitin, Sonia
Wolff, Tobias 1945- .... **CLC 39, 64, 172; SSC
63**
See also AAYA 16; AMWS 7; BEST 90:2;
BYA 12; CA 114; 117; CAAS 22; CANR
54, 76, 96, 192; CN 5, 6, 7; CSW; DA3;
DLB 130; EWL 3; INT CA-117; MTCW
2; MTFW 2005; RGAL 4; RGSF 2; SSFS
4, 11
Wolitzer, Hilma 1930- .... **CLC 17**
See also CA 65-68; CANR 18, 40, 172; INT
CANR-18; SATA 31; YAW
Wollstonecraft, Mary 1759-1797 .... **LC 5, 50,
90, 147**
See also BRWS 3; CDBLB 1789-1832;
DLB 39, 104, 158, 252; FL 1:1; FW;
LAIT 1; RGEL 2; TEA; WLIT 3
Wonder, Stevie 1950- .... **CLC 12**
See also CA 111
Wong, Jade Snow 1922-2006 .... **CLC 17**
See also CA 109; 249; CANR 91; SATA
112; SATA-Obit 175
Wood, Ellen Price
See Wood, Mrs. Henry
Wood, Mrs. Henry 1814-1887 ...... **NCLC 178**
See also CMW 4; DLB 18; SUFW
Wood, James 1965- .... **CLC 238**
See also CA 235
Woodberry, George Edward
1855-1930 .... **TCLC 73**
See also CA 165; DLB 71, 103
Woodcott, Keith
See Brunner, John (Kilian Houston)
Woodruff, Robert W.
See Mencken, H. L.
Woodward, Bob 1943- .... **CLC 240**
See also CA 69-72; CANR 31, 67, 107, 176;
MTCW 1
Woodward, Robert Upshur
See Woodward, Bob
Woolf, (Adeline) Virginia 1882-1941 .. **SSC 7,
79; TCLC 1, 5, 20, 43, 56, 101, 123,
128; WLC 6**
See also AAYA 44; BPFB 3; BRW 7;
BRWC 2; BRWR 1; CA 104; 130; CANR
64, 132; CDBLB 1914-1945; DA; DA3;
DAB; DAC; DAM MST, NOV; DLB 36,
100, 162; DLBD 10; EWL 3; EXPS; FL
1:6; FW; LAIT 3; LATS 1:1; LMFS 2;
MTCW 1, 2; MTFW 2005; NCFS 2; NFS
8, 12, 28; RGEL 2; RGSF 2; SSFS 4, 12;
TEA; WLIT 4
Woollcott, Alexander (Humphreys)
1887-1943 .... **TCLC 5**
See also CA 105; 161; DLB 29
Woolman, John 1720-1772 .... **LC 155**
See also DLB 31
Woolrich, Cornell
See Hopley-Woolrich, Cornell George
Woolson, Constance Fenimore
1840-1894 .... **NCLC 82; SSC 90**
See also DLB 12, 74, 189, 221; RGAL 4
Wordsworth, Dorothy 1771-1855 . **NCLC 25,
138**
See also DLB 107
Wordsworth, William 1770-1850 .. **NCLC 12,
38, 111, 166, 206; PC 4, 67; WLC 6**
See also AAYA 70; BRW 4; BRWC 1; CD-
BLB 1789-1832; DA; DA3; DAB; DAC;
DAM MST, POET; DLB 93, 107; EXPP;
LATS 1:1; LMFS 1; PAB; PFS 2; RGEL
2; TEA; WLIT 3; WP
Wotton, Sir Henry 1568-1639 .... **LC 68**
See also DLB 121; RGEL 2

Wouk, Herman 1915- .... **CLC 1, 9, 38**
See also BPFB 2, 3; CA 5-8R; CANR 6,
33, 67, 146; CDALBS; CN 1, 2, 3, 4, 5,
6; CPW; DA3; DAM NOV, POP; DLBY
1982; INT CANR-6; LAIT 4; MAL 5;
MTCW 1, 2; MTFW 2005; NFS 7; TUS
Wright, Charles 1932-2008 ... **BLC 1:3; CLC
49**
See also BW 1; CA 9-12R; 278; CANR 26;
CN 1, 2, 3, 4, 5, 6, 7; DAM MULT,
POET; DLB 33
Wright, Charles 1935- ... **CLC 6, 13, 28, 119,
146**
See also AMWS 5; CA 29-32R; CAAS 7;
CANR 23, 36, 62, 88, 135, 180; CP 3, 4,
5, 6, 7; DLB 165; DLBY 1982; EWL 3;
MTCW 1, 2; MTFW 2005; PFS 10
Wright, Charles Penzel, Jr.
See Wright, Charles
Wright, Charles Stevenson
See Wright, Charles
Wright, Frances 1795-1852 .... **NCLC 74**
See also DLB 73
Wright, Frank Lloyd 1867-1959 .... **TCLC 95**
See also AAYA 33; CA 174
Wright, Harold Bell 1872-1944 .... **TCLC 183**
See also BPFB 3; CA 110; DLB 9; TCWW
2
Wright, Jack R.
See Harris, Mark
Wright, James (Arlington)
1927-1980 .... **CLC 3, 5, 10, 28; PC 36**
See also AITN 2; AMWS 3; CA 49-52; 97-
100; CANR 4, 34, 64; CDALBS; CP 1, 2;
DAM POET; DLB 5, 169, 342; EWL 3;
EXPP; MAL 5; MTCW 1, 2; MTFW
2005; PFS 7, 8; RGAL 4; TUS; WP
Wright, Judith 1915-2000 ... **CLC 11, 53; PC
14**
See also CA 13-16R; 188; CANR 31, 76,
93; CP 1, 2, 3, 4, 5, 6, 7; CWP; DLB 260;
EWL 3; MTCW 1, 2; MTFW 2005; PFS
8; RGEL 2; SATA 14; SATA-Obit 121
Wright, L(aurali) R. 1939- .... **CLC 44**
See also CA 138; CMW 4
Wright, Richard 1908-1960 .. **BLC 1:3; CLC
1, 3, 4, 9, 14, 21, 48, 74; SSC 2, 109;
TCLC 136, 180; WLC 6**
See also AAYA 5, 42; AFAW 1, 2; AMW;
BPFB 3; BW 1; BYA 2; CA 108; CANR
64; CDALB 1929-1941; DA; DA3; DAB;
DAC; DAM MST, MULT, NOV; DLB 76,
102; DLBD 2; EWL 3; EXPN; LAIT 3,
4; MAL 5; MTCW 1, 2; MTFW 2005;
NCFS 1; NFS 1, 7; RGAL 4; RGSF 2;
SSFS 3, 9, 15, 20; TUS; YAW
Wright, Richard B. 1937- .... **CLC 6**
See also CA 85-88; CANR 120; DLB 53
Wright, Richard Bruce
See Wright, Richard B.
Wright, Richard Nathaniel
See Wright, Richard
Wright, Rick 1945- .... **CLC 35**
Wright, Rowland
See Wells, Carolyn
Wright, Stephen 1946- .... **CLC 33**
See also CA 237; DLB 350
Wright, Willard Huntington
1888-1939 .... **TCLC 23**
See also CA 115; 189; CMW 4; DLB 306;
DLBD 16; MSW
Wright, William 1930- .... **CLC 44**
See also CA 53-56; CANR 7, 23, 154
Wroblewski, David 1959- .... **CLC 280**
See also CA 283
Wroth, Lady Mary 1587-1653(?) .... **LC 30,
139; PC 38**
See also DLB 121

PC Cumulative Nationality Index

Heine, Heinrich **25**
Hölderlin, (Johann Christian) Friedrich **4**
Mueller, Lisel **33**
Rilke, Rainer Maria **2**
Sachs, Nelly **78**
Stramm, August **50**

GREEK

Cavafy, C(onstantine) P(eter) **36**
Elytis, Odysseus **21**
Homer **23**
Pindar **19**
Sappho **5**
Seferis, George **66**
Sikelianos, Angelos **29**

HUNGARIAN

Illyés, Gyula **16**
Szirtes, George **51**

INDIAN

Das, Kamala **43**
Kabir **56**
Kalidasa **22**
Mirabai **48**
Tagore, Rabindranath **8**

IRISH

Boland, Eavan **58**
Day Lewis, C(ecil) **11**
Goldsmith, Oliver **77**
Heaney, Seamus (Justin) **18, 100**
Joyce, James (Augustine Aloysius) **22**
Kavanagh, Patrick (Joseph) **33**
Kinsella, Thomas **69**
MacNeice, Louis **61**
Mahon, Derek **60**
McGuckian, Medbh **27**
Ní Chuilleanáin, Eiléan **34**
Swift, Jonathan **9**
Yeats, William Butler **20, 51**

ISRAELI

Amichai, Yehuda **38**

ITALIAN

Ariosto, Ludovico **42**
Carducci, Giosue **46**
Dante **21**
Gozzano, Guido **10**
Leopardi, Giacomo **37**
Martial **10**
Montale, Eugenio **13**
Pasolini, Pier Paolo **17**
Pavese, Cesare **13**
Petrarch **8**
Quasimodo, Salvatore **47**
Stampa, Gaspara **43**
Ungaretti, Giuseppe **57**
Zanzotto, Andrea **65**

JAMAICAN

Goodison, Lorna **36**

JAPANESE

Hagiwara, Sakutaro **18**
Ishikawa, Takuboku **10**
Matsuo Basho **3**
Nishiwaki, Junzaburō **15**
Yosano Akiko **11**

LEBANESE

Gibran, Kahlil **9**

MARTINICAN

Césaire, Aimé (Fernand) **25**

MEXICAN

Juana Inés de la Cruz **24**
Paz, Octavio **1, 48**
Urista, Alberto H. **34**

NEW ZEALAND

Curnow, (Thomas) Allen (Monro) **48**

NICARAGUAN

Alegria, Claribel **26**
Cardenal, Ernesto **22**
Darío, Rubén **15**

NIGERIAN

Okigbo, Christopher (Ifenayichukwu) **7**

PALESTINIAN

Darwish, Mahmoud **86**

PERSIAN

Khayyam, Omar **8**
Rumi, Jalâl al-Din **45**

POLISH

Herbert, Zbigniew **50**
Mickiewicz, Adam **38**
Milosz, Czeslaw **8**
Szymborska, Wisława **44**
Zagajewski, Adam **27**

PORTUGUESE

Camões, Luís de **31**
Pessoa, Fernando (António Nogueira) **20**

PUERTO RICAN

Cruz, Victor Hernández **37**

ROMAN

Horace **46**
Martial **10**
Ovid **2**
Vergil **12**

ROMANIAN

Cassian, Nina **17**
Celan, Paul **10**
Tzara, Tristan **27**

RUSSIAN

Akhmadulina, Bella **43**
Akhmatova, Anna **2, 55**
Bely, Andrey **11**
Blok, Alexander (Alexandrovich) **21**
Brodsky, Joseph **9**
Lermontov, Mikhail Yuryevich **18**
Mandelstam, Osip (Emilievich) **14**
Pasternak, Boris (Leonidovich) **6**
Pushkin, Alexander (Sergeyevich) **10**
Shvarts, Elena **50**
Tsvetaeva (Efron), Marina (Ivanovna) **14**
Yevtushenko, Yevgeny (Alexandrovich) **40**

SALVADORAN

Alegria, Claribel **26**
Dalton, Roque **36**

SCOTTISH

Burns, Robert **6**
Dunbar, William **67**
Henryson, Robert **65**
Macpherson, James **97**
Muir, Edwin **49**
Scott, Walter **13**
Spark, Muriel **72**
Stevenson, Robert Louis **84**

SENEGALESE

Senghor, Léopold Sédar **25**

SINGAPORAN

Thumboo, Edwin Nadason **30**

SOUTH AFRICAN

Brutus, Dennis **24**

SPANISH

Castro, Rosalia de **41**
Cernuda, Luis **62**
Fuertes, Gloria **27**
García Lorca, Federico **3**
Guillén, Jorge **35**
Jiménez (Mantecón), Juan Ramón **7**

ST. LUCIAN

Walcott, Derek **46**

SWEDISH

Ekeloef, (Bengt) Gunnar **23**

SWISS

Jaccottet, Philippe **98**

SYRIAN

Gibran, Kahlil **9**

WELSH

Abse, Dannie **41**
Dafydd ap Gwilym **56**
Thomas, Dylan (Marlais) **2, 52**
Thomas, R. S. **99**

Nationality Index

PC-100 Title Index

ISBN-13: 978-1-4144-4177-1
ISBN-10: 1-4144-4177-0

207